UNEQUAL
SISTERS

UNEQUAL SISTERS

A Multicultural Reader in U.S. Women's History

Third Edition

edited by Vicki L. Ruiz & Ellen Carol DuBois

Routledge
New York • London

Published in 2000 by
Routledge
29 West 35th Street
New York, NY 10001

Published in Great Britain by
Routledge
11 New Fetter Lane
London EC4P 4EE

Copyright © 2000 by Routledge

Printed in the United States of America on acid free paper.

10 9 8 7 6 5 4 3 2 1

Library of Congress Cataloging-in-Publication Data

Unequal sisters: a multicultural reader in U.S. women's history /
edited by Vicki L. Ruiz and Ellen Carol DuBois.—3rd ed.
p. cm.
Includes bibliographical references and index.
ISBN 0-415-92516-9.—ISBN 0-415-92517-7 (pbk.)
1. Women—United States—History Cross-cultural studies.   2. Sex
role—United States—History Cross-cultural studies.   3. Afro
-American women—History.   I. Ruiz, Vicki.   II. DuBois, Ellen
Carol, 1947-   .

HQ1410.U54   2000   99-16825
305.4' 0973—dc21   CIP

Contents

Acknowledgments

First of all, we would like to thank all of the authors who have contributed essays to this volume and to the first and second editions of *Unequal Sisters*. We are also grateful to Nancy Hewitt, who provided a preface to accompany her classic 1985 article "Beyond the Search for Sisterhood" especially for this third edition. Thanks also to Enedina Casarez Vásquez for graciously allowing us to reprint her inspiring artwork, the emblem for *Unequal Sisters*. While collaborating on these three volumes has not always been easy, what has remained constant is that each edition represents a collective labor of love. Deirdre Mullane, Brendan O'Malley, and Derek Krisoff, the Routledge team, have been terrific advocates for the book; their patience and support certainly hastened production of this volume. We commend Susan Warga for the skillful copyediting of the manuscript. On the Arizona State side, the administrative staff in the Department of Chicana and Chicano Studies, Susan Alameda and Araceli Albarrán, protected blocks of office time so Vicki could focus on the volume. In addition, ASU doctoral students in history Laura Muñoz and Timothy Hodgdon were superlative assistants. Vicki adds a personal note of acknowledgment to her compañero, Victor Becerra, who weathered a major health crisis with humor, love, and quiet courage. Finally, we gratefully thank our students, past and present, for both their enthusiasm and their challenges. We hope the conversations continue as we live in the present and mentor for the future. *¡Adelante!*

Introduction to the Third Edition

Vicki L. Ruiz and Ellen Carol DuBois

> A lack of courage allows us to remain blinded to our history and deaf to the cries of our past.
> —Maya Angelou

In the introduction to the first edition of *Unequal Sisters*, we wrote:

Well into its second decade, the field of women's history stands at a crossroads. Growing demands for the recognition of "difference"—the diversity of women's experiences—can no longer be satisfied by token excursions into the histories of minority women, lesbians, and the working class. The journey into women's history itself has to be remapped. From many corners comes the call for a more complex approach to women's experiences, one that explores not only the conflicts between women and men but also the conflicts among women; not only the bonds among women but also the bonds between women and men. Only such a multifaceted perspective will be sufficient "to illuminate the interconnections among the various systems of power that shape women's lives."[1]

In *Unequal Sisters* we seek to address such issues in the context of American women's history. In particular, this anthology highlights scholarship on women of color, from which we draw more than half our articles. In addition, other selections explore "difference" with respect to class and sexual orientation. The dynamics of race and gender, however, are the pivotal point of this collection.

Most of the early work on U.S. women's history paid little attention to race, and assumed instead a universal women's experience, defined in contrast to "men's" history. While a stark focus on the difference between the male and female past helped to legitimize women's history, the past it explored was usually only that of middle-class white women. In this uniracial model, the universal man of American history was replaced with the universal woman.

For instance, much of nineteenth-century women's history scholarship rests on the assumption that women's lives were lived in a separate domestic women's "sphere," on which basis they were able to claim a kind of social power distinct from that of men. This concept grew out of the historical experience of white, leisured women. And despite historians' earnest efforts to include less privileged women—notably female slaves and immigrant wives—the narrative line of women's history could not help but marginalize them. These other histories came across either as exotic or deviant, providing no clue to the larger history of American womanhood. In this uniracial model, race and gender cannot be brought into the same theoretical field. White women appear "raceless," their historical experiences determined solely by gender. By contrast, the distinct historical experiences of women of color, to the degree that they are acknowledged, are credited solely to race. The uniracial framework leads women's historians, eager to expand their range, right into the trap of "women-and-minorities," a formula that accentuates rather than remedies the invisibility of women of color.

While the notion of a universal female past focuses on power relations between men and women, scholarship has begun to appear that explores power relations *between women*—of different races, classes, and cultures. Slave owner and slave, mistress and maid, reformer and immigrant, and social worker and client are some of the many relationships of inequality that run through women's history. When focused on questions of race, we term this sort of approach "biracial." Scholarship in this biracial mode benefits from a paradigm for examining power, not only between men and women but also within women's history itself. This biracial approach shatters the notion of a universal sisterhood. Simply stated, it permits feminist historians to discard celebration for confrontation, and allows them to explore the dynamics through which women have oppressed other women.

While the biracial approach has effectively broken though the notion of a universal female experience, it has its limits. The framework itself leads the historian to focus her examination on the relation between a powerful group, almost always white women, and minority women, the varieties of whose experiences are too often obscured. In other words, the historical emphasis is on white power, and women of color have to compete for the role of "other." The historical testimonies of women of color thus tend to be compacted into a single voice. The biracial framework has helped create a situation in which the demand for greater understanding of race can be reduced to a black-and-white analysis—literally and figuratively.

Much as the uniracial framework in women's history is closely associated with the Northeast, the biracial model has its own regional bias, and seems best to describe the Southeast. For the possibilities of describing a richer palette for painting women's history, we turn to the West. Western women's historians are taking the lead in moving beyond biracialism, if only because the historical experiences of the region require a multifaceted approach. Given the confluence of many cultures and races in this region—Native American, Mexican, Asian, black, and Anglo—grappling with race at all requires a framework that has more than two positions. Nor is white history always center stage. Even the term "the West" reflects only one of several historical perspectives; the Anglo "West" is also the Mexican "North," the Native American "homeland," and the Asian "East." Nor are the possibilities for such an approach limited to one region. Even in areas that seem racially homogeneous or in which the struggle between two races understandably preoccupies historians, there are other peoples and positions to consider.

To describe this third framework, the one we seek to elaborate in *Unequal Sisters*, we use the term *multicultural*. We choose the term *multicultural* over *multiracial* because we seek to focus on the interplay of many races and cultures, because we acknowledge that not all white women's histories can be categorized under one label, and because we seek to suggest that the term *race* needs to be theorized rather than assumed. As a framework for women's history, a multicultural approach poses a variety of challenges to scholarship. Many groups of women, rarely explored or incorporated into women's history, await further study. There are distinctions to note and comparisons to be made among different groups of women with respect to family life, forms of work, definitions of womanhood, sources of power, and bonds among women. The various forms of white domination must be examined for their impact on women's history: the dispossession of Mexican land after 1848; the genocide and relocation of Native Americans; the legal exclusion of Asian Americans. Even slavery takes on multiple meanings for women's history through a multicultural lens. Finally, a multicultural approach to women's history invites the study of cultural contact and transformation, so important in understanding the development of family patterns, child-rearing practices, sexuality, and other cultural arenas crucial to women's history concerns.

In U.S. history, race has coincided closely with class. The segmentation of people of color into lower-echelon industrial, service, and agricultural jobs has served to blunt their opportunities for economic mobility. The multicultural framework allows for an analysis that takes class into account not as a separate entity, but as an intertwined component of both race and gender. The history of women cannot be studied without considering both race and class. Many of the essays in this volume provide insight into the structural and ideological components of class as it interplays with race and gender in the formations of women's consciousness.

At the risk of overreaching, it does seem that a multicultural approach, one in which many pasts can be explored simultaneously, may be the only way to organize a genuinely national, truly inclusive history of women. As Jacquelyn Dowd Hall has written, women's history must develop "a historical practice that turns on partiality, that is self-conscious about perspective, that releases multiple voices rather than competing orthodoxies, and that, above all, nurtures an 'internally differing but united political community.'"[2] To allow for overlapping narratives and to recognize multiple forms of power—this is both an old populist dream and a postmodern challenge.

Such a kaleidoscopic approach undoubtedly runs the risk of fragmentation. But in moving beyond the notion of women's history as a monolith, coherence need not be abandoned. "We should not have to choose between a common legacy and cultural diversity, especially in a nation where diversity is a legacy" writes James Quay, director of the California Council of the Humanities.[3] We hope, in this volume and in future scholarship it may encourage, to contribute to a reconceptualization of American women's history, as a series of dialectical relations among and across races and classes of women, representing diverse cultures and unequal power.

Creating and reclaiming a multicultural U.S. women's history remains a great adventure and an unfinished journey. The first two editions of *Unequal Sisters* may have contributed to the popularity of "race, class, and gender" as a shorthand for a through reenvisioning of American history, a history of multiple and overlapping narratives. Given the confines of a single volume, this edition represents but a small sampling of this current scholarship. We, however, remain committed to the challenge of keeping race, class, and gender equally and simultaneously in play as we seek a fuller recounting of women's lives over time. After ten years and three editions, we have a clearer idea of the shared perspectives that have allowed us to look beyond our differences and work together. Each time we set out to make *Unequal Sisters* happen, we struggle—in our selections, in our deliberate choice of words for the introduction—to achieve a shared voice. Our disagreements over adjectives and adverbs can reach monumental proportions. Nonetheless, a common understanding links our selections for the third edition to a larger historical and political vision, one predicated in community engagement and gender equality. In the eloquent words of historian George Lipsitz, "We do not choose our color, but we do choose our commitments. We do not choose our parents, but we do choose our politics."[4]

In compiling this latest edition, we reminded ourselves of three principles of inclusion. First, the articles should advance an ongoing political tradition of progressive feminist, antiracist, and social justice activism, which links our subjects, our narrators, and ourselves. The articles highlight the histories of women as conscious agents for social change and/or examine the competing and conflicting identities that shape women's actions. As a totality, the anthology represents both insider and outsider perspectives on historically dominant forms of feminism. *Unequal Sisters* chronicles both the legacies of struggle among women of color and the antiracist efforts of Euro-American women.

Second, when possible, we privilege the analytical and historical voices of women of color to recast the narrative core of U.S. women's history. With our roots in women's history and Chicano/a history, we remain committed to expanding the range of perspectives from which American history is both understood and experienced. The assertion that multiple narratives make synthesis and narrative well nigh impossible does not fit with our own paths as educators and scholars. Indeed, an underlying premise of *Unequal Sisters* is that these multiple narratives are linked to each other through relations of power, of exchange, and of conflict. These webs of interactions form the very basis of a national narrative.

Third, the articles continue to expand the parameters of possibilities while challenging "baseline narratives" in our own field of U.S. women's history—it is not a question of "culture as the consolation prize," but of remembering the dances of resistance.[5] In the first edition, especially, this meant challenging the analytic primacy of the paradigm of separate spheres, which has since come under intellectual scrutiny from several quarters. Now our obligation is to resist the temptation to fossilize multicultural women's history into the next orthodoxy where the same set of assumptions and problems is worked and reworked over and over. This revised edition further reflects our continuing conviction that, despite obligatory lip service in many women's history collections and much feminist theory, integrated work on race, class, gender, and sexuality remains underrepresented. It is much easier to chant the mantra than to produce the scholarship to do it justice.

Let us turn now to the articles selected for the third edition. In our attempt to represent the florescence of writings by and about women of color over the last decade, we have enlarged the collection to include thirty-nine articles, twenty-eight of which directly address the experiences of women of color. Furthermore, we particularly recognize the need to offer our readers an expanded view into scholarship on lesbian history and to diversify our coverage of Jewish American women.

While the basic elements of voice, agency, and unequal power that characterized the first and second editions of *Unequal Sisters* remain, the selections for this third edition also emphasize emerging scholarly concerns that seem significant for a dynamic and fluid multicultural women's history. Indeed, we hope that that the third edition complicates the very categories of analysis it places in the forefront for studying U.S. women's history through these new directions. Therefore, we include essays that address the following concerns and areas:

Masculinity. Following the expansion of women's history into the history of gender, several articles begin to map the variety of contexts in and the ways by which men assert masculine identities and ideologies, sometimes in the presence of women and sometimes in their absence. How did miners, who flocked to California in search of gold, for example, constitute community and redefine domesticity?

Transnationalism. While our center remains the United States, our geographic reach now includes movements of people and ideas over national borders. Given the importance of migration/immigration, it is imperative to start placing U.S. women's history within a global context (for example, the complex relationship between East Indian women reformers and their American patrons). The whole multicultural project, so to speak, turns on situating stories and their meanings across borders.

Racialized sexuality. From a women's history perspective, it has long been clear that the creation and re-creation of race requires the policing of women's sexuality and reproduction as well as the exploiting of women's bodies for pleasure and profit. We have included new scholarship that examines both the enabling and prohibiting of sexuality across racial lines. Marriage and miscegenation laws go hand in hand in maintaining these boundaries, delineating, for instance, the impact of these statutes on the property rights of racial/ethnic women who married Euro-American men.

Memory. The act of remembering is both individual and collective. Even as community identity is built upon collective memory and shared experiences, each story reminds us of our inescapable individuality. Oral histories offer a vibrant personalization of the past, a compelling, immediate connection between readers and narrators. And yet as some memories are revealed, others are silenced. A room of one's own has many closets, not all of which are equally accessible. Revelations of sexual orientation seem particularly strategic for the narrator, matters of when and to whom are carefully weighed. The third edition considers the dialectic between reminiscence and reticence as well as the process by which the past becomes memory and then memory becomes history. In the words of Norma Cantú: "The stories mirror how we live our life in our memories."[6]

Cultural representations. Popular culture carries within it the imprints of collective memory. Cultural representations—music, literature, movies, and other media—speak volumes about social location. Immigrant women and their daughters negotiate U.S. popular culture as they watch a silent movie in a segregated California theater in the 1920s or learn about "American customs" in a Vietnamese refugee camp at a Florida airbase in the 1970s. Strikingly parallel, both instances reveal the packaging of a gendered American dream and women's responses to consumer promises in the face of discrimination and economic segmentation.

The feminist project undergirding *Unequal Sisters* has one foot in the past and one foot in the present—reclaiming stories long silenced and striving toward social justice. The scholars whose works are assembled within these covers not only open up social categories including gender, race, class, culture, region, generation, and sexual orientation but bring them together through comparative analyses, studies of unequal power dynamics, and explorations of intercultural borders and tactical coalitions. Valerie J. Matsumoto, whose own work illuminates the aspirations and simple courage of Japanese American women, has insightfully observed: "Perhaps scholars should be reminded that we, no less than those we study, are actors in history, making choices that affect the lives of others."[7]

We envision this third edition as the capstone edition, perhaps the last of the *Unequal Sisters* series for some time, and as such, we encourage the readers' critical engagement with history, an engagement that centers on continuing conversations with the past and the present. Multicultural women's history, when done well, encourages students to visualize worlds outside their own, to reflect on their own individual positionality, and to make connections with a collective historical past. Multivalent representations of memory, difference, voice, and engagement resonate throughout this volume. *Unequal Sisters* illuminates not only the *mascaras y muros* (masks and walls) embedded in women's narratives, but also their *ánimo y sueños* (spirit and dreams). We hope that this third edition not only expands our historical knowledge across race, ethnicity, sexual orientation, class, and gender, but helps foster for all of us a stronger civic culture of mutual regard and recognition. We continue to learn from each other's stories.

Notes

1. We want to thank Joanne Meyerowitz for this phrasing of our project in personal correspondence with the editors.
2. Jacquelyn Dowd Hall, "Partial Truths," *Signs: Journal of Women in Culture and Society* 14, 4 (1989): 908.
3. James Quay, "The Learning Society and the New American Legacy," *Humanities News* 11 (spring 1989): 4.
4. George Lipsitz, *The Possessive Investment in Whiteness: How White People Profit from Identity Politics* (Philadelphia: Temple University Press, 1998), viii.
5. Patricia Nelson Limerick, "Has 'Minority History' Transformed the Historical Discourse?" *Perspectives: The Newsletter of the American Historical Association* 35, 8 (1997): 23.
6. Norma Cantú, *Canícula: Snapshots of Girlhood en La Frontera* (Albuquerque: University of New Mexico Press, 1995), xiii.
7. Valerie J. Matsumoto, *Farming the Home Place: A Japanese American Community in California, 1919–1982* (Ithaca: Cornell University Press, 1993), 224.

1

Beyond the Search for Sisterhood: American Women's History in the 1990s

Nancy A. Hewitt

The opening article of this volume was originally published in 1985. The author has added the following introduction, looking back at the article she wrote a decade and a half ago and setting it in a larger and later context.

In 1984, when I was asked by editors of the British journal *Social History* to write an article reviewing the field of American women's history, I was a young assistant professor with an agenda. Like most of my generation of feminist scholars, professional ambitions were fired by political awakenings. Converted, and I do mean converted, to antiwar politics and radical feminism as a first-year student at Smith College in the late 1960s, I became convinced that history offered a critical lever for opening the minds of women and men to the oppressive character of American military, political, and social institutions and attitudes. The American history survey course I took in my sophomore year, in which Dr. Allen Weinstein catalogued a national tradition of racism and militarism from the colonial era through the Vietnam War, convinced me that if Americans had truly understood their history, they would not continue to support U.S. interventions in the domestic and economic affairs of other nations. The consciousness-raising that would be provided by a more accurate—that is, antiracist, anti-imperialist, and feminist—national history was critical, I thought, to mobilizing movements for progressive social change.

By the time I completed my Ph.D. in 1981, I was even more convinced that writing and teaching history was an important form of political engagement. From this perspective, the invitation to publish an article on the state of American women's history provided the opportunity to craft a manifesto. Manifestos are an important academic genre as well as an activist one. They highlight certain aspects of a situation in order to sharpen their political points, and they are intended as inspirations to action. The article that follows was written in that spirit, as a response to what I saw as a troublesome trend within both the feminist movement and feminist scholarship: the desire for, sometimes insistence on, a shared sisterhood among women that obscured, ignored, or denied differences of race, class, sexual orientation, and ideology.

At the time, challenging the sisterhood model of women's history seemed a bold step. Since the late 1980s, however, difference has become the watchword of much feminist scholarship, and studies of the varied and often conflicting histories of women in the United States, and North America more generally, continue to multiply. The publication, reprinting, and updating of *Unequal Sisters* throughout the 1990s offers exciting evidence of just how rich and varied the field of American women's history has become. In 1984–85, however, the future success of the "difference paradigm" would have been hard to predict. Instead, women's separate sphere, the cults of domesticity and true womanhood, and

1

female worlds of love and ritual flourished, each representing distinct and compelling visions of commonality and community.

To challenge what I saw as an overly homogeneous and singular history of American women seemed risky when I sent my article off to *Social History*. I was more than a little nervous over its reception, particularly among more senior scholars. As it turned out, it was not as bold or unique a stance as I had feared (and hoped). Instead, it was part of wave of scholarship that rather swiftly dislodged earlier efforts to root American women's history in the lives of middle-class, white, northeastern women. The notes to the original version of "Beyond the Search for Sisterhood" trace the beginnings of that wave. Over the next decade, as illustrated by the articles and bibliographies contained in *Unequal Sisters*, a flood of articles, monographs, and anthologies appeared. Thus, in many ways, my article now seems a rather moderate proposal, a statement of some obvious truths, an intervention soon overwhelmed by the wealth of new work on African American, Native American, immigrant, working-class, southern, and western women. At the same time, the history of sexuality opened up other vistas of difference that crosscut categories of race, region, and class, reminding us of both the difficulties involved in creating neat categories of difference and the excitement of recognizing connections between and across categories.

As my friend and colleague Jacquelyn Dowd Hall reminds us, historical scholarship never reveals more than "partial truths."[1] This is particularly so for review essays, which seek to capture the main threads of a field at a particular moment in time and in doing so highlight certain issues and interpretations, thereby ignoring others. The "partial truths" that seemed so important to me in the mid-1980s have now taken on new and problematic meaning. And this is so not only because I did not anticipate the complications and conflicts that would be created by the embrace of difference among American women's historians, but also because I inadvertently contributed to a portrait of the field that negated pioneering work on working-class, African American, immigrant, and southern women. That is, my article not only recognized the centrality of white, middle-class, northeastern women to American women's history of the 1970s and early 1980s, but also helped to create it by obscuring the important work that had already been published on other groups of women. Like critiques of second-wave feminism that declare it a white, middle-class women's movement by excluding from its pantheon of foremothers all those African American, Native American, Asian American, Latina, and working-class women who embraced women's liberation in the 1960s and 1970s, my critique of women's history failed to capture the diversity of the field at its origins.

Six years after "Beyond the Search for Sisterhood" was first published, Lise Vogel wrote a compelling article that pointed out the dangers posed to women's history by re-creations, including mine, that treated "partial truths" as the whole story.[2] These dangers now echo through popular media and through undergraduate and even many graduate courses in women's history, where over and over again feminism (first- and second-wave) is dismissed as simply a white, middle-class movement and women's history is claimed to ignore all but middle-class and affluent white women. While these critiques offer important reminders of the limits of certain types of activism and certain types of scholarship, they can function only by excluding the rich and diverse traditions from which feminism and women's history emerged.

Rosalyn Baxandall and Linda Gordon are now compiling materials from second-wave feminist groups and organizations that document the pioneering efforts of working-class and African American women. The context for their work is constituted by the many studies of American women activists produced by scholars such as Vicki Ruiz, Ellen DuBois, Elsa Barkley Brown, Rosalyn Terborg-Penn, Peggy Pascoe, Ardis Cameron, Susan Glenn,

Deborah Gray White, Theda Perdue, Jacquelyn Dowd Hall, Yamila Azize-Varga, Alma Garcia, Sucheng Chan, Evelyn Nakano Glenn, Clara Sue Kidwell, Devon Abbott Mihesuah, Chana Kai Lee, and dozens of other historians.[3] Dissertations recently completed or in progress will only expand our understanding of the richness and diversity within both women's activism and feminist movements.

The stories told by historians and other scholars documenting differences among women have not been limited to celebratory tales of struggle against racial, ethnic, sexual, and economic oppression. Instead, a growing body of work now explores tensions within, as well as between, particular communities—the class tensions that disrupt racial and ethnic solidarities, the homophobia that poisons minority as well as majority cultures, the racism that shatters class-based alliances. Thus, the exclusive and hegemonic dimensions of "community" are now explored along with the power relations that often inhere in supposedly collaborative efforts when one group of women controls more economic, political, and cultural resources than another.

Recent work on conservative and right-wing women only illustrates more dramatically the ways that sisterhood or a common set of values can constrain as well as liberate women. The communities forged by nativist and proslavery women in the mid-nineteenth century, by antisuffragists in the early 1900s, by women of the Ku Klux Klan and female advocates of military growth in the 1920s, by segregationists and antibusing advocates in the 1960s, and by antiabortion/prolife and antifeminist groups since the 1970s are just as powerful in their emotional and ideological bonds as the more progressive groups so often studied by women's historians.[4] Sisterhoods rooted in racism, militarism, nativism, and traditional patriarchal values may be less inspiring to most scholars, but they remind us that our history and our heritage are truly multicultural and that only by incorporating the full range of women into American history can we come to grips with where we have been and where we still need to go.

Yet the profusion of work published in the late 1980s and throughout the 1990s cannot correct the sense left by "Beyond the Search for Sisterhood" that prior to 1985, the field of American women's history was the bastion of privileged white northern women. While it is true that in the years when the field was being created, both women's historians and those they studied were most likely to be white, middle-class, and northern, alternative paths were being carved out from the very beginning. Eleanor Flexner, who never held a regular academic appointment but who pioneered in the writing of women's history, incorporated black and working-class women into her now-classic *Century of Struggle*, published in 1959. In the 1970s Anne Firor Scott opened up the field of southern women's history with *From Pedestal to Politics;* Gerda Lerner offered a powerful critique of whites-only women's history in her pathbreaking anthology *Black Women in White America;* Rayna Green introduced feminists to Native American women's history; and Sarah Eisenstein offered working-class perspectives in *Give Us Bread, but Give Us Roses.* These are only a few of the most oft-cited and well-known early efforts to create a racially, economically, and regionally diverse history of American women.

Unequal Sisters builds on this legacy. As this volume demonstrates, feminist scholars have moved well beyond a search for sisterhood, probing instead the myriad intertwined differences that characterize American women's past and present. Yet we still seek common ground. If historians less often look for universal connections among women across time and place, many of us are still eager to explore those moments when women have worked collectively to sustain communities within particular race, class, or ethnic enclaves. Most feminist scholars also cherish those instances where women reach across such barriers to establish, if only temporarily, cross-racial, cross-class, and cross-national alliances. And though truly interracial, international, or interclass efforts are even harder to unearth, they do arise now and then, often inspired by struggles for family and community survival. They remind us that the search for sisterhood is still a valuable enterprise as long as those of us searching recognize the inequalities that must be overcome to achieve it.

One of the principal projects of the contemporary feminist movement in the United States has been the development of a sense of community among women, rooted in their common oppression and expressed through a distinctive women's culture. This project is premised on the patriarchal assumptions accepted by the majority of North America's early feminist leaders: that gender is the primary source of oppression in society and is the model for all other forms of oppression.[1] American women's historians of the 1960s and 1970s not only accepted the premises and projects of the women's movement but also helped to establish them. The bonds that encircled past generations of women were initially perceived as restrictive, arising from female victimization at the hands of patriarchs in such institutions as medicine, education, the church, the state, and the family. Historians soon concluded, however, that oppression was a double-edged sword; the counterpart of subordination in or exclusion from male-dominated domains was inclusion in an all-female enclave. The concept of womanhood, it soon appeared, bound women together even as it bound them down.[2] The formative works in American women's history have focused on the formation of these separate sexual spheres, particularly among the emerging urban bourgeoisie in the first half of the nineteenth century. Reified in prescriptive literature, realized in daily life, and ritualized in female collectivities, this "woman's sphere" came to be seen as the foundation of women's culture and community in antebellum America.[3]

Though feminists, including scholars, have perceived community as a source of support and solidarity for women, both history and politics affirm that a strong sense of community can also be a source of exclusion, prejudices, and prohibitions. For the past decade the women's movement itself has been accused of forming its own exclusive community, characterized by elitism, ethnocentrism, and a disregard for diversity. At the same time, students of black and working-class women's lives have argued that the notion of a single women's community rooted in common oppression denies the social and material realities of caste and class in America.[4] Yet as the concept of community has become increasingly problematic for women's historians, it has also become increasingly paradigmatic. This article will evaluate the current paradigm in American women's history—premised on patriarchy and constructed around community—by comparing the creation, conditions, and practices of communal life among black and white working-class women with that among the white bourgeoisie in the nineteenth and early twentieth centuries.

The community that has become the cornerstone of North American women's history was discovered within the Victorian middle class. There a "rich female subculture" flourished "in which women, relegated to domesticity, constructed powerful emotional and practical bonds with each other."[5] Three distinct but related investigations converged to illuminate this enclave of sisterhood. Barbara Welter first identified the construction of a new ideology of gender in the years 1820 to 1860 that defined the "true woman" as pious, pure, domestic, and submissive. Nancy Cott correlated this ideology with a separation of women and men into distinct spheres of activity, at least among New England's middle classes. For this group, commercial and industrial developments in the late eighteenth and early nineteenth centuries simultaneously consigned married women to domesticity and launched men on public careers. Carroll Smith-Rosenberg then discovered within the private domain a dynamic "world of love and ritual" in which a distinct set of values was elaborated into a richly textured women's culture.[6]

Though each of these authors regarded her work as speculative and carefully noted parameters of time, region, and class, the triad of true woman, separate spheres, and woman's culture became the most widely used framework for interpreting women's past in the United States. The articles and arguments presented by the architects of the paradigm are widely quoted, reprinted frequently, summarized in textbooks and popular histories, reproduced in curriculum packets, and elaborated upon in an array of scholarly studies. By gendering the Victorian landscape and evaluating historical patterns and processes in women's own terms, the historians of bourgeois womanhood have established concepts and categories that now shape the analysis of all groups of American women.[7]

Historians soon traced the bonds of womanhood into public arenas and across race and class barriers. According to Cott, the "doctrine of woman's sphere opened to women (reserved for them) the avenues of domestic influence, religious morality, and child nurture. It articulated a social power based on their special female qualities."[8] That social power first was revealed in church and charitable societies and in educational missions, then was gradually expanded into campaigns for moral reform, temperance, the abolition of slavery, and even women's rights.[9] By the late nineteenth century, domestic skills and social power would converge in "social housekeeping," embracing and justifying women's participation in urban development, social welfare programs, social work, the settlement house movement, immigrant education, labor reform, and electoral politics.[10]

At the same time that middle-class wives reached across the domestic threshold, they also apparently, though more haltingly, stepped across the moat dividing them from women of other classes and races. Some plantation mistresses, for instance, decried, at least in their private diaries, the sexual double standard reflected in white men's abuse of slave women. In at least one southern town, free black and white women seemed to adopt a common set of values grounded in personalism: Both races were "more attuned to the needs and interests of other women, more concerned with economic security, more supportive of organized charity, and more serious about the spiritual life than men."[11] White working-class women were also soon caught in the web of womanhood. One historian noted that this web could be paralyzing for an individual working woman, but added that "when a strong enough wind is blowing, the whole web and all the women in it can be seen to move and this is a new kind of movement, a new source of power and connectedness."[12] Those connections, moreover, stretched across economic strata as industrialization created "an oppressive leisure life" for affluent women and "an oppressive work life" for their laboring sisters, forging a "bond of sisterhood" across classes.[13]

Elaborations on and extensions of female community multiplied rapidly. Women on wagon trains heading west, worshipers in evangelical revivals and in Quaker meetinghouses, prostitutes on the Comstock Lode, mill workers in Lowell boardinghouses, and immigrants on the streets of Lawrence and the stoops of Providence loved and nurtured one another, exchanged recipes, gossip, and herbal remedies, swapped food and clothing, shared child-rearing and domestic chores, covered for each other at work, protected one another from abusive fathers, husbands, lovers, and bosses, and supported each other in birth and death.[14] For each group, these "friendship and support networks" could also become "crucibles in which collective acts of rebellion were formed."[15] Middle-class "rebels" formed single-sex public associations to ameliorate social ills and eradicate social evils. Quaker farm wives, in Seneca Falls, Waterloo, and Rochester, New York, attacked the "repeated injuries and usurpations on the part of man toward woman."[16] Lowell mill operatives on strike for higher wages vowed that "none will go back, unless they receive us all as one."[17] In Lawrence, Massachusetts, New York City's Lower East Side, Cripple Creek, Colorado, and Tampa, Florida, immigrant women—as wives and wage earners—

united shop-floor struggle with neighborhood discontent and employed the resources of their everyday life as weapons in the class struggle.

How could the bonds of womanhood, first forged in the domestic enclaves of the Victorian bourgeoisie, have filtered through the walls dividing private and public domains, affluent and poor, native-born and immigrant, black and white? The answer provided by the authors of the women's community construct was a combination of patriarchy and modernization. Patriarchy explained what women held in common—sexual vulnerability, domestic isolation, economic and educational deprivation, and political exclusion. Modernization served as the causal mechanism by which the ideology of separate spheres and the values of "true womanhood" were dispersed throughout the society.[18] Employing modernization as the mechanism of change allowed North American scholars to recognize broad forces (industrialization, urbanization and class stratification) and collective psychological developments (the growth of individualism and the search for autonomy) while maintaining the primacy of gender.[19] In addition, the "trickle-down" method by which societies supposedly become modern suggested that the analysis of elite women could provide an appropriate framework for understanding and predicting the experiences of all women. Finally, the teleological bent of modernization obscures conflict and thereby reinforced the notion that bonds among women based on gender are stronger than barriers between women based on class or race.

The adoption of modernization by leading social historians, including women's historians, has carried us a great distance from Jesse Lemisch's early plea for a history written "from the bottom up."[20] As more feminist scholars pursued studies of black and white working-class life, however, they demanded renewed attention to the complexity of women's experience and recognition of the conflict that it engenders. At the same time, students of bourgeois women began debating woman's specific role in modernization: Was she the repository of traditional values, the happy humanizer of modernity, a victim of male-dominated forces, or an eager agent of Progress? Those who compared the experiences of privileged and poor women in the Victorian era concluded that if modernization occurred, it led not to the inclusion of women in a universal sisterhood but rather to the dichotomization of women along class lines into the pious and pure "modern" woman and the prurient and parasitical "premodern" woman.[21] Students of the Third World were even more adamant that women, rather than gaining by the development of a new domesticated ideal, lost "traditional forms of power and authority on the road to 'emancipation' from premodern lifeways."[22]

In addition, some women's historians attacked the concept of modernization itself as vague, untested, "nebulous," "both one-dimensional and elastic," or "a piece of postcapitalist ideology."[23] This last criticism focused on the cornerstone of the current paradigm—the separation of spheres—suggesting that it may have been culturally prescribed by dominant sectors of society to divide classes against themselves. It is not clear, however, that either the working classes or the bourgeoisie itself actually patterned their lives according to such prescriptions. Certainly bourgeois women were not so separated from same-class men as to disengage them from the prejudices and power inherent in their class position. Evidence of this appears in white suffragists' use of racist rhetoric, Protestant charitable ladies' denial of aid to Catholics, affluent women's refusal to support working women's strikes, moral reformers' abhorrence of working-class sexual mores, and settlement house educators' denigration of immigrant culture.[24] Finally, students of black women's history reject the teleological design of modernization. Like contemporary black feminists, they argue that the concept of a woman's community derived from white women's experience distorts the reality of black lives and ignores the ways that white solidarity, including sisterhood, has served to deny rights to blacks, including women.[25]

We can most fully illuminate the value and limits of women's community by examining the bonds of womanhood among that group furthest removed from the Victorian parlor, southern slaves. Slave women functioned within two communities in the antebellum era: one structured by white masters, the other by slaves themselves. The key to women's roles in both was work. In the former, labor was imposed upon blacks as their principal obligation; in the latter, labor was a primary concern by necessity. In both arenas, women's work embraced the production of goods and services and the production of human beings.[26] In both worlds and in both forms of work, the sexual division of labor encouraged women to band together for sustenance, security, and sociability.

In the fields, the master's house, and the slave quarters, black women often performed sex-specific tasks and worked in sex-segregated groups. Plantation owners generally differentiated field work by gender—"women hoed while men plowed"—though such lines were frequently ignored when the need arose.[27] Then, women carted manure, shoveled, cut trees, hauled lumber, drove teams, and cleared land. Even when performing tasks similar to those of men, women did not always work side by side with slaves. The "trash gang" was one form of an all-female work group. It was composed of pregnant women, nursing mothers, young girls, and old women, who were assigned the lighter work of raking stubble or pulling weeds while other female teams hoed and picked the cotton.[28] On rice plantations, the division of labor by gender was probably even more regularized and rigid.

Within the master's house, on all plantations, work was highly sex-segregated.[29] Female slaves cooked and sewed, nursed and reared children, and performed a wide array of domestic chores. Here, even more than in the fields, women worked in all-female circles in which the older trained the younger in work-related skills and survival techniques. The latter had a specific meaning for house slaves, who were trapped by the division of sexual labor and by their proximity to white men in a highly charged and potentially abusive situation. The "passionlessness" of "true women" was counterposed, by white males, to the sexual insatiability of blacks, justifying the rape of female slaves and enhancing white profits if coercion led to conception. The testimony of ex-slaves suggests that they rarely found refuge in the sympathies of white mistresses, who were as likely to take out their frustrations on the victim as on the victimizer, and thus slave women learned early the importance of self-reliance and of black sisterhood.[30]

Once slaves were safely ensconced in their own quarters, they joined in the collective performance of essential labors, such as food preparation, household maintenance, and child care. Here as in the fields, women and men performed some overlapping tasks, but they often did so in sex-segregated circles. Other chores they specifically divided along gender lines: Fishing and hunting were for men, gardening and cooking were for women. However, the value placed on men's and women's work was more equal among blacks than whites. Certain female skills, such as cooking, sewing, quilting, or healing, were highly regarded since knowledge in these areas was essential to the survival of the slave community. Midwives were of particular importance. Though male physicians were reshaping the birth process among affluent whites, childbirth remained an all-female ritual among blacks and one that occurred with much greater frequency and hazard.[31] Child rearing was probably also more clearly defined as black women's rather than white women's work, especially since slave women often nursed and cared for the children of their owners as well as their own family. The emphasis on the slave mother's role was reinforced by both white masters and slaves themselves. As masters imposed a matrifocal structure on slave families, black women drew on their own self-identification with maternity to cement their central position in the slave family and community.[32]

Slave women, like their bourgeois counterparts, functioned in a sex-segregated world; but without access to land, cash, or the fruits of one's labor, slave women and men were denied the measures that defined status in bourgeois society. In general, the absence of such measures equalized men's and women's status and allowed women in particular to develop criteria for determining self-worth that were relatively independent of men, white or black.[33] Yet despite this development of a woman's sphere and a set of women's values, slave women did not define themselves in opposition to their male counterparts. Rather, black women forged bonds of sisterhood and then wielded them as weapons in the fight for black community survival. Moreover, though defined in part by women's roles in reproduction and domesticity, black womanhood was not an extension of white womanhood, nor did sisterly feelings among slaves extend, except on rare occasions, to white mistresses.[34]

From the perspective of the slave experience, then, strong communal ties among women were rooted not in the culture-bound concept of the separation of spheres but in the material realities of the sexual division of labor. That division assigned men and women distinct but complementary roles. In this context, strong bonds among women strengthened the community as a whole, providing support for the interests of slave men and a defense against domination by white women and men. This same dynamic—of a sexual division of labor resulting in complementary roles, the development of bonds among women and the use of those bonds in defense of community interests, and the formation of a strong sense of identity among same-class women that served as a barrier to universal sisterhood—can be traced for other groups of nineteenth-century working women. In western mining and eastern mill towns at midcentury and in northern immigrant and southern industrial centers at the turn of the century, women banded together to perform essential labor and then wielded their collective power in defense of same-class men and in defiance of other-class women.[35]

In towns where the primary form of work was rigidly sex-typed, such as deep-shaft mining or textile manufacturing, women and men formed distinct circles of association in the workplace as well as in the household and community. Yet even in industrial centers of the late nineteenth century, where both men and women worked for wages, sex segregation within factories and the continued assignment of domestic chores to females assured the development of a sense of community based on gender. A variety of work-related experiences shaped the bonds of womanhood among wage earners. In Lowell, Massachusetts, for instance, young mill operatives taught each other skills, substituted for each other at work, warned each other of a foreman's approach, and shared meals, leisure hours, and even beds at company-owned boardinghouses. A half century later in nearby Lawrence, immigrant daughters gathered at an appointed corner in the predawn hours to "walk each other to the mills"—talking all the way and sharing information on wages and working conditions in the different factories. On returning home in the evening, the bonds were tightened further. As one worker recounted: "Back then you see this is how you lived—you slept in shifts, we all lived like one then. One kitchen we all used and we all knew each other."[36]

Working-class housewives shared similar burdens across communities and across time. Combining their efforts and expertise in cooking, child care, sewing, nursing, and laundry, housewives provided each other with advice, missing items for recipes, hand-me-down clothes, soap flakes, a moment's respite from child minding, and an extra pair of hands.[37] Communal spaces, such as stoops, streets, churches, groceries, and bathhouses, became forums for the exchange of "gossip," including the latest information on wages, prices, and rents. These women were also in charge of providing emotional support, food, and general assistance during life crises, organizing social functions for children and adults, supplying welfare services to widows and orphans, and socializing young girls into proper patterns of family, work, and courtship.

The importance of these bonds of womanhood was strikingly visible when workers walked off their jobs; the ability of a community to survive without wages was often related to women wage earners' militancy and to the resources hoarded and distributed by non-wage-earning housewives. Triumphs on the shop floor were directly tied to the tenaciousness of working-class women in keeping their families and neighborhoods fed and functioning. Evidence now abounds that striking women "often outdid men in militancy." It was "harder to induce women to compromise"; they were " more likely to hold out to the bitter end . . . to obtain exactly what they want."[38] This militancy was strengthened when men joined women in unions and on picket lines.

It is true that skilled craftsmen and male union leaders sought to exclude women from the benefits they enjoyed and that women in the garment industry and elsewhere called strikes over the objections of male advisors. The most virulent sexism of union men, however, surfaced when the sexual division of labor appeared to be breaking down and consequently threatened wage scales set by skilled men. In this situation it was often women of different racial or ethnic backgrounds who challenged existing male jobs, and skilled workers were hostile to any intrusions from these groups, whether by women or by men. When the sexual division of labor placed men and women in different industries or in different jobs in the same industry, thus eliminating the threat of job loss and wage cuts, men and women joined forces to protect their common economic interests.[39] In Massachusetts, for instance, the Lowell Female Labor Reform Association and the New England Working-man's Association combined efforts to gain a law mandating ten-hour days for industry. In Troy and Cohoes, New York, iron molders and laundresses supported each other in alternating strikes. In western Pennsylvania, miners and textile operatives often contributed to the same family income, and so received benefits from better contracts in either industry. In North Carolina, women finally overcame opposition of union leaders, joined the Textile Workers Union of America and the Tobacco Workers International Union, and played significant and militant roles in numerous strikes and labor actions.[40]

Moreover, both male and female workers benefited from the community networks woven by non-wage-earning women that served as a safety net in times of economic crisis. In Cripple Creek, Colorado, for instance, where there were few wage-earning possibilities for women, miners' wives ran soup kitchens, boycotted antiunion merchants, walked picket lines, defended union offices against soldiers, continued the printing of union papers when editors were jailed, raised bail bonds, and provided food for incarcerated members of the Western Federation of Miners. In 1912 the housewives of Lawrence extended their customary communal cooking efforts to provide meals for strikers' families, and older women shouldered more than their normal burden of child care so younger women could join picket lines. Housewives also went door to door and store to store collecting food, clothing, and funds, using their power as consumers to pressure merchants into supporting strike activities. Standard household items became weapons against union foes, with scalding water, red pepper, and household shears always at the ready. The "gossip" networks of more peaceful periods and the communal spaces where women daily congregated became the communication centers for strike organization. The strategies developed there were often put into effect by the women themselves. They paraded through the neighborhoods jeering, hooting, and hissing at potential scabs; cornered strikebreakers and stripped them on the streets; and brandished sewing scissors to cut the backs of soldiers' uniforms, thus "exposing their yellow insides."[41] In addition, in all striking communities, it was women, in individual families and neighborhood circles, who stretched the available food, nursed the sick and wounded, exchanged essential items, and sustained the emotional as well as physical resources of strikers and their families.

The sisterly bonds that bolstered working-class communities, like those among slaves, extended from the domestic enclave into the public domain, were forged from material necessity, and were employed in the interests of men as well as women. The very tightness of the web thus formed often served as a wall against women of other social, economic, ethnic, or racial groups. In western mining camps, for instance, prostitutes and dance hall girls formed their own sisterly circles through the exchange of "small favors, the sharing of meals, fashion advice, and sewing," yet miners' wives recognized no common bonds. Here the division of sexual labor between "good" girls and "bad" girls served to divide working-class women against themselves. Yet at the same time, miners' wives refused to support women of the merchant and professional families in the "civic housekeeping" crusades against gambling houses and brothels since crusade leaders sided with employers and against workers whenever strikes occurred.[42]

Lowell mill operatives were less hostile to the town's "ladies," who they believed would be "compassionate" to any who were "in want"; but they claimed nonetheless that " we prefer to have the disposing of our charities in our own hands."[43] While willing to dispense that charity to Yankee sisters and brothers, native-born mill operatives refused to extend it to the Irish and French Canadian women who began flooding the mills at midcentury. An even more direct confrontation between communities of working women occurred in Atlanta in 1896. There it was the attempt to introduce black women into textile jobs that led to a strike and the formation of a union by previously unorganized white women. The union's first victory was the ouster of the newly recruited black employees. In the tobacco towns of North Carolina, the lines between black and white communities were subtler but no less definitively drawn, and they were clearly rooted in the racial and sexual divisions of labor. Black women, who suffered from lower wages and more frequent layoffs than whites, were hired by white women coworkers as domestic servants during slack seasons.[44] This practice eased the tension between white working-class husbands and wives, as the latter suffered under the double burden of wage work and housework, while also reinforcing, both symbolically and pragmatically, the racial specificity of southern sisterhood.

If we take these experiences of community among women and project them back upon the Victorian bourgeoisie, we find important parallels. The separation of spheres that supposedly arose from an ideological barrier between men's and women's worlds may be more usefully analyzed as a transformation in the sexual division of labor. Occurring in the midst of commercial and industrial development, the new division provided for more specialized roles for each sex and thereby ensured their mutual dependency in the production of goods and services and the reproduction of human beings. Bourgeois women, rather than retreating into an isolated domestic enclave that was a haven from class concerns and conflicts, became central actors in the family and the community; in both arenas their labor was essential to class formation.[45] Still, they performed their tasks in sex-segregated groups, and a particular set of female rituals and values did emerge from these groups, as it did among women in other economic, ethnic, and racial enclaves.

The sexual division of labor became rigidified among the emerging bourgeoisie by the mid-nineteenth century as middle-class, and especially married, women retreated from the cash nexus and from the fecundity of their foremothers. Homebound wives were not idle, however. They continued to produce children's and women's clothing and a variety of other goods, and they provided a wide range of services for their families—laundry, cleaning, food preparation, shopping, and child care. The assistance of domestic servants relieved privileged women of some of the most arduous physical labor, but the majority of middle-class women were confronted with ever-expanding duties as furniture became more elaborate, home entertainments more prevalent, and consumerism more pervasive.[46] Overall, the "felicity of families" was increasingly dependent on wives who were "properly methodical and economical in their distributions and expenditures of time."[47]

The greatest transformation for these women in the use of time was the shift in emphasis from the production of goods to the production of human beings. The declining birthrate affected bourgeois women in two ways. First, they assumed a greater role in policing sexual activity, both their own and others', accepting in the process a new sexual identity of "passionlessness." Second, the nurturing and socialization of bourgeois children became more complex in this period, and mothers shouldered most of the added burden.[48] From the first months of an infant's life, mothers were admonished to begin "instructing their sons in the principles of liberty and government," preparing them for service in a new array of white-collar and professional careers, and protecting sons and daughters from the "contamination of the streets" and the corruption of their souls.[49] To educate mothers for their new role, advice books, magazines, and mothers' associations flourished; the price of successful progeny was eternal maternal vigilance.

The concern for the maintenance and upward mobility of the family was shared by husbands and wives even as their roles in that achievement were rendered more distinct. This was true in the public sphere as well as the private. It proved impossible to protect children from contaminants and corruption without active community involvement, and bourgeois mothers, with the approval of their husbands, banded together to fight delinquency, destitution, prostitution, profligacy, intemperance, and impiety. Such endeavors extended the sexual division of labor into the public arena, where men proffered cash donations and financial and legal advice and women raised and distributed funds and supplied the voluntary labor to establish the first urban welfare systems.[50]

As in the working class, middle-class women were not a unified body in the mid-nineteenth century, and here too, the critical divisions were along lines not of gender but of economic and social interest. And again, these divisions were most visible in the public domain, where conflicts among three distinct segments of the emerging bourgeoisie revealed that sibling rivalry was as characteristic as sisterhood. The conflicts, moreover, embraced both the goals and the styles of social activism. In Rochester, New York, for instance, the wives of the city's wealthiest and most powerful men labored "economically, noiselessly, and consistently" to ameliorate the worst effects of rapid urban growth. At the other end of the middle-class spectrum, the wives of farmers and small traders, outside the circles of local political influence, asserted that "commotion shows signs of vitality" and organized demonstrations, wore bloomers instead of long skirts, and socialized in mixed-race company in their attempt to foment a "thorough Re-organization of Society."In between these extremes, the wives of upwardly mobile entrepreneurs insisted that there was a proper role for women "between the doll and the Amazon," apparently located in orphan asylums, homes for delinquent boys and "friendless" women, temperance crusades, and female auxiliaries to men's political associations.[51] In each case, the women had the support of male kin and neighbors; together, the men and women of each class segment sought to channel social change in the direction of their own material and social interests.[52]

It was those in between the Amazons and the dolls who most fully embraced the tenets of true womanhood, yet it was precisely these upwardly mobile, public-minded women who most often substituted class hegemony for sisterly harmony. The "contradiction in the exercise of bourgeois women's historical agency" was most evident for this group: "that women both wielded power and that their power was not always progressive."[53] Indeed, the adherence of privileged women to a narrow and class-bound definition of women's proper sphere, while a boon to their own sense of community, was a barrier to their inclusion of women from other social and economic circumstances. Bourgeois women's new roles in production and reproduction were rooted in a "decentralized home system" in which each married woman was wholly responsible for the care and nurture of her own individual family, "passionlessness" combined with vigilant maternity, moral and spiritual superiority that justified women's power in the family and entry into the public domain, voluntary labor, and the belief in the natural and universal differentiation of the sexes in biological, intellectual, emotional, and economic terms.[54] When "true women" attempted to extend these "benefits" and beliefs to all women, they failed to recognize the value that white and black working-class women placed on their own carefully constructed communities, and therefore created antipathy in their search for unity.

"True women," as educators, writers, dispensers of charity, and missionaries to the heathen, touted their own lifestyle, expressed and covered its contradictions in their public espousals of privatized domesticity, and took little cognizance of the values and mores of those being aided.[55] Even those female reformers who demonstrated genuine concern for the problems faced by women across classes did not necessarily offer solutions that were more attentive to cultural and social differences among women. In the desire to eliminate the sexual double standard, for instance, middle-class moral reformers offered prostitutes the wages of domestic servants as a substitute for the wages of sin and sought to replace sexual pleasure with passionlessness in order to curb what they saw as the dangers of unbridled lust. Their marginal concern for fertility control became the primary focus of female activists by the late nineteenth century. In family planning campaigns, the economic burden of large numbers of children and the technical control of conception led women to advocate the small nuclear family as the model for all groups, without attention to different cultural and social meanings of motherhood. Similarly, affluent wives claimed solidarity with working-class sisters in the fight against alcohol, yet few temperance leaders helped working-class women organize on their own behalf or supported divorce as an option for abused wives. All three groups of bourgeois reformers advocated state regulation of the vices they abhorred, the use of charity to aid deserving victims, and the intervention of male physicians to apply scientific solutions to moral dilemmas. In each case, these solutions lessened working-class women's control over their own lives and instead increased the powers of the dominant class in shaping the most intimate aspects of working-class women's lives.[56]

In the attempt to free working women from the hazards of long hours and poor working conditions, middle-class women again rejected the strategy of supporting grassroots organizational efforts. Instead, they aligned themselves, sometimes inadvertently, with concerned politicians and chauvinistic union leaders in demanding protective legislation to reduce the hours and workload of female wage earners. Even those privileged women with more progressive views, who established working alliances with laboring sisters through such associations as the Women's Trade Union League, often supported an activist agenda that placed the priorities of the women's movement—suffrage—above the bread-and-butter issues crucial to the workers.[57] Also, most middle-class women genuinely believed that the "family wage," by which the male head of household received a salary sufficient to support his wife and children, was the best hope for society and for working women. Yet, as upwardly mobile black and immigrant women discovered, when women's wages and their domestic labor became or were perceived as less essential to the family, the household became more clearly a den of inequity.[58]

This domesticated den, however, was the centerpiece of most bourgeois reform efforts. Aid was offered to individual families that most closely resembled the privatized ideal. Thus, alms were distributed to "respectable" families in impoverished neighborhoods. Birth control was dispensed to married women in stable relationships to remove the taint of promiscuity from family planning clinics. Poor women in urban and rural areas were forced to hide, limit, or relinquish their communal modes of child care and healing to gain access to public health programs, nursing services, and well-baby clinics. Americanization courses taught immigrant daughters to emulate bourgeois lifestyles and to evacuate the crowded stoops and communal kitchens for the privatized home.[59]

Finally, middle-class women, believing that they were essentially different from men, advocated the establishment of single-sex associations and thereby created divisions within the working-class communities they had entered supposedly to assist.[60] They were aided, no doubt, by working-class men who alternately excluded women from their class-based organizations, attempted to gain control of potentially successful working-class women's campaigns, or ignored women's issues in pursuit of their own agenda. Thus, in the garment workers' strike of 1908, union leaders offered support only after the women had walked off the job. In the tenants'-rights movement and the kosher-meat boycotts in New York City, women "pioneered as the organizers of protests," but men took over "when the higher levels of the structure first emerged."[61] In antilynching campaigns in the South, it was black women who fought to safeguard their male kin against false rape accusations and vigilante justice, while black men concentrated on gaining property and political rights.[62] Yet even the difficulties of organizing with same-class men did not necessarily ensure the success of women's cross-class alliances. Some working-class women remained in organizations dominated by men; some forged temporary alliances with more affluent women to achieve limited goals; and some struggled with the advantages and ambiguities of dual affiliations with same-class men and middle-class women. For instance, despite male takeover of the leadership positions in the tenant's-rights movement and the kosher-meat boycotts, women remained active in large numbers in both movements. Many black and white working-class women who joined forces with more affluent women in the antilynching crusade or the Women's Trade Union League remained active only until their immediate goal was achieved. Those working-class women who attempted to maintain dual affiliations with same-class men and other-class women did so at great personal cost.[63]

Whichever path working-class women chose, they demonstrated the limits of any universal notion of sisterhood. That women attempted cross-class alliances more frequently than men cannot be doubted and does indicate certain commonalities in the experience of womanhood in North America in the nineteenth and early twentieth centuries. Yet evidence from the lives of slaves, mill operatives, miners' wives, immigrants, and southern industrial workers as well as from "true women" indicates that there was no single woman's culture or sphere. There was a culturally dominant definition of sexual spheres promulgated by an economically, politically, and socially dominant group. That definition was firmly grounded in the sexual division of labor appropriate to that class, just as other definitions developed based on the sexual division of labor in other class and racial groups. All of these divisions were characterized by sufficient sex stereotyping to ensure the formation of distinct female circles of labor and distinct rituals and values rooted in that laboring experience. To date historians have focused on the parallels in the establishment of women's spheres across classes, races, and ethnic groups and have asserted certain commonalities among them, assuming their common origin in the modernization of society during the nineteenth century. A closer examination now reveals that no such universal sisterhood existed, and that in fact the development of a sense of community among various classes of women served as a barrier to an all-embracing bond of womanhood. Finally, it is now clear that privileged women were willing to wield their sex-specific influence in ways that, intentionally or unintentionally, exploited other women in the name of "true womanhood."

The quest to integrate women into historical analysis has already moved beyond the search for sisterhood. Yet like charitable ladies, plantation mistresses, settlement house residents, and Women's Trade Union League founders of the nineteenth and early twentieth centuries, women's historians continue to employ the rhetoric of community despite the reality of conflict. In highlighting the importance of collective action for women and the centrality of woman-constructed networks for community-wide campaigns, feminist scholars have demonstrated women's historical agency. Now we must recognize that that agency is not only our legacy but also our labrys, and like any double-edged weapon, it cuts both ways: Women influenced and advocated change, but they did so within the context of their particular social and material circumstances.

Sisterhood—the sharing of essential emotional and economic resources among females—was central to the lives of nearly all groups of American women from the antebellum era to the early twentieth century and was rooted in the sexual division of labor in the family, the workplace, the community, and the political arena. It was during this same period that cultural elites sought to impose a universal definition of the female character on society at large through the "cult of true womanhood." If women's historians now accept that ideology as the basis for cross-class and interracial sisterhood, we only extend the hegemony of the antebellum bourgeoisie. To recognize and illuminate the realities of all women's historical experience, we must instead acknowledge that for most nineteenth- and early-twentieth-century women, and their modern counterparts, community was more a product of material conditions and constraints than of ideological dictates, and that therefore diversity, discontinuity, and conflict were as much a part of the historical agency of women as of men.

Notes to Introduction

1. Jacquelyn Dowd Hall, "Partial Truths," *Signs* 14, 4 (1989): 902–11.
2. Lise Vogel, "Telling Tales: Historians of Their Own Lives," *Journal of Women's History* 2 (winter 1991): 94–96. Her essay was part of a larger forum entitled "Dialogue: History and Theory."
3. This is obviously a very partial list compiled to highlight the diverse backgrounds of women activists documented in historical literature today. References to the work of these authors, and many others, can be found in the selected bibliographies at the end of this volume.
4. See, for example, Kathleen Blee, *Women of the Klan: Racism and Gender in the 1920s* (Berkeley: University of California Press, 1991); Rebecca E. Klatch, *Women of the New Right* (Philadelphia: Temple University Press, 1987); Nancy MacLean, *Behind the Mask of Chivalry: The Making of the Second Ku Klux Klan* (New York: Oxford University Press, 1994); and Kirsten Delegard, "Women Patriots: Female Anti-Radicals and the Politics of Nationalism, 1919–1939" (Ph.D. diss., Duke University, 1999).

Notes

I would like to thank Ron Atkinson, Ardis Cameron, Wendy Goldman, Steven Lawson, and Marcus Rediker for their thoughtful readings of many drafts of this article and for their faith in its completion. Geoff Eley and the participants in the "Communities of Women" session at the Sixth Berkshire Conference on the History of Women were also essential sources of encouragement and ideas.
1. The classic statements include Kate Millett, *Sexual Politics* (Garden City, N.Y.: Doubleday, 1970); Shulamith Firestone, *The Dialectic of Sex: The Case for Feminist Revolution* (New York: William Morrow, 1970); Susan Brownmiller, *Against Our Will: Men, Women, and Rape* (New York: Simon and Schuster, 1975); Robin Morgan, ed., *Sisterhood Is Powerful: An Anthology* (New York: Vintage, 1970); and Shulamith Firestone and

Anne Koedt, eds., *Notes from the Second Year: Major Writings of Radical Feminists* (New York: Radical Feminist Publications, 1979). Only in the late 1970s did significant numbers of feminist scholars in the United States begin seriously to consider socialist perspectives in their discussions of women's oppression; an integrated socialist-feminist analysis is distant and, moreover, is not a goal of a major portion of American feminist scholars. See, for example, Lydia Sargent, ed., *Women and Revolution: A Discussion of the Unhappy Marriage of Marxism and Feminism* (Boston: South End Press, 1981), and Zillah Eisenstein, ed., *Capitalist Patriarchy and the Case for Socialist Feminism* (New York: Monthly Review Press, 1979).

2. The quote and the clearest statement of its implications can be found in Nancy Cott, *The Bonds of Womanhood: "Woman's Sphere" in New England, 1780–1835* (New Haven: Yale University Press, 1977), 1. For examples of early historical studies of patriarchy and patriarchal institutions, see Lois Banner and Mary Hartman, eds., *Clio's Consciousness Raised* (New York: Harper and Row, 1974); Berenice A. Carroll, ed., *Liberating Women's History: Theoretical and Critical Essays* (Chicago: University of Illinois Press, 1976); and the entire issue of *Feminist Studies* 3, 1–2 (1975).

3. The antebellum period, roughly 1820 to 1860, has received the most attention from women's historians.

4. This position has been articulated most clearly with reference to race. See, for example, Bonnie Thornton Dill, "Race, Class, and Gender: Prospects for an All-Inclusive Sisterhood," *Feminist Studies* 9 (spring 1983): 131–50; Phyllis Marynick Palmer, "White Women/Black Women: The Dualism of Female Identity and Experience in the United States," *Feminist Studies* 9 (spring 1983): 151–70; Berenice Fisher, "Guilt and Shame in the Women's Movement: The Radical Idea of Action and Its Meaning for Feminist Intellectuals," *Feminist Studies* 10 (summer 1984): 185–212. For a debate on the concept of women's culture by leading women's historians, see Ellen DuBois, Mari Jo Buhle, Temma Kaplan, Gerda Lerner, and Carroll Smith-Rosenberg, "Politics and Culture in Women's History: A Symposium," *Feminist Studies* 6 (spring 1980): 26–84. While most black women are also working women or working-class women, the studies of black women in the United States have generally focused specifically on slavery or on cultural aspects of black life. Studies of working-class women, on the other hand, have almost always focused on white women. A recent exception is Dolores Janiewski, *Sisterhood Denied: Race, Class, and Gender in a New South Community* (Philadelphia: Temple University Press, 1985).

5. The quote is from Sara Evans, "Rethinking Women's Lives," *In These Times*, January 1983, 19–25, who was summarizing the current state of women's history for readers of this popular socialist weekly.

6. Barbara Welter, "The Cult of True Womanhood, 1820–1860," *American Quarterly* 18 (summer 1966): 151–74; Cott, *Bonds of Womanhood*; and Carroll Smith-Rosenberg, "The Female World of Love and Ritual: Relations between Women in Nineteenth-Century America," *Signs* 1 (autumn 1975): 1–29.

7. These concepts, though supposedly linked to the economic and social developments of the early 1800s, have been projected back into analyses of colonial women and forward to twentieth-century studies. See, for example, Mary Beth Norton, *Liberty's Daughters: The Revolutionary Experience of American Women, 1750–1800* (Boston: Little, Brown, 1980); Linda K. Kerber, "Daughters of Columbia: Educating Women for the Republic, 1787–1805, " in Stanley Elkins and Eric McKitrick, eds., *The Hofstadter Aegis: A Memorial* (New York: Alfred A. Knopf, 1974); Leslie Woodcock Tentler, *Wage-Earning Women: Industrial Work and Family Life in the United States, 1900–1930* (New York: Oxford University Press, 1979). Feminist anthropologists initially suggested that the division of men and women into public and private spheres might be even more timeless. See Michelle Zimbalist Rosaldo, "Woman, Culture, and Society: A Theoretical Overview," in Michelle Zimbalist Rosaldo and Louise Lamphere, eds., *Woman, Culture, and Society* (Stanford: Stanford University Press, 1974).

8. Cott, *Bonds of Womanhood*, 200.

9. The earliest suggestions of this position appear in Eleanor Flexner, *A Century of Struggle: The Women's Rights Movement in the United States* (Cambridge, Mass.: Harvard University Press, 1959), and Andrew Sinclair, *The Emancipation of the American Woman* (New York: Harper and Row, 1965). More detailed studies based on the doctrine of woman's sphere can be found in Barbara Epstein, *The Politics of Domesticity: Women, Evangelicalism, and Temperance in Nineteenth-Century America* (Middletown, Conn.: Wesleyan University Press, 1981); Blanche Glassman Hersh, *The Slavery of Sex: Feminist-Abolitionists in America* (Urbana: University of Illinois Press, 1978); Keith E. Melder, *Beginnings of Sisterhood: The American Woman's Rights Movement, 1800–1849* (New York: Schocken, 1977); and Carroll Smith-Rosenberg, *Religion and the Rise of the City: The New York City Mission Movement, 1812–1870* (Ithaca, N.Y.: Cornell University Press, 1971).

10. See, for example, Flexner, *Century of Struggle*; Allen F. Davis, *Spearheads for Reform: The Social Settlements and the Progressive Movement, 1890–1914* (New York: Oxford University Press, 1967); Maxine Seller, "The Education of the Immigrant Woman, 1900–1935," in Linda Kerber and Jane Mathews, eds., *Women's America: Refocusing the Past* (New York: Oxford University Press, 1982); Ruth Borden, *Women and Temperance: The Quest for Power and Liberty, 1873–1900* (Philadelphia: Temple University Press, 1980); Mari Jo

Buhle, *Women and American Socialism, 1870–1920* (Urbana: University of Illinois Press, 1981); and Anne Firor Scott, *Making the Invisible Woman Visible* (Urbana: University of Illinois Press, 1984).

11. Quote from Suzanne Lebsock, *The Free Women of Petersburg: Status and Culture in a Southern Town, 1784–1860* (New York: W. W. Norton,1984), xix. See also Anne Firor Scott, "Women's Perspective on Patriarchy in the 1850s," in Jean E. Friedman and William G. Shade, eds., *Our American Sisters: Women in American Life and Thought*, 3rd ed. (Lexington, Mass.: D. C. Heath, 1982); for an overstated example, see Catherine Clinton, *The Plantation Mistress: Woman's World in the Old South* (New York: Pantheon, 1983).

12. Meredith Tax, *The Rising of the Women: Feminist Solidarity and Class Conflict, 1880–1917* (New York: Monthly Review Press, 1980), 7.

13. Quote from the middle-class leaders of the Women's Trade Union League in Robin Miller Jacoby, "The Women's Trade Union League and American Feminism," in Milton Cantor and Bruce Laurie, eds., *Class, Sex, and the Woman Worker* (Westport, Conn.: Greenwood Press, 1971), 205, 206.

14. Johnny Mack Faragher and Christine Stansell, "Women and Their Families on the Overland Trail to California and Oregon, 1842–1867," in Nancy Cott and Elizabeth Pleck, eds., *A Heritage of Her Own: Towards a New Social History of American Women* (New York: Simon and Schuster, 1979); Julie Roy Jeffrey, review in *Signs* 8 (autumn 1982): 143–46; Nancy Cott, " Young Women in the Second Great Awakening in New England," *Feminist Studies* 3 (fall 1975): 15–29; Anne M. Boylan, "Evangelical Womanhood in the Nineteenth Century: The Role of Women in Sunday Schools," *Feminist Studies* 4 (October 1978): 62–80; Anne M. Boylan, "Women in Groups: An Analysis of Women's Benevolent Organizations in New York and Boston, 1797–1840," *Journal of American History* 71 (December 1984): 497–523; Marion B. Goldman, *Gold Diggers and Silver Miners: Prostitution and Social Life on the Comstock Lode* (Ann Arbor: University of Michigan Press, 1981); Thomas Dublin, "Women, Work and Protest in the Early Lowell Mills: 'The Oppressing Hand of Avarice Would Enslave Us,'" in Milton Cantor and Bruce Laurie, eds., *Class, Sex, and the Woman Worker* (Westport, Conn.: Greenwood Press, 1971); Ardis Cameron, "Women 's Culture and Working-Class Activism" (paper presented at the annual meeting of the Social Science History Association, Washington, D.C., November 1983); and Judith Smith, "Our Own Kind: Family and Community Networks in Providence," *Radical History Review* 17 (spring 1978): 99–120. Similar patterns for England and France are traced in Ellen Ross, "Survival Networks: Women's Neighborhood Sharing in London before World War I," *History Workshop* 15 (spring 1983): 4–27; Olwen Hufton, "Women and the Family Economy," *French Historical Studies* 9 (spring 1975): 1–22; and Bonnie G. Smith, *Ladies of the Leisure Class: The Bourgeoises in Northern France in the Nineteenth Century* (Princeton: Princeton University Press, 1981).

15. Quote from Rayna Rapp, Ellen Ross, and Renata Bridenthal, "Examining Family History," in Judith Newton, Mary Ryan, and Judith Walkowitz, eds., *Sex and Class in Women's History* (New York: Routledge and Kegan Paul, 1983), 244.

16. Quote from *Report of the Woman's Rights Convention, Held at Seneca Falls, N.Y., 19 and 20 July 1848* (Rochester, N.Y.: John Dick, 1848). See also Carroll Smith-Rosenberg, "Beauty, the Beast and the Militant Woman: A Case Study in Sex Roles and Social Stress in Jacksonian America," *American Quarterly* 23 (October 1971): 562–84; Melder, *Beginnings of Sisterhood*; and Nancy A. Hewitt, *Women's Activism and Social Change: Rochester, New York, 1822–1872* (Ithaca, N.Y.: Cornell University Press, 1984).

17. Quoted in Dublin, "Women, Work and Protest," 52. See also Cameron, "Women's Culture"; Tax, *Rising of the Women*, chs. 8 and 9; and Elizabeth Jameson, "Imperfect Unions: Class and Gender in Cripple Creek, 1894–1904," in Milton Cantor and Bruce Laurie, eds., *Class, Sex, and the Woman Worker* (Westport, Conn.: Greenwood Press, 1971).

18. Among the most influential works using a modernization framework are Cott, *Bonds of Womanhood*; Smith-Rosenberg, "Beauty, the Beast and the Militant Woman"; Carl Degler, *At Odds: Women and the Family in America from the Revolution to the Present* (New York: Oxford University Press, 1980); Aileen S. Kraditor, ed., *Up from the Pedestal* (New York: Quadrangle, 1968); and Daniel Scott Smith, "Family Limitation, Sexual Control, and Domestic Feminism in Victorian America," *Feminist Studies* 1 (winter–spring 1973): 40–57. Cott is the most explicit in acknowledging her debt to historical modernization literature (*Bonds of Womanhood*, 3–5).

19. For examples of historical modernization literature, see Richard D. Brown, "Modernization and the Modern Personality in Early America, 1600–1865, " *Journal of Interdisciplinary History* 11 (1972): 201–28; and Fred Weinstein and Gerald Platt, *The Wish to Be Free: Society, Psyche, and Value Change* (Berkeley: University of California Press, 1969). For a statement of the general theory, see Cyril E. Black, *The Dynamics of Modernization* (New York: Free Press, 1966); and Alex Inkeles, "Making Men Modern: On the Causes and Consequences of Individual Change in Six Developing Countries, " *American Journal of Sociology* 75 (1969): 208–25.

20. Jesse Lemisch, "The American Revolution Seen from the Bottom Up, " in Barton J. Bernstein, ed., *Towards a New Past: Dissenting Essays in American History* (New York: Vintage, 1967).

21. This dichotomization has affected both European and American women. See, for example, Barbara Ehren-reich and Deirdre English, *For Her Own Good: 150 Years of Advice to Women* (Garden City, N.Y.: Doubleday, 1979), ch. 2, and Leonore Davidoff, "Class and Gender in Victorian England," in Judith Newton, Mary Ryan and Judith Walkowitz, eds., *Sex and Class in Women's History* (New York: Routledge and Kegan Paul, 1983).

22. Quote from Jean E. Jackson, review in *Signs* 9 (winter 1983), 304. See also Karen Sacks, *Sisters and Wives: The Past and Future of Sexual Equality* (Westport, Conn.: Greenwood Press, 1979); and Lourdes Benéria and Gita Sens, "Class and Gender Inequalities and Women's Role in Economic Development: Theoretical and Practical Implications," *Feminist Studies* 8 (spring 1982): 152–76.

23. See, for example, Alice Kessler-Harris, *Out to Work: A History of Wage-Earning Women in America* (New York: Oxford University Press, 1982), preface; Rapp, Ross, and Bridenthal, "Examining Family History," 233; Jean E. Friedman, "Women's History and the Revision of Southern History," in Joanne Hawks and Sheila Skemp, eds., *Sex, Race, and the Role of Women in the South* (Jackson: University of Michigan Press, 1983); and Elizabeth H. Pleck, "Women's History: Gender as a Category of Historical Analysis," in James B. Gardner and George Rollie Adams, eds., *Ordinary People and Everyday Life: Perspectives on the New Social History* (Nashville, Tenn.: American Association of State and Local History, 1983).

24. Among those questioning the degree of separation between men's and women's spheres in the middle class are Hewitt, *Women's Activism and Social Change*; Mary P. Ryan, *Cradle of the Middle Class: Family and Commu-nity in Oneida County, New York, 1780–1865* (Cambridge: Cambridge University Press, 1981); Tyler May, "Expanding the Past: Recent Scholarship on Women in Politics and Work," *Reviews in American History* (December 1982): 216–33; and Ellen K. Rothman, "Sex and Self-control: Middle-class Courtship in Amer-ica, 1770–1870," *Journal of Social History* 15 (spring 1982): 409–25. On evidence of class prejudice among women, see Aileen S. Kraditor, *The Ideas of the Woman Suffrage Movement, 1890–1920* (New York: Columbia University Press, 1965), chs. 6 and 7; Hewitt, *Women's Activism*, ch. 5; Jacoby, "The Women's Trade Union League," 218–21; and Linda Gordon and Ellen DuBois, "Seeking Ecstasy on the Battlefield: Danger and Pleasure in Nineteenth-Century Feminist Sexual Thought," *Feminist Studies* 9 (spring 1983): 7–25.

25. See, for example, Angela Y. Davis, *Women, Race, and Class* (New York: Random House, 1981); Dill, "Race, Class and Gender"; Edwards, *Rape, Racism, and the White Women's Movement: An Answer to Susan Brown-miller* (Chicago: Sojourner Truth Organization, n.d.); Friedman, "Women's History and the Revision of Southern History"; Sharon Harley and Rosalyn Terborg-Penn, eds., *The Afro-American Woman: Struggles and Images* (Port Washington, N.Y.: Kennikat Press, 1978); bell hooks, *Ain't I a Woman: Black Women and Feminism* (Boston: South End Press, 1981); Gloria T. Hull, Patricia Bell Scott, and Barbara Smith, eds., *All the Women Are White, All the Men Are Black, but Some of Us Are Brave: Black Women's Studies* (Old Westbury, N.Y.: Feminist Press, 1982); Gerda Lerner, *The Majority Finds Its Past* (New York: Oxford University Press, 1979), chs. 5, 6, and 7; Palmer, "White Woman/Black Women"; and Rennie Simson, "The Afro-American Woman: The Historical Context of the Construction of Sexual Identity," in Ann Snitow, Christine Stansell, and Sharon Thompson, eds., *Powers of Desire* (New York: Monthly Review Press, 1983).

26. Throughout this article I will be employing Frederick Engels's definition of production, which has a dual character; "on the one side, the production of the means of existence, of food, clothing, and shelter and the tools necessary for that production; on the other side, the production of human beings themselves, the propagation of the species." Under this latter, I also include social reproduction, which embraces child rear-ing and domestic labor as well as childbearing. Quoted in Frederick Engels, *The Origin of the Family, Private Property and the State*, ed. Eleanor Leacock (New York: International Publishers, 1972).

27. Quote from Deborah White, "Female Slaves: Sex Roles and Status in the Antebellum Plantation South," *Journal of Family History*, fall 1983, 248–61. I am indebted to White's analysis throughout the section on slave women. See also Davis, *Women, Race and Class*; John W. Blassingame, *The Slave Community: Plantation Life in the Antebellum South* (New York: Oxford University Press, 1972); Herbert Gutman, *The Black Family in Slavery and Freedom, 1750–1925* (New York: Pantheon, 1976); Eugene Genovese, *Roll, Jordan, Roll: The World the Slaves Made* (New York: Vintage, 1972); and Gerda Lerner, ed., *Black Women in White America* (New York: Vintage, 1972), 7–72.

28. White, "Female Slaves," 251–53.

29. While black women were assigned to men's work in the fields, especially during busy seasons, black men were apparently never assigned to women's work in the household, even under dire circumstances.

30. For slave testimony, see Linda Brent [Harriet Brent Jacobs], *Incidents in the Life of a Slave Girl*, ed. Lydia Maria Child (Boston, 1861); and Elizabeth Keckley, *Behind the Scenes* (New York: G. W. Carleton, 1868). Both are analyzed in Simson, "Afro-American Woman." See also Lerner, *Black Women*, 47–51, 150–63; and Lebsock, *Free Women of Petersburg* (1984), introduction.

31. On the transition to male physicians among affluent whites and the resulting effects on female rituals, see Catharine M. Scholten, "'On the Importance of the Obstetrick Art' : Changing Customs of Childbirth in America, 1760–1825," *William and Mary Quarterly* 34 (1977): 426–45.

32. On black motherhood, see White, "Female Slaves," 256–58; Cheryll Ann Cody, "Naming, Kinship, and Estate Dispersal: Notes on Slave Family Life on a South Carolina Plantation, 1786 to 1833," *William and Mary Quarterly* 31 (1982): 192–211; Genovese, *Roll, Jordan, Roll*; and Gutman, *The Black Family*. For a comparison of southern white men's and women's roles in child rearing, see Smith, "Autonomy and Affection" (1983). On contemporary black women's views of mothering, see Carol Stack, *All Our Kin: Strategies for Survival in a Black Community* (New York: Harper, 1974), and Black Women's Liberation Group, "Statement on Birth Control," in Robin Morgan, ed., *Sisterhood Is Powerful: An Anthology* (New York: Vintage, 1970).

33. See White, "Female Slaves," 256–58. On similar patterns in African cultures, see Sacks, *Sisters and Wives*.

34. See Simson, "Afro-American Woman," and Lebsock, *Free Women of Petersburg*, 139–40.

35. Throughout the rest of this article, *same-class* will be used to identify women and men of the same ethnicity and race as well as the same economic status.

36. Quote from Cameron, "Women's Culture," 6. See also Dublin, "Women, Work, and Protest."

37. See, for example, Cameron, "Women's Culture"; Jameson, "Imperfect Unions"; Ross, "Survival Networks"; and Smith, "Our Own Kind."

38. Kessler-Harris, *Out to Work*, 160. For other examples, see 247–48.

39. For a brilliant analysis of the conflicts between male unionists and women workers, see Alice Kessler-Harris, "Where Are the Organized Women Workers?" *Feminist Studies* 3 (fall 1975): 92–110. See also Patricia Cooper, "From Hand Craft to Mass Production: Men, Women, and Work Culture in American Cigar Factories, 1900–1919" (Ph.D. diss., University of Maryland, 1981). For a discussion of male-female cooperation, see Johanna Brenner and Maria Ramas, "Rethinking Women's Oppression," *New Left Review* 144 (March–April 1984): 44–49.

40. See, for example, Dublin, "Women, Work and Protest," 58–61; Daniel J. Walkowitz, *Worker City, Company Town: Iron and Cotton Worker Protest in Troy and Cohoes, New York, 1855–1884* (Urbana: University of Illinois Press, 1978), chs. 3–5; Kessler-Harris, "Where Are the Organized Women Workers?" 100 and n. 34; and Dolores Janiewski, "Sisters under Their Skins: Southern Working Women, 1880–1950," in Joanne Hawks and Sheila Skemp, eds., *Sex, Race, and the Role of Women in the South* (Jackson: University of Mississippi Press, 1983).

41. Quote from Cameron, "Women's Culture," 10–11. See also Jameson, "Imperfect Unions," especially 191–93.

42. On prostitutes, quote is from Jeffrey, review in *Signs*, 146. On miners' wives' responses, see Jameson, "Imperfect Unions," 180, 184–86, and 188–89.

43. Quoted in Dublin, "Women, Work and Protest," 53.

44. Janiewski, "Sisters under Their Skins," 26, 29–30.

45. See Ryan, *Cradle of the Middle Class*, chs. 4 and 5; and Hewitt, *Women's Activism*, ch. 7.

46. On changes in domestic work and domestic servitude, see Susan Strasser, *Never Done: A History of American Housework* (New York: Pantheon, 1982); and Faye Dudden, *Serving Women: Household Service in Nineteenth-Century America* (Middletown, Conn.: Wesleyan University Press, 1983). In addition, women had less help from children with the expansion of public education. For an analysis of the variation in (or lack of) hours spent on housework as a result of technological changes, see Heidi Hartmann, "The Family as a Locus of Gender, Class, and Political Struggle: The Example of Housework," *Signs* 6 (spring 1981): 366–94, and Joann Vanek, "Time Spent in Housework," *Scientific American*, November 1974, 116–21.

47. Judith Sargent Murray, a late-eighteenth-century educator, quoted in Kerber, "Daughters of Liberty," 91.

48. On the first effect, see Nancy Cott, "Passionlessness: An Interpretation of Victorian Sexual Ideology, 1790 to 1850," *Signs* 55 (1978): 219–36; and Smith, "Family Limitation." On the second, see Anne L. Kuhn, *The Mother's Role in Childhood Education: New England Concepts, 1830–1860* (New Haven: Yale University Press, 1974); Nancy Folbre, "Of Patriarchy Born: The Political Economy of Fertility Decisions," *Feminist Studies* 9 (summer 1983): 261–84; Wanda Minge-Kalman, "The Industrial Revolution and the European Family: The Institutionalization of 'Childhood' as a Market for Family Labor," *Comparative Studies in Society and History* 20 (July 1978): 454–67; and Ryan, *Cradle of the Middle Class*, ch. 5.

49. Quote from Dr. Benjamin Rush in Kerber, "Daughters of Columbia," 91, and Ryan, *Cradle of the Middle Class*, 148.

50. Numerous community studies, both published and in progress, make this point clearly. See particularly Hewitt, *Women's Activism*; Scott, *Making the Invisible Woman Visible*; and Ryan, *Cradle of the Middle Class*. Current research on Cincinnati by Caroline Blum and on St. Louis by Marion Hunt provides further evidence.

51. Quoted in Hewitt, *Women's Activism*, 17, 189–90, 209; see also 243–52 generally.

52. See Hewitt, *Women's Activism*, ch. 7; Ryan, *Cradle of the Middle Class*, ch. 3.

53. Judith L. Newton, Mary P. Ryan, and Judith R. Walkowitz, eds., *Sex and Class in Women's History* (New York: Routledge and Kegan Paul, 1983), 9.

54. On the development of the "decentralized home system," see Hartmann, "The Family as the Locus of Gender, Class and Political Struggle."

55. See, for example, Kathryn Kish Sklar, *Catharine Beecher: A Study in American Domesticity* (New Haven: Yale University Press, 1973); Mary Kelley, *Private Woman, Public Stage: Literary Domesticity in Nineteenth-Century America* (New York: Oxford University Press, 1984); and Mary E. Young, "Women, Civilization, and the Indian Question," in Linda Kerber and Jane Mathews, eds., *Women's America: Refocusing the Past* (New York: Oxford University Press, 1982).

56. See Gordon and DuBois, "Seeking Ecstasy on the Battlefield"; Mary P. Ryan, "The Power of Women's Networks: A Case Study of Female Moral Reform in America," *Feminist Studies* 4 (spring 1979): 66–86; Linda Gordon, *Woman's Body, Woman's Right: A Social History of Birth Control in America* (New York: Grossman, 1976); and Borden, *Women and Temperance*. The outstanding example of moral reform studies, focused on England, is Judith R. Walkowitz, *Prostitution and Victorian Society: Women, Class and the State* (New York: Cambridge University Press, 1980). Early investigations into working-class and minority groups suggest that they construct their sexuality and morality differently than the bourgeoisie. See, for instance, Jed Dannenbaum, "The Origins of Temperance Activism and Militancy among American Women," *Journal of Social History* 14 (winter 1981): 235–52; Martin B. Duberman, Fred Eggan, and Richard Clemmer, "Documents in Hopi Sexuality: Imperialism, Culture, and Resistance," *Radical History Review* 20 (spring–summer 1979): 99–130; Kathy Peiss, "'Charity Girls' and City Pleasures: Historical Notes on Working-Class Women's Sexuality, 1880–1920," in Ann Snitow, Christine Stansell, and Sharon Thompson, eds., *Powers of Desire* (New York: Monthly Review Press, 1983); and Simson, "Afro-American Woman."

57. See Kessler-Harris, "Where Are the Organized Women Workers?"; Jacoby, "Women's Trade Union League"; and Nancy Schrom Dye, "Creating a Feminist Alliance: Sisterhood and Class Conflict in the New York Women's Trade Union League, 1903–1914," in Milton Cantor and Bruce Laurie, eds., *Class, Sex, and the Woman Worker* (Westport, Conn.: Greenwood Press, 1971).

58. Cameron has found evidence of immigrant women's opposition to the "family wage" in Lawrence, Massachusetts, in the 1880s based on women's fear of losing power in the family (personal correspondence with the author). On changes in status with upward mobility, see especially Rosalyn Terborg-Penn, "Black Male Perspectives on the Nineteenth-Century Woman," in Sharon Harley and Rosalyn Terborg-Penn, eds., *The Afro-American Woman: Struggles and Images* (Port Washington, N.Y.: Kennikat Press, 1978), and Lerner, *Black Women*, 290–94. For the importance of women's control of economic resources to their status in society, see Sacks, *Sisters and Wives*, and Judith K. Brown, "Iroquois Women: An Ethnohistoric Note," in Rayna B. Reiter, ed., *Toward an Anthropology of Women* (New York: Monthly Review Press, 1975).

59. See Hewitt, *Women's Activism*, ch. 7; Gordon, *Woman's Body*, chs. 9 and 10; Sondra Zeidenstein, ed., *Learning about Rural Women* (New York: Population Council, 1979), introduction; and Seller, "Education of the Immigrant Woman" (1982).

60. The vast majority of charitable, missionary, moral reform, temperance, and antislavery societies were single-sex associations in the antebellum era, as were the largest such organizations at the turn of the century—the women's clubs, temperance societies, and suffrage associations. For this same pattern in these and other movements, see Estelle Freedman, "Separation as Strategy: Female Institution Building and American Feminism, 1870–1930," *Feminist Studies* 5 (fall 1979): 512–29.

61. Quote from Ronald Lawson and Stephen E. Barton, "Sex Roles in Social Movements: A Case Study of the Tenant Movement in New York City," *Signs* 6 (winter 1980), 231. See also Tax, *Rising of the Women*, ch. 6, and Paula Hyman, "Immigrant Women and Consumer Protest: The New York City Kosher Meat Boycott of 1902," *American Jewish History* 70 (September 1980): 91–105.

62. See Davis, *Women, Race, and Class*, ch. 11. On black women's struggles to work with black men and/or white women, see Cynthia Neverdon-Morton, "The Black Women's Struggle for Equality in the South, 1895–1925," in Sharon Harley and Rosalyn Terborg-Penn, eds., *The Afro-American Woman: Struggles and Images* (Port Washington, N.Y.: Kennikat Press, 1978); Ida B. Wells Barnett, *On Lynching* (New York: Arno Press, 1969); and Jacquelyn Dowd Hall, *Revolt against Chivalry: Jessie Daniel Ames and the Women's Campaign against Lynching* (New York: Columbia University Press, 1979). An excellent summary of differences in black men's and women's approach to public activism was presented by Darlene Clark Hines at the Southern Historical Association meetings in Charleston, South Carolina, in November 1983.

63. See, for example, Kessler-Harris, "Organizing the Unorganizable" (1971).

2

"This Evil Extends Especially to the Feminine Sex": Captivity and Identity in New Mexico, 1700–1846

James F. Brooks

Late in the summer of 1760, a large Comanche raiding party besieged the fortified *placita* of Pablo Villalpando in the village of Ranchos de Taos, New Mexico. After a day-long fight, the Comanches breached the walls and killed most of the male defenders. They then seized fifty-seven women and children, among whom was twenty-one-year-old María Rosa Villalpando, Pablo's second daughter, and carried them into captivity on the Great Plains. María's young husband, Juan José Xacques, was slain in the assault, but her infant son, José Juliano Xacques, somehow escaped both death and captivity.

The Comanches apparently traded María shortly thereafter to the Pawnees, for by 1767 she was living in a Pawnee village on the Platte River and had borne another son, who would come to be known as Antoine. In that year, the French trader and cofounder of St. Louis, Jean Salé dit Leroie, visited the Pawnees and began cohabiting with María. About a year later she bore Salé a son, whom they named Lambert. This arrangement apparently suited Salé's trading goals, for it wasn't until 1770 that he ended María's Indian captivity and brought her to St. Louis, where they married.

Jean and María (now Marie Rose Salé) had three more children before, for reasons unknown, Jean returned to France, where he remained the rest of his life. María stayed in St. Louis to become the matriarch of an increasingly prominent family. She died at the home of her daughter Helene in 1830, at well over ninety years of age. For María Rosa, captivity had yielded a painful, yet ultimately successful, passage across cultures into security and longevity.[1]

This chapter explores the role captive women such as María Rosa played in promoting conflict and accommodation between colonial Spanish (and later Mexican) society and the indigenous people of greater New Mexico. During the Spanish and Mexican occupation of the region, thousands of Indian and hundreds of Spanish women and children "crossed cultures" through the workings of a captive-exchange system that knit diverse communities into vital, and violent, webs of interdependence. These captives, whether of Spanish origin or Native Americans "ransomed" by the Spanish at *rescates* (trade fairs), proved crucial to a borderlands political economy that utilized human beings in far-reaching social and economic exchange.

Developing in the wake of Spanish slave raids and Indian reprisals, over time this commerce in captives provided the basis for a gradual convergence of cultural interests and identities at the village level, emerging in borderlands communities of interest by the middle years of the nineteenth century. Seen as both the most valuable "commodities" in intersocietal trade *and* as key transcultural actors in their own right, captive women and children participated in a terrifying, yet at times fortuitous, colonial dialectic between exploitation and negotiation. Until now, their histories have lain in the shadows of border-lands historiography.[2] An examination of their lives may alter our understanding of colonial processes in New Mexico and elsewhere in North America.

Whatever the large-scale antagonisms between European colonists and Native Americans, at the local level problems of day-to-day survival required methods of cross-cultural negotiation. Prolonged, intensive interaction between New Mexican *pobladores* (village settlers) and nomadic-pastoral Indian societies required some mutually intelligible symbols through which cultural values, interests, and needs could be defined. Horses, guns, and animal hides spring immediately to mind as traditional symbols of exchange, but women and children proved even more valuable—and valorized—as both agents and objects of cultural negotiation. In New Mexico, as elsewhere in North America, the exchange of women through systems of captivity, adoption, and marriage provided European and native men with mutually understood symbols of power with which to bridge cultural barriers.[3]

Rival men had exchanged women and seized captives long before European colonialism in North America. The exogamous exchange of women between "precapitalist" societies appears to represent a phenomenon by which mutual obligations of reciprocity are established between kindreds, bands, and societies, serving both to reinforce male dominance and to extend the reproductive (social and biological) vigor of communities.[4] The capture and integration of women and children seems the most violent expression along a continuum of such exchange traditions. This patriarchal subordination of women and children, it has been argued, served as a foundation upon which other structures of power and inequality were erected. Gerda Lerner contends that the assertion of male control over captive women's sexual and reproductive services provided a model for patriarchal ownership of women in "monogamous" marriages by which patrilineal bloodlines remained "pure." From this sense of proprietorship grew other notions of property, including the enslavement of human beings as chattels.[5]

In New Spain, under the *Recopilación* of 1680, Spanish subjects had been encouraged to redeem indigenous captives from their captors, baptize them into the Catholic faith, and acculturate them as new "detribalized" colonial subjects.[6] These redemptions occurred in roughly two forms: either through formal "ransoming" at annual trade fairs (*ferias* or *rescates*) or through small-scale bartering (*cambalaches*) in local villages or at trading places on the Great Plains. Trade fairs at Taos, Pecos, and Picuris Pueblos had long fostered the exchange of bison meal for corn, beans, and squash between Plains Indians and the Río Grande pueblos and had probably included some exchanges of people as well.[7]

These seasonal events continued after the Spanish conquest. Throughout the eighteenth century, Spanish church and secular authorities vied to gain control of this trade, variously blaming each other or local alcaldes for "the saddest of this commerce." In 1761 Fray Pedro Serrano chided the Spanish governors, who "when the fleet was in" scrambled to gather as many horses, axes, hoes, wedges, picks, bridles, and knives as possible in order to "gorge themselves on the great multitude of both sexes offered for sale."[8] Fifteen years later, Fray Atanasio Domínguez reported that the Comanches brought to Taos for sale "pagan Indians, of both sexes, whom they capture from other nations." The going rate of exchange, which seems to have held quite steady until the mid-nineteenth century, was "two good horses and some trifles" for an "Indian girl twelve to twenty years old." Captive boys usually brought a "she mule" or one horse and a "poor bridle . . . garnished with red rags." The general atmosphere, according to Domínguez, resembled a "second hand market in Mexico, the way people mill about."[9]

After 1800 formal *rescates* seem to decline, replaced with smaller, more frequent on-the-spot bartering. This seems to be due to several factors—Plains Indians' wish to avoid possible

Table 2.1 Baptisms of Selected Non-Pueblo Indians, 1700–1850

Tribe	1700–1750	1750–1800	1800–1850	Total
Apaches	632	260	87	979
Pawnees	18	2	3	23
Aas (Crows)	8	62	20	80
Kiowas	17	18	32	67
Comanches	14	179	33	226
Utes	11	63	551	625
Navajos	211	124	422	757
Total	911	708	1,148	2,757

Adapted from David M. Brugge, *Navajos in the Catholic Church Records of New Mexico, 1694–1875* (Tsaile, Ariz.: Navajo Community College Press, 1985), 22–23.

exposure to European American disease, a desire on the part of New Mexican villagers to escape taxation of their trade, and a geographical expansion of the borderlands economy. By the 1850s local traders such as José Lucero and Powler Sandoval would purchase Mexican captives from Comanches at Plains outposts including Quitaque in Floyd County, Texas, giving, for example, "one mare, one rifle, one shirt, one pair of drawers, thirty small packages of powder, some bullets, and one buffalo robe" in exchange for ten-year-old Teodoro Martel of Saltillo, Mexico.[10]

Judging from extant New Mexican parochial registers (Table 2.1), between 1700 and 1850 nearly three thousand members of nomadic or pastoral Indian groups entered New Mexican society as *indios de rescate*, *indios genízaros*, *criados*, or *huérfanos*, primarily through the artifice of "ransom" by colonial purchasers.[11] Ostensibly the cost of ransom would be retired by ten to twenty years of service to the redeemers, after which time these individuals would become *vecinos* (tithe-paying citizens). In practice, these people experienced their bondage on a continuum that ranged from near-slavery to familial incorporation, an issue that will be addressed at length in this essay.

Ransomed captives constituted an important component in colonial society, averaging some 10 to 15 percent of the colonial population. In the peripheral villages, they may have represented as much as 40 percent of the "Spanish" residents.[12] Girls and boys under the age of fifteen composed approximately two thirds of these captives, and some two thirds of all captives were women "of serviceable age," or prepubescent girls.[13]

This commerce in women and children was more than a one-way traffic, however. Throughout the period under consideration, nomadic groups such as the Comanches and Navajos made regular raids on the scattered *poblaciones*, at times seizing as many as fifty women and children.[14] In 1780 Spanish authorities estimated that the Naciones del Norte alone held more than 150 colonial subjects captive, and by 1830 the figure for the Comanches alone may have exceeded 500.[15] Among the Navajos, as late as 1883 Agent Dennis M. Riordan estimated that there were "300 slaves in the hands of the tribe," many of whom were "Mexicans captured in infancy."[16] Like their Indian counterparts, these women and children found themselves most often incorporated into their host society, apparently through indigenous systems of adoption. As fictive kin, they too experienced a range of treatment. It is impossible to arrive at precise numbers of New Mexican captives in Indian societies, but their representation becomes increasingly significant in a discussion of the workings of the captive system and of the personal experiences of captives themselves.

Although the captive-exchange system seems overwhelmingly complex when examined through particular cases, certain overall patterns seem consistent. First, captive taking and trading represented the most violent and exploitative component of a long-term pattern of militarized socioeconomic exchange between Indian and Spanish society. Second, it seems that New Mexican captives and *indios de rescate* generally remained in their "host" societies throughout their lifetimes. Third, female captives often established families within the host society, and their descendants usually became full culture-group members. Male captives, on the other hand, either suffered a quick retributive death or, if young, grew to become semiautonomous auxiliary warriors within their new society. Finally, it appears that many captives found ways to transcend their subordinate status by exercising skills developed during their "cross-cultural" experience. In doing so, they negotiated profound changes in the cultural identity of the societies within which they resided, changes that continue to reverberate in the borderlands today.

The Captive Experience

Torn from their natal societies in "slave" raids, treated like *piezas* (coins) in a volatile system of intercultural exchange, and finally the "property" of strangers, captive and ransomed women seem unlikely subjects as historical actors. But their experiences show them negotiating narrow fields of agency with noteworthy skill. From positions of virtual powerlessness, captive women learned quickly the range of movement allowed by the host culture, especially in regard to adoption and *compadrazgo* (godparenthood) practices. This first phase of integration gave them "kin" to whom they could turn for protection and guidance. But this security remained limited, and many faced coercive conjugal relationships, if not outright sexual exploitation by their new masters.

Whether of Spanish or Indian origin, two factors seem essential to understanding the lives of captives. First, captive status and treatment within the host society established the "structures of constraint" within which individuals might pursue their goals.[17] Second, sheer luck and the individual captive's personal resources determined the actual lived experience, ranging from terror and exploitation to a few remarkable cases of deft negotiation and good fortune, into which María Rosa Villalpando's story certainly falls. Overall, the interplay of structural constraints, contingency, and skills can be seen in most captives' lives. Another Nueva Mexicana, Juana Hurtado Galván, proved so adept at the cross-cultural enterprise that her story exemplifies successful adaptation.

Early in the summer of 1680, shortly before the conflagrations of the Pueblo Revolt, a band of "Apaches del Nabajo" swept down upon the rancho of Captain Andrés Hurtado and took captive his seven-year-old daughter, Juana.[18] For the next twelve years, her life among the Navajos lies concealed, a blank in the historical record that can only be reconstructed by inference and imagination. But those years of captivity seem to hold the key to understanding much of Juana's subsequent life, a long and controversial career that ended in 1753. When she died, Juana owned a rancho with three houses and extensive herds and flocks, and her illegitimate son Juan Galván served as the *teniente* (assistant magistrate) of the Zia district.[19] Nativity had given Juana linkages to both Spanish and Pueblo society, and in her captivity she developed linguistic and kinship ties with the Navajos. Throughout her life, her experience as a captive woman would afford her special negotiating skills with which she pursued security for her lineage.

Juana's mother had come from the pueblo of Zia, probably as a *criada* (domestic servant) of the *encomendero* Hurtado, but we know little more about her life.[20] No doubt sexually used by the *español*, she bore a daughter in 1673, just one among hundreds of such *coyotas* (children of mixed Spanish-Indian parentage) resulting from the Spanish colonization of

New Mexico. The mother's connection with Zia Pueblo, however, remained central to her daughter's story. After Juana's half-brother Martín, a soldier in the Spanish *reconquista* of 1692, ransomed Juana from captivity, the young woman petitioned for and received a private *merced* (land grant) at the northwest corner of the Zia Pueblo lands, near the village known today as San Ysidro.[21] This rancho proved a key locus of trade between Navajos, Pueblos, and Spanish *pobladores* for the next half century—and the source of Juana's wealth and influence.[22]

Although restored to colonial society, Juana never severed connections with her one-time captors. Frequent visits by Navajos to her rancho suggest that she had experienced adoption into a Navajo clan. She may even have married in captivity; she never formalized any future conjugal relationship. Kinship aside, her trilingual skills and cultural intermediacy facilitated economic exchanges between potential enemies. Her affinity with Navajos remained so close that Fray Miguel de Menchero commended her usefulness in assisting proselytization efforts: "They had kept her for so long [that] the Indians of said Nation make friendly visits to her, and in this way the father of the said mission has been able to instruct some of them."[23]

Juana's conduct, however, also attracted criticism from church authorities. Throughout her life, she persisted in maintaining a long-term liaison with a married man of Zia, presumably named Galván. By 1727, this relationship had resulted in four children and charges of scandalous behavior leveled against her by the padres. When authorities sought to place Juana in stocks, however, the people of Zia "threatened that the whole pueblo would move to the mesa tops, rather than have her mistreated."[24] Like the Navajos, the people of Zia saw tangible benefits in the presence of this kinswoman on their borders. Defining kinship more broadly than did the Spanish, they seemed willing to provoke conflict in defense of their relationship with someone who provided a bridge across three cultures. Drawing upon her qualities and talents as a negotiator, Juana "La Galvana" utilized her experience as a captive to carve out an intermediate niche in the complex power relations of colonial New Mexico.

Juana's intermediacy was accentuated by her mixed-blood status, and her paternal linkage to a Spanish *encomendero* probably allowed her the opportunity to occupy a privileged niche compared with many captives. Since one aspect of the captive system originates in indigenous, precontact exogamous exchange traditions, we need to look at gender and social hierarchies within native societies to begin to understand the structures of constraint that Juana and other captives might have experienced. Although they display variation, women's and captives' status within Indian societies of the borderlands (Navajo, Apache, Ute, and Comanche) may be generally described as subordinate to that of men and holders of the "cultural franchise" but enhanced by traditions of matrilineality and social mobility.[25]

Navajo patterns of gender and social hierarchies show a blending of Athabascan traditions and cultural adaptations to Spanish colonialism near their homelands. Navajo women owned the flocks of sheep and wove the textiles that formed the core of their pastoral economy. Matrilineal descent, therefore, conferred important productive resources as well as kin reckoning through women. Navajo men, however, prevailed in "public" decisions involving warfare and diplomacy.[26]

Captives taken in warfare with other tribes or the Spanish again experienced a range of treatment. If not killed in vengeance satisfaction, the captive invariably suffered a period of harsh and terrifying treatment. This "taming" process probably formed the first phase in adoption ritual.[27] After taming, most captives were inducted into the clan of their captor, or of the "rich man" who purchased them from the successful warrior. Once a captive had become a clan member, it seems few barriers stood in the way of social advancement. The

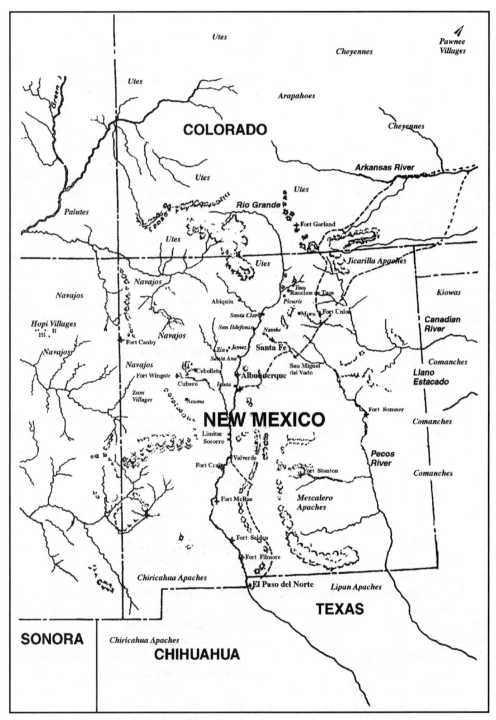

Figure 2.1. New Mexico, circa 1847

New Mexican captive Nakai Na'dis Saal, raised in a clan on Black Mesa, "became a singer of the Nightway," an important Navajo ceremony.[28] The Sonoran captive Jesús Arviso, taken by Chiricahua Apaches in 1850 as a boy and traded to the Navajo Kla clan, served as the principal interpreter for his host society throughout the Fort Sumner–Long Walk era. Marrying into the Nanasht'ezhii clan, he chose to remain a Navajo, welcoming a congressional delegation to Fort Defiance in 1919 and living at Cubero until his death in 1932.[29]

Captive women usually became clan members and married exogamously. Even if not inducted into clan membership, their children by Navajo men were considered members of the father's clan.[30] Although we can only speculate, these clan and kin affiliations probably provided Juana Hurtado with the networks that allowed her to act as an intermediary between Zia Pueblo and Spanish society. Indeed, Juana seems noteworthy among captives for having chosen to return to her birthright, for some sources indicate that many captives when "set free . . . immediately took the shortest trail back to the hogans of their masters."[31]

Captives seem to have fared less well among the Jicarilla Apaches, a semisedentary people who practiced a seasonal economy that balanced hunting and collecting with extensive horticulture. Apache women, however, benefited from matrilineality and ownership of fields and crops that "were planted, weeded, and harvested by the joint labors of the entire family." This gender-integrated labor diverged when men hunted or raided and women engaged in the life-cycle labor of family reproduction. While subordinate to men, women made important ritual contributions to the success of hunters: "[A] man and his wife pray together and smoke ceremonially before the husband leaves for the hunt. After his departure the woman continues a series of ritual duties." Likewise, before men departed for warfare or raiding, "a woman [was] chosen to represent each man to serve as proxy in group decisions, [and she] obeyed many restrictions in matters of dress, food, and behavior to ensure his safe return."[32]

Warfare among the Jicarillas often involved the seizure of captives, either for vengeance satisfaction or for cultural integration. Adult male captives "were tied to posts and slain by women with lances," but captive women and children found themselves incorporated into the band. A captive woman "could not be molested until she had been brought back and a ceremony . . . performed over her," probably some form of adoption that established her subordination within the Apachean levirate. Even with this adoption, captive women "were not considered fit wives. They were sexually used, and sent from camp to camp to do the heavy work. Their children by Apache men, however, were recognized as Jicarilla" and "accepted into Apache life."[33] We shall see that this second-generation integration appears nearly universal among the indigenous groups in question, and proves an important factor in captive women's decisions to remain within the host society even when offered their "freedom."

These patterns of gender and social subordination, mitigated by adoption and generational enfranchisement, are reiterated in an examination of Comanche society. Jane Collier has argued that women's status in Comanche society, as reflected through the dynamics of bridewealth marriage, "may best be understood in the context of relations between men."[34] Certainly the Comanches represent the most noteworthy case of Plains Indian individualism and status competition between men, where wife stealing often served as an intraband expression of a general cultural pattern.[35] E. A. Hoebel pointed out earlier, however, that although "before the law, [the] Comanche woman was a quasi-chattel," social custom allowed women a considerable degree of choice in extralegal activity.[36]

Both Collier and Hoebel overlooked evidence of women-centered status competition, a stretching of patriarchal structures of constraint. In half of the marital disputes Hoebel recorded, women had left their husbands for other men, often joining their lovers on war parties. In one case, the couple stayed away from the band for two years, and when they returned, the woman had fifteen horses in her personal string.[37] Women could also obtain horses (next to captives the most prestigious "commodity" in Comanche society) through the institution of the Shakedown Dance, whereby successful raiders were shamed into giving a part of their herd to young, unmarried women.[38] Status and prestige also accrued to women through the matrilineal transfer of medicine powers, as in the case of Sanapia, a Comanche Eagle Doctor.[39] These examples suggest that within male-defined structures of constraint, Comanche women exploited opportunities for competitive mobility and status enhancement. Captives, although initially lower in status, appear to have negotiated similar avenues of social mobility.

No other Plains society engaged in captive raiding as vigorously as did the Comanches. This seems a result of both individual status competition and the need to replace a population ravaged by warfare and epidemic disease.[40] Comanche society offered several social locations into which captives could be integrated, ranging from chattels to kinsmen and kinswomen.[41] Ralph Linton suggests that the prestige value of captives reflected their "importance in the social and economic life of the tribe. Mostly Mexican, they tended the horse herds and practiced most of the specialized industries such as gun repairing and saddle-making." The honored position of center-pole cutter in the Comanche Sun Dance went to either a "virtuous Comanche woman, a virtuous captive woman, [or] a captive man who had a number of war-deeds to his credit."[42] Among the Kiowas, a Plains group closely allied with the Comanches after 1805, captives such as Loki-Mokeen, a Mexican mulatto, could become officers of the Sun Dance and protectors of the sacred Taimé Bundle.[43] Andrés Martinez, called by the Kiowa "Andali," was seized from his family's pastures near Las Vegas, New Mexico, and grew to adulthood as a Kiowa warrior. In 1889 he converted to Methodism and told his story to the Reverend J. J. Methven.[44] Likewise, the "captive-friend" who fought alongside his Comanche warrior-brother appears prominently as a type in Hoebel's ethnography.[45]

Captive women often found themselves under the protection of Comanche women. Rosita Rodríguez, writing in 1846, reported she "remained a prisoner among the Comanche Indians about one year, during which time I was obliged to work very hard, but was not otherwise badly treated as I became the property of an old squaw who became much attached to me."[46] Similarly, Sarah Ann Horn, taken captive in 1837, reported that she was taken in "by an old widow woman . . . a merciful exception to the general character of these merciless beings." Although she was "set to work to dress buffalo hides," she did not suffer sexual abuse.[47] It appears that at least some captive women were informally adopted by older women, by which action they received the protection of the Comanche incest taboo.[48]

Rodrígues and Horn are among the very few women who, when repatriated, wrote of their experiences among the Comanche. Most captive women seem to have remained with their captors, marrying and establishing families in the host society.[49] Rodrígues herself had left a son behind among the Comanche, reporting that "I heard from him a short time ago—he is well and hearty but he is pure Indian now."[50] Josiah Gregg noted the presence of Mexican women among the Comanches when he began traveling the Santa Fe Trail in the 1830s. He remarked with surprise that some of these "preferred remaining with [their captors], rather than encounter the horrible ordeal of ill-natured remarks on being restored to civilized life." One woman refused to return even after the offer of one thousand dollars for her ransom. She sent word that the Comanches "had disfigured her by tattooing; that she was married, and perhaps *enceinte* [pregnant], and she would be more unhappy returning . . . under these circumstances than remaining where she was."[51]

These women had good reason to fear social opprobrium if they returned to Spanish society. When authorities introduced an alms-gathering plan in 1780 to raise funds for the ransom of Spanish captives, Teodoro de Croix declared with alarm that "this evil extends especially . . . to the feminine sex . . . on account of the lascivious vice of sensuality in which they are now afforded the greatest liberty to indulge themselves."[52] This may have been a rhetorical flourish to heighten interest in the plan, but it suggests that the conjugal arrangements of Comanche women might entail certain attractions to captive Spanish women as well.

Cultural and Social Accommodation in Captivity

Spanish concerns about the influence of Indian lifeways on their subjects went beyond anxieties about the behavior of "their" women in captivity. The very fact that thousands of Indian captives and their descendants now resided in Spanish society stimulated a growing polemic of caste-conscious distancing by elite *españoles* from the culturally mixed village people. Ramón Gutiérrez has argued that eighteenth-century New Mexico developed as a "timocracy," where "differences between aristocrats and landed peasants were of degree rather than kind. Spaniards, whatever their estate, were men of honor in comparison to the vanquished Indians." Gutiérrez contends that the *genízaro* caste, formed from the mass of *indios de rescate* obtained by the Spanish through ransom, constituted a "dishonored" status against which all Spanish, regardless of economic position, could define their own *calidad* (status).[53]

While Gutiérrez offers strong evidence for this honor/dishonor distinction among elite *españoles*, his use of prescriptive sources generated by these elites tends to leave on-the-ground relations between mestizo *pobladores* and their *genízaro* neighbors somewhat obscure. As we will see, by the end of the eighteenth century, Spanish ecclesiastics and administrators spoke of their colonial villagers in terms usually associated with *los indios bárbaros,* often referring to them as "indolent," "rude," "independent," and "lewd." Captive exchange lay at the heart of this blurring of cultural boundaries.

New Mexico seems similar to other cultural borderlands, where patterns of cultural accommodation appear beneath colonial structures of conflict, as the exigencies of day-to-day survival promote periods of relatively peaceful coexistence.[54] Always uncertain, and often punctuated by violent exchanges, *poblador* (village settler) and nomadic-pastoral Indian relations seem to have begun to converge in regionally defined communities of interest by late in the eighteenth century, especially after formal negotiations of Spanish, Comanche, Ute, and Navajo peace treaties during 1786. This movement, however, distanced the village people of New Mexico from their colonial administrators, a trend that would lead to internal conflict by the nineteenth century.

Foreshadowing this turmoil, in 1794 Don Fernando de la Concha complained to the incoming governor, Don Fernando Chacón, that the village people of the province seemed "indolent": "They love distance which makes them independent; and if they recognize the advantages of union, they pretend not to understand them, in order to adopt the liberty and slovenliness they see . . . in their neighbors, the wild Indians."[55]

Concern on the part of Spanish administrators had increased throughout the preceding decades. In 1776 Antonio Bonilla had found the "settlements of the Spaniards . . . scattered and badly defended," protecting neither themselves nor "contributing to the defense of the province."[56] Two years later, Fray Augustín de Morfi attributed this situation to the fact that the "*pobladores* liked to live apart, far from the prying eyes of neighbors and the restraining influence of authorities," where they could "commit with impunity all manner of immoral and criminal acts, and . . . were not ashamed to go about nude so that lewdness was seen here more than in the brutes."[57]

Like Morfi, Concha felt that social intercourse with the *indios bárbaros* lay at the heart of this problem. Life in the villages, he told his successor, had become so distanced from colonial control that he recommended "the removal of more than two thousand [villagers]," whose "bad upbringing results from . . . the proximity and trade of the barbarous tribes." This trade appears to have become increasingly a part of the borderlands economy in New Mexico, and one which villagers sought to conceal from colonial control. Concha complained that the villagers, "under a simulated appearance of ignorance or rusticity . . . conceal the most refined malice."[58]

A decade later Chacón would note that the villagers were "little dedicated to farming," surviving instead on a vigorous trade with nomadic Indians. In exchange for the *pobladores'* manufactured goods and agricultural products, nomads such as the Comanches gave them "Indian captives of both sexes, mules, moccasins, colts, mustangs, all kinds of hides and buffalo meat."[59] As the Bourbon reforms brought efforts to incorporate New Mexico within the economic sphere of New Spain, especially in a developing sheep and textile industry, the informal economic autonomy of villagers seemed a barrier to progress.[60]

Tensions between administrators in Santa Fe and their backcountry subjects exploded in August 1837. The villagers of Río Arriba descended upon the villa and seized the government, executing Governor Albino Pérez in the process.[61] Infuriated by rumored direct taxation under Santa Ana's *centralismo* of 1835, which threatened to interfere with their autonomous indigenous trade, the rebels identified themselves "with the savage tribes . . . making the same cause and their same interests."[62] Mexico restored central authority by 1838, but the "community of interest" between New Mexican villagers and their native neighbors persisted. In 1847 the villages again rose in rebellion, this time against the American military government of occupation. Pueblo Indians and *pobladores* killed Governor Charles Bent in Taos, while Manuel Cortés of Mora joined with Apache and Cheyenne allies to raid U.S. military and commercial supply lines on the eastern frontier.[63] This ability to build strategic linkages across cultural boundaries was a consequence of long experience in economic and human exchange.

The seeds of these linkages were both cultural and biological, as revealed in a village-level intermingling of status groups. In Ranchos de Taos, for example, the Colonial Census of 1750 reported nine Spanish households of fifty-seven persons, six *coyote* households of fifty-five persons, and eight *genízaro* households of twenty-five persons. Even the Spanish households showed a blurring of caste category: the house of Antonio Atiensa included his *coyota* wife, María Romero; their son, Domingo Romero *(castizo)*; and the widow Juana with her daughter Manuela, no doubt *criadas*. Likewise, the house of Juan Rosalio Villapando, an important *español*, included his wife, María Valdes, and their six children, all of whom are termed *coyote*, suggesting that María may have been an *india de rescate*. Pablo Francisco Villalpando's household, from which María Rosa would be seized ten years later, contained three female and two male *sirvientes*, two of whom carried the family name. Mixing may have crossed class as well as caste lines in some village families.[64]

The fact that the census arranged households by caste category reveals a conscious concern about *casticidad* on the part of Spanish administrators, but the data also demonstrate how informally these categories might be arranged at the village level. Census findings from a cluster of plazas at Belén show a somewhat different, yet consistent, pattern. In 1790 the third plaza, Nuestra Señora de los Dolores de los Genízaros, contained thirty-three households, all designated as *genízaro*, a strong indication that in some cases true communities developed among some *indios de rescate*. But the adjacent second plaza of Jarales held thirty Spanish, twelve mestizo, four *coyote*, and two *genízaro* households. The marriage patterns from these communities reveal little caste-anxious endogamy; of the twenty-eight unions, only one is *español-española*. Six marriages involved *genízaro-genízara*, and five mestizo-mestiza. The remaining sixteen show a crossing of caste lines. In most of these, hypogamy seems the rule, with women marrying men of "lower" status. Children of these unions, for example, *genízaro-coyota*, seem to follow the father's status and are later enumerated as *genízaros*.[65]

By the late eighteenth century, however, this designation for children born of captive Indian women may not have carried the strictly "dishonored" quality that Gutiérrez proposes. Instead, it may imply a movement toward identity formation on the part of the *genízaros* themselves. As early as 1744 sources report that *genízaro* men played an important role as military auxiliaries for the Spanish.[66] By 1780 a group of thirty-three *genízaros* negotiated with Spanish authorities from a position of some power, threatening that if their lands in the Barrio de Analco in Sante Fe were not protected, they might go "in search of relief to our lands and nation."[67] An official Tropa de Genízaros was organized in 1808 to patrol the eastern frontier of New Mexico in response to Zebulon Pike's adventurism of the previous year.[68] And in 1837, following the Río Arriba rebellion noted earlier, the revolutionary *canton* elected as their new governor José Gonzales, a *poblador* and *cibolero* from Taos who may have been a *genízaro*.[69] As subordinate yet militarily skilled members of New Mexican society, *genízaro* men found themselves valued in a colony always in need of men-at-arms. Once established on the outer marches of the province, they managed to assert an intermediate negotiatory identity.

Gradual movement toward borderlands communities of interest emerged as a consequence of the presence of captive Indian women in colonial New Mexico. Initially little more than pawns in a distinctive slave trade, these *indias de rescate* established families within the host society whose members eventually owned land, served in the military, and even led major rebellions. In their case, maternity provided avenues of agency, especially as they manipulated structural constraints to establish increasing security for their offspring and, consequently, for themselves.

Two structures of constraint apply particularly to women in colonial New Mexico; marriage and *compadrazgo* (godparent) relations. For Spanish women, and for mixed-blood or captive women who had internalized their conversion to Christianity, the dictates of the Catholic Church constrained their agency within marriage. Gutiérrez has shown how caste-endogamous marriages served to "purify" the bloodlines of New Mexico's ruling elite.[70] The gender hierarchy of the church also firmly established women's subordination as dependents under the patriarchal authority of husbands and the church, with preservation of family honor through legitimate offspring their principal social role. Unlike women in the English colonies, however, Spanish women maintained separate property throughout their marriage(s) and could bequeath their estates independent of their husbands' wills.[71]

Spanish women's "property" often included *indias de rescate*, who found themselves transferred to daughters as servants or "emancipated" with the condition that they continue to "watch over and assist my daughter as if she were her mother."[72] Others received clear title to parcels of land "in appreciation of years of service to me without salary."[73] When José Riano contested the will of Gregoria Gongora in 1739, he explicitly excepted from the disputed property "a piece of land for the *india* who raised my youngest and other children."[74]

Although these cases suggest a familial quality to the relations between Spanish and Indian women, few masters or mistresses actually formalized this quality in godparent relations. Of the 3,294 "slave" baptisms in New Mexico between 1693 and 1849, only 14 percent featured "owners" as *padrinos*, and the vast majority (65 percent) showed "no apparent relationship," involving simply members of the local Spanish community. Gutiérrez argues that these figures reflect the internal contradictions between the benign character of *compadrazgo* and the exploitative character of master-slave relations.[75]

An alternative explanation might see these baptismal data as representative of mutually supportive relationships between the *pobladores* of New Mexico and *indios de rescate*, a variation upon traditions of adoption that we have seen as ubiquitous in nomadic-pastoral Indian society. Frances Quintana argues that in New Mexico, *compadrazgo* relations show two patterns, an "old world" tradition that "intensified existing kin relationships" among colonial elites and a "new world" innovation that "helped to stabilize relationships between native Indian populations and Spanish and mestizo groups."[76]

In addition to the baptisms of *indios de rescate* noted above, during the same period we see the baptism of 1,984 "illegitimate" children born of the women of the *genízaro* caste. In fact, Gutiérrez has recorded only twenty church-sanctioned marriages among members of this group and suggests that this reveals the continuing control by masters over the sexual services of "slave" women.[77] Certain of his cases support Gutiérrez's conclusion, but we should also recognize that refusal to "consecrate" a conjugal union also served as an act of resistance among both Pueblo and nomadic Indian groups.[78] At Zia Pueblo, and among the Navajos, a refusal to name the parents of "illegitimate" children continually frustrated Spanish authorities.[79] It seems reasonable to conclude that here existed a mixed pattern of sexual exploitation of *indias de rescate* by Spanish masters and a collective strategy of identity maintenance that, by refusing Catholic structures, retained the offspring of those and voluntary unions with Indian men as members of the cultural community.

Although conceived in grossly unequal relationships, the children born of unions with captors often served to strengthen the status of captive women. As full culture-group members of either Indian or *genízaro* communities, these daughters and sons provided social access and security to their mothers. As Marietta Morrissey has found for slave women in the Caribbean, concubinage with dominant men often involved a painful balancing of shame and hope. If they acceded to sexual relations with masters, their children were born free and in a position to assist in the dream of manumission.[80] In some cases as well, real bonds of affection and respect developed between sugar planters and slave women, a factor that seems likely in some of the New Mexican examples.

Although the creation of kinship seems the primary avenue by which captive women sought security and identity, we may also discern other facets of their lives from within the historical record. In addition to the life-cycle labor of family reproduction, these women engaged in subsistence and market production. The eighteenth and nineteenth centuries saw dramatic shifts in the status and work of Plains Indian women as peoples such as the Comanches, Kiowas, and Cheyennes began participating in the European fur and hide trade. With the horse and gun, one Indian man could procure fifty to sixty buffalo hides per season, twice as many as one Indian woman could tan for use or exchange. An increase in polygyny, and in raiding for captive women, served to counteract this labor shortage.[81] The captivity narratives quoted earlier make it clear that captive women were "set to work to tan hides" almost immediately. The appearance of polygynous households probably made this work more efficient, for "co-wives" might process hides while the "first wife" performed higher-status production and distribution such as cooking, clothing manufacture, and ceremonial activities.

In New Mexico, *indias de rescate* appear most often as household servants, but to consider their work entirely "domestic" is probably misleading. Since both Apache and Navajo captive women came from societies in which women were the principal horticulturalists, they may have found themselves gardening and even tending flocks. We are only beginning to develop an understanding of women's economic life in colonial New Mexico, but Angelina Veyna's work with women's wills suggests that both Spanish and Indian women may have been more involved in farming than previously thought. The fact that women owned *rejas* (plowshares) and willed them not to their sons but to their daughters suggests either a farming orientation or a means of attracting potential husbands.[82]

Navajo and Apache women also worked as weavers, both of basketry and of textiles. H. P. Mera has described the nineteenth-century "slave blanket" as a crossover style between Navajo and New Mexican techniques, using New Mexican yarns and designs but produced on the distinctive upright looms of Navajo women.[83] These early New Mexican serapes were important trade items at *rescates*, given in exchange for buffalo hides and dried pemmican. Although today in villages such as Chimayo men weave the distinctive Rio Grande blankets, this seems the result of a concerted effort early in the nineteenth century to develop a commercial textile industry.[84]

Captive women and children played important roles in one last area, that of Spanish-Indian diplomacy. Their cross-cultural experience made them valuable as interpreters, translators, and envoys for Spanish military leaders. By 1750 the Comanches had obtained French guns, and Governor Vélez declared that unless a peace was negotiated, the Comanches might prove "the ruin of this province."[85] In order to communicate with several Comanche hostages held in Santa Fe, Vélez utilized the interpretive services of a Kiowa woman who had been captured by the Comanches, lost to the Utes in a raid, then purchased as a *criada* by Antonio Martín. This negotiation resulted in a temporary truce, sealed by the exchange of several prisoners.[86]

When the peace collapsed in 1760, captive women again served in a diplomatic capacity, this time as emissaries. Unable to find the appropriate Comanche leaders with whom to bargain, Vélez "dispatched six Comanche women prisoners as ambassadors to their nation." Within a month, four of the women had returned, along with nine Comanche captains, and another truce was affirmed by the return to the Comanches of "thirty-one women and children, among whom, fortunately, were their relatives."[87] Likewise, when Governor Juan Bautista de Anza and Ecueracapa negotiated the Spanish-Comanche Peace of 1786, which lasted until 1846, they sealed their agreement by exchanging a Comanche boy, "José Chiquito," for Alejandro Martín, "eleven years a captive among the band of Captain Tosapoy."[88]

Captivity and Identity in New Mexico

Often deemed invisible commodities in the "slave trade" of the Spanish borderlands, the captive women and children discussed here emerge as human actors engaged in a deeply ambivalent dialectic between exploitation and negotiation. Their stories begin in a moment of abject powerlessness, where subordination serves as a substitute for violent death. But from that moment forward, we see them taking tentative steps toward autonomy and security. Captive women worked within the limits set by their captors, yet through the creation of kinship, their daily labors, and their diplomatic usefulness, they managed to carve out a future for themselves and their lineages. Although fewer in number, captive boys became men who utilized their military skills to attain status and limited autonomy.

Beginning in an indigenous tradition of captive taking, and intensified by Spanish military and economic exploitation, the captive-exchange system developed as the high-stakes component of a borderlands political economy that produced conflict *and* coexistence.

Maria Mies has conceptualized the interlinkage of men's militarism and the forcible exchange of women as a universal "predatory mode of appropriation," a paradigm for "all exploitative relations between human beings."[89] In New Mexico, Spanish and Indian men found that even more than horses, guns, or hides, their counterparts valued women and children, and they established a nominal agreement that these would serve as objects and agents of intersocietal exchange. Conflict and accommodation patterns, therefore, between these rival societies may represent attempts by differing forms of patriarchal power to achieve external economic and military objectives while reinforcing the stability of internal social and gender hierarchies.

Yet despite the exploitative quality of the captive-exchange system, its victims found ways to exercise agency and achieve some measure of security and comfort for themselves and their descendants. Within the structures of constraint lay some opportunity, at times more opportunity than that available in their natal societies. María Rosa Villalpando of Taos found herself traded to the Pawnees, married there, then remarried to become the "matriarch" of a French fur-trading enterprise in St. Louis. When her New Mexican son, José Juliano, visited her there in 1802 and attempted to establish a claim as heir, she paid him off with two hundred pesos and sent him packing. José Juliano took a long route home, for by 1809 New Mexican authorities contacted administrators in San Antonio, Texas, and suggested José be forcibly sent home, for he had a wife and children "without support" in the village of Ojo Caliente.[90] Juana Hurtado received the support of the Zias and Navajos in her role as cultural centerperson. Likewise, a Crow woman might be sold at a *rescate* by the Comanches, escape to find her way homeward, and end up leading a French trading expedition back to New Mexico.[91] Finally, a Pawnee woman in Santa Fe could discover that her master had settled land upon her in his will, for the consideration that she continue to serve as *criada* to his son.[92]

In time, the mixed-blood descendants of captive women and children exhibited new collective interests that influenced their choice of cultural identification. Although this essay is only a preliminary examination, it seems reasonable to suggest that the collective interests of second-generation and subsequent descendants blurred the boundaries between New Mexican *pobladores* and their Indian neighbors. Plains Indian societies became increasingly militarized and market-oriented during this period, and New Mexican villagers increasingly mobile. By the 1830s, New Mexican *ciboleros* (bison hunters) and *comancheros* (traders and raiders) appeared regularly in travel accounts.[93] Plains societies displayed new forms of collective action, and villagers rose in radically democratic rebellions.

Although the American conquest of 1846–48 resulted in the erosion of shared values and interests between New Mexicans and southwestern Indians, vestiges of the borderlands community of interest still survive. Miguel Montoya, historian of the village of Mora, defines the historical identity of his neighbors in this way: "We were Spanish by law, but Indian by thought-world and custom. We respected *los viejos* [the elders], who looked after our spiritual health. We have relatives in the Pueblos, and out there, in Oklahoma [pointing east, to the reservations of the Comanche and Southern Cheyennes]."[94]

Notes

1. Jack B. Tykal, "Taos to St. Louis, the Journey of Maria Rosa Villalpando," *New Mexico Historical Review* 65, 3 (April 1990): 161–74.

2. Treatments of "slavery" in New Mexico are L. R. Bailey's *The Indian Slave Trade in the Southwest* (Los Angeles: Western Lore Press, 1966), which contains no analysis of gender differentiation nor any of captivity among

Indian groups; David M. Brugge's *Navajos in the Catholic Church Records of New Mexico, 1694–1875* (Tsaile, Ariz.: Navajo Community College Press, 1985), an important piece of documentary research upon which this essay relies heavily but which does not attempt a unifying analytical framework; and the recent work of Ramón Gutiérrez, *When Jesus Came, the Corn Mothers Went Away: Marriage, Sexuality and Power in New Mexico, 1500–1846* (Stanford, Calif.: Stanford University Press, 1991), whose analysis relies on an exploitation paradigm drawn from chattel slavery in the southern United States. Gutiérez does not consider the experience of Spanish captives in Indian societies.

3. For an in-depth treatment of this question, see the author's "Captives and Cousins: Bondage and Identity in New Mexico, 1700–1837" (master's thesis, University of California, Davis, 1991), and Ph.D. dissertation, "Captives and Cousins; Violence, Kinship, and Community in the New Mexico Borderlands 1680–1880" (University of California, Davis, 1995).

4. Friedrich Engels, *The Origin of the Family, Private Property, and the State* (New York: Pathfinder Press, 1972 [1884]); Gerda Lerner, *The Creation of Patriarchy* (Oxford: Oxford University Press, 1986); Claude Lévi-Strauss, *The Elementary Structures of Kinship* (Boston: Beacon Press, 1969 [1949]); Gayle Rubin, "The Traffic in Women: Notes on the 'Political Economy' of Sex," in Rayna Reiter, ed., *Toward an Anthropology of Women* (New York: Monthly Review Press, 1975); Verena Martínez-Alier (Stolke), *Marriage, Class, and Colour in Nineteenth Century Cuba* (Cambridge: Cambridge University Press, 1974); Jane Fishburne Collier, *Marriage and Inequality in Classless Societies* (Stanford, Calif.: Stanford University Press, 1988).

5. Lerner, *Creation of Patriarchy*; Martínez-Alier (Stolke), in *Marriage, Class, and Colour*, applies this argument to nineteenth-century Cuba. Claude Meillassoux makes the case for the patrimony-to-property transition in his synthesis of indigenous-domestic African slave systems in *The Anthropology of Slavery: The Womb of Iron and Gold* (Chicago: University of Chicago Press, 1991).

6. While reiterating the ban on Indian slavery first set forth in 1542, the *Recopilación* reinforced the "just war" doctrine, whereby hostile Indians might be enslaved if taken in conflict. *Indios de rescate* (ransomed Indians), on the other hand, were "saved" from slavery among their captors and owed their redeemers loyalty and service. See Silvio Zavala, *Los Esclavos Indios en Nueva España* (Mexico City: Edician de Colegio Nacional Luis Gonzáles Obregón, 1967), for a complete treatment of these policies.

7. For theoretical and empirical cases, see the essays in Katherine Spielmann, ed., *Farmers, Hunters, and Colonists: Interaction between the Southwest and the Southern Plains* (Tucson: University of Arizona Press, 1991).

8. "Report of the Reverend Father Provincial, Fray Pedro Serrano . . . to the Marquis de Cruillas . . . 1761," in Charles Wilson Hackett, trans. and ed., *Historical Documents Relating to New Mexico, Nueva Vizcaya, and Approaches Thereto, to 1773* (Washington, D.C.: Smithsonian Institution, 1937), 3:486–87.

9. Eleanor B. Adams and Fray Angélico Chávez, trans. and eds., *The Missions of New Mexico, 1776: A Description by Fray Francisco Atanasio Domínguez* (Albuquerque: University of New Mexico Press for Cultural Properties Review Committee, 1956), 252. See also Amando Represa, "Las Ferias Hispano-Indias del Nuevo México," in *La España Ilustrada en el Lejano Oeste* (Valladolid: Junta de Castillay León, Consejería de Cultura y Bienestan Social, 1990), 119–25.

10. James S. Calhoun to Commissioner Brown, 31 March 1850, in Annie Heloise Abel, ed., *The Official Correspondence of James S. Calhoun, Indian Agent at Santa Fe* (Washington, D.C.: U.S. Government Printing Office, 1915), 181–83. For the archaeology of *comanchero* sites on the plains, see Frances Levine, "Economic Perspectives on the Comanchero Trade," in Spielmann, ed., *Farmers, Hunters, and Colonists*, 155–69.

11. Since only some 75 percent of baptismal registers still exist, the actual figures are probably somewhat higher. Brugge, *Navajos in Catholic Church Records*, 2.

12. Analysis of the Spanish Colonial Census of 1750, New Mexico State Records Center, indicates a rural village population of 1,052, of whom 447 are recorded as having some Indian blood. In the "urban" areas of Santa Fe and Albuquerque, a total population of 2,757 contained only 400 individuals similarly designated.

13. Brugge, *Navajos in Catholic Church Records*, 116, estimates a 60-40 female-male ratio for the Navajo captives he studied. Working again with the Spanish Colonial Census of 1750, where individuals are designated either by proper name or by a gendered noun (*criada/o, genízara/o india/o*), I find that women total 153 of 282 individuals, or 54 percent. Since some bondswomen, for example, are designated simply "cinco indias criadas y ocho coyotitos" (*Spanish Archives of New Mexico* [hereafter SANM] I, roll 4, frame 1175, State Record Center, Santa Fe), we cannot determine a precise gender breakdown. Nineteenth-century figures demonstrate continuity: Lafayette Head's 1865 census of Indian captives held in Costilla and Conejos Counties, Colorado Territory, shows females numbering 99 of 148 captives (67 percent), with children under age fifteen 96 of those 148 (65 percent); *National Archives, New Mexico Superintendency*, Microcopy 234, roll 553. In 1770, Don Augustín Flores de Vergara donated "for the sermon of the day" at the Chapel of San Miguel in Santa Fe "one Indian girl of serviceable age valued at 80 pesos." See "Certified Copy of the Expenditures Made by Captain Don Augustín Flores de Vargara for the Chapel of Glorious San Miguel," Crawford Buel Collection, New Mexico State Records Center, Santa Fe.

14. In 1760 a Comanche band attacked what is now Ranchos de Taos and carried fifty-seven women and children into captivity. See "Bishop Tamarón's Visitation of New Mexico, 1760," Eleanor B. Adams, ed. and trans., *Historical Society and New Mexico Publications in History* 15 (1954): 58. In a raid on Abiquiu in 1747, twenty-three women and children were carried off, as documented in "An Account of Conditions in New Mexico, Written by Fray Juan Sanz de Lezuan, in the Year 1760," in Hackett, *Historical Documents*, 3:477.

15. "*Bando* of Don Phelipe de Neve, Governor and Commandant-general of the Interior Provinces of New Spain, May 8, 1784," in the Bexar Archives, Barker History Center, University of Texas, Austin. For the 1830s estimate, see Jean Luis Berlandier, *The Indians of Texas in 1830*, ed. John C. Ewers (Washington, D.C.: Smithsonian Institution Press, 1969), 119. The 1933 Comanche Ethnographic Field School out of Santa Fe estimated that 70 percent of Comanche society at that time were mixed-bloods of primarily Mexican Comanche descent; see E. Adamson Hoebel, "The Political Organization and Law Ways of the Comanche Indians," *Memoirs of the American Anthropological Association*, no. 54 (Menasha, Wisc., 1940).

16. Riordan to commissioner, 14 August 1883, *Annual Report of the Commissioner of Indian Affairs for the Year 1883* (U.S. Department of the Interior, Washington, D.C.); it should be noted that here, twenty years after the Emancipation Proclamation, U.S. officials were still attempting to extinguish Indian slavery in New Mexico.

17. Nancy Folbre defines "structures of constraint" as "sets of assets, rules, norms, and preferences that shape the interests and identities of individuals or social groups." In doing so the structures "define the limits and rewards to individual choice." This conceptualization allow us to recognize the *simultaneity* of exploitation and agency, a key element in this essay. Nancy Folbre, *Who Pays for the Kids? Gender and the Structure of Constraint* (New York: Routledge, 1994).

18. See Fray Angélico Chávez, *Origins of New Mexico Families* (Santa Fe: Museum of New Mexico Press, 1992 [1954]), 49–50, for reference to Hurtado's *encomienda* holdings, including Santa Ana Pueblo.

19. "Inventory and settlement of the estate of Juana Galvana, *genízara* of Zia Pueblo, 1753," SANM I, no. 193. I thank Frances Quintana for suggesting Juana Hurtado as a case study in captivity and for sharing her notes with me. Her essay "They Settled by Little Bubbling Springs," (*El Palacio* 84, 3 [1978]: 19–49) treats the history of the Santísima Trinidad Grant at Los Ojitos Hervidores.

20. SANM II, no. 367, reel 6, frames 1010–23.

21. The journal of Don Diego de Vargas records Martín's ransom of Juana at the Zuni pueblo of Halona, along with her fourteen-year-old daughter, María Naranjo, as well as a younger daughter and a son "about three years old." This raises some confusion as to Juana's age at her capture in 1680 and suggests that at least one and probably two of her children were born to her during her captivity. As we will see, if true, this would have given Juana and her "Navajo" children membership in a Navajo clan and may help explain her long-term good relations with Navajos in the years to come. See J. Manuel Espinosa, trans. and ed., *First Expedition of Vargas into New Mexico, 1692* (Albuquerque: Quivira Society, 1940), 237.

22. Archdiocesan Archives of Santa Fe (hereafter AASF), Burials, reel 43, frame 371; SANM II, no. 406.

23. "Declaration of Fray Miguel de Menchero, Santa Bárbara, May 10, 1744," in Hackett, *Historical Documents*, 3:404–5.

24. Abandonment of the pueblo for defensible mesa-top positions often preceded Pueblo-Spanish conflict. Quintana, "They Settled." See SANM II, no. 345, for details of the incident. For treatment in broader historical context, see Frances Leon Swadesh, "The Structure of Hispanic-Indian Relations in New Mexico," in Paul M. Kutsche, ed., *The Survival of Spanish American Villages* (Colorado Springs: Colorado College Press, 1979), 53–61.

25. See Morris E. Opler, "The Kinship Systems of the Southern Athabaskan-Speaking Tribes," *American Anthropologist* 38 (1936): 622–33; M. E. Opler, "Cause and Effect in Apachean Agriculture, Division of Labor, Residence Patterns, and Girl's Puberty Rites," *American Anthropologist* 74 (1972): 1133–46; Harold E. Driver, "Reply, to Opler . . . ," *American Anthropologist* 74 (1972): 1147–51; Collier, *Marriage and Inequality*.

26. See W. W. Hill, "Some Navaho Culture Changes during Two Centuries, with a Translation of the Early Eighteenth Century Rabal Manuscript," in *Smithsonian Miscellaneous Collections* 100 (1939): 395–415. For Navajo kinship and marriage systems, see Gary Witherspoon, *Navajo Kinship and Marriage* (Chicago: University of Chicago Press, 1975).

27. See Arnold van Gennep, *The Rites of Passage* (Chicago: University of Chicago Press, 1960 [1909]), for a treatment of the common attributes of integration rituals.

28. Brugge, *Navajos in Catholic Church Records*, 138, citing a conversation with Bruce Yazzi, a son of Nakai Na'dis Saal.

29. Ibid., app. B, 175; David M. Brugge, "Story of Interpreter for Treaty of 1868," *Navajo Times*, 21 August 1968.

30. Brugge, *Navajos in Catholic Church Records*, 139. This seems an anomaly in the matrilineal reckoning of kin by Navajo clans, but given the nonkin status of an unadopted captive, it would be the only method of integrating her progeny.

31. "Agent Bowman to the Commissioner of Indian Affairs, Sept. 3, 1884," in *Annual Report of the Commissioners of Indian Affairs for the Year 1884,* quoted with extensive corroborative evidence in Brugge, *Navajos in Catholic Church Records,* 142.

32. Morris E. Opler, "A Summary of Jicarilla Apache Culture," *American Anthropologist* 38 (1936): 206, 208, 209.

33. Ibid., 213. This information, gathered by Opler in the 1930s, may reflect an intensification of social stratification following the American conquest of the 1850s.

34. Collier, *Marriage and Inequality,* 23.

35. Hoebel, "Political Organization," 49ff.

36. Ibid., 49.

37. Ibid., 51, 62. Absconding cases constituted twenty-two of the forty-five marital disputes recorded by Hoebel.

38. See Ernest Wallace and E. Adamson Hoebel, *The Comanche: Lords of the Southern Plains* (Norman: University of Oklahoma Press, 1952), 72.

39. David E. Jones, *Sanapia: Comanche Medicine Woman* (Prospect Heights, Ill.: Waveland Press, 1984 [1972]). Sanapia received her medicine powers through her mother and maternal uncle, consistent with the Shoshonean levirate. Her powers became fully developed only after she experienced menopause.

40. Stanley Noyes, *Los Comanches: The Horse People* (Albuquerque: University of New Mexico Press, 1993); Brooks, "Captives and Cousins" (Ph.D. diss.), 133–35; Dan Flores, "Bison Ecology and Bison Diplomacy: The Southern Plains from 1800 to 1850," *Journal of American History* 78, 2 (September 1991): 465–85.

41. Wallace and Hoebel, *Comanche,* 241–42.

42. Ralph Linton, "The Comanche Sun Dance," *American Anthropologist* 37(1935): 420–28; quotes, 421. For a detailed description of captives in the Sun Dance, see J. J. Methven, *Andele, or the Mexican-Kiowa Captive: A Story of Real Life among the Indians,* ed. James F. Brooks (Albuquerque: University of New Mexico Press, 1996 [1899]), 58–69.

43. For Loki-Mokeen's story and others, see Maurice Boyd, "The Southern Plains: Captives and Warfare," in *Kiowa Voices: Myths, Legends, and Folktales* (Forth Worth: Texas Christian University Press, 1983), 2:155–82.

44. For Martínez's life story, see Brooks, ed., *Andele: The Mexican-Kiowa Captive.*

45. Hoebel, "Political Organization," 68.

46. "Rosita Rodrígues to Don Miguel Rodrígues, January 13, 1846," letter in the Bexar Archives, Barker History Center, University of Texas, Austin.

47. "A Narrative of the Captivity of Mrs. Horn and Her Two Children" (St. Louis, 1839) reprinted in C. C. Rister, *Comanche Bondage* (Glendale, Calif.: Western Lore Press, 1955), 157.

48. On the incest taboo, see Hoebel, "Political Organization," 108. I am indebted to Tressa Berman for suggesting the association between captive women's low incidence of sexual abuse and the adoptive incest taboo. For similar examples among other Indian groups, see James Axtell, "The White Indians of Colonial America," in *Colonial America* (New York: W. W. Norton, 1983), 16–47, esp. 27.

49. Cynthia Ann Parker, the mother of Quanah Parker, the last Comanche war chief, is the most famous example. See Margaret Schmidt Hacker, *Cynthia Ann Parker* (El Paso: University of Texas at El Paso Press, 1990). Parker lived thirty-four years among the Comanches and died "of heartbreak" shortly after her "rescue."

50. Rodrígues letter, 13 January 1846.

51. Josiah Gregg, *The Commerce of the Prairies,* ed. Milo Milton Quaife (Lincoln: University of Nebraska Press, 1967 [1844]), 208.

52. "*Expediente* of de Croix, June 6, 1780; Bonilla's Certification of June 15, 1780," in the Bexar Archives, Barker History Center, University of Texas, Austin.

53. Gutiérrez, *When Jesus Came,* 190, 206. The *genízaros* remain the center of scholarly debate as to their true status in New Mexican society. This focuses on whether they constituted a caste category, defined from without, or if in time they developed as an "ethnogenetic" identity group. See Tibo Chavez, *El Rio Abajo,* ch. 10, "The *Genízaro,*" (Albuquerque: Pampa Print Shop, date unknown); Fray Angélico Chávez, "*Genízaros,*" in *The Handbook of North American Indians* (Washington, D.C.: Smithsonian Institution Press, 1980), 9:198–200; Robert Archibald, "Acculturation and Assimilation in Colonial New Mexico," *New Mexico Historical Review* 53, 3 (July 1978): 205–17; Stephen M. Horvath, "The *Genízaro* of Eighteenth Century New Mexico: A Re-examination," in *Discovery* (Santa Fe: School of American Research, 1977), 25–40; Russell M. Magnaghi, "Plains Indians in New Mexico: The *Genízaro* Experience," *Great Plains Quarterly* 10 (spring 1990): 86–95.

54. See Richard White's *The Middle Ground: Indians, Empires, and Republics in the Great Lakes Region, 1640–1820* (Cambridge: Cambridge University Press, 1991), and Gregory Evans Dowd, *Spirited Resistance: The North American Indian Struggle for Unity, 1745–1815* (Baltimore: Johns Hopkins University Press, 1991), for new, though divergent, conceptualizations of these relationships. Other authors preceded White and Dowd in

stressing the importance of intermarriage in promoting these patterns of accommodation, principally Sylvia Van Kirk in her *Many Tender Ties: Women in Fur-Trade Society in Western Canada, 1670–1870* (Norman: University of Oklahoma Press, 1980) and Jennifer S. H. Brown in *Strangers in Blood: Fur Trade Company Families in Indian Country* (Vancouver: University of British Columbia Press, 1980).

55. "Don Fernando de la Concha to Lieutenant Colonel Don Fernando Chacón, Advice on Governing New Mexico, 1794," trans. Donald E. Worcester, *New Mexico Historical Review* 24, 3 (1949): 236–54; quote, 250.

56. Alfred B. Thomas, ed. and trans., "Antonio de Bonilla and the Spanish Plans for the Defense of New Mexico, 1777–1778," in *New Spain and the West* (Lancaster, Penn.: Lancaster Press, 1932), 1:196.

57. Fray Juan Agustín de Morfi, Desóordenes que se advierten en el Nuevo Mexico, 1780, *Archivo General de la Nación (AGN)*, Historia, 25.

58. "Don Fernando de la Concha," 251.

59. Marc Simmons, ed. and trans., "The Chacón Economic Report of 1803," *New Mexico Historical Review* 60, 1 (1985): 81–83; quotes, 83, 87.

60. The economic "modernization" of New Mexico has usually been attributed to the influence of the St. Louis–Santa Fe–Chihuahua trade that began in 1821. For a much earlier emergence, see Ross H. Frank, "From Settler to Citizen: Economic Development and Cultural Change in Late Colonial New Mexico, 1750–1820" (Ph.D. diss., University of California, Berkeley, 1992); for this aspect in the sheep commerce, see John O. Baxter, *Las Carneradas: Sheep Trade in New Mexico, 1700–1860* (Albuquerque: University of New Mexico Press, 1987).

61. Janet Lecompte has collected and interpreted most of the primary source material on this revolt, in *Rebellion in Río Arriba, 1837* (Albuquerque: University of New Mexico Press, 1985). Her class interpretation stresses tensions between *ricos* and *pobres* and neglects to consider the obvious cultural issues at work.

62. Governor Manuel Armijo, "Diario del Gobierno de la República Mexicana, Vol. 9. No. 45, Nov. 30, 1837," trans. in Locompte, *Rebellion*, 139.

63. For the extensiveness of the 1847 Taos revolt, see *Insurrection against the Military Government in New Mexico and California, 1847 and 1848* (U.S. Senate, 56th Congress, First Session, Document No. 442, 1901); Michael McNierney, ed. and trans., *Taos 1847: The Revolt in Contemporary Accounts* (Boulder: University of Colorado Press, 1980); James W. Goodrich, "Revolt at Mora, 1847," *New Mexico Historical Review* 47, 1 (1972): 49–60.

64. See the Spanish Colonial Census of 1750, New Mexico State Records Center, Santa Fe, 47–48.

65. Analysis drawn from Stephen M. Horvath, "The Genízaro of Eighteenth Century New Mexico: A Re-examination," in *Discovery* (Santa Fe: School of American Research, 1977), 25–40.

66. Fray Miguel de Menchero claimed in 1744 that the "*genízaro* Indians . . . engage in agriculture and are under obligation to go out and explore the country in pursuit of the enemy, which they are doing with great bravery and zeal." See "Declaration of Menchero," in Hackett, *Historical Documents*, 3:401.

67. See "Appeal of Bentura Bustamante, Lieutenant of Genízari Indians," 20 June 1780, SANM I, no. 1229, roll 6, frames 323–35.

68. "José Manrique, Draft of a Report for Nemesio Salcedo y Salcedo, Nov. 26, 1808," in the Pinart Collection, Bancroft Library, University of California, Berkeley.

69. Lecompte, *Rebellion*, 36–40, n. 54.

70. Gutiérrez, *When Jesus Came*, 7–9.

71. Angelina F. Veyna, "Hago, dispongo, y ordeno mi testamento: Reflections of Colonial New Mexican Women," paper presented at the annual meeting of the Western History Association, October 1991, in possession of author.

72. SANM I, no. 344, cited in Veyna, "Hago, dispongo, y ordeno."

73. "Testament of Don Santiago Roibal, 1762," fragment in New Mexico State Records Center, Santa Fe.

74. SANM II, no. 427, roll 7, frames 1023–25.

75. Gutiérrez, *When Jesus Came*, 182.

76. Frances Quintana, *Pobladores: Hispanic Americans of the Ute Frontier* (South Bend, Ind.: University of Notre Dame Press, 1974; reprint, Aztec, N.M.: privately published, 1991), 206–10.

77. Gutiérrez, *When Jesus Came*, 252.

78. As early as 1714, Spanish authorities were ordering "married" couples in the Río Grande pueblos to establish neolocal households rather than reside with their parents, a clear attempt to break matrilocal residence patterns and assert colonial control over the institution of marriage. (See SANM II, reel 4, frame 1014, as an example.)

79. Swadesh, "They Settled," 44.

80. Marietta Morrissey, *Slave Women in the New World: Gender Stratification in the Caribbean* (Lawrence: University of Kansas Press, 1989), 13–15. The ambiguous benefits of maternity to women held captive in patrilineal societies is borne out by looking at women under indigenous African systems of captivity and slavery.

Among the Margi of Nigeria, for example, social integration of captive-descended children could result in the elevation of mothers, if those children achieved social prominence in trade or warfare. See James H. Vaughan, "*Mafakur:* A Limbic Institution of the Margi," in Suzanne Miers and Igor Kopytoff, eds., *Slavery in Africa* (Madison: University of Wisconsin Press, 1977), 85–102.

81. Alan M. Klein, "The Political Economy of Gender: A Nineteenth Century Plains Indian Case Study," in Patricia Albers and Beatrice Medicines eds., *The Hidden Half: Studies of Plains Indian Women* (Washington, D.C.: University Press of America, 1983), 143–74; for a study of the bison economy, see Flores, "Bison Ecology."

82. Veyna, "Hago, dispongo, y ordeno," 9. Veyna also notes that "when tools were distributed to the settlers of Santa Cruz de la Cañada in 1712, only women were allotted *rejas.*"

83. H. P. Mera, *The Slave Blanket*, General Series Bulletin No. 5, Laboratory of Anthropology, Santa Fe, 1938.

84. See Lansing Bloom, "Early Weaving in New Mexico," *New Mexico Historical Review* 2 (1927): 228–38; Baxter, *Las Cameradas*, 60. See also Suzanne Baizerman, "Textile Traditions and Tourist Art: Hispanic Weaving in New Mexico" (Ph.D. diss., University of Minnesota, St. Paul, 1987), esp. 76–79, 130–31.

85. "General Campaign: Report of Governor Vélez Cachupín to Conde de Revilla Gigedo, Nov. 27, 1751," in A. B. Thomas, *The Plains Indians and New Mexico, 1751–1778* (Norman: University of Oklahoma Press, 1940), 74.

86. "Juan José Lobato to Vélez, August 28, 1752," in Thomas, *Plains Indians*, 114–15.

87. "Report of Vélez to Marqués de Cruillas, 1762," in Thomas, *Plains Indians*, 152–53.

88. "Abstract of Report Offered by de Anza, as Written by Pedro Garrido y Durran, Chihuahua, December 21, 1786," in Alfred B. Thomas, *Forgotten Frontiers: A Study of the Spanish Indian Policy of Don Juan Bautista de Anza, Governor of New Mexico, 1777–1787* (Norman: University of Oklahoma Press, 1932), 296; Elizabeth A. John, *Storms Brewed in Other Men's Worlds* (Lincoln: University of Nebraska Press, 1975), 732.

89. Maria Mies, "Social Origins of the Sexual Division of Labor," in Maria Mies, Veronika Bennholdt-Thomsen, and Claudia Von Werlhof, eds., *Women: The Last Colony* (London: Zed Books, 1988), 67–95; quote, 87.

90. Tykal, "From Taos to St. Louis"; "Report of Governor Vélez to Marqués de Cruillas . . . 1762," in Thomas, *Plains Indians*, 151. Vélez had asked the Comanche leader Nimiricante of the whereabouts of the women and children seized at Ranchos de Taos in 1760. Nimiricante replied that "they might have died, or been traded to the French and Jumanos." For José Juliano's problems in San Antonio, see Salcedo to Manrique, July 27, 1809, SANM II, no. 2239.

91. The French traders Jean Chapuis and Luis Fueilli were guided to Santa Fe in 1752 by "an Indian woman of the Aa tribe, who had fled to the house of her master [in Santa Fe] four months before and was following the road to her country." See "Vélez to Revilla Gigedo, Sept. 18, 1752," in Thomas, *Plains Indians*, 109.

92. See SANM I, no. 657, "Demanda puesta por Lucia Ortega contra Roque Lovato sobre una Donacion—Ano del 1769."

93. See Gregg, *Commerce of the Prairies*, 86, 208, 219.

94. Author's interview with Miguel Montoya, Las Vegas, N.M., 17 August 1990.

3

Distress and Discord in Virginia Slave Families, 1830–1860

Brenda Stevenson

The family was an institution that was by all measures vitally important to every faction of the population of antebellum Virginia, white and black, slave and free. Moreover, the family was important to these various groups of southerners for quite similar reasons. They believed that a positive family life was necessary to both individual and group survival—emotional, physical, cultural, economic, and social. For many, its existence implied an assurance of comfort in a world that more often than not proved to be harsh, unpredictable, and violent. Regardless of one's racial or cultural identity, political status, social class, or religious beliefs, family was an ideal and a reality that antebellum southerners prodigiously sought and fought to protect. Family was for them the most natural of institutions, and within its confines the most fundamental human events—birth, life, marriage, and death—took on a legitimacy that guaranteed one's humanity and immortality. The family institutions that antebellum southerners erected provided organization and structure to their lives and resources.[1]

Yet for many residents of pre–Civil War Virginia, the opportunity to live, act, and take comfort within the physical and emotional boundaries of one's family were privileges that were often elusive, if not impossible to obtain. No group of early-nineteenth-century Virginians found it more difficult to create and maintain stable marriages and families than did slaves. This essay is an examination of Virginia slave families during the latter half of the antebellum era. Of primary concern are the problems that adult slaves encountered within their families, particularly as marital partners and parents.

Blacks suffered greatly from the constant pressures attendant to living and working within a slave society. Ideologies of race differences and hierarchy were so popular that few whites, even those who did not benefit directly from the slave system, could conceive of any roles for blacks in their communities other than as exploited, dehumanized workers—and producers of workers. As members of a numerical minority defined by racial difference, they were the targets of profound sociocultural, political, and economic oppression that was meant to create and maintain the financial success and social prestige of elite whites in antebellum society. Moreover, white Virginians tried to impose their authority on every aspect of slave life, including the family, in order to fulfill their need to control the labor of their human chattel. It was not unusual for slave masters to choose their slaves' marital partners, to separate couples they had united, to force extramarital sexual partners on them, and even to sell off their children when it became economically advantageous, promoted discipline in the quarters, or helped to secure their own authority.

The negative implications of such actions for slaves who were trying to maintain functional family groups were, of course, substantial. An acutely detrimental phenomenon was the forced outmigration of slaves from Virginia in the antebellum period to other parts of the South as part of the lucrative domestic slave trade. This mandatory and often indiscriminate exodus that separated husband from wife and mother from child stripped many slaves of the kin- and community-based networks that they had managed to construct over generations of residence in Virginia. Slave owners sold and shipped literally hundreds of thousands of slave men, women, and children, representing all age groups, with various family and marriage commitments, out of the state. Richard Sutch conservatively estimates that during the decade from 1850 to 1860 alone, slaveholders and traders exported almost sixty-eight thousand Virginia slaves to the lower South and Southwest.[2] More often than not, masters sold their slaves without regard to family groups or marital status. Even those slaveholders who wanted to keep slave families united had little control over their future unity once the slave family was purchased by someone else. Donald Sweig's survey of the marital histories of slaves in northern Virginia, for example, indicates that as many as 74 percent of those exported left the state without accompanying family members.[3] Moreover, one can reasonably surmise that since most of the slaves exported were between twenty and forty-nine years old, many of them were spouses and parents at the time of their departure.[4] Regional studies substantiate this generalization. When Jo Ann Manfra and Robert Dykstra reviewed a survey of late-antebellum slave marriages in southern Virginia, for example, they found that at least one-third of those couples who separated did so as a result of slaveholder demands.[5] Manfra and Dykstra's analysis also documents that mandatory division was the predominant reason young married slave couples separated.[6] Separated slave couples and the breakup of families also produced orphans. The disruption of family ties and its consequences (such as orphaned children) were especially serious problems for Virginia bondsmen and -women during the latter half of the antebellum period.

Other information descriptive of Virginia slave life in the last decades before the Civil War also documents these phenomena. When one considers the recollections of ex-slaves, many of which record the personal histories of the last generation of slave children, adolescents, and young adults, the scope of these problems is obvious. Charles Perdue, Thomas Barden, and Robert Phillips provide the largest collection of published Virginia slave narratives in *Weevils in the Wheat: Interviews of Virginia Ex-Slaves* (1976). Of the 142 autobiographical statements found in this compilation, 87 include both impressionistic and detailed statistical information that ex-slaves provided about their parents. Among this group of former slaves, fully 18 percent suggested that neither their mothers nor their fathers contributed significantly to their rearing.[7] While some of these children lived with other kin, such as grandparents and aunts, others were less fortunate. The details they offer of their lives elucidates the painful consequences of orphan status in a society where individual slave survival was almost synonymous with family and community support. Consider the personal history of Armaci Adams, a slave born at the very end of the antebellum era who suffered parental loss.

"I was bawn in Gates County, North Carolina but I ain't stayed down dere long," Adams began her account of her life. The ex-slave implied in her statement that as an infant she lived with both of her parents in a domestic unit that was similar in structure and function to a nuclear family. Isaac Hunter, "an ole Methodist preacher," owned Armaci and her parents. When she was only three years old, two catastrophic events drastically changed Armaci's family situation and tore her away from the nurturing world of her parents' home forever: In the same year that her mother died of an unspecified cause, Isaac Hunter decided to sell most of his other slaves south. Among the first group to leave was Armaci's father. The Reverend Mr. and Mrs. Hunter then moved their much-reduced agricultural unit, including Armaci, to a farm in Huntersville, Virginia. Instead of placing the child in a slave home for rearing, however, the Hunters kept Armaci in their house and raised her themselves. Within a few months, Armaci had suffered the loss of both of her parents and most of her slave community.[8]

In addition to having to cope with what must have been a tremendous sense of loss, displacement, and abandonment, the young child found herself in the precarious position of having to rely solely on her white owners for care and guidance. Unfortunately, it was not a situation that Armaci or her new caretakers appreciated or adjusted to well. The Hunters never developed a close or affectionate attachment to their small ward. They obviously doubted that Armaci, a young child growing up during the era of a civil war that might well mean an end to slavery, would ever be worth the minimal material support they supplied her. At one point, their uneasiness about gaining a financial return on their investment even prompted them to try to sell her. Yet they were unable to do so because the potential buyer thought her physically handicapped—much of Armaci's body was covered with extensive burn scars that she had received while trying to cook her food in a fireplace without adult supervision. "De . . . man wouldn' buy me 'cause he 'fraid I won' be no good on account o' de burn scars," she explained.[9]

When the Civil War ended, the Hunters refused to free Armaci. By that time she had become an important domestic laborer in their household and the only one of their slaves who remained with them. Armaci was only seven years old at war's end and did not know that she was free. Her master and mistress continued to hold and treat her as a slave for six more years. They even conspired to discourage her father's attempts to find and to take the young girl home with him. Skillfully employing well-honed techniques of psychological and physical intimidation, they were able to gain and maintain control of Armaci. They developed an emotional hold over her even though they treated her harshly. (Years later Adams did not hesitate to characterize both Mr. and Mrs. Hunter as "hell cats," yet it was difficult for her to leave them.)[10]

Without the presence of her own black family or fictive kin, Armaci became the kind of slave Mr. and Mrs. Hunter wanted. She was passive, submissive, and hardworking. Acting out of a profound belief that she had no other alternative, Armaci met the Hunters' demands for hard work, accepted their meager material aid, and submitted to the beatings that she received from them for any mistake or misunderstanding. Over the years, her emotional dependency became acute. For example, when her father arrived at the Hunters' home some time after the end of the war to take Armaci back to his new family, Armaci was confused as to whether or not she should leave and eventually was convinced to stay with her owners. Mrs. Hunter told the child stories about her stepmother, and Armaci was afraid to leave with her father. Mrs. Hunter's lies apparently held more credibility for the frightened Armaci than her father's obvious desire to have her reunited with his family. She understandably feared life away from the small plantation that had defined her worldview for most of her life. "When paw come ter git me," she noted, "dey wouldn' let 'im see me so he went on 'way." It was not until she was a young adolescent that Armaci realized that she was "free" and finally was able to break the bonds she had with Mr. and Mrs. Hunter.[11]

Slave kin groups and communities on large holdings ideally provided alternative means for slaves to exchange and share emotional and economic support with loved ones in spite of the potentially destructive power of the owners to separate slave families. Regardless of the many Virginia slave family groups that had some characteristics of a nuclear structure, extended families and stepfamilies persisted in slave communities as innovative sources of socialization, social intercourse, material aid, and cultural expression.

Within the arena of the slave community, child rearing was a shared responsibility. In the absence of a parent, other nuclear and extended family members and sometimes fictive kin took on the major responsibility of rearing children. Adult female siblings or maternal female kin were the first choices as surrogate primary caregivers. When Robert Bruce constructed a list of slaves located on his plantation in Charlotte County, Virginia, during the late 1830s, he noted that three maternal grandmothers served as the primary caregivers for small children whose mothers either were dead or had been sold away.[12] Hannah Valentine, a domestic servant to Governor David Campbell of Abingdon, Virginia, took on the care and rearing of her grandchildren when her daughter, Eliza, accompanied the governor's family to Richmond. Writing to her in 1838, the surrogate mother noted reassuringly: "Your Children are all . . . doing very well and have never suffered from sickness one moment since you Left here. [T]hey talk some Little about you but do not appear to miss you a great deal."[13]

The importance of any one person's particular contribution to the rearing of children within slave families was determined by a number of variables. Generally, physical proximity to the child, the closeness of the consanguinal tie, and gender implied one's responsibility in this familial matter. Another important variable was the size of the slave child's nuclear and extended family. Slave children who were members of large families and slave communities, for example, were surrounded by a number of kin who could serve as child rearers. Other considerations that affected this decision were the age of possible caregivers and the status of these nurturers' physical and mental health, the other domestic responsibilities of these potential rearers, and, relatedly, their willingness to accept the responsibility of helping to raise the youngsters. Ideally, adult slave kin and friends fully embraced these additional commitments of time, energy, and material resources if it was necessary to do so. Yet there certainly were some slaves who were reluctant to cooperate. The opinions of other family members and the larger slave community also helped to assess how child-rearing tasks were to be distributed. Slave owners, however, ultimately decided who would assume such responsibilities, and slaves, in general, had to act accordingly.

Slave masters insisted on the importance of the slave mother in the slave family, particularly in regard to child rearing. In so doing, they helped to sustain both African and European cultural traditions that slaves drew upon when deciding how to order their social world. Accordingly, slave mothers took on the most significant long-term obligations of child care. Virginia slave owners promoted matrifocal and matrilocal families among their slaves in several ways.[14] First, a Virginia law dated 1662 stipulated that black children take the status of their mothers.[15] This legal association between slave mother and child reinforced, within the slaveholder's perception of an ordered domestic world, the cultural dictates of their society concerning gender-differentiated responsibility. Masters believed that slave mothers, like white women, had a natural bond with their children and that therefore it was their responsibility—more so than that of slave fathers—to care for their offspring. Consequently, young slave children routinely lived with their mothers or female maternal kin, thus establishing the matrilocality of slave families. Moreover, masters compiling lists of their human property routinely identified the female parent of slave children but only sometimes indicated paternity. Also, when prompted to sell a group of slaves that might include parents and their children, owners sometimes tried to sell a mother with her small children as a single unit but rarely afforded slave fathers this same consideration.

At the same time that slaveholders promoted a strong bond between slave mothers and their children, they denied to slave fathers their paternal rights of ownership and authority, as well as denying them their right to contribute to the material support of their offspring. Undoubtedly, slave masters felt that if it became necessary for them to challenge the power that slave parents had in the lives of their children, it would be much easier to do so if the parent with whom the child most readily identified as an authority figure was a female rather than a male. Slaveholders' insistence on the importance of the slave mother by identifying her as the head of the slave family and primary caregiver of the children, along with the derivation of the slave child's status from that of the mother, firmly established the matrifocality of most slave families. Thus, while slave fathers had a significant presence in the consciousness of their children, mothers obviously were much more physically and psychologically present in the children's lives.

A review of the slave narratives can elucidate further these issues of slave family structure and membership. If one considers the sample Perdue provides in his compilation, it is clear that the large majority of Virginia ex-slaves identified their mothers as the primary providers of care and socialization during their childhood. Significantly, 82 percent spoke of the physical presence of their mothers during most of their childhood years, while only 42 percent recalled continuous contact with their fathers. Moreover, fully one-third of those who did make mention of the presence of their fathers during their childhood indicated that these men did not live with them but only visited on their days off.[16]

The absence of slave fathers was not a problem that was restricted to the latter part of the antebellum period. Since the colonial period, young male slaves were the primary targets of intrastate and interstate trading in Virginia. As such, their arbitrary removal from wives and children always was a source of difficulty plaguing slave families. Of course, the numbers of young male slaves exported increased over time. Their continual decline on some farms and plantations in Virginia meant a decrease in the number of slave families with both parents present. (Significantly, only 42 percent of the ex-slaves interviewed as part of the Virginia Federal Writers' Project suggested in their autobiographical accounts that they had close physical contact with both of their parents.)[17] Moreover, the removal of adult male slaves from their Virginia kin networks robbed even slave families that were matrifocal, since they, too, had benefited significantly from material and emotional resources that fathers, husbands, and other male relatives who lived close by routinely provided. Many Virginia slave children born in the last decades before the Civil War, therefore, grew up without fathers or black male role models and nurturers, while women bore and reared children without the comfort and support of their husbands or other male kin.

Virginia Bell, an ex-slave from Louisiana, recalled her parents' personal histories: "Both of them was from Virginny, but from diff'rent places, and was brought to Louisiana by nigger traders and sold to Massa Lewis. I know my pappy was lots older than my mother and he had a wife and five chillun back in Virginny and had been sold away from them out there. . . . I don' know what become of his family back in Virginny, 'cause when he was freed he stayed with us."[18] Katie Blackwell Johnson was a Virginia ex-slave who never had the privilege of living with her father. As an adult, Johnson recalled very little about her male parent. "I only remember seeing him once," she stated. "He was stretched on the floor. He took me in his arms and I went to sleep. My mother said he was a great gambler and he never came to see us without a jug of liquor."[19]

Although many of the ex-slaves interviewed obviously knew and lived with their mothers, some slaves also grew up without their mothers. This was particularly so for the last generations of Virginia slaves, those born and reared between 1830 and 1860, when masters increasingly were selling women to traders who took them out of the state. Information descriptive of the slave exports from the state documents this activity. Richard Sutch estimates that by 1850, slaveholders were selling equal numbers of adult women and men and actually more adolescent and young adult females than males within those broad age cohorts.[20] Because the average age at first birth for Virginia slave women was between nineteen and twenty,[21] large numbers exported were probably young mothers, many of whom were forced to leave without their young. Liza McCoy recalled that her aunt Charlotte, a slave who lived in Matthews County, "was sold to Georgia away from her baby when de chile wont no more three months."[22] Ex-slave Fannie Berry included in her autobiographical account of life in late antebellum Virginia a tragic scene of slave mothers separated from their infants:

> Dar was a great crying and carrying on 'mongst the slaves who had been sold. Two or three of dem gals had young babies taking with 'em. Poor little things. As soon as dey got on de train dis ol' new master had de train stopped an' made dem poor gal mothers take babies off and laid dem precious things on de groun' and left dem behind to live or die. . . . [The] master who bought de mothers didn't want gals to be bothered wid dese chillun 'cause he had his cottonfields fer new slaves to work.[23]

Berry went on to explain the fate of the abandoned infants that "some po' white man would take dem an' raise dem up as his slaves and make 'em work on his plantation and if he wanted to, would sell 'em."[24]

Unfortunately, the socialization of slave youth was a difficult task for slaves regardless of the composition of their individual families. Slave child rearers faced obstacles to success that most whites did not. The most important deterrent was a legal one that had negative implications for all aspects of the relationship between rearer and child. Simply, slave parents were not the legal guardians of their children—white owners were. Moreover, since slaveholders were quite willing to share their authority with persons other than slave kin, particularly nurses, overseers, drivers, and other whites residing on their property, slave family members had many threats to their influence over the lives of their youngsters. Slave children were confronted with a variety of authority figures, white and black, each with his or her own priorities, demands, and contributions to their upbringing. These youths had to learn to assess the power and value of each of these adults as well as to appease their demands, often simultaneously.

Slave kin and white owners held the most important positions of power in the lives of slave children. Yet, as the balance of power was both a delicate and complex phenomenon that could shift quite suddenly, slave kin had to work diligently to retain some control in the face of unsolicited interference from others. White owners balked at attempts by slave kin to gain control over the lives or allegiances of black children in opposition to their authority as masters. They understood that such challenges to their authority showed that their slaves did not accept their assigned inferior status and were teaching their slave children to resist as well. Masters met such trials with extreme hostility and often open brutality. Also, since most antebellum Virginia slaveholders were white and male and most slave child caregivers were bondswomen, masters, especially, were incensed at the notion that their authority and power might be questioned by someone they viewed as three times their inferior—that is, black, female, and slave. A slave mother's successful defiance of an owner's authority would have meant a weakening of the control that the slaveholder hoped to exert over his other slaves—a situation few Virginia masters would tolerate.[25]

Matilda Carter was an ex-slave who lived on a farm near Newport News. She recalled that her master, John Wynder, even refused to allow his wife to interfere with his command over his slaves. "My sister Sally was a favorite of my mistress," Carter noted. "She didn' have to wuk in de fields. She ain't had nottin' to do 'ceptin play wid de chillun all day. But de Marser he try to make lil sis wuk. So my mistress she jes' hide her when she think Marser goin git her." Wynder was determined to end his wife's attempts to undermine his decision-making power with regard to his property. He remedied the situation by selling his wife's favored slave to the Deep South. "Mother never did get over dis ack of sellin' her baby to dem slave drivers down New Orleans," Carter concluded.[26]

Caroline Hunter's recollections about her life as a child with her slave mother and three brothers on a small farm near Suffolk, Virginia, at the end of the antebellum era include a telling example of the frustration that slave kin felt in response to the intrusion of white authority in the lives of their children. The scene she describes also suggests important questions about the slave child's general perception of black adult authority:

> During slavery it seemed lak yo' chillun b'long to ev'ybody but you. Many a day my ole mama has stood by an' watched massa beat her chillun 'till dey bled an' she couldn' open her mouf. Dey didn' only beat us, but dey useta strap my mama to a bench or box an' beat her wid a wooden paddle while she was naked.[27]

Stripped naked and beaten before her daughter, other family members, and the slave community, Caroline Hunter's mother must have known that such an example of her obvious helplessness in the face of slaveholder power would jeopardize her authority within her own domestic sphere—authority that she needed in order to rear Caroline and her other children. Nevertheless, the owner's demonstration of control did not destroy the bond between child and parent or the respect that Caroline had for her mother. On the contrary, the experience seemed to have deepened the young girl's appreciation for her mother's plight and helped to further instill in the daughter a profound hatred for their cruel owner. Yet these expressions of white dominion and control repeatedly witnessed by slave youth had some impact on the ways in which slaves differentially identified and related to white and black authority.

Ex-slave Nancy Williams of Yanceville, Virginia, recounted an experience that demonstrates the influence owners could have on a slave child's perspective of parental authority. Williams explained that as a young child, she was a favorite of her master, who consequently did not beat her and frowned on the strict disciplinary policy of her parents. Her parents probably believed that their master was spoiling Nancy and resented his intrusion in their domestic affairs. It was clear to slave parents that children reared in such a manner eventually would face harsh confrontations with whites and also risk alienation from their slave peers. Consequently, slave child rearers such as the Williamses had to fight a war of wits with their owners to gain the necessary authority to properly socialize their own children.

Not surprisingly, slave children did not always cooperate with their parents' efforts. Nancy Williams sometimes tried to manipulate her master's "benevolence" in order to avoid the stinging punishments that her parents often inflicted. The ex-slave recalled that on one such occasion, she had refused to do a task that her mother had assigned her. Nancy was fleeing her parent and the inevitable beating she was to receive when she decided that the best place to hide was between her owner's legs. Nancy, mindful of her master's fondness for her, knew that her mother would not whip her in his presence. "I run up de stairs rit 'tween marsa's legs," Williams remembered, "an ask him for 10 [cents]. She couldn't ketch me den." Mrs. Williams, however, was not about to let her child get away with this obvious act of disrespect or her original offense. Years later, the errant daughter noted her mother's eventual triumph: "[W]hen she did [catch me,] she beat de debil outa me."[28]

One can expect that with the decline of the viability of the extended slave family and the nonrelated surrogate kin network in the wake of increased exportation of slaves, the overall socialization of many slave youth suffered. One must also concede, however, that even under optimum conditions for success, slave kin rarely were able to rear children that were not affected to some degree by the actions and ideologies of whites who held so much power over their physical, psychological, and intellectual development. Obviously, slaves sometimes internalized prevalent racist views, which created tension within their families and communities. Color stratification was a problem that posed particularly negative consequences for those slaves touched by it, because of the explosive issues of force, sex, female purity, and marital sanctity that it evoked. Color consciousness and stratification among blacks resulted from a combination of factors, such as a consistently high rate of miscegenation and, relatedly, a large biracial population among slaves and free blacks, as well as the popularity of racist ideologies concerning race difference and hierarchy and their practical application in antebellum Virginia society.

Much of the interracial sexual activity that resulted in the state's biracial population involved white males' coercion and rape of black females. Consequently, the children born of these assaults were potent symbols of the immense power that whites held over the most intimate spheres of black life. They were a constant reminder to their mothers and her kin of their powerlessness in the face of white male domination and violence. "My mama said that in dem times a nigger 'oman couldn't help herself," May Satterfield recalled, "fo she had to do what de marster say. . . . [S]he had to go."[29] Consequently, the presence of racially mixed children in homes of slaves sometimes engendered feelings of shame, humiliation, and anger.

Slave families and communities usually attached an even deeper stigma to those children conceived as a result of voluntary sexual relations between black women and white men. Although slaves were very empathetic to those women who were the victims of coercion, they often ostracized slave women who openly consorted with white men. Many bondswomen and bondsmen viewed these concubines as promiscuous and disloyal. Their children shared, to a certain extent, the dishonor of their mothers.

It is not surprising, therefore, that many racially mixed children felt shame and confusion about their white parentage. Patience Richardson Avery, for example, immediately rejected the notion that Thomas Hatcher Jr., a white resident of some prominence in Chesterfield County, was her father. When her mother first introduced Mr. Hatcher to their small daughter. Patience remembered that she screamed: "I ain't got no father; . . . He no father o' mine! He white!"[30] Although she was only a few years old at the time, Patience profoundly understood the sociopolitical distinction between "black" and "white" and was horrified that she might be related to a white man. Some of her kin were equally horrified. Their rejection of Patience because of her racially mixed heritage caused her a great deal of physical and emotional pain as she grew older. Moreover, her account of her extended family's response remains as an important illustration of the kinds of conflict miscegenation brought to slave families. It also demonstrates the failures of some extended families to fully embrace those persons who were born outside of the nuclear core.

Forced to live with a maternal uncle (Robert Richardson) and his wife and children after the death of both her mother and maternal grandmother, Patience was the victim of discrimination and ill treatment at her uncle's home. Mrs. Richardson's attitude toward the girl was especially cruel. She not only assigned Patience excessively heavy workloads and blamed her for things beyond her control but also viciously beat her when displeased with her performance or overall behavior. The manner in which the aunt chose to discipline Patience is clearly indicative of her disdain for the child. Also, Mrs. Richardson's beatings acutely resembled the type of punishment that slaveholders inflicted on blacks in their attempts to humiliate and "break" them. Surely her intent was similar to that of a slave master. "Ev'ry time dat ole 'oman would whip me she would strip me nacked an' cut me wid a strip 'till I was whelped all over, an' de blood blister was everywhere," Mrs. Avery remembered. "I couldn' walk, neither set down," she added.[31]

Patience Avery emphatically believed that the lack of consideration and harsh beatings her aunt gave her were due to her white paternity. Obviously, Mrs. Richardson resented

Patience's parentage and presence in her home. Recalling the time when she lived with her uncle's family, the ex-slave noted: "Four years I stayed wid a mean 'oman, an' she was de meanes' . . . 'oman I ever saw. Mean an' cruel. You see, I was treated cruelly 'cause I was dis white man's chile."[32] Eventually, Patience sought refuge from Mrs. Richardson's violent beatings and verbal assaults with a neighboring white farmer and his wife, who provided the girl with minimal material support for her domestic labor. Rejected and brutalized by her black kin, Patience Avery ironically found greater acceptance in the homes of those whites toward whom she initially felt so much hostility.

Mothers and other family members were sensitive to the kinds of teasing, insults, and rough treatment that their mulatto children might receive at the hands of blacks and whites. They often lied to them about their paternity or taught them to avoid the issue when questioned about it. "Who's yo' pappy?" was the question that slaves often asked Candis Goodwin, the illegitimate daughter of a neighboring slave owner and a slave woman. Goodwin often quipped back at those teasing her, "Tuckey buzzard lay me an' de sun hatch me," but she secretly knew her "pappy" was "Massa Williams."[33]

Despite the obvious hostility with which many slaves responded to miscegenation, the reaction in the slave quarters to racially mixed children often was a complex and contradictory one. While many felt uneasy with the presence of these children and a few openly rejected them, unresolved feelings of black inferiority caused some to treat racially mixed and generally light-skinned children as superior to their darker peers. Many slaves also respected the operative class system in antebellum southern society. The combination of color and class stratification caused some slaves to afford the mulatto offspring of elite whites a particularly elevated status. Biracial slaves sometimes also held themselves aloof from other blacks. Consider the personal history and behavior of Ary, an octoroon woman who came to work for the missionaries at Craney Island, Virginia, in 1863.

Ary was the proud daughter of a Virginia planter and a mulatto house servant. By young adulthood she had become the concubine of her young master, who also was her first cousin. She eventually bore him a child, who died during the Civil War. Convinced that she was the favorite child of her wealthy father and that her young master's feelings of affection were genuine, Ary believed that she was superior to her darker peers. While on Craney Island, she often boasted of her elite white parentage and insisted that she was better than the other "contraband."[34] Remembering her lover's pronouncement that she was to have nothing to do with "colored men" because they "weren't good enough" for her, Ary was determined not to associate too closely with any blacks. Yet even before she had told her story, her physical appearance, especially her long, straight hair, had gained the octoroon a measure of status even among those "contraband" who resented her air of superiority.[35]

Certainly, many male and female slaves viewed African Americans with light skin and eye color, straight hair and noses, and thin lips as exceedingly attractive. When the mulatto Candis Goodwin was a young woman living on the Eastern Shore, she was considered "de purties'" girl in the area.[36] Virginia Haynes Shepherd of Churchland was the daughter of a domestic slave and a white doctor. Although she was embarrassed when asked about her paternity, Mrs. Shepherd was quite forthcoming with her impressions of black feminine beauty. Describing one slave woman of local acclaim, Shepherd noted: "Diana was a black beauty if there ever was one. She had this thin silk skin, a sharp nose, thin lips, a perfect set of white teeth and beautiful long coal-black hair."[37]

Thus, while Patience Avery and other mulattoes were uncomfortable with an ancestry that was partially white, other racially mixed African Americans, such as Ary, were proud of it, considered themselves superior to other blacks, and believed they were the elite within their families and their communities. Many blacks must have accepted these notions of entitlement that some light-skinned slaves promoted—few racially mixed slaves could have afforded to prolong such pretensions of superiority otherwise.

Of course, other problems related to the flaws in the antebellum South also haunted the families of bondsmen and bondswomen. Reared in a society that was extremely violent, even by the standards of the nineteenth century, slaves sometimes also chose brutal force as a means of control of their families and among their peers. (Recall the description of the beatings that Patience Richardson Avery stated her aunt gave her.) Privy to some of these events, whites from the South and North did not hesitate to comment on what they perceived as violent behavior that some slave child rearers exhibited when they punished their children.

Indeed, the stories regarding widespread violence of slaves toward each other were prevalent enough to warrant discussions of this issue in nineteenth-century guides outlining appropriate measures of treatment and control of slave property. Authors writing on the subject of slave management, on one hand, routinely advised masters to carefully scrutinize the domestic relations of their slaves in order to prevent physical abuse within the quarters.[38] Slaves, on the other hand, drew on both West African and European cultural dictates concerning the issue of corporal punishment. Most believed that "a few licks now and then, does em good," and whippings in response to numerous offenses were an important part of their children's socialization.[39]

The violence and brutality that whites imposed on their slaves undoubtedly influenced the ways in which bondsmen and bondswomen treated their own children and other dependents. The ability to beat someone, to hold that kind of physical control over another human, was a sadistic expression of power that blacks learned repeatedly from their interaction with and observation of white authority figures. This expression of control was meant to impress children with their parents' ability to command some power over their offspring's behavior. Also, adult slave kin wanted to demonstrate to whites, who often tried to usurp or demean slave parental authority, that they claimed a right to control and chastise their own children regardless of the legal guardianship that white owners possessed. Perhaps it was this demonstration of black slave power within their own domestic sphere rather than the concern for the actual physical pain the children endured that really offended whites.

As "contraband of war," for example, Virginia slaves who took refuge behind Union lines and went to reside in the federal army and freedmen aid-society camps quickly claimed their freedom, which in part they defined as a right to make vital decisions regarding their own children. It is obvious that they were no more receptive to the judgments that northern teachers and missionaries made about their methods of child discipline and rearing than they were of their former owners' "interference." One northern white teacher of the "contraband" in Virginia's southern coastal area wrote in 1864, "[W]e have our sympathies called out, almost every day, for the innocent children who are harshly beaten by their willful enemies[,] their harsh mamas. . . . [C]lose by us lives a black woman who lashes her little boy with a rawhide. We have remonstrated repeatedly, but she 'Reckons I shall beat my boy just as much as I please'; . . . and she does beat him till his cries wring the anguish from our hearts."[40]

Ex-slave Nancy Williams recalled that both of her parents gave her severe beatings when they thought that her behavior warranted it. Williams's mother sometimes feared that her husband was too harsh when he punished the mischievous girl. Nancy remembered one incident in which her father became particularly incensed with one of her pranks. After her father detected that she had stolen money from him and had then tried to disguise her crime with a lie, he exploded. Placing her in an old guano bag, Williams hung his daughter up on a rack in the meat house and began to "smoke" her. He hoped that this type of torture would induce the child to tell the truth. Instead, the odor and smoke from the burning tobacco along with her physical discomfort made Nancy "drunk." Angered even more by his failure to get her to confess, Mr. Williams then dumped the disoriented child onto the floor and began to beat her "somepin awful," all the while demanding that she recant her lie. The combination of pain, fear, and smoke caused Nancy to faint briefly. When she regained consciousness, she fled her father's whipping, calling on members of her family and community to intervene.[41]

The severity of the physical abuse that Nancy Williams's father inflicted on his child was probably unusual among slaves. Most ex-slaves recalling relationships with their parents spoke of receiving much more moderate discipline. One must not discount, however, the tremendous emotional stress under which adult slaves lived; it definitely affected their relationships with each other, sometimes even to the point of gross maltreatment. Yet one must also note that while Nancy's father's response was undoubtedly severe, he thought that his actions, regardless of their obvious harshness, would help his daughter to become a more responsible adult. Moreover, Mr. Williams believed that it was his duty and right as a Christian father to ensure that he reared his children with strong moral character, and therefore he felt that he had acted appropriately. "Father said he'd rather die an' go to hell an' burn den to live agin in heaven roun' Christ robe an' leave a passel o' tongue tied niggers to steal," Nancy Williams explained.[42] Still, Mr. Williams's behavior on that occasion indicated that he sometimes could lose control and that his anger and frustration could expose his family to acts that would hurt and humiliate as much as teach and protect.

Abuse in slave families was not limited to children alone. Spousal ill treatment was another serious problem. Relationships between husbands and wives suffered from slaveholders' usurpation of control in slave marriages even more profoundly than those relationships between parents and children. Verbal and physical abuse among married partners were sometimes responses to complex issues of discord within slave marriages. This prevalence of mistreatment among some antebellum blacks toward their spouses prompted one ex-slave to comment that "some good masters would punish slaves who mistreated womenfolk and some didn't."[43]

Unfounded in Virginia law, slave marriages were tenuous relationships in which couples struggled to survive among the immense and divisive pressures of slave life. Slaveholders had the final say as to which slaves would marry, whom they could marry, and when, and therefore exercised immense dominion over this most intimate of decisions affecting adult slaves. Because they controlled vital aspects of slave marriage, owners' actions often meant the success or failure of these relationships.

Concerned with economic and logistic issues that slaves were not privy to, masters sometimes imposed marriage partners on slaves whom the individual bondswoman or bondsman might not have chosen if given the opportunity to decide otherwise. Charles Grandy, an ex-slave from Norfolk, recalled that on the farm where he resided,

> Marsa used to sometimes pick our wives fo' us. If he didn't have on his place enough women for the men, he would wait on de side of de road till a big wagon loaded with slaves come by. Den Marsa would stop de ole nigger-trader and buy you a woman. Wasn't no use tryin' to pick one cause Marsa wasn't gonna pay but so much for her. All he wanted was a young healthy one who looked like she could have children, whether she was purty or ugly as sin.[44]

Although Grandy spoke specifically of the lack of choice male slaves had in acquiring wives, it is evident from his description of the process that the women involved—young women recently sold away from families and perhaps husbands—had absolutely no choice in the matter. Apparently the sexist perspectives of many male owners persuaded them to be more solicitous of the desires of male slaves in the matter than those of female slaves. Ex-slave Katie Blackwell Johnson explained that the slave women she knew "had no choice in the matter as to whom they would marry. If a man saw a girl he liked he would ask his master's permission to ask the master of the girl for her. If his master consented and her master consented, then they came together."[45] The emotional and sexual exploitation of some women slaves forced to marry men they did not love undoubtedly increased their resentment toward their masters and their husbands, which then sparked marital discord. Likewise, those males forced to marry women they did not know or even think physically appealing hindered the development of a loving, respectful marital relationship.

On some rare occasions, the preferential treatment that white male owners allowed bondsmen with regard to their choice of marriage partners (along with other salient variables such as the depletion of the young male slave population in some areas and an emphasis on slave breeding) contributed to polygamous marital relations among slaves. Israel Massie of Emporia, Virginia, noted that he knew of a few male slaves who were married to several women simultaneously. Usually these wives lived on different farms, yet Massie also recalled a polygamous marital situation where the husband and his wives lived on the same plantation. "When Tom died dar wuz Ginny, Sarah, Nancy, an' Patience," the Reverend Mr. Massie explained. "All four dar at de grave crying over dat one man. Do ya kno' chile, dem women never fou't fuss, an' quarrel over dem men folks? Dey seemed to understood each other."[46]

Massie's description of polygamous marriages among Virginia slaves provides important documentation of the existence of alternative and, perhaps, competitive marriage forms in Virginia at the end of the antebellum era ("competitive" because it is obvious that many slaves embraced monogamy rather than polygamy as the appropriate manner to orient their marriages). Given the paucity of information regarding the persistence of polygamy as a viable form of marital organization, however, it is difficult to discern whether it existed throughout the era or emerged as a response to slaveholder-engineered breeding schemes. Yet the cooperation of the women married to the slave Tom that Massie describes suggests that there were sociocultural and perhaps historical bases for the continual manifestation of polygamy among slaves.

Clearly, the marital forms and relationships of slaves were related in part to their owners' desires to increase their slave holdings. Many antebellum Virginia slaveholders insisted that their slaves exercise their procreative powers to the fullest extent and encouraged various forms of marriage or sociosexual bonding between male and female slaves to ensure high birthrates. Slave breeding in Virginia is well documented through child-to-woman ratios, the personal papers of owners, and the testimonies of slaves. As one ex-slave noted: "The masters were very careful about a good breedin' woman. If she had five or six children she was rarely sold."[47] A comparison of white and slave child-to-woman ratios from the period 1820 to 1860 as an indicator of fertility, for example, documents that slave women began having children at an earlier age than white females, although Anglo American women eventually did bear more children than black slave women. An analysis of several slave lists from Virginia, which include information descriptive of the age at first birth of slave mothers, further substantiates these findings. The average age at first birth for Virginia slaves was approximately twenty years. White women, on the other hand, began to have children later, at about twenty-two.[48] Moreover, while white child-to-woman ratios for both the considered age cohorts 0–14 years (child) : 15–49 years (mother) and 0–9 years : 10–49 years declined over the antebellum era, child-to-woman ratios for slave women considered in the cohorts 0–14 years (child) : 15–49 years (mother) increased noticeably during the same time period.[49] This evidence, along with a review of the changes in demographic patterns among slaves over time, documents that slave breeding was in some cases an important priority among Virginia slave owners.

The slave register of William Bolling and his heirs of Goochland County, Virginia, offers just such information for analysis.[50] William Bolling's register is a particularly valuable document because of the long time period it details (1752 to 1860) and the numbers of mothers whose children's birth dates were recorded. The Bolling list includes 103 mothers who had 493 children (an additional six were reported as stillborn) born to them during this 108-year period. Careful scrutiny of this document indicates that although the age at the mother's first birth did not change significantly, the time between the live births of slave children declined significantly. For the period 1800 to 1820, for example, the average time between slave births on the Bolling plantations was about thirty-three months. By the decade beginning in 1850, however, slave mothers were giving birth to a live child approximately every twenty-two months. In other words, the average time between live births had decreased by one third from 1820 to 1860.

While the information is less conclusive regarding the change in the average number of live children these women bore, it is clear that women in the last years of the antebellum era were having more children than those in the earlier decades. Within the ten-year period from 1850 to 1860 alone, the slave mothers on the Bolling plantations bore an average of four live children. Significantly, this figure conservatively represents only one half of the childbearing years of these mothers. When one analyzes the numbers of children that Bolling slave women had during the period 1820 to 1850 (which represents a more complete childbearing cycle), an average of five live births is calculated. Clearly, those slave women who were beginning to bear children at the end of the antebellum era demonstrated a greater potential for natural increase than those of earlier generations. That this demographic change came at a time when slave marriages and families were so threatened by substantial exportations of adult slaves of childbearing age speaks to the resolve of owners to encourage procreation among their slaves. In order to promote the rapid birth of slave children, slave masters not only offered material incentives and may have threatened those slaves who refused to cooperate, but also usurped the slaves' decision as to whether or not to participate in monogamous marital relationships. Some slaveholders forced slave women and men to have several sexual partners outside of their marriage. Elige Davisson of Richmond, for example, stated that he was married once before he became free, but his owner still brought "some more women to see" him. Davisson insisted that his master would not let him have "just one woman" but mandated that the young male slave have sexual relations with several other female slaves so that they would bear children.[51] Such demands to participate in their owner's breeding schemes brought a great deal of pain and anger to the individual slaves and to the couples involved.

Undoubtedly slave marriages varied in terms of quality, length, and ideals even in the most supportive environment. Most slaves wanted long-standing, loving, affectionate, monogamous relationships with their spouses. Yet they could not expect that their partners would be able to protect them from some of the most violent and abusive aspects of slave life. Most could only hope that their spouses would understand the lack of choices they had with regard to labor, attention to domestic responsibilities, and their relationships with whites. The inability of slave wives and husbands to actualize their ideals of gender-differentiated behavior, even those that were obviously unrealistic given their positions as slaves, often was the source of marital discord.

Slave women with "abroad marriages" usually had no alternative but to take on the role of the central authority figure within their immediate families, especially as child rearers, while their husbands lived on separate plantations. In doing so, however, they challenged Western traditions concerning gender-specific behavior and power in nineteenth-century households that slaves often respected. Consequently, matrifocal families were common among late-antebellum Virginia slaves but were not always acceptable to the couples who comprised them. Since many slave women and men hoped to function in their families according to the proposed ideal of the larger southern society, their inability to do so engendered resentment, frustration, and anger.

Thomas Harper, for example, a slave blacksmith in Alexandria, Virginia, decided to escape to Canada because he was not allowed to support his family. It was, he explained, too "hard to see them in want and abused when he was not at liberty to aid or protect them."[52] Another Virginia slave confessed that he traded stolen goods in order to provide material support for his wife and children. "There were, in our vicinity," he noted, "plenty of 'poor white folks,' as we contemptuously called them, whom we cordially despised, but with whom we carried on a regular traffic at our master's expense."[53] Dangerfield Newby became so frustrated in his attempts to secure his family's freedom that he helped plan and execute the raid of John Brown on Harpers Ferry in 1859. His need to offer his wife and children the security of freedom was enhanced by his wife's constant appeal. "I want you to buy me as soon as possible," she wrote to him in August 1859, "for if you do not get me somebody else will. . . . Do all you can for me, which I have no doubt you will," she begged.[54] The blacksmith's desire to "protect" and "support" his family as well as the Newbys' feelings about the husband's duty to provide the security of freedom to his family suggest that some slaves held ideals of manhood also popular in some European and African cultures.

Slave husbands sometimes imposed nearly impossible ideals of womanhood on their wives as well. Some were reluctant to commit themselves to women who did not meet their standards of beauty. Charles Grandy stated that slave men resented slaveholders who chose wives for them that were "ugly" instead of "purty." Ralph, a slave from Richmond, commented that when he first met his future wife (a free black), he thought that she "was one of the most beautiful of women." According to the Richmond bondsman, her beauty was one of the principal reasons that he "soon became madly in love."[55] Of course, no one wanted to marry someone as "ugly as sin," and certainly many slave women were physically attractive. Nevertheless, their harsh work routines, nutritionally deficient diets, poor material support, and limited access to medical attention robbed many slave women of their vitality and beauty when they were still young. Moreover, white men often reserved the most attractive slave women for themselves, refusing to let them marry slaves, or violated slave marriages whenever they chose to do so. Not surprisingly, ideals concerning female purity and marital chastity presented extreme challenges to slave couples.

The instances of white male sexual aggression toward married slave women created a great deal of tension and discord in the marital relationships of slaves. Although slave husbands theoretically understood the inability of their wives to protect themselves against the sexual overtures and attacks of white men, they resented and were angered by such occurrences. Their reactions were in response equally to their own sense of powerlessness to defend their wives and to a recognition of the physical and psychological pain their spouses experienced. When slave husbands did intervene, they suffered harsh retaliation—severe beatings, sometimes permanent separation from their family, or even murder. Many probably felt, as did Charles Grandy, who spoke of the murder of a male slave who tried to protect his wife from the advances of their overseer, that a "nigger ain't got no chance."[56]

Consequently, some slave husbands targeted their helpless wives to be the recipients of their frustration, pain, guilt, and rage rather than the white men who attacked them. Regardless of whom the slaves struck out at, however, their responses had little effect on the behavior of those white men who raped female slaves. "Marsters an' overseers use to make slaves dat wuz wid deir husbands git up, [and] do as they say," Israel Massie noted. "Send husbands out on de farm, milkin' cows or cuttin' wood. Den he gits in bed wid slave himself. Some women would fight an tussel. Others would be 'umble—feared of dat beatin.' What we saw, couldn't do nothing 'bout it. . . . My blood is bilin' now [at the] thoughts of dem times. Ef dey told dey husbands he wuz powerless."[57]

Many slave women were ashamed that they had been victimized by their white masters and were afraid of the consequences for themselves, their families, and the children they might have conceived. They tried to conceal the sexual assault from their husbands. "When babies came," Massie went on to explain, "dey [white fathers] ain't exknowledge 'em. Treat dat baby like 'tothers—nuthing to him. Mother feard to tell 'cause she know'd what she'd git. Dat wuz de concealed part."[58] Some slave wives went to great lengths to keep the truth from their husbands, claiming that mulatto children actually belonged to their spouses. "Ole man, . . . stop stedin' [studying] so much foolishness," responded one frightened slave wife when her husband noted that their youngest child was very physically distinct from their other children.[59] She was able to end her husband's open suspicions by constructing a story, but few could hide the obvious.

Faced with such overwhelming problems, some slave couples responded in ways that further augmented the destruction of their marriages and families. Alcoholism, domestic violence, jealousy, and adultery were internal problems that sometimes plagued these relationships. More than a few slave couples voluntarily separated. Manfra and Dykstra's review of a survey of late-antebellum slave couples who resided in the south of Virginia, for example, indicates that of those marriages terminated before general emancipation, 10.1 percent ended as a result of mutual consent and another 10.8 percent because of the desertion of a spouse.[60]

Given the degradation of monogamous marriage relations among slaves, it is not surprising that some slaves had limited respect for the institution. Ralph (mentioned earlier) noted that when he first met his future wife, he realized that she was married and a mother but persisted in his pursuit of her. Explaining his behavior, he noted:

> And how can the slave be expected to observe the marriage vows? In most cases they make none—plight no troth—have a sort of understanding that their agreement shall continue until one or both choose to form some other tie. And even if wishing to continue faithful unto death, they know their master deems their vows null and void, if he chooses to separate them; and he often does without scruple, by selling one or both. When their superiors disregard their slaves' obligations, the slaves will think lightly of them, too; and this utter contempt of the whites for the sacredness of marriage amongst slaves has done more to demoralize and brutalize the slave than all the personal wrongs he suffers. . . . The *sentiment* that should exist in marriage is excluded or crushed by the necessity of their condition; and the tie becomes a mere *liaison*, founded upon the instinct of the brute.[61]

Perhaps Ralph's impressively erudite critique of slave marriages derived principally from his attempt to justify his own adulterous actions. Yet his analysis of the marital commitment between slaves is suggestive of the demoralizing effect that slavery must have had on some couples. Ralph did not hesitate to ignore the bounds of propriety when he sought and succeeded in winning another man's wife as his own. "For a good while," the slave noted, "she might be said to have two husbands: but finally her first husband went . . . and Sally became my acknowledged wife."[62]

Most slaves certainly respected the institution and believed that to interfere with the relations between a husband and a wife was wrong. Even Ralph felt that he was morally wrong in so doing. His inevitable guilt regarding the matter surfaced several years later. Trying to comprehend the reason for his wife's untimely death, the mourning slave concluded that he "deserved to lose her" because of the immoral way he had won her—"a just retribution and requital of her first husband's wrongs."[63]

The forced separation of slave couples, of course, had the most devastating impact on slave marriages. Large numbers of loving commitments ended in this manner. When slaveholders separated husbands and wives by long distances, it was almost impossible for these couples to retain close ties to each other. The difficulty was a result of the emotional and sociosexual needs of adult slaves as well as of the insistence of their owners that they remain sexually active and thus naturally reproductive. Some masters expected these separated couples to form new relationships as soon as possible. Many did eventually remarry, but the pain and sense of loss that they felt must have been a source of continual anguish for them and their children, who had to adjust to the authority of stepparents and to their inclusion in stepfamilies.

When one Virginia "contraband" woman found her first husband in a refugee camp in 1864, she testified that the two "threw [them]selves into each others arms and cried." The husband as well as the woman, however, had remarried since their forced separation. While his new wife looked on the touching scene of reunion with obvious jealousy, the older wife was disturbed for other reasons. Although she described her present husband as "very kind" and she was determined not to leave him, she had to admit that she could no longer be happy after seeing her first husband. The thought of the source of their permanent separation still angered and frustrated her, even though she claimed she was pleased with her present spouse. "White folk's got a heap to answer for the way they've done to colored folks! So much they wont never *pray* it away!" she concluded in disgust.[64]

The voice of this one ex-slave in condemning those slaveholders who purposely destroyed slave marriages and families is no doubt representative of the voices of many who were similarly hurt. Their personal testimonies as well as the plantation records of their owners document the destruction that came to many Virginia slave families during the last decades of the antebellum era. Involuntary separation and the dispersal of husbands and wives from the rest of their families, sexual abuse, material deprivation, and forced marriages were some of the tremendous problems faced by slave families. Domestic violence, color stratification, spousal abandonment, and adultery were some of the manifestations of the internal strife within black slave families and marriages, caused in large measure by their oppressive living conditions.

Late-antebellum southern society was indeed a harsh environment within which slaves tried to establish and maintain successful marriages and families. Many were able to do so, yet others failed in their efforts to sustain viable slave marriages and kin networks. The lives of Virginia slaves were too precarious to guarantee the complete and constant success of any social institution, including marriage and the family. Consequently, the slave family emerged in the postbellum South as a viable but battered institution, threatened by new forms of economic and social oppression as well as the internal strife inherited from the previous era.

Notes

1. Several important works are available which are discussions of the general lifestyles as well as family and marriage problems of antebellum Southerners. For free blacks in antebellum Virginia, see Luther P. Jackson, *Free Negro Labor and Property Holding in Virginia, 1830–1860* (New York: Athenaeum, 1969 [c. 1942]; reprint ed., 1986). See also: "Free Women of Color" in Suzanne Lebsock, *The Free Women of Petersburg: Status and*

Culture in a Southern Town, 1784–1860 (New York: W. W. Norton, 1984), 87–111. For a general discussion of free blacks in the antebellum lower South, see Ira Berlin, *Slaves Without Masters: The Free Negro in the Antebellum South* (New York: Vintage Books, 1976), 174.

Concerning slavery and the slave family, the most impressive, scholarly treatments are found in John W. Blassingame, *The Slave Community: Plantation Life in the Antebellum South* (New York: Oxford Univ. Press, 1972), Deborah Gray White, *Ar'n't I A Woman? Female Slaves in the Plantation South* (New York: W. W. Norton, 1985); Eugene Genovese, *Roll, Jordan, Roll: The World the Slaves Made* (New York: Pantheon Books, 1974), and particularly Herbert G. Gutman, *The Black Family in Slavery and Freedom, 1750–1925* (New York: Pantheon Books, 1976).

For the most thoughtful descriptions of antebellum white familial relations, see Elizabeth Fox-Genovese *Within the Plantation Household: Black and White Women in the Old South* (Chapel Hill: Univ. of North Carolina Press, 1988); Catherine Clinton *The Plantation Mistress: Woman's World in the Old South* (New York: Pantheon Books, 1982); Bertram Wyatt-Brown, *Southern Honor: Ethics and Behavior in the Old South* (New York: Oxford Univ. Press, 1982); Anne Firor Scott, *The Southern Lady: From Pedestal to Politics, 1830–1930* (Chicago: Univ. of Chicago Press, 1970); and Lebsock, *Free Women of Petersburg.*

2. Richard Sutch, "The Breeding of Slaves for Sale and the Westward Expansion of Slavery, 1850–1860," in Stanley L. Engerman and Eugene Genovese, eds., *Race and Slavery in the Western Hemisphere: Quantitative Studies* (Princeton: Princeton Univ. Press, 1975), Appendix, Table 4, p. 207.

3. Donald M. Sweig, "Northern Virginia Slavery: A Statistical and Demographic Investigation" (Ph.D. dissertation, College of William and Mary, 1982), 206.

4. Sutch, "The Breeding of Slaves for Sale," Appendix, Tables 4 and 5, pp. 207, 209.

5. JoAnn Manfra and Robert R. Dykstra, "Serial Marriage and the Origins of the Black Stepfamily: The Rowanty Evidence," *Journal of American History* 72 (June 1985): 32. These authors state that 35.3 percent of slave marriages terminated in their sample from Dinwiddie County, Virginia was due to involuntary separation. Comparatively, Blassingame in his compilation of causes of slave marriage termination records that 39 percent in Mississippi, 26.8 percent in Tennessee, and 29.2 percent in Louisiana ended as a result of forced separation. Blassingame, *Slave Community*, Table 2, p. 90.

6. Manfra and Dykstra, "Serial Marriage," p. 36.

7. The slave narrative which comprise this sample were the 142 included in Charles L. Perdue, Jr., Thomas E. Barden, and Robert K. Phillips, eds., *Weevils in the Wheat: Interviews with Virginia Ex-Slaves* (Charlottesville: Univ. Press of Virginia, 1976).

8. Ibid,. p. 1.

9. Ibid., p.3.

10. Ibid., pp. 1, 3.

11. Ibid., pp. 3–4.

12. "Slave List," Bruce Family Papers, Virginia Historical Society, Richmond, hereafter referred to as VHS.

13. Robert S. Starobin, ed., *Blacks in Bondage: Letters of American Slaves* (reprinted, New York: Markus Wiener Publishing, 1988), 72.

14. Anthropologist Nancy Tanner offers one of the most viable definitions for matrifocality. She describes the term in part as "(1) kinship systems in which (a) the role of the mother is structurally, culturally, and affectively central and (b) this multidimensional centrality is legitimate; and (2) the societies in which these features coexist, where (a) the relationship between the sexes is relatively egalitarian and (b) both women and men are important actors in the economic and ritual spheres." Matrilocal families are those in which the majority of the functional members reside in the home of the mother. Nancy Tanner, "Matrifocality in Indonesia and Africa and Among Black Americans," in Michele Zimbalist Rosaldo and Louise Lamphere, eds., *Woman, Culture and Society* (Stanford: Stanford Univ. Press, 1974), 131.

15. William Waller Hennings, ed., *The Statutes at Large: Being a Collection of All the Laws of Virginia*, vol. 2 (Richmond: Samuel Pleasants, 1832), 170.

16. Perdue et al., eds., *Weevils in the Wheat*, passim. See, for example, Frank Bell's description of his Uncle Moses Bell's relationship with his family, p. 26.

17. Perdue et al., eds., *Weevils in the Wheat*, passim.

18. Norman Yetman, ed., *Voices from Slavery* (New York: Holt, Rinehart and Winston, 1970), 26.

19. Perdue et al., eds., *Weevils in the Wheat*, p. 161.

20. Sutch, "Breeding of Slaves for Sale," Appendix, Table 5, p. 209.

21. Information for computation of the average age of Virginia slave mothers at first birth, 19.71 years, was compiled from slave lists dated during the period 1800–1865, located in the William H. Gray Farm Book, Gray Family Papers, VHS; Ledger of George Saunders, Saunders Family Papers, Virginia State Library, Richmond, Virginia. Ledger of William Gatewood and Samuel Vance Gatewood, Gatewood Family Papers, VHS; Stringfellow Family Bible, Stringfellow Family Papers, VHS; Allen T. Caperton Family Papers, VHS;

Slave Lists, John Young Mason Papers, VHS; Slave Lists, William Bolling Papers, VHS; Slave List, Baskerville Family Papers, VHS.

Trussel and Steckel estimate that the mean age of first birth for slave mothers throughout the antebellum South was 20.6 years. James Trussel and Richard Steckel, "The Age of Slaves at Menarche and Their First Birth" *Journal of Interdisciplinary History*, 8 (Winter 1978): 492.

22. Perdue et al., eds., *Weevils in the Wheat*, p. 199.

23. Ibid., p. 33.

24. Ibid.

25. Eugene Genovese also argues, and rightfully so, that "inherent" in the "paternalism" of slave owners, "were dangerously deceptive ideas of 'gratitude,' 'loyalty,' and 'family.' Inherent also was an intimacy that turned every act of impudence and insubordination—every act of unsanctioned self-assertion—into an act of treason and disloyalty, for by repudiating the principle of submission it struck at the heart of the master' moral self-justification and therefore at his self-esteem." Genovese, *Roll, Jordan, Roll*, p. 91.

For more detailed discussions of these issues, see Thomas L. Weber, *Deep Like the Rivers: Education in the Slave Quarter Community, 1831–1865* (New York: W. W. Norton, 1978), 63–79, passim; and Brenda Stevenson, "'Seemed Like Your Children Belonged to Everyone But You': The Rearing of Slave Children in Antebellum Virginia," presented at the annual conference of the Organization of American Historians, Apr. 12, 1987, Reno, Nevada.

26. Perdue et al., eds., *Weevils in the Wheat*, p. 68.

27. Ibid., p. 150.

28. Ibid., p. 317.

29. Ibid., p. 245.

30. Ibid., p. 15.

31. Ibid., pp. 16–17.

32. Ibid.

33. Ibid., p. 108.

34. In late May 1861, General Benjamin F. Butler of the United States Army, then commander of Fortress Monroe at Old Point Comfort, Virginia, decided to accept slaves escaping from Confederate owners as "contraband" of the Civil War, that is, property which belonged to the enemy that could have been used against the Union in the war effort. His decision set an important precedent in the war, and before its end, thousands of slaves escaped and sought protection in Union-held camps and forts as "contraband." See, for example, Robert Francis Engs's discussion in *Freedom's First Generation: Black Hampton, Virginia, 1861–1890* (Philadelphia: Univ. of Pennsylvania Press, 1979), 18–22.

35. Henry Swint, ed., *Dear Ones At Home: Letters from Contraband Camps* (Nashville: Vanderbilt Univ. Press, 1966), 39, 55–56, 73.

36. Perdue et al., eds., *Weevils in the Wheat*, pp. 108–9.

37. Ibid., pp. 255–57.

38. James O. Breeden, ed., *Advice to Masters: The Ideal in Slave Management in the Old South* (Westport, Conn.: Greenwood Press, 1980), 282.

39. Swint, ed., *Dear Ones at Home*, p. 161.

40. Ibid., p. 123.

41. Perdue et al., eds., *Weevils in the Wheat*, p. 317.

42. Ibid.

43. Ibid., p. 161.

44. Quoted in *The Negro in Virginia*. Compiled by the Virginia Federal Writers' Project of the Work Projects Administration in the state of Virginia (New York: Hastings Publishers, 1940), 83–84.

45. Perdue et al., eds., *Weevils in the Wheat*, p. 161.

46. Ibid., p. 209.

47. Ibid., p. 161.

48. For information on sources consulted in the computation of the average age of Virginia slave mothers at first birth, see note 21 above. James Trussell and Richard Steckel estimate that the mean age at first birth for antebellum Southern white women was "about two years" later than the projected 20.6 years they estimated for age at first birth for slave mothers in the antebellum South. Trussell and Steckel, "The Age of Slaves at Menarche and Their First Birth," p. 492.

49. Consider, for example, the child:woman ratios for slaves and whites in Virginia when distributed in the age cohorts 1–14 years (children) and 14/15–49 years (women) represented in Table A.

Table B includes child:woman ratios for slaves and whites in Virginia distributed in the age cohorts 0–9 years (children) and 10–49 years (women).

50. William Bolling Slave Register, 1752–1865, Bolling Family Papers, VHS.

Table A

Census Year	Slave	White
1820	1.916678	2.499881
1830	1.818838	1.358570*
1840	1.960139	2.172618
1850	2.057590	2.162029
1860	2.012159	2.191168

* The unusually low ratio produced from census information available for 1830 is probably indicative of a substantial undercount of white children age 0–14 years old. This error also is reflected in the white child : woman ratio for 1830 descriptive of the age cohorts 0–9 years (children) and 10–49 years (women), and to a lesser extent for blacks during this census year in both categories of compilation.

Table B

Census Year	Slave	White
1820	—	1.237707
1830	1.311458	.950202*
1840	1.346319	1.226515
1850	1.079547	1.3326
1860	1.047343	1.015537

* This ratio probably reflects an undercount of children aged 0–9 years during this census year.

Sources: Census for 1820 (Washington, D.C.: G504, 512, 518, Gales and Seaton, 1821), 23–26; Fifth Census or Enumeration of the Inhabitants of the United States, 1830 (Washington, D.C.: Duff Green, 1832), 87, 89; Compendium of the Enumeration of the Inhabitants of the Unites States (Washington, D.C.: Department of the Interior, 1841), 32–33, 36–38; J. D. B. DeBow, Statistical View of the United States . . . Being a Compendium of the Seventh Census . . . (Washington, D.C.: A. O. P. Nicholson, 1854), 215, 253–55, 257; Joseph G. Kennedy, Population of the United States in 1860, Compiled from the Original Returns of the Eighth Census (Washington. D.C.: Government Printing Office, 1864), 507–8, 512.

51. Yetman, ed., Voices from Slavery, p. 92.
52. William Still, ed., Underground Railroad (New York: Arno Press, 1968), 411.
53. "A Slave's Story," Putnam Monthly Magazine 9 (June 1957): 617.
54. John W. Blassingame, ed., Slave Testimony: Two Centuries of Letters, Speeches, Interviews and Autobiographies (Baton Rouge: Louisiana State Univ. Press, 1977), 118.
55. Negro in Virginia, p. 84; "A Slave's Story," p. 617.
56. Perdue et al., eds., Weevils in the Wheat, p. 117.
57. Ibid., p. 207.
58. Ibid.
59. Ibid.
60. Manfra and Dykstra, "Serial Marriage," p. 32.
61. "A Slave's Story," p. 617.
62. Ibid.
63. Ibid., pp. 617–18.
64. Swint, ed., Dear Ones At Home, pp. 123–24.

4

Gender, Race, and Culture: Spanish Mexican Women in the Historiography of Frontier California

Antonia I. Castañeda

Historians, whether writing for a popular or a scholarly audience, reflect contemporary ideology with respect to sex, race, and culture. Until the mid-1970s, when significant revisionist work in social, women's, and Chicano history began to appear, the writing of California history reflected an ideology that ascribed racial and cultural inferiority to Mexicans and sexual inferiority to women.[1] Not only do ideas about women form an integral part of the ideological universe of all societies, but the position of women in society is one measure by which civilizations have historically been judged.[2] Accordingly, California historians applied Anglo, middle-class norms of women's proper behavior to Mexican women's comportment and judged them according to their own perceptions of Mexican culture and of women's positions within that culture.

This essay pays a good deal of attention to the popular histories of frontier California because of the inordinate influence they have had on the more scholarly studies. In particular, the factual errors and stereotypes in the work of Hubert Howe Bancroft, Theodore H. Hittell, and Zoeth Skinner Eldredge have been propagated not only by other nineteenth- and twentieth-century popularizers but also by scholars—in the few instances where they include women at all. Although historians of the Teutonic, frontier hypothesis, and Spanish borderlands schools barely mention women, an implicit gender ideology influences their discussions of race, national character, and culture. The more recent literature in social, women's, and Chicano history breaks sharply with the earlier ideology and corollary interpretations with respect to race and culture or gender and culture, but it has yet to construct an integrative interpretation that incorporates sex-gender, race, and culture.

The Popular Histories of the Late Nineteeth Century

> Women were not treated with the greatest respect: in Latin and in savage countries they seldom are; hence, as these were half Latin and half savage, we are not surprised to learn that the men too often idled away their time, leaving the women to do all the work and rear the family.[3]

Written by lawyers, bankers, and other prominent men who came to California in the aftermath of the Mexican War and the gold rush, the multivolume popular histories of the late nineteenth century provide the first composite description and interpretation of Spanish Mexican California.[4] These histories fundamentally reflect the political and socioracial ideology that informed both the war with Mexico and the subsequent sociopolitical and economic marginalization of Mexicans in California.[5] With respect to women, they reaffirm the contradictory but stereotypic images found in the travel journals and other documents

58

written by entrepreneurs, merchants, adventurers, and other members of the advance guard of expansion between the 1820s and 1840s.[6]

In the tradition of the patrician historians whose romantic literary style set the standards and popular patterns from the end of the nineteenth century until well into the twentieth, Bancroft, Hittell, and other popularizers intersperse their voluminous histories of California with musings about race, religion, national character, savagery, and civilization.[7] Riddled with the nationalistic fervor of the post–Civil War decades and with an unquestioning belief in Nordic racial superiority, these historians predictably conclude that the Anglo-Saxon race and civilization are far superior to the Latin race and Spanish Mexican civilization that had produced in California, according to Bancroft, "a race halfway between the proud Castillian and the lowly root digger," existing "halfway between savagery and civilization."[8] Only Amerindians ranked lower than the minions of Spain.

In the works on early colonial development, the discussion of women is only incidental to the larger consideration of specific institutions—the mission, presidio, and pueblo—or of great men, the governors. Thus, for example, a brief discussion of the maltreatment of Amerindian women in the mission system has no importance beyond its illustration of institutional development and Spanish brutality, which, in the tradition of the "Black Legend," spared not even women.[9] Similarly, Bancroft treats sexual and other violence against native women primarily in relation to the bitter conflict between the institutions of church and state, and attributes it to the moral degeneration of the racially mixed soldier-settler population.

Bancroft and his colleagues also introduce individual elite women to their readers. The portraits of two in particular set the tone for the consistent romanticization of "Spanish" as opposed to "Mexican" women. A prototype of the tempestuous Spanish woman, Eulalia Callis, the high-born Catalán wife of the doughty Governor Fages, was dubbed the "infamous *governadora*" (governor's wife) for refusing Fages her bed upon his refusal to relinquish the governorship and return the family to Mexico.[10]

Even more important in the development of the "Spanish" stereotype was Concepción Arguello, the young daughter of Don José Arguello, commandant at the Presidio of San Francisco. Prototype of the tragic maiden, Doña Concepción became betrothed to the Russian ambassador and chamberlain Nickolai Petrovich Resanov in 1806.[11] Resanov had sailed to California from Alaska aboard the brig *Juno*, seeking to trade the ship's entire cargo for foodstuffs desperately needed to stave off starvation and mass desertions in Sitka. But Governor Arrillaga, bound by Spain's policy of prohibiting trade with foreigners, refused to negotiate. Undaunted, Resanov wooed the young Concepción and, upon her acceptance of his proposal of marriage, persuaded her father to intercede with the governor, who finally agreed to the trade.

Resanov left for Alaska and thereafter for Russia, promising to return as soon as he had the czar's permission to marry, but he died while in Russia. Doña Concepción continued to await his return, for she did not learn of his death until many years later. After a life spent in nursing and charitable work, she became, in 1851, the first novice in the newly established Dominican convent in Monterey. She took her vows as Sister María Dominica in 1852 and died five years later at age sixty-six.[12]

Bancroft's commentary addresses not only the diplomatic and political strategy evident in Resanov's courtship and proposal of marriage but also the character of the Californians, both male and female: "What wonder that court life at St. Petersburg was fascinating, or that this child, weary of the sun-basking indolence of those about her, allowed her heart to follow her ambitions."[13] This aura of exotic drama and romance informs all later descriptions of "Spanish" women, in popular and scholarly works alike.

Bancroft also briefly discusses women in the context of colonial settlement and the family. He records the arrival of the first group of Spanish Mexican women and families in 1774 and the overland journeys of the Anza and Rivera soldier-settler families in 1775–76 and 1781 respectively. He also comments on Governor Borica's efforts to attract single women to the distant frontier and on the arrival of the *niñas de cuna*, the ten orphan girls brought to Alta California in 1800 as future marriage partners for single presidial soldiers.[14]

In general, the popular historical accounts of the Spanish period (1769–1821) are notable for their absence of pejorative gender-specific sexual stereotypes. Instead, pejorative stereotypes are generalized to the entire group and focus on race. In accounts of Mexican California (1822–46), the popular historians divide women into two classes: "Spanish" and "Mexican." Although the vast majority of Californians, including the elite, were *mestizo* or *mulato* and Mexican, not Spanish, in nationality, women from longtime Californian elite, landowning families, some of whom married Europeans or Euro-Americans, were called "Spanish." Women from more recently arrived or nonelite families were called "Mexican." "Spanish" women were morally, sexually, and racially pure; "Mexican" women were immoral and sexually and racially impure. These sexual stereotypes not only reveal the convergence of contemporary political and social ideological currents but also underscore the centrality of the politics of sex to the ideological justification of expansion, war, and conquest. The dominant social Darwinism of the late nineteenth century, which used scientific theory to rationalize Nordic racial superiority and male sexual supremacy, also held that a society's degree of civilization could be judged by the status and character of its women. The Victorian true woman, like her predecessor the republican mother, represented the most advanced stage of civilized society.[15] Physically and mentally inferior to men but possessed of the cardinal female virtues—piety, purity, submissiveness, and domesticity—she was confined to the home, where she could neither threaten nor challenge the existing order. She was the norm by which historians judged Mexican women, individually and collectively, and thus one of the norms by which they judged Mexican society. Like other reductionist representations of Mexicans in the literature that treats the Mexican period as a "backdrop to the coming of Old Glory," pejorative stereotypes of Mexicanas thus served a political purpose.[16] The worst stereotypes of women appeared in the histories of the Mexican rather than the Spanish period not just because the primary sources were written largely by white men who visited and/or lived in Mexican, not Spanish, California, but because the war was fought with Mexico.

The most extensive treatment of Mexican women appears in Bancroft's interpretative social history, *California Pastoral,* in which he devotes an entire chapter to "Woman and Her Sphere."[17] By virtue of publishing the earliest work of this genre, Bancroft became the main source for the stereotypes of women in Mexican California in subsequent histories.

In the work of Bancroft, Hittell, and their modern successors, the portrayals of Mexican men, the wartime foes, are uniformly stereotypic and pejorative, focusing both on their racial origins and on a national character formed by Spanish tyranny, absolutism, and fanaticism. Bancroft describes Mexicans as "droves of mongrels" deriving from a "turgid racial stream" and concludes that they were "not a strong community either physically, morally, or politically." He depicts life in Mexican California as a long, happy holiday in a lotus land where "to eat, to drink, to make love, to smoke, to dance, to ride, to sleep seemed the whole duty of man."[18]

His stereotypes of women, however, are contradictory and reveal greater gradation. Women's position in Mexican society, especially, is treated contradictorily. "The Californians, violent exercise and lack of education makes them rough and almost brutal. They have little regard for their women, and are of a jealous disposition . . . they are indifferent husbands, faithless and exacting and very hard taskmasters," Bancroft says at one point. Yet several pages later he comments, "[T]here was strong affection and never a happier family than when a ranchero, dwelling in pastoral simplicity saw his sons and his sons' sons bringing to the paternal roof their wives and seating them at the ever-lengthening table."[19]

Bancroft's Mexican women are dunces and drudges. They work laboriously and continuously; bear twelve, fifteen, and twenty children; and are subject to being prostituted by their husbands, who "wink at the familiarity of a wealthy neighbor who pays handsomely for his entertainment." Women have no recourse to laws, which men make and women obey. At the same time, however, Bancroft quotes earlier writers to the effect that "the women are pretty, but vain, frivolous, bad managers, and extravagant. They are passionately fond of fine, showy dresses and jewelry . . . their morality is none of the purest; and the coarse and lascivious dances show the degraded tone of manners that exist." Nevertheless, infidelity is rare because Californianas fear the swift and deadly revenge exacted by jealous husbands.[20]

Bancroft based his negative images of Mexican women on the accounts of Richard Henry Dana and others who visited California in the 1840s, on the eve of the war with Mexico. But he also recorded a positive image derived from the writings of Alfred Robinson and other Euro-Americans who traveled to California in the 1820s and 1830s to ply the hide and tallow trade and who married elite Californianas and settled there.[21]

Robinson's accounts expressed similar negative stereotypes of men but presented positive portrayals of "Spanish" or "Californio" women. Robinson, who married María Teresa de la Guerra y Noriega, wrote that "the men are generally indolent and addicted to many vices . . . yet . . . in few places of the world . . . can be found more chastity, industrious habits and correct deportment than among the women."[22] Similar images appeared in literary pieces written on the eve of the Mexican War by individuals who had no firsthand experience of California. In this literature, Spanish-speaking women invited the advances of Euro-American men, whom they anxiously awaited as their saviors from Mexican men. For example, "They Wait for Us," published in Boston at the time that John C. Frémont's outlaw band was raising the Bear Flag at Sonoma in June 1846, treats Mexican women as the symbol for the country about to be conquered:

> They Wait for Us
>
> The Spanish maid, with eyes of fire
> At balmy evening turns her lyre,
> And, looking to the Eastern sky,
> Awaits our Yankee Chivalry
> Whose purer blood and valiant arms,
> Are fit to clasp her budding charms.
>
> The *man*, her mate, is sunk in sloth—
> To love, his senseless heart is loth:
> The pipe and glass and tinkling lute,
> A sofa, and a dish of fruit;
> A nap, some dozen times by day;
> Sombre and sad, and never gay.[23]

The meaning is clear—Mexicans cannot appreciate, love, direct, or control their women/country.

Forty years later, Bancroft and Hittell underscored this theme in the primary sources. "It was a happy day," writes Bancroft, "for the California bride whose husband was an American." According to Hittell, Californian *señoritas* eagerly sought American husbands, who "might not touch the guitar as lightly," but "made better husbands than those of Mexican blood."[24] The chaste, industrious Spanish beauty who forsook her inferior man and nation in favor of the superior Euro-American became embedded in the literature. The negative image that Bancroft and others picked up from the English-language primary sources was reserved for Mexican women: *fandango*-dancing, *monte*-dealing prostitutes, the consorts of Mexican bandits.[25] These dual stereotypes became the prototypic images of Spanish-speaking women in California. They were the grist of popular fiction and contemporary newspapers throughout the latter part of the nineteenth and early twentieth centuries, and they resurfaced in the popular historical literature of the twentieth century, including the few works that focused specifically on women of Spanish California.

The Makers of Modern Historiography: The Teutonic Historians

While Bancroft, Hittell, and other popularizers stereotyped women in their sweeping general histories of California, their scholarly contemporaries, the Teutonic historians, barely mentioned women at all. As professional historical scholarship took root in the post–Civil War era, the question of gender became a nonissue.[26]

Rather, the new scientific historians, reflecting the period's conservative, organic nationalism, were concerned principally with explaining the origin, nature, and Old World antecedents of Euro-American institutions in the United States. Their studies focused on political institutions, the pivotal structures perceived both as the sources of a nation's order and coherence and as the hallmarks that distinguished one civilization from another. They dichotomized such institutions into free and nonfree, defining democratic institutions based on representative government as free and superior, and institutions based on monarchies as unfree and inferior.[27] The Teutonics divided contemporary New World civilizations deriving from European origins accordingly.

For these historians, deification of the national state was closely linked to glorification of Anglo-Saxon people and institutions. Euro-American civilization in the United States, according to the Teutonic germ theory of history, was characterized by superior, free institutions transplanted from medieval England and Germany by Anglo-Saxons, the superior Caucasian race, and destined to expand to the entire North American continent. The Teutonics did not question the earlier romantic historians' interpretation of continental expansion as God-ordained manifest destiny; instead, they recast the same view in terms of evolutionary theory.[28] In the inexorable sweep of Anglo-Saxons across the continent, inferior races and civilizations were to be swept aside.

The Teutonic historians' emphasis on Old World antecedents focused their attention on the eastern region of the United States rather than on the Far West, which had but recently been incorporated into the Union. The few early scholarly studies of colonial California and the Southwest focused on Spanish institutional development.[29] For post–Civil War historians concerned with nationalism and national unification, the important question was how to explain the Spanish-Mexican institutions rooted in California and the Southwest. A corollary question was how to incorporate the new region intellectually and ideologically into the history of the United States.[30]

While imbued with the more objective scientific approach to historical research being taught at Johns Hopkins and other graduate schools, scholarly studies were nevertheless informed by the racist attitudes that saturated the primary sources and popular histories, particularly those of the Mexican War era, and by the colonial legacy of the Black Legend. In explaining the Spanish presence and institutions in the region ceded to the United States, the

Teutonic historians concluded that Spain had failed to implant permanent institutions in this area, for two reasons. First, Spanish political institutions were not free. Second, Spanish cohabitation with inferior Amerindian and Negroid races in the Americas had produced an even more inferior, mongrelized population incapable of self-government.[31] The low level of population across New Spain's vast northern region, its inability to pacify Amerindian groups fully, and its lack of strong agricultural, commercial, or industrial development were offered as proof positive that Spanish institutions had been a dismal failure. Spain's colonizing institutions, the missions, presidios, and pueblos, were not adequate to develop the region, nor did they leave a lasting influence on the people or landscape.

While the Teutonics' major documentary sources were Euro-American, they also cited French, English, and Russian travel accounts to California and the writings of Franciscan missionaries.[32] The anti-Spanish sentiments of French, English, and Euro-American expeditionary forces, as well as these countries' continued interest in acquiring California, are obvious in the logs, journals, and reports of Jean François Galaup de La Perouse, George Vancouver, William Shaler, and other foreigners who visited Spanish California.[33] The reports, petitions, and correspondence of the mission priests, most of whom were peninsular Spaniards, cast aspersions on the racially mixed soldiers and settlers sent to this remote outpost of the empire. Historian Manuel Servín suggests that in California, prejudice and discrimination against persons of mixed blood can be traced to the pejorative racial attitudes of peninsular Franciscans and other *españoles* during the Spanish colonial era.[34]

Since women were not a formal part of institutional life, the Teutonic historians did not discuss them.[35] Frank W. Blackmar, for example, who relies heavily on Bancroft for his description of colonial California, makes only passing reference to women in his discussion of the institution of the mission and the social and political life of the Spanish colonies.[36] But popular and amateur historians of the time continued to include women in their works, stereotyping Mexican women on the basis of both sex and race, as we have seen. These stereotypes take on additional significance when we recognize that, as Rodman Paul recently stated, the West, particularly California, that most romanticized, mythologized, and distorted of western states, "is a primary meeting ground of professional historiography, popular interests, and popular writers."[37]

Throughout the late nineteenth and early twentieth centuries, then, even as Frederick Jackson Turner successfully challenged the germ theory of Euro-American history, the history of California remained the province of popular historians, journalists, and writers. Professional historians, now writing within the developing frontier hypothesis school of historiography, continued the Teutonics' neglect of women.

Nonetheless, ideas about gender and race formed a part of their intellectual subsoil. As the United States moved from expansionism to imperialism by going to war against Spain and by preparing to absorb former Spanish colonies, race and culture became pivotal political issues for imperialists and anti-imperialists alike. In addition, increased immigration from southern and eastern Europe occasioned considerable discussion about the assimilability of certain races and ethnic groups as well as alarm over the high birthrate among the new immigrants. At the same time, social and political theorists were alarmed by the decline in the birthrate among the white middle class, the potential threat that women's greater economic independence posed to the existing social order, and the women's rights movement. The survival and destiny of the Anglo-Saxon race, they determined, rested with women. In particular, eugenicist theorists like such as Pearson and Havelock Ellis glorified an ideal of motherhood that required women's self-sacrifice for the good of the race. Though it rested on social function rather than on biological constraint, the eugenicist ideal denied women's individuality, removed them as potential economic competitors, and silenced their potential political voices.[38]

Turner's Frontier Hypothesis and the Fantasy Spanish Heritage

As the mission revival movement and the rediscovery of California's "Spanish" past gained force toward the end of the nineteenth century, Frederick Jackson Turner's presidential address to the American Historical Association in 1893 redefined Euro-American history and civilization. By the early twentieth century, Turner's concept, the "frontier hypothesis," had supplanted the Teutonic germ theory of history and American institutions.[39]

Instead of looking to Old World antecedents to explain the development of representative government and Euro-American civilization, Turner focused on the New World itself, whose environment alone explained the differences between the civilizations of Europe and America. In his view, expansion into new areas re-created the conditions of primitive social organization as successive waves of trappers, traders, miners, farmers, and cattlemen adapted to and molded the environment on continuous frontiers—"the meeting point between savagery and civilization." The men engaged in this continuous process were imbued with a "rugged individualism" that, combined with frontier conditions, promoted democracy and representative government. From the very beginning, then, the frontier was a democratizing agent. Departing from the Teutonic emphasis on Anglo-Saxon racial origins, Turner argued that "in the crucible of the frontier [redemptioners of non-English stock] were Americanized, liberated and fused into a mixed race, English in neither nationality nor characteristic."[40] American development represented a severance, a discontinuity with European origins, patterns, and institutions.

While on one hand Turner conceived of Euro-American history as discontinuous from European origins, on the other hand his reinterpretation merely shifted the emphasis on institutional origins from the Old World to the New World—from the German forest to the American wilderness—and stressed the impact of the new environment on diverse groups of Caucasian males. It left intact the Teutonics' basic assumptions about representative government, democratic institutions, race, culture, gender, and economics. In both interpretations, neither women nor non-Caucasian men were active participants in the creation of democratic institutions. That both were legally prohibited from direct participation in such institutions was not an issue; rather, their exclusion was consistent with theories of biological and social evolution.

Joan Jensen and Darlis Miller have identified four major stereotypes of Euro-American women in the Turnerian literature of the western frontier: gentle tamers, sunbonneted helpmeets, hell raisers, and bad women.[41] The first two types were extolled as bastions of the pioneer family; the second two were condemned as libertines, created by the same frontier influence that liberated men. But in the Turnerian studies that extol and stereotype Euro-American women, Spanish Mexican women were entirely absent—a fact hardly surprising in view of the school's racist attitudes toward non-Caucasian peoples and its ignoring of what Richard Hofstadter called "the shameful aspects of Western development, including the arrogance of American expansion, the pathetic tale of the Indians, anti-Mexican [and] anti-Chinese nativism."[42]

With respect to Mexicans, the revisionist frontier historians, if they addressed the pre-American period at all, retained the Teutonic interpretation of Spanish institutional failure while dismissing the Mexican period as an unimportant interlude between the Spanish and North American eras. Maintaining the stereotype of indolent Mexicans, Frederic L. Paxson argued that in losing California, Mexico had "paid the penalty under that organic law of politics which forbids a nation to sit still when others are moving," and thus "determined the inevitability of the United States War with Mexico and the Conquest of California and the South West."[43]

Having thus easily dismissed the obstacles that Indians and Mexicans, as prior occupants, represented to acquisition of the land base, the frontier historians focused their white, male-centered studies on the "Westward Movement" of Anglo American pioneers into Oregon, Utah, the Pacific Northwest, and, most particularly, gold-rush California. Most recently, historians reexamining the literature of the frontier and the West have concluded that the initial success of Turner's thesis was due largely to the fact that he told an emerging industrial nation rising to world power what it wanted to hear. "Turner," states Michael Malone, "told a maturing nation . . . that it was not an appendage of a decadent Europe, but rather was a unique and great country in its own right."[44]

Meanwhile, Anglo westerners were searching for roots in the land they now occupied. To collect, exhibit, and publish their past the new westerners organized local county and state historical societies, museums, and journals during the late nineteenth and early twentieth centuries. And, in the tradition of the earlier historical literature, the histories published by these institutions were romantic, provincial, nationalistic, and rife with filial piety.[45]

But in California, the search for roots that fit into national history ran into hardpan—the Indians and Mexicans on the land. While the United States Army and the federal government had largely removed the Indians from their midst, historically minded Californians still had to deal with Mexicans and with the fact of Spanish Mexican colonization and institutions on the slopes that they now called home.[46] Whereas their scholarly Teutonic forebears had dismissed Spain and its institutions, the new westerners now took an interest in the region's "Spanish" past. In Spain's Caucasian racial origins and former imperial grandeur they found an acceptable European past for one particular class of the former Mexican citizens in their midst, whose blood flowed in some of their own veins. In the now decaying Spanish missions and their "laudable" effort to Christianize the native population they found one institution worthy of preserving—at least structurally—for posterity.

The mission revival movement, which initiated a Spanish-Mediterranean architectural style for public and private buildings, dates from this period. Historical societies and journals published histories of the missions and pueblos, along with reminiscences of the halcyon days in the former Spanish colony.[47] Preservationists targeted first the missions, then the adobes. Leading Anglo denizens in towns up and down the state organized "fiesta days" that included parades, music, food, rodeos, and a *fandango* (dance) or two. In Santa Barbara, Helen Hunt Jackson's novel *Ramona* was converted into a play that was performed year after year. Some of the descendants of California's "best Spanish families," who aided and abetted both the creation and the perpetuation of the Spanish myth, joined these celebrations.[48]

The majority of Anglo Californians seeking to understand their past probably did not read the scholarly studies of the frontier historians. The newspapers, novels, and non-professional histories that they did read continued the romanticized "Spanish" stereotypes first applied to mestizas in the primary sources and in Bancroft. In these works, women were featured prominently, and even males were now romanticized.[49]

The gratuitous determination that Mexican California's landowning class, some of whom still had kinship and/or economic ties to the new westerners, were pure-blooded Spaniards was a principal feature of the newly fabricated "fantasy Spanish heritage," to use Carey McWilliams's term.[50] Taking some of their cues from contemporary newspaper stories that "the best families were of Castillian stock, many of them pure in blood and extremely fair of skin," the new popularizers created a new racial and social history for the landowning class that the Euro-American conquest had displaced and now appropriated. In these fabulous histories, "the men went to Old Spain or Mexico for their wives and there was but little mixture of the high-bred Spanish families with the Mexicans and Indians." In *Spanish Arcadia*, which focuses on the Mexican period, Nellie Van de Grift Sánchez wrote that the Californios "kept their white blood purer than did the Mexicans or South Americans," and thus, "as a race, are greatly superior to the Mexicans."[51]

Dispossessed of their lands and politically disenfranchised, the former rancheros represented no threat to Euro-American supremacy and thus could be safely romanticized. The new popular histories converted Mexican rancheros into "the California dons," dashing, silver-saddled caballeros who roamed baronial estates from dawn to dusk in a remote Spanish past. The new dons, however, continued to be inept; incapable of hard work, they lacked the genius or moral strength to develop California's lush, fertile land. (Gertrude Atherton, who published short stories, novels, and popular histories in the late nineteenth and early twentieth centuries, entitled one collection of short stories about Mexican California *The Splendid Idle Forties*.)[52]

The women of Spanish California, however, according to these novels and histories, surpassed the men. Like the primary sources of the 1840s, the new popularizers concluded that women were men's superiors in "modesty, moral character, and sound common sense."[53] California's "Spanish" (read Caucasian) daughters were industrious, chaste, and morally as well as racially pure. In short, they could be claimed as the pure-blooded "Spanish" grandmothers of many a Euro-American frontier family. But Mexican women fared less well. While the literature seldom specifically discusses Mexican women, a designation that included nonelite Californianas and Mexicanas who came during the gold rush, it implies that they were licentious women—common prostitutes who, like their male counterparts, deserved to be wiped out. Thus popular historical interpretations of California's Spanish Mexican past essentially dichotomized Californianas the same way the scholarly frontier historians dichotomized and stereotyped Anglo American women—as good and bad women. For Californianas, however, the values of good and bad were explicitly related to their race and culture or class.

Meanwhile, among professional historians, Spain's presence in the American Southwest resurfaced as a historiographical issue. In the early decades of the twentieth century a reexamination of the history of colonial institutions in the old Spanish borderlands by a young scholar named Herbert Eugene Bolton led to a reinterpretation of those institutions and to a "new" school of historiography.

The Spanish Borderlands School

In the 1930s Turner's frontier thesis came under increasing scrutiny and attack. A new generation of revisionist historians argued that national development resulted not from a single cause but from many, from economic and class forces as well as from ideas rooted in East Coast intellectualism rather than western individualism.

The Great Depression, too, provoked a reexamination of the social unanimity implicit in Turner's interpretation of United States history. The climate of national questioning, internationalism, and the Good Neighbor Policy toward Mexico and Latin America prompted scholars to tackle once more the history of California, the Southwest, and the Far West. At the University of California at Berkeley, Herbert Eugene Bolton and his students developed a new revisionist school, the Spanish borderlands school of historiography. The new school revised the Teutonics' original theory of Spanish institutional failures by turning it on its head. Basing their arguments on a concept of "a Greater America" and on archival research in unmined Spanish-language collections, Bolton and his students argued that, contrary to prevalent scholarly wisdom, which they characterized as nationalistic, chauvinistic, and distorted, Spanish institutions had not failed.[54]

Examining the Spanish borderlands in the broad context of European exploration, exploitation, and colonization of the American continents from the sixteenth to the nineteenth centuries, Bolton conceptualized Spain's far northern frontiers as integral parts of Euro-American history. He concluded that, with the exception of New Mexico, Spain's movement into its far northern frontier was defensive in nature. He argued further that Spain's frontier institutions—the mission, presidio, and pueblo—not only were admirably suited to frontier conditions and defensive needs but also had exerted a lasting impact on the landscape and had paved the way for subsequent Euro-American colonizers. Missions and ranchos had broken ground for subsequent Anglo American agricultural and pastoral development. Spanish pueblos had been the nucleus of major urban centers throughout the West. Spanish laws had influenced western mining, water, and community property rights, and Spanish terminology continued in use throughout the western states.[55]

Rejecting both the Hispanophobia of the Teutonics and the strident nationalism of the Turnerians, the borderlands school effectively refuted the allegation of Spain's institutional failure. Nevertheless, Bolton and his students retained their predecessors' definitions of the makers and nature of history. Caucasian males engaged in exploration and in the development of religious, political, military, and economic institutions make history. But the Spaniards whom the Teutonics had disparaged as a cruel, greedy, bigoted nonwhite lot of miscreants the Boltonians lauded as valiant, daring, heroic Europeans.[56] Where the Teutonics had seen institutional failure, the Boltonians saw a seedbed for Spanish civilization.

In either view, however, women and nonwhite males do not contribute to history. While the Boltonians did address the exploitation of the Indians, their discussion revolved around the mission's efficacy as a frontier institution, not around the lot of the Indian.[57] The early Spanish borderlands studies rarely mention racially mixed soldiers and settlers. When Bolton does briefly discuss California's mestizo and *mulato* colonists, he reaffirms Bancroft's views of their idle but kindly, hospitable, and happy character. Like the contemporary popular historians, he makes a racial distinction between Californians and Mexicans: "Californians were superior to other Spanish colonists in America, including Mexicans," a superiority that he attributes to "the greater degree of independence, social at least if not political," caused by their isolation from Mexico and to their "good Castillian blood."[58] Women, who (to the historians) were neither intrepid explorers, barefooted black-robed missionaries, nor valiant lancers for the king, do not figure in Spanish borderlands studies. Until very recently, mention of women was limited to scattered references to intermarriage in the Americas, to women's relationship to the men who founded Spanish institutions, or, in the case of Amerindian women, to the institution of the mission itself.

Though Bolton touches briefly on the cultural significance of marriage between Spanish *conquistadores* and Amerindian women in the early conquest of the Americas, borderlands discussions of California native women center on their relation to the mission. Borderlands descriptions of rapacious attacks on Amerindian women by soldiers focus not on the women but on the conflict over authority that these attacks exacerbated between officials of church and state.[59] Until recently borderlands historians, like the Teutonics, attributed the problems of Spanish institutional development to the despicable behavior of the common soldiers, which was in turn blamed on their socioracial origins. In the 1970s, however, borderlands historians began to examine the experiences and contributions of the racially mixed *soldado de cuera* (leather-jacket soldier) and *poblador* (settler), who derived largely from the lower social classes of colonial Spanish society. Although this new generation of historians has dealt more equitably with the issue of race, it has still focused exclusively on soldiers and male settlers.[60]

Just as the early Boltonians dismissed the common soldier, so they dismissed the racially mixed wives of the artisans, soldiers, settlers, and convicts—women who endured difficult ocean voyages or who trekked over desert wastelands to settle Alta California. The only women systematically included are the wives of the governors, principally Eulalia Callis, with her marital strife, her "scandalous behavior," and the problems that she caused the missionaries.[61]

Although the borderlands school studies end with the close of the Spanish colonial era, Bolton makes brief reference to Mexican women in connection with Euro-American expansion into the old Spanish borderlands in the 1820s and 1830s. Though he shows an awareness of the importance of intermarriage and miscegenation to frontier development, and of the significance of Mexican women's economic roles as property owners and consumers on the borderlands, he joins the popular historians in his uncritical acceptance of Euro-American males' claims that Mexican women preferred them to Mexican males.[62] While noting that James Ohio Pattie was a notorious braggart, Bolton nevertheless paraphrases Pattie's report that "at a *fandango* in Taos, the gateway to New Mexico, the American beaux captured not only all the señoritas, but the señoras as well. The jealous *caballeros* drew their knives." And "in California, long before the Mexican War," wrote Bolton, "it was a customary boast of a señorita that she would marry a blue-eyed man."[63] Thus Bolton accepts the distorted view that equated California women with the land that promised "freedom-loving, adventure-loving, land-hungry Americans" romance, exoticism, and adventure.[64]

Presidarias, Pobladoras, Californianas, Chicanas: Reinterpreting Spanish Mexican Women in Frontier California

Within the last two decades, social historians and feminist historians have illuminated nineteenth-century U.S. social, women's, Chicano, borderlands, and family history; recent studies on colonial women in Mexico and Latin America have yielded information and analysis pertinent to women in Spanish Mexican California.[65] Yet even this new body of literature fails to deal directly with Spanish Mexican women on the remote outposts of empire. There are no published book-length scholarly studies of Mexicanas on nineteenth-century frontiers, and the periodical literature is sketchy and impressionistic rather than grounded in substantive primary research.

Recent studies of women in the Far West reflect a historiography in the initial stages of development. Current works include edited and annotated compilations of primary materials, most specifically of "westering" Anglo women's diaries and journals; descriptive works with varying degrees of analysis within the context of social, economic, and family history; and edited anthologies.[66]

Descriptive studies, including those of Sandra L. Myres and Julie Roy Jeffrey, have emphasized the perspective of Euro-American women and, in a neo-Turnerian version of the frontier as place (environment) and process, have viewed Amerindian and Mexican women as part of the new environment to which Yankee, midwestern, and southern white women pioneers must adapt.[67] Glenda Riley and Annette Kolodny have probed Euro-American women's images of Amerindians; and Sandra Myres has described Anglo women's response to Mexicans.[68] These works find that Anglo women generally shared Anglo men's racial antipathy to Amerindians and Mexicans, though they tended to be more sympathetic to women of other racial and cultural groups.[69] Proximity sometimes served to break down barriers, and in some instances Anglo women struck up friendships with Amerindians and Mexican women based on "mutual respect and trust."[70] Three anthologies, *New Mexico Women: Intercultural Perspectives* (1986), *The Women's West* (1987), and *Western Women: Their Land, Their Lives* (1988), address the critical, albeit thorny, issues of race, sex, class, and cultural interaction in the frontier West and Southwest.[71]

In many respects, however, these initial efforts continue to mirror the larger problems of the earlier historiography. That is, the new scholarship lacks a clear framework to examine the historical experience of women whose race and culture are not Anglo North American. Moreover, it often reflects the underlying assumptions and race and class biases of the earlier historiography. Historians of women in the frontier West, for example, have not yet grappled with defining the term *frontier* from a non-Anglo perspective, nor have they yet tackled the roles of English-speaking women in the imposition of Anglo hegemony. The new scholarship has indeed focused on gender, but its concept of gender ignores non-white, non-middle-class experiences on the frontier. And the lack of an integrative conceptual framework particularly hampers attempts to address the question of race and the nature of interracial contact, including interracial marriage.

Thus Myres, Riley, and Susan Armitage find a "more peaceful version of Indian-white contact" in the diaries and journals of literate Anglo women, but they fail to reconcile this version with the brutality and violence that Amerindian and Mexican women experienced during the Anglo North American conquest of the western frontier.[72] Although the underlying assumption that westering Anglo women were less violent than Anglo men may in fact be true, it is also true that Anglo women benefited directly from male violence that occurred before their own arrival in a particular region: frontier wars, army massacres, and the violence during the California gold rush.[73] Anglo women may have neither committed nor witnessed this violence, but they reaped its fruits: removal of Amerindians and Mexicans from the land base. And in addition to general violence rife in a society under conquest, Amerindian and Mexican women also suffered sexual violence.[74] Gerda Lerner and other feminist scholars have concluded that under conditions of military and/or political conquest, rape, abduction, and other acts of sexual violence against women of the conquered group are acts of domination.[75] Although Albert Hurtado and other scholars studying the history of Amerindian people in California have begun to address sexual violence, historians of women in the frontier West have not examined this subject, which is pivotal to the history of Amerindian and Mexican women.[76] While certainly women of all races and classes in the West experienced domestic violence, conquest and racism intensified sexual assault. Because racial inferiority was equated with sexual impurity—even prostitution—nonwhite women could be raped with impunity, just as they could be enslaved, killed, or worked to death like beasts of burden.

Anglo attitudes toward Mexican women have been the subject only of brief essays. In "Californio Women and the Image of Virtue," David Langum concludes that the pejorative stereotypes of Mexican women were class-based, derived from the perceptions of lower-class Mexican women by upper-class Yankees such as Richard Henry Dana.[77] But Dana did have the opportunity to observe elite Californianas, and Langum does not address Dana's underlying gender ideology. Furthermore, Langum's class explanation is merely an extension to women of Cecil Robinson's earlier interpretation of pejorative stereotypes of Mexicanos, an interpretation that has already been refuted.[78] In "The Independent Women of New Mexico," Janet Lecompte attributes Anglos' negative views of Nuevo Mexicanas' morality to sexist Anglo behavioral norms conditioned by the relatively constricted position of women in North American society and culture, and by the corollary view of womanhood as the upholder and symbol of American morality.[79] Unfortunately Lecompte does not develop the gender-based argument, nor does she fully address the issue of race.

Jane Dysart, Darlis Miller, and Rebecca Craver have published the only studies to date on the subject of interracial marriage.[80] These works describe but do not analyze significant historical, political, economic, and cultural issues inherent in interracial marriage and assimilation; and despite their recognition that intermarriage existed before the Anglo North American conquest, their point of departure is generally North American culture and society. Yet intercultural contact, interracial marriage, and mestizo children were part of Mexican women's historical reality long before the arrival of Anglo Americans on the landscape; this subject, especially, requires examination within a broader context.[81] Moreover, in the early periods of contact, when whites sought to establish trapping, trading, and other commercial relations with Indians and Mexicans, intermarriage and consensual unions were as much economic as they were sexual or romantic alliances. White men who married or lived with nonwhite women were assimilated into the women's culture. This pattern was conditioned by the sex ratio, itself a manifestation of the particular stage of contact, which we must take into account before we can generalize about intermarriage and assimilation. In her exemplary study of the Spanish Mexican women of Santa Fe, 1820–80, Deena González grounds her examination of interracial marriage in Spanish Mexican patterns of racial and cultural contact, while also charting the economic changes that her subjects experienced with the change of legal and political institutions from Mexican to Anglo American patterns.[82]

Earlier studies of nineteenth-century Chicano history include general discussions of Chicanas, particularly in relation to labor and the family, but they do not incorporate gender as a category of analysis. Those of Albert Camarillo, Richard Griswold del Castillo, and Ricardo Romo begin on the eve of the Mexican-American War and center on the development of Chicano communities in California's urban centers during the latter half of the nineteenth and early twentieth centuries.[83] Griswold del Castillo's more recent study on the Chicano family also begins after the U.S. war with Mexico, as does the earliest social history of the Californios; Roberto Alvarez's anthropological examination of family migration in Baja and Alta California focuses mainly on the period after 1880.[84] Recent social and frontier histories of Spanish and Mexican California and the Southwest, whether they derive from the Spanish borderlands school or from Mexican historical studies, either ignore women entirely or discuss them in very general terms.[85] For colonial California, one unpublished dissertation and three brief articles on marriage and child-rearing patterns and on race, all by Gloria Miranda, constitute the totality of recent scholarly studies.[86]

But there is new scholarship in colonial Mexican and Latin American women's and family history that is invaluable to the study of Spanish-speaking women in eighteenth- and nineteenth-century California. Ramón Gutiérrez's *When Jesus Came, the Corn Mothers Went Away* offers a singularly important point of departure for an examination of gender and marriage in colonial New Mexico.[87] Although Gutiérrez's is the only recent study that focuses on New Spain's northern frontier, Patricia Seed's *To Love, Honor, and Obey in Colonial Mexico* examines the changing laws and conflicts over marriage choice.[88] Sylvia Arrom's *The Women of Mexico City, 1790–1857*, and Asunción Lavrin's work on nuns and women's wills address the status of colonial women in law, in the patriarchal family, in religious orders, and in social, economic, and political life.[89] The new scholarship revises earlier interpretations of Mexicanas as passive, male-dominated, and powerless. While most of these studies do not focus on frontier women, they provide a well-defined sociocultural and political context for such discussion by illuminating gender-specific Spanish colonial and Mexican laws and policies.

And there are rich sources for the study of frontier Spanish Mexican women.[90] Though the standard archival sources for the Spanish colonial period are official reports, correspondence, diaries, and journals written by male missionaries and military authorities, they yield factual information about women's work and life in the missions and presidios, as well as insights into the gender ideology of the era. And although few Spanish-speaking women were literate, they did have petitions and letters penned for them.[91] There are also quantifiable sources: censuses, court records, and mission registers of baptisms, marriages, and deaths. The marriage registers reveal the extent of interracial marriage between Amerindian women and Spanish mestizo men. Both ecclesiastical and military records document the violence that soldiers committed against Amerindian women.[92]

For the Mexican period, civil, criminal, and ecclesiastical court records reveal that women sued and were sued for divorce (legal separation), for land, and for custody of children and godchildren, as well as for numerous social transgressions.[93] Court records document a significant increase in domestic violence against women; they also document violence by women. Court records, official reports, and correspondence yield information about race relations. *Libros de solares* (books of lots) record women's ownership of town lots, and there are also documents proving women's receipt and ownership of Mexican land grants. Before secularization in 1836, interracial marriages—now of Mexican women with European and European American men—may be traced through mission registers.

For the era just before and after the American conquest, there are further quantifiable sources, in addition to the journals and correspondence of Anglo men and women, contemporary newspapers, and the literature of the gold rush. The records of the Land Grant Commission detail Mexican women's loss and retention of land grants. Extant Ayuntamiento (later City Council) records and Sole Trader records permit examination of Mexican women's economic life, as do the federal manuscript censuses. Women's wills and probate court records reveal the nature and disposition of women's property. Justice of the peace and parish records document interracial marriage. Justice of the peace and superior court records document crimes with which women were charged, crimes of which women were the victims, and indentures of children. Hubert Howe Bancroft's collection includes narratives from eleven Mexican women that provide significant information and insight into women's lives, work, family, race relations, and politics up to the 1870s, when the women were interviewed. Finally, family collections and papers in various repositories throughout the state contain women's correspondence, diaries, and journals of elite, literate Californianas and, in some cases, middle-class Mexican women who came to California in the latter half of the nineteenth century.[94]

The threads of Spanish Mexican women's history run throughout these sources. What is missing is an approach to the history of the frontier that integrates gender, race, and culture or class as categories of historical analysis. An integrative ethnohistorical approach would enable us to examine women's roles and lives in their societies of origin, as well as to describe and interpret how conquest changed their lives and restructured economic and social relationships not only between the sexes but also among persons of the same sex. For example, although we know that Spanish Mexican and Anglo American societies were stratified along gender, as well as racial and class lines, research is wanting on the nature or extent of male domination and the subordination of women in Amerindian societies before

1769. Feminist anthropologists have suggested that male domination was not universal in the Americas, and that foraging societies—such as those that existed in California—were essentially egalitarian, but this hypothesis has not been tested. Nor have historians compared gender stratification and patriarchy in Spanish Mexican and European American frontier California. I have suggested here that violence toward women is part of the politics of domination. Likewise, pejorative stereotypes and the deracination of *mestiza* women reveal the intersection of ideologies of gender, sexuality, and race in the politics of conquest. But it is premature to generalize about women and race relations, intermarriage, and assimilation on the frontiers of expansion. We have not yet done the research.

For three centuries American frontiers were bloody battlegrounds of European and Amerindian expansion and conquest and of Amerindian resistance. Impoverished Spanish-speaking mestiza, *mulata*, and other *casta* women who migrated to Alta California in the eighteenth century came as part of soldier-settler families recruited and subsidized to populate the military forts in imperial Spain's most remote outpost. These women began the process of reproducing Hispanic culture and society on this frontier. Their daughters and granddaughters continued it as the region changed from Spanish to Mexican political control. A developing agropastoral economy built on trade and Amerindian labor gave rise to greater social stratification and the beginning of class distinctions. By the mid-1840s the great-granddaughters of the first generation of women, then in the midst of their own childbearing years, themselves experienced war, conquest, and displacement. Many of them became part of the menial wage labor force of a new, expanding capitalist economy and society that bought their labor as cheaply as possible while it devalued their persons racially, culturally, and sexually. It is time to reexamine the history of these women within a conceptual framework that acknowledges the sex-gender, race, and culture or class issues that inhered in the politics and policies of frontier expansion, and to reinterpret the terms that define our changing reality on this frontier—*presidarias, pobladoras*, Californianas, Chicanas.

Notes

1. For comprehensive bibliographies on the Spanish Mexican frontier see John Francis Bannon, *The Spanish Borderlands Frontier, 1531–1821* (New York: Holt, Rinehart, and Winston, 1970), 257–87; Oakah L. Jones Jr., *Los Paisanos: Spanish Settlers on the Northern Frontiers of New Spain* (Norman: University of Oklahoma Press, 1979), 309–32; David J. Weber, *The Mexican Frontier, 1821–1846* (Albuquerque: University of New Mexico Press, 1982), 377–407; Weber, "Mexico's Far Northern Frontier, 1821–1846: A Critical Bibliography," *Arizona and the West* 19 (autumn 1977): 225–66; Weber, "Mexico's Far Northern Frontier: Historiography Askew," *Western Historical Quarterly* 7 (July 1976): 279–93.

    The following (not exhaustive) list includes titles discussing Spanish Mexican women in early biographies, family histories, and histories of ranchos: Susanna Bryant Dakin, *A Scotch Paisano: Hugo Reid's Life in California, 1832–1852* (Berkeley: University of California Press, 1939); Bess Adams Garner, *Windows in an Old Adobe* (Claremont, Calif.: Bronson Press, 1970 [1939]); Henry D. Hubbard, *Vallejo* (Boston: Meador Publishing Company, 1941); Terry E. Stephenson, "Tomas Yorba, His Wife Vicenta, and His Account Book," *The Quarterly Historical Society of Southern California* 23 (March 1944): 126–55; Myrtle McKittrick, *Vallejo: Son of California* (Portland, Ore.: Bindfords and Mort Publishers, 1944); Susanna Bryant Dakin, *The Lives of William Hartnell* (Stanford, Calif.: Stanford University Press, 1949); Angustias de la Guerra Ord, *Occurrences in Hispanic California*, trans. Francis Price and William Ellison (Washington, D.C.: Academy of Franciscan History, 1956); Edna Deu Pree Nelson, *The California Dons* (New York: Appleton-Century-Crofts, 1962); *The 1846 Overland Trail Memoir of Margaret M. Hecox*, ed. Richard Dillon (San Jose, Calif.: Harlan-Young Press, 1966); Madie Brown Emparan, *The Vallejos of California* (San Francisco: Gleeson Library Association, 1968); Virginia L. Carpenter, *The Ranchos of Don Pacífico Ontiveros* (Santa Ana, Calif.: Friis Pioneer Press, 1982).

    For a discussion of race as a central theme in the history of the West and a review of the most recent historical literature, see Richard White, "Race Relations in the American West," *American Quarterly* 38 (1986):

396–416. Herbert Eugene Bolton criticized American historiography for its nationalistic chauvinism in "The Epic of Greater America," *American Historical Review* 38 (April 1933): 448–74. See also White, "Race Relations in the American West," and Weber, "Mexico's Far Northern Frontier: Historiography Askew." For a review of pervasive ideas about female inferiority, see Rosemary Agonito, *History of Ideas on Women: A Sourcebook* (New York: Perigree Brooks, 1977).

2. Eileen Power, *Medieval Women*, ed. by M. M. Postan (London, New York, Melbourne: Cambridge University Press, 1975), 9.

3. Hubert Howe Bancroft, *California Pastoral, 1769–1848* (San Francisco: The History Company, 1888), 305; Theodore S. Hittell, *History of California* (San Francisco: The History Company, 1897), 2:469–511; see especially Hubert Howe Bancroft, *History of California*, 7 vols. (San Francisco: History Company, 1886–1890); Zoeth Skinner Eldredge, *History of California*, 5 vols. (New York: Century Company, 1915).

4. Franklin Tuthill, *The History of California* (San Francisco: H. H. Bancroft and Company, 1866); Lucia Norman, *A Popular History of California from the Earliest Period of Its Discovery to the Present Time* (San Francisco: A. Roman, AGT, Publisher, 1883 [1867]); J. M. Guinn, *A History of California and an Extended History of Los Angeles and Environs Also Containing Biographies of Well Known Citizens of the Past and Present*, 3 vols. (Los Angeles: Historic Record Company, 1915).

5. Thomas R. Hietala, *Manifest Design: Anxious Aggrandizement in Late Jacksonian America* (Ithaca, N.Y., and London: Cornell University Press, 1985); Reginald Horsman, *Race and Manifest Destiny: The Origins of Racial Anglo-Saxonism* (Cambridge and London: Harvard University Press, 1981); Frederick Merk, *A Reinterpretation of Manifest Destiny and Mission in American History* (New York: Alfred A. Knopf, 1963); Ramon Eduardo Ruiz, ed., *The Mexican War: Was It Manifest Destiny?* (New York: Holt, Rinehart and Winston, 1963).

6. For a discussion of the contradictory but stereotypic images of women in European American travel literature, see Antonia I. Castañeda "Anglo Images of Nineteenth Century Californianas: The Political Economy of Stereotypes," in Adelaida del Castillo, ed., *Between Borders: Essays on Mexicana/Chicana History* (Los Angeles: Floricanto Press, 1990).

7. For a discussion of the early traditions of United States historical writing, see Michael Kraus and Davis D. Joyce, *The Writing of American History*, rev. ed. (Norman: University of Oklahoma Press, 1985), 92–135; John Higham, *History: Professional Scholarship in America* (New York, Evanston, San Francisco, London: Harper and Row, 1965), 3–25, 68–74, 148–49; David Levin, *History as Romantic Art: Bancroft, Prescott, Motley and Parkman* (Stanford, Calif.: Stanford University Press, 1959).

8. Bancroft, *California Pastoral*, 180; see also Edward N. Saveth, "The Conceptualization of American History," in Edward N. Saveth, ed., *American History and the Social Sciences* (London: The Free Press of Glencoe, 1964), 10–11.

9. The Black Legend refers to an anti-Spanish policy perpetrated by Spain's European enemies accusing the Spanish monarch of brutal tyranny more extreme than that of their own absolutist regimes. See James J. Rawls, *Indians of California: The Changing Image* (Norman and London: University of Oklahoma Press, 1984), 42–43, 55, 64; Charles Gibson, ed., *The Black Legend: Anti-Spanish Attitudes in the Old World and the New* (New York: Alfred A. Knopf, 1971); Phillip Wayne Powell, *Tree of Hate: Propaganda and Prejudice Affecting United States Relations with the Hispanic World* (New York and London: Basic Books, 1971).

10. For discussion of Eulalia Callis, see Bancroft, *History of California*, 1:389–93, and Eldredge, *History of California*, 1:5–8.

11. Bancroft, *History of California*, 2:64–78, 78 n. 23; Bancroft, *California Pastoral*, 331–32; Richard A. Pierce, *Resanov Reconnoiters California: A New Translation of Resanov's Letters, Parts of Lieutenant Khvostov's Log of the Ship Juno, and Dr. Georg von Langsdorff's Observations* (San Francisco: The Book Club of San Francisco, 1972), 15–23, 69–72.

12. Bancroft, *History of California*, 2:77–78, 78 n. 23; Susanna Bryant Dakin, *Rose, or Rose Thorn? Three Women of Spanish California* (Berkeley: The Friends of the Bancroft Library, 1963), 25–56.

13. Bancroft, *History of California*, 2:72.

14. Bancroft, *History of California*, 1:224, 257–69, 341–45, 603, 603 n. 6, 606 n. 13.

15. For discussion of Nordic superiority in North American history, see Kraus and Joyce, *The Writing of American History*, 136, 145, 165; Bert James Lowenberg, *American History in American Thought* (New York: Simon and Schuster, 1972), 347–49, 371–75, 380–98, 458–65; Levin, *History as Romantic Art*, 85–87; and Edward Saveth, *American Historians and European Immigrants, 1875–1925* (New York: Russell and Russell, 1965), 90–92.

  For discussion of male supremacy, see Mary P. Ryan, *The Empire of the Mother: American Writing about Domesticity, 1830–1860* (New York and London: Harrington Park Press, 1985); Carroll Smith-Rosenberg, *Disorderly Conduct: Visions of Gender in Victorian America* (New York and Oxford: Oxford University Press, 1985); Mary Beth Norton, "The Evolution of White Women's Experience in Early America," *The American Historical Review* 89 (June 1984): 593–619; Lorna Duffin, "Prisoners of Progress: Women and Evolution," in Sara Delamont and Lorna Duffin, eds., *The Nineteenth Century Woman: Her Cultural and Physical World* (New York: Barnes and Noble Books, 1978), 57–91; Agonito, *History of Ideas on Women,* 251–63; Susan Phinney Conrad, *Perish the Thought: Intellectual Women in Romantic America, 1830–1860* (New York: Oxford University Press, 1976), 15–41; Linda K. Kerber, *Women of the Republic: Intellect and Ideology in Revolutionary America* (New York and London: W. W. Norton & Company, 1986 [1980]).

16. Weber, *The Mexican Frontier, 1821–1846,* 17.

17. Bancroft, *California Pastoral,* 305–34; Bancroft, *History of California,* vols. 2, 3, and 4.

18. Bancroft, *California Pastoral,* 76–79, 292–93; Bancroft, *History of California,* 2:69.

19. Bancroft, *California Pastoral,* 279–80, 305.

20. Bancroft, *California Pastoral,* 279–80, 322; Hittell, *History of California,* 2:491.

21. With few exceptions, Euro-Americans who left published accounts of Mexican California in their memoirs, journals, and correspondence described Mexican men in racist terms and consistently expressed expansionist sentiments toward U.S. acquisition of California. Bancroft draws heavily upon these published sources, and he also had access to numerous unpublished manuscripts of similar sentiment. See Castañeda, "Anglo Images of Nineteenth Century Californianas"; see also notes 78 and 79.

22. Alfred Robinson, *Life in California* (Santa Barbara: Peregrine Press, 1970 [1846]), 51, and as quoted in Bancroft, *California Pastoral,* 326.

23. "They Wait for Us," as quoted in Horsman, *Race and Manifest Destiny,* 233.

24. Bancroft, *California Pastoral,* 312; Hittell, *History of California,* 2:179.

25. In Spanish Mexican California, *el fandango* was a specific dance, while *un fandango* referred to an informal dancing party. Euro-Americans used the term loosely and applied it to all dances and any dancing occasion. *Monte* is a card game. See Lucille K. Czarnowski, *Dances of Early California Days* (Palo Alto: Pacific Books, 1950), 16, 22.

26. For early critiques of sexism in the historical scholarship, see "Part I: On the Historiography of Women," in Berenice A. Carroll, ed., *Liberating Women's History: Theoretical and Critical Essays* (Urbana: University of Illinois Press, 1976), 1–75; Gerda Lerner, *The Majority Finds Its Past: Placing Women in History* (New York and Oxford: Oxford University Press, 1979).

27. Discussion of the Teutonic hypothesis is based primarily on Kraus and Joyce, *The Writing of American History;* Lowenberg, *American History in American Thought;* George Callcott, *History in the United States, 1800–1860: Its Practices and Purpose* (Baltimore and London: John Hopkins University Press, 1970); John Higham, *Writing American History: Essays on Modern Scholarship* (Bloomington and London: University of Indiana Press, 1970); Holt W. Stull, *Historical Scholarship in the United States and Other Essays* (Seattle: University of Washington Press, 1967); Saveth, *American Historians and European Immigrants.*

28. Kraus and Joyce, *The Writing of American History,* 165; Callcott, *History in the United States, 1800–1860,* 154, 162, 165–72; Levin, *History as Romantic Art,* 78, 82–85, 121–37.

29. Frank W. Blackmar, *Spanish Institutions in the Southwest* (Glorieta, N. M.: Rio Grande Press, 1976 [1891]).

30. Kraus and Joyce, *The Writing of American History,* 92–135, 164–209; Higham, *History,* 151–52, 167; Lowenberg, *American History in American Thought,* 131–32, 200–20, 328, 424.

31. Blackmar, *Spanish Institutions in the Southwest;* Lewis Hanke, ed., *Do the Americas Have a Common History? A Critique of the Bolton Theory* (New York: Alfred A. Knopf, 1964).

32. Rawls, *Indians of California,* 32–43.

33. *Jean Francois Galaup de La Perouse, A Voyage round the World in the Years 1785, 1786, 1787, and 1788,* ed. M. L. A. Milet-Mureau, 3 vols (London: J. Johnson, 1798), esp. 2:202–4; George Vancouver, *Vancouver in California, 1792–1794: The Original Account of George Vancouver,* Early California Travel Series, nos. 9, 10, and 22, ed. Marguerite Eyer Wilbur (Los Angeles: Glen Dawson, 1953–54), 19, 243–48; William Shaler, *Journal of a Voyage between China and the Northwestern Coast of America Made in 1804 by William Shaler* (Claremont, Calif.: Saunders Studio Press, 1935).

34. Manuel Patricio Servín, "California's Hispanic Heritage," *The Journal of San Diego History* 19 (1973): 1–9.

35. Trained in the Teutonic school, Henry Adams sometimes rebelled against its canons; see "The Primitive Rights of Women," in his *Historical Essays* (New York: Charles Scribner's Sons, 1891), 1–41.

36. Blackmar, *Spanish Institutions in the Southwest,* 112–51, 255–79.

37. Rodman W. Paul and Michael P. Malone, "Tradition and Challenge in Western Historiography," *Western Historical Quarterly* 16 (January 1985):27.

38. Saveth, *American Historians and European Immigrants,* 32–65; Richard Hofstadter, *Social Darwinism in American Thought* (New York: George Braziller, Inc., 1959 1944]), 170–200; Duffin, "Prisoners of Progress: Women and Evolution," 57–91.

39. Frederick Jackson Turner, *The Frontier in American History* (New York: Robert E. Krieger Publishing Company, 1976 [1920]), 1–38. Turner's "The Significance of the Frontier in American History" first appeared in the *American Historical Association, Annual Report of the Year 1893* (Washington, D.C., 1894), 199–227. Dis-

cussion of Turner and the frontier hypothesis of American history is based on the following: Ray Allen Billington, *America's Frontier Heritage* (New York, Chicago, and San Francisco: Holt, Rinehart, and Winston, 1966); Ray Allen Billington, ed., *The Frontier Thesis: Valid Interpretation of American History?* (New York: Robert E. Krieger Publishing Company, 1977 [1966]); George Rogers Taylor, ed., *The Turner Thesis: Concerning the Role of the Frontier in American History*, (Lexington: D. C. Heath and Company, 1956); Richard Hofstadter, *The Progressive Historians: Turner, Beard, Parrington* (New York: Alfred A. Knopf, 1968); Earl Pomeroy, "The Changing West," in *The Reconstruction of American History*, edited by John Higham (London: Hutchinson & Co., 1962), 64–81.

40. Turner, *The Frontier in American History*, 3, 23.

41. Joan M. Jensen and Darlis A. Miller, "The Gentle Tamers Revisited: New Approaches to Women in the American West," *Pacific Historical Review* 49 (May 1980): 173–213.

42. Hofstadter, *The Progressive Historians*, 104.

43. Frederick Logan Paxson, *The Last American Frontier* (New York: Macmillan Company, 1910), 107.

44. Michael P. Malone, ed., *Historians and the American West* (Lincoln and London: University of Nebraska Press, 1983), 5.

45. See, for example, "California Historical Society, 1852–1922," *California Historical Society Quarterly* 1 (July–October 1922): 9–22.

46. Rawls, *Indians of California*, 137–70; Patricia Nelson Limerick, *The Legacy of Conquest: The Unbroken Past of the American West* (New York and London: Norton, 1987), 44–45, 82.

47. See, for example, "Society of Southern California: Fifteen Years of Local History Work," *Historical Society of Southern California Publications* (hereafter cited as *HSSCP*) 4 (1898): 105–10; Walter Bacon, "Value of a Historical Society," *HSSCP* 4 (1899): 237–42; Marion Parks, "In Pursuit of Vanished Days: Visits to the Extant Historic Adobe Houses of Los Angeles County," Part 1, *Historical Society of Southern California Annual Publications* (hereafter cited as *HSSCAP*) 14 (1928): 7–63; Part 2, *HSSCAP* 14 (1929): 135–207.

48. Helen Hunt Jackson, *Ramona* (Boston: Little, Brown and Company, 1922 [1884]); Richard Griswold del Castillo, "The del Valle Family and the Fantasy Heritage," *California History* 59 (spring 1980): 2–15.

49. Tirey L. Ford, *Dawn and the Dons: The Romance of Monterey* (San Francisco: A. M. Robertson, 1926); Nellie Van de Grift Sánchez *Spanish Arcadia* (San Francisco, Los Angeles, Chicago: Powell Publishing Company, 1929); Sydney A. Clark, *Golden Tapestry of California* (New York: Robert M. McBride and Company, 1937).

50. Carey McWilliams, *North from Mexico: The Spanish-Speaking People of the United States* (New York: Greenwood Press, 1968 [1948]), 35–47.

51. Mabel Clare Craft, "California Womanhood in 1848," *San Francisco Chronicle*, 23 January 1898, 12–13; Van de Grift Sánchez, *Spanish Arcadia*, 237.

52. Charlotte S. McClure, *Gertrude Atherton* (Boston: Twayne Publishers, 1979); Lawrence Clark Powell, *California Classics: The Creative Literature of the Golden State* (Los Angeles: Ward Ritchie Press, 1971), 103–14. For discussion of Anglo images and stereotypes of Californianos that mention but do not focus on women, see James D. Hart, *American Images of Spanish California* (Berkeley: Friends of the Bancroft Library, 1960); Harry Clark, "Their Pride, Their Manners, and Their Voices: Sources of the Traditional Portrait of Early Californians," *California Historical Society* 52 (spring 1974): 71–82; David J. Langum, "Californios and the Image of Indolence," *Western Historical Quarterly* 9 (April 1978): 181–96; David J. Weber, "Here Rests Juan Espinosa: Toward a Clearer Look at the Image of the 'Indolent' Californios," *Western Historical Quarterly* 10 (January 1979), 61–68.

53. Van de Grift Sánchez, *Spanish Arcadia*, 375.

54. Bolton, "The Epic of Greater America"; Bolton, *Wider Horizons of American History* (New York and London: D. Appleton-Century Company, 1939 [1930]), 55–106. For a critique of the Bolton theory, see Hanke, *Do the Americas Have a Common History?*

55. Bolton, "The Mission as a Frontier Institution in the Spanish American Colonies," in his *Wider Horizons of American History*, 107–48; Bolton, *The Spanish Borderlands: A Chronicle of Old Florida and the Southwest* (New Haven, Conn.: Yale University Press, 1921), 7–10; Bolton, "Defensive Spanish Expansion and the Significance of the Spanish Borderlands," in John Francis Bannon, ed., *Bolton and the Spanish Borderlands* (Norman: University of Oklahoma Press, 1964), 32–66.

56. John W. Caughey, "Herbert Eugene Bolton," in Wilbur Jacobs, John W. Caughey, and Joe B. Frantz, eds, *Turner/Bolton/Webb: Three Historians of the American Frontier* (Seattle and London: University of Washington Press, 1965), 49; David J. Weber, "Turner, the Boltonians, and the Borderlands," *American Historical Review* 91 (February 1986): 68.

57. Bolton, "The Mission as a Frontier Institution"; Bolton, *The Spanish Borderlands*, 188–91; 192–202, 215–17, 279–87; Charles E. Chapman, *A History of California: The Spanish Period* (New York: Macmillan Company, 1930), 352–96.

58. Bolton, *The Spanish Borderlands*, 294. The reciprocal influence between popular and scholarly history is worth noting in the case of Bolton and Van de Grift Sánchez, professional and popular historians who worked together. See John Francis Bannon, *Herbert Eugene Bolton: The Historian and the Man* (Tucson: University of Arizona Press, 1978), 171, 173.

59. Bolton, "Defensive Spanish Expansion and the Significance of the Borderlands," 61, 63; Bolton, "The Epic of Greater America," 452.

60. Jones, *Los Paisanos*; Max L. Moorhead, "The *Soldado de Cuera:* Stalwart of the Spanish Borderlands," and Leon G. Campbell, "The First *Californios:* Presidial Society in Spanish California, 1769–1822," in Oakah L. Jones Jr., ed., *The Spanish Borderlands: A First Reader* (Los Angeles: Lorrin L. Morrison, 1974), 85–105 and 106–18.

61. Donald A. Nuttall, "The Gobernantes of Upper California: A Profile," *California Historical Quarterly* 51 (fall 1972): 253–80.

62. Bolton, "Epic of Greater America," 452; Bolton, "Significance of the Borderlands," 56–58. Bolton, "Spanish Resistance to Carolina Traders," in *Bolton and the Spanish Borderlands*, edited by John Francis Bannon (Norman: University of Oklahoma Press, 1964), 148.

63. Bolton, "Significance of the Borderlands," 56, 58.

64. Ibid., 54.

65. For theories of gender and discussion of gender as a category of social and historical analysis in women's history, see Linda J. Nicholson, *Gender and History: The Limits of Social Theory in the Age of the Family* (New York: Columbia University Press, 1986); Smith-Rosenberg, *Disorderly Conduct*, 11–52; Linda Gordon, "What's New in Women's History," and Carroll Smith-Rosenberg, "Writing History: Language, Class, and Gender," in Teresa de Lauretis, ed., *Feminist Studies—Critical Studies* (Bloomington: Indiana University Press, 1986), 20–30 and 31–54; Joan Kelly-Gadol, "The Social Relation of the Sexes: Methodological Implications of Women's History," in Judith L. Norton, Mary P. Ryan, and Judith Walkowitz, eds., *Sex and Class in Women's History* (London: Routledge and Kegan Paul, 1983), 1–15; Catharine A. MacKinnon, "Feminism, Marxism, Method, and the State: An Agenda for Theory," in Nannerl O. Keohane, Michelle Z. Rosaldo, and Barbara C. Gelpi, eds., *Feminist Theory: A Critique of Ideology* (Chicago: University of Chicago Press, 1982), 1–30.

   For early discussion of Chicana history, see Rosaura Sánchez, "The History of Chicanas: Proposal for a Materialist Perspective," in Adelaida del Castillo, ed., *Between Borders: Essays on Mexicana/Chicana History* (Los Angeles: Floricanto Press, 1989); Mario García, "The Chicana in American History: The Mexican Women of El Paso, 1880–1920—A Case Study," *Pacific Historical Review* 49 (May 1980): 315–37; María Linda Apodaca, "The Chicana Woman: An Historical Materialist Perspective," in *Women in Latin America: An Anthology from Latin American Perspectives* (Riverside, Calif.: Latin American Perspectives, 1979), 81–100.

   For studies that use gender as a category of historical analysis with respect to Spanish-speaking women in the present West and Southwest, see Ramón Gutiérrez, *When Jesus Came, the Corn Mothers Went Away: Marriage, Sexuality and Power in New Mexico, 1500–1846* (Stanford, Calif.: Stanford University Press, 1990); Sarah Deutsch, *No Separate Refuge: Culture, Class and Gender on an Anglo-Hispanic Frontier in the American Southwest, 1880–1940* (New York: Oxford University Press, 1987); Salomé Hernández, "Nuevo Mexicanas as Refugees and Reconquest Settlers," in Joan M. Jensen and Darlis Miller, eds., *New Mexico Women: Intercultural Perspectives* (Albuquerque: University of New Mexico Press, 1986), 41–70; Deena González, "The Spanish-Mexican Women of Santa Fe: Patterns of Their Resistance and Accommodation, 1820–1880" (Ph.D. diss., University of California, Berkeley, 1985); Antonia I. Castañeda, "*Presidarias y Pobladoras:* Spanish-Speaking Women in Monterey, California, 1770–1821" (Ph.D. diss., Stanford University, 1990).

66. For a review of the historical literature and citations relative to new approaches to the history of women in the frontier West, see Glenda Riley, "Frontier Women," in Roger L. Nichols, ed., *American Frontier and Western Issues: A Historiographical Review* (New York: Greenwood Press, 1986), 179–98; Sandra L. Myres, "Women in the West," in Michael Malone, ed., *Historians and the American West* (Lincoln: University of Nebraska Press, 1983), 369–86; Jensen and Miller, "The Gentle Tamers Revisited"; Glenda Riley, "Images of the Frontierswoman: Iowa as a Case Study," *Western Historical Quarterly* 8 (1977): 189–202. For a discussion of literary stereotypes in historical portraits of frontier women, see Sandra L. Myres, *Westering Women and the Frontier Experience, 1800–1915* (Albuquerque: University of New Mexico Press, 1982), 1–11; see also William Cronon, Howard Lamar, Katherine G. Morrissey, and Joy Gitlin, "Women and the West: Rethinking the Western History Survey Course," *Western Historical Quarterly* 17 (July 1986): 269–90; and Susan Armitage, "Women and Men in Western History: A Stereoptical Vision," *Western Historical Quarterly* 16 (October 1985):381–95.

   For studies taking more inclusive, multicultural approaches to women in the West, see del Castillo, ed., *Between Borders*; Lillian Schlissel, Vicki Ruiz, and Janice Monk, eds., *Western Women: Their Land, Their Lives* (Albuquerque: University of New Mexico Press, 1988); Susan Armitage and Elizabeth Jameson, eds., *The*

Women's West (Norman and London: University of Oklahoma Press, 1987); Joan M. Jensen and Gloria Ricci Lothrop, *California Women: A History* (San Francisco: Boyd and Fraser Publishing Company, 1987); and Jensen and Miller, eds., *New Mexico Women*.

    For examples of edited and annotated source material on women in the West, see Sandra L. Myres, ed., *Ho for California: Women's Overland Diaries from the Huntington Library* (San Marino: Henry E. Huntington Library and Art Gallery, 1980); *A Victorian Gentlewoman in the Far West: The Reminiscences of Mary Hallock Foote*, edited by Rodman W. Paul (San Marino: The Huntington Library, 1980); Christine Fischer, ed., *Let Them Speak for Themselves: Women in the American West, 1849–1900* (New York: E. P. Dutton, 1977); Dame Shirley (Louise A. K. S. Clappe), *The Shirley Letters* (Santa Barbara and Salt Lake City: Peregrine Smith, Inc., 1970 [1854–55]).

67. For generally descriptive studies see Myres, *Westering Women;* Lillian Schlissel, *Women's Diaries of the Westward Journey* (New York: Schocken Books, 1982); Julie Roy Jeffrey, *Frontier Women: The Trans-Mississippi West, 1840–1900* (New York: Hill and Wang, 1979).

    For women and the family in California and the Far West, see Richard Griswold del Castillo, *La Familia: Chicano Families in the Urban Southwest, 1848 to the Present* (Notre Dame, Ind.: University of Notre Dame Press, 1984); Robert L. Griswold, *Family and Divorce in California, 1850–1890* (Albany: State University of New York Press, 1982); and John Mack Faragher, *Women and Men on the Overland Trail* (Yale University Press, 1979).

68. Annette Kolodny, *The Land before Her: Fantasy and Experience of the American Frontiers, 1630–1860* (Chapel Hill and London: University of North Carolina Press, 1984); Glenda Riley, *Women and Indians on the Frontier, 1825–1915* (Albuquerque: University of New Mexico Press, 1984); Sandra L. Myres, "Mexican Americans and Westering Anglos: A Feminine Perspective," *New Mexico Historical Review* 57 (1982): 414–30.

69. Ibid.

70. Riley, *Women and Indians on the Frontier*, 224.

71. Jensen and Miller, eds., *New Mexico Women;* Armitage and Jameson, eds., *The Women's West;* Schlissel, Ruiz, and Monk, eds., *Western Women: Their Land, Their Lives.*

72. Susan Armitage, "Through Women's Eyes: A New View of the West," in Susan Armitage and Elizabeth Jameson, eds., *The Women's West* (Norman and London: University of Oklahoma Press, 1987), 17.

73. Limerick, *The Legacy of Conquest.*

74. Albert L. Hurtado, *Indian Survival on the California Frontier* (New York and London: Yale University Press, 1989), 169–92; Antonia I. Castañeda, "Sexual Violence in the Politics and Policies of Conquest: Amerindian Women and the Spanish Conquest of Alta California," in Adela de la Torre and Beatriz M. Pesquera, eds., *Building with Our Hands: New Directions in Chicana Scholarship* (Berkeley: University of California Press, 1993); Castañeda, "Anglo Images of Nineteenth Century *Californianas.*"

75. Gerda Lerner, *The Creation of Patriarchy* (New York and Oxford: Oxford University Press, 1986); see also Susan Brownmiller, *Against Our Will: Men, Women and Rape* (Toronto, New York, London, Sydney, Auckland: Bantam Books, 1976 [1975]); Christine Ward Gailey, "Evolutionary Perspectives on Gender Hierarchy," in Beth B. Hess and Myra Marx Ferree, eds., *Analyzing Gender: A Handbook of Social Science Research* (Newbury Park, Beverly Hills, London, New Delhi: Sage Publications, 1987), 32–67; Carole J. Sheffield, "Sexual Terrorism: The Social Control of Women," in Hess and Ferree, *Analyzing Gender*, 171–89; Jalna Hanmer and Mary Maynard, "Introduction: Violence and Gender Stratification," in Jalna Hanmer and Mary Maynard, eds., *Women, Violence and Social Control* (Atlantic Highlands, N.J.: Humanities Press International, Inc., 1987), 1–12; see also Anne Edwards, "Male Violence in Feminist Theory: An Analysis of the Changing Conceptions of Sex/Gender Violence and Male Dominance," and David H. J. Morgan, "Masculinity and Violence," in Hanmer and Maynard, eds., *Women, Violence and Social Control*, 13–29 and 180–92.

76. See note 74.

77. David Langum, "Californio Women and the Image of Virtue," *Southern California Quarterly* 59 (fall 1977): 245–50.

78. Cecil Robinson, *With the Ears of Strangers: The Mexican in American Travel Literature* (Tucson: University of Arizona Press, 1963); Ramond A. Paredes, "The Mexican Image in American Travel Literature, 1831–1869," *New Mexico Historical Review* 52 (January 1977): 5–29; Paredes, "The Origins of Anti-Mexican Sentiment in the United States," *New Scholar* 6 (1977): 139–65; Doris L. Meyer, "Early Mexican American Responses to Negative Stereotyping," *New Mexico Historical Review* 53 (January 1978): 75–91; David J. Weber, "Scarce More than Apes: Historical Roots of Anglo-American Stereotypes of Mexicans in the Border Region," in David J. Weber, ed., *New Spain's Far Northern Frontier: Essays on Spain in the American West, 1540–1821,* (Albuquerque: University of New Mexico Press, 1979), 295–307.

79. Janet Lecompte, "The Independent Women of Hispanic New Mexico, 1821–1846," *Western Historical Quarterly* 12 (January 1981): 17–35; see also James H. Lacy, "New Mexico Women in Early American

Writings," *New Mexico Historical Review* 34 (January 1959): 41–51; Beverly Trulio, "Anglo American Attitudes toward New Mexican Women," *Journal of the West* 12 (April 1973): 229–39.

80. Jane Dysart, "Mexican Women in San Antonio, 1830–1860: The Assimilation Process," *Western Historical Quarterly* 7 (October 1976): 365–75; Darlis A. Miller, "Cross-Cultural Marriages in the Southwest: The New Mexico Experience, 1846–1900," *New Mexico Historical Review* 57 (October 1982): 335–59; Rebecca McDowell Craver, *The Impact of Intimacy: Mexican-Anglo Intermarriage in New Mexico, 1821–1846*, Southwestern Studies monograph no. 66 (El Paso: Texas-Western Press, 1982); see also Kathleen Crawford, "María Amparo Ruíz Burton: The General's Lady," *Journal of San Diego History* 30 (summer 1984): 198–211.

81. González, "The Spanish-Mexican Women of Santa Fe," 111–53; Antonia I. Castañeda, *"Presidarias y Pobladoras,"* ch. 5.

82. González, "The Spanish-Mexican Women of Santa Fe"; for comparative purposes and studies of differing quality, see Sylvia Van Kirk, *Many Tender Ties: Women in Fur Trade Societies, 1670–1870* (Norman: University of Oklahoma Press, 1980); Walter O'Meara, *Daughters of the Country: The Women of the Fur Traders* (New York: Harcourt, Brace, and World, 1968); William R. Swagerty, "Marriage and Settlement Patterns of Rocky Mountain Trappers and Traders," *Western Historical Quarterly* 49 (1980): 159–80.

83. Albert Camarillo, *Chicanos in California: A History of Mexican Americans in California* (San Francisco: Boyd and Fraser Publishing Company, 1984); Ricardo Romo, *East Los Angeles: History of a Barrio* (Austin: University of Texas Press, 1983); Camarillo, *Chicanos in a Changing Society: From Mexican Pueblos to American Barrios in Santa Barbara and Southern California, 1848–1930* (Cambridge, Mass., and London: Harvard University Press, 1979); Richard Griswold del Castillo; *The Los Angeles Barrio, 1850–1890: A Social History* (Berkeley and Los Angeles: University of California Press, 1979); see also Leonard Pitt, *The Decline of the Californios: A Social History of the Spanish-Speaking Californians, 1846–1890* (Berkeley and Los Angeles: University of California Press, 1971); Gloria E. Miranda, "Racial and Cultural Dimensions in Gente de Razón Status in Spanish and Mexican California," *Southern California Quarterly* 70 (Fall 1988): 235–64; Miranda, "Hispano-Mexicano Childrearing Practices in Pre-American Santa Barbara," *Southern California Historical Quarterly* 65 (1983): 307–20; Miranda, "Gente de Razón Marriage Patterns in Spanish and Mexican California: A Case Study of Santa Barbara and Los Angeles," *Southern California Historical Quarterly* 63 (1981): 1–21.

   For Chicano histories that treat pre-twentieth-century New Mexico, Texas, or the entire Southwest and include discussion of women, see David Montejano, *Anglos and Mexicans in the Making of Texas, 1836–1986* (Austin: University of Texas Press, 1987); Arnoldo De León, *They Called Them Greasers: Anglo Attitudes toward Mexicans in Texas, 1821–1900* (Austin: University of Texas Press, 1983); Gilberto Miguel Hinojosa, *A Borderlands Town in Transition: Laredo, 1755–1870* (College Station: Texas A&M University Press, 1983); Mario T. García, *Desert Immigrants: The Mexicans of El Paso, 1880–1920* (New Haven, Conn., and London: Yale University Press, 1981); Alicia V. Tjarks, "Comparative Demographic Analysis of Texas, 1777–1793," *Southwestern Historical Quarterly* 77 (January 1974): 291–338.

84. Griswold del Castillo, *La Familia*; Pitt, *The Decline of the Californios*; Roberto Alvarez, Jr., *Familia: Migration and Adaption in Baja and Alta California, 1800–1975* (Berkeley, Los Angeles, London: University of California Press, 1987).

85. See note 60.

86. Gloria Elizarraras Miranda, "Family Patterns and the Social Order in Hispanic Santa Barbara, 1784–1848" (Ph.D. diss., University of Southern California, Los Angeles, 1978); Miranda, "Racial and Cultural Dimensions in Gente de Razón Status"; Miranda, "Hispano-Mexicano Childrearing Practices"; Miranda, "Gente de Razón Marriage Patterns."

87. Gutiérrez, *When Jesus Came the Corn Mothers Went Away*; see also Ramón Gutiérrez, "Honor Ideology, Marriage Negotiation, and Class-Gender Domination in New Mexico, 1690–1846," *Latin American Perspectives* 44 (winter 1985): 81–104.

88. Patricia Seed, *To Love, Honor, and Obey in Colonial Mexico: Conflicts over Marriage Choice, 1574–1821* (Stanford: Stanford University Press, 1988).

89. Sylvia M. Arrom, *The Women of Mexico City, 1790–1857* (Stanford: Stanford University Press, 1985); Asunción Lavrin, "Women in Convents: Their Economic and Social Roles in Colonial Mexico," in *Liberating Women's History: Theoretical and Critical Essays*, edited by Berenice A. Carroll (Urbana: University of Illinois Press, 1976), 250–77; Asunción Lavrin and Edith Couturier, "Dowries and Wills: A View of Women's Socioeconomic Role in Colonial Guadalajara and Puebla, 1640–1790," *Hispanic American Historical Review* 59 (May 1979): 280–304); *Latin American Women: Historical Perspectives*, edited by Asunción Lavrin (Westport, Connecticut: Greenwood Press, 1978).

90. The sources identified in the following discussion are selective and representative. Each archival repository, including city and county libraries, museums, and historical societies, must be examined and/or reexamined for materials pertinent to women and must be approached with gender-specific questions.

91. The standard archival sources for Spanish-Mexican California history that contain transcripts and/or abstracts of government reports and correspondence, censuses, transcripts of hearings, petitions, letters, testimonies, etc. include the bound volumes of *The Archives of California*, 63 vols., and the microfilm copy of the multivolume *Archivo de la Nación*, Bancroft Library, University of California, Berkeley, California; see also *The Writings of Junipero Serra*, 4 vols., edited by Antonine Tiebesar (Washington, D.C.: Academy of Franciscan History); *Writings of Francisco de Lasuen*, 2 vols., edited by Finbar Kinneally (Washington, D.C.: Academy of American Franciscan History, 1965).

92. The Mission Archives at Mission Santa Barbara, Santa Barbara, California, include, among numerous other sources, the extant *Books of Marriage*, *Books of Baptism*, and *Books of Death* for each mission, marriage testimonies, petitions for dispensation of consanguinity, mission censuses, sermons, official reports, and correspondence. Also, individual missions may have additional archival material.

93. For the Mexican period, see *Archives of California*, as well as the "Vallejo Collection" and the reminiscences of individual women in the manuscript collection, including Catarina Avila de Ríos, Angustias de la Guerra Ord, Apolinaria Lorenzana, Felipa Osuna de Marrón, Juana Machado de Ridington, Eulalia Pérez, María Inocenta Pico, Mariana Torres, Dorotea Valdez, Rosalía Vallejo de Leese, Bancroft Library, Berkeley, California. For the civil and criminal court records for the northern district of Mexican California, and the Libros de Solares for Monterey, see *The Monterey Archives*, 16 vols., Office of the County Recorder and Clerk, Salinas, California; see also the Monterey Collection, San Marino, California.

94. María Ignacia Soberanes de Bale, Papers and Correspondence, Bale Family Papers, Manuscript Collection, Bancroft Library, Berkeley, California; *Records of the Land Grant Commission*, Archives of the State of California, Sacramento, California.

5

To Earn Her Daily Bread: Housework and Antebellum Working-Class Subsistence

Jeanne Boydston

In 1845, in a volume entitled *The Sanitary Condition of the Laboring Population of New York*, former city health inspector John H. Griscom published his observations on the health of New York City's working poor. He sketched a bleak scene. Forced into crowded, tinder-box tenements that lacked adequate light or ventilation, and subjected daily to the waste that leached in from streets, outhouses, and animal yards, the laboring classes seemed to Griscom bound for extinction.[1]

Middle-class reformers such as Griscom tended to raise these specters as a way of deploring the alleged sloth and intemperance of the poor, rather than as a means of examining the economy that created the poverty.[2] Nevertheless, the conditions they so vividly documented have remained a subject of special interest to American historians, for these were the transitional generations—the households that lived the lurching transformations toward wage dependency. By the late 1870s, the number of people working solely for wages in manufacturing, construction, and transportation alone was almost equivalent to the size of the entire population in 1790.[3] The strategies that enabled working-class households to survive the intervening period tell us much, not only about the making of the American working classes, but, equally important, about the making of American industrial capitalism itself.

Historians have generally described the coming of industrialization in terms of changes in paid work. The transformation has been framed as one from a community of comparatively independent producers to a class of wage workers, forced for their survival to sell labor as a commodity on the capitalist market. This approach defines the problem of antebellum working-class subsistence as a question of pay. Wages are taken to correspond to "means of support" along the lines of Paul Faler's conclusion that by 1830 Lynn shoemakers "were full time wage earners with no important means of support other than . . . their income from shoemaking."[4]

Certainly, this emphasis reflects the way in which paid workers themselves formulated the problem of household survival. When the Philadelphia cordwainers complained in 1805 that the "pittance of subsistence" they received in wages was inadequate to provide "a fair and just support for our families," they expressed a conflation of "subsistence" and "wages" that was common among antebellum wage earners.[5] The clearest and most consistent statement of that conflation was in the growing insistence upon a "family wage." The "family wage," a wage for husbands high enough to eliminate the need for daughters and wives to work for pay, was based on an assumption that cash income constituted the entirety of the family subsistence: a "family wage" to the male head would, workingmen insisted, permit the mechanic to provide "a livelihood for himself and [his family]" from his "earnings" alone.[6]

Nevertheless, recent work in American social history suggests that this strict equation of wages with "means of support" does not accurately describe the range of strategies through which the nineteenth-century working classes pieced together their livelihoods. Christine Stansell has pointed to the importance of casual labor—"peddling, scavenging, and the shadier arts of theft and prostitution"—in "making ends meet" in the households of the laboring poor in mid-nineteenth-century New York City.[7] Judith E. Smith has noted the dense networks of resource sharing (including the sharing of food) that existed among immigrant families in turn-of-the-century Providence, Rhode Island.[8] Examining the grassroots politics of socialism in early-twentieth-century New York City, Dana Frank has demonstrated the power of housewives, in their work as shoppers, to force down food prices through community-based boycotts.[9] Each of these studies offers a vision of a survival economy based not solely on the cash income of waged labor, but on a far larger and more intricate fabric of resources.

In this essay, I will argue that the antebellum working classes did indeed rely for their subsistence upon means of support other than their wages. Among the key economic resources of antebellum working-class households was housework itself—the unwaged (although not always unremunerated) labor that wives performed within their own families. Working-class women understood their obligations as mothers and wives to extend from such unpaid labor as child rearing, cooking, and cleaning to such casualized forms of cash earning as taking in boarders and vending. In the course of this work, their labor represented a substantial economic benefit—both to their families and to the employers who paid their husbands' wages. Within the household, wives' labor produced as much as half of the family subsistence. Beyond the household, the value of housework accrued to the owners of mills and factories and shops, who were able to pay "subsistence" wages at levels that in fact represented only a fraction of the real price of workers' survival.

The distinctive value of housewives' labor lies largely unrecognized in the traditional Marxist analysis that has informed so much of the study of working-class history. This results from the way in which Marx formulated the concept of "means of subsistence." Marx defined "subsistence" as "the labour-time necessary for the production [and reproduction] of labour-power"—that is, the labor time required to ensure the survival of the wage earner both from day to day and from generation to generation.[10] But Marx assumed that the working class bought its entire subsistence on the market, with cash. In his discussion of the sale of labor power, for example, he identified "the means of subsistence" as "articles" that "must be bought or paid for," some "every day, others every week, others every quarter and so on."[11] He mentioned food, fuel, clothing, and furniture as examples. Having thus conceptually limited "subsistence" to what had to be purchased with income, Marx made a parallel limitation of the concept of "necessary labour-time" to labor time that earned money.

Limiting the definition of subsistence to that which had to be purchased with cash was a convenience for Marx, whose focus was on the potential of money to obscure inequalities in the buying and selling of labor. He reasoned that the price of labor, the wage, represented very different values to the worker and to the capitalist. The worker received the cost of subsistence; the capitalist purchased all that labor could produce in a given period of time. As the capitalist was able to increase the value labor produced over the cost of keeping labor alive, he gained for himself a "surplus value" that was the origin of new capital. Formulated in this way, the cash exchange—money, with its "inherent" "possibility . . . of a quantitative incongruity between price and magnitude of value"—became key to Marx's analysis.[12]

Marx was not entirely consistent in this formulation, however. One sometimes glimpses in *Capital* his own acknowledgment of the limitations of his analysis. His original definition of the value of labor power as "the labour-time necessary for the production, and consequently also the reproduction" of labor in no way excludes the labor time required to search the docks or borrow food in a period of shortage, for example.[13] At one point, moreover, he defined "subsistence" as the variety of resources "physically indispensable" to survival.[14] This definition might well include the labor of processing food into a digestible state, of nursing the sick back to health, and of tending small children—all of this routine in the labor of working-class housework. Finally, in his analysis of surplus value, Marx acknowledged that the wage might not always represent the value of subsistence. The capitalist could increase his margin of surplus value "by pushing the wage of the worker down below the value of his labour-power"—that is, below subsistence level.[15] This was not a mere hypothetical possibility for Marx, who acknowledged "the important part which this method plays in practice." But he found himself "excluded from considering it here by our assumption that all commodities, including labour-power, are bought and sold at their full value."[16]

Housework, however, was not bought and sold at its full value. Indeed, it was not bought and sold at all, but rather was exchanged directly for subsistence, in the manner of barter, within the family. Nonetheless, the cooking and cleaning, scavenging and borrowing, nursing and mending and child rearing that made up housework was clearly necessary to produce a husband's labor power. In other words, it was constituent in the total labor time represented by the commodity—labor power—the husband would sell on the market. At one point in his discussion of money, Marx noted that the *quantitative* contradiction expressed by the price could also become a *qualitative* one—that "a thing can, formally speaking, have a price without having a value."[17] The history of housework had left this labor in just the opposite position: It had a value without having a price. This distinguished housework from the forms of labor Marx was examining, but it did not exclude it from the process through which the surplus value of industrial capitalism was realized.

Indeed, for the northwestern United States at least, evidence suggests that the denial of the economic worth of housework was a historical process integral to the development of industrial capitalism.[18] The Europeans who settled the region in the seventeenth century appear to have recognized the economic contribution of wives' work. A largely subsistence-oriented people, New England Puritans defined the household as the "economical society" and understood that family survival required the wife's work in the garden, the barnyard, and the larder as much as it required the husband's work in the fields and meadows and barn.[19] Court records bear testimony to the perceived importance of wives' labor, in the form of actions to overturn a husband's will when magistrates concluded that the wife's share did not accurately reflect her "diligence and industry" in "the getting of the Estate."[20]

At the same time, colonial society contained the ideological foundations for later denial of the economic worth of wives' labor. As ministers reminded women, husbands—not wives—were the public representatives of the household: "Our Ribs were not ordained to be our Rulers."[21] Wives' subordination was embedded in the English common law that the Puritans brought with them to New England. As *feme covert*, a wife's legal identity was subsumed under that of her husband, who was recognized as the owner of her labor time, the products of that labor time, and any cash realized from the sale of either the labor or its products. However much individual males acknowledged individual wives' economic worth, the tradition of law identified that worth with the husband. Thus, Marx's assumption throughout *Capital* that the "possessor" of labor power and "the person whose labour-power it is" were one and the same person was historically inaccurate for housework in America from the beginning of English settlement.[22]

Mediated early on by the local nature of economic activity, wives' coverture became a more critical factor in the history of housework during the eighteenth century. Over the course of that century, the elaboration of cash markets and the growing competition among males for wages and property served to enhance the importance of money as a primary socially recognized index of economic worth. In public discussions of the economy, that is to say, industriousness was increasingly associated with moneymaking, while work that did not bring cash payment came scarcely to be recognized as work at all. This changing perception applied even to discussions of farming, still a largely subsistence-oriented activity. As Jared Eliot contended, the absence of a cash market "tends to enervate and abate the Vigor and Zeal" of the farmer and "renders him Indolent."[23] Working for the most part without prospect of payment, and unable to lay legal claim to payment even when it was made, the prototype of the free worker who labored outside of the cash marketplace was the wife.

This is not to say that wives never sold their labor, or the products of their labor, directly for cash.[24] But wives' formal relationship to the market remained ambiguous at best—as men's was not. Over the course of the eighteenth century, as the importance of cash markets increased, the absence of a formal relationship with those markets rendered women *as a group* less visible as participants in and contributors to the economy. Remunerated or not, their labor was conceptually subsumed under the labor of the person who owned it, their husbands. Laurel Thatcher Ulrich has suggested that by the mid-eighteenth century, the husband who would acknowledge the individuality of his wife's paid labor (as distinct from his own claim as head of household) was a rare exception.[25]

The growing equation of cash with economic value created for women palpable contradictions between experience and ideology. At a time when even the comparatively prosperous Esther Edwards Burr numbered among her labors cooking, cleaning, baking, seeing to her family's provision of vegetables, fruits, beverages, and dairy products, whitewashing walls, spinning, raising two children, covering chair bottoms, and making, remaking, and mending clothes,[26] colonial newspapers taunted that wives "want[ed] sense, and every kind of duty" and spent their time "more trifling than a baby."[27] From merely "owning" the family labor pool, husbands had now been ideologically identified as the *whole* of the family labor pool.

But the growing cultural invisibility of the economic value of the wife's labor in the family was not limited to the well-off. Indeed, by the end of the eighteenth century, the material conditions of survival in poor households provided a solid foundation, within the experience of working-class families themselves, for this new conception of the relation of men's paid labor or household support. As Ruth Schwartz Cowan has argued, one of the first effects of the coming of industrialization was the removal of men's labor from the household.[28] As poorer families could no longer provide land to their sons and as the growing power of masters and retailing middlemen undercut the traditional lines of advancement for journeymen in the trades, men experienced a dislocation in their ability to provide their share of the household maintenance. Under economic siege in the provision of their traditional portion of the family's subsistence, working-class men responded by conflating that part with the whole of the family economy. Certainly this conflation was made easier by the general and growing invisibility of the economic value of housework among the middle classes. But working-class men appear to have first expressed the conflation in the course of attempting to articulate and protest changes in the nature and status of their own labor. Like the Philadelphia cordwainers, early-nineteenth-century journeymen hatters complained that the erosion of the apprenticeship system was preventing them from "gain[ing] an honest livelihood for themselves and families," and the seamen who gathered at New York's City Hall to protest the Embargo Act in 1808 sought "wages which may enable them to support their families."[29]

Similarly, it was in this context that the demand for the family wage was forged; as Martha May has observed, workingmen recognized that under existing conditions, "the working-class family would be unable to maintain a tolerable standard of living or retain its customs and traditions."[30] But in the context of a society in which men's "ownership" of the family labor time had already been transformed into a perception that men were the only laborers in the family economy, the "family wage" ideal worked to reinforce the invisibility of the wife's contribution. As workingmen searched for a language through which to express concretely the brutalization of the paid workplace and the deterioration of their standard of living, the "family wage" ideal incorporated an ideal of female domesticity, including a distinction between women's household activities and economic labor. Workingmen's newspapers contrasted the "odious, cruel, unjust and tyrannical system" of the factory to the rejuvenative powers of the home.[31] *The Northern Star and Freeman's Advocate* agreed: "It is in the calm and quiet retreat of domestic life that relaxation from toil is obtained."[32] Early trade unionist William Sylvis waxed sentimental about the charm of women's mission:

> To guide the tottering footsteps of tender infancy in the paths of rectitude and virtue, to smooth down the wrinkles of our perverse nature, to weep over our shortcomings, and make us glad in the days of our adversity, to counsel, and console us in our declining years.[33]

In working-class as well as middle-class representations, counsel, comfort, and consolation had become the products of women's labor in the home.

Behind the rhetoric of female domesticity, however, antebellum working-class wives continued to engage in a complex array of subsistence-producing labor. They worked primarily as unpaid laborers in the family, where their work was of two general types. On the first level, wives (as well as children) were responsible for finding ways to increase the household provisions without spending cash. The most common form of this labor was scavenging—for food, for discarded clothing, for household implements, and for fuel. On the outskirts of cities and in smaller communities, wives and daughters collected bullrushes (which could be used to make chair bottoms), cattails (which could be used to stuff mattresses), and broom straw.[34] In the cities, women of the laboring poor haunted docks and wharves in search of damaged goods, and examined the refuse of the streets and marketplaces for food, cloth, or furniture that would be useful to their families.

Often carried out as an entirely legal enterprise, in practice the work of scavenging sometimes shaded into theft, another of the strategies through which families of the laboring poor added to their larders.[35] Throughout the antebellum period, both black and white women appeared in court to face charges of the theft of common and basic household implements: washtubs, frying pans, kettles, clothing, and other items that seem destined not for resale but for immediate consumption. When Mary Brennan stole a $3 pair of shoes from Percy S. White in 1841, "[s]he assigned her great destitution as the sole cause of the theft."[36]

Among more prosperous working-class families, shopping, household manufacturing, and gardening also functioned as means of avoiding cash outlays. Food bought in quantity was cheaper; grown in a garden, it was virtually free.[37] While the labor of gardening was often shared among family members, by the antebellum period marketing (which men had often done in earlier times) was women's work. In addition, some women continued to manufacture their own candles and make their own soap, and most women manufactured mattresses, pillows, linen, curtains, and clothing, and repaired furniture and garments.

Working-class wives worked not only to avoid spending money altogether, but also to reduce the size of necessary expenditures. Important for both of these ends was the maintenance of friendly contacts with neighbors, to whom one might turn for goods or services either as a regular supplement to one's own belongings or in periods of emergency. New to a building, neighborhood, or community, a woman depended upon her peers for information on the cheapest places to shop, the grocers least likely to cheat on weights and prices, and the likely spots for scavenging. Amicable relations with one's neighbors could yield someone to sit with a sick child or a friend from whom to borrow a pot or a few pieces of coal. In the event of fire, women often found that it was neighboring females who "exerted themselves in removing goods and furniture, and also in passing water" through the bucket brigade.[38] A history of friendly relations motivated one woman "to [go] herself to Whitehall after a load [of wood provided as public support], and . . . to see it delivered" when her neighbor's family was in danger of going without heat.[39]

Scarcity created tensions between cooperation and competition that required careful calculation. Boston's Mary Pepper complained that a neighbor had her run in as a drunk for no other reason than to get her evicted: "An its all along of your wanting my little place becaise ye cant pay the rent for your own," she charged.[40] Pepper was a single mother, responsible for the entirety of the household economy. Perhaps she had not had time to develop the bonds of mutual aid and obligation that might have prompted her neighbors to protect rather than complain of her. On the other hand, perhaps no amount of friendliness could have overridden a neighbor's need for her apartment. Indeed, Pepper herself may have acquired it by similar means.

Working-class wives also provided the bulk of the labor necessary to transform raw materials into items that the family could consume. That is to say, they hauled coal and wood, laid fires, and cooked the raw cornmeal, beans, onions, potatoes, and occasional meat that comprised the mainstay of working-class diets. Among working-class households able to afford cloth, wives made many of the family's garments and linens. Where clothing was scavenged and/or handed down, wives did the mending, the lengthening, the letting out and taking in. They lugged water into the dwelling—or else they carried laundry out—so that the family clothing could be washed. They carried the garbage from the building—or, more convenient and less backbreaking, sometimes simply threw it out of a window onto the streets.

Poverty simplified this labor. Since there was seldom enough money to buy food ahead or in large quantities, poorer wives spent relatively less time than middle-class wives in either food preparation or preservation. A table, a chair, some blankets and rags for mattresses, a cooking pot, and a few utensils might well constitute the sum of the household furnishings, requiring little of the general upkeep that occupied so much of the time of wives in wealthier families or even in more prosperous working-class households. Among the working poor, providing warmth, food, and clothing took precedence over providing a scrubbed and scoured environment. Moreover, exacting standards of cleanliness were to little avail in city tenant houses in which there were no outlets for the soot and fumes of cooking and into which water might run "at every storm."[41]

It was not uncommon for working-class wives also to be responsible for bringing some cash into the household economy. The regularity of this labor varied from household to household, depending not only on the size but also on the reliability of the husband's wage packet. Facing systemic economic hardship, married black women were more likely to undertake regular outside work as cooks, nurses, washerwomen, and maids. (Among whites, paid domestic service was commonly limited to single women.) Both black and white married women became seamstresses. Both sometimes became street vendors. If they lacked the 25-cents-a-day fee to rent a market stall, then from sidewalks and carts they hawked roots and herbs they had dug themselves, or fruits, vegetables, candy, eggs, peanuts, coffee, or chocolate.[42] Some women collected rags to sell to paper manufacturers, "poking into the gutters after rags before the stars go to bed."[43] If their husbands had employment building canals and railroads, wives sometimes took jobs for a season as cooks and laundresses for the entire work camp.[44]

But much of the cash earning of working-class wives was even less visible than these examples suggest. Virtually every wife whose husband worked in close proximity to the household (be he a tailor or a tavern keeper) was expected to contribute labor as his assistant. In this capacity, her portion of the labor was seldom distinguished by a separate wage or fees paid directly in her name. Rather, her work was subsumed under her husband's pay, or absorbed into an enterprise identified as exclusively his. For example, it was only in the course of a criminal prosecution in 1841 that it became clear on the record that John Cronin's wife "generally tended the junk shop" that bore his name.[45] Equally invisible was the cash that women earned by taking boarders into the household. In this instance, they exchanged their labor as cooks and maids, and sometimes as washerwomen and seamstresses, for a payment to the household. Virtually indistinguishable in nature from the labor they performed for free for their families, and enmeshed in that work in the course of the daily routine, boarding could nonetheless add as much as $3 or $4 a week to the household budget.

Through all of this, wives also took primary responsibility for nursing elderly or sick household members and for child rearing. In the conditions of the nineteenth-century city, the latter was a responsibility that brought special anxieties. The dangers of the city to children were legion—fires, horses running out of control, unmarked wells, unfenced piers, and disease, as well as temptations to theft and prostitution as means of making some money. In families where the household economy required that the mother or children go out to work, or that the mother focus her attention on needlework, for example, within the household, close supervision was impossible. This is not to suggest, as did the middle-class reformers of the period, that these parents were negligent. Within the demand for the family wage, and for working-class female domesticity, was a demand for a household in which children could be protected and better cared for. Wage-earning men longed for the day when "our wives, no longer doomed to servile labor, will be . . . the instructors of our children."[46]

The distinction between "paid labor" and "housework" implied in working-class men's yearning for the domestic ideal persisted in later-nineteenth-century analyses of women's unpaid labor and was eventually replicated in *Capital*. Because wives' work was largely unpaid, and because husbands came to the marketplace as the "possessors" of their wives' labor, Marx did not address the role of housework in the labor exchange that led to surplus value. Neither did he attend to the dynamics that permitted the husband to lay claim, in the price of his own labor, to the value of his wife's work.

The exchange value of housework is elusive, but it is not impossible to calculate. Some of it was directly paid, even when done by a wife in the context of her family duties—vending and needlework, for example. But even that labor for which wives were *not* paid when they worked in the context of their own families *was* paid when performed in the context of someone else's family, that is, as domestic service. The equivalence was direct, for in the antebellum period paid domestic service and unpaid housework were the same labor, often performed by the same woman, only in different locations and in different parts of her workday or workweek. Since paid domestic servants were customarily provided with room and board in addition to their wages, moreover, their earnings represented a price over and above food, shelter, and warmth, or, understood as an equivalent for housework, over and above the wife's basic maintenance.

In northeastern cities in 1860, cooks (who frequently also did the laundry) earned between $3 and $4 a week. Seamstresses averaged $2.50 a week, and maids made about the same amount. On the market, caring for children was at the lower end of the pay scale, commanding perhaps $2 a week. Taken at an average, this puts the price of a wife's basic housework at about $3 a week—or $150 a year—excluding the value of her own maintenance.[47]

To this should be added the value of goods a wife might make available within the family for free or at a reduced cost. Among poorer households, this was the labor of scavenging. A rag rug found among the refuse was worth 50 cents, an old coat several dollars. Flour for a week, scooped from a broken barrel on the docks, could save the household almost $1 in cash outlay.[48] When Mary Brennan stole the pair of shoes, she avoided a $3 expenditure (or would have, had she been successful). In these ways, a wife with a good eye and a quick hand might easily save her family $1 a week—or $50 or so over the course of the year.

Not all working-class wives scavenged. In households with more cash, wives were likely to spend that labor time in other forms of purchase-avoidance work. By shopping carefully, buying in bulk, and drying or salting extra food, a wife could save 10 to 50 percent on the family food budget, or about $1 a week on an income of $250 a year.[49] Wives who kept kitchen gardens could, at the very least, produce and preserve potatoes worth 25 cents a week, or some $10 to $15 a year.[50]

But there was also the cash that working-class wives brought into the household—in the form of needlework, vending, taking in boarders, running a grocery or a tavern from her kitchen, or working unpaid in her husband's trade. A boarder might pay $4 a week into the family economy. Subtracting $1.50 for food and rent, the wife's labor time represented $2.50 of that sum, or $130 a year.[51] Needlewomen averaged about $2 a week, or $100 a year.[52] Calculated on the basis of a "helper" in a trade, the wife's time working in her husband's occupation (for example, alongside her shoemaker husband for the equivalent of a day a week) was worth some $20 a year.[53]

The particular labor performed by a given woman depended on the size and resources of her household. In this way, housework remained entirely embedded within the family. Yet we can estimate a general market price of housework by combining the values of the individual activities that made it up: perhaps $150 for cooking, cleaning, laundry, and child rearing, even in poor households another $50 or so saved through scavenging and wise shopping, another $50 or so in cash brought directly into the household. This would set the price of a wife's labor time among the laboring poor at roughly $250 a year beyond maintenance, or in the neighborhood of $400 a year when the price of a single woman's maintenance purchased on the market (about $170 a year) is included. In households with more income, where the wife could focus her labor on saving money and on taking in a full-time boarder, that price might reach over $500 annually, or between $600 and $700 including maintenance.

The shift in the nature of and increase in the value of wives' work as a husband's income increased seems not to have been entirely lost on males, who advised young men that if they meant to get ahead, they should "get married."[54] This difference by income may also further explain the intersection of gender and economic interests that informed working-men's ideal of female domesticity. Women's wages were low—kept that way in part by the rhetoric surrounding the family wage ideal. Given this, a wife working without pay at home may have been more valuable to the family maintenance than a wife working for pay inside or outside the home. Similarly, the low levels of women's wages meant that few women could hope to earn the $170 a year necessary to purchase their maintenance on the market. This was true even for women in industrial work. While a full-time seamstress who earned $2.50 a week and was employed year-round would earn only $130 a year, an Irishwoman with ten years' seniority in the Hamilton mills earned only about $2.90 a week in 1860, or about $150 a year.[55]

Because of her need for access to cash, the wife's dependence on a wage earner within the family was particularly acute. She was not the only member benefiting from the amalgamation of labors that the household represented, however. A single adult male living in New York City in 1860 could scarcely hope to get by on less than $250 a year: $4 a week for room and board ($208 a year) and perhaps $15 a year for minimal clothing meant an outlay of almost $225 before laundry, medicines, and other occasional expenses.[56] Many working-class men did not earn $225 a year, and for them access to the domestic labor of a wife might be the critical variable in achieving maintenance. Even men who did earn this amount might find a clear advantage in marrying, for a wife saved money considerably over and above the cost she added for her own maintenance.

Historians have frequently analyzed the working-class family as a collectivity, run according to a communal ethic. But by both law and custom the marital exchange was not an even one. Finally the husband owned not only the value of his own labor time, but the value of his wife's as well—as expressed, for example, in cash or cooked food, manufactured or mended clothing, scavenged dishes or food, and children raised to an age at which they, too, could contribute to the household economy. There is no evidence that working-class males were prepared to give up the prerogatives of manhood. To the contrary, as we have seen, the rhetoric of the family wage suggests that they were engaged in a historical process of strengthening those claims.

Perhaps it would seem absurd to quibble over who owned the poverty or near-poverty that so often characterized working-class households. There were things to be owned, however, and ownership could prove the determining factor of subsistence or destitution if the household broke up. First, the husband possessed his own maintenance and any improvements in it that became possible as a result of the labor of his wife and children. He also owned whatever furnishings the family had accumulated. Although a table, a chair, clothing, bedding, and a few dishes seem (and were) scant enough property, they were the stuff of which life-and-death transactions were made in the laboring classes; pawned overnight, for example, clothes were important "currency" to cover the rent until payday. The husband also owned the children his wife raised; their wages (when they reached their mid-teens) might amount to several hundred dollars a year—almost as much as his own. Even while they were quite young, children might be helpful in scavenging fuel and food.

To be sure, wives commonly benefited from some or all of these sources of value, and both personal and community norms tended to restrain husbands from taking full advantage of their positions. Not only the affectional bonds of the family, but the expanding cultural emphasis on the husband as the "protector" and "provider" may have helped mediate emotionally the structural inequities of the household.

At the same time, community norms did not prevent the expression of individual self-interest in marriage, and the stresses of material hardship were as likely to rend as to create mutualities of concern. The frequency of incidents in which a wife had her husband arrested for battery and then "discharged at her request" suggests a complex, and less than romantic, dynamic of dependence in antebellum families. The continuing development of cash exchange networks throughout the antebellum period and the relegation of barter largely to domestic transactions had heightened that dynamic. A man could wear dirty clothes or look for cheaper accommodations or eat less to reduce his cash outlay, even if these choices might prove destructive in the long run. But the mariner's wife who stood with her four children on New York's docks, begging her husband for half of his wages, was in a far more extreme position of dependency. Her husband preferred to remain on board ship—with his wages.[57]

Husbands were not the only ones to benefit from the economic value of housework and from its invisibility. Employers were enabled by the presence of this sizeable but uncounted labor in the home to pay both men and women wages that were, in fact, below the level of subsistence. At a time when the level of capital accumulation in the Northeast remained precariously low and when, as a result, most new mills did not survive ten years, the margin of profit available from sub-subsistence wages was crucial.

Occasionally mill owners acknowledged that the wages they paid did not cover maintenance. One agent admitted:

> I regard my work-people just as I regard my machinery. So long as they can do my work *for what I choose to pay them*, I keep them, getting out of them all I can. . . . [H]ow they fare outside my walls I don't know, nor do I consider it my business to know. They must look out for themselves.[58]

More often, however, both capitalists and the political economists who rose in their defense maintained that they did indeed care about their workers, and that the wages they paid represented the true value of the labor they received, including the value of producing that labor. In 1825, for example, John McVickar caused to be reprinted in the United States the *Encyclopaedia Britannica* discussion of political economy, which asserted that "the cost of producing artificers, or labourers, regulates the wages they obtain."[59] Eleven years later, in *Public and Private Economy*, Theodore Sedgwick carried this optimism about the relationship of wages to subsistence one step further—at the same time revealing the dangerous uses to which the belief that wages represented subsistence could be put. Since "a little, a very little only" was required to maintain labor, Sedgwick argued, even at current levels of payment "in the factories of New England, very large numbers [of workers] may annually lay up half their wages; many much more."[60] Presumably wages not only covered but exceeded the value of maintenance. The other shoe would fall, again and again, as employers used the fact of working-class survival to justify further cuts in wages. The value of unpaid housework in mediating those cuts would remain invisible.

Although there is no evidence that capitalists consciously thought of it in this way, it was clearly in the interests of capital for housework to remain invisible. Following the lines of Marx's analysis, some scholars have concluded that, since it was unwaged, housework could not have created surplus value—that there must be a discrete exchange of money for that process to occur. Marx recognized, though, that the nature of the individual transaction was less important than its part in the general movement of capital. In the case of housework, which Marx did not examine, it was the very unwaged character of the labor that made it so profitable to capital. Traded first to the husband for partial subsistence, it then existed in the husband's labor as an element of subsistence made available to capital for free. Indeed, housework had achieved just the reverse of the qualitative contradiction Marx predicted: It had a value without having a price. Excluding the cash that working-class wives brought into the household, housework added several hundred dollars a year to the value of working-class subsistence—several hundred dollars that the employer did not have to pay as a part of the wage packet. Had the labor of housework been counted, wages would have soared to roughly twice their present levels. And as factory and mill owners knew well, "profits must vary inversely as wages, that is, they must fall as wages rise, and rise as wages fall."[61]

It is important to recognize that employers were able to appropriate the value of housework in part because the people they were paying *also* appropriated it. Paid workers protested many things during the antebellum period—long hours, pay cuts, production speedups—but there is no evidence that they objected to the fiction that wages were meant to cover the full value of household maintenance. Indeed, to have questioned that premise would have been to question the very structure of the gender system and of the family as socially constituted in the history of the northeastern United States. In this way, capital's claim to the surplus value of the wife's labor existed through and was dependent upon the husband's claim to that same value. So long as husbands understood their status as men (and so as heads of households) to depend upon the belief that they were the primary, if not the sole, "providers" of the family, the value of housework would remain unacknowledged by—and profitable to—their employers.

The history of industrialization in the United States and elsewhere has been written largely as a history of paid work. Housework, where it has been included at all, has been fitted into the historical scheme merely as an ancillary factor: Family life felt the shock waves of industrialization, but the epicenter of the quake was elsewhere, in the realm of "productive" labor. Marx himself drew the distinction between "productive" and "reproductive" work. He realized, however, as historians since have tended to forget, that the lines between these spheres were artificial: "[E]very social process of production is at the same time a process of reproduction."[62] The case of women's unpaid labor in the antebellum northeastern United States suggests that the opposite is also accurate. Only when we make the changing conditions and relations of housework integral parts of the narrative of economic and social transformation will our telling of the story become complete.

Notes

I would like to thank Betsy Blackmar, Carol Karlsen, Lori Ginzberg, Ileen DeVault, Nancy F. Cott, and the Columbia Seminar on Working-Class History for their helpful criticisms of various drafts of this article. I am also grateful to Rutgers University for its support, through the Henry Rutgers Research Fellowship.

1. John H. Griscom, *The Sanitary Condition of the Laboring Population of New York* (New York: Arno Press, 1970 [1845]).
2. For discussions of the attitudes of middle-class reformers toward the poor in the antebellum period, see Carroll Smith-Rosenberg, *Religion and the Rise of the American City: The New York City Mission Movement, 1812–1870* (Ithaca: Cornell University Press, 1971), and Paul Boyer, *Urban Masses and Moral Order in America, 1820–1920* (Cambridge: Harvard University Press, 1978). For a contemporary example, in addition to Griscom's, see Charles Loring Brace, *The Dangerous Classes of New York, and Twenty Years' Work, among Them* (New York: WynKoop and Hallenbeck, 1872).
3. U.S. Bureau of the Census, *Historical Statistics of the United States, Part I* (Washington, D.C.: United States Government Printing Office, 1975), Series A 6–8, 8, and Series D 167–181, 139.
4. Paul G. Faler, *Mechanics and Manufacturers in the Early Industrial Revolution: Lynn, Massachusetts, 1780–1860* (Albany: State University of New York Press, 1981), 84.
5. "The Address to the Working Shoemakers of the City of Philadelphia to the Public," as quoted in John Commons et al., *History of Labor in the United States* (New York: Macmillan Company, 1918), 1:141–42.
6. As quoted in Martha May, "Bread before Roses: American Workingmen, Labor Unions and the Family Wage," in Ruth Milkman, ed., *Women, Work and Protest: A Century of U.S. Women's Labor History* (Boston: Routledge and Kegan Paul, 1985), 3.
7. Christine Stansell, "Women, Children, and the Uses of the Streets: Class and Gender Conflict in New York City, 1850–1869," *Feminist Studies* 8, 2 (1982): 312–13.
8. Judith E. Smith, "Our Own Kind: Family and Community Networks in Providence," *Radical History Review* 17 (spring 1978): 99–120.

9. Dana Frank, "Housewives, Socialists, and the Politics of Food: The 1917 New York Cost-of-Living Protests," *Feminist Studies* 11, 2 (1985): 255–85.

10. Karl Marx, *Capital*, trans. Ben Fowkes (New York: Vintage Books, 1977), 1:274.

11. Ibid., 1:276.

12. Ibid., 1:196.

13. Ibid., 1:274.

14. Ibid., 1:277.

15. Ibid., 1:431.

16. Ibid., 1:431.

17. Ibid., 1:197.

18. For a more detailed discussion of the transformation of housework as an aspect of industrialization, see Jeanne Boydston, "Home and Work: The Industrialization of Housework in the Northeastern United States from the Colonial Period to the Civil War" (Ph. D. diss., Yale University, 1984).

19. For example, William Perkins gave his 1631 sermon on "oeconomie" the subtitle "Or, Household-Government: A Short Survey of the Right Manner of Erecting and Ordering a Family."

20. William Brigham, *The Compact with the Charter and Laws of the Colony of New Plymouth* (Boston: Dutton and Wentworth, 1836), 281.

21. William Secker, "*A Wedding Ring for the Finger . . .*" (Boston: Samuel Green, 1690), n.p.

22. See, for example, Marx's discussion of the sale of labor power in *Capital*, 1:271.

23. Jared Eliot, *Essays upon Field Husbandry in New England and Other Papers, 1748–1762*, eds. Harry J. Carman and Rexford G. Tugwell (New York, 1942), as quoted in Richard L. Bushman, *From Puritan to Yankee: Character and the Social Order in Connecticut, 1690–1765* (New York: W. W. Norton and Company, 1967), 26–27.

24. See, for example, Laurel Thatcher Ulrich, "'A Friendly Neighbor': Social Dimensions of Daily Work in Northern Colonial New England," *Feminist Studies* 6,2 (1980): 392–405; and Joan M. Jensen, "Cloth, Butter and Boarders: Women's Household Production for the Market," *The Review of Radical Political Economics* 12,2 (1980): 14–24.

25. Ulrich, "'A Friendly Neighbor,'" 394–95.

26. Carol F. Karlsen and Laurie Crumpacker, eds., *The Journal of Esther Edwards Burr, 1754–1757* (New Haven: Yale University Press, 1984).

27. "A-La-Mode, for the Year 1756," *Boston Evening Post*, Supplement, 8 March 1756; "By the Ranger," *Boston Evening Post*, 16 October 1758.

28. Ruth Schwartz Cowan, *More Work for Mother: The Ironies of Household Technology from the Open Hearth to the Microwave* (New York: Basic Books, 1983), 63–67.

29. *American State Papers, 1789–1815*, vol. 2, *Finance* (Washington: Gales and Seaton, 1832), 257; George Daitman, "Labor and the 'Welfare State' in Early New York," *Labor History* 4 (fall 1963): 252.

30. May, "Bread before Roses," 4.

31. *The Man*, 13 May 1835, as quoted in Commons, *History of Labor*, 388.

32. *The Northern Star and Freeman's Advocate*, January 2, 1843.

33. James C. Sylvis, ed., *Life, Speeches, Labors, and Essays of William H. Sylvis* (Philadelphia: Claxton, Remsen, and Haffelfinger, 1872), 120.

34. Susan May Strasser, *Never Done: A History of American Housework* (New York: Pantheon, 1982), 18.

35. For an excellent discussion of the uses of theft as an economic tool among the antebellum laboring poor, see Stansell, "Women, Children, and the Uses of the Streets."

36. For examples, see the *New York Tribune*, 12, 14, 19, and 20 April 1841, and 17 May 1841. The quotation is from 20 April 1841.

37. See below, n. 48.

38. *Boston Evening Transcript*, 20 September 1830.

39. Ezra Stiles Ely, *Visits of Mercy*, 6th ed. (Philadelphia: S. F. Bradford, 1829), 1:88.

40. *Boston Evening Transcript*, 27 July 1830.

41. Griscom, *Sanitary Condition*, 9.

42. See, for example, Solon Robinson, *Hot Corn: Life Scenes in New York Illustrated* (New York: Dewitt and Davenport, 1854), 31; and Thomas F. DeVoe, *The Market Book, Containing a Historical Account of the Public Markets in the Cities of New York, Boston, Philadelphia and Brooklyn* (New York: Burt Franklin, 1862), 370.

43. Robinson, *Hot Corn*, 198.

44. DeVoe, *The Market Book*, 463; Robert Ernst, *Immigrant Life in New York City, 1825–1863* (New York: King's Crown Press, 1949), 66.

45. *New York Tribune*, 22 April 1841.

46. William English, as quoted in Martha May, "Bread before Roses," 5.

47. Wages are from Edgar W. Martin, *The Standard of Living in 1860: American Consumption Levels on the Eve of the Civil War* (Chicago: University of Chicago Press, 1942), 177, and Faye E. Dudden, *Serving Women: Household Service in Nineteenth-Century America* (Middletown, Conn.: Wesleyan University Press, 1983), p. 149.

48. This is calculated on the basis of an average weekly budget for a working-class family of five, as itemized in the *New York Tribune* in 1851. According to that budget, flour could be bought in bulk at $5 a barrel, a barrel lasting a family of five about eight weeks. Since the *Tribune* budget assumes a family with an annual income over $500 (and therefore able to benefit from the savings of buying in bulk), I have increased the cost by 30 percent. See Norman Ware, *The Industrial Worker, 1840–1860: The Reaction of American Industrial Society to the Advance of the Industrial Revolution* (New York: Quadrangle/The New York Times Book Company, 1974), 33. On savings from buying in bulk, see Griscom, *Sanitary Condition*, 8. Other cash values are found in Martin, *Standard of Living*, 122, and in Richard Osborn Cummings, *The American and His Food: A History of Food Habits in the United States* (Chicago: University of Chicago Press, 1941), 75.

49. See above, n. 48.

50. Based on figures provided in Ware, *The Industrial Worker*, 33.

51. Martin, *Standard of Living*, 168.

52. Martin, *Standard of Living*, 177.

53. This calculation is based on wages in Carroll D. Wright, *Comparative Wages, Prices, and Cost of Living* (Boston: Wright and Potter Printing Company, 1889), 47, 55. It provides a very conservative index for wives' work; wives frequently had skills far beyond the "helper" level.

54. Grant Thorburn, *Sketches from the Note-book of Lurie Todd* (New York: D. Fanshaw, 1847), 12. Thorburn recommended marriage as a sensible economic decision for young men earning as little as $500 a year—more than males of the laboring poor, but within the range of better-paid workingmen.

55. Thomas Dublin, *Women at Work: The Transformation of Work and Community in Lowell, Massachusetts, 1826–1860* (New York: Columbia University Press, 1979), Table 11.12.

56. See Martin, *Standard of Living*, 168, for the average weekly cost of room and board for a single, adult male living in New York City.

57. Ely, *Visits of Mercy*, 194.

58. Quoted in Ware, *The Industrial Worker*, 77. Emphasis mine.

59. John McVickar, *Outlines of Political Economy* (New York: Wilder and Campbell, 1825), 107.

60. Theodore Sedgwick, *Public and Private Economy* (New York: Harper and Brothers, 1836), 30, 225.

61. McVickar, *Outlines*, 144.

62. Marx, *Capital*, 1:711.

6

Cherokee Women and the Trail of Tears

Theda Perdue

More than 150 years ago, in 1839, the United States forced the Cherokee Nation west of the Mississippi River to what later would become the state of Oklahoma. The Cherokees primarily occupied territory in the Southeast that included northern Georgia, northeastern Alabama, southeastern Tennessee, and southwestern North Carolina. In the three decades preceding removal, they experienced a cultural transformation. Relinquishing ancient beliefs and customs, the leaders of the nation sought to make their people culturally indistinguishable from their white neighbors, in the hope that through assimilation they could retain their ancestral homeland. White land hunger and racism proved too powerful, however, and the states in which the Cherokees lived, particularly Georgia, demanded that the federal government extinguish the Indians' title and eject them from the chartered boundaries of the states. The election of Andrew Jackson in 1828 strengthened the states' cause.

While President Jackson promoted the policy of removing eastern Indians to the west, he did not originate the idea. Thomas Jefferson first suggested that removal beyond the evils of "civilization" would benefit the Indians and provide a justification for his purchase of Louisiana. Between 1808 and 1810 and again between 1817 and 1819, members of the Cherokee Nation migrated to the west as the Cherokee land base shrank. But the major impetus for total removal came in 1830 when Congress, at the urging of President Jackson, passed the Indian Removal Act, which authorized the president to negotiate cessions of Indian land in the east and transportation of native peoples west of the Mississippi. Although other Indian nations, such as the Choctaws, signed removal treaties right away, the Cherokees refused. The Cherokee Nation's leaders retained legal counsel and took their case against repressive state legislation to the United States Supreme Court (*Cherokee Nation v. Georgia*, 5 Peters 1). The Cherokee Nation won on the grounds that the Cherokees constituted a "domestic dependent" nation—not a foreign state under the U.S. Constitution. The state's failure to respond to the decision and the federal government's refusal to enforce it prompted an unauthorized Cherokee faction to negotiate removal. In December 1835 these disaffected men signed the Treaty of New Echota, by which they exchanged the Cherokee Nation's territory in the Southeast for land in the West. The United States Senate ratified the treaty, and in the summer of 1838 soldiers began to round up Cherokees for deportation. Ultimately, the Cherokees were permitted to delay until fall and to manage their own removal, but this leniency did little to ameliorate the experience the Cherokees called the "trail of tears." The weather was unusually harsh that winter; cold, disease, hunger, and exhaustion claimed the lives of at least four thousand of the fifteen thousand people who traveled the thousand miles West.[1]

The details of Cherokee removal have been recounted many times by scholars and popular writers. The focus of these accounts has tended to be political: They have dealt primarily with the United States' removal policy, the negotiation of removal treaties, and the political factionalism that the removal issue created within Cherokee society. In other words, the role of men in this event has dominated historical analysis. Yet women also were involved, and it seems appropriate to reexamine the "trail of tears" using gender as a category of analysis. In particular, what role did women play in removal? How did they regard the policy? Did their views differ from those of men? How did the removal affect women? What were their experiences along the "trail of tears"? How did they go about reestablishing their lives in their new homes in the West? How does this kind of analysis amplify or alter our understanding of the event?

The Treaty of New Echota, by which the Cherokee Nation relinquished its territory in the Southeast, was signed by men.[2] Women were present at the rump council that negotiated the treaty, but they did not participate in the proceedings. They may have met in their own council—precedents for women's councils exist—but if they did, no record remains. Instead, they probably cooked meals and cared for children while their husbands discussed treaty terms with the United States commissioner. The failure of women to join in the negotiation and signing of the Treaty of New Echota does not necessarily mean that women were not interested in the disposition of tribal land, but it does indicate that the role of women had changed dramatically in the preceding century.

Traditionally, women had a voice in Cherokee government.[3] They spoke freely in council, and the War Woman (or Beloved Woman) decided the fate of captives. As late as 1787 a Cherokee woman wrote Benjamin Franklin that she had delivered an address to her people urging them to maintain peace with the new American nation. She had filled the peace pipe for the warriors, and she enclosed some of the same tobacco for the United States Congress in order to unite symbolically her people and his in peace. She continued:

> I am in hopes that if you Rightly consider that woman is the mother of All—and the Woman does not pull Children out of Trees or Stumps nor out of old Logs, but out of their Bodies, so that they ought to mind what a woman says.[4]

The political influence of women, therefore, rested at least in part on their biological role in procreation and their maternal role in Cherokee society, which assumed particular importance in the Cherokees' matrilineal kinship system. In this way of reckoning kin, children belonged to the clan of their mother, and their only relatives were those who could be traced through her.[5]

Not only were the Cherokees matrilineal, they also were matrilocal. That is, a man lived with his wife in a house that belonged to her, or, perhaps more accurately, to her family. According to the naturalist William Bartram, "Marriage gives no right to the husband over the property of his wife; and when they part she keeps the children and property belonging to them."[6] The "property" that women kept included agricultural produce—corn, squash, beans, sunflowers, and pumpkins—stored in the household's crib. Produce belonged to women because they were the principal farmers. This economic role was ritualized at the Green Corn Ceremony every summer, when an old woman presented the new corn crop. Furthermore, eighteenth-century travelers and traders normally purchased corn from women instead of men, and in the 1750s the garrison at Fort Loudoun, in present-day eastern Tennessee, actually employed a female purchasing agent to procure corn.[7] Similarly, the fields belonged to the women who tended them, or rather to the women's lineages. Bartram observed that "their fields are divided by proper marks and their harvest is gathered separately."[8] While the Cherokees technically held land in common and anyone could use unoccupied land, improved fields belonged to specific matrilineal households.

Perhaps this explains why women signed early deeds conveying land titles to the "Proprietors of Carolina." Agents who made these transactions offered little explanation for the signatures of women on these documents. In the early twentieth century a historian speculated that they represented a "renunciation of dower," but it may have been that the women were simply parting with what was recognized as theirs, or they may have been representing their lineages in the negotiations.[9]

As late as 1785 women still played some role in the negotiation of land transactions. Nancy Ward, the Beloved Woman of Chota, spoke to the treaty conference held at Hopewell, South Carolina, to clarify and extend land cessions stemming from Cherokee support of the British in the American Revolution. She addressed the assembly as the "mother of warriors" and promoted a peaceful resolution to land disputes between the Cherokees and the United States. Under the terms of the Treaty of Hopewell, the Cherokees ceded large tracts of land south of the Cumberland River in Tennessee and Kentucky and west of the Blue Ridge Mountains in North Carolina. Nancy Ward and the other Cherokee delegates to the conference agreed to the cession not because they believed it to be just but because the United States dictated the terms of the treaty.[10]

The conference at Hopewell was the last treaty negotiation in which women played an official role, and Nancy Ward's participation in that conference was somewhat anachronistic. In the eighteenth century, the English as well as other Europeans had dealt politically and commercially with men, since men were the hunters and warriors in Cherokee society and Europeans were interested primarily in military alliances and deerskins. As relations with the English grew increasingly important to tribal welfare, women became less significant in the Cherokee economy and government. Conditions in the Cherokee Nation following the American Revolution accelerated the trend. In their defeat, the Cherokees had to cope with the destruction of villages, fields, corn cribs, and orchards that had occurred during the war, and the cession of hunting grounds that accompanied the peace. In desperation, they turned to the United States government, which proposed to convert the Cherokees into replicas of white pioneer farmers in the anticipation that they would then cede additional territory (presumably hunting grounds they no longer needed).[11] While the government's so-called civilization program brought some economic relief, it also helped produce a transformation of gender roles and social organization. The society envisioned for the Cherokees, one that government agents and Protestant missionaries zealously tried to implement, was one in which a man farmed and headed a household composed only of his wife and children. The men who gained power in eighteenth-century Cherokee society—hunters, warriors, and descendants of traders—took immediate advantage of this program in order to maintain their status in the face of a declining deerskin trade and pacification, and then diverted their energy, ambition, and aggression into economic channels. As agriculture became more commercially viable, these men began to farm or to acquire African slaves to cultivate their fields for them. They also began to dominate Cherokee society, and by example and legislation they altered fundamental relationships.[12]

In 1808 a council of headmen (there is no evidence of women participating) from Cherokee towns established a national police force to safeguard a person's holdings during life and "to give protection to children as heirs to their father's property, and to the widow's share," thereby changing inheritance patterns and officially recognizing the patriarchal family as the norm. Two years later, a council representing all seven matrilineal clans, but once again apparently including no women, abolished the practice of blood vengeance. This action ended one of the major functions of clans and shifted the responsibility for punishing wrongdoers to the national police force and tribal courts. Matrilineal kinship clearly did not have a place in the new Cherokee order.[13]

We have no record of women objecting to such legislation. In fact, we know very little about most Cherokee women because written documents reflect the attitudes and concerns of a male Indian elite or of government agents and missionaries. The only women about whom we know very much are those who conformed to expectations. Nancy Ward, the Beloved Woman who favored peace with the United States, appears in the historical records, while other less cooperative Beloved Women are merely unnamed, shadowy figures. Women such as Catherine Brown, a model of Christian virtue, gained the admiration of missionaries, and we have a memoir of Brown's life; other women who removed their children from mission schools incurred the missionaries' wrath, and they merit only brief mention in mission diaries. The comments of government agents usually focused on those native women who demonstrated considerable industry by raising cotton and producing cloth (in this case, Indian men suffered by comparison), not those who grew corn in the matrilineage's fields.[14] In addition to being biased and reflecting only one segment of the female population, the information from these sources is secondhand; rarely did Indian women, particularly traditionalists, speak for themselves.

The one subject on which women did speak on two occasions was land. In 1817 the United States sought a large cession of Cherokee territory and removal of those who lived on the land in question. A group of Indian women met in their own council, and thirteen of them signed a message that was delivered to the National Council. They advised the council:

> The Cherokee ladys now being present at the meeting of the Chiefs and warriors in council have thought it their duties as mothers to address their beloved Chiefs and warriors now assembled.
>
> Our beloved children and head men of the Cherokee nation we address you warriors in council.[W]e have raised all of you on the land which we now have, which God gave us to inhabit and raise provisions.[W]e know that our country has once been extensive but by repeated sales has become circumscribed to a small tract and never have thought it our duty to interfere in the disposition of it till now, if a father or mother was to sell all their lands which they had to depend on[,] which their children had to raise their living on[,] which would be bad indeed and to be removed to another country. [W]e do not wish to go to an unknown country which we have understood some of our chidren wish to go over the Mississippi but this act of our children would be like destroying your mothers. Your mother and sisters ask and beg of you not to part with any more of our lands.[15]

The next year, the National Council met again to discuss the possibility of allotting Cherokee land to individuals, an action the United States government encouraged as a preliminary step to removal. Once again, Cherokee women reacted:

> We have heard with painful feelings that the bounds of the land we now possess are to be drawn into very narrow limits. The land was given to us by the Great Spirit above as our common right, to raise our children upon, & to make support for our rising generations. We therefore humbly petition our beloved children, the head men and warriors, to hold out to the last in support of our common rights, as the Cherokee nation have been the first settlers of this land; we therefore claim the right of the soil. . . . We therefore unanimously join in our meeting to hold in our country in common as hitherto.[16]

Common ownership of land meant in theory that the United States government had to obtain cessions from recognized, elected Cherokee officials who represented the wishes of the people. Many whites favored allotment because private citizens then could obtain individually owned tracts of land through purchase, fraud, or seizure. Most Cherokees recognized this danger and objected to allotment for that reason. The women, however, had an additional incentive for opposing allotment. Under the laws of the states in which the

Cherokees lived and of which they would become citizens if land were allotted, married women had few property rights. A married woman's property, even property she held prior to her marriage, belonged legally to her husband.[17] Cherokee women and matrilineal households would have ceased to be property owners.

The implications for women became apparent in the 1830s, when Georgia claimed its law was in effect in the Cherokee country. Conflicts over property arose because of uncertainty over which legal system prevailed. For example, a white man, James Vaught, married the Cherokee Catherine Gunter. She inherited several slaves from her father, and Vaught sold two of them to General Isaac Wellborn. His wife had not consented to the sale, and so she reclaimed her property and took them with her when the family moved west. General Wellborn tried to seize the slaves just as they were about to embark, but a soldier, apparently recognizing her claim under Cherokee law, prevented him from doing so. After removal, the general appealed to Principal Chief John Ross for aid in recovering the slaves, but Ross refused. He informed Wellborn: "By the laws of the Cherokee Nation, the property of husband and wife remain separate and apart and neither of these can sell or dispose of the property of the other." Had the Cherokees accepted allotment and come under Georgia law, Wellborn would have won.[18]

The effects of the women's protests in 1817 and 1818 are difficult to determine. In 1817 the Cherokees ceded tracts of land in Georgia, Alabama, and Tennessee, and in 1819 they made an even larger cession. Nevertheless, they rejected individual allotments and strengthened restrictions on alienation of improvements. Furthermore, the Cherokee Nation gave notice that they would negotiate no additional cessions—a resolution so strongly supported that the United States ultimately had to turn to a small unauthorized faction in order to obtain the minority treaty of 1835.[19]

The political organization that existed in the Cherokee Nation in 1817 and 1818 had made it possible for women to voice their opinion. Traditionally, Cherokee towns were politically independent of one another, and each town governed itself through a council in which all adults could speak. In the eighteenth century, however, the Cherokees began centralizing their government in order to restrain bellicose warriors whose raids jeopardized the entire nation, and to negotiate as a single unit with whites. Nevertheless, town councils remained important, and representatives of traditional towns formed the early National Council. This National Council resembled the town councils in that anyone could address the body. Although legislation passed in 1817 created an Executive Committee, power still rested with the council, which reviewed all committee acts.[20]

The protests of the women to the National Council in 1817 and 1818 were, however, the last time women presented a collective position to the Cherokee governing body. Structural changes in Cherokee government more narrowly defined participation in the National Council. In 1820 the council provided that representatives be chosen from eight districts rather than from traditional towns, and in 1823 the committee acquired a right of review over acts of the council. The more formalized political organization made it less likely that a group could make its views known to the national government.[21]

As the Cherokee government became more centralized, political and economic power rested increasingly in the hands of a few elite men who adopted the planter lifestyle of the white antebellum South. A significant part of the ideological basis for this lifestyle was the cult of domesticity, in which the ideal woman confined herself to home and hearth while men contended with the corrupt world of government and business.[22] The elite adopted the tenets of the cult of domesticity, particularly after 1817, when the number of Protestant missionaries, major proponents of this feminine ideal, increased significantly, and their influence on Cherokee society broadened.

The extent to which a man's wife and daughters conformed to the idea quickly came to be one measure of his status. In 1818 Charles Hicks, who later served as principal chief, described the most prominent men in the Cherokee Nation as "those who have for the last 10 or 20 years been pursuing agriculture & kept their women & children at home & in comfortable circumstances." Eight years later, John Ridge, one of the first generation of Cherokees to have been educated from childhood in mission schools, discussed a Cherokee law that protected the property rights of a married woman and observed that "in many respects she has exclusive & distinct control over her own, particularly among the less civilized." The more "civilized" presumably left such matters to men. Then Ridge described suitable activities for women: "They sew, they weave, they spin, they cook our meals and act well the duties assigned them by Nature as mothers." Proper women did not enter business or politics.[23]

Despite the attitudes of men such as Hicks and Ridge, women did in fact continue as heads of households and as businesswomen. In 1828 the *Cherokee Phoenix* published the obituary of Oo-dah-less, who had accumulated a sizeable estate through agriculture and commerce. She was "the support of a large family," and she bequeathed her property "to an only daughter and three grandchildren." Oo-dah-less was not unique. At least one-third of the heads of household listed on the removal roll of 1835 were women. Most of these were not as prosperous as Oo-dah-less, but some were even more successful economically. Nineteen owned slaves (190 men were slaveholders), and two held over twenty slaves and operated substantial farms.[24]

Nevertheless, these women had ceased to have a direct voice in Cherokee government. In 1826 the council called a constitutional convention to draw up a governing document for the nation. According to legislation that provided for election of delegates to the convention, "No person but a free male citizen who is full grown shall be entitled to vote." The convention met and drafted a constitution patterned after that of the United States. Not surprisingly, the constitution that male Cherokees ratified in 1827 restricted the franchise to "free male citizens" and stipulated that "no person shall be eligible to a seat in the General Council, but a free Cherokee male, who shall have attained the age of twenty-five." Unlike the United States Constitution, the Cherokee document clearly excluded women, perhaps as a precaution against women who might assert their traditional right to participate in politics instead of remaining in the domestic sphere.[25]

The exclusion of women from politics certainly did not produce the removal crisis, but it did mean that a group traditionally opposed to land cession could no longer be heard on the issue. How women would have voted is also unclear. Certainly by 1835 many Cherokee women, particularly those educated in mission schools, believed that men were better suited to deal with political issues than women, and a number of women voluntarily enrolled their households to go west before the forcible removal of 1838 and 1839. Even if women had united in active opposition to removal, it is unlikely that the United States and aggressive state governments would have paid any more attention to them than they did to the elected officials of the nation who opposed removal or the fifteen thousand Cherokees, including women (and perhaps children), who petitioned the United States Senate to reject the Treaty of New Echota. While Cherokee legislation may have made women powerless, federal authority rendered the whole nation impotent.

In 1828 Georgia had extended state law over the Cherokee Nation and white intruders who invaded its territory. Georgia law prohibited Indians, both men and women, from testifying in court against white assailants, and so they simply had to endure attacks on person and property. Delegates from the nation complained to Secretary of War John H. Eaton about the lawless behavior of white intruders:

Too many there are who think it an act of trifling consequence to oust an Indian family from the quiet enjoyment of all the comforts of their own firesides, and to drive off before their faces the stock that gave nourishment to the children and support to the aged, and appropriate it to the satisfaction of avarice.[26]

Elias Boudinot, editor of the bilingual *Cherokee Phoenix*, even accused the government of encouraging the intruders in order to force the Indians off their lands, and he published the following account:

A few days since two of these white men came to a Cherokee house, for the purpose, they pretended, of buying provisions. There was no person about the house but one old woman of whom they inquired for some corn, beans etc. The woman told them she had nothing to sell. They then went off in the direction of the field belonging to this Cherokee family. They had not gone but a few minutes when the woman of the house saw a heavy smoke rising from that direction. She immediately hastened to the field and found the villains had set the woods on fire but a few rods from the fences, which she found already in a full blaze. There being a very heavy wind that day, the fire spread so fast, that her efforts to extinguish it proved utterly useless. The entire fence was therefore consumed in a short time. It is said that during her efforts to save the fence the men who had done the mischief were within sight, and were laughing heartily at her.

The Georgia Guard, established by the state to enforce its law in the Cherokee country, offered no protection and, in fact, contributed to the lawlessness. The *Phoenix* printed the following notice under the title "Cherokee women, Beware":

It is said that the Georgia Guard have received orders, from the Governor we suppose, to inflict corporeal punishment on such females as shall hereafter be guilty of insulting them. We presume they are to be the judges of what constitutes *insult*.[27]

Despite harassment from intruders and the Guard, most Cherokees had no intention of going west, and in the spring of 1838 they began to plant their crops as usual. Then United States soldiers arrived, began to round up the Cherokees, and imprisoned them in stockades in preparation for deportation. In 1932 Rebecca Neugin, who was nearly a hundred years old, shared her childhood memory and family tradition about removal with historian Grant Foreman:

When the soldier came to our house my father wanted to fight, but my mother told him that the soldiers would kill him if he did and we surrendered without a fight. They drove us out of our house to join other prisoners in a stockade. After they took us away, my mother begged them to let her go back and get some bedding. So they let her go back and she brought what bedding and a few cooking utensils she could carry and had to leave behind all of our other household possessions.[28]

Rebecca Neugin's family was relatively fortunate. In the process of capture, families were sometimes separated and sufficient food and clothing were often left behind. Over fifty years after removal, John G. Burnett, a soldier who served as an interpreter, reminisced:

Men working in the fields were arrested and driven to stockades. Women were dragged from their homes by soldiers whose language they could not understand. Children were often separated from their parents and driven into the stockades with the sky for a blanket and the earth for a pillow.

Burnett recalled how one family was forced to leave the body of a child who had just died and how a distraught mother collapsed of heart failure as soldiers evicted her and her three children from their homes.[29] After their capture, many Cherokees had to march miles over rugged mountain terrain to the stockades. Captain L. B. Webster wrote his wife about moving eight hundred Cherokees from North Carolina to the central depot in Tennessee: "We were eight days in making the journey (80 miles), and it was pitiful to behold the women & children, who suffered exceedingly—as they were all obliged to walk, with the exception of the sick."[30]

Originally the government planned to deport all the Cherokees in the summer of 1838, but the mortality rate of the three parties that departed that summer led the commanding officer, General Winfield Scott, to agree to delay the major removal until fall. In the interval, the Cherokees remained in the stockades, where conditions were abysmal. Women in particular often became individual victims of their captors. The missionary Daniel Butrick recorded the following episode in his journal:

> The poor Cherokees are not only exposed to temporal evils, but also to every species of moral desolation. The other day a gentleman informed me that he saw six soldiers about two Cherokee women. The women stood by a tree, and the soldiers with a bottle of liquor were endeavoring to entice them to drink, though the women, as yet were resisting them. He made this known to the commanding officer but we presume no notice was taken of it, as it was reported that those soldiers had those women with them the whole night afterwards. A young married woman, a member of the Methodist society was at the camp with her friends, though her husband was not there at the time. The soldiers, it is said, caught her, dragged her about, and at length, either through fear, or otherwise, induced her to drink; and then seduced her away, so that she is now an outcast even among her own relatives. How many of the poor captive women are thus debauched, through terror and seduction, that eye which never sleeps, alone can determine.[31]

When removal finally got under way in October, the Cherokees were in a debilitated and demoralized state. A white minister who saw them as they prepared to embark noted: "The women did not appear to as good advantage as did the men. All, young and old, wore blankets which almost hid them from view."[32] The Cherokees had received permission to manage their own removal, and they divided the people into thirteen detachments of approximately one thousand each. While some had wagons, most walked. Neugin rode in a wagon with other children and some elderly women, but her older brother, mother, and father "walked all the way."[33] One observer reported that "even aged females, apparently nearly ready to drop in the grave, were traveling with heavy burdens attached to the back." Proper conveyance did not spare well-to-do Cherokees the agony of removal, the same observer noted:

> One lady passed on in her hack in company with her husband, apparently with as much refinement and equipage as any of the mothers of New England; and she was a mother too and her youngest child, about three years old, was sick in her arms, and all she could do was to make it comfortable as circumstances would permit. . . . She could only carry her dying child in her arms a few miles farther, and then she must stop in a strangerland and consign her much loved babe to the cold ground, and that without pomp and ceremony, and pass on with the multitude.[34]

This woman was not alone. Journals of the removal are largely a litany of the burial of children, some born "untimely."[35]

Many women gave birth alongside the trail: at least sixty-nine newborns arrived in the West.[36] The Cherokees' military escort was often less than sympathetic. Daniel Butrick wrote in his journal that troops frequently forced women in labor to continue until they collapsed and delivered "in the midst of the company of soldiers." One man even stabbed an expectant mother with a bayonet.[37] Obviously, many pregnant women did not survive such treatment. The oral tradition of a family from southern Illinois, through which the Cherokees passed, for example, includes an account of an adopted Cherokee infant whose mother died in childbirth near the family's pioneer cabin. While this story may be apocryphal, the circumstances of Cherokee removal make such traditions believable.[38]

The stress and tension produced by the removal crisis probably accounts for a postremoval increase in domestic violence, of which women usually were the victims. Missionaries reported that men, helpless to prevent seizure of their property and assaults on themselves and their families, vented their frustrations by beating wives and children. Some women were treated so badly by their husbands that they left them, and this dislocation contributed to the chaos in the Cherokee Nation in the late 1830s.[39]

Removal divided the Cherokee Nation in a fundamental way, and the Civil War magnified that division. Because most signers of the removal treaty were highly acculturated, many traditionalists resisted more strongly the white man's way of life and distrusted more openly those Cherokees who imitated whites. This split between "conservatives," those who sought to preserve the old ways, and "progressives," those committed to change, extended to women. We know far more, of course, about "progressive" Cherokee women, who left letters and diaries that in some ways are quite similar to those of upper-class women in the antebellum South. In letters, they recounted local news such as "they had Elick Cockrel up for steeling horses" and "they have Charles Reese in chains about burning Harnages house" and discussed economic concerns: "I find I cannot get any corn in this neighborhood, and so of course I shall be greatly pressed in providing provision for my family." Nevertheless, family life was the focus of most letters: "Major is well and tryes hard to stand alone he will walk soon. I would write more but the baby is crying."[40]

Occasionally we even catch a glimpse of conservative women who seem to have retained at least some of their original authority over domestic matters. Red Bird Smith, who led a revitalization movement at the end of the nineteenth century, had considerable difficulty with his first mother-in-law. She "influenced" her adopted daughter to marry Smith through witchcraft and, as head of the household, meddled rather seriously in the couple's lives. Interestingly, however, the Kee-Too-Wah society, which Red Bird Smith headed, had little room for women. Although the society had political objectives, women enjoyed no greater participation in this "conservative" organization than they did in the "progressive" republican government of the Cherokee Nation.[41]

Following removal, the emphasis of legislation involving women was on protection rather than participation. In some ways, this legislation did offer women greater opportunities than the law codes of the states. In 1845 the editor of the *Cherokee Advocate* expressed pride that "in this respect the Cherokees have been considerably in advance of many of their white brethren, the rights of their women having been amply secured almost ever since they had written laws." The nation also established the Cherokee Female Seminary to provide higher education for women, but like the education women received before removal, students studied only those subjects considered to be appropriate for their sex.[42]

Removal, therefore, changed little in terms of the status of Cherokee women. They had lost political power before the crisis of the 1830s, and events that followed relocation merely confirmed new roles and divisions. Cherokee women originally had been subsistence-level farmers and mothers, and the importance of these roles in traditional society had made it possible for them to exercise political power. Women, however, lacked the economic resources and military might on which political power in the Anglo American system rested. When the Cherokees adopted the Anglo American concept of power in the eighteenth and nineteenth centuries, men became dominant. But in the 1830s the chickens came home to roost. Men, who had welcomed the Anglo American basis for power, now found themselves without power. Nevertheless, they did not question the changes they had fostered. Therefore, the tragedy of the "trail of tears" lies not only in the suffering and death the Cherokees experienced but also in the failure of many Cherokees to look critically at the political system they had adopted—a political system dominated by wealthy, highly acculturated men, and supported by an ideology that made women (as well as others defined as "weak" or "inferior") subordinate. In the removal crisis of the 1830s, men learned an important lesson about power; it was a lesson women had learned well before the "trail of tears."

Notes

1. The standard account of Cherokee removal is Grant Foreman, *Indian Removal: The Emigration of the Five Civilized Tribes of Indians* (Norman, Okla., 1932), 229–312. Also see Ronald N. Satz, *American Indian Policy in the Jacksonian Era* (Lincoln, Neb., 1975); Dale Van Every, *Disinherited: The Lost Birthright of the American Indian* (New York, 1966); William G. McLoughlin, "Thomas Jefferson and the Beginning of Cherokee Nationalism, 1806 to 1809," *William and Mary Quarterly*, 3d ser., 32 (1975): 547–80; Thurman Wilkins, *Cherokee Tragedy: The Story of the Ridge Family and the Decimation of a People* (New York, 1970); Gary E. Moulton, *John Ross: Cherokee Chief* (Athens, Ga., 1978); Russell Thornton, "Cherokee Population Losses during the Trail of Tears: A New Perspective and a New Estimate," *Ethnohistory* 31 (1984); 289–300. Other works on the topic include Gloria Jahoda, *The Trail of Tears* (New York, 1975); Samuel Carter, *Cherokee Sunset: A Nation Betrayed* (Garden City, N.Y., 1976); and John Ehle, *The Trail of Tears: The Rise and Fall of the Cherokee Nation* (New York, 1988). A good collection of primary documents can be found in the *Journal of Cherokee Studies* 3 (1978). For the context in which the removal policy developed, see Francis Paul Prucha, *American Indian Policy in the Formative Years: The Indian Trade and Intercourse Acts, 1790–1834* (Cambridge, Mass., 1962). Not all Cherokees went west; see John R. Finger, *The Eastern Band of Cherokees, 1891–1900* (Knoxville, Tenn., 1984).
2. Charles J. Kappler, ed., *Indian Affairs: Laws and Treaties* (Washington, D.C., 1904–1941), 2:439–49.
3. While some similarities to the role of women among the Iroquois exist, the differences are significant. Both had matrilineal kinship systems and practiced the same fundamental sexual division of labor, but the Cherokees had no clan mothers who selected headmen, an important position among the Iroquois of the Five Nations. The Cherokees were an Iroquoian people, but linguists believe that they separated from the northern Iroquois thousands of years ago. Certainly, the Cherokees had been in the Southeast long enough to be a part of the southeastern cultural complex described by Charles Hudson in *The Southeastern Indians* (Knoxville, Tenn., 1976). Yet where women were concerned, the Cherokees differed from other southeastern peoples. James Adair, an eighteenth-century trader, gave the following analysis: "The Cherokees are an exception to all civilized or savage nations in having no laws against adultery; they have been a considerable while under a petticoat-government, and allow their women full liberty to plant their brows with horns as oft as they please, without fear of punishment" (James Adair, *Adair's History of the American Indian*, ed. Samuel Cole Williams [Johnson City, Tenn., 1930], 152–53). Adair was correct that Cherokee women enjoyed considerable sexual autonomy. Furthermore, they seem to have exercised more political power than other eighteenth-century native women in the Southeast. Earlier sources, however, describe "queens" who ruled southeastern peoples other than the Cherokee. See Edward Gaylord Bourne, ed., *Narratives of the Career of Hernando de Soto* (New York, 1922), 1:65–72. Consequently, the unusual role of women in Cherokee society cannot be attributed definitively to either Iroquoian or southeastern antecedents.
4. Samuel Hazard, ed., *Pennsylvania Archives, 1787* (Philadelphia, 1852–56), 11:181–82. See also Theda Perdue, "The Traditional Status of Cherokee Women," *Furman Studies* (1980): 19–25.
5. The best study of the aboriginal Cherokee kinship system is John Phillip Reid, *A Law of Blood: The Primitive Law of the Cherokee Nation* (New York, 1970). Also see William H. Gilbert, *The Eastern Cherokees* (Washington, D.C., 1943) and Alexander Spoehr, *Changing Kinship Systems: A Study in the Acculturation of the Creeks, Cherokee, and Choctaw* (Chicago, 1947).
6. William Bartram, "Observations on the Creek and Cherokee Indians, 1789," *Transactions of the American Ethnological Society* 3, part 1 (1954): 66.
7. William L. McDowell, ed., *Documents Relating to Indian Affairs, 1754–1765* (Columbia, S.C., 1970), 303; Henry Timberlake, *Lieu. Henry Timberlake's Memoirs, 1756–1765*, ed. Samuel Cole Williams (Johnson City,

Tenn., 1927), 89–90; Benjamin Hawkins, *Letters of Benjamin Hawkins, 1796–1806*, vol. 9 of *Georgia Historical Society Collections* (Savannah, Ga., 1916), 110; Adair, *Adair's History*, 105–17.

8. William Bartram, *The Travels of William Bartram*, ed. Mark Van Doren (New York, 1940), 90.

9. Alexander S. Salley, ed., *Narratives of Early Carolina, 1650–1708* (New York, 1911), 90.

10. *American State Papers*, Class 2: *Indian Affairs* (Washington, D.C., 1832), 1:41. For Nancy Ward, see Ben Harris McClary, "Nancy Ward: Last Beloved Woman of the Cherokees," *Tennessee Historical Quarterly* 21 (1962): 336–52; Theda Perdue, "Nancy Ward," in Catherine Clinton and Ben Barker-Benfield, eds., *Portraits of American Women* (New York, 1991).

11. Prucha, *American Indian*, 213–49; Bernard W. Sheehan, *Seeds of Extinction: Jeffersonian Philanthropy and the American Indian* (Chapel Hill, N.C., 1973); Robert F. Berkhofer Jr., *Salvation and the Savage: An Analysis of Protestant Missions and American Indian Response* (Lexington, Ky., 1965).

12. William G. McLoughlin, *Cherokee Renascence in the New Republic* (Princeton, 1986); William G. McLoughlin, *Cherokees and Missionaries, 1789–1839* (New Haven, Conn., 1984); Henry T. Malone, *Cherokees of the Old South: A People in Transition* (Athens, Ga., 1956); Theda Perdue, *Slavery and the Evolution of Cherokee Society, 1540–1866* (Knoxville, Tenn., 1979).

13. *Laws of the Cherokee Nation: Adopted by the Council at Various Times, Printed for the Benefit of the Nation* (Tahlequah, Cherokee Nation, 1852), 3– 4.

14. Rufus Anderson, *Memoir of Catherin Brown, A Christian Indian of the Cherokee Nation* (Philadelphia, 1832); Hawkins, *Letters*, 20.

15. Presidential papers microfilm: Andrew Jackson (Washington, 1961), Series 1, Reel 22; also mentioned in Journal of Cyrus Kingsbury, 13 February 1817, Papers of the American Board of Commissioners for Foreign Missions, Houghton Library, Harvard University, Cambridge, Mass. (hereafter cited as American Board papers).

16. Brainerd Journal, 30 June 1818 (American Board papers).

17. For women's property rights in the United States, see Mary Beard, *Woman as a Force in History: A Study in Traditions and Realities* (New York, 1946); Marylynn Salmon, "Women and Property in South Carolina: The Evidence from Marriage Settlements, 1730–1830," *William and Mary Quarterly*, 3d ser., 39 (1982): 655–85; Marylynn Salmon, "Equality or Submersion? *Feme Covert* Status in Early Pennsylvania," in Carol Berkin and Mary Beth Norton, eds., *Women of America* (Boston, 1979); Marylynn Salmon, "'Life Liberty and Dower': The Legal Status of Women after the Revolution," in Carol Berkin and Clara Lovett, eds., *Women, War and Revolution* (New York, 1980); Norma Basch, "Invisible Women: The Legal Fiction of Marital Unity in Nineteenth-Century America," *Feminist Studies* 5 (1979): 346–66; Norma Basch, *In the Eyes of the Law: Women, Marriage, and Property in Nineteenth-Century New York* (Ithaca, N.Y., 1982); Albie Sachs and Joan Hoff-Wilson, *Sexism and the Law: A Study of Male Beliefs and Legal Bias in Britain and the United States* (New York, 1979); Suzanne Lebsock, *The Free Women of Petersburg: Status and Culture in a Southern Town, 1784–1860* (New York, 1984).

18. Louis Wyeth to R. Chapman and C. C. Clay, 16 May 1838; Memorial of Isaac Wellborn to Martin Van Buren, n.d.; Writ of the Morgan County (Alabama) Court, 9 1838 (Letters Received by the Office of Indian Affairs, 1824–1881, RG 75, National Archives, Washington, D.C.). Joel R. Poinsett to Mathew Arbuckle, 17 December 1838; John Ross to Joel R. Poinsett, 18 July 1839 (John Ross Papers, Thomas Gilcrease Institute, Tulsa, Okla.).

19. Charles C. Royce, *Indian Land Cessions in the United States* (Washington, D.C., 1900), 684–85, 696–97.

20. V. Richard Persico Jr., "Early Nineteenth-Century Cherokee Political Organization," in Duane H. King, ed., *The Cherokee Indian Nation: A Troubled History* (Knoxville, Tenn., 1979), 92–109.

21. *Laws of the Cherokee Nation*, 14–18, 31–32.

22. The classic article is Barbara Welter, "The Cult of True Womanhood, 1820–1860," *American Quarterly* 18 (1966): 151–74. Also see Glenna Matthews, *"Just a Housewife": The Rise and Fall of Domesticity in America* (New York, 1987). In *The Plantation Mistress: Woman's World in the Old South* (New York, 1982), Catherine Clinton points out that southern women, particularly from the planter class, did not exactly fit the model for northern women. Yet Cherokee women may have conformed more closely to that model than many other southern women because of the influence of northern missionaries. See Theda Perdue, "Southern Indians and the Cult of True Womanhood," in Walter J. Fraser Jr., R. Frank Saunders Jr., and Jon L. Wakelyn, eds., *The Web of Southern Social Relations: Essays on Family Life, Education, and Women* (Athens, Ga., 1985), 35–51. Also see Anne Firor Scott, *The Southern Lady: From Pedestal to Politics, 1830–1930* (Chicago, 1970), 3–21; Mary E. Young, "Women, Civilization, and the Indian Question," in Mabel E. Deutrich and Virginia C. Purdy, eds., *Clio Was a Woman: Studies in the History of American Women* (Washington, D.C., 1980).

23. Ard Hoyt, Moody Hall, William Chamberlain, and D. S. Butrick to Samuel Worcester, 25 July 1818 (American Board Papers); John Ridge to Albert Gallatin, 27 February 1826 (John Howard Payne Papers, Newberry Library, Chicago, Ill. [hereafter cited as Payne Papers]).

24. *Cherokee Phoenix*, 2 July 1828; Census of 1835 (Henderson Roll), RG 75, Office of Indian Affairs, National Archives, Washington, D.C.; R. Halliburton Jr., *Red over Black: Black Slavery among the Cherokee Indians* (Westport, Conn., 1977), 181–92. Robert Bushyhead, a native Cherokee-speaker from Cherokee, North Carolina, identified the gender of names on the Henderson Roll.

25. *Laws of the Cherokee Nation*, 79, 120–21.

26. George Lowrey, Lewis Ross, William Hicks, R. Taylor, Joseph Vann, and W. S. Shorey to John H. Eaton, 11 February 1830, Letters Received, Office of Indian Affairs, 1824–1881, National Archives, Washington.

27. *Cherokee Phoenix*, 26 March 1831; 16 July 1831.

28. Foreman, *Indian Removal*, 302–3.

29. John G. Burnett, "The Cherokee Removal through the Eyes of a Private Soldier," *Journal of Cherokee Studies* 3 (1978): 183.

30. Capt. L. B. Webster, "Letters from a Lonely Soldier," *Journal of Cherokee Studies* 3 (1978): 154.

31. Journal of Daniel S. Butrick, n.d., Payne Papers. There is another Butrick journal in the American Board Papers. The one in the Payne Papers is as much a commentary as a personal narrative.

32. J. D. Anthony, *Life and Times of Rev. J. D. Anthony* (Atlanta, 1896).

33. Foreman, *Indian Removal*, 302–3.

34. "A Native of Maine, Traveling in the Western Country," *New York Observer*, 26 January 1839.

35. A good example is B. B. Cannon, "An Overland Journey to the West (October–December 1837)," *Journal of Cherokee Studies* 3 (1978): 166–73.

36. "Emigration Detachments," *Journal of Cherokee Studies* 3 (1978): 186–87.

37. Butrick Journal, Payne Papers.

38. Story related by unidentified member of an audience at Warren Wilson College, Black Mountain, N.C., January 1983.

39. Butrick Journal, 30 April 1839, 2 May 1839 (American Board Papers).

40. Edward Everette Dale and Gaston Litton, eds., *Cherokee Cavaliers: Forty Years of Cherokee History as Told in the Correspondence of the Ridge-Watie-Boudinot Family* (Norman, Okla., 1939), 20–21, 37–38, 45–46. For comparison, see Scott, *Southern Lady*, and Clinton, *Plantation Mistress*.

41. *Indian Pioneer History* (Oklahoma Historical Society, Oklahoma City), 9:490–91; Robert K. Thomas, "The Redbird Smith Movement," in William N. Fenton and John Gulick, eds., *Symposium on Cherokee and Iroquois Culture* (Washington, D.C., 1961).

42. *Cherokee Advocate*, 27 February 1845; Rudi Halliburton Jr., "Northeastern Seminary Hall," *Chronicles of Oklahoma* 51 (1973–74): 391–98; *Indian Pioneer History*, 1:394.

7

"Domestic" Life in the Diggings: The Southern Mines in the California Gold Rush

Susan Lee Johnson

In 1853 Helen Nye wrote from California to her mother in Massachusetts: "I have heard of Miners at some diggins subsisting for days on Acorns of which we have a very fine kind in this Country." Nye was a white woman whose husband was a merchant at Don Pedro's Bar, in the area known during the gold rush as the Southern Mines. She explained to her mother how newcomers learned to make use of the oak tree's bounty by watching native people during their autumn harvest. In general, though, gold rush immigrants saw the food that Indians most valued as something to be eaten only in dire circumstances. As Charles Davis explained to his daughter in Massachusetts, while acorns, grass, and wild oats abounded in the Sierra Nevada foothills, these were suitable only for "Wild Indians and Wild Animals."[1] Davis's disdain for native sustenance suggests that cooking and eating became sites of contestation in the diggings. In fact, this was the case all over the gold region, given the relative absence of women there. But it was especially true in the Southern Mines, which was both the homeland of Miwok Indians and the destination for a majority of non–Anglo American immigrants to gold rush California, including Mexicans, Chileans, French, Chinese, and some African Americans.[2] In the Southern Mines, culinary practices fit into a larger constellation of activities that signaled for many a world of confusion—men mending trousers and caring for the sick, Anglos dining on acorns and frijoles. As Edmund Booth complained to his wife back in Iowa, "Cal. is a world upside down—nothing like home comforts and home joys."[3]

To understand why California seemed like a world standing on its head, one must ponder the multiple meanings of such everyday practices as eating acorns, digging gold, and inhabiting a race or a gender.[4] Even in so short a time as the gold rush years and even in so small a place as the Southern Mines, meanings proliferated, evolved, collided. While native people there lived in communities with roughly equal numbers of women and men, among immigrant peoples skewed sex ratios meant drastically altered divisions of labor in which men took on tasks that their womenfolk would have performed back home. Analyzing how men parceled out such work and how they thought about what they were doing tells us much about the content of gender in the gold rush. Crucial too are the meanings of the domestic and personal service work that the small number of non-native women did in California, and the perceptions native and immigrant peoples held of one another's ways of manufacturing material life.

Skewed sex ratios in the diggings were accompanied by an extraordinary demographic diversity: people came to California from all over the world, producing and reproducing ideas about color, culture, and nation that, on U.S. soil, often coalesced into conversations about race. Race, like gender, is a set of changing ideas about human difference and hierarchy, and a relation in which those ideas are put into practice.[5] In a time and place like gold rush California, its meanings pulsed through everyday life like an erratic heartbeat. For instance, the way that certain tasks, such as cooking or laundry, came to be associated with certain non-Anglo men demonstrates how constructions of race could be mapped onto constructions of gender in the diggings.

Indeed, in the boom years of the gold rush, relations of class were often obscured or even subsumed by the day-to-day salience of gender and race. This was in part because the means of getting gold during the initial boom was by "placer" (surface, individualized) mining rather than "quartz" (underground, industrialized) mining.[6] Placer mining required almost no capital and did not necessarily entail a hierarchy among workers—claims could be staked for free, the necessary tools were simple and easily built or acquired, and the work could be done (though it was not always done) by a small group of people who rotated tasks. Later, entrepreneurs developed "hydraulic" mining, a more capital-intensive means of exploiting surface deposits, whereby men shot powerful streams of water against hills assumed to be rich in "deep gravels." When hydraulic and quartz mining took hold, they were accompanied by an elaboration of class hierarchies. Class relations followed a different course in areas—like much of the Southern Mines—where insufficient water and underground deposits thwarted development of hydraulic and quartz mining. In such areas, the making of class was often signaled by the growth of local water companies, whereby capitalists bought up rights to scarce water and then sold use of the water to placer miners who needed it to wash gold-bearing dirt. But all of these developments—water monopolies and hydraulic and quartz operations—came about as the initial boom, which was predicated on rich surface diggings, began to give way to a bust. In the early years of the gold rush—roughly 1848 to 1853—class contests and solidarities often had as much to do with immigrants' memories of class in their homelands as with actual social relations structured through divisions of labor in the mines. Gold-rush California was an unusual time and place.

This, though, is not news; historians have long noted the social peculiarities of the gold rush. Indeed, while not all histories of the event and its context have been self-consciously social histories, all have attended to key social dimensions of the demographic cataclysm that followed the 1848 discovery of gold in the Sierra Nevada foothills. Most have noted that "society" in the diggings was, first, mostly male and, second, significantly multiracial and multiethnic.[7] These two demographic realities, along with the initial absence of state power in the foothills, the social implications of that absence, and the suspension of some class distinctions, are among the most oft-mentioned aspects of gold-rush California. Yet with one exception—an important new cultural history that compares arguments about the meanings of gold in both American California and Australian Victoria—twentieth-century scholarship has stressed questions of social structure over those of social meaning. Newer work, then, must build on these earlier accounts, employing interrelated modes of analysis developed in ethnic studies, feminist studies, and cultural studies. That is, to the concern with demography we must add a concern for the *content* of social categories such as gender or race.[8]

In this essay, I explore some social meanings and cultural consequences of two of the peculiarities that have interested historians of the gold rush—that is, the relative absence of women and the overwhelming presence of polyglot peoples. I do so by concentrating on what might be thought of as "domestic" life in the diggings—and especially on practices relating to cooking, serving, and eating meals.[9] Not everyone in the Southern Mines dug gold, but everyone did perform, or relied on others to perform, life-sustaining and life-enhancing tasks such as procuring provisions and preparing food. Since few could reproduce the divisions of labor that made performance of these tasks seem more or less predictable and culturally coherent back home, gold-rush participants devised new ways to provide for their needs and wants. But all the while they wondered about what it meant that Anglo American men were down on their knees scrubbing their shirts in a stream, that Mexican women were making money hand over fist selling tortillas in the gold town of Sonora, or that French men seemed so good at creating homey cabins in the diggings.

Distinguishing between two kinds of work—domestic and personal service work, on one hand, and work in the mines, on the other—may seem to reify categories of labor. In making such distinctions, one invokes the discursive division between home and workplace that accompanied the growth of industrial capitalism in the nineteenth century. One also echoes more recent Marxist-feminist delineations of productive and reproductive labor, which have placed "reproductive" chores (often women's work) on a par with those "productive" chores (often men's work) assumed to constitute true economic activity.[10]

But impulses similar to those that split home life off from labor in the nineteenth century—impulses scrutinized by twentieth-century feminists—also led most gold-rush participants to view mining as qualitatively different from and more important than their other daily tasks. This makes intuitive sense, since immigrants traveled hundreds or thousands of miles to dig gold or to profit from those who did. Yet performing this privileged economic activity required that miners pay attention to the exigencies of everyday life. Then, too, for one group in the Southern Mines—Miwok Indians—gold digging rarely became the most important, community-defining kind of labor performed. So the dichotomy drawn here between mining labor and domestic and personal service work is at once heuristic *and* grounded in some, but not all, relevant historical circumstances.

In the end, though, the distinction serves another purpose. During the 1980s historians learned to use poststructuralist analyses of language that show how binary oppositions work—oppositions such as the one between productive and reproductive labor. In the productive/reproductive labor distinction, for example, the leading term (productive or "breadwinning" work) takes primacy, while its partner (reproductive or "domestic" work) is weaker or derivative. This hierarchical relation mirrors some social relations of dominance and subordination based on gender, and also on race.[11] So foregrounding "reproductive" or "domestic" labor in a history of a mining area, where mining labor might be assumed to take precedence, is itself a gesture toward unsettling that hierarchical relation. I begin, then, not in the mines, but in the canvas dwellings of gold-rush participants.

Though most immigrants lived in such homes, the word *tent* actually described a wide variety of structures. Some people lived in cramped quarters, such as the Chinese men Scottish traveler J. D. Borthwick saw, who were organized "in a perfect village of small tents." But when miners stayed still for any length of time, they built more elaborate shelters. For instance, though Belgian miner Jean-Nicolas Perlot and his French companions lived at first in a small tent and a brush hut, within a year they constructed a sturdy log cabin covered with a canvas roof. In such cabins, immigrants built bedsteads and fireplaces, though some men remembered how improvised chimneys forced smoke inside instead of drawing it out. Heavy rain in the foothills could impair the draft of even a well-built fireplace, and Welsh-born Angus McIsaac noted in his diary that men living with such irritants often compared their smoky cabins to scolding wives or leaky ships.[12]

McIsaac's observation suggests how readily gold-rush participants saw in their material world metaphoric possibilities, how easily the frustrations of camp life took on gendered meanings. McIsaac himself thought a smoky home was "ill compared" to a scolding spouse or a leaky vessel, noting, "[W]ere I compelled to take charge of either, I would on all [occasions] choose the former." While McIsaac considered a woman the most pleasing ward, he took for granted the gender hierarchy his words implied. Meanwhile, he and his neighbors took charge of their more immediate surroundings by christening their cabins with names that suggested, even celebrated, the absence of sharp-tongued spouses: Loafers' Retreat, Temperance Hole, and Jackass Tent. Like the white miners who called their camp Whooping-boys Hollow, McIsaac and friends took a certain pleasure in the canvas-covered world-without-women they created.[13]

Not all shelters in the Southern Mines bespoke the ambivalent bachelorhood of men such as McIsaac. Among immigrant peoples, more Mexican men than others came to California with their womenfolk. So some Mexican communities in the diggings celebrated different social possibilities than did Whooping-boys Hollow. One observer of such communities was William Perkins, a Canadian merchant in the town of Sonora, which was founded in 1848 by miners from the state of the same name in northern Mexico. Perkins was rhapsodic in his descriptions of Mexican camp life there:

> I had never seen a more beautiful, a wilder or more romantic spot. The Camp . . . was literally embowered in the trees. The habitations were constructed of canvas, cotton cloth, or of upright unhewn sticks with green branches and leaves and vines interwoven, and decorated with gaudy hangings of silks, fancy cottons, flags, brilliant goods of every description; the many-tinted Mexican *zarape*, the rich *manga*, with its gold embroidery, Chinese scarves and shawls of the most costly quality.

For Perkins, the scene recalled "descriptions we have read of the brilliant bazaars of oriental countries." Whatever the orientalizing eyes of Perkins saw, there is no reason to doubt that Mexicans did indeed decorate their dwellings with bright flags and fabrics and serapes. Perkins noted that it was Mexican men who built the houses, and who, "leaving their wives and children in charge," went off during the week to dig gold. However few and far between, then, even in gold-rush California there were eye-catching, well-tended worlds-without-men.[14]

For the most part, though, miners fended for themselves. Once they built cabins or pitched tents, inhabitants had to organize domestic labor such that all stayed well-fed and healthy. The most common type of household in the boom years of the gold rush was that of two to five men who constituted an economic unit; they worked together in placer claims held in common, alternating tasks and placing the gold in a fund from which they purchased provisions. This generalization holds for most white men, both North American and European, and most free African Americans during the gold rush. It may hold for many Mexican and Chilean men, and perhaps some Chinese men as well. But for those North Americans, Latin Americans, and Chinese who went to California under conditions of slavery, debt peonage, or contract labor, other domestic arrangements were probably obtained. And whenever women were present in the camps or whenever men lived in or near towns with boardinghouses and restaurants, daily subsistence was a different matter.[15]

All gold-rush households, save those of Miwoks, relied on tenuous market relations to supply most of their basic needs. Out in the camps, men traded gold dust for supplies at the nearest store, generally a tent or cabin a fair hike from home stocked with freight hauled overland from the supply town of Stockton, in the San Joaquin Valley. Beef, pork, beans, flour, potatoes, and coffee ranked high on miners' lists of items purchased. In flush times they might also be able to buy onions, dried apples, or a head of cabbage, though fresh fruits and vegetables were the hardest items to find.[16]

Limited foodstuffs spelled monotonous meals for most, but also encouraged people to exchange cooking techniques. Men from Europe and the United States, for example, sometimes adopted Mexican practices. Perlot and his companions, en route to the mines in 1851 and low on provisions, met up with a party of Mexicans who were eating what looked to Perlot like turnips dipped in salt and pepper, fresh tortillas, and hearty beef-steaks cooked over an open flame. The Mexican men gave Perlot some raw meat, and he returned with it to his own party, proclaiming, "Messieurs . . . in this country, this is how beefsteak is cooked." Howard Gardiner, from Long Island, was less enthusiastic about the Mexican meals he learned to prepare during lean times, such as those based around *pinole*, recalling that he and his partners lived "more like pigs than human beings." Just as gold-rush shelters took on gendered meanings, so too could gold-rush food become racialized in its procurement, preparation, or consumption.[17]

Among Latin Americans, men might try to appeal to one another's tastes, especially when commercial interests were at stake. Vicente Pérez Rosales, a small-time Chilean *patrón* who went to California with his brothers and five laborers, learned in mid-1849 that non-Anglos were being driven from the mines. So he turned his attention to trade, setting up a store filled with Chilean cheese and beef jerky, toasted flour, dried peaches, candied preserves, and barrels of brandy. All items sold well except the jerky, which was full of what looked like moth holes. So the Chilean merchants laid the jerky out in the sun and coated it with hot lard to fill up the apertures. Then they piled it up in a pyramid shape and doused it with Chilean hot sauce. The pungent smell caught the attention of some Mexicans, and so the traders told the customers that it was the kind of jerky "served to the aristocracy in Santiago." Pérez Rosales recalled, "We lied like experienced mer-chants who assure a trusting female customer that they are losing money on an item, and would not sell it at such a low price to anyone but her." Here and elsewhere Pérez Rosales turned Mexican unfamiliarity with Chilean foodstuffs to his advantage, playing on envy of aristocratic privilege and, in his own mind, making women of Mexican men, thereby underscoring Chilean manliness. Such interethnic episodes, which were charged with taken-for-granted notions of gender and tinged with class meanings, must have occurred frequently in the Southern Mines.[18]

Most immigrants, like these Mexican customers, preferred to purchase their provisions. But during the first few winters of the gold rush, floods and treacherously muddy roads between Stockton and the foothills brought severe shortages of supplies.[19] So many miners tried to supplement store-bought food by hunting and fishing, and a few gathered greens or planted small gardens. Not all who hunted met with success. New Englander Moses Little brought down some quail just in time for Christmas dinner in 1852, but he spent most of his shot at target practice. William Miller, also from New England, had better luck. He and his white partners were camped near a group of free black miners, and in addition to joining forces to dam the river and work its bed, the two parties went out deer hunting together and otherwise shared provisions. Heavy rains foiled the mining plans, but the African American and Anglo American residents of the camp continued to exchange gifts of fresh venison—despite harassment from white southerners who resented the presence of free blacks. By Christmas, one of the black men, Henry Garrison (born in New York but emigrated from Hawaii), had moved into Miller's tent. All parties spent the holiday together indulging in a "Splendid Dinner" of venison and the trimmings, and dancing to the music of Garrison's fine fiddle playing. Though men were not always successful hunters—given both the in-experience of immigrants from towns and cities and the decline in foothill animal popula-tions wrought by the gold rush—cultural memory of hunting as a male pursuit encouraged men to give it a try.[20]

Fewer men planted gardens or gathered greens, so visitors were astonished by Perlot's singular store of herbs and vegetables. After serving salad to an incredulous miner in the mid-1850s, Perlot took him on a stroll: "I led him a hundred paces from the house . . . where I gathered chervil; a few steps farther to a place where cress was growing well . . . ; a little farther, I found lamb's lettuce." One of Perlot's partners, Frenchman Louvel, had planted the garden the year before. On seeing it, the newcomer exclaimed, "My God, . . . how stupid can you be! to suffer four years as I have, without having had an idea as simple as that."[21]

Still, most immigrant men suffered from the dietary deficiencies created by their ignorance of the wild plants that Miwok women gathered and their unwillingness to grow more familiar crops.[22] Perhaps they hesitated to plant vegetables because their campsites were temporary, or because kitchen gardens were generally women's responsibility back home. Whatever the reason, their reluctance made them sick. George Evans, for example, could not fathom why he was too ill to work in the mines, until doctors told him he had scurvy. So he had friends gather wild cabbage and onions, and he bought some potatoes and a bottle of lime juice. His health took a turn for the better.[23]

Evans, given his condition, was wise to eat his vegetables raw, but most miners cooked their food and had to decide among themselves how to share culinary duties. The evidence for such divisions of labor says more about Anglo men than other gold seekers, but Europeans and free blacks, at least, seem to have followed similar practices. The Belgian Perlot claimed, in fact, that most men organized cooking in like fashion: "The rule generally observed between miners in partnership . . . was to do the cooking by turns of a week." Similarly, John Doble, from rural Indiana, explained, "[S]ometimes one does the cooking and sometimes another and one only cooks at a time and cooks for all who are in the Cabin."[24]

A man's "cook week" began on Sunday, when he prepared for the days ahead, as Moses Little recorded: "It being my week to cook I have been somewhat busy—more so than on other Sabbath—Coffee to burn A box full of nuts to fry Bread to bake & Beef to cut up & take care of." During the week, the cook continued to make large quantities of staple foods like bread and beans, in addition to getting up three meals a day. The days around New Year's 1850 must have been the cook week of Henry Garrison, the fiddle player who lived with William Miller and his dancing partners, because Miller's journal for that period is filled with references to Garrison cooking breakfast, making apple pudding, and stirring up a "Beautiful Stew" of squirrel meat. Miller must have looked forward to Garrison's cook weeks, because at least one of his other partners had trouble even lighting a fire, say nothing of preparing meals. Domestic competence was hardly universal in the diggings, but men valued it when they found it among their comrades.[25]

While it is more difficult to determine from English-language and translated sources whether most gold seekers adopted similar divisions of labor, such sources do provide some evidence of Chinese domestic habits. Yet white observers were more apt to note how odd they found Chinese foods, cookware, and eating implements than to describe how Chinese men divided up domestic work. When J. D. Borthwick visited Chinese camps, the miners invited him to eat with them, but he declined, finding their dishes "clean" but "dubious" in appearance. He added that he much preferred "to be a spectator," a role chosen by many a white man in his dealings with Chinese miners. The spectacle Borthwick described was that of a Chinese camp at dinnertime, with men "squatted on the rocks in groups of eight or ten round a number of curious little black pots and dishes, from which they helped themselves with their chopsticks." Borthwick's word picture evoked white men's visions of the Chinese; there was something both delicate and animal-like in the circle of men with their curious cookware. While his words said as much about white visions as about Chinese practices, they did suggest that Chinese miners working in large parties broke into smaller groups who shared meals, and that they used cooking and eating utensils from their homeland.[26]

Some white men were more gracious than Borthwick when invited to join Chinese circles. John Marshall Newton was camped near five hundred Chinese miners in 1852. After helping the Chinese secure their title to a claim that had been challenged by English miners,

Newton fancied himself a "hero" in his neighbors' eyes. The Chinese men did give him gifts and invite him for meals; no doubt they appreciated Newton's assistance in what often proved for them an inhospitable local world. But however much they credited his actions, they also relished making him the butt of dinnertime jokes. Invariably when Newton sat down to eat, someone would hand him chopsticks. "Of course I could do nothing with them," Newton recalled, and so "the whole 500 seeing my awkwardness would burst out into loud laughter."[27]

To the Chinese miners, their neighbor must have looked a bit like an overgrown child fumbling with his food. Still, despite this momentary reversal of a dynamic in which white men disproportionately held the power and resources necessary to ensure survival in the diggings, more often Chinese men found it expedient to curry favor with whites. In a situation where white men missed more than anything "home comforts and home joys," Chinese men could turn such longings to their advantage. Howard Gardiner, for example, lived for a time by himself near a Chinese man. Sometimes Gardiner would stay late working on his claim, and when he went home, he recalled, "I found that the Celestial had preceded me and prepared supper." Gardiner's neighbor must have found some benefit in looking after the white man. Meanwhile, for Gardiner the arrangement seemed so unremarkable—so familiar—that he granted it only passing mention. In everyday events like these, where men of color performed tasks white men associated with white women, gold-rush race relations became gender relations as well.[28]

Among some men in the diggings, such domestic practices were institutionalized. Timothy Osborn, a white man from Martha's Vineyard, lived in 1850 near a party headed by a Mississippi planter. The white planter brought four of his thirty black slaves with him from home, whom Osborn observed were "prompt in executing the commands of their master." Osborn, who did his own domestic work, remarked that the African American men "were very useful fellows about a camp . . . in cooking and keeping everything 'decently and in order.'" Northerners sometimes complained about slave labor in the mines, but if Osborn's sentiments were at all common, the idea of having someone else prepare meals for white men and clean up around their camps had its appeal. After all, this was a culturally intelligible division of labor, even if back home it usually followed what were understood as lines of gender rather than race.[29]

Osborn did not stop to think why his black neighbors were so "prompt" in obeying their master—after all, California was admitted to the union as a "free" state as part of the Compromise of 1850. The New Englander later learned that at least one of the men had left behind a wife and children in Mississippi; this could have provided good motivation for helping the master achieve his goals as quickly as possible. Then, too, although four black men accompanied the planter to California, by the time the group left for home, only three joined the return party. Maybe one of the men had been able to buy his way out of bondage after a few months of diligent work in the diggings. This was a common occurrence in California, where the price of freedom was generally around a thousand dollars. Whatever motivated the African American men's behavior, Osborn himself could not help but look longingly at the services they provided.[30]

In still other camps, men who were not in hierarchical relationships with one another nevertheless chose divisions of labor that bore resemblance to the habits of home. When Perlot teamed up with Louvel, the Frenchman who gardened behind the cabin, the two came up with such an agreement. According to Perlot, Louvel had a "refined palate" and was a superb cook. So the men decided to forgo cooking in weekly rotations: "Louvel . . . consented to do it alone, on condition that I would go hunting every Sunday. He concocted the stew, I furnished the hare; each one found his satisfaction in this arrangement."

In the long run, the plan had its costs. During the summer, both Louvel and Perlot spent their time digging a ditch for water to make it easier to wash gold-bearing dirt once the rains began. When they finished and found the skies still clear, Louvel grew restless. As Perlot recalled, Louvel "had nothing for distraction but his culinary occupations," while Perlot kept busy hunting. After weeks of inactivity, Louvel left to join a fellow countryman further north. Perlot was on his own for several months until he found a new partner, for whom he immediately prepared a welcoming feast. This partner was the fellow who was impressed by Perlot's succulent salads—so taken that the newcomer, like Louvel before him, agreed to take on cooking duties indefinitely. Perlot had a way with men.[31]

No doubt similar domestic arrangements existed elsewhere in the diggings. But most who could rely on someone to make all their meals by definition either lived in or near a boarding-house, owned a slave, or had a wife. Thomas Thorne lived in the best of all possible gold-rush worlds. An Anglo immigrant from Texas, Thorne came to the Southern Mines with both enslaved women and men *and* a white wife. Together Thorne's wife Mary and the enslaved Diana Caruthers and her daughters ran a boardinghouse that was renowned for delicacies such as buttermilk and fresh eggs. A few miners lived with the Thornes, while others took their meals at the cabin for a weekly fee. Neighbors such as Charles Davis ate there only on occasion, as Davis explained to his daughter: "[H]ere in California we can get . . . a great plenty of common food of every kind. . . . But no eggs, no Turkey, no Chickens no pies no doughnuts no pastry . . . unless we take a meal at Mrs. Thornes."[32]

Even when black labor helped to create such plenitude, white men associated domestic comfort largely with white women—in this case, with Mary Thorne. When Mary was ill, Davis acknowledged that there was "nobody except the Old darkey Woman & her two daughters to serve up for the boarders." But his preface of "nobody except" defined the presence of the Caruthers women as a sort of absence. Indeed, while white men might credit the usefulness of slaves for housework, it was white women's domestic abilities that most enthralled them. After eighteen months of cooking for himself, Lucius Fairchild, a future governor of Wisconsin, moved into a sturdy frame dwelling where one of the residents lived with a wife and child. The Vermont woman kept house for the men, and Fairchild was ecstatic: "You can't imagine," he wrote to his family, "how much more comfortable it is to have a good woman around." Or, as a similarly situated Anglo gold seeker put it, "A woman about a house produces a new order of things."[33]

It was not only family homes that triggered gendered and racialized imaginings. Roadside houses where white women cooked for travelers also proved good sites for conflating things culinary and things female. Consider how P. V. Fox described his stop at such an establishment: "Had beef steak, Pickled Salmon, Hash, Potatoes, Bread, biscuit, Griddle cakes & Sirrup, Tea & coffee. Pies & cakes, Peach sauce, and a chat with the land lady (The rarest dish)." It was indeed the case that meals at white women's boardinghouses were more elaborate than white miners' usual fare. In particular, where an Anglo woman served food, milk and eggs were sure to be found—not surprising, since cows and chickens had long been a special province of women in rural American divisions of labor. In California, the prospect of indulging in such items could take on the urgency of romance. On one occasion, Samuel Ward—brother of soon-to-be-famous Julia Ward Howe—was traveling to Stockton from the mines and hesitated to stop at a new wayside inn rather than the one kept by a male acquaintance on the Tuolumne River. But, he recalled, "a smiling hostess in the doorway and a tethered cow hard by tempted me." Then he completed the metaphor: "This infidelity to my friend, the landlord of the Tuolumne, was recompensed by the unusual luxury of eggs and milk, for which I felt an eager longing."[34]

As Ward's turn of phrase suggests, men's longings and men's loyalties could be confusing in California. Domestic concerns were somehow female (were they not?) and so it was only natural (was it not?) that men would prove inept at caring for themselves in the diggings. Often enough, such was the case. But for every case of scurvy, for every burned loaf of bread, for every man who could not cook a decent meal for his partners, there were daily domestic triumphs in the diggings. When he first arrived in the mines, for example, Pennsylvanian Enos Christman complained that his flapjacks "always came out heavy doughy things" that no one could eat. But trial and error brought good results, as Christman proudly noted: "We can now get up some *fine dishes!*" What were men to make of the domestic contentment they found in the diggings? What did it mean when a New Englander sat down to his journal after a sumptuous trout dinner and wrote, "French cooks we consider are totally eclipsed and for the reestablishment of their reputation we . . . recommend a visit to our camp"?[35]

For English-speaking men to liken themselves to French cooks was no empty gesture. Anglo American and British immigrants seem to have considered exaggerated domesticity a national trait among French men. Englishman Frank Marryat was delighted to find a large French population in the town of Sonora, "for where Frenchmen are," he wrote, "a man can dine." Likewise, A. Hersey Dexter, who suffered through the hard winter of 1852–53, claimed he was saved by "the little French baker" next door, who allowed neighboring miners a loaf of bread each day. Yet it was the traveler Borthwick who best elaborated this vision. Borthwick described a French dwelling in Calaveras County that bore resemblance to that of Perlot and Louvel—a "neat log cabin," behind which was a "small kitchen-garden in a high state of cultivation." Alongside stood a "diminutive facsimile of the cabin itself," inhabited by a "knowing-looking little terrier-dog." Along with Dexter, Borthwick insisted on fashioning French men and things French as somehow dainty (small, little, diminutive)—echoing Borthwick's descriptions of Chinese men huddled around their "curious little black pots."[36]

But in French domestic lives Borthwick found nothing exotic—the cabin was neat; the garden was cultivated; even the dog had an intelligent face. Instead, Borthwick found among the French a magic ability to create a homelike atmosphere: "[W]ithout really . . . taking more trouble than other men about their domestic arrangements, they did 'fix things up' with such a degree of taste . . . as to give the idea that their life of toil was mitigated by more than a usual share of ease and comfort."[37] The experience of Perlot and Louvel, of course, indicates that some French-speaking men were more inclined to "fix things up" than others. But the Anglo propensity for casting all French men as a sort of collective better half in the diggings is telling. More explicitly than back home, where gender could be mapped predictably onto bodies understood as male and female, gender in California chased shamelessly after racial and cultural markers of difference, heedless of bodily configurations.

California *was*, for many, a "world upside down." Lucius Fairchild, for example, worked for a time waiting tables and felt compelled to explain the situation to his family: "Now in the states you would think that a person . . . was broke if you saw him acting the part of *hired Girl* . . . but here it is nothing, for all kinds of men do all kinds of work." Besides, he went on, "I can *bob around the table*, saying 'tea or Coffee Sir.' about as fast as most *hombres*." Though Fairchild insisted it meant nothing in California, his explanation suggested that it meant a great deal—white men bobbing around tables waiting on other white men. If he could act the part with such enthusiasm, did gender and race have less to do with bodies and essences than with performing tasks and gestures? No doubt Fairchild thought he could tell a "natural" hired girl from a "made-up" one. But the anxiety such situations produced could be striking.[38] Fairchild, for example, compared his own performance not to those of "real" women but to those of other *"hombres"*—as if the English word might not adequately insist upon his own essential manhood.

It was true that people who thought of themselves as *"hombres"* rather than "men" had less call to wait on or be waited on by other male gold seekers. Mexican men, as noted, arrived with their womenfolk more often than other gold-rush immigrants. Mexican women did domestic work in California not just for husbands and brothers but often—at a price—for larger communities. Consider, for example, the party assembled in 1848 by Antonio Franco Coronel, a southern California ranchero. Coronel went to the diggings with four servants, two native men and two Sonorans, a woman and her husband, who were indebted to their *patrón* for the cost of the journey north. The Californio gave the woman a half ounce of gold each day to buy provisions for the group. Of her own accord, she started preparing more food than her party could eat; the extra she sold. She charged a peso a plate for tortillas and frijoles, and eventually earned three or four ounces of gold (fifty dollars or more) per day.[39]

Likewise, in the town of Sonora, Mexican women made a magnificent display of their culinary talents, cooking in open-air kitchens huge quantities of wheat and corn tortillas to serve along with a *sopa* of meat cooked in chile sauce. William Perkins recalled that both Indian and Spanish Mexican women sold their wares in this manner, while native men who had once lived in Spanish missions passed through the weekend crowds carrying buckets of iced drinks on their heads and singing out *"agua fresca, agua fresca, quatro reales."*[40] A few white women also sold food in quantity—one gold seeker met a woman from Oregon "who cooked and sold from early morn to dewy eve dried apple pies for $5.00 each." But nowhere did Anglos create the extensive commercial domestic world that Mexican women, along with Mission Indian men, set up on the streets of Sonora. It was a world that was reminiscent of Mexican cities, where women supported themselves by hawking tortillas, tamales, and fresh produce. Even Hermosillo and Ures in northern Mexico could not have produced as many willing customers for women's wares as the gold-rush town of Sonora, however. There is no way to quantify how much gold dust passed from men's to women's hands in this domestic marketplace, but it must have been considerable.[41]

Still, as Fairchild's waitressing suggests, this commercial sphere included men who provided goods and services as well. Fairchild was not alone in serving his fellow (white) man, but more often men who did such work were not Anglo American. Helen Nye, the woman who lived at Don Pedro's Bar, was in a good position to keep track of the demand, in particular, for non-Anglo cooks. Her home was also a boardinghouse, but she did not prepare the meals. In letters to her mother and sisters, Nye explained her absence from the kitchen in a number of ways. Once she intimated that her husband had decided to hire a French cook, seemingly over her objections. On another occasion, she wrote that although she wanted to help out, "about all who hire as Cooks prefer to do the whole and have the regular price." In yet another letter, she complained that her cook Florentino had "left in a kind of sulky fit" and that his job landed in her hands. This, she wrote, "was too much as it kept me on my feet all the day."

The shifting ground of Nye's explanation suggests that she worried about what her female relatives might think of her circumstances. Still, the male cooks kept on coming. Florentino got over his fit and returned, and he was preceded and followed by others, including an African American man. And though Nye implied that her husband made hiring decisions, she once revealed her own hand in the process by writing to her sister, "I think I shall try a Chinese cook next they are generally liked." Nye's compulsion about explaining her relationship to domestic duties and her inconsistent descriptions indicate that novel divisions of labor could unsettle notions of womanliness as well as manliness.

What *did* it mean for a white woman to turn over cooking to a French man, a black man, a Chinese man?[42]

It was confusing—the way that gender relations, race relations, and labor relations coursed into and out of customary channels in California, here carving gullies out of hard ground, there flowing in familiar waterways, whereby women waited on men, darker-skinned people served lighter-skinned people, and a few held control over the labor of many. Beyond food preparation, other kinds of domestic and personal service work became sites of confusion and contestation—especially laundry, sewing, and the care of convalescing men, activities that were often gendered female in immigrants' homelands.[43] Washing clothes, for example, was generally the province of individual miners in the diggings, but in more densely populated areas, women and and men of color often took in laundry for a price of twenty-five to fifty cents per piece. White men's letters and diaries indicate that Mexican women, African American men, and, most especially, Chinese men all opened wash houses in the Southern Mines. But however often white men scrubbed their own shirts or handed them over to people of color to wash, they were haunted by memories of white women who did this work back home. A bit of gold-rush doggerel entitled "We Miss Thee, Ladies" called white men in California "a banished race," and lamented to "ladies" left behind:

> We miss thee at the washing tub,
>   When our sore and blistered digits,
> Hath been compelled to weekly rub,
>   Giving us blues, hysterics, figits.[44]

One of the more serious indications that life in the diggings did indeed give immigrant men "figits" about race and gender is the extent to which gold-rush personal accounts, written primarily by Anglo-Americans and Europeans, are filled with painstaking descriptions of native sexual divisions of labor. No other people's daily habits so interested white men, and no aspect of those habits proved so fascinating as the seemingly endless round of Miwok women's work. This was not a new fascination. For nearly three centuries, Europeans and then white Americans had commented on native divisions of labor, concluding that Indian women did most of the work while Indian men frittered away their time hunting and fishing. Historians have studied the actual differences between native and white divisions of labor that gave rise to such perceptions, as well as the ways in which such perceptions bolstered Euro-American ideologies of conquest. These elements infuse descriptions of California Indian practices as well.[45]

But gold-rush accounts were written in a particular historical context—one where men far outnumbered women, where a stunningly diverse population inhabited a relatively small area, and where most turned their attention to an economic activity that offered potential (however seldom realized) for quick accumulation of capital. In this context, where differences based on maleness and femaleness, color and culture, and access to wealth and power were so pronounced and yet so unpredictable, curiosity about the habits of native peoples took on a special urgency. In particular, men who recently had assumed responsibility for much of their own domestic work now seemed preoccupied with how differently native women maintained themselves and their communities.

White men were especially interested in how Indian women procured and prepared acorns, perhaps the single most important food Miwoks ate. In 1852, for example, John Doble watched as a nearby Miwok encampment grew from three bark huts to four hundred in preparation for what he called "a big Fandango." As he approached the camp, he found a half dozen Miwok women at work. Suddenly he realized why he had seen in the foothills so many flat stone outcrops filled with round indentations. It was on such surfaces that women sat pounding acorns with oblong rocks; the holes were created by the repeated impact of stone against stone. Once the acorns were hulled and ground, Doble observed, women leached the meal to remove the bitter-tasting tannic acid. Then they made it into bread or else boiled it, which involved dropping red-hot rocks into tightly woven baskets filled with water.[46]

Other men's descriptions of this process shared Doble's obsession with detail, an obsession matched rarely in gold-rush personal accounts save in explanations of placer mining techniques. Even miners' own culinary efforts did not receive as much attention as those of native women. It was almost as if, in their diligent representations of the seemingly reproductive work of Miwok women and the seemingly productive work of mining men, diary and letter writers tried to reinscribe ideas about gender difference that life in the diggings had so easily unsettled. But ideas about gender difference were always already ideas about race difference, and Miwok women were not the "ladies" whose absence made white men fidget. Indeed, in California, difference piled upon difference until it was hard for gold-rush participants to insist upon any one true order of things. After all, no one could deny that white miners also performed "reproductive" tasks. Nor could anyone deny that native women's customary chores were "productive"—or that Miwok women now panned for gold as well. Besides, there were few simple parallels between Indian women's labor and the Euro-American category of "domestic" work. Try as men might to remember the comfort of customary gender relations, discomfort and disorientation were far more common in the diggings. In response, immigrant men tried to make sense of what they saw by drawing on an older discourse that opposed native women's drudgery and native men's indolence.

It was a familiar refrain. French journalist Étienne Derbec knew the tune: "It is generally believed that the Indians live from the hunt; but, mon Dieu! they are too lazy." Derbec claimed that Indian women always struggled under heavy burdens—either baskets of seeds and nuts when out gathering or family provisions when traveling—while men carried only their bows and arrows. Enos Christman, watching Miwoks pass through Sonora, noted this too: "The women appeared to do all of the drudgery, having their baskets . . . well filled with meat." A more thoughtful diarist might have noted whose work produced the animal flesh the women carried.[47]

Friedrich Gerstäcker, a German traveler, assessed native divisions of labor differently. He acknowledged that a woman had to collect seeds, catch insects, cook meals, rear children, and bear heavy loads, while a man merely walked about "at his leisure with his light bow and arrow." But Gerstäcker thought he understood why: "[T]hough this seems unjust," he wrote, "it is necessary." He went on, "[I]n a state of society where the lives of the family depend on the success of the hunter, he must have his arms free." Still, the seemingly contradictory impulse either to castigate native men for their sloth or to elevate their economic role to a position of dominance arose from a common, culturally specific concern about the meanings of manhood.[48]

This concern had its roots in the changing social and economic order that sent such letter, diary, and reminiscence writers off to California in the first place—one in which the transformation from a commercial to an industrial capitalism was accompanied by an increasing separation of home and workplace and by shifting distinctions between male and female spheres. White men who aspired to middle-class status were quickly caught up in this whirlwind of change, and the uncertainty of their own positions in the emerging economic system made the potential for quick riches in California all the more enticing.[49] What most found in the diggings was no shortcut to middle-class manhood, but rather a bewildering array of humanity that confounded whatever sense of a natural order of things they could find in mid-nineteenth-century Western Europe or eastern North America. They might try to reinscribe gender difference through ritual descriptions of Miwok women's "domestic" chores and their own "breadwinning" labor. But, in the self-same gesture, that reinscription produced and reproduced race difference as well. Besides, the content of both immigrant and Indian lives in the diggings defied such easy oppositions.

Then, too, Miwok people talked back. Native women in particular looked with disbelief at how immigrant peoples organized their lives. Leonard Noyes, for example, recalled that an older Indian woman one day gave him "quite a Lecture on White Women working [too] little and Men [too] much." "She became very much excited and eloquant over it," Noyes remembered, "saying it was all wrong." In exchanges like these, gold-rush contests over the meanings of gender and race—always close to the surface of everyday life—were articulated emphatically.[50]

And Miwok sexual divisions of labor were not unchanging; they were dynamic constructions that shifted according to the exigencies of local economies impinged upon by market forces. At times native people resisted the changes, continuing older practices to an extent that bewildered immigrant observers. As Timothy Osborn exclaimed, "[S]o long as a fish or a squirrel can be found . . . they will not make any exertions towards supplying themselves with any of the luxuries so indispensable to the white man!" He watched as Miwok women gathered acorns, and wondered why they did so, "while with the same labor expended in mining they could realize gold enough to keep them supplied with flour and provisions for the entire winter!"[51]

Elsewhere, immigrants saw different strategies. Friedrich Gerstäcker noted that the "gold discovery has altered [Indians'] mode of life materially." On one hand, he thought, "they have learned to want more necessaries," while on the other, "the means of subsistence diminishes." More and more, Miwoks supplemented customary ways of getting food with gold mining in order to buy nourishment. Perlot recalled that in 1854 he regularly saw Indian women traveling to immigrant towns in Tuolumne and Mariposa counties to purchase flour with gold they had dug. At Belt's Ferry on the Merced River, where Samuel Ward lived, Miwoks probably spent *more* time mining than they did gathering and hunting. Following an Indian-immigrant conflict in 1851 known as the Mariposa War, merchant George Belt received a federal license to trade with local Miwoks as well as a contract to furnish them with flour and beef in order to keep the peace. Ward watched over Belt's ferry and store, and got to know native people who felt their best chance for survival lay in setting up camp near an Indian trader. Mining, performed by both women and men, supplied the gold they used to buy goods at the store. Still, problems multiplied in the contract for provisions, and even goods for purchase failed to appear on the shelves. So Miwok women frequently fanned out in search of seeds and nuts, and Miwok men watched for salmon runs or headed down to the San Joaquin Valley to hunt for wild horses.[52]

The more things stayed the same, the more they changed. Miwok men watched for salmon, but found the fish had been waylaid by dams built downstream. Miwok women gathered, but just as their menfolk had added horse raiding to hunting duties decades before, so might women now pan for gold as often as they collected acorns. White men looked for women to wash their clothes, but instead of wives or mothers, they found a market for laundry dominated by Chinese men. White women, few in number, set up housekeeping in California, but learned that there were plenty of men for hire to help lighten the burdens of everyday life. African Americans who came to the mines enslaved worked as hard as ever, but found, too, that the gold rush opened up new possibilities for freedom. Mexican women sold tortillas on the street, just as they had in Sonoran towns and cities, but discovered that in California the market for their products seemed as if it could not be glutted. And Chilean, French, and Mexican men engaged in one more strategy to help themselves and their families out of precarious situations back home. Given racial and ethnic tensions in the mines and Anglo American efforts to assert dominance in California, some such men were not lucky enough to escape with their lives. If they did, though, they learned that mining the white miners—with their incomparable nostalgia for "home comfort and home joys" and their sense of entitlement to the same—was both safer and more lucrative than washing gold-bearing dirt.

Still, as often as Anglo men patronized a commercial domestic sphere peopled largely by non-Anglos, they also turned inward to create for themselves the comforts and joys of home. Some men reveled in what one man called the " fellow-feeling" that grew out of shared domestic tasks.[53] Many more bemoaned the absence of white women—for whom household chores increasingly were considered not only a responsibility but a natural vocation—and belittled their own, often manifest, abilities to sustain life.[54] Indeed, in the diggings, the process of idealizing the home and woman's place in it was uncomplicated by the day-to-day tensions of actual family households. Thus, gold or no gold, newly married Moses Little could write confidently that there were "riches far richer" back home with his "companion in Domestic Happiness." Benjamin Kendrick was similarly emphatic in his recommendation: "I would not advise a single person that has a comfortable home in New England to leave its comforts and pleasures for any place such as California with all its gold mines." But New Yorker A. W. Genung went farthest in giving the gold country's missing quality—domestic comfort—an explicit gender and, implicitly, a race. Acknowledging its advantageous physiography, fine climate, and economic potential, Genung nonetheless was adamant about California's chief deficiency: "The country cannot be a great country nor the people a happy people unblessed by woman's society and woman's love." The society of Miwok or Mexican women did not figure in Genung's equation; the woman whose love California lacked was white. For men such as these, the more things changed, the more things stayed the same.[55]

For many, then, the gold boom created what seemed an unnatural state of affairs—even so, a state of affairs to which they were ineluctably drawn. Benjamin Kendrick might not advise a single person to leave an eastern home, but he and thousands upon thousands of men did just that. While gold-rush California was an unusual time and place, it was a time and place of its historical moment and geopolitical position. Thus the New Englander Kendrick, no less than the Californio Antonio Franco Coronel and the Belgian Jean-Nicolas Perlot, felt compelled to risk the journey. The United States had just achieved continental breadth when gold was "discovered" in the Sierra Nevada foothills—that is, not just when someone saw it in a sawmill's tailrace, but when it took on meaning in an expanding nation and an imminent industrial capitalist world order. The representatives of this emerging order were busy sending tentacles out about the globe, linking peoples, places, and products to each other in their pursuit of wealth. In this world of commerce and now of industry, gold was money, or wealth, that could be turned with human labor and tools of manufacture into capital. Not all who rushed for gold were capitalists—far from it—but all had been touched by capitalism's dynamic tendencies. Some sought gold to create capital; others to ward off that dynamism and its habit of turning human energy into labor power.[56]

Those who sought gold, however, discovered much more than buried treasure. They discovered a "world upside down." It was not just the white men who boasted about feather-light flapjacks, or the Mexican women who managed a domestic market, or the

French men who tidied their tasteful cabins, or the Miwok women who panned for gold; it was a world turned by a spasmodic fiasco of meanings. As time went by in the Southern Mines, Anglo American men—and their womenfolk, who arrived in large numbers only after the initial boom—found more reliable ways to assert dominance in the diggings. As even more time went by, and as the gold rush passed into popular memory, Anglo Americans, and particularly Anglo American men, found ways to claim the event as a past that was entirely their own.[57] In so doing, they buried a past in which paroxysms of gender and race brought daily discomfort to participants, but also glimpses of whole new worlds of possibility. If we are to find in the gold rush a usable past at this present time, when changing relations of race and gender so bewilder those accustomed to power, we must dig deeply in the meanings as well as the structures of the "world upside down" that Edmund Booth described to his wife in 1850.[58] We must understand a time and place wherein white men wept when they thought about what they believed they had left behind.

Consider an episode Enos Christman recorded in his diary in 1852. One night, two Mexican women happened by a group of Anglo miners who were settling into their blankets at Cherokee Camp, near Sonora. The traveling musicians produced guitars and a tambourine, and the men set aside their bedding, listened to the serenade, and then got up to dance with each other. As the night wore on, the music's tempo slowed, until finally the women started strumming the chords of "Home, Sweet Home." They did not intone the lyrics; these women had watched Anglo miners long enough to know that the familiar tune alone would evoke the desired reaction. The men responded apace: "Suddenly a sob was heard, followed by another, and yet another, and tears flowed freely down the cheeks of the gold diggers." The musicians walked away, their tambourine filled with pieces of gold.[59]

Notes

1. Helen Nye to Mother, January 6, 1853, Helen Nye Letters, Beinecke Library, Yale University, New Haven, Connecticut; Charles Davis to Daughter, January 1, 1852, Charles Davis Letters, Beinecke Library. I use the term *immigrant* to refer to all newcomers in the Sierra Nevada foothills, including those from the eastern United States.

2. For elaboration, see Susan Lee Johnson, "'The Gold She Gathered': Difference, Domination and California's Southern Mines, 1848–1853" (Ph.D. diss., Yale University, 1993). See also Rodman Paul, *California Gold: The Beginning of Mining in the Far West* (Lincoln: University of Nebraska Press, 1965 [1947]), esp. pp. 91–115.

3. Edmund Booth, *Edmund Booth, Forty-Niner: The Life Story of a Deaf Pioneer* (Stockton, Calif.: San Joaquin Pioneer and Historical Society, 1953), 31.

4. Conceptually, I have been helped here by Denise Riley, *"Am I that Name?" Feminism and the Category of "Women" in History* (Minneapolis: University of Minnesota Press, 1988), esp. 6; and Evelyn Brooks Higginbotham, "African-American Women's History and the Metalanguage of Race," *Signs* 17, 2 (winter 1992): 251–74, esp. 253–56.

5. Much of the important scholarship on this and related points is summarized and critiqued in Thomas C. Holt, "Making: Race, Race-Making, and the Writing of History," *American Historical Review* 100, 1 (February 1995): 1–20. See esp. Barbara Jeanne Fields, "Race and Ideology in American History," in J. Morgan Kousser and James M. McPherson, eds., *Region, Race, and Reconstruction: Essays in Honor of C. Vann Woodward*, (New York: Oxford University Press, 1982).

6. For years, the best overview of California mining has been Paul, *California Gold*, and of western mining more generally, Rodman Paul, *Mining Frontiers of the Far West, 1848–1880* (Albuquerque: University of New Mexico Press, 1974 [1963]). Recently a wonderful new overview appeared: Malcolm J. Rohrbough, *Days of Gold: The California Gold Rush and the American Nation* (Berkeley: University of California Press, 1997). Scholarship on industrialized mining in the Far West has burgeoned of late, while work on placer mining has lagged behind. On hard-rock mining, see, e.g., David M. Emmons, *The Buttle Irish: Class and Ethnicity in an American Mining Town, 1875–1925* (Urbana: University of Illinois Press, 1989); A. Yvette Huginnie, "'Mexican Labor' in a 'White Man's Town': Race, Class and Copper in Arizona, 1840–1925"

(book manuscript, forthcoming); Elizabeth Jameson, *All that Glitters: Class, Culture and Community in Cripple Creek* (Urbana: University of Illinois Press, 1998); Mary Murphy, *Mining Cultures: Men, Women, and Leisure in Butte, 1914–1941* (Urbana: University of Illinois Press, 1997). A work that will shed light on the impact of placer mining regionally is Elliot West, *Visions of Power: The Colorado Gold Rush and the Transformation of the Great Plains* (Lawrence: University Press of Kansas, forthcoming). On changes over time in class relations in California's Southern Mines, see Johnson, "'The Gold She Gathered,'" esp. 382–412. I have elaborated on the assertions made therein in the book version of this study, which is forthcoming from W. W. Norton.

7.   For a discussion of the meanings of "the social" in this historical context, see Susan Lee Johnson, "Bulls, Bears, and Dancing Boys: Race, Gender, and Leisure in the California Gold Rush," *Radical History Review* 60 (fall 1994): 4–37.

8.   The earliest scholarly work on the gold rush appeared in the 1880s: Charles Howard Shinn, *Mining Camps: A Study in American Frontier Government*, ed. Rodman Wilson Paul (Gloucester, Mass.: Peter Smith, 1970 [1884]); and Josiah Royce, *California from the Conquest in 1846 to the Second Vigilance Committee in San Francisco, A Study of American Character* (Santa Barbara, Calif.: Peregrine, 1970 [1886]). Shinn's was a happy account of the special genius of Anglo-Saxons for self-government. Royce took a darker view, indicting gold-rush participants for their "social irresponsibility" and their "diseased local exaggeration of [Americans'] common national feeling toward foreigners." The 1940s brought two more publications—Paul, *California Gold*, and John Walton Caughey, *The California Gold Rush* [formerly titled *Gold Is the Cornerstone*] (Berkeley: University of California Press, 1975 [1948])—of which Paul's proved most enduring. Paul, too, rejected Shinn's notion of "race-instinct" and saw the managerial talents of white miners as something that developed over time, particularly as placer mining gave way to hydraulic and quartz mining. Starting in the 1960s, another group of historians began to situate the gold rush in larger narratives of racial domination, racial resistance, and the making of race and class in California, thereby centering the experiences of ethnic Mexicans, native peoples, Chinese immigrants, and African Americans in stories of mining and community formation that had long represented them as marginal characters; see Leonard Pitt, *The Decline of the Californios: A Social History of the Spanish-Speaking Californians, 1846–1890* (Berkeley: University of California Press, 1966); Alexander Saxton, *The Indispensable Enemy: Labor and the Anti-Chinese Movement in California* (Berkeley: University of California Press, 1971); Rudolph M. Lapp, *Blacks in Gold Rush California* (New Haven, Conn.: Yale University Press, 1977); Albert L. Hurtado, *Indian Survival on the California Frontier* (New Haven, Conn.: Yale University Press, 1988); Ronald Takaki, *Strangers from a Different Shore: A History of Asian Americans* (Boston: Little, Brown, 1989); Sucheng Chan, *Asian Americans: An Interpretive History* (Boston: Twayne, 1991); Tomás Almaguer, *Racial Fault Lines: The Historical Origins of White Supremacy in California* (Berkeley: University of California Press, 1994). The classic "new social history" of the gold rush is Ralph Mann's study of two towns in the Northern Mines: *After the Gold Rush: Society in Grass Valley and Nevada City, California, 1849–1870* (Stanford, Calif.: Stanford University Press, 1982). For Mann, the absence of women, the abundance of foreign-born peoples, and the emergence of clear class hierarchies come to life in the analysis of quantifiable data. Mann demonstrates the process by which Nevada City became a center of Anglo American commerce and county government, while Grass Valley became a community of working-class Cornish and Irish miners. For a more recent account of social and religious themes in the gold-rush period, see Laurie F. Maffly-Kipp, *Religion and Society in Frontier California* (New Haven, Conn.: Yale University Press, 1994). Along with Rohrbough, *Days of Gold*, the most important new work on the gold rush to appear in over a decade is David Goodman, *Gold Seeking: Victoria and California in the 1850s* (Stanford, Calif.: Stanford University Press, 1994). Goodman's is a history of ideas about wealth, republicanism, order, agrarianism, the pastoral, domesticity, and excitement, and the ways in which those ideas helped people make sense of their participation in the Australian and American gold rushes.

9.   See Johnson, "'The Gold She Gathered,'" esp. ch. 3, for full consideration of these and other "domestic" tasks, including laundry, sewing, and care of the sick. For a trenchant analysis of related themes among cowboys, see Blake Allmendinger, *The Cowboy: Representations of Labor in an American Work Culture* (New York: Oxford University Press, 1992), esp. 50–59. For helpful, but different, accounts of "domestic" concerns in gold-rush California, see Goodman, *Gold Seekings*, esp. 149–87, and Maffly-Kipp, *Religion and Society*, esp. 148–80, both of which emphasize gender over race and ethnicity in their analyses of "domesticity."

10.   Analyses of productive versus reproductive labor particularly characterized Marxist-feminist thought of the 1970s and 1980s. A culminating explication and critique appears in Joan Kelly, "The Doubled Vision of Feminist Theory," in *Women, History and Theory* (Chicago: University of Chicago Press, 1984). See also the essays collected in Zillah Eisenstein, ed., *Capitalist Patriarchy and the Case for Socialist Feminism* (New York: Monthly Review Press, 1979); and Heidi Hartmann, "The Family as the Locus of Gender, Class, and Political Struggle: The Example of Housework," *Signs* 6, 3 (1981): 366–94.

11. See Evelyn Nakano Glenn, "From Servitude to Service Work: Historical Continuities in the Racial Division of Paid Reproductive Labor," *Signs* 18, 1 (1992): 1–43; and Joan Scott, "Deconstructing Equality-versus-Difference: Or, the Uses of Poststructuralist Theory for Feminism," *Feminist Studies* 14, 1 (1988): 33–50.

12. J. D. Borthwick, *The Gold Hunters* (Oyster Bay, N.Y.: Nelson Doubleday, 1917 [1857]), 252, and see 143, 302; Jean-Nicolas Perlot, *Gold Seeker: Adventures of a Belgian Argonaut during the Gold Rush Years*, trans. Helen Harding Bretnor, ed. Howard R. Lamar (New Haven, Conn.: Yale University Press, 1985), 100–1, 153; journal entry, 18 December 1852, Angus McIsaac Journal, Beinecke Library.

13. Journal entry, 18 December 1852, McIsaac Journal; Jesse R.Smith to Sister Helen, 23 December 1852, Lura and Jesse R. Smith Correspondence, Huntington Library, San Marino, California.

14. William Perkins, *Three Years in California: William Perkins' Journal of Life at Sonora, 1849–1852*, ed. Dale L. Morgan and James R. Scobie (Berkeley: University of California Press, 1964), 101, 103. On orientalism, see Edward W. Said, *Orientalism* (New York: Pantheon, 1978).

15. These generalizations are based on wide reading in gold-rush personal accounts that describe household organization; an adequate citation of the evidence would run several pages. But see, e.g., Moses F. Little Journals, Beinecke Library, items 12 and 14; John Amos Chaffee and Jason Palmer Chamberlain Papers, Bancroft Library, University of California, Berkeley, Chamberlain Journals 1 and 2; Alfred Doten, *The Journals of Alfred Doten, 1849–1903*, 3 vols., ed. Walter Van Tilburg Clark (Reno: University of Nevada Press, 1973), esp. 1:91–250: Perlot, *Gold Seeker*, esp. 89–292. Secondary accounts that address such issues include Paul, *California Gold*, 72–73; Caughey, *California Gold Rush*, 177–201; Mann, *After the Gold Rush*, 17. While I have not undertaken a full statistical analysis of the 1850 census, even a spot check through the microfilm reels for Calaveras, Tuolumne, and Mariposa Counties supports my contentions about household size. See U.S. Bureau of the Census, Seventh Federal Population Census, 1850, National Archives and Records Service, RG-29, N. 432, reels 33, 35, 36 [hereafter cited as 1850 Census].

16. See, e.g., John Doble, *John Doble's Journal and Letters from the Mines: Mokelumne Hill, Jackson, Volcano and San Francisco, 1851–1865*, ed. Charles L. Camp (Denver: Old West Publishing, 1962), 38–39, 58; Doten, *Journal*, 1:115–27 (Doten kept a store in Caleveras County, and these pages record the patronage of Chinese, Mexicans, and Chileans); Helen Nye to Mother, 6 January 1853, Nye Letters (Nye's husband was a merchant at Don Pedro's Bar Toulumne County); account book entries, 1852–53, Little Journals, item 13; Charles Davis to Daughter, 5 January [1852], Davis Letters; Perlot, *Gold Seeker*, 153, 154, 159–60; Howard C. Gardiner, *In Pursuit of the Golden Dream: Reminiscences of San Francisco and the Northern and Southern Mines, 1849–1857*, ed. Dale L. Morgan (Stoughton, Mass.: Western Hemisphere, 1970), 95, 107, 164–65.

17. Perlot, *Gold Seeker*, 56–57; cf. George W. B. Evans, *Mexican Gold Rush Trail: The Journal of a Forty-Niner*, ed. Glenn S. Dumke (San Marino, Calif.: Huntington Library, 1945), 200. Gardiner, *In Pursuit of the Golden Dreams*, 95; cf. Perkins, *Three Years*, 106.

18. Vicente Pérez Rosales, "Diary of a Journey to California," in *We Were 49ers! Chilean Accounts of the California Gold Rush*, trans. and ed. Edwin A. Beilharz and Carlos U. López (Pasadena, Calif.: Ward Ritchie Press, 1976), 3–99, esp. 70–77. This event actually took place in Sacramento, entrepôt for the Northern Mines and some camps in the northern part of the Southern Mines.

19. See, e.g., journal entries, 20 October, 15 November, and 19 December 1852, Little Journals, item 12; Perlot, *Gold Seeker*, 155–60; A Hersey Dexter, *Early Days in California* (Denver: Tribune-Republican Press, 1886), 20–26.

20. Journal entries, 21, 24, and 25 December 1852, Little Journals, item 12; journal entries, 25 and 27 November 1851, Timothy C. Osborn Journal, Bancroft Library; journal entries, 13 October–25 December 1849, William W. Miller Journal, Beinecke Library; Perlot, *Gold Seeker*, 272.

21. Perlot, *Gold Seeker*, 272. And see journal entry, 26 November 1849, Miller Journal; Doten, *Journals*, 1:85, 147–48, 151; Doble, *Journal and Letters*, 94.

22. On Miwok women's gathering, see Richard Levy, "Eastern Miwok," in *Handbook of North American Indians*, vol. 8, *California*, ed. Robert F. Heizer (Washington, D.C.: Smithsonian Institution, 1978), 398–413, esp. 402–5.

23. Evans, *Mexican Gold Rush Trail*, 260–61. Cf. Perkins, *Three Years*, 262; Borthwick, *Gold Hunters*, 57; Doble, *Journal and Letters*, 58; journal entries, 12–24 August 1851, Chamberlain Journal no. 1; Benjamin Butler Harris, *The Gila Trial: The Texas Argonauts and the California Gold Rush*, ed. Richard H. Dillon (Norman: University of Oklahoma Press, 1960), 123 (on scurvy among Mexican miners); Étienne Derbec, *A French Journalist in the California Gold Rush: The Letters of Étienne Derbec* (Georgetown, Calif.: Talisman Press, 1964), 40–41, 121–22, 140–41.

24. Perlot, *Gold Seeker*, 260; Doble, *Journal and Letters*, 245. See also journal entries, 24 August and 6 September 1852, Little Journals, item 12.

25. Journal entries, 24 October, 22 and 24 November 1852, Little Journals, item 12; journal entries, 22 and 30 December 1849, 1, 4, and 5 January 1850, Miller Journal. And see journal entries, 14 July 1850, 12 January and 9 February 1851, George W. Allen Journals, Beinecke Library.

26. Borthwick, *Gold Hunters*, 255–56, 302–3.

27. John Marshall Newton, *Memoirs of John Marshall Newton* (n.p.: John M. Stevenson, 1913), 48–50.

28. Gardiner, *Pursuit*, 166. Although Gardiner spent most of his time in the Southern Mines, this actually took place in the Northern Mines.

29. Journal entries, 26 July and 23 August 1850, Osborn Journal. See also Josiah Foster Flagg to Mother, 9 March 1851, Josiah Foster Flagg Letters, Beinecke Library.

30. Journal entries, 26 July and 23 August 1850, Osborn Journal. For background on slavery in the diggings, see Lapp, *Blacks in the Gold Rush California*, esp. 64–77; Johnson, "'The Gold She Gathered,'" chs. 2 and 5.

31. Perlot, Gold Seeker, 258–71, esp. 259–60, 271.

32. Census 1850, reel 35; Samuel Ward, *Sam Ward in the Gold Rush*, ed. Carvel Collins (Stanford, Calif.: Stanford University Press, 1949) pp. 28, 149–52, 167; Charles Davis to Daughter, 5 January [1852], and 6 January 1854, Davis Letters.

33. Charles Davis to Daughter, 5 January [1852], and 6 January 1854, Davis Letters; Lucius Fairchild, *California Letters of Lucius Fairchild*, ed. Joseph Schafer (Madison: State Historical Society of Wisconsin, 1931), 48, 63; Enos Christman, *One Man's Gold: The Letters and Journal of a Forty-Niner*, ed. Florence Morrow Christman (New York: Whittlesey House, McGraw-Hill, 1930), esp. 187.

34. Journal entry, 18 April 1852, P. V. Fox Journals, Beinecke Library; Ward, *Sam Ward in the Gold Rush*, 168 (Julia Ward Howe would become a prominent participant in the U. S. women's movement and the author of "Battle Hymn of the Republic"). See also journal entry, 3 July 1850, Osborn Journal; Journal entry, 30 March 1851, Allen Journals; Mrs. Lee Whippple-Haslam, *Early Days in California: Scenes and Events of the '50s as I Remember Them* (Jamestown, Calif.: Mother Lode Magnet [c. 1924]), 11. On women in dairy and poultry production, see, e.g., Joan M. Jensen, *Loosening the Bonds: Mid-Atlantic Farm Women, 1750–1850* (New Haven, Conn.: Yale University Press 1986); Jensen, "Cloth, Butter and Boarders: Women's Household Production for the Market," *Review of Radical Political Economics* 12, 2 (1980): 14–24; John Mack Faragher, *Women and Men on the Oveland Trail* (New Haven, Conn.: Yale University Press, 1979), esp. 51; and Faragher, *Sugar Creek: Life on the Illinois Prairie* (New Haven, Conn.: Yale University Press, 1968), esp. 101–5.

35. On domestic failures, see, e.g., journal entry, 22 December 1849, Miller Journal; Doble, *Journal and Letters*, 54. For the triumphs, see Christman, *One Man's Gold*, 126; journal entry, 12 July 1850, Osborn Journal.

36. Frank Marryat, *Mountains and Molehills; or, Recollections of a Burnt Journal* (Philadelphia: J. B. Lippincott, 1962 [1855]), p. 136; Dexter, *Early Day*, 23–24; Borthwick, *Gold Hunters*, 342–44.

37. Borthwick, *Gold Hunters*, 342–44.

38. Fairchild, *California letters*, 139. On gender as performative, see Judith Butler, *Gender Trouble: Feminism and the Subversion of Identity* (New York: Routledge, 1990), esp. 24–25, 33, 134–41, and Butler, *Bodies that Matter: On the Discursive Limits of "Sex"* (New York: Routledge, 1993), esp. 1–23, 223–42.

39. Antonio Franco Coronel, "Cosas de California," trans. and ed. Richard Henry Morefield, in *The Mexican Adaptation in American California, 1846–1875* (1955; San Francisco: R & E Research Associates, 1971), pp. 76–96, esp. 93–94. And see Derbec, *French Journalist*, 128. Coronel may have exaggerated his cook's profits, but even if he doubled the amount she took in each day, her earnings would have been greater than those of the average miner in 1848. See "Appendix B: Wages in the California Gold Mines," in Paul, *California Gold*, 349–50.

40. Perkins, *Three Years*, 105–6.

41. Harris, *The Gila Trial*, 124; Silvia Marina Arrom, *The Women of Mexico City, 1790–1857* (Stanford, Calif.: Stanford University Press, 1985), 158–59, 192–93.

42. Helen Nye to Sister Mary, 26 December 1852, 8 February and 14 March 1853, 20 May 1855, Nye Letters.

43. For elaboration, see Johnson, "'The Gold She Gathered,'" 179–96.

44. Doble, *Journal and Letters*, 58; Derbec, *French Journalist*, 142; Christman, *One Man's Gold*, 132; Gardiner, *Pursuit*, 69, 188–89; Perkins, *Three Years*, 157–58; Friedrich W. C. Gerstäcker, *Narrative of a Journey around the World* (New York: Harper and Row, 1853), 225; Borthwick, *Gold Hunters*, 82, 361. On Chinese laundry workers, see Takaki, *Strangers from a Different Shore*, 92–94; Paul Ong, "An Ethnic Trade: The Chinese Laundries in Early California," *Journal of Ethnic Studies* 8, 4 (1981): 95–113. For the poem, see "The Miners' Lamentations," California Lettersheet Facsimiles, Huntington Library.

45. See, e.g., William Cronon, *Changes in the Land: Indians, Colonists, and the Ecology of New England* (New York: Hill and Wang, 1983), 52–58, 92; Glenda Riley, *Women and Indians on the Frontier, 1825–1915* (Albuquerque: University of New Mexico Press, 1984), esp. 76–81.

46. Doble, *Journal and Letters*, 42–50. See also journal entries, 16 and 17 November 1852, Little Journals, item 12; Ward, *Sam Ward in the Gold Rush*, 136; Derbec, *French Journalist*, 154–56; Gerstäcker, *Narrative*, 210–11; Doten, *Journals*, 1:212.

47. Derbec, *French Journals*, 155; Christman, *One Man's Gold*, 180.

48. Gerstäcker, *Narrative*, 217.

49. See, e.g., Mary Ryan, *Cradle of the Middle Class: The Family in Oneida County, New York, 1790–1865* (Cambridge: Cambridge University Press, 1981); Charles E. Rosenberg, "Sexuality, Class, and Role in Nineteenth-Century America," *American Quarterly* 35 (May 1973): 131–53; E. Anthony Rotundo, *American Manhood: Transformations in Masculinity from the Revolution to the Modern Era* (New York: Basic Books, 1993); Mark C. Carnes and Clyde Griffen, eds., *Meanings for Manhood: Constructions of Masculinity in Victorian America* (Chicago: University of Chicago Press, 1990); J. A. Mangan and James Walvin, eds., *Manliness and Morality: Middle-Class Masculinity in Britain and America, 1800–1940* (Manchester: Manchester University Press, 1987).

50. Leonard Withington Noyes Reminiscences, Essex Institute, Salem, Massachusetts, transcription at Calaveras County Museum and Archives, San Andreas, California, p. 75.

51. Journal entry, 20 October 1849, Osborn Journal.

52. Gerstäcker, *Narrative*, 217–18; Perlot, *Gold Seeker*, 181; Ward, *Sam Ward in the Gold Rush*, 51–52, 111, 125, 126–27, 136–37. On the Mariposa War, see Johnson, "'The Gold She Gathered,'" ch. 5.

53. William McCollum, *California as I Saw It. Pencillings by the Way of Its Gold and Gold Diggers. And Incidents of Travel by Land and Water*, ed. Dale L. Morgan (Los Gatos, Calif.: Talisman Press, 1960 [1850]), 160–61. Cf. Harris, *The Gila Trial*, 113, 123, 132–34, 136.

54. On vocational domesticity, see, e.g., Nancy F. Cott, *The Bonds of Womanhood: "Woman's Sphere" in New England, 1780–1835* (New Haven, Conn.: Yale University Press, 1977), esp. 74. Catharine Beecher popularized the idea in her *Treatise on Domestic Economy* (1841), which was in its ninth printing at the time of the gold rush; see Kathryn Kish Sklar, *Catharine Beecher: A Study in American Domesticity* (New York: W. W. Norton, 1976), 151–67.

55. Journal entry, 31 August 1852, Little Journals, item 12; Benjamin Kendrick to Father, 25 September 1849, Benjamin Franklin Kendrick Letters, Beinecke Library; A. W. Genung to Mr. and Mrs. Thomas, 14 February 1852, A. W. Genung Letters, Beinecke Library.

56. For elaboration of these themes, see Johnson, "'The Gold She Gathered,'" ch. 2.

57. For discussion of collective memory of the gold rush, see ibid., ch. 1 and Epilogue; and Susan Lee Johnson, "History, Memory, and the California Gold Rush," paper presented at the "Power of Ethnic Identities in the Southwest" conference, Huntington Library, San Marino, California, 23 September 1994, and the annual meeting of the American Historical Association, Chicago, 8 January 1995.

58. I completed this essay at the historical moment (during the summer of 1995) when affirmative action policies came under unprecedented attack across the United States, but especially in the State of California.

59. Christman, *One Man's Gold*, 204–5.

8

To Catch the Vision of Freedom: Reconstructing Southern Black Women's Political History, 1865–1880

Elsa Barkley Brown

After emancipation, African American women, as part of black communities throughout the South, struggled to define on their own terms the meaning of freedom. Much of the literature on Reconstruction-era African American women's political history has focused on the debates at the national level over the Fifteenth Amendment, which revolved around the question of whether the enfranchisement of African American men or the enfranchisement of women should take precedence.[1] Such discussions, explicitly or not, contribute to a political framework that assumes democratic political struggles in the late-nineteenth-century United States were waged in pursuit of constitutional guarantees of full personhood and citizenship. A careful investigation of the actions of African American women between 1865 and 1880, however, leads one to question that framework. Historians seeking to reconstruct the post–Civil War political history of African American women have first to determine whether the conceptualizations of republican representative government and liberal democracy, which are the parameters of such a discussion, are the most appropriate ones for understanding southern black women's search for freedom—even political freedom—following the Civil War.

The family and the concept of community as family offered the unifying thread that bound African Americans together in the postslavery world. The efforts to reunite family and to establish ways of providing for all community members occupied much of freed people's time and attention. In their June 1865 petition to President Andrew Johnson, black men and women in Richmond, Virginia, for example, took note of the considerable efforts many had undergone in the two months since emancipation to reunite "long estranged and affectionate families." It was probably in recognition of the hope inherent in emancipation's possibility of family units existing physically together that the city's African Baptist churches replaced the prewar seating patterns, which had placed men and women separately, with families sitting together.[2]

Family members provided a variety of support—physical, economic, emotional, and psychological. Camilla Jones cared for her husband and two children and for the home and son of her widowed brother, who lived in a separate apartment in the same tenement. Rachel and Abraham Johnson, who had no children, shared their home with Mary Jones, Rachel's widowed sister, and her three children. While the thirty-four-year-old widow Catherine Green went to work in a tobacco factory, her thirty-five-year-old single sister, Laura Gaines, cared for Catherine's son and took in washing to add to the family income. Elderly parents moved in with children, as did Mariah Morton, who lived in the 1870s with her two daughters, one a widow as well and the other single. Parents opened bank accounts for their children, even those who were adult, away from home, married, and employed. And children who left Richmond to search for work elsewhere provided for the money in their savings accounts to be used by other relatives, if needed, during their absence.[3] In all these ways African American women and men testified to the notion of family members as having a mutual and continuing responsibility to help each other and to prepare for hard times.

This sense of shared responsibility extended past blood ties to include in-laws and even fictive kin. Thus Eliza Winston, a sixty-year-old washerwoman, took in a fourteen-year-old girl, saw to it that she was able to attend school rather than seek employment, and made her the beneficiary of her savings account. Those who had a place to live made room in their homes for those with whom they had labored as "fellow servants" during slavery. Unmarried or widowed mothers moved in with other single mothers in order to provide mutual support.[4]

Churches and secret societies, based on similar ideas of collective consciousness and collective responsibility, served to extend and reaffirm notions of family throughout the black community. Not only in their houses but also in their meeting halls and places of worship, they were brothers and sisters caring for each other. The institutionalization of this notion of family cemented the community. Community/family members recognized that the understanding of collective responsibility had to be maintained from generation to generation. Such maintenance was in part the function of the juvenile branches of the mutual benefit associations, as articulated by the statement of purpose of the Children's Rosebud Fountains, Grand Fountain United Order of True Reformers:

> Teaching them . . . to assist each other in sickness, sorrow and afflictions and in the struggles of life; teaching them that one's happiness greatly depends upon the others. . . . Teach them to live united. . . . The children of different families will know how to . . . talk, plot and plan for one another's peace and happiness in the journey of life.
>
> Teach them to . . . bear each other's burdens . . . to so bind and tie their love and affections together that one's sorrow may be the other's sorrow, one's distress be the other's distress, one's penny the other's penny.[5]

The institutions that ex-slaves developed give testament to the fact that their vision of freedom was not merely an individual one or, as historian Thomas C. Holt has put it, "that autonomy was not simply personal" but "embraced familial and community relationships as well." While Fanny Jackson, a student at the Lincoln Institute in Richmond in 1867, might declare, "I am highly animated to think that slavery is dead, and I am my own woman," the vision of autonomy which she then articulated embraced her husband, her children, and her community at large.[6] African Americans throughout the South in the post–Civil War period emphatically articulated their understanding that freedom and autonomy could not be independently achieved. In 1865 women in Richmond who attempted to support themselves and their families through domestic work noted the impossibility of paying the "rents asked for houses and rooms," given "the prices paid for our labor." They feared that many would be led "into temptation" out of economic necessity.[7] Mutual benefit societies and churches sought to provide some relief; a number of single black women banded together in homes and in secret societies. Despite these efforts, their worst fears were realized and an unknown number of black women were reduced to prostitution in order to feed, shelter, and clothe themselves and their loved ones. Ann Lipscomb, a single mother who worked, when possible, as a seamstress, was one such woman. Yet in 1872 when she joined with other single mothers to organize the Mutual Benevolent Society, they elected her president and entrusted their bank account to her.[8] Thus they quite emphatically demonstrated the notion of collective autonomy; they understood that none of them would be free until and unless Ann Lipscomb was also free. Their fates were intimately tied together; individual freedom could be achieved only through collective autonomy.

This understanding of autonomy was shared by those who had been slave and those who had been free.[9] In fact, the whole process of emancipation may have, at least momentarily, reaffirmed the common bonds of ex-slave and previously free, for, despite their individual freedom in law, "freedom" in actuality did not come to free black men and women until the emancipation of slaves. Thus their own personal experiences confirmed for previously free men and women as well as ex-slaves the limitations of personal autonomy and affirmed the idea of collective autonomy.[10]

The vision of social relations that Ann Lipscomb and her fellow black Richmonders articulated was not the traditional nineteenth-century notion of possessive individualism whereby society is merely an aggregation of individuals, each of whom is ultimately responsible for herself or himself.[11] In this individual autonomy, "whether one eats or starves depends solely on one's individual will and capacities." According to liberal ideology, it is the self-regulating impersonality of contractual relations that makes social relations just.[12] Such a notion of freedom and social responsibility was diametrically opposed to the one that undergirded black institutional developments in Richmond and elsewhere in the post–Civil War period, where the community and each individual in the community were ultimately responsible for every other person. Whether one eats or starves in this setting depends on the available resources within the community as a whole. Individuals must each do their part and are free to make decisions about their lives, but ultimately it is the resources of the whole that determine the fate of the individual. This vision of social responsibility was expressed in the Richmond Humane Society's September 1865 proposal that the approximately eighteen thousand black Baptists and Methodists in the city contribute twenty cents each to a coffer of $3,600 that could be the basis for providing relief for the poor in the community.[13] Black Richmonders were proud of their communal consciousness. In their 1865 petition to President Johnson they asserted that "none of our people are in the alms-house and when we were slaves, the aged and infirm who were turned away from the homes of hard masters, who had been enriched by their toil, our benevolent societies supported while they lived, and buried them when they died." Because of this assumption of communal responsibility, they proudly proclaimed, "comparatively few of us found it necessary to ask for Government rations, which have been so bountifully bestowed upon the unrepentant Rebels of Richmond."[14]

It is a striking example of the different vision held by white Freedmen's Bureau officials throughout the South that they regarded this ethos of mutuality as one of the negative traits that had to be curtailed in the process of preparing freedpeople for life in a liberal democratic society. One South Carolina bureau agent, John De Forest, lamented the tendency among freedpeople to assume obligations to "a horde of lazy relatives and neighbors, thus losing a precious opportunity to get ahead on their own." A case in point was Aunt Judy, who, though supporting herself and her children on her meager income as a laundress, had "benevolently taken in, and was nursing, a sick woman of her own race . . . The thoughtless charity of this penniless Negress in receiving another poverty-stricken creature under her roof was characteristic of the freedmen. However selfish, and even dishonest, they might be, they were extravagant in giving."[15] As historian Jacqueline Jones has pointed out, De Forest's notion that the willingness to share constituted a "thoughtless" act was a product of assumptions "that a 'rational' economic being would labor only to enhance her own material welfare."[16] The different vision of African American women, and of freedpeople in general, posed a persistent problem for northern white men and women, who consistently sought to reeducate and assimilate freedpeople to the requirements of the free labor ideology by introducing a different cultural worldview as a means of imposing a different economic and political worldview as well.

Recent historical explorations of the transition from slavery to freedom have provided substantial evidence that the economic vision of many African American women and men differed fundamentally from that imposed even by freedpeople's most supportive white allies. Northern white men and women assumed that ex-slaves would, in the postwar world, form a disciplined working class. Ex-slaves, in large part, shared a different economic vision.[17] They were "always on the move," searching for family, denying their labor to "dishonest or oppressive employers," and asserting their independence through their mobility. Rather than staying in place, working as much as possible for as high a wage as possible, and thus possibly accumulating a greater array of material goods, a large number of freedpeople sought not to maximize income but to minimize the amount of "time spent at work on other people's behalf." Domestic workers who moved from employer to employer, thus exasperating white women who despaired of ever finding reliable—that is, stable, permanent— servants, showed elements of this pattern.[18] Black men and women throughout the South, whether laboring on small farms or plantations or in homes or factories, generally made economic decisions based on family priorities rather than individual aspirations. For many men and women, higher wages served as an incentive not to more work but to less, for they allowed one to obtain the basic necessities in shorter periods of time and thus eliminate the need for long-term employment under someone else's control. Such behavior appeared lazy or irrational to those who assumed freedpeople should adopt naturally those habits of thrift, diligence, and acquisitiveness that were a cornerstone of free labor ideology.[19]

In a larger society that assumed economic behavior to be a reflection of innate human characteristics rather than socially defined ones, freedwomen's behavior, like freedmen's, left them subject to a variety of assumptions about their inherent "nature," in light of their obvious nonconformity to what was presented as normal human behavior. Racist ideology was thus fed ex-slaves' adoption of a different economic worldview than that which was increasingly becoming the norm in the late-nineteenth-century United States. So deeply embedded are these assumptions that historians, too, have often assumed the imperative of a free wage labor system to be the equivalent of normal behavior and thus either have berated ex-slaves for not voluntarily adopting these modes of behavior at emancipation or, more sympathetically, have tried to defend ex-slaves against charges of being lazy by arguing that they did follow this norm but racist white people just did not admit it. As the works of historians Barbara Fields and Thomas Holt point out, both of these sets of interpretations stem from a framework much like that adopted by post–Civil War white northerners.[20] Rather than accepting ex-slaves' behavior as evidence of a different and equally valid consciousness that refutes our socially defined assumptions about innate economic behavior, both interpretations assume an absolute norm and then proceed to demonstrate how well ex-slaves either did or did not measure up. While the purpose of one may be proving the inferiority of African Americans, and of the other rescuing ex-slaves from such declarations of inferiority, both begin with the same externally imposed parameters and thus miss the ex-slaves' experiences altogether.

The ex-slaves' economic worldview developed from different criteria than those of the larger white society. The worldview that defined the black community's notions of the function of labor equally defined its image of freedom and the approach to secure it. It is this worldview from which all social, political, and economic institutions took shape. If an understanding of the different worldviews from which African Americans and Euro-Americans operated in the post–Civil War South is necessary to analyze work, family, and community behavior, then a similar understanding is also fundamental to an analysis of the political position of African American women in this same time period. Relatively little has been written about southern black women's participation in Reconstruction-era politics; what has been cited has often been descriptive and anecdotal. The few efforts at analysis have failed to consider the possibility of a radically different political worldview in the African American community. For example, Jacqueline Jones notes the fundamental difference in Aunt Judy's "ethos of mutuality" and John De Forest's "possessive individualism" as it pertained to Aunt Judy's economic behavior, but she then fails to adopt a similar logic in her political analysis. Instead, she falls back on notions of republican representative government that stem from the same theory of possessive individualism she has rejected as inappropriate to her economic analysis. Thus Jones "searches in vain for any mention of women delegates in accounts of formal black political conventions . . . local and state gatherings during which men formulated and articulated their vision of a just postwar society." Jones does note that "freedwomen sometimes spoke up forcefully at meetings devoted to specific community issues." But she concludes that "black men . . . like other groups in nineteenth century America . . . believed that males alone were responsible for—and capable of—the serious business of politicking." Freedwomen, Jones tells us, "remained outside the formal political process" and thus occupied "in this respect . . . a similarly inferior position" as white women.[21] Jones's analysis assumes a universal meaning to the fact that men—black and white—were able to cast a vote and women—black and white—were not. She thus invests the meaning in the act of voting itself rather than in the relations in which that act is embedded. As this essay will demonstrate, just what, in any given case, voting or not voting means has to be investigated and determined, not presumed. Having looked for and not found women delegates, women officeholders, or women otherwise exercising a *legal* franchise—all the important political liberties in a republican representative government—Jones misses what she does see: women participating in democracy in a most fundamental way. Jones's perspective rests on a common contemporary assumption, drawn from nineteenth-century political ideology, that the key political right, and responsibility, is the exercise of a legally granted franchise. The obsession in African American women's political history with questions of legal enfranchisement thus stems from this larger preconception.[22]

A thorough effort to uncover evidence of southern black women's political behavior during the latter half of the nineteenth century is vitally needed. In addition, there is a need to develop an interpretative framework consistent with the alternative economic, institutional, and cultural worldview of freedpeople. The following analysis is based on my ongoing research on Richmond, Virginia, and on published materials on the postwar years in other areas of the South.[23]

The Reconstruction Act of 1867 required all the former Confederate states, except Tennessee, to hold constitutional conventions. Black men were enfranchised for the delegate selection and ratification ballots. In Virginia, Republican ward clubs elected delegates to the party's state convention, where a platform was to be adopted. On 1 August, the day the Republican state convention opened in Richmond, thousands of African American men, women, and children absented themselves from their employment and joined the delegates at the convention site, the First African Baptist Church. Tobacco factories, lacking a major portion of their workers, were forced to close for the day. This pattern persisted whenever a major issue came before the state and city Republican conventions held during the summer and fall of 1867 or the state constitutional convention that convened in Richmond from December 1867 to March 1868. A *New York Times* reporter estimated that "the entire colored population of Richmond" attended the October 1867 local Republican convention, where delegates to the state constitutional convention were nominated.

Noting that female domestic servants composed a large portion of those in attendance, the correspondent reported: "[A]s is usual on such occasions, families which employ servants were forced to cook their own dinners, or content themselves with a cold lunch. Not only had Sambo gone to the Convention, but Dinah was there also."[24]

It is important to note that these men and women did not absent themselves from work just to be onlookers at the proceedings. Rather, they intended to be active participants. They assumed as equal a right to be present and participate as the delegates themselves, a fact they made abundantly clear at the August 1867 Republican state convention. Having begun to arrive four hours before the opening session, African American women and men had filled the meeting place long before the delegates arrived. Having shown up to speak for themselves, they did not assume delegates had priority—in discussion or in seating. Disgusted at the scene, as well as unable to find seats, the conservative white Republican delegates removed to the Capitol Square to convene an outdoor session. That was quite acceptable to the several thousand additional African American men and women who, unable to squeeze into the church, were now able to participate in the important discussions and to vote down the proposals of the conservative faction.[25]

Black Richmonders were also active participants throughout the state constitutional convention. A *New York Times* reporter commented on the tendency for the galleries to be crowded "with the 'unprivileged,' and altogether black." At issue was not just these men's and women's presence but also their behavior. White women, for example, certainly on occasion sat in the convention's gallery as visitors silently observing the proceedings; these African Americans, however, participated from the gallery, loudly engaging in the debates. At points of heated controversy, black delegates turned to the crowds as they made their addresses on the convention floor, obviously soliciting and relying upon mass participation. Outside the convention hours, mass meetings were held to discuss and vote on the major issue. At these gatherings vote was either by voice or by rising, and men, women, and children voted. These meetings were not mock assemblies; they were important gatherings at which the community made plans for freedom. The most radical black Republican faction argued that the major convention issues should actually be settled at these mass meetings with delegates merely casting the community's vote on the convention floor. Though this did not occur, black delegates were no doubt influenced by the mass meetings in the community and the African American presence in the galleries, both of which included women.[26]

Black Richmonders were, in fact, operating in two political arenas—an internal one and an external one. Though these arenas were related, each proceeded from different assumptions, had different purposes, and therefore operated according to different rules. Within the internal political process women were enfranchised and participated in all public forums—the parades, rallies, mass meetings, and conventions themselves.[27] Richmond is not atypical in this regard.[28]

It was the state constitutional convention, however, that would decide African American women's and men's status in the political process external to the African American community. When the Virginia convention began its deliberations regarding the franchise, Thomas Bayne, a black delegate from Norfolk, argued the inherent link between freedom and suffrage and contended that those who opposed universal suffrage were actually opposing the freedom of African American people:

> If the negro was out of the question, I think it would be admitted that it [suffrage] was a God-given right. . . . [T]he State of Virginia [has] no rights to give to the black man. . . . How can any man assume to give me a right. . . . I want this Convention to understand that the right of suffrage and the right of liberty cannot be separated. . . . When one ceases, the other ceases. . . . No sooner did separation take place between these rights,

than the strong began to oppress and predominate over the weak. . . . I repeat it as the sincere conviction of my heart, that this is an inherent right, this right of suffrage. . . . If you tell a man that this right is a privilege that you have to confer upon him, he will want to know where you got it. . . . If it is a right that men can confer, that power of the right to confer is because of their strength. . . . When we have the right to exercise this right of suffrage . . . the weak can stand up in their manhood and in their knowledge that it is God-given, and bear down all opposition.[29]

In rejoinder, E. L. Gibson, a conservative white delegate, enunciated several principles of republican representative government. Contending that "a man might be free and still not have the right to vote," Gibson explained the fallacy of assuming that this civil right was an inherent corollary to freedom: If the right were inherent, then it would belong to both sexes and to all from "the first moment of existence" and to foreigners immediately. This was "an absurdity too egregious to be contemplated."[30] And yet this "absurd" notion of political rights was in practice in the Richmond black community, where males and females voted without regard to age and the thousands of rural migrants who came into Richmond were subject to no waiting period but immediately possessed the full rights of the community.[31] What was absurd to Gibson and most white men—Republican or Democrat—was obviously quite rational to many black Richmonders. Two different conceptions of freedom and public participation in the political process were in place.

Gibson's arguments relied on several assumptions that were by then basic to U.S. democracy.[32] First were the ideas that freedom and political liberty were not synonymous and that people could be free without having political liberty. In fact, not all free people were entitled to political liberty because some persons were not capable, that is, not "fit" to exercise political liberty. Thus only those persons who had acquired the manners and morals that enabled them to exercise their freedom responsibly and properly were entitled to political liberty. A certain uniformity was expected; persons who had not yet learned to regulate their lives appropriately—to be thrifty, industrious, and diligent—were not yet capable of responsibly exercising this liberty. Those not capable of political liberty would rely on those capable of it to protect their freedom.[33]

Although Gibson did not specifically articulate this next point, the logic of his assumptions leads to the conclusion that even those with political liberty—as indicated by the right of suffrage—were not equally capable of political decision making. Thus the majority of the people, including the majority of those with suffrage, were expected to leave political decision making to those more qualified. Such political assumptions required that an individual, having once achieved freedom, hand over to others the responsibilities and rights of preserving her or his freedom. In fact, late-nineteenth-century assumptions concerning republican representative government required that the majority of people be passive in their exercise of freedom for the proper operation of democracy. Suffrage granted people not the right to participate in political decision making but the right to participate in choosing political decision makers. Having become accustomed to this political process by now, we often act as if the two are synonymous. Freedpeople knew they were not.

In a frequently noted observation on women in Reconstruction-era politics, Elizabeth Botume, a northern white teacher in Beaufort, South Carolina, made clear that the political view many white northerners tried to impose was consistent with a particular economic view, too:

Most of the field-work was done by the women and girls; their lords and masters were much interrupted in agricultural pursuits by their political and religious duties. When the days of "*conventions*" came, the men were rarely at home; but the women kept steadily at work in the fields. As we drove around, we saw them patiently "cleaning up their ground," "listing," "chopping down the old cotton stalks and hoeing them under," gathering "sedge" and "trash" from the riverside, which they carried in baskets on their heads, and spread over the land. And later, hoeing the crops and gathering them in.

We could not help wishing that since so much of the work was done by the colored women,—raising the provisions for their families, besides making and selling their own cotton, they might also hold some of the offices held by the men. I am confident they would despatch business if allowed to go to the polls; instead of listening and hanging around all day, discussing matters of which they knew so little, they would exclaim,—

"Let me vote and go; I've got work to do."[34]

Botume's analysis hinged on several assumptions: that adoption of habits of thrift and diligence were the factors that qualified one for suffrage; that voting equaled political participation; and that "listening and hanging around all day, discussing matters," were not important forms of political participation. Botume, like so many northern allies, thought free black people were to earn the rights of freedom by adopting the proper habits of responsibility and industry. Her lament was that these African American women, who had been "reconstructed" in that sense, were not rewarded by the franchise.[35] Central to her complaint about African American women's disfranchisement is her exasperation at African American men's assumption that political rights included the right to participate in political discussions (and thereby political decision making). She believed these industrious women, having come to exercise their proper economic role, would also adopt their appropriate role in the political system and would properly exercise the suffrage. They would vote and get on back to work rather than hang around engaging in political issues that, she thought, neither they nor the men had capacity to understand. Botume would leave it to others more capable to make the important political decisions. Thus even the slight support southern black women mustered among white northerners for their enfranchisement came in a context that would have preferred to leave them far less active in the political process than they had been in the most immediate post–Civil War days.

The history of African American women's political involvement in South Carolina and elsewhere leaves one dubious about Botume's predictions regarding how black women would exercise the franchise. Nevertheless, Botume's observations do point to the fact that in the end only men obtained the legal franchise. The impact of this decision is neither inconsequential nor fully definitive. African American women were by law excluded from the political arena external to their community. Yet this does not mean that they were not active in that arena—witness Richmond women's participation in the Republican and the constitutional conventions.

Southern black men and women debated the issue of woman suffrage in both the external and internal political arenas, with varying results. Delegates to the South Carolina convention, 56 percent of whom were black, adopted a constitution that included "male" as a qualification for voting, despite a stirring argument for woman suffrage from William J. Whipper, a black delegate from Beaufort. Nevertheless, a significant proportion of South Carolina's Reconstruction-era black elected officials favored woman suffrage or were at least open to a serious discussion of the issue. It was the South Carolina House of Representatives, which was 61 percent black, that allowed Louisa Rollin to speak on the floor of the assembly in support of woman suffrage in March 1869. Several black male representatives argued in favor of the proposal then and again two years later, when Lottie Rollin led a woman suffrage rally at the state capital. In March 1872 Beverly Nash, a state senator, and Whipper, then a state representative, joined with other delegates to propose a woman suffrage amendment to the state constitution. Alonzo J. Ransier, U.S. congressman from South Carolina and later the state's first black lieutenant governor, presented his argument on the floor of the U.S. House of Representatives in 1874: "[U]ntil [women as well as men have the right to vote] the government of the United States cannot be said to rest upon the 'consent of the governed.'" According to historian Rosalyn Terborg-Penn, Ransier, who was president of the South Carolina Woman's Rights Association, was widely supported by his black South Carolinian colleagues. In fact, six of the eight black men who represented South Carolina in the U.S. Congress during the Reconstruction era supported woman suffrage.[36]

The question of woman suffrage was a subject of discussion in other southern legislative chambers as well. It was often raised by white men to demonstrate the absurdity of black delegates' argument for the inherent right of suffrage. Black delegates, even when they rejected woman suffrage, were far more likely to treat it as a matter for serious discussion. If not expressing support, which they often did, black delegates were far more likely to express at least ambivalence rather than firm conviction of the absurdity of female electorates. Thomas Bayne, the Virginia delegate who so articulately delineated the argument for suffrage as an inherent right, presents one of the more complex cases. Unsupported by white Republicans in his assertion of inherent right and jeered by Gibson and other white conservative delegates, Bayne retorted,

> In speaking of the right to women to vote, I thought it an inherent right, and that women were wrongfully deprived of it. While I do not say that this is my opinion, yet I would simply say, in answer to that, that woman's right is a right to stay home. It is woman's right to raise and bear children, and to train them for their future duties in life. When she does that she is performing high duties which God himself has imposed upon her, in order that those children may carry out and exercise this very God-given right.[37]

Thus Bayne followed the logic of his "inherent right" argument, rejected his opponents' belief that woman suffrage was an absurdity, and conceded that as an inherent right "women were wrongfully deprived of it." He then, however, proceeded to what on the surface appears a very traditional statement of women's roles as confined to the domestic arena. But, by stating domestic roles as "rights," given the context of Reconstruction labor relations, he perhaps implies that his quarrel was not with those who supported woman suffrage but with those who would deny black women the right to domestic duties by obligating them to labor outside the home. Bayne did not, for example, say that a woman's right to stay home was her only right, nor did he suggest that training children was her highest duty or only duty. Historian Michael Hucles has pointed out that Bayne himself, in a discussion of his own terminology, said he often used the word *men* to stand for all human beings, male and female, thus affirming the possibility that his arguments for suffrage were intended as statements regarding universal suffrage, as in fact they were taken by Gibson and other white conservatives and radicals. Until more detailed research is done, determining Bayne's true meaning is well-nigh impossible. He does, however, clarify the problems with simplistic gender analyses of black male and female behavior in a time period when all economic, political, and social relations were in a state of redefinition. Black women and men had to redefine their relationships within the context of their own worldview and the realities of late-nineteenth-century U.S. society. Bayne may well have found himself confronted with the ambiguities inherent in such a situation, and his own position may be as contradictory as it sounds. Alternatively, he may have been stating quite clearly two distinct and contradictory rights of black women—rights in what historians would call both the public and private spheres—thus making clear the artificiality of the distinctions that historians make.[38] Whatever

Bayne's particular position, it is clear that serious discussion of woman suffrage in southern legislative chambers during the Reconstruction era seemed to depend upon a strong African American representation.

The debate over woman suffrage occurred in the internal arena as well, with varying results. In Nansemond County, Virginia, a mass meeting held that women should get the legal franchise; in Richmond, while a number of participants in a mass meeting held for female suffrage, the majority opinion swung against it.[39] But the meaning of that decision was not as straightforward as it may seem. The debate as to whether women should be given the vote in the external political arena occurred in internal political arena mass meetings where women participated and voted not just before and during *but also after* the negative decision regarding legal enfranchisement. This mass meeting's decision maintained the status quo in the external community; ironically enough, the status quo in the internal community was maintained as well—women continued to have a vote. Both African American men and women clearly operated within two distinct political systems. Eventually the external system would have its effect and the debate over women's enfranchisement would come to be more fully related to the internal political system. When this occurred, it had ramifications far into internal community institutions as well. Thus African American women sitting in Richmond's First African Baptist Church in the 1880s had to fight for the right to vote in church meetings and were in the 1890s even asked to defend their presence at these meetings.[40]

Focusing on formal disfranchisement, however, obscures the larger story. The economic and political circumstances of African Americans underwent significant change in the years following emancipation. We may imagine that the political frameworks thus significantly changed as well. Black women's vision of freedom and democracy, like that of black people as a whole, may never have been that expansive again. Yet we must be alert to the persistence of old patterns along with the adoption of new. In the changing political frameworks one might expect to find a continuing thread of women's political participation even at the same time as one finds them more and more fundamentally excluded from both the external and the internal political process.

In Richmond and throughout the South exclusion from legal enfranchisement did not prevent African American women from affecting the vote and the political decisions. They organized political societies such as the Rising Daughters of Liberty, which actively engaged in political campaigns by educating the community on the issues, raising funds for candidates, and getting out the vote. Coal miners' wives living outside Manchester, Virginia, played a similar role through the United Daughters of Liberty. Mississippi freedwomen placed themselves in potentially dangerous positions by wearing Republican campaign buttons during the 1868 election. In some instances the women walked "all the way to town, as many as twenty or thirty miles," to "buy, beg, or borrow one, and thus equipped return and wear it openly in defiance of . . . master, mistress, or overseer" and sometimes of husband as well. Domestic servants also risked job and perhaps personal injury by wearing their buttons to work. "To refuse, neglect, or lack the courage to wear that badge . . . amounted almost to a voluntary return to slavery," according to many freedwomen and freedmen.[41]

Black women initially took an active role in the South Carolina political meetings. Those disfranchised women whom Botume imagined would vote and go home, not involving themselves in political discussion, displayed a particular insistence on continued *public* political activity. The assumptions that underlay these women's activities are instructive. Laura Towne, a northern white teacher, tells us it was the white Republicans who first announced to the freedpeople that "women and children ought to stay at home on such occasions." Yet it does not appear to be merely the presence of females that disturbed these white men, for they quickly made it clear that Towne, of course, was welcome. Their announcement was meant to exclude "outsiders who were making some noise." Probably because of protests or disregard of the exclusion notice, the white Republicans modified their initial ban to state that "the *females* can come or not as they choose, . . . but the meeting is for men voters." It was clearly the women's failure to take the position of passive observers that was being censured.[42] Some black men took their cue, one even using the occasion to prompt women to "'stay at home and cut grass,' that is, hoe the corn and cotton fields—clear them of grass!" while the men were at the political meetings.[43]

Even though they were excluded from further participation in the Republican meetings by the late 1860s, African American women in South Carolina, Louisiana, and elsewhere were still attending the meetings in the 1870s.[44] Although women were never elected delegates, it does appear that occasionally women were sent to the political meetings on behalf of their community. Lucy McMillan, a South Carolina widow, reported that her attendance at a political meeting was the result of community pressure: "They all kept at me to go. I went home and they quizzed me to hear what was said, and I told them as far as my senses allowed me."[45]

Women's presence at the meetings was often anything but passive. In the violent political atmosphere of the last years of Reconstruction, they had an especially important—and dangerous—role. While the men participated in the meeting, the women guarded the guns—thus serving in part as the protectors of the meeting. This was not a symbolic or safe role in a time when "men are shot at, hunted down, trapped and held till certain meetings are over, and intimidated in every possible way." During the violent times of late Reconstruction, African American women in South Carolina were reported "in arms, carrying axes or hatchets in their hands hanging down at their sides, their aprons or dresses half-concealing the weapons." One clergyman, contending African Americans could defend themselves if necessary, noted that "80,000 black men in the State . . . can use Winchesters and 200,000 black women . . . can light a torch and use a knife." At times women as well as men actually took up arms. In 1878 Robert Smalls, attacked by redshirts* while attempting to address a Republican meeting in Gillisonville, sought refuge and later reported that "every colored man and woman seized whatever was at hand—guns, axes, hoes, etc., and ran to the rescue." Some of these women probably had double incentive, as the redshirts had "slap[ped] the faces of the colored women coming to the meeting."[46]

African American women took the political events to heart and took dramatic steps to make their political sentiments known. They also expressed their outrage when the political tide turned against their interests. Alabama women reportedly "were converted to Radicalism long before the men and almost invariably used their influence strongly for the purpose of the League." South Carolina Democrats believed African American women to be "the head and fount of the opposition." Thomas Holt has suggested that the South Carolina black woman's "reputation for political partisanship was . . . enhanced by her frequent appearance at the head of angry Charleston mobs, like the one which wreaked havoc on the German merchants after the Republican defeat in the municipal elections of 1871."[47]

African American women in South Carolina and elsewhere understood themselves to have a vital stake in African American men's franchise. The fact that only men had been granted the vote did not mean that only men should exercise that vote. Women reportedly

---

* Rifle clubs organized to intimidate black voters and secure Wade Hampton's election as governor in 1876; sometimes used to describe any armed white supremacist group in late 1870s South Carolina.

initiated sanctions against men who voted Democratic. One South Carolina witness reported that "no mens were to go to the polls unless their wives were right alongside of them; some had hickory sticks; some had nails—four nails drive in the shape of a cross—and dare their husbands to vote any other than the Republican ticket." In the highly charged political atmosphere of the late 1870s it was no small matter for these women to show up at the election site carrying weapons. Armed Democrats patrolled the polling areas, and Republicans were often "driven from the polls with knives and clubs. Some of them were badly wounded."[48] We might wonder whether the weapons the women carried were for use on their husbands or on the Democratic opponents, but in either case these women very publicly declared their stake in their husband's vote.

Black Republican politicians throughout the South took women's participation seriously and publicly encouraged them to abstain from sexual relations with any man who voted Democratic. Some women left their Democratic husbands. Engaged women were encouraged to postpone the wedding until after the election, when they could obtain assurance that their future husband was not a Democrat. In Alabama women banded together in political clubs to enforce these sanctions collectively. Some politicians also endorsed women's use of weapons to influence their husbands' vote.[49] It is likely that, rather than initiating these actions on the part of African American women, Republican legislators merely recognized and endorsed actions initiated by the women themselves. These examples all suggest that African American women and men understood the vote as a collective possession, not an individual one, and furthermore that African American women, unable to cast a separate vote, viewed African American men's vote as equally theirs. Their belief that the franchise should be cast in the best interest of both was not the nineteenth-century patriarchal notion that men voted on behalf of their wives and children. By the latter assumption, women had no individual wills; rather, men operated in women's best interest because women were assumed to have no right of input. African American women assumed the political rights that came with being a member of the community, even though they were not granted the political rights they thought should come with being citizens of the state.

The whole sense of the ballot as collectively owned is most eloquently presented by Violet Keeling, a tobacco worker who testified in February 1884 before a Senate committee investigating the violence in the previous year's elections in Danville, Virginia. Assenting in her husband's decision not to vote in that election for fear he might be killed, she made it clear that she would not, however, assent in his or anyone else's voting Democratic: "[A]s for my part, if I hear of a colored man voting the Democratic ticket I stay, as far from him as I can; I don't have nothing in the world to do with him. . . . No, sir; I don't 'tallow him to come in my house." Asked why she should "have such a dislike to a colored man that votes the Democratic ticket," she replied:

> I think that if the race of colored people that has got no friends nohow, and if they don't hang together they won't have none while one party is going one way and another the other. I don't wish to see a colored man sell himself when he can do without. Of course we all have to live, and I always like to have a man live even if he works for 25 cents a day, but I don't want to see him sell himself away. . . . I think if a colored man votes the Democratic ticket he has always sold himself. . . . If I knew a colored man that voted the Democratic ticket to come to my house, I would tell him to go somewhere else and visit.

Asked "suppose your husband should go and vote a Democratic ticket," she responded: "I would just picke up my clothes and go to my father's, if I had a father, or would go to work for 25 cents a day."[50]

Violet Keeling clearly articulated the notion that a black man could not exercise his vote only in his own behalf. If he sold his vote, he sold hers. The whole issue of the ostracism of black Democrats reveals very clearly the assumptions regarding suffrage that were operative throughout African American communities. Black Democrats were subject to the severest exclusion: disciplined within or quite often expelled from their churches, kicked out of mutual benefit societies, not allowed to work alongside others in the fields or accepted in leadership positions at work or in the community. Ministers were dismissed from their churches or had their licenses to preach revoked; teachers who voted Democratic found themselves without pupils. Democrats' children were not allowed in schools. And, perhaps the most severe sanction of all, black Democrats found themselves unaided at the time of a family member's death. Women participated in all of these actions as well as in the mobs that jeered, jostled, and sometimes beat black Democrats or rescued those who were arrested for such behavior. In fact, women were often reported to be the leaders of such mob involvements.[51] One historian noted that "the average negro . . . believed it was a crime 'to vote against their race.'"[52]

From the perspective of liberal democratic political ideology, these activities might be perceived as "unconscionable" "interference with the [individual voter's] expression of . . . political preference."[53] But African Americans in the post–Civil War South understood quite clearly that the actions of one member of the community affected, and in this instance endangered, all others in that community. Thus they understood there was no such thing as an individual action or a "possessive individual," owing nothing to society. This understanding was most clearly put by Robert Gleed, a Mississippi state senator, in his 1871 testimony before the U.S. Senate:

> [I]t is traitorous in these men to acquiesce with a party who says we have no rights in the community in common with other citizens. . . . They [black Democrats] have the right [to vote Democratic] just like Benedict Arnold had a right to trade off the army just like he did; but that does not make it justice and equity because he did.[54]

The issue, as Gleed and many black men and women understood it, was not autonomy but responsibility. It was that sense of suffrage as a collective possession, not an individual one, that was the foundation of much of women's political activities.[55]

Sarah Nash, Nancy Hodges, and the other female hucksters who gathered in Portsmouth, Virginia, in May 1866 "to consult each other and talk our troubles over" made that collective possession clear. Nash and Hodges, along with seven other women "representing many hundreds" of others "who huckster for a living," signed a petition to General O. O. Howard complaining about the unfair taxation policies that were driving them out of business, about their husbands' and children's loss of jobs, and about the general "obbitrary power" controlling them in many matters regarding which they had "never been consulted." These women were speaking, however, not of whether each individually had voice and representation but of whether their community had a voice. Thus they noted that "their husbands, though called upon to pay a head tax of ($4.00) four dollars, have no voice in making city, State or national government."[56] This is not to suggest that African American women did not desire the vote or that they did not often disagree with the actions taken by some black men. One should, however, be careful about imposing presentist notions of gender equality on these women. Clearly for them the question was not an abstract notion of individual gender equality but rather one of community. That such a vision might over time lead to a patriarchal conception of gender roles is not a reason to dismiss the equity of its inception.

Women's presence at the polls was not just a negative sanction; it was also a positive expression of the degree to which they understood the men's franchise to be a new political opportunity for themselves as well as their children. They reinforced this idea of black men's voting as a new freedom that they had all achieved by turning the occasion into a public festival and celebration, bringing lemonade and ginger cakes and spending the day at the polls. Of course, the principal reason for the group presence at the polls was protection. The tendency for "crowds" of freedmen to go to the polls together was seen by their white contemporaries and by some historians as evidence that they were forced to vote the Republican ticket or that they did not take seriously the franchise but instead saw election day as an opportunity for a picnic or other entertainment. Henderson Hamilton Donald, for example, noting that freedmen "always voted in companies," found this behavior "odd and sometimes amusing." Yet his own description suggests the real meaning: "When distances were great, crowds of them under leaders went to the polling places a day in advance and *camped out like soldiers on the march*."[57] Women and children often went along, their presence reflecting their excitement about the franchise but also their understanding of the dangers involved in voting. Women may have gone for additional protection of the voters, like those women in South Carolina who carried weapons, or to avoid potential danger to those left alone in the countryside while the men were gone. But, in any case, the necessity for a group presence at the polls reinforced the sense of collective enfranchisement. What may have been chiefly for protection was turned into festivity as women participated in a symbolic reversal of the meaning of the group presence.

African American women throughout the South in the Reconstruction era assumed *publicly* the right to be active participants in the political process long after they had been formally removed—and they did so, in part, through their husbands. They operated out of an assumption that his vote was theirs. Unlike many northern white middle-class women, southern black women in the immediate post–Civil War era did not base their political participation in justifications of superior female morality or public motherhood. They did not need to; their own cultural, economic, and political traditions provided rationale enough—"autonomy was not simply personal."

One of the ramifications of liberal democratic political theory is that our notion of politics is severely circumscribed. In a context where only certain persons have the rights and abilities to participate fully, the *formal* political process takes on an exclusivity and sanctity all its own. Historians operating from this perspective often ascribe the totality of politics to the formal political arena. With this assumption, Jacqueline Jones asserts that "the vitality of the political process, tainted though it was by virulent racial prejudice and violence, provided black men with a public forum distinct from the private sphere inhabited by their womenfolk."[58] But these women's actions were fundamentally *political*. That African American women did not operate inside the formal political process does not negate the intensely political character of their actions. These actions represented a continuous significant political participation on their part. Black women, therefore, were hardly confined (even without the franchise or elective office) to a private sphere.[59] They were certainly not confined to any less bloody sphere.[60]

African American women understood "that freedom meant above all the right to participate in the process of creating it."[61] Being denied this right in the external political arena and having this right increasingly circumscribed in the internal arena as well, these women created their own political expression, thus inventing the power their freedom required. Their actions were not merely a grievance against their own lack of political rights or lack of rights of the black community but, more important, a critique of the absence of freedom and democracy, as they understood it, in the society at large. By their actions and assumptions they challenged the fundamental assumptions of the U.S. political process itself.

Citizenship entails constitutionally granted political rights and privileges that make one a full-fledged and active member of the body politic. Thus one must be granted the right to be active in the political process. But these women operated out of a notion of community, wherein all—men, women, and children; freeborn and formerly slave; native and migrant—had inherent rights and responsibilities requiring no higher authority than their commitment to each other. Their sense of community, related to the collective character of their notion of freedom, had foundation in their understanding that freedom, in reality, would accrue to each of them individually only when it was acquired by all of them collectively. It was this very sense of community rather than citizenship, of peoplehood rather than personhood, that was the basis for their activities. In other words, it was their vision of freedom that granted them the right to assume the political responsibilities that neither the state nor some members of their own community acknowledged to be theirs.

It is clear that to understand southern black women's political history in the post–Civil War era requires that we develop alternative political definitions to those defined by liberal democratic thought. Even the terminology by which we understand African American women's political struggle must be rethought, for we currently have no language in which to express the concepts that these women understood. The significance of this may be difficult to contemplate—both for black women historically and for our notions of how far we have progressed today. For understanding African American women's involvement in the political process in the post–Civil War era, even without the franchise, requires us at least to consider the possibility that when black women, such as those in Richmond, obtained the legal franchise in the 1920s they may actually have been far less involved in the political decision-making process than were their unenfranchised foremothers in the immediate post–Civil War period.[62]

Ultimately northern and southern white men may have denied African American women the freedom fully to shape their own lives in the post–Civil War era. But we, trapped in our own mental prisons, have denied them their freedom as well, insisting instead that they accept our very limited and pessimistic vision of human possibilities. There is an enormous amount of work yet to be done on southern black women's political history in the last four decades of the nineteenth century. Just as African American women, as part of black communities throughout the South, struggled in the post–Civil War era to catch, that is, to make real, their vision of freedom, we, as historians, must now struggle to catch, that is, to understand, their vision of freedom. In the process we need not only to refine our base of information but also to reconstruct our frameworks, creating new ones that allow us to interpret these women's lives in ways that do justice to their vision of freedom.

Notes

This essay had its origins in my students' questions and insights as we explored definitions of freedom in African American Studies 100 and History 202 at Emory University, 1986–87. Their excitement about the ideas and their willingness to challenge not only my assumptions but their own deeply held convictions were inspirational as well as informative. Earlier versions of this essay were presented at the "Afro-American Women and the Vote, 1837 to 1965" conference, University of Massachusetts at Amherst, 14 November 1987, where I benefited from the comments of Ena Farley; the Social History Seminar, Newberry Library, Chicago, Illinois, 16 October 1991; and the workshop on "Historical Perspectives on Race and Racial Ideologies" Postemancipation Studies Project, Center for Afroamerican and African Studies, University of Michigan, 22 November 1991. I would like to thank Thea Arnold, Jacquelyn Dowd Hall, Nancy Hewitt, Thomas C. Holt, Lillian Jones, Dee Dee Joyce, Joseph Reidy, Leslie S. Rowland, Rebecca Scott, David Thelen, and Dale Tomich for their careful readings and critiques of this essay.

1. See, for example, Angela Davis, *Women, Race, and Class* (New York: Random House, 1981), 70–86; Paula Giddings, *When and Where I Enter: The Impact of Black Women on Race and Sex in America* (New York: William Morrow, 1984), 64–71; Rosalyn Terborg-Penn, "Afro-Americans in the Struggle for Woman

Suffrage" (Ph.D. diss., Howard University, 1977), ch. 2; Bettina Aptheker, "Abolitionism, Woman's Rights, and the Battle over the Fifteenth Amendment," in *Woman's Legacy: Essays on Race, Sex, and Class in American History* (Amherst: University of Massachusetts Press, 1982).

2. *New York Tribune*, 17 June 1865; Peter Randolph, *From Slave Cabin to Pulpit* (Boston: Earle, 1893). For discussions of freedpeople's efforts to reunite families throughout the South, see Robert H. Abzug, "The Black Family during Reconstruction;" in Nathan I. Huggins, Martin Kilson, and Daniel M. Fox, eds., *Key Issues in the Afro-American Experience*, vol. 2, *Since 1865* (New York: Harcourt Brace Jovanovich, 1971), 32–34; Ira Berlin, Steven F. Miller, and Leslie S. Rowland, "Afro-American Families in Transition from Slavery to Freedom," *Radical History Review* 42 (1988): 89–121; Eric Foner, *Reconstruction: America's Unfinished Revolution, 1863–1877* (New York: Harper and Row, 1988), 82–85; Leon F. Litwack, *Been in the Storm So Long: The Aftermath of Slavery* (New York: Random House, 1979), 229–47; Peter J. Rachleff, *Black Labor in the South: Richmond, Virginia, 1865–1890* (Philadelphia: Temple University Press, 1984), 15–16.

3. Using the records of the Freedman's Savings and Trust Company and the manuscript census, Peter J. Rachleff has done an extensive job of re-creating this family network (*Black Labor in the South*, 15–23).

4. Rachleff, *Black Labor in the South*, 17, 22, 26; *Freedmen's Record* 2, 3 (March 1866): 53.

5. W. P. Burrell and D. E. Johnson Sr., *Twenty-five Years History of the Grand Fountain of the United Order of True Reformers, 1881–1905* (Richmond: Grand Fountain, United Order of True Reformers, 1909), 76–77.

6. Thomas C. Holt, "'An Empire over the Mind': Emancipation, Race, and Ideology in the British West Indies and the American South," in J. Morgan Kousser and James McPherson, eds., *Region, Race, and Reconstruction: Essays in Honor of C. Vann Woodward* (New York: Oxford University Press, 1982), 299; Fanny Jackson to Friends of the North, 22 March 1867, in *Freedmen's Record* 3, 6 (June 1867): 106. See also David Montgomery, *The American Civil War and the Meanings of Freedom: An Inaugural Lecture Delivered before the University of Oxford on 24 February 1987* (Oxford: Clarendon Press, 1987), 11–13: "[T]he former slaves' own conception of freedom . . . was above all a collective vision, rooted in generations of common experience in the United States. . . . The point is not simply that former slaves lacked experience in bourgeois ways but rather that they did not define either freedom or property in the same individualistic and market-oriented terms that their northern liberators employed."

7. Rachleff, *Black Labor in the South*, 37–38.

8. Ibid., 26–27.

9. Locating the origins of this collective worldview is beyond the scope of this essay, but several works are suggestive of both African origins and the degree to which this democratic ethos was a response to the necessities of life for black people—slave or free—in a slave society. On the African origins of one of the primary institutional expressions of this collective worldview, see Betty M. Kuyk, "The African Derivation of Black Fraternal Orders in the United States," *Comparative Studies in Society and History* 25 (October 1983): 559–92. Lawrence Levine offers evidence of a collective worldview, African in origin but transformed to meet the needs of life under slavery and freedom; see *Black Culture and Black Consciousness: Afro-American Folk Thought from Slavery to Freedom* (New York: Oxford University Press, 1977). One of the most striking evidences of the democratic ethos under slavery comes to us from a study of children at play. David K. Wiggins tells us that slave children played no games that eliminated players: The rules they devised for their various games of dodge ball and tag prevented the removal of any participants. When one of the main fears of daily life was being removed from the community—sold or hired out—slaves chose not to duplicate that fear in their own social structure. Slave children attempted to provide some security by ensuring that none of them would be excluded from participating and thus through their play reinforced the basic communal values of the slave community. See "The Play of Slave Children in the Plantation Communities of the Old South, 1820–1860," in N. Ray Hiner and Joseph M. Hawes, eds., *Growing Up in America: Childhood in Historical Perspective* (Urbana: University of Illinois Press, 1985), 181–82. See also Thomas L. Webber, *Deep like the Rivers: Education in the Slave Quarter Community, 1831–1865* (New York: W. W. Norton, 1978), esp. 63–70, 144, 224–44; Herbert G. Gutman, *The Black Family in Slavery and Freedom, 1750–1925* (New York: Pantheon Books, 1976), esp. ch. 5; Ira Berlin, *Slaves without Masters: The Free Negro in the Antebellum South* (New York: Pantheon Books, 1974), ch. 9.

10. My effort in this essay is to distinguish the collective vision of these African Americans from the individualistic vision of the government officials, businessmen, missionaries, and teachers who developed and implemented Reconstruction policies. This is not to suggest that there was a monolithic "black" versus a monolithic "white" vision of freedom. Northern white industrial workers and southern white yeoman farmers also often expressed a collectivist vision and understood the individualistic assumptions of free labor ideology in a market economy as detrimental to their collective (and individual) self-interest (Montgomery, *American Civil War*). Contemporary U.S. historians' own socialization often leads them to assume individualism as natural human behavior and thus to assume that collective identity is the "peculiarity" that needs explaining, when in fact collective identity has been the foundation of many people's understanding of self.

"Throughout most of human history the antithesis of slavery has not been autonomy but belonging; defining freedom as individual autonomy is a phenomenon of the modern era" (Thomas C. Holt, "Of Human Progress and Intellectual Apostasy," *Reviews in American History* 15 [March 1987]: 58).

11. C. B. Macpherson, *The Political Theory of Possessive Individualism: Hobbes and Locke* (Oxford: Oxford University Press, 1962).

12. Holt, "'An Empire over the Mind,'" 287.

13. John Thomas O'Brien Jr., "From Bondage to Citizenship: The Richmond Black Community, 1865–1867" (Ph.D. diss., University of Rochester, 1974), 78, 174–75, 277–78. For a discussion of institutional developments in Richmond's black community as an outgrowth of this collective consciousness and its attendant understandings of social responsibility, see Rachleff, *Black Labor in the South*. For similar discussions regarding other southern black communities in the post–Civil War era, see Edward Magdol, *A Right to the Land: Essays on the Freedmen's Community* (Westport, Conn.: Greenwood Press, 1977); Herbert G. Gutman, "Schools for Freedom: The Post-Emancipation Origins of Afro-American Education," in Herbert G. Gutman, *Power & Culture: Essays on the American Working Class*, ed. Ira Berlin (New York: Pantheon Books, 1987), 260–97.

14. *New York Tribune*, 17 June 1865.

15. John William De Forest, *A Union Officer in the Reconstruction* (Hamden, Conn.: Archon Books, 1968 [1948]), 97–99. For an extended discussion of the ways in which this ethos of mutuality shaped a variety of freedpeople's communities, see Magdol, *Right to the Land*. Habits of mutuality are not exclusive to persons of African descent. For similar discussions of European and Euro-American working-class and rural communities, see, for example, E. P. Thompson, *The Making of the English Working Class* (London: Victor Gollancz, 1963); Jacquelyn Dowd Hall, James Leloudis, Robert Korstad, Mary Murphy, LuAnn Jones, and Christopher B. Daly, *Like a Family: The Making of a Southern Cotton Mill World* (Chapel Hill: University of North Carolina Press, 1987); Steven Hahn, *The Roots of Southern Populism: Yeoman Farmers and the Transformation of the Georgia Upcountry, 1850–1890* (New York: Oxford University Press, 1983).

16. Jacqueline Jones, *Labor of Love, Labor of Sorrow: Black Women, Work, and the Family from Slavery to the Present* (New York: Basic Books, 1985), 65–66. Assumptions of individual autonomy permeate the conceptual frameworks that shape much contemporary discussion of African American women's economic conditions as well. Consider, for example, analyses of women's wages that treat the closing gap between the earnings of full-time black and white female employees as evidence of increasing economic parity among women. Such analyses extract women from their families and communities, assuming they are "possessive individuals" whose well-being and status are determined solely by their individual resources. Yet in reality the economic base and status of black and white full-time wage-earning women are markedly different, since the majority of these white women live in households in which there are two full-time wage earners and the majority of these black women live in households in which they are the only full-time wage earners. A critique of such analyses was presented by Linda Burnham, "Struggling to Make the Turn: Black Women and the Transition to a Post-Industrial Society," at the Schomburg Center for Research in Black Culture Symposium "Survival and Resistance: Black Women in the Americas," 9 June 1989.

17. Gerald David Jaynes, *Branches without Roots: Genesis of the Black Working Class in the American South, 1862–1882* (New York: Oxford University Press, 1986); Barbara Jeanne Fields, *Slavery and Freedom on the Middle Ground: Maryland during the Nineteenth Century* (New Haven: Yale University Press, 1985); Holt, "'An Empire over the Mind,'" 283–314; Julie Saville, "A Measure of Freedom: From Slave to Wage Laborer in South Carolina, 1860–1868" (Ph.D. diss., Yale University, 1986); Ira Berlin, Steven Hahn, Steven F. Miller, Joseph P. Reidy, and Leslie S. Rowland, "The Terrain of Freedom: The Struggle over the Meaning of Free Labor in the U.S. South," *History Workshop Journal* 22 (autumn 1986): 108–30; Armstead L. Robinson, "'Worser dan Jeff Davis': The Coming of Free Labor during the Civil War, 1861–1865," in Thavolia Glymph and John J. Kushma, ed., *Essays on the Postbellum Southern Economy* (Arlington: University of Texas, 1985), 11–47; Harold D. Woodman, "The Reconstruction of the Cotton Plantation in the New South," in Glymph and Kushma, eds., *Postbellum Southern Economy*, 95–119; Lawrence N. Powell, *New Masters: Northern Planters during the Civil War and Reconstruction* (New Haven: Yale University Press, 1980), esp. ch. 6.

18. Fields, *Slavery and Freedom*, 157–65.

19. Ibid., 157–66; Saville, "Measure of Freedom"; Holt, "'An Empire over the Mind.'"

20. Fields, *Slavery and Freedom*, 165–66; Holt, "'An Empire over the Mind.'"

21. Jones, *Labor of Love*, 66–67.

22. For studies of black women's struggle for legal enfranchisement, see note 1 above; see also Beverly Lynn Guy-Sheftall, "Books, Brooms, Bibles and Ballots: Black Women and the Public Sphere," in *"Daughters of Sorrow": Attitudes toward Black Women, 1880–1920* (Brooklyn, N.Y.: Carlson Publishing, 1990).

23. This analysis is necessarily generalized. Further research will no doubt reveal important distinctions in black women's political activism across regions within the South, within states, and between rural and urban areas.

24. *Richmond Dispatch*, 1, 2 August, 30 September, 9 October 1867; *New York Times*, 1, 2, 6 August, 15, 18 October 1867. My discussion of these events follows closely Rachleff, *Black Labor in the South*, 45–46. See also Richard L. Morton, *The Negro in Virginia Politics*, 1865–1902, Publications of the University of Virginia Phelps-Stokes Fellowship Papers, no. 4 (Charlottesville: University of Virginia Press, 1919), 40–43. Similar reports issued from other areas throughout the South, causing one chronicler to report that "the Southern ballot-box" was as much "the vexation of housekeepers" as it was of farmers, businessmen, statesmen, or others: "Elections were preceded by political meetings, often incendiary in character, which all one's servants must attend." Election day itself could also be a problem. As one Tennessean reported in 1867, "Negro women went [to the polls], too; my wife was her own cook and chambermaid" (Myrta Lockett Avary, *Dixie after the War: An Exposition of Social Conditions Existing in the South, during the Twelve Years Succeeding the Fall of Richmond* [1906 New York: Negro Universities Press, 1969], 282–84). For similar occurrences in Florida, see Susan Bradford Eppes, *Through Some Eventful Years* (Gainesville: University of Florida Press, 1968 [1926]), 282–86.

25. *Richmond Dispatch*, 1, 2 August 1867; *New York Times*, 2, 6 August 1867; see also Rachleff, *Black Labor in the South*, 45; Morton, *Negro in Virginia Politics*, 40–43.

26. The October 1867 city Republican ward meetings and nominating convention adopted the practice common in the black community's mass meetings: a voice or standing vote that enfranchised men, women, and children. See, for example, the 8 October Second Ward meeting for delegate selection: "All who favored Mr. Washburne were first requested to rise, and forty were found on the floor, including women." *Richmond Dispatch*, 30 September, 9 October 1867, 2, 4, 14, 23, 24 January, 15, 25 February, 3, 8, 25 April 1868; *New York Times*, 6 August, 15, 18 October 1867, 11 January 1868; Rachleff, *Black Labor in the South*, 45–49; Avary, *Dixie after the War*, 229–31, 254.

    Throughout the state of Virginia, the internal community political gatherings adopted measures by a voice or standing vote that could often enfranchise not only women but children as well. See, for example, the minutes of the mass meeting of colored citizens of Elizabeth City County, Virginia, 5 December 1865: "When upon this motion the entire audience rose to their feet and remained standing some time"; Brig. Gen. S. Brown to Brig. Gen. B. C. Card, Washington, D.C., 19 December 1865, "Negroes, Employment of," Consolidated Correspondence File, ser. 225, Central Records, Records of the Office of the Quartermaster General, Record Group 92, National Archives, Washington, D.C. [Y-719]. (Bracketed numbers refer to file numbers of documents in the Freedmen and Southern Society Project, University of Maryland. I thank Leslie S. Rowland, project director, for facilitating my access to these files.)

    The issue of children's participation is an interesting one, suggestive of the means by which personal experience rather than societal norms shaped ex-slaves' vision of politics. A similarly telling example was in the initial proposal of the African National Congress that the new South African constitution set the voting age at fourteen, a testament to the young people, such as those in Soweto, who experienced the ravages of apartheid and whose fight against it helped bring about the political negotiations to secure African political rights and self-determination.

27. Compare southern black women's active participation in formal politics—internal and external—in the first decades after the Civil War to Michael McGerr's assessment that nineteenth-century "women were allowed in to the male political realm only to play typical feminine roles—to cook, sew, and cheer for men and to symbolize virtue and beauty. Men denied women the central experiences of the popular style: not only the ballot but also the experience of mass mobilization." McGerr's analysis fails to acknowledge the racial basis of his study, that is, that it is an assessment of white women's political participation. Michael McGerr, "Political Style and Women's Power, 1830–1930," *Journal of American History* 77 (December 1990): 864–85, esp. 867. My analysis also differs substantially from Mary P. Ryan, *Women in Public: Between Banners and Ballots, 1825–1880* (Baltimore: Johns Hopkins University Press, 1990). Ryan gives only cursory attention to African Americans but finds black women's political expression in the Civil War and Reconstruction eras restricted "with particular severity" and "buried beneath the surface of the public sphere"; see esp. 146–47, 156.

28. For women's participation in political parades in Louisville, Kentucky, Mobile, Alabama, and Charleston, South Carolina, see Gutman, *Black Family in Slavery and Freedom*, 380; *Liberatora*, 21 July 1865, and *New York Daily Tribune*, 4 April 1865, both reprinted in Dorothy Sterling, ed., *The Trouble They Seen: Black People Tell the Story of Reconstruction* (Garden City, N.Y.: Doubleday, 1976), 2–4. In other areas of Virginia besides Richmond, and in South Carolina, Louisiana, and Arkansas, men and women participated in the political meetings. See, for example, Vincent Harding, *There Is a River: The Black Struggle for Freedom in America* (New York: Harcourt Brace Jovanovich, 1981), 294–97; Laura M. Towne, *Letters and Diary of Laura M. Towne Written from the Sea Islands of South Carolina, 1862–1884*, ed. Rupert sargent Holland New York: Negro Universities Press, 1969 [1912]), 183; testimony of John H. Burch given before a Senate committee appointed to investigate the exodus of black men and women from

Louisiana, 46th Cong., 2d Sess., S. Rept. 693, pt. 2, 232–33, reprinted in Herbert Aptheker, ed., *A Documentary History of the Negro People in the United States* (New York: Citadel Press, 1951), 2:721–22; Thomas Holt, *Black over White: Negro Political Leadership in South Carolina during Reconstruction* (Urbana: University of Illinois Press, 1977), 34–35; Randy Finley, "Freedperson's Identities and the Freedmen's Bureau in Arkansas, 1865–1869," paper presented at the annual meeting of the Southern Historical Association, Orlando, Florida, 11 November 1993 (cited with permission of Finley). Graphic artists recognized the participation of women as a regular feature of parades, mass meetings, and conventions, as evidenced by their illustrations; see "The Celebration of Emancipation Day in Charleston" from *Leslie's Illustrated Newspaper*, reprinted in Francis Butler Simkins and Robert Hilliard Woody, *South Carolina During Reconstruction* (Gloucester, Mass.: Peter Smith, 1966 [1932]), facing 364; "Electioneering at the South," *Harper's Weekly*, 25 July 1868, reprinted in Foner, *Reconstruction*, fol. 386; "Colored People's Convention in Session," reprinted in Sterling, *The Trouble They Seen*, 65.

29. *New York Times*, 11 January 1868; *The Debates and Proceedings of the Constitutional Convention of the State of Virginia, Assembled at the City of Richmond* (Richmond, 1868), 524–27.

30. *New York Times*, 11, 22 January 1868; *Debates and Proceedings, Virginia*, 505–7.

31. Estimates of the number of black people who migrated into Richmond in the immediate postemancipation period run as high as fifteen thousand. Rachleff, *Black Labor in the South*, 14; Virginius Dabney, *Richmond: The Story of a City* (Garden City, N.Y.: Doubleday, 1976), 208; Randolph, *From Slave Cabin to Pulpit*, 59.

32. My discussion of liberal democratic political ideology draws on Macpherson, *Political Theory of Possessive Individualism*; C. B. Macpherson, *Democratic Theory: Essays in Retrieval* (Oxford: Oxford University Press, 1973), and *The Life and Times of Liberal Democracy* (Oxford: Oxford University Press, 1977).

33. For a similar and extended discussion focused on Jamaica and Britain, see Thomas C. Holt, *The Problem of Freedom: Race, Labor, and Politics in Jamaica and Britain, 1832–1938* (Baltimore: Johns Hopkins University Press, 1992); also Thomas C. Holt, "'The Essence of the Contract': The Articulation of Race, Gender, and Political Economy in British Emancipation Policy, 1838–1866," paper presented at "Seminar on Racism and Race Relations in the Countries of the African Diaspora," Rio de Janeiro, Brazil, 6 April 1992 (cited with permission of Holt).

34. Elizabeth Hyde Botume, *First Days amongst the Contrabands* (New York: Arno Press and New York Times, 1968 [1893]), 273. See Jones, *Labor of Love*, 66–67; Margaret Washington Creel, "Female Slaves in South Carolina," *TRUTH: Newsletter of the Association of Black Women Historians*, summer 1985.

35. For a discussion of the idea of emancipated slaves earning freedom and political liberties through proper orientation to a market economy, see Holt, "'An Empire over the Mind.'" An explicit statement of that assumption was given by white Republicans during the Virginia constitutional convention debates. Disagreeing with Bayne's argument regarding the inherent right of suffrage, Judge John Underwood contended, "I hold that the colored men . . . ought to have the right of suffrage. . . . [T]hey have shown themselves competent . . . they have shown their industry and their effort and desire to elevate themselves. . . . I do not think that the Indians, wandering upon the plains, . . . having no fixed homes, no habits of industry—I do not think that such a class of people should be entitled to vote. . . . Just so soon as they become settled and industrious in their habits like the colored men of this State, then I will go for giving the Indians the right to vote." Bayne, on the other hand, supported suffrage for Indians. *Debates and Proceedings, Virginia*, 527.

36. Percentages computed from figures given by Holt, *Black over White*, 35, 97. *Proceedings of the Constitutional Convention of South Carolina, held at Charleston, South Carolina, beginning January 14 and ending March 17, 1868* (Charleston: Denny and Perry, 1868), 836–38; *New York Times*, 3 April 1869; Terborg-Penn, "Afro-Americans in the Struggle for Woman Suffrage," 52–54; Rosalyn Terborg-Penn, "The Rollin Sisters," in Darlene Clark Hine, Elsa Barkley Brown, and Rosalyn Terborg-Penn, eds., *Black Women in America: An Historical Encyclopedia* (Brooklyn, N.Y.: Carlson Publishing, 1993), 990–91. There are some reports that black women actually voted in Reconstruction-era South Carolina. Benjamin Quarles states that in some "districts in the South Carolina elections of 1870 colored women under the encouragement of Negro election officials, exercised the privilege of voting. By this act the Negro became the first practical vindicator of woman's right to the ballot" ("Frederick Douglass and the Woman's Rights Movement," *Journal of Negro History* 25 [January 1940]: 35). Others have suggested that whenever black men were ill and unable to come to the polls to cast their ballot, their wives or other female relatives were allowed to vote in their place.

37. *Debates and Proceedings, Virginia*, 254.

38. Eric Foner sees Bayne as a primary example of the "distinction between the public sphere of men and the private world of women" that developed with freedom. Quoting only Bayne's comment "It is woman's right to raise and bear children, and to train them for their future duties in life," Foner sees this "militant

Virginia political leader" as having a "severely restricted definition of women's rights" (*Reconstruction*, 87). This may be true, but such a conclusion is not necessarily the meaning of Bayne's statement when taken in its full context; only further research on Bayne and his colleagues will clarify these issues. But Bayne's self-conscious explication of his own terminology further reinforces my reading of his discussion of domestic roles of women as in addition to, not instead of, political roles. (Hucles, having pointed out Bayne's terminology, still accepts Foner's reading of Bayne's statement about domestic roles and thus accepts Foner's conclusions regarding Bayne's sexism and exclusion of women from political rights; Michael Hucles, "Many Voices, Similar Concerns: Traditional Methods of African-American Political Activity in Norfolk, Virginia, 1865–1875," *Virginia Magazine of History and Biography* 100 [October 1992]: 543–66.)

I am not ignoring the importance of language but emphasizing the importance of historicizing and investigating language. Bayne, like other Afro-Virginians, used a conventional political language, just as they used conventional political forms, but gave each larger meaning than conventionally intended. A recent literary study that takes these questions of language, gender, citizenship, and freedom as its core is Claudia Tate, *Domestic Allegories of Political Desire: The Black Heroine's Text at the Turn of the Century* (New York: Oxford University Press, 1992). Like most studies, however, its concentration on northern middle-class black women and its reading of the postemancipation period through late-nineteenth-century eyes and texts ignore the different language and meanings of the immediate postemancipation era among ex-slaves in the South. Tate thus assumes that "discourses of citizenship . . . were *inherently* gendered until the ratification of the Twenty second [*sic*] Amendment in 1920" (21, 243 n; emphasis mine). My effort is to understand how an explicitly gendered discourse on citizenship and rights *developed* within late-nineteenth-century black communities, rather than assuming it was either inherently there at emancipation or immediately and uncontestedly assumed thereupon. For a fuller explication of this, see Elsa Barkley Brown, "Negotiating and Transforming the Public Sphere: African American Political Life in the Transition from Slavery to Freedom," *Public Culture* 7 (fall 1994): 107–46.

39. *Richmond Dispatch*, 18 June 1867; Rachleff, *Black Labor in the South*, 48.

40. First African Baptist Church, Richmond, Virginia, Minutes, Books II and III, Virginia State Library Archives, Richmond. These developments are explored in Barkley Brown, "Negotiating and Transforming the Public Sphere." The whole question of the operating procedures of internal community institutions such as churches and mutual benefit and fraternal societies needs investigation; surviving church minute books and denominational minutes offer a promising source for future analyses. In any case, the question of women's participation in the external political arena should be analyzed in the context of developments within internal community institutions. These debates over gender roles within black churches occurred at congregational and denominational levels. For studies that examine these debates at the state and/or national level in the late nineteenth and early twentieth centuries, see Evelyn Brooks Higginbotham, *Righteous Discontent: The Women's Movement in the Black Baptist Church* (Cambridge, Mass.: Harvard University Press, 1993); Glenda Gilmore, "Gender and Jim Crow: Women and the Politics of White Supremacy in North Carolina, 1896–1920" (Ph.D. diss., University of North Carolina, Chapel Hill, 1992); Cheryl Townsend Gilkes, "'Together and in Harness': Women's Traditions in the Sanctified Church," *Signs: Journal of Women in Culture and Society* 10 (summer 1985): 678–99.

41. Rachleff, *Black Labor in the South*, 31–32; A. T. Morgan, *Yazoo; or, On the Picket Line of Freedom in the South: A Personal Narrative* (New York: Russell and Russell, 1884), 231–33; W. L. Fleming, *The Civil War and Reconstruction in Alabama* (New York: Peter Smith, 1905), 777.

42. This censuring of women's political participation was part of a larger pattern whereby northern white men attempted to teach southern black men and women "proper" relations. Towne noted that "several speakers have been here who have advised the people to get the women into their proper place" (Towne, *Letters and Diary of Laura M. Towne*, 183–84). It was the participation, not merely the presence, of black women at political meetings that was the issue elsewhere as well. In Richmond, for example, white women certainly on occasion sat in the convention's gallery as visitors, merely watching the proceedings. The problem with the black women and men, as many white observers saw it, was that they participated from the gallery. Avary, *Dixie after the War*, 254–57.

43. Towne, *Letters and Diary of Laura M. Towne*, 183. Despite this example, the various continued activities of women, often with the approval of men, makes clear that ex-slaves' compliance with these norms of "proper" relations was not immediately forthcoming. However, more detailed investigations of the ways in which freedmen and freedwomen came to work out family and community relationships—political, economic, and social—in various areas of the South are needed. Until then, the various formulations that lay out a well-developed public/private dichotomy and patriarchal construction of black family and community life as a fairly immediate occurrence after emancipation amount to nothing more than a presentist reading of an as yet not fully explored past.

44. Holt, *Black over White*, 34–35. A witness before the Senate investigating committee testified in 1872 that the women "have been very active since 1868 in all the political movements; they form a large number in all the political assemblages" in Louisiana. Testimony of John H. Burch in Aptheker, *Documentary History*, 2:721.

45. Lucy McMillan testimony taken at Spartanburg, South Carolina, 10 July 1871, in U.S. Congress, *Testimony Taken by the Joint Select Committee to Inquire into the Condition of Affairs in the Late Insurrectionary States*, 42d Cong., 2d sess., S. Rept. v. 2, n. 41, pt. 4: *South Carolina* (Washington, D.C.: Government Printing Office, 1872), 2:605 (hereafter cited as *Ku Klux Klan Testimony*).

46. Holt, *Black over White*, 35; Avary, *Dixie after the War*, 362; Towne, *Letters and Diary of Laura M. Towne*, 284–91.

47. Fleming, *Civil War and Reconstruction in Alabama*; Joel Williamson, *After Slavery: The Negro in South Carolina during Reconstruction, 1861–1877* (Chapel Hill: University of North Carolina Press, 1965), 344; Holt, *Black over White*, 35.

48. U.S. Congress, *Smalls v. Tillman*, 45th Cong., 1st sess., H. Misc. Doc. no. 11 (1877), quoted in Dorothy Sterling, ed., *We Are Your Sisters: Black Women in the Nineteenth Century* (New York: W. W. Norton, 1984), 370; Towne, *Letters and Diary of Laura M. Towne*, 284.

49. *Smalls v. Tillman*, in Sterling, *We Are Your Sisters*, 370; Fleming, *Civil War and Reconstruction in Alabama*, 564–65, 776.

50. Violet Keeling's testimony before the Senate investigating committee, 18 February 1884, 48th Cong., 1st sess., S. Rept. no. 579, reprinted in Aptheker, *Documentary History*, 2:739–41.

51. Avary, *Dixie after the War*, 285–86, 347; Fleming, *Civil War and Reconstruction in Alabama*, 564–65, 776–78; *Ku Klux Klan Testimony: North Carolina*, 9, 289, *Georgia*, 236, 248, 290, 1184, *Alabama*, 684, 878, 1072–73, 1078–80, *Mississippi*, 725, *Florida and Miscellaneous*, 50; Thomas I. Evans, Alexander H. Sands, N. A. Sturdivant, et al., Richmond, to Major General Schofield, 31 October 1867, reprinted in *Documents of the Constitutional Convention of the State of Virginia* (Richmond: Office of the New Nation, 1867), 22–23; John H. Gilmer to Schofield, reprinted in the *New York Times*, 30 October 1867; Joe M. Richardson, *The Negro in the Reconstruction of Florida, 1865–1877* (Tallahassee: Florida State University, 1965), 237–38; Lerome Bennett Jr., *Black Power U.S.A.: The Human Side of Reconstruction, 1867–1877* (Chicago: Johnson Publishing, 1967), 359; Frenise A. Logan, *The Negro in North Carolina, 1876–1894* (Chapel Hill: University of North Carolina Press, 1964), 22–23; Henderson Hamilton Donald, *The Negro Freedman: Life Conditions of the American Negro in the Early Years after Emancipation* (New York: Cooper Square Publishers, 1971 [1952]), 203–5; Charles Nordhoff, *The Cotton States in the Spring and Summer of 1875* (New York: Burt Franklin, 1876), 11, 22; Simkins and Woody, *South Carolina during Reconstruction*, 512; Sir George Campbell, *White and Black: The Outcome of a Visit to the United States* (New York: Negro Universities Press, 1969 [1879]), 181, 317; *New York Times*, 3 November 1867; Proceedings before Military Commissioner, City of Richmond, 26 October 1867, in the case of Winston Jackson, filed as G-423 1867, Letters Received, ser. 5068, 1st Reconstruction Military District, Records of the U.S. Army Continental Commands, Record Group 393, pt. 1, National Archives [SS-1049].

52. Fleming, *Civil War and Reconstruction in Alabama*, 776.

53. Quote is from James E. Sefton, "A Note on the Political Intimidation of Black Men by Other Black Men," *Georgia Historical Quarterly* 52 (December 1968): 448. My analysis here leans heavily on an unpublished essay by Joseph Reidy on Reconstruction-era politics.

54. Robert Gleed testimony before Mississippi Subcommittee, 10 November 1871, *Ku Klux Klan Testimony: Mississippi*, 725. Gleed's statement also challenges feminist theory that attempts to dichotomize men and women's ideas of justice by arguing that men accept a more abstract equal application of the law as justice, whereas women insist upon a notion of justice more closely tied to issues of morality and outcome. See Carol Gilligan, *In a Different Voice* (Cambridge, Mass.: Harvard University Press, 1982). This is, of course, a problematic argument, as it assumes gender to be an analytical category removable from the context of race and class. For a critique of Gilligan that emphasizes the degree to which the elements she sees as female might also be seen as African American, common to both males and females in black communities, see Carol Stack, "The Culture of Gender: Women and Men of Color," *Signs: Journal of Women in Culture and Society* 11 (winter 1986): 321–24. See also Carol B. Stack, "Different Voices, Different Visions: Gender, Culture, and Moral Reasoning," in Maxine Boca Zinn and Bonnie Thornton Dill, eds., *Women of Color in U.S. Society* (Philadelphia: Temple University Press, 1994), 291–301.

55. The larger society reinforced this sense of collective ownership of the vote. Black women (and children) were included in the retribution black men faced when they cast a Republican vote. Harriet Hernandes, a South Carolina woman, testified that her entire community lay out at night to avoid whippings or murder. "Mighty near" everyone in her neighborhood had been whipped "because [when] men . . . voted radical tickets they [the Ku Klux Klan] took the spite out on the women when they could get at them. . . . Ben

Phillips and his wife and daughter; Sam Foster; and Moses Eaves, they killed him—I could not begin to tell all—Ann Bonner and her daughter, Manza Surratt and his wife and whole family, even the least child in the family, they took it out of bed and whipped it. They told them if they did that they would remember it." Violet Keeling reported that on election day she carried a knife with her as she walked to and from work for fear that if the Republicans were victorious, black women as well as black men would be held responsible. Harriet Hernandes' testimony taken at Spartanburg, South Carolina, 10 July 1871, in *Ku Klux Klan Testimony: South Carolina*, 586; Keeling testimony in Aptheker, *Documentary History*, 2:739.

56. Petition from Nancy Hodges and other hucksters filed as Geo. Teamoh to Gen. O. O. Howard, 21 May 1866, T-173 1866, Letters Received, ser. 15, Washington Headquarters, Records of the Bureau of Refugees, Freedmen, and Abandoned Lands, Record Group 105, National Archives [A-7619].

57. Avary, *Dixie after the War*, 282–83; Donald, *Negro Freedman*, 207 (emphasis mine).

58. Jones, *Labor of Love*, 66. Jones is not alone in her assessment. In his generally rigorous analysis, Eric Foner, apparently adopting Jones's analysis, also suggests the public/private dichotomy between black men and women, based in part on men's participation in the formal political process; Nell Irvin Painter assumes that since black women were unenfranchised in the Reconstruction era, "they could not act politically as men could." Foner, *Reconstruction*, 87; Nell Irvin Painter, "Comment," in Darlene Clark Hine, ed., *The State of Afro-American History: Past, Present, and Future*, (Baton Rouge: Louisiana State University Press, 1986), 82.

59. My work here and elsewhere questions the usefulness of the public/private dichotomy for understanding African American women's history. Others have also raised questions in relation to the larger fields of women's history and women's studies. Linda Kerber, acknowledging the degree to which conceptualizing this dichotomy opened up many avenues of women's lives to historical investigation, also suggests that such a dichotomy has probably outlived its usefulness. Elsa Barkley Brown, "Womanist Consciousness: Maggie Lena Walker and the Independent Order of Saint Luke," *Signs: Journal of Women in Culture and Society* 14 (spring 1989): 610–33; Linda K. Kerber, "Separate Spheres, Female Worlds, Woman's Place: The Rhetoric of Women's History," *Journal of American History* 75 (June 1989): 9–39. See also Alice Kessler-Harris, "Gender Ideology in Historical Reconstruction: A Case Study from the 1930s," *Gender and History* 1 (spring 1989): 31–49. Kerber echoes Michele Rosaldo's critique of oppositional modes of thought in general and transhistoric conceptions of home versus public life in particular. Linda Nicholson provides a basis for understanding the reification of these categories as a product of Western liberalism. She argues that liberalism as a political theory rests on the assumption that the family, as the sphere of the private, and the political, as the sphere of the public, are "inherently demarcatable." M. Z. Rosaldo, "The Use and Abuse of Anthropology: Reflections on Feminism and Cross-Cultural Understanding," *Signs: Journal of Women in Culture and Society* 5 (spring 1980): 389–417; Linda Nicholson, *Gender and History: The Limits of Social Theory in the Age of the Family* (New York: Columbia University Press, 1986). For an example of the ways in which those challenging public/private dichotomies often reinvent the same dichotomy, see Elsa Barkley Brown, "Imaging Lynching: African American Women, Communities of Struggle, and Collective Memory," in Geneva Smitherman, ed., *African American Women Speak Out: Responses to Anita Hill–Clarence Thomas* (Detroit: Wayne State University Press, 1995).

60. Even a cursory reading of Reconstruction-era documents makes this clear. The thirteen volumes of *Ku Klux Klan Testimony*, for example, are filled with reports of whipping and/or raping of black women—for their refusal to work in the fields or in white men's and women's homes, for their husbands' political activities, or for their families' efforts to acquire land. One North Carolina man, Essic Harris, reported that the rape of black women by the Ku Klux Klan was so common in his community that "[i]t has got to be an old saying." Some women, such as Lucy McMillan, reported violent attacks as a direct result of their own political activities. McMillan's house was burned after she attended a political meeting and reported back to her community. She was accused of being a "d——d radical," "making laws" and "bragging and boasting that I wanted the land." Essic Harris testimony, 1 July 1871, *Ku Klux Klan Testimony: North Carolina*, 100; McMillan testimony, ibid., 604–11.

61. Harding, *There Is a River*, 296.

62. The point, of course, is that the meaning cannot be presumed merely from the act. The implications of this are far-reaching, for it recalls to our attention the fact, as stated by Michele Rosaldo, "[t]hat woman's place in human social life is not in any direct sense a product of the things she does . . . but of the meaning her activities acquire through concrete social interactions. And the significances women assign to the activities of their lives are things that we can only grasp through an analysis of the relationships that women forge, the social contexts they (along with men) create—and within which they are defined. Gender in all human groups must . . . be understood in political and social terms, with reference . . . to local and specific forms of social relationship" (Rosaldo, "Use and Abuse of Anthropology," 400). Ignoring this is analytically problematic. See, for example, Susan Mann's explication of black women's status under the sharecropping

system. Mann, by design, lifts her exploration of economic roles out of the context of political and cultural roles and ideology and thus explores the meaning of labor removed from its social context. More important, her exploration of economic roles assumes that the distinctions between women laboring in the home and men laboring in the field have inherent universal implications rather than ones embedded in a particular historical context. See Susan A. Mann, "Slavery, Sharecropping, and Sexual Inequality," *Signs: Journal of Women in Culture and Society* 14 (summer 1989): 774–98. One point of my essay is to demonstrate that variables such as enfranchisement/disfranchisement (or work in the fields/work in the home) mean different things in different social and historical contexts. Our tendency to attribute inherent meaning to certain activities obscures rather than explains historically specific developments of social relations between black men and black women.

9

Deference and Defiance: Labor Politics and the Meanings of Masculinity in the Mid-Nineteenth-Century New England Textile Industry

Mary H. Blewett

The recent appearance of historical studies of masculinity is a welcome response to the feminist insistence that gender is a useful category of historical analysis. Some historians, however, have described working-class masculinity as stable across time and cultures or as essentially similar to middle-class masculinity.[1] When interrogated, gender meanings prove far more volatile than many historians suspect. The analysis of male gender and its contested meanings in labor politics can benefit from the perspective and methods of feminist history that treat gender as relational, link conceptions of masculinity with femininity, examine the class relations of economic power, identify female agency in historical process, and, while historicizing masculinity, continue to analyze the central issue of gender inequality.[2]

The unstable meaning of working-class masculinity became central to specific political struggles among groups of men (employers and workers, spinners and weavers) and among working-class men and women during the turbulent 1870s in the New England textile industry. Working-class women from Lancashire, England, contributed in significant and provocative ways to the definitions of manhood and womanhood by their voiced expectations, their organizational activities, their memories of history, and their views on politics. Definitions of masculinity became a part of working women's collective assertion.[3] Struggles over gender meanings thus reflected not only conflicts among employers and male workers over economic power and social authority but also conflicts within the culture and politics of immigrant, working-class life.[4] These conflicts symbolized powerful interrelationships that intimately connected the public and the private, linking workplace and community life with sexual identity and family position. These contests, which divided working-class men and women, also suggest historical possibilities that might have been chosen to avoid the marginalization of women at work, in labor protest, and within working-class families.

Men and women textile workers from Lancashire, similar to those studied by Sonya Rose, immigrated in successive waves before and after the American Civil War to southeastern New England: specifically to the cities of Fall River and New Bedford, Massachusetts, and to the mill villages north of Providence, Rhode Island.[5] They tried to make their political experience in Lancashire the basis for a new labor politics in New England. The intense conflict that occurred in the decade of the 1870s reminds us that many immigrant cultures transferred vital traditions of radical politics to industrializing America.[6] The redefinition of working-class gender ideology and the defeat of Lancashire radicalism contributed to the growing conservatism of the American labor movement in the late nineteenth century. In addition, evidence on working-class emigrants from Lancashire can contribute to the ways historians interpret the dynamics of working-class reformism in mid-Victorian England and demonstrate how studies of gender relations can clarify the disputed question of working-class respectability.

Men and women of Lancashire came to Fall River in the late 1860s and 1870s as individual men, as brothers and sisters, or as husbands and wives, some perhaps in pursuit of the elusive family wage. Most left behind them the networks of kin who formed such an important part of Lancashire culture and politics.[7] Those who chose to emigrate and seemed reluctant to return to England had also left behind the reformism and stability as well as the established systems of paternalism and deference adopted by the Victorian textile industry.[8]

Following the American Civil War, the textile mills in Fall River grew enormously. The vast scale of the new corporate enterprises, their heavily indebted capitalization, and their integration of all processes of textile work differed significantly from the operations in the smaller, family-owned, often single-process textile mills of Lancashire. After scouring the region of New England for native-born American workers to fill up these new mills, Fall River employers actively recruited additional textile workers from Lancashire in the early 1870s.[9] British textile unions, faced with an overcrowded labor market, strongly encouraged the emigration of workers.[10] Many of the structural elements of Lancashire work and kinship that supported employee paternalism, union organization, and its family wage rhetoric in mid-century England did not survive the voyage to New England.

Immigrants faced ruthless American managers intent on dominating the domestic market for cheap printed cotton cloth through their massive productive capacity to glut that market with the cheapest standardized goods. From the moment that Lancashire immigrants entered Fall River factories, mill managers continuously challenged their customary measures of manly skill and strength. Agents bought the cheapest raw cotton and the best machinery and paid the lowest piece rates in the region while demanding the highest productivity, thus requiring ever more intensive physical exertions from the operatives. Mule spinners who, in contrast with Lancashire practice, labored without the help of piecers worked at an especially intense pace to produce massive quantities of yarn for inferior gray goods, whose defects would be concealed by the printing process. Piece rates for weaving, cut again and again in the 1870s, exacted similar efforts from weavers. Fall River agents glutted the domestic market with the cheapest possible goods.

In addition to facing competitive challenges to their dominance of this lucrative post–Civil War market, Fall River managers found themselves responsible in the early 1870s for paying off very heavy corporate debts for highly inflated land values and for expensive new buildings (including desperately needed worker housing) and machinery. As a group and unlike mill owners in Lancashire, they and their sons, nephews, and sons-in-law often relied on managerial or financial skills acquired in commerce rather than experience in textile production. This background made them indifferent to and contemptuous of English work traditions and labor protest. Capitalists in Fall River regarded the doffed caps of Lancashire men, their politeness, and references to their employers as "masters" as marks of unmanly servility. In nineteenth-century American society, only black slaves had masters. Much of this courteous English demeanor rested on midcentury behaviors that had been worked out in deferential relationships with employers who agreed to negotiate with union men. In Fall River, however, Lancashire men faced both their employers' immense market power and a dismissive, open contempt for their deferential manhood.[11]

In Lancashire, English mule spinners in the 1830s and 1840s had joined with short-time reformers to define working-class male respectability through skill and the family wage, and female respectability through domesticity and sexual propriety.[12] Both spinners and hand loom weavers had opposed the employment of women and children in textile factories, viewing them as cheap labor, easily coerced. By midcentury both sexes commonly tended the steam-driven looms in Lancashire, but spinners had successfully prevented women from working on self-acting mules. Male textile workers had also gradually shed their public image as "Lancashire brutes" for that of sober, conscientious, self-educated, and serious men who ran consumer cooperatives like small businesses and negotiated respectably and reasonably with their employers.

English spinners and weavers developed different organizational strategies to defend their interests. Spinners tried to limit the trade to young men and boys whose work as piecers and minders required male supervisory authority. Lancashire spinners brought to New England their conviction that the effective organization of small numbers of skilled male workers in key communities would enable them to counteract the mill agents' insistence that market forces of supply and demand determined wages. In contrast, the weavers' organizations accepted both men and women, who received the same piece rates for weaving. Their goal had been the establishment of a standard list of wages in Lancashire. For the weavers, regional organization had become more important than the sex composition of the craft.[13]

Beginning in the 1850s, labor protest in Fall River had been led sporadically by small groups of mule spinners from Lancashire, of both English and Irish birth. They supported the campaign for the ten-hour day and contributed to the Preston strike fund in 1854. Until 1875, the weavers deferred to the spinners' style of resistance in Fall River. A strike in 1870 after a general wage cut demonstrated how immigrant spinners tried to establish their public stance as respectable men of skill to maneuver their employers into Lancashire-style negotiations. The mill agents attempted to provoke violent reactions by the striking spinners to demonstrate to the community that union leaders were reckless and irresponsible. The spinners were determined to prevent any association of male unionists with acts of violence against strikebreakers that might justify the employers' refusal to negotiate. Spinners tried to avoid this by assigning responsibility for tough confrontations in the streets to sympathetic weavers (both men and women) and to the spinners' own women and children. The spinners' union thus implicitly endorsed public activity for women that involved rude, violent behavior: yelling, pummeling strikebreakers, and throwing stones, behavior antithetical to that of respectable working-class men.[14] While the union spinners remained respectable and law-abiding, their women could, at the direction of the men on whom they depended for support, exhibit violent behavior in league with others against strikebreakers in contests with employers.[15]

The only incident of violence toward a strikebreaker in 1870 illustrates how the spinners' allies assumed responsibility for intimidation. The victim was a Scottish immigrant farmer who had worked as a spinner for only three years. He had refused to join the union and expected trouble but identified no attacker. To make an example of him, noisy members of a crowd waiting outside the mill kicked, stoned, and gave him "a tremendous pounding" as he left for the night after two days' work. The street crowds were composed mostly of women and children, and his attackers probably included weavers. They supplied the howls and jeers, the fists and blows, to humble a disloyal male. They were backed up by the tenants of corporation housing nearby, armed with stones and dirt clods and ready to shower the strikebreakers at a signal. Most were women sitting at their windows with stones concealed in their aprons.[16] Male authority in labor protest prevailed, while peaceable manly behavior and female unruliness served class politics. However peaceable they remained, the striking spinners could not persuade the agents to negotiate.

During the 1870 strike mill agents impugned the manliness of spinning by claiming that elsewhere in Massachusetts, "girls run mules easily and successfully." In response, the spinners argued that they worked harder and faster at their Fall River machines than anyone else in New England, walking twenty-five miles and more per day over eleven hours with only one young back boy to help piece up broken yarns: "a pretty good day's work for any man." The striking spinners insisted that the exhausting work was "not a fitting employment for females."[17]

Fall River employers rejected negotiations in 1870, successfully imported strikebreakers from other textile cities in the region, and used their control of municipal government to break the strike.[18] Leaders of the spinners' union were blacklisted and forced to leave Fall River to look elsewhere for work or give up spinning. Protest strategies based on manly respectability and deferential behavior might have offered hope in Lancashire, but they did not work in Fall River. Instead, after losing strikes, respectable union spinners faced the further loss of both craft and union brotherhoods.

In some cases women's involvement in the 1870 strike represented more than support for their husbands. Unlike the general pattern in Lancashire, where mule spinners' wives were not employed, some Fall River spinners' wives were weavers.[19] In 1871 an English-born spinner described to a state investigator a pattern that he claimed was familiar to the families of mule spinners. Each working day he rose at 5 A.M. to start the breakfast while his children and wife slept, then helped to put the dinner into the pails, and after work started the supper "until she gets home."[20] He explained that shared housework made it possible for his wife with the help of her twelve-year-old daughter, to tend ten looms, more than the usual six to eight looms of women weavers, and thus earn more on piecework. Public testimony by a head of family about his choice to participate in routine housework alongside a working wife did not contradict a spinner's sense of manliness. Other families who immigrated with kin could rely on relatives for help with housework, thus releasing the mother for employment. As the mills continued to expand production in the early 1870s and supply plenty of work, some wives of spinners wove in Fall River mills.

During a frenzy of mill building between 1870 and 1873, Lancashire immigration to Fall River increased, providing reinforcements for the spinners union and recruits for similar activities among weavers. Like the spinners, immigrant weavers in the Fall River mills faced low wages, long hours, and opposition to labor protest unheard of in Lancashire since the 1840s. One Fall River manufacturer confided to an overseer his eagerness to employ "green horns" from Lancashire. "Yes," the overseer said, "but you'll find that they have brought their horns with them."[21] Still, Fall River agents were confident that they could dominate these historically unruly people as easily as the national market for print cloth. While organizing in secret, Lancashire immigrants joined other Massachusetts textile workers and labor reformers in the successful campaign for the ten-hour day in 1874. In response, Fall River managers ignored statutory limitations (weakened by a legal loophole) and significantly sped up work processes throughout the 1870s while pushing daily operations beyond the legal limit. State policy made no real difference inside the mills. Productive capacity remained Fall River's key to dominating the market.

During the depression years of 1873–75, intensifying workloads sapped physical strength and stamina, those customary measures of a man's worth, especially for spinners. Working-class men regarded these pressures on their bodily strength as an assault on their physical capacity to support their families. Denied their customary piecers and minders, Fall River spinners had only their back boys to ease the pressures of repairing the flimsy yarns spun from cheap cotton during the back-and-forth motions of the huge frames. These pressures, added to low piece rates, produced a characteristically brisk "Fall River walk." Few spinners, even the young and vital ones, had the stamina to work the full month of six-day weeks, eleven hours a day, in the brutally hot spinning rooms, without laying off as "sick" for several days to regain their strength. A roster of "sick spinners" routinely filled the jobs of exhausted men for several days each month. When employers defined a spinner's work as just beyond the extent of a man's physical powers, an abuse the operatives called "the grind,"they undermined a man's pride in strength and skill.[22]

Wage cuts during the deepening depression after 1873 meant less income to spend on food to sustain overtaxed vitality. Lancashire spinners and weavers had legendary appetites for beef and beer. Workers concealed the cheese and bread in their dinner pails that hard times forced them to substitute for their customary cold meat. Employers, with the support of temperance organizations, criticized all alcohol consumption as drunkenness and argued that "more sickness is caused by beer than by overwork."[23] Still, textile workers believed that a man's physical well-being, especially under the grueling terms he faced in Fall River factories, required red meat and plenty of beer.

Overseers also denied spinners their customary time to oil and clean their machines by setting the piece rate so low as to require almost total concentration on machine operations. In September 1874, when a half-trained young man in the Granite Mills neglected his mules to keep up with his more experienced fellow spinners, his unoiled gears sparked into cotton waste and caused a fatal fire. Unlike English practice, the Granite Mill overseers posted the daily work records of each spinner to encourage competition. As one Lancashire immigrant said, "If a man is not able to get as much off his mules as the others, he is . . . a butt of ridicule to his fellow-workmen. A boy of seventeen likes to feel like a man . . . and will be tempted to neglect his machinery."[24] The power of the mill agents to define the pace of work allowed the measure of manhood to assume a new and deadly potential.

As the depression worsened, worker resistance seemed hopeless. Since the lost strike in 1870, the ten-hour law had failed to limit overwork, while the pace of work intensified and wages fell. Mill managers used the blacklist and the piece rate to discipline the workforce, and sought to isolate and humiliate the leaders of resistance. Spinners defended their control of the craft and their leadership of labor protest as the best foundation for their respectable manhood, but employers allowed no interference with the ways they sought to dominate the market. Any successful challenge to the power of the mills would galvanize labor politics.

In late 1874 the mill agents decided to stimulate the depressed prices in the market by cutting production, but when other New England mills shifted from their regular goods into print cloth to meet the shortfall, Fall River returned to full capacity and cut wages by 10 percent. Manufacturers flooded the market and undercut their upstart competitors. In retaliation, the weavers led by rebellious women workers revived Lancashire traditions of popular radicalism.[25] They challenged the control of labor protest by deferential, respectable spinners and won the only strike victory for weavers in nineteenth-century Fall River. In doing so, they called into question the meanings of working-class masculinity and femininity.

The strike was started by angry women weavers who had been excluded from union meetings where male weavers had capitulated to the 10 percent wage cut in early 1875. Led by rebellious Lancashire women, working women denounced deference and respectability as cowardly and unmanly. Never a part of the dialogue of deference, the women ignored the mid-century compromise between capital and labor in the old country and its language of paternalism and the family wage. Instead the women turned to alternative forms of popular radicalism as more appropriate to the ruthless character of Fall River–style corporate capitalism. They cited historic precedents of the long-term expedience of resistance—win, lose, or draw—on the relationship between labor and capital, specifically using the Preston strike in the mid-1850s as an example. The lessons of history and politics were plain to them and informed their views of masculinity.

The 16 January meeting called by women weavers reverberated with direct challenges to working-class manhood.

> Dissatisfied with the dilatory, shilly-shally and cowardly action of many of the chief conductors of our late meetings, we, the female operatives have decided to meet together and speak and act for ourselves, as we and our children are as much interested in, and are as great sufferers by, this late movement of the manufacturers. . . . Every reduction they succeed in establishing, renders us less liable to resist the next.[26]

Women shouted insults during their meeting: "Come on, you cowards! You were [be]got in fear, though you were born in England!" They were reminding the male weavers in public that they were the freeborn sons of the handloom weavers of Lancashire who had fought tenaciously and boldly for their rights.[27] They ascribed to masculinity the qualities that they themselves were exhibiting: aggressiveness and defiance. They saw New England as a new Lancashire where the old battles needed to be refought by working men and women together.

The activities of the women weavers in the 1875 strike drew upon but significantly expanded their former participation in labor protest both in Fall River and in Lancashire. They organized female textile workers across skill, ethnic, and religious lines.[28] In contrast with their more subordinated role in Lancashire labor politics, women strikers appeared regularly on public platforms with men, agitating at strike meetings, and traveling to other textile cities in southern New England to raise money. They called for the removal of all children under fourteen from the mills, and (perhaps most provocatively) they urged the mule spinners to organize into their union and support equal pay for those young women who were being recruited by the mills to operate primitive ring spinning frames.[29] Speaking for themselves as working women and for children, they defined new ways in which women workers might represent joint family interests in labor protest apart from family wage rhetoric. Their leaders formulated the successful strategy of targeting the three most obnoxious mills, a strategy that after three months forced the employers to rescind the wage cut. In all of this, women were challenging the hegemony of respectable, deferential men over the conduct of labor protest.

Before joining the women's strike, the male weavers, discouraged by past failures and current hard times, took their caps in their hands and tried once again to negotiate with their employers. On 17 January a group of male weavers approached Robert Borden, treasurer of the Crescent Mill. When Borden protested that the manufacturers suffered more than the weavers from hard times, their barely concealed anger flared briefly. As the men went away disappointed, a reporter remarked to Borden: "That's a gentlemanly set of strikers." "Yes," Borden replied, "I make them gentlemanly." The next day, the male weavers and the spinners—some perhaps persuaded by their working wives, either weavers or carders—joined the women's strike.[30]

The decision to support the women's strike and thereby tolerate their independent activism created immediate dissension among the Lancashire men of Fall River. Men who went along with the women's plucky assertiveness were accused in print of being manipulated as "Adam in the garden of old" by "babbling Amazons." As one Lancashire immigrant put it: "Let us have family altars, not demoralizing harems."[31] At issue were the prerogatives of sober and careful men weighing the possibilities and tactics of labor protest against men who might permit themselves to be misguided and potentially unmanned by emotional, rebellious Eves. But the behaviors and tactics of deferential manhood had failed in the 1870 strike. Could earlier forms of resistance be used to confront the market power of the Fall River managers? Other Lancashire men found in the women's reading of the lessons of history and politics and its gender representations a satisfying if more unruly, physical core to masculine militancy. As one man put it: "If a man cannot knock down his oppressor, you at least like to see him try; and if you cannot knock the tyrant down who would oppress you, you can at least give him a welter!"[32] Whatever the rancor or misgivings among those male weavers and spinners who reluctantly joined the strike, once it was won in April and the wage cut restored, the weavers controlled local labor politics.[33] Their aggressiveness and success had empowered labor protest and defeated the arrogant employers.

After the strike, the weavers' first goal was to make New England the "Lancashire of America" through regional associations of textile workers organized to obtain a standard list of wages and ten-hour legislation for all New England states.[34] For union mule spinners, such a strategy offered a solution to strikebreaking and the blacklist, but it also required the sharing of labor protest and the definition of its goals with the weavers and their contingent of activist women. Spinners had tolerated female participation in strike activities, such as in 1870, only as long as skilled men directed labor protest and controlled spinning. The success of the 1875 strike had created a dilemma for mule spinners. An alliance with the weavers represented the tantalizing prospect of a powerful combination against the mills that might lead to union recognition. But such an alliance might also undermine the spinners' dominance of their union and their leadership of local protest as respectable men. Still, with their own style of contention a failure, the prospect of gaining a position of power to use against the mills must have seemed irresistible to union manhood.

Defeated employers also weighed the implications of the success of the weavers' strike. During the summer of 1875, as the weavers organized throughout southern New England, the Fall River mill agents decided that continuing hard times and competition in print cloth production from small firms in Rhode Island required them once again to glut the market with cheap cloth. They cut wages to the level they had been at before the weavers' strike in January and threatened the operatives with a general lockout.[35]

The weavers responded by resurrecting the Lancashire tradition that rejected the impersonal marketplace ideology of supply and demand and substituted a moral economy with workers as active judges of right and wrong.[36] This represented an extraordinary challenge to the power of the Fall River mill agents to control production and thus dominate the market. Lancashire weavers persuaded the spinners and carders to withhold their labor collectively from the mill, not in a strike, but by deliberately taking a one-month "vacation" in August. They meant this unilateral withdrawal of their labor to be a conscious effort to influence print cloth prices for their own benefit. Weavers widely applauded a resolution that if the Fall River mills could not pay decent wages for weaving, they had no moral right to the print goods market. They agreed that if other manufacturers could pay more for the work, then "they have the best right to it," and the Fall River mills "must stand their chance of being burst up."[37] Convinced that the mills would inevitably be forced to halt overproduction, the weavers timed the shutdown for the summer months, when their cost of living was relatively low.

This defiant act denied the validity of a morally neutral market run by natural economic laws that masked the dominant position of the Fall River mills. By early August thirty-five mills and fifteen thousand operatives stood idle, while political activities, led by Fall River weavers, for a ten-hour day in Rhode Island intensified. In response, the mill owners became absolutely determined to crush at any cost this unprecedented threat to their power. The ferocity of this struggle exposed the spinners and weavers to the old charges against their manhood of brutality and recklessness.

After one month's vacation and with no increase in cloth prices even with all the Fall River mills shut down, the weavers and spinners sought to return to work, but they were met with a month-long lockout designed to starve them into submission.[38] When it was over at the end of September, the mill agents, eager to demolish any hope for a Lancashire in America, required the hungry and desperate workers to sign away their union member-ship before the mills would employ them. This was unthinkable, as one spinner expressed it: "We mun ask for oor roights the same as thae gie em in Englan'."[39] He characterized the mill agents' response as: "Noo, mind yea thae toorn upon em and insoolt em by declarin' thae'll never soobmit to the rooles here as thae ay doone in Englan'." This requirement produced a response by Lancashire people that harkened back to the bread riots of the late eighteenth century.[40]

A seventy-five-year-old agitator and former hand loom weaver reminded an emotional mass meeting of thousands about food riots in England and Wales. He told them that "as good men as you have been unable to contain themselves in times past . . . while there was bread in the town I would go and take it."[41] Hundreds of men and women strikers marched to city hall cheering and yelling, "Bread! Tyranny!" Twenty boys bore poles on which were impaled loaves of bread stolen from a bakery. An American flag hung upside-down as a distress signal preceded a sign that read "15,000 white slaves for auction" topped with a loaf of bread. To underscore their anger at being told at city hall to return to work or face as noncitizens the miseries of the state poor farm, one woman striker hit the mayor on the head with a loaf of bread. As their forebears had done, the crowd demanded to be fed and if refused threatened to take food wherever they might find it.[42] English men and women joined together out of desperation to demand from American authorities their customary right to feed their families.[43]

Lancashire people well understood the historic and cultural significance of the crowd activities, but all others in Fall River were baffled and frightened. Only editors of the con-servative press in Boston and Providence recognized the historic import of Manchester-style bread riots in New England, while labor reformer Jennie Collins appreciated the "extraordinary proof of English cool-headed control" that indicated disciplined, ritualized crowd action.[44]

The spectacle of the bread riot, the rumors and threats of arson and looting, and the emotional displays of rage and pain directed at city authorities by Lancashire working-class men and women threw labor politics into disarray. Native-born American workers and French Canadian immigrants who had supported the weavers' strike in January were confused, appalled, and alienated.[45] Labor reformers expressed embarrassment and con-cern. These cultural divisions and the crushing defeat of the vacation strategy convinced the spinners that the weavers' union with its contingent of female agitators had led the strikers into utter disaster. The employers seemed able to withstand all the resources that Lancashire workers had thrown against them.[46]

The collapse of the weavers' strategy, the loss of the strike, the disaster of the lockout, and the activities of the bread rioters laid bare the tensions over gender meanings and styles of resistance that divided textile workers in 1875. Lancashire immigrant Robert Howard, who emerged as the leader of the spinners' union, later described the tensions leading up to the vacation strike: "[E]mbers of discontent, which had been smoldering all summer, burst suddenly into a blaze." He depicted women weavers and their male allies as dangerous conflagrations that raged out of control, consuming and destroying.[47] Begging city authorities for bread, with violence as the only alternative to the horrors of the state

Figure 9.1. An artist's sketch of various events surrounding the bread riot on 27 September, *The Daily Graphic* (New York), 2 October 1875, p. 713.

poor farm, was not a manly way to behave in public or deal with employers. Uncontrolled women workers had instigated riotous actions, and their emotional, public displays of anger and dependency had emasculated the male weavers. Simon Morgan, secretary of the weavers' committee, was embarrassed by public revelations of a recent drunken spree that ended when his wife had him put into police custody.[48] The press represented the women strikers as "the most excited" and as "more violent and vulgar than the men."[49] The activism of the men and women weavers challenged the authority of spinners in labor protest, threatened male control of the spinning trade, and now undercut the respectable masculinity of spinners by association with public riot. Passion had overcome reason.[50]

Guided by a failed heritage, the efforts of weavers to wrest away the mills' market power resulted in a concerted attack on all union activity. To the dismay of the spinners, mill owners used the disorderly conduct of bread rioters to identify both the spinners and weavers as Lancashire "brutes" and later to dismiss all union men as "English and Irish scum."[51] When the strikers were forced to sign away their union memberships before returning to work in October, the weavers' union disappeared and union spinners went underground.

With the Lancashire past feminized and rendered perilous in 1875, spinners regained the leadership of labor politics in Fall River. Robert Howard, who, like many moderates, had emigrated in the early 1870s, won acceptance as a leader who first made his own men "as obedient and docile and harmonious as the parts of a mule frame."[52] Later Howard personally expunged all memory of the bread riots of 1875 from the official history of the textile workers.[53] The spinners' union adopted moderate and cautious policies that restored a proper sense of respectable manhood through stern control of its members. These policies, however, offered workers no real means to confront either the power of their employers to set wages and the pace of work or their employers' ability to replace mule spinners by hiring strikebreakers or using young women on the rapidly advancing technology of ring spinning frames. But even as new technology began to threaten their craft, the mule spinners refused to organize the female ring spinners. Instead these women (and working wives in general) became the mule spinners' enemy and nemesis. The weavers' dream of a Lancashire in America was abandoned as respectable union spinners identified unruly working women as disreputable females tainted by association with a vulnerable radical heritage.

A lost spinners' strike in 1879 demonstrated the weaknesses of abandoning the weavers' popular radicalism and regional organization. Waiting with patience and courtesy for three long years for the market to rise, spinners reminded the mill owners of their promises to rescind the wage cuts when good times returned. The mill managers, however, refused to negotiate and recruited operatives from other textile cities and from Canada. As passions against strikebreakers rose in the streets of Fall River, French Canadian men, women, and children were stoned by strikers. More important for the spinners, the mills increased the numbers of ring spinning frames run by women and boys. The reality of unskilled ring spinners producing quantities of warp yarn in the Pocasset Mill during the 1879 strike prepared the spinners to accept arguments in favor of "thinning" the labor market by the withdrawal of all women or at least all married women from factory work.[54]

In the aftermath of that struggle, Robert Howard brought social reformer Lillian Chace Wyman to Fall River to interview blacklisted spinners. They visited the home of one elderly English spinner, "Mr. W." He complained to Wyman about his experience with the blacklist as an assault on his manhood. As with many spinners, Mr. W had been told only that he was being fired for poor work, forcing him to spend weeks seeking another place, only to be discharged again and again until by chance he discovered his name on the blacklist in some mill office. He was relieved, however, to find it was in retaliation for union activity and not a judgment on his ability to spin. As Mr. W put it: "You may think it a weakness in me but that pleased me, and it pleased the old woman [his wife] and made her proud to think they couldn't find fault with me."[55]

Mr. W had also been proud of his activities as a union leader in Lancashire and spoke with great bitterness about the strikebreakers of New England who had defeated the 1879 strike. After months of being blacklisted, poverty forced him to sign away his union membership and return to work, promising to remain silent about grievances and never again participate in strikes. This act signaled a shameful abandonment of the traditions of union activity that formed the basis of his resistance. Remembering the sting of this, he sprang to his feet and cried out: "I'm humiliated,—I'm less of a man than I was!" Mr. W's sense of humiliation and loss of manhood also reflected the defeat of Lancashire militancy that was the aftermath of that bitter decade of class struggle in Fall River.

In spite of a keen sense of loss among some spinners, such as Mr. W, who cherished their militant Lancashire heritage as essential to their manliness and who as strikers in 1870 and 1875 had rejected market forces as the measure of a man's wage, the national mule spinners' union, organized in 1880, advocated a family wage paid to respectable and dispassionate union men. Adopting as their motto "Defense Not Defiance," the union endorsed the exclusive control of mule spinning by men, the acceptance of market forces to determine wage levels with special provision for skilled workers, and the abandonment of radical Lancashire political traditions for American-style electoral politics.

When union men embraced partisan politics and labor reform policies as the key to the resolution of worker grievances, the involvement of disfranchised women in labor politics appeared not only undesirable but irrelevant. Womanhood connoted political isolation and dependence, while respectable manhood operated within the new American economic and political context. The national mule spinners union became central to New England labor politics and to the development of the American Federation of Labor in the late nineteenth century.[56] It offered protection to mule spinners but abandoned coalitions with weavers. As male unionists from Lancashire withdrew from political collaboration with women workers, they defended their cultural identity by building highly nationalistic but sex-segregated recreational activities such as cricket and soccer clubs, and joined fraternal organizations such as the Odd Fellows, the Foresters, and the Sons of St. George.[57]

The struggle in Fall River over the meanings of masculinity took place in two overlapping arenas: the working-class community and the textile mill. After years of defeat, the weavers had seized control of labor politics and struck defiant blows at the mills' control of the national market. Initial success had repudiated the past failures of respectable men, but later this strategy produced a humiliating defeat and the destruction of established organizations. Dissension within the working-class community seemed as divisive to the cause of labor politics as the power of the mills.[58] The key issue that divided workers was the meaning of being a Lancashire workingman in America and the ensuing style of resistance.

Spinners and weavers in New England went their separate ways. Memories of the defeat in 1875 haunted strikes in Fall River throughout the late nineteenth century and restricted the potential of activist women weavers, their male allies, and Lancashire-style militancy.[59] These struggles over the appropriate role of men and women in labor protest clearly demonstrate both female agency and the significance of gender to working-class politics and culture. It is important to historicize gender for both sexes and to identify those moments of conflict, choice, and possibility before gender meanings hardened and sexual difference became rigidly embedded in discourse and institutions. In doing so, historians can uncover how and why the meanings of masculinity and femininity are made and remade in a changing world.

Notes

My thanks to Ava Baron, Donna Gabaccia, Bruce Laurie, John Cumbler, Tessie Liu, Joy Parr, Hal Benenson, Joe Trotter, Sonya Rose, Keith McClelland, and an anonymous reader for *Gender & History* for their helpful criticism of earlier versions.

1. For a critique of essentialism as the basis of two studies of masculinity in the workplace, see Steven Maynard, "Rough Work and Rugged Men: The Social Construction of Masculinity in Working-Class History," *Labour/Le Travail* 23 (spring 1989): 159–69.

2. One good example is the introduction to Michael Roper and John Tosh, eds., *Manful Assertions: Masculinities in Britain since 1800* (London: Routledge, 1991).

3. Personal correspondence with Hal Benenson, 28 August 1991.

4. For a critique of studies of ethnic groups that ignore issues of gender, see Donna Gabaccia, "The Transplanted: Women and the Family in Immigrant America," *Social Science History* 12 (fall 1988): 243–53, and Donna Gabaccia, "Immigrant Women: Nowhere at Home," *Journal of American Ethnic History* 10 (summer 1991): 59–85.

5. Fall River became the leading post–Civil War center of the lucrative print cloth trade, which shifted the balance of wealth and productive power from northern Massachusetts cities such as Lowell to southeastern New England. Unlike many immigrants to the United States, Lancashire immigrants came with industrial skills and class consciousness. Roland Berthoff's characterization of British immigrants as politically conservative in *British Immigrants in Industrial America, 1790–1950* (Cambridge, Mass.: Harvard University Press, 1953) has been contradicted by John T. Cumbler, *Working-Class Community in Industrial America: Work, Leisure, and Struggle in Two Industrial Cities* (Westport, Conn.: Greenwood Press, 1979), and Cynthia Shelton, *The Mills of Manayunk: Industrialization and Social Conflict in the Philadelphia Region, 1787–1837* (Baltimore: Johns Hopkins University Press, 1986), which trace the transfer of Lancashire radicalism by nineteenth-century textile workers. See also Mary H. Blewett, "Traditions and Customs of Lancashire Popular Radicalism in Late Nineteenth-Century Industrial America," *International Labor and Working-class History* 42 (fall 1992): 5–19.

6. Virginia Yans-McLaughlin, ed., *Immigration Reconsidered* (New York: Oxford University Press, 1990), and Dirk Hoerder, ed., *"Struggle a Hard Battle": Essays on Working-class Immigrants* (DeKalb: Southern Illinois University Press, 1986).

7. This conclusion is based on preliminary data on Fall River's Ward 2 in the 1870 United States Census of Population manuscripts. On kin networks, see Michael Anderson, *Family Structure in Nineteenth Century Lancashire* (Cambridge: Cambridge University Press, 1971). On the relationship of men and women in Lancashire working-class culture, see Harold Benenson, "The 'Family Wage' and Working Women's Consciousness in Britain, 1880–1914," *Politics and Society* 19 (1991): 71–118.

8. For recent debates among English historians over the emergence of reformism and respectability, see Neville Kirk, *The Growth of Working Class Reformism in Mid-Victorian England* (Urbana: University of Illinois Press, 1985). Some of the Lancashire immigrants to Fall River clearly remembered the Preston strike, where traditions of radical politics challenged local paternalists; H. I. Dutton and J. E. King, *"Ten Per Cent and No Surrender": The Preston Strike, 1853–1854* (Cambridge: Cambridge University Press, 1981).

9. Thomas Russell Smith, *The Cotton Textile Industry of Fall River, Massachusetts* (New York, 1944), 50–65, and Frederick M. Peck and Henry H. Earl, *Fall River and Its Industries* (Fall River, 1877), 68.

10. Charlotte Erickson, "The Encouragement of Emigration by British Trade Unions, 1850–1900," *Population Studies* 3 (1949): 248–73. On the small size of Lancashire firms, see William Lazonick, "Competition, Specialization, and Industrial Decline," *Journal of Economic History* 41 (March 1981): 31–38. On midcentury labor-capital relations, see Patrick Joyce, *Work, Society and Politics: The Culture of the Factory in Later Victorian England* (Brighton: Harvester Press, 1980).

11. My argument emphasizes the instrumentality of deference, as does Neville Kirk's critique of Patrick Joyce's work in the *Bulletin of the Society for the Study of Labour History* 42 (spring 1981): 41–43.

12. Mariana Valverde, "'Giving the Female a Domestic Turn': The Social, Legal and Moral Regulation of Women's Work in British Cotton Mills, 1820–1850," *Journal of Social History* 21 (spring 1988): 619–34.

13. H. A. Turner, *Trade Union Growth, Structure, and Policy* (Toronto: University of Toronto Press, 1962), 108–68. See also Carol E. Morgan, "Women, Work and Consciousness in the Mid-nineteenth-century English Cotton Industry," *Social History* 17 (January 1992): 23–41.

14. These acts, observed by state police and reported in the press, were illegal under English law. On the 1870 strike, see Massachusetts Bureau of Labor Statistics (hereafter MBLS), *Second Annual Report* (1871): 47–93; *Fall River News*, July–September 1870; *Boston Herald*, 26–30 August 1870.

15. Keith McClelland, "Some Thoughts on Masculinity and the 'Representative Artisan' in Britain, 1850–1880," *Gender & History* 1 (summer 1989):164–77. If British working-class men represented themselves as independent and respectable, then working-class women could be represented as dependent and disreputable. Such representation seemed of tactical use to the spinners' union in 1870.

16. MBLS (1871), 68–74, 84.

17. *Fall River News*, 8 August 1870.

18. The Lancashire immigrant Robert Howard, who arrived in Fall River in 1873 and later became the secretary of the mule spinners' union, later wrote an overview of the New England textile trades that cited activities that "nearly caused a riot" in 1870, and commended the strikers when "reason triumphed over passion." "Progress in the Textile Trades," in George E. McNeill, ed., *The Labor Movement: The Problem of To-Day* (Boston, 1887), 219.

19. How many spinners' wives were weavers or carders is impossible to know; population census manuscripts in 1870 and 1880 identify all textile operatives simply by "works in a cotton mill." Women, married and single, represented about half of the Fall River weaving workforce of eight thousand in 1875.

20. MBLS (1871), 476–81.

21. This story was told during a meeting of rebellious female weavers who were calling on their male coworkers to use their "horns." *Fall River News*, 18 January 1875.

22. MBLS (1871), 482; MBLS (1882), 348–54.

23. MBLS (1871), 49, 469–70, 476–86; MBLS (1882), 209, 219, 254–60.

24. *Labor Journal*, 26 September and 3 October 1874.

25. According to one observer who was personally acquainted with these Lancashire activists in Fall River, "almost without exception these men were the sons of English Chartists." Jonathan Thayer Lincoln, *The Factory* (Boston: Houghton Mifflin, 1912), 95. Memories of their own mothers' and grandmothers' activism may have inspired Lancashire women.

26. *Fall River News*, 18 January 1875.

27. Ibid. A committee of four women met with the Weavers' Union after the meeting to convince them to join the strike.

28. Women who dominated carding operations had organized over one thousand members in late 1874; Howard, "Progress in the Textile Trades," 221–22. The women's meetings included weavers and carders, native-born Yankees, and French Canadian immigrant women as well as Lancashire women; *Fall River News*, 18 Jan., 22 Feb., 8 and 17 March 1875. By the mid-1870s, the work force in Fall River was 33.9% English immigrants, 25.2% native-born Americans, 20.7% Irish immigrants, and 17.3% French Canadian immigrants. The figures are from 1878, cited in MBLS (1882), 204–5.

29. As one young striker put it: "Women should have as good pay as men. Female operatives ought to set a high value on themselves." *Boston Herald*, 25 April 1875. See also *Fall River News*, 15 and 22 Feb., 1, 8, 13, 15 and 17 Mar., 5 April 1875; *Boston Herald*, 1 Feb., 25 April 1875. For intriguing but undeveloped evidence on women's involvement in Lancashire radical politics, see James Epstein, "Understanding the Cap of Liberty: Symbolic Practice and Social Conflict in Early Nineteenth-Century England," *Past and Present* 122 (February 1989): 75–118, and Dorothy Thompson, "Women and Nineteenth-Century Radical Politics: A Lost Dimension," in *The Rights and Wrongs of Women*, ed. Juliet Mitchell and Ann Oakley (Penguin Books, 1976), 112–38.

30. *Boston Globe*, 18 January 1875.

31. *Fall River News*, 22 Feb. 1875. The writer was Thomas Stephenson, a labor reformer from Lawrence, Massachusetts, who had witnessed the Preston strike and supported the spinners' approach to labor politics.

32. The speaker was Henry Sevey, a Lancashire immigrant who published the *Labor Journal* in Fall River and supported the weavers' strike. *Fall River News*, 22 Feb. 1875. "Welter" is defined in the *Oxford English Dictionary* XII (1961), 311, as "a state of confusion, upheaval, or turmoil," a usage that dates from around 1870.

33. In the official history of the strike written by "A Workingman" and published by the Weavers' Union in the spring of 1875, tensions among strikers over deference and defiance shaped the language of the document. The role of women weavers in initiating the strike was acknowledged, but no female names or activities appeared in the text. The political importance of resistance to wage cuts and the strike's successful strategy was credited to the male leadership who used the publication to attempt to pressure the employers into accepting wage arbitration. *History of the Fall River Strike*, by A Workingman (Fall River, 1875).

34. *Fall River News*, 5 April 1875; *History of the Fall River Strike*, 25–29.

35. *Fall River News*, 19, 22, 24, and 30 July 1875.

36. I agree with William Reddy that "not learning the rules of the game . . . refusing to accept them [is] the true meaning of Thompson's notion of a 'moral economy.'" "The Textile Trade and the Language of the Crowd at Rouen, 1752–1871," *Past and Present* 74 (February 1977): 88.

37. *Fall River News*, 2 August 1875.

38. Even sympathetic observers of the vacation strike warned that a shutdown in Fall River alone would have no impact on the severely depressed market; *Providence Sun*, 7 and 14 Aug. 1875.

39. The spinner was a fifty-year-old emigrant from Preston in 1857; *New York Herald*, 26 Sept. 1875.

40. For the distinctive role of British women as instigators of food riots, see Malcolm I. Thomis and Jennifer Grimmet, *Women in Protest, 1800–1850* (New York: St. Martin's Press, 1982), chapter 2. For the food riot as a pre-industrial, mixed-sex event, see John Bohstedt, "Gender, Household and Community Politics: Women in English Riot 1790–1810," *Past and Present* 120 (August 1988): 88–122.

41. *New York Herald*, 25 Sept. 1875. On the importance of memories about the triumph of the customary over the market, see Andrew Charlesworth and Adrian J. Randall, "Morals Markets and the English Crowd in 1766," *Past and Present* 114 (1987): 200–13.

42. *Fall River News*, 27 and 29 September, 2 Oct. 1875; *New York Times*, 28 and 29 Sept. 1875; *New York Herald*, 25–29 Sept. 1875; *Providence Journal*, 29 Sept. 1875. For a review by E. P. Thompson of the uses of the moral economy by historians, see *Customs in Common* (New York: New Press, 1991), 259–351. I agree with John Bohstedt's call for an examination of the ways food riots acted as responses to changing economic and political contexts; "The Moral Economy and the Discipline of Historical Context," *Journal of Social History* 26 (Winter 1992): 265–84.

43. Some of the most radical weavers were men perhaps unused to paternalism and deference who had emigrated in the 1850s. Before 1875, however, they had followed the leadership of the spinners.

44. *Providence Journal*, 29 Sept. 1875; *Commercial Bulletin*, 2 Oct. 1875; *Boston Globe*, 4 Oct. 1875.

45. *L'Echo du Canada*, 2 Oct. 1875; *Fall River News*, 13, 16 and 19 Oct. 1875; *New York Herald*, 13, 16 and 19 Oct. 1875.

46. Unrevealed until 1878 and 1879 were the heavy financial losses sustained by the mills in 1875 that led to bankruptcies and charges of embezzlement as the result of speculation in cotton futures.

47. Howard, "Progress in the Textile Trades," 223.

48. *Boston Herald, Fall River News*, 11 Sept. 1875.

49. *Fall River News, Boston Globe, New York Times*, 29 Sept. 1875.

50. Howard, "Progress in the Textile Trades," 219.

51. On the mill owners' attitudes and insults, MBLS (1882), 341.

52. *Boston Globe*, 18 Aug. 1879.

53. Howard, "Progress in the Textile Trades," 223. Patrick Joyce's distinctly masculinist populism in *Visions of the People: Industrial England and the Question of Class, 1840–1914* (Cambridge: Cambridge University Press, 1991) is based in part on his reading of *The Cotton Factory Times*, whose editors eagerly accepted Howard's version of union politics in New England.

54. On the 1879 strike, *Boston Herald*, 16 June–7 Oct. 1879; *Boston Globe*, 13 June–25 Aug. 1879; and MBLS (1880), 53–68.

55. Lillian Chace Wyman, "Studies of Factory Life," *Atlantic Monthly* (November 1888): 605–12.

56. Cumbler, *Working-Class Community*, 173–94. As head of the Mule Spinners Union, Robert Howard was elected to the Massachusetts legislature in the 1880s as a labor reformer and became a major figure in the Knights of Labor and the AFL.

57. Workingmen from Lancashire with Irish Catholic backgrounds were absorbed into Democratic party politics in Fall River and into Catholic fraternal and charitable organizations, while French Canadian workers withdrew into religious and cultural activities in their own communities.

58. Isaac Cohen's otherwise fine study, "American Management and British Labor: Lancashire Immigrant Spinners in Industrial New England," *Journal for the Comparative Study of Society and History* 27 (1985): 608–50, ignores the political conflicts between spinners and weavers.

59. The last strike in Fall River that divided Lancashire spinners and weavers occurred in 1894.

10

Miscegenation Law, Court Cases, and Ideologies of "Race" in Twentieth-Century America

Peggy Pascoe

On 21 March 1921 Joe Kirby took his wife, Mayellen, to court. The Kirbys had been married for seven years, and Joe wanted out. Ignoring the usual option of divorce, he asked for an annulment, charging that his marriage had been invalid from its very beginning because Arizona law prohibited marriages between "persons of Caucasian blood, or their descendants" and "negroes, Mongolians or Indians, and their descendants." Joe Kirby claimed that while he was "a person of the Caucasian blood," his wife, Mayellen, was "a person of negro blood."[1]

Although Joe Kirby's charges were rooted in a well-established—and tragic—tradition of American miscegenation law, his court case quickly disintegrated into a definitional dispute that bordered on the ridiculous. The first witness in the case was Joe's mother, Tula Kirby, who gave her testimony in Spanish through an interpreter. Joe's lawyer laid out the case by asking Tula Kirby a few seemingly simple questions:

> *Joe's lawyer:* To what race do you belong?
> *Tula Kirby:* Mexican.
> *Joe's lawyer:* Are you white or have you Indian blood?
> *Tula Kirby:* I have no Indian blood.
> *Joe's lawyer:* Do you know the defendant [Mayellen] Kirby?
> *Tula Kirby:* Yes.
> *Joe's lawyer:* To what race does she belong?
> *Kirby:* Negro.

Then the cross-examination began.

> *Mayellen's lawyer:* Who was your father?
> *Tula Kirby:* Jose Romero.
> *Mayellen's lawyer:* Was he a Spaniard?
> *Tula Kirby:* Yes, a Mexican.
> *Mayellen's lawyer:* Was he born in Spain?
> *Tula Kirby:* No, he was born in Sonora.
> *Mayellen's lawyer:* And who was your mother?
> *Tula Kirby:* Also in Sonora.
> *Mayellen's lawyer:* Was she a Spaniard?
> *Tula Kirby:* She was on her father's side.
> *Mayellen's lawyer:* And what on her mother's side?
> *Tula Kirby:* Mexican.
> *Mayellen's lawyer:* What do you mean by Mexican, Indian, a native [?]
> *Tula Kirby:* I don't know what is meant by Mexican.
> *Mayellen's lawyer:* A native of Mexico?

161

Tula Kirby: Yes, Sonora, all of us.
Mayellen's lawyer: Who was your grandfather on your father's side?
Tula Kirby: He was a Spaniard.
Mayellen's lawyer: Who was he?
Tula Kirby: His name was Ignacio Quevas.
Mayellen's lawyer: Where was he born?
Tula Kirby: That I don't know. He was my grandfather.
Mayellen's lawyer: How do you know he was a [S]paniard then?
Tula Kirby: Because he told me ever since I had knowledge that he was a Spaniard.

Next the questioning turned to Tula's opinion about Mayellen Kirby's racial identity.

Mayellen's lawyer: You said Mrs. Mayellen Kirby was a negress. What do you know about Mrs. Kirby's family?
Tula Kirby: I distinguish her by her color and the hair; that is all I do know.[2]

The second witness in the trial was Joe Kirby, and by the time he took the stand, the people in the courtroom knew they were in murky waters. When Joe's lawyer opened with the question "What race do *you* belong to?" Joe answered, "Well . . . ," and paused, while Mayellen's lawyer objected to the question on the ground that it called for a conclusion by the witness. "Oh, no," said the judge, "it is a matter of pedigree." Eventually allowed to answer the question, Joe said, "I belong to the white race I suppose." Under cross-examination, he described his father as having been of the "Irish race," although he admitted, "I never knew any one of his people."[3]

Stopping at the brink of this morass, Joe's lawyer rested his case. He told the judge he had established that Joe was "Caucasian." Mayellen's lawyer scoffed, claiming that Joe had "failed utterly to prove his case" and arguing that "[Joe's] mother has admitted that. She has [testified] that she only claims a quarter Spanish blood; the rest of it is native blood." At this point the court intervened. "I know," said the judge, "but that does not signify anything."[4]

From the Decline and Fall of Scientific Racism to an Understanding of Modernist Racial Ideology

The Kirbys' case offers a fine illustration of Evelyn Brooks Higginbotham's observation that although most Americans are sure they know "race" when they see it, very few can offer a definition of the term. Partly for this reason, the questions of what "race" signifies and what signifies "race" are as important for scholars today as they were for the participants in *Kirby v. Kirby* seventy-five years ago.[5] Historians have a long—and recently a distinguished—record of exploring this question.[6] Beginning in the 1960s, one notable group charted the rise and fall of scientific racism among American intellectuals. Today their successors, more likely to be schooled in social than intellectual history, trace the social construction of racial ideologies, including the idea of "whiteness," in a steadily expanding range of contexts.[7]

Their work has taught us a great deal about racial thinking in American history. We can trace the growth of racism among antebellum immigrant workers and free-soil northern Republicans; we can measure its breadth in late-nineteenth-century segregation and the immigration policies of the 1920s. We can follow the rise of Anglo-Saxonism from Manifest Destiny through the Spanish-American War and expose the appeals to white supremacy in woman suffrage speeches. We can relate all these developments (and more) to the growth and elaboration of scientific racist attempts to use biological characteristics to scout for racial hierarchies in social life, levels of civilization, even language.

Yet the range and richness of these studies all but end with the 1920s. In contrast to historians of the nineteenth- and early-twentieth-century United States, historians of the nation in the mid- to late twentieth century seem to focus on racial ideologies only when they are advanced by the far Right (as in the Ku Klux Klan) or by racialized groups themselves (as in the Harlem Renaissance or black nationalist movements). To the extent that there is a framework for surveying mainstream twentieth-century American racial ideologies, it is inherited from the classic histories that tell of the post-1920s decline and fall of scientific racism. Their final pages link the demise of scientific racism to the rise of a vanguard of social scientists led by the cultural anthropologist Franz Boas: When modern social science emerges, racism runs out of intellectual steam. In the absence of any other narrative, this forms the basis for a commonly held but rarely examined intellectual trickle-down theory in which the attack on scientific racism emerges in universities in the 1920s and eventually, if belatedly, spreads to courts in the 1940s and 1950s and to government policy in the 1960s and 1970s.

A close look at such incidents as the *Kirby* case, however, suggests a rather different historical trajectory, one that recognizes that the legal system does more than just reflect social or scientific ideas about race; it also produces and reproduces them.[8] By following a trail marked by four miscegenation cases—the seemingly ordinary *Kirby v. Kirby* (1922) and *Estate of Monks* (1941) and the pathbreaking *Perez v. Lippold* (1948) and *Loving v. Virginia* (1967)—this article will examine the relation between modern social science, miscegenation law, and twentieth-century American racial ideologies, focusing less on the decline of scientific racism and more on the emergence of new racial ideologies.

In exploring these issues, it helps to understand that the range of nineteenth-century racial ideologies was much broader than scientific racism. Accordingly, I have chosen to use the term *racialism* to designate an ideological complex that other historians often describe with the terms *race* or *racist*. I intend the term *racialism* to be broad enough to cover a wide range of nineteenth-century ideas, from the biologically marked categories scientific racists employed to the more amorphous ideas George M. Fredrickson has so aptly called "romantic racialism."[9] Used in this way, the notion of racialism helps counter the tendency of twentieth-century observers to perceive nineteenth-century ideas as biologically "determinist" in some simple sense. To racialists (including scientific racists), the important point was not that biology determined culture (indeed, the split between the two was only dimly perceived), but that race, understood as an indivisible essence that included not only biology but also culture, morality, and intelligence, was a compellingly significant factor in history and society.

My argument is this: During the 1920s, American racialism was challenged by several emerging ideologies, all of which depended on a modern split between biology and culture. Between the 1920s and the 1960s, those competing ideologies were winnowed down to the single, powerfully persuasive belief that the eradication of racism depends on the deliberate nonrecognition of race. I will call that belief *modernist racial ideology* to echo the self-conscious "modernism" of social scientists, writers, artists, and cultural rebels of the early twentieth century. When historians mention this phenomenon, they usually label it "antiracist" or "egalitarian" and describe it as in stark contrast to the "racism" of its predecessors. But in the new legal scholarship called critical race theory, this same ideology, usually referred to as "color blindness," is criticized by those who recognize that it, like other racial ideologies, can be turned to the service of oppression.[10]

Modernist racial ideology has been widely accepted; indeed, it compels nearly as much adherence in the late-twentieth-century United States as racialism did in the late nineteenth century. It is therefore important to see it not as what it claims to be—the nonideological end of racism—but as a racial ideology of its own, whose history shapes many of today's arguments about the meaning of race in American society.

The Legacy of Racialism and the *Kirby* Case

Although it is probably less familiar to historians than, say, school segregation law, mis-cegenation law is an ideal place to study both the legacy of nineteenth-century racialism and the emergence of modern racial ideologies.[11] Miscegenation laws, in force from the 1660s through the 1960s, were among the longest-lasting of American racial restrictions. They both reflected and produced significant shifts in American racial thinking. Although the first miscegenation laws had been passed in the colonial period, it was not until after the demise of slavery that they began to function as the ultimate sanction of the American sys-tem of white supremacy. They burgeoned along with the rise of segregation and the early-twentieth-century devotion to "white purity." At one time or another, forty-one American colonies and states enacted them; they blanketed western as well as southern states.[12]

By the early twentieth century, miscegenation laws were so widespread that they formed a virtual road map to American legal conceptions of race. Laws that had originally prohib-ited marriages between whites and African Americans (and, very occasionally, American Indians) were extended to cover a much wider range of groups. Eventually, twelve states targeted American Indians, fourteen Asian Americans (Chinese, Japanese, and Koreans), and nine "Malays" (or Filipinos). In Arizona, the *Kirby* case was decided under categories first adopted in a 1901 law that prohibited whites from marrying "negroes, Mongolians or Indians"; in 1931, "Malays" and "Hindus" were added to this list.[13]

Although many historians assume that miscegenation laws enforced American taboos against interracial sex, marriage, more than sex, was the legal focus.[14] Some states did for-bid both interracial sex and interracial marriage, but nearly twice as many targeted only marriage. Because marriage carried with it social respectability and economic benefits that were routinely denied to couples engaged in illicit sex, appeals courts adjudicated the legal issue of miscegenation at least as frequently in civil cases about marriage and divorce, inheritance, or child legitimacy as in criminal cases about sexual misconduct.[15]

By the time the *Kirby* case was heard, lawyers and judges approached miscegenation cases with working assumptions built on decades of experience. There had been a flurry of challenges to the laws during Reconstruction, but courts quickly fended off arguments that miscegenation laws violated the Fourteenth Amendment guarantee of "equal protection." Beginning in the late 1870s, judges declared that the laws were constitutional because they covered all racial groups "equally."[16] Judicial justifications reflected the momentum toward racial categorization built into the nineteenth-century legal system and buttressed by the racialist conviction that everything from culture, morality, and intelligence to heredity could be understood in terms of race.

From the 1880s until the 1920s, lawyers whose clients had been caught in the snare of miscegenation laws knew better than to challenge the constitutionality of the laws or to dis-pute the perceived necessity for racial categorization; these were all but guaranteed to be losing arguments. A defender's best bet was to do what Mayellen Kirby's lawyer tried to do: to persuade a judge (or jury) that one particular individual's racial classification was in error. Lawyers who defined their task in these limited terms occasionally succeeded, but even then the deck was stacked against them. Wielded by judges and juries who believed that setting racial boundaries was crucial to the maintenance of ordered society, the criteria used to determine who fit in which category were more notable for their malleability than for their logical consistency. Genealogy, appearance, claims to identity, or that mystical quality "blood"—any of these would do.[17]

In Arizona, Judge Samuel L. Pattee demonstrated that malleability in deciding the *Kirby* case. Although Mayellen Kirby's lawyer maintained that Joe Kirby "appeared" to be an Indian, the judge insisted that parentage, not appearance, was the key to Joe's racial classification:

> Mexicans are classed as of the Caucasian Race. They are descendants, supposed to be, at least of the Spanish conquerors of that country, and unless it can be shown that they are mixed up with some other races, why the presumption is that they are descendants of the Caucasian race.[18]

While the judge decided that ancestry determined that Joe Kirby was "Caucasian," he simply assumed that Mayellen Kirby was "Negro." Mayellen Kirby sat silent through the entire trial; she was spoken about and spoken for but never allowed to speak herself. There was no testimony about her ancestry; her race was assumed to rest in her visible physical characteristics. Neither of the lawyers bothered to argue over Mayellen's racial designation. As Joe's lawyer later explained,

> The learned and discriminating judge . . . had the opportunity to gaze upon the dusky countenance of the appellant [Mayellen Kirby] and could not and did not fail to observe the distinguishing characteristics of the African race and blood.[19]

In the end, the judge accepted the claim that Joe Kirby was "Caucasian" and Mayellen Kirby "Negro" and held that the marriage violated Arizona miscegenation law; he granted Joe Kirby his annulment. In so doing, the judge resolved the miscegenation drama by adding a patriarchal moral to the white supremacist plot. As long as miscegenation laws regulated marriage more than sex, it proved easy for white men involved with women of color to avoid the social and economic responsibilities they would have carried in legally sanctioned marriages with white women. By granting Joe Kirby an annulment rather than a divorce, the judge not only denied the validity of the marriage while it had lasted but also in effect excused Joe Kirby from his obligation to provide economic support to a divorced wife.[20]

For her part, Mayellen Kirby had nothing left to lose. She and her lawyer appealed to the Arizona Supreme Court. This time they threw caution to the winds. Taking a first step toward the development of modern racial ideologies, they moved beyond their carefully limited argument about Joe's individual racial classification to challenge the entire racial logic of miscegenation law. The Arizona statute provided a tempting target for their attack, for under its "descendants" provision, a person of "mixed blood" could not legally marry anyone. Pointing this out, Mayellen Kirby's lawyer argued that the law must therefore be unconstitutional. He failed to convince the court. The appeals court judge brushed aside such objections. The argument that the law was unconstitutional, the judge held,

> is an attack . . . [Mayellen Kirby] is not entitled to make for the reason that there is no evidence that she is other than of the black race. . . . It will be time enough to pass on the question she raises . . . when it is presented by some one whose rights are involved or affected.[21]

The Culturalist Challenge to Racialism

By the 1920s, refusals to recognize the rights of African American women had become conventional in American law. So had refusals to recognize obvious inconsistencies in legal racial classification schemes. Minions of racialism, judges, juries, and experts sometimes quarreled over specifics, but they agreed on the overriding importance of making and enforcing racial classifications.

Lawyers in miscegenation cases therefore neither needed nor received much courtroom assistance from experts. In another legal arena, citizenship and naturalization law, the use of experts, nearly all of whom advocated some version of scientific racism, was much more common. Ever since the 1870s, naturalization lawyers had relied on scientific racists to help them decide which racial and ethnic groups met the United States naturalization requirement of being "white" persons. But in a series of cases heard in the first two decades of the twentieth century, this strategy backfired. When judges found themselves drawn into a heated scientific debate on the question of whether "Caucasian" was the same as "white," the United States Supreme Court settled the question by discarding the experts and reverting to what the justices called the opinion of the "common man."[22]

In both naturalization and miscegenation cases, judges relied on the basic agreement between popular and expert (scientific racist) versions of the racialism that permeated turn-of-the-century American society. But even as judges promulgated the common sense of racialism, the ground was shifting beneath their feet. By the 1920s, lawyers in miscegenation cases were beginning to glimpse the courtroom potential of arguments put forth by a pioneering group of self-consciously "modern" social scientists willing to challenge racialism head on.

Led by cultural anthropologist Franz Boas, these emerging experts have long stood as the heroes of histories of the decline of scientific racism (which is often taken to stand for racism as a whole). But for modern social scientists, the attack on racialism was not so much an end in itself as a function of the larger goal of establishing "culture" as a central social science paradigm. Intellectually and institutionally, Boas and his followers staked their claim to academic authority on their conviction that human difference and human history were best explained by culture. Because they interpreted character, morality, and social organization as cultural rather than racial phenomena and because they were determined to explore, name, and claim the field of cultural analysis for social scientists, particularly cultural anthropologists, sociologists, and social psychologists, they are perhaps best described as culturalists.[23]

To consolidate their power, culturalists had to challenge the scientific racist paradigms they hoped to displace. Two of the arguments they made were of particular significance for the emergence of modern racial ideologies. The first was the argument that the key notion of racialism—race—made no biological sense.

This argument allowed culturalists to take aim at a very vulnerable target. For most of the nineteenth century, scientific racists had solved disputes about who fit into which racial categories by subdividing the categories. As a result, the number of scientifically recognized races had increased so steadily that by 1911, when the anthropologist Daniel Folkmar compiled the intentionally definitive *Dictionary of Races and Peoples*, he recognized "45 races or peoples among immigrants coming to the United States." Folkmar's was only one of several competing schemes, and culturalists delighted in pointing out the discrepancies between them, showing that scientific racists could not agree on such seemingly simple matters as how many races there were or what criteria—blood, skin color, hair type—best indicated race.[24]

In their most dramatic mode, culturalists went so far as to insist that physical characteristics were completely unreliable indicators of race; in biological terms, they insisted, race must be considered indeterminable. Thus, in an influential encyclopedia article on "race" published in the early thirties, Boas insisted that "it is not possible to assign with certainty any one individual to a definite group." Perhaps the strongest statement of this kind came from Julian Huxley and A. C. Haddon, British scientists who maintained that "the term *race* as applied to human groups should be dropped from the vocabulary of science." Since

Huxley was one of the first culturalists trained as a biologist, his credentials added luster to his opinion. In this and other forms, the culturalist argument that race was biologically indeterminable captured the attention of both contemporaries and later historians.[25]

Historians have paid much less attention to a second and apparently incompatible argument put forth by culturalists. It started from the other end of the spectrum, maintaining not that there was no such thing as biological race but that race was nothing more than biology. Since culturalists considered biology of remarkably little importance, consigning race to the realm of biology pushed it out of the picture. Thus Boas ended his article on race by concluding that although it remained "likely" enough that scientific study of the "anatomical differences between the races" might reveal biological influences on the formation of personality, "the study of cultural forms shows that such differences are altogether irrelevant as compared with the powerful influence of the cultural environment in which the group lives."[26]

Following this logic, the contrast between important and wide-reaching culture and unimportant (but biological) race stood as the cornerstone of many culturalist arguments. Thus the cultural anthropologist Ruth Benedict began her influential 1940 book *Race: Science and Politics* with an analysis of "what race is *not*," including language, customs, intelligence, character, and civilization. In a 1943 pamphlet coauthored with Gene Weltfish and addressed to the general public, she explained that real "racial differences" occurred only in "nonessentials such as texture of head hair, amount of body hair, shape of the nose or head, or color of the eyes and the skin." Drawing on these distinctions, Benedict argued that race was a scientific "fact," but that racism, which she defined as "the dogma that the hope of civilization depends upon eliminating some races and keeping others pure," was no more than a "modern superstition."[27]

Culturalists set these two seemingly contradictory depictions of race—the argument that biological race was nonsense and the argument that race was merely biology—right beside each other. The contradiction mattered little to them. Both arguments effectively contracted the range of racialist thinking, and both helped break conceptual links between race and character, morality, psychology, and language. By showing that one after another of these phenomena depended more on environment and training than on biology, culturalists moved each one out of the realm of race and into the province of culture, widening the modern split between culture and biology. Boas opened his article on race by staking out this position. "The term race is often used loosely to indicate groups of men differing in appearance, language, or culture," he wrote, but in his analysis, it would apply "solely to the biological grouping of human types."[28]

In adopting this position, culturalist intellectuals took a giant step away from popular common sense on the issue of race. Recognizing—even at times celebrating—this gap between themselves and the public, they devoted much of their work to dislodging popular racial assumptions. They saw the public as lamentably behind the times and sadly prone to race "prejudice," and they used their academic credentials to insist that racial categories not only did not rest on common sense, but made little sense at all.[29]

The *Monks* Case and the Making of Modern Racial Ideologies

This, of course, was just what lawyers challenging miscegenation laws wanted to hear. Because culturalist social scientists could offer their arguments with an air of scientific and academic authority that might persuade judges, attorneys began to invite them to appear as expert witnesses. But when culturalists appeared in court, they entered an arena where their argument for the biological indeterminacy of race was shaped in ways neither they nor the lawyers who recruited them could control.

Take, for example, the seemingly curious trial of Marie Antoinette Monks of San Diego, California, decided in the Superior Court of San Diego County in 1939. By all accounts, Marie Antoinette Monks was a woman with a clear eye for her main chance. In the early 1930s she had entranced and married a man named Allan Monks, potential heir to a Boston fortune. Shortly after the marriage, which took place in Arizona, Allan Monks declined into insanity. Whether his mental condition resulted from injuries he had suffered in a motorcycle crash or from drugs administered under the undue influence of Marie Antoinette, the court would debate at great length. When Allan Monks died, he left two wills: an old one in favor of a friend named Ida Lee and a newer one in favor of his wife, Marie Antoinette. Ida Lee submitted her version of the will for probate, Marie Antoinette challenged her claim, and Lee fought back. Lee's lawyers contended that the Monks marriage was illegal. They charged that Marie Antoinette Monks, who had told her husband she was a "French" countess, was actually "a Negro" and therefore prohibited by Arizona law from marrying Allan Monks, whom the court presumed to be Caucasian.[30]

Much of the ensuing six-week-long trial was devoted to determining the "race" of Marie Antoinette Monks. To prove that she was "a Negro," her opponents called five people to the witness stand: a disgruntled friend of her husband, a local labor commissioner, and three expert witnesses, all of whom offered arguments that emphasized biological indicators of race. The first so-called expert, Monks's hairdresser, claimed that she could tell that Monks was of mixed blood from looking at the size of the moons of her fingernails, the color of the "ring" around the palms of her hands, and the "kink" in her hair. The second, a physical anthropologist from the nearby San Diego Museum, claimed to be able to tell that Monks was "at least one-eighth negroid" from the shape of her face, the color of her hands, and her "protruding heels," all of which he had observed casually while a spectator in the courtroom. The third expert witness, a surgeon, had grown up and practiced medicine in the South and later served at a Southern Baptist mission in Africa. Having once walked alongside Monks when entering the courthouse (at which time he tried, he said, to make a close observation of her), he testified that he could tell that she was of "one-eighth negro blood" from the contour of her calves and heels, from the "peculiar pallor" on the back of her neck, from the shape of her face, and from the wave of her hair.[31]

To defend Monks, her lawyers called a friend, a relative, and two expert witnesses of their own, an anthropologist and a biologist. The experts both started out by testifying to the culturalist position that it was impossible to tell a person's race from physical characteristics, especially if that person was, as they put it, "of mixed blood." This was the argument culturalists used whenever they were cornered into talking about biology, a phenomenon they tended to regard as so insignificant a factor in social life that they preferred to avoid talking about it at all.

But because this argument replaced certainty with uncertainty, it did not play very well in the *Monks* courtroom. Seeking to find the definitiveness they needed to offset the experts who had already testified, the lawyers for Monks paraded their own client in front of the witness stand, asking her to show the anthropologist her fingernails and to remove her shoes so that he could see her heels. They lingered over the biologist's testimony that Monks's physical features resembled those of the people of southern France. In the end, Monks's lawyers backed both experts into a corner; when pressed repeatedly for a definite answer, both reluctantly admitted that it was their opinion that Monks was a "white" woman.[32]

The experts' dilemma reveals the limitations of the argument for racial indeterminacy in the courtroom. Faced with a conflict between culturalist experts, who offered uncertainty and indeterminacy, and their opponents, who offered concrete biological answers to racial questions, judges were predisposed to favor the latter. To judges, culturalists appeared frustratingly vague and uncooperative (in other words, lousy witnesses), while their opponents seemed to be good witnesses willing to answer direct questions.

In the *Monks* case, the judge admitted that his own "inexpert" opinion—that Marie Antoinette "did have many characteristics that I would say . . . [showed] mixed negro and some other blood"—was not enough to justify a ruling. Turning to the experts before him, he dismissed the hairdresser (whose experience he was willing to grant, but whose scientific credentials he considered dubious); he passed over the biologist (whose testimony, he thought, could go either way); and he dismissed the two anthropologists, whose testimonies, he said, more or less canceled each other out. The only expert the judge was willing to rely on was the surgeon, because the surgeon "seemed . . . to hold a very unique and peculiar position as an expert on the question involved from his work in life."[33]

Relying on the surgeon's testimony, the judge declared that Marie Antoinette Monks was "the descendant of a negro" who had "one-eighth negro blood . . . and 7/8 caucasian blood"; he said that her "race" prohibited her from marrying Allan Monks and from inheriting his estate. The racial categorization served to invalidate the marriage in two overlapping ways. First, as a "negro," Marie Antoinette could not marry a white under Arizona miscegenation law; and second, by telling her husband-to-be that she was "French," Marie Antoinette had committed a "fraud" serious enough to render the marriage legally void. The court's decision that she had also exerted "undue influence" over Monks was hardly necessary to the outcome.[34]

As the *Monks* case suggests, we should be careful not to overestimate the influence culturalists had on the legal system. And, while in courtrooms culturalist experts were trying—and failing—to convince judges that biological racial questions were unanswerable, outside the courts their contention that biological racial answers were insignificant was faring little better. During the first three decades of the twentieth century, scientists on the "racial" side of the split between race and culture reconstituted themselves into a rough alliance of their own. Mirroring the modern dividing line between biology and culture, its ranks swelled with those who claimed special expertise on biological questions. There were biologists and physicians; leftover racialists such as physical anthropologists, increasingly shorn of their claims to expertise in every arena *except* that of physical characteristics; and, finally, the newly emerging eugenicists.[35]

Eugenicists provided the glue that held this coalition together. Narrowing the sweep of nineteenth-century racialist thought to focus on biology, these modern biological experts then expanded their range by offering physical characteristics, heredity, and reproductive imperatives as variations on the biological theme. They were particularly drawn to arenas in which all these biological motifs came into play; accordingly, they placed special emphasis on reforming marriage laws. Perhaps the best-known American eugenicist, Charles B. Davenport of the Eugenics Record Office, financed by the Carnegie Institution, outlined their position in a 1913 pamphlet, *State Laws Limiting Marriage Selection Examined in the Light of Eugenics*, which proposed strengthening state control over the marriages of the physically and racially unfit. Davenport's plan was no mere pipe dream. According to the historian Michael Grossberg, by the 1930s, forty-one states used eugenic categories to restrict the marriage of "lunatics," "imbeciles," "idiots," and the "feebleminded"; twenty-six states restricted the marriages of those infected with syphilis and gonorrhea; and twenty-seven states passed sterilization laws. By midcentury, blood tests had become a standard legal prerequisite for marriage.[36]

Historians have rather quickly passed over the racial aspects of American eugenics, seeing its proponents as advocates of outmoded ideas soon to be beached by the culturalist sea change. Yet until at least World War II, eugenicists reproduced a modern racism that was biological in a particularly virulent sense. For them, unlike their racialist predecessors (who tended to regard biology as an indicator of a much more expansive racial phenomenon), biology really was the essence of race. And unlike nineteenth-century scientific racists (whose belief in discrete racial dividing lines was rarely shaken by evidence of racial intermixture), twentieth-century eugenicists and culturalists alike seemed obsessed with the subject of mixed-race individuals.[37]

In their determination to protect "white purity," eugenicists believed that even the tightest definitions of race by blood proportion were too loose. Setting their sights on Virginia, in 1924 they secured passage of the most draconian miscegenation law in American history. The act, entitled "an Act to preserve racial integrity," replaced the legal provision that a person must have one-sixteenth "negro blood" to fall within the state's definition of "colored" with this provision:

> It shall hereafter be unlawful for any white person in this State to marry any save a white person, or a person with no other admixture of blood than white and American Indian. For the purpose of this act, the term "white person" shall apply only to the person who has no trace whatsoever of any blood other than Caucasian; but persons who have one-sixteenth or less of the blood of the American Indian and have no other non-Caucasic blood shall be deemed to be white persons.

Another section of the Virginia law (which provided for the issuance of supposedly voluntary racial registration certificates for Virginia citizens) spelled out the "races" the legislature had in mind. The list, which specified "Caucasian, Negro, Mongolian, American Indian, Asiatic Indian, Malay, or any mixture thereof, or any other non-Caucasic strains," showed the lengths to which lawmakers would go to pin down racial categories. Within the decade, the Virginia law was copied by Georgia and echoed in Alabama. Thereafter, while supporters worked without much success to extend such laws to other states, defenders of miscegenation statutes added eugenic arguments to their rhetorical arsenal.[38]

Having been pinned to the modern biological wall and labeled as "mixed-race," Marie Antoinette Monks would seem to have been in the perfect position to challenge the constitutionality of the widely drawn Arizona miscegenation law. She took her case to the California Court of Appeals, Fourth District, where she made an argument that echoed that of Mayellen Kirby two decades earlier. Reminding the court of the wording of the Arizona statute, her lawyers pointed out that "on the set of facts found by the trial judge, [Marie Antoinette Monks] is concededly of Caucasian blood as well as negro blood, and therefore a descendant of a Caucasian." Spelling it out, they explained:

> As such, she is prohibited from marrying a negro or any descendant of a negro, a Mongolian or an Indian, a Malay or a Hindu, or any of the descendants of any of them. Likewise . . . as a descendant of a negro she is prohibited from marrying a Caucasian or descendant of a Caucasian, which of course would include any person who had any degree of Caucasian blood in them.

Because this meant that she was "absolutely prohibited from contracting valid marriages in Arizona," her lawyers argued that the Arizona law was an unconstitutional constraint on her liberty.[39]

The court, however, dismissed this argument as "interesting but in our opinion not tenable." In a choice that speaks volumes about the depth of attachment to racial categories, the court narrowed the force of the argument by asserting that "the constitutional problem would be squarely presented" only if one mixed-race person were seeking to marry another mixed-race person, then used this constructed hypothetical to dodge the issue:

> While it is true that there was evidence that appellant [Marie Antoinette Monks] is a descendant of the Caucasian race, as well as of the Negro race, the other contracting party [Allan Monks] was of unmixed blood and therefore the hypothetical situation involving an attempted alliance between two persons of mixed blood is no more present in the instant case than in the Kirby case. . . . The situations conjured up by respondent are not here involved. . . . Under the facts presented the appellant does not have the benefit of assailing the validity of the statute.

This decision was taken as authoritative. Both the United States Supreme Court and the Supreme Judicial Court of Massachusetts (in which Monks had also filed suit) refused to reopen the issue.[40]

Perhaps the most interesting thing about the Monks case is that there is no reason to believe that the public found it either remarkable or objectionable. Local reporters who covered the trial in 1939 played up the themes of forgery, drugs, and insanity; their summaries of the racial categories of the Arizona law and the opinions of the expert witnesses were largely matter-of-fact.[41]

In this seeming acceptability to the public lies a clue to the development of modern racial ideologies. Even as judges narrowed their conception of race, transforming an all-encompassing phenomenon into a simple fact to be determined, they remained bound by the provisions of miscegenation law to determine who fit in which racial categories. For this purpose, the second culturalist argument, that race was merely biology, had far more to offer than the first, that race was biologically indeterminable. The conception of race as merely biological seemed consonant with the racial categories built into the laws, seemed supportable by clear and unequivocal expert testimony, and fit comfortably within popular notions of race.

The Distillation of Modernist Racial Ideology: From *Perez* to *Loving*

In the *Monks* case we can see several modern racial ideologies—ranging from the argument that race was biological nonsense to the reply that race was essentially biological to the possibility that race was merely biology—all grounded in the split between culture and biology. To distill these variants into a unified modernist racial ideology, another element had to be added to the mix, the remarkable (in American law, nearly unprecedented) proposal that the legal system abandon its traditional responsibility for determining and defining racial categories. In miscegenation law, this possibility emerged in a case that also, and not coincidentally, featured the culturalist argument for biological racial indeterminacy.

The case was *Perez v. Lippold*. It involved a young Los Angeles couple, Andrea Perez and Sylvester Davis, who sought a marriage license. Turned down by the Los Angeles County clerk, they challenged the constitutionality of the California miscegenation law directly to the California Supreme Court, which heard their case in October 1947.[42]

It was not immediately apparent that the *Perez* case would play a role in the development of modernist racial ideology. Perhaps because both sides agreed that Perez was "a white female" and Davis "a Negro male," the lawyer who defended the couple, Daniel

Marshall, did not initially see the case as turning on race categorization. In 1947 Marshall had few civil rights decisions to build on, so he tried an end-run strategy: He based his challenge to miscegenation laws on the argument that because both Perez and Davis were Catholics and the Catholic Church did not prohibit interracial marriage, California miscegenation law was an arbitrary and unreasonable restraint on their freedom of religion.

The freedom-of-religion argument made some strategic sense, since several courts had held that states had to meet a high standard to justify restrictions on religious expression. Accordingly, Marshall laid out the religion argument in a lengthy petition to the California Supreme Court. In response, the state offered an even lengthier defense of miscegenation laws. The state's lawyers had at their fingertips a long list of precedents upholding such laws, including the *Kirby* and *Monks* cases. They added eugenic arguments about racial biology, including evidence of declining birth rates among "hybrids" and statistics that showed high mortality, short life expectancies, and particular diseases among African Americans. They polished off their case with the comments of a seemingly sympathetic Roman Catholic priest.[43]

Here the matter stood until the California Supreme Court heard oral arguments in the case. At that session, the court listened in silence to Marshall's opening sally that miscegenation laws were based on prejudice and to his argument that they violated constitutional guarantees of freedom of religion. But as soon as the state's lawyer began to challenge the religious-freedom argument, one of the court's associate justices, Roger Traynor, impatiently interrupted the proceedings. "What," he asked, "about equal protection of the law?"

> *Mr. Justice Traynor:* . . . it might help to explain the statute, what it means. What is a negro?
> *Mr. Stanley:* We have not the benefit of any judicial interpretation. The statute states that a negro [Stanley evidently meant to say, as the law did, "a white"] cannot marry a negro, which can be construed to mean a full-blooded negro, since the statute also says mulatto, Mongolian, or Malay.
> *Mr. Justice Traynor:* What is a mulatto? One-sixteenth blood?
> *Mr. Stanley:* Certainly certain states have seen fit to state what a mulatto is.
> *Mr. Justice Traynor:* If there is 1/8 blood, can they marry? If you can marry with 1/8, why not with 1/16, 1/32, 1/64? And then don't you get in the ridiculous position where a negro cannot marry anybody? If he is white, he cannot marry black, or if he is black, he cannot marry white.
> *Mr. Stanley:* I agree that it would be better for the Legislature to lay down an exact amount of blood, but I do not think that the statute should be declared unconstitutional as indefinite on this ground.
> *Mr. Justice Traynor:* That is something anthropologists have not been able to furnish, although they say generally that there is no such thing as race.
> *Mr. Stanley:* I would not say that anthropologists have said that generally, except such statements for sensational purposes.
> *Mr. Justice Traynor:* Would you say that Professor Wooten of Harvard was a sensationalist? The crucial question is how can a county clerk determine who are negroes and who are whites.[44]

Although he addressed his questions to the lawyers for the state, Justice Traynor had given Marshall a gift no lawyer had ever before received in a miscegenation case: judicial willingness to believe in the biological indeterminacy of race. It was no accident that this argument came from Roger Traynor. A former professor at Boalt Hall, the law school of the University of California, Berkeley, Traynor had been appointed to the court for his academic expertise rather than his legal experience; unlike his more pragmatic colleagues, he kept up with developments in modern social science.[45]

Marshall responded to the opening Traynor had provided by making sure that his next brief included the culturalist argument that race was biological nonsense. In it, he asserted that experts had determined that "race, as popularly understood, is a myth"; he played on the gap between expert opinion and laws based on irrational "prejudice" rooted in "myth, folk belief, and superstition"; and he dismissed his opponents' reliance on the "grotesque reasoning of eugenicists" by comparing their statements to excerpts from Adolf Hitler's *Mein Kampf*.[46]

Marshall won his case. The 1948 decision in the *Perez* case was remarkable for many reasons. It marked the first time since Reconstruction that a state court had declared a state miscegenation law unconstitutional. It went far beyond existing appeals cases in that the California Supreme Court had taken the very step the judges in the *Kirby* and *Monks* cases had avoided—going beyond the issue of the race of an individual to consider the issue of racial classification in general. Even more remarkable, the court did so in a case in which neither side had challenged the racial classification of the parties. But despite these accomplishments, the *Perez* case was no victory for the culturalist argument about the biological indeterminacy of race. Only the outcome of the case—that California's miscegenation law was unconstitutional—was clear. The rationale for this outcome was a matter of considerable dispute.

Four justices condemned the law and three supported it; altogether, they issued four separate opinions. A four-justice majority agreed that the law should be declared unconstitutional but disagreed about why. Two justices, led by Traynor, issued a lengthy opinion that pointed out the irrationality of racial categories, citing as authorities a virtual who's who of culturalist social scientists, from Boas, Huxley, and Haddon to Gunnar Myrdal. A third justice issued a concurring opinion that pointedly ignored the rationality or irrationality of race classifications to criticize miscegenation laws on equality grounds, contending that laws based on "race, color, or creed" were—and always had been—contrary to the Declaration of Independence, the Constitution, and the Fourteenth Amendment; as this justice saw it, the Constitution was color-blind. A fourth justice, who reported that he wanted his decision to "rest upon a broader ground than that the challenged statutes are discriminatory and irrational," based his decision solely on the religious-freedom issue that had been the basis of Marshall's original argument.[47]

In contrast, a three-justice minority argued that the law should be upheld. They cited legal precedent, offered biological arguments about racial categories, and mentioned a handful of social policy considerations. Although the decision went against them, their agreement with each other ironically formed the closest thing to a majority in the case. In sum, although the *Perez* decision foreshadowed the day when American courts would abandon their defense of racial categories, its variety of judicial rationales tells us more about the range of modern racial ideologies than it does about the power of any one of them.[48]

Between the *Perez* case in 1948 and the next milestone miscegenation case, *Loving v. Virginia*, decided in 1967, judges would search for a common denominator among this contentious variety, trying to find a position of principled decisiveness persuasive enough to mold both public and expert opinion. One way to do this was to back away from the culturalist argument that race made no biological sense, adopting the other culturalist argument that race was biological fact and thus shifting the debate to the question of how much biological race should matter in determining social and legal policy.

In such a debate, white supremacists tried to extend the reach of biological race as far as possible. Thus one scientist bolstered his devotion to white supremacy by calling Boas "that appalling disaster to American social anthropology whose influence in the end has divorced the social studies of man from their scientific base in physical biology."[49] Following the lead of eugenicists, he and his sympathizers tried to place every social and legal superstructure on a biological racial base.

In contrast, their egalitarian opponents set limits. In their minds, biological race (or "skin color," as they often called it), was significant only because its visibility made it easy for racists to identify those they subjected to racial oppression. As Myrdal, the best-known of the mid-twentieth-century culturalist social scientists, noted in 1944 in his monumental work, *An American Dilemma:*

> In spite of all heterogeneity, the average white man's unmistakable observation is that *most Negroes in America have dark skin and woolly hair*, and he is, of course, right. . . . [The African American's] African ancestry and physical characteristics are fixed to his person much more ineffaceably than the yellow star is fixed to the Jew during the Nazi regime in Germany.[50]

To Myrdal's generation of egalitarians, the translation of visible physical characteristics into social hierarchies formed the tragic foundation of American racism.

The egalitarians won this debate, and their victory paved the way for the emergence of a modernist racial ideology persuasive enough to command the kind of widespread adherence once commanded by late-nineteenth-century racialism. Such a position was formulated by the United States Supreme Court in 1967 in *Loving v. Virginia*, the most important miscegenation case ever heard and the only one now widely remembered.

The *Loving* case involved what was, even for miscegenation law, an extreme example. Richard Perry Loving and Mildred Delores Jeter were residents of the small town of Central Point, Virginia, and family friends who had dated each other since he was seventeen and she was eleven. When they learned that their plans to marry were illegal in Virginia, they traveled to Washington, D.C., which did not have a miscegenation law, for the ceremony, returning in June 1958 with a marriage license, which they framed and placed proudly on their wall. In July 1958 they were awakened in the middle of the night by the county sheriff and two deputies, who had walked through their unlocked front door and right into their bedroom to arrest them for violating Virginia's miscegenation law. Under that law, an amalgam of criminal provisions enacted in 1878 and Virginia's 1924 "Act to preserve racial integrity," the Lovings, who were identified in court records as a "white" man and a "colored" woman, pleaded guilty and were promptly convicted and sentenced to a year in jail. The judge suspended their sentence on the condition that "both accused leave . . . the state of Virginia at once and do not return together or at the same time to said county and state for a period of twenty-five years."[51]

In 1963 the Lovings, then the parents of three children, grew tired of living with relatives in Washington, D.C., and decided to appeal this judgment. Their first attempts ended in defeat. In 1965 the judge who heard their original case not only refused to reconsider his decision but raised the rhetorical stakes by opining:

> Almighty God created the races white, black, yellow, malay and red, and he placed them on separate continents. And but for the interference with his arrangement there would be no cause for such marriages. The fact that he separated the races shows that he did not intend for the races to mix.

But by the time their argument had been processed by the Supreme Court of Appeals of Virginia (which invalidated the original sentence but upheld the miscegenation law), the case had attracted enough attention that the United States Supreme Court, which had previously avoided taking miscegenation cases, agreed to hear an appeal.[52]

On the side of the Lovings stood not only their own attorneys, but also the National Association for the Advancement of Colored People (NAACP), the NAACP Legal Defense and Education Fund, the Japanese American Citizens League (JACL), and a coalition of Catholic bishops. The briefs they submitted offered the whole arsenal of arguments developed in previous miscegenation cases. The bishops offered the religious-freedom argument that had been the original basis of the *Perez* case. The NAACP and the JACL stood on the opinions of culturalist experts, whose numbers now reached beyond social scientists well into the ranks of biologists. Offering both versions of the culturalist line on race, NAACP lawyers argued on one page, "The idea of 'pure' racial groups, either past or present, has long been abandoned by modern biological and social sciences," and on another, "Race, in its scientific dimension, refers only to the biogenetic and physical attributes manifest by a specified population. It does not, under any circumstances, refer to culture (learned behavior), language, nationality, or religion." The Lovings' lawyers emphasized two central points: Miscegenation laws violated both the constitutional guarantee of equal protection under the laws and the constitutional protection of the fundamental right to marry.[53]

In response, the lawyers for the state of Virginia tried hard to find some ground on which to stand. Their string of court precedents upholding miscegenation laws had been broken by the *Perez* decision. Their argument that Congress never intended the Fourteenth Amendment to apply to interracial marriage was offset by the Supreme Court's stated position that congressional intentions were inconclusive. In an attempt to distance the state from the "white purity" aspects of Virginia's 1924 law, Virginia's lawyers argued that since the Lovings admitted that they were a "white" person and "colored" person and had been tried under a section of the law that mentioned only those categories, the elaborate definition of "white" offered in other sections of Virginia law was irrelevant.[54]

On only one point did the lawyers for both parties and the Court seem to agree: None of them wanted to let expert opinion determine the outcome. The lawyers for Virginia knew only too well that during the twentieth century the scientific foundations of the eugenic biological argument in favor of miscegenation laws had crumbled, so they tried to warn the Court away by predicting that experts would mire the Court in "a veritable Serbonian bog of conflicting scientific opinion." Yet the Lovings' lawyers, who seemed to have the experts on their side, agreed that "the Court should not go into the morass of sociological evidence that is available on both sides of the question." "We strongly urge," they told the justices, "that it is not necessary." And the Court, still reeling from widespread criticism that its decision in the famous 1954 case *Brown v. Board of Education* was illegitimate "sociological jurisprudence," was not about to offer its opponents any more of such ammunition.[55]

The decision the Court issued was, in fact, carefully shorn of all reference to expert opinion; it spoke in language that both reflected and contributed to a new popular common sense on the issue of race. Recycling earlier pronouncements that "distinctions between citizens solely because of their ancestry" were "odious to a free people whose institutions are founded upon the doctrine of equality" and that the Court "cannot conceive of a valid legislative purpose . . . which makes the color of a person's skin the test of whether his conduct is a criminal offense," the justices reached a new and broader conclusion. Claiming (quite inaccurately) that "[w]e have consistently denied the constitutionality of measures which restrict the rights of citizens on account of race," the Court concluded that the racial classifications embedded in Virginia miscegenation laws were "so directly subversive of the principle of equality at the heart of the Fourteenth Amendment" that they were "unsupportable." Proclaiming that it violated both the equal protection and the due process clauses of the Fourteenth Amendment, the Court declared the Virginia miscegenation law unconstitutional.[56]

Legacies of Modernist Racial Ideology

The decision in the *Loving* case shows the distance twentieth-century American courts had traveled. The accumulated effect of several decades of culturalist attacks on racialism certainly shaped their thinking. The justices were no longer willing to accept the notion that race was the all-encompassing phenomenon nineteenth-century racialist thinkers had assumed it to be; they accepted the divisions between culture and biology and culture and race established by modern social scientists. But neither were they willing to declare popular identification of race with physical characteristics (like "the color of a person's skin") a figment of the imagination. In their minds, the scope of the term *race* had shrunk to a point where biology was all that was left; *race* referred to visible physical characteristics significant only because racists used them to erect spurious racial hierarchies. The Virginia miscegenation law was a case in point; the Court recognized and condemned it as a statute clearly "designed to maintain White Supremacy."[57]

Given the dependence of miscegenation laws on legal categories of race, the Court concluded that ending white supremacy required abandoning the categories. In deemphasizing racial categories, they joined mainstream mid-twentieth-century social scientists, who argued that because culture, rather than race, shaped meaningful human difference, race was nothing more than a subdivision of the broader phenomenon of ethnicity. In a society newly determined to be "color-blind," granting public recognition to racial categories seemed to be synonymous with racism itself.[58]

And so the Supreme Court promulgated a modernist racial ideology that maintained that the best way to eradicate racism was the deliberate nonrecognition of race. Its effects reached well beyond miscegenation law. Elements of modernist racial ideology marked many of the major mid-twentieth-century Supreme Court decisions, including *Brown v. Board of Education*. Its effects on state law codes were equally substantial; during the 1960s and 1970s, most American states repealed statutes that had defined "race" (usually by blood proportion) and set out to erase racial terminology from their laws.[59]

Perhaps the best indication of the pervasiveness of modernist racial ideology is how quickly late-twentieth-century conservatives learned to shape their arguments to fit its contours. Attaching themselves to the modernist narrowing of the definition of race to biology and biology alone, conservative thinkers began to contend that unless their ideas rested solely and explicitly on a belief in biological inferiority, they should not be considered racist. They began to advance "cultural" arguments of their very own, insisting that their proposals were based on factors such as social analysis, business practicality, or merit—on anything, in other words, except biological race. In their hands, modernist racial ideology supports an Alice-in-Wonderland interpretation of racism in which even those who argue for racially oppressive policies can adamantly deny being racists.

This conservative turnabout is perhaps the most striking indication of the contradictions inherent in modernist racial ideology, but it is not the only one. Others run the gamut from administrative law to popular culture. So while the U.S. Supreme Court tries to hold to its twentieth-century legacy of limiting racial categories when it cannot eradicate them, U.S. government policies remain deeply dependent on them. In the absence of statutory definitions of race, racial categories are now set by the U.S. Office of Management and Budget, which in 1977 issued a "Statistical Directive" that divided Americans into five major groups—American Indian or Alaskan Native, Asian or Pacific Islander, black, white, and Hispanic. The statistics derived from these categories help determine everything from census counts to eligibility for inclusion in affirmative action programs to the drawing of voting districts.[60] Meanwhile, in one popular culture flashpoint after another—from the Anita Hill/Clarence Thomas hearings to the O. J. Simpson case, mainstream commentators insist that "race" should not be a consideration even as they explore detail after detail that reveals its social pervasiveness.[61]

These gaps between the (very narrow) modernist conception of race and the (very wide) range of racial identities and racial oppressions bedevil today's egalitarians. In the political arena, some radicals have begun to argue that the legal system's deliberate nonrecognition of race erodes the ability to recognize and name racism and to argue for such policies as affirmative action, which rely on racial categories to overturn rather than to enforce oppression. Meanwhile, in the universities, a growing chorus of scholars is revitalizing the argument for the biological indeterminacy of race and using that argument to explore the myriad of ways in which socially constructed notions of race remain powerfully salient. Both groups hope to do better than their culturalist predecessors at eradicating racism.[62]

Attaining that goal may depend on how well we understand the tortured history of mid-twentieth-century American ideologies of race.

Notes

This article was originally presented at the 1992 annual meeting of the Organization of American Historians, and it has benefited considerably from the responses of audiences there and at half a dozen universities. For especially helpful readings, suggestions, and assistance, I would like to thank Nancy Cott, Karen Engle, Estelle Freedman, Jeff Garcilazo, Dave Gutierrez, Ramon Gutierrez, Eric Hinderaker, Marcia Klotz, Dorothee Kocks, Waverly Lowell, Valerie Matsumoto, Robyn Muncy, David Roediger, Richard White, the Brown University women's history reading group, and the editors and anonymous reviewers of the *Journal of American History*.

1. Ariz. Rev. Stat. Ann. sec. 3837 (1913); "Appellant's Abstract of Record," 8 Aug. 1921, pp. 1–2, *Kirby v. Kirby*, docket 1970 (microfilm: file 36.1.134), Arizona Supreme Court Civil Cases (Arizona State Law Library, Phoenix).

2. "Appellant's Abstract of Record," 12–13, 13–15, 15, *Kirby v. Kirby*.

3. Ibid., 16–18.

4. Ibid., 19.

5. Evelyn Brooks Higginbotham, "African-American Women's History and the Metalanguage of Race," *Signs* 17 (winter 1992): 253. See Michael Omi and Howard Winant, *Racial Formation in the United States: From the 1960s to the 1990s* (New York, 1994); David Theo Goldberg, ed., *Anatomy of Racism* (Minneapolis, 1990); Henry Louis Gates Jr., ed., *"Race," Writing, and Difference* (Chicago, 1986); Dominick LaCapra, ed., *The Bounds of Race: Perspectives on Hegemony and Resistance* (Ithaca, 1991); F. James Davis, *Who Is Black? One Nation's Definition* (University Park, 1991); Sandra Harding, ed., *The "Racial" Economy of Science: Toward a Democratic Future* (Bloomington, 1993); Maria P. P. Root, ed., *Racially Mixed People in America* (Newbury Park, 1992); and Ruth Frankenberg, *White Women, Race Matters: The Social Construction of Whiteness* (Minneapolis, 1993).

6. Among the most provocative recent works are Higginbotham, "African-American Women's History"; Barbara J. Fields, "Ideology and Race in American History," in J. Morgan Kousser and James M. McPherson, eds., *Region, Race, and Reconstruction: Essays in Honor of C. Vann Woodward* (New York, 1982), 143–78; Thomas C. Holt, "Marking: Race, Race-Making, and the Writing of History," *American Historical Review* 100 (February 1995): 1–20; and David R. Roediger, *Towards the Abolition of Whiteness: Essays on Race, Politics, and Working Class History* (London, 1994).

7. On scientific racism, see Thomas F. Gossett, *Race: The History of an Idea in America* (Dallas, 1963); George W. Stocking Jr., *Race, Culture, and Evolution: Essays in the History of Anthropology* (Chicago, 1982 [1968]); John S. Haller Jr., *Outcasts from Evolution: Scientific Attitudes to Racial Inferiority, 1859–1900* (Urbana, 1971); George M. Fredrickson, *The Black Image in the White Mind: The Debate on Afro-American Character and Destiny, 1817–1914* (New York, 1971); Thomas G. Dyer, *Theodore Roosevelt and the Idea of Race* (Baton Rouge, 1980); Carl N. Degler, *In Search of Human Nature: The Decline and Revival of Darwinism in American Social*

Thought (New York, 1991); and Elazar Barkan, *Retreat of Scientific Racism: Changing Concepts of Race in Britain and the United States between the World Wars* (Cambridge, Eng., 1992). On the social construction of racial ideologies, see the works cited in note 6, above, and Ronald T. Takaki, *Iron Cages: Race and Culture in Nineteenth-Century America* (New York, 1979); Reginald Horsman, *Race and Manifest Destiny: The Origins of American Racial Anglo-Saxonism* (Cambridge, Mass., 1981); Alexander Saxton, *The Rise and Fall of the White Republic: Class Politics and Mass Culture in Nineteenth-Century America* (London, 1990); David R. Roediger, *The Wages of Whiteness: Race and the Making of the American Working Class* (London, 1991); Audrey Smedley, *Race in North America: Origin and Evolution of a Worldview* (Boulder, 1993); and Tomás Almaguer, *Racial Fault Lines: The Historical Origins of White Supremacy in California* (Berkeley, 1994).

8.   On law as a producer of racial ideologies, see Barbara J. Fields, "Slavery, Race, and Ideology in the United States of America," *New Left Review* 181 (May–June 1990): 7; Eva Saks, "Representing Miscegenation Law," *Raritan* 8 (fall 1988): 56–60; and Collette Guillaumin, "Race and Nature: The System of Marks," *Feminist Issues* 8 (fall 1988): 25–44.

9.   See especially Fredrickson, *Black Image in the White Mind.*

10.   For intriguing attempts to define American modernism, see Daniel J. Singal, ed., *Modernist Culture in America* (Belmont, 1991); and Dorothy Ross, ed., *Modernist Impulses in the Human Sciences, 1870–1930* (Baltimore, 1994). For the view from critical race theory, see Brian K. Fair, "Foreword: Rethinking the Colorblindness Model," *National Black Law Journal* 13 (spring 1993): 1–82; Neil Gotanda, "A Critique of 'Our Constitution Is Color-Blind,'" *Stanford Law Review* 44 (November 1991): 1–68; Gary Peller, "Race Consciousness," *Duke Law Journal* (September 1990): 758–847; and Peter Fitzpatrick, "Racism and the Innocence of Law," in Goldberg, ed., *Anatomy of Racism*, 247–62.

11.   Many scholars avoid using the word *miscegenation*, which dates to the 1860s, means "race mixing," and has, to twentieth-century minds, embarrassingly biological connotations; they speak of laws against "interracial" or "cross-cultural" relationships. Contemporaries usually referred to "anti-miscegenation" laws. Neither alternative seems satisfactory, since the first avoids naming the ugliness that was so much a part of the laws and the second implies that "miscegenation" was a distinct racial phenomenon rather than a categorization imposed on certain relationships. I retain the term *miscegenation* when speaking of the laws and court cases that relied on the concept, but not when speaking of people or particular relationships. On the emergence of the term, see Sidney Kaplan, "The Miscegenation Issue in the Election of 1864," *Journal of Negro History* 24 (July 1949): 274–343.

12.   Most histories of interracial sex and marriage in America focus on demographic patterns rather than legal constraints. See, for example, Joel Williamson, *New People: Miscegenation and Mulattoes in the United States* (New York, 1980); Paul R. Spickard, *Mixed Blood: Intermarriage and Ethnic Identity in Twentieth-Century America* (Madison, 1989); and Deborah Lynn Kitchen, "Interracial Marriage in the United States, 1900–1980" (Ph.D. diss., University of Minnesota, 1993). The only historical overview is Byron Curti Martyn, "Racism in the United States: A History of the Anti-Miscegenation Legislation and Litigation" (Ph.D. diss., University of Southern California, 1979). On the colonial period, see A. Leon Higginbotham Jr. and Barbara K. Kopytoff, "Racial Purity and Interracial Sex in the Law of Colonial and Antebellum Virginia," *Georgetown Law Journal* 77 (August 1989): 1967–2029; George M. Fredrickson, *White Supremacy: A Comparative Study in American and South African History* (New York, 1981): 99–108; and James Hugo Johnston, *Race Relations in Virginia & Miscegenation in the South, 1776–1860* (Amherst, 1970), 165–90. For later periods, see Peter Bardaglio, "Families, Sex, and the Law: The Legal Transformation of the Nineteenth-Century Southern Household" (Ph.D. diss., Stanford University, 1987), 37–106, 345–49; Peter Wallenstein, "Race, Marriage, and the Law of Freedom: Alabama and Virginia, 1860s–1960s," *Chicago-Kent Law Review* 70, 2 (1994): 371–437; David H. Fowler, *Northern Attitudes towards Interracial Marriage: Legislation and Public Opinion in the Middle Atlantic and the States of the Old Northwest, 1780–1930* (New York, 1987); Megumi Dick Osumi, "Asians and California's Anti-Miscegenation Laws," in Nobuya Tsuchida, ed., *Asian and Pacific American Experiences: Women's Perspectives* (Minneapolis, 1982), 2–8; and Peggy Pascoe, "Race, Gender, and Intercultural Relations: The Case of Interracial Marriage," *Frontiers* 12, 1 (1991): 5–18. The count of states is from the most complete list in Fowler, *Northern Attitudes*, 336–439.

13.   Ariz. Rev. Stat. Ann. sec. 3092 (1901); 1931 Ariz. Sess. Laws ch. 17. Arizona, Idaho, Maine, Massachusetts, Nevada, North Carolina, Oregon, Rhode Island, South Carolina, Tennessee, Virginia, and Washington passed laws that mentioned American Indians. Arizona, California, Georgia, Idaho, Mississippi, Missouri, Montana, Nebraska, Nevada, Oregon, South Dakota, Utah, Virginia, and Wyoming passed laws that mentioned Asian Americans. Arizona, California, Georgia, Maryland, Nevada, South Dakota, Utah, Virginia, and Wyoming passed laws that mentioned "Malays." In addition, Oregon law targeted "Kanakas" (native Hawaiians), Virginia "Asiatic Indians," and Georgia both "Asiatic Indians" and "West Indians." See Fowler, *Northern Attitudes*, 336–439; 1924 Va. Acts ch. 371; 1927 Ga. Laws no. 317; 1931 Ariz. Sess. Laws ch. 17; 1933 Cal. Stat. ch. 104; 1935 Md. Laws ch. 60; and 1939 Utah Laws ch. 50.

14. The most insightful social and legal histories have focused on sexual relations rather than marriage. See, for example, Higginbotham and Kopytoff, "Racial Purity and Interracial Sex"; Karen Getman, "Sexual Control in the Slaveholding South: The Implementation and Maintenance of a Racial Caste System," *Harvard Women's Law Journal* 7 (spring 1984): 125–34; Martha Hodes, "Sex across the Color Line: White Women and Black Men in the Nineteenth-Century American South" (Ph.D. diss., Princeton University, 1991); and Martha Hodes, "The Sexualization of Reconstruction Politics: White Women and Black Men in the South after the Civil War," in John C. Fout and Maura Shaw Tantillo, eds., *American Sexual Politics: Sex, Gender, and Race since the Civil War* (Chicago, 1993), 59–74; Robyn Weigman, "The Anatomy of Lynching," in Fout and Tantillo, eds., *American Sexual Politics,* 223–45; Jacquelyn Dowd Hall, "'The Mind that Burns in Each Body': Women, Rape, and Racial Violence," in Ann Snitow, Christine Stansell, and Sharon Thompson, eds., *Powers of Desire: The Politics of Sexuality* (New York, 1983), 328–49; Kenneth James Lay, "Sexual Racism: A Legacy of Slavery," *National Black Law Journal* 13 (spring 1993): 165–83; and Kevin J. Mumford, "From Vice to Vogue: Black/White Sexuality and the 1920s" (Ph.D. diss., Stanford University, 1993). One of the first works to note the predominance of marriage in miscegenation laws was Mary Frances Berry, "Judging Morality: Sexual Behavior and Legal Consequences in the Late Nineteenth-Century South," *Journal of American History* 78 (December 1991): 838–39. On the historical connections among race, marriage, property, and the state, see Saks, "Representing Miscegenation Law," 39–69; Nancy F. Cott, "Giving Character to Our Whole Civil Polity: Marriage and the Public Order in the Late Nineteenth Century," in Linda K. Kerber, Alice Kessler-Harris, and Kathryn Kish Sklar, eds., *U.S. History as Women's History: New Feminist Essays* (Chapel Hill, 1995), 107–21; Ramon A. Gutierrez, *When Jesus Came, the Corn Mothers Went Away: Marriage, Sexuality, and Power in New Mexico, 1500–1846* (Stanford, 1991); Verena Martinez-Alier, *Marriage, Class, and Colour in Nineteenth-Century Cuba: A Study of Racial Attitudes and Sexual Values in a Slave Society* (Ann Arbor, 1989); Patricia J. Williams, "Fetal Fictions: An Exploration of Property Archetypes in Racial and Gendered Contexts," in Herbert Hill and James E. Jones Jr., eds., *Race in America: The Struggle for Equality* (Madison, 1993): 425–37; and Virginia R. Dominguez, *White by Definition: Social Classification in Creole Louisiana* (New Brunswick, 1986).

15. Of the forty-one colonies and states that prohibited interracial marriage, twenty-two also prohibited some form of interracial sex. One additional jurisdiction (New York) prohibited interracial sex but not interracial marriage; it is not clear how long this 1638 statute was in effect. See Fowler, *Northern Attitudes,* 336–439. My database consists of every appeals court case I could identify in which miscegenation law played a role: 227 cases heard between 1850 and 1970, 132 civil and 95 criminal. Although cases that reach appeals courts are by definition atypical, they are significant because the decisions reached in them set policies later followed in more routine cases and because the texts of the decisions hint at how judges conceptualized particular legal problems. I have relied on them because of these interpretive advantages and for two more practical reasons. First, because appeals court decisions are published and indexed, it is possible to compile a comprehensive list of them. Second, because making an appeal requires the preservation of documents that might otherwise be discarded (such as legal briefs and court reporters' trial notes), they permit the historian to go beyond the judge's decision.

16. Decisions striking down the laws include *Burns v. State,* 48 Ala. 195 (1872); *Bonds v. Foster,* 36 Tex. 68 (1871–72); *Honey v. Clark,* 37 Tex. 686 (1873); *Hart v. Hoss,* 26 La. Ann. 90 (1874); *State v. Webb,* 4 Cent. L. J. 588 (1877); and *Ex parte Brown,* 5 Cent. L. J. 149 (1877). Decisions upholding the laws include *Scott v. State,* 39 Ga. 321 (1869); *State v. Hairston,* 63 N.C. 451 (1869); *State v. Reinhardt,* 63 N.C. 547 (1869): *In re Hobbs,* 12 F. Cas. 262 (1871) (No. 6550); *Lonas v. State,* 50 Tenn. 287 (1871); *State v. Gibson,* 36 Ind. 389 (1871); *Ford v. State,* 53 Ala. 150 (1875); *Green v. State,* 58 Ala. 190 (1877); *Frasher v. State,* 3 Tex. Ct. App. R. 263 (1877); *Ex Parte Kinney,* 14 F. Cas. 602 (1879) (No. 7825); *Ex parte Francois,* 9 F. Cas. 699 (1879) (No. 5047); *Francois v. State,* 9 Tex. Ct. App. R. 144 (1880); *Pace v. State,* 69 Ala. 231 (1881); *Pace v. Alabama,* 106 U.S. 583 (1882); *State v. Jackson,* 80 Mo. 175 (1883); *State v. Tutty,* 41 F. 753 (1890); *Dodson v. State,* 31 S.W. 977 (1895); *Strauss v. State,* 173 S.W. 663 (1915); *State v. Daniel,* 75 So. 836 (1917); *Succession of Mingo,* 78 So. 565 (1917–18); and *In re Paquet's Estate,* 200 P. 911 (1921).

17. Individual racial classifications were successfully challenged in *Moore v. State,* 7 Tex. Ct. App. R. 608 (1880); *Jones v. Commonwealth,* 80 Va. 213 (1884); *Jones v. Commonwealth,* 80 Va. 538 (1885); *State v. Treadaway,* 52 So. 500 (1910); *Flores v. State,* 129 S.W. 1111 (1910); *Ferrall v. Ferrall,* 69 S.E. 60 (1910); *Marre v. Marre,* 168 S.W. 636 (1914); *Neuberger v. Gueldner,* 72 So. 220 (1916); and *Reed v. State,* 92 So. 511 (1922).

18. "Appellant's Abstract of Record," 19, *Kirby v. Kirby.*

19. "Appellee's Brief," 3 Oct. 1921, p. 6, *Kirby v. Kirby.*

20. On the theoretical problems involved in exploring how miscegenation laws were gendered, see Pascoe, "Race, Gender, and Intercultural Relations"; and Peggy Pascoe, "Race, Gender, and the Privileges of Property: On the Significance of Miscegenation Law in United States History," in Susan Ware, ed., *New Viewpoints in Women's History: Working Papers from the Schlesinger Library 50th Anniversary Conference, March 4–5, 1994* (Cambridge, Mass., 1994), 99–122. For an excellent account of the gendering of early

miscegenation laws, see Kathleen M. Brown, *Good Wives and Nasty Wenches: Gender, Race, and Power in Colonial Virginia* (Chapel Hill, 1996).

21. "Appellant's Brief," 8 Sept. 1921, *Kirby v. Kirby; Kirby v. Kirby*, 206 P. 405, 406 (1922). On *Kirby*, see Roger Hardaway, "Unlawful Love: A History of Arizona's Miscegenation Law," *Journal of Arizona History* 27 (winter 1986): 377–90.

22. For examples of reliance on experts, see *In re Ah Yup*, 1 F. Cas. 223 (1878) (No. 104); *In re Kanaka Nian*, 21 P. 993 (1889); *In re Saito*, 62 F. 126 (1894). On these cases, see Ian F. Haney Lopez, *White by Law: The Legal Construction of Race* (New York, New York University Press, 1996). For reliance on the "common man," see *U.S. v. Bhagat Singh Thind*, 261 U.S. 204 (1923). On *Thind*, see Sucheta Mazumdar, "Racist Responses to Racism: The Aryan Myth and South Asians in the United States," *South Asia Bulletin* 9, 1 (1989): 47–55; Joan M. Jensen, *Passage from India: Asian Indian Immigrants in North America* (New Haven, 1988), 247–69; and Roediger, *Towards the Abolition of Whiteness*, 181–84.

23. The rise of Boasian anthropology has attracted much attention among intellectual historians, most of whom seem to agree with the 1963 comment that "it is possible that Boas did more to combat race prejudice than any other person in history"; see Gossett, *Race*, 418. In addition to the works cited in note 7, see I. A. Newby, *Jim Crow's Defense: Ante-Negro Thought in America, 1900–1930* (Baton Rouge, 1965), 21; and John S. Gilkeson Jr., "The Domestication of 'Culture' in Interwar America, 1919–1941," in JoAnne Brown and David K. van Keuren, eds., *The Estate of Social Knowledge* (Baltimore, 1991), 153–74. For more critical appraisals, see Robert Proctor, "Eugenics among the Social Sciences: Hereditarian Thought in Germany and the United States," in Brown and van Keuren, eds., *The Estate of Social Knowledge*, 175–208; Hamilton Cravens, *The Triumph of Evolution: The Heredity-Environment Controversy, 1900–1941* (Baltimore, 1988); and Donna Haraway, *Primate Visions: Gender, Race, and Nature in the World of Modern Science* (New York, 1989), 127–203. The classic—and still the best—account of the rise of cultural anthropology is Stocking, *Race, Culture, and Evolution*. See also George W. Stocking Jr., *Victorian Anthropology* (New York, 1987), 284–329.

24. U.S. Immigration Commission, *Dictionary of Races or Peoples* (Washington, D.C., 1911), 2. For other scientific racist classification schemes, see *Encyclopaedia Britannica*, 11th ed., s.v. "Anthropology"; and *Encyclopedia Americana: A Library of Universal Knowledge* (New York, 1923), s.v. "Ethnography" and "Ethnology."

25. Franz Boas, "Race," in *Encyclopaedia of the Social Sciences*, ed. Edwin R. A. Seligman (New York, 1930–35), 13:27; Julian S. Huxley and A. C. Haddon, *We Europeans: A Survey of "Racial" Problems* (London, 1935), 107.

26. Boas, "Race," 34. For one of the few instances when a historian has noted this argument, see Smedley, *Race in North America*, 275–82.

27. Ruth Benedict, *Race: Science and Politics* (New York, 1940), 12; Ruth Benedict and Gene Weltfish, *The Races of Mankind* (Washington, D.C., 1943), 5.

28. Boas, "Race," 25–26.

29. See, for example, Huxley and Haddon, *We Europeans*, 107, 269–73; Benedict and Weltfish, *Races of Mankind*; Benedict, *Race*; and Gunnar Myrdal, *An American Dilemma: The Negro Problem and Modern Democracy* (New York, 1944), 91–115.

30. The Monks trial can be followed in *Estate of Monks*, 4 Civ. 2835, Records of California Court of Appeals, Fourth District (California State Archives, Roseville); and *Gunn v. Giraudo*, 4 Civ. 2832, ibid. (Gunn represented another claimant to the estate). The two cases were tried together. For the seven-volume "Reporter's Transcript," see *Estate of Monks*, 4 Civ. 2835, ibid.

31. "Reporter's Transcript," 2:660–67, 3:965–76, 976–98, *Estate of Monks*.

32. Ibid., 5:1501–49, 6:1889–1923.

33. Ibid., 7:2543, 2548.

34. "Findings of Fact and Conclusions of Law," in "Clerk's Transcript," 2 Dec. 1940, *Gunn v. Giraudo*, 4 Civ. 2832, p. 81. One intriguing aspect of the *Monks* case is that the seeming exactness was unnecessary. The status of the marriage hinged on the Arizona miscegenation law, which would have denied validity to the marriage whether the proportion of "blood" in question was "one-eighth" or "one drop."

35. For descriptions of those interested in biological aspects of race, see Stocking, *Race, Culture, and Evolution*, 271–307; I. A. Newby, *Challenge to the Court: Social Scientists and the Defense of Segregation, 1954–1966* (Baton Rouge, 1969); and Cravens, *Triumph of Evolution*, 15–55. On eugenics, see Proctor, "Eugenics among the Social Sciences," 175–208; Daniel J. Kevles, *In the Name of Eugenics: Genetics and the Uses of Human Heredity* (New York, 1985): Mark H. Haller, *Eugenics: Hereditarian Attitudes in American Thought* (New Brunswick, 1963); and William H. Tucker, *The Science and Politics of Racial Research* (Urbana, 1994), 54–137.

36. Charles B. Davenport, *Eugenics Record Office Bulletin No. 9: State Laws Limiting Marriage Selection Examined in the Light of Eugenics* (Cold Spring Harbor, 1913); Michael Grossberg, "Guarding the Altar: Physiological Restrictions and the Rise of State Intervention in Matrimony," *American Journal of Legal History* 26 (July 1982): 221–24.

37. See, for example, C[harles] B[enedict] Davenport and Morris Steggerda, *Race Crossing in Jamaica* (Westport, Conn., 1970 [1929]); Edward Byron Reuter, *Race Mixture: Studies in Intermarriage and Miscegenation* (New York, 1931); and Emory S. Bogardus, "What Race Are Filipinos?" *Sociology and Social Research* 16 (1931–32), 274–79.

38. 1924 Va. Acts ch. 371; 1927 Ga. Laws no. 317; 1927 Ala. Acts no. 626. The 1924 Virginia act replaced 1910 Va. Acts ch. 357, which classified as "colored" persons with one-sixteenth or more "negro blood." The retention of an allowance for American Indian "blood" in persons classed as white was forced on the bill's sponsors by Virginia aristocrats who traced their ancestry to Pocahontas and John Rolfe. See Paul A. Lombardo, "Miscegenation, Eugenics, and Racism: Historical Footnotes to *Loving v. Virginia*," *U.C. Davis Law Review* 21 (winter 1988): 431–52; and Richard B. Sherman, "'The Last Stand': The Fight for Racial Integrity in Virginia in the 1920s," *Journal of Southern History* 54 (February 1988): 69–92.

39. "Appellant's Opening Brief," *Gunn v. Giraudo*, 12–13. This brief appears to have been prepared for the California Supreme Court but used in the California Court of Appeals, Fourth District. On 14 February 1942 the California Supreme Court refused to review the Court of Appeals decision. See *Estate of Monks*, 48 C. A. 2d 603, 621 (1941).

40. *Estate of Monks*, 48 C. A. 2d 603, 612–15 (1941); *Monks v. Lee*, 317 U.S. 590 (*appeal dismissed*, 1942), 711 (*reh'g denied*, 1942); *Lee v. Monks*, 62 N.E. 2d 657 (1945); *Lee v. Monks*, 326 U.S. 696 (*cert. denied*, 1946).

41. On the case, see *San Diego Union*, 21 July 1939–6 Jan. 1940. On the testimony of expert witnesses on race, see ibid., 21 Sept. 1939, 4A; 29 Sept. 1939, 10A; and 5 Oct. 1939, 8A.

42. *Perez v. Lippold*, L.A. 20305, Supreme Court Case Files (California State Archives). The case was also known as *Perez v. Moroney* and *Perez v. Sharp* (the names reflect changes of personnel in the Los Angeles County clerk's office). I have used the title given in the *Pacific Law Reporter*, the most easily available version of the final decision: *Perez v. Lippold*, 198 P. 2d 17 (1948).

43. "Petition for Writ of Mandamus, Memorandum of Points and Authorities and Proof of Service," 8 Aug. 1947, *Perez v. Lippold*; "Points and Authorities in Opposition to Issuance of Alternative Writ of Mandate," 13 Aug. 1947, ibid.; "Return by Way of Demurrer," 6 Oct. 1947, ibid.; "Return by Way of Answer," 6 Oct. 1947, ibid.; "Respondent's Brief in Opposition to Writ of Mandate," 6 Oct. 1947, ibid.

44. "[Oral Argument] on Behalf of Respondent," 6 Oct. 1947, pp. 3–4, ibid.

45. Stanley Mosk, "A Retrospective," *California Law Review* 71 (July 1983): 1045; Peter Anderson, "A Remembrance," California Law Review 71 (July 1983): 1066–71.

46. "Petitioners' Reply Brief," 8 Nov. 1947, pp. 4, 44, 23–24, *Perez v. Lippold*.

47. *Perez v. Lippold*, 198 P. 2d at 17–35, esp. 29, 34.

48. Ibid., 35–47.

49. For the characterization of Franz Boas by Robert Gayres, editor of the Scottish journal *Mankind Quarterly*, see Newby, *Challenge to the Court*, 323. On *Mankind Quarterly* and on mid-twentieth-century white supremacist scientists, see Tucker, *Science and Politics of Racial Research*.

50. Myrdal, *American Dilemma*, 116–17.

51. *Loving v. Commonwealth*, 147 S.E. 2d 78, 79 (1966). For the *Loving* briefs and oral arguments, see Philip B. Kurland and Gerhard Casper, eds., *Landmark Briefs and Arguments of the Supreme Court of the United States: Constitutional Law* (Arlington, 1975), 64:687–1007. Edited cassette tapes of the oral argument are included with Peter Irons and Stephanie Guitton, eds., *May It Please the Court: The Most Significant Oral Arguments Made before the Supreme Court since 1955* (New York, 1993). For scholarly assessments, see Wallenstein, "Race, Marriage, and the Law of Freedom"; Walter Wadlington, "The Loving Case: Virginia's Antimiscegenation Statute in Historical Perspective," in Kermit L. Hall, ed., *Race Relations and the Law in American History: Major Historical Interpretations*, (New York, 1987), 600–634; and Robert J. Sickels, *Race, Marriage, and the Law* (Albuquerque, 1972).

52. *Loving v. Virginia*, 388 U.S. 1, 3 (1967); Wallenstein, "Race, Marriage, and the Law of Freedom," 423–25, esp. 424; *New York Times*, 12 June 1992, B7. By the mid-1960s, some legal scholars had questioned the constitutionality of miscegenation laws, including C. D. Shokes, "The Serbonian Bog of Miscegenation," *Rocky Mountain Law Review* 21 (1948–49): 425–33; Wayne A. Melton, "Constitutionality of State Anti-Miscegenation Statutes," *Southwestern Law Journal* 5 (1951): 451–61; Andrew D. Weinberger, "A Reappraisal of the Constitutionality of Miscegenation Statutes," *Cornell Law Quarterly* 42 (winter 1957): 208–22; Jerold D. Cummins and John L. Kane Jr., "Miscegenation, the Constitution, and Science," *Dicta* 38 (January–February 1961): 24–54; William D. Zabel, "Interracial Marriage and the Law," *Atlantic Monthly* 216 (October 1965): 75–79; and Cyrus E. Phillips IV, "Miscegenation: The Courts and the Constitution," *William and Mary Law Review* 8 (fall 1966): 133–42.

53. Kurland and Casper, eds., *Landmark Briefs*, 741–88, 847–950, 960–72, esp. 898–99, 901.

54. Ibid., 789–845, 976–1003.

55. Ibid., 834, 1007.

56. *Loving v. Virginia*, 388 U.S. at 12.

57. Ibid., 11.

58. The notion that American courts should be "color-blind" is usually traced to Supreme Court Justice John Harlan. Dissenting from the Court's endorsement of the principle of "separate but equal" in *Plessy v. Ferguson*, Harlan insisted that "[o]ur Constitution is color-blind, and neither knows nor tolerates classes among citizens." *Plessy v. Ferguson*, 163 U.S. 537, 559 (1896). But only after *Brown v. Board of Education*, widely interpreted as a belated endorsement of Harlan's position, did courts begin to adopt color blindness as a goal. *Brown v. Board of Education*, 347 U.S. 483 (1954). On the history of the color-blindness ideal, see Andrew Kull, *The Color-Blind Constitution* (Cambridge, Mass., 1992). On developments in social science, see Omi and Winant, *Racial Formation in the United States*, 14–23.

59. *Brown v. Board of Education*, 347 U.S. 483 (1954). The Court declared distinctions based "solely on ancestry" "odious" even while upholding curfews imposed on Japanese Americans during World War II; see *Hirabayashi v. United States*, 320 U.S. 81 (1943). It declared race a "suspect" legal category while upholding the internment of Japanese Americans; see *Korematsu v. United States*, 323 U.S. 214 (1944). By 1983, no American state had a formal race-definition statute still on its books. See Chris Ballentine, "'Who Is a Negro?' Revisited: Determining Individual Racial Status for Purposes of Affirmative Action," *University of Florida Law Review* 35 (fall 1983): 692. The repeal of state race-definition statutes often accompanied repeal of miscegenation laws. See, for example, 1953 Mont. Laws ch. 4; 1959 Or. Laws ch. 531; 1965 Ind. Acts ch. 15; 1969 Fla. Laws 69–195; and 1979 Ga. Laws no. 543.

60. The fifth of these categories, "Hispanic," is sometimes described as "ethnic" rather than "racial." For very different views of the current debates, see Lawrence Wright, "One Drop of Blood," *New Yorker*, 25 July 1994, 46–55; and Michael Lind, *The Next American Nation: The New Nationalism and the Fourth American Revolution* (New York, 1995), 97–137.

61. *People v. O. J. Simpson*, Case no. BA 097211, California Superior Court, L.A. County (1994).

62. See, for example, Kimberle Williams Crenshaw, "Race, Reform, and Retrenchment: Transformation and Legitimation in Antidiscrimination Law," *Harvard Law Review* 101 (May 1988): 1331–87; Dana Y. Takagi, *The Retreat from Race: Asian-American Admissions and Racial Politics* (New Brunswick, 1992), 181–94; and Girardeau A. Spann, *Race against the Court: The Supreme Court and Minorities in Contemporary America* (New York, 1993), 119–49. See note 5, above. On recent work in the humanities, see Tessie Liu, "Race," in Wightman Fox and James T. Kloppenberg, eds., *A Companion to American Thought* (Cambridge, Mass., 1995), 564–67. On legal studies, see Richard Delgado and Jean Stefancic, "Critical Race Theory: An Annotated Bibliography," *Virginia Law Review* 79 (March 1993): 461–516.

11

"Too Dark to Be Angels": The Class System among the Cherokees at the Female Seminary

Devon A. Mihesuah

The Cherokee Female Seminary was a nondenominational boarding school established by the Cherokee Nation at Park Hill, Indian Territory, in order to provide high-quality education for the young women of its tribe. The curriculum was based on that of Mount Holyoke Seminary in South Hadley, Massachusetts, and it offered no courses focusing on Cherokee culture. The seminary first opened in 1851, but in 1887 it was destroyed by fire. Two years later a larger, three-story seminary building was erected on the outskirts of the Cherokee Nation's capital, Tahlequah. By 1909, when the building was converted into Northeastern State Normal School by the new state of Oklahoma, approximately three thousand Cherokee girls had attended the seminary. A male seminary was built at the same time, three miles from the female seminary; it educated Cherokee youth until it burned in 1910.[1]

While the female seminary was indeed a positive influence on many of its pupils, there is much evidence to suggest that the social atmosphere at the seminary contributed to the rift between Cherokee girls from progressive, mixed-blood families and those from more traditional, uneducated backgrounds. Although many of the girls hailed from traditional families, the seminary did nothing to preserve or reinforce Cherokee customs among its students. But retention of ancestral Cherokee values was not the purpose of the school's establishment.

The Cherokee National Council was controlled by progressive, educated, mixed-blood tribesmen, many of whom subscribed to the value system of the upper-class antebellum South. Their decisions regarding the seminary were supported by most of the mixed-bloods of the tribe—white men and their Cherokee spouses (for the most part mixed-bloods)—and, to a lesser extent, by the progressive full-bloods. The prime interest of these progressive tribal members was indeed education, but also the proper "refinement" of their daughters so that they could serve as knowledgeable, but dutiful, wives in the Cherokee Nation. Another reason for the seminary was the acculturation of the poor full-blood girls, but apparently this idea did not come about until 1871, after the council was pressured by disgruntled tribesmen to establish a "primary department" to provide education free of charge to poorer full-blood children who could not afford the five-dollar-per-semester tuition charged beginning in 1872.[2]

The social aspects of the seminary are intriguing. Regardless of social, economic, and ancestral backgrounds, all the girls (with the exception of a few white pupils and girls of other tribes) identified themselves as Cherokees. Because of these socioeconomic differences, within the seminary walls a definite class system evolved, creating tension much like that which existed throughout the Cherokee Nation between the mixed-bloods and the full-bloods, between the traditionalists and the progressives, and between those tribal members who were proslavery and those who were not.[3]

Figure 11.1. The second Cherokee Female Seminary Building (circa 1902) was closer to Tahlequah, with a better water supply. It measured 246' × 69', with an eastern wing measuring 70' × 100', and it cost $78,000 to build. (All photos in this article courtesy of the University Archives, John Vaughan Library , Northeastern State University, Tahlequah, Oklahoma.)

During the seminary's early years (1851–56) there was no tuition fee, but money undoubtedly determined who entered the seminary. In the 1850s, according to the laws of the Cherokee Nation, the only prerequisite for admittance was an acceptable score on the entrance examination (except during the summer sessions, when all students paid), combined, perhaps, with a first-come-first-served priority. But daughters of politically prominent and affluent families (Adair, Bushyhead, Hicks, McNair, Ross, and Thompson, to name a few) were always enrolled.[4] These girls were from acculturated, educated households, had already attended good public schools, and had no difficulty passing the written examination. Most full-bloods who wanted to enroll did not have the educational background that enabled them to pass the test. The schools they attended in the distant reaches of the Cherokee Nation were not as well equipped as those closer to the capital, Tahlequah, nor were there enough Cherokee-speaking teachers to help them learn English.

In 1856 the seminary closed because of financial difficulties. After it reopened in 1872, the enrollment situation changed somewhat, but money still gave students an advantage. Some students who failed courses semester after semester were repeatedly granted readmittance—as long as they could pay the tuition.[5] Indicative of the lenient standards of English for tuition payers is an excerpt from a student's letter to her sister in 1889:

> I seat myself this evening to right you a few lines to let you know that I am well at the present and hope this to find you the same I was glad to hear frome you this evening I haven't got but 2 letters frome home and one frome you and I have writen 6 letters since I have been here and this is the 7 I aint rooming with no body yet here is the picture of the jail house.[6]

Although many students were indeed from affluent families, wealthy students were in the minority.[7] It is true that the majority of the students came from families who could manage to pay the tuition, but they were not necessarily from the monied class. In fact, daughters of the wealthier families were sent to schools outside the Cherokee Nation and never attended the female seminary.[8] And each year dozens of primary-school students went to the school free of charge. The class system at the seminary, then, was based on money from 1851 to 1856, but from 1872 until 1910 was apparently based more on race (Cherokee and white blood quantums), appearance (Indian or Caucasian), and degree of acculturation.

Acculturated students and teachers took tremendous pride in their education and appearance. Mixed-blood students frequently scorned those girls who had less white blood and darker skin. A few progressive full-bloods also belittled those who had limited understanding of white ways. It was the general consensus among the mixed-blood students that the full-blood girls were "a little bit backward," and the full-bloods were well aware of their inferior status at the seminary.[9]

Many factors contributed to the feelings of inferiority and alienation experienced by the full-bloods and "unenlightened" mixed-bloods at the school. Since most full-bloods and some poor mixed-bloods worked for their room and board, they were assigned to the third floor with the primary-school students. Because they were often lagging academically, many were placed in classes with the younger girls. They were left behind on social excursions, because only those in the high-school grades were allowed to attend events in Tahlequah and the male seminarians' ball games. Unlike the pupils whose parents sent them spending money, the poorer students were unable to afford party clothes, nor could they buy after-dinner snacks from the local vendors—also a social occasion.

The attitudes of some of the teachers also led to resentment among many of the full-bloods. The National Council employed many qualified mixed-blood instructors, but there were no traditional Cherokee teachers. Despite the instructors' sympathies for the traditional girls, they rarely understood the problems the full-bloods faced. In 1908, for example, mixed-blood seminary superintendent Albert Sydney Wyly (an 1890 graduate of the male seminary) expressed his impatience with the full-blood girls by referring to the mixed-bloods as "whiter" and therefore "more intellectual." He criticized the full-bloods for their "pathetic attachment to home" and remarked patronizingly that at least they "possess a great deal of artistic ability."[10]

Another example of insensitivity is cited by teacher Dora Wilson Hearon, who in 1895 noted that she and her aunt, principal Ann Florence Wilson, took the third-floor inspection duty because the other teachers were repelled by the students' head lice.[11] In 1907, prior to the school's first rehearsal of the annual Shakespeare production (*A Midsummer Night's Dream*), a mixed-blood senior responded to the administration's concerned query, "Full-blood girls to do Shakespeare? Impossible!" by saying, "You don't know [teachers] Miss Allen and Miss Minta Foreman!" implying that these instructors were indeed miracle workers.[12]

The teachers also relentlessly reinforced the importance of learning and retaining the values of white society. At the same time they repressed Cherokee values, thereby causing confusion among the more traditional students. One instructor, Kate O'Donald Ringland, later recalled that in regard to seminary philosophy, "anything 'white' was ideal";[13] an alumna remembers learning in the primary grades that the "white way was the only acceptable way."[14] DeWitt Clinton Duncan spoke for his fellow National Council members in a lengthy *Cherokee Advocate* (the Cherokee Nation newspaper) diatribe when he asked, "Can the mental wants of an Indian youth be satisfied . . . by resources less fruitful than that which caters to the Anglo-Saxon mind? The Cherokee language, at the present advanced

Figure 11.2. The fourteen members of the Cherokee Female Seminary class of 1905.

period of their [Cherokees'] civilization, cannot meet the exigencies of our people."[15] With the National Council advocating white education, the traditionalists were continually pressured to adopt a different culture if they wanted to attend the seminary.

But not all seminary full-bloods felt ostracized. At least 165 full-bloods enrolled in the seminary (about 11 percent of the fifteen hundred students whose blood quantums can be ascertained), and they stayed enrolled an average of four semesters, two semesters longer than the mixed-bloods, but five semesters less than the graduates.[16] This was probably because girls of one family frequently attended school together, which helped to alleviate homesickness. Some were even adopted into the "big happy seminary family," a phrase used by a mixed-blood (1/32 Cherokee blood) to refer to the upper echelons of the student hierarchy.[17] Because of interruptions such as the Civil War, the destruction of the school by fire, smallpox epidemics, and alternative educational opportunities, not one student, not even a graduate (many of whom enrolled for more than ten semesters), remained in the seminary from first grade through graduation.[18]

Full-bloods who enrolled in the common schools usually learned to speak and read Cherokee, but many were not particularly happy about it and wanted the type of education offered at the seminary. A student at the Cave Springs common school who desired to attend the seminary stated that the common schools could not compete with the female seminary because "we can only interpret Sequoyah's alphabet."[19] After the 1870s many of the neighborhood common schools taught in the Cherokee language for the benefit of the full-bloods; therefore, high-school-age children who could not afford the seminary tuition were limited in their educational choices.

Some full-bloods who wanted a seminary education were willing to work for their tuition, but only a limited number of workers were allowed each semester. Some of the more acculturated full-blood girls at the seminary were from families that could afford the tuition. Thus these students were able to live with the mixed-bloods on the second floor and enjoyed an elevated status. Many of them did not speak Cherokee, nor did they have any interest in traditional Cherokee customs. As seminary alumna Charlotte Mayes Sanders recalls, the "full-bloods went to Tahlequah to become like the white folk."[20] Indeed, many of their families had already succeeded, and the children came to the seminary armed with the knowledge of white society necessary to function among their acculturated peers.

Especially in the early years, citizens of the Cherokee Nation charged that elitism and prejudice against the full-bloods existed at the seminary. But in 1854 progressive full-blood student Na-Li eloquently defended her seminary by stating in *The Cherokee Rose Buds* (the newspaper of the seminary in the 1850s) that "it is sometimes said that our Seminaries were made only for the rich and those who were not full Cherokee; but it is a mistake. . . . Our Chief and directors would like very much that they [full Cherokees] should come and enjoy these same privileges as those that are here present."[21] Na-Li, however, had been adopted by a mission at an early age, had had a thorough primary education, and easily passed the admittance examination.

In further defense of her heritage and skin color, Na-Li asserted that although her parents were "full Cherokees . . . belonging to the common class," she felt it "no disgrace to be a full Cherokee. My complexion does not prevent me from acquiring knowledge and being useful hereafter. . . . [I will] endeavor to be useful, although I sometimes think that I cannot be."[22] It appears that the more Cherokee blood a girl had, or the more Indian she looked, the more she felt she had to prove herself as a scholar and as a useful member of a society that (she believed) valued only those women who were white in appearance and in attitude.

Na-Li probably was not entirely incorrect in her interpretation of the values of the mixed-bloods. Even progressive mixed-blood girls who were dark-skinned faced prejudice. Florence Waters (5/16 Cherokee) was told by a lighter-skinned classmate that she could not participate in the elocution class production of *The Peri* because "angels are fair-haired and you are too dark for an angel."[23] When the full-blood girls did go to Tahlequah, and especially outside the Cherokee Nation, they had more difficulty adapting to society's "whiteness." In 1899 the preponderance of mixed-blood Cherokees in Tahlequah was illustrated by *Twin Territories* writer Ora Eddleman, who expressed dismay over the wealthy Cherokees and the "blond Cherokee women."[24]

The seminarians were indeed defensive about their hair and skin coloring. In an 1855 issue of *A Wreath of Cherokee Rose Buds*, girls complained in an editorial about the Townsend, Massachusetts, female seminary's paper, *The Lesbian Wreath*, which referred to the Cherokee girls as their "dusky sisters."[25] A popular practice of the Cherokee seminary's paper was to tell anecdotes and stories in which appearance was a prominent factor, particularly blue eyes. For example, one story tells of the consequences that young "Kate M." faced after plagiarizing a poem for literature class. "Fun and abundance," student Lusette writes, "peeped from her blue eyes . . . and the crimson blush stole upon her cheeks." In the same issue, author Inez writes about what her schoolmates might be doing in four years. One student is described as a "fair, gay, blue-eyed girl," and another is a "fairy-like creature with auburn hair." Still another story by student Icy, entitled "Two Companions," pairs Hope ("the very personification of loveliness") with a "tiny, blue-eyed child" named Faith.[26] Evidently, to the seminary students, blue eyes were the epitome of enlightenment and civilization.

Unquestionably ethnocentric, the seminarians were convinced of their superiority over individuals of other tribes. After a group of Osage men visited the seminary in 1855, student Irene wrote a romantic essay—not unlike those of white authors of the day—about

Figure 11.3. Female seminarians on the school's front porch, 1897.

the "lofty, symmetrical forms, and proud, free step, of these sons of nature just from their wild hunting ground." She found their war dance amusing ("those tall, dusky forms stomping and stooping around . . . making a wailing sound"). In comparing her tribe and theirs, she pointed out that the Osages listened attentively to the seminarians sing "Over There," because, she figured, at least the "wild and untutored Savage has an ear for music as well as the cultivated and refined."[27]

Other essays in *Rose Buds* include anecdotes about "hostile Indians" attacking peaceful Cherokees in the "wild and unknown regions" on the way to the California gold fields, and about "barbarous Camanches [sic]" living in their "wild wilderness." A student named Cherokee described a Seneca Dog Dance in which the drum "made a very disagreeable noise. . . . What there was in such music to excite the Senecas' belles is more than I can imagine." Although she judged the dancers to be graceful, she believed they "ought to have been at something better."[28]

Many of the girls came from slaveholding families, yet the issue of slavery was not mentioned in any issues of the *Rose Buds*, nor in any of the female students' or teachers' memoirs. (A male seminarian later referred to a black man as a "nigger.") Separation of the Cherokee and black races was a fact, however, and the children of the black freedmen could only attend the "Negro High School."[29]

Yet at the same time that the "upper-class" Cherokees believed themselves to be elevated above the unenlightened members of their tribe and above other tribes as a whole, these same girls and teachers felt inferior to the whites, despite the fact that many of them had more "white blood" than Cherokee.[30] So they took every opportunity to flaunt their white ancestry. Female seminary superintendent and male seminary graduate Spencer Seago Stephens, for example, proclaimed in 1889 that "it is the white blood that has made us what we are. . . . If missionaries wish to lift up Indian tribes . . . let them encourage intermarriage with whites." Unsure that the Cherokees could obtain a high level of civilization by themselves, he asserted that "intermarriage will accomplish the purpose quickly."[31]

Commentary from Cherokee citizens who shared Stephens's belief in the productive influence of association with whites appeared in the *Cherokee Advocate*. Writer "Cherokee" observed that "the gloom that pervades the red man's mind is fast disappearing: instead of darkness and doubt, his countenance is being lit up with intelligence." To indicate that the traditionalists of the tribe were perhaps heathenistic compared to their progressive peers, he further asserted that "those who cling with death-like tenacity to our old rites and ceremonies do not consider that a moral change is taking place in the Cherokee world."[32]

The attitude that the Cherokees needed a moral change was also illustrated in *The Sequoyah Memorial*, the newspaper of the Cherokee Male Seminary. One student wrote that "the bow and arrow have been laid aside," and that until the Cherokees reached the "summit of civilization and refinement," they could never be happy and contented.[33] Female seminary student Estelle stated, "O! that all, especially among the Cherokees could but learn the vast importance of a good education. This and this only will place us on equality with other enlightened and cultivated nations."[34]

Students were profoundly influenced by the comments of their chiefs. At the annual May picnic in 1877 celebrating the opening of the seminaries, acculturation advocate William Potter Ross expressed his fears that his tribe would be outdone by other tribes in Indian Territory: "While our neighboring Tribes and Nations are pressing forward in the pursuit of knowledge, let not the Cherokee . . . be second in the race." The last thing his tribe needed, he warned the seminarians, was "lazy and useless men" and "slouchy and slip-shod women."[35] And to make it clear that the Cherokees still had not reached that summit of equality with whites by 1884, Chief Dennis Bushyhead earnestly spoke of the importance of praying at the same altar with "our whiter and stronger brothers [giving] our common thanks to God . . . [that they] will show magnanimity and justice to their weaker brethren."[36]

Students also took pleasure in comparing the old Cherokee ways with the new and improved lifestyles of the tribe to show that many tribal members had progressed past savagery and were on their way to equality with whites. In an 1854 issue of the *Cherokee Rose Buds*, student Edith championed the virtues of nineteenth-century white society and boasted the progress the Cherokees had made: "Instead of the rudely constructed wigwams of our forefathers which stood there [the Park Hill area] not more than half-a-century ago," she wrote, "elegant white buildings are seen. Everything around denotes taste, refinement, and progress of civilization among our people."[37]

The prolific Na-Li collaborated with another student in 1855 to illustrate their uneducated ancestors' backwardness and, more important, to emphasize the vast improvements the tribe had made. In scene one of the essay "Two Scenes in Indian Land," Na-Li describes a "wild and desolate" estate of a Cherokee family composed of "whooping, swarthy-looking boys" and plaited-haired women, all of whom "bear a striking resemblance to their rude and uncivilized hut." She concludes that the poor imbeciles "pass the days of their wild, passive, uninteresting life without any intellectual pleasure or enjoyment," except, she adds, to attend the Green Corn Dance, a "kind of religious festival."[38]

Scene two, by author Fanny, paints a completely different picture of Cherokee life. In her commentary, even the environment around the family's home has magically blossomed from the influence of the missionaries. "Civilization and nature are here united," she expounds. "Flowers, music, and even better, the *Holy Word of God* is here to study, showing that religion has shed its pure light over all." The Indian lad, "in place of his bow and arrow, is now taught to use the pen and wield the powers of eloquence." The girl, "instead of keep-

Figure 11.4. Female and male seminary drama club members performing in blackface, 1896. This skit was entitled "De Debatin' Club."

ing time with the rattling of the terrapin shells [around her ankles], now keeps time with the chalk as her fingers fly nimbly over the blackboard." Fanny then professes her hope that "we may advance, never faltering until all the clouds of ignorance and superstition, and wickedness flee from before the rays of the Suns of Knowledge and Righteousness."[39] In these tales, then, there was the possibility that the "wild Cherokee Indian" could be changed and become a new person. The seminarians were not shy in vocalizing their hope that their unsophisticated peers would do the same.

Other passages reflect the students' feelings of inferiority to whites. The same *Rose Buds* issue that discusses "elegance and civilization" of the Cherokee Nation also compares the tribe unfavorably with the eastern United States by stating that the new bride of Chief John Ross, Mary Stapler, admirably left her more civilized surroundings in Philadelphia in order to "dwell with him in his *wild* prairie home."[40] Another editorial, commenting on the completed 1855 spring term, declares, "We present you again with a collection of Rosebuds, gathered from our Seminary garden. If, on examining them, you chance to find a withered or dwarfish bud, please pass it by. . . . We hope for lenient judgement, when our efforts are compared with those of our white sisters."[41] Another editorial, "Exchanges," acknowledges the newspapers received from other girls' schools in New England. But the Cherokee seminarians did not send copies of *Rose Buds* in return, because, as an editor explains, "we feel ourselves entirely too feeble to make any adequate recompense. . . . We are simply Cherokee school girls."[42]

In light of the reverence held for the Cherokee Female Seminary by the progressive tribal members, and considering the reason for its establishment, it is little wonder that the 212 girls who graduated from the seminary and, to a lesser extent, those who did not graduate but used their seminary education to obtain degrees from other institutions were considered the crème de la crème of the Cherokee Nation.[43] But that narrow-minded attitude ignores the more than 2,770 girls who did not graduate from the female seminary or from any other school.[44] Granted, many girls left the seminary before they had completed their first semester, and some left after only one week. But their early departures do not necessarily indicate an inability to handle the workload or the social atmosphere of the school.

Some dropouts had had problems with the course of study, but not all of them had been unable to master the difficult subjects. According to the student grade lists from 1876 to 1903, most were able to cope with the Mount Holyoke–style curriculum.[45] Prior to their enrollment in the female seminary, many of the pupils had attended the Cherokee common schools, the Cherokee Orphan Asylum, or one of the missionary schools or other high schools outside the Cherokee Nation, and had reasonably good educational backgrounds.[46] In addition, many mixed-blood parents hired private tutors if their daughters had difficulty with their studies or if the common-school teachers were incompetent.

The graduates, of course, made high grades (80s to 90s) throughout their careers at the seminary. Most of those who graduated were from comparatively affluent families, which enabled them to visit their homes more often than students from remote areas.[47] Many of the graduates were related and attended the school at the same time as their relatives, which helped to alleviate homesickness.[48] And, like successful students today, the girls who performed best received encouragement from their parents. Of the parents whose records could be examined, graduates' fathers had a 98 percent literacy rate and their mothers 100 percent, compared to the 82 percent and 86 percent literacy rate of the nongraduates' fathers and mothers, respectively. Most of the full-bloods' parents could not write in English, and just 69 percent of their fathers and 55 percent of their mothers could read.[49] Only two of the graduates were full-bloods, and they had been adopted by white and mixed-blood parents and were educated in mission schools prior to seminary enrollment.[50]

Most of those who dropped out after one semester still made medium to high grades (70s to 90s). These dropouts usually left because of personal or family illness, an impending marriage, or homesickness. Other factors, such as the seminary's closure in 1856, the destructive fire in 1887, the departure of Principal Wilson in 1901, and the creation of Northeastern State Normal School in 1909, caused students to enroll in other schools. In 1893 several girls voluntarily went home because of the crowded living conditions. In 1902, because of the increased prosperity of the nation's farmers and the need for a "large force" to harvest crops, many students returned to the farm to do "home work."[51] A large number of these dropouts (except those who married immediately) enrolled in and graduated from other institutions.

Dropouts who had made low grades (50 or below) were in the minority. These students often left soon after enrolling (within the first day or month). Most were traditional full-bloods, or mixed-bloods of one-half to three-quarters Cherokee, who had attended distant Cherokee-language common schools and were not prepared for the difficult curriculum or the oppressive white atmosphere of the school.

Indeed, while some Cherokees did want to send their children to the school but could not afford to, some full-bloods opposed the seminaries and did not send their children to them even if they had the money. Prejudice against traditional Cherokees was the parents' main argument, but they also had doubts about the practicality of the school's curriculum. The seminary met the expectations of the National Council, the teachers, and most of the nation's citizens, but some Cherokees protested that the academic curriculum was not applicable to the needs of the students.

This attitude was expressed in a letter to the *Cherokee Advocate* in 1881 signed "Bood Guy." The writer stated, "What our youngsters ought to be . . . are farmers and stock raisers." He doubted that the students heard "the words 'farm' or 'farming' during the entire three or four years' course of instruction." Preferring practical training over academic courses, the writer asked, "What sense or good is there in preparing our youth for their [white] business?" He concluded that both seminaries were merely "pieces of imitation, with the high schools of the United States for models," and therefore served no practical purpose in a nation composed mainly of farmers. The education that the students received, he believed, "ought to conform to, and fit them for, what they expect to become."[52] In 1880—out of a population of approximately 25,438—3,550 Cherokees were farmers, 135 were mechanics, and 82 were teachers.[53]

The debate over educational priorities had begun as early as 1823, when Chief John Ross and Second Principal Chief Charles Hicks disagreed over the type of "national academy" the tribe should establish. Ross advocated the traditional, New England–style school, while Hicks championed what he believed was the most practical education for the tribe, a vocational school.[54] The council disregarded Hicks's suggestion, and thirty-three years later Indian agent W. A. Duncan reported that the seminaries still "were only producing intellectuals . . . but not everyone can become a professional . . . [or] live here without manual labor."[55] Because of pressure from tribal members who wanted vocational training to be available, the National Council gave the board of education permission to declare the boarding schools "industrial or manual labor boarding schools."[56]

Within the next few years, principal chiefs Dennis Bushyhead and Joel B. Mayes took a strong interest in the accomplishments of the seminaries. Bushyhead acknowledged the "gratifying results" of the seminaries' curriculum, but in 1881 he advocated using more of the tax revenue for a mandatory "system of manual labor" for the primary-grade students (who were usually from poor, farming families) that would be "optionary" for the upper grades. In the 1890s Chief Mayes tried to persuade the National Council to purchase Fort Gibson for use as an industrial school, but the council was not receptive to the idea, presumably because most of the councilmen's children attended the seminaries and had no intention of becoming farmers or laborers.[57]

The Department of the Interior's annual report for 1899 stated that instead of "being taught the domestic arts [girls] are given . . . Latin and mathematics while branches of domestic economy are neglected. The dignity of work receives no attention at their hands."[58] The seminary administrators yielded to the pressure, and by 1905 the school's "domestic science" department included lessons in cooking, cleaning (dusting and making their beds; a laundress washed their clothes), sewing (usually to mend torn clothes; only a few girls became skilled seamstresses), and a modest agricultural program that featured botany, gardening, and flower arrangement.[59]

Many alumnae did become agriculturalists, but others had a profound interest in the whites' more lucrative businesses. Because many of their parents and siblings owned and operated stores in Tahlequah or other parts of the Cherokee Nation, the girls already had developed the confidence to pursue careers in the business world and were not afraid to interact with whites. In addition, many of the more progressive girls came from families who had hired help to perform domestic chores.

The girls who graduated were, as a whole, the most acculturated and affluent students at the seminary. After graduation, they became, among other things, educators, businesswomen, physicians, stock raisers, and prominent social workers.[60] They also followed their mothers' examples and "married well." Of the 212 graduates, at least 189 eventually married. Most of them married white men or men who had a smaller amount of Cherokee blood than they had. In a few cases, the husbands had a greater degree of Indian blood, but in every such instance they were either physicians, politicians, or members of prominent (usually wealthy) Cherokee families.[61] Clearly, the more white blood the woman had, the more apt she was to marry a non-Cherokee, a tribal member with high social status, or a man who had at least the same degree of white blood that she possessed. Indicative of the latter were the fifteen women who married graduates of the male seminary.[62]

Another interesting aspect was (and is) the value placed upon blood quantums as a source of identity. Many of the girls who went to the seminaries often had brothers and sisters who did not attend. In a comparison of the quantums of entire families, it is apparent that the women who married white men, or men with a lesser degree of Cherokee blood than they had, had tended during enrollment to claim a lesser degree of Cherokee blood than their siblings—perhaps in an attempt to appear "whiter," while at the same time retaining their Cherokee identity. In contrast to the value systems of the seminarians, many of their descendants today claim a Dawes Roll error and argue that their ancestors were much more Cherokee than they said they were. It appears that there is now a movement among many Americans to find or inflate their Cherokee roots, a distinct contrast to many of the seminarians, who were more interested in their non-Indian backgrounds.[63]

Despite the differences of opinion between the traditional and the progressive Cherokees over education, and despite the school's class system, the Cherokee Female Seminary survived as a tribal institution for over five decades.[64] The hundreds of Cherokee girls who passed through its halls were profoundly influenced—both positively and negatively—by their experiences at the school.

The girls' seminary experiences helped to strengthen their identities as Cherokees, although there were differences in opinion as to what a Cherokee really was. At least 30 percent were of one-sixteenth degree or less Cherokee blood, yet they still considered themselves to be Cherokees.[65] Many girls had never even heard the Cherokee language. One student admitted years later, "I did not realize what my Indian heritage meant to me when I attended the Cherokee Female Seminary."[66] All she heard was the word *Cherokee*, and she assumed that all tribal members lived like the seminarians. But the full-bloods who were fluent in their native language and who participated in tribal ceremonies also saw themselves as Cherokees, and their tenure at what they regarded as an oppressive school only strengthened their ties to their traditional families.

Both the progressive and the traditional tribal members considered themselves to be more Cherokee than the other group. The progressives believed that because of their enlightening educational and religious experiences, their intermarriage with whites, and their successful reestablishment in Indian Territory after their removal from the East, they were the new and improved Cherokees. The traditionalists, on the other hand, viewed the mixed-bloods not as Cherokees but as non-Indian "sellouts" or, at best, "white Cherokees." Interestingly, just like many mixed-bloods today, the Cherokee women who looked Caucasian found that their appearance, in combination with their educational backgrounds, gave them an advantage: They were able to slip back and forth between the white and Cherokee cultures (or at least the Cherokee culture they were used to), depending on their needs.

Not all tribal members subscribed to the school's philosophy, but a large portion of them did. Although there undoubtedly was prejudice against the traditional girls—and these students were often devastated by their seminary experiences—full-bloods were at least exposed to the ways of white society, and the mixed-blood girls had the opportunity to interact for a short time with less acculturated tribal members.

The female seminary is remembered for what it stood for: acculturation, assimilation, enlightenment, or survival, depending on the needs and values of the alumnae. The school

Figure 11.5. Members of the class of 1903, left to right: Leola "Lee" Ward Newton, Grace Wallace Richards, Caroline "Carri" Freeman Baird, and Laura Effie Duchworth Boatright. All four were 1/32 Cherokee blood.

was not meant for every female Cherokee; the seminary's atmosphere and attitude were white, and the progressive Cherokees were attempting to acculturate their peers. While the school contributed to a detrimental class system, the education it offered gave a strong educational background to those who went on to colleges and universities and was invaluable to the acculturated girls' success in business and in social circles within and outside of the Cherokee Nation.

Despite its shortcomings, the Cherokee Female Seminary was unquestionably the catalyst for the prosperity of many Cherokee women and their families. To many Cherokees, the old female seminary building, which now stands on the campus of Northeastern State University in Tahlequah, remains a symbol of adaptation and progress in a changing, and often inhospitable, world.

Notes

1. See Devon I. Abbott, "The History of the Cherokee Female Seminary: 1851–1910" (Ph.D. dissertation, Texas Christian University, 1989) and "'Commendable Progress': Acculturation at the Cherokee Female Seminary," *American Indian Quarterly* 11 (summer 1987): 187–201. The total enrollment is estimated, because ten years of seminary rolls are missing. Although thirty years of rolls are available, my estimate of the enrollment is lower than the apparent totals on the rolls, because many girls attended the seminary for more than one year. For this study, their names were recorded only once—for a total of almost three thousand different names.
2. "An Act in Relation to the Male and Female Seminaries, and Establishing Primary Departments Therein for the Education of Indigent Children," 28 November 1873, in *Constitutions and Laws of the Cherokee Nation* (St. Louis: R. and T. A. Ennis Stationers, Printers and Book Binders, 1975), reprinted as vol. 7 of *Constitutions and Laws of the American Indian Tribes* (Wilmington, Del.: Scholarly Resources, Inc., 1973), 267–69.
3. Not all full-bloods were traditional and/or poor, nor were all mixed-bloods progressive and/or wealthy.

4. Thomas Lee Ballenger, *Names of Students of Cherokee Male and Female Seminaries, Tahlequah, Oklahoma, from 1876 to 1904*, in Special Collections, Northeastern State University (NSU), Tahlequah, Oklahoma.

5. "Ann Florence Wilson's Grade Book" or "Cherokee Female Seminary Records of Grades, 1876–1909," in NSU's Office of Admissions and Records, Administration Building, Tahlequah.

6. Letter dated 10 September 1889, in Cherokee Female Seminary Miscellaneous Box, archives, NSU.

7. The students' socioeconomic backgrounds were compiled by the author, using the Index to the Five Civilized Tribes, the Final Dawes Roll, M1186, roll 1, and the Enrollment Cards for the Five Civilized Tribes, 1898–1914, rolls 2–15, cards 1–11,132, at the Federal Archives in Fort Worth, Texas.

8. Ibid., in combination with Emmett Starr, *History of the Cherokee Indians, Their Legends and Folklore* (Muskogee: Hoffman Printing, Inc., 1984), 489–680.

9. Personal interview with Pearl Mayes Langston, 6 June 1989, Fort Gibson, Oklahoma.

10. Albert Sydney Wyly to John D. Benedict (1908), letter in Miscellaneous Female Seminary Box, archives, NSU.

11. For information on Ann Florence Wilson, see Devon I. Abbott, "Ann Florence Wilson, Matriarch of the Cherokee Seminary," *Chronicles of Oklahoma* 67 (winter 1989–90): 426–37.

12. Maggie Culver Fry, comp., *Cherokee Female Seminary Years: A Cherokee National Anthology by Many Tribal Authors* (Claremore, Okla.: Rogers State College Press, 1988), 83.

13. Kate O'Ringland to Abraham Knepler, 21 April 1938 (Knepler, Ph.D. dissertation, "Digest of the Education of the Cherokee Indians," Yale University, 1939, 323).

14. Personal interview with Rick Corley, 27 December 1988, Arlington, Texas.

15. *Cherokee Advocate*, 23 August 1873, 2.

16. "Wilson's Grade Book."

17. Personal interview with Charlotte Mayes Sanders, 20 October 1988, Tahlequah, Oklahoma.

18. "Wilson's Grade Book."

19. *Cherokee Advocate*, 2 May 1884.

20. Interview with Sanders.

21. *The Cherokee Rose Buds*, 2 August 1854, 2.

22. Ibid.

23. Fry, *Cherokee Female Seminary Years*, 104–5.

24. *Twin Territories*, June 1899.

25. *Wreath of Cherokee Rose Buds*, 14 February 1855, 2, at Anthropological Archives, Smithsonian Institution, Washington, D.C.

26. Ibid., 5; *Cherokee Rose Buds*, 2 August 1854, 6, at archives, NSU.

27. *Wreath of Cherokee Rose Buds*, 14 February 1855, 5.

28. Ibid., 4, 6.

29. Thomas L. Ballenger, "The Colored High School of the Cherokee Nation," *Chronicles of Oklahoma* 30 (winter 1952–53): 454–62.

30. The students' blood quantums were derived by the author from the census records and the Index to the Five Civilized Tribes, the Final Dawes Roll, M1186, roll 1, and the Enrollment Cards for the Five Civilized Tribes, 1898–1914, M1186, rolls 2–15, cards 1–11,132, at the Federal Archives. The Final Dawes Roll has many errors in regard to the Cherokees' blood quantums, so cross-references of other family members were used. If the student died prior to the opening of the rolls, the quantum was found via either siblings, children, or parents. Married names were located on the census records, in newspapers, and in Emmett Starr, *History of the Cherokees*. A few of the early students, graduates, and husbands had died, leaving no progeny and thus no clue as to their degree of Cherokee blood, but only two were reported to be full-bloods. Some of the students during the later years (1903–9) were not enrolled, because they were recent arrivals to Indian Territory.

31. *Kansas City Times*, 29 July 1889, 2. Stephens's comment almost echoes Thomas Jefferson's speech to Indians visiting Washington, D.C., in 1808, when he said, "You will unite yourselves with us, join in our great councils and form one people with us, and we shall all be Americans; you will mix with us by marriage, your blood will run in our veins, and will spread with us over this great continent." In Saul K. Padover, *Thomas Jefferson on Democracy* (New York: Mentor, New American Library, Appleton-Century Co., 1939), 106–7, quoted in William G. McLoughlin, *Cherokee Renascence in the New Republic* (Princeton: Princeton University Press, 1986), 37.

32. *Cherokee Advocate*, 4 February 1851, 2.

33. *The Sequoyah Memorial*, 2 August 1855, in archives, NSU.

34. *Wreath of Cherokee Rose Buds*, 14 February 1855, 3.

35. *The Journal*, 17 May 1877, 1.

36. Cited in V. A. Travis, "Life in the Cherokee Nation a Decade after the Civil War," *Chronicles of Oklahoma* 4 (March 1926), 30.

37. *Cherokee Rose Buds*, 2 August 1854, 3.

38. *Wreath of Cherokee Rose Buds*, 1 August 1855, 1–2.
39. Ibid.
40. *Cherokee Rose Buds*, 2 August 1854, 3.
41. *Wreath of Cherokee Rose Buds*, 1 August 1855, 4.
42. Ibid.
43. Statement by Professor Rudi Halliburton at the Seventeenth Annual Symposium on the American Indian, 3–8 April 1989, at NSU.
44. See Abbott, "History of the Cherokee Female Seminary," Appendix A, for some of the nonseminary graduates and the colleges and universities they enrolled in.
45. "Wilson's Grade Book."
46. See N. B. Johnson, "The Cherokee Orphan Asylum," *Chronicles of Oklahoma* 34 (summer 1956): 159–82.
47. The students' home districts were compiled from the 1880 Cherokee Census and Index, schedules 1–6, 7RA-07, rolls 1–4, and the 1890 Cherokee Census (no index), schedules 1–4, 7RA-08, rolls 1–4, at the Federal Archives; "Wilson's Grade Book"; "Mary Stapler's Class Book" at archives, NSU; *Catalog of the C.N.F.S., 1896 and Announcements for 1897 and 1898*, 3–6, at archives, NSU; *Souvenir Catalog: 1850–1905*, at archives, NSU; "Register and Accounts of Female Seminary Primary and Boarding School Students," bound ledger in archives, NSU.
48. At least one hundred families sent three or more children—including sisters and cousins—to attend the seminary at the same time.
49. The parents' literacy rates were compiled from the 1880 Cherokee Census and Index, schedules 1–6, 7RA-07, rolls 1–4, and the 1890 Cherokee Census (no index), schedules 1–4, 7RA-08, rolls 1–4, at the Federal Archives.
50. Catherine Hastings Maxfield, 1855, and Martha Whiting Fox, 1856. The 1880 Cherokee Census and Index, schedules 1–6, 7RA-07, rolls 1–4.
51. *Cherokee Advocate*, 9 September 1893, 2; ibid., 16 September 1893, 2; ibid., 30 September 1893, 2; ibid., 7 October 1893, 2; ibid., 14 October 1893, 2; Cop-pock to Benedict, 11 July 1901, *Report of the Commissioner of Indian Affairs (RCIA)*, 57th Cong., 1st sess., H. Doc. 5 (serial 4291), 318–19; CHN 97, Cherokee Schools: *Female Seminary, Documents 2735–2777*, 11 May 1887-December 1902, at the Oklahoma Historical Society, Oklahoma City.
52. *Cherokee Advocate*, 31 August 1881, 1.
53. Leslie Hewes, *Occupying the Cherokee Country of Oklahoma* (Lincoln: University of Nebraska, 1978), 39.
54. Ard Hoyt to Jeremiah Evarts, 14 August 1823, American Board Commissioners Foreign Missions, letter 104, ABC, 18.3.1, vol. 3, quoted in William McLoughlin's *The Cherokee Ghost Dance* (Macon, Ga.: Mercer University Press, 1984), 494.
55. Report of W. A. Duncan, 25 September 1856, *RCIA for 1853*, 34th Cong., 3rd sess., H. Exec. Doc. 1 (serial 893), 692.
56. Sec. 20 of "An Act Relating to Education," in *Compiled Laws of the Cherokee Nation* (Tahlequah, I.T.: National Advocate Print, 1881), reprinted as vol. 9 of *Constitutions and Laws of the American Indian Tribes* (Wilmington, Del.: Scholarly Resources, Inc., 1973), 236.
57. "Fourth Annual Message of Chief Dennis W. Bushyhead," in *Annual Messages of Hon. Chief D. W. Bushyhead*, 33, Special Collections, NSU; *Cherokee Advocate*, 17 November 1889, 1; message of Chief Joel B. Mayes to National Council, 17 November 1889, in *Cherokee Letter Book*, vol. 14, p. 4, and J. B. Mayes to T. J. Morgan, 18 October 1890, in *Cherokee Letter Book*, vol. 3, p. 11, Phillips Collection, Western History Collection, University of Oklahoma, Norman.
58. *RCIA for 1899*, 56th Cong., 2d sess., H. Doc. 5 (serial 3915), 92.
59. *Cherokee Female Seminary Souvenir Catalog: 1850–1906*, at archives, NSU.
60. See Abbott, "History of the Cherokee Female Seminary," 181–89, and Appendices B–E.
61. See ibid., 212–13, for the girls' husbands.
62. See ibid., Appendix G for seminarians who married each other.
63. These assertions are based on findings in the 1880 and 1890 Cherokee Census Records, and the Dawes Rolls and Enrollment Cards. Additionally, in almost every interview I conducted during my study of the history of the female seminary, the subjects asserted that they were indeed more Cherokee than they appeared, because, "the Dawes Roll is wrong." My comment regarding Americans' affinity towards the Cherokee tribe is based on the startling numbers of students, colleagues, and acquaintances who have told me that they have a "full-blood Cherokee" mother or grandmother. Unfortunately, few of these individuals can substantiate their claims, since their ancestors were invariably "out of town" during the enrollment.
64. The female seminary was open for business for forty academic years.
65. Statistics compiled from the 1880 Cherokee Census and Index, schedules 1–6, 7RA-07, rolls 1–4, and the 1890 Cherokee Census (no index), schedules 1–4, 7RA-08, rolls 1–4, at Federal Archives.
66. M. Fry, *Cherokee Female Seminary Years*, 157.

12

Going for the Jugular of Hindu Patriachy: American Women Fund-Raisers for Ramabai

Kumari Jayawardena

> I beg of my Western sisters not to be satisfied with . . . the outside beauties of the grand philoso-
> phies . . . and the interested discourse of our educated men, but to open the trap doors of the
> great monuments of the ancient Hindu intellect, and enter into the dark cellars where they will
> see the real working of the philosophies they admire so much.
>
> —Ramabai (1896)

> The Christian ladies, trying to infiltrate our society under the cloak of women's education and
> their supporters—however learned—would be regarded by us as enemies of the people, of
> Hinduism and also of the cause of women's education.
>
> —B. G. Tilak (1892)

An important area of "women's work for women" was fund-raising by Western women
for good causes abroad, including missionary work. One of the famous campaigns in
America, carried out by women of various denominations, was in support of Pandita
Ramabai's project for the education of child widows and orphans in India. I chose this
particular case because it provides an early example of the dilemmas of "global sisterhood" and the predicaments caused by policy disagreements between Western fund-
raisers and Eastern recipients. Important issues of feminist consciousness among Indian
and American women arise in considering Ramabai's fierce challenge to Hindu patriarchy. But her feminism and Christianity came into conflict with emerging Hindu
nationalism and led her into serious problems with both local nationalists and foreign
funders. Feminism, nationalism, and Christianity, then, became the key issues in the
famous cause of Ramabai.

Pandita Ramabai (1858–1922) was the daughter of a Sanskrit scholar of Maharashtra, of
the exclusive caste of Chitpavan Brahmins, who had deviated from orthodoxy by teaching
his wife and children to read Sanskrit, the classical language of India. By the age of twelve
Ramabai was highly proficient in the Hindu texts. The family lived a nomadic life, moving
all over the country visiting sacred sites.[1] One aspect of Ramabai's unorthodox upbringing
was that, contrary to tradition, she had not been married off in childhood. Instead, Ramabai married Bipin Bihari Madhavi, a graduate of Calcutta University, who also belonged
to the reformist Brahmo Samaj. He was of a lower caste than Ramabai, and the marriage
was a civil ceremony, because both had liberal views and rejected Hindu orthodoxy. The
two had a daughter, but Madhavi died suddenly of cholera, leaving Ramabai in the unfortunate position of being a sonless widow in India. Rather than crushing her, this setback
led to the beginning of "her career as an Indian widow."[2] Ramabai returned to Pune, where
she had relatives, and by 1883 she was active in the reformist group Prarthana Samaj and
began speaking out on women's education, condemning child marriage and urging that

women be instructed in Sanskrit and their own local language. Several women from leading high-caste Pune families joined her in forming a women's association, the Arya Mahila Samaj. Because of her erudition, Ramabai was honored with the title Pandita. Proceeds from her book *Stree Dharma Nithi* (Moral Law for Women) enabled her to travel to England, where she lived with the sisters of St. Mary's Home, Wantage. She converted to Christianity in 1883 and taught Sanskrit at the Cheltenham Ladies' College, a school that became a model for girls' high schools in South Asia.

In India, Ramabai's conversion caused shock because she was appropriating the religion of the imperial rulers during a revival of Hinduism. To Ramabai, the situation in the 1880s seemed bleak for women. There was little evidence of social reform, with Indians and British rulers reluctant to make radical changes affecting women's position in society. Moreover, the plight of women seemed without hope as long as they were bound by the constraints of Hindu tradition. A sharp break was needed, and she made this by converting to Christianity. After four years in England, Ramabai went to Philadelphia to attend the graduation of a relative, Anandibai Joshi, who had completed her medical studies at the Women's Medical College of Pennsylvania. The college dean, Rachel Bodley, was impressed by Ramabai and assisted her in the publication, in 1887, of *The High Caste Hindu Woman*.[3] The book discusses in detail certain discriminatory aspects of Hinduism, especially child marriage and widow's status, and traces them back to Hindu theological texts, particularly the Code of Manu. Ramabai referred to the need for self-reliance (rather than lifelong dependency on men) for education, and for Indian women teachers in a country where "caste and the seclusion of women are regarded as essential tenets." The goal would be to create a body of Indian women who would teach other women "by precept and example."[4] Ramabai urged that a useful beginning could be made by concentrating on high-caste women, because these women had "quickness of perception and intelligence," and needed only education to become "competent teachers."[5]

Pandita Ramabai's feminism was way ahead of her time. Her challenge was not merely a demand for the abolition of a few social evils, but an attempt to expose and reject the patriarchal basis of religion and culture. In this she differed from the male social reformers who were highlighting the need for reforms through legislation and education, without themselves challenging the structures of oppression. Many of the reformers did not practice what they preached, some of them even taking child brides or marrying off their children while campaigning against the system.[6] As Kosambi has pointed out, Ramabai "was a solitary woman leader of the women's cause" who has long been "eclipsed by the storm over her conversion to Christianity and her consequent neglect by contemporary mainstream Hindu society, which was acutely vulnerable to assaults on its religious identity."[7]

The Formation of the Ramabai Association

Pandita Ramabai's book aroused interest among Christian circles in America. In a message to the readers Ramabai said, "Tell them to help me educate the high-caste child widows; for I solemnly believe that this hated and despised class of women, educated and enlightened, are, by God's grace, to redeem India!"[8] Ramabai's proposal was for homes for child widows, "where they can take shelter without the fear of losing their caste or being disturbed in their religious belief" and could become teachers, nurses, and housekeepers. Ramabai appealed for funds from abroad since "the great majority of my country-people being most bitterly opposed to the education of women, there is little hope of my getting from them either good words or pecuniary aid."[9] She asked for help for a period of ten years, to prove that her project could succeed, and made an emotional appeal to Americans to free Indian child widows from "life-long slavery and infernal misery" and from their tormentors: "Let the cry of India's daughters reach your ears and stir your hearts."[10] In the introduction to Ramabai's book, Rachel Bodley referred to the English missionary William Carey, who said on his departure to India in 1793, "I will go down into the deep mine, but remember that you must hold the ropes." Bodley hoped "that among the favoured women of this Christian land there might be found a sufficient number to hold the ropes for Ramabai," and added:

> When in that great Hindu nation about to come to birth, the women are moved to arise in their degradation, and cry "Help or we perish" . . . a corresponding multitude of women must be found elsewhere, willing . . . to send this help.[11]

In 1887 at a large public meeting, the Ramabai Association was formed in Boston and addressed by Ramabai under the auspices of the Unitarians, because they were "free from sectarianism"; it was reported that the "audience was moved to tears and laughter by Ramabai's pathos and keen wit."[12] Membership in the Ramabai Association entailed a pledge to give not less than one dollar a year for ten years. Provision was also made for a scholarship of one hundred dollars annually for ten years, and for donations to the building fund. From the outset there was strong liberal influence on the workings of the Ramabai Association, whose first president was the leading Unitarian clergyman of Boston, the Rev. Edward E. Hale, a doctor of divinity. He was known for his open-minded views on other religions and was involved in social reform in Boston.[13]

The women vice presidents of the Ramabai Association included Frances E. Willard, who had been president of the Evanston College for Ladies and in 1888 wrote *Women in the Pulpit*, arguing the case for women's ordination.[14] She was active in temperance, women's rights, and socialist movements. The Ramabai Association also had a board of trustees of ten persons "equally unsectarian" and composed of "some of the best business and professional men of Boston."[15] The "men" included three women, Phoebe Adam, Ellen Mason, and Pauline Agassiz Shaw.[16] The important work of the Ramabai Association was carried out by the nine women of the Executive Committee. They were of all denominations, and associated with a variety of church, humanitarian, and philanthropic activities. Thus, while the main work of the association was done by activist women, many of them veterans of earlier struggles for the abolition of slavery, the necessary status and legitimacy for fund-raising were provided by men who were the "pillars" of ecclesiastical and secular Boston society. The Ramabai Association also had two Indian advisory boards in Pune and Bombay, consisting entirely of distinguished Indian reformers and professionals.

In 1887 and 1888 Ramabai toured the United States, speaking, forming groups, and observing new methods of education. By December 1889 there were fifty-seven Ramabai Circles all over the United States and Canada with a membership of 4,069, the largest contributors being those of Brooklyn, Chicago, Cornell University, Indianapolis, New York, Smith College, Philadelphia, Richmond (Virginia), the Pacific Coast, and Toronto.[17] All these Ramabai Circles were affiliated with the main association in Boston. At the end of the second year of its activities the association reported that it was in a "strong position," having a balance of $27,000 from an income of $36,000.[18] The Ramabai Association also published a bulletin, *Lend a Hand*, which gave details of the work of the association and news about Ramabai.

Ramabai's Return to India

Ramabai returned to India via Hong Kong, where she received a rousing reception from the Indian community.[19] In Bombay she started Sharada Sadan, a school for high-caste widows. Helping her was Miss Dennison, a young American who had traveled back with her. The opening ceremonies were described as "rather novel" because Ramabai rejected advice to invite an important British official or a local dignitary to preside, choosing instead a woman writer, Kashibai Kanitkar. The school was specifically intended to be for child widows of the three high castes, the restriction ensuring that women would not refuse to come to the school on grounds of caste taboos about eating and living with those of low castes. The caste restriction, however, prevented Ramabai from applying to the government for a grant and land for school buildings. The school began with two pupils, increasing to twenty-two in three months. The number gradually grew, and after ten years 350 child widows and girls had attended the school, of whom fourteen were trained to be teachers, eight to be nurses, seven as missionary assistants, seven as matrons, two as house-keepers, and ten "of the once despised widows were happy wives in homes of their own."[20]

Sharada Sadan was shifted in 1891 to Pune, one of the innovations being the kinder-garten training class based on the Froebel system.[21] After the famine of the mid-1890s, the school was again shifted, this time to Kedgaon. There in 1896, with help from her daughter, Manorama, Ramabai started a new school, the Mukti Sadan, for famine victims of the lower castes. But by this time the ideology of the Ramabai project had narrowed. For ten years the Sharada Sadan had been run as a secular school, according to the wishes of the American funders, but "the Kedgaon establishment became openly Christian, with a church and regu-lar missionary activity."[22] Up to her death in 1922, Ramabai remained in Kedgaon and was active in educational work, vocational training in teaching, nursing, weaving, printing, and tailoring, and translating the Bible into Marathi. By this time she and her daughter had found solace in a revivalist type of Christianity. Nevertheless, the project had achieved world fame; missionaries had publicized her work, and every winter tourists were "daily at the gates" wanting to look around the school. There were, in 1907, six English, American, and Swedish women residents. In other parts of Asia, women were also inspired by Ram-abai, one notable case being Kartini, the Indonesian pioneer of female education.[23]

But in India the reactions to Ramabai were mixed, especially in view of her hesitation to ally publicly with nationalist causes. For Christians in India and their supporters abroad, the crucial question of social reform was linked to British rule. It was not merely that "enlightenment" and progress were thought of as part of the blessings the British had con-ferred upon India, but also that the end of British rule was seen as a reversion to conflict, ignorance, and superstition. Ramabai, who had been attacked by B. G. Tilak and the polit-ical extremists, was particularly aware of this issue. As the agitation in India increased, especially the ferment in Bengal around 1905, Ramabai was faced with a dilemma: Is benevolent foreign rule in any circumstance preferable to self-government? Her answer was that Christianity had to continue its noble work in India, and for this, British rule was necessary. In 1909 she described the "makers of this unrest in India" as "fine well-educated people, trying to do good to the country in their own way"; but she faulted them for failing to see that India was not a nation.[24] She added that because it took the British many cen-turies of "Christian training" to arrive at their "love of the right principle," it would take Indians some centuries to "come up to the mark."[25] What is ironic, however, is that by this date the American funders and the American public may have been more sympathetic to Indian nationalism than Ramabai was. During the last decade of her life, Ramabai had moved toward a more fundamentalist Christianity, being also preoccupied with Bible translations and constant prayer sessions, while Ramabai's American funders were more interested in possible political changes in India.[26]

The Funders versus the Funded

Relations between funders and recipients of funds are inevitably complex, and the case of the Ramabai Association and Ramabai was no exception. The officials of the association were anxious initially to emphasize their advanced attitudes and the liberal content of their activities, and to disassociate themselves from the more fundamentalist and crude evangelical aspects of missionary activity abroad. Ramabai's strength had been that she was Indian and not the typical foreign missionary preaching Christianity to "natives."[27] Although anxious that Indians should create their own forms, the Ramabai funders occasionally felt compelled to intervene. Even by 1889, the Ramabai Association agreed that Ramabai could not cope alone with all the problems of running the school. It spoke of her "lack of experience in teaching, organizing, and in business matters" and of the need for "help and sympathy of a woman of experience, judgement and courage." The committee sent Sarah Hamlin, who was "a woman of cultivation and refinement, of experience in teaching, organizing and traveling" and who had been Ramabai's "most loyal friend" on the Pacific Coast, to help her.[28]

The Ramabai Association was also clearly worried that "even the *appearance* of breaking faith" was to be avoided, as "the Hindus have put such confidence in the word of Ramabai and of the American people that the school shall be strictly secular, countenancing no interference with Hindu beliefs and customs."[29] Sarah Hamlin took a close look at the school and made frequent reports on Ramabai to the committee in Boston. While praising Ramabai's work, Hamlin was also conscious of the possible dangers of the school's becoming too closely associated with Christianity. The question arose because several pupils used to participate with Ramabai in morning prayers in her room.[30] But Ramabai defended her right to openly practice Christianity and to have prayer meetings in her room, and because the school was dominated by her charismatic personality, it was difficult to prevent pupils from being attracted to Ramabai's religious practices. The issue was an explosive one, and in 1892 and 1893 there was a crisis in India over the proselytization of child widows in Ramabai's school, leading to the resignation of the Indian advisory board.[31] The controversy became public, and well-known reformers and the press were involved. The most damaging attack came from leading nationalists, such as B. G. Tilak, who alleged that Ramabai's Sharada Sadan was merely a cover for proselytizing.

There were two considerations that affected the American funders' attitude toward Ramabai's strong Christian views. One was the general liberal climate of interest in Asian religions and a reaction against dogmatic and fundamentalist Christianity. Second, the Unitarians, Methodists, and other nonconformist Christians of the association were disconcerted, if not disappointed, by Ramabai's dogmatism. They asked whether Ramabai had broken her pledge to the American funders that she would run the school in a nondenominational and nonsectarian manner, where students could worship as they pleased. As a result, significant changes occurred in the relationship between Ramabai and her American funders in 1898; ten years had elapsed since the formation of the Ramabai Association, and Pandita Ramabai went to the United States for the annual meeting in 1898. The association dissolved itself and a new one, the American Ramabai Association, was formed, to which the property was transferred.[32] The next crisis for the funders occurred in 1902 when Ramabai, without the approval of the American Ramabai Association, took the Sharada

Sadan from Pune to Kedgaon (because of the bubonic plague and "other plagues"). In Ramabai's words, "This action of mine has naturally displeased many of my friends in America, and consequently the subscriptions for the Sharada Sadan have fallen off."[33] By 1902 the issue of Christian proselytization at Ramabai's school again became a matter of controversy.

But perhaps the most disturbing question for the funders was the way in which the Ramabai issue became a confrontational one with Hindus and theosophists at a time when liberal Christians were trying to promote a new approach to non-Christians. Ramabai's project was obviously unacceptable to orthodox Hindus from the outset. Because she was a Brahmin widow, her conversion, denunciations of Hinduism, attack on caste taboos, and promotion of Christianity in her schools were seen as scandalous. Ramabai was also strong in her advocacy of women's rights long before such ideas were generally acceptable in either the West or India, and she was ahead of her time in her challenge to patriarchy. By focusing mainly on the condition of child widows, Ramabai was choosing an area of action that hit out against Hinduism, Brahmin oppression, and male domination. To her, the condition of Hindu widows was not merely a social evil to be reformed; rather, it was a symptom of a disease that had to be eradicated. Her challenge was thus a basic one, questioning Hinduism; even Indians who might have agreed with Ramabai on the condition of Hindu women could not agree with her appeal "to take the Real Remedy, the Gospel of Christ, to millions of India's women."[34] Moreover, Ramabai's conversion and her denunciation of Hinduism as the root cause of women's oppression occurred at a time when nationalism and Hindu revivalism were growing in strength. It was also a period during which the West was becoming acquainted at first hand with the views of leading Hindus, such as Swami Vivekananda.

The popularity of Ramabai in the United States caused a problem for Vivekananda, and when he criticized Ramabai's activities, there were accusations and counter accusations of misrepresentation. This conflict between Americans was an interesting confrontation along gender lines—American women coming out in defense of Ramabai against the Indian "man of the hour," Vivekananda, and his sponsor, Dr. Lewis James of the Brooklyn Ethical Society. The problem began when, at this society's invitation, Vivekananda spoke in December 1894 on "Indian Religions." This led to a controversy in the pages of the *Brooklyn Eagle* between Dr. James and Mrs. McKeen of the Brooklyn Ramabai Association, alleging that Vivekananda in his public lecture had denied that Hindu widows were suffering. Vivekananda's intervention clearly caused some anguish among the Boston Ramabai Association, which in 1895 referred to "the grave misstatements made by some of the Hindus visiting this country, not only in regard to child wives and widows, but concerning Ramabai and her school."[35] While foreign missionaries living in India were very supportive of Ramabai, it was to be expected that foreign women theosophists and women followers of Swami Vivekananda were highly ambivalent, if not critical of her.

In turn, Ramabai regarded Westerners such as Annie Besant and Sister Nivedita, who were championing the cause of Hinduism, with feelings bordering on contempt. There was no open confrontation between Annie Besant and Ramabai, but when Besant gave a lecture on theosophy in Pune "Ramabai consented to depart from her usual custom of not appearing in public, and attended the lecture where she was cheered by the audience."[36] But she was critical of Besant and other Westerners who were attracted by Hinduism; writing to her American funders, Ramabai described the horrors of child widows and remarked that the world was going backward since Mrs. Besant had the nerve to say that Hindu widows should never remarry. "Let us hope that better days are coming for the poor, despised Hindu widows," Ramabai wrote, "in spite of all the seeming obstacles in their way of progress."[37] On her part, Annie Besant alleged that Ramabai's conversion to Christianity and her use of the widows' school for making converts had been a setback for female education in India. On her first visit to India in 1893, Besant had wanted to concern herself "with the question of the education of girls" but had been discouraged by "thoughtful Indians" because of Ramabai's Christianity and her attempts at converting child widows and orphans under the guise of education.[38]

How much did Ramabai's conversion harm the cause of women's education? It certainly provided an ideal excuse for traditionalists to warn against female education—linking it with the dangers of exposure to Christian influences and westernized behavior and the rejection of Hindu religion and culture. It also, in the 1890s, made theosophists extremely cautious about moving ahead to start girls' schools. But although Ramabai's conversion was an excuse, it is also true that Ramabai, who started so fearlessly in her challenge to Hindu patriarchy, destroyed her chances of leading women's struggles by her narrow preoccupation with Bible translation and conversion. The women of India could hardly benefit by moving from the patriarchal domination of the Brahmins to the patriarchal ideology of Christian fundamentalism. Moreover, in seeing British rule as the protector of Christianity, Ramabai lost the opportunity to emerge as a truly national woman leader who could also challenge colonialism. What her American funders could clearly see—namely, the need for secular institutions and a sympathy for Indian nationalism—bypassed Ramabai and proved to be a real setback for women's rights in India. But Ramabai's pioneering work for women was not forgotten, and the voice of Indian women in protest, which she articulated as early as the 1880s, was kept alive by succeeding generations of Indian women for whom her attacks on the "jugular" of Hindu patriarchy made her a true hero and a pioneer feminist.

Notes

1. For a time they lived in a forest, but her parents and sister died of starvation during the great famine of 1876–77. Ramabai, age sixteen, and her brother then traveled on foot to north and east India searching for food and work. Helen S. Dyer, *Pandita Ramabai: The Story of Her Life* (New York: Fleming H. Revell Co., 1900).

2. Ibid., 29.

3. Rachel Little Bodley had the chair of chemistry at the Women's Medical College, Philadelphia, becoming its dean in 1874, a post she held for fourteen years. She was involved in supporting medical missionary work, keeping in touch with Dr. Clara Swain and Dr. Anna Kugler, who worked in India. E. T. James, J. W. James, and P. Boyer, *Notable American Women: A Biographical Dictionary, 1607–1950* (Cambridge, Mass.: Harvard University Press, 1971).

4. Pandita Ramabai, *The High Caste Hindu Woman* (Philadelphia and London: George Bell, 1887), 130.

5. Ibid., 131.

6. The reformer M. G. Ranade first married at the age of thirteen. His second marriage, at thirty-one, was to a girl of eleven, in order to please his father; T. T. Telang, a critic of child marriage, had his daughter married off at a young age; and Deshmukh, who publicly called for widow remarriage, refused to attend such a wedding due to family pressure. Meera Kosambi, "Women, Emancipation and Equality: Pandita Ramabai's Contribution to Women's Causes," *Economic and Political Weekly* (Bombay), 29 October 1988, 45.

7. Ibid., 38.

8. Ramabai, *The High Caste Hindu Woman*, xxiv.

9. Ibid., 139.

10. Ibid., 142.

11. Ibid., xxii.

12. Ramabai Association, *Report of the Annual General Meeting, 1897* (Boston: Ramabai Association, 1897), 14.

13. One of the vice presidents was the Rev. Phillips Brooks, whose Trinity Church was a "social landmark in Boston" (H. A. I. Goonetileke, *Images of Sri Lanka Through American Eyes* [Colombo: United States Information Service, 1976], 180–81). He had traveled in India and Sri Lanka, and in 1891 he became bishop of Massachusetts. He was a liberal Christian, "ever open to the cry of the distressed and oppressed of whatever nation" (Ramabai Association, *Report of the Annual General Meeting, 1893* [Boston: Ramabai Association, 1893], 24–25).

14. Nancy A. Hardesty, *Great Women of Faith* (Grand Rapids, Mich.: Baker Book House, 1980), 109.

15. Ramabai Association, *Report of the Annual General Meeting, 1987*, 14.

16. Pauline Agassiz Shaw was a well-known educational philanthropist, active in social work, including day nurseries and training schools in the poorer parts of Boston; in the 1890s she became a suffragist and a supporter of peace movements. James, James, and Boyer, *Notable American Women*, 13:278.

17. Ramabai Association, *Report of the Annual General Meeting, 1890* (Boston: Ramabai Association, 1890), 12.

18. Ibid., 11.

19. "I was delighted to see the chivalrous spirit rising in the hearts of my young countrymen, who thus manifested their desire to honour woman. . . . I felt very proud to think that the time was not far distant when my sisters would be honoured by our brothers, not because they were mothers or superior beings, but because they were women." Ramabai Association, *Report of the Annual General Meeting, 1890*, 15.

20. American Ramabai Association, *Report of the Annual General Meeting, 1903* (Boston: American Ramabai Association, 1903), 15–16.

21. Ramabai Association, *Report of the Annual General Meeting, 1892* (Boston: Ramabai Association, 1892), 25.

22. Kosambi, "Women, Emancipation and Equality," 42.

23. Raden Adjeng Kartini in 1902 wrote: "I read of her in the paper. I trembled with excitement; not alone for the white woman is it possible to attain an independent position, the brown Indian too can make herself free. . . . For days I thought of her. . . . See what one good example can do." Quoted in Kartini, *Letters of a Javanese Princess*, trans. Agnes Louise Symmers, ed. Hildred Geertz (New York: W. W. Norton, 1964), 177–78.

24. "We are wanting, first and foremost, in UNITY. We are so many castes . . . clans . . . families and . . . individuals." Ramabai posed a rhetorical question to Hindus: "Why did you not go to England to trade . . . and establish Hindu rule? Why could we not be masters and mistresses of a glorious empire?" The answer was that British rule was not based on "lies and deceitfulness of a few unprincipled traders, bu on right Christian principles." American Ramabai Association, *Report of the Annual General Meeting, 1909* (Boston: American Ramabai Association, 1909).

25. Ibid., 16–21.

26. The president of the American Ramabai Association referred to the slogan "India for the Indians" and predicted that "the great movements of the future" would be those with great and powerful native leaders," while also sympathizing with "difficulties that confront the people there from a religious point of view." Ibid., 39.

27. As the Rev. Lyman Abbot said, Christians "should be more wise than we have been in our missionary movements" and should concentrate on "spontaneous and indigenous movements like that of Ramabai"; Christianity, he said, had been confounded with "that particular form which it has taken on in our Anglo-Saxon race." Ramabai Association, *Report of the Annual General Meeting, 1892*, 36–37.

28. Ramabai Association, *Report of the Annual General Meeting, 1890*, 22.

29. Ibid., 28.

30. Hamlin had been bold enough to ask whether this was not in violation of the pledge of nonsectarianism given to the American funders. Ibid., 28.

31. Allegations that pupils were being converted led to a crisis. Thirty pupils were withdrawn and the school "seemed in danger of annihilation." Ramabai was accused "of disloyalty to her own people, of obtaining money from American people under false pretences, of defiantly interfering with the religious customs of her pupils, and of dismissing the Managing Board that she might openly teach Christianity in her school" (Ramabai Association, *Report of the Annual General Meeting, 1892*, 14). Allowance was made for both the enthusiasm of the convert and Ramabai's "Indian" ways. Judith Andrews in the executive committee report for 1900 wrote: "Her oriental nature leads her to more ardent utterances than some of her Occidental sisters are accustomed to hearing. Might it not be well to ask ourselves if some of our restrained and seasoned utterances may not seem as inadequate to her as hers seem extravagant to us?" American Ramabai Association, *Report of the Annual General Meeting, 1900* (Boston: American Ramabai Association, 1900). 30.

32. While the Sharada Sadan remained overtly secular, the school at Kedgaon, called Mukti (salvation), with 365 women and girls, was "Christian pure and simple." American Ramabai Association, *Report of the Annual General Meeting, 1899* (Boston: American Ramabai Association, 1899), 13.

33. American Ramabai Association, *Report of the Annual General Meeting, 1904* (Boston: American Ramabai Association, 1904), 18.

34. Jenny Fuller, *The Wrongs of Indian Womanhood* (New York: F. H. Revell and Co., 1899), 13.

35. Ramabai Association, *Report of the Annual General Meeting, 1896* (Boston: Ramabai Association, 1896), 28.

36. American Ramabai Association, *Report of the Annual General Meeting, 1899*, 19–20.

37. American Ramabai Association, *Report of the Annual General Meeting, 1904*, 21–22.

38. Annie Besant, "The Education of Indian Girls." [1904], in Besant, *Essays and Addresses*, vol. 4, *India* (London and Madras: Theosophical Publishing Society), 318.

13

Ilse Women and the Early Korean American Community: Redefining the Origins of Feminist Empowerment

Alice Yang Murray

While constituting less than one-fourth of the approximately eight thousand Koreans who immigrated to Hawaii and the mainland between 1903 and 1924, Ilse (first-generation) women were a vital force in shaping the development of Korean American history. Women who immigrated with their husbands or arrived as picture brides combated poverty and discrimination and participated in the resistance campaign against Japanese imperialism in Korea. Confronting harsh conditions, immigrant women developed economic, social, and political roles to address the needs of their families and immigrant society. Manifesting strength, initiative, and leadership skills, Ilse women demonstrated the importance of women's individual and collective contributions to the Korean American community.

An examination of the history of Ilse women's struggles and accomplishments may help modern Korean American women recover feminist models and strategies. According to Eui-Young Yu, surviving Ilse women retain a strong ethnic identity and enjoy matriarchal status in the community.[1] Yu even suggests that the first group of Ilse women achieved greater status and higher positions than women in contemporary society. An analysis of the experiences of these immigrant women provides insight into how they dealt with adversity, established leadership roles within the community, and reconceptualized the "proper sphere" of women's activities. While traditional Confucian ideology dictated that a "woman's place" was within the home, economic necessity and patriotism caused women to counter these restrictions and assert their ability to both sustain and direct immigrant society.

The history of Korean American women therefore challenges traditional views of "feminist" agency and consciousness, which are based primarily on the experiences of middle-class white women and the campaign for suffrage. Nancy Cott has noted that in most works on women's history, the term *feminism* fails to capture the diverse ways in which women have "protested male domination or attempted to redefine gender hierarchy."[2] Criticizing the tendency to define feminism in purely gendered terms, Chandra Talpade Mohanty urges researchers to develop more nuanced approaches for exploring how minority women experience intersecting gender, race, and class systems.[3] An analysis of how racial/ethnic women responded to patriarchy must also examine their struggles against racism, colonialism, and imperialism.[4] Ilse women's experiences in the early Korean American community exemplify how in the process of defending their families and the community, women constructed new definitions of women's power inside and outside the home.

Korean American women immigrated in two waves between 1903 and 1924. The first wave of Ilse women arrived in America between 1903 and 1910. Most of the 637 women who came with 6,048 immigrant men to Hawaii between 1903 and 1905 accompanied husbands who planned to work on sugar and pineapple plantations. These immigrants left Korea to escape the poverty caused by famine, heavy taxation, and exploitation by Japanese merchants. Recruited by Hawaiian plantation interests to break the strikes of Japanese laborers, these Korean migrants entered America with, on average, less than two dollars. Between 1906 and 1910, 222 Korean students and political exiles, including a group of forty women, were admitted to the mainland. Women thus accounted for only one-tenth of the entire Korean community in America in 1910.[5]

While Korea was a primarily rural society, most immigrants came from urban port cities such as Inchon, Chinnampo, Wonsan, Pusan, Masan, and Mokpo, and the large cities of Seoul and Pyongyang. Many Ilse women came from the northwestern part of Korea, Pyongan-do, where Protestant missionaries had been active since the 1890s. Consequently, while nearly 40 percent of all early immigrants were Christian converts, some scholars believe an even higher percentage of women who came had a Christian background and were less influenced by Confucian patriarchy.[6] A few so-called warrior women emigrated as a form of rebellion against husbands who kept concubines. Hei-won Sarah Kim described how her mother, Maria Hwang, left her husband in 1905: "She said, 'I can no longer live under this circumstance with you. I am taking the children to America and will shame you in the future. These children shall become educated and I shall become a wonderful person. You can remain as you are.'"[7]

The second wave of Ilse women arrived between 1910 and 1924. Male immigration had declined rapidly after Korea became a Japanese protectorate in 1905. Between 1905 and 1910 the Japanese government pressured Korea to halt the emigration of male laborers. Plantation owners in Hawaii had recruited Korean male laborers to break the strikes of Japanese immigrant laborers. On the mainland, groups like the Asiatic Exclusion League also began denouncing Korean "cheap labor" as part of a larger campaign against Japanese laborers. After officially annexing Korea in 1910, Japan barred Korean male emigration but authorized exit permits for "picture brides" because of a mistaken assumption that the presence of women and the formation of families would reduce Korean immigrant activities against Japanese colonialism in Korea. Consequently before the Immigration Act of 1924 ended Japanese and Korean immigration to the United States, 951 picture brides went to Hawaii and 115 went to the mainland.

Picture brides came to America to relieve impoverished families, to escape political and religious oppression by Japanese imperialists, and to explore educational and occupational opportunities denied them in Korea. These women chose their prospective husbands after examining pictures they received in their hometowns. They were usually younger, better-educated, and more politically active than the first wave of women immigrants. Many of these women were attending high school in Korea, and a few even went to college before they emigrated. In fact, many of these picture brides were better-educated than the men they married.[8] One woman described how she became a picture bride because she hoped to find economic, social, and political freedom in America:

> That time girls in my village can't walk around . . . can't go any place, only to Sunday school. . . . Girls always only were home their whole life before they marry . . . cooking, sewing, working. That time, a girl very seldom went out to a foreign country. Under the Japanese, no freedom. People can't talk. . . . I thinking when I grow up I like going Hawaii. Hawaii's a free place, everybody living well. . . . If you like talk, you can talk; you like work, you can work.[9]

Most of these women, who believed that America was a country of unlimited opportunity, where the streets were paved with gold, were greeted by husbands who were much older and much poorer than they had been led to expect. While most picture brides were between the ages of seventeen and twenty-five, the men they married were on average eighteen years older. Anna Choi, who came to Hawaii in 1915 at the age of fifteen in defiance of her family's wishes, recalled the shock and disappointment she felt when she saw her forty-six-year-old fiancé:

> I could not believe my eyes. His hair was grey and I could not see any resemblance to the picture I had. He was a lot older than I had imagined. I had a very big decision to make of whether or not to listen to my uncle. If my fiancé had been a little bit younger, I would have listened to my uncle readily, but I did not have it in my heart to disappoint or hurt such a middle-aged man like him.[10]

Encountering an unfamiliar environment, a new language, and different customs, many women experienced adjustment problems. After coming to America to study nursing and serve as a missionary for the poor, Do Yun Yoon declared that every day of her life she regretted her decision to become a picture bride: "I have been unable to carry out my purpose to have an education, my husband, who hasn't an education, hasn't been a good provider, so I felt I came for nothing!"[11]

While a few women refused to accept their marriages and returned to their homeland, most stayed and helped their husbands and children confront poverty and discrimination. Denied naturalization rights until 1952, Korean immigrants were considered an "unassimilable" and inferior people. They were refused service in restaurants, barber shops, and public recreation facilities. Many white landlords refused to rent or lease property to Koreans. Agitating for an end to all Asian immigration, racist white labor activists inflamed hostility against Koreans with images of a supposedly dirty, immoral, and treacherous "yellow peril." In one race riot, Korean orange pickers at Mary Steward's orchard in Upland, California, were attacked by white farmers and workers wielding stones and rocks.[12]

Immigrants also suffered from a discriminatory wage system that provided male sugarcane workers with an average daily wage of only sixty-five cents. Since male wages were so low, many families could not survive without the income provided by working women. Laboring alongside their husbands for an average of ten hours a day, six days a week, Ilse women received a daily wage of fifty cents.[13] Many immigrant women also earned money by cooking, cleaning, and sewing for the Korean bachelor community. Since most immigrant men refused to help their wives with household chores, Ilse women also worked long hours attending to the needs of the family. In her autobiography, Mary Paik Lee recalled how her entire family lived in a former chicken shack in Riverside, California, and relied on the money her mother earned by waking up at 3 A.M. to cook for thirty to forty bachelors.[14]

Individually and collectively, women devised strategies to help their families. Ilse women's paid and unpaid labor played an important role in improving the social mobility of Korean immigrants. Women ran boardinghouses and accumulated enough capital to help their families establish small businesses in Honolulu and other urban areas. According to Eui-Young Yu, Ilse women "successfully led their men out of the sugar and pineapple plantations to urban entrepreneurship and raised children to become professional workers."[15] Since most picture brides married men who were much older, many found themselves widowed at an early age. Women from the same home village, province, or church, however, supported each other emotionally and financially by forming *kyes*, or mutual financing associations. These *kyes* helped many widows buy homes, invest in businesses, and pay for their children's education.[16]

Women's networks also influenced the development of the Korean American church as the central community institution attending to immigrants' social, cultural, and political needs. As "Bible women" in Korea, some Ilse women had led women's Bible classes and conducted missionary work.[17] In America immigrant women attended Sunday worship services, Bible classes, and prayer meetings. They also served as church stewardesses, deaconesses, and committee members. Teaching Sunday-school classes and Korean-language programs, Ilse women helped the second generation gain knowledge of Korean culture and a sense of pride in their ethnic heritage.

The first woman's organization, the Korean Women's Association (Hankuk Puin Hoe), was founded in 1908 in San Francisco by a small group of women who wanted to promote Korean-language programs, support church activities, and encourage community solidarity. Established with similar goals in Hawaii in 1913, the Korean Women's Society (Taehanin Puin Hoe) also urged women to resist Japanese colonialism by boycotting Japanese products.[18]

These organizations did not set out to help women fight against patriarchy. On the contrary, one can argue that by emphasizing women's responsibility for taking care of children and for purchasing merchandise for the family, these groups reinforced and affirmed women's domestic roles. And yet while the founders may not have initially attacked or even questioned the doctrine that women's primary place was within the home, women's activism in these organizations challenged the Confucian exclusion of women from the public sphere. Ilse women activists reformulated the Confucian concept of the "good wife" and the "wise mother" by extending their defense of home and family into the public realm.

Assuming leadership roles in the campaign to free Korea from Japanese control, immigrant women so expanded the parameters of women's "traditional sphere" that the concept became anachronistic. These women believed that Japan's ruthless suppression of the March 1919 peaceful demonstrations in Korea obligated all immigrants, men and women alike, to support the independence movement. Between March 1919 and December 1920 the seven thousand Korean immigrants living in America and Mexico raised more than two hundred thousand dollars in independence funds. Bong-Youn Choy thus estimates that every Korean resident made an average contribution of thirty dollars, the equivalent of a month's wages for the average Korean laborer.[19] Women proudly pointed out that 531 women church members were arrested in Korea for participating in the protests.[20] Accounts of how women resistance workers suffered imprisonment, torture, and death at the hands of the Japanese police further intensified immigrant women's commitment to liberate their homeland.

Korean women in Hawaii organized a parade to demonstrate their support of the March 1919 protests. Dressed in traditional clothing, these women proudly marched to downtown Honolulu singing patriotic songs. On 15 March 1919, forty-one representatives of women's societies throughout the Hawaiian islands met in Honolulu to consolidate their efforts, founding the Korean Women's Relief Society (Taehan Puin Kujehoe). Although the organization was supposed to supplement the work of the Korean National Association (Taehanin Kungminhoe), women elected their own officers and formulated their own agenda. The organization supported the nationalist campaign by training emergency nurses for anti-Japanese actions and by raising funds for the provisional government in China, the Korean Independence Army, and especially the families of the thirty-three signers of the Declaration of Korean Independence.[21] These dedicated activists raised two hundred thousand dollars by reprinting and selling the declaration's manifesto, selling rice cakes and kimchi, working extra hours in the plantation fields, and donating family savings.[22]

Women on the mainland also united to support the independence movement. On 2 August 1919 women throughout California met in Dinuba to establish the Korean Women's Patriotic Society (Taehan Yoja Aikukdan). The founders agreed to coordinate their activities with the Korean National Association, to boycott Japanese goods, and to raise funds for the needy in America and Korea. Even though the society never included more than one-fourth of the female population on the mainland, it has been credited as the most important fund-raising organization within the Korean community.[23]

The Korean Women's Patriotic Society exemplifies how women's domestic roles could be politicized. Women manifested their patriotism by selling food and crafts at bazaars. Advocating meatless days, no-soy-sauce days, and the wearing of simple clothing, members demonstrated how women's influence over family spending could assume political significance. Testifying to the effectiveness of the group's efforts to mobilize Korean women on the mainland, the society quickly established branch offices wherever there was a sizable immigrant community: San Francisco, Los Angeles, Sacramento, Willows, Delano, and Reedley.

Women's organizations, of course, were not immune to the factional infighting that weakened the nationalist movement. Personal and ideological disputes between nationalist leaders Ahn Chang-ho, Park Yong-man, and Syngman Rhee divided the immigrant community. Ahn Chang-ho urged Koreans to cultivate the spiritual regeneration and educational development of patriotic leaders. Advocating a more militant strategy, Park Yong-man advised immigrants to establish military training academies. Syngman Rhee emphasized the importance of strengthening diplomatic ties to gain support for Korean liberation. Instead of providing a unified campaign against Japan, adherents to the three leaders and their different strategies became rivals for power and recognition within the community. Factional conflict also diminished the effectiveness of the women's organizations, and in 1929 members of the Korean Women's Relief Society separated into three different organizations.[24]

Nevertheless, women in the Korean Women's Relief Society and Korean Women's Patriotic League demonstrated that women could institute, plan, and operate their own organizations. Both groups gained more supporters and became more active when the advent of the Sino-Japanese War in 1937 unleashed new hopes for Korean independence. By expanding their fund-raising and relief projects, these organizations helped revive the nationalist movement during and after World War II. Under the auspices of the United Korean Committee, the Korean Women's Patriotic Society sent to Korea in February 1946 over a thousand tons of relief goods. On 10 March 1946 the Korean Women's Relief Society also contributed to the United Korean Committee relief project by sending seven hundred tons of goods to Korea.[25]

Women's contributions to the independence movement received some public recognition inside and outside the ethnic community. A 1919 *New Korea* editorial celebrated the "courageous" efforts of the Korean Women's Patriotic Society. The paper also noted how a woman helped raise $370 when her play, *The Tragedy of Korea*, became a major attraction during a four-day patriotic conference.[26] On 11 April 1942 the *Korean National Herald* proclaimed that the Korean Women's Relief Society was "one of the outstanding Korean organizations in the territory in both local and patriotic activities." Even the mainstream *Honolulu Advertiser* honored members of the Korean Women's Relief Society for their "tireless" work to publicly express the "unanimous desire on the part of Koreans in this community to be of concerted help in the war program" (22 April 1944).

In April 1941 six women were elected to serve with male leaders on various committees as part of the United Korean Committee. This represented the first official recognition of women in a unified campaign for Korean independence.[27] Yet while a few individual women and certain women's groups gained public praise, it is clear that women were not treated as equals within the nationalist movement. For the most part, Korean immigrant men encouraged and accepted women's services to the community without affirming women's right to lead the community.

Denied decision-making roles in the Korean National Association, women asserted themselves as leaders within their own organizations. A picture bride interviewed in 1975 provides some insight into how independence activists believed they could mobilize women to effect social and political change:

> Korean women in Hawaii wanted to do something for the patriots in Korea who were sacrificing their lives. We thought it was a matter of life and death for all Korean women to unite our forces . . . The Honolulu Korean women held their general meeting first; in the Island of Maui we had seventy-two women elect officers at our general meeting. Then we met every day to decide on how to organize and what kinds of work we should do.[28]

This woman became president of her group in 1922, although she was only twenty years old. She made speeches to women's groups and attempted to "politically awaken other Korean women and mobilize them to collect funds and relief goods." She described how her experiences in church organizations helped her become more confident: "When I look back now, the reason that I could come up with such independent ideas and could express my honest opinions even to strange men was that I had learned to express my thoughts in the church groups by having Bible study meetings and by visiting strangers' houses."[29] This committed activist continued her fund-raising work even while pregnant and went door to door carrying one child on her back and holding another child's hand.[30]

As women gained political and leadership skills, at least some began to demand that women had both the duty and the right to assume larger public roles. One picture bride declared in a 1921 article that "women should work like men" and that men and women had an equal responsibility in the independence movement. In the process of urging women to join the nationalist campaign, the author also provided a ringing attack on the social restrictions women faced:

> Sisters! Stop dreaming in a family which is actually an invisible prison. Stand up and unshackle our utmost task to free ourselves of bondage, to build our wealth, to enlist our soldiers, and to obtain an education. If we are prepared, there will be no discrimination against us women in political participation or legal activities. . . . Recently, magazines have spoken about women's liberation. We should educate ourselves so that we can gain equality with men [in the independence movement].[31]

The author exhorted women to become active not only to fulfill their "national duty" but also to help women fight for leadership roles within the community. The Korean Women's Patriotic Society reflected this new consciousness of women's abilities and needs when in 1924 it amended the organization's primary goal, which became to "better prepare women for the independence of Korea by extending their social awareness from individual to family, and from family to community, based on the norms and moral principles of civilized society."[32] Promoting greater education for women, the organization also advocated that women should exert more power within the independence movement.

Some women asserted that women were more qualified than men to lead the community. In her *Korean National Herald* column "A Woman Knows," Cynicia Cynn argued that Koreans needed to "openly admit that the he-diplomats have failed completely." Indicting men for cheating and selfishness, she claimed that they were "slower in maturing than women." Citing such "past masters" of diplomacy as Queen Elizabeth and Queen Victoria, Cynn concluded that "when it comes to bargaining a woman can always best a man."[33]

Cynn was not the only one to challenge the notion that women were inferior to men. In an article published by *The Korean Evangel*, Mrs. Hae-soo Whang of San Francisco criticized Korean patriarchal traditions for denying women access to higher education. She argued that women who were better-educated would do a superior job of planning for their family's future and raising their children. Whang, however, attacked the idea that women should seek an education only "to serve others." Advising women to seek higher education "for your own good," she declared, "You have to be happy before you can make others happy and you have to feel full before you can feed others." Whang concluded that obtaining a higher education would help women "escape from those looking down on us" and enable them to gain the "equality with men which was given by God."[34]

If a few women spoke out for equality for themselves, many more were devoted to helping their sons and daughters improve their status. The recollections of second-generation women who were born and raised during this period demonstrate Ilse women's significant influence on their children's identity. Jean Park, for example, remembered how after her father lost his job her mother became "the dominant one in the family"; she "wore the pants in the family and made all the important decisions." Jean's mother raised chickens and earned enough money from bootlegging to invest in a trucking business before the Great Depression forced her to work as a farm laborer. Even while struggling to help her family survive these tough times, Mrs. Park still found the energy to support the independence movement and to teach her children how to speak, read, and write Korean.[35]

In her book *The Dreams of Two Yi-min*, Margaret K. Pai also recounted the courage and determination of her mother, Hee Kyung Kwon. Pai proudly described how Mrs. Kwon, an ardent nationalist, returned to Korea in 1918 to participate in the peace demonstrations and was imprisoned by the Japanese police. During World War II Mrs. Kwon rolled bandages for the Red Cross and went from house to house selling U.S. war bonds. According to Pai, her mother's "practical common sense" made it possible for her father to develop a successful drapery business. Mrs. Kwon also demanded acknowledgment of her decisive role in the family during Margaret's wedding rehearsal, when she exclaimed to her husband: "I don't see why you have to be in this wedding procession at all. What have *you* done for your daughter? *I'm* the one who should be taking her up the altar!"[36]

Kim Ronyoung's novel *Clay Walls* also pays tribute to the endurance and tenacity of Ilse women. In an interview, Kim Ronyoung (Gloria Hahn) revealed that the character of Haesu Chun was based on her mother, Helen Kim. Helen Kim's hopes that an education would help her break away from the traditional role of Korean women were destroyed when she was forced to accept an arranged marriage. While staying home to raise her children, she broke the "monotony of homemaking" by working actively in her church, writing for Korean newspapers, and helping found the Korean Women's Patriotic Society. After her husband lost his business and died, she began sewing day and night to sustain the family. Hahn credited her mother with serving as an inspiring role model: "If the measure of one's life is in his response to the human condition under ordinary circumstances, the measure of my mother's life is in her response under extraordinary circumstances. Her response has been heroic."[37]

Gloria Hahn's novel celebrates Ilse women such as her mother, who, despite their small numbers, played an essential role in the growth of the early Korean community in the United States. These women came to America hoping to find economic prosperity, educational opportunity, and religious and political freedom. Instead they had to confront poverty and racial discrimination. Persevering, they helped their families survive and establish small businesses. Immigrant women expanded women's traditional sphere by establishing women's organizations to provide social services for the community and to fight for the liberation of Korea. Acquiring organizational and decision-making skills, women activists became more confident and assertive. Some women even publicly expressed their anger at continued gender discrimination and called for greater rights for women. Ilse women thus left their children and the community a legacy of women's endurance, strength, and leadership under difficult conditions.

Notes

1. Eui-Young Yu, "Korean-American Women: Demographic Profiles and Family Roles," in E.-Y. Yu and E. Phillips, eds., *Korean Women in Transition: At Home and Abroad* (Los Angeles: Center for Korean American and Korean Studies, California State University, Los Angeles, 1987), 183–97.

2. Nancy Cott, "What's in a Name? The Limits of 'Social Feminism,' or, Expanding the Vocabulary of Women's History," *Journal of American History* 76, 3 (December 1989): 827.

3. Chandra Talpade Mohanty, "Cartographies of Struggle: Third World Women and the Politics of Feminism," in C. T. Mohanty, Ann Russo, and Lourdes Torres, eds., *Third World Women and the Politics of Feminism* (Bloomington and Indianapolis: Indiana University Press, 1991), 11.

4. Norma Alarcón, "The Theoretical Subject(s) of this Bridge Called My Back and Anglo-American Feminism," in H. Calderón and J. D. Saldívar, eds., *Chicana Criticism in a Social Context* (Durham, N.C.: Duke University Press, 1989); Gloria Anzaldúa, ed., *Making Face, Making Soul/Haciendo Caras: Creative and Critical Perspectives by Women of Color* (San Francisco: Aunt Lute Books, 1990); Nancy Hewitt, "Beyond the Search for Sisterhood: American Women's History in the 1990s," in this volume.

5. Eun Sik Yang, "Korean Women in America: 1903–1930," in E.-Y. Yu and E. Phillips, eds., *Korean Women in Transition: At Home and Abroad* (Los Angeles: Center for Korean American and Korean Studies, California State University, Los Angeles, 1987), 167–81.

6. Eun Sik Yang, "Korean Women of America: From Subordination to Partnership, 1903–1930," *Amerasia* 11, 2 (1984): 1–28.

7. Sonia Shinn Sunoo, ed., *Korean Kaleidoscope* (Davis, Calif.: Korean Oral History Project. Sierra Mission Area, United Presbyterian Church, U.S.A., 1982), 156.

8. Eui-Young Yu, "Women in Traditional and Modern Korea," in E.-Y. Yu and E. Phillips, eds., *Korean Women in Transition: At Home and Abroad* (Los Angeles: Center for Korean American and Korean Studies, California State University, Los Angeles, 1987), 15–27.

9. Alice Chai, "Korean Women in Hawaii, 1903–45," in N. Tsuchida, ed., *Asian and Pacific American Experiences: Women's Perspectives* (Minneapolis: Asian/Pacific American Learning Resources Center and General College, 1982), 77–78.

10. Bong-Youn Choy, *Koreans in America* (Chicago: Nelson-Hall, 1979), 321.

11. Sunoo, *Korean Kaleidoscope*, 71.

12. Choy, *Koreans in America*, 109.

13. Yang, "Korean Women in America," 169.

14. Mary Paik Lee, *Quiet Odyssey: A Pioneer Korean Women in America*, ed. Sucheng Chan (Seattle: University of Washington Press, 1990), 14.

15. Yu, "Korean-American Women: Demographic Profiles and Family Roles," 195.

16. Chai, "Korean Women in Hawaii, 1903–45."

17. Esther K. Arinaga, "Contributions of Korean Immigrant Women," in N. F. Young and J. R. Parrish, eds., *Montage: An Ethnic History of Women in Hawaii* (Honolulu: General Assistance Center for the Pacific College of Educational Foundations, University of Hawaii, 1977), 74.

18. Eui-Young Yu, "The Activities of Women in Southern California Korean Community Organizations," in E.-Y. Yu and E. Phillips, eds., *Korean Women in Transition: At Home and Abroad* (Los Angeles: Center for Korean American and Korean Studies, California State University, Los Angeles, 1987), 276.

19. Choy, *Koreans in America*, 158.

20. Yong-Ock Park, "The Women's Modernization Movement in Korea," in S. Mattielli, ed., *Virtues in Conflict: Tradition and the Korean Woman Today* (Seoul: Royal Asiatic Society, 1977), 105.

21. Kingsley K. Lyu, "Korean Nationalist Activities in Hawaii and the Continental United States, 1900–1945," part 1, *Amerasia* 4, 1 (1977): 23–85, part 2, *Amerasia* 4, 2 (1977): 53–100.

22. Chai, "Korean Women in Hawaii, 1903–1945," 83.

23. Yang, "Korean Women in America: 1903–1930," 177.

24. Lyu, "Korean Nationalist Activities in Hawaii and the Continental United States, 1900–1945," part 2, 60.

25. Warren Y. Kim, *Koreans in America* (Seoul: Po Chin Chai Printing Co., 1971), 67–68.

26. Yang, "Korean Women in America: 1903–1930," 176–77.

27. Yang, "Korean Women of America: From Subordination to Partnership, 1903–1930," 21.

28. Chai, "Korean Women in Hawaii, 1903–1945," 83.

29. Ibid., 84.

30. Ibid.

31. Yang, "Korean Women in America: 1903–1930," 178.

32. Ibid.

33. Cynicia Cynn, "A Woman Knows," *Korean National Herald*, Honolulu, Hawaii, 29 April 1942.

34. Hae-soo Whang, "Higher Education for Korean Women," *The Korean Evangel* (San Francisco: Korean Mission Methodist Episcopal Church, 1911).

35. Ronald Takaki, *Strangers from a Different Shore: A History of Asian Americans* (Boston: Little, Brown and Company, 1989), 288–91.

36. Margaret K. Pai, *The Dreams of Two Yi-min* (Honolulu: University of Hawaii Press, 1989), 130.

37. Choy, *Koreans in America*, 311. The novel is Kim Ronyoung, *Clay Walls* (Seattle: University of Washington Press, 1987).

14

Black and White Visions of Welfare: Women's Welfare Activism, 1890–1945

Linda Gordon

One of the pleasures of historical scholarship is that it may lead into unexpected paths, and what begins as a frustration—say, from an apparent shortage of sources—may end as a new opening. This essay began as an attempt to examine gender differences in visions of public welfare among reformers. Having compiled material about women welfare activists who were mainly white, I found I could not distinguish the influence of gender from that of race in their perspectives. (Indeed, to many white historians, the racial characteristics of the white people we studied were invisible until we began to learn from minority historians to ask the right questions.) So I set up a comparison between black and white women welfare activists, with results that were illuminating about both groups. Three major areas of difference between black and white women's ideas emerged: first, about the nature of entitlement, between a black orientation toward universal programs and a white orientation toward supervised, means-tested ones; second, in the attitude toward mothers' employment; third, in strategies for protecting women from sexual exploitation. In what follows I want both to show how those differences were manifest and to suggest their roots in historical experience.[1]

Several historians have recently studied black women's civic contributions, but black women's reform campaigns have not usually been seen as part of welfare history. How many discussions of settlement houses include Victoria Earle Matthews's White Rose Mission of New York City, Margaret Murray Washington's Elizabeth Russell Settlement at Tuskegee, Alabama, Janie Porter Barrett's Locust Street Social Settlement in Hampton, Virginia, or Lugenia Burns Hope's Neighborhood Union in Atlanta, Georgia, among many others? In examining this activism from a welfare history perspective, I came to understand how the standard welfare histories had been by definition white-centered. It was possible to make the widespread welfare reform activity of minority women visible only by changing the definition of the topic and its periodization.[2]

The white experience has defined the very boundaries of what we mean by welfare. Whites were by 1890 campaigning for government programs of cash relief and for regulations such as the Pure Food and Drug Act and anti-child-labor laws. These welfare programs had racial content not only in the perspectives of the reformers (white), but also in the identification of their objects (largely the immigrant working class, which, although white, was perceived as racially different by turn-of-the-century reformers). The programs also had class content, visible, for example, in their rejection of traditional working-class cooperative benevolent societies. Moreover, because of these orientations, welfare in the late nineteenth century was increasingly conceived as an *urban* reform activity.[3]

By contrast, African Americans, still concentrated in the South and in rural communities, had been largely disfranchised by this time, and even in the North had much less power than whites, certainly less than elite whites, to influence government. Southern states had smaller administrative capacities and were paltrier in their provision of public services, even to whites. African Americans did campaign for governmental programs and had some success; at the federal level, they had won an Office of Negro Health Work in the United States Public Health Service, and they had gotten some resources from the extension programs of the United States Department of Agriculture. Nevertheless, black welfare activity, especially before the New Deal, consisted to a great extent of building private institutions. Black women welfare reformers created schools, old people's homes, medical services, and community centers. Attempting to provide for their people what the white state would not, they even raised private money for public institutions. For example, an Atlanta University study of 1901 found that in at least three southern states (Virginia, North Carolina, and Georgia) the private contribution to Negro public schools was greater than that from tax monies.[4] For example, a teacher in Lowndes County, Alabama, appealed for funds in 1912:

> Where I am now working there are 27,000 colored people. . . . In my school district there are nearly 400 children. I carry on this work eight months in the year and receive for it $290, out of which I pay three teachers and two extra teachers. The State provides for three months' schooling. . . . I have been trying desperately to put up an adequate school building for the hundreds of children clamoring to get an education. To complete it . . . I need about $800.[5]

Thus a large proportion of their political energy went to raising money, and under the most difficult circumstances—trying to collect from the poor and the limited middle class to help the poor. White women raised money, of course, but they also lobbied aldermen and congressmen, attended White House conferences, and corresponded with Supreme Court justices; black women had less access to such powerful men and spent proportionally more of their time organizing bake sales, rummage sales, and church dinners. The detailed example of the Gate City Kindergartens, established in Atlanta in 1905, may illustrate this:

> Another method of raising funds was through working circles throughout the city. . . . From Bazaars held at Thanksgiving time, lasting as long as a week, when every circle was responsible for a day, one day of which a turkey dinner was served. Money was made by sales in items of fancy work, aprons, etc., canned fruit, cakes and whatever could be begged. The association realized as much as $250.00 at a Bazaar. From track meets sponsored by colleges, and participated in by the children of the public school, $100.00 gate receipts were cleared. Food and cake sales brought at times $50.00. April sales brought $50.00, and one time the women realized as much as $100.00 from the sale of aprons. Sales of papers, magazines and tin foil brought as much as $50.00. A baby contest brought $50.00. Intercollegiate contest brought $100. Post-season baseball games realized as much as $25.00. Sales of soap wrappers, soap powder wrappers, saved and collected from housewives, and baking powder coupons brought $25.00. . . . [The list goes on.]

It cost twelve hundred dollars in cash to maintain the kindergartens each year. In addition, donations in kind were vital—all five kindergartens were housed in donated locations, clothes were constantly solicited for the needy children, and for several years Procter & Gamble gave five boxes of Ivory soap annually.[6] Some black welfare activists were adept at raising white money but had to accept sometimes galling strings, and even the most successful tried to shift their economic dependence to their own people.[7] No doubt some of these money-raising activities were also pleasurable and community-building social occasions, but often they were just drudgery, and those doing the work hated it. Jane Hunter, a Cleveland black activist, wrote that "this money getting business destroys so much of ones real self, that we cannot do our best."[8]

This essay uses a limited comparison—between black and white women reformers—to alter somewhat our understanding of what welfare is and to bring into better visibility gender and race (and class) influences on welfare thinking. The essay uses two kinds of data: written and oral-history records of the thoughts of these activists, and a rudimentary collective biography of 145 black and white women who were national leaders in campaigns for public welfare between 1890 and 1945.[9] This method emerges from the premise expressed by the feminist slogan "The personal is political": that political views and activities are related not only to macroeconomic and social conditions but also to personal circumstances such as family experiences and occupational histories.

My approach uses a broad definition of welfare. I include reformers who sought regulatory laws, such as the Pure Food and Drug Act, compulsory education, and anti-child-labor regulations. I do not include reformers who worked mainly on labor relations, civil rights, women's rights, or a myriad of other reform issues not centrally related to welfare.[10] In categorizing many different activists, I had to ignore many differences in order to make broad generalization possible. This method inevitably obscures context and some fascinating personalities. Many more monographs are necessary, but I notice that historical thinking develops through a constant interplay between monographs and syntheses; I hope that this essay, because of its very breadth, will stimulate more monographs.

I did not form this sample according to a random or other formal selection principle. Instead I identified members of my sample gradually, during several years of research on welfare campaigns, and then tracked down biographical information. The process is a historian's form of snowball sampling, because often tracking down one activist produces references to another. Naturally, there are many bits of missing information because biographical facts are difficult to find for many women, especially minority women. I make no claim to having created a representative sample or an exhaustive list. But, on the methodological principle of saturation, I doubt that my generalizations would be much altered by the addition of more individuals.

To bound my sample, I included only those who were national leaders—officers of national organizations campaigning for welfare provision or builders of nationally important institutions, such as hospitals, schools, or asylums. (For more on the sample, see the Appendix.) These leaders were not typical welfare activists; more typical were those who worked exclusively locally, and their personal profiles might be quite different. But the national leaders had a great deal of influence on the thinking of other women. I included only activists prominent chiefly after 1890 because it was in the 1890s that such key national organizations as the National Association of Colored Women (NACW) began and that white women welfare activists began a marked emphasis on public provision. I followed welfare activism until 1945 because I wanted to look at broad patterns of ideas across a long period of policy debate; I ended in 1945 because among white women there was a marked decline in such agitation after that date, and among blacks there was a shift in emphasis to civil rights.

My approach sacrifices, of course, change over time. Substantial generational as well as individual differences among women had to be put aside. For example, the early black activists were, on average, more focused on race uplift and the later ones more on integration; during this period the mass northward migration of blacks shifted reformers' concerns not only away from the South but also increasingly toward urban problems. The white women welfare activists of the 1890s tended to divide between Charity Organization Society devotees and settlement advocates; by the 1930s, they were more united in promoting professionalism in public assistance. Nevertheless, I am convinced that there are enough continuities to justify this periodization, continuities that will emerge in the discussion below.

The two groups thus formed were in many ways not parallel. For example, the white women were mainly from the Northeast or Midwest, and there were few southern white women—only 16 percent of the group were either born or active in the South, whereas a majority of the black women were born in the South. For another example, many of the black women were educators by occupation, while white women who were educators were few. But these divergences are part of what I am trying to identify, part of the differences in black and white women's perspectives. Among whites, northerners contributed more to national welfare models than did southerners. And education had particular meanings for African Americans and was integrated into campaigns for the welfare of the race in a distinctive way. Generalizing among a variety of women of several generations, the comparison naturally eclipses some important distinctions, but it does so to illuminate others that are also important.[11]

I identified sixty-nine black women as national leaders in welfare reform. Separating the white from the black women was not my decision: The networks were almost completely segregated. First, the national women's organizations were segregated; those that included blacks, such as the Young Women's Christian Association (YWCA), had separate white and black locals. Second, since black women rarely held government positions, they rarely interacted with white women officially. Third, the national network of white women reformers usually excluded black women even when they could have been included.[12] The exclusion of black women from the white women's clubs and the ignoring or trivializing of life-and-death black issues, such as lynching, have been amply documented.[13] To cite but one example, one of the most important women in the New Deal—Mary McLeod Bethune—was not a part of the tight, if informal, caucus that the white New Deal women formed.[14] There were important counterexamples, interracial efforts of significant impact, particularly local ones: In Chicago, for instance, white settlement and charity workers joined black reformers in campaigning for public services for dependent children, establishing the Chicago Urban League, and responding to the 1919 race riot. In the South interracial efforts arose from evangelical religious activity. Some white members of this sample group worked with the Commission of Interracial Cooperation, forming its Women's Council, which had 805 county-level groups by 1929.[15] The national YWCA became a forum for communication between black and white women. But these efforts were marked by serious and sometimes crippling white prejudice, and the core networks of women remained segregated.

While the black group was created in part by white racism, it was also created from the inside, so to speak, by personal friendships. Often these relationships were born in schools and colleges and continued thereafter, strengthened by the development of black sororities after 1908. The creation of national organizations and networks extended relationships and ideas among these black women leaders across regional boundaries. For example, the Phillis Wheatley Home for the protection of single black urban women, established by Jane Hunter in Cleveland in 1911, spurred the opening of similar homes in Denver, Atlanta, Seattle, Boston, Detroit, Chicago, Greenville, Winston-Salem, Toledo, and Minneapolis by 1934. When Fannie Barrier Williams spoke in Memphis in 1896, she had never been in the South before, having grown up in upstate New York and settled in Chicago.[16] More and more the women began to travel widely, despite the difficult and humiliating conditions of travel for black women. Friendships could be intense, despite distance; black women early in the twentieth century, like white women, sometimes spoke openly of their strong emotional bonds. Darlene Clark Hine quotes Jane Hunter writing Nannie Burroughs, "It was so nice to see you and to know your real sweet self. Surely we will . . . cultivate a lasting friendship. I want to be your devoted sister in kindred thought and love." At other times Hunter wrote to Burroughs of her loneliness "for want of a friend."[17] Mutual support was strong. When in the 1930s the president and trustees of Howard University, led by Abraham Flexner, tried to force Howard's dean of women, Lucy D. Slowe, to live on campus with her girls (something the dean of men was not, of course, required to do) and she refused to comply, a whole network of women interceded on her behalf. A group of five asked for a meeting with Flexner, which he refused. Another group of women interviewed trustees in New York and reported to Slowe their perceptions of the situation. Mary McLeod Bethune urged her to be "steadfast" and campaigned for her among sympathetic Howard faculty.[18] The network was divided by cliques and encompassed conflicts and even feuds. Yet it had a bottom line of loyalty. Even those who criticized Bethune for insufficient militance understood her to be absolutely committed to the network of black women.[19]

The black women's network was made more coherent by its members' common experience as educators and builders of educational institutions. Education was the single most important area of activism for black women. The majority of women in this sample taught at one time or another, and 38 percent were educators by profession. For many, reform activism centered around establishing schools, from kindergartens through colleges, such as Nannie Burroughs's National Training School for Women and Girls in Washington, D.C., Lucy Laney's Haines Institute in Augusta, Georgia, or Arenia Mallory's Saints' Industrial and Literary Training School in Mississippi. In his 1907 report on economic cooperation among Negro Americans, for example, W. E. B. Du Bois counted 151 church-connected and 161 nonsectarian private Negro schools. Although he did not discuss the labor of founding and maintaining these institutions, we can guess that women contributed disproportionately.[20]

Another black welfare priority was the establishment of old people's homes, considered by Du Bois the "most characteristic Negro charity." These too, according to the early findings of Du Bois, were predominantly organized by women.[21] But if we were to take the period 1890 to 1945 as a whole, the cause second to education was health. Black hospitals, while primarily initiated by black and white men, depended on crucial support from black women. Between 1890 and 1930 African Americans created approximately two hundred hospitals and nurse-training schools, and women often took charge of the community organizing and fund-raising labor. Over time black women's health work changed its emphasis, from providing for the sick in the 1890s to preventive health projects after about 1910. Yet even in the first decade of the century, Du Bois found that most locations with considerable black populations had beneficial and insurance societies that paid sickness as well as burial benefits; these can be traced back a century before Du Bois studied them. In several cities the societies also paid for medicines and actually created their own health maintenance organizations (HMOs). With the dues of their members they hired physicians, annually or on a quarterly basis, to provide health care for the entire group.[22]

Many women's clubs made health work their priority. The Washington, D.C., Colored YWCA built a program around visiting the sick. The Indianapolis Woman's Improvement Club focused on tuberculosis, attempting to make up for the denial of service to blacks by the Indianapolis board of health, the city hospital, and the Marion County tuberculosis society. The preventive health emphasis was stimulated in part by educational work. For example, Atlanta's Neighborhood Union did a survey of conditions in the black schools in 1912 to 1913 that revealed major health problems; in 1916 this led the Neighborhood

Union to establish a clinic that offered both health education and free medical treatment. Possibly the most extraordinary individual in black women's public health work was Modjeska Simkins, who used her position as director of Negro work for the antituberculosis association of South Carolina to inaugurate a program dealing with the entire range of black health problems, including maternal and infant mortality, venereal disease (VD), and malnutrition as well as tuberculosis. Perhaps the most ingenious women's program was Alpha Kappa Alpha's Mississippi Health Project. These black sorority women brought health care to sharecroppers in Holmes County, Mississippi, for several weeks every summer from 1935 to 1942. Unable to rent space for a clinic because of plantation owners' opposition, they turned cars into mobile health vans, immunizing over fifteen thousand children and providing services such as dentistry and treatment for malaria and VD for between twenty-five hundred and four thousand people each summer.[23]

These reformers were united also through their churches, which were centers of networking and of activism, in the North as well as the South. Indeed, more locally active, less elite black women reformers were probably even more connected to churches; the national leadership was moving toward more secular organization, while remaining more church-centered than white women welfare leaders. Black churches played a large role in raising money, serving in particular as a conduit for appeals for white money, through missionary projects.[24]

The YWCA also drew many of these women together. Victoria Matthews's White Rose Mission influenced the YWCA, through its leader Grace Dodge, to bring black women onto its staff, which experience groomed many black women leaders.[25]

And despite the fact that these were national leaders, they shared a regional experience. At least 57 percent were born in the South. More important, perhaps, two-thirds of these migrated to the Northeast, Midwest, and mid-Atlantic regions, thus literally spreading their network as they fled Jim Crow and sought wider opportunity.[26]

Most members of this network were married—85 percent. More than half of the married women had prominent men as spouses, and their marriages sometimes promoted their leadership positions.[27] Lugenia Burns Hope was the wife of John Hope, first black president of Atlanta University; Irene Gaines was the wife of an Illinois state legislator. Ida Wells-Barnett's husband published Chicago's leading black newspaper. George Edmund Haynes, husband of Elizabeth, was a Columbia Ph.D., a professor at Fisk, an assistant to the secretary of labor from 1918 to 1921, and a founder of the Urban League. George Ruffin, husband of Josephine, was a Harvard Law graduate, a member of the Boston City Council, and Boston's first black judge. Most of the women, however, had been activists before marriage, and many led lives quite independent of their husbands. (Of these married women, 20 percent were widowed, divorced, or separated.)

Their fertility pattern was probably related to their independence. Of the whole group, 43 percent had no children; and of the married women, 34 percent had no children (there were no unmarried mothers).[28] (In comparison, 31 percent of the white married women in this sample were childless.) It thus seems likely that these women welfare activists used birth control, although long physical separations from their husbands may have contributed to their low fertility.[29] In their contraceptive practices these women may have been as modern as contemporary white women of comparable class position.

For most African American women a major reason for being in the public sphere after marriage was employment, due to economic necessity; but for this group of women, economic need was not a driving pressure. A remarkable number had prosperous parents.[30] Crystal Fauset's father, although born a slave, was principal of a black academy in Maryland. Elizabeth Ross Haynes's father went from slavery to ownership of a fifteen-hundred-acre plantation. Addie Hunton's father was a substantial businessman and founder of the Negro Elks. Mary Church Terrell's mother *and* father were successful in business. Most black women in the sample had husbands who could support them; 51 percent of the married women had high-professional husbands—lawyers, physicians, ministers, educators.[31] The women of this network were also often very class-conscious, and many of the clubs that built their collective identity were exclusive, such as the sororities, the Chautauqua Circle, and the Twelve in Atlanta. The fact that about 40 percent were born outside the South provides further evidence of their high status, since the evidence suggests that the earlier northward migrants were the more upwardly mobile.[32] In all these respects, this group probably differed from typical local activists, who were less privileged. Yet even among this elite group only a tiny minority—12 percent—were not employed.[33] To be sure, this economic privilege was only relative to the whole black population; on average, the black women's network was less wealthy than the white women's. Even those who were born to middle-class status were usually newly middle-class, perhaps a generation away from slavery and without much cushion against economic misfortune. Still, among many whites the first and most important emblem of middle-class status was a woman's domesticity. One can safely conclude that one meaning of these women's combining of public and family lives was the greater acceptance among African Americans, for many historical reasons, of the public life of married women.

The black women's national network was made more homogeneous by educational attainment, high social status, and a sense of superiority to the masses that brought with it obligations of service. Of the black women, 83 percent had a higher education, comparable to the proportion of white women, and 35 percent had attended graduate school. These figures may surprise those unfamiliar with the high professional achievement patterns of black women between 1890 and 1945. The full meaning of the statistics emerges when one compares them with the average educational opportunities for blacks in the United States at this time. In the earliest year for which we have figures, 1940, only 1 percent of African Americans, male and female, had four or more years of college. Moreover, only 41 percent of the women in this sample attended black colleges, whereas those colleges conferred 86 percent of all black undergraduate degrees in the period from 1914 to 1936.[34] Several women in this sample who were born into the middle class described learning for the first time in adulthood of the conditions of poverty in which most African Americans lived—an ignorance characteristic of prosperous whites but rarer among blacks. As Alfreda Duster, Ida Wells-Barnett's daughter, recalled, "It was difficult for me to really empathize with people who had come from nothing, where they had lived in cottages, huts in the South, with no floor and no windows and had suffered the consequences of the discrimination and the hardships of the South."[35] Many black women joined Du Bois in emphasizing the importance of building an intellectual and professional elite, calling upon the "leading" or "intelligent" or "better class of" Negroes to take initiatives for their people. Class and status inequalities, measured by such markers as money, occupation, and skin color, created tensions in this network, as comparable inequalities did in the white network.[36] Some thought of their obligations in the eugenic terms that were so fashionable in the first three decades covered by this study. "I was going to multiply my ability and my husband's by six," Alfreda Duster said in describing her decision to have six children.[37] Such thinking had somewhat different meanings for blacks than for whites, however, reflecting their awareness that race prejudice made it difficult for educated, prosperous blacks to escape the discrimination and pejorative stereotyping that held back all African Americans. As Ferdinand Barnett, later to become the husband of Ida B. Wells, put it in 1879, "One vicious, ignorant Negro is readily conceded to be a type of all the rest, but a Negro educated and refined is said to be an exception. We must labor to reverse this rule; education and moral excellence must become general and characteristic, with ignorance and depravity the exception."[38]

Indeed, the high social status and prosperity common in this group should not lead us to forget the discrimination and humiliation that they faced. Their high levels of skills and education were frustrated by lack of career opportunity. Sadie Alexander, from one of the most prominent black families in the United States, was the first black woman Ph.D., with a degree from the University of Pennsylvania. But she could not get an appropriate job because of her color, and was forced to work as an assistant actuary for a black insurance company. Anna Arnold Hedgeman, one of the youngest women in this sample, from a small Minnesota town where she had attended integrated schools and churches, graduated from Hamline University in St. Paul and then discovered that she could not get a teaching job in any white institution. Instead she went to work in Holly Springs, Mississippi, until she found the Jim Crow laws intolerable. Despite the relatively large black middle class in Washington, D.C., African American women there could not generally get clerical jobs in the federal government until the 1940s.[39]

Moreover, this black activism was born in an era of radically worsening conditions for most African American women, in contrast to the improving conditions for white women. The older women in this network had felt segregation intensify in their adult lifetimes; there was widespread immiseration and denial of what political power they had accumulated after the emancipation. In the 1920s the second Ku Klux Klan attracted as many as six million members. These experiences, so rarely understood by whites, further reinforced the bonds uniting black women and influenced their welfare visions.[40]

The seventy-six white women, like the blacks, constituted a coherent network. Most of them knew each other, and their compatibility was cemented by a homogeneous class, religious, and ethnic base. Most had prosperous, many even prominent parents; virtually all were of north European, Protestant backgrounds, from the Northeast or Midwest. The nine Jewish members were hardly representative of Jewish immigrants: Five had wealthy German-Jewish parents (Elizabeth Brandeis Raushenbush, Hannah Einstein, Josephine and Pauline Goldmark, and Lillian Wald). There were three Catholics (Josephine Brown, Jane Hoey, and Agnes Regan), but they were hardly typical of Catholics in the United States in the period: They were all native-born of prosperous parents. The shared Protestantism of the others was more a sign of similar ethnic background than of avid religious commitment, for few were churchgoers or intense believers, and churches did not organize their welfare activities.

The great majority (86 percent) were college-educated, and 66 percent attended graduate school. By contrast, in 1920 fewer than 1 percent of all American women held college degrees. It is worth recalling, however, that 83 percent of the black women were college-educated, and their disproportion to the black population as a whole was even greater. The white women had attended more expensive, elite schools; 37 percent had graduated from one of the New England women's colleges.

The white women had even more occupational commonality than the blacks. The great majority were social workers.[41] To understand this correctly we must appreciate the changing historical meanings of social work. Prior to the Progressive Era, the term referred not to a profession but to a range of helping and reform activity; the word *social* originally emphasized the reform, rather than the charity, component. Here it is relevant that many had mothers active in social reform.[42] The early-twentieth-century professionalization of social work has often been conceptualized as creating a rather sharp break both with amateur friendly visiting and with political activism. The experience of the women I am studying suggests otherwise: Well into the 1930s they considered casework, charity, and reform politics as "social work." By contrast to the African American women, very few were educators, a pattern that suggests that creating new educational institutions was no longer a reform priority for white women and that other professional jobs, especially governmental ones, were open to them.[43]

The whites had at least as much geographical togetherness as the black women. Sixty-eight percent worked primarily in the New England and mid-Atlantic states—hardly surprising since the national headquarters of the organizations they worked for were usually located there. Moreover, 57 percent had worked in New York City during the Progressive Era or the 1920s. New York City played a vanguard role in the development of public services and regulation in the public interest, and women in the network were influential in that city's welfare programs. New York City settlement houses specialized in demonstration projects, beginning programs on a small, private scale and then getting them publicly funded. The settlements initiated vocational guidance programs, later adopted by the public schools; they initiated use of public schools for after-hours recreation programs and public health nursing. Lillian Wald, head of the Henry Street Settlement, coordinated the city's response to the 1919 influenza epidemic. The settlements lobbied for municipal legislation regulating tenements and landlord-tenant relations, and milk purity and prices. In 1917 the Women's City Club of New York City opened a Maternity Center in Hell's Kitchen, where they provided prenatal nursing care and education and housekeeping services for new mothers. Expanded to ten locations in Manhattan, this effort served as a model for the bill that eventually became the Sheppard-Towner Act. The Women's City Club provided an important meeting place for many of these women, and it can serve as an indicator of their prosperity: Members had to pay substantial dues and an initiation fee, and the club purchased a mansion on Thirty-fifth Street and Park Avenue for $160,000 in 1917.[44]

Some of these white women had been active in party politics even before they had the vote. Some had been in the Socialist Party, and many were active in the 1912 Progressive Party campaign. Most, however, preferred nonpartisan public activism. During the late 1920s and 1930s they became more active in political parties, and transferred their allegiance to the Democratic Party. Here too New York was important, because the political figure who most attracted these women to the Democrats was Franklin D. Roosevelt, in his governorship and then his presidency. Several women who had been active in reform in the city, notably Belle Moskowitz, Rose Schneiderman, and Eleanor Roosevelt, took on statewide roles. The Al Smith campaign of 1928 promoted more division than unity, however, because most women social workers were critical of his "wet" positions and his association with machine politics. The reassuring presence of his aide Moskowitz and Franklin Roosevelt's "aide" Eleanor Roosevelt was critical in bringing their network into the Democratic Party.[45]

The black network also underwent a political realignment from Republican to Democratic, but with different meanings, largely associated with migration northward, because the southern Democratic Party was essentially closed to blacks. Ironically, this transition was also in part effectuated by Eleanor Roosevelt, who became the symbol of those few white political leaders willing to take stands on racial equality.[46] Nevertheless Eleanor Roosevelt did not create an integrated network, nor was she able to swing the white network to support the leading black demand during the Roosevelt administration: a federal antilynching law.

Women in both networks taught, mentored, even self-consciously trained each other. Among blacks this occurred in colleges, in white-run organizations such as the YMCAs, and in black organizations such as sororities, the National Association of Colored Women, and many local groups. A higher proportion of the white women than of the black women worked in settlement houses—probably partly because so many of the white women were single. That experience strongly encouraged intergenerational connections and intimacy, because the younger or newer volunteers actually lived with their elders, seeing them in action. In the civic organizations, leaders groomed, protected, and promoted their protégées: Jane Addams did this with Alice Hamilton, Lillian Wald, and Florence Kelley; Sophonisba Breckinridge launched her student Grace Abbott's career by placing her at the head of the newly formed Immigrants' Protective League; the whole network campaigned for Abbott and then for Frances Perkins to become secretary of labor.[47] Such involvements continued when network members became federal or state officials, with other members as their employees. The chiefs of the Children's and Women's Bureaus—the two key federal agencies run by women—exercised extraordinary involvement in the personal lives of their employees. Mary Anderson, for example, head of the Women's Bureau, corresponded frequently with her employees in other parts of the country about their family lives, advising them about the care of aging parents, among other things.[48]

It is quite possible that black women's personal and professional support networks were just as strong; there is less evidence because, as several historians of African American women have suggested, black women left fewer private papers than did white women.[49] Given this caveat, the white women's network does appear to differ in one measure of mutual dependence. The great majority of the white women were single— only 34 percent had ever been married, and only 18 percent remained married during their peak political activity (42 percent of those who ever married were divorced, separated, or widowed). Only 28 percent had children. In this respect they are probably quite different from many local welfare activists, a group that included fewer elite women and more who were married. Moreover, 28 percent were in relationships with other women that might have been called "Boston marriages" a few decades before.[50] (My figure is a conservative one since I counted only those women for whom I could identify a specific partner. It does not include such women as Edith Rockwood, who lived until her death in 1953 with Marjorie Heseltine of the Children's Bureau and Louise Griffith of the Social Security Agency and who built and owned a summer house jointly with Marion Crane of the Children's Bureau.)[51] At the time these relationships were mainly not named at all, although Mary ("Molly") Dewson referred to her mate as "partner." Contemporaries usually perceived them as celibate.[52] Today some of these women might be called lesbian, but there is much controversy among historians as to whether it is ahistorical to apply the word to that generation, a controversy I wish to avoid here since it is not relevant to my argument. What is relevant is not their sexual activity but their dependence on other women economically, for jobs; for care in grief, illness, and old age; for vacation companionship; for every conceivable kind of help. Despite their singleness, their efforts were very much directed to family and child welfare. It is remarkable to contemplate that so many women who became symbols of matronly respectability and asexual "social motherhood" led such unconventional private lives.

Moreover, they turned this mutual dependency into a political caucus. When lesbian history was first being written, these relationships between women were seen, first, in exclusively private and individual terms, and, second, as a lifestyle that isolated them from the heterosexual social and cultural mainstream. Recently, Estelle Freedman and Blanche Wiesen Cook have helped change that paradigm.[53] The women's female bonding did not disadvantage them but brought them political power, and they got it without making the sacrifices of personal intimacy that men so often did. Privileged women that they were, several of them had country homes, and groups would often weekend together; we can be sure that their conversation erased distinctions between the personal and the political, between gossip and tactics.

In truth, we do not know how different these white women's relationships were from black women's. Many black married women, such as Bethune and Charlotte Hawkins Brown, lived apart from their husbands (but so did several white women counted here as married, such as Perkins); and a few back women, such as Dean Lucy Slowe of Howard, lived in Boston marriages. Many blacks in this sample spoke critically not only of men but of marriage, and feared its potential to demobilize women. Dorothy Height lamented that the "over-emphasis on marriage has destroyed so many people."[54]

Both white and black women, if single, experienced a sense of betrayal when a friend married; and both, if about to marry, feared telling their single comrades.[55] In time, particularly from the 1930s on, the white women's sense that marriage and activity in the public sphere were incompatible choices diminished, and more married activists appeared.[56] This change, however, only makes it the more evident that throughout the period, black women had greater willingness, necessity, or ability to combine marriage and public activism, through coping strategies that may have included informal marital separations.

The white women's friendship network was particularly visible among the most prominent women because they took it with them to their prominent and well-documented jobs. Their friendships transcended boundaries between the public and private sectors, between government and civic organization. In this way they created what several historians have begun calling a "women's political culture"—but again we must remember that this concept has referred primarily to white women. The powerful settlement houses, Hull House and the Henry Street Settlement, for example, became virtually a part of municipal government and were able to command the use of tax money when necessary. When women gained governmental positions, there was as much extra-agency as intra-agency consultation and direction. In its first project, collecting data on infant mortality, the Children's Bureau used hundreds of volunteers from this organizational network to help. In 1920 Florence Kelley of the National Consumers' League (NCL) listed investigations the Women's Bureau should undertake, and these were done. Mary Anderson of the Women's Bureau arranged for the NCL to draft a bill for protection of female employees for the state of Indiana, and Anderson herself wrote comments on the draft. In 1922 Anderson wrote Mary Dewson of the NCL asking her to tone down her critical language about the National Woman's Party, and Dewson complied; in 1923 Dewson asked Anderson to help her draft a response to the National Woman's Party that was to appear in *The Nation* under Dewson's name.

Such cooperation continued throughout the New Deal. A good example was the Women's Charter, an attempt made in 1936, in response to the increased intensity of the campaign for the Equal Rights Amendment (ERA), to negotiate a settlement between the two sides of the women's movement. An initial meeting was attended by representatives of the usual white women's network civic organizations—YWCA, League of Women Voters, Women's Trade Union League, American Association of University Women (AAUW), Federation of Business and Professional Women—as well as several state and federal government women. The first draft of the charter was written by Anderson, still head of the Women's Bureau; Frieda Miller, then head of the women's section of the New York State Department of Labor; Rose Schneiderman, formerly of the National Recovery Administration (until the Supreme Court overruled it) and soon to become head of the New York State Department of Labor; and Mary Van Kleeck. The drafting of the charter exemplifies two of the findings regarding this network: the importance of New York and the predominance of single women.[57]

Singleness did not keep these women from useful connections with men, however. These connections came with kinship and class, if not with marriage. Clara Beyer got her "in" to the network because Felix Frankfurter recommended her to administer the 1918 District of Columbia minimum wage law. She then brought in Elizabeth Brandeis, the daughter of Louis Brandeis, to share the job with her. Brandeis's two sisters-in-law, Josephine and Pauline Goldmark, were also active in this network. Sophonisba Breckinridge, Florence Kelley, Julia Lathrop, and Katherine Lenroot were daughters of senators or congressmen. Loula Dunn's father and two grandfathers had been in the Alabama legislature. Susan Ware computed, about a different but overlapping group of New Deal women, that almost 50 percent (thirteen of twenty-eight) were from political families.[58] These women often learned politics in their households, and knew where to get introductions and referrals to politically influential people when they needed them. When Beyer said, "It was my contacts that made [me] so valuable, that I could go to these people," she was speaking about both her women's network and her male connections.[59]

With these group characteristics in mind, I want to examine the welfare ideas of these two networks.

One major difference in the orientation of the two groups was that the whites, well into the Great Depression, more strongly saw themselves as helping others—people who were "other" not only socially but often also ethnically and religiously. The perspective of the white network had been affected particularly by large-scale immigration, the reconstitution of the urban working class by people of non-WASP origin, and residential segregation, which grouped the immigrants in ghettos not often seen by the white middle class. Much has been written about the arrogance and condescension these privileged social workers showed their immigrant clients. Little has been done to discover the impact of the immigrant population on the reformers' own ideas. The black/white comparison suggests that ethnic difference between the white poor and white reformers not only discouraged identification but also slowed the reformers' development of a structural understanding of the origins of poverty, as opposed to one that blamed individual character defects, however environmentally caused. Thus into the 1940s, the great majority of the white women in this sample supported welfare programs that were not only means-tested but also "morals-tested," continuing a distinction between the worthy and the unworthy poor. They believed that aid should always be accompanied by expert supervision and rehabilitation so as to inculcate into the poor work habits and morals that they so often lacked, or so the reformers believed. (And, one might add, they did not mind the fact that this set up a sexual double standard in which women aid recipients would be treated differently and more severely than men recipients.)[60]

In comparison, black women were more focused on their own kind. Despite the relative privilege of most of them—and there was criticism from blacks of the snobbery of some of these network members—there was less distance between helper and helped than among white reformers. There was less chronological distance, for all their privileges were so recent and so tenuous. There was less geographical distance, for residential segregation did not allow the black middle class much insulation from the black poor. Concentrating their efforts more on education and health, and proportionally less on charity or relief, meant that they dealt more often with universal needs than with those of the particularly unfortunate, and sought to provide universal, not means-tested, services.

These were differences of degree and should not be overstated. Most of the white women in this sample favored environmental analyses of the sources of poverty. Many black women's groups engaged in classic charity activity. In the 1890s Washington, D.C., black women volunteered to work with the Associated Charities in its "stamp work," a program designed to inculcate thrift and saving among the poor. In the depression of 1893 these relatively prosperous black "friendly visitors" donated supplies of coal and food staples. The Kansas Federation of Women's Clubs, Marilyn Brady found, clung to all the tenets of the "cult of true womanhood" except, perhaps, for fragility. As Ena Farley wrote of the Boston League of Women for Community Service, "Their patronage roles toward others less fortunate than themselves not only dramatized their relative superiority within the minority structure, but also gave them the claim to leadership and power positions." But these programs must be understood in a context in which the needy were far more numerous, and the prosperous far fewer, than among whites.[61]

This does not mean that there was no condescension among black women. Black leaders shared with white ones the conviction that the poor needed training, to develop not only skills but also moral and spiritual capacities. Mary Church Terrell could sound remarkably like a white clubwoman:

> To our poor, benighted sisters in the Black Belt of Alabama we have gone and we have been both a comfort and a help to these women, through the darkness of whose ignorance of everything that makes life sweet or worth the living, no ray of light would have penetrated but for us. We have taught them the ABC of living by showing them how to make their huts more habitable and decent with the small means at their command and how to care for themselves and their families.[62]

Like the Progressive Era white female reformers, the blacks emphasized the need to improve the sexual morals of their people.[63] Fannie Barrier William declared that the colored people's greatest need was a better and purer home life—that slavery had destroyed home ties, the sanctity of marriage, and the instincts of motherhood.[64]

Concern for sexual respectability by no means represented one class or stratum imposing its values on another; for black women as for white women, it grew also from a feminist, or womanist, desire to protect women from exploitation, a desire shared across class lines. But this priority had profoundly different meanings for black women reformers. Not only were black women more severely sexually victimized, but combating sexual exploitation was for blacks inseparable from race uplift in general, as white sexual assaults against black women had long been a fundamental part of slavery and racial oppression. Indeed, black activists were far in advance of white feminists in their campaigns against rape and their identification of that crime as part of a system of power relations, and they did not assume that only *white* men were sexual aggressors. The historian Darlene Clark Hine suggests that efforts to build recreational programs for boys also reflected women's strategies for protecting girls from assault. Nevertheless, given the difficulties of effecting change in the aggressors, many black welfare reformers focused on protecting potential victims. Many of the earliest black urban institutions were homes designed to protect working women. Black women's considerable contribution to the founding and development of the Urban League had such motives. Just as the efforts by white welfare reformers to protect girls and women contained condescending and victim-blaming aspects, particularly inasmuch as they were directed at different social groups (immigrants, the poor), so victim-blaming was present among black reformers, too. The problem of sex exploitation could not be removed from intrarace class differences that left some black women much more vulnerable than others, not only to assault but also to having their reputations smeared; black women, like white women, defined their middle-class status in part by their sexual respectability. But their sexual protection efforts were so connected to uplift for the whole race, without which the reformers could not enjoy any class privileges, that the victim blaming was a smaller part of their message than among whites.[65]

Moreover, despite the sense of superiority among some, the black women reformers could not easily separate their welfare-related activities from their civil rights agitation.[66] As Deborah White puts it, "The race problem . . . inherently included the problems of poverty."[67] Race uplift work was usually welfare work by definition, and it was always conceived as a path to racial equality. And black poverty could not be ameliorated without challenges to white domination. A nice example: In 1894 Gertrude Mossell, in a tribute to black women's uplift activity, referred to Ida Wells's antilynching campaign as "philanthropy." Several of these women, notably Terrell and Anna J. Cooper, were among the first rebels against Booker T. Washington's domination because of their attraction both to academic educational goals for their people and to challenges to segregation.[68] Those who considered themselves women's rights activists, such as Burroughs, Terrell, and Cooper, particularly protested the hypocrisy in the white feminists' coupling of the language of sisterhood with the practice of black exclusion—as in Terrell's principled struggle, as an elderly woman, to gain admission to the District of Columbia chapter of the American Association of University Women.

To be sure, there was a shift in emphasis from race uplift and thus institution building in the first part of this long period under study to the struggle against segregation in the second. But the shift was visible only in overview, because many women activists had been challenging racism from early in their careers. Williams, for example, as early as 1896 insisted that white women needed to learn from blacks.[69] YWCA women such as Eva Bowles, Lugenia Burns Hope, and Addie Hunton struggled against discrimination in the YWCA soon after the first colored branch opened in 1911. Charlotte Hawkins Brown, who was noted and sometimes criticized for her snobbery and insistence on "respectability," nevertheless "made it a practice, whenever insulted in a train or forced to leave a pullman coach and enter the Jim Crow car, to bring suit." At least one lawyer, in 1921, tried to get her to accept a small settlement, but she made it clear that her purpose was not financial compensation but justice.[70] Cooper, whose flowery and sentimental prose style might lead one to mistake her for a "soft," accommodating spirit, rarely let a slur against Negroes go unprotested. She wrote to the Oberlin Committee against Al Smith in 1928 that she could not "warm up very enthusiastically with religious fervor for Bible 'fundamentalists' who have nothing to say about lynching Negroes or reducing whole sections of them to a state of peonage."[71]

The many women who had always challenged racism made a relatively smooth transition to a civil rights emphasis in their welfare work. There were conflicts about separatist versus integrationist strategies from the beginning of this period, not only in women's participation in leading black discourse but also in women's own projects. For example, Jane Hunter's establishment of a black YWCA in Cleveland evoked much black criticism, especially from those who thought her success in raising white money sprang from her decision not to challenge the white YWCA. Yet most black women in this network used separate institution-building and antisegregation tactics at the same time. Nannie Burroughs, noted for her work as an educator promoting black Christian and vocational education, urged a boycott of the segregated public transportation system of Washington, D.C., in 1915.[72] (Burroughs was Hunter's model.) In the 1930s Burroughs denounced the Baptist leadership and resisted its control so strongly that that church almost cut off financial support for the National Training School for Girls that she had worked so hard and long to build. "'Don't wait for deliverers,' she admonished her listeners. . . . 'There are no deliverers. They're all dead. . . . The Negro must serve notice . . . that he is ready to die for justice.'" The Baptists relented, but Burroughs was still provoking white churchmen a decade later. In 1941 she canceled an engagement to speak for the National Christian Mission because the hierarchy insisted on precensoring her speech.[73] "The Negro is oppressed not because he is a Negro—but because he'll take it."[74] Bethune, who began her career as founder of a black college and was criticized by some for her apologias for segregated New Deal programs, was walking a picket line in front of Peoples Drugs in the District of Columbia, demanding jobs for colored youth, in 1939 even while still at the National Youth Administration.[75]

Moreover, the greater emphasis on civil rights never eclipsed uplift strategies. From the New Deal on, black government leaders were simultaneously trying to get more black women hired, protesting the passing over of qualified black applicants, and working to improve the qualifications and performance of black individuals. In 1943 Corinne Robinson of the Federal Public Housing Authority organized a skit, entitled *Lazy Daisy*, that called upon black government workers to shed slothful habits.[76] Nannie Burroughs in 1950 complained that the average Negro "gets up on the installment plan—never gets dressed fully until night, and by then he is completely disorganized." But that is because, she explained, "He really has nothing to get up to." To repeat: There was for these women no inherent contradiction between race uplift and antidiscrimination thinking.[77]

These black welfare activists were also militant in their critique of male supremacy, that militance, too, arising from their work for the welfare of the race. Deborah White has argued that the black women's clubs, more than the white ones, claimed leadership of the race for women. Charlotte Hawkins Brown declared her own work and thoughts were just as important as Booker T. Washington's.[78] Moreover, their ambitions were just as great as those of the white women: African Americans spoke of uplifting their race; white women described themselves as promoting the general welfare, but only because their focus on their own race was silent and understood. Whether or not these women should be called feminists (and they certainly did not call themselves that), they shared characteristics of the white group that has been called "social feminists"; their activism arose from efforts to advance the welfare of the whole public, not just women, in a context where, they believed, men did not or could not adequately meet the needs.[79]

Black and white women welfare reformers also differed in their thinking about women's economic role. The white women, with few exceptions, tended to view married women's economic dependence on men as desirable, and their employment as a misfortune; they accepted the family wage system and rarely expressed doubts about its effectiveness, let alone its justice. There was substantial variation within this network and change over time in its members' view of the family wage. There was also substantial contradiction. Beginning in the 1890s, women social investigators repeatedly demonstrated that the family wage did not work, because most men did not earn enough, because some men became disabled, and because others were irresponsible toward their families. Sybil Lipschultz has shown that between two key Supreme Court briefs written by women in the white network—for *Muller v. Oregon* in 1908, and for *Adkins v. Children's Hospital* in 1923—the grounds for protective legislation changed considerably. The brief for *Muller* privileged sacred motherhood and treated women's wage labor as an anomaly that should be prevented; the brief for *Adkins* argued from women's weaker position in the labor market and the need for government to intervene because it was not an anomaly.[80] Yet when the women's welfare network moved away from protective labor legislation toward public assistance or family policy, its recommendations presupposed that the desirable position for women was as domestic wives and mothers dependent on male earnings. The many unmarried women in the network viewed their own singleness as a class privilege and a natural condition for women active in the public sphere, and felt that remaining childless was an acceptable price for it. They were convinced that single motherhood and employment among mothers meant danger. They feared other than temporary relief to single mothers if no counseling or employment was offered, because they resisted establishing single-mother families as durable institutions.[81]

This is where the social work legacy is felt. The white reformers were accustomed to, and felt comfortable with, supervising. Long after Jane Addams with her environmentalist, democratic orientation became their hero, they continued to identify with the Charity Organization Society fear of "pauperizing" aid recipients by making it too easy for them and destroying their work incentive—and they feared that too much help to deserted women, for example, would do just this, let men off the hook. They did not share the belief of many contemporary European socialists that aid to single mothers should be a matter of right, of entitlement. Even Florence Kelley, herself a product of a European socialist education, defended the family wage as the appropriate goal of reform legislation. A divorced mother herself, she nevertheless lauded "the American tradition that men support their families, the wives throughout life," and lamented the "retrograde movement" that made the man no longer the breadwinner. The U.S. supporters of mothers' pensions envisioned aid as a gift to the deserving, and felt an unshakable responsibility to supervise single mothers and restore marriages and wives' dependency on husbands whenever possible. This "white" view was clearly a class perspective as well. A troubling question is unavoidable: Did these elite white women believe that independence was a privilege of wealth to which poor women ought not aspire?[82]

The black women reformers also held up breadwinner husbands and nonemployed wives as an ideal; black and white women spoke very similarly about the appropriate "spheres" of the two sexes, equally emphasizing motherhood.[83] The difference I am describing here is not diametric. Lucy D. Slowe, dean of women at Howard, believed that working mothers caused urban juvenile delinquency, and she called for campaigns to "build up public sentiment for paying heads of families wages sufficient to reduce the number of Negro women who must be employed away from home to the detriment of their children and of the community in general."[84] Personally, many of the married black activists had trouble prevailing upon their husbands to accept their activities, and some were persuaded to stay home. Ardie Halyard, recollecting the year 1920, described the process:

> Interviewer: How did your husband feel about your working?
> Halyard: At first, he thought it was very necessary. But afterwards, when he became able to support us, it was day in and day out, "When are you going to quit?"[85]

Dorothy Ferebee's husband could not tolerate her higher professional status. Inabel Lindsay promised her husband not to work for a year and then slid into a lifelong career by taking a job that she promised was only temporary.[86]

Mixed as it was, acceptance of married women's employment as a long-term and widespread necessity was much greater among blacks than among whites. Fanny Jackson Coppin had argued in the 1860s for women's economic independence from men, and women were active in creating employment bureaus. We see the greater black acknowledgment of single mothers in the high priority black women reformers gave to organizing kindergartens, then usually called day nurseries. In Chicago, Cleveland, Atlanta, Washington, and many other locations, daytime child-care facilities were among the earliest projects of women's groups. Terrell called establishing them her first goal, and her first publication was the printed version of a speech she had delivered at a National American Woman Suffrage Association convention, which she sold for twenty-five cents a copy to help fund a kindergarten.[87] In poor urban white neighborhoods the need for child care may have been nearly as great, and some white activists created kindergartens, but proportionally far fewer. Virtually no northern white welfare reformers endorsed such programs as long-term or permanent services until the 1930s and 1940s; until then even the most progressive, such as Kelley, opposed them even as temporary solutions, fearing they would encourage the exploitation of women through low-wage labor.[88]

Black women decried the effects of the "double day" on poor women as much as did white reformers. They were outspoken in their criticism of men who failed to support families. Burroughs wrote, "Black men sing too much 'I Can't Give You Anything But Love, Baby.'"[89] But their solutions were different. From the beginning of her career, Burroughs understood that the great majority of black women would work all their lives, and she had to struggle against continuing resistance to accepting that fact to get her National Training School funded. And most black women activists projected a favorable view of working women and women's professional aspirations. Elizabeth Ross Haynes wrote with praise in 1922 of "the hope of an economic independence that will some day enable them [Negro women] to take their places in the ranks with other working women."[90] Sadie Alexander directly attacked the view that a married woman's ideal should be domesticity. She saw that in an industrial society the work of the housewife would be increasingly seen as "valueless consumption" and that women should "place themselves again among the producers of the world."[91]

This high regard for women's economic independence is also reflected in the important and prestigious role played by businesswomen in black welfare activity. One of the best-known and most revered women of this network was Maggie Lena Walker, the first woman bank president in the United States. Beginning work at the age of fourteen in the Independent Order of St. Luke, a mutual benefit society in Richmond, Virginia, that provided illness and burial insurance as well as social activity for blacks, in 1903 she established the St. Luke Penny Savings Bank. Walker became a very wealthy woman. She devoted a great deal of her money and her energy to welfare activity, working in the National Association for the Advancement of Colored People (NAACP), the National Association of Wage Earners, and local Richmond groups. In the context of African American experience, Walker's business was itself a civil rights and community welfare activity; many reformers, including prominently Bethune and Du Bois, believed that economic power was a key to black progress. The St. Luke enterprise stimulated black ownership and employment. They opened a black-owned department store in Richmond, thus threatening white economic power, and met intense opposition from white businessmen; indeed, a white Retail Dealers' Association was formed to crush the store. Several noteworthy businesswomen-activists got rich manufacturing cosmetics for blacks: the mother-daughter team of C. J. Walker and A'Lelia Walker (not related to Maggie Walker) of Pittsburgh and Indianapolis, and Annie Turnbo Malone of St. Louis. Reformer Jane Hunter was respected not only because of her welfare contributions but also because, though once penniless, she left an estate of over four hundred thousand dollars at her death; as was Sallie Wyatt Stewart, who left over one hundred thousand dollars in real estate.[92]

These factors suggest considerable differences in orientations (among the numerous similarities) between white and black women activists, although the preliminary stage of research on this topic requires us to consider the differences more as hypotheses than as conclusions. First, black women claimed leadership in looking after the welfare of their whole people more than did comparable whites. Because of this assumption of race responsibility, and because for blacks welfare was so indistinguishable from equal rights, black women emphasized programs for the unusually needy less, and universal provision more, than did white women. Perhaps in part because education was so important a part of the black women's program, and because education developed for whites in the United States as a universal public service, blacks' vision of welfare provision followed that model. Among whites, a relatively large middle class encouraged reformers to focus their helping efforts on others, and kept alive and relatively uncriticized the use of means and morals testing as a way of distributing help, continuing the division of the "deserving" from the "undeserving" poor. Among the black reformers, despite their relatively elite position, welfare appeared more closely connected with legal entitlements, not so different from the right to vote or to ride the public transportation system.[93] Had their ideas been integrated into the white women's thinking, one might ask, would means testing and humiliating invasions of privacy have been so uniformly accepted in programs such as Aid to Families with Dependent Children (AFDC), over which the white women's network had substantial influence?

Another difference is the black women's different attitude toward married women's employment. Most of the white women welfare reformers retained, until World War II, a distinctly head-in-the-sand and even somewhat contradictory attitude toward it: It was a misfortune, not good for women, children, or men; helping working mothers too much would tend to encourage it. Thus they were more concerned to help—sometimes to force—single mothers to stay home than to provide services that would help working mothers, such as child care or maternity leave. Black women were much more positive about women's employment. Despite their agreement that a male family wage was the most desirable arrangement, they doubted that married women's employment would soon disappear, or that it could be discouraged by making women and children suffer for it. In relation to this race difference, it is hard to ignore the different marital status of the majority of the women in the two groups: Most of the black women had themselves had the experience of combining public-sphere activism with marriage, if less often with children.[94] Perhaps the fact that most of the white women had dispensed with marriage and family, probably largely by choice, made them see the choice between family and work as an acceptable one, oblivious to the different conditions of such "choice" among poorer women.

Third, black and white welfare reformers differed considerably about how to protect women from sexual exploitation. Black welfare reformers were more concerned to combine the development of protective institutions for women with an antirape discourse. Among whites, rape was not an important topic of discussion during this period, and in protective work for women and girls, male sexuality was treated as natural and irrepressible. It is not clear how the black activists would have translated antirape consciousness into welfare policy had they had the power to do so, but it seems likely that they would have tried.

There were also substantial areas of shared emphases between white and black women. Both groups oriented much of their welfarist thinking to children, rarely questioning the unique responsibility of women for children's welfare. Neither group questioned sexual "purity" as an appropriate goal for unmarried women. Both groups used women's organizations as their main political and social channels. Both emphasized the promotion of other women into positions of leadership and jobs, confident that increasing the numbers of women at the "top" would benefit the public welfare. Both believed that improving the status of women was essential to advancing the community as a whole. Yet in the 1920s both groups were moving away from explicitly feminist discourse and muting their public

criticisms of what we would today call sexism. Moreover, they shared many personal characteristics: low fertility, relatively high economic and social status, very high educational
attainment.

These impressions raise more questions than they answer. I wonder, for example, what
the relation was between the national leaders and local rank-and-file activists: Were the
leaders "representative" of "constituencies"? One might hypothesize that local activists
were more often married and less elite, since singleness and prosperity were probably
among the factors that allowed women to travel and to function nationally. To what extent
were the black/white differences functions of chronology? White reformers were, for
instance, active in building educational institutions in the nineteenth century; by the early
twentieth century the institutions they needed were in place. Further research might also
make it possible to identify historical circumstances that contributed to these race differences, circumstances such as migration, changing demand for labor, and immigration and
its closure.

I approached this evidence as part of a general inquiry into welfare thinking in the
United States in this century. In this project I found, as have several other historians, that
the white women's reform network—but not the black women's—had some influence on
welfare policy, particularly in public assistance programs. I have tried to show here that
this influence was as much colored by race as by gender. The white women's influence
supported the legacies in our welfare programs of means testing, distinguishing the deserving from the undeserving, moral supervision of female welfare recipients, failing to criticize men's sexual behavior, and discouraging women' s employment. Black women's
influence on federal welfare programs was negligible in this period; indeed, the leading
federal programs—old-age insurance, unemployment compensation, workmen's compensation, and the various forms of public assistance such as AFDC—were expressly constructed to exclude blacks. It is not too late now, however, to benefit from a review of black
women's welfare thought as we reconsider the kind of welfare state we want.[95]

Appendix

The women in these samples were selected because they were the leaders of national organizations that lobbied for welfare programs (such as the National Consumers' League, the
National Child Labor Committee, the National Association of Colored Women, or the
National Council of Negro Women), or government officials responsible for welfare programs who were also important advocates of such programs, or builders of private welfare
institutions. Women who were simply employees of welfare programs or institutions were
not included; for example, educators were included only when they were builders of educational institutions. For the blacks, this sample of welfare activists overlaps extensively with a
sample one might construct of clubwomen and political activists, but not exactly; for example, Ida Wells-Barnett is not here because she must be categorized as primarily a civil rights,
not a welfare, campaigner. Among the whites this sample overlaps somewhat with "social
feminists," but those who were primarily labor organizers, for example, are not included.

Some of what appear to be race differences are differences of historical time and circumstance. Thus a study of women between, say, 1840 and 1890 would have included
more white women educators (because white women were then working to build educational institutions, as black women were later) and more white married women (because
the dip in the marriage rate among college-educated white women occurred later).
Regional differences are also produced by this definition of the samples: a focus on local or

Table 14.1 Selected Black Women Welfare Activists

Name	Main Reform	Name	Main Reform
Alexander, Sadie Tanner Mossell	Civil rights	Jones, Verina Morton	Social work
Anthony, Lucille	Health	Laney, Lucy Craft	Education
Ayer, G. Elsie	Education	Lawton, Maria Coles Perkins	Education
Barnes, Margaret E.	Education	Lindsay, Inabel Burns	Education
Barrett, Janie Porter	Education	Lyle, Ethel Hedgeman	Club
Bearden, Bessye	Civil rights	Mallory, Arenia Cornelia	Education
Bethune, Mary McLeod	Education	Malone, Annie M. Turnbo	Education
Bowles, Eva Del Vakia	Social work	Marsh, Vivian Osborne	Club
Brawley, Ruth Merrill	Social work	Matthews, Victoria Earle	Social work
Brown, Charlotte Hawkins	Education	Mays, Sadie Gray	Social work
Brown, Sue M.	Education	McCrorey, Mary Jackson	Social work
Burroughs, Nannie Helen	Education	McDougald, G. Elsie Johnson	Education
Callis, Myra Colson	Employment	McKane, Alice Woodby	Health
Carter, Ezella	Education	Merritt, Emma Frances Grayson	Education
Cary, Alice Dugged	Child welfare	Nelson, Alice Ruth Dunbar	Social work
Cook, Coralie Franklin	Education	Pickens, Minnie McAlpin	Civil rights
Cooper, Anna Julia Haywood	Education	Randolph, Florence	Club
Davis, Belle	Health	Ridley, Florida Ruffin	Club
Davis, Elizabeth Lindsey	Club	Ruffin, Josephine St. Pierre	Club
Dickerson, Addie W.	Club	Rush, Gertrude E.	Social work
Faulkner, Georgia M. DeBaptiste	Social work	Saddler, Juanita Jane	Civil rights
Fauset, Crystal Bird	Civil rights	Snowden, Joanna Cecilia	Social work
Ferebee, Dorothy Boulding	Health	Stewart, Sallie Wyatt	Social work
Gaines, Irene McCoy	Civil rights	Talbert, Mary Barnett	Civil rights
Harris, Judia C. Jackson	Social work	Taylor, Isabelle Rachel	Social work
Haynes, Elizabeth Ross	Civil rights	Terrell, Mary Eliza Church	Civil rights
Hedgeman, Anna Arnold	Civil rights	Walker, A'Lelia	Social work
Height, Dorothy I.	Civil rights	Walker, Maggie Lena	Social work
Hope, Lugenia Burns	Social work	Warren, Sadie	Social work
Hunter, Jane Edna Harris	Social work	Washington, Margaret Murray	Education
Hunton, Addie D. Waites	Civil rights	Wells, Eva Thornton	Social work
Jackson, Juanita Elizabeth	Civil rights	Wheatley, Laura Frances	Education
Jeffries, Christina Armistead	Civil rights	Williams, Fannie Barrier	Social work
Johnson, Bertha La Branche	Education	Young, Mattie Dover	Social work
Johnson, Kathryn Magnolia	Civil rights		

state, as opposed to national, activity would have led to the inclusion of more western and southern women, for example; women in the Northeast and mid-Atlantic were more likely to be important in national politics because New York and Washington, D.C., were so often the headquarters of national activities

In order to simplify this list, only a single, general, major area of welfare activism is given for each woman. Because many women were active in several areas, the identifications given here do not necessarily conform to some figures in the text, for example, how many women were social workers or educators. The categories for the white and black women are not the same. Among the whites I gave more specific identifications to indicate the importance of several key arenas, such as the National Consumers' League and the United States Children's Bureau. To use such specific identifications among the black women would have been uninformative, since virtually all were, for example, active in the NACW. Furthermore, a few black women participated in such a variety of welfarist activity organized through the NACW, sororities, or other women's organizations that I could define their major sphere as simply club work.

Table 14.2 Selected White Women Welfare Activists

Name	Main Reform	Name	Main Reform
Abbott, Edith	Social work	Kelley, Florence Molthrop	Consumers' League
Abbott, Grace	Children's Bureau	Kellor, Frances (Alice)	Immigrant welfare
Addams, Jane	Settlement	Lathrop, Julia Clifford	Childrens' Bureau
Amidon, Beulah Elizabeth	Social work	Lenroot, Katherine Frederica	Children's Bureau
Anderson Mary	Women's Bureau	Loeb, Sophie Irene Simon	Mothers' pensions
Armstrong, Barbara		Lundberg, Emma Octavia	Children's Bureau
Nachtrieb	Social Security	Maher, Amy	Social Security
Armstrong, Florence Arzelia	Social Security	Mason, Lucy Randolph	Consumers' League
Beyer, Clara Mortenson	Children's Bureau	McDowell, Mary Eliza	Settlement
Blair, Emily Newell	Democratic Party	McMain, Eleanor Laura	Settlement
Bradford, Cornelia Foster	Settlement	Miller, Frieda Segelke	Women's Bureau
Breckinridge, Sophonisba		Moskowitz, Belle Israels	Democratic Party
Preston	Social work	Newman, Pauline	Women's Bureau
Brown, Josephine Chapin	Social work	Perkins, Frances	Social Security
Burns, Eveline Mabel	Social Security	Peterson, Agnes L.	Women's Bureau
Cannon, Ida Maud	Medical social work	Pidgeon, Mary Elizabeth	Women's Bureau
Colcord, Joanna	Social work	Rankin, Jeannette Pickering	Congresswoman
Coyle, Grace Longwood	Social work	Raushenbush, Elizabeth	
Crane, Caroline Bartlett	Sanitation reform	Brandeis	Unemployment
Deardorff, Neva Ruth	Social work	Regan, Agnes Gertrude	Social work
Dewson, Mary W. (Molly)	Democratic Party	Richmond, Mary Ellen	Social work
Dinwiddie, Emily Wayland	Housing reform	Roche, Josephine Aspinall	Consumers' League
Dudley, Helena Stuart	Settlement	Roosevelt, (Anna) Eleanor	Social work
Dunn, Loula Friend	Social work	Schneiderman, Rose	Labor
Eastman, Crystal (Catherine)	Industrial health	Sherwin, Belle	Club
Einstein, Hannah Bachman	Mothers' pensions	Simkhovitch, Mary Kingsbury	Settlement
Eliot, Martha May	Children's Bureau	Springer, Gertrude Hill	Social work
Ellickson, Katherine Pollak	Social Security	Switzer, Mary Elizabeth	Social work
Elliott, Harriet Wiseman	Democratic Party	Taft, (Julia) Jessie	Social work
Engle, Lavinia Margaret	Social Security	Thomas, M. Carey	Education
Evans, Elizabeth Glendower	Consumers' League	Towle, Charlotte Helen	Social work
Fuller, Minnie Ursula	Child welfare		(academic)
Goldmark, Josephine Clara	Consumers' League	Ville, Gertrude	Social work
Goldmark, Pauline Dorothea	Consumers' League	Van Kleeck, Mary Abby	Women's Bureau
Gordon, Jean Margaret	Consumers' League	Wald, Lillian D.	Settlement
Hall, Helen	Settlement	White, Sue Shelton	Democratic Party
Hamilton, (Amy) Gordon	Social work	Wood, Edith Elmer	Housing reform
Hamilton, Alice	Industrial health	Woodbury, Helen Laura	
Hoey, Jane Margueretta	Social Security	Sumner	Children's Bureau
Iams, Lucy Virginia Dorsey	Housing reform	Woodward, Ellen Sullivan	Social work
Keller, Helen	Health reform		

Notes

For critical readings of this article in draft I am indebted to Lisa D. Brush, Nancy Cott, Elizabeth Higginbotham, Evelyn Brooks Higginbotham, Jacquelyn D. Hall, Stanlie James, Judith Walzer Leavitt, Gerda Lerner, Adolph Reed Jr., Anne Firor Scott, Kathryn Kish Sklar, Susan Smith, David Thelen, Susan Traverso, Bill Van Deburg, Deborah Gray White, and anonymous readers for *The Journal of American History*. I could not meet all the high standards of these scholars, many of whom took a great deal of time and care with this sprawling essay, but several of them not only offered valuable insights but also saved me from some errors resulting from my venture into a new field, and I am extremely grateful.

1. For a critique of gender bias in existing welfare scholarship and an explanation of the need for further research about the influence of gender, see the introduction to Linda Gordon, ed., *Women, the State, and Welfare* (Madison, 1990), 9–35.

2. One of the subjects of this study, Inabel Burns Lindsay, former dean of the Howard University School of Social Work, wrote a dissertation on this topic at the University of Pittsburgh in 1952, and published it as "Some Contributions of Negroes to Welfare Services, 1865–1900," *Journal of Negro Education* 25 (winter 1956): 15–24. Her publication did not spark others, however. A valuable collection of documents is Edyth L. Ross, ed., *Black Heritage in Social Welfare, 1860–1930* (Metuchen, 1978). Neither publication considers the particular role of women. For suggestions that black women participated more in organized activity than did white women, see Anne Firor Scott, "Most Invisible of All: Black Women's Voluntary Associations," *Journal of Southern History* 56 (February 1990): 5; and Ena L. Farley, "Caring and Sharing since World War I: The League of Women for Community Service—A Black Volunteer Organization in Boston," *Umoja* 1 (summer 1977): 1–12. Victoria Earle Matthews's surname is sometimes spelled "Mathews." Ralph E. Luker, "Missions, Institutional Churches, and Settlement Houses: The Black Experience, 1885–1910," *Journal of Negro History* 69 (summer/fall 1984): 101–13; Dorothy C. Salem, *To Better Our World: Black Women in Organized Reform, 1890–1920* (Brooklyn, 1990), 44–45; Sharon Harley, "Beyond the Classroom: The Organizational Lives of Black Female Educators in the District of Columbia, 1890–1930," *Journal of Negro Education* 51 (summer 1982): 262; Jacqueline Anne Rouse, *Lugenia Burns Hope: Black Southern Reformer* (Athens, Ga., 1989); Elizabeth Lasch, "Female Vanguard in Race Relations: 'Mother Power' and Blacks in the American Settlement House Movement," paper delivered at the Berkshire Conference on the History of Women, Rutgers University, June 1990 (in Linda Gordon's possession). Since the black settlements were often called missions and were often more religious than typical white settlements, historians have not clearly recognized the broad range of services they provided and the organizational/agitational centers they became.

3. On public social welfare programs attacking working-class self-help programs in England, see Stephen Yeo, "Working-Class Association, Private Capital, Welfare, and the State in the Late Nineteenth and Twentieth Centuries, " in Noel Parry et al., eds., *Social Work, Welfare, and the State* (London, 1979). Self-help associations of the poor were probably as common in the United States as in England.

4. Charles L. Coon, "Public Taxation and Negro Schools," quoted in W. E. B. Du Bois, ed., *Efforts for Social Betterment among Negro Americans* (Atlanta, 1909), 29. The tax money spent on black schools was, of course, proportionally and absolutely far less than that spent on white.

5. Cynthia Neverdon-Morton, *Afro-American Women of the South and the Advancement of the Race, 1895–1925* (Knoxville, 1989), 79.

6. Louie D. Shivery, "The History of the Gate City Free Kindergarten Association" (from a 1936 Atlanta University M.A. thesis), in Ross, ed., *Black Heritage in Social Welfare*, 261–62.

7. Tera Hunter, "'The Correct Thing': Charlotte Hawkins Brown and the Palmer Institute," *Southern Exposure* 11 (Sept./Oct. 1983): 37–43; Sandra N. Smith and Earle H. West, " Charlotte Hawkins Brown," *Journal of Negro Education* 51 (summer 1982): 191–206.

8. Darlene Clark Hine, "'We Specialize in the Wholly Impossible': The Philanthropic Work of Black Women," in Kathleen D. McCarthy, ed., *Lady Bountiful Revisited: Women, Philanthropy, and Power* (New Brunswick, 1990), 84.

9. For help in gathering and analyzing biographical data, I am indebted to Lisa Brush, Bob Buchanan, Nancy Isenberg, Nancy MacLean, and Susan Traverso.

10. For a discussion of the definition of welfare, see Gordon, ed., *Women, the State, and Welfare*, 19–35; and Linda Gordon, "What Does Welfare Regulate?" *Social Research* 55 (winter 1988): 609–30. Child labor is an issue of both welfare and labor reform. I have included it here because, for so many women active in this cause, it seemed a logical, even inevitable, continuation of other child welfare activity; opposition to child labor was a much-used argument for mothers' pensions and Aid to Families with Dependent Children.

11. Although my focus is on welfare, a similar predominance of northern whites and southern blacks occurred among the national women's organizations. For example, Margaret (Mrs. Booker T.) Washington was the first southerner to be head of any national secular women's group—in her case, the National Association of Colored Women (NACW). See Darlene Rebecca Roth, "Matronage: Patterns in Women's Organizations, Atlanta, Georgia, 1890–1940" (Ph.D. diss., George Washington University, 1978), 81. On the integration of education into campaigns for welfare by African Americans, see, for example, Elizabeth Higginbotham, "Too Much to Ask: The Costs of Black Female Success," ch. 3, "Socialized for Survival" (in Elizabeth Higginbotham's possession).

12. Of the sixty-nine black women, five held governmental positions: Mary McLeod Bethune was director of the Division of Negro Affairs at the National Youth Administration under Franklin D. Roosevelt; Alice Cary was a traveling advisor to the Department of Labor during World War I; Crystal Fauset was a state

legislator from Philadelphia and race relations advisor to the Works Progress Administration during the New Deal; Anna Hedgeman was assistant to the New York City commissioner of welfare in 1934. By contrast, 53 percent of the white women held federal government positions, and 58 percent held state positions.

13. Neverdon-Morton, *Afro-American Women of the South*, 191–236; Rosalyn Terborg-Penn, "Discrimination against Afro-American Women in the Woman's Movement, 1830–1920," in Sharon Harley and Rosalyn Terborg-Penn, eds., *The Afro-American Woman: Struggles and Images* (Port Washington, 1978), 17–27.

14. These white reformers were not more racist than the men engaged in similar activity and often less so. Eight white women from this sample were among the founding members of the National Association for the Advancement of Colored People (NAACP): Jane Addams, Florence Kelley, Julia Lathrop, Sophonisba Breckinridge, Mary McDowell, Lillian Wald, and Edith and Grace Abbott.

15. Steven J. Diner, "Chicago Social Workers and Blacks in the Progressive Era," *Social Service Review* 44 (December 1970): 393–410; Sandra M. Stehno, "Public Responsibility for Dependent Black Children: The Advocacy of Edith Abbott and Sophonisba Breckinridge," *Social Service Review* 62 (September 1988): 485–503; Gerda Lerner, *Black Women in White America: A Documentary History* (New York, 1972), 459; Salem, *To Better Our World*, 248–50; Jacquelyn Dowd Hall, *Revolt against Chivalry: Jessie Daniel Ames and the Women's Campaign against Lynching* (New York, 1979), 66.

16. Jacqueline Rouse, biographer of Lugenia Burns Hope of Atlanta, lists ten other black activists who, with Hope, formed a close southern network by about 1910—Bethune in Florida, Nettie Napier and M. L. Crosthwait in Tennessee, Jennie Moton and Margaret Washington in Alabama, Maggie Lena Walker in Virginia, Charlotte Hawkins Brown and Mary Jackson McCrorey in North Carolina, and Lucy Laney and Florence Hunt, also in Georgia. Rouse, *Lugenia Burns Hope*, 5. Rouse also identifies an overlapping group of black southern women educators—Hope, Hunt, McCrorey, Washington, Moton, and Bethune, with the addition of Marion B. Wilkinson of South Carolina State College; Julia A. Fountain of Morris Brown College in Atlanta; and A. Vera Davage of Clark College in Atlanta; ibid., 55. Paula Giddings, *In Search of Sisterhood: Delta Sigma Theta and the Challenge of the Black Sorority Movement* (New York, 1988). Darlene Rebecca Roth found that black clubwomen retained closer ties with their schools than did white clubwomen; Roth, "Matronage," 183. Hine, "'We Specialize in the Wholly Impossible,'" 70–93; Fannie Barrier Williams, "Opportunities and Responsibilities of Colored Women," in James T. Haley, ed., *Afro-American Encyclopaedia; or, the Thoughts, Doings, and Sayings of the Race* (Nashville, 1896), 146–61.

17. Hine, "'We Specialize in the Wholly Impossible,'" 83.

18. On the attempt to force Lucy D. Slowe to live in the women's dormitory, see the letters in folder 59, box 90-3, and folder 100, box 90-4, Lucy D. Slowe Papers (Moorland-Spingarn Research Center, Howard University, Washington, D.C.), esp. Coralie Franklin Cook et al. to Lucy D. Slowe, 9 June 1933, folder 9, box 90-2; Clayda J. Williams to Slowe, 23 August 1993; and Mary McLeod Bethune to Slowe, 23 November 1933, folder 28. Howard University was notorious for its discriminatory treatment of women, backward even in relation to other colleges at the time. On Howard, see Giddings, *In Search of Sisterhood*, 43.

19. For remarks made about Bethune at the 1938 National Conference of Negro Women White House Conference, praising her for not being satisfied to be the token black but struggling to increase black representation in the New Deal, see folder 4, box 1, series 4, 27–28, National Council of Negro Women Papers (Mary McLeod Bethune Museum and Archives, Washington, D.C.).

20. Tullia Brown Hamilton also found this focus on education predominant among the black women reformers she studied. Tullia Brown Hamilton, "The National Association of Colored Women, 1896–1920" (Ph.D. diss., Emory University, 1978), 45–46. Similarly Roth found that even among Atlanta's most elite organization of black women, the Chautauqua Circle, all had been employed as teachers; Roth, "Matronage," 181. Melinda Chateauvert found that women graduates of Washington, D.C.'s elite black Dunbar High School (who outnumbered males two to one around 1910) were overwhelmingly likely to go on to the district's free Miner Teacher's College to become teachers; Melinda Chateauvert, "The Third Step: Anna Julia Cooper and Black Education in the District of Columbia," *Sage* 5, student supplement (1988): 7–13. For the same conclusion, see Carol O. Perkins, "The Pragmatic Idealism of Mary McLeod Bethune," *Sage* 5, student supplement (fall 1988): 30–36. W. E. B. Du Bois, ed., *Economic Cooperation among Negro Americans* (Atlanta, 1907), 80–88.

21. Du Bois, ed., *Efforts for Social Betterment among Negro Americans*, 65–77. For a northern local example, see Russell H. Davis, *Black Americans in Cleveland: From George Peake to Carl B. Stokes, 1796–1969* (Cleveland, 1972), 192.

22. Darlene Clark Hine, *Black Women in White: Racial Conflict and Cooperation in the Nursing Profession, 1890–1950* (Bloomington, 1989), xvii; Edward H. Beardsley, *A History of Neglect: Health Care for Blacks and Mill Workers in the Twentieth-Century South* (Knoxville, 1987), 101; Susan L. Smith, "The Black Women's Club Movement: Self-Improvement and Sisterhood, 1890–1915" (M.A. thesis, University of Wisconsin, Madison, 1986); Susan L. Smith, "Black Activism in Health Care, 1890–1950," paper delivered at the con-

ference "Black Health: Historical Perspectives and Current Issues," University of Wisconsin, Madison, April 1990 (in Gordon's possession); Salem, *To Better Our World*, 74; Du Bois, *Economic Cooperation among Negro Americans*, 92–103; Du Bois, *Efforts for Social Betterment among Negro Americans*, 17–22; Scott, "Most Invisible of All," 6; Claude F. Jacobs, "Benevolent Societies of New Orleans Blacks during the Late Nineteenth and Early Twentieth Centuries," *Louisiana History* 29 (winter 1988): 21–33; Kathleen C. Berkeley, "'Colored Ladies Also Contributed': Black Women's Activities from Benevolence to Social Welfare, 1866–1896," in Walter J. Fraser Jr., R. Frank Saunders Jr., and Jon L. Wakelyn, eds., *The Web of Southern Social Relations: Women, Family, and Education* (Athens, Ga., 1985), 181–203.

23. Colored YWCA, *Fifth and Sixth Years Report, May 1909–May 1911* (Washington, D.C., n.d.), 10–11 (Library, State Historical Society of Wisconsin, Madison); I am indebted to Bob Buchanan for this reference. Earline Rae Ferguson, "The Woman's Improvement Club of Indianapolis: Black Women Pioneers in Tuberculosis Work, 1903–1938," *Indiana Magazine of History* 84 (September 1988): 237–61; Darlene Clark Hine, *When the Truth Is Told: A History of Black Women's Culture and Community in Indiana, 1875–1950* (Indianapolis, 1981). The Atlanta Neighborhood Union also worked against tuberculosis. Cynthia Neverdon-Morton, "Self-Help Programs as Educative Activities of Black Women in the South, 1895–1925: Focus on Four Key Areas," *Journal of Negro Education* 51 (summer 1982): 207–21; Walter R. Chivers, "Neighborhood Union: An Effort of Community Organization," *Opportunity* 3 (June 1925): 178–79. Modjeska Simkins's work is briefly summarized in Beardsley, *History of Neglect*, 108–12. Smith, "Black Women's Club Movement"; Smith, "Black Activism in Health Care."

24. Fannie Barrier Williams, "Social Bonds in the 'Black Belt' of Chicago: Negro Organizations and the New Spirit Pervading Them," *Charities*, October 7, 1905: 40–44; Scott, "Most Invisible of All," 8.

25. The Young Women's Christian Association (YWCA) was segregated, and these activists fought that segregation. Nevertheless, as Dorothy Height points out forcefully in her interview, "It was unmatched by any other major group drawn from the major white population" in the opportunities it offered to black women; Dorothy Height interview by Polly Cowan, 11 February 1974–6 November 1976, 173, Black Women Oral History Project (Schlesinger Library, Radcliffe College, Cambridge, Mass.). See also descriptions of YWCA opportunities in Frankie V. Adams interview by Gay Francine Banks, 26 and 28 April 1977, 9, (Schlesinger Library); Salem, *To Better Our World*, 46.

26. I could not identify birthplaces for all the women, and those with missing information include some likely to have been southern-born.

27. Others have reached similar conclusions. See Marilyn Dell Brady, "Kansas Federation of Colored Women's Clubs, 1900–1930," *Kansas History* 9 (spring 1986): 19–30; Linda Marie Perkins, *Black Feminism and "Race Uplift," 1890–1900* (Cambridge, Mass., 1981), Bunting Institute Working Paper (ERIC microfiche ED 221445), 4; Salem, *To Better Our World*, 67.

28. In the black population in general, 7 percent of all married women born between 1840 and 1859 were childless, and 28 percent of those born between 1900 and 1919 were childless. U.S. Department of Commerce, Bureau of the Census, *Historical Statistics of the United States: Colonial Times to 1970* (Washington, 1975), 1:53.

29. Black women's overall fertility was declining rapidly in this period, falling by one-third between 1880 and 1910, and southern black women had fewer children than southern white women. Some of this low fertility was attributable to poor health and nutrition. Moreover, the women in this network were virtually all urban, and the fertility of urban black woman was only half that of rural black women. See Jacqueline Jones, *Labor of Love, Labor of Sorrow: Black Women, Work, and the Family from Slavery to the Present* (New York, 1985), 122–23. Supporting my view of black women's use of birth control, see Jessie M. Rodrique, "The Black Community and the Birth-Control Movement," in Christina Simmons, eds., *Passion and Power: Sexuality in History* (Philadelphia, 1989), 138–54. This article offers a convincing criticism of my own earlier work, which overstated black hostility to birth control campaigns because of their genocidal implications. I also learned from Elizabeth Lasch's unpublished paper that Margaret Murray Washington's settlement at Tuskegee offered a course of study on sex hygiene that included birth control; this suggests the need for further research on black women's advocacy of birth control. Lasch, "Female Vanguard in Race Relations," 4.

30. I was able to identify 25 percent (seventeen) with prosperous parents.

31. Marilyn Dell Brady found the same marital patterns for black women reformers in her study of Kansas. Brady, "Kansas Federation of Colored Women's Clubs, 1900–1930," 19–30. The major figures she studied were married and supported by their husbands.

32. Anna Arnold Hedgeman, *The Trumpet Sounds: A Memoir of Negro Leadership* (New York, 1964), 25, 74; Farley, "Caring and Sharing since World War I," 317–37. Hamilton, "National Association of Colored Women," 41; Paula Giddings, *When and Where I Enter: The Impact of Black Women on Race and Sex in America* (New York, 1984), 108; Berkeley, "'Colored Ladies Also Contributed,'" 185–86.

33. For corroboration on the employment of well-to-do black women, see Roth, "Matronage," 180–81. On black women's socialization toward employment, see Inabel Burns Lindsay interview by Marcia Greenlee, 20 May–7 June 1977, 4, 40, Black Women Oral History Project.

34. Charles S. Johnson, *The Negro College Graduate* (Chapel Hill, 1938), 18–20; U.S. Department of Commerce, Bureau of the Census, *The Social and Economic Status of the Black Population in the United States: An Historical View, 1790–1978* (Washington, 1979), 93.

35. Alfreda Duster interview by Greenlee, 8–9 March 1978, 9, Black Women Oral History Project; Hedgeman, *Trumpet Sounds*, 3–28.

36. In my comments on the class attitudes of black women welfare reformers, I am mainly indebted to the interpretations of Deborah Gray White, especially in Deborah Gray White, "Fettered Sisterhood: Class and Classism in Early Twentieth Century Black Women's History," paper delivered at the annual meeting of the American Studies Association, Toronto, November 1989 (in Gordon's possession). See also Williams, "Social Bonds in the 'Black Belt' of Chicago." On black discrimination against relatively dark-skinned women, see, for example, Nannie Burroughs, "Not Color but Character," *Voice of the Negro* 1 (July 1904): 277–79; Duster interview, 52; Giddings, *In Search of Sisterhood*, 105; Perkins, *Black Feminism and "Race Uplift,"* 4; and Nancy Weiss, *Farewell to the Party of Lincoln: Black Politics in the Age of FDR* (Princeton, 1983), 139. Berkeley argues against the importance of class differences in the NACW, but I found them substantial. See Berkeley, "'Colored Ladies Also Contributed.'" On class development among blacks, see August Meier and David Lewis, "History of the Negro Upper Class in Atlanta, Georgia, 1890–1958," *Journal of Negro Education* 28 (spring 1959): 128–39.

37. Duster interview, 37.

38. Philip S. Foner, ed., *The Voice of Black America: Major Speeches by Negroes in the United States, 1797–1971* (New York, 1972), 462.

39. Hedgeman, *Trumpet Sounds*, 1–28; Chateauvert, "The Third Step"; Height interview, 40; Caroline Ware interview by Susan Ware, 27–29 January 1982, 94, Women in Federal Government Oral Histories (Schlesinger Library).

40. Robert Alan Goldberg, *Hooded Empire: The Ku Klux Klan in Colorado* (Urbana, 1981), vii.

41. Of the white women reformers, 78 percent had been social workers at some time; 68 percent had social work as their major reform area. I checked to see if the social work background could have been a characteristic of the less prominent women, but this was not the case. The most prominent two-thirds of the group were even more frequently social workers (84 percent).

42. Stanley Wenocur and Michael Reisch, *From Charity to Enterprise: The Development of American Social Work in a Market Economy* (Urbana, 1989), p. 33.

43. Of the white women, 18 percent had held academic jobs at one time; 9 percent were mainly employed as educators. For only 1 percent was education their major reform area.

44. Lillian Wald, *Windows on Henry Street* (Boston, 1934); Mary Kingsbury Simkhovitch, *Neighborhood: Story of Greenwich House* (New York, 1938); William W. Bremer, *Depression Winters: New York Social Workers and the New Deal* (Philadelphia, 1984); George Martin, *Madame Secretary: Frances Perkins* (Boston, 1976), 134–35; Elisabeth Israels Perry, "Training for Public Life: ER and Women's Political Networks in the 1920s," in Joan Hoff-Wilson and Marjorie Lightman, eds., *Without Precedent: The Life and Career of Eleanor Roosevelt* (Bloomington, 1984), 30.

45. Elisabeth Israels Perry, *Belle Moskowitz: Feminine Politics and the Exercise of Power in the Age of Alfred E. Smith* (New York, 1987), 76–77; Walter Trattner, "Theodore Roosevelt, Social Workers, and the Election of 1912: A Note," *Mid-America* 50 (January 1968): 64–69. On pre-woman-suffrage women's electoral participation, see, for example, S. Sara Monoson, "The Lady and the Tiger: Women's Electoral Activism in New York City before Suffrage," *Journal of Women's History* 2 (fall 1990): 100–135.

46. I thank Anne Firor Scott for pointing out this similarity to me.

47. On settlement house relationships, see Virginia Kemp Fish, "The Hull House Circle: Women's Friendships and Achievements," in Janet Sharistanian, ed., *Gender, Ideology, and Action: Historical Perspectives on Women's Public Lives* (Westport, Conn., 1986); and Kathryn Kish Sklar, "Hull House in the 1890s: A Community of Women Reformers," *Signs* 10 (summer 1985): 658–77. Lela B. Costin, *Two Sisters for Social Justice: A Biography of Grace and Edith Abbott* (Urbana, 1983), 38–40; Martin, *Madame Secretary*, 233.

48. See, for example, Ethel Erickson to Mary Anderson, 14 July 1938; Anderson to Erickson, 4 August 1938; Erickson to Anderson, 29 July 1942; Anderson to Erickson, 1 August 1942, box 1263, Women's Bureau Papers, RG 86 (National Archives).

49. Darlene Clark Hine, "Rape and the Inner Lives of Black Women in the Middle West: Preliminary Thoughts on the Culture of Dissemblance," in Vicki L. Ruiz and Ellen Carol DuBois, eds., *Unequal Sisters: A Multicultural Reader in U.S. Women's History*, 2nd ed. (New York: Routledge, 1994), 342–47; Deborah Gray White, "Mining the Forgotten: Manuscript Sources for Black Women's History," *Journal of American History* 74 (June 1987): 237–42; Elsa Barkley Brown, comment at Berkshire Conference on the History of Women, 1990.

50. The singleness of the white women reformers was characteristic of other women of their race, class, and education in this period. In 1890, for example, over half of all women doctors were single. Of women earning Ph.D.'s between 1877 and 1924, three-fourths remained single. As late as 1920, only 12 percent of all professional women were married. See, for example, Carl N. Degler, *At Odds: Women and the Family in America from the Revolution to the Present* (New York, 1980), 385. Roth corroborates the significance of marital breaks in the lives of activists, finding that civically active white women in Atlanta in this period were more likely to be widows. Roth, "Matronage," 182. On Boston marriages, see Micaela di Leonardo, "Warrior Virgins and Boston Marriages: Spinsterhood in History and Culture," *Feminist Issues* 5 (fall 1985): 47–68.

51. Mrs. Tilden Frank Phillips, memoir, 22 February, 26 February 1953, folder 22, Edith Rockwood Papers (Schlesinger Library); will of Edith Rockwood, folder 20, ibid.

52. Blanche Wiesen Cook, "The Historical Denial of Lesbianism," *Radical History Review* 20 (spring/summer 1979): 60–65. For quotations from a (hostile) contemporary source, see James Johnson, "The Role of Women in the Founding of the United States Children's Bureau," in Carol V. R. George, ed., *"Remember the Ladies": New Perspectives on Women in American History: Essays in Honor of Nelson Manfred Blake* (Syracuse, 1975), 191.

53. Cook, "Historical Denial of Lesbianism"; Blanche Wiesen Cook, "Female Support Networks and Political Activism: Lillian Wald, Crystal Eastman, Emma Goldman," in Nancy F. Cott and Elizabeth H. Pleck, eds., *A Heritage of Her Own* (New York, 1979), 412–44; Estelle B. Freedman, "Separatism as Strategy," *Feminist Studies* 5 (fall 1979): 512–29.

54. Slowe lived with Mary Burrill, who is treated as a partner in letters to and from Slowe and in letters of condolence to Burrill after Slowe's death in 1937. See letters in box 90–1, Slowe Papers. Height interview, 52.

55. Duster interview, 11; Wendy Beth Posner, "Charlotte Towle: A Biography" (Ph.D. diss., University of Chicago School of Social Service Administration, 1986), 47, 77–78.

56. Mary Dewson to Clara Beyer, 12 October 1931, folder 40, box 2, Clara Beyer Papers (Schlesinger Library); Ware interview, 40–42; Janice Andrews, "Role of Female Social Workers in the Second Generation: Leaders or Followers," 1989 (in Gordon's possession). The possibility of combining marriage and career had been debated intensely starting in the 1920s, but it was in the 1930s that the change began to be evident. See Lois Scharf. *To Work and to Wed: Female Employment, Feminism, and the Great Depression* (Westport, 1980).

57. Florence Kelley to Anderson, 28 June 1920; Anderson to Dewson, 23 August 1920; Anderson to Dewson, 23 October 1922; Dewson to Anderson, 1 June 1923; all box 843, Women's Bureau Papers. Anderson to Mary Van Kleeck, 8 January 1937, folder 22, box 1, Mary Anderson Papers (Schlesinger Library); Judith Sealander, "Feminist against Feminist: The First Phase of the Equal Rights Amendment Debate, 1923–1963," *South Atlantic Quarterly* 81 (spring 1982): 154–56. Mary R. Beard participated in the early meeting to draft the charter but ultimately did not sign it. I thank Nancy Cott for clarification on this point.

58. Susan Ware, *Beyond Suffrage: Woman in the New Deal* (Cambridge, Mass., 1981), 156–57.

59. Vivien Hart, "Watch What We Do: Women Administrators and the Implementation of Minimum Wage Policy, Washington, D.C., 1918–1923," paper delivered at the Berkshire Conference on the History of Women, 1990, 31 (in Gordon's possession).

60. Gordon, "What Does Welfare Regulate?"; Barbara Nelson, "The Origins of the Two-Channel Welfare State: Workmen's Compensation and Mothers' Aid," in Gordon, ed., *Women, the State, and Welfare*, 123–57.

61. Brady, "Kansas Federation of Colored Women's Clubs"; Lindsay, "Some Contributions of Negroes to Welfare Services," 15–24; Constance Greene, *The Secret City: A History of Race Relations in the Nation's Capital* (Princeton, 1967), 144–46; Neverdon-Morton, *Afro-American Women of the South*; Neverdon-Morton, "Self-Help Programs as Educative Activities of Black Women in the South"; Farley, "Caring and Sharing since World War I," esp. 4.

62. Mary Church Terrell, "Club Work among Women," *New York Age*, January 4, 1900, p. 1. Although this speech was given in 1900, another given in 1928 uses virtually the same rhetoric. See Mary Church Terrell, "Progress and Problems of Colored Women," *Boston Evening Transcript*, December 15, 1928, folder 132, box 102–4, Mary Church Terrell Papers (Moorland-Spingarn Research Collection).

63. For just a few examples, see Elise Johnson McDougald, "The Task of Negro Womanhood," in *The New Negro: An Interpretation*, ed. Alain Locke (New York, 1925), pp. 369–84; Mary Church Terrell, "Up-To-Date," *Norfolk Journal and Guide*, November 3, 1927, folder W, box 102–2, Terrell Papers; Williams, "Opportunities and Responsibilities of Colored Women"; and many speeches by Slowe, box 90–6, Slowe Papers. See also Perkins, *Black Feminism and "Race Uplift."*

64. Williams, "Opportunities and Responsibilities of Colored Women," p. 150.

65. White, "Fettered Sisterhood"; Hine, "Rape and the Inner Lives of Black Women in the Middle West." White reformers rhetoric about protecting women named prostitution, not rape, as the problem. See Ellen DuBois and Linda Gordon, "Seeking Ecstasy on the Battlefield: Nineteenth-Century Feminist Views of Sexuality," *Feminist Studies* 9 (spring 1983): 7–25; Lillian Wald, "The Immigrant Young Girl," in *Proceedings of the National Conference of Charities and Correction at the Thirty-sixth Annual Session Held in the City of Buffalo,*

N.Y., June 9th to 16th, 1909 (Fort Wayne, n.d.), 264. Jane Edna Hunter, *A Nickel and a Prayer* (Cleveland, 1940); Marilyn Dell Brady, "Organizing Afro-American Girls' Clubs in Kansas in the 1920s," *Frontiers* 9, 2 (1987): 69–73; Greene, *Secret City*, 144–46; Salem, *To Better Our World*, 44–46; Scott, "Most Invisible of All," 15; Monroe N. Work, " Problems of Negro Urban Welfare" (from *Southern Workman*, January 1924) in Ross, ed., *Black Heritage in Social Welfare*, 383–84; "Foreword" (from *Bulletin of National League on Urban Conditions among Negroes*, Report 1912–13), ibid., 241; Guichard Parris and Lester Brooks, *Blacks in the City: A History of the National Urban League* (Boston, 1971), 3–10; Hine, "'We Specialize in the Wholly Impossible,'" 73.

66. Evelyn Brooks, "Religion, Politics, and Gender: The Leadership of Nannie Helen Burroughs," *Journal of Religious Thought* 44 (winter/spring 1988): 7–22; Cheryl Townsend Gilkes, "Building in Many Places: Multiple Commitments and Ideologies in Black Women's Community Work," in Ann Bookman and Sandra Morgen, eds., *Women and the Politics of Empowerment* (Philadelphia, 1988), 53–76.

67. White, "Fettered Sisterhood," 5.

68. Mrs. N. F. Mossell, *The Work of the Afro-American Woman* (Sharon Harley Freeport, 1971 [1894]), 32. Ida Wells-Barnett is the woman most associated with this challenge to Booker T. Washington, but she was not included in this sample because she was primarily a civil rights, rather than a welfare, activist. On Anna J. Cooper, see Sharon Harley, "Anna J. Cooper: A Voice for Black Women," in Sharon Harley and Rosalyn Terborg-Penn, eds., *Afro-American Woman*, 87–96; and Louise Daniel Hutchinson, *Anna J. Cooper: A Voice from the South* (Washington, 1981). On Mary Church Terrell, see Dorothy Sterling, *Black Foremothers* (New York, 1979); and Elliott Rudwick, *W.E.B. Du Bois: Voice of the Black Protest Movement* (Urbana, 1982), 129–30.

69. Williams, "Opportunities and Responsibilities of Colored Women," 157.

70. Story told in Lerner, *Black Women*, 375–76. On the complexity of Brown's attitudes, see Tera Hunter, "'The Correct Thing'"; and Smith and West, "Charlotte Hawkins Brown."

71. Anna J. Cooper to A. G. Comings. 1 October Rosalyn Terborg-Penn,1928, folder 5, box 32-1, Anna J. Cooper Papers (Moorland-Spingarn Research Collection). Cooper was another one of those figures who tirelessly challenged racism even in its apparently small or accidental varieties. For example, she wrote to the *Atlantic Monthly* complaining about an article mentioning a poor Negro with lice. *Atlantic Monthly* editors to Cooper, 31 January 1935, folder 5, box 23-1, ibid.

72. Hine, "'We Specialize in the Wholly Impossible'"; Evelyn Brooks Barnett, "Nannie Burroughs and the Education of Black Women," in Sharon Harley and Rosalyn Terborg-Penn, eds., *Afro-American Woman*, 97–108; Brooks, "Religion, Politics, and Gender," 12.

73. Burroughs, speech at Bethel AME Church in Baltimore, reported in "Baptists May Oust Nannie H. Burroughs," *Chicago Defender*, 9 September 1939; "Nannie Burroughs Refuses to Speak on National Christian Mission," *Pittsburgh Courier*, 1 February 1941, Burroughs Vertical File (Moorland-Spingarn Research Collection).

74. Burroughs's 1943 remark is quoted in Lerner, *Black Women*, 552.

75. On criticism of Bethune, see B. Joyce Ross, "Mary McLeod Bethune and the National Youth Administration: A Case Study of Power Relationships in the Black Cabinet of Franklin D. Roosevelt," *Journal of Negro History* 60 (January 1975): 1–28. On her defense of the New Deal, see Mary McLeod Bethune, "'I'll Never Turn Back No More!'" *Opportunity* 16 (November 1938): 324–26; "Mrs Bethune Praises NYA Courses as 'Bright Ray of Hope for Rural Negroes,'" *Black Dispatch*, 1 May 1937; Bethune, Vertical File (Moorland-Spingarn Research Collection); "Mrs Bethune Hails Achievements of the New Deal," *Washington Tribune*, 12 November 1935, ibid.; "55,000 Aided by the NYA Program, Says Dr. Bethune," *Washington Tribune*, 23 April 1938, ibid. On her picketing, see photo and caption, "Give US More Jobs," *Washington Afro-American*, 12 August 1939, ibid.

76. Corinne Robinson to Jeanetta Welch Brown, with script of *Lazy Daisy* enclosed, 22 September 1943, folder 274, box 17, series 5, National Council of Negro Women Papers.

77. Era Bell Thompson, "A Message from a Mahogany Blond," *Negro Digest* 9 (July 1950): 31.

78. White, "Fettered Sisterhood"; Smith and West, "Charlotte Hawkins Brown," 199.

79. I am in sympathy with Cott's critique of the use of the concept "social feminism," but it remains descriptive of a widely understood phenomenon, and we have as yet no terms to substitute. Nancy F. Cott, "What's in a Name? The Limits of 'Social Feminism'; or, Expanding the Vocabulary of Women's History," *Journal of American History* 76 (December 1989): 809–29.

80. Sybil Lipschultz, "Social Feminism and Legal Discourse: 1908–1923," *Yale Journal of Law and Feminism* 2 (Fall 1989): 131–60.

81. Linda Gordon, *Heroes of Their Own Lives: The Politics and History of Family Violence, Boston, 1880–1960* (New York, 1988), 82–115.

82. Florence Kelley, "Minimum-Wage Laws," *Journal of Political Economy* 20 (December 1912): 1003.

83. See, for examples, Roth, "Matronage," 87; Brady, "Kansas Federation of Colored Women's Clubs," 19–31; and Marilyn Dell Brady, "Organizing Afro-American Girls' Clubs in Kansas in the 1920s."

84. Lucy D. Slowe, "Some Problems of Colored Women and Girls in the Urban Process" [probably 1930s], folder 143, box 90-6, Slowe Papers.

85. Ardie Clark Halyard interview by Greenlee, 24, 25 August 1978, transcript, p. 15, Black Women Oral History Project.

86. Dorothy Boulding Ferebee interview by Merze Tate, 28–31 December 1979, transcript, p. 9, ibid.; Lindsay interview, 4–5.

87. Sharon Harley, "For the Good of Family and Race: Gender, Work, and Domestic Roles in the Black Community, 1880–1930," *Signs* 15 (winter 1990): 336–49; Helen A. Cook, "The Work of the Woman's League, Washington, D.C.," in W. E. B. Du Bois, ed., *Some Efforts of American Negroes for Their Own Social Betterment*, (Atlanta, 1898), 57; Du Bois, ed., *Efforts for Social Betterment among Negro Americans*, 119–20, 126–27; Giddings, *When and Where I Enter*, 100–101; Hine, *When the Truth Is Told*, 52–54; Ross, ed. *Black Heritage in Social Welfare*, 233–34; Perkins, *Black Feminism and "Race Uplift"*, 7–8; Allan Spear, *Black Chicago: The Making of a Ghetto, 1890–1920* (Chicago, 1967), 102; Stehno, "Public Responsibility for Dependent Black Children"; Harley, "Beyond the Classroom," 254–65; Rouse, *Lugenia Burns Hope*, 28; Davis, *Black Americans in Cleveland*, 195; Stetson, "Black Feminism in Indiana"; Greene, *Secret City*, 144–46; Mary Church Terrell, *A Colored Woman in a White World* (Washington, 1940), 153.

88. The white reformers in the first decades of the twentieth century were campaigning hard for mothers' pensions and feared that daytime child care would be used as an alternative, forcing mothers into poor jobs. But they continued to see mothers' employment as a misfortune. For example, Florence Kelley in 1909 argued that day nurseries should be acceptable only for temporary emergencies and that the social cost of mothers' employment was always too high. "A friend of mine has conceived the monstrous idea of having a night nursery to which women so employed might send their children. And this idea was seriously described in so modern a publication as Charities and the Commons . . . without a word of editorial denunciation." Florence Kelley, "The Family and the Woman's Wage," *Proceedings of the National Conference of Charities and Correction . . . 1909*, 118–21.

89. Giddings, *When and Where I Enter*, 205.

90. Barnett, "Nannie Burroughs and the Education of Black Women." For Elizabeth Ross Haynes's statement of 1922, see Lerner, *Black Women*, 260.

91. Giddings, *When and Where I Enter*, 196.

92. My discussion of Walker is based on Elsa Barkley Brown, "Womanist Consciousness: Maggie Lena Walker and the Independent Order of Saint Luke," *Signs* 14 (spring 1989): 610–33. On the significance of black banks and other businesses, see also Du Bois, *Economic Cooperation Among Negro Americans*, 103–81. Hedgeman, *Trumpet Sounds*, 47–48; *Who's Who in Colored America* (New York, 1927), 209; Hine, "'We Specialize in the Wholly Impossible,'" 86; Hine, *When the Truth Is Told*, 51.

93. This orientation toward entitlement was evident *despite* the southern state governments' relatively smaller size, and it casts doubt on state capacity explanations for reformers' strategies.

94. Although many of the African American women leaders were legally married, it does not necessarily follow that they lived their daily lives in close partnerships with their husbands or carried much domestic labor responsibility.

95. Gordon, "What Does Welfare Regulate?"

15

Partisan Women in the Progressive Era: The Struggle for Inclusion in American Political Parties

Melanie Gustafson

> The female politician is unexpected; her presence provokes a brief digression during which the public wanders off into internal musing about how this woman is like a man and yet not like a man.
>
> —Madeline Kunin, former governor of Vermont

On 4 August 1912 the *New York Times* reported the "strange sight" of women taking on the "role of politician." Their presence on a chartered train traveling from New York to the first national Progressive Party convention in Chicago changed the normal course of political events, according to the *Times*. Half of every car was full of women, and for once men "were not going down the aisles with their hats on, flicking cigar ashes on the carpet, no indeed." Decorum ruled the day. Even at the Progressive Party convention, where "about a quarter of the seats were taken by women . . . nobody smoked."[1] The women of the Progressive Party, as well as the presence of women in the Democratic and Republican Parties, had, as the *Times* phrased it, "suddenly . . . feminized" the presidential campaign of 1912.[2]

While women's suffrage was not yet universal, over 4 million women could vote in municipal and state elections, while almost 1.5 million women could vote in presidential elections.[3] Because the campaign of 1912 was predicted to be a close three-way race between Theodore Roosevelt, William Howard Taft, and Woodrow Wilson, no political party believed it could take women's support for granted. Nor could the parties completely ignore nonvoting women. As the *New York Times* put it, the parties not only were looking to enlist women voters into their ranks but also hoped to win the aid of "just the kind of woman who can influence votes, if they don't actually cast them."[4]

Many prominent women—including Jane Addams, Frances Kellor, and Margaret Dreier Robins—were visible supporters of the new Progressive Party because it was the first national party to endorse woman suffrage and pledge that women would "have an equal voice with men in every phase of party management."[5] These women believed that the time had come to work alongside influential men to reshape the political landscape.[6]

Women also worked in the Republican and Democratic campaigns of 1912. Their efforts followed traditions set in the late nineteenth century. Republican and Democratic women joined auxiliaries and clubs that complemented the work of the national committees. Helen Varick Boswell led the Republican women, and Florence Jaffray Harriman led the Democratic women, both organizing women's political work with unprecedented enthusiasm.

The most prominent women in the press reports were white social reformers. African American women supported the parties, but their activism was less celebrated by the press and less welcome by the parties. After the 1912 national party conventions, with the hardening of the color line in the parties, African American women faced restrictions similar to those faced by African American men. They were excluded from party committees and had limited roles in the parties.[7]

In their initial efforts to mobilize women supporters, all three parties ignored two decades of women's auxiliary work with the Republican and Democratic Parties. Because women's auxiliaries were institutionally marginalized, parties had no direct experience with sharing political power with women. As a "separate sphere" for women, auxiliaries also did not disrupt the general view that women were nonpartisan. Thus, the inclusion of women in 1912 was possible only because this was not seen as threatening traditional partisan power structures.

As voters and as vote gatherers, women were of great interest to all the political parties in 1912, but was the *New York Times* correct in its assessment of women's impact on the rituals and process of partisan politics? The answer is no. The *Times* exaggerated the impact women's presence had in transforming the parties and the party system. However, the campaign of 1912 was a critical one for women, not because women determined the electoral fates of their parties or actually "feminized" party structures, but because the allegiance given to parties by leading women reformers accelerated and intensified debates among women about partisanship as practice and identity. These debates occurred just as the efforts of a generation of women activists working for important reforms seemed to be nearing success. A combination of a sense of urgency about implementing solutions to social problems, an optimism about the transformation of governments into principled vehicles for the public good, and a concern about the significance for women of the transfer of power from public institutions, such as settlement houses, to governmental agencies provided the context for women's partisan efforts and debates.[8]

The story of women's partisan activism involves more than the establishment of auxiliaries, the winning of committee and delegate positions, and the public acknowledgment of women's place in the parties. Women's struggle for inclusion in political parties raised serious questions about the meaning of partisanship as a political identity for women and, in turn, influenced decisions regarding political arguments, tactics, and goals. Women wanted to use the parties to enhance their influence in the political world, but they also did not want to lose themselves in the parties. The history of these partisan women, then, is about both separation and integration, difference and equality.[9] Partisan women did not simply argue for or against separation or integration; rather, they oscillated between the two as they demanded the right to be partisan. Their battles for acceptance in the parties would resonate for the rest of the decade and into the 1920s.

The year 1920, with the passage of the Nineteenth Amendment, is generally described by U.S. historians as a political watershed for women, the moment when women's political identity and women's relationships to the public sphere and politics were forever changed. The argument that the federal suffrage amendment opened the floodgates to women's partisanship has often relegated the subject of female partisanship to the post suffrage era. Yet, as some historians have already demonstrated, diverse groups of women in the presuffrage era developed and acted on partisanship identities. Women worked to make the party of their choice responsive to a female constituency by building alliances with male political party leaders and by creating coalitions between women's organizations and political parties. After 1920 women continued to question the advantages and disadvantages of separatist and integrationist strategies, the boundaries between women's and men's public work, and the dilemma of defining citizenship. This examination of women's partisan activism prior to 1920 is an attempt to contribute to a framework for connecting these eras and showing the continuity between them.

Gender and Partisanship

In the nineteenth century gender became crucial in organizing the U.S. political world and in reading others' political interests. Partisanship and nonpartisanship became a way to distinguish political roles in terms of gender identity. Women were considered to be nonpartisan. They were viewed and presented themselves as motivated by issues, not elections, and by principles, not a search for power. The idea of women as inherently nonpartisan was reinforced by the vital female-centered political culture of benevolent and reform organizations, as well as by women's exclusion from the rituals of electoral politics, including the continuing disfranchisement of women at the national level.[10] Intended as a compliment to the women voters of his state, Congressman Edward Taylor of Colorado noted: "Women's interests cannot, generally speaking, be roused very much by mere partisan strife."[11]

Men, on the other hand, were identified as inherently partisan. Partisanship was not simply an attachment to a particular political organization, but, as historian Michael McGerr writes, a "lens through which to view the world."[12] Men supported their bosses and machines, friends and allies. They understood ideas of patronage, rewards for loyalty, and personal and group power. Political parties and elections shaped their political culture and separated them from women.

The changing contours of nineteenth-century political culture, particularly the establishment of women's party auxiliaries, brought into question the gendered meanings of nonpartisanship and partisanship. However, late-nineteenth-century transgressions of the gendered border of politics actually reinforced the accepted definition of the political woman as nonpartisan. Thus, the nonpartisan political woman and the partisan political man remained important representations of the division of the political world even when individuals or groups, in their actions or ideas, transgressed the division. Not until 1912 would actual political practice challenge this definition and provide women with more opportunities for partisanship. By 1916 the limitations on those opportunities were evident as men resisted women's efforts to transform their political identities, agendas, and modes of activism. When women entered the postsuffrage era, nonpartisanship was still equated with women's political culture.[13]

Women's Historical Involvement in Political Parties

Political parties were quasi-private institutions in the nineteenth century, guided by individual citizens and largely unregulated by the state. This allowed for women's informal access to their operations. Party leaders encouraged interested women to attend party-sponsored meetings and work on behalf of party candidates. Despite their political activism and party involvement, women retained their reputation for nonpartisanship even while developing partisan identities.

The importance of nonpartisanship to the representation and actions of political women can be seen in the case of Judith Ellen Foster, who established two important organizations in 1888—the Woman's National Republican Association (WNRA) and the Non-Partisan Woman's Christian Temperance Union (Non-Partisan WCTU).[14] Believing that the alliance between the National Woman's Christian Temperance Union (National WCTU) and the Prohibition Party "brought confusion of thought concerning Prohibition as a principle and party Prohibition as a policy," Foster opposed Frances Willard's move to dedicate the resources of the National WCTU to the Prohibition Party.[15] At the same time, Foster used her connections to James Clarkson, president of the

National League of Republican Clubs, to gain entrée to her favored party. She proposed the formation of a woman's auxiliary and established the WNRA as the female complement to male clubs.[16] As president of the auxiliary, Foster addressed the Republican national convention of 1892, proclaiming: "We are here to help you and we have come to stay."[17] A few years later the Women's National Democratic League was founded by Nellie Fassett Crosby in New York City.[18] Both these organizations were auxiliaries to the national parties.

Political parties welcomed women because women embodied nonpartisanship even when they acted in partisan ways. The Republican party's formal recognition of a women's auxiliary gave party men something they desperately needed in an era when they felt besieged by social reformers who increased the importance of nonpartisan, issue-oriented coalitions in the political realm. These social reformers defined parties as corrupt entities that harmed or, at best, were irrelevant to the needs of society. Party leaders also felt besieged by internal factionalism when insurgents demanded limitations on machines and bosses.[19] In response, party leaders made concessions to nonpartisan reformers and insurgent men in their parties and, at the same time, welcomed women, who contributed to the legitimacy of the parties.

When Judith Ellen Foster founded the Non-Partisan WCTU at the same time that she formed the WNRA, she reinforced rather than recast the public perception of the political woman as nonpartisan. By the turn of the century, women worked on behalf of the Republican and Democratic Parties, as well as in other parties, but continued to present themselves and be perceived as principled political actors in an unprincipled political world.[20] Women's suffrage campaigns, their municipal anticorruption efforts, and gains of partial suffrage in the western states did not challenge this perception. Partisan women strengthened the gendered division of politics by holding before their faces a nonpartisan mask even as their bodies struck a partisan pose. In part, they did this by reassuring men and the general public that their primary goal was the success of the party itself, not political offices for themselves or for other women, especially in suffrage states.[21]

The Role of Women in Founding the Progressive Party

Women were still strongly identified by the public as nonpartisan in 1912 when the fifteenth Republican national convention opened in June at Chicago's Coliseum. Auxiliary women's presence there followed tradition. They cheered for their favorite candidates from the balcony and the floor. Women also attended the Democratic national convention, which met in Baltimore later that same month. However, at neither convention did women influence the proceedings.[22] Even the three women who attended the Republican convention in an official capacity—Florence Collins Porter and Isabella Blaney, delegates from the new suffrage state of California, and Helen Varick Boswell, representing the WNRA—lacked any power or authority.[23]

It was the suffragists, not the female party activists, who captured the most attention at the Republican convention. Suffragists had attended party conventions since 1868, actively watching the proceedings and waiting for their invitation to present a suffrage plank to the national platform committees. As the first national convention of the year, and as one with numerous male suffrage supporters in attendance, the Republican convention was of special interest to the suffragists. Moreover, the nomination battle placed Theodore Roosevelt, who had recently become more vocal in his support of woman suffrage, against President William Howard Taft, who continued to oppose the extension.[24]

Representatives of the National American Woman Suffrage Association, including Jane Addams, Louise DeKoven Bowen, and Lillian Wald, were disappointed when their seven-minute presentation did not result in the adoption of a platform plank supporting women's enfranchisement. But their attendance had its reward when hundreds of progressive Republicans walked out of the Coliseum in protest over the nomination of Taft as the party's candidate for president.

Roosevelt, angry and confrontational but with his finger correctly taking the pulse of assembled supporters, announced the immediate formation of a new party, appropriated the name Progressive, and welcomed into it all self-proclaimed progressives.[25] The call for supporters encouraged women to participate. Promised their voices would be heard and their issues endorsed, women seized the moment.[26] Within days it became known that some of the most prominent female social reformers in the nation, including Jane Addams, Margaret Dreier Robins, Frances Kellor, Maud Nathan, and Sophonisba Breckinridge, were supporting the new party and contributing to the provisional committee's work in writing the Progressive party platform.[27]

Although the women and men of the new Progressive Party differed in their stands on substantial political issues and varied in their political goals, they were united by their overall dedication to formulating and implementing a progressive agenda that focused on a government for and by the people. They believed that party platforms could be transformed from uninteresting or ignored promises and rhetoric into principled and practical agendas for achieving social justice. Progressive party members also believed that the purpose of political parties should not be simply to place candidates before the electorate, but also to research and draft bills for presenting to legislatures. Political party organizations, therefore, would have a purpose and a mission both before and after elections.

The case of the Progressive Party highlights the ironic advantage of white partisan women's political and racial invisibility. In the press and at the public hall where the Progressive Party held its national convention, white women delegates and supporters were welcomed with fanfare, while in the private chambers of the provisional committee meeting rooms, African American Progressives from contested southern delegations were excluded from party participation.[28] As Patricia Gurin has written, African American men in southern states were effectively disfranchised by the early 1900s. While northern African American men had the right to vote, they were "generally denied access to elective office" and formed "clientage relationships, usually with the Republican party, to have any political influence."[29] White women, also facing widespread disfranchisement, employed similar strategies. Both African Americans and white women formed their own separate local and national political organizations. In 1912, both groups wanted to break out of the clientage/auxiliary relationship to parties without losing their independent identity and power. White women had more initial success, but in the long term, the predominantly white party did not advance racial or gender equality, and white men continued to hold the positions of most authority and power.[30]

In spite of the Progressive party's exclusion of southern African American men, some African Americans did support the party.[31] Mrs. Lydia Smith of Brooklyn, New York, was the "only woman of color," according to the *New York Age*, to attend the New York State Progressive Convention in Syracuse, New York, and there were "heated arguments among women as to women's voting and the merits of the respective parties."[32] Grace Johnson organized Progressive women in the Boston area, including ten "colored women."[33] African American women also supported the Democratic Party. On 17 August 1912, Woodrow Wilson addressed the first public gathering of Democratic women at Sea Girt, New Jersey. The *New York Times* reported that nearly a thousand women attended to organize the Democratic woman's auxiliary and "among the members are nearly a score of negro women."[34]

Women's Participation in the Three Parties, 1912–1920

Reports on the numbers of women delegates and participants at the national Progressive convention and at the state conventions vary, and accuracy is difficult.[35] Estimates range from sixteen to forty women delegates and five to twenty women alternates elected to the national convention.[36] The relative scarcity of women in the party can be traced through its organizational changes. The national committee pledged that women would be equally represented in all councils of the party, but that never occurred. Each state was to have 50 percent representation of women on its state committee, but only in New York, Illinois, Pennsylvania, and California were women prominent, and they never neared the 50 percent mark.[37] Only three women, Jane Addams, Isabella Blaney, and Frances Kellor, held positions on the national committee;[38] Jean Gordon of Louisiana declined;[39] and Alice Carpenter of Massachusetts sat on the platform committee. The press's fascination with this "new sight in politics" often led to an exaggeration of the numbers of women who held official positions in the party, but the emphasis on women breaking new ground in the partisan arena was correct. Compared to the Republican and Democratic Parties, the Progressives took the lead by making equality an issue.

Republican and Democratic women chose to continue in the auxiliary mode. Republican women, led by Helen Boswell, transformed the Woman's National Republican Association into the Women's Bureau of the Republican National Committee. The *New York Times* reported that it was the best equipped of the women's party organizations, "knows just how to go about to get the best results with the least amount of effort," and was "as well entrenched as the regular Republican machine."[40]

It took a new organization to bring Democratic women into the campaign. The Woman's Democratic Club and the Women's National Democratic League, founded by Nellie Fassett Crosby, were the most established Democratic organizations for women.[41] But as male Democrats fought one of the most interesting and bitter precampaign battles over the party's presidential candidate, the Woman's Democratic Club was involved in raising funds for the establishment of a memorial to Thomas Jefferson, and the Women's National Democratic League was promoting a "harmony affair," the Dolly Madison Breakfast, whose purpose was to bring together the wives of Democratic leaders.[42] The lack of leadership in the two older organizations and the initiative of the dynamic Florence Harriman led to the creation of the Women's National Wilson and Marshall Organization. This Democratic woman's auxiliary coordinated women's efforts in 1912 and, as the Democratic Women's Bureau, was the backbone of women's work in the party for the remainder of the decade.[43]

Jane Addams and the Debate on Partisanship

When Jane Addams, the founder of Hull House and one of the most prominent women of her day, seconded Theodore Roosevelt's nomination for president at the Progressive Party national convention, she propelled women onto the front pages of the newspapers across the country. Arthur Ruhl wrote that a delegation of women escorted "to the convention hall its one figure perhaps—next to the protagonist himself—of greatest interest and significance. Some were girls in cap and gown, some 'our very best people.' . . . Most of them carried 'Votes for Women' flags; most were for the new party, and two or three were not, but all were there to do honor to Miss Jane Addams, who had consented to be a delegate at large from Illinois and to second the nomination of Col. Roosevelt."[44] Newspaper headlines declared "Women as a Factor in Political Campaign," and "New Party Gives Women a Chance," and the papers followed the daily activities of women in all the parties.[45] As the *Woman's Journal* reported, times had certainly changed "since Mary Livermore was elected as a delegate to the Republican State Convention in Massachusetts only to have her credentials rejected on the grounds of her sex, and to have a politician ask whether, if a trained monkey had been regularly accredited as a delegate to the Convention, it would have been necessary to accept him."[46]

Jane Addams, because of her prominence, and the Progressive women, because of the party's promise of equality, set the tone among women for public and private debates over their party activism. In 1912 women's partisan work was controversial among women not so much because women were seen as stepping beyond a proper political role but because it raised two interrelated concerns: women's relationship to changes in the implementation of public policy, and their allegiance to a distinct women's political culture and set of issues.

Public Policy

Recognition of "the transfer of primary responsibility for social policy from the state to the federal level" made women focus on new locations for political decision-making, writes Eileen L. McDonagh.[47] As women's reform activism expanded in the twentieth century, women grew frustrated with the control over public policy held by officeholders who had benefited from the "spoils system." Women reformers, motivated by what historian Robyn Muncy calls a "genuine and profound concern for those disadvantaged by unregulated industrial capitalism," had found that "patronage effectively blocked them from competition for any position within governmental agencies."[48] Thus, women challenged patronage and championed further civil service reform. They also sought positions in existing agencies and the creation of a professional social welfare culture. Their goal was to change the process of initiating and guiding public policy and to place experts, rather than political cronies, in charge. The founding of the Progressive Party, which was promoted by supporters as "a well-defined program of social legislation with resolute leaders of courage and political experience," was seen as a further step toward this goal.[49]

Jane Addams called on women to recognize that indirect influence and nonpartisanship had limited the scope and reach of female reform movements. She argued that the time had come for women to reject the position of assistant in the political world. Throughout the campaign she dedicated much of her work on behalf of the party to explaining not only why women should support the Progressive Party, but why women should engage in party work and why partisanship was an acceptable political identity for women. Addams argued that women "were not changing their interest in taking up politics"; rather, the "interest of women in philanthropy is exactly the same but they find they can reach the desired ends more directly through a political party."[50] She felt that women would benefit if suffrage was advanced by a Progressive victory, but to her it was more important that the campaign meet its "educational purpose" in teaching the public "about social reform, of which many are ignorant."[51] This sentiment was echoed by Mary Dreier, who wrote to Lillian Wald that the Progressives were "to have the biggest educational campaign the country has ever seen except perhaps before the Civil War."[52]

In her decades-long work as a social reformer, Addams had come to recognize that "enterprises carefully developed by public-spirited women . . . languish and fail of their highest usefulness because their founders and promoters could have no further part in them," and that a "worthy code of social legislation can only be secured through the cooperation of the nation and states, held to a common purpose through party unity."[53] In essence, Addams believed that political parties held enormous power in the public world and that women needed formal places within them to have the influence necessary to implement their social vision.

Allegiance to Women's Political Culture and Issues

Ida Husted Harper of the National American Woman Suffrage Association (NAWSA) was especially critical of Addams, arguing that women's partisan activities would siphon off energy from the suffrage movement and divert women's loyalties.[54] Criticisms also came from the antisuffragist editors of the *Woman's Protest*, from Mabel Boardman of the National Red Cross, and from Harriot Stanton Blatch of the Woman's Political Union, who stated that it was "suicidal" for women to affiliate with a political party and work for political candidates.[55] These women believed that party affiliation would, as Manuela Thurner has pointed out in her article on antisuffragists, rob a woman of "her political neutrality and nonpartisanship and consequently diminish her influence with legislative or other governmental authorities that had so far been responsive to women's requests on the very grounds of their political disinterestedness."[56] Thus for some, partisan activism served to undermine rather than enhance women's political power.[57]

However, Addams claimed her right to act as an individual when she became a supporter of the Progressive Party. To the public and to the suffragists she stated that individuals should be allowed to join political parties but "should, in no case, urge their suffrage associations to such action."[58] Addams and other partisan women moved cautiously and with great respect for women who decided to remain nonpartisan because the future of female partisan activism was largely unknown.[59] Still, Addams could not help noting that Harper, in her public criticism of Roosevelt and the Progressive Party, had herself "departed from the nonpartisan attitude."[60]

One of the strongest arguments for female partisanship was that women's political culture was, in fact, already fragmented. Race, ethnicity, religion, region, and the party loyalties of kin divided women on issues and allegiances, as well as on means and ends. When Addams argued that every individual should have the freedom to choose her or his own political values without interference from others, she expressed the idea that partisan activism was about individual political opportunity rather than group power.[61] In 1912 the *Woman's Journal* conducted polls of its leaders to prove that women differed in their political ideologies and commitments and to show that all women would not vote the same in the upcoming election. The purpose in publicizing the lack of a female voting bloc was twofold. It was proof that no one, not even the national organization of suffragists, could "deliver" the woman's vote. Further, the divided opinions of its members showed it was "absolutely necessary" for the NAWSA to remain nonpartisan if it was going to survive. By a vote of ten to one at the subsequent national NAWSA convention, the organization reaffirmed that it was an "absolutely nonpartisan, non-sectarian body."[62] More important, members also defeated a resolution that called for all officers of the association to remain nonpartisan. Women members and officeholders, the NAWSA stated, could join political parties *as individuals* but could not invoke the name of the organization on behalf of their party.[63] This important change promised that partisan activists would not be punished for their party work.

Partisan Women Continue to Form Auxiliaries

Although the Progressives lost the election in 1912 and in the next few years their coalition would break apart, the women who chose the partisan path had demonstrated their seriousness about playing party politics, transforming some men's views about women's place in politics.[64] After the campaign, in a widely circulated letter, Theodore Roosevelt thanked Jane Addams for seconding his nomination. "I prize your action," he wrote, "not only because of what you are and stand for, but because of what it symbolized for the new movement.... Women have thereby shown to have their places to fill precisely as men have, and on an absolute equality. It is idle now to argue whether women can play their part in politics, because in this convention we saw the accomplished fact."[65]

Despite the Progressive Party's attempts at equality, the auxiliary mode for women was firmly in place by 1916. As Democrat Florence Harriman argued in her 1923 autobiography, women worked in auxiliaries because they wished to work on women's behalf and to organize women, and this was true both before and after 1920.[66] But because of the acceptance of the auxiliary mode, women had to tread carefully to be treated seriously as politicians. Roosevelt may have been convinced that by 1912 women had proven they could be equal participants in partisan politics but, as we are well aware, gender equality in the parties continues to be an elusive goal.

As peripheral to the party, auxiliaries created the impression that women were less dedicated or interested in parties and voting than men, an image reinforced by the continuation of nonpartisanship as a very important component within the political culture of women, for example, in women's suffrage organizations and later in the League of Women Voters and other female-only political groups. These organizations allowed women to continue the process of formulating a political vision outside the dominance of strong parties but also kept the idea of the nonpartisan woman alive.

In 1940 Mary Simkhovitch wrote in her autobiography that women on the whole "hold their political allegiance with a sense of proportion lacking in the total electorate. Their loyalties are to the country first, and if their party loyalty seems to be in conflict with their convictions, they do not hold tenaciously to a party line." Women's political identity could still be counted on to be a variable factor because, as Simkhovitch argued, women's "party spirit is held with independence of spirit."[67] Independence—as a spirit or as a separate auxiliary— while potentially powerful, could also be limiting by reinforcing the idea that women were less loyal than men to their party and thus could not be trusted with positions of power.

Conclusion

In 1920, with the passage of the Nineteenth Amendment, women were officially "welcomed" into the political parties, and the entire nation began to question how women would vote, in what numbers, and whether women would run for office. Those issues had been partially explored and partially settled during the 1912 campaign—but only partially. In 1928, Carrie Chapman Catt, in response to an inquiry about what women had done with the vote, wrote that women had engaged in "agitation concerning their own place in political parties which is not yet complete."[68] As a self-described "old time suffragist," Catt was neither mystified nor disappointed that women had not found places of equality in political parties. Men, she declared, "are reconciled, on the whole, to women voters, but not to women in politics"; women, on the whole, were determined to change these circumstances of exclusion, subordination, and silence.[69] She was correct. In the years surrounding the suffrage victory, African American and white women continued their struggle for inclusion in political parties. Ruth McCormick, Cornelia Pinchot, Hallie Q. Brown, and Lethia Fleming led women's struggle for greater inclusion in the Republican Party in a race against the Democrats, who were led by Emily Newell Blair and Elizabeth

Bass. Inclusion and power continued to be an ongoing issue for partisan women after 1920 because neither party excelled at organizing its women.

In 1940, Emily Newell Blair wrote that when she went to National Democratic Headquarters in 1922 to organize Democratic women "not so much as a scrap of paper remained from all the splendid work of Mrs. Elizabeth Bass, Chairman of the first Democratic Women's Bureau. After the defeat of 1920, office space had been curtailed and files destroyed."[70] Women must have often felt that their struggle for greater inclusion and power in political parties was a process of continually starting over. The knowledge they shared with those who went before them was that women had initiated and fought for every gain they had made in the partisan sphere of politics. In this degree, the eras before and after suffrage look very much the same.

Notes

Earlier versions of this study were presented at the Organization of American Historians Annual Meeting, April 1994; Third Annual American Heritage Center Symposium, University of Wyoming, September 1994; Upstate New York Women's History Conference, SUNY at Binghamton, November 1994; and American Historical Association Annual Meeting, January 1995. I am grateful to all who attended those sessions for their comments and suggestions. Nancy Hewitt, Elisabeth Perry, and an anonymous reviewer for the *Journal of Women's History* provided careful readings of an earlier draft, and I thank them for their help. This is part of a larger work in progress that began as a dissertation at New York University under the direction of Susan Ware, to whom I am very thankful for all she has taught me and continues to teach me about women and history. I am grateful to the Huntington Library for a summer fellowship that allowed me to immerse myself in nineteenth-century women's history.

1. *New York Times*, 4 August 1912.
2. *New York Times*, 11 August 1912.
3. Anne F. and Andrew M. Scott, *One Half the People: The Fight for Woman Suffrage* (Philadelphia: J. B. Lippincott, 1975).
4. *New York Times*, 11 August 1912.
5. Ibid.; Edith Hooker to Jane Addams, 6 August 1912, Reel 6, The Jane Addams Papers, ed. Mary Lynn McCree Bryan (Ann Arbor, Mich.: University Microfilm International, 1984), cited hereafter as Addams Papers, Microfilm Edition.
6. For more discussion, see Melanie Gustafson, "Partisan Women: Gender, Politics, and the Progressive Party of 1912" (Ph.D. diss., New York University, 1993).
7. On African-American women's political activism, see Bess Beatty, "Perspectives on American Women: The View from Black Newspapers, 1865–1900," *Maryland Historian* 9 (fall 1978): 39–50; Rosalyn Terborg-Penn, "Discrimination Against Afro-American Women in the Woman's Movement, 1830–1920," in Sharon Harley and Rosalyn Terborg-Penn, eds., *The Afro-American Woman: Struggles and Images*, (Port Washington, N.Y.: Kennikat Press, 1978), 17–27; Paula Giddings, *When and Where I Enter: The Impact of Race and Sex in America* (New York: William Morrow, 1984); Elsa Barkley Brown, "Womanist Consciousness: Maggie Lena Walker and the Independent Order of Saint Luke," *Signs* 14, 3 (spring 1989): 610–33; Marjorie Spruill Wheeler, *New Women of the New South: The Leaders of the Woman Suffrage Movement in Southern States* (New York: Oxford University Press, 1993); and Elisabeth Lasch-Quinn, *Black Neighbors: Race and the Limits of Reform in the American Settlement House Movement, 1890–1945* (Chapel Hill: University of North Carolina Press, 1993). *The Crisis* publicized the suffrage struggles and voting actions of black women. See, for example, *The Crisis*, October 1911, November 1911, June 1912; *New York Tribune*, 19 January 1910. For more discussion, see Melanie Gustafson, "Jane Addams and the Construction of Race and Gender in the Progressive Party of 1912," paper presented at the Tenth Berkshire Conference on the History of Women, University of North Carolina at Chapel Hill, 7 June 1996.
8. Useful studies on women and politics include Kristi Andersen, *After Suffrage: Women in Partisan and Electoral Politics before the New Deal* (Chicago: University of Chicago Press, 1996); Paula Baker, "The Domestication of Politics: Women and American Political Society, 1780–1920," *American Historical Review* 89 (June 1984): 620–47; Suzanne Lebsock, "Women and American Politics, 1880–1920" and Nancy Cott, "Across the Great Divide: Women in Politics before and after 1920," both in Louise Tilly and Patricia Gurin, eds., *Women, Politics, and Change* (New York: Russell Sage Foundation, 1990), 33–62, 153–76.

9. See, for example, Joan Scott, "Deconstructing Equality-versus-Difference; or the Uses of Poststructuralist Theory for Feminism," *Feminist Studies* 14 (spring 1988): 33–50; Nancy Cott, *The Grounding of Modern Feminism* (New Haven, Conn.: Yale University Press, 1987); Estelle Freedman, "Separatism as Strategy: Female Institution Building and American Feminism, 1870–1930," *Feminist Studies* 5 (fall 1979): 512–29; Kathryn Kish Sklar, "Hull House in the 1890s: A Community of Women Reformers," *Signs* 10 (summer 1985): 658–77; Joan Hoff, *Law, Gender and Injustice: A Legal History of U.S. Women* (New York: New York University Press, 1991); Mary Dietz, "Context Is All: Feminism and Theories of Citizenship," *Daedalus* 116 (fall 1987): 1–24; and Joan Cocks, *The Oppositional Imagination: Feminism, Critique, and Political Theory* (New York: Routledge, 1989).

10. Susan B. Anthony preferred the word *all-partisan* to *nonpartisan*. See Susan B. Anthony to Jessie Anthony, 1 August 1896, Susan B. Anthony Memorial Collection, Huntington Library, San Marino, California. Correspondence in this collection and in the Elizabeth Harbert Collection, also at the Huntington Library, reveals some of the vitality and complexity of disfranchised women's relationships to political parties.

11. "Speech of Hon. Edward T. Taylor of Colorado in the House of Representatives, Wednesday, April 24, 1912," *Congressional Record*, vol. 48, pt. 12, Appendix, 63rd Congress, 2nd Sess., 176–93. Taylor underestimated the partisan commitments and enthusiasms of Colorado women. Since their enfranchisement in 1893, Colorado women were active in political parties. Democratic, Republican, and Populist women established party clubs, supported women for electoral and appointed political positions, and constantly struggled for more representation in party structures and governments. Their efforts can be traced through various Denver, Colorado, newspapers, including the *Rocky Mountain News*.

12. Michael McGerr, *The Decline of Popular Politics: The American North, 1865–1928* (New York: Oxford University Press, 1986), 13. See also Jean Baker, *Affairs of Party: The Political Culture of Northern Democrats in the Mid-Nineteenth Century* (Ithaca: Cornell University Press, 1983).

13. For an excellent discussion of women's political culture, see Kathryn Kish Sklar, *Florence Kelley and the Nation's Work: The Rise of Women's Political Culture, 1830–1990* (New Haven: Yale University Press, 1995).

14. The Woman's National Republican Association was also known for a while as the Woman's Republican Association of the United States. Mrs. Thomas W. Chace of Rhode Island was secretary of this organization. Frank L. Byrne, "Judith Ellen Foster," in Edward James, et al., eds., *Notable American Women, 1607–1950*, 3 vols. (Cambridge, Mass.: Harvard University Press, 1971); Elmer Adams and Warren Foster, *Heroines of Modern Progress* (New York: Macmillan, 1926); David C. Mott, "Judith Ellen Foster," *Annals of Iowa* 19, 2 (October 1933): 127–38.

15. Minutes of the 1885 annual meeting of the Woman's Christian Temperance Union, Series 3, Reel 2, National Woman's Christian Temperance Union Papers, Temperance and Prohibition Papers, Microfilm Edition; Judith Ellen Foster, Letter to the Editor, *Boston Journal*, 9 September 1884. This debate can be followed through the minutes of the 1886, 1887, and 1888 annual meetings of the National Woman's Christian Temperance Union, Series 3, Reel 2, Woman's Christian Temperance Union Papers, Microfilm Edition. See also the Non-Partisan National Woman's Christian Temperance Union Collection, Sophia Smith Collection, Smith College.

16. According to Michael McGerr, these clubs were "centers of political education and exchange." Michael McGerr, *The Decline of Popular Politics*, 82. Interestingly, in the same year that Clarkson and Foster formed a political alliance, Clarkson was embroiled in a Republican party controversy involving another Republican woman supporter, Anna Dickinson. See Anna Dickinson Papers and James Clarkson Papers, Library of Congress. Also see Kathleen Berkeley, "Partisan Politics Makes for Strange Bedfellows: The Political Career of Anna Elizabeth Dickinson, 1842–1932" (paper presented at the annual meeting of the Southern Historical Association, New Orleans, Louisiana, November 1995); and Rebecca Edwards, "Gender in American Party Politics, 1880–1900" (Ph.D. diss., University of Virginia, 1994). I am grateful to Rebecca Edwards for talking with me about these early years.

17. Henry H. Smith, comp., *All the Republican National Conventions from Philadelphia, June 17, 1856 to and Including St. Louis, June 16, 1896* (Washington, D.C.: Robert Beall, 1896); Francis Curtis, *The Republican Party* (New York: G. P. Putnam's Sons, 1904), 251–53; *California Outlook*, 4 May 1912, 13 and 21.

18. Mrs. John Sherwin Crosby (Nellie Fassett) was known as the "Mother of New York Women Democrats." According to Crosby's obituary in the *New York Times*, the Women's National Democratic League was founded in 1904, and in 1920 Crosby was a New York delegate to the National Democratic Convention. See *New York Times*, 31 January 1924.

19. Richard L. McCormick, *The Party Period and Public Policy* (New York: Oxford University Press, 1986); Richard L. McCormick, "The Discovery that Business Corrupts Politics: A Reappraisal of the Origins of Progressivism," *American Historical Review* 86 (April 1981): 247–74; Philip VanderMeer, "Bosses, Machines and Democratic Leadership: Party Organization and Managers in Indiana, 1880–1910," *Social Science History* 12 (winter 1988): 395–428; Peter Odegard, *Pressure Politics: The Story of the Anti-Saloon League* (New York: Columbia University Press, 1966).

20. Judith Ellen Foster, *The Republican Party and Temperance* (n.p., n.d. [1888?]); Frances Willard, *Glimpses of Fifty Years* (Chicago: Woman's Christian Temperance Publication Association, 1889); Barbara Epstein, *Politics of Domesticity: Women, Evangelism, and Temperance in Nineteenth-Century America* (Middletown, Conn.: Wesleyan University Press, 1981); Mary Ryan, "The American Parade: Representations of the Nineteenth-Century Social Order," in Lynn Hunt, ed., *The New Cultural History* (Berkeley: University of California Press, 1989); Steven Buechler, "Elizabeth Boynton Harbert and the Woman Suffrage Movement, 1870–1896," *Signs* 13 (autumn 1987): 78–97; Michael Goldberg, "An Army of Women: Gender, Politics and Power in Kansas Populism, the Woman Movement, and the Republican Party, 1879–1896" (Ph.D. diss., Yale University, 1992).

21. Certainly women held political offices in the late nineteenth century, but overall the emphasis was on cooperation with men rather than competition. Helen L. Sumner Woodbury, *Equal Suffrage: The Results of an Investigation in Colorado* (New York: Arno Press, 1972 [1909]); Paula Petrik, *No Step Backward: Women and Family on the Rocky Mountain Mining Frontier, Helena, Montana, 1865–1900* (Helena: Montana Historical Society Press, 1987); Beverly Beeton, *Women Vote in the West: The Woman Suffrage Movement, 1869–1896* (New York: Garland, 1986); Rosalind Urbach Moss, "The 'Girls' from Syracuse: Sex Role Negotiations of Kansas Women in Politics, 1887–1890," in Susan Armitage and Elizabeth Jameson, eds., *The Women's West* (Norman: University of Oklahoma Press, 1987); Anne Scott, *Natural Allies: Women's Associations in American History* (Urbana: University of Illinois Press, 1991); and Elizabeth M. Cox, *Women State and Territorial Legislators, 1895—1995* (Jefferson, N.C.: McFarland & Company, 1996).

22. Republican National Committee, *Official Report of the Proceedings of the Fifteenth Republican National Convention, 1912* (New York: Tenny Press, 1912); George Mowry, *The Era of Theodore Roosevelt and the Rise of Modern America* (New York: Harper and Brothers, 1958); Josephine L. Good, *Republican Womanpower: The History of Women in Republican National Conventions and Women in the Republican National Committee* (Washington, D.C.: Women's Division, Republican National Committee, 1963); National Federation of Republican Women, *NFRW: Fifty Years of Leadership, 1938–1988* (Washington, D.C.: NFRW, 1987); Democratic National Committee, *Democratic Text-Book, 1912* (New York: Isaac Goldmann, Co., Printers, 1912).

23. For information on Florence Collins Porter and Isabella Blaney, see *California Outlook*, 30 March and 13 April 1912. See also Judith Raftery, "Los Angeles Clubwomen and Progressive Reform," in William Deverell and Tom Sitton, eds., *California Progressivism Revisited* (Berkeley: University of California Press, 1994). Helen Varick Boswell had taken over the presidency of the WNRA after Judith Ellen Foster's death in 1910. Helen V. Boswell, "Political Episodes," *Woman Republican*, March, April, May, and June 1935.

24. Susan B. Anthony and Ida Husted Harper, eds., *History of Woman Suffrage* (Salem, N.H.: Ayer Company, 1883–1900), vol. 4, ch. 23; vol. 5, ch. 23; *Woman's Journal*, 29 June 1912, 201–4; "Minutes of the Official Board Meeting of the NAWSA," 5 June 1912, National American Woman Suffrage Association Records, Library of Congress, Reel 42, Addams Papers, Microfilm Edition.

25. The history of the Progressive Party has been covered in numerous books and articles. Among those used for background in this article are: Allen Davis, "Social Workers and the Progressive Party, 1912–1916," *American Historical Review* 69 (1964): 671–88; John Gable, *Bull Moose Years: Theodore Roosevelt and the Progressive Party* (Port Washington, N.Y.: Kennikat Press, 1978); Amos Pinchot, *History of the Progressive Party 1912–1916*, ed. Helene Maxwell Hooker (New York: New York University Press, 1958); John Milton Cooper Jr., *The Warrior and the Priest: Woodrow Wilson and Theodore Roosevelt* (Cambridge: Harvard University Press, 1984); John Reynolds, *Testing Democracy: Electoral Behavior and Progressive Reform in New Jersey, 1880–1920* (Chapel Hill: University of North Carolina Press, 1988); James Wright, *The Progressive Yankees: Republican Reformers in New Hampshire, 1906–1916* (Hanover, N.H.: University of New England Press, 1987). See also Theodore Roosevelt, "Two Phases of the Chicago Convention," *Outlook*, 20 July 1912, 620–30.

26. "The Call for the New Party," *Outlook*, 20 July 1912, 601–2. It is not exactly clear when or by whom these promises were made. Correspondence between Ben Lindsay and Jane Addams indicates that from the time it became known Roosevelt and his supporters would create a new party, the understanding was that women were welcome and the new party would endorse suffrage. Jane Addams to Ben Lindsay, 25 June 1912; Ben Lindsay to Jane Addams, 6 July 1912, Reel 6, Addams Papers, Microfilm Edition.

27. William Allen White, "Noted Men Work on Platform," clipping, n.p., n.d. [Boston, 6 August 1912?], Grace Allen Johnson Papers, Woman's Rights Collection, Schlesinger Library, Radcliffe College; Chester Rowell, "The Building of the Progressive Platform," *California Outlook*, 17 August 1912, 5; "A Contract with the People: Platform of the Progressive Party," reprinted in Theodore Roosevelt, ed., *Progressive Principles* (New York: Progressive National Service, 1913); Maud Nathan, *Once upon a Time and Today* (New York: G. P. Putnam's Sons, 1933), 142–44. I am grateful to Jacqueline Dirks for the Nathan citation.

28. The provisional committee heard from the contested delegations of Hawaii, Alaska, and the District of Columbia first and then moved on to discuss Alabama, Florida, and Mississippi. "Resolutions Committee," Progressive Party Papers, Theodore Roosevelt Collection, Harvard College Library, Harvard University;

"Official Report of the Proceedings of the Provisional National Progressive Committee," *Progressive Party Papers*, Theodore Roosevelt Collection, Harvard College Library, Harvard University; *The Crisis*, November 1912, 30–31; Paul D. Casdorph, *Republicans, Negroes, and Progressives in the South, 1912–1916* (University, Ala.: University of Alabama Press, 1981).

29. Patricia Gurin et al., *Hope and Independence: Blacks' Response to Electoral and Party Politics* (New York: Russell Sage, 1989), 23.

30. W. E. B. DuBois, along with the African American delegates from the contested southern delegations, led both the challenge within the Progressive Party and the African American exodus from it. Some African American leaders were furious at those who continued to support the party. William M. Trotter sent a telegram to Addams stating that "woman suffrage will be stained with negro blood unless women refuse alliance with Roosevelt." W. M. Trotter to Jane Addams, 6 August 1912, Swarthmore College Peace Collection, Reel 6, Addams Papers, Microfilm Edition. Trotter was a founder of the National Independent Political League, of which Ida B. Wells-Barnett was the director of Women's Auxiliary. See *Pittsburgh Courier*, 29 July 1911. For Addams's continued support of the Progressives, see Jane Addams, "The Progressive Party and the Negro," *The Crisis*, November 1912, 30–31 and *New York Times*, 13 October 1912. See also *New York Times*, 7 August 1912; *The Crisis*, October 1912, 282–83; George Mowry, "The South and the Progressive Lily White Party of 1912," *Journal of Southern History* 6 (May 1940): 237–47; Arthur S. Link, "Theodore Roosevelt and the South in 1912," *North Carolina Historical Review* 23 (July 1946): 313–24.

31. "Know the Truth!" "What Southern Colored Men Say About Roosevelt and the Progressive Party," and "The Negro Question," *Progressive Party Papers*, Theodore Roosevelt Collection, Harvard College Library, Harvard University. Also, J. F. Ransom to Jane Addams, 6 August 1912; May Childs Nervey to Jane Addams, 17 August 1912; George William Cook to Jane Addams, 17 August 1912; Swarthmore College Peace Collection, Reel 6, Addams Papers, Microfilm Edition. Will Hays, Republican Party chairman, noted that "fifty of the leading Negroes of Indiana" were "all active Progressive workers in 1912." Will Hays, *The Memoirs of Will Hays* (Garden City, N.Y.: Doubleday, 1955), 144.

32. May Martel, "Woman's Part in the Campaign," *New York Age*, 7 November 1912.

33. Grace Johnson to Mrs. Child, n.d., Grace Allen Johnson Papers, Woman's Rights Collection, Schlesinger Library, Radcliffe College.

34. *New York Times*, 18 August 1912.

35. No roll call votes were taken at the convention and the platform and nominees were accepted by acclamation. *National Progressive Program, 1912*, Progressive Party Papers, Theodore Roosevelt Collection, Harvard; Ernest Hamlin Abbott, "The Progressive Convention," *Outlook*, 17 August 1912, 857–64; Edward Lowry, "With the Bull Moose in Convention," *Harper's Weekly*, 17 August 1912.

36. The *Woman's Journal* reported there were thirty to forty women delegates. The *Progressive Bulletin* listed thirty-four women as "A Few of the Women Progressives." John Gable counted eighteen or nineteen women delegates using two documents that were issued by the party after the convention. My own calculations lead me to estimate that there were sixteen women delegates and five alternates. *Woman's Journal*, 10 August 1912, 249; *Progressive Bulletin*, September 1912. 11; Progressive Party Papers, Theodore Roosevelt Collection, Harvard; Gable, *Bull Moose Years*, 267.

37. Membership Rolls and *Progressive Bulletin*, Progressive Party Papers, Theodore Roosevelt Collection, Harvard; Chauncey Dewey to Mrs. Raymond Robbins (sic), 9 September 1912, Reel 22, Woman's Trade Union League Papers, Microfilm Edition; *New York Times*, 4 August 1912. 4; Pinchot, *History of the Progressive Party*.

38. Allen F. Davis, *American Heroine: The Life and Legend of Jane Addams* (New York: Oxford University Press, 1973); John Farrell, *Beloved Lady: A History of Jane Addams' Ideas on Reform and Peace* (Baltimore: Johns Hopkins University Press, 1967); Daniel Levine, *Jane Addams and the Liberal Tradition* (Madison: State Historical Society of Wisconsin, 1971); Ellen Fitzpatrick, *Endless Crusade: Women Social Scientists and Progressive Reform* (New York: Oxford University Press, 1990); and Elisabeth Lasch-Quinn, *Black Neighbors*.

39. Gordon wrote Jane Addams that she did not trust Roosevelt on the woman suffrage question. Jean M. Gordon to Jane Addams, 10 August 1912, Swarthmore College Peace Collection, Reel 6, Addams Papers, Microfilm Edition. See also Marjorie Spruill Wheeler, *New Women of the New South*, 102; Kathryn W. Kemp, "Jean and Kate Gordon: New Orleans Social Reformers, 1898–1933," *Louisiana History* 24 (1983): 389–401. Roosevelt's attitudes toward women and woman suffrage can be traced through his private and public writings. His views going into the 1912 election can be seen in Theodore Roosevelt, "Women's Rights; and the Duties of Both Men and Women," *Outlook*, 3 February 1912, 262–66.

40. *New York Times*, 11 August 1912 and 20 August 1912.

41. Mrs. John S. Crosby, "The Right of the Ballot" (speech given at the Equal Suffrage League of the City of New York meeting, 2 May 1912), National American Woman Suffrage Association Records, Rare Books and Manuscripts Division, The New York Public Library, Astor, Lenox and Tilden Foundations; *New York Times*, 31 March 1912; U.S. Congress, "Extension of Remarks of Hon. Steven B. Ayers, of New York, in the

House of Representatives, Monday, August 5, 1912," *Congressional Record*, vol. 48, pt. 12, Appendix, 62nd Congress, 2nd Sess., 509–11.

42. *New York Times*, 31 March 1912, 17 May 1912, and 25 September 1912.

43. Harriman wrote to Democratic National Committee Chairman William F. McCoombs to ask whether allowing women to work in the campaign would be acceptable. McCoombs responded positively and by early August women were actively working in the Democratic Party. Florence Jaffray Harriman, *From Pinafores to Politics* (New York: Henry Holt and Co., 1923); *New York Times*, 7 August 1912.

44. *Collier's*, 24 August 1912.

45. *Boston Journal*, n.d., Grace Allen Johnson Papers, Woman's Rights Collection, Schlesinger Library, Radcliffe College.

46. *Woman's Journal*, 31 August 1912, 276.

47. Eileen L. McDonagh, "Issues and Constituencies in the Progressive Era: House Roll Call Voting on the Nineteenth Amendment, 1913–1919," *Journal of Politics* 51 (February 1989): 119–36; Stephen Skowronek, *Building a New American State: The Expansion of National Administrative Capacities, 1887–1920* (New York: Cambridge University Press, 1982).

48. Robyn Muncy, *Creating a Female Dominion in American Reform, 1890–1935* (New York: Oxford University Press, 1991), 33.

49. Herbert Croly, "Progressives' Dilemma?: The New Party," *American Magazine*, November 1912, 12–14; Jane Addams, "My Experiences as a Progressive Delegate," *McClure's* November 1912, 12.

50. *Woman's Journal*, 27 September 1912, 6.

51. *New York Times*, 26 September 1912; Jane Addams, "Pragmatism in Politics," *Survey*, 5 October 1912, 11–12; Jane Addams, "Why I Became a Progressive," *Progressive Bulletin* 1, 15 (28 December 1912): 2.

52. Mary Dreier to Lillian Wald, n.d. [1912?], Reel 8, Lillian Wald Papers, Rare Books and Manuscripts Division, The New York Public Library, Astor, Lenox and Tilden Foundations.

53. Jane Addams, "Why I Went into Politics," *Ladies Home Journal*, January 1913; "Jane Addams Relates the Steps by which She Became a Progressive," *Progressive Bulletin* 1, 15 (28 December 1912): 2. Addams also attempted to counter the arguments that parties were corrupting influences. She explained that she had taken stands against what she perceived as political and partisan corruption, defining corruption in the way that Peter Burke has done as "behavior deviating from the formal duties of a public role." Peter Burke, *History and Social Theory* (Ithaca: Cornell University Press, 1992), 74. See Jane Addams, "Ethical Survivals in Municipal Corruption," *International Journal of Ethics* 8 (April 1898): 372–91; Jane Addams, *Democracy and Social Ethics* (New York: Macmillan, 1902).

54. Ida Husted Harper, Letter to the Editor, *New York Times*, 10 August 1912; Ida Husted Harper to Jane Addams, n.d., Swarthmore College Peace Collection, Reel 7, Addams Papers, Microfilm Edition; "The Crisis of the Woman Suffrage Party," *Outlook*, August 1912. Harper's criticisms continued in 1916. See *New York Times*, 15 October 1916.

55. *Woman's Political Union*, 6 January 1913, 2; Harriot Stanton Blatch to Jane Addams, 12 August 1912, Swarthmore College Peace Collection, Reel 6, Addams Papers, Microfilm Edition; *New York Times*, 6 September 1912; *Woman's Protest*, September 1912 and August 1913; *Chicago Daily Tribune*, 15 August 1912.

56. Manuela Thurner, "'Better Citizens Without the Ballot': American Antisuffrage Women and Their Rationale during the Progressive Era," *Journal of Women's History* 5, 1 (spring 1993): 41.

57. The issue of divided loyalties had also been raised in the election year of 1894 when Kansas suffragists began working for the Republican party. According to Eleanor Flexner, the suffrage fight in Kansas "confirmed Miss Anthony's deep-seated distrust of 'partial' suffrage. . . . The difficulty was that women promptly aligned themselves with a political party." Eleanor Flexner, *Century of Struggle: The Woman's Rights Movement in the United States* (Cambridge: Harvard University Press, 1975), 229. After 1894, the NAWSA disavowed suffragists who worked for political parties. Anthony and Harper, eds., *History of Woman Suffrage*, 4: 645.

58. Jane Addams, "Why I Seconded Roosevelt's Nomination," *Woman's Journal*, 17 August 1912, 257; *New York Times*, 11 August 1912; Jane Addams to Anna Howard Shaw, 20 August 1912, Elizabeth G. Evans Papers, Schlesinger Library, Radcliffe College, Reel 6, Addams Papers, Microfilm Edition; *New York Times*, 26 November 1912.

59. In Addams's case, she carefully split her time between suffrage-only work and party work. She made rules for herself. She refused to speak to women-only groups after the National Progressive Convention and before the election. She believed that separate women's groups were useful only for organization and then only for organizing around specific issues. Addressing and working alongside men was a step in translating those issues into legislation. Work on those issues involved propaganda, which required speaking in public, including to mixed audiences. *New York Times*, 13 October 1912; Jane Addams to Julia Kent, 12 December 1911, Susan B. Anthony Memorial Collection, University of Rochester Library, Reel 6, Addams Papers,

Microfilm Collection; Jane Addams to Alde Blake, 13 July 1912, Michigan Historical Collections, Bentley Historical Library, University of Michigan, Reel 6, Addams Papers, Microfilm Edition.

60. Jane Addams, Letter to the Editor, *New York Times*, 23 August 1912; Ida Husted Harper to Jane Addams, n.d., Reel 7, Addams Papers, Microfilm Edition.

61. *Chicago Daily Tribune*, 15 August 1912, clipping, Grace Allen Johnson Papers, Schlesinger Library, Radcliffe College; Jane Addams, "Pragmatism in Politics," *Survey*, 5 October 1912, 12.

62. *Woman's Journal*, 14 September 1912, 292; 12 October 1912, 324; and 2 November 1912, 345.

63. Anthony and Harper, eds., *History of Woman Suffrage*, 5:332–36; Jane Addams, "Communion of the Ballot," *Woman's Journal*, 14 December 1912; Carrie Chapman Catt, "Political Parties and Women Voters," 14 February 1920, Carrie Chapman Catt Papers, Woman's Rights Collection, Schlesinger Library, Radcliffe College.

64. Woodrow Wilson and the Democrats won the election with 42 percent of the popular vote; Roosevelt and the Progressives followed with 27 percent; Taft came in third with 23 percent.

65. Theodore Roosevelt to Jane Addams, 5 November 1912, Swarthmore College Peace Collection, Reel 7, Addams Papers, Microfilm Edition. Or, as Louis Seibold put it in the *New York World* in a story about Republican women: "Never again will the swish of a skirt startle Congress." *New York World*, 25 November 1916, clipping in Carrie Chapman Catt Scrapbook, Carrie Chapman Catt Collection, New York Public Library.

66. Florence Harriman, *From Pinafores to Politics*, 352–53.

67. Mary Simkhovitch, *Here Is God's Plenty: Reflections on American Social Advance* (New York: Macmillan, 1940), 138.

68. Carrie Chapman Catt to Miss London, 18 October 1928, Carrie Chapman Catt Papers, New York Public Library.

69. Carrie Chapman Catt, "What Women Have Done with Suffrage," n.d., Carrie Chapman Catt Papers, Reel 7, Library of Congress.

70. Emily Newell Blair, "Advance of Democratic Women," *Democratic Digest*, April 1940, 15.

16

Unbound Feet: Chinese Women in the Public Sphere

Judy Yung

Immigration to the United States proved to be a double-edged sword for Chinese women in the early twentieth century. Saddled by cultural restrictions, racial and gender discrimination, and labor exploitation, many suffered undue hardships and led strenuous lives in San Francisco. Yet sociohistorical conditions in their homeland and community at the time also afforded them opportunities to unbind their feet and their lives, to reshape gender roles and change their circumstances for the better. For most working-class immigrant women, family and work responsibilities consumed all their time and energy, leaving little left over for self-improvement or leisure activities, and even less for community involvement. However, there was a growing number of educated, middle-class women who, inspired by Christianity, Chinese nationalism, and Progressivism, began to take the first steps toward social activism in Chinatown. Prominent among these early leaders and activists were the wives and daughters of merchants and Chinese Christians.

Chinese women's efforts to organize for self-improvement and community service paralleled those of the white and black women's club movements, although Chinese women's clubs developed much later and followed a different course in certain respects. While white and black women started their clubs in the early and late nineteenth century, respectively, the first major Chinese women's club in America—the Chinese Women's Jeleab [Self-Reliance] Association—did not appear until 1913. As Gerda Lerner points out, women's organizations usually got going only after a sizable group of educated, middle-class women with some leisure emerged.[1] Given their later arrival and smaller numbers in America, Chinese women were slower than white and black women in developing the leadership necessary for organized activity. The organizational structure of these women's clubs was similar, though, since black and Chinese women patterned their clubs after those of white women. Indeed, one of the reasons black and Chinese women's clubs formed in the first place was that both groups were excluded from white women's clubs. Middle-class values such as support for education, socioeconomic mobility, and community improvement formed the basis for most women's organizations, but white women were more interested in self-improvement and gender equality, black women in racial equality, and Chinese women in national salvation for China.[2] The driving force behind Chinese immigrant women's entry into the public sphere was the well-being of their family, community, and nation.

The Protestant churches were the first to encourage Chinese women's participation in organized activities outside the home, as evidenced by the small but visible number of Chinese women who attended Sunday services, English classes, meetings, outings, and Christmas programs sponsored by churches in the early 1900s. At a time when respectable women were still seldom seen in public, these regular outings were often the only occasion on which women left their homes. This point was made in a *San Francisco Chronicle* interview with Foo Tai, "a Christianized Chinese woman." According to the reporter, Foo Tai spent her day at home cooking, sewing, and caring for her baby while her husband worked outside as a cook. An educated woman, she seldom went out *except* to attend church meetings as president of the Chinese Women's Society of the Baptist Mission or to shop at the local stores.[3] A number of other churches helped organize similar Chinese women's societies to encourage involvement in Christian activities. Members of the (Congregational) Mothers and Daughters Society, (Presbyterian) Circle of the King's Daughters, and (Methodist) Missionary Society met regularly to have lunch or socialize, and paid dues to help support the work of Bible women in their home villages in China.[4]

Chan Fuk Tai, an educated woman who was married to a pharmacist, also seldom went out except to teach Bible study, Chinese language, and embroidery to Chinese girls at the Baptist church. According to her daughter Dora Lee Wong, it was the one chance she had to mingle with other Chinese women, many of whom were the wives of Chinese ministers. "And she had quite a large class of students—girls who came from well-to-do merchant families," Dora added.[5] The church thus provided educated, middle-class women such as Foo Tai and Chan Fuk Tai entry into the public sphere, an opportunity to interact with other women of like mind, and a means to develop leadership skills. Indeed, Chinese women committed to the Christian cause were among the earliest women leaders in the community to organize events on behalf of women, the church, and national salvation. For example, Mrs. Ng Poon Chew (aka. Chun Fah), who was brought up and educated at the Presbyterian Mission Home, was indispensable to her husband in his role as minister, editor of the *Chung Sai Yat Po (CSYP)* newspaper, and champion for civil rights and Chinese nationalism. She was also actively involved in the establishment of the Chinese YWCA in 1916, led many fund-raising drives on behalf of China and the Chinese community, and, along with other Chinese Christian wives, took the initiative to sponsor community forums on nationalist and women's issues.[6]

Chinese women's involvement in church activities expanded their gender roles, in effect. The Won family, for example, was first exposed to Christianity when a Chinese missionary came to their house to tell them Bible stories. The five daughters in the family were encouraged to attend an embroidery class at the Methodist church, and all were baptized at the Congregational church. They then persuaded their mother, Wong Ho, to attend church as well. "We were very fortunate that mother listened to us and was willing to go to church and to some of the meetings," said one of the five daughters, Won King Yoak. "By associating with other church members, my mother became more open-minded. We were all well read and up-to-date with the latest news."[7] The women in the family later became the first Chinese American women to join Dr. Sun Yat-sen's revolutionary party and to be married in the Western tradition.

One of the earliest Christian organizations to serve Chinese American women, and certainly the longest-lasting, was the Chinese YWCA, established in 1916 and still functioning today in San Francisco Chinatown.[8] Its homogeneous membership, reflecting the segregated living patterns in existence even today, is indicative of a time when Chinese women were excluded from both white female and Chinese male organizations. Unlike YWCA branches in the South, however, the Chinese YWCA worked from the very beginning to garner the involvement and support of Chinese women and the Chinatown community in all aspects of its operations—a strategy more in keeping with the national organization's goals of inclusiveness, local autonomy, and indigenous programs.[9] It also paralleled the YWCA's efforts in China at the time, which sought to improve literacy, health care, and job and leadership skills among women who were assuming new roles because of industrialization.[10] In San Francisco, Chinese Christians, particularly educated middle-class women

Figure 16.1. Chinese YWCA Board of Directors, 1920s. Emily Fong (Mrs. B. S. Fong) and Chun Fah (Mrs. Ng Poon Chew) are in the first row, second and third from left; Won King Yoak (Mrs. Daniel Wu) is in the back row, fourth from left. *(Courtesy of Chinese YWCA, San Francisco)*

such as Mrs. Ng Poon Chew, Mrs. Theodore Chow, the wife of a Methodist pastor, and Mrs. H. Y. Chang, the wife of the secretary of the Chinese Legation, were involved in the planning stages of the Chinese YWCA. Although the local branch was headed by white women until Rose Chew was appointed in 1932, a predominantly Chinese board of directors and bilingual staff set policies, implemented programs, and handled casework. By 1929 all but one of the board members were Chinese women—the wives of merchants and ministers as well as single women with professional backgrounds.

The YWCA was well regarded by progressive elements in the Chinese community because of the organization's promotion of Chinese nationalism. According to an editorial in *CSYP*, "The hand that rocks the cradle rules the world. . . . By helping our women develop morally, intellectually, physically, and socially . . . the YWCA is benefiting the family and the future citizens of tomorrow and, therefore, the Chinese community as well as our country."[11] The YWCA nurtured this positive image by making extensive use of the Chinese press to publicize its programs and by maintaining direct involvement in community and fund-raising activities, such as Red Cross work, benefits for Chinese Hospital, famine and war relief work for China, receptions for Chinese dignitaries, and Chinese Independence Day parades. The YWCA also took the leadership role in promoting better housing, health, and child-care services and countering negative images of Chinese Americans in movies and Chinatown tours. Its repeated successful drives for new members, the Community Chest, and the YWCA capital fund speak well of the relentless efforts of Chinese women who were committed to the organization and reflect the wide support the YWCA enjoyed in the community. During the first year of its operation, 1916, the organization attracted 280 members. By 1920 it had grown to 500 members, and five years later to 699

Figure 16.2. Participants in Well Baby Contest sponsored by Chinese YWCA and Department of Public Health, 1928. *(Courtesy of Chinese YWCA, San Francisco)*

members. But its programs and services reached beyond these numbers, serving an average of 15,000 persons a year in the 1920s. Even in the midst of the Depression, women who were earning only $1.25 a day gave $1.00 to renew their annual membership, and the community came through with $25,000 to help build a new facility to be designed by architect Julia Morgan and built at 965 Clay Street.

During its first fifteen years, and before the emergence of the second generation, the Chinese YWCA focused on serving immigrant women with home visits, English classes, advice on household sanitation and baby care, interpreting services, and help with employment, immigration, and domestic problems. Similar to the YWCA's program in China, the purpose of these services was less to convert souls than to Americanize the foreign-born and improve their working and living conditions. At a time when social workers were not yet on the scene, the YWCA, along with the Methodist and Presbyterian Mission Homes, was an important resource for women in need. As the following case shows, Chinese staff were sensitive to the needs of their clients and effective in helping them resolve their problems. During the time that Florence Chinn Kwan was associate secretary of the Chinese YWCA, from 1921 to 1923, she encountered a young woman who had been forced into an arranged marriage. The husband had died of tuberculosis early on in the marriage, and the mother-in-law was intolerable. The widow asked Florence to help her escape to the Presbyterian Mission Home. "So, little by little, when she came to the YWCA for English class, she'd bring her jewelry to me and I would keep it for her. Then one day I took her to the home. She taught Chinese there, became a Christian, and never remarried."[12] Immigrant women also came to the YWCA for help when they needed an interpreter or when they felt unfairly treated at work.

Americanization efforts on the part of the YWCA were directed much more strongly at second-generation daughters than at immigrant mothers. Yet one area where the American way was pushed was child care, as exemplified by the Well Baby Contest that the YWCA cosponsored with the city's Public Health Department in 1928. Part of a national campaign promoted by the National Council of Mothers to lower infant mortality by educating mothers about infant hygiene, the contest was distinctly mainstream American.[13] Even so, Chinese women responded enthusiastically because of the pride they took in their children's well-being as well as the community effort that went into the event. More than sixty mothers entered 176 babies ranging in age from six months to five years in the contest. Three babies were chosen as the healthiest by physicians of Chinese Hospital and awarded prizes. Follow-up workshops were held at the YWCA on baby care, and the book used by the winning baby's mother, *Baby Diet*, was translated into Chinese for the benefit of other immigrant mothers. Through such cooperative programs and the day-to-day services it offered immigrant women, the Chinese YWCA succeeded in helping them with their personal problems, changing their attitudes toward Western institutions, and drawing some out of their homes into the public arena for self-improvement and social interaction.

Christian organizations such as the YWCA were not the only force having an impact on Chinese women's lives during this time; the intense nationalistic spirit that took hold in the early twentieth century also affected Chinese women in far-reaching ways. Not only did the call for modernization include the need to improve conditions for Chinese women, but reformers also solicited women's active participation in national salvation work. Fundraising for disaster relief and the revolution in China opened up opportunities for women to become involved in the community, develop leadership abilities, and move into the male-dominated public sphere. In 1907, for example, *CSYP* printed an article about flood and famine in the lower Yangtze River area, appealing specifically to Chinese women in the United States to follow the example of American women in other cities, who had already donated over $430,000. The article encouraged the growing numbers of literate Chinese women to take heed and help spread the word among women everywhere.[14] When the same area was hard hit by another natural disaster in the early part of 1911, women participated in a program of songs and drama sponsored by the Presbyterian Church and, later, by the Chinese Six Companies to raise money.[15] These efforts on the part of Chinese women established a pattern of community involvement that would repeat itself each time a nationalist or community cause demanded their help, thus furthering women's participation in public affairs.

Chinese American women first entered the political arena in support of the 1911 revolution. The Tongmenghui, the revolutionary party founded by Dr. Sun Yat-sen to overthrow the Qing dynasty and establish a republic in China, was the earliest organization to accept them into its ranks. Several dozen women—primarily relatives of Tongmenghui men—are known to have joined the San Francisco branch in 1910, making it the first sexually integrated organization in San Francisco's Chinatown.[16] Among them were Wong Ho and her five daughters, who had harbored Sun in their home during one of his secret visits to San Francisco. Wong Ho's son, Won Hongfei, was one of the founding members of the San Francisco branch of the Tongmenghui, and he later served as Dr. Sun's personal secretary in China. It was he who encouraged his mother to allow all the girls to attend church, become educated, and contribute to the revolutionary effort. Despite the objections of relatives who believed that women should not be seen in public, Wong Ho later allowed her daughters to sit on a decorated float during the 1912 celebration of the founding of the Chinese Republic. Soon after, Lilly King Gee Won, one of the daughters, followed the revolution to China, where she spent the next sixty-eight years of her life helping to build a new China.[17]

In support of the revolution, women in China participated in benefit performances, enlisted in the army, and engaged in dangerous undercover work. Although far from the war front, Chinese women in San Francisco, gripped by the same patriotic fervor, moved into the public arena to do their share. They made "speeches of fire and patriotism" that called for the destruction of the Manchu dynasty and for woman's suffrage in China; they donated money and jewelry for the cause; and they helped with Red Cross work—doing

fund-raising, preparing bandages and medicines, and sewing garments for the war effort—
sometimes under the auspices of Protestant churches, other times under the banner of the
Women's Young China Society.[18] A core group of women, including the Won sisters,
attended political rallies, helped roll bandages at the Congregational church, and made
handcrafted items to sell at fund-raising events.

The national crisis encouraged changes in gender roles for women in China and America,
inspiring them to become "new women" like Qiu Jin. Born into the gentry class, Qiu Jin was
an accomplished poet, horseback rider, and fencer. In response to the failure of the 1898
reforms and the Allied sacking of Beijing during the Boxer Rebellion, she resolved to help
save China and to fight for women's rights. When her arranged marriage proved a failure,
she left her conservative husband and went to study in Japan. There she became involved in
radical politics and the Tongmenghui.[19] Qui Jin was both a nationalist and a feminist, as evidenced in her actions and her writings. For example:

Women's Rights

We want our emancipation!
For our liberty we'll drink a cup,
Men and women are born equal,
Why should we let men hold sway?
We will rise and save ourselves,
Ridding the nation of all her shame.
In the steps of Joan of Arc,
With our own hands will we regain our land.[20]

While organizing for the revolution in Zhejiang, Qiu Jin was arrested and put to death; she
was only thirty-two. Newspapers in both China and the United States expressed outrage
over her execution; she was equally mourned by revolutionaries on both sides of the Pacific
Ocean.[21] Dr. Sun, in his many talks to overseas Chinese, often pointed to Qiu Jin as a role
model for Chinese women—a far cry from the traditional model of passivity and subservience. His words did not go unheeded. A few women in San Francisco followed her
example and cut their hair as a revolutionary gesture; others redoubled their commitment
to the revolutionary cause.[22]

Although the success of the revolution and the establishment of a republic in China
failed to bring peace and prosperity to the country, it did have a lasting impact on the
lives of Chinese American women. Jane Kwong Lee later commented, "After the establishment of the Republic of China, Chinese women in this country picked up the
forward-looking trend for equality with men. They could go to school, speak in public
places, have their feet freed from binding, and go out to work in stores and small factories
if they needed to work."[23]

Indeed, the ultimate symbol of subjugation—the crippling practice of foot binding—
was brought to an end. The new republican government, linking the elimination of foot
binding with women's emancipation, halted the practice by issuing prohibition orders
against it and by promoting women's education. Following the example of women in
China, Chinese women in America also began to unbind their feet (a process that was often
just as painful as having the feet bound) and to stop binding their daughters' feet. By the
1920s, the only trace of foot binding that remained was the unnaturally small feet of older
women encased in specially made leather shoes.[24]

Women also began to leave the confines of the home for wage work, community activities, and political involvement. The following story of how the 1911 revolution changed

one woman's life in Butte, Montana, is applicable to Chinese women's experience in San Francisco:

> When I came to America as a bride, I never knew I would be coming to a prison. Until the Revolution, I was allowed out of the house but once a year. That was during New Year's when families exchanged New Year calls and feasts. We would dress in our long, plaited, brocaded, hand-embroidered skirts. These were a part of our wedding dowry brought from China. Over these we wore long-sleeved, short satin or damask jackets. We wore all of our jewelry, and we put jeweled ornaments in our hair.
>
> The father of my children hired a closed carriage to take me and the children calling. Of course, he did not go with us, as this was against the custom practiced in China. The carriage would take us even if we went around the corner, for no family women walked. The carriage waited until we were ready to leave, which would be hours later, for the women saw each other so seldom that we talked and reviewed all that went on since we saw each other.
>
> The women were always glad to see each other; we exchanged news of our families and friends in China. We admired each other's clothes and jewels. As we ate separately from the men, we talked about things that concerned women. When the New Year festivals were over, we would put away our clothes and take them out when another feast was held. Sometimes, we went to a feast when a baby born into a family association was a month old. Otherwise, we seldom visited each other; it was considered immodest to be seen too many times during the year.
>
> After the Revolution in China, I heard that women there were free to go out. When the father of my children cut his queue he adopted new habits; I discarded my Chinese clothes and began to wear American clothes. By that time my children were going to American schools, could speak English, and they helped me buy what I needed. Gradually the other women followed my example. We began to go out more frequently and since then I go out all the time.[25]

Meanwhile in San Francisco, Mrs. Owyang and Mrs. Chu Chin Shung, wives of the outgoing and incoming Chinese consuls, respectively, caused quite a stir when they attended a Chinese banquet with their husbands. "The fact that women were present was taken as an indication of the democracy of the new China," the reporter covering the event wrote.[26] A year later, the same newspaper found it newsworthy to report that not only had Chinese women marched in a parade through Chinatown for the first time, but at a banquet hosted by the Chinese Nationalist League of America "they made speeches just as the men did."[27] Because of the changes wrought by the revolution, Chinese women in San Francisco were beginning to flex their political muscles.

In keeping with this new image of women, the Chinese Women's Jeleab [Self-Reliance] Association was established in 1913. As indicated by its name, this organization was unique in that it was started by Chinese American women unaffiliated with a church or nationalist cause. Its origin, purpose, and membership were a combination of San Francisco and Oakland, of Chinese nationalism and Western progressivism, of immigrant mothers and American-born daughters. According to a full-page story that appeared in the *San Francisco Chronicle*—complete with a photograph of the group's members holding the American flag and their club banner inscribed with its Chinese name—the Jeleab Association was inspired by the Chinese revolution and American progressivism. In the words of its "thoroughly Americanized" president, Mrs. C. G. Lee (Clara Lee):

> How did it start? It's hard to say exactly. It's one of those things that grow out of a need. For two years the women of the Chinese quarters of San Francisco and Oakland have watched the progress of the men and encouraged them all they could. They were interested in what the men were doing and were yearning to do something themselves, but so

few of them had any education at all. Why some couldn't even read and write their own language. Many were too poor to afford an education; and others couldn't be spared from family duties. It didn't look very bright at first.[28]

The organization, she continued, was patterned after the Chinese Native Sons of the Golden State, which excluded female membership.[29] It was also broadened to include foreign-born women:

> The idea first started with the Chinese Native Sons' parlor. If a Native Sons' parlor, why not a Native Daughters? But we soon found that that wouldn't do [since many of the members were not native-born], so we concluded to have simply a woman's club for the purpose that had brought us together. Then we had to have an American name, for we intended to incorporate and have a charter. It was impossible, however, to find an English word that would combine all the reasons for which the club was formed. . . . The name would have to stand for independence, educational and progressive. We finally decided to take a Chinese word *[jeleab]*, and, by using it, Anglicize it.[30]

Led by educated, middle-class women such as Clara Lee, the Jeleab Association chose to follow the example of other American clubs and file incorporation papers in Sacramento, stating its purpose as "social intercourse, benevolent work, educational advantages, and mutual assistance and benefit, and not for pecuniary profit."[31] But a more elaborate purpose was given in a statement by member Liu Yilan published in the *Sai Gai Yat Po*, or *Chinese World*, on 22 September 1913. Liu Yilan pressed the point that Chinese women's subordination was due to their lack of education and self-reliance. That could change for Chinese women in America, "where education flourishes and women's rights are allowed to develop," she said. "Women who are born and raised here have the chance to enter school when young and receive the same education as men. Even the older women who came from China have been inspired, after being continuously exposed to talk of freedom and equality, and after seeing for themselves the elevated status enjoyed by women here as opposed to the inferior position of women back home." The key, she concluded, was for women to band together and learn from each other:

> It is important that we broaden our contacts by making new friends and not keep to ourselves and become limited to our own little world. If we women are to become independent, we must form a big group so we can cull and share ideas and benefit from each other. Therefore, those of us who are of like mind have decided to form this group and to call it Lumei Zhongguo Nüjie Zili Hui [Chinese Women's Jeleab Association]. Our goal is to cultivate self-reliance in each of us and, further, to promote and propagate this concept in China, so as to strip away the black curtain that has blocked our [women's] view of the sky for thousands of years. This, then, is the purpose of our group.[32]

Herein was a new ideology concerning Chinese women's emancipation, one that combined Chinese nationalist thought on women's right to education with American ideals of freedom and equality. Equally important, it advocated self-improvement through social interaction in line with the progressive views of women's clubs in America. Indeed, the self-initiated Jeleab Association represented a new awakening in the social consciousness of Chinese immigrant women, a recognition of a higher status of womanhood to which they could aspire in America.

According to the newspaper article, in 1913 the Jeleab Association boasted a membership of two hundred Chinese women from San Francisco and Oakland, all immigrant mothers and American-born daughters, who met regularly in the parlor of the Chinese Native Sons of the Golden State in Oakland. As the immediate need was to educate the

Figure 16.3. Clara Lee, founder and president of the Chinese Women's Jeleab [Self-Reliance] Association, 1913. *(Courtesy of Dr. Lester Lee)*

illiterate, an evening class was established for the study of Chinese under the direction of Mrs. T. L. Lee, a Baptist minister's wife, with plans to tackle English next. Seventy-five years later, Clara Lee noted in an interview that the Jeleab Association, despite its auspicious beginnings, disbanded a few years later. "It didn't last very long," she said. "Some lived [too far away] in San Francisco, and some moved away later."[33] The other successful program, she recalled, was a class that met every Monday afternoon for instruction in using American sewing patterns. But even without the organization, progressive women such as Clara Lee continued to practice self-reliance while influencing others to become "new women." Aside from being the first Chinese woman to register to vote in 1911 and the founder of the Jeleab Association, Clara was also an active member of the YWCA, the International Institute, and Fidelis Coterie, and she devoted much of her life to volunteer work on behalf of immigrant women and the Chinese community.[34]

Immigration to the United States proved to be a double-edged sword for Chinese women in the early twentieth century. Saddled by cultural restrictions, racial and sex discrimination, and labor exploitation, many suffered undue hardships and led strenuous lives. Yet socioeconomic conditions and historical forces at the time afforded women like Wong Ah So, Law Shee Low, and Jane Kwong Lee opportunities to unbind their lives and reshape gender roles—in essence, to change their circumstances for the better. Their daughters, second-generation women born and raised in the United States, would benefit by their experiences. Without bound feet and bound lives but still fettered by race, gender, and class oppression, their challenge would be to break the double binds of cultural conflict at home and discrimination in the larger society, and take the first steps toward realizing their full potential as Chinese American women.

Notes

This essay is taken, with minor revisions, from Judy Yung, *Unbound Feet: A Social History of Chinese Women in San Francisco* (Berkeley and Los Angeles: University of California Press, 1995).

1. See Gerda Lerner, *The Majority Finds Its Past: Placing Women in History* (Oxford: Oxford University Press, 1979), ch. 5.
2. See ibid., ch. 6; Anne Firor Scott, *Natural Allies: Women's Associations in American History* (Urbana: University of Illinois Press, 1991); Karen J. Blair, *The Clubswoman as Feminist: True Womanhood Redefined, 1868–1914* (New York: Holmes & Meier, 1980); Paula Giddings, *When and Where I Enter: The Impact of Black Women on Race and Sex in America* (New York: William Morrow, 1984); and Evelyn Brooks Higginbotham, *Righteous Discontent: The Women's Movement in the Black Baptist Church, 1880–1920* (Cambridge, Mass.: Harvard University Press, 1993).
3. *San Francisco Chronicle*, 18 January 1903, 2.
4. Wesley Woo, "Protestant Work among the Chinese in the San Francisco Bay Area, 1850–1920" (Ph.D. diss., University of California, Berkeley, 1983), 231, 264.
5. Dora Lee Wong, interview with author, 5 October 1982.
6. Ira M. Condit, *The Chinaman as We See Him and Fifty Years of Work for Him* (Chicago: Fleming H. Revell Co., 1900), 209–10; Corinne K. Hoexter, *From Canton to California: The Epic of Chinese Immigration* (New York: Four Winds Press, 1976); and *CSYP*, 25 and 28 May 1911.
7. King Yoak Won Wu, interview with Genny Lim, 27 October 1982, Chinese Women of America Research Project, Chinese Culture Foundation of San Francisco.
8. I am indebted to Teresa Wu of the Chinese YWCA, historian and architect Philip P. Choy of the Chinese Historical Society of America, and Yee Ling Fong of the International Institute of San Francisco for sharing past correspondence, board minutes, and staff reports of the Chinese YWCA with me.
9. According to Giddings, *When and Where I Enter*, 155–58, black women in the South resented the discriminatory policies of the national board, particularly the lack of black women on the board and local black input on the establishment and running of YWCA branches in the South.
10. See Alison R. Drucker, "The Role of the YWCA in the Development of the Chinese Women's Movement, 1890–1927," *Social Services Review*, September 1979, 421–40; Mary S. Sims, "The Natural History of a

Social Institution: The Y.W.C.A." (Ph.D. diss., New York University, 1935); Jean McCown, "Women in a Changing China: The Y.W.C.A." (5 April 1970), YWCA of the U.S.A., National Board Archives, New York; Emma Sarepta Yule, "Miss China," *Scribner's* 71 (January 1922): 66–79; and Kwok Pui-lan, *Chinese Women and Christianity, 1860–1927* (Atlanta: Scholars Press, 1992), 126–32.

11. *CSYP*, 28 September 1929.
12. Florence Chinn Kwan, interview with author, 12 October 1988.
13. For an analysis of the baby contest in the larger context of maternal and infant care in the United States, see Alisa Klaus, *Every Child a Lion: The Origins of Maternal and Infant Health Policy in the United States and France, 1890–1920* (Ithaca: Cornell University Press, 1993).
14. *CSYP*, 4 May 1907.
15. *CSYP*, 21 April, 12 and 17 May 1911. Also known as the Chinese Consolidated Benevolent Association, the Chinese Six Companies was formed in 1862 to protect the general interests of the Chinese on the Pacific Coast. It originally consisted of six *huigan* (united clans of people from the same region or district in China), thus its name.
16. Zeng Bugui, "Sun Zhongshan yu Jiujinshan nü Tongmenghui yuan" (Sun Yat-sen and the women members of San Francisco's Tongmenghui), in *Zhongshan xiansheng yishi* (Anecdotes of Sun Yat-sen) (Beijing: Zhong-guo Wenshi Chubanshe, 1986), 141–42.
17. See Lilly King Gee Won, "My Recollections of Dr. Sun Yat-sen's Stay at Our Home in San Francisco," *Chinese America: History and Perspectives 1990*, 67–82.
18. *San Francisco Call*, 13 February 1911, 1; 29 October 1911, 34; and *CYSP*, 25 May, 21 and 27 November 1911; 12 January 1912.
19. See Mary Backus Rankin, "The Emergence of Women at the End of the Ch'ing: The case of Ch'iu Chin," in Margery Wolf and Roxane Witke, eds., *Women in Chinese Society* (Stanford: Stanford University Press, 1975), 39–66; and Leslie Eugene Collins, "The New Women: A Psychological Study of the Chinese Feminist Movement from 1900 to the Present" (Ph.D. diss., Yale University, 1976), 351–60.
20. Quoted in Elizabeth Croll, *Feminism and Socialism in China* (New York: Schocken Books, 1980), 68–69.
21. *CSYP*, 22 and 31 August, 9, 11, 12, 13, 16, and 17 September 1907.
22. Zeng, "Sun Zhongshan," 141; *San Francisco Call*, 29 October 1911, 34.
23. Jane Kwong Lee, "Chinese Women in San Francisco," *Chinese Digest*, June 1938, 8.
24. Howard S. Levy, *Chinese Footbinding: The History of a Curious Exotic Custom* (New York: Walton Rawls, 1966), 275–80; Dora Lee Wong, interview; Florence Chinn Kwan, interview; Fred Schulze interview with author, 26 January 1989; Clara Lee, interview with author, 2 October 1986; Connie Young Yu, "The World of Our Grandmothers," in Asian Women United, eds., *Making Waves: Anthology of Writings By and About Asian American Women* (Boston: Beacon Press, 1989), 33–42.
25. Rose Hum Lee, "The Growth and Decline of Chinese Communities in the Rocky Mountain Region" (Ph.D. diss., University of Chicago, 1947), 252–53.
26. *San Francisco Examiner*, 10 May 1914, 78.
27. Ibid., 26 July 1915, 6.
28. *San Francisco Chronicle*, 8 February 1914, 5.
29. The Chinese Native Sons of the Golden State changed its name to the Chinese American Citizens Alliance in 1928 after the Native Sons of the Golden West refused to give them affiliated status. See Sue Fawn Chung, "The Chinese American Citizens Alliance: An Effort in Assimilation, 1895–1965," *Chinese America: History and Perspectives 1988*, 30–57.
30. *San Francisco Chronicle*, 8 February 1914, 5.
31. Ibid.
32. *Sai Cai Yat Po*, 22 September 1913, 12.
33. Clara Lee, interview with author, 31 July 1989.
34. The daughter of liberal parents Rev. Chan Hon Fun and Ow Muck Gay, Clara Lee was born in 1886. The family moved to Oakland before the 1906 earthquake, and Clara remained there after her marriage to Dr. Charles Lee, the first Chinese licensed dentist in California. She had just turned 100 when I interviewed her in 1986. Clara Lee passed away in 1993 at the age of 106.

17

The Emergence of Feminism in Puerto Rico, 1870–1930

Yamila Azize-Vargas

Without a doubt, the twentieth century can be named the century of feminism. Economic, political, and social transformations interacted to significantly change women's status. Puerto Rico was no exception. Here I discuss the principal factors and events that were fundamental to improving women's situation in Puerto Rico during the first three decades of the twentieth century.

First I give a brief summary of women's education in Puerto Rico during the nineteenth century and then contrast it with the historical changes brought about by the U.S. invasion of Puerto Rico in 1898. U.S. military intervention had a major impact on women's work, particularly with the establishment of the tobacco and needlework industries, which employed thousands of women between 1900 and 1930 in Puerto Rico.

Women's work outside the home and their access to more education contributed to creating the conditions for the emergence of feminism in Puerto Rico. Two major groups emerged: one consisting of working-class women, and the second of formally educated and more affluent women. I discuss their conflicts and struggles to achieve recognition for women in Puerto Rican society.

Spanish Colonialism and Education

Education stands out as one of the most important forces that molded women's lives. There is little to be said about formal education during the first half of the nineteenth century. The Spanish government was not interested in providing any education to women. What efforts were undertaken were made possible by private institutions and individuals. A very small number of privileged girls were taught exclusively by women professors, as men were prohibited from teaching at or visiting girls' schools, but there were very few women professors or girls' schools. In 1860, for example, there were 122 schools for boys and 25 for girls. Ten years later the unequal proportion of schools still persisted: 246 schools for boys, 67 for girls.[1]

The quality of women's education was very poor. As Cuesta Mendoza, a historian of this period, has said, "Education for Puerto Rican women in the nineteenth century condemned them to living between saucepans and sewing cases for the rest of their lives."[2] Several prominent Puerto Rican intellectuals spoke out on this issue, among them intellectuals such as Eugenio María de Hostos, Salvador Brau, Manuel Fernández Juncos, and Alejandro Tapia y Rivera. Eugenio María de Hostos was one of the very first to endorse educational equity, not only in Puerto Rico, but also in Latin America. In a speech entitled "Scientific Education for Women," Hostos argued that women's inferiority was caused by "social, intellectual and moral restraints" together with "men's monopoly of social power." He proposed that society give women a "scientific" education; that is the only way women "will be emancipated from error and slavery." Exiled from Puerto Rico for political reasons, he worked in Chile and the Dominican Republic to establish educational institutions for women.[3]

After the United States Invasion

The end of the century brought significant changes to Puerto Rico and to women's education and status. After the United States Army invasion in 1898, education became one of the priorities of the metropolitan power. Education was envisioned as an instrument to Americanize the population.[4] More schools were opened, and the number of students and teachers in public education increased dramatically. Coeducation was established and more girls attended school, but their education remained quite different from the boys'. Women's educational inequality was planned and imposed by the United States government, based on U.S. economic interests and needs. World War I was also a determining factor in the implementation of educational policy for women.

During the first two decades of the twentieth century, a significant transformation of the Puerto Rican economy took place. The devaluation of the Spanish peso immediately after the U.S. invasion created a serious economic crisis on the island. Poor women were forced into jobs based on their traditional education and skills; female employment increased significantly in the needlework and tobacco industries, and in professions such as nursing and teaching. By 1910 women made up more than half the labor force in the field of education and the tobacco industry. In 1919 more then thirty-five thousand women did needlework at home.[5]

World War I severely interrupted commercial relations between the United States and the Philippines, which at the time was the garment industry's main supplier. Puerto Rico, recently become a colony, provided a new source of cheap labor for the garment industry. There was a desperate need for jobs on the island and, given the critical economic situation, workers' wages were extremely low. Garment firms started to train people, mainly women who traditionally had learned this kind of sewing at home. The training then became institutionalized, as home economics, taught by North Americans, became part of the public school's curriculum for all girls. Several commercial needlework corporations, interested in establishing their developing business in Puerto Rico, financed these programs or opened their own schools. By 1918, according to the commissioner of education, home economics was "so popular" that course in embroidery and drawn work became part of the curriculum in all Puerto Rican schools.[6]

Along with needlework, U.S. investment was concentrated in tobacco. In contrast to needlework, tobacco production revolved around the factory.[7] Thus while women's work in the tobacco industry, like needlework, capitalized on their supposed manual abilities, women in the tobacco industry faced quite a different work experience. They had to leave their homes, work with other women and men in a common space, and deal with terrible working conditions.

Women experienced various kinds of discrimination in the needlework and tobacco industries, as well as in education and the other occupations in which they were concentrated. They were paid less than men even when they did the same kind of work. Historical testimonies document women complaining about sexual harassment from their male bosses. The Puerto Rico Employment Bureau reported and denounced the inhumane working conditions in the garment industry. In the teaching profession, where they constituted a majority, women were forbidden to be members of, or even vote for, the School Board.

Women's oppression in the needlework and tobacco industries contributed to the conditions for the emergence of class and feminist consciousness. Women faced double exploitation, as workers and as women. They were paid less than men, while they continued to be responsible for their households.

Women's Struggles and the Federación Libre de Trabajadores (Free Workers' Union)

The first clear signs of protest came from women who worked in the tobacco industry. From the beginning of the twentieth century, newspapers published women's testimonies demanding help from the leaders of the Federación Libre de Trabajadores (FLT), then the main labor organization in Puerto Rico. Women demanded the right to organize, to be educated and to be protected from discrimination and harassment. The FLT's first response was rejection. But despite opposition from several male leaders, the women began their organizing drive. By 1904 there were eight women's unions with more than five hundred members.[8] In 1906 and 1907 newspapers reported several strikes by women in the tobacco industry.[9]

The presence of the "lector" (reader) in the tobacco factories played a significant role in the process of women's growing awareness and organization. The reader, paid by the workers, read daily newspapers and major literary works to workers in the factory. Oral testimonies and research document that this "lector" was an agitator who promoted unionization among the tobacco workers.

The high point of these struggles came in 1908, when two women delegates to the fifth annual congress of the FLT presented a resolution demanding an official campaign to promote the unionization of working women in Puerto Rico. Other resolutions approved in that meeting dealt with the right to education, to right to better working conditions, and the first formal demand for women's suffrage.[10] The leaders of the tobacco unions, who years before had complained about women's participation in the industry, finally recognized that "they couldn't do anything to stop women in the industry . . . we must then, help them to get organized in unions, to get education; they can't be our enemies, they have to be our allies."[11] Soon after, women also became part of the board of directors of the Federación Libre de Trabajadores.[12]

Luisa Capetillo

One of the most outstanding women leaders in this movement was Luisa Capetillo. Born in Arecibo, of a Spanish father and French mother, she received a liberal education. Her involvement in the labor movement began in 1907 when she became a "lectora" in one of the tobacco factories. She became actively involved in meetings and strikes, and then worked as a reporter for *Unión Obrera*, the main labor newspaper in Puerto Rico at the time. As a writer she published several books: *Ensayos libertarios* (Libertarian essays, 1907), *La humanidad del futuro* (The humanity of the future, 1910), *Mi opinión sobre las libertades, derechos y deberes de la mujer* (My opinion about women's freedom, rights and duties, 1911), and her last, *Influencia de las ideas modernas* (The influence of modern ideas, 1916). She wrote on education and the importance of women working outside the home, on the benefits of a Communist society free from oppression and religion, on love, and on the future of society. In all her writings she insisted on her affiliation with socialism, on her support for women's liberation, and particularly her defense of "free love." She never married, and had three children in open relationships. Capetillo traveled to New York, Cuba, the Dominican Republic, and Florida, and published the feminist magazine *La Mujer*. She was arrested in Cuba for wearing slacks. In Puerto Rico she is remembered in a popular song that says: "Doña Luisa Capetillo, intentionally or not, has created a tremendous uproar because of her culottes."[13]

The Suffragist Movement

Several years after the working women's feminist campaigns, another group of women organized the Liga Femínea de Puerto Rico (Puerto Rican Feminine League). Founded in 1917 by Ana Roqué de Duprey, its main objective was to fight for women's right to vote. Ana Roqué's commitment to women's rights had begun at the end of the nineteenth century. As the founder and editor of several feminist newspapers, she consistently demanded the right to vote, to education, and to the active participation of women in society.[14]

In contrast to the feminist working women, the suffragists from Liga Femínea demanded the restricted vote. This meant that only those women twenty-one years old and over who knew how to read and write could participate in general elections. In Puerto Rico just one-sixth of the female population met those requirements. The suffragist organization, though contemporary with the working women's organization, had a different ideology and different strategies. Working women in labor unions were active in strikes, demanded universal suffrage, and discussed issues affecting the working class as a whole. In contrast, the majority of the suffragists who favored the restricted vote did not share working women's problems or situation, and avoided involvement in militant demonstrations such as strikes or other kinds of protests.[15]

The Nineteenth Amendment: Colonialism, Feminism, and the Fight for Universal Suffrage

As early as 1908, the impact of feminist polemics was evident in the political arena. Nemesio Canales, writer and legislator, expressed his solidarity with the resolutions approved at the Federación Libre de Trabajadores assembly, and presented a bill demanding "legal emancipation for Puerto Rican women," including universal suffrage. The bill was not approved.[16] This was the first of a series of twelve different bills presented over a twenty-year period.

Besides male opposition, an additional obstacle to women's suffrage involved Puerto Rico's colonial status. Given Puerto Rico's subordination to the United States, several suffragists expected that the Nineteenth Amendment to the U.S. Constitution (passed in 1919, granting universal suffrage to all U.S. women citizens twenty-one years or over) would extend to Puerto Rico. Since Puerto Ricans had been granted U.S. citizenship in 1917, there was a legal basis for this expectation.

Events were more complicated, however. Once Congress approved the law, the Puerto Rican Legislature was uncertain about its validity in Puerto Rico. The confusion over the amendment's applicability was clarified by a solitary but militant action by one woman: Genera Pagán.

Born in San Juan at the end of the nineteenth century, Genera Pagán became a tobacco stripper in one of the largest tobacco factories. As a working woman, she faced miserable

wages and terrible working conditions. Like other women, Genera realized the importance of syndicalism and militancy to achieve social change. She emerged as a leader during a working women's strike in 1914. Years later, after losing her husband in World War
I, she emigrated to New York, where she worked in the garment industry. The feminist
movement in the United States was at its height, particularly around the issue of universal
suffrage. Shortly after the approval of the Nineteenth Amendment, Genera became
involved in the fight for the extension of the new law to Puerto Rico. When she learned
about the confusion over the new law, she decided to go back to Puerto Rico and fight for
women's rights.[17]

Genera Pagán believed that because she was a U.S. citizen, the 1919 law applied to
her—and to all Puerto Rican women—and so she attempted to register to vote. The
Puerto Rican government did not know what to do, so it requested an opinion from the
Bureau of Insular Affairs in Washington, D.C. Several months later, the Bureau of Insular
Affairs decided that the Nineteenth Amendment was not applicable to Puerto Rico.[18]

Several considerations shaped this outcome. As Ana Roqué pointed out in 1920, in one
of the last issues of her feminist newspaper, Puerto Rican legislators feared approving universal suffrage in Puerto Rico for three hundred thousand women. The majority of women
were poor, and potential supporters of the Socialist Party, the first political party to support both suffrage for women and working women's labor struggles. Several legislators
were quoted in a few newspapers saying that they were afraid of a possible victory by the
Socialist Party due to women's electoral support. This explains why Ana Roqué wrote in
her newspaper: "[I]f you [the legislators] are afraid of the political power the illiterate class
could gain with the vote, *you should restrict the right to vote to literate women.*" Several years
later her statement became a prophecy.[19]

The challenge raised by Genara Pagán showed that suffragists were overconfident
about the extension of the Nineteenth Amendment to Puerto Rico. Disillusioned with the
negotiations, their militancy decreased significantly. Liga Femínea disappeared and its
leader, Ana Roqué, announced in 1920 that she was temporarily quitting, proclaiming that
the "only hope in the universal suffrage struggle lay with working women's organizations."
Mercedes Solá, another distinguished suffragist writer and leader, also recognized the
importance of solid organizations "like the one built by working women in the struggle for
women's rights."[20]

Working Women's Struggle for Universal Suffrage

Working women were, again, the first to raise the banner of feminism at the beginning of
the new decade. By 1920 the Socialist Party had organized the Asociación Feminista Popular (AFP, Popular Feminist Association). One of its first activities was a mass rally with a
special guest speaker, Betty Hall, a very well known North American suffragist.[21] This liaison between Puerto Rican and North American feminists was an important precedent that
influenced future feminist strategies.

Several months after the foundation of the AFP, the suffragists decided to reorganize.
A new organization, Liga Social Sufragista (Suffragist Social League), was founded. Milagros
Benet Newton, an active suffragist who held more conservative views than prior leaders, was
elected president. She disapproved of Genera Pagán's defiant acts, and stood in favor of the
restricted vote.[22] Her presidency, however, did not last long. She was followed by Ricarda
López, one of the founders of the Teachers Federation, who brought significant changes to
the league, particularly the defense of universal suffrage.

Subsequently, women's struggles for universal suffrage gained momentum. Two other suffragist groups were organized: Asociación Puertorriqueña de Mujeres Sufragistas (Puerto Rican Association of Suffragist Women) and Liga Panamericana de Mujeres Votantes (Pan-American Women's League), which followed the conservative direction promoted by Benet Newton. These new organizations took a firm stand in favor of restricted suffrage. The majority of the legislators shared this conservative position. Thus, of the eleven proposals presented for legislation, none was as liberal and comprehensive as the one that had been presented by Nemesio Canales in 1908. The majority asked for restricted suffrage, fearing the party preference of poor women—the Socialist Party. The Liberal Party, the party in power, of course opposed universal suffrage for women.

The political battle was on, and the debate reached other institutions: civic and religious associations, magazines, and newspapers. For example, cartoons mocking women's demand for suffrage appeared in popular magazines such as *El Carnaval* and *El Diluvio*.[23] The Catholic Church leaders opposed women's vote because it "could interrupt women's destiny, according to God and Nature, to be mothers and housewives."[24] *El Mundo*, one of the leading newspapers at that time, conducted a survey in which the majority of people who responded favored universal suffrage for women.[25] The Teachers Federation approved a resolution demanding women's suffrage.

Building Solidarity with North American Feminists and the Pressure from Washington, D.C.

Over the following years, suffrage was one of the most widely discussed issues in the political arena. By 1927 there was a general consensus among several important civic, professional, and political organizations favoring women's right to vote, but the debate over universal versus restricted suffrage constituted a major obstacle to passing legislation. This debate initially divided the politicians and the feminists. A temporary coalition was formed between the conservative suffragist groups, which supported restricted suffrage, and feminist working women from both the Socialist Party and labor unions, which defended and insisted on universal suffrage. But the issue of restricted versus universal suffrage dissolved this united front. However, liberal suffragists in the Liga Social Sufragista, who supported universal suffrage, created a different strategy: lobbying in Washington, D.C.[26]

These liberal suffragists developed an ongoing relationship with the National Woman's Party. (It should be pointed out, however, that before the Liga began to seek help from North American suffragists, working women from the Socialist Party had contacted them.) Through their North American contacts, the Puerto Rican suffragists were able to lobby several congressmen. Their efforts paid off; they were able to convince two congressmen to present legislation. In January 1929 the bill moved up to the Committee for Insular Possessions and Territories of the United States Congress, which gave it a favorable recommendation.[27] This legislation then put pressure on the Puerto Rican Legislature to approve women's suffrage. Several months later a new bill, Number 12, was presented in Puerto Rico. If this bill, granting restricted suffrage for women, was not approved soon, the U.S. legislation would be enacted. The bill passed, and protests arose immediately. Leaders of the Suffragist Social League, the Socialist Party, and other groups vigorously attacked the discriminatory law.[28]

In 1932 approximately fifty thousand women participated in general elections, the first elections in which a group of women exercised their right to vote. Ironically, María Luisa Arcelay, who was not a feminist and was not involved in feminist struggles, was the first woman elected to the legislature. She had economic power as an owner of several needle-work factories, hence her record as a legislator who lacked interest in feminist issues and in some instances opposed women's interests. For example, she did not support a bill to raise wages for women in the needlework industry, and did not initiate the bill to grant universal suffrage to women. It was clear that when she had to take sides, she defended her personal economic interests.

Feminist struggles waned during the period following the passage of the suffrage bill. This was also the trend in other countries. Thirty years passed before we witnessed a new wave of feminist activism.

Conclusion

One of the major achievements of contemporary feminist movements has been the redis-covery of their forgotten history. Women can learn many lessons from their predecessors' fights. The history of women's struggles, as this essay on Puerto Rican feminism shows, widens the discussions and perspectives on the current situation for women. Three major issues should be underlined: first, the inexorable relationship between feminism and social class, evident, for example, in the restricted versus universal suffrage polemic and the selec-tion of María Luisa Arcelay as the first, "token" woman in the Puerto Rican Legislature; second, the tremendous importance of international solidarity among women, as was demonstrated by the support and collaboration between Puerto Rican and U.S. feminists; and third, women's obtaining of rights and equality when they unite and organize, when they develop a collective commitment to struggle for their rights.[29]

Notes

1. For more information on the history of women's education in Puerto Rico, see Cayetano Coll y Toste, *Histo-ria de la instrucción pública en Puerto Rico hasta el año 1898* (Spain: Editorial Vasco Americana, 1970). Statistics quoted were taken from Juan José Osuña, *A History of Education in Puerto Rico* (Editorial U.P.R., 1949), 56.

2. A. Cuesta Mendoza, *Historia de la educación en el Puerto Rico colonial de 1821–1898*, 2 vols. (Dominican Republic: Imprenta Arte y Clue, 1948).

3. For more information on Hostos, see E. Rodíguez Demoncci, ed., *Hostos en Santo Domingo, Homenaje de la República Dominicana con motivo del Centenario de Eugenio María de Hostos*, 1939, 214–15; Eugenio María de Hostos, "La educación cientifica de la mujer," *Páginas Escogidas* (Selected pages) (Argentina: Colección Estrada, 1952), 81.

4. Aida Negrón de Montilla, *Americanization in Puerto Rico and the Public School System, 1900–1930* (P.R.: Edi-torial Edil, 1971).

5. "Major Female Occupations in Puerto Rico, 1899–1930," in United States Department of Labor, *The Employment of Women in Puerto Rico* (Washington, D.C.: U.S. Government Printing Office, 1934).

6. Report of the Governor of Puerto Rico, *Informe del Comisionado de Instrucción*, Años 1911, 175, 467; Ana L. Reyes de Martínez, *El Desarrollo del programa de economía doméstica en Puerto Rico 1903–1964* (San Juan: Departamento de Instrucción Pública, Junta Estatal de Instrucción Vocacional, 1964).

7. Angel Quintero Rivera, "Socialista y tabaquero: La proletización de los artesanos," *Sin Nombre*, January–March 1978, 13.

8. Igualdad Iglesias, "La mujer en la organización obrera," in *El obrerismo en Puerto Rico* (Workmanship in Puerto Rico) (Spain: Ed. Juan Ponce de León, 1973), 323–27.

9. *Unión Obrera*, 1 September 1910, 26 September 1910, 26 August 1911, 14 July 1911.

10. Federación Libre de Trabajadores, *Procedimientos de Sexto Congreso de la Federación Libre de Trabajadores de Puerto Rico* (San Juan, 1910).

11. A. Torres, *Espíritu de clase* (San Juan: Imprenta F.L.T., 1917), 43–44.

12. *Unión Obrera*, 1 September 1906.

13. N. Valle, *Luisa Capetillo* (San Juan, 1975).

14. For more information on Ann Roqué, see A. Negrón Muñoz, *Mujeres de Puerto Rico* (San Juan: Imprenta Venezuela, 1935); C. Meléndez, "Ana Roqué de Duprey: Biografia en cuatro tiempos," *Figuraciones de Puerto Rico* (San Juan: Instituto de Cultura Puertorriqueña, 1958).

15. For more information on the suffragist organizations, see their newspapers *Pluma de mujer* (for 1915) and *Album puertorriqueño* (for 1918).

16. N. Canales, *Paliques* (San Juan: Edit. Coquí, 1968).

17. *El Mundo*, 3 September 1920.

18. Ibid., 17 September 1920, 6 January 1921.

19. *Heraldo de la mujer*, October 1919. Emphasis added.

20. M. Solá, *Feminismo* (P.R.: Imprenta Cantero, 1922).

21. *Unión Obrera*, 14 December 1920.

22. *El Mundo*, 3 September 1920.

23. *El Carnaval*, 12 September, 1920, cartoon entitled "Cuando las mujeres voten"; 19 September 1920, "Cosas del sufragio femenino"; 26 September 1920, "Y quieren que uno las apoye."

24. *El Mundo*, 4 September 1920.

25. Ibid., March, April, and May 1923.

26. Ibid., 28 November 1927.

27. "Confer the right to vote to women of Porto Rico," U.S. House of Representatives, report no. 1895, 70th Congress, May 1928; "Conferring the Right to Vote upon Porto Rican Women," U.S. Senate, report no. 1454, 70th Congress, 18 January 1929.

28. *El Mundo*, 29 May 1929.

29. For more information on the history of feminism in Puerto Rico, see Y. Azize, *La mujer en la lucha. Historia del feminismo en Puerto Rico 1898–1930* (San Juan: Editorial Cultural, 1985); Y. Azize, ed., *La mujer en Puerto Rico. Ensayos de investigación* (P.R.: Editorial Huracán, 1987).

18

Woman Suffrage around the World: Three Phases of Suffragist Internationalism

Ellen Carol DuBois

Even with the revival of modern feminism and women's history, woman suffrage movements have been a curiously understudied phenomenon. There are two related explanations for this lack of scholarly attention. One is the assumption that, with the exception of a few very well known and highly dramatic cases such as England and the United States, women have been "granted" the vote by friendly (or calculating) governments, rather than because of their own organized demand for it. The movement's first historian, New Zealand progressive William Pember Reeves, observed, scarcely before the first women had returned from the polls in that country in 1893, that chivalrous politicians had granted women the vote without their having to mobilize significantly on its behalf.[1]

The claim that woman did not fight for their own political equality is closely related to another dismissive evaluation of women's enfranchisement and barrier to interested scholars. This is the very commonly made claim that the enfranchisement of women has been, on balance, a conservative development, both with respect to the forces responsible for achieving votes for women and the ultimate impact that women's votes have had on political life. This charge is unsubstantiated by empirical research, which has had remarkably little to contribute to our understanding of the impact of gender on voting behavior, since men's and women's votes are rarely counted separately. Whether or not women vote differently from men and whether that difference is tilted to the right or the left seem to vary a great deal and to reflect not only the general political environment within which voters act but whether or not there are political factors working on women and not on men, especially whether there is an active and widespread feminist movement at work.

Perhaps the most remarkable thing about the claim of conservatism with respect to woman suffrage movements is that it predates not only the actual enfranchisement of women, but even the heyday of the woman suffrage movement. The charge that women would vote more conservatively than men was an important element in the debate itself, coming largely from leftists, as an argument against votes for women. During the 1875 debate over whether to endorse woman suffrage in the founding documents of the German Social Democratic Party, opponents cited the allegedly reactionary political tendencies of women, especially their ties to the church. William Leibnicht defended them: "Opponents of female suffrage often maintain that women have no political education but there are plenty of men in the same position, and by this reasoning they ought not to be allowed to vote either. The 'herd of voters' which has figured at all elections did not consist of women."[2]

The general consensus as to the movement's conservatism is very widespread. Consider, for example, Richard Evans's classic survey, *The Feminists*.[3] Evans argues that while the demand for woman suffrage has its origins in classical liberalism, its achievement in the late nineteenth and early twentieth centuries coincided with and partook of the decline and contraction of that tradition. Led by elite and conservative "ladies," Evans argued, the turn-of-the-century movement abandoned its roots in universal suffrage traditions and struck a Faustian bargain in which it accepted property restrictions in order to get the vote for privileged women. Particularly in Germany, he argues, "[t]he enfranchisement of women was seen, both by politicians and by the suffragists themselves, as a means of controlling society in the interests of the 'stable' part of the population, the middle classes."[4]

At the beginning of the women's history revival even feminists seemed to embrace their own version of the tendency to dismiss woman suffrage as a conservative development, especially with respect to issues of women's sexual and social freedom. From this perspective, the campaign for political equality appeared to be the least interesting and narrowest aspect of women's historical efforts for self-liberation. Here the argument was that the drive for votes for women substituted formal, legal equality for other, more radical aspects of the women's movement—for instance, a challenge to conservative sexual morality. Among United States historians, both Aileen Kraditor and William O'Neill set the tone for this type of argument.[5] Feminists such as Aleksandra Kollontai and Emma Goldman were invoked as alternative heroines of women's emancipation to bourgeois suffrage leaders. Pember Reeves's categorical dismissal of the role of any organized women's movement in winning votes for women was replaced with a second set of interpretations that focused on the woman suffrage leadership taken by groups such as the Woman's Christian Temperance Union (WCTU). The WCTU's suffrage activism was seen not as a positive force for women's emancipation, but rather as a reinforcement of the confining notions of separate spheres and women's responsibilities for morality, conservative in terms of both women's roles and larger social relations of class and power. This approach restored women's agency to the suffrage story but paid the price of conceding the movement's fundamental conservatism.[6] Is this price necessary?

I would like to offer an alternative, revisionist overview of woman suffrage movements around the world, which stresses two aspects. One is the internationalism of these movements: the cooperation among women of various nations, the influence that actions of women in one country have had on those in another, and the way that women's international cooperation gave them resources to combat their marginalization in the politics of their own nations. Woman suffrage can be usefully conceptualized as an international protest movement, or perhaps more accurately a series of such movements. Usually suffragism is studied in the context of a single country, in my case the United States, in order to demonstrate how much women's drive for political equality was shaped by, indeed was part and parcel of, a particular national political history and cannot be understood without reference to that history.[7] Yet a national focus alone underplays the rich international circulation of ideas, personalities, organizations, and inspiration that sustained woman suffragism over its very long history and that in many cases has been a crucial element in the actual achievement of women's enfranchisement. Ian Tyrrell suggests instead a more international history (he uses the term *transnational* so as not to assume global harmony and equality) that takes into account, without taking for granted, the national framework of the political life from which women were excluded and which they wished to enter.[8]

The other and related aspect of this approach is to challenge the conservative hypothesis, to argue that woman suffrage has been, on balance, a progressive development, drawing on and adding to left-wing political forces, albeit frequently in an embattled fashion. This is an argument I have been putting forth ever since my first piece on suffragism in the United

States, entitled "The Radicalism of the Woman Suffrage Movement," but here I want to reframe this claim in international terms.[9]

Most obviously, in the years of international woman suffragism's greatest strength, from 1890 through World War I, the movement was influenced and spread by women associated with the Second Socialist International. However, especially given the substantial antifeminist and antisuffrage countertradition within international socialism, the leftism of suffrage activism need not be limited to women working within the framework of organized socialist parties. On either side (chronologically speaking) of the suffragism of the Second International, we can find the impact of the World's Woman's Christian Temperance Union and the international character of the independent militant suffragettes, who had their beginnings in Britain. Such a reconceptualization and a global survey can, in addition, help to expand our definition of progressive politics to incorporate more women operating outside of male-dominated, left-wing environments.

This review takes place from a deliberately and self-consciously socialist-feminist perspective. A corollary to the conservative thesis is the insistence that there has historically been a fundamental antagonism between socialism and feminism. By contrast, modern socialist-feminists try to tolerate the tension between the two movements and to make of it a creative and powerful progressive politics. Describing United States women's theoretical and scholarly efforts in the 1970s to reconcile the two traditions, or at least put them on speaking terms with each other, Mary Bailey characterized the hyphen that separates the two sides of the term *socialist-feminism* as a metaphor for the unresolved tension, the creative conflicts, that this wing of the modern feminist movement strives to tolerate, explore, and advance. Movingly, Bailey writes, "What intervenes in this relationship of two terms is desire, on every level. Hyphen as wish. We have heard its whisperings."[10]

While modern socialist-feminism is uniquely self-aware, it is possible to trace such politics back into the nineteenth century and to argue that they have consistently been a radicalizing force in the movement for women's emancipation. This essay can be read, therefore, as a contribution to the reconstruction of the socialist-feminist tradition, as part of a contest over the meaning and political direction of the contemporary women's movement. This argument can—and has—been directed to either side of the hyphen: to the feminist audience, the emphasis is on the importance of socialist influences in our tradition; to the socialists, the message is the existence of a rich women's emancipatory vein in our history.

Woman's Temperance and Woman Suffrage: The First Internationalism

The first international woman suffrage movement was organized by the World's Woman's Christian Temperance Union. The WCTU, formed in the United States in 1874, began as a conventional Protestant women's organization with a narrow moral reform focus but soon became an amazingly ambitious, politically aggressive women's organization. The leading figure in this transformation was Frances Willard, and one of the distinctive marks of her leadership was her brilliant work at enlisting the organization in the fight for woman suffrage.

Willard profoundly expanded the WCTU by introducing what she called her "Do Everything Policy," a complex structure in which separate issues were pursued within semiautonomous "departments," each under the authority of its own "superintendent." Within this framework, and fueled by Willard's deeply political sensibilities, woman suffrage flourished. By convincing WCTU women that temperance itself was a political issue, she led her constituency to advocate woman suffrage, which had previously been taken up only by small and politically isolated groups of advanced women. Indeed, it is not too much to say that under Willard's leadership the WCTU was one of the first environments within which woman suffrage was made comprehensible and compelling to substantial numbers of women.[11]

In 1884, in conjunction with her companion, Lady Henry Somerset, Willard declared the formation of the World's Woman's Christian Temperance Union, an international companion organization to the American WCTU. The temperance movement had long been transatlantic, following British lines of international influence, and the formation of the World's WCTU reflected Willard's deepening bonds with British temperance women. Still, what is striking about the World's WCTU is its movement in western and southern, rather than eastern and northern, directions. WCTU organizers in the western United States, who were working to "uplift" Asian women immigrants from prostitution and opium addiction, began to see that if populations, workers, and vices migrated from nation to nation, perhaps virtue and organized movements of upstanding women could do the same.[12]

The World's WCTU was spread by American organizer/missionaries. Two of the most intrepid of these missionaries to the "world's women" were Jessie Ackerman and Mary Leavitt, who planted the World's WCTU's first truly successful seeds in Australia and New Zealand. Leavitt's WCTU career had begun as suffrage superintendent in Massachusetts. WCTUs already existed in South Australia and New Zealand before Leavitt arrived, but what she brought with her was the broader, "do everything" vision of the organization that Willard had developed, and particularly the commitment to securing political equality for women. In her pioneering examination of the New Zealand woman suffrage movement, Patricia Grimshaw argues that the international links of WCTU suffragists in that country gave them considerable cachet, as well as access to the whole range of Anglo-American suffrage thought, including the advanced ideas of John Stuart Mill. In the far-flung outposts of "Western civilization," affiliation with the international women's temperance movement was a way to combat the sense of isolation on the periphery. Kate Sheppard touted the case of Wyoming, the sole locale of woman suffrage in the United States in her first New Zealand propaganda.[13]

The internationalism of the woman suffrage movement in this early stage did not all go in one direction, carrying political authority and innovation only from the center to the periphery. Early victories in Australia and New Zealand sent sophisticated women activists back to England and the United States, where they helped to move suffrage movements there into new directions. Dora Montefiore, leader of New South Wales suffragism, moved from Australia to England, where Sylvia Pankhurst credited her with encouraging Pankhurst in the early 1900s to make her first outdoor suffrage speech.[14] Australian suffragism sent Alice Henry to the United States, where, her biographer, Diane Kirkby, argues, she was one of the earliest to insist that wage-earning women must be made the center of an expansive, modern woman suffrage movement.[15]

As suggested above, historians' recognition of the role of the WCTU in the early enfranchisement of women was at first accompanied by a consensus that this temperance/suffrage movement was basically conservative in thrust—in Ian Tyrrell's words, intended to "advance the women's culture of evangelical domesticity" rather than to move women into politics or politics in a progressive direction.[16] This judgment has begun to give way in two directions. One interpretive strategy has been to learn more about the diversity of women's suffrage activism in this early period. Audrey Oldfield, in her detailed study of Australian suffragism state by state, emphasizes the substantial number of suffrage leaders who were secularists, not WCTU evangelicals, associated with the Australian Labor Party, and linked to wage-earning women.[17] Thus, she shifts the emphasis from the WCTU to the larger political environment, and demonstrates that woman suffragism in Australia and New Zealand flourished as part of a political context of expanding reform ambition and maturing working-class activism. These same elements contributed, at about the same time, to the rise of populism in the United States.

A second analytic strategy has been to reexamine the political and ideological content of the WCTU itself. As Tyrrell argues, the WCTU's evangelical roots lent it a critical perspective on the commercial and material preoccupations of advancing capitalism. In England, temperance/suffragists and leaders of the World's WCTU were women like Margaret Bright Lucas and Hannah Whitehall Smith, from families long at the cutting edge of British liberalism. In the western United States, where the WCTU was an important and progressive locale for women's activism in the late 1880s, the WCTU was a substantial source for the political upsurge of populism. Willard herself played a significant role in the early stages of the People's Party and state WCTU leaders included fiery populist radicals like Mary Lease of Kansas. In the United States, these political links were crucial to (although not always credited with) the first successes of woman suffrage. The first genuinely popular political campaigns for woman suffrage, in the 1890s, were in states where insurgent populist parties were strong. Colorado was the first state (as opposed to territory) in which voters authorized woman suffrage in a popular referendum; this took place in 1893, the same year as women won the vote in New Zealand. The second successful voter referendum was in Idaho, the next year. There were also important campaigns in Kansas (1894) and California (1896) which reflected populist support.

While the WCTU's class and economic politics demonstrated a significant left-leaning bent, its moralistic approach to the family and to sexuality justifies the label conservative. Granting this, it is important to observe that similarly conservative sexual and familial politics also characterized the Socialist parties of the period. Indeed, for the United States Mari Jo Buhle has demonstrated that populist moralism was crucial to the translation of socialism, which had been marginalized in German immigrant communities, into a genuinely American idiom.[18] For native-born women, she demonstrates that the WCTU was frequently a conduit into socialism: Ella Reeve Bloor, legendary founder of the U.S. Communist Party, got her political start in the WCTU. In the U.S., in Australia, and elsewhere, the Victorian, traditional perspective of moral reform movements on sex roles and the family was welcomed by socialists as a way to reinforce domestic peace in the working-class family; it may even have eased the way for working-class feminism.

Similar limits operated in temperance/suffragism with respect to race. With the notable exception of New Zealand, where the woman suffrage campaign included Maori women, the WCTU's record on women of color was disappointing. Over and over, the alleged inclusiveness of the WCTU's vision of a worldwide reform movement of politically empowered women gave way to claims about the barbarism or political incapacity of nonwhite peoples. On tour around England to raise international awareness of the plight of her people in the United States, African American suffragist Ida B. Wells charged Frances Willard with aiding and abetting the epidemic of lynchings in the southern states by her readiness to accept the portrait of black people as fundamentally immoral.[19] In Australia, as Oldfied describes. a superficial racial universalism quickly gave way to the refusal to include Aboriginal women in the 1902 federal act of enfranchisement. But again, these same limitations were true of working-class, socialist and left-leaning politics. Queensland, where the racialism of the suffragists was the most explicit and aggressive, was the Australian state with the closest ties between suffragists and the Labor Party.[20]

Cheryll Walker's work on South Africa is most revealing of this pattern. Woman suffragism, which was first brought to the Cape Colony in 1895 by the World's WCTU, was aided and supported by the rise of the South African Labor Party. For several decades, woman suffragists negotiated the treacherous waters of South African racial politics by taking the position that women should vote according to the same rules as men; in the Cape, this would have included colored and Indian women. Finally, in the 1920s, when the Labor Party enrolled in the campaign to remove Cape Coloreds from the voting rolls, woman suffragists easily gave in on principle and acceded to this exclusion, earning the aid of the ascendant National Party and the rapid resolution of their demands. Despite what she judges to be the ultimate conservatism of these developments, Walker nonetheless comments on the fact that the movement's "early sponsorship was from the left."[21] Ian Tyrrell has thoughtfully explored the contradictions between the WCTU's decided commitment to Anglo-Saxon superiority and the fact that its deepest criticisms were reserved for the moral failings of British and American society. But here too, this constitutes a similarity to rather than a difference from socialism in the age of empire.

Woman Suffrage in the Second Socialist International

In the early twentieth century, an even more openly and aggressively feminist movement began to develop within international socialism, with political equality one of its most consistent demands. The largest socialist women's movements were in Germany, the United States, and Austria, but there was also activity in Italy, France, Russia, all of Scandinavia, the Netherlands, Australia, Ireland, South Africa, Central and Eastern Europe, the southern cone of Latin America, and elsewhere.[22]

The figure most identified with this international socialist women's effusion was Clara Zetkin. Through the 1890s Zetkin forged within the German Social Democratic Party a socialist women's program and practice that became the prototype for women in socialist parties around the world. To take just one example, a socialist women's organization, the Feminist Center, operated in Argentina from 1906 through 1912, advocating the Second International feminist platform, which included woman suffrage and special labor legislation for women.[23] From 1907 to 1915, the size and vigor of this worldwide socialist women's network constituted a sort of informal Women's International, with annual conferences. International Women's Day, which is now celebrated around the world, and Women's History Month, which American feminists celebrate in March, are the lineal descendants of the International Proletarian Women's Day first authorized by the 1910 international socialist women's conference.

Socialists first celebrated "Women's Day" in the United States in 1909, as part of their internationally-authorized campaign for woman suffrage.[24] Zetkin picked it up and institutionalized the practice within the International in 1910. The holiday became a solely Communist observance in the 1920s, until the American women's liberation movement, itself inspired by international Communist women activists, reimported the celebration to the United States in the 1960s. In the late 1970s the holiday went through one more political transformation in the United States, and it became the federally mandated Women's History Month.[25]

Most accounts of the embattled socialist-feminists of the early twentieth century emphasize either their struggles with the sexism of male socialists or their challenge to middle-class women's movements, but it was really the *balance* they struck, always fragile and often upset, between these two political forces that determined their political environment.[26] In several of the leading socialist parties, the tension between socialism and feminism led to open conflict among socialist women leaders themselves. Among German socialist women, for instance, Zetkin's loyalty to international socialism was counterpoised to (and balanced by) Lily Braun's greater inclination to the independent women's movement. There were similar sororal antagonisms in the French party between Elizabeth Renaud and Louise Saumoneau, and in Italy between Anna Kulisckoff and Anna Mozzoni.[27] But resisting the temptation to choose sides or to designate one position alone as correct, one can read such conflicts as an expression of the creative tension buried within socialist feminism and of the shifting and unstable but distinct and authentic political territory it occupied.

The issue of woman suffrage was at the very center of—the virtual expression of—the balance socialist women struck between the nonsocialist women's movement and the male-dominated socialist left. Had these women not forced their perspective forward within their parties, woman suffrage would have languished as a principle tainted by socialism but not really sustained by it. On the other hand, had it not been for the degree of autonomy socialist women were able to sustain within their parties from the mid-1890s on, and the new classes of women to whom they brought the issue, the demand for woman suffrage probably would not have been revived and placed at the center of a militant, mass modern women's movement.

Zetkin first succeeded in getting the German Social Democratic Party to adopt the explicit endorsement of political rights "without distinction of sex" in 1891. For decades, socialist men had been thwarting suffrage petitioners by objecting that women were too reactionary to risk enfranchising. This time Zetkin responded that the vote "was a means to assemble the masses, to organize and educate them," and that it was precisely political organizing, including working for the vote, that would "educate" women out of whatever relative "backwardness" they suffered.[28] Within the International, the first pro-woman-suffrage resolution was passed in 1900, but particular national parties continued to set aside demands for woman suffrage to concentrate on universal manhood suffrage. The campaign led by Zetkin to strengthen organized socialism's commitment to woman suffrage coincided with the first all-women's international socialist conference, at Stuttgart, Germany in 1907. There the International finally accepted the principle that political equality for women was a noncontingent, fundamental demand that socialist parties must pursue "strenuously." A plank was adopted insisting "the socialist parties of all countries have a duty to struggle energetically for the introduction of universal suffrage for women."[29]

Women working from within socialist parties liked to argue that the bourgeois case for woman suffrage was a defense of property and individual privilege, while they demanded the vote as a weapon of working-class power. While full discussion of this issue cannot be included here, two points should be noted: first, that property qualifications on women's voting had at least as much to do with marital status as class; and second, that many of the leading nonsocialist suffragists called for universal woman suffrage, without property restrictions.

What really distinguished socialist woman suffragism from the bourgeois variant was the link it made between women workers and political equality. The distinctively socialist argument for woman suffrage rested on the recognition that the increasingly public character of women's labor had to be matched with an equally public political role. Charlotte Perkins Gilman, whose historical account of women's evolution toward emancipation is indistinguishable from Frederick Engels's, was a major force in popularizing the socialist approach to women's equality throughout the nonsocialist women's movement in America.[30] "The demand for woman suffrage results from the economic and social revolutions provoked by the capitalist mode of production," resolved a socialist women's conference in 1904, "but in particular from the revolutionary change in labor and the status and consciousness of women."[31] In the United States, England, and elsewhere, such economic arguments came to be widely accepted among nonsocialist suffragists, which is an indication of the degree to which socialist women led the larger suffrage movement into new territory.

Substantive support for woman suffrage within socialism required overcoming the powerful heritage of socialist and trade union hostility to wage-earning women. Previously, female wage earning had generally been decried as an index of working-class degradation; in the socialist utopia, adult women would be relieved of the necessity to earn a wage. After the 1890s this was much less the case. The tradition of "proletarian sexism" left its mark, however, in the policy of special regulation of women workers, offered as protection for the most vulnerable in the labor market but actually functioning to keep women in a separate and unequal sector of the labor force.[32]

Through the 1880s, laws to regulate the wage relation only for women workers were advocated in male-dominated trade unions and socialist movements, but women activists, including those who concentrated on organizing wage earners and who accepted the desirability of state regulation of the wage relation, opposed such selective legislation for women only. In England, the conflict between these two positions occurred in the Fabian Society over the 1896 Factory Act. Socialist–feminists, among them Elizabeth Cady Stanton's daughter Harriot Stanton Blatch, criticized the limitation of hours among women workers, while Beatrice Webb, representing the classic trade union position and the leading faction within the Fabians, argued (successfully) for laws against exploitation but only of women workers.[33] In the complex interactions on behalf of suffragism within the Second International, support for sex-based labor legislation seems to have been the price extracted from women for substantive support from socialist men for woman suffrage. Zetkin, who had attacked special restrictions on working women in 1889, changed her position in 1893, now faithfully advocating special labor legislation for women.

Organizationally, the intermediate position of socialist suffragists led to the twin principles of autonomy for women's organizing in socialist parties and antagonism to collaboration with nonsocialist suffragists. Of these, hostility to bourgeois women's efforts was the more intensely expressed, perhaps because they represented such serious competition. The initial impulse for the international socialist movement to organize working women in the 1890s, after decades of inactivity, was the necessity of countering the organizational inroads that nonsocialist women were making among female wage earners. Barbara Clements argues that the great Russian socialist Aleksandria Kollantai was drawn to the organizing of working women and to feminist issues by the fear that the bourgeois women's movement was becoming too influential among working-class women.[34]

In 1896 Zetkin made hostility to the nonsocialist women's movement a fundamental principle of socialist women's organizing in Germany. Despite the fact that their programs were largely the same, Zetkin argued fiercely against any collaboration between women in the proletarian and bourgeois movements and struggled constantly (if futilely) to draw the line between the two. In 1907, Zetkin overcame strong opposition from Austrians and Americans to establish noncooperation with bourgeois suffragists as the official policy for socialist women around the world. Like the concessions that Zetkin and other socialist women made to sex-based labor legislation, anticollaborationism helped to offset the innovation represented by strong support for woman suffrage from a socialist platform. Anticollaborationism was more important rhetorically than organizationally, and was honored as frequently in the breach as in the observance. In the United States socialist women kept their sectarian distance from their "enemy sisters" only in New York City; elsewhere there was considerable cooperation throughout the 1910s, especially around votes for women.[35]

Although Zetkin's strongest rhetorical challenges were directed at bourgeois suffragists, she also fought to keep socialist women from being overwhelmed organizationally by men within socialism. In structural terms, this commitment to autonomy within socialism was expressed by organizing women separately from men within the Socialist Party, a corollary to the practice of organizing them separately from the nonsocialist women's movement. The most vigorous and powerful of the national socialist women's movements—those in the United States, Austria, and Scandinavia—followed the lead of the Germans and organized women separately from men. In the United States, socialist women had their own organization, the Socialist Women's National Union, even before Eugene V. Debs formed the Socialist Party in 1901; in 1908 it metamorphosed into the Women's National Committee of the Socialist Party, USA. To be sure, in Germany this strategy was dictated by laws that prohibited women from engaging in political activities.[36] (By definition, an all-female organization could not be political.) But the separate organization of women within socialism served an enormously important positive function as well, making it possible to set up the infrastructure of a semiautonomous women's movement and to nurture an entire generation of socialist women leaders. Indeed, when in 1908 the repeal of the German anti-association laws led the leaders of the Social Democratic Party to abolish separate women's organizations, Zetkin fought furiously against this action, which she felt would lead to women's eventual disempowerment within German socialism. She lost, and her own power within the Social Democratic Party declined.

Such semiautonomous socialist women's organizations never developed in France or Italy, which may be one of the reasons why woman suffrage did not come to either country in the years immediately after World War I. Despite the fact that the socialist parties in both countries formally supported woman suffrage and that, at least in France, there was a nonsocialist woman suffrage movement of some size, the absence of the link between the two may well have been critical. Finland serves as a fitting counterexample. There the Social Democratic Party was unusually hospitable to feminists within the party, and a large socialist women's network developed, which played a major role in the first victory for woman suffrage in Europe, in 1906.

Feminist Internationalism: Militant Suffragism around the World

The emergence of a newly militant suffragism, influenced by the upsurge of socialist politics after 1890 but ideologically and organizationally independent of it, is the third source for the great growth of the woman suffrage movement internationally. While WCTU suffragists translated the goal of political equality into a familiar, female-friendly idiom, and suffragists within socialist parties prepared the way for wage earners' suffragism, these independent militant suffragists made their contribution to the revival of suffragism by linking it to a fundamental challenge to gender definitions and relations, and adding a whole new level of tactical radicalism to suffrage agitation. This independent militancy was decidedly internationalist, both in spirit and in substance. Its roots were in England, but its branches reached out not only to Western Europe and North America but also to China, South America, Central Europe, and elsewhere.

This phenomenon of independent militant suffragism had its origins in the activity of disruptive suffrage radicals who surfaced in England about 1906 and who were dismissed by the press as "suffragettes," originally a term of opprobrium that the women themselves embraced and inverted. The British suffragettes are one of the few aspects of the international woman suffrage movement that has entered general historical consciousness, but study of them has until recently been limited largely to the complex and contradictory Pankhurst family, whose turn to conservative patriotism during the war added considerable fuel to the thesis of suffragism's ultimate conservatism. However, a new generation of women's historians is offering a revisionist history of suffrage militance in England that better appreciates its links with the left. They emphasize that the radicalization of the suffrage movement in Britain reached far beyond the Pankhurst family; also that its roots lay in the organization of working-class women and the dedication of activists inspired by, but independent of, organized socialism.[37]

The militant revival of British suffragism predates the involvement of the Pankhursts and can be traced to a suffrage movement among Lancashire textile workers in the 1890s. Middle-class suffragists with socialist inclinations turned to organizations of working-class women, notably the female textile workers' unions, to generate a working-women's suffrage movement. The tactics of this new kind of suffragism were borrowed from trade unionism and emphasized "open-air campaigning, factory-gate meetings and street corner speaking."[38] Politically, its goal was to pressure the fledgling Labour Party to provide a parliamentary route for woman suffrage. The Pankhursts, a family closely associated with Labour, began their suffrage work within this framework. In 1903 they organized the Women's Social and Political Union (WSPU), which initially emphasized public agitation, working-class organization, and Labour Party political links.

In 1906 the WSPU moved its operations from Manchester to London to concentrate on organizing mass public demonstrations, the likes of which had never been seen in any women-led movement.[39] Soon other British suffrage societies, including the once conventional National Union of Women's Suffrage Societies (NUWSS), were organizing their own "monster demonstrations" for suffrage. By 1911 militant modern tactics under various organizational labels dominated the British suffrage movement.

As the WSPU moved away from its working-class origins, it developed its own highly influential form of civil disobedience, borrowed from the "political law breaking" tradition of Irish nationalism.[40] Christabel Pankhurst, referring in 1908 to the "Fenian outrages in Manchester and the blowing up of Clerkenwell Gaol," wondered "how anybody after that can say that militant methods are not effectual."[41] This civil disobedience strain took on an increasingly violent air, culminating in firebombs and martyrdom on the part of the suffragettes and punitive forced feeding on the part of the British state. Sandra Holton argues that the shift from mass action to illegal tactics alienated many working-class women, who expressed their suffragism at giant demonstrations rather than in prison. Nonetheless, the political theater of arrests and forced feedings intensified women's militance around the world.

These independent suffrage militants came to stand for a modern, post-Victorian approach to building a mass woman-suffrage movement. The term *suffragette* conjured up radical challenges to dominant definitions of womanhood. Until this point, bourgeois femininity—in Europe, North America, and their cultural outlands—was marked by a devotion to the separation of the domestic and private world of women and the public and political world of men. Suffragette militance literally took women out of the parlor and into the streets. Parades, outdoor demonstrations, street-corner meetings—these were the marks of modern suffrage agitation. Inasmuch as wage-earning women provided the female army that first breached the walls around the public realm, suffragette militance was initially "viewed as a specifically working-class initiative." But the challenge to cloistered femininity that it expressed eventually drew women of all classes.[42] Indeed, the more upper-class the women who made the challenges to traditional sex roles, the more effective the challenges were.

In the same way as they had pioneered mass suffrage demonstrations, the Pankhursts inaugurated and then abandoned to other British suffragists the strategy of pressuring the

Labour Party to support woman suffrage. This meant countering the Labour Party's insistence that so long as votes for men were bound by property limitation, it could not support the suffragists' position of votes for women on the same terms as men; it would only endorse expansion of suffrage to all adults of both sexes. About the same time as the WSPU shifted from Manchester to London, from mass demonstrations to civil disobedience, and from a working-class base to elite cadres, the WSPU repudiated Labour as a lost cause and started to move to the right, a shift that has weighed heavily in most histories British suffrage militance. But the NUWSS took up the paths that the Pankhursts pioneered, hammering away at Labour's objections to woman suffrage. In 1911 this persistence was rewarded by Labour's agreement to support a compromise bill, which set the level of female enfranchisement at an intermediate position, between propertied and adult. The bill failed when the Liberal Party deserted it, but the détente between suffrage and Labour held firm.

The example of the British suffragettes had tremendous international influence, attributable to the extensive worldwide publicity they worked so hard to get. The International Woman Suffrage Association (IWSA), established in 1902, provided a conduit for their influence, much as the Second International did for the socialist suffragism of Zetkin and Kollontai. The IWSA had been designed to meet every five years, but it soon found itself meeting much more frequently, infused with the spirit of suffragette militance.[43] In 1906 the IWSA met in Copenhagen, and delegates brought back news of the British militants to Hungary, Russia, and elsewhere.[44] In 1909 it met in London, and delegates were treated to various demonstrations of militant tactics—mass marches, civil disobedience, hunger strikes. In 1913, in conjunction with IWSA meetings in Budapest, Sylvia Pankhurst toured Central Europe to talk about her working-class-based version of militance.[45]

Socialist women of the Second International, who had helped to inspire the formation of the IWSA by their example, were in turn much influenced by the feminist militance it spread. Despite their oft-repeated opposition to "collaboration" with "bourgeois suffragists," they could not resist the energy of the suffragette example; the mass demonstrations of International Proletarian Women's Day from 1911 through 1913 may have been imitations of the "monster parades" organized earlier by British militants.[46]

American suffragists were especially quick to pick up the inspiration of the British militants. Many of them were influenced by and sympathetic to socialism, although they were not party members. Harriot Stanton Blatch, herself a veteran of British Fabianism in the 1890s, returned to the United States to organize a working-class-based, tactically militant, independent woman suffrage insurgency. After American women won the vote, Blatch became an active member of the Socialist Party and ran for office on its ticket. In San Francisco, trade union activist Maud Younger ("the millionaire waitress") organized the Working Women's Suffrage Society.[47] By 1913 tens of thousands of women were marching in New York City, and the example of suffrage parades was spreading across the country. Despite the dictums of the Second International, American socialist women cooperated closely with these independent militants. In California in 1911, in Wisconsin in 1912, and even in New York, it was often difficult to distinguish the two groups or to predict which feminists would show up inside the Socialist Party and which would be outside. In 1913 this suffrage revival culminated with a mass suffrage parade in Washington, D.C., and the creation of a national suffragette society, the National Woman's Party.[48]

The suffragette example also shaped the Irish woman suffrage movement, which was only fitting, given the role that Irish nationalists played in holding up a final parliamentary solution to votes for women in England. The Catholicism of France and Italy is often cited as an explanation for their outrageously delayed enfranchisement of women there, but the influence of Catholicism proved no serious barrier to the flourishing of militant suffragism in Ireland. The leading figure here was Hanna Sheehy-Skeffington, a socialist, friend of Irish labor, and militant suffragist. Inspired by the Pankhursts, she organized the Irish Women's Franchise League, which heckled politicians, held demonstrations, and engaged in that signature suffragette activity, breaking windows with stones. In their struggle to influence the shape of the coming Irish nation, the suffragists eventually gained the support of the Irish Labour Party. In 1922, in their new republic, Irish women got the vote on equal terms with men, six years before the British.[49]

Nor was it only Europeans and North Americans who responded to the feminist excitement of the British suffragettes. In 1912 in Nanking, China, the Woman Suffrage Alliance, an independent feminist group, petitioned the provisional parliament to "enact equality of the sexes and recognize women's right to vote." Convinced that the men would not take their demand seriously, they armed themselves with pistols, stormed the parliament building three days in a row, and had to be dragged off by guards. In imitation of the WSPU, they broke windows, "drenching their hands in fresh blood." Around the world, suffragette sisters celebrated their dedication. The WSPU itself sent a message of support, and in New York, the president of the suffrage organization paraded under a sign declaring "Catching Up with China."[50] Argentinian suffragists, exasperated with a ridiculously limited municipal suffrage, organized the Partido Feminista Nacional, in imitation of the British WSPU.[51]

World War I and Votes for Women: Moving into a New Era

The women of most European and North American countries won the formal right to vote in the years during and immediately after World War I. But to grant the war itself responsibility for enfranchising women is, in the words of French suffrage historians Steven Hause and Anne Kenney, a way of denying the "generations of feminist labor that made enfranchisement possible."[52] Nor is the correlation quite so precise. Combatant countries (France, Italy, and Belgium) did not enfranchise women at that time, while neutral nations (the Netherlands and the Scandinavian countries) were among the first to do so. In some countries, such as Denmark and Iceland, the war held up the enfranchisement of women, the forces for which were already in place by 1914. In England and the United States, the war provided time (and a suprapartisan environment) for the maturation of the political forces necessary to enfranchise women. In Germany and Austria, where defeat and revolution brought in socialist governments that enfranchised women, a more direct causal role can be attributed to the war. But a case can be also made that the war had a negative impact on existing woman suffrage movements. In France, the war was actually "a setback for the woman suffrage movement."[53] The majority of suffragists in combatant countries advocated preparedness, war work, and service to the state. In Germany, socialist and nonsocialist suffrage women both formally embraced the war. In England, Christabel and Emmeline Pankhurst became intensely prowar, renaming their *Suffragette* magazine *Britannia*. Conservative political forces were set in motion that dominated European politics for the next twenty-five years and in which reaction against the gains made with respect to sexual equality was a significant component. In Italy, in 1923, Mussolini briefly played the prosuffrage card, instituting municipal suffrage for women just as local elections were being undermined. By 1930 woman suffrage and Italian feminism in general had collapsed.[54] In Italy and France, women had to wait until the end of a *second* world war to gain the vote.

While most suffragists became prowar enthusiasts, a minority were determinedly antiwar. In England, Sylvia Pankhurst broke with her mother and sister to become a leading antiwar feminist. Outside of England, independent militants tended to the antiwar camp.

In the United States, the National Woman's Party resisted prowar jingoism, becoming the first American organization to run afoul of antisedition laws. In Ireland, Hanna Sheehy-Skeffington became a militant pacifist. The international feminist pacifist network formed by these suffrage activists named itself the Women's International League for Peace and Freedom, and constitutes one of the most important legacies of the prewar suffrage movement.[55] Among women leaders within organized socialism, Clara Zetkin, who had long since been driven from the German Social Democratic Party's leadership, was notable for her opposition to the war.

In the 1920s and 1930s the dynamic of international suffragism shifted away from Europe and North America toward Latin America, the Middle East, and Asia. These post-1920 movements for women's enfranchisement continued to develop in connection with larger working-class movements. Despite the fact that Communists disdained the parliamentary politics that had allowed prewar socialist suffragists to argue their case, left-wing advocates of political equality for women were still able to make some gains. In Indochina and throughout Latin America, for instance, political equality for women was advocated in conjunction with working-class militancy beginning in the 1920s.[56] International networks established before World War I—notably the International Woman Suffrage Association, renamed the International Alliance of Women—also continued to provide a medium for the ideas and legacy of women's enfranchisement to move between nations.

However, it was a new political force, anticolonial nationalist movements, that provided the major crucible for organized efforts for women's enfranchisement after World War I. Important preliminary work has been done in this area by Kumari Jayawardena with respect to Asia, and by Asunción Lavrin and Francesca Miller with respect to Latin America.[57] They have convincingly demonstrated that revolutionary nationalism incubated women's ambitions for political equality in this new period and within this expanded global territory; Asian, Latin American, and Middle Eastern women political activists were both inspired and frustrated by the rising expectations of male-dominated elites, who sought to challenge imperial power and to cultivate political and cultural renewal in their new nations. More research is needed to build on this pioneering scholarship.

Moving the history of woman suffrage movements into the age of revolutionary nationalism would seem to pose a major challenge to the international framework I am advocating, but even here I think we will find that there is much to be gained by tracing the circulation of ideas, individuals, resources, and inspirations between nations. New transnational women's organizations were formed, pan-American and pan-Pacific women's networks linking advocates of women's political equality; first the League of Nations and then the United Nations also facilitated the international spread of ideas of women's political equality. Finally, it is significant to recall the impact that images of fighting women activists from Asia and Latin America, women guerrilla fighters carrying babies on one side and rifles on the other, had in the 1960s on American and European women, who had become alienated from their own traditions of political activism and of struggles for sexual equality. It was as if these historical traditions, set in motion long ago in one part of the globe, returned to their origins several epochs later, able to inspire and educate anew.

Notes

1. Audrey Oldfield, *Woman Suffrage in Australia: A Gift or a Struggle?* (Cambridge: Cambridge University Press, 1992), 212–14; Patricia Grimshaw, *Women's Suffrage in New Zealand* (Auckland: Auckland University Press, 1972); and Katie Spearitt, "New Dawns: First Wave Feminisms 1880–1914," in Kay Saunders and Raymond Evans, eds., *Gender Relations in Australia: Domination and Negotiations* (San Diego: Harcourt, Brace, 1992).

2. Quoted in Werner Thonnesson, *The Emancipation of Women: The Rise and Decline of the Women's Movement in German Social Democracy, 1863–1993* (Bristol: Pluto Press, 1969), 32.

3. Richard J. Evans, *The Feminists: Women's Emancipation Movements in Europe, America, and Australasia, 1840–1920* (London: Croom Helm, 1977).

4. Ibid., 217. See also Ross Evans Paulson, *Women's Suffrage and Prohibition: A Comparative Study of Equality and Social Control* (Glenview, Ill.: Scott, Foresman, 1973), for a similar evaluation of woman suffrage, which applauds rather than criticizes its alleged conservatism.

5. Aileen S. Kraditor, *The Ideas of the Woman Suffrage Movement, 1890–1920* (New York: Columbia University Press, 1965); and William O'Neill, *Everyone Was Brave: The Rise and Fall of Feminism in America* (Chicago: Quadrangle Books, 1969). Ian Tyrrell reexamines Kraditor's influential thesis that over time suffragists shifted from "justice" to "expediency" claims to the vote in *Woman's World, Woman's Empire: The Woman's Christian Temperance Union in International Perspective, 1800–1930* (Chapel Hill: University of North Carolina Press, 1991).

6. Bunkle, "The Origins of the Women's Movement in New Zealand," in Bunkle and Beryl Hughes, eds., *Women in New Zealand Society* (Auckland: George Allen and Unwin, 1980), 52–76.

7. Ellen Carol DuBois, *Feminism and Suffrage: The Emergence of an Independent Women's Movement in America, 1848–1869* (Ithaca: Cornell University Press, 1978).

8. Ian Tyrrell, "American Exceptionalism in an Age of International History," *American Historical Review*, 96, 4 (1991): 1031–55.

9. Ellen C. DuBois, "The Radicalism of the Woman Suffrage Movement: Notes toward the Reconstruction of American Feminism," *Feminist Studies* 3 (1975): 63–71.

10. Quoted in Rosalind Petchevsky, "Dissolving the Hyphen: A Report on Marxist-Feminist Groups," in Zillah Eisenstein, ed., *Capitalist Patriarchy and the Case for Socialist Feminism* (New York: Monthly Review Press, 1979), 375.

11. Ruth Bordin, *Women and Temperance: The Quest for Power and Liberty, 1873–1900* (Philadelphia: Temple University Press, 1981).

12. Tyrrell, *Woman's World*, 19.

13. Grimshaw, *Women's Suffrage in New Zealand*, 37.

14. Sylvia Pankhurst, *The Suffragette Movement*, (London: Virago, 1977 [1931]), 178.

15. Diane Kirkby, *Alice Henry: The Power of Pen and Voice* (Melbourne: Cambridge University Press, 1991).

16. Tyrrell, *Woman's World*, 221.

17. Oldfield, *Woman Suffrage in Australia*, 21. This was made most clear to me in Diane Kirkby's excellent biography of Alice Henry, which begins with a portrait of the Australian suffrage movement.

18. Mari Jo Buhle, *Women and American Socialism, 1870–1920* (Urbana: University of Illinois Press, 1981).

19. Vron Ware, *Beyond the Pale: White Women, Racism, and History* (London and New York: Verso, 1992), ch. 2.

20. Oldfield, *Woman Suffrage in Australia*, 63.

21. Cheryll Walker, *The Women's Suffrage Movement in South Africa* (Cape Town: University of Cape Town Press, 1979), 26.

22. Marilyn J. Boxer and Jean H. Quataert, eds., *Socialist Women: European Socialist Feminism in the Nineteenth and Early Twentieth Centuries* (New York: Elsevier North-Holland, 1978); Richard J. Evans, *Comrades and Sisters: Feminism, Socialism and Pacifism in Europe, 1870–1945* (New York: St. Martin's, 1987); Evans, *The Feminists*; Charles Sowerwine, "The Socialist Women's Movement from 1850 to 1940," in Renate Bridenthal, Claudia Koontz, and Susan Stuard, eds., *Becoming Visible: Women in European History*, 2nd ed. (Boston: Houghton Mifflin, 1987); Jane Slaughter and Robert Kern, eds., *European Women on the Left: Socialist, Feminism and the Problems Faced by Political Women, 1880–Present* (Westport, Conn.: Greenwood Press, 1981).

23. Cynthia Little, "Education, Philanthropy, and Feminism: Components of Argentine Womanhood, 1860–1926," in Asunción Lavrin, ed., *Latin American Women: Historic Perspectives* (Westport, Conn.: Greenwood Press, 1978). On Second International feminism in South Africa, see Cheryll Walker, *The Women's Suffrage Movement in South Africa*. On Galicia, see Martha Boyachevsky-Chomiak, "Socialism and Feminism: The First Stages of Women's Organizations in the Eastern Part of the Austrian Empire," in Tova Yedlin, ed., *Women in Eastern Europe and the Soviet Union* (Ottawa: Carleton University Press, 1975).

24. Meredith Tax, *Rising of the Women: Feminist Solidarity and Class Conflict, 1880–1917* (New York: Monthly Review Press, 1980), 188.

25. Temma Kaplan, "On the Socialist Origins of International Women's Day," *Feminist Studies* 11 (1985).

26. Mari Jo Buhle, "Women and the Socialist Party, 1901–1914," *Radical America* 4 (1970); Boxer and Quataert, eds., *Socialist Women*.

27. Sowerwine, "The Socialist Women's Movement from 1850 to 1940," 409.

28. Jean H. Quataert, *Reluctant Feminists in German Social Democracy, 1885–1917* (Princeton: Princeton University Press, 1979), 94.

29. Sowerwine, "The Socialist Women's Movement from 1850 to 1940," 416.

30. Buhle, *Women and American Socialism*, ch. 2.

31. Thonnesson, *The Emancipation of Women*, 63.

32. Alice Kessler Harris, *Out to Work: A History of Wage-Earning Women in the United States* (New York: Oxford University Press, 1982), ch. 7. In her later work, Kessler Harris has backed away from this assessment to some degree; see Alice Kessler Harris, *A Woman's Wage: Historical Meanings and Social Consequences* (Lexington: University of Kentucky Press, 1989).

33. Polly Beals, "Fabian Feminism: Gender, Politics and Culture in London, 1880–1930" (Ph.D. diss., Rutgers University, 1989).

34. Barbara Clements, *Bolshevik Feminist: The Life of Aleksandria Kollontai* (Bloomington: Indiana University Press, 1979), 59. Similarly, Linda Edmonson argues that "such was the abhorrence felt by Orthodox Marxists toward the idea of separate women's organisations that the potential value of the female proletariat went almost unnoticed" until the nonbourgeois women's movement forced it upon socialists' attention; see Linda Edmonson, *Feminism in Russia, 1900–1917* (Stanford: Stanford University Press, 1984), 171.

35. John D. Buenker, "The Politics of Mutual Frustration: Socialists and Suffragists in New York and Wisconsin," in Sally Miller, ed., *Flawed Liberation: Socialism and Feminism* (Westport, Conn.: Greenwood Press, 1981).

36. Kollontai's biographer says that when Kollontai discovered that the separate organizing of socialist women, to which she was passionately committed in Russia, was the child of German necessity, she was astonished; Clements, *Bolshevik Feminist*, 64.

37. Sandra Stanley Holton, *Feminism and Democracy: Women's Suffrage and Reform Politics in Britain, 1900–1918* (Cambridge: Cambridge University Press, 1986); Jill Liddington and Jill Norris, *One Hand Tied behind Us: The Rise of the Women's Suffrage Movement* (London: Virago, 1978); Lisa Tickner, *The Spectacle of Women: Imagery of the Suffrage Campaign, 1907–1914* (London: Chatto and Windus, 1987). In addition, there is another group of contemporary feminist historians of British suffragism who have emphasized instead the sexual politics—as anticipating modern antipornography feminism—especially under Christabel Pankhurst's leadership. See Susan Kingsley Kent, *Sex and Suffrage in Britain 1860–1914* (Princeton: Princeton University Press, 1987); and Sheila Jeffreys, *The Spinster and Her Enemies: Feminism and Sexuality, 1880–1930* (London: Pandora Press, 1985).

38. Holton, *Feminism and Democracy*, 33.

39. Sylvia Pankhurst, *The Suffragette Movement*, 195.

40. Rosemary Cullen Owens, *Smashing Times: A History of the Irish Woman Suffrage Movement, 1889–1922* (Dublin: Attic Press, 1984), 40.

41. Quoted in Jane Marcus, ed., *Suffrage and the Pankhursts* (London: Routledge and Kegan Paul, 1987), 48.

42. Holton, *Feminism and Democracy*, 35; Ellen Carol DuBois, "Working Women, Class Relations and Suffrage Militance: Harriot Stanton Blatch and the New York Woman Suffrage Movement, 1894–1907," *Journal of American History* 74, 1 (1987): 34–58.

43. Evans, *The Feminists*, 248–53; Edith F. Hurwitz, "The International Sisterhood," in Renate Bridenthal and Claudia Koontz, eds., *Becoming Visible: Women in European History*, 1st ed. (Boston: Houghton Mifflin, 1977).

44. International Council of Women, *Women in a Changing World: The Dynamic Story of the International Council of Women since 1888* (London: Routledge and Kegan Paul, 1966).

45. Pankhurst, *The Suffragette Movement*, 535.

46. Evans, *Comrades and Sisters*, 68–75.

47. Susan L. Englander, *Class Conflict and Coalition in the California Woman Suffrage Movement, 1907–1917* (Lewiston, N.Y.: Mellen Research University Press, 1992); DuBois, "Working Women."

48. Buhle, *Women and American Socialism*; Meredith Tax, *Rising of the Women*; Christine Lunardini, *From Equal Suffrage to Equal Rights: Alice Paul and the National Woman's Party, 1910–1928* (New York: New York University Press, 1986).

49. Leah Levenson and Jerry H. Natterstad, *Hanna Sheehy-Skeffington: Irish Feminist* (Syracuse: Syracuse University Press, 1986), 37.

50. Ono Kazuko, *Chinese Women in a Century of Revolution, 1850–1950* (Stanford: Stanford University Press, 1989), 80–92.

51. Ann Pescatello, *Power and Pawn: The Female in Iberian Families, Societies and Cultures* (Westport, Conn.: Greenwood Press, 1976), 191.

52. Steven C. Hause and Anne R. Kenney, *Women's Suffrage and Social Politics in the French Third Republic* (Princeton: Princeton University Press, 1984).

53. Hause and Kenney, *Women's Suffrage and Social Politics*; Evans, *The Feminists*, 223.

54. Donald Meyer, *Sex and Power: The Rise of Women in America, Russia, Sweden and Italy* (Middletown, Conn.: Wesleyan University Press, 1987), 37.

55. Gertrude Bussey and Margaret Tims, *Pioneers for Peace: Women's International League for Peace and Freedom, 1915–1965* (Oxford: Alden Press, 1980 [1967]).

56. Sonia Kruks, Rayna Rapp, and Marilyn Young, eds., *Promissory Notes: Women in the Transition to Socialism* (New York: Monthly Review Press, 1987).

57. The English-language scholarship on post-1920 suffrage movements is just beginning to be accumulated. Kumari Jayawardena, *Feminism and Nationalism in the Third World* (London: Zed Books, 1986); Francesca Miller, *Latin American Women and the Search for Social Justice* (Stanford: Stanford University Press, 1992); Asuncíon Lavrin, ed., *Latin American Women: Historic Perspectives.*

19

In Politics to Stay: Black Women Leaders and Party Politics in the 1920s

Evelyn Brooks Higginbotham

Between 1900 and 1930 more than 1.5 million black men and women migrated from the South to the urban North. The massive trek, actually begun in the last decade of the nineteenth century, shifted into high gear during World War I, when wartime demands from northern industry promised employment and, most of all, escape from the southern way of life—from its boll-weevil-ravaged sharecrop farming and from its segregation, disfranchisement, and lynching. In the decade between 1910 and 1920 the black population soared in such cities as Chicago (from 44,103 to 109,458), Detroit (from 5,741 to 40,878), Cleveland (from 8,448 to 34,451), New York (from 91,709 to 152,467), and Philadelphia (from 84,459 to 134,229).[1] Concentrated in the ghettos of urban centers, the migrants soon transformed their restricted residential opportunities into political opportunity.

With migration stepped up to even higher levels between 1920 and 1930, the growing significance of the black vote did not escape the attention of machine politicians. Blacks played an especially influential role in Chicago's machine politics. For instance, in the city's closely contested mayoral race in 1915, the black vote was critical to the victory of Republican William Hale Thompson. Moreover, growing black populations in the northern cities and border states precipitated the rise of black officeholders. In the first three decades of the twentieth century blacks increasingly sent their own to state legislatures, city councils, judgeships, and clerkships. In 1928 the political clout of Illinois blacks carried Oscar DePriest, the first northern black congressman, to the House of Representatives.[2]

Invisible Politics

Black women played an active and valuable role in the electoral politics of the 1920s, but their role is, too often, overlooked as if an unimportant, even impotent factor in the profound political changes under way. Black political behavior during the early decades of the twentieth century has certainly been analyzed in a number of excellent studies. Unfortunately, the overwhelming majority treat black women as invisible participants, silent members of the black electorate. The literature, much of which was written between the 1930s and 1970s, fails to investigate, to any meaningful extent, either the black female vote or the role of black women leaders in getting out the vote.[3]

While the significance of the female vote has not received serious attention from the traditional literature on black politics, it also has been too easily dismissed by the recent scholarship in women's history. And though a growing body of research has appeared on the suffragist activities among black women leaders, very little is known about their political participation in the decade after the ratification of the Nineteenth Amendment.[4] Feminist scholarship has placed black women's club work firmly within the context of the organizational history of suffragism and has identified such individual leaders as Mary Church Terrell, Ida B. Wells Barnett, and Nannie Helen Burroughs as outspoken champions of women's suffrage in the first two decades of the twentieth century, but this scholarship fails to recognize their continuing political activism after 1920. The passage of the Nineteenth Amendment, according to this research, appears to portend the end rather than the starting point of black women's involvement in electoral politics for the next decade. This assumption is based on the following realities.

On the eve of ratification, the handwriting on the wall boldly read, "The full meaning of the Nineteenth Amendment would be denied to black women." Historians of the woman's suffrage movement have exposed the racist and class biases of white women suffragists.[5] In a deliberate effort to win southern white support, they disassociated their cause from black voting rights issues. The white women's movement abandoned its earlier nineteenth century ties with the black freedom struggle in favor of an alliance with white supremacy. The reversal reflected a fundamental shift not only in strategy, but also in the rationale upon which suffragism had rested. By the late nineteenth and early twentieth centuries, white suffragists argued from the position of expediency rather than justice. The National American Woman Suffrage Association, having adopted a states' rights policy toward its member organizations in 1903, paved the way for its southern wing to argue the expediency of woman's suffrage in nullifying the intent of the Fifteenth Amendment and buttressing the cause of white supremacy in general. An assent, if not a direct contributor to the disfranchisement and segregation of southern blacks of both sexes, the strategy assured the denial of black women's ballots. Carrie Chapman Catt, Alice Paul, Ida Husted Harper, and other luminaries of the women's movement added insult to injury by expressing their racist sensibilities in correspondence, segregated marches, and various public statements. The press reported the hard facts once ratification became reality. In state after state in the South, large numbers of black women turned out to register only to be turned back.[6]

Historian Rosalyn Terborg-Penn draws attention to the suffrage clubs of black women in the states that ratified the woman's vote prior to 1920, but she concludes that the postscript to the passage of the Nineteenth Amendment was one of frustration and disillusionment. By the mid-1920s discontented black feminists, Terborg-Penn posits, turned their eyes away from mainstream electoral politics to the renewed antilynching crusade, social service efforts, and separatist or Third World causes such a the International Council of Women of the Darker Races, Pan-Africanism, and the Marcus Garvey movement.[7] Although her assessment correctly emphasizes the hostile, racially charged environment that black women faced, it underestimates the continuing interest of black women leaders in the electoral process.

The work of Ida Wells Barnett, the great black feminist and antilynching crusader, illustrates the potential of black women leaders in mobilizing voters. Her autobiography tells of her activities with the Alpha Suffrage Club for black women soon after Illinois adopted woman's suffrage in 1913. She credited her club with the election of Oscar DePriest in 1915 as Chicago's first black alderman. The large black turnout also played the decisive role in the victory of William Hale Thompson.[8]

Migration and Woman Suffrage

When America returned to normalcy after World War I, the combined realities of Jim Crow and southern disfranchisement, of northern discrimination in housing and jobs, and of pervasive racism both customary and institutionalized created a set of social conditions as inimical to black progress as had existed in previous generations. Although their grievances were just as pronounced, black women, like their men, did not greet these objective conditions with the same degree of resignation and accommodation that had characterized the era of Booker T. Washington. Rather, their response was one of optimism, reflecting a reevaluation of their circumstances and a transformed subjective perception of their own power to bring about change. This subjective transformation was conditioned by new forces at work—namely, migration and the woman's vote. Both appeared to signal a break with the past.

Thousands upon thousands of migrants of voting age annually left states in the Deep South, where voting restrictions had been most repressive. That these states simultaneously imposed the greatest economic and social restrictions upon blacks accounts for the eagerness of so many to uproot themselves and search for greater economic and political freedom. Unskilled and semiskilled jobs in the northern cities offered wage rates considerably higher than the southern agricultural work in which most of the migrants previously had been engaged. Florette Henri's study of the Great Migration observes that "to farm workers in the South who made perhaps $.75 a day, to urban female domestics who might earn from $1.50 to $3.00 a week, the North during the war years beckoned with factory wages as high as $3.00 to $4.00 a day, and domestic pay of $2.50 a day." Despite the higher cost of living and the drastic reduction of factory employment for blacks after the war ended, the urban North's higher wages and greater economic opportunity relative to the South continued to lure hundreds of thousands of black migrants throughout the 1920s. For black southern migrants, the ballot box, no less than heightened employment opportunity and greater social mobility, served as a badge of freedom from the Jim Crow world they fled.[9]

When viewed as an indicator of voting behavior, employment suggests its positive role within the critical mix of urban opportunities that encouraged black women's political integration. Women constituted a sizable proportion of the northern black labor force. In 1920 the black married women's employment rate stood at five times that of white married women. In the largest northern cities in 1930 between 34 and 44 percent of black households had two or more members employed. Moreover, successive waves of migrants contributed to the growth of economic and social differentiation within the black urban community. The appearance of a black male and female elite composed of lawyers, educators, physicians, ministers, and entrepreneurs reflected a leadership ever mindful of black political interests and the importance of voter mobilization for the realization of those interests.[10]

Harold Gosnell indicates the political consciousness of black women in his classic *Negro Politicians* (1935), the earliest systematic study of urban black political behavior. More attentive to women than subsequent works by social scientists, Gosnell's several studies on Chicago politics were written in the 1920s and 1930s, when the implications of woman's recently acquired right to vote were more consciously observed. Gosnell notes that black women "shared with their men folks an intense interest in politics." He reveals that in the 1923 local election relatively fewer black women than white used the antisuffragist argument as an excuse for not voting. While Gosnell does not dwell on the political mobilization of black women, he clearly acknowledges their importance in augmenting the black vote: "The huge increment in the absolute number of the estimated eligible colored voters between 1910 and 1920 was due largely to the adoption of woman suffrage in 1913 and to the flood of newcomers after 1914."[11] The conflation of woman's suffrage and black urban migration made possible greater political opportunity and leverage for blacks as a group. It also served to broaden black women's perceptions of their own influence and activism. Throughout the 1920s black women leaders, far from abandoning the electoral process, envisioned themselves in politics to stay.

The Black Press and Women's Political Consciousness

The black press served as an important vehicle for promoting the political concerns of black women. Varying in form from lengthy informative articles to mere blurbs, its news announced and promoted organizational activities and noteworthy persons and events rarely covered by the white press. Its pages featured the election or appointment of blacks to prominent and, just as often, quite obscure positions across the nation. Papers such as the *Chicago Defender, New York Age, Pittsburgh Courier, Norfolk Journal and Guide*, and *Baltimore Afro-American* served not only their local markets, but a national one hungry for "race news." The *Chicago Defender*, which had the largest readership of all, is often cited for its influential role in the Great Migration out of the South during World War I. The importance of the black press did not go unrecognized by campaigning politicians. Robert L. Vann, editor of the *Pittsburgh Courier*, was appointed chairman of the publicity committee of the Colored Voters' Division of the Republican National Committee during the 1928 presidential race. Claude A. Barnett, of the Associated Negro Press, was secretary. In fact, the Hoover forces enlisted practically every black news editor on this committee.[12]

Black newspapers frequently reprinted or cited each other's stories along with those from such national magazines as the National Association for the Advancement of Colored People's *Crisis*, the National Urban League's *Opportunity*, and the National Association of Colored Women's *National Notes*. Through the Associated Negro Press important news releases were syndicated in the different papers. Hanes Walton draws attention to the historical role of the black press as a transmitter of political culture—as an agent of political socialization. Its role combated the negative black images presented in the white newspapers. The black press provided the counterorientation to forces affirming black inferiority. In its coverage of women's political activities during the 1920s, it also reinforced the idea of a prominent place for women within black political culture.[13]

The *Baltimore Afro-American*, a weekly during the twenties, concisely illustrates the way black women's political activities were portrayed. In the four issues appearing between 17 September and 16 October 1920, twenty-two articles covered one or another aspect of women's newly acquired right to vote. Three articles presented congratulatory responses by various black and white notables to the ratification of the Nineteenth Amendment. One noted the appointment of Lethia Fleming as head of the black woman's advisory committee to the national Republican Party during the 1920 presidential campaign, while another covered Daneva Donnell's appointment as the only black on the first all-woman jury in an Indianapolis court. Five articles exposed the thwarted attempts of black women to register in the southern states. Nine reported political activities among women in Baltimore. Most of these activities took the form of meetings and rallies. One of the local stories featured the results of the first two days of registration in the city's predominantly black wards and concluded that "where the colored women are organized as in the 14th and 17th wards their registration nearly equals that of the men."[14]

The final three articles on black women and politics were represented in the column "A Primer for Women Voters," written by Augusta T. Chissell. Chissell, a member of the Colored Women's Suffrage Club of Maryland, designed the weekly column as a tool for political education. Readers were invited to write in questions, which she in turn answered.

Question—There are some men who will be up for election in this state in November who have bitterly opposed woman suffrage. What do you think of supporting them?

Answer—Women should weigh this question very carefully, not from the standpoint of resentment but from the standpoint of justice.[15]

Question—What is meant by party platform? And where may I go to be taught how to vote?

Answer—Party platform simply means what either candidate promises to do after he is elected. The Just Government League is conducting a polling booth at its headquarters. . . . You may go there and become acquainted with the whole order of things. You will also do well to attend the Thursday night meetings of the YWCA under the auspices of the Colored Women's Suffrage Club.[16]

Black women leaders used the press to voice their political concerns and programs throughout the 1920s.

Clubwomen and Politics

Even more important to the political activism of black women leaders was the organizational network already in place on the eve of the ratification of the Nineteenth Amendment. The National Association of Colored Women (NACW) had stood at the forefront of the suffragist cause among black women and became the logical springboard for future political work. By the 1920s the NACW came to represent the organizational hub of the women's club movement. It was the linchpin that united hundreds of women's clubs throughout the nation in shared goals and strategies of social service and racial uplift. Divided into districts, under which fell regional and state federations, the elaborate infrastructure established linkages and opened channels of communication between women's organizations in every black community in America. Through its national leaders and committees, plans were centralized and tasks divided. Through its biennial meetings and national magazine, *National Notes*, the NACW functioned as a clearinghouse, providing a communications network for the dissemination of information and the promotion of collective action.[17]

NACW members, largely of middle-class status, received wide coverage in the black press, and the leaders at the state and national levels were, more often than not, prominent in other progressive groups with respect to racial advancement, such as the National Association for the Advancement of Colored People (NAACP), the National Urban League, and the Commission on Interracial Cooperation. Some of these same leaders also occupied high places of influence within major religious organizations.[18] Tullia Hamilton's study of the first generation of NACW leaders reveals their privileged status vis-à-vis the great majority of black women. Most of the 108 leaders identified by Hamilton had been born in the South between 1860 and 1885 but had settled in the North a decade or two prior to the onslaught of migrants during the World War I period. Unlike the masses of uneducated and unskilled black women who were restricted to domestic service and other menial employment, NACW leaders enjoyed the benefits of education and greater employment opportunities. Approximately three-quarters of them were married. Most of the clubwomen were career-oriented; about two-thirds were teachers and a small proportion were clerical workers and entrepreneurs.[19]

In 1926 the NACW boasted affiliated clubs in forty-one states. Its vast scope and influence prompted Mary McLeod Bethune, national president between 1924 and 1928, to remark: "Every organization is looking to the National Association of Colored Women for assistance in some line of advancement."[20] One organization that looked to the NACW for assistance was the Republican National Committee, which had enlisted outgoing president Hallie Q. Brown to direct its voters' drive among black women in 1924.[21] During the presidential race, the NACW's usual social service activities took a backseat to intense partisan politics. Its magazine, *National Notes*, encouraged political consciousness, shared ideas and strategies, and followed the progress of the campaign in the various states. The selection of Brown, NACW president between 1920 and 1924, reflected the Coolidge forces' recognition of her command over hundreds of thousands of black women.

As director of the Colored Women's Department of the Republican National Committee, Brown built her campaign network on the foundation of the existing regional, state, and local structures of her organization. She recruited her army of workers from the NACW's leadership—from women who had already proved their organizing abilities. Brown appointed Maria C. Lawton of Brooklyn to head the eastern division of the Republican campaign and Myrtle Foster Cook of Kansas to head the western division. At the time, Lawton held the presidency of the Empire State Federation, the association of clubwomen at the New York state level. Her mobilizing ability had been responsible for the tremendous growth in affiliated clubs since 1912. As organizer of the Empire State Federation in 1912 and president from 1916 to 1926, Lawton had expanded the number of clubs from a small concentration mostly in New York City and Buffalo to 103 in all parts of the state. Cook afforded the Republican Party another strong mobilizing resource. As editor-manager of *National Notes*, she transformed the nationally read magazine into a political organ for the Republican Party.[22]

Black women's Republican clubs sprang up everywhere—led by clubwomen already in the vanguard of the civic and political affairs of their communities. The overall operation included precinct captains; ward chairmen; city, county, and district chairmen; state chairmen: and national organizers and speakers. Each state chairman developed circulars and bulletins for her own territory and sent reports to the black press "with accurate and encouraging accounts of women's campaign activities." Their reports highlighted their cooperation in a cause that "has added to our lives a rich chapter of wider friendships with the mutual confidence born of close acquaintance and hard work." The campaign had a tremendous psychological effect on these workers, who described it as rewarding and personally enriching. Lawton referred to the campaign's emotionally fulfilling impact on black women workers. It became an "outlet for their pent up aspirations and ambitions to be counted as integral parts of the body politic."[23]

Reports from state chairmen and organizers revealed optimism in politics and a belief that their efforts were decisive to the electoral outcome. Although the Republican Party had utilized black women leaders in the past, the election in 1924 involved their participation in more extensive, visible, and official ways. The state organizer from Rhode Island typified this attitude in her reflections on Coolidge's victory: "I am sure the work our colored women did during the last campaign helped materially to give the National ticket the large plurality it had in the Nation." Campaign reports indicate that there were hundreds of Coolidge-Dawes clubs and meetings in halls, churches, fraternal lodges, schools, homes, and on the streets. House-to-house canvassing appeared to be their most effective strategy, but bringing in speakers of national reputation also received a good response. Other interesting techniques were employed. The organizer for upstate New York outlined the following activities based on her tour of Elmira, Rochester, Auburn, Buffalo, and Niagara Falls:

> We found the forming of Coolidge-Dawes Clubs using pledge cards an excellent method for tabulating new voters and bringing in old voters who were in the class of stay-at-homes. Another method found very effective was Block Captains in every

district. These, with their assistants, kept a list of new voters and registrants of old, in turn. These were given to the chairman of our Get-Out-The-Vote Committee. This committee of twenty women did Yeoman work on election day; no voter of their district was omitted.[24]

Organizers in West Virginia noted the role of special circular letters—one with an appeal to the ministry and another to women directly. West Virginia women also found the question box helpful in identifying issues of concern to voters. The report from Minnesota relied heavily on mass distributions—pamphlets entitled "Important Information for All Legal Voters," "Register Today" cards, and sample ballots. Iowa was the only state to cite telephone canvassing among its techniques. Kentucky reported its least successful technique—getting women to answer mailed questionnaires.[25]

Florie Pugh of Oklahoma City held instructional meetings in the evenings and lectured on how to organize a precinct and district, the duty of a precinct committeewoman, how to poll, how to get the voters registered, new voters, the necessity of voting by 10:00 A.M. on election day, and why black people should be Republicans. Lillian Browder, a precinct captain in Chicago, stressed the need to discuss gender politics in house-to-house canvassing. She found that women exhibited greater responsiveness and interest when told of legislation and political affairs vital to home life. Thus Browder talked to women about laws that touched upon their lives—for example, the Child Labor Law, the Pure Food Act, and the law regulating working hours for women, and she associated passage of this legislation with the Republican Party.[26]

The presidential race of 1924 and Coolidge's ultimate victory reinforced a growing sense of political efficacy among black clubwomen. They interpreted their role as crucial to the Republican victory, and they expected a continued relationship with the party and with political organizations among white women. Estele R. Davis, who served on the Speakers' Bureau during the Coolidge campaign, captured the perceived interconnection between their club movement and political participation:

> How little have we realized in our club work for the last twenty-five years that it was God's way of preparing us to assume this greater task of citizenship. I often wonder what would have happened without our organized club work which has not only trained us for service, but has created a nation-wide sisterhood through which we know the outstanding women of each state who are able to serve our race in the time of need.[27]

The National League of Republican Colored Women

Throughout the summer of 1924 women came to value the need for permanent organization at the state and national levels. In some states political clubs had operated since the adoption of women's suffrage, but in most the presidential campaign had spurred the desire for continued political work. Mamie Williams (Mrs. George S. Williams) and Mary Booze, both NACW women and also the Republican national committeewomen from Georgia and Mississippi, respectively, urged the practicality of uniting black women's Republican clubs in a national organization.[28] On 7 August 1924, hours after the adjournment of the biennial meeting of the NACW, Williams and Booze reconvened a number of the clubwomen for the purpose of forming the National League of Republican Colored Women (NLRCW). Booze and Williams were named honorary presidents, while the official roster also included Nannie Burroughs of the District of Columbia, president; Sue M. Brown (Mrs. S. Joe Brown) of Iowa, vice president; Daisy Lampkin of Pennsylvania, treasurer and chairman of the executive committee; Mary Church Terrell of the District of

Columbia, treasurer; and Mrs. Elizabeth Ross Hanes, parliamentarian. These women were well known for their visibility in political affairs and for their work with the NAACP and the Urban League.[29]

The NLRCW sought to become a permanent political force among black women, adopting the slogan "We are in politics to stay and we shall be a stay in politics." It distinguished its goals from that of the NACW and other groups that adopted partisan political activities on a temporary basis and specifically at election time.[30] While endorsing the Republican National Committee's appointment of Brown as director of colored women for the presidential campaign, the members of the NLRCW criticized the NACW for abandoning its nonpartisan image and expressed disapproval of its heavy coverage of the Republican campaign through the pages of *National Notes*.

There are several explanations for this reaction on the part of women whose roles as leaders overlapped both organizations. First, the NLRCW ensured continuation of a partisan political emphasis by taking it out of the hands of an organization whose intentions and objectives had historically been to unite black women of all affiliations and persuasions in the work of social service. The NACW's Citizenship and Legislative departments constituted integral parts of the organization's "lifting as we climb" philosophy, but they were designed to inspire civic duty and legislative study for race and sex advancement, not to advance specific political parties.[31] Second, rivalries existed between women. Some of the NLRCW women claimed that certain NACW leaders had used their position during the presidential campaign to further their own selfish personal ambitions.[32] On the other hand, individuals in the NLRCW might have perceived the new organization as a stepping-stone to a political appointment that had bypassed them in the last campaign.

The crossover of membership in the two organizations invariably blurred distinctions. Reports of campaign activities during the 1924 election were sent to Nannie Burroughs as well as to the NACW officials working with the Republican National Committee.[33] Members of the NLRCW often quoted the slogan of the NACW when confirming their attendance at an event sponsored by the former. In 1928 Daisy Lampkin wrote to Burroughs about Lethia Fleming, an outstanding Republican organizer in Ohio and leader in both the NLRCW and the NACW: "She seemed to confuse the two National organizations, but I made it clear to her that they are in no way connected." By 1926 the NACW, while continuing to urge women's political participation, had relinquished overt partisanship to the NLRCW.[34]

In 1924 Burroughs sent out a questionnaire to black women leaders throughout the country. The exact number mailed is unknown, and only twenty-three responses appear to exist, representing respondents from eleven states. While this number is too small to be representative of black women in general, the questions themselves reveal the major concerns of the NLRCW in the building of its program. Some of the questions read as follows:

> —Did you hear of any vote selling among the women?
> —What is being done to educate women as to the value of the ballot?
> —Are Negro women taking an active part in local politics?
> —Is it true that a number of women failed to register and vote because their husbands are opposed to woman suffrage?
> —Did you hear that Whites who hire servants tried to influence their votes?
> —What is the general attitude of the White women of your city toward Negro women since they have suffrage?
> —Give the names of Congressmen from your State who have poor records on the Negro question.
> —What should the Negro demand of the incoming administration?
> —Who are the women in your city and State best qualified to organize political clubs to assist in the work?[35]

Meeting in Oakland in August 1926, the executive committee of the NLRCW presented its goals and intentions in the form of a resolution—copies of which were sent to Sallie Hert, a vice chairman of the Republican National Committee and head of its Women's Division, and to the Associated Negro Press for distribution in all the black newspapers. The resolution requested formal and active affiliation with the Women's Division of the Republican National Committee and offered the services and counsel of its state leaders in the upcoming congressional election.[36]

The response by the Women's Division of the Republican National Committee could not have been more promising. Sallie Hert invited Burroughs to represent the NLRCW at its first national conference of women leaders. Eighty-five women from thirty-three states met in Washington between 12 and 14 January 1927 to discuss their role in the Grand Old Party. The group included national committeewomen (Booze of Mississippi and Williams of Georgia being the only other blacks present), state vice chairmen, and Republican women's clubs. The women discussed a variety of issues of direct interest to Burroughs: maintaining a functioning organization throughout the year, women's representation in the party organization, problems of organizing and fund-raising, party integrity and loyalty, and overcoming differences among Republican women.[37]

Burroughs was among seventy-five women from the group who visited the White House and received greetings from President and Mrs. Coolidge. She also heard talks by Secretary of War Dwight Davis and secretary of commerce Herbert Hoover. The high point for Burroughs was the opportunity to address the gathering. She began her remarks by stating: "I'm glad to be able to give a touch of color to this meeting. No political party in America is 100 percent American without this touch of color." She proceeded to inform her seemingly quite receptive audience of the work of her own organization.[38]

In May 1927 the NLRCW called its own three-day conference in Washington, D.C. Leaders from twenty-three states came together to discuss their concerns and to hear high-ranking officials in the GOP discuss issues and policies. Included among the array of speakers were Sallie Hert of the Women's Division, Virginia White Speel of the Republican Central Committee for the District of Columbia, Secretary of Labor James Davis, and Secretary of the Interior Hubert Work. Feelings of efficacy continued to run high among black women.[39]

The presidential election in 1928 witnessed NLRCW leaders in prominent campaign positions. Lampkin, chairman of its executive committee, was appointed by the Republican high command to direct the mobilization of black women voters in the East. Burroughs had deeply wanted the position, but her nonvoting status as a District of Columbia resident operated to her disadvantage. An eloquent orator, Burroughs was appointed to the National Speakers' Bureau and became one of the most highly sought-after speakers on the campaign trail.[40] Many NLRCW members journeyed to Washington for the inauguration of Hoover. They rejoiced in his victory. It seemed just as much their own.

By 1932 the honeymoon had ended between the black women and the Republican Party. The Depression focused the attention of black leaders, male and female, on questions of economic survival. The Hoover administration had little to say to most Americans, least of all to blacks, on economic relief. Burroughs, like most blacks, continued to support Hoover in that year, but with increasing criticism of his policies toward the black poor. Nor had the party of Lincoln fared well in its civil rights record during Hoover's term. In the throes of unprecedented economic suffering, blacks came to challenge their traditional loyalty to the party responsible for their emancipation from slavery.[41]

Black leaders denounced the various racist actions of the Hoover administration. His efforts to render the Republican Party in the South "lily-white," his segregation of the

Gold Star Mothers, and his nomination of an avowed advocate of black disfranchisement to the Supreme Court incurred the wrath of black leaders throughout the nation.[42] However, for members of the NLRCW, the unhappy alliance between blacks and the administration was foreshadowed as early as Hoover's inauguration. In March 1929 the chairman of the Inaugural Charity Ball requested that Burroughs retrieve tickets "accidentally" sent to black women workers in the Hoover campaign. Burroughs acquiesced to Republican wishes for a segregated ball, but not without registering the protest of her coworkers: "It is not easy for me to get the others reconciled to embarrassments for which they are not responsible. One has said already, 'They use us in the crisis and humiliate us at will.'" In 1932 Sallie Hert's replacement by Lena Yost as head of the Republican Women's Division further alienated the black women. Yost lacked the sincerity and interest that had characterized Hert's relationship with the NLRCW. Burroughs's correspondence discloses increasing frustration with the party's solicitation of her support at election time, while at all other times treating her suggestions with "silent contempt."[43]

The League of Women Voters

Another organization that captured the interest of black clubwomen during the 1920s was the League of Women Voters (LWV). Lines of communication remained open between the NACW and black units of the LWV. While individual blacks held membership in some of the predominantly white state leagues, separate black leagues operated in Oakland, San Francisco, Los Angeles, Chicago, and St. Louis. Delegates from the Oakland, Chicago, and St. Louis groups were represented at the league's national conferences in the 1920s. They were also represented on the state boards of the California and Illinois leagues. Leaders of the black leagues were, at the same time, leaders of their state federated clubs—the constituent members of the NACW.

Hettie Tilghman, leader among black California women in the LWV, referred to the overlap in membership for the NACW and two black leagues, the Alameda County League of Colored Women Voters and the San Francisco Colored League. She cited their political activities from the dual role of federated women and League of Women Voters. Delilah Beasley, an active member of the NACW and the Alameda County League of Colored Women Voters, devoted press coverage to both in her column, "Activities among Negroes," which ran in the white daily, the *Oakland Tribune*. On 25 November 1925 she announced the interest of the Alameda County League of Colored Women Voters in the observance of World Court Day, scheduled for 17 December. Her column also cited an article written by the president of the Alameda County League for the magazine of the NACW. The article, which had appeared a few weeks earlier in *National Notes*, praised the California State League and National League of Women Voters for their efforts in securing the passage of specific legislation affecting women and children.[44]

On 6 October 1920 the St. Louis League of Women Voters organized a "Colored Committee" to bring before the larger body racial concerns related to education, health, child welfare, and citizenship. Nine years later, B. F. Bowles headed the committee, which functioned as an important liaison between the league and the large black female population in St. Louis. Under Bowles's leadership, the committee assumed a number of projects: gathering data on southern election laws and policies, offering lectures on pending legislation, holding citizenship schools, providing scholarships to black students, entertaining national league officers at gatherings in the black community, forming junior leagues among black girls, and contributing financially to the budget of the

St. Louis league. In an editorial in the *St. Louis American,* Carrie Bowles, another black league member and member of the NACW, praised the St. Louis league for being "one of the very few leagues in the U.S. in which the colored members enjoy every privilege of the organization on terms of absolute equality." Writing in the national magazine of the NACW in 1928, Bowles again praised her city league for sending a black delegate to the eighth annual conference.[45]

Illinois black clubwomen also contributed to the work of the league. In 1926 the Illinois State League of Women Voters elected a black woman, Margaret Gainer, to membership on its board of directors. Gainer, also a member of the Illinois State Federation of Colored Women's Clubs, directed the latter's citizenship department, which included the program of the Illinois League of Women Voters. The Illinois State Federation constituted an extensive network of black clubwomen. It organized in 1899 and by 1926 comprised ninety two clubs with 2,074 members divided into three districts: the Chicago and Northern, the Central, and the Southern.[46]

Several clubwomen in the Chicago area were league members. The Douglass League of Women Voters, the black unit of the league in the city, was headed by Irene Goins, a leader of the Illinois State Federation as well. On 18 June 1924 Florence Harrison of the national league met with the black members to discuss their plans for the development of citizenship schools. Attached to Harrison's report were the black women's plans for the national "Get-Out-the-Vote Campaign." In addition to incorporating the campaign into the citizenship program of the Illinois State Federation of Colored Women's Clubs, the Douglass League proposed:

1. Frequent meetings open and advertised, to be held in the Community Center . . . to which the League hopes to rally colored women from a large surrounding territory. At its meetings there will be from time to time (a) Ballot demonstrations (repeated); (b) Importance of registration (repeated); (c) Issues of the Campaign; (d) Candidates' meetings.
2. A system of home teaching for the colored women who cannot come to the Community Center . . . will be carried into the homes by members of the Douglass League.
3. "Excursion tickets" indicating a trip to the polls and asking "have you voted?" will be hung on tags on the doors in the neighborhood.[47]

News of league activities encouraged politically minded black women to seek membership in either separate or integrated units. However, they were usually discouraged. Delilah Beasley of Oakland expressed her frustration in establishing a black league in Los Angeles. Her efforts encountered prejudice throughout the state and especially in Los Angeles itself. Urging the formation of "full Colored Leagues" and auxiliaries to the white leagues, she stressed the need for black women to develop their own leadership, separate from whites so that "they do not antagonize the members of the White league by their presence." Yet Beasley did not demur from strongly recommending black representation on the general state board.[48]

On the other hand, Ohio black women opposed racial separatism in league work. Members of the Ohio Federation of Colored Women's Clubs had hoped to integrate various local leagues, after Sybil Burton, president of the state league, addressed their meeting and solicited their cooperation in mobilizing the vote. Ohio black women were ripe for participation. Burton admitted that the Ohio league found it unnecessary to sponsor educational classes for black women in the state because J. Estelle Barnett, a league member and black woman editor of the newspaper *In the Queen's Garden,* had used her paper to disseminate information on ballot marking and the necessity for voting.[49]

With no uniform guidelines, Burton preferred to leave the decision of accepting blacks to the individual leagues, whose racial policies varied by community. Oberlin accepted blacks freely and equally. Zanesville received black members but made them unwelcome at their luncheons and other social gatherings. The Toledo league sought advice from the national league when black women desired membership. The general consensus of the Toledo league was against integration, but they encouraged black women to form their own separate units. The Cincinnati league likewise contemplated the formation of an all-black unit. The reply from the national league tended to be discouraging in every way. While acknowledging that a few of the states had black leagues and a few others actually integrated individual black women into their ranks, Anne Williams Wheaton, press secretary, asserted: "Those who have expertise in this matter think it is far better not to encourage organizations of colored Leagues."[50] Rather than formal organization, the national league sought to address black issues through its Committee on Negro Problems—the name later being changed, at the request of black members, to the Committee on Interracial Problems.

In 1921 the committee formed in response to a petition by southern black women whose suffrage rights were denied. Interracial in composition, the committee included representatives from states where "the colored vote is a material and accepted fact." Its purpose was to implement educational and citizenship training programs, not augment black league membership. Although plans were devised by its three successive chairmen, Julia Lathrop (1921), Minnie Fisher Cunningham (1921–25), and Adele Clark (after 1925), the small committee left little in the way of accomplishment. A questionnaire was sent out to the states in 1927, but most did not reply, nor did the states that responded always do so thoughtfully and accurately. The ineffectiveness of the committee was evidenced in the infrequency of its meetings, all of which occurred informally at the national conventions and did not carry over into the interim period.[51] By the end of the decade the League of Women Voters had lost, largely by its own choice, the potential for being an important mobilizing force among black women.[52]

Conclusion

At the dawning of the 1930s, blacks found themselves on the brink of a political transition that would greatly accelerate in the next five years. The more dramatic collective action of blacks during the Depression and their strategic placement in the New Deal hierarchy have overshadowed the contribution of the previous decade to their political mobilization and increased political leverage. The ratification of the Nineteenth Amendment in 1920 lent significant impetus to black women's interest in the American political process, although the continuing legacy of racism conditioned the nature and extent of their participation. The racist policies of the National American Woman Suffrage Association continued in the 1920s with its successor organization, the League of Women Voters, to discourage black participation. Black women leaders, while organizing their own separate organizations, encountered racism from the very elected officials for whom they campaigned. Yet black women's discontent and frustration with white women's organizations, with the Republican Party, and with a racist society in general during the 1920s translated not into an abandonment of politics but into the emergence of new leaders, alliances, and strategies.

In 1936, when the majority of black voters shifted to the Democratic Party, the unswerving Republican allegiance of such leaders as Nannie Burroughs and Mary Church Terrell no longer won the applause of the black electorate. The Democratic Party had shed its long-worn garb of white supremacy, its image as the party of the "solid South," segregation, and black disfranchisement. Under Franklin Roosevelt's New Deal, the Democrats came to be perceived as the party most receptive to black opportunity. Mary McLeod Bethune's visibility in the Roosevelt administration and Crystal Bird Fauset's membership on the Democratic National Committee expressed both the continuation of women's political activism and shifting opportunities for black women leaders. In 1932 Bethune sat on the board of counselors of the Women's Division of the Republican National Committee with such notable Republican stalwarts as Mrs. Theodore Roosevelt and Mrs. William Howard Taft. In 1936 she presided over Roosevelt's Black Cabinet.[53] Bethune 's shifting allegiance symbolized the changed mood of the black electorate and, certainly not least of all, woman's prerogative to change her mind.

Notes

1. Florette Henri, *Black Migration* (Garden City, N.Y.: Anchor/Doubleday, 1975), 50–59, 68–69; Martin Kilson, "Political Change in the Negro Ghetto, 1900–1940," in Nathan I. Huggins, Martin Kilson, and Daniel M. Fox, eds., *Key Issues in the Afro-American Experience* (New York: Harcourt Brace Jovanovich, 1971), 2:175; Jacqueline Jones, *Labor of Love, Labor of Sorrow: Black Women, Work, and the Family from Slavery to the Present* (New York: Basic Books, 1985), 152–60.

2. Harold F. Gosnell, *Negro Politicians* (Chicago: University of Chicago Press, 1935), 13–92, 180–90.

3. Paul Lewinson, *Race, Class, and Party: A History of Negro Suffrage and White Politics in the South* (New York: Oxford University Press, 1932); Harold F. Gosnell, "The Negro Vote in Northern Cities," *National Municipal Review* 30 (1941): 264–67, 268; St. Clair Drake and Horace R. Cayton, *Black Metropolis* (New York: Harper and Row, 1945); James Q. Wilson, *Negro Politics: The Search for Leadership* (New York: Free Press, 1960); Kilson, "Political Change in the Negro Ghetto"; Ira Katznelson, *Black Men, White Cities* (Chicago: University of Chicago Press, 1976).

4. See, for example, Rosalyn Terborg-Penn, "Discontented Black Feminists: Prelude and Postscript to the Passage of the Nineteenth Amendment," in Lois Scharf and Joan M. Jensen, eds., *Decades of Discontent: The Women's Movement, 1920–1940* (Westport, Conn.: Greenwood Press, 1983), 261–78.

5 Aileen S. Kraditor, *The Ideas of the Woman Suffrage Movement, 1890–1920* (Garden City, N.Y.: Anchor/Doubleday, 1971), 138–71; Rosalyn Terborg-Penn, "Discrimination against Afro-American Women in the Woman's Movement, 1830–1920," in Sharon Harley and Rosalyn Terborg-Penn, eds., *The Afro-American Woman: Struggles and Images* (Port Washington, N.Y.: Kennikat Press, 1978), 17–27; Paula Giddings, *When and Where I Enter: The Impact of Black Women on Race and Sex in America* (New York: William Morrow, 1984), 129–30, 165–69, 177, 218–20.

6. "The Woman Voter Hits the Color Line," *Nation*, 6 October 1920.

7. Terborg-Penn, "Discontented Black Feminists."

8. Ida B. Wells-Barnett, *Crusade for Justice: The Autobiography of Ida B. Wells*, ed. Alfreda M. Duster (Chicago: University of Chicago Press, 1970), 345–53.

9. Henri, *Black Migration*, 52–80; Doug McAdam, *Political Process and the Development of Black Insurgency, 1930–1970* (Chicago: University of Chicago Press, 1982), 77–81; Gosnell, *Negro Politicians*, 16–19.

10. Henri, *Black Migration*, 54–55; Kilson, "Political Change in the Negro Ghetto," 170–82; Jones, *Labor of Love*, 162–80, 190, 193–94.

11. Interview with Harold F. Gosnell, 17 March 1986, Bethesda, Maryland; also see Gosnell, *Negro Politicians*, 15, 19, 374; Gosnell, *Machine Politics: Chicago Model* (Chicago: University of Chicago Press, 1968).

12. "Negro Republican Campaign Division," *Norfolk Journal and Guide*, 11 August 1928; also see press release, "Republican National Committee, for Release Thursday, 2 August 1928," Nannie Helen Burroughs Papers, Library of Congress.

13. Hanes Walton, *Invisible Politics: Black Political Behavior* (Albany: State University of New York Press, 1985), 51.

14. See the *Baltimore Afro-American* for "Equal Rights League Sends Congratulations to Women"; "Colored Woman Sits on Jury," and "Committee of Women Named—Mrs. Lethia G. Fleming of Cleveland Is Approved Chairman," 17 September 1920; "Women Hit Color Line," 8 October 1920; "Vital Meeting—Come and Hear Why We Should Stand by Our Race Candidate," 1 October 1920; "Women Spring Big Surprise," 24 September 1920; "Women Make Good," 16 October 1920.

15. Augusta T. Chissell, "A Primer for Women Voters," *Baltimore Afro-American*, 24 September 1920.

16. *Baltimore Afro-American*, 1 October 1920.

17. National Association of Colored Women, *National Notes*, April 1923, 18; Charles H. Wesley, *The History of the National Association of Colored Women's Clubs, Inc.: A Legacy of Service* (Washington, D.C.: National Association of Colored Women's Clubs, 1984), 55–100.

18. Giddings, *When and Where I Enter*, 107–9, 135–36; Evelyn Brooks, "Religion, Politics, and Gender: The Leadership of Nannie Helen Burroughs," *Journal of Religious Thought* 44 (1988): 7–22.

19. Tullia Kay Brown Hamilton, "The National Association of Colored Women" (Ph.D. diss., Emory University, 1978), 53.

20. Mary McLeod Bethune, "Biennial Report of the National Association of Colored Women, 1924–1926," *National Notes*, July and August 1926, 3–4.

21. Hallie Q. Brown, "Republican Colored Women of America," *National Notes*, December 1924, 1.

22. "Report from the Western Division and the Eastern Division," *National Notes*, December 1924, 2–3; Wesley, *History of the National Association*, 91, 201–2.

23. "Report," *National Notes*, December 1924, 2–3.

24. Ibid., 4.

25. Ibid.

26. Gosnell notes a higher percentage of women precinct captains in the black wards. His roster showed as much as one-fourth of the captains to be women in the black Third Ward in Chicago. See Gosnell, *Machine Politics*, 61–63; "Campaign Experiences," *National Notes*, January 1925, 13–14.

27. "Campaign Experiences," *National Notes*, January 1925, 13.

28. In the southern states black disfranchisement and Democratic hegemony combined to effectively nullify any hope of amassing votes for state and local office, but posts within the Republican party as well as federal patronage positions were still available to southern Republicans by virtue of the votes they delivered at the national conventions. The influence of black Republicans and their female officeholders such as Mary Booze of Mississippi and Mamie Williams of Georgia lay largely with the ability of the black Republican organization in each southern state to achieve recognition at the Republican national convention. Termed "black and tans," these organizations distinguished themselves from the Republican organizations with overwhelmingly white membership—"lily-whites." The influence of the black and tans was keenly felt in the presidential nominations of McKinley in 1896, Taft in 1908 and 1912, and Hoover in 1928. See Lewinson, *Race, Class, and Party*, 170–76; V. O. Key, *Southern Politics in State and Nation* (New York: Vintage Books, 1949), 286–89; and Hanes Walton, *Black Republicans: The Politics of the Black and Tans* (Metuchen, N.J.: Scarecrow Press, 1975), 133–35.

29. "Minutes of the Temporary Organization of the National League of Republican Colored Women, 7 August 1924," and "Minutes of the Subsequent Meeting of the NLRCW, 11 August 1924," Burroughs Papers.

30. "The National League of Republican Colored Women," *National Notes*, July 1928, 10.

31. Mary Church Terrell, "An Appeal to Colored Women to Vote and Do Their Duty in Politics," *National Notes*, November 1925, 1; Mary Church Terrell, "What Colored Women Can and Should Do at the Polls," *National Notes*, March 1926, 3.

32. Mazie Griffin to Burroughs, n.d.; Mamie Williams to Burroughs, 5 January 1925, Burroughs Papers; also see "Departments and Their Functions," *National Notes*, January 1925, 2.

33. See, for example, Frannie Givens, of the East-End Colored Women's Political Clubs, to Burroughs, 20 October 1924; Mary E. Gardiner, of the Women's Republican Club of Cambridge, to Burroughs, 21 October 1924; Susan B. Evans, state director of colored women's activities of the St. Paul, Minn., Republican State Central Committee, 22 October 1924; Elizabeth L. Gulley, of the Colored Division, Wayne County Coolidge–Groesbeck Club, Republican State Central Committee of Michigan, 29 October 1924; and Mrs. Charles W. French, Parliamentarian, Kansas State Federation of Colored Women, to Burroughs, 30 October 1924, Burroughs Papers.

34. However, the NACW's *National Notes* carried articles promoting the National League of Republican Colored Women. See "Republican Call," April 1927, 6; "The National League of Republican Colored Women," July 1928, 10.

35. "Colored Women in Politics Questionnaire," Burroughs Papers.

36. "Meeting of the Executive Committee of the National League of Republican Colored Women, Oakland, Calif., 6 August 1926"; and Burroughs to Mrs. Alvin Hert, 11 August 1926, Burroughs Papers.

37. "Summarized Report of the Conference of the Republican National Committeewomen, State Vice-Chairmen, and State Club Presidents, January 12, 13, 14, 1927," Burroughs Papers.

38. Ibid.

39. "G.O.P. Women from Twenty-three States in Session," *Afro-American* (Washington ed.), 21 May 1927.

40. Daisy Lampkin to Burroughs, 2 and 17 July, 8 October 1928, Lampkin to Mrs. Paul FitzSimmons, 8 October 1928; Lampkin to Fellow Republican, 17 July 1928, Burroughs Papers.

41. Nancy J. Weiss, *Farewell to the Party of Lincoln: Black Politics in the Age of FDR* (Princeton: Princeton University Press, 1983), 3–33.

42. Gold Star Mothers were the mothers and widows of men buried in Europe who had died in active service during World War I. The U.S. government sponsored the women's passage to Europe in order to place wreaths on the graves. Black Gold Star Mothers were sent over in separate and blatantly inferior ships; ibid., 16–17.

43. Burroughs to Mrs. John Allen Dougherty, Chairman, Inaugural Charity Ball, 2 March 1929; Burroughs to Sallie Hert, 19 August 1929, 14 April 1930; Susie M. Myers to Burroughs, 3 May 1932; Burroughs to Mrs. Ellis Yost, 27 September 1932, 30 June 1934; Burroughs to Maude B. Coleman, 8 September 1936, Burroughs Papers.

44. Delilah L. Beasley, "Activities among Negroes," *Oakland Tribune*, 22 November 1925; Hettie Tilghman, "What the Study of Legislative Work Has Meant to Our Group," *National Notes*, November 1925, 3; "Miss Delilah L. Beasley," *National Notes*, March 1928, 8; Beasley, "California Women Preparing for Biennial Convention," *National Notes*, April 1926; Belle Sherwin to Sybil R. Burton, 31 March 1925, League of Women Voters Papers, Library of Congress (hereafter cited as LWV Papers).

45. Mrs. B. F. Bowles and Mrs. E. C. Grady, "The Colored Committee of the League of Women Voters of St. Louis: The First Nine Years"; Gladys Harrison to Ruth Siemer, 14 October 1929; Siemer to Beatrice Marsh, 30 June 1930; and Marsh to Adele Clark, 2 July 1930; also written sometime in the late 1920s but undated is Carrie Bowles, "Defends League of Women Voters," *St. Louis American*; clipping and aforementioned letters in LWV Papers; Carrie Bowles, "Women Voters' National League," *National Notes*, May 1928, 15.

46. "Mrs. Elizabeth Lindsay Davis . . .," *National Notes*, April 1926, 1; "Illinois Federation of Colored Women's Clubs," *National Notes*, July 1926, 24.

47. "Excerpt from letter from Florence Harrison to Miss Sherwin dated 18 June 1924" and attached page, "Sent by Mrs. Rich to B.S. 1924," LWV Papers.

48. Delilah L. Beasley to Mrs. Warren Wheaton, 23 March 1926; Wheaton to Beasley, 25 March 1926, LWV Papers.

49. Sybil R. Burton to Belle Sherwin, 27 March 1925, LWV Papers.

50. Agnes Hilton to Gladys Harrison, 9 August 1928; Anne Williams Wheaton to Hilton, 17 August 1928, LWV Papers.

51. "Special Committee on Inter-Racial Problems, 17 April 1934"; "Report of the Special Committee on Interracial Problems to the Board of Directors, December 1927"; "National League of Women Voters—Report for the Committee on Negro Problems, April 1924–April 1925"; and "Committee on Negro Problems—Chairman Mrs. Minnie Fisher Cunningham, 11 July 1924," LWV Papers.

52. See, for example, a letter written by a black woman, Eva Nichols Wright, of Washington, D.C., to Belle Sherwin: "In reply to the question 'Are colored women of your city interested as members, in the League of Women Voters or the National Woman's Party? If not, why not?' The replies with two exceptions were negative. To the question, 'To what extent do white women and colored women work together politically?' The same negative reply was received with three or four exceptions, and many expressed themselves as being discouraged." Wright to Sherwin, 25 April 1927, LWV Papers.

53. Republican National Committee, Women's Division, *Organization News*, 22 October 1932, 2, in Burroughs Papers; Weiss, *Farewell to the Party of Lincoln*, 137–48, 180–84.

20

Sexual Geography and Gender Economy: The Furnished-Room Districts of Chicago, 1890–1930

Joanne Meyerowitz

The broad outlines of the early twentieth-century sexual revolution in the United States are now well known.[1] From roughly 1890 to 1930 public discussions and displays of sexuality multiplied in popular magazines, newspapers, and entertainments. At the same time, women began to adopt more sexual, or at least less modest, styles; shorter skirts, cosmetics, bobbed hair, and cigarettes, once the styles of prostitutes, all seemed evidence of a larger change in mores when adopted by "respectable" working- and middle-class women. Men and women mingled freely in new commercialized recreation industries and in workplaces. And surveys of the middle class revealed increases in premarital intercourse.

Historians have now written at least three versions of this sexual revolution. In the oldest and now standard account, young, middle-class "flappers" rebelled against the repressive standards of their parents by engaging in shocking behavior, such as petting in automobiles, dancing to jazz music, and using bawdy language.[2] A second version of the sexual revolution developed with the growth of the field of U.S. women's history. In this rendition, young feminist bohemians, or independent "new women," influenced by the writings of Freud and other sexologists, experimented sexually and rejected the homosocial sisterhood of earlier women's rights activists.[3] A third variation points to a working-class component. Urban, working-class "rowdy girls" appear as early as the 1830s but seem to enter historical center stage in precisely the same years that the middle-class "new women" and "flappers" self-consciously rejected Victorian mores. In the workplace and in dance halls, theaters, and amusement parks, young, working-class women adopted an overtly sexual style that dismayed both their parents and middle-class reformers.[4]

This article is a case study of working-class women's sexuality in the furnished-room districts of turn-of-the-century Chicago. In a particular setting, how did women participate in the sexual revolution, and how was their behavior interpreted and publicized? This approach modifies the various versions of the sexual revolution. For one, it locates neglected geographical centers of urban sexual activity—the furnished-room districts—and early active participants in the sexual revolution, the women lodgers. Second, it highlights economic imperatives that motivated and shaped at least part of the sexual revolution. And, finally, it shows how middle-class observers reshaped the experiences of sexually active working-class women and broadcast them to a larger national audience.

Recently U.S. feminists have engaged in heated debates over the meaning of twentieth-century sexual expression. The debates are polarized between those who emphasize the sexual dangers, such as rape, that oppress women and those who focus on the sensual pleasures that await women.[5] While this article does not enter these debates directly, it suggests the importance of studying sexuality in context. Sexual behavior, of course, is neither inherently dangerous for women nor inherently pleasurable. Like other socially constructed behaviors, its meanings derive from the specific contexts in which it is enacted. This study examines how and why a particular group of women adopted the freer modes of sexual expression that characterized the early-twentieth-century sexual revolution. It finds that neither sexual danger nor sensual pleasure provides adequate explanation.

Most major American cities today have a distinct geography of sexuality. That is, one could locate districts and neighborhoods known as the institutional and social centers of various sexual subcultures. Take San Francisco, for example, a city known for its celebration of sexual variety. Upscale heterosexual singles live in apartments and frequent bars in the Marina district. Downscale heterosexual men go to porn shops and massage parlors in the Tenderloin. Female prostitutes sell their services at the corner of Eighteenth and Mission Streets; male prostitutes sell their services on Polk Street. Gay men congregate in the Castro district, and lesbians meet in the bars and coffeehouses in the vicinity of Valencia Street.

A lesser-known geography of sexuality also existed in early-twentieth-century American cities. In 1916 sociologist Robert Park identified what he called "moral regions" of the city, "detached milieus in which vagrant and suppressed impulses, passions, and ideals emancipate themselves from the dominant moral order."[6] Park was not the first to define neighborhoods by sexual behavior. At the end of the nineteenth century, a few urban investigators identified the furnished-room districts, or areas where rooming houses abounded, as "moral regions" of sorts, distinct neighborhoods where unconventional sexual behavior flourished.[7] By the early twentieth century, reformers defined a "furnished-room problem" more precisely. In 1906, for example, in a study of Boston's furnished-room district, Albert Benedict Wolfe lamented the "contamination of young men, the deterioration in the modesty and morality of young women, the existence of actual houses of prostitution in the guise of lodging-houses, the laxity of landladies, the large number of informal unions, the general loosening of moral texture."[8] By the late 1910s and 1920s, more dispassionate sociologists explored "a new code of sex relationships" in the furnished-room districts of Chicago.[9] Evidence from newspapers, autobiographies, vice reports, and social surveys also suggests that the furnished-room districts were indeed the centers of sexually unconventional subcultures.[10]

By the end of the nineteenth century, most major American cities had furnished-room districts. These often first appeared in the city center and later, as business displaced downtown housing, moved out farther along major transportation lines. The large proportion of adult residents and the small proportion of children distinguished these districts demographically from other neighborhoods of the city. A residential street in a furnished-room district usually resembled others in the city: A typical block would consist of single-family homes, buildings of flats, large tenements, or older mansions. The owners of the buildings, however, converted the interiors into one- or two-room dwellings. They might divide a flat into two or three smaller units or divide a large tenement into an "apartment hotel" with as many as a hundred furnished rooms.

In Chicago three such districts emerged in the late nineteenth century. On the South Side, the furnished-room district included major portions of the Chicago black community and also what was, before the 1912 raids, the segregated vice district of the city. On the West Side, the district housed a population of predominantly white service and factory workers. A transient male hobo population congregated on the inner boundaries. On the North Side, where rents were slightly higher, clerical and sales workers lived in rooming houses alongside white service and manufacturing workers, artists, bohemians, and radicals of all stripes. In the early twentieth century, the North Side district included substantial numbers of Irish and Swedish roomers.[11]

These districts burgeoned in the early 1890s, when migrants and visitors streamed to Chicago for the World's Columbian Exposition. They continued to grow in the first decades of the twentieth century. By 1923 the Illinois Lodging House Register reported over eighty-five thousand lodgers in about five thousand rooming houses in the three major furnished-room districts. By 1930 residents of the new small unit apartments (with private bathrooms and kitchenettes) joined lodgers in these neighborhoods.[12]

Several distinctive features of the furnished-room districts fostered the development of extramarital sexual relationships. Most obviously, women and men lived together in houses where most people did not live in families. In these neighborhoods, lodgers found numerous opportunities to create social and sexual ties with their peers. Further, the high geographic mobility in the furnished-room districts made informal, transient relationships the norm. One writer went so far as to claim that the entire population of Chicago's North Side furnished-room district changed every four months.[13] This high turnover rate created an atmosphere of anonymity in which lodgers rarely knew their neighbors well. Community pressures to conform to conventional familial roles were weaker than in more settled neighborhoods, and parental authorities were absent. Many rooming-house keepers, eager to keep their tenants, refrained from criticizing or interfering with roomers' sexual behavior.[14] In addition, the predominance of men in the North and West Side districts may have encouraged women to participate in extramarital heterosexual relationships: It would have been easy to meet men and difficult to avoid them.[15]

In any case, the prevalence of prostitution in the furnished-room districts created a climate where open expressions of sexuality were common. In the first decade of the twentieth century, the most prominent vice district of Chicago lay in the South Side furnished-room district. Brothels were tolerated in sections of the West and North Side districts as well.[16] In addition, on the South, West, and North Sides, some keepers of rooming houses and hotels rented rooms by the hour or night to prostitutes and their customers.[17] After the municipal government closed the brothels in the 1910s, social investigators repeatedly found rooming houses and hotels used for prostitution.[18]

In addition to hotels and rooming houses, the "bright-light" centers of the furnished-room districts provided settings in which men and women could socialize. Investors who hoped to profit from the demand by lodgers opened cafeterias, cheap restaurants, tearooms, soft-drink parlors, saloons, dance halls, cabarets, and movie theaters. Residents of the districts turned these institutions into social centers. As one observer noted: "Considerable companionship grows up around these resorts. One is struck by the fact that the same people visit and re-visit the same cabaret time and again."[19]

On the North Side, Clark Street and, on the West Side, Halsted Street were well known for their nightlife. In 1918 Clark Street alone housed fifty-seven saloons, thirty-six restaurants, and twenty cabarets.[20] On the South Side, the State Street "Stroll" and Thirty-fifth Street emerged as the "bright-light" centers of the black community. Dance halls, restaurants, movies, and saloons for black customers coexisted with "black and tan" cabarets, which offered racially integrated recreation.[21] When young men and women who lived with their parents were out for a night on the town, and when wealthier people went "slumming," they often went to the furnished-room districts of the city.

These areas, it seems, were geographic settings where behavior considered unacceptable elsewhere was accepted matter-of-factly and even encouraged. In residential communities of Chicago, neighbors often stigmatized sexually active unmarried women. For example, Mamie, a young woman who lived with her parents in a working-class neighborhood of

Chicago, first encountered problems in 1918 when a policewoman reported her for "unbecoming conduct with sailors." Later, rumor had it that her neighbors talked of signing a petition to expel her from the neighborhood.[22] Contrast Mamie's brief case history with the comment of a student of Chicago's South Side furnished-room district: "It is said that an attractive woman who does not 'cash in' is likely to be considered a fool by her neighbors, instead of any stigma being attached to a woman who 'hustles' in this neighborhood."[23]

By the early twentieth century the furnished-room districts of Chicago and other large cities were known as havens for women and men who chose to defy conventions.[24] In addition to migrants and transients, they attracted women and men seeking adventure and a chance to break taboos in a community without parental supervision.[25] Here interested lodgers could enter peer-oriented subcultures that sanctioned extramarital sexual behavior. A 1918 account of Chicago's North Side shows the complex and casual nature of social and sexual relationships:

> [J. and V.] went to the North Clark Street section where they posed as man and wife. They took a couple of furnished rooms, . . . and remained there for two years. Both of them worked, often bringing in as much as $30.00 a week together. They took their meals out and got along very well.
>
> Then two of the girl's sisters came to Chicago to find work and rented rooms next to them. These girls had good intentions but not securing very lucrative positions, they soon learned how to supplement their wages by allowing young men to stay with them.
>
> These girls struck up an acquaintanceship with another girl who used to remain overnight with them now and again when they had been out to a dance or cabaret. J. liked this new girl and as he put it could not "help monkeying with her" and when V. found it out she became extremely jealous and shortly afterwards left him. Her sisters and the other girl followed her.[26]

Other accounts provide additional glimpses of how women formed social networks in the furnished-room districts. In 1911 two women, seventeen and twenty years old, met at a South Side dance hall. The older woman persuaded the younger to room with her on Chicago's North Side. After they moved in together, they made "pick up acquaintances" with men at dance halls and on the street.[27] Around 1913 Myrtle S., who roomed on the North Side, made friends with a woman at the restaurant where she ate her meals. This woman introduced her to a man, Lew W., with whom she spent several evenings drinking beer. Myrtle testified that she lost her virginity when Lew took advantage of her: "[O]ne night she lost consciousness after her drink of beer and awoke next morning in the Superior Hotel." Despite this betrayal, she returned to the hotel with Lew on two other occasions. Later, Myrtle met another man at a "chop suey" restaurant.[28]

Some of the social circles that developed in the furnished-room districts were distinguished by unconventional lifestyles, sexual preferences, or political leanings. In the North Side district, for example, a subculture of hoboes congregated in and around Washington, or Bughouse, Square. In her autobiography, hobo "Box-Car Bertha" wrote, "Girls and women . . . seemed to keep Chicago as their hobo center. . . . They are centered about the Near North Side, in Bughouse Square, in the cheap roominghouses and light housekeeping establishments, or begged or accepted sleeping space from men or other women there before them." The women hoboes whom Bertha described engaged casually in sexual relationships. One woman, she wrote, had "a group of sweethearts," others lived and traveled with men "to whom by chance or feeling they had attached themselves," and still others engaged in "careless sex relations."[29]

By the 1920s lesbian communities were also visible.[30] According to blues singer Ma Rainey, a black bisexual, lesbians frequented State Street, in the South Side rooming-house area. A song she recorded in 1924 included the following among other more sexually suggestive verses:

> Goin' down to spread the news
> State Street women wearing brogan shoes
> Hey, hey, daddy let me shave 'em dry. . . .
> There's one thing I don't understand
> Some women walkin' State Street like a man,
> Eeh, hey, hey, daddy let me shave 'em dry.[31]

According to Box-Car Bertha, "several tea shops and bootleg joints on the near-north side . . . catered to lesbians," including many among the Chicago hobo population.[32] Another observer found lesbians in the somewhat less transient population of the North Side furnished-room district's bohemian circles. He, too, noted that homosexual women and men frequented the tearooms of the area and held parties in their rented rooms.[33]

The best-known subcultures of the furnished-room districts were undoubtedly the bohemian circles of artists, intellectuals, and political radicals. In Chicago, black bohemians congregated in the South Side furnished-room district, and some white socialists and anarchists lived in the West Side district.[34] But the heart of Chicago's bohemia was on the North Side, where one study found that "[m]ost of the experimenters are young women."[35] In most respects, Chicago's bohemians resembled those of New York's Greenwich Village. Chicago, though, had its own distinctive institutions. The informal Dill Pickle Club provided a setting for lectures, plays, and jazz performances.[36] And the anarchist tradition of soapbox oratory in Washington Square provided a public forum for unconventional speakers.[37]

As in the other subcultures of the furnished-room districts, women who joined bohemian circles expected and often wanted to participate in extramarital sexual activities. For example, Natalie Feinberg, the daughter of working-class Jewish immigrants from Russia, expressed an interest in "free love" before she moved away from her family in Chicago, changed her name to Jean Farway, and "frequented the various gathering places" of the bohemians. According to the sociologist who described her, "She won the reputation of wishing to become a great courtesan."[38]

Historians remember the furnished-room districts primarily for the articulate, "emancipated" middle- and upper-class members of bohemian communities. Such people are often seen as vanguards of modern sexuality, women and men who experimented freely with new sexual possibilities learned from Sigmund Freud, Havelock Ellis, and other sexologists.[39] The geography of sexuality helps place the bohemians in context, as only one subculture among several. The furnished-room districts housed working-class women and men as well as middle- and upper-class bohemians. There is no evidence that the "revolution" of a bohemian and middle-class vanguard trickled down to the working class. In fact, it seems more likely that bohemians learned of new sexual possibilities not only from the "highbrow" writings of the sexologists but also from the "lowbrow" behavior of their less intellectual neighbors.[40]

Furnished-room districts not only provide a setting for observing various participants in the sexual revolution; they also reveal the social and economic context that shaped changing sexual mores. Heterosexual relationships in the furnished-room districts included "dating," "pickups," "occasional prostitution," and "temporary alliances." Like professional prostitution and marriage, these were economic as well as sexual and social relationships. Because employers paid self-supporting women wages intended for dependent daughters and wives, many women lodgers worked in low-paying jobs that barely covered subsistence.[41] In an era of rapidly expanding urban consumerism, these women were forced into scrimping and self-denial. By entering sexual relationships, however, they could supplement their wages with free evenings on the town, free meals in restaurants, and sometimes gifts and money. In many cases, the new sexual expression allowed women to participate in the urban consumer economy.

Even in the most innocent dating, men customarily paid for the evening's entertainment. Women, in return, gave limited sexual favors, ranging from charming companionship to sexual intercourse. A 1910 federal report on self-supporting working women stressed the economic value of dating:

> Even if most of the girls do not spend money for amusements, it is no proof that they go without them. Many of the girls have "gentlemen friends" who take them out. "Sure I go out all the time, but it doesn't cost me anything; my gentleman friend takes me," was the type of remark again and again. . . . Girls who have "steadies" are regarded as fortunate indeed.[42]

A woman need not have a "steady," however, to benefit from dating. In "pickups," "women met male strangers casually on street corners or in dance halls, restaurants, and saloons. They then spent the evening and sometimes the night with them." In Chicago women attempted to pick men up in dance halls and on the streets. In 1911, for example, a vice investigator in a North Side dance hall encountered several women who asked him "to take them to shows or dances."[43] Ten years later, in the heart of the South Side furnished-room district, Gladys B., an eighteen-year-old black woman, "went cabareting" with James P. after she picked him up at the corner of Thirty-fifth and State Streets. They ended the evening in a hotel room.[44] Presumably James paid for the cabarets, the room, and perhaps Gladys's sexual services. (In this case, he paid more than he bargained for: This mundane pickup became newsworthy only when Gladys escaped in the night with James's wad of money.)

In the early twentieth century, young working-class women who lived in their parents' homes also participated avidly in the new urban dating patterns promoted by commercialized recreation facilities.[45] For many women lodgers in the furnished-room districts, though, the necessity of supporting themselves on low wages added a special imperative. Lodgers themselves were highly aware of the economic benefits of dating. A waitress said bluntly, "If I did not have a man, I could not get along on my wages."[46] And a taxi dancer stated, "It's a shame a girl can't go straight and have a good time but I've got to get what I get by 'Sex Appeal.'"[47] One male resident of the North Side furnished-room district concluded: "[Women] draw on their sex as I would on my bank account to pay for the kind of clothes they want to wear, the kind of shows they want to see."[48]

"Occasional prostitution" resembled dates and pickups, but here the economic benefits were even clearer. Women asked men explicitly to pay for the sexual services provided them. These women worked in stores, offices, factories, and restaurants by day and sold their sexual services on occasional nights for extra money. While many women who dated probably exchanged only companionship, flirtation, and petting for evenings on the town, the smaller group of occasional prostitutes stepped up the barter, exchanging sexual intercourse for gifts or money. These women did not necessarily see themselves as prostitutes; they simply played the "sex game" for somewhat higher stakes.[49]

Without watchful relatives nearby, women lodgers could engage in occasional prostitution more easily than working women who lived in their parents' homes. Accordingly, vice investigators in search of occasional prostitutes went to the furnished-room districts to find them. In a North Clark Street saloon, for example, a vice investigator met two women who lived in the North Side district. They worked in a department store for $5.50 per week. "They can't live on this," he reported, "so they 'hustle' on the side." In another case, the investigator reported on a nineteen-year-old migrant from Indiana who worked in a South Side restaurant: "Is not a regular prostitute, goes with men for presents or money. Is poorly paid at restaurant."[50]

With pickups and occasional prostitution, the relationships usually lasted for one night only. In a "temporary alliance," a woman maintained a sexual relationship with one or more "steady" boyfriends, or lived with a man as if she were married. Amy, a twenty-year-old woman who lived on the South Side, worked as a cashier in a downtown restaurant until she met a streetcar conductor who agreed to "keep" her. He had given her a new fall hat and promised to buy her a new winter coat. Amy occasionally went out with other men "to get a little more spending money."[51] Another account of temporary alliances in furnished rooms stated tersely, "For ten months, Marion lived a hand-to-mouth existence, dependent upon the bounty of several men with whom she became intimate."[52] Such alliances were motivated in some cases by "genuine and lasting regard," but in others, "the motive of the girl is simply to find support, and that of the man gratification."[53]

From the limited evidence available, it seems that economic concerns also shaped sexual relationships in the lesbian subculture. Some lesbians depended on men, earning money as prostitutes. Others found higher-paid or wealthier women to support them. For example, in the North Side district in the late 1890s, one lesbian, Beatrice, was supported by her lover Peggy, who earned money as a prostitute. Peggy had "had a dozen sweethearts, all lesbian" and had "always supported them." On at least one occasion, some lesbians also adopted a form of gold digging or, more precisely, veiled blackmail. After a North Side party, some lesbians persuaded the wealthier women attending to pay for their companionship: "The lesbians would get their names and addresses and borrow money by saying, 'I met you at . . . [the] [party]?'" Some lesbians also prostituted themselves to other women.[54]

This emphasis on the economics of sexual relationships should not obscure the sexual dangers or the sensual pleasures that many women experienced. On one hand, some women lodgers encountered undeniable sexual violence, including rape, and others found themselves betrayed by false promises of marriage.[55] On the other hand, many women clearly enjoyed real relationships in which they found physical pleasure, excitement, and companionship. As one woman stated bluntly, "Frankly, I like intercourse!"[56] Further, the economic dependency in these relationships was not necessarily more exploitative or more oppressive than wives' traditional dependence on husbands or daughters' traditional dependence on fathers.

The financial imperatives are important, though, for they point to a neglected economics of the early-twentieth-century sexual revolution. The exchange of sexual services for monetary support moved beyond the marital bedroom and the brothel and into a variety of intermediate forms including dating, pickups, temporary alliances, and occasional prostitution. The sexual revolution was not simply, as one historian has written, "prosperity's child."[57] In the furnished-room districts, economic need shaped sexual experimentation. "What I get is mine. And what they have is mine, too, if I am smart enough to get it," said one self-avowed gold digger. "I'll show you how to take their socks away."[58] "Modern" sexual expression, then, not only threatened women with danger and promised women pleasure; in a variety of forms, it also offered financial reward.

Contemporary feminists who debate the meanings of sexual expression are not the first to define sexuality in terms of danger and pleasure. In the past century and a half, middle-class American commentators, including feminists, have often invested sexual expression with one of two opposing meanings. On one side, many observers, especially in the nineteenth century, have described nonmarital sexual expression with various stories of danger, disease, decay, and disorder. On the other side, some observers, primarily in the twentieth century, have represented nonmarital sexuality with stories of pleasure, vitality, adventure, and freedom.[59] In both constructions, sexuality was stripped of its everyday contexts and inflated with symbolic meaning. In the early twentieth century, the bourgeois attack on Victorian "sexual repression" marked a self-conscious shift in the dominant discourse from sex as danger to sex as pleasure.[60] As this conception of sexuality changed, the woman lodger played a central symbolic role. Through local and national media, a variety of commentators constructed conflicting interpretations of her unconventional sexual behavior. Reformers, manufacturers of popular culture, and sociologists dominated these debates.[61]

At the turn of the century, reformers presented the woman lodger as a symbol of endangered womanhood. In the organized boarding-home movement, the antiprostitution crusade, and the campaign to improve women's wages, reformers wrote with genuine concern for poorly paid, self-supporting women. With a sense of female solidarity, they deplored the economic hardships faced by the wage-earning woman, but they reserved their greatest distress for her sexual vulnerability.[62] Like most middle-class Americans of their day, they lamented female sexual expression outside marriage, but, unlike many, they rarely blamed the women involved."[63] Following earlier female moral reformers, they read sexual expression as a symbol of female victimization in an increasingly ruthless urban world.[64] These writers portrayed sexually active women lodgers as passive, pure, and impoverished orphans duped, forced, or unduly tempted by scheming men. While they occasionally criticized women lodgers for their "tendency . . . to drift away from sweet and tender home influences," most often they condemned the "vampires" who trapped "poor, innocent little girls."[65] The reformers acknowledged that a woman lodger might enjoy the companionship she found in the furnished-room districts, but "the glare of cheap entertainments and the dangers of the street," they feared, would overpower her.[66] In short, they adopted a stereotype of female weakness and innocence that absolved the woman lodger of responsibility for her own sexual behavior.

The reformers appointed themselves as maternal protectors. In Chicago and other cities, they opened subsidized boarding homes—"veritable virtue-saving stations"—to lure women from commercial rooming houses.[67] By the 1920s Chicago had over sixty organized homes managed by Protestant, Catholic, Jewish, African American, German, Swedish, Polish, and Norwegian-Danish middle-class women for working women of their own religious, racial, and ethnic background.[68] They established room registries that placed women lodgers with private families in residential neighborhoods. They campaigned for minimum-wage laws because they saw the low pay of women lodgers as a major cause of "immorality." To "outwit evil agents, who would deceive the innocent," they placed charity workers in train stations and police matrons in public dance halls.[69] While they helped women in need of support, they obscured the actions that women lodgers took on their own behalf, and elaborated instead an image of weak-willed women in sexual danger. In fact, well after most reformers had acknowledged the competence of working women living with parents, the "woman adrift," who lodged on her own, bereft of protectors, remained a symbol of endangered womanhood.

A variant of the reformers' discourse reached into popular culture. In the late nineteenth and early twentieth centuries, popular "working-girl" romance novels, printed as cheap books or story-paper serials, adopted the image of orphaned, innocent, and imperiled "women adrift."[70] In these melodramatic stories, young, virtuous, native-born, white women endured countless agonies when alone in the city, and eventually married wealthy men. Here the language of female victimization reached its most sensational. Listen to

Charlotte M. Stanley, the author of "Violet, the Beautiful Street Singer; or, an Ill-Starred Betrothal": "Oh, what cruel fate was it that had so suddenly altered the safe, smooth current of her young existence and cast her adrift in this frightful seething whirlpool of vice and crime?"[71] In romance novels, the gravest dangers a woman faced were threats to her sexual purity, generally seduction, abduction, procurement, and forced marriage. The queen of romance was probably Laura Jean Libbey, the author of over sixty novels in the late nineteenth century. Libbey created especially naive heroines who endured unusually frequent and frightening perils. In the opening chapters of one Libbey novel, beautiful Junie, an "artless little country lass" alone in the city, spurns the advances of a cad, follows a seemingly kind male stranger "without the least thought of her danger," and falls into the clutches of the cruel Squire Granger, who abducts her.[72] Like the reformers, Libbey publicized the perils of life in the city and sympathized with the lone woman, whom she portrayed as passive, innocent, and endangered.

The reformers and romance novelists, though, were fighting a losing battle, in part because the women they hoped to help belied the image of helpless victim. In fact, some women lodgers themselves directly attacked the reformers who treated them as pathetic orphans. In 1890, several "self-respecting and self-supporting" residents of the Chicago YWCA home wrote a blistering letter to a local newspaper:

> The idea seems to be in circulation that we who are unfortunate enough to be independent, are a collection of ignorant, weak-minded young persons, who have never had any advantages, educational or otherwise, and that we are brought here where we will be philanthropically cared for, and the cold winds tempered for us. A matron is provided, and a committee of women who happen to be blessed with a few thousand dollars worth of aristocracy, has charge of the matron.

The women also complained of the furniture and food, and referred to themselves as the "victims of the home."[73]

By the early twentieth century, some reformers began to reassess their outlook. Managers of organized homes and other astute observers could not help note that many women lodgers were competent, assertive, and sexual by choice. Using the fact-gathering methods of the new social science, social investigators met face-to-face with women who pursued sexual companionship actively.[74] While reformers' concern for the woman lodger continued, they dropped their earlier emphasis on her passivity. Some also began to recognize that wage-earning women had sexual feelings. In 1910 one Chicago antivice crusader, who described self-supporting women as innocent, naive, and unprotected, admitted that "every normal girl or woman has primal instincts just as strong as her brother's."[75] Jane Addams, Louise DeKoven Bowen, and other Chicago reformers rejected earlier images of female passionlessness, and instead blamed overwork, commercialized recreation, and alcohol for bringing out natural yearnings and instincts that they preferred to see repressed.

As reformers observed women lodgers, their fears about sexual danger diminished. They saw that women in the furnished-room districts lived in a world that attached less stigma to female sexual activity. Reformers interviewed women who had given up their chastity without an inkling that they had chosen "a fate worse than death," and they saw that a wage-earning woman might choose to sell or exchange sexual services without ruining her life. "The fact that she has earned money in this way does not stamp her as 'lost,'" a 1911 federal report stated. "And the ease with which, in a large city, a woman may conceal a fall of this kind, if she desires to do so, also helps make a return to virtuous ways easy.... [O]ccasional prostitution holds its place in their minds as a possible resource, extreme, to be sure, but not in the least unthinkable."[76]

By the mid-1910s the observations of reformers coincided with broader changes in middle-class thought and behavior. In the years before World War I, increasing numbers of middle-class urban women adopted the more open sexual behavior of women in the furnished-room districts. This change in middle-class morals further undermined the older image of female innocence and passionlessness, and challenged reformers' fear that female sexual behavior denoted female victimization. After World War I, in a conservative political climate, reformers suffered further from declining public interest and from government repression and indifference.[77]

Ultimately reformers' views on sexuality could not compete with a newer discourse emerging in popular culture. In the early twentieth century, cabaret reviews and movies attracted audiences by using the woman lodger as an appealing symbol of urban vitality, allure, and adventure. In these newer texts, the woman lodger, headstrong and openly sexual, lived freely in a fast-paced urban environment. In the earlier romance novels, unfortunate circumstance—poverty or death in the family—forced timid young women, soon to be victims, from happy parental homes. Or foolish young women left home and soon regretted it. In the newer scenarios, opportunistic women, such as Theodore Dreiser's Sister Carrie, chafed at the restriction of domesticity and the dullness of the small town. As one writer concluded, "[The city] is her frontier and in it she is the pioneer."[78] In the earlier discourse, the woman victim's suffering signified the high cost of urban living; in the newer, the woman pioneer's pleasure pointed to its rewards.[79]

By the first decade of the twentieth century, the new image reached national audiences in stories of chorus girls who achieved stardom and married wealth.[80] These women strutted boldly across the stage, displaying their bodies and commanding attention through their sexual appeal. They won wide publicity in 1908 when the trial of Henry Thaw made sensational headlines and reached larger audiences still in a movie, *The Great Trial.* Thaw had murdered architect Stanford White in a jealous rage over White's affair with Thaw's wife, Evelyn Nesbit. During the trial, Nesbit, a former chorus girl, told how wealthy men entertained, courted, and, in her case, married the sexually attractive dancers in cabarets and theaters. As she recounted her rise from the life of a hardworking chorus girl to a life of luxury and extravagance, she announced the material and romantic pleasures available to the sexual, independent wage-earning woman.[81]

In the following years, as the number of movie theaters expanded rapidly and the size of audiences grew, the woman lodger emerged as a central character in the new feature films. At first, in early "white slavery" films, the heroines faced threats to their virtue and sometimes eventual victimization. At the same time, though, in early serials—*The Perils of Pauline* and *The Hazards of Helen*—the heroines, independent from family, were "healthy, robust, and self-reliant." They met available and often monied men whom they attracted with their native allure. While they encountered dangers and difficulties, they also enjoyed a daring nightlife in cabarets and dance halls, as well as the high life in opulent villas.[82] By 1915 Mary Pickford, the first major movie queen, was portraying women lodgers who flirted, danced, wore revealing clothing, and enjoyed energetic activities. Always chaste, she combined the purity of the Victorian orphan with the healthy sexuality of the chorus girl. Her exuberance and spunk attracted male suitors, leading to upwardly mobile marriages.[83]

By the 1920s, the movies drew clear connections between independence from family, on one side, and female sexuality and material gain, on the other. In some movies, the woman lodger was the stock heroine in rags-to-riches stories. *At the Stage Door* typifies the formula: "Mary leaves home to become a chorus girl in New York, and soon she achieves stardom. Philip Pierce, a young millionaire, is attracted to her."[84] As the heterosexual activities and assertive behavior of the independent working woman became more explicit in movies, so did the threat she posed to men.[85] The woman lodger as "gold digger" appeared at least as early as 1915. In *The Model: Or, Women and Wine*, wealthy young Dick Seymour pursues an independent working woman, Marcelle Rigadont, an artist's model. Marcelle, as one character advises her, wants to "play him for a sucker . . . and bleed him for every cent he's got." She finally confesses, "I never loved you—It was only your money I was after."[86] In the 1920s at least thirty-four films included the "gold digger" with her "aggressive use of sexual attraction."[87]

Although unrecorded forms of entertainment are harder to document, it seems that similar themes appeared in chorus revues at cabarets and theaters. In the opening number of the Midnight Frolic's *Just Girls*, staged in 1915, "girls from 24 cities and one small home town came to New York for adventure, men, and a new life." *Sally*, a Ziegfield revue staged in 1920, told the story of a working-class orphan who climbed from "the chorus to theatrical fame, wealthy admirers, and riches."[88] By the 1920s, variations on these plot lines appeared repeatedly in new monthly pulp romance magazines such as *True Story* and *True Romances*.

In the late 1910s and 1920s the new image of women lodgers achieved academic legitimacy in writings by urban sociologists at the University of Chicago. Inaugurated in the 1890s, the academic discipline of sociology moved quickly from an antiurban moralism to more rarefied theoretical questions. In Chicago, sociologists, predominantly male, undertook intensive investigations of urban life, using census data, interviews, and observation. They showed little interest in women or in sexuality per se; rather, they used sexual behavior in the furnished-room districts to bolster their theories of "urban evolution." Sociologist Robert Park wrote, "Everywhere the old order is passing, but the new has not arrived. . . . This is particularly true of the so-called rooming-house area."[89] In this view, the furnished-room districts became the vanguard of urban change, characterized by "disorganization" and "individuation." As these terms suggest, some sociologists saw the furnished-room districts as disturbed, soulless, and lonely.[90] For the most part, though, sociologists had a stronger faith in progress. As the vanguard of urban evolution, the furnished-room districts were, in a sense, the most advanced development of urban life. With a marked ambivalence, sociologists described the residents of furnished-room districts as "emancipated" as frequently as they called them "disorganized."[91]

For sociologists, the woman of the furnished-room districts represented the freedom of urban life. As in movies, the urban woman was seen as released from the "monotony of settled family life" in the small town.[92] From a barren, restricted existence, she moved to "a section of the old frontier transplanted to the heart of the modern city" where, competent and self-seeking, she could pursue her individual desires and ambitions.[93] One particularly blunt sociology student stated, "The homeless woman of modern cities is the emancipated woman."[94] In areas where earlier reformers had discovered sexual exploitation of unprotected women, sociologists now found willing participation. Of dating for money, Frances Donovan wrote, "She is not . . . exploited nor driven into it, but goes with her eyes wide open."[95] Another sociologist asserted, more dubiously, that prostitutes were no longer exploited by procurers or pimps.[96] And, as in the movies, some sociologists depicted the sexually "emancipated" woman as a potential threat to men: "In the quest after the material equipment of life . . . the girl becomes not only an individualist but also—frankly—an opportunist."[97] In earlier reformers' portrayals, men exploited naive women; in sociologists' constructions, women lodgers, like Hollywood "gold diggers," took advantage of men.

No less than earlier images of the innocent victim, new images of the urban pioneer reduced women in furnished-room districts to stereotypes, exaggerating certain features of their lives and neglecting others. Sociologists used self-supporting women as examples of uniquely urban personalities, emphasizing those traits that supported their theories of urban evolution: individualism, unconventional sexual behavior, transient personal relationships, and freedom from social control. Their commitment to the idea of evolutionary progress encouraged them to view these urban features as at least somewhat positive and liberating. At the same time, sociologists undermined reform efforts to alleviate female poverty. They downplayed the negative constraints of low wages, sexual harassment, and economic dependence, and thus suggested that reformers were superfluous, even meddling.

Reformers and romance novelists portrayed women lodgers as passive, passionless, and imperiled, while sociologists, moviemakers, and pulp magazine writers depicted them as active, pleasure-seeking, and opportunistic. The changing discourse marks the waning influence of moral reformers and the rise to cultural power of manufacturers of mass entertainment and academic social scientists. It also highlights a larger change in the portrayal of women in America, from the Victorian angel to the sexy starlet. In the late nineteenth century women lodgers, alone in the city, epitomized the purity of endangered womanhood; in the early twentieth century the same women were among the first "respectable" women broadcast as happy sexual objects.

The sexual behavior of women in turn-of-the-century furnished-room districts is not an isolated episode in women's history. Other U.S. historians also describe sexual expression among women lodgers. From at least the 1830s to at least the 1960s, women who supported themselves in the cities sometimes explored the boundaries of sexual convention.[98] In other societies as well, "modern" sexual behavior has reflected in part the changing social and economic relations wrought by wage work and urbanization. The migration of labor to cities has removed some women workers from traditional forms of community or family control and protection, thus opening possibilities for both sexual experimentation and sexual coercion. At the same time, the worldwide gender gap in wages has sustained women's dependence on others, especially on men. In new urban, industrial settings, the traditional exchange of services for support has taken on extrafamilial, sexual forms, including temporary alliances and occasional prostitution.[99]

In turn-of-the-century Chicago, the volume of migrants led entrepreneurs to invest in restaurants, furnished-rooming houses, theaters, cabarets, and dance halls. Women and men flocked to and shaped these institutions, creating new peer-oriented subcultures in specific urban districts. In these districts, most women could not afford to view sex solely in terms of sexual danger or sensual pleasure, for sexual expression was also tied inextricably to various forms of economic reward. In this context, the sexual revolution was, most likely, sometimes oppressive, sometimes exciting, and often an exchange.

The history of women lodgers in the furnished-room districts is important, for these women helped shape the modern sexual expression that other women later adopted. In the furnished-room districts themselves, middle- and upper-class bohemian "new women" observed the unconventional behavior of working-class women who were their neighbors. Middle-class pleasure-seekers and "flappers" may have copied the blueprints of "sexy" behavior they observed while slumming in the districts' cabarets and dance halls. And moviegoers and magazine readers learned from the portrayals of women lodgers, as films, cabarets, and romance magazines used the sexuality of independent wage-earning women to attract and titillate viewers and readers. In these ways, turn-of-the-century women lodgers helped chart the modern American sexual terrain.

Notes

1. This article is reprinted in slightly revised form from Nancy Hewitt, ed., *Women, Families, and Communities: Readings in American History* (New York: Scott Foresman, 1990). It draws on material in Joanne Meyerowitz, *Women Adrift: Independent Wage-Earners in Chicago, 1880–1930* (Chicago: University of Chicago Press,

1988). Thanks to Estelle Freedman, Zane Miller, Leila Rupp, Christina Simmons, and Bruce Tucker for their helpful comments. And special thanks to Nancy Hewitt, who helped sustain this article through its strange publication history.

2. Frederick Lewis Allen, *Only Yesterday* (New York: Harper and Brothers, 1931); William Leuchtenburg, *The Perils of Prosperity, 1914–1932* (Chicago: University of Chicago Press, 1958); James McGovern, "The American Woman's Pre–World War I Freedom in Manners and Morals," *Journal of American History* (September 1968); Gerald F. Critoph, "The Flapper and Her Critics," in Carol V. R. George, ed., *"Remember the Ladies": New Perspectives on Women in American History* (Syracuse: Syracuse University Press, 1975). See also Paula S. Fass, *The Damned and the Beautiful: American Youth in the 1920s* (New York: Oxford University Press, 1977); John Modell, "Dating Becomes the Way of American Youth," in Leslie Page Moch and Gary Stark, eds., *Essays on the Family and Historical Change* (College Station: Texas A & M University Press, 1983).

3. June Sochen, *The New Woman: Feminism in Greenwich Village, 1910–1920* (New York: Quadrangle Books, 1972); Elaine Showalter, ed., *These Modern Women: Autobiographical Essays from the Twenties* (Old Westbury, N.Y.: Feminist Press, 1978); Carroll Smith-Rosenberg, "The New Woman as Androgyne: Social Disorder and Gender Crisis, 1870–1936," in Smith-Rosenberg, ed., *Disorderly Conduct: Visions of Gender in Victorian, America* (New York: Alfred A. Knopf, 1985); Esther Newton, "The Mythic Mannish Lesbian: Radclyffe Hall and the New Woman," *Signs: Journal of Women in Culture and Society* (summer 1984); Ellen Carol DuBois and Linda Gordon, "Seeking Ecstasy on the Battlefield: Danger and Pleasure in Nineteenth-Century Feminist Sexual Thought," in Carole S. Vance, ed., *Pleasure and Danger: Exploring Female Sexuality* (Boston: Routledge and Kegan Paul, 1984); Leila J. Rupp, "Feminism and the Sexual Revolution in the Early Twentieth Century: The Case of Doris Stevens," *Feminist Studies* (summer 1989). For an earlier account, see Henry F. May, *The End of American Innocence: A Study of the First Years of Our Own Time, 1912–1917* (New York: Alfred A. Knopf, 1986).

4. Kathy Peiss, *Cheap Amusements: Working Women and Leisure in Turn-of-the-Century New York* (Philadelphia: Temple University Press, 1986); for the nineteenth century, see Christine Stansell, *City of Women: Sex and Class in New York, 1789–1860* (New York: Alfred A. Knopf, 1986).

5. For a summary of these debates, see "Forum: The Feminist Sexuality Debates," *Signs: Journal of Woman in Culture and Society* (autumn 1984); Carole S. Vance, "Pleasure and Danger: Toward a Politics of Sexuality," in Vance, ed., *Pleasure and Danger*.

6. Robert Park, "The City: Suggestions for the Investigation of Human Behavior in Urban Environment," in Richard Sennett, ed., *Classic Essays on the Culture of Cities* (New York: Meredith Corporation, 1969), 128–29.

7. Robert Woods, ed., *The City Wilderness: A Settlement Study* (Boston: Houghton Mifflin, 1898); see especially William I. Cole's article, "Criminal Tendencies," 166–69.

8. Albert Benedict Wolfe, *The Lodging House Problem in Boston* (Boston: Houghton Mifflin, 1906), 171. See also Franklin Kline Fretz, *The Furnished Room Problem in Philadelphia* (Ph.D. diss., University of Pennsylvania, 1912); S. P. Breckinridge and Edith Abbott, "Chicago's Housing Problems: Families in Furnished Rooms," *American Journal of Sociology* (November 1910): 289–308.

9. Harvey Warren Zorbaugh, *Gold Coast and Slum: A Sociological Study of Chicago's Near North Side* (Chicago: University of Chicago Press, 1929), 153.

10. To avoid being unduly influenced by the sociologists' discourse, I have accepted the sociologists' conclusions only when I could corroborate them with evidence from other sources, such as newspapers accounts, reports of reformers, and memoirs.

11. In the 1910s the South Side district ran from Sixteenth to Thirty-third Streets and from Clark Street to Prairie Avenue; the West Side district ran from Washington to Harrison Streets and from Ashland Boulevard to Halsted Street; the North Side district went from Division Street to the Chicago River and from Wells to Rush Streets. Edith Abbott, *The Tenements of Chicago, 1908–1935* (Chicago: University of Chicago Press, 1936).

    Information on the population of the furnished room districts was derived from sociological studies and from the Federal Manuscript Census, Meyerowitz's samples of Chicago "women adrift," 1880 and 1910, and the tract-by-tract census data found in Ernest W. Burgess and Charles Newcomb, eds., *Census Data of the City of Chicago, 1920* (Chicago: University of Chicago Press, 1931), and Ernest W. Burgess and Charles Newcomb, eds. *Census Data of the City of Chicago, 1930* (Chicago: University of Chicago Press, 1933).

12. On growth of districts, see Abbott, *Tenements of Chicago*, ch. 10; also Kimball Young, "Sociological Study of a Disintegrated Neighborhood" (M.A. thesis, University of Chicago, 1918). On the number of lodgers, see T. W. Allison, "Population Movement in Chicago," *Journal of Social Forces* (May 1924): 529–33. The lodging houses included in the 1923 register were only those with more than ten roomers.

13. Zorbaugh, *Gold Coast and Slum*, 72.

14. See Wolfe, *The Lodging Problem in Boston*; for examples of permissive landladies in Chicago, see Louise DeKoven Bowen, *The Straight Girl on the Crooked Path: A True Story* (Chicago: Juvenile Protective Association of Chicago, 1916).

15. In 1920 the sex ratio in the North Side district was 1.4 and in the West Side district 1.6. In 1930 the ratio in the North Side district was 1.3 and in the West Side district 2.0. In both years, the South Side district, which was more dispersed over a larger area, had a sex ratio of 1.0. These sex ratios were derived from tract-by-tract census data found in Burgess and Newcomb, eds., *Census Data of the City of Chicago, 1920* and *Census Data of the City of Chicago, 1930*.

16. Vice Commission of Chicago, *The Social Evil in Chicago: A Study of Existing Conditions with Recommendations by the Vice Commission of Chicago* (Chicago: Vice Commission of Chicago, 1911), 87–91.

17. *The Social Evil in Chicago*, 73, 74, 92–94.

18. "Investigation of Commercialized Prostitution," December 1922, Juvenile Protective Association of Chicago Papers 5:92, University of Illinois at Chicago Manuscript Collections.

19. Young, "Sociological Study of a Disintegrated Neighborhood," 52.

20. Ibid., 42; Abbott, *The Tenements of Chicago*, 322.

21. James R. Grossman, *Land of Hope: Chicago, Black Southerners, and the Great Migration* (Chicago: University of Chicago Press, 1989), 117; E. Franklin Frazier, *The Negro Family in Chicago* (Chicago: University of Chicago Press, 1932), 103. See also Carroll Binder, "Negro Active in Business World," *Chicago Daily News*, 5 August 1927; Junius B. Wood, *The Negro in Chicago* (reprint of articles in *Chicago Daily News*, 11–27 December 1916), 25.

22. Reckless, "The Natural History of Vice Areas," 381.

23. E. H. Wilson, "Chicago Families in Furnished Rooms" (M.A. thesis, University of Chicago, 1929), 100.

24. See Young, "Sociological Study of a Disintegrated Neighborhood," 54; also Zorbaugh, *Gold Coast and Slum*. As early as 1898, Frederick Bushee suggested that "The lodging houses themselves [in Boston's South End district] are the homes of the queer and questionable of every shade," in Woods, ed., *The City Wilderness*, 50.

25. See, for example, Walter C. Reckless, *Vice in Chicago* (Chicago: University of Chicago Press, 1933), 53–54. I use Claude Fischer's definition of subcultures: "social worlds . . . inhabited by persons who share relatively distinctive traits (like ethnicity or occupation), who tend to interact especially with one another, and who manifest a relatively distinct set of beliefs and behaviors." Claude S. Fischer, *The Urban Experience* (New York: Harcourt, Brace, Jovanovich, 1976), 36.

26. Young, "Sociological Study of a Disintegrated Neighborhood," 79.

27. Case record from Chicago Vice Study File, cited in Walter C. Reckless, *Vice in Chicago*, 53, 54.

28. *Chicago Examiner*, 12 April 1913.

29. Box-Car Bertha as told to Dr. Ben L. Reitman, *Sister of the Road: The Autobiography of Box-Car Bertha* (New York: Macauley, 1937), 68, 70, 62, 29.

30. There is some evidence of a lesbian community among prostitutes in Paris as early as the 1880s, and also evidence suggesting that some lesbians in New York participated in the male homosexual subculture there by the 1890s. In general, though, American lesbian communities were not visible until the 1920s, perhaps because the majority of women had fewer opportunities than men to leave family life. Moreover, romantic attachments between women were not usually labeled deviant in America until the early twentieth century. Middle- and upper-class women who lived together as couples in "Boston marriages," for example, were not segregated as outcasts from heterosexual family and friends. On early male homosexual subcultures in American cities, see Jonathan Katz, ed., *Gay American History: Lesbians and Gay Men in the U.S.A.* (New York: Avon Books, 1976), 61–81; John D'Emilio, "Capitalism and Gay Identity," in Ann Snitow, Christine Stansell, and Sharon Thompson, eds., *Powers of Desire: The Politics of Sexuality* (New York: Monthly Review Press, 1983), and George Chauncey Jr., "Christian Brotherhood or Sexual Perversion? Sexual Boundaries in the World War One Era," *Journal of Social History* (winter 1985). On lesbian prostitutes in Paris and on turn-of-the-century tolerance for lesbianism, see Lillian Faderman, *Surpassing the Love of Men: Romantic Friendship and Love Between from the Renaissance to the Present* (New York: William Morrow and Co., 1981), 282, 298.

31. Paul Oliver, *Screening the Blues: Aspects of the Blues Tradition* (London: Cassell and Co., 1968), 225, 226.

32. Box-Car Bertha, *Sister of the Road*, p. 65.

33. "A nurse told me of being called on night duty in an apartment in the 'village' and of being entertained every night by the girls in the apartment across the well, some of whom would put on men's evening clothes, make love to the others, and eventually carry them off in their arms into the bedrooms." Zorbaugh, *Gold Coast and Slum*, 100.

34. Frazier, *The Negro Family in Chicago*, 103; interview with Eulalia B., conducted by author, 16 October 1980.

35. Zorbaugh, *Gold Coast and Slum*, 91.

36. "Dill Pickle Club," in Vivien Palmer, "Documents of History of the Lower North Side," vol. 3, pt. 2, doc. 52, Chicago Historical Society.

37. Zorbaugh, *Gold Coast and Slum*, 114–15.

38. Walter Reckless, "The Natural History of Vice Areas in Chicago" (Ph.D. diss., University of Chicago, 1925), 374, 375. For a similar rejection of social background, see the story of Christina Stranski (aka

DeLoris Glenn) in Paul G. Cressey, *The Taxi-Dance Hall: A Sociological Study in Commercialized Recreation and City Life* (Chicago: University of Chicago Press, 1932), 56.

39. On bohemians as a vanguard of sex radicalism, see May, *The End of American Innocence.*

40. A few other historians have suggested that working-class women were pioneers in changing sexual mores. See, for example, Nathan G. Hale Jr., *Freud and the Americans: The Beginnings of Psychoanalysis in the United States, 1876–1917* (New York: Oxford University Press, 1971), 477; Lewis A. Erenberg, *Steppin' Out: New York Nightlife and the Transformation of American Culture, 1890–1930* (Westport, Conn.: Greenwood Press, 1981); Daniel Scott Smith, "The Dating of the American Sexual Revolution: Evidence and Interpretation," in Michael Gordon, ed., *The American Family in Social-Historical Perspective* (New York: St. Martin's Press, 1973).

41. On women's wages, see Leslie Woodcock Tentler, *Wage-Earning Women: Industrial Work and Family Life in the United States, 1900–1930* (New York: Oxford University Press, 1979).

42. Charles P. Neill, *Wage-Earning Women in Stores and Factories*, vol. 5, *Report on Condition of Woman and Child Wage-Earners in the United States* (Washington, D.C.: Government Printing Office, 1910), 75.

43. *The Social Evil in Chicago*, 186.

44. *Chicago Defender*, 20 August 1921.

45. See Kathy Peiss, "'Charity Girls' and City Pleasures: Historical Notes on Working-Class Sexuality, 1880–1920," in Stansell, and Thompson, eds., *Powers of Desire.*

46. Louise DeKoven Bowen, *The Girl Employed in Hotels and Restaurants* (Chicago: Juvenile Protective Association of Chicago, 1912).

47. "Alma N. Z——r," Paul Cressey notes, c. 1926, 5, Ernest Burgess Papers 129:6, University of Chicago Manuscript Collections.

48. Zorbaugh, *Gold Coast and Slum*, 86.

49. Frances Donovan, *The Woman Who Waits* (New York: Arno Press 1974, [1920]), 211–20.

50. *The Social Evil in Chicago*, 133, 95.

51. Ibid., 188.

52. Ruth Shonle Cavan, *Suicide* (Chicago: University of Chicago Press, 1928), 206.

53. Wolfe, *The Lodging House Problem in Boston*, 142. In these accounts of heterosexual relationships, most of the women lodgers seem to be under thirty years of age. Older women lodgers were probably somewhat less attractive to the predominantly young male suitors. They also seemed to tire of the nightlife, preferring the more stable support and companionship sometimes provided in marriage. In fact, most women lodgers in Chicago did eventually marry. For a revealing interview with an older woman, see Anderson, "Life History of a Rooming House Keeper," c. 1925, Ernest Burgess Papers 127:2, University of Chicago Manuscript Collections.

54. Box-Car Bertha, *Sister of the Road*, 223, 66, 69, 288. This limited evidence of dependent relationships is corroborated by other evidence that early twentieth-century working-class lesbians often adopted somewhat traditional gender roles, with one partner assuming a masculine role. See Katz, *Gay American History*, 383–90. See also Joan Nestle, "The Fem Question," in Vance, ed., *Pleasure and Danger*, and Elizabeth Lapovsky Kennedy and Madeline Davis, "The Reproduction of Butch-Fem Roles: A Social Constructionist Approach," in Kathy Peiss and Christina Simmons, eds., *Passion and Power: Sexuality in History* (Philadelphia: Temple University Press, 1989).

55. See, for example, Louise DeKoven Bowen, *A Study of Bastardy Cases* (Chicago: Juvenile Protective Association, 1914).

56. Lillian S. W—n," Paul Cressey Notes, 18, Ernest Burgess Papers 129:6, University of Chicago Manuscript Collections.

57. Kenneth Yellis, "Prosperity's Child: Some Thoughts on the Flapper," *American Quarterly* (spring 1969).

58. *Chicago Daily Times*, 31 January 1930.

59. I'm not suggesting that the contemporary feminist sexuality debates replicate the earlier discourse, only that contemporary debates are a new, different, and interesting variant of older associations. On sex as danger, see Caroll Smith-Rosenberg, "Sex as Symbol in Victorian Purity: An Ethnohistorical Analysis of Jacksonian America," in John Demos and Sarane Spence Boocock, eds., *Turning Points: Historical and Sociological Essays on the Family* (Chicago: University of Chicago Press, 1978); Paul Boyer, *Urban Masses and Moral Order in America, 1820–1920* (Cambridge, Mass.: Harvard University Press, 1978); on sex as pleasure, see Paul Robinson, *The Modernization of Sex: Havelock Ellis, Alfred Kinsey, William Masters and Virginia Johnson* (New York: Harper and Row, 1976). For a general history of the changing dominant discourses on sexuality, see John D'Emilio and Estelle Freedman, *Intimate Matters: A History of Sexuality in America* (New York: Harper and Row, 1988). On late-nineteenth- and early-twentieth-century feminist variants of the shift from sex as danger to sex as pleasure, see DuBois and Gordon, "Seeking Ecstasy on the Battlefield," in Vance, ed., *Pleasure and Danger*. For formulations in Britain, see Judith Walkowitz, *Prostitution and Victorian Society: Women, Class, and the State* (Cambridge: Cambridge University Press, 1980); Susan Kingsley Kent, *Sex and Suffrage*

in Britain, 1860–1914 (Princeton: Princeton University Press, 1987); Frank Mort, *Dangerous Sexualities: Medico-Moral Politics in England Since 1830* (London: Routledge and Kegan Paul, 1987). In general, representations of sex as vitality, pleasure, adventure, and freedom have not been studied as closely by historians as representations of sex as danger, disease, decay, and disorder.

60. On the attack on Victorian "sexual repression," see Christina Simmons, "Modern Sexuality and the Myth of Victorian Repression," in Peiss and Simmons, eds., *Passion and Power.* See also Michel Foucault, *The History of Sexuality*, vol. 1 (New York: Vintage Books, 1980).

61. For psychiatrists' contribution to these public discussions, see Elizabeth Lunbeck, "'A New Generation of Women': Progressive Psychiatrists and the Hypersexual Woman," *Feminist Studies* (fall 1987).

62. On late-nineteenth-century reformers' interest in working women, see Mari Jo Buhle, "The Nineteenth-Century Woman's Movement: Perspectives on Women's Labor in Industrializing America," Bunting Institute of Radcliffe College, 1979.

63. For a more detailed discussion of the reformers' position, see Meyerowitz, *Women Adrift*, ch. 3. For a similar combination of feminist sympathy and middle-class moralism in the early to mid-nineteenth century, see Stansell, *City of Women*, 70–74.

64. On earlier reformers, see especially Mary P. Ryan, "The Power of Women's Networks: A Case Study of Female Moral Reform in Antebellum America," *Feminist Studies* (spring 1979); Carroll Smith-Rosenberg, "Beauty, the Beast, and the Militant Woman: A Case Study of Sex Roles and Social Stress in Jacksonian America," in Nancy F. Cott and Elizabeth H. Pleck, eds., *A Heritage of Her Own: Toward a New Social History of American Women* (New York: Simon and Schuster, 1979).

65. Women's Christian Association of Chicago, *Fifth Annual Report* (1881), 12; Charles Bryon Chrysler, *White Slavery* (Chicago: n.p., 1909), 13.

66. Annie Marion MacLean, "Homes for Working Women in Large Cities," *Charities Review*, July 1899, 228.

67. MacLean, "Homes for Working Women," 228.

68. Josephine J. Taylor, "Study of YWCA Room Registry," 1928, Ernest Burgess Papers 138:9, University of Chicago Manuscript Collections: Essie Mae Davidson, "Organized Boarding Homes for Self-Supporting Women in the City of Chicago" (M.A. thesis, University of Chicago, 1914); Ann Elizabeth Trotter, *Housing Non-Family Women in Chicago: A Survey* (Chicago: Chicago Community Trust, c. 1921).

69. YWCA of Chicago, *18th Annual Report* (1894), 33. On the national Travelers' Aid movement, see Lynn Y. Weiner, *From Working Girl to Working Mother: The Female Labor Force in the United States, 1820–1980* (Chapel Hill: University of North Carolina Press, 1985). On reforming the dance halls, see Elisabeth I. Perry, "'The General Motherhood of the Commonwealth': Dance Hall Reform in the Progressive Era," *American Quarterly* (winter 1985).

70. For a brief description of the "working-girl" novel, see Cathy N. Davidson and Arnold E. Davidson, "Carrie's Sisters: The Popular Prototypes for Dreiser's Heroine," *Modern Fiction Studies* (autumn 1977).

71. Charlotte M. Stanley, "Violet, the Beautiful Street Singer; or An Ill-Starred Betrothal," *New York Family Story Paper*, 5 September 1908. See also T. W. Hanshew, "Alone in New York: A Thrilling Portrayal of the Dangers and Pitfalls of the Metropolis," *New York Family Story Paper*, 30 April 1887.

72. Laura Jean Libbey, *Junie's Love Test* (New York: George Munro, 1883), 66.

73. *Sunday Inter Ocean*, 16 November 1890. The women who lived in this YWCA home tended to be white, native-born women who held more middle-class jobs in offices and stores. Black women and immigrant women also expressed displeasure with forms of housing that invaded their privacy and reduced their initiative. See Meyerowitz, *Women Adrift*, ch. 4.

74. See, for example, Louise DeKoven Bowen, *Safeguards of City Youth at Work and at Play* (New York: Macmillan, 1914), 23; Clara E. Laughlin, *The Work-a-Day Girl* (New York: Arno Press, 1974 [1913]), 51.

75. Leona Prall Groetzinger, *The City's Perils* (n.p., c. 1910), 110.

76. Mary Conyngton, *Relation between Occupation and Criminality of Women*, vol. 15, *Report on Condition of Woman and Child Wage-Earners in the United States* (Washington, D.C.: Government Printing Office, 1911), 102–3.

77. Other factors undermining the reformers' image of passive, endangered women included the WWI venereal disease campaign, the decline in the number of women immigrants arriving from Europe, and a slight rise in women's real wages in the 1920s. As these changes occurred, most reformers lost interest in women lodgers; those who maintained their interest lost the power to shape cultural images.

78. Donovan, *The Woman Who Waits*, 9.

79. For a more detailed discussion of this newer image, see Meyerowitz, *Women Adrift*, ch. 6.

80. Lois Banner, *American Beauty* (Chicago: University of Chicago Press, 1983), 180–84.

81. On the Thaw trial, see Lewis Erenberg, *Steppin' Out*, 53; Lary May, *Screening Out the Past: The Birth of Mass Culture and the Motion Picture Industry* (New York: Oxford University Press, 1980), 34, 43.

82. May, *Screening Out the Past*, 108.

83. Ibid., 119, 142, 143. For a discussion of "heterosocial culture" in earlier films, see Peiss, *Cheap Amusements*, 153–58.

84. Kenneth Munden, ed., *The American Film Institute Catalog, Feature Films, 1921–1929* (New York: R. R. Bowker Co., 1971), 29.

85. The 1920s stories that represented sexual expression as pleasurable and adventurous often had a subtext of potential danger (especially to men), as the "gold digger" movies attest.

86. "The Model; or, Women and Wine," *Picture-Play Weekly*, 12 June 1915, 12–16.

87. Mary P. Ryan, "The Projection of a New Womanhood: The Movie Moderns in the 1920s," in Jean E. Friedman and William G. Shade, eds., *Our American Sisters: Women in American Life and Thought*, 2nd ed. (Boston: Allyn and Bacon, 1976), 376.

88. Erenberg, *Steppin' Out*, 210, 223.

89. Robert E. Park, "Introduction," in Zorbaugh, *Gold Coast and Slum*, viii.

90. Cavan, *Suicide*, 81; Robert E. L. Faris, *Chicago Sociology, 1920–1932* (Chicago: University of Chicago Press, Midway Reprint, 1979 [1967]), 35.

91. See, for examples, Ernest Mowrer, *Family Disorganization: An Introduction to Sociological Analysis* (Chicago: University of Chicago Press, 1927), 111; Faris, *Chicago Sociology*, 79.

92. Walter C. Reckless, "The Natural History of Vice Areas in Chicago," 211.

93. Zorbaugh, *The Gold Coast and the Slum*, 199.

94. Reckless, "The Natural History of Vice Areas," 209.

95. Donovan, *The Woman Who Waits*, 220.

96. W. I. Thomas, *The Unadjusted Girl, with Cases and Standpoint for Behavioral Analysis* (Boston: Little, Brown, and Co., 1923), 150.

97. Cressey, *The Taxi-Dance Hall*, 47.

98. Stansell, *City of Women*, 83–101, 171–192; Linda Gordon, *Woman's Body, Woman's Right: A Social History of Birth Control in America* (New York: Penguin Books, 1977), 203–4; Barbara Ehrenreich, Elizabeth Hess, and Gloria Jacobs, *Re-Making Love: The Feminization of Sex* (Garden City, N.Y.: Anchor Press/Doubleday, 1986), 39–42, 54–62.

99. There is a recent and growing literature on contemporary women migrants in Third World nations. For a good introduction, see the special issue of *International Migration Review* (winter 1984), and Annette Fuentes and Barbara Ehrenreich, *Women in the Global Factory* (Boston: South End Press, 1983). For additional references to sexuality, see also Ilsa Schuster, "Marginal Lives: Conflict and Contradiction in the Position of Female Traders in Lusaka, Zambia," in Edna G. Bay, ed., *Women and Work in Africa* (Boulder: Westview Press, 1982), and Sharon Stichter, *Migrant Laborers* (Cambridge: Cambridge University Press, 1985). On capitalism, urbanization, migration, and sexuality in Europe, see the now-classic accounts of the eighteenth century in Edward Shorter, "Illegitimacy, Sexual Revolution and Social Change in Modern Europe," *Journal of Interdisciplinary History* (autumn 1971), and Louise A. Tilly, Joan W. Scott, and Miriam Cohen, "Women's Work and Fertility Patterns," *Journal of Interdisciplinary History* (winter 1976). Shorter emphasizes the sexual pleasure pursued by women, while Tilly, Scott, and Cohen underscore women's sexual vulnerability. For a more recent account, see Nicholas Rogers, "Carnal Knowledge: Illegitimacy in Eighteenth-Century Westminster," *Journal of Social History* (winter 1989).

21

Making Faces: The Cosmetics Industry and the Cultural Construction of Gender, 1890–1930

Kathy Peiss

In the late nineteenth and early twentieth centuries, American women began to purchase and wear face powder, rouge, lipstick, and other kinds of visible cosmetics. A society that had scorned Victorian women's makeup as a mark of disrepute and illegitimacy had, by the early decades of the twentieth century, embraced powder and paint as essential signs of femininity. Once marking the prostitute and the aristocratic lady as symbols of rampant sexuality and materialistic excess, cosmetics became understood as respectable and indeed necessary for women's success and fulfillment.

Cosmetics, of course, are nothing new. Throughout history and in many cultures, women and men have colored, distorted, and exaggerated their physical features. In the early twentieth century, however, cosmetics took on new meaning in American culture. They became part of an ongoing discourse on femininity that made problematic women's identity in an increasingly commercial, industrial, and urban world. Women linked cosmetics use to an emergent notion of their own modernity, which included wage-work, athleticism, leisure, freer sexual expressiveness, and greater individual consumption. At the same time, new forms of mass culture shaped this discourse, as women began to see their faces differently in a number of novel cultural mirrors: in motion pictures, in mass-market women's magazines and advertising, in shop windows, on fashion runways, and across the counters of department stores.[1]

This essay focuses, however, on the crucial role of the cosmetics and beauty business in popularizing cosmetics and shaping gender definitions. In this century, cosmetics use has been inextricably tied to the emergence of a mass consumer industry. From the 1870s onward, American business has aggressively developed consumer markets, utilizing new techniques of mass production and distribution. In search of expanded and predictable profits, capitalism has promoted the redefinition and commodification of everyday social needs. The cosmetics business, whose financial success lay in defining the outward appearance of femininity, exemplifies this history. In the cosmetics industry, we can see how specific processes of mass production, distribution, marketing, and advertising rendered new social meanings about female identity and made them compelling to women consumers.

Complicating this story, however, is the segmentation of the industry from its inception into three distinct lines of trade. In modern marketing parlance, the industry has long been divided into the "class," "mass," and "ethnic" markets. The "class market" represents high-priced cosmetic lines, both domestic and imported, whose aura is one of exclusivity and social status. Sold in department stores and exclusive salons, these products are marketed to wealthy and upwardly mobile middle-class women. "Mass" cosmetic products, the low-priced lines available in drugstores, variety stores, and discount beauty outlets, are marketed to a wide range of consumers, but particularly targeted toward working-class and lower-middle-class women, as well as teenagers. The ethnic market is a contemporary euphemism for the African American beauty industry, although this market includes Hispanic Americans, Asian Americans, and other women of color.

Historically the class, mass, and African American segments of the industry shared certain problems in fostering the popular use of cosmetics, especially in their need to convince women that being "painted" was not only respectable but a requirement of womanhood. In some respects they came up with similar solutions, which they projected through techniques of mass marketing and advertising. Each appropriated and manipulated a complex set of images about womanhood during a historic period that witnessed major changes in women's experience and status. However, they represented gender in different and contradictory ways that bespeak the divisions of class and race within the industry and, more broadly, within American society. Thus in this essay I first trace the commercialization of cosmetics and their popularization in each segment of the industry. I then turn to the ideological definition of womanhood, focusing on the ways that class and race were inextricably implicated in the cosmetics industry's projections of gendered appearance.

The Commercialization of Cosmetics

Women's cosmetics use in the nineteenth-century United States is difficult to determine with any exactness. Creams, lotions, and tonics—that is, external cosmetic applications involving skin care or therapeutic treatment—were widespread. From the 1840s, family keepsakes and formularies offered recipes to soften and whiten skin, cure freckles, and remove unwanted hair, and were distributed to a wide range of Americans, from middle-class ladies and gentlemen to farmers and mechanics. Many advice books also instructed women in the simple home manufacture of "make-up," that is, cosmetics involving the application of color to the face: pulverized chalk for face powder, beet root for rouge, burnt cloves or green walnut juice for eyebrow and lash coloring. As was the case with medicinal remedies, an oral tradition concerning hair and skin care probably comprised an aspect of women's culture.[2]

Yet the use of makeup was problematic for many nineteenth-century women. Among fashionable middle- and upper-class women, the obvious use of powder and paint came into vogue in the 1850s and 1860s, only to decline in the late nineteenth century. For the vast majority of middle-class women, however, enameling the face with a white liquid or visibly tinting it with rouge were objectionable practices. By 1900 the use of face powder seems to have become more common among urban middle-class women, judging from advice books and commentators; even the subtle application of rouge and eyebrow pencil, if concealed, was deemed acceptable.[3]

The use of cosmetics by white working-class and black women in the latter half of the nineteenth century is even more difficult to determine. Many working-class women refrained from makeup use, given religious beliefs, ethnic cultural traditions, concepts of respectability, and the cost of the products. Probably the most frequent working-class consumers of cosmetics were prostitutes, who signaled their trade to potential customers through the visible use of face powder and rouge. But other working women used these products as well, particularly the subculture of "disorderly" women oriented toward urban nightlife and sexual pleasure. Their use of cosmetics, as well as fancy dress and hairpieces, marked a distinctive and provocative cultural style, if not an oppositional aesthetics. For example, a ruddy complexion, either naturally or artificially induced, seems to have been an ideal among some working women. Reddish cheeks accompanied their boisterous, high-spirited behavior, and offered a sharp contrast to the pale faces of middle-class women. Other working women, who played with the ideal of being "ladies," powdered themselves so much that various employers, from department store managers to household mistresses, barred the use of face powders.[4] While there is even less evidence concerning cosmetics use among black women, stylishness and adornment were ideals cultivated by postbellum African Americans, signifying freedom and respectability. Although the issue of personal grooming for black women centered more around hair care, some use of cosmetics, particularly homemade products, is probable.[5]

Whatever the patterns of cosmetic use, consumer resistance to commercially manufactured cosmetics was very high in the nineteenth century. One fear concerned the potential health hazards of so-called patent cosmetics, a term that associated cosmetics with the extravagant claims and often ruinous results of patent medicines. American consumers were increasingly sensitive to the dangers of adulterated products and the substitutions of unscrupulous dealers; in the case of cosmetics, such fears were heightened by the centuries-old tradition of using arsenic, white lead, and other toxic substances in powders and enamels. Advice books often cautioned women, in the words of one, to become their "*own manufacturer*—not only as a matter of *economy*, but of *safety*." Indeed, cosmetics were ideologically linked to a larger critique of commerce and its practice of artifice and deception.[6]

The critique of cosmetics on grounds of health and safety was linked to another powerful, if less specific, set of concerns about what it meant to be "painted." On the one hand, for many Americans, cosmetics were associated with aristocratic excess, undemocratic luxury, and female self-indulgence. Artifice was the mode of parasitical ladies of fashion, who sacrificed health and familial duty in frivolous, self-centered pursuits. On the other hand, the "painted woman" most powerfully signified the prostitute, the immoral, public woman who lived outside the sanction of a middle-class society that valorized women's purity and the home. "Paint" demarcated the boundary between respectability and promiscuity, bourgeois gentility and lower-class vulgarity. If cultural definitions of gender were shaped and bounded by the cultural construction of class and race, then cosmetics contributed significantly to the external marking of those boundaries. Thus, handling social divisions and their cultural markers proved a special problem for the nascent cosmetics industry.[7]

The production of commercial cosmetics remained quite limited in the late nineteenth century. The census of manufactures of 1889 lists only 157 companies whose primary business was perfume and cosmetics. In a period when many consumer goods found a national market, the cosmetics industry was slow to take off. A comparison might be made with patent medicines and soaps, two products that, like cosmetics, were related to physical care and appearance. Sale of these goods gave rise to large corporations that had developed mass production, national distribution, and national advertising by the 1880s. Cosmetics, however, remained a small-scale business, highly entrepreneurial and without a distinctive identity. It was not until the years immediately before and after World War I that the industry experienced substantial growth. In 1914 there were 496 companies manufacturing perfume and cosmetics, and the value of their products was nearly $17 million; by 1919, although the number of companies had risen only to 569, the value of products climbed dramatically, to almost $60 million.[8]

The Segmentation of the Industry

Commercial manufacture of cosmetics emerged from several distinct lines of trade in the mid-nineteenth century: the manufacture of pharmaceuticals and drugstore supplies, the local business activity of druggists, and commercial beauty culture. Patent medicine makers produced some cosmetic products, particularly those with therapeutic claims. In addition, companies manufacturing perfumery, flavoring extracts, essential oils, and druggists' sundries also included a few cosmetics in their product lines. These were placed before the public through traditional routes of distribution, including drugstores, general stores, and peddlers. Relatively few of them—such as Pond's Extract and Hagan's Magnolia Balm— achieved national distribution or brand name recognition.

More commonplace were the hundreds of local druggists and hairdressers who compounded their own powders and creams, purchasing raw ingredients through wholesalers and jobbers. The catalogs of leading wholesale druggists, for example, contained only a few commercially made preparations but carried a full line of oils, waxes, powders, chemicals, dyes, and perfumes required in cosmetic formulas. In the late nineteenth century, cosmetics manufactured solely for a local or regional market far outnumbered those that achieved national distribution.[9]

Although drugstores were the primary purveyors of commercial cosmetics to the public, it was "beauty culture"—and its commercial exploitation by beauty parlor owners, cosmetic manufacturers, women's magazines, advertisers, and retailers—that fundamentally altered the market for cosmetics. Beauty culture became the crucial intermediary between a women's culture suspicious of powder and paint to one that delighted in them. Beginning in the 1880s, beauty culturists popularized the notion of ritualizing beautification for women. Beauty salons were initially places for the dressing and ornamentation of hair, but by the 1890s they had expanded their services to include facial treatments, manicures, and massage. At their most grand, these salons were service stations for elite and middle-class women's enhancement and relaxation.[10] But on a more modest scale, beauty culture was also available to women of lesser means, and was particularly important to African American women; indeed, the latter pioneered in the development of hair and skin treatments and products, creating one of the leading black-owned businesses in the United States.

The origins of the "class" segment of the cosmetics industry lie in the development of beauty culture for elite and upwardly mobile white women. In salons located on prestigious commercial streets and at expensive resorts, beauty culturists consciously created a paradoxical world of discipline and indulgence, therapy and luxury.[11] For women who had long been enjoined to sacrifice their own desires on behalf of husband and family, the message was irresistible: Women could fulfill the old prescription of "beauty a duty" while at the same time giving in to the siren call of a newer consumerist message. In the words of cosmetologist Susanna Cocroft, "Don' be ashamed of your desire for beauty."[12]

Ironically, beauty culturists generally did not approve of makeup, stressing breathing, exercise, diet, and bathing as the route to natural beauty. Madame Yale, a typical popularizer, warned women to avoid "fashion's glamor and the artificer's whims." For beauty culturists, as for many nineteenth-century Americans, the face was a window into the soul, and complexion problems were indicative of a life that was disordered, out of balance. Thus Susanna Cocroft asked women: "Is your complexion *clear?* Does it express the clearness of your life? Are there discolorations or blemishes in the skin—which symbolize imperfections within?" Beauty culture promised self-transformation that was both internal and external, an idea that resonated powerfully in American middle-class culture (Fig. 21.1).[13]

Beauty culturists initially offered face powder, rouge, and other makeup somewhat apologetically, or even with a tone of exasperation: "Outward applications only have the office of assisting in, and completing, the process which must begin *within*." Madame Yale in the 1890s sold a liquid powder, rouge, and lip tint that she termed "Temporary Beautifiers." She rather grudgingly noted their purchase by "many ladies . . . too indolent to cultivate

What New York
and Paris Society
and Stage Women
are Doing to
Keep Young Looking

Figure 21.1. Detail from Susanna Cocroft's "Success Face Lifters" pamphlet. Warshaw Collection of Business Americana, Archives Center, National Museum of American History, Smithsonian Institution. Photo No. 89-14354.

natural beauty by the Yale System of Beauty Culture" or by "actresses and all whose inclinations or pursuits render 'makeup' necessary."[14]

Nevertheless, the dynamics of beauty culture led to the greater acceptance of cosmetics. By making the complexion, rather than bone structure or physical features, more central to popular definitions of beauty, it popularized the democratic idea that beauty could be achieved by all women if only they used the correct products and treatment. This logic led to the assertion that every woman *should* be beautiful—as a duty to her husband and children, in order to achieve business success, or to find romance—and those who were not beautiful had only themselves to blame.

Beauty culturists also foregrounded the *process* of achieving beauty, not just the end product, and moved that process into popular discourse—in the semipublic environment of beauty salons and in the widely read pages of women's magazines and newspapers. The development of beauty "systems" or "methods" was particularly important. Such "systems" replaced apprenticeship and oral tradition with formal instruction in beauty culture and cosmetology, and proved quite profitable for a number of entrepreneurs who developed beauty schools and correspondence courses. But the notion of a beauty "system" or "method" also changed the consumer's relationship to cosmetics by encouraging the systematic, step-by-step process of beauty application. Beauty culturists, that is, replaced all-purpose creams and lotions with a series of specialized products, each designed to perform a single function. The more entrepreneurial of them not only manufactured these products for the home use of their clients but also began to market them to women who did not have direct access to exclusive urban salons, largely through department stores, drugstores, and mail order. By the early twentieth century, beauty culturists' ambivalence toward powder and paint diminished as they saw the possibilities for profit in makeup product lines.[15]

The career of Elizabeth Arden, born Florence Nightingale Graham, illustrates a dominant pattern of entrepreneurship in beauty culture that led to the development of the "class market." She began her career in Eleanor Adair's beauty salon in New York City, first as a receptionist and then as a beauty operator specializing in facials. Soon she became partners with cosmetologist Elizabeth Hubbard, opening a Fifth Avenue salon in 1909 on the strength of Hubbard's products and her own treatment techniques. When their partnership dissolved, Graham took over the salon, lavishly decorated it for an elite clientele, and began to improve on Hubbard's formulas. It was at this time that she transformed herself into Miss Elizabeth Arden, a name she perceived to be romantic and high class. After the first salon was successful, she opened others in a number of cities. Initially the salons offered the usual complexion cures, facials, massage, and hairdressing, but by 1915 Arden had begun to make up her customers, although she did not advertise this service. In 1918 Arden decided to expand sales by going after store orders in fancy retail shops and department stores, often giving them exclusive rights to sell her line in a particular locality. She sent trained representatives or "demonstrators" to teach saleswomen how to sell her products. By 1920 she had developed an extensive product line that included skin care treatments and a full line of face makeup, using Ardena and Venetian as tradenames. According to her biographer, by 1925 Arden's domestic wholesale division was grossing two million dollars each year, from sales to women whose families had incomes in the top 3 percent in the United States.[16]

Other beauty culture entrepreneurs, such as Helena Rubinstein and Dorothy Gray, followed the same route to success: first establishing salons for society women, then developing nationally distributed product lines that conveyed a sense of exclusivity and richness to their clientele. At this time, importers also increased the number and variety of products they offered to wholesalers and retailers. Fine-quality imported goods from France and England had long been available to elite women, but by the 1910s firms (such as Coty) from these countries had begun to open branches and offices in the United States to exploit the growing demand for cosmetics. Department store buyers also were increasingly important in providing high-priced goods to the public. Along with beauty culturists, these were critical figures in expanding the class market for cosmetics, countering the image of the painted woman with connotations of gentility, refinement, and social status.

In contrast, the "mass" segment of the cosmetics industry grew out of the pharmaceutical and drugstore trade after 1900, when a few products broke out of their local market and secured national distribution and brand name recognition. Usually these were creams and lotions, often used by both women and men. Hinds' Honey and Almond Cream, for example, was formulated in 1872 by a Portland, Maine, drugstore owner who gradually went into manufacturing full time and entered the Boston and New York City markets. In 1905 Aurelius S. Hinds conducted his first nationwide advertising campaign, and five years later added vanishing cream and other products to his line.[17] While Hinds and other skin care products achieved success in the national market, visible makeup such as rouge and lipstick had more limited distribution before World War I.

The outlets for mass market cosmetics were varied. Independent drugstores and general stores remained important, especially in small towns, but sales of cosmetics were boosted by emergent forms of national distribution: chain drugstores and variety stores, department stores, and large mail-order outfits, as well as systematized house-to-house selling.[18] The new chain stores aggressively pushed a full range of inexpensive brand name products, as well as private label cosmetics. Both independent and chain merchandisers sought to base drugstore profits not only on the dispensing of medicines and drugs but on the sale of goods consumers needed on an everyday basis, including toiletries. Department store merchandisers similarly found that toiletries and sundries, including soaps, brushes, and rubber goods as well as cosmetics and perfumes, could draw women into the stores; some carried both class and mass products, displaying them in eye-catching cases on the main selling floor.[19]

Mail-order houses were initially conservative in the lines they carried, reflecting their small-town and rural clientele of housewives and older women. Catalogs of the late nineteenth century tended to group cosmetics inconsequentially with food, patent medicines, and soaps. Yet as early as 1897 Sears offered its own line of toilet preparations, including rouge, eyebrow pencil, and face powder in three colors, as well as such brand names as Ayer's, Pozzoni's, and Tetlow's. The Larkin Company, which began as a soap manufacturer and expanded into general catalog sales, buried cosmetics in the back pages of the

1907 catalog, but by the early 1920s had begun to feature them in the opening pages, accompanied by flowery descriptions and color illustrations.[20]

The advertising of mass-market cosmetics also underwent important changes in this period. Since few companies in the nineteenth century saw cosmetics as their primary product, relatively little money was spent on developing marketing or advertising strategies. Cosmetics were advertised mainly on trade cards, displays, and posters, as well as almanacs, sample envelopes, sheet music, and broadsides. Some firms advertised at expositions and world's fairs; Lundborg's perfume fountain, for example, was a popular attraction at the 1893 Columbian Exposition in Chicago.[21]

Magazine advertising, however, was quite limited before 1900: Only a few firms advertised in women's magazines, and their advertisements (usually for creams and powders, rarely rouge) were set in small type in the back pages—in contrast, for example, to soap advertisements, which often appeared on full pages or magazine covers. In the 1910s, however, large-scale national advertising of cosmetics began in earnest, and by the early 1920s it had become a dominant force in women's magazines.[22]

In the late nineteenth century manufacturers and advertisers of mass-market cosmetics responded to widespread consumer resistance in several ways. They took pains to stress the safety of their products, seeking to identify them with the widespread cult of health and cleanliness. Some made therapeutic claims for face powders and liquid tints; Stoddart's Peerless Face Powder, for example, was touted as "approved by the medical Profession." The invisibility of the products, moreover, guaranteed that a woman would not be perceived as painted and immoral. Ricksecker's powder, for example, was "*modestly invisible* when used with discrimination." Manufacturers such as Pozzoni's stressed the naturalness and purity of their preparations by using angelic children in their advertising (Fig. 21.2). Even a tag like "Just a Kiss," featured on Tetlow's packaging, played coquetry off against innocence (Fig. 21.3).[23]

While a logical response to consumers' fears, this advertising tactic was ultimately a self-defeating one. The industry's growth depended on its ability to convince women not only to use cosmetics but to buy as many different products as possible. Making appeals to the naturalness and invisibility of cosmetics could not accomplish this; rather, manufacturers needed to convince women of the acceptability of artifice and visible color.

Many companies in the early twentieth century found this a difficult idea to promote; like the beauty culturists, most of them argued that their products merely "improved on nature." Yet the growing importance of color can be seen in the expansion of product lines.

Figure 21.2. Pozzoni's Face Powder advertising card. Warshaw Collection of Business Americana, Archives Center, National Museum of American History, Smithsonian Institution.

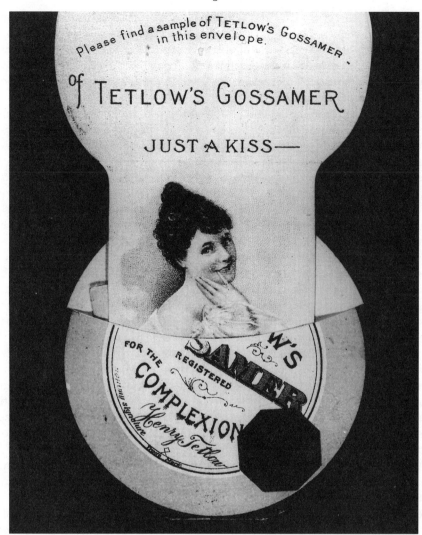

Figure 21.3. Tetlow's Gossamer "Just a Kiss" powder sample envelope. Warshaw Collection of Business Americana, Archives Center, National Museum of American History, Smithsonian Institution. Photo No. 88-1157.

Some manufacturers who had succeeded in marketing a cream or lotion began to create coordinated sets of products, somewhat akin to the beauty culturists' notion of "system." Propounding a domino theory of cosmetics use, they argued that once a woman started using face powder, she would inevitably be drawn to complementary, although more daring, products such as rouge and lipstick. Increasingly they appealed to artifice in the pursuit of "natural beauty." Women were urged to buy several face powders and blend them for a natural look; or buy specialized powders, such as a violet tint to wear under artificial light; or wear matching lip tints and rouge to achieve the "bloom of youth."[24]

At this time, a number of entrepreneurs began to produce and market new cosmetic products that asserted and even celebrated artifice. Lipsticks and eyeshadows in colorful shades, for example, made their appearance on the market after World War I. "Mascaro," which in the nineteenth century had been a general-purpose touch-up for light or graying hair used by both men and women, became specialized as "mascara," a woman's cosmetic for eyelashes. Manufacturers sold cosmetics in luxurious sets to be seen on dressing tables, but even more popular were goods packaged in portable containers. Compacts for face powder and rouge and the lipstick cylinder were marketed in the 1910s, suggesting the increasingly public place of cosmetics.

Manufacturers of mass-market goods often developed a single product, one that was socially unacceptable or controversial, and aggressively promoted it in the trade press and in national advertising. In so doing, they turned to sources of cultural legitimation other than that of middle-class and elite beauty culture.

Social definitions of womanhood were strongly contested from the late nineteenth century onward. The ideal of the "New Woman" represented a departure from concepts of female identity constituted solely in domestic pursuits, sexual purity, and moral motherhood. Yet this new ideal was an unstable one. For some, the New Woman was a mannish, political, and professional woman who had entered the public sphere on her own terms. For others, the New Woman was a sensual, free-spirited girl—in the 1880s a "Daisy," by the 1910s and 1920s a flapper. The latter figure embodied another set of contradictions: She was at once an independent wage earner, making her own way in the world, and a beautiful, romantic girl, seeking marital fulfillment. This image became increasingly important in the selling of mass-market cosmetics, as manufacturers and advertisers sought to appeal particularly to the rising number of young working women of both middle-class and working-class origins.[25]

An important tactic of the industry was to link cosmetics to emergent forms of popular entertainment and leisure, especially the motion pictures. Mary Pickford's screen image of youthful innocence sold such mass-market creams and lotions as Pompeian in general-circulation periodicals and traditional women's magazines (Fig. 21.4). The cosmetics of artifice, in contrast, were heavily advertised in the new confession magazines and "fanzines," such as *True Story* and *Photoplay*, directed at young working-class and middle-class women. Drugstore promotions and display windows also capitalized on the movie craze. Maybelline, for example, marketed its sole product, mascara, by using close-up photographs of movie stars with heavily painted eyes and eyelashes in its magazine advertising and on display cards (Fig. 21.5).[26]

The connection between motion pictures and cosmetics was in some cases quite direct: The movie industry's makeup experts often made technological breakthroughs in products that were then applied to everyday cosmetics. Max Factor, a Russian immigrant, is the most prominent example of a "makeup artist to the stars" who went into cosmetics manufacturing for the mass market. But as important to the cosmetics industry were the "look" and style of female screen stars who promoted the use of color and artifice. Although the theater may have affected everyday makeup practices, the movies were far more influential because of their enormous popularity, and because close-up cinematography could magnify heavily painted lips, eyes, and cheeks. Certainly the cultural style of many working women and early flappers who wore provocative makeup, hair styles, and fashionable clothing was legitimized and reinforced by what they saw on the screen. By the late 1920s, as the Payne Fund studies indicate, young women from a range of socioeconomic backgrounds modeled their cosmetics use, and manners generally, on the movie images they saw. Exploiting the movie industry tie-in, mass-market manufacturers promoted glamor as an integral part of women's identity.[27]

The African American segment of the industry emerged in the late nineteenth century, part of the more general development of an African American consumer market. Constrained even more than white working people by poverty, most blacks had little spending

Figure 21.4. Mary Pickford, 1917, Pompeian Beauty Panel. Warshaw Collection of Business Americana, Archives Center, National Museum of American History, Smithsonian Institution.

Figure 21.5. Maybelline advertisement, *Photoplay* (1920). *Courtesy Maybelline, Inc.*

money for anything beyond the goods essential for survival. Yet a nascent middle class, black migration, and the growing racial segregation of cities spurred some entrepreneurs to develop businesses serving black consumers.[28] Some white-owned firms cultivated this market for cosmetics in the black community as early as the 1890s. The Lyon Manufacturing Company, for example, a Brooklyn-based firm that sold patent medicines, advertised its Kaitharon hair tonic to blacks through almanacs and ad cards. The product was touted as a straightener for kinky hair, with testimonials from African American ministers, political leaders, and schoolteachers.[29]

Far more important at this time, however, was the development of African American beauty culture and a hair and skin care industry owned by blacks. Such figures as Anthony

Overton, Annie Turnbo Malone, and Madame C. J. Walker were among the most successful African American entrepreneurs to market face creams, hair oils, and other products. Several black-owned firms developed out of the drugstore supplies trade or began as small cosmetics companies. Anthony Overton, who by 1916 had built up one of the largest black-owned businesses in the United States, began his career as a peddler and baking powder manufacturer. He shifted into cosmetics when his daughter's formula for a face powder proved popular in their community. Using networks of distribution he had already established, Overton sold his High Brown Face Powder through an army of door-to-door agents.[30]

Even more significant, however, were the women entrepreneurs who developed African American beauty culture. Beauty culture offered black women good employment opportunities in the sex- and race-segregated labor market: It required low capitalization, was an easy trade to learn, and was much in demand. Beauty parlors could be operated cheaply in homes, apartments, and small shops, and hair and skin care products could be mixed in one's kitchen to be sold locally. Since drugstores, chain stores, and department stores often refused to locate in the black community, door-to-door and salon sales were the dominant forms of distribution. Advertising was generally limited to black-owned newspapers, although large companies such as Poro purchased space in many of them throughout the country, achieving a kind of "national" advertising.[31]

Annie Turnbo Malone (the founder of Poro), Madame C. J. Walker, and others pioneered in the development of beauty systems that would ensure black women smooth, manageable hair. White racism had symbolically linked the supposedly "natural" inferiority of blacks to an appearance marked by unruly, "kinky" hair and slovenliness in dress. As Gwendolyn Robinson has argued in her study of the African American cosmetics industry, the dominant culture's ascription of promiscuity to black women led them to stress the importance of looking respectable. For black women, hair care, including straightening, was one external marker of personal success and racial progress, signifying a response to the white denigration of black womanhood. The beauty culturists asserted and exploited this view in their advertising. Madame Walker, for example, ran a full-page newspaper ad in 1928 whose headline announced "Amazing Progress of Colored Race—Improved Appearance Responsible."[32]

Like the white beauty culturists, the leading black entrepreneurs had developed extensive product lines in skin care and cosmetics by World War I, including face creams, bleaches, and powders. Some of these products and beauty systems, especially hair straightening and skin bleaching, were highly controversial in the black community. They sparked debate over black emulation of dominant white aesthetics, and over the issue of color differences among African Americans. The use of cosmetics not only rendered gender definitions (that is, what constituted female respectability) problematic but tied those definitions to "race consciousness" and black resistance to white domination as well.

The response of African American beauty culturists was complex, adhering to the dominant aesthetic while asserting the centrality of the industry to collective black advancement. Unlike the white industry, African American beauty culturists evidenced a genuine commitment to work on behalf of their community. Walker and Malone trained thousands of black women in their methods to become sales agents, salon owners, and beauty operatives; their promotional literature and handbooks continually emphasized their commitment to black women's employment and the economic progress of African Americans. In the absence of many commercial outlets, Walker sought a relationship with women's clubs and churches, offering promotions, beauty shows, and product sales to help raise funds for these organizations. Moreover, the sales methods—salon operatives and door-to-door agents selling to friends and neighbors—probably enhanced the web of mutual support and assistance integral to black women's culture. The integration of this industry with aspects of black community life and politics sets it apart from the white industry.[33]

Cultural Constructions of Gender, Class, and Race

Despite the difference in their origins, patterns of distribution, and markets, the three segments of the cosmetics industry developed a number of similar products and encountered many of the same issues. The industry converged in certain ways in its handling of gender, responding to social and cultural changes affecting women's attitudes toward appearance, redefining popular notions of female sexual and social respectability to include cosmetics use, and then revising definitions of female beauty into ideals that could be achieved only through cosmetics. Whatever the class and race of cosmetics consumers, all segments of the industry in their advertising and marketing reshaped the relationship between appearance and feminine identity by promoting the externalization of the gendered self, a process much in tune with the tendencies of mass culture.[34]

What to beauty culturists had been a simultaneous process of transforming the interior self and external appearance became in the hands of the twentieth-century cosmetics industry the "makeover." Makeup promised each woman the tools to express her "true" self, indeed, to experiment until she found it. Cosmetics communicated the self to others and infused the self with a sense of esteem and legitimacy. In this new attention to personality and novelty, being able to find yourself and change yourself, cosmetics manufacturers began to reorient their industry away from beauty culture and toward "fashion," allowing for an endless number of "looks" and an endless proliferation of products.[35]

But the linkage of female individuality, self-expression, and respectability held different meanings in the different contexts under which cosmetics were sold. While a full-scale analysis of the divisions of class and race embedded in the industry's cultural messages cannot be attempted here, I will suggest one route such an analysis might take: the tension between the appearance of Anglo-Saxon gentility and the exploitation of "foreign" exoticism.

While invoking ideas of female self-expression through the use of makeup, the cosmetics industry in the 1910s and 1920s never transcended the problem of class that had been raised in the nineteenth-century identification of "paint" with immorality. The "class" end of the industry had long stressed the gentility and refinement possible through skin care regimens; they now applied this argument to the use of makeup and artifice. The French cachet of imported goods was especially important in conveying status and "chic." Until the 1906 Food and Drug Act prohibited misbranding and false labeling, U.S. companies frequently identified their products as made in Paris.[36] After 1906 they used foreign-sounding, aristocratic trade names, such as Rubinstein's Valaze line and Arden's Ardena, or they claimed the use of French formulas. Although manufacturing their products in the United States, Arden and Rubinstein commonly made reference to the cosmetic practices of Parisian women as examples American women should emulate. By 1919 national advertisers of cosmetics, particularly of imported brands, had adopted "atmosphere advertisements" depicting the lifestyles of the rich and famous. Dorin face powders and compacts, for example, were associated with Saratoga Springs, the Paris Opera, and the races at Ascot: "Not all the users of La Dorine can be members of smart clubs but they are all eager to enjoy as much of the dainty refinement of the fashionable world as they can."[37]

Companies selling cosmetics to blacks also used images of refinement and social improvement to sell their products, but this strategy must be placed in the overall context of racial stereotyping and black aspirations. The advertising for the highly successful Overton-

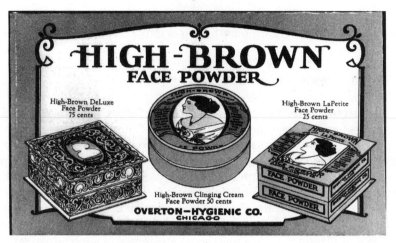

Figure 21.6. Overton-Hygienic High Brown Face Powder packet. Curt Teich Postcard Archives, Lake County Museum, Wauconda, Illionois.

Hygienic Manufacturing Company, for example, featured light-skinned, refined-looking women and appealed more to respectability and gentility than elitism (Fig. 21.6). In contrast, Kashmir Chemical Company, a black-owned firm with a brief life in the late 1910s and early 1920s, frequently used advertising with very fashionably dressed women sitting at dressing tables or in automobiles—ads that emulated the elite images common in mainstream magazines.[38]

Mass-market manufacturers stressed the makeover as a route to upward mobility, arguing that a woman's personal success relied on her appearance. As one manufacturer's pamphlet observed, "You can select ten ordinary girls from a factory and by the skillful use of such preparations as Kijja and proper toilet articles . . . you can in a short time make them as attractive and good-looking as most any ten wealthy society girls. . . . [I]t is not so much a matter of beauty with different classes of girls as it is how they are fixed up." A similar story is told in a 1924 trade advertisement for Zip depilatory: A dark-skinned woman, her appearance suggesting an eastern or southern European immigrant, is able to achieve social acceptance, implicitly among her Americanized friends, by ridding herself of superfluous hair (Fig. 21.7).[39]

Some manufacturers, particularly at the class end of the industry, sought to dissociate themselves from any cosmetic practices that might be understood as working-class and "vulgar." The trade press, for example, editorialized against putting on makeup in public places, that is, *showing* the artifice; one writer even wanted to start a campaign among sales personnel to advise their customers against the use of too much face powder. Advice books and women's magazines were particularly directive about extreme cosmetic use: Powdering one's nose in restaurants or shops "stamps you as having poor breeding," noted one; another condemned "girls on the streets everyday with their faces daubed like uncivilized Indians." Of vivid red lips, yet another observed, "You cannot afford to make yourself ridiculous if you have started for success, or you want to attract a REAL man."[40] Much of this was a response to young women's cosmetic practices, particularly the "made-up" look of working-class women.

As the reference above to "uncivilized Indians" suggests, manufacturers not only dealt with the cultural identification of "paint" and artifice with class but also with a deeply embedded set of resonances concerning race, ethnicity, and color in American society.

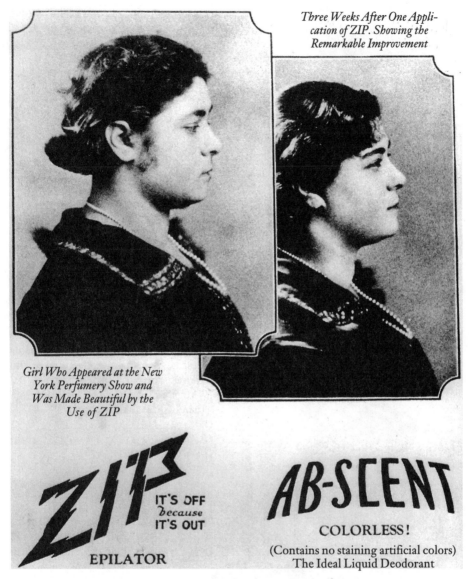

Three Weeks After One Application of ZIP. Showing the Remarkable Improvement

Girl Who Appeared at the New York Perfumery Show and Was Made Beautiful by the Use of ZIP

ZIP
IT'S OFF
because
IT'S OUT
EPILATOR

AB-SCENT
COLORLESS!
(Contains no staining artificial colors)
The Ideal Liquid Deodorant

Figure 21.7. Detail from Zip advertisement, in *Toilet Requisites* (April 1924).

Mass-market manufacturers, for example, often employed exotic images of foreign peoples to advertise products that did not have a distinct place in white bourgeois culture. An instructive comparison might be made with the soap industry, which created advertisements associating cleanliness with colonization and Anglo American supremacy (Fig. 21.8). Cosmetics manufacturers, in contrast, used images of American Indian, Egyptian, Turkish, and Japanese women as well as European women to link reluctant Americans to a global cosmetic culture (Fig. 21.9). Versions of "Little Egypt," who caused a furor at the 1893 Columbian Exposition, sold rouge and other cosmetics of artifice. This fascination with the foreign and exotic, fueled by Western imperialism, can be seen throughout American culture in the late nineteenth century.[41]

Figure 21.8. Higgins and Foweler trade card. Warshaw Collection of Business Americana, Archives Center, National Museum of American History, Smithsonian Institution. Photo No. 89-14352.

Figure 21.9. Murray and Lanham's Florida Water advertising card. Warshaw Collection of Business Americana, Archives Center, National Museum American History, Smithsonian Institution.

In the hands of cosmetics manufacturers, exoticism continued to be powerful long into the twentieth century. Advertisers created narratives about beauty culture through the ages, bypassing the Greco-Roman tradition in favor of Egypt and Persia. Cleopatra was virtually a cult figure, displayed in advertising to all segments of the market. Kashmir's Nile Queen line, for example, juxtaposed images of genteel black womanhood with frankly sensual representations of naked and semiclothed women (Fig. 21.10). Promotions of lower-priced makeup, particularly rouge, eye shadow, and mascara, frequently used exotic "vamp" images.[42]

Advertisers also linked "foreign types" to the realization of women's identity through cosmetics. The Armand complexion powder campaign of 1928–29 instructed women to "find yourself," using a question-and-answer book written by a "famous psychologist and a noted beauty expert"; however, individuality was submerged into a typology that coded appearance and personality together according to ethnic euphemisms—Godiva, Colleen, Mona Lisa, Sheba, Sonya, Cherie, Lorelei, and, of course, Cleopatra (Fig. 21.11).[43]

At the same time, the cosmetics industry at all levels projected contradictory cultural messages linking whiteness with social success and refinement. With the sale of bleach cream and light-colored face powders, this issue became a particularly controversial one within the black community. Products with names like Black-No-More and Tan Off, many of which were manufactured by white-owned companies as well as black-owned ones, baldly appealed to European aesthetic standards and the belief that light-skinned African Americans were more successful and, if women, more desirable as wives. Others struck a more ambivalent tone: Golden Brown Ointment, for example, instructed consumers, "Don't be fooled by so-called 'Skin Whiteners.'" The company admonished that its product "won't whiten your skin—as that can't be done," yet claimed that the ointment produced a "soft, light, bright, smooth complexion" that would "help in business or social life."[44]

It is crucial to note, however, that bleach creams, produced by class and mass manufacturers, were also widely advertised to white women. Until the mid-1920s, when the sun-tanning craze swept the United States, bleach creams were touted as a means of acquiring a whiteness that connoted gentility, female domesticity, "protection" from labor, the exacting standards of the elite, and Anglo-Saxon superiority. Most of the time advertisers treated such issues obliquely, but they could be quite direct. One series of silhouettes, appearing in a late-nineteenth-century advertisement for Hagan's Magnolia Balm, a skin bleach sold to white women, used physiognomic signifiers to convey that light skin meant Anglo-Saxon gentility. In these images, not only does the woman's skin color lighten upon using the product, but her features undergo a transformation from a stereotyped rural black woman to a genteel lady (Fig. 21.12). Several decades later, manufacturer Albert F. Wood could declare quite openly: "A white person objects to a swarthy brown-hued or mulatto-like skin, therefore if staying much out of doors use regularly Satin Skin Varnishing Greaseless Cream to keep the skin normally white."[45]

Such explicit and covert attention to race and ethnicity in a business devoted in large part to coloration should not be surprising if we recall the history of this period: the extensive immigration of peoples who looked "different" from earlier Western European immigrants and threatened to be unassimilable; intensified consciousness about "race" spurred by legal segregation, heightened violence against blacks, and northern migration; and the growing acceptance of scientific racism, which ordered human progress, including the attainment of physical beauty, according to racial-ethnic types, with white Anglo-Saxons at the top of that hierarchy. What I would suggest is that the cosmetics industry has historically taken discourses of class, ethnicity, race, and gender—discourses that generate deeply held conscious and unconscious feelings of fear, anxiety, and even self-hatred—and displaced

Figure 21.10. Front cover of Kashmir Chemical Company's Nile Queen pamphlet, 1919. Chicago Historical Society.

Figure 21.11. "Which of These Alluring Types Are You?" Detail from the Armand Complexion Powder as proof, 1929 N. W. Ayer Collection, Archives Center, National Museum of American History, Smithsonian Institution. Photo No. 89-14353.

Figure 21.12. Detail from Lyon's Manufacturing Company, "The Secret of Health and Beauty" pamphlet. Warshaw Collection of Business Americana, Archives Center, National Museum of American History, Smithsonian Institution. Photo No. 89-14351.

them onto safe rhetorical fields, in this case, a language of "color" and "type," a rhetoric of "naturalness," "expressiveness," and "individuality."[46]

The cosmetics industry played a crucial role in defining the appearance of femininity in the early twentieth century, but it was not the only player. How women consumers of different social groups shaped those definitions remains an open question for historical research. The profound changes in women's lives in this period may well have spurred women to indulge new fantasies of beauty and calculate differently its material and psychological benefits. Undoubtedly many women did not receive the intended messages of manufacturers and advertisers passively, but how they used cosmetics and understood their meaning must, at this point, be left to speculation.[47]

Clearly the cosmetics industry responded to a larger cultural field of established and emergent images and definitions of femininity, crosscut by class and race. In various ways the industry worked with those images, reshaping them in response to its perceptions of women's fears and desires. If, in the early twentieth century, some Americans sought to define female selfhood in meaningful ways (through the act of thinking or through productive labor, for example), the cosmetics industry foregrounded the notion that one's "look" was not only the expression of female identity but its essence as well. In this, the mass, class, and African American ends of the industry converged. Although the cosmetics industry may not have controlled the discourse over femininity, the multibillion-dollar industry that exists today is testimony to its ability to convince women to purchase, as Charles Revson cynically put it, "hope in a jar."

Notes

1. See, e.g., Lary May, *Screening Out the Past: The Birth of Mass Culture and the Motion Picture Industry* (New York: Oxford University Press, 1980); Roland Marchand, *Advertising the American Dream: Making Way for Modernity* (Berkeley: University of California Press, 1985), 176–88; Lewis A. Erenberg, *Steppin' Out: New York Nightlife and the Transformation of American Culture, 1890–1930* (Westport, Conn: Greenwood Press, 1981); Martha Banta, *Imaging American Women: Idea and Ideals in Cultural History* (New York: Columbia University Press, 1987); William R. Leach, "Transformations in a Culture of Consumption: Women and Department Stores, 1890–1925," *Journal of American History* 71 (September 1984): 319–42.

2. Lois Banner, *American Beauty* (Chicago: University of Chicago Press, 1983). Among the many advice books and formularies, see, e.g., *The American Family Keepsake of People's Practical Cyclopedia* (Boston, 1849); Smith and Swinney, *The House-Keeper's Guide and Everybody's Hand-Book* (Cincinnati, 1868); *The American Ladies' Memorial: An Indispensable Home Book for the Wife, Mother, Daughter* (Boston, 1850); Emily Thornwell, *The Lady's Guide to Perfect Gentility* (New York: Derby and Jackson, 1857). See also Cosmetics files in the Warshaw Collection of Business Americana, Archives Center, National Museum of American History, Smithsonian Institution (hereafter cited as Warshaw), a rich collection of advertising graphics, posters, pamphlets, and ephemera.

3. Banner, *American Beauty*, 42–44, 119; Arnold James Cooley, *Instructions and Cautions Respecting the Selection and Use of Perfumes, Cosmetics and Other Toilet Articles* (Philadelphia: J. B. Lippincott and Company, 1873), 428.

4. On working women's subculture, see Christine Stansell, *City of Women: Sex and Class in New York, 1789–1860* (New York: Knopf, 1986); and Kathy Peiss, *Cheap Amusements: Working Women and Leisure in Turn-of-the-Century New York* (Philadelphia: Temple University Press, 1986).

5. Gwendolyn Robinson, "Class, Race and Gender: A Transcultural, Theoretical and Sociohistorical Analysis of Cosmetic Institutions and Practices to 1920" (Ph.D. diss., University of Illinois at Chicago, 1984), ch. 2.

6. Lola Montez, *The Art of Beauty: or Secrets of a Lady's Toilet* (New York: Dick and Fitzgerald, 1853), xii–xiii, 47; Cooley, *Instructions and Cautions;* Karen Haltunen, *Confidence Men and Painted Women: A Study of Middle-Class Culture in America, 1830–1870* (New Haven: Yale University Press, 1982).

7. For analyses that speak to the intersection of class and gender in the nineteenth century, see Stansell, *City of Women,* and Nancy Hewitt, "Beyond the Search for Sisterhood: American Women's History in the 1980s," *Social History* 10 (1985): 299–321.

8. For statistics on the cosmetics industry, see U.S. Bureau of the Census, *Census of Manufactures: Patent & Proprietary Medicines and Compounds & Druggists' Preparations* (Washington, D.C.: U.S. Government Printing Office, 1919); and *Toilet Requisites* 6 (June 1921): 26. On the patent medicine industry, see James Harvey Young, *The Toadstool Millionaires: A Social History of Patent Medicines in America before Federal Regulation* (Princeton: Princeton University Press, 1961); and Sarah Stage, *Female Complaints: Lydia Pinkham and the Business of Women's Medicine* (New York: Norton, 1979). On soap, see Richard L. Bushman and Claudia L. Bushman, "The Early History of Cleanliness in America," *Journal of American History* 74 (1988): 1213–38.

9. For druggists' formularies, see John H. Nelson, *Druggists' Hand-Book of Private Formulas,* 3rd ed. (Cleveland, 1879); Charles E. Hamlin, *Hamlin's Formulae, or Every Druggist His Own Perfumer* (Baltimore: Edward B. Read and Son, 1885). Trade catalogs document wholesale druggists' goods: see, e.g., W. H. Schieffelin and Company, *General Prices Current of Foreign and Domestic Drugs, Medicines, Chemicals . . .* (New York, March 1881); and Bolton Drug Company, *Illustrated Price List* (ca. 1890), both in Archives Center, National Museum of American History; Brown, Durrell and Company, *The Trade Monthly* (Boston, January 1895) and others in *Trade Catalogues at Winterthur, 1750–1980* (Clearwater Publishing Company microfilm collection). For a general history, see Edward Kremers and George Urdang, *Kremer's and Urdang's History of Pharmacy,* 4th ed. (Philadelphia: J. B. Lippincott Company, 1976).

10. Banner, *American Beauty*, 28–44, 202–25. See also Anne Hard, "The Beauty Business," *American Magazine* 69 (November 1909): 79–90.

11. For general background on female cosmetics entrepreneurs, see Margaret Allen, *Selling Dreams: Inside the Beauty Business* (New York: Simon and Schuster, 1981); Maxene Fabe, *Beauty Millionaire: The Life of Helena Rubinstein* (New York: Thomas Y. Crowell, 1972); Patrick O'Higgins, *Madame: An Intimate Biography of Helena Rubinstein* (New York: Viking Press, 1971); Alfred Allan Lewis and Constance Woodworth, *Miss Elizabeth Arden* (New York: Coward, McCann, and Geoghegan, 1972). The latter two biographies, written in breathless prose, include fascinating gossip but are questionable histories.

12. Susanna Cocroft, *How to Secure a Beatiful Complexion and Beautiful Eyes: A Practical Course in Beauty Culture* (Chicago: James J. Clarke and Company, 1911) in Cosmetics, Warshaw. See also her *Beauty a Duty: The Art of Keeping Young* (Chicago: Rand McNally, 1915).

13. Madame Yale, *The Science of Health and Beauty* (n.p., 1893), 6, in Cosmetics, Warshaw; Cocroft, *Beautiful Complexion.*

14. Yale, *Science of Health and Beauty,* 26.

15. See n. 11, and also Paulette School, *Beauty Culture at Home* (Washington, D.C.: n.p., 1914); E. Burnham, *The Coiffure,* catalog no. 37 (Chicago, 1908), in Hair files, Warshaw.

16. Lewis and Woodworth, *Elizabeth Arden.*

17. *Toilet Requisites* 10 (October 1925): 64. *Toilet Requisites,* later *Beauty Fashion,* was the trade journal for buyers and retailers of cosmetics, toiletries, and druggists' sundries; founded in 1916, it is an excellent source for developments in the industry.

18. Alfred D. Chandler Jr., *The Visible Hand: The Managerial Revolution in American Business* (Cambridge: Harvard University Press, 1977), ch. 7. See also Susan Strasser, "'Refuse All Substitutes': Branded Products and

the Relationships of Distribution, 1885–1920" (paper presented at the annual meeting of the American Studies Association, New York, November 1987).

19. See *Fancy Goods Graphics*, 1879–1890; and catalogs from B. Altman and Company, John Wanamaker, Siegel-Cooper, Simpson Crawford Company, and R. H. Macy and Company, ranging in date from 1880 to 1920, all in Dry Goods files, Warshaw. *Toilet Requisites* carried extensive coverage of department store counter and window displays. For a general discussion, see William R. Leach, "Transformations in a Culture of Consumption," and Susan Porter Benson, *Counter Cultures: Saleswomen, Managers and Customers in American Department Stores, 1890–1940* (Urbana: University of Illinois Press, 1986).

20. *Sears General Catalogue*, no. 105 (fall 1897); Larkin Company Catalogues, no. 55 (1907) and no. 86 (fall and winter 1921), in Soap files, Warshaw.

21. For late-nineteenth-century advertising, see the material culture sources in Cosmetics, Patent Medicines, and Hair files, in Warshaw. For discussions of the changes in advertising, see Daniel Pope, *The Making of Modern Advertising* (New York: Basic Books, 1983); Robert Jay, *The Trade Card in Nineteenth-Century America* (Columbia: University of Missouri Press, 1987); and for a later period, Marchand, *Advertising the American Dream*.

22. See such mass circulation women's magazines as *Ladies Home Journal* and *Delineator*, 1890–1920.

23. Ricksecker's Products brochure; Stoddart's Peerless Liquid and Stoddart's Peerless Face Powder trade cards; Harriet Hubbard Ayer, Recamier Cream, and Recamier Balm advertising cards, all in Cosmetics files, Warshaw.

24. For these trends, and those stated in the following paragraph, see *Toilet Requisites*, 1916–25.

25. For discussions of this new cultural ideal among middle-class women, see Banta, *Imaging American Women*; Carroll Smith-Rosenberg, "New Woman as Androgyne," in *Disorderly Conduct: Visions of Gender in Victorian America* (New York: Oxford University Press, 1985); Sheila Rothman, *Women's Proper Place: A History of Changing Ideals and Practices* (New York: Basic Books, 1979). On working-class women, see Peiss, *Cheap Amusements*; and Elizabeth Ewen, *Immigrant Women in the Land of Dollars* (New York: Monthly Review Press, 1985).

26. See *Photoplay* and *True Story*, 1920–25. Also Photoplay Magazine, *The Age Factor in Selling and Advertising: A Study in a New Phase of Advertising* (Chicago and New York: Photoplay, 1922).

27. See, for example, *Toilet Requisites* 9 (March 1925): 46, on using a scene from the film *Male and Female* in a window display. On women's response to the movies, see Herbert Blumer, *Movies and Conduct* (New York: Macmillan, 1933), 30–58; and Peiss, *Cheap Amusements*.

28. Vanessa Broussard, "Afro-American Images in Advertising, 1880–1920" (M.A. thesis, George Washington University, 1987).

29. Lyon Manufacturing Company, *What Colored People Say* (n.p., n.d.) and *Afro-American Almanac 1897* (n.p.), Patent Medicine files, Warshaw.

30. For the most extensive discussion of the black cosmetics industry, see Robinson, "Class, Race and Gender"; for her treatment of Overton, see 313–39.

31. For insights into cosmetics advertising in black newspapers, see Claude A. Barnett Papers, Archives and Manuscripts Department, Chicago Historical Society, esp. box 262.

32. Robinson, "Class, Race and Gender," 280–82, 347–411, 515. The Walker advertisement appeared in the *Oklahoma Eagle*, 3 March 1928, rotogravure section, in Barnett Papers, box 262, f4. See also Black Cosmetics Industry File, Division of Community Life, National Museum of American History; "Poro Hair & Beauty Culture" handbook (St. Louis, 1922), Barnett Papers. There were many other African American beauty culturists: see, e.g., Mrs. Mattie E. Hockenhull, *Imported Method in Beauty Culture. First Lessons* (Pine Bluff, Ark.: Gudger Printing Company, 1917); and W. T. McKissick and Company, *McKissick's Famous Universal Agency or System* (Wilmington, Del.: n.p., n.d.), in Hair files, Warshaw.

33. Robinson, "Class, Race and Gender," 449–551.

34. See Warren I. Susman, *Culture as History: The Transformation of American Society in the Twentieth Century* (New York: Pantheon, 1984), especially "'Personality' and the Making of Twentieth-Century Culture," 271–85.

35. For an example of this reorientation, see the Armand complexion powder and proofs, 1916–32, in Armand Co., N. W. Ayer Collection, Archives Center, National Museum of American History, Smithsonian Institution.

36. See *American Perfumer*, 1906–8, for detailed reporting on the effects of the Food and Drug Act, also Bureau of Chemistry, General Correspondence, Record Group 97, Entry 8, National Archives. For a general discussion, see James Harvey Young, *The Medical Messiahs: A Social History of Health Quackery in Twentieth-Century America* (Princeton: Princeton University Press, 1967), chs. 1–3.

37. *Toilet Requisites* 4 (August 1919): 10, and 4 (April 1919): 3.

38. Overton-Hygienic Manufacturing Company, High Brown Face Powder sample envelope, in Curt Teich Postcard Collection, Lake County Museum, Wauconda, Illinois; Kashmir Chemical Company, Nile

Making Faces   345

Queen Cosmetics advertising, box 4, f1 and f2, in Claude A. Barnett Collection, Prints and Photographs Department, Chicago Historical Society.

39. Countess Ceccaldi (Tokolon Company), *Secrets and Arts of Fascination Employed by Cleopatra, the Greatest Enchantress of All Time* (ca. 1920s), in Cosmetics file, Warshaw; Zip advertisement, *Toilet Requisites* 9, 1 (April 1924).

40. *The Secret of Charm and Beauty* (New York: Independent Corporation, 1923), 19, 22–23; Nell Vinick, *Lessons in Loveliness: A Practical Guide to Beauty Secrets* (New York: Longmans, Green and Company, 1930), 46; *Toilet Requisites* 5 (April 1920): 21, and 6 (June 1921): 30–31.

41. Cf. trade cards for Hoyt's German Soap and Murray and Lanham's Florida Water, in Soap and Cosmetics files, respectively, Warshaw. John Kasson in *Amusing the Millions: Coney Island at the Turn of the Century* (New York: Hill and Wang, 1978) discusses middle-class interest in exoticism; thanks also to James Gilbert for his helpful insights on this subject.

42. See e.g., Ceccaldi, *Secrets and Arts of Fascination;* Kashmir Chemical Company, Nile Queen Cosmetics, Barnett Papers. The King Tut craze in 1923 proved profitable to the cosmetics industry: see *Toilet Requisites* 12 (March 1923): 25, and unnumbered page following 32.

43. Armand ad proofs, Ayer Book 382, especially Advt. No. 10039, 1929. N. W. Ayer Collection.

44. Golden Brown Ointment advertisement, *New York Age,* 7 February 1920, 5. These advertisements abound in the African American press; see e.g., Crane and Company, *New York Age,* 5 January 1905, 4; M. B. Berger and Company, *New York Age,* 14 January 1909, 3; Black-No-More, *New York Age,* 16 July 1914.

45. Lyon's Manufacturing Company, *The Secret of Health and Beauty* (n.p, n.d.) in Patent Medicines file, Warshaw; Albert F. Wood, *The Way to a Satin Skin* (Detroit, 1923), 8–9, in Archives Center, National Museum of American History.

46. Cf. Frederic Jameson, "Reification and Utopia in Mass Culture," *Social Text* 1 (1979): 130–48.

47. Reception analysis is fraught with difficulties for the historian, but for a theoretical model, see Janice A. Radway, *Reading the Romance: Women, Patriarchy and Popular Literature* (Chapel Hill: University of North Carolina Press, 1984); and Michael Denning, *Mechanic Accents: Dime Novels and Working Class Culture in America* (New York: Meuthuen, 1987).

22

"Star Struck": Acculturation, Adolescence, and Mexican American Women, 1920–1950

Vicki L. Ruiz

Siga las estrellas
[Follow the stars]
—Max Factor cosmetic ad in *La Opinion*, 1927

Ethnic identity, Americanization, and generational tension first captured the historical imagination during the 1950s with the publication of Oscar Handlin's *The Uprooted* and Alfred Kazin's *A Walker in the City*.[1] These issues continue to provoke discussion among both humanists and social scientists. Within the last decade, feminist scholars have expanded and enriched our knowledge of acculturation through the study of immigrant daughters. Cross-class analysis of adolescent culture provides another window into the world of ethnic youth.[2] This vibrant discourse on generation, gender, and U.S. popular culture has a decidedly East Coast orientation. Are patterns typical of working-class immigrants in New York City applicable to those in Los Angeles?

This essay discusses the forces of Americanization and the extent to which they influenced a generation of Mexican American women coming of age during the 1920s and 1930s. The adoption of new cultural forms, however, did not take place in a vacuum. The political and economic environment surrounding Mexican immigrants and their children would color their responses to mainstream U.S. society. The Spanish-speaking population in the United States soared between 1910 and 1930 as over a million Mexicanos* migrated northward. Pushed by the economic and political chaos generated by the Mexican Revolution and lured by jobs in U.S. agribusiness and industry, they settled into the existing barrios and forged new communities in both the Southwest and the Midwest, in small towns and cities. For example, in 1900 only 3,000 to 5,000 Mexicans lived in Los Angeles, but by 1930 approximately 150,000 persons of Mexican birth or heritage had settled into the city's expanding barrios. On a national level, by 1930 Mexicans formed the "third largest 'racial' group," outnumbered only by Anglos and blacks.[3]

Pioneering social scientists, particularly Manuel Gamio, Paul Taylor, and Emory Bogardus, examined the lives of these Mexican immigrants, but their materials on women are sprinkled here and there, at times hidden in unpublished field notes. Among Chicano historians

---

Mexicano(-a) designates someone of Mexican birth residing in the United States. *Mexican American* denotes a person born in the United States with at least second-generation status. *Mexican* is an umbrella term for both groups. I use the term *Chicano(-a)* only for the contemporary period, as most of the older women whose oral interviews contributed to this study did not identify as Chicanas. *Latino(-a)* indicates someone of Latin American birth or heritage. I refer to "Americanization" within the context of immigration history, that is, as an idealized set of assumptions pushed by state agencies and religious groups to "transform" or "anglicize" newcomers. Bureaucrats and missionaries narrowly defined "America" as signifying only the United States.

Figure 22.1. My mother as a young woman, Erminia Ruiz, ca. 1941. *Collection of the author.*

and writers there appears a fascination with second-generation Mexican American men, especially as *pachucos.*[4] The lifestyles and attitudes of their female counterparts have gone largely unnoticed, even though women may have experienced deeper generational tensions.[5] "Walking in two worlds," they blended elements of Americanization with Mexican expectations and values.[6] To set the context, I will look at education, employment, and media as agents of Americanization and assess the ways in which Mexican American women incorporated their messages. Drawing on social science fieldwork and oral interviews, I will discuss also the sources of conflict between adolescent women and their parents as well as the contradictions between the promise of the American dream and the reality of restricted mobility and ethnic prejudice.

This study relies extensively on oral history. The memories of thirteen women serve as the basis for my reconstruction of adolescent aspirations and experiences (or dreams and routines). Of the thirteen full-blown life histories, ten are housed in university archives, eight as part of the Rosie the Riveter collection at California State University, Long Beach. I became familiar with most of these interviews during the course of my research for *Cannery Women, Cannery Lives*, and two surfaced as student oral-history projects. I personally interviewed three of the narrators.

The women themselves are fairly homogeneous by nativity, class, residence, and family structure. With one exception, all are U.S. citizens by birth and attended southwestern schools. Ten of the interviewees were born between 1913 and 1929.[7] Although two came from families once considered middle-class in Mexico, all can be considered working-class in the United States. Their fathers' typical occupations included farm work, day labor, and busing tables. Two women had fathers with skilled blue-collar jobs (a butcher and a surveyor), and two were the daughters of small family farmers. The informants usually characterized their mothers as homemakers, although several remembered that their mothers took seasonal jobs in area factories and fields. The mother of the youngest interviewee (Rosa Guerrero) supported her family through domestic labor and fortune-telling. Eleven grew up in urban barrios, ten in Los Angeles. Most families were nuclear rather than extended, although kin usually (but not always) resided nearby. Rich in detail, these interviews reveal the complex negotiations across generations and across cultures.

Education and employment were the most significant agents of Americanization. Educators generally relied on an immersion method in teaching the English language to their Mexican pupils. In other words, Spanish-speaking children had to sink or swim in an English-only environment. Even on the playground, students were enjoined from conversing in their native Spanish. Admonishments such as "Don't speak that ugly language, you are an American now" not only reflected a strong belief in Anglo conformity but also denigrated the self-esteem of Mexican American children and dampened their enthusiasm for education.[8] Ruby Estrada remembered that corporal punishment was a popular method for teaching English: "The teacher was mean and the kids got mean."[9] At times children internalized these lessons, as Mary Luna reflected: "It was rough because I didn't know English. The teacher wouldn't let us talk Spanish. How can you talk to anybody? If you can't talk Spanish and you can't talk English, what are you going to do? . . . It wasn't until maybe the fourth or fifth grade that I started catching up. And all along that time I just felt I was stupid."[10]

Students also became familiar with U.S. history and holidays (e.g., Thanksgiving). In recounting her childhood, Rosa Guerrero elaborated on how in her own mind she reconciled the history lessons at school with her own heritage. "The school system would teach everything about American history, the colonists and all of that," she explained, "then I would do a comparison in my mind of where my grandparents came from, what they did, and wonder how I was to be evolved and educated."[11]

Schools, in some instances, raised expectations. Imbued with the American dream, young women (and men) believed that hard work would bring material rewards and social acceptance. In fact, a California grower disdained education for Mexicans because it would give them "tastes for things they can't acquire."[12] Some teenage women aspired to college; others planned careers as secretaries. "I want to study science or be a stenographer," one Colorado adolescent informed Paul Taylor. "I thinned beets this spring, but I believe it is the last time. The girls who don't go to school will continue to top beets the rest of their lives."[13]

Courses in typing and shorthand were popular among Mexican American women even though few southwestern businesses hired Spanish-surnamed office workers. In 1930 only 2.6 percent of all Mexican women wage earners held clerical jobs. Anthropologist Ruth

Tuck noted the contradiction between training and placement. When she asked one teacher why Mexican women were being trained for clerical positions largely closed to them, the educator replied, "To teach them respect for the white collar job." Skin color also played a role in obtaining office work. As one typing teacher pointed out to young Julia Luna, "Who's going to hire you? You're so dark."[14]

Many young Mexican women never attended high school but took industrial or service-sector jobs directly after the completion of the eighth grade. Like the Eastern European and French Canadian workers studied by John Bodnar and Tamara Hareven, they gave family needs priority over individual goals. Family obligations and economic necessity propelled Mexican women into the labor force. One government study appearing in a 1931 issue of *Monthly Labor Review* revealed that in Los Angeles over 35 percent of the Mexican families surveyed had wage-earning children.[15] By 1930 approximately one-quarter of Mexicana and Mexican American female wage earners in the Southwest obtained employment as industrial workers. In California, they labored principally in canneries and garment firms.[16] Like many female factory workers in the United States, most Mexican operatives were young, unmarried daughters whose wage labor was essential to the economic survival of their families. As members of a "family wage economy," they relinquished all or part of their wages to their elders. According to a 1933 University of California study, of the Mexican families surveyed with working children, the children's monetary contributions comprised 35 percent of the total household income.[17]

At times working for wages gave women a feeling of independence. Historian Douglas Monroy asserted that outside employment "facilitated greater freedom of activity and more assertiveness in the family for Mexicanas." Some young women went a step farther and used their earnings to leave the family home. Facing family disapproval, even ostracism, they defied parental authority by sharing an apartment with female friends.[18] Conversely, kin networks, particularly in canneries and packing houses, reinforced a sense of family. Working alongside female kin, adolescents found employment less than liberating. At the same time the work environment afforded women the opportunity to develop friendships with other Spanish-surnamed operatives and occasionally with their ethnic immigrant peers. They began to discuss with one another their problems and concerns, finding common ground both as factory workers and as second-generation ethnic women. Teenagers chatted about fads, fashions, and celebrities.[19]

Along with outside employment, the media also influenced the acculturation of Mexican women. Movie and romance magazines enabled adolescents (and older women as well) to experience vicariously the middle-class and affluent lifestyles heralded in these publications, and thus to nurture a desire for consumer goods. Radios, motion pictures, and Madison Avenue advertising had a profound impact on America's cultural landscape. According to historians John D'Emilio and Estelle Freedman, "Corporate leaders needed consumers . . . who were ready to spend their earnings to purchase a growing array of goods designed for personal use. . . . Americans did not automatically respond to factory output by multiplying their desire for material goods; an ethic of consumption had to be sold."[20] The Mexican community was not immune to this orchestration of desire, and there appeared a propensity toward consumerism among second-generation women. In his 1928 study of Mexican women in Los Angeles industry, Paul Taylor contended that second to economic need, the prevalent motive for employment among single women was a desire to buy the "extras"—a radio, a phonograph, jazz records, fashionable clothes. As Carmen Bernal Escobar revealed, "After I started working, I liked the money. I love clothes—I used to buy myself beautiful clothes."[21] As members of a "consumer wage economy," daughters also worked in order to purchase items for their families' comfort, such as furniture, draperies, and area rugs.[22] Other teenagers had more modest goals. After giving most of her wages to her mother, Rosa Guerrero reserved a portion to buy peanut butter and shampoo. "Shampoo to me was a luxury. I had to buy shampoo so I wouldn't have to wash my hair with the dirty old Oxydol. I used to wash my hair with the soap for the clothes."[23]

The American cinema also made an impression. Although times were lean, many southern California women had dreams of fame and fortune, nurtured in part by the proximity to Hollywood. Movies, both Mexican and American, provided a popular form of entertainment for barrio residents. It was common on Saturday mornings to see children and young adults combing the streets for bottles so that they could afford the price of admission—ten cents for the afternoon matinee. Preteens would frequently come home and act out what they had seen on the screen. "I was going to be Clara Bow," remembered Adele Hernández Milligan. Another woman recounted that she had definitely been "star struck" as a youngster and attempted to fulfill her fantasy in junior high by "acting in plays galore." The handful of Latina actresses appearing in Hollywood films, such as Dolores Del Rio and Lupe Velez, also whetted these aspirations. Older star-struck adolescents enjoyed afternoon outings to Hollywood, filled with the hope of being discovered as they strolled along Hollywood and Vine with their friends.[24]

The influential Spanish-language newspaper *La Opinión* encouraged these fantasies in part, by publishing gossipy stories about movie stars such as Charlie Chaplin and Norma Shearer as well as up-to-the-minute reports on the private lives and careers of Latino celebrities. It also carried reviews of Spanish-language films, concerts, and plays.[25] Although promoting pride in Latino cultural events, the society pages reflected the public fascination with Hollywood. One week after its first issue, *La Opinion* featured a Spanish translation of Louella Parsons's nationally syndicated gossip column. Furthermore, the Los Angeles–based newspaper directly capitalized on the dreams of youth by sponsoring a contest with Metro-Goldwyn-Mayer. "Day by day we see how a young man or woman, winner of some contest, becomes famous overnight," reminded *La Opinion* as it publicized its efforts to offer its readers a similar chance. Touted as "the unique opportunity for all young men and women who aspire to movie stardom," this promotion held out the promise of a screen test to one lucky contestant.[26]

For many, show business had obvious appeal; it was perceived as a glamorous avenue for mobility. One could overcome poverty and prejudice as a successful entertainer. As an article on Lupe Velez optimistically claimed, "Art has neither nationalities nor borders."[27]

Americanization seemed to seep into the barrios from all directions—from schools, factories, and even from the ethnic press. Parental responses to the Americanization of their children can be classified into two distinct categories—accommodation and resistance. These responses seem rooted more in class than in gender. In the sample of thirteen interviews and in my survey of early ethnographies, I can find no indication that intergenerational tension occurred more frequently among fathers and daughters than among mothers and daughters. Although parents cannot be viewed as a monolithic group, certainly both took an active interest in the socialization of their children. While resistance was the norm, some parents encouraged attempts at acculturation, and at times entire families took adult-education courses in a concerted effort to become "good Americans." Paul Taylor argues that middle-class Mexicans desiring to dissociate themselves from their working-class neighbors had the most fervent aspirations for assimilation. Once in the United States, middle-class Mexicanos found themselves subject to ethnic prejudice that did not discriminate by class. Because of restrictive real estate covenants and segregated schools, these immigrants had lived in the barrios with people they considered their inferiors.[28] By passing as "Spanish," they cherished hopes of melting into the American social landscape. Sometimes mobility-minded parents sought to regulate their children's choice of friends and later their marriage partners. "My folks never allowed us to go around with Mexicans," remembered Alicia Mendeola Shelit. "We went sneaking around, but my Dad wouldn't allow it. We'd always be with white." Interestingly, Shelit was married twice, both times to Anglos. As anthropologist Margarita Melville has concluded in her contemporary study of Mexican women immigrants, "aspirations for upward mobility" emerged as the most distinguishing factor in the process of acculturation.[29] Of course, it would be unfair to characterize all middle-class Mexican immigrants as repudiating their *mestizo* identity. Or as one young woman cleverly remarked, "Listen, I may be a Mexican in a fur coat, but I'm still a Mexican."[30]

Although enjoying the creature comforts afforded by life in the United States, Mexican immigrants retained their cultural traditions, and parents developed strategies to counteract the alarming acculturation of their young. Required to speak only English at school, Mexican youngsters were then instructed to speak only Spanish at home. Even in families that permitted the use of English, parents took steps to ensure the retention of Spanish among their children. Rosa Guerrero fondly remembered sitting with her father and conjugating verbs in Spanish "just for the love of it."[31] Proximity to Mexico also played an important role in maintaining cultural ties. Growing up in El Paso, Texas, Guerrero crossed the border into Ciudad Juárez every weekend with her family in order to partake of traditional recreational events, such as bullfights. Her family, moreover, made yearly treks to visit relatives in central Mexico. Those who lived substantial distances from the border, resisted assimilation by building ethnic pride through nostalgic stories of life in Mexico.[32] As one San José woman related:

> My mother never . . . tired of telling us stories of her native village in Guanajuato; she never let us children forget the things that her village was noted for, its handicrafts and arts, its songs and its stories. . . . She made it all sound so beautiful with her descriptions of the mountains and the lakes, the old traditions, the happy people, and the dances and weddings and fiestas. From the time I was a small child I always wanted to go back to Mexico and see the village where my mother was born.[33]

Though many youngsters relished the folk and family lore told by their parents or grandparents, others failed to appreciate their elders' efforts: "Grandmother Pérez's stories about the witches and ghosts of Los Conejos get scant audience, in competition with Dick Tracy and Buck Rogers."[34]

In bolstering cultural consciousness, parents found help through youth-oriented community organizations. Church, service, and political clubs reinforced ethnic awareness. Examples included the Logia "Juventud Latina" of the Alianza Hispano Americana, the Mexican American Movement initially sponsored by the YMCA, and the youth division of El Congreso de Pueblos de Hablan Española. Bert Corona, a leading California civil rights advocate for over four decades, began his career of activism as a leader in both the Mexican American Movement and the youth auxiliary of the Spanish-speaking Peoples Congress.[35]

Interestingly, only two of the thirteen women mentioned Catholicism as an important early influence. The Catholic church played more of a social role; it organized youth clubs and dances and it was the place for baptisms, marriages, and funerals.[36] For others, Protestant churches offered a similar sense of community. Establishing small niches in Mexican barrios, Protestant missionaries envisioned themselves as the harbingers of salvation and Americanization. Yet some converts saw their churches as reaffirming traditional Mexican values. "I was beginning to think that the Baptist church was a little too Mexican. Too much restriction," remembered Rose Escheverria Mulligan. Indeed, this woman longed to join her Catholic peers, who regularly attended church-sponsored dances: "I noticed they were having a good time."[37] Whether gathering for a Baptist picnic or a Catholic dance, teenagers seemed more attracted to the social rather than the spiritual side of their religion. Certainly more research is needed to assess the impact of Protestant social workers and missionaries on the attitudes of adolescent women. Mary Luna, for example, credited her love of reading to an Anglo educator who converted a small house in the barrio into a makeshift community center and library. The dual thrust of Americanization, education, and consumerism, can be discerned in the following excerpt from Luna's oral history. "To this day I just love going to libraries. . . . There are two places that I can go in and get a real warm, happy feeling; that is, the library and Bullock's in the perfume and make-up department."[38]

Blending new behavior with traditional ideals, young women also had to balance family expectations with their own need for individual expression. Within families, young women, perhaps more than their brothers, were expected to uphold certain standards. Indeed, Chicano social scientists have generally portrayed women as "the 'glue' that keeps the Chicano family together" as well as the guardians of "traditional culture."[39] Parents therefore often assumed what they perceived as their unquestionable prerogative to regulate the actions and attitudes of their adolescent daughters. Teenagers, on the other hand, did not always acquiesce in the boundaries set down for them by their elders. Intergenerational tension flared along several fronts.

Generally, the first area of disagreement between a teenager and her family would be over her personal appearance. During the 1920s a woman's decision to bob or not bob her hair assumed classic proportions within Mexican families. After considerable pleading, Belen Martínez Mason was permitted to cut her hair, though she soon regretted her decision: "Oh, I cried for a month."[40] Differing opinions over fashions often caused ill feelings. One Mexican American woman recalled that when she was a young girl, her mother dressed her "like a nun," and she could wear "no make-up, no cream, no nothing" on her face. Swimwear, bloomers, and short skirts also became sources of controversy. Some teenagers left home in one outfit and changed into another at school. Once María Fierro arrived home in her bloomers. Her father asked, "Where have you been dressed like that, like a clown?" "I told him the truth," Fierro explained. "He whipped me anyway. . . . So from then on whenever I went to the track meet, I used to change my bloomers so that he wouldn't see that I had gone again."[41] The impact of flapper styles on the Mexican community was clearly expressed in the following verse taken from a *corrido* (ballad) appropriately entitled "Las Pelonas [The Bobbed-Haired Girls]":

> Red Bandannas
> I detest,
> And now the flappers
> Use them for their dress.
> The girls of San Antonio
> Are lazy at the *metate*.
> They want to walk out bobbed-haired,
> With straw hats on.
> The harvesting is finished,
> So is the cotton;
> The flappers stroll out now
> For a good time.[42]

With similar sarcasm, another popular ballad chastised Mexican women for applying makeup so heavily as to resemble a piñata.[43]

Once again bearing the banner of glamour and consumption, *La Opinión* featured sketches of the latest flapper fashions as well as cosmetic ads from both Latino and Anglo manufacturers. The most elaborate layouts were those of Max Factor. Using celebrity testimonials, one advertisement encouraged women to "follow the stars" and purchase "Max Factor's Society Make-up." Factor, through an exclusive arrangement with *La Opinión*, went even further in courting the Mexican market by answering beauty questions from readers in a special column—"Secretos de Belleza [Beauty Secrets]."[44]

The use of cosmetics, however, cannot be blamed entirely on Madison Avenue ad campaigns. The innumerable barrio beauty pageants, sponsored by *mutualistas*, patriotic societies, churches, the Mexican Chamber of Commerce, newspapers, and even progressive labor unions encouraged young women to accentuate their physical attributes. Carefully chaperoned, many teenagers did participate in community contests, from La Reina de Cinco de Mayo to Orange Queen. They modeled evening gowns, rode on parade floats, and sold raffle tickets.[45] Carmen Bernal Escobar remembered one incident when, as a contestant, she had to sell raffle tickets. Every ticket she sold counted as a vote for her in the pageant. Naturally the winner would be the woman who had accumulated the most votes. When her brother offered to buy twenty-five dollars' worth of votes (her mother would not think of letting her peddle the tickets at work or in the neighborhood), Escobar, on a pragmatic note, asked him to give her the money so that she could buy a coat she had spotted while window-shopping.[46]

The commercialization of personal grooming made additional inroads into the Mexican community with the appearance of barrio beauty parlors. Working as a beautician conferred a certain degree of status, "a nice, clean job," in comparison with factory or domestic work. As one woman related:

> I always wanted to be a beauty operator. I loved makeup; I loved to dress up and fix up. I used to set my sisters' hair. So I had that in the back of my mind for a long time, and my mom pushed the fact that she wanted me to have a profession—seeing that I wasn't thinking of getting married.[47]

Although further research is needed, one can speculate that neighborhood beauty shops reinforced women's networks and became places where they could relax, exchange *chisme*, and enjoy the company of other women.[48]

Conforming to popular fashions and fads cannot be construed as a lack of ethnic or political consciousness. In 1937 Carey McWilliams spoke before an assembly of fifteen hundred walnut workers in Los Angeles and was "profoundly stirred" by this display of grassroots labor militancy by Eastern European and Mexican women. Describing the meeting, he wrote, "And such extraordinary faces—particularly the old women. Some of the girls had been too frequently to the beauty shop, and were too gotten up—rather amusingly dressy."[49] I would argue that dressing up for a union meeting could be interpreted as an affirmation of individual integrity. Although they worked under horrendous conditions (actually cracking walnuts with their fists), their collective action and personal appearance give evidence that they did not surrender their self-esteem.

The most serious point of contention between an adolescent daughter and her parents, however, centered on her behavior toward young men. In both cities and rural towns, girls had to be closely chaperoned by a family member every time they attended a movie, dance, or even church-related events. Recalling the supervisory role played by her "old-maid" aunt, María Fierro laughingly explained, "She'd check on us all the time. I used to get so mad at her." Ruby Estrada recalled that in a small southern Arizona community, "all the mothers" escorted their daughters to the local dances. Even talking to male peers in broad daylight could be grounds for discipline.[50] Adele Hernández Milligan, a resident of Los Angeles for over fifty years, elaborated, "I remember the first time that I walked home with a boy from school. Anyway, my mother saw me and she was mad. I must have been sixteen or seventeen. She slapped my face because I was walking home with a boy."[51] Describing this familial protectiveness, one social scientist aptly remarked that the "supervision of the Mexican parent is so strict as to be obnoxious."[52]

Faced with this type of situation, young women had three options: They could accept the rules set down for them, they could rebel, or they could find ways to compromise or circumvent traditional standards. "I was *never* allowed to go out by myself in the evening; it just was not done." In rural communities where restrictions were perhaps even more stringent, "nice" teenagers could not even swim with their male peers: "We were ladies and wouldn't go swimming out there with a bunch of boys." Yet many seemed to accept these limits with equanimity. "It wasn't devastating at all," reflected Ruby Estrada. "We took it in stride. We never thought of it as cruel or mean. . . . It was taken for granted that that's the way it was."[53] In Sonora, Arizona, as in other small towns, relatives and neighbors kept close watch over adolescent women and quickly reported any suspected indiscretions. "They were always spying on you," Estrada remarked. Women in cities had a distinct advantage over their rural peers in that they could venture miles from their neighborhood into the anonymity of dance halls, amusement parks, and other places of commercialized leisure. With carnival rides and the Cinderella Ballroom, the Nu-Pike Amusement Park of Long Beach proved a popular hangout for Mexican youth in Los Angeles.[54] It was more difficult to abide by traditional norms when excitement beckoned just on the other side of the streetcar line.

Some women openly rebelled. They moved out of their family homes and into apartments. Considering themselves freewheeling single women, they could go out with men unsupervised, as was the practice among their Anglo peers. "This terrible freedom in the United States," one Mexicana lamented. "I do not have to worry because I have no daughters, but the poor *señoras* with many girls, they worry."[55] Those Mexican American adolescents who did not wish to defy their parents openly would sneak out of the house in order to meet their dates or to attend dances with female friends. A more subtle form of rebellion was early marriage. By marrying at fifteen or sixteen, these women sought to escape parental supervision; yet it could be argued that many of these child brides exchanged one form of supervision for another in addition to the responsibilities of child rearing.[56]

The third alternative sometimes involved quite a bit of creativity as these young women sought to circumvent traditional chaperonage. Alicia Mendeola Shelit recalled that one of her older brothers would always accompany her to dances, ostensibly as a chaperone. "But then my oldest brother would always have a blind date for me." Carmen Bernal Escobar was permitted to entertain her boyfriends at home, but only under the supervision of her brother or mother. The practice of "going out with the girls," though not accepted until the 1940s, was fairly common. Several Mexican American women, often related, would escort one another to an event (such as a dance), socialize with the men in attendance, and then walk home together. In the sample of thirteen interviews, daughters negotiated their activities with their parents. Older siblings and extended kin appeared in the background either as chaperones or as accomplices. Although unwed teenage mothers were not unknown in the Los Angeles barrios, families expected adolescent women to conform to strict standards of behavior.[57] As one might expect, many teenage women knew little about sex other than what they picked up from friends, romance magazines, and the local theater. As Mary Luna remembered, "I thought that if somebody kissed you you could get pregnant." In *Singing for My Echo*, New Mexico native Gregorita Rodríguez confided that on her wedding night, she knelt down and said her rosary until her husband gently asked, "Gregorita, *mi esposa*, are you afraid of me?" At times this naïveté persisted beyond the wedding. "It took four days for my husband to touch me," one woman revealed. "I slept with dress and all. We were both greenhorns, I guess."[58]

Of course, some young women did lead more adventurous lives. A male interviewer employed by Mexican anthropologist Manuel Gamio recalled his "relations" with a woman he met in a Los Angeles dance hall. Though born in Hermosillo, Elisa "Elsie" Morales considered herself Spanish. She helped support her family by dancing with strangers. Although she lived at home and her mother and brother attempted to monitor her actions, she managed to meet the interviewer at a "hot-pillow" hotel. To prevent pregnancy, she relied on contraceptive douches provided by "an American doctor." Although Morales realized her mother would not approve of her behavior, she noted that "she [her mother] is from Mexico. . . . I am from there also but I was brought up in the United States, we think about things differently." Just as Morales rationalized her actions as "American," the interviewer perceived her within a similar though certainly less favorable definition of Americanization. "She seemed very coarse to me. That is she dealt with one in the American way."[59] In his field notes, Paul Taylor recorded an incident in which a young woman had moved in with her Anglo boyfriend after he had convinced her that such living arrangements were common among Americans. Popular *corridos*, such as "El Enganchado" and "Las Pelonas," also touched on the theme of the corrupting influence of U.S. ways on Mexican women.[60]

Interestingly, both Anglo and Mexican communities held almost identical preconceptions of each other's young female population. While Mexicanos viewed Anglo women as morally loose, Latina actresses in Hollywood found themselves typecast as hot-blooded women of low repute. For example, Lupe Velez starred in such films as *Hot Pepper*, *Strictly Dynamite*, and *The Mexican Spitfire*.[61] The image of loose sexual mores as distinctly American probably reinforced parental fears as they watched their daughters apply cosmetics and adopt the apparel advertised in fashion magazines. In other words, "If she dresses like a flapper, will she then act like one?" Seeds of suspicion reaffirmed the penchant for traditional supervision.

Tension between parents and daughters, however, did not always revolve around adolescent behavior. At times teenagers questioned the lifestyles of their parents. "I used to tell my mother she was a regular maid," Alicia Shelit recalled. "They [the women] never had a voice. They had to have the house clean, the food ready for the men . . . and everything just so."[62] As anthropologist Tuck observed, "Romantic literature, still more romantic movies, and the attitudes of American teachers and social workers have confirmed the Pérez children in a belief that their parents do not 'love' each other; that, in particular, Lola Pérez is a drudge and a slave for her husband."[63]

However I would argue that the impact of Americanization was most keenly felt at the level of personal aspiration. "We felt if we worked hard, proved ourselves, we could become professional people," asserted Rose Escheverria Mulligan.[64] Braced with such idealism, Mexican Americans faced prejudice, segregation, and economic segmentation. Though they considered themselves Americans, others perceived them as less than desirable foreigners. During the late 1920s the *Saturday Evening Post*, exemplifying the nativist spirit of the times, featured inflammatory characterizations of Mexicans in the United States. For instance, one article portrayed Mexicano immigrants as an "illiterate, diseased, pauperized" people who bear children "with the reckless prodigality of rabbits."[65] Racism was not limited to rhetoric; between 1931 and 1934 an estimated one-third of the Mexican population in the United States (over five hundred thousand people) were either deported or repatriated to Mexico even though many were native U.S. citizens. Mexicans were the only immigrants targeted for removal. Proximity to the Mexican border, the physical distinctiveness of *mestizos*, and easily identifiable barrios influenced immigration and social-welfare officials to focus their efforts solely on the Mexican people, people whom they viewed as both foreign usurpers of American jobs and unworthy burdens on relief rolls. From Los Angeles, California, to Gary, Indiana, Mexicans were either summarily deported by immigration agencies or persuaded to depart voluntarily by duplicitous social workers who greatly exaggerated the opportunities awaiting them south of the border.[66] According to historian George Sánchez:

> As many as seventy-five thousand Mexicans from southern California returned to Mexico by 1932. . . . The enormity of these figures, given the fact that California's Mexican population was in 1930 slightly over three hundred and sixty thousand . . . , indicates that almost every Mexican family in southern California confronted in one way or another the decision of returning or staying.[67]

By 1935 the deportation and repatriation campaigns had diminished, but prejudice and segregation remained. Historian Albert Camarillo has demonstrated that in Los Angeles restrictive real estate covenants and segregated schools increased dramatically between 1920 and 1950. The proportion of Los Angeles area municipalities with covenants prohibiting Mexicans and other minorities from purchasing residences in certain neighborhoods climbed from 20 percent in 1920 to 80 percent in 1946. Many restaurants, theaters, and public swimming pools discriminated against their Spanish-surnamed clientele. In southern California, for example, Mexicans could swim at the public plunges only one day out of the week (just before they drained the pool).[68] Small-town merchants frequently refused to admit Spanish-speaking people into their places of business. "White Trade Only" signs served as bitter reminders of their second-class citizenship.[69]

In 1933 a University of California study noted that Mexicans in southern California were among the most impoverished groups in the United States. Regardless of nativity, they were often dismissed as cheap, temporary labor and were paid "from 20 to 50 percent less per day for . . . performing the same jobs as other workers."[70] This economic segmentation did not diminish by generation. Writing about San Bernardino, California, in the 1940s, Ruth Tuck offered the following illustration:

> There is a street . . . on which three families live side by side. The head of one family is a naturalized citizen, who arrived here eighteen years ago; the head of the second is an alien who came . . . in 1905; the head of the third is the descendant of people who came . . . in 1843. All of them, with their families, live in poor housing; earn approximately $150 a month as unskilled laborers; send their children to "Mexican" schools; and encounter the same sort of discriminatory practices.[71]

Until World War II Mexicans experienced restricted occupational mobility, as few rose above the ranks of blue-collar labor. Scholars Mario García and Gilbert González have convincingly argued that the curricula in Mexican schools helped to perpetuate this trend. Emphasis on vocational education served to funnel Mexican youth into the factories and building trades.[72] In the abstract, education raised people's expectations, but in practice, particularly for men, it trained them for low-status, low-paying jobs. Employment choices were even more limited in rural areas. As miners or farm workers, Mexicans usually resided in company settlements where almost every aspect of their lives was regulated, from work schedules to wage rates to credit with local merchants. In 1925 a newspaper editor in Greeley, Colorado, bluntly advocated "a caste system," even though he alleged such a system "will be worse upon us, the aristocracy, than upon the Mexicans in their serfdom."[73] In both urban and rural areas, ethnicity became not only a matter of personal choice and heritage but also an ascribed status imposed by external sources.[74]

Considering these circumstances, it is not surprising that many teenagers developed a shining idealism as a type of psychological ballast. Some adolescents, like the members of the Mexican American Movement, believed that education was the key to mobility; while others placed their faith in the application of Max Factor's bleaching cream.[75] Whether they struggled to further their education or tried to lighten their skin color, Mexican Americans sought to protect themselves from the damaging effects of prejudice.

Despite economic and social stratification, many Mexicanas believed that life in the United States offered hope and opportunity. "Here woman has come to have place like a human being," reflected Señora _____.[76] More common, perhaps, was the impact of material assimilation: the purchase of an automobile, a sewing machine, and other accoutrements of the U.S. consumer society. The accumulation of these goods signaled the realization of (or the potential for realizing) the American dream. As Margaret Clark eloquently commented:

> In Sal si Puedes [a San José barrio] where so many people are struggling to escape poverty and want, a "luxury item" like a shiny new refrigerator may be the source of hope and encouragement—it may symbolize the first step toward the achievement of a better way of life.

One of Clark's informants aired a more direct statement: "Nobody likes to be poor."[77]

The era of World War II ushered in a set of new options for Mexican women. In southern California some joined unions in food-processing plants and negotiated higher wages and benefits. Still others obtained more lucrative employment in defense plants. As "Rosie the Riveters," they gained self-confidence and the requisite earning power to improve their standard of living. A single parent, Alicia Mendeola Shelit, purchased her first home as the result of her employment with Douglas Aircraft.[78] The expansion of clerical jobs also provided Mexican American women with additional opportunities. By 1950, 23.9 percent of Mexican women workers in the Southwest held lower white-collar positions as secretaries or salesclerks.[79] They could finally apply the office skills they had acquired in high school or at storefront business colleges. Although beyond the scope of this study, intermarriage with Anglos may have been perceived as a potential avenue for mobility.[80]

Most of the thirteen interviewees continued in the labor force, combining wage work with household responsibilities. Only the oldest (Ruby Estrada, of Arizona) and the youngest (Rosa Guerrero, of Texas) achieved a solid, middle-class standard of living. Though one cannot make facile correlations, both women are the only narrators who attained a college education. Six of the eleven California women took their places on the shop floor in the aerospace, electronics, apparel, and food-processing industries. Two became secretaries and one a salesclerk at Kmart. The remaining two were full-time homemakers. Seven of these eleven informants married Anglo or Jewish men, yet their economic status did not differ substantially from those who chose Mexican spouses.[81] With varying degrees of financial security, the California women are now working-class retirees. Their lives do not exemplify rags-to-riches mobility but rather upward movement within the working class. Though painfully aware of prejudice and discrimination, people of their generation placed faith in themselves and faith in the system. In 1959 Margaret Clark asserted that the second-generation residents of Sal si Puedes "dream and work toward the day when Mexican Americans will become fully integrated into American society at large."[82] The desire to prove oneself appears as a running theme in twentieth-century Mexican American history. I should hasten to add that in the process, most people refused to shed their cultural heritage: "Fusion is what we want—the best of both ways."[83]

358 Vicki L. Ruiz

In this essay I have attempted to reconstruct the world of adolescent women, taking into account the broader cultural, political, and economic environment. I have given a sense of the contradictions in their lives—the lure of Hollywood and the threat of deportation. The discussion gives rise to an intriguing question. Can one equate the desire for material goods with the abandonment of Mexican values? I would argue that the ideological impact of material acculturation has been overrated. For example, a young Mexican woman may have looked like a flapper as she boarded a streetcar on her way to work at a cannery, yet she went to work (at least in part) to help support her family, as one of her obligations as a daughter. The adoption of new cultural forms certainly frightened parents but did not of itself undermine Mexican identity. The experiences of Mexican American women coming of age between 1920 and 1950 reveal the blending of the old and the new: fashioning new expectations, making choices, and learning to live with those choices.

Notes

I gratefully acknowledge the research assistance of Amagda Pérez and Christine Marin. I appreciate the generosity and long-standing support of Sherna Gluck, who has given me permission to quote from eight volumes of the Rosie the Riveter Revisited Oral History Collection housed at California State University, Long Beach. I also wish to thank the American Council of Learned Societies and the Committee on Research, University of California, Davis, for financial support of this project. Roland Marchand, Ramón Gutiérrez, and Howard Shorr provided incisive comments on earlier drafts, and I appreciate their interest in my work.

1. Oscar Handlin, *The Uprooted* (New York: Grosset and Dunlap, 1951); Alfred Kazin, *A Walker in the City* (New York: Harcourt Brace Jovanovich, 1951).
2. Examples of this rich literature include John Bodnar, *The Transplanted* (Bloomington: Indiana University Press, 1985); Kathy Peiss, *Cheap Amusements: Working Women and Leisure in Turn-of-the-Century New York* (Philadelphia: Temple University Press, 1986); Paula S. Fass, *The Damned and the Beautiful: American Youth in the 1920s* (New York: Oxford University Press, 1977), and John D'Emilio and Estelle B. Freedman, *Intimate Matters* (New York: Harper and Row, 1988).
3. Albert Camarillo, *Chicanos in a Changing Society: From Mexican Pueblos to American Barrios in Santa Barbara and Southern California, 1848–1930* (Cambridge, Mass.: Harvard University Press, 1979), 200–1; Ricardo Romo, *East Los Angeles: History of a Barrio* (Austin: University of Texas Press, 1983), 61; T. Wilson Longmore and Homer L. Hitt, "A Demographic Analysis of First and Second Generation Mexican Population of the United States: 1930," *Southwestern Social Science Quarterly* 24 (September 1943): 140.
4. Manuel Gamio, *Mexican Immigration to the United States. A Study of Human Migration and Adjustment* (New York: Arno Press, 1969 [1930]); Paul S. Taylor, *Mexican Labor in the United States*, 2 vols. (Berkeley: University of California Press, 1928, 1932); Emory S. Bogardus, *The Mexican in the United States* (Los Angeles: University of Southern California Press, 1934). Pachucos were young men who adopted the zoot suit, a badge of adolescent rebellion in Mexican and African American communities during World War II. Because of their dress and demeanor, they were subject to verbal and physical abuse by law enforcement officials and servicemen. Mauricio Mazón, *The Zoot Suit Riots: The Psychology of Symbolic Annihilation* (Austin: University of Texas Press, 1984) and the Luis Valdez play and feature film *Zoot Suit* provide examples of the literature on *pachucos*.
5. Works that focus on Mexican women during this period include Rosalinda M. González, "Chicanas and Mexican Immigrant Families 1920–1940: Women's Subordination and Family Exploitation," in Lois Scharf and Joan Jensen, eds., *Decades of Discontent: The Women's Movement, 1920–1940* (Westport, Conn.: Greenwood Press, 1983), 59–83, and Vicki L. Ruiz, *Cannery Women, Cannery Lives: Mexican Women, Unionization, and the California Food Processing Industry, 1930–1950* (Albuquerque: University of New Mexico Press, 1987).
6. Ruth Zambrana, "A Walk in Two Worlds," *Social Welfare* 1 (spring 1986): 12.
7. The age breakdown for the thirteen interviewees is as follows: Two women were born between 1910 and 1912; six between 1913 and 1919; four between 1920 and 1929; and one after 1930.
8. Adelina Otero, "My People" [1931] in Carlos Cortés, ed., *Aspects of the Mexican American Experience* (New York: Arno Press, 1976), 150; Ruth Tuck, *Not with the Fist* (New York: Arno Press, 1974 [1946]), 185–88; Vicki L. Ruiz, "Oral History and La Mujer: The Rosa Guerrero Story," in Vicki L. Ruiz and Susan Tiano, eds., *Women on the United States–Mexico Border: Responses to Change* (Boston: Allen and Unwin, 1987), 226–27; interview with Belen Martínez Mason, in Sherna Berger Gluck, ed., *Rosie the Riveter Revisited: Women and the World War II Work Experience* (Long Beach, Calif.: CSULB Foundation, 1983), 23:24–25.

9. Interview with Ruby Estrada conducted by María Hernández, 4 August 1981, The Lives of Arizona Women, Oral History Project, Special Collections, Hayden Library, Arizona State University, Tempe, 6.

10. Mary Luna interview, *Rosie the Riveter*, 20:10. During the 1940s, bilingual education appeared as an exciting experiment in curriculum reform. See George I. Sanchez, eds., "First Regional Conference on the Education of Spanish-Speaking People in the Southwest" [1945], in Cortés, ed., *Aspects of the Mexican American Experience*.

11. Margarita B. Melville, "Selective Acculturation of Female Mexican Migrants," in Margarita B. Melville, ed., *Twice a Minority: Mexican American Women* (St. Louis: C. V. Mosby, 1980), 161; Ruiz, "Oral History and La Mujer," 222.

12. Rose Escheverria Mulligan interview, *Rosie the Riveter*, 27:16–17, 24; Ruiz, "Oral History and La Mujer," 227–28; Taylor, *Mexican Labor*, 1:79, 205–6.

13. Tuck, *Not with the Fist*, 162–63, 190–91; Paul S. Taylor, "Women in Industry," field notes for *Mexican Labor*, Bancroft Library, University of California, 1 box; Estrada interview, 10–15; Escheverria Mulligan interview, 40; Taylor, *Mexican Labor*, 1:205. A synthesis of the Taylor study has been published. See Paul S. Taylor, "Mexican Women in Los Angeles Industry in 1928," *Aztlán* 11 (spring 1980): 99–131.

14. Lois Rita Helmbold, "The Work of Chicanas in the United States: Wage Labor and Work in the Home, 1930 to the Present" (seminar paper, Stanford University, 1977), 53; Taylor, field notes; Tuck, *Not with the Fist*, 190–91; interview with Julia Luna Mount, 17 November 1983, conducted by the authors.

15. John Bodnar, "Immigration, Kinship and the Rise of Working-Class Realism in Industrial America," *Journal of Social History* 14 (fall 1980): 53–55; Tamara K. Hareven, "Family Time and Industrial Time: Family and Work in a Planned Corporation Town, 1900–1924," in Tamara K. Hareven, ed., *Family and Kin in Urban Communities* (New York: New Viewpoints, 1977), 202; Taylor, notes; U.S. Department of Labor, Bureau of Labor Statistics, "Labor and Social Conditions of Mexicans in California," *Monthly Labor Review* 32 (January–June 1931): 89.

16. Mario Barrera, *Race and Class in the Southwest* (Notre Dame, Ind.: University of Notre Dame Press, 1979), 131; Taylor, notes. The percentage of Mexican women workers employed in industry was comparable to the participation of European immigrant women in eastern industry, where one-third of ethnic women who worked outside the home labored as blue-collar employees (Alice Kessler-Harris, *Out to Work: A History of Wage Earning Women in the United States* [New York: Oxford University Press, 1982], 127).

17. Heller Committee for Research in Social Economics of the University of California and Constantine Panuzio, *How Mexicans Earn and Live*, University of California Publications in Economics 13, 1, Cost of Living Studies (Berkeley: University of California, 1933), 5:11, 14–17; Taylor, notes; Luna Mount interview; Alicia Shelit interview, *Rosie the Riveter*, 37:9. For further delineation of the family wage and the consumer wage economy, see Louise A. Tilly and Joan W. Scott, *Women, Work and Family* (New York: Holt, Rinehart, and Winston, 1978).

18. Taylor, notes; Helmbold, "Work of Chicanas," 15, 30–31, 36; Douglas Monroy, "An Essay on Understanding the Work Experience of Mexicans in Southern California, 1900–1939," *Aztlán* 12 (spring 1981): 70; González, "Chicanas and Mexican Immigrant Families," 72.

19. Discussing popular magazines and movies helped build important cross-cultural bridges—bridges that would facilitate union-organizing drives among southern California food-processing workers during the late 1930s and early 1940s. See Ruiz, *Cannery Women, Cannery Lives*.

20. Roland Marchand, *Advertising the American Dream: Making Way for Modernity, 1920–1940* (Berkeley: University of California Press, 1985), 197–99, 219; D'Emilio and Freedman, *Intimate Matters*, 278.

21. Taylor, notes; Richard G. Thurston, "Urbanization and Sociocultural Change in a Mexican-American Enclave" (Ph.D. diss., University of California, Los Angeles, 1957; reprint, San Francisco: R and E Research Associates, 1974), 128; Helmbold, "Work of Chicanas," 42–44; interview with Carmen Bernal Escobar, 15 June 1986, conducted by the author.

22. Elizabeth Fuller, *The Mexican Housing Problem in Los Angeles*, Studies in Sociology, Sociological Monograph 5, 17 (New York: Arno Press, 1974 [1920]), 4–5.

23. Ruiz, "Oral History and La Mujer," 226.

24. Shelit interview, 4; Adele Hernández Milligan interview, *Rosie the Riveter*, 26:14; Martínez Mason interview, 59–60; Luna interview, 18, 26; Clint C. Wilson II and Felix Gutiérrez, *Minorities and Media* (Beverly Hills: Sage Publications, 1985), 85–86.

25. For examples, see *La Opinión*, 16 and 18 September 1926, 13 and 15 May 1927, 3 and 4 June 1927.

26. Ibid., 23, 24, 27, and 30 September, 1926.

27. Ibid., 2 March 1927.

28. Taylor, notes. Referring to Los Angeles, two historians have argued that "Mexicans experienced segregation in housing in nearly every section of the city and its outlying areas" (Antonio Ríos-Bustamante and Pedro Castillo, *An Illustrated History of Mexican Los Angeles 1781–1985* [Los Angeles: Chicano Studies Research Center/University of California, 1986], 135). Ruth Tuck noted that Anglo Americans also employed the term *Spanish* in order to distinguish individuals "of superior background or achievement" (Tuck, *Not with the Fist*, 142–43).

29. Shelit interview, 32; Mulligan interview, 14; Melville, "Selective Acculturation," 155, 162.

30. Tuck, *Not with the Fist*, 133.

31. Gamio, *Mexican Immigration*, 172–73; Bogardus, *The Mexican in the United States*, 75; Romo, *East Los Angeles*, 142; Ruiz, "Oral History and La Mujer," 224. "Some adolescents are stimulated to play the dual roles of being good Mexicans at home and good 'Americans' at school" (Bogardus, 75).

32. Ruiz, "Oral History and La Mujer," 221, 224–25; Margaret Clark, *Health in the Mexican American Culture* (Berkeley: University of California Press, 1959), 21.

33. Clark, *Health*, 21.

34. Tuck, *Not with the Fist*, 108.

35. Ríos-Bustamante and Castillo, *Illustrated History*, 139; George Sánchez, "The Rise of the Second Generation: The Mexican American Movement" (unpublished paper, courtesy of the author), 26–27; interview with Luisa Moreno, 12–13 August 1977, conducted by Albert Camarillo.

36. Sociologist Norma Williams contends that contemporary Mexican Americans view the Catholic Church almost solely in terms of social, life-cycle functions, such as baptisms and funerals. See Norma Williams, *The Mexican American Family: Tradition and Change* (New York: G. K. Hall, 1990).

37. Vicki L. Ruiz, "Dead Ends or Gold Mines? Using Missionary Records in Mexican American Women's History," *Frontiers* 12 (June 1991): 33–56; Mulligan interview, 24. For an interesting collection of Protestant missionary reports for this period, see Carlos Cortés, ed., *Church Views of the Mexican American* (New York: Arno Press, 1974).

38. Luna interview, 9.

39. George Sanchez, "'Go after the Women': Americanization and the Mexican Immigrant Woman 1915–1929," Stanford Center for Chicano Research, working paper no. 6, 2.

40. Bogardus, *The Mexican in the United States*, 74; Martínez Mason interview, 44. During the 1920s, Mexican parents were not atypical in voicing their concerns over the attitudes and appearance of their "flapper adolescents." A general atmosphere of tension between youth and their elders existed—a generation gap that cut across class, race, ethnicity, and region. See Fass, *Damned and Beautiful*.

41. Shelit interview, 18; Taylor, *Mexican Labor*, 2:199–200; María Fierro interview, *Rosie the Riveter*, 12:10.

42. Gamio, *Mexican Immigration*, 89; the verse is taken from "Las Pelonas" in the original Spanish:

> Los paños colorados
> Los tengo aborrecidos
> Ya hora las pelonas
> Los usan de vestidos.
> Las muchachas de S. Antonio
> Son flojas pa'l metate
> Quieren andar pelonas
> Con sombreros de petate.
> Se acabaron las pizcas,
> Se acabó el algodón
> Ya andan las pelonas
> De puro vacilón.

43. Taylor, *Mexican Labor*, 2:vi–vii.

44. *La Opinión*, 18 September 1926, 3 May 1927, 5 June 1927. Using endorsements from famous people was a common advertising technique. See Marchand, *Advertising the American Dream*, 96–102.

45. Rodolfo F. Acuña, *A Community under Siege: A Chronicle of Chicanos East of the Los Angeles River 1945–1975* (Los Angeles: UCLA Chicano Studies Research Center Publications, 1984), 278, 407–8, 413–14, 418, 422; *FTA News*, 1 May 1945; Escobar interview. For an example of the promotion of a beauty pageant, see issues of *La Opinion*, June and July 1927.

46. Escobar interview.

47. Sherna B. Gluck, *Rosie the Riveter Revisited: Women, the War and Social Change* (Boston: Twayne, 1987), 81, 85.

48. *Chisme* means "gossip."

49. Letter from Carey McWilliams dated 3 October 1937, to Louis Adamic, Adamic File, carton l, Carey McWilliams Collection, Special Collections, University of California, Los Angeles.

50. Martínez Mason interview, 29–30; Escobar interview; Fierro interview, 15; Estrada interview, 11–12. Chaperonage was also common in Italian immigrant communities. Indeed, many of the same conflicts between parents and daughters had surfaced a generation earlier among Italian families on the East Coast (Peiss, *Cheap Amusements*, 69–70, 152).

51. Hernández Milligan interview, 17.

52. Evangeline Hymer, "A Study of the Social Attitudes of Adult Mexican Immigrants in Los Angeles and Vicinity: 1923" (M.A. thesis, University of Southern California, 1924; reprint, San Francisco: R and E Research Associates, 1971), 24–25.

53. Escobar interview; Estrada interview, 11, 13.

54. Estrada interview, 12; Shelit interview, 9; Ríos-Bustamante and Castillo, *Illustrated History*, 153.

55. Taylor, notes; Thurston, "Urbanization," 118; Bogardus, *The Mexican in the United States*, 28–29, 57–58.

56. Martínez Mason interview, 30; Beatrice Morales Clifton interview, *Rosie the Riveter*, 8:14–15.

57. Shelit interview, 9, 24, 30; Escobar interview; Martínez Mason interview, 30; Hernández Milligan interview, 27–28; Taylor, notes.

58. Luna Mount interview; Fierro interview, 18; Luna interview, 29; Gregorita Rodriguez, *Singing for My Echo* (Santa Fe, N.M.: Cota Editions, 1987), 52; Martínez Mason interview, 62.

59. "Elisa Morales," Manuel Gamio field notes, Bancroft Library, University of California, 1 box.

60. Taylor notes; Taylor, *Mexican Labor*, 2:vi–vii; Gamio, *Mexican Immigration*, 89. The *corrido* "El Enganchado" in vol. 2 offers an intriguing glimpse into attitudes toward women and Americanization.

61. Wilson and Gutiérrez, *Minorities and Media*, 86.

62. Tuck, *Not with the Fist*, 115; Shelit interview, 26.

63. Tuck, *Not with the Fist*, 115.

64. Taylor, *Mexican Labor*, 1:205–6; Ruiz, "Oral History and La Mujer," 227–28; Sanchez, "Mexican American Movement," 7–10, 12; Escheverria Mulligan interview, 17.

65. Kenneth L. Roberts, "The Docile Mexican," *Saturday Evening Post*, 10 March 1928, as quoted in Sanchez, "'Go After the Women,'" 8.

66. Rodolfo F. Acuña *Occupied America: A History of Chicanos*, 2nd ed. (New York: Harper and Row, 1981), 138, 140–41; Albert Camarillo, *Chicanos in California* (San Francisco: Boyd and Fraser, 1984), 48–49; Abraham Hoffman, *Unwanted Mexican Americans in the Great Depression* (Tucson: University of Arizona Press, 1974), 43–66; Francisco E. Balderrama, *In Defense of La Raza: The Los Angeles Mexican Consulate and the Mexican Community, 1929–1936* (Tucson: University of Arizona Press, 1982), 16–20; Neil Betten and Raymond A. Mohl, "From Discrimination to Repatriation: Mexican Life in Gary, Indiana, during the Great Depression," in Norris Hundley, ed., *The Chicano* (Santa Barbara: ABC-Clio Press, 1975), 132, 138–39.

67. Sánchez, "Mexican American Movement," 10.

68. Albert Camarillo, "Mexican American Urban History in Comparative Ethnic Perspective" (Distinguished Speakers Series, University of California, Davis, 26 January 1987); Acuña, *Occupied America*, 310, 318, 323, 330–31; Romo, *East Los Angeles*, 139; Tuck, *Not with the Fist*, 51, 53; Shelit interview, 15.

69. Taylor, *Mexican Labor*, 1:221–24; interview with María Arredondo, 19 March 1986, conducted by Carolyn Arredondo.

70. Heller Committee Study, *How Mexicans Earn and Live*, 68–69, 72; Camarillo, *Chicanos in a Changing Society*, 215.

71. Tuck, *Not with the Fist*, 209–10.

72. Barrera, *Race and Class*, 82–91; Mario T. García, *Desert Immigrants: The Mexicans of El Paso, 1880–1920* (New Haven, Conn.: Yale University Press, 1981), 110–26; Gilbert González, "Racism, Education, and the Mexican Community in Los Angeles, 1920–30," *Societas* 4 (autumn 1974): 287–300.

73. González, "Chicanas and Mexican Immigrant Families," 63–66; Taylor, *Mexican Labor*, 1:162–66, 176–79, 190–91, 217, 220, 227–28 (quote from 220).

74. Melville, "Selective Acculturation," 159–60; John García, "Ethnicity and Chicanos," *Hispanic Journal of Behavioral Sciences* 4 (1982): 310–11.

75. Sanchez, "Mexican American Movement," 7–9; Guadalupe San Miguel Jr., "Culture and Education in the American Southwest: Towards an Explanation of Chicano School Attendance," *Journal of American Ethnic History* 7 (spring 1988): 15, 17; *La Opinión*, 5 June 1927.

76. "Sra_____," Manuel Gamio, field notes.

77. Clark, *Health*, 92.

78. Ruiz, *Cannery Women, Cannery Lives*; Shelit interview, 52–55; Sherna Berger Gluck, "Interlude or Change: Women and the World War II Work Experience," 14, 32–34 (rev. version, courtesy of author; originally published in *International Journal of Oral History* 3 [1982]); see also Gluck, *Rosie the Riveter Revisited*.

79. William H. Chafe, *The American Woman: Her Changing Social, Economic, and Political Roles, 1920–1970* (New York: Oxford University Press, 1972), 137–43, 146; Barrera, *Race and Class*, 131, 140–45.

80. Shelit interview, 32; Escheverria Mulligan interview, 14; Richard Griswold del Castillo, *La Familia: Chicano Families in the Urban Southwest, 1848 to the Present* (Notre Dame, Ind.: University of Notre Dame Press, 1984), 120–22.

81. Many of the husbands were skilled workers in the aerospace industry. The most prestigious occupation for a spouse was firefighter.

82. Clark, *Health*, 20.

83. Tuck, *Not with the Fist*, 134. According to historian Richard Griswold del Castillo, "[P]resent-day Chicano families are a bridge between the social and cultural heritages of Anglo and Latin America" (*La Familia*, 126).

23

Crossed Boundaries in Interracial Chicago: Pilipino American Families since 1925

Barbara M. Posadas

On an often snowy, blustery, cold, winter night each December 30, for almost seventy years, the Pilipino community of Chicago has gathered to commemorate the execution of Philippine patriot Jose Rizal. In recent years, attendance at the dance has been dominated by Pilipino couples newly arrived in the country; the doctors, nurses, accountants, engineers, and other professionals whose emigration from the islands has boosted the group's population in the city from 1,740 in 1940 to 9,428 in 1970—a pattern resembling that of the United States as a whole, where the number rose from 45,563 to 336,731 in the same period. Today, men in tuxedos, their wives in elaborate gowns brought with them from their homeland, and a sprinkling of small children never left with a baby-sitter dominate at the community festival in which the sounds of many different dialects color the pauses between sets.[1]

In years long past, much was different. The young men who arrived from the Philippines in the 1920s, when the Charleston was the rage, and danced more sedately in the 1930s and 1940s to the big-band sounds of Tommy and Jimmy Dorsey, Benny Goodman, and Glenn Miller rarely held professional employment. Though many had come to the United States as self-supporting students to finish high school and obtain an American college degree, few had persisted long enough to accomplish the goals of their youth. They commonly found work in clubs, restaurants, hotels, and private homes—the lucky few won enhanced prestige with higher pay and more regularized employment as post office clerks or as attendants on Pullman railway cars, where more than four hundred were hired between 1925 and 1940. At Rizal Day dances throughout these years, these men, now known in Chicago as the "old-timers," were typically accompanied by white, American-born sweethearts and wives, dressed in chiffon, satin, and silk, whose knowledge of the dialects spoken by their partners rarely extended beyond one or two words. Their community has always been interracial.[2]

Though the body of writing on Asian immigrants and their descendants has grown considerably in recent years, historical scholarship continues to slight the Pilipinos in the United States. Over two decades ago, Roger Daniels remarked:

> The history of the Filipino-American should be written soon while the memories of the pioneers can still be tapped. The young men of the 1920s are just a little younger than the century, and the table of mortality is reaping a larger harvest every year.[3]

More recently, in surveying works published in the late 1970s, he noted: "An overwhelming majority of the essays deal with . . . either Chinese or Japanese: other Asian immigrant groups are still largely neglected by scholarship."[4] Only H. Brett Melendy's cross-national study, *Asians in America: Filipinos, Koreans, and East Indians*, offers a useful survey.[5] For additional detail on the first (pre-1934) wave of Pilipino immigration, those interested in their history must turn either to brief, early portraits that emphasize or react against viewing Pilipinos as a social problem[6] or to more modern treatments oriented toward an assessment of service needs or toward group consciousness-raising.[7]

Moreover, scholars focusing on the Pilipino experience have concentrated on California and Hawaii, the areas to which most migrated, and have thereby stressed the immigrants' agricultural employment in farm fields and sugar plantations.[8] Given this emphasis on West Coast and Hawaiian Pilipinos, many of whom either never married or failed to form durable family ties, conventional wisdom portrays the old-timer Pilipino, in his later years, as "lonely and alone."[9] Victimization emerges as the common denominator of this generation's life in the United States:

> [M]ost old-timers will sit and talk to a sympathetic ear about their life in America. Their story is pierced not only with humor, but also with bitterness, for many of them have only poverty-line incomes, callous and weather-beaten faces to show for their toil in American farm fields and existence in urban hotels, restaurants and apartments. By material standards, so highly held by American society, the first generation of Philippine Americans has achieved little or left little.[10]

Virtually nothing has yet appeared on Pilipinos who moved permanently from West Coast ports of arrival to major cities in the Midwest and on the East Coast.[11] These Pilipinos, while numerically smaller as a group than the Pacific Coast residents, constitute nonetheless an important element in the generation's history, for they experienced the problems of accommodation and acculturation to American life in an economic and social setting somewhat different from that of the West Coast, and in addition confronted these challenges with a significantly higher level of education.[12]

Similarly, the interracial marriages contracted by the old-timers have received scant attention since the 1930s, when these unions were used by advocates of Pilipino exclusion to justify immigration restrictions on moral grounds—that the Asian newcomers posed a danger to American society because of their "preference" for white women. Ignoring the demographic reality of an immigrant population overwhelmingly young, single, and male, critics stereotyped Pilipinos as aggressive, uneducated, irresponsible, and prone to fighting and gambling; the women they married were "near-moron white girls."[13] More careful analyses of the social bases of intermarriage, such as those appearing in *Sociology and Social Research* during these years, discussed the topic in legal and statistical terms, or from the perspective of male needs and susceptibilities. The women remained anonymous creatures of ignorance, acquisitiveness, and passion.[14] Their thoughts, actions, and feelings have rarely emerged.[15]

This essay seeks to examine the interracial community formed in Chicago during the late 1920s and early 1930s through a composite utilizing interviews with husbands and wives now in their seventies, for it is through the memories of these couples that the processes of cultural adaptation and racial interaction over an almost fifty-year period can best be analyzed. Through their words, the familial values they brought to and modified during their marriages can be identified. Through their stories, the support and survival mechanisms they utilized in combating both familial and social disapproval of their marriages can be assessed.[16]

The Pilipino population in Illinois grew steadily, albeit on a small scale, between 1920, when 164 island migrants were located by the federal census, and 1930, when their total reached 2,011. By 1940, after a decade of national economic hardship and the virtual

Table 23.1. Pilipinos in Chicago and California, 1940: Education and Occupation

	Chicago	Los Angeles	San Francisco	California
Population	1,097	2,912	1,936	22,636
Median Years of Schooling	12.2	9.0	8.9	6.8
Professional and Semiprofessional	3.8	2.2	0.8	0.7
Farmer & Farm Manager	—	0.4	—	1.5
Proprietor, Manager, and Official	1.0	1.4	1.1	1.1
Clerical/Sales	11.5	2.0	3.1	1.0
Craftsman/Foreman	3.2	1.8	2.4	.7
Operative	10.5	7.1	6.2	3.1
Domestic Service	4.6	10.3	12.8	4.8
Service	59.1	65.0	69.5	23.4
Farm Laborer	—	2.5	0.3	60.8
Nonfarm Laborer	6.2	7.0	3.0	2.7
No Occupation Reported	0.2	0.3	0.7	0.3
Total	100.0	100.0	100.0	100.0

Source: U.S. Bureau of the Census, *1940 Census of Population: Characteristics of the Nonwhite Population by Race*, 112; ibid., *Population*, vol. 3, "The Labor Force: Occupation, Industry, Employment, and Income," 874–75.

stoppage of further mass immigration from the Philippines in 1934 under the terms of the Tydings-McDuffie Act, the state population had declined slightly, to 1,930. Thus, the first wave of immigration from the Philippines had produced in Illinois a population less than one-tenth the size of California's 22,636. Other differences were more striking than sheer size, however. More than 90 percent of the Illinois residents lived in Chicago, whereas only 21.4 percent of the California Pilipinos were recorded as living in Los Angeles or San Francisco. This urban-rural dichotomy, clearly reflected in dissimilar occupational distributions, fixed a different group identity in each area. In Chicago, 64 percent of the Pilipinos labored as service workers. In California, over 60 percent of the state's much larger Pilipino population worked as agricultural hands, though in Los Angeles and San Francisco, the numbers concentrated in the service sector—75 and 82 percent, respectively—actually exceeded the Chicago figure (Table 23.1).[17]

Drastically different levels of schooling for Pilipinos living in Illinois and California further enhanced the contrast. Among Chicagoans, median years of schooling stood at 12.2; for Californians, 6.8. Even in Los Angeles and San Francisco, the figures hovered at 9 years. In contrast with the typical West Coast Pilipino, the average Chicago migrant was a high-school graduate with some college experience.[18] It is difficult to determine precisely why Chicago drew a more highly educated population, though several factors were undoubtedly important. Many came to continue their schooling. By the mid-1920s Pilipinos were arriving in Chicago to attend specific colleges and universities in the area. In 1924, 103 students were enrolled at the University of Chicago, Northwestern University, DePaul University, and Crane Junior College. Downstate in Urbana, 25 Pilipinos studied at the University of Illinois.[19] These immigrants probably came with a high-school diploma from the Philippines in hand.[20] Like other Pilipinos seeking an American education, most in Chicago expected to be self-supporting. But they quickly found that the low pay and the long hours of most available service jobs—and the temptations of life in Chicago—limited their successful continuation in school. Caught in the United States by their deeply felt shame at having failed to attain an American degree, many remained in the city, thereby fixing the educational level of the group at a high level.[21] On the other hand, many Pilipinos migrated to Hawaii and the West Coast specifically to find work in agriculture. Like the students, they too hoped to return to their homeland—with money rather than a degree—but found their dreams also limited by American conditions. California's lower educational level is a measure of their entrapment.[22]

These basic patterns also produced a chain migration phenomenon in both areas. In Hawaii and on the West Coast, literate farm laborers wrote home with news of opportunities in agriculture; company recruiters, cognizant of varying economic conditions in different Philippine provinces, sought additional workers in areas where poor prospects and a labor surplus continued. Hence, a steady stream of less-educated Pilipinos, often from the economically depressed Ilocos provinces, flowed into California and Hawaii. Chicagoans, on the other hand, set in motion far smaller chains among relatives and friends who were probably of the same educational level. Because the original Pilipino population came from a variety of provinces, these chains ultimately produced a community of diverse provincial loyalties in Chicago.[23]

The Chicago to which almost 1,800 Pilipinos had migrated by 1930 was an overwhelmingly "ethnic" city of 3.4 million inhabitants, almost 90 percent of whom were either foreign-born whites or their children. More than half a million claimed Polish ancestry; slightly fewer were of German heritage. Russian Jews, Italians, Swedes, Irish, and Czechs all boasted populations of more than a hundred thousand. Distinctive neighborhoods, identified by national background, created a patchwork urban landscape of tongues and customs. Minorities comprised a scant 7.1 percent of the city's residents. Most of Chicago's 234,000 blacks were concentrated in the South Side "Black Belt." Among Asians, almost 2,800 Chinese, identified with a bustling Chinatown at Twenty-second and Wentworth, outnumbered both Pilipinos and the fewer than 500 Japanese. During the Depression decade, these figures changed little. In 1940, the total population remained at 3.4 million; 44,000 additional   black residents expanded ghetto borders; Pilipinos declined by 56.[24]

Among Chicago's white males, unlike Pilipinos, a high-school education had not yet become the norm in 1940. The median length of schooling for native-born white males, 9.4 years, indicated completion of at least a grammar school course by more than half; for foreign-born white males, a lower figure, 7.5 years, pertained.[25] These figures reflected an age bias: Older men had left school earlier in their lives than their sons. Because few Pilipinos were older than forty-five, they were more likely statistically to have gone farther in school than other Chicagoans. Yet a correction removing the post-forty-five generation from the calculation would probably not raise the white median to that of the Pilipinos. In 1920 only 32 percent of America's high-school-age youth were enrolled in school; in 1930, the figure had just passed 50 percent for the nation as a whole.[26]

But their additional years of schooling gave Pilipinos little competitive advantage in Chicago. The young men soon found that their skin color defined the occupations they might enter, the income they might earn, and the mobility they might experience. Those in Chicago's service sector, where three-fifths of the Pilipinos worked, had a median yearly income of $824 in 1940; those classified as "operatives" in the city's numerous industries, the 22 percent of the population most likely to contain a heavy concentration of white ethnics, took home a median income of $1,092 in that year.[27] While it is true that Pilipinos employed by the Pullman Company—the only Chicago occupational group as yet studied in detail—earned over $1,200 per year, not including tips, after the Brotherhood of Sleeping Car Porters signed its first contract with the company in 1937, even the Pullman attendants experienced racial barriers on the job. Like black porters, Pilipino attendants found themselves barred from more responsible, more highly paid conductor positions because Pullman restricted these jobs to whites.[28] Thus, if Chicago provided Pilipinos with

Table 23.2. Chicago, 1940: Male Education and Occupation

	Pilipino	White	Black	Other
Median Years of Schooling		7.5FB[a]		
	12.2	9.4NB	7.7	NA
Professional and Semiprofessional	3.8	7.0	3.3	6.1
Farmer and Farm Manager	—	0.1	0.1	—
Proprietor, Manager, and Official	1.0	10.7	2.7	20.9
Clerical/Sales	11.5	22.3	10.1	8.9
Craftsman/Foreman	3.2	20.3	9.2	2.6
Operative	10.5	22.2	20.1	27.3
Domestic Service	4.6	0.1	1.4	2.0
Service	59.1	8.8	32.8	29.9
Farm Laborer	—	0.1	0.1	—
Nonfarm Laborer	6.2	8.1	20.1	2.6
No Occupation Reported	0.2	0.5	0.4	0.1
Total	100.0	100.0	100.0	100.0

[a]FB = foreign-born; NB = native-born.
Source: U.S. Bureau of the Census, *1950 Census of Population: Characteristics of the Nonwhite Population by Race*, 111–12; ibid., *Population*, vol. 2, "Characteristics of the Population," 642; ibid., *Population*, vol. 3, "The Labor Force," 874–75, 898.

the best opportunities available in the United States, it is only in comparison with the West Coast situation. By 1940 Pilipinos in Chicago had moved into "clerical" and "craftsmen" categories more rapidly than Los Angeles and San Francisco residents (Table 23.1). But the disadvantages experienced by Chicago Pilipinos are obvious when the comparison is made with the city's whites (Table 23.2).

Pilipinos experienced similar problems in housing and recreation. Newcomers in the 1920s found most neighborhoods closed to brown men with low incomes. By this decade, inventive Chicagoans had begun covering the city with restrictive covenants specifically designed to foreclose black penetration of white areas; other minorities were also excluded. Declared constitutional in 1926, these covenants gave legal teeth to pervasive prejudice. During the 1920s white Chicago still smarted from the aftermath of the black-white race riot of 1919. Many white Chicagoans supported the *Chicago Tribune*'s policy: "Black Man, Stay South."[29]

Unlike blacks, Pilipinos were never ghettoized. Many first found housing on the near West Side, in an Italian-dominated, polyglot ethnic area near the factories and warehouses bordering the central business district. Here, the "Pinoys" frequently clashed with young Italians who viewed brown-skinned men as a challenge to white "turf."[30] Seventy-six-year-old Philip A. Lontoc recalled the dangers of walking alone. Conrado Ocampo remembered that groups of Pilipinos would send one of their number down the street alone while the rest hid. After that brave soul drew an attack, the others would rush to do battle.[31] When Domingo C. Manzon arrived in the city in the mid-1920s, young Pilipinos on the West Side had already formed the Filipino Association of Chicago, an umbrella organization under which the various provincial clubs functioned.

During the next decade, the focus on Chicago's Pilipino community shifted from the near West Side to the near North Side, into an area less linked with a particular ethnic group, an area closer to the "Gold Coast" mansions where many were employed. As on the West Side, Pilipinos found housing in declining apartment buildings, often living in groups to save on expenses. Here too, by 1930, a clubhouse with pool hall, barbershop, and frequent dances appeared. In return for permitting Protestant church services on its premises, the overwhelmingly Catholic Pilipino population secured an annual contribution of approximately two hundred dollars from the board of directors of the Chicago Theological Seminary, which extended its appropriation into the 1940s.[32] Despite this support, however, most Pilipinos remained nominally Catholic. Some traveled to the southern end of the Chicago Loop where, as members of the CYO (Catholic Youth Organization), they attended meetings and movies at the Paulist mission, Old St. Mary's Church. But for most, church attendance was irregular.

On the near North Side, Pilipinos found Chinese restaurants, pool halls, and dance halls that welcomed the money they spent. No specific ethnic group consistently challenged their presence. But around the city and even in the neighborhood where most Pilipinos lived, no one could guarantee Pilipinos freedom from insult or physical violence on the streets. This situation, one may speculate, flowed from Chicago's own racial climate, rather than from knowledge of the confrontations occurring between Pilipinos and whites on the West Coast. A city that had succeeded in confining a once-scattered black population to specific enclaves in the years since 1910 found little need to base its treatment of brown men on the attitudes of white Californians.[33] This basic racial tension was heightened whenever a Pilipino appeared in public with a white woman, and in the 1920s and 1930s virtually all Chicago Pilipinos found their female contact limited to women who were white.

In 1940, six years after unrestricted immigration by Pilipinos to the United States had been halted by law, Chicago's Pilipino community held 1,298 residents over the age of twenty, of whom only 61 were female. This striking sexual imbalance, a ratio of 21:1, had already forced a significant number of men in the community to find wives outside their own group. By 1940, 532 men had married, only 54 to Pilipinas; 478, or 90 percent, of the marriages within the community, were "mixed."[34]

From the perspective of the men, the choice of an "American" wife is readily understandable, given the likely alternative—remaining single. In addition, in the racially charged atmosphere of Chicago, Pilipinos took pride in their individual ability to date and marry white women despite their persistent dream of returning to the Philippines. But the motivation underlying the women's choice of nonwhite spouses requires more careful consideration. From interviews, a general portrait emerges. The women, in their early twenties when they married, were most frequently the daughters of immigrant parents of the working class. Their educations generally ended after eighth grade, when family custom and financial circumstances dictated their entry into the labor force. As with working-class daughters in general, the earnings of these young women from light factory work, waitressing, and, less frequently, office work were turned over to their parents, who returned to the girls a small allowance for clothing, recreation, and other necessities. One elderly woman recalled her own situation in the Polish household in which she grew up:

> I got fifteen dollars a week [filling bottles at a flavoring extract company]. You had to turn your pay over to your mother. Mom gave me five dollars back. It was so hard. If you wanted a pair of silk stockings, the cheapest was a dollar ninety-nine. . . . And if you lost your job, there was hell to pay from Pa until you found another.

While she and her sisters had been sent to work at age fourteen or fifteen, her brothers had attended high school; the youngest, college. Yet if the work was dull, the pay poor, and the conditions hard both on the job and at home, these young women did win a measure of independence remarkable within the authoritarian confines of the ethnic household. Once the day's work was finished and their household chores were completed, they ranged far throughout the city in search of recreation; movies and dancing were favored pastimes.[35] In time, through word passed by sisters, friends, and coworkers, many heard of what seemed a remarkable opportunity. At the Plaza "Dancing School" on North Clark Street, they might earn money while dancing. Another Polish woman reminisced:

> We used to go to the Riverview Ballroom. We loved dancing. All of us girls loved danc-ing. So we used to go and pay to dance at the Riverview Ballroom and the Trianon. So when we could go to the Plaza School and dance for nothing and make money that was a great thing for us. We thought, "Oh, how wonderful. We can make money and enjoy ourselves," because we just loved dancing. . . . What we earned at the school, that was for our clothes.

Taxi-dance halls such as the Plaza on Chicago's near North Side enabled a young woman to triple her weekly spending money in several evenings; each ten-cent dance ticket collected was split between the proprietor and the dancers.[36]

The dance halls were frequented by men of many nationalities, but among the most regu-lar in attendance were Chicago's Pilipinos, who found that money might buy the feminine companionship their skin color prevented elsewhere. Plaza rules forbade after-hours contact between dancers and patrons, but "you always found a way." In the absence of an outright legal ban against cross-racial unions, even the stringent social taboos then in force failed to prevent relationships from forming. Dating began, and interracial marriage followed.

Immaculately dressed and frequently well-spoken, the Pilipinos presented a level of cul-ture and refinement that the women had not generally experienced. With their courtly ways, the Pilipinos were lavish with attention, good times, and gifts. Those who were still in school or who held regular employment seemed to promise secure futures—at least in the immediate months ahead. Most important, first contacts with the Pilipinos came as a stark contrast with the Americans they had dated. One woman recalled:

> I was going out with a Polish fellow . . . but him and his buddy . . . tried to rough me up a little bit, and I lost all faith in him, almost in all men, but when we met the Pilipinos they were so gentle. They were such gentlemen.

Another remembered the trauma of an engagement to an Irish lad, broken only three weeks before the wedding after a mysterious conference between the young man and a priest. Marriage to a Pilipino appeared an escape from the world of their mothers—a world of authoritarian husbands, multiple childbirths, and daughters consigned to a recapitula-tion of the experience. Like the women's fashionable clothing, their Pilipino husbands were a "modern" choice. Potential problems never crossed their minds: "What did we know! We were green!" And they were in love.

Not all found their future husbands while working as taxi dancers, but most involve-ments came through situations in which contact with Pilipinos, if not encouraged, was at least tolerated. Forty-nine years ago a Czech girl from an Iowa farm community, working as a waitress in the city and sharing an apartment with her sister and brother-in-law, began dating a fellow building resident, a Pilipino, and married him a year later. While Protestant reformers debated "bring[ing in] high-type American girls from outside communities" to counteract "exploitation by women of bad character, 'gold-diggers,'" the Pilipinos' typical pattern of residence, employment, and recreation made likely their choice of working-class, ethnic wives.[37]

The actual decision to marry was often made with speed and on impulse. Though both parties were frequently Catholic, none of the interviewees considered a church wedding necessary or possible at that point.[38] After a five-month courtship, during which they "didn't see each other that often," one couple joined another in eloping to Crown Point, Indiana, the site favored by most interracial couples for the ease with which a license and a ceremony could be obtained. On a wintry Sunday evening in November 1931, the four hired a taxi for the nearly hundred-mile round-trip, found a justice of the peace, and returned that same night to dinner at a Chinese restaurant and a shared apartment. Purchase of rings and thoughts of problems came later.

Confrontations with ethnic families they had seemingly abandoned became a chronic difficulty for the women. Though several marriages met acquiescence—"*You* have to live with him!"—parents more frequently reacted with anger and a tenacious refusal to accept the interracial union for years to come. In one instance, a Polish couple discovered that two daughters, a seventeen-year-old and a twenty-year-old, had both married Pilipinos. Both girls had gone their own way for some time, living at home and working daytime factory jobs to keep a regular sum flowing to the family each week, but also dancing for pay in secret. The parents adamantly refused to meet their new sons-in-law, yet encouraged the girls to visit frequently, hoping that their regard for their mother would eventually draw them back into the family—and away from their unacceptable husbands. The youngest succumbed within a year and chose a Polish lad for her second matrimonial venture. The eldest continued torn for five years, making weekly visits, before her family relented and, in a symbolic gesture, gave the couple a blanket for their fifth anniversary. But for three more decades the couple could never be certain that invitations to family gatherings would arrive addressed to both husband and wife.

Another continuing problem facing the couples was the search for a place of residence. The ease with which the couples had been accepted as they socialized at the taxi-dance hall, at Pilipino clubhouse activities, at cafés on the near North Side and in Chinatown, and at nightclubs in Chicago's Black Belt evaporated all too quickly with the reality of life as husband and wife. Rejection after rejection greeted their answering of "apartment for rent" advertisements and signs. Once a landlord willing to accept a Pilipino and his white wife was found, his building quickly became a haven for other interracial couples, thereby reinforcing the ties among them. In one instance, a large courtyard apartment building in the 900 block of Cornelia Avenue in Chicago's Lake View neighborhood sheltered at least fifteen Pilipino-American families during a twenty-five-year period extending into the 1950s.[39] While not all these residents occupied apartments simultaneously, the effect of even successive occupancy was considerable. Similarly, on the city's near Northwest Side, in the aging Wicker Park district, at least seven families found apartments within a two-block radius, most in another courtyard building whose owner, a sympathetic Polish widow, had come to value the Pilipino-American couples as good tenants. Yet one white wife recalls "begging" for an apartment for friends—another interracial couple—in the 1950s; the landlady's figurative mental quota had already been reached. Although she relented in this case, she vowed that it would be the last.

Like these buildings, most locations where Pilipino-American couples found apartments in Chicago were in white neighborhoods characterized by ethnic mixture rather than identification with a single group. By conscious choice, partners scrupulously avoided black areas in the belief that residence in the ghetto would further diminish their tenuous status in white society.[40] In their white, multiethnic neighborhoods, couples generally found neighbors to be sociable in the halls and on the sidewalks. Residents of whatever race shared an implicitly understood inability to secure more expensive quarters, though topics of conversation remained explicitly impersonal, and close friendships between white and interracial couples rarely formed. As they came to be known and recognized on their blocks, Pilipino husbands and white wives could more comfortably appear together in this limited sphere.

Such security was not abandoned lightly, and families often remained in their apartments for over a decade, seeking to avoid the anxiety that the search for a new home might bring. During the mid-1950s one couple attempted to purchase a home near the wife's sister on the far Northwest Side of Chicago, only to be informed after having cashed their savings bonds for the down payment that the willing seller had come under severe pressure from neighbors unwilling to see the block integrated. For years after the incident the husband remained so traumatized by the event that neither the pressure of his wife nor that of his family could induce him to leave an increasingly dangerous locale. When he did consent to a change, he moved his family to a flat above his widowed father-in-law, knowing that in this way he might avoid the rejection of strangers. Few Pilipino-American couples of the "old-timer" generation secured the American dream of the new home in the suburbs, which captured so many in the years after World War II. Home ownership, when attained, generally meant the purchase of an older home in a city neighborhood, or in a less-developed, often unincorporated, suburban area.

Years after their marriages, other ventures into the wider community remained cautious, as in California, where the daughter of an interracial couple recalled: "Father never walked beside us. He was always either ahead of us or behind us."[41] Chicagoans sometimes sat apart on buses in the early years, and refrained from dining in "American" restaurants for most of their lives.

As they confronted familial and social rejection, the women understandably turned to each other for companionship and understanding. Dinners and parties at each other's apartments, group ventures to Pilipino-sponsored dances at clubs and hotels, outings to Chinese restaurants where prejudice was never a problem—such activities sustained a sense of community. Though "community" never comprised the entire interracial population in any effective sense, smaller cliques formed on the basis of provincial loyalties carried with the men from the islands, because of work-related contact among husbands at the Pullman Company or in specific hotels, and from residential proximity.

Additionally, the women felt most comfortable with wives originally met just before or immediately after their own marriages—women whose circumstances while single were similar to their own. These women came to be closest friends, capable of discussing openly the frequent "wounds" delivered by outsiders to participants in interracial marriages. And, more important, their conversations with female friends helped them to adjust, individually and collectively, to the new culture they encountered in marriage to men from the Philippines. The individual traits exhibited by their husbands, when ascribed to the group, seemed more comprehensible, if not less irritating. Seemingly excessive hospitality, demanding hours in the kitchen from both husband and wife and a virtual open-door policy with regard to the frequency of "company," became the accepted norm as "something we all did." And while their husbands' tendency to lapse into native dialect when together forced gatherings into a sex-segregated pattern, the women found some relief in collective criticism. These avenues of support were particularly important to women whose husbands worked for the Pullman Company and were customarily away from home for three- to six-day periods at least half the time. With their husbands gone, visiting among the women took on added importance; in emergencies, friends were nearby, and in ordinary times, lonely hours were filled.[42]

The ability to define and continue more fundamental values was ultimately of greater importance to the endurance of their interracial marriages. Faithfulness to one's spouse and devotion to one's children—traditional moral and familial values—constituted basic norms for those whose marriages survived. For example, couples with children exhibited nearly uniform agreement that wives should not work outside the home since husbands working for Pullman were out of the city for days at a time. As one wife commented:

> I worked twelve weeks . . . when my kids were small . . . in a plastic place. . . . I liked that better than housework. . . . The youngest ones were going to grammar school. But it never worked out with the kids. It's hard. He's out on the road. . . . If you have kids, you should stay around home.

Tacit agreement was also achieved in other areas. In keeping with the customs of both Pilipino and ethnic cultures, wives exercised considerable control over their husbands' wages, knowing the exact amount of earnings, savings, and expenditures. Decisions regarding purchases were made jointly, and wives never "asked" for money. In contrast with the perpetuation of this tradition, spouses generally abandoned explicit cultural identification in the raising of their children, preferring instead to define a new "American" emphasis. Both Pilipino husbands and ethnic wives believed that becoming "American" would assist their offspring in achieving success. Wives raised in non-English-speaking homes and educated in ethnic parochial schools vowed that their children would not be handicapped by a second language and accented English; most sent their children to public schools. Thus, mestizo children knew few words in either their mother's or their father's native tongue. Similarly, husbands and wives never learned the original language of the other, a fact that severely limited the Pilipino husbands' communication with their wives' elderly ethnic relatives; conversations between white wives and visitors from the Philippines were conducted in English. In the era during which most of their children grew to maturity, an era before ethnic consciousness came to be emphasized, cultural identity was most visible in the food served at the family table. At parties, husbands' and wives' ethnic specialties appeared side by side; potatoes and rice competed at daily dinners.[43]

These broad spheres of agreement coexisted with areas of subtle tension as well, areas in which agreement or compromise emerged only over time. Trust between marriage partners was sometimes clouded not only by personal incidents, but also by group reputation. For one wife, the dismay and the anger involved in finding that her husband had not made her the beneficiary of his insurance policy after several years of marriage loomed as a grievance even after more than forty years. His explanation—that many Pilipinos had been "taken" by American women met at "dancing schools"—had been rejected as irrelevant. Yet, at the same time, she remembered wondering in those early years if he could really "settle down"; "the boys were pretty wild when they were single." And she recalled stalking out of a dance one evening when his attentions to another woman became too obvious. But, as might be expected in marriages that persisted over decades, trust and acceptance grew. Husbands who "strayed" and wives who "ran around" were judged immoral—foolish at best.

Concerns over the planning of a family and the disciplining of children needed resolution as well. While ethnicity and race divided the spouses, many couples "practiced" a common Catholicism. Yet the large-family norm, rarely questioned in the Philippines, found direct challenge from the American wives. Though her husband wanted six children, and maintains his wish to this day, one forceful wife countered effectively:

> I wanted three. I put a stop to it. . . . I could have had a dozen, like my grandma had fifteen. I said forget it. No way. . . . If had had my way, I would have had one.

In another instance, a wife in her late forties sought support from her gynecologist against a husband who maintained that the religious ceremony performed twenty-five years after their elopement now precluded the use of birth control; they and their only child, an eleven-year-old born fourteen years after their marriage, then occupied a two-and-a-half-room apartment and had few prospects for a quick move to more commodious quarters. In this case, as in the first, the wife's more realistic assessment of economic conditions outweighed her husband's preference for tradition. Similarly, most Pilipino-American families were small; American women bore an average of 1.38 children during their marriages to the Pilipinos of this study. Only the rare family unit contained four or five offspring.

Just as the topic of family limitation sometimes caused tension between husbands and wives, so too could differing standards of acceptable behavior for growing children provoke disagreement. In one family, while their daughter was small, the mother accused the father of excessive permissiveness—showering the child with toys, buying the girl high heels before her eighth-grade graduation, and allowing her to "talk back" without severe reprimand. In contrast, once the child reached adolescence, he attempted to enforce a strict code of conduct derived from his own youthful experience with sisters and sweethearts back in the islands—a code that his wife believed would only encourage their daughter to rebel. Long discussions, late into many nights, debated recurring conflicts over dating and curfew that continued until their daughter accepted a job offer in another city and left the family home. In most families, the mothers took responsibility for setting disciplinary norms, partly because they remained at home while their Pullman husbands traveled. In addition, given the families' emphasis on Americanization, mothers born in the United States seemed more able to guide the adolescents than fathers born abroad, and fathers generally acquiesced in accepting the contention "That's the way things are done here."

As they aged and as their families grew to maturity, the sources of support for these interracial couples began to change. With the passage of time, both societal and familial antagonisms began to diminish. In the climate of the emerging civil rights movement of the 1960s, and with the migration of a professional population from the Philippines in the years after 1965, the Pilipino old-timers rediscovered their racial heritage and took pride in their survival in a hostile environment for so many years. As their children formed families of their own, without exception marrying men and women of ethnic origins other than Pilipino, and as they frequently found a "success," defined by education and income, that had eluded the Pilipino immigrants and their white wives, the older couples took comfort in a vicarious, ultimate integration into American life. Though many of their children were easily identifiable as Asian in heritage, their culture had become an amalgam of old and new. In the 1960s and 1970s, as they gathered at the Dr. Jose Rizal Community Center in Chicago with the newer, younger, and often more prosperous professionals who had immigrated since 1965, the old-timers sometimes discovered that their attitudes toward politics, family life, and nationality had become more "American" than those of their countrymen.

During the lengthy marriages of the couples surveyed for this study, the social and economic pressures they faced consistently linked husbands and wives together against the society around them; for this reason, the determination to succeed in their marriages became, for several wives, an explicit and vital goal. Of course, not all interracial marriages formed in these years endured. Many women, once married to Pilipinos, have disappeared completely from view, and without their experiences this picture of interracial life must necessarily remain tentative and incomplete. Yet, in a sense, in seeking the basis of Chicago's Pilipino-American community, theirs is not the critical story, for the community derives its heritage from those who formed lasting bonds across racial lines.

Notes

This article, an earlier version of which was presented at the Fifth Berkshire Conference on the History of Women, Vassar College, June 1981, has benefited from the comments and criticism generously offered by Professors Roger Daniels of the University of Cincinnati and Roland L. Guyotte of the University of Minnesota, Morris.

1. U.S. Bureau of the Census, *1940 Census of Population: Characteristics of the Nonwhite Population by Race* (Washington, D.C., 1943), 5–6; U.S. Bureau of the Census, *1970 Census of Population, Subject Reports: Japanese, Chinese, and Filipinos in the United States* (Washington, D.C., 1973), 119, 169; *Associated Filipino P   r   e   s   s   ,* 30 December 1934, in Bessie Louise Pierce Notes, Chicago Historical Society.

2. U.S., *1940 Census*, 112. See also Barbara M. Posadas, "The Hierarchy of Color and Psychological Adjustment in an Industrial Environment: Filipino Immigrants, the Pullman Company and the Brotherhood of Sleeping Car Porters" (paper delivered at the Eighth Annual Conference on Ethnic and Minority Studies, University of Wisconsin–LaCrosse, 25 April 1980).

3. Roger Daniels, "Comments by Roger Daniels: Filipino Immigration in Historical Perspective," in Josefa M. Saniel, ed., *The Filipino Exclusion Movement: 1927–1935* (Quezon City, 1967), 49.

4. Roger Daniels, "North American Scholarship and Asian Immigrants, 1974–1979," *Immigration History Newsletter* 11 (May 1979). Important contributions since the publication of Daniels's article include: Sucheng Chan, *Asian Americans: An Interpretive History* (Boston, 1991); Fred Cordova, *Filipinos: Forgotten Asian Americans* (Dubuque, Ia., 1983); and Ronald T. Takaki, *Strangers from a Different Shore: A History of Asian Americans* (Boston, 1989).

5. H. Brett Melendy, *Asians in America: Filipinos, Koreans, and East Asians* (Boston, 1977).

6. See, for example, Emory S. Bogardus, "The Filipino Immigrant Problem," *Sociology and Social Research* 13 (May–June 1929): 472–79, and "American Attitudes toward Filipinos," *Sociology and Social Research* 14 (September–October 1929): 59–69; Bruno Lasker, *Filipino Immigration to the Continental United States and Hawaii* (Chicago, 1931); Honorante Mariano, *The Filipino Immigrant in the United States* (San Francisco, 1972 [1933]); Trinidad A. Rojo, "Social Maladjustment among Filipinos in the United States," *Sociology and Social Research* 21 (1937): 447–57; Benicio T. Catapusan, "The Social Adjustment of Filipinos in the United States" (Ph.D. diss., University of Southern California, 1940); Carey McWilliams, "The Little Brown Brother," in *Brothers Under the Skin* (Boston, 1951 [1943]), 229–49; John H. Burma, "The Background of the Current Situation of Filipino-Americans," *Social Forces* 30 (October 1951): 42–48.

7. Bok Lim C. Kim and Margaret E. Andon, *A Study of Asian Americans in Chicago: Their Socio-Economic Characteristics, Problems and Service Needs* (Washington, D.C., 1975); Wayne S. Wooden and J. H. Monane, "Cultural Community, Cohesion and Constraint: Dynamics of Life Satisfaction among Aged Filipino Men of Hawaii," *Explorations in Ethnic Studies* 3 (July 1980): 25–39; Royal F. Morales, *Makibaka: The Pilipino American Struggle* (Los Angeles, 1973); Jovina Navarro, ed., *Diwang Pilipino: Pilipino Consciousness* (Davis, Calif., 1974); Jesse Quinsaat, ed., *Letters in Exile: An Introductory Reader on the History of Pilipinos in America* (Los Angeles, 1976); Jovina Navarro, ed., *Lahing Pilipino: A Pilipino American Anthology* (Davis, Calif., 1977).

8. Sonia E. Wallovits, "The Filipinos in California" (M.A. thesis, University of Southern California, 1966); H. Brett Melendy, "California's Discrimination against Filipinos, 1927–1935," in Saniel, ed., *The Filipino Exclusion Movement*, 3–10; Ruben R. Alcantara, "The Filipino Community in Waialua" (Ph.D. diss., University of Hawaii, 1973); Adelaida Castillo, "Filipino Migrants in San Diego, 1900–1946," *Journal of San Diego History* 22 (1976): 26–35; Edwin B. Almirol, "Ethnic Identity and Social Negotiation: A Study of a Filipino Community in California" (Ph.D. diss., University of Illinois at Urbana-Champaign, 1977), and "Filipino Voluntary Associations: Balancing Social Pressures and Ethnic Images," *Ethnic Groups* 2 (1978): 65–92; Miriam Sharma, "Pinoy in Paradise: Environment and Adaptation of Pilipinos in Hawaii, 1906–1946," *Amerasia* 7, 2 (fall–winter 1980): 91–117.

9. Morales, *Makibaka*, 118.

10. Juanita Tamayo Lott, "An Attempt," in Navarro, *Diwang Pilipino*, 9.

11. Exceptions are Albert W. Palmer, *Orientals in American Life* (New York, 1934), which contains an eight-page section on the Chicago community, and Benny F. Feria's memoirs, *Filipino Son* (Boston, 1954). See also Roberto V. Valangca, *Pinoy: The First Wave (1898–1941)* (San Francisco, 1977), which includes the brief reminiscences of several Pilipinos who lived in Chicago; and Precioso M. Nicanor, *Profiles of Notable Filipinos in the U.S.A.* (New York, 1963), which contains biographical sketches of New York Pilipinos.

12. *1940 Census*, 5, 111–12; *1960 Census of Population: Characteristics of the Population* 1:15, *Illinois* (Washington, D.C., 1963), 58.

13. C. M. Goethe, quoted in Melendy, *Asians in America*, 61.

14. On intermarriage, see Alida C. Bowler, "Social Hygiene in Racial Problems—The Filipino," *Journal of Social Hygiene* 18 (1932): 452–57; Nellie Foster, "Legal Status of Filipino Intermarriages in California," *Sociology and Social Research* 16 (May–June 1932): 441–54; Romanzo Adams, *Interracial Marriage in Hawaii: A Study of the Mutually Conditioned Processes of Acculturation and Amalgamation* (Montclair, N.J., 1969 [1937]); Benicio T. Catapusan, "Filipino Intermarriage Problems in the United States," *Sociology and Social Research* 22 (January–February 1938): 265–72; Severino F. Corpus, "Second Generation Filipinos in Los Angeles," *Sociology* and *Social Research* 22 (May–June 1938): 446–51; Constantine Panunzio, "Intermarriage in Los Angeles, 1924–1933," *American Journal of Sociology* 47 (March 1942): 690–701; Randall Risdon, "A Study of Interracial Marriages Based on Data for Los Angeles County," *Sociology and Social Research* 39 (1954): 92–95; and John H. Burma, "Interethnic Marriage in Los Angeles, 1948–1959," *Social Forces* 42 (December 1963): 156–65. See also the discussion of cultural adaptation and conflict in Catapusan, "The Social Adjustment of Filipinos in the United States," 76–88. On U.S. laws governing interracial marriage, see Milton L. Barron, ed., *The Blending American: Patterns of Intermarriage* (Chicago, 1972), 77–84.

15. Iris Brown Buaken, "My Brave New World," *Asia and the Americas* 43 (May 1943), 268–70; Iris Brown Buaken, "You Can't Marry a Filipino: Not If You Live in California," *Commonweal* 41 (16 March 1945): 534–37; Manuel Buaken, *I Have Lived with the American People* (Caldwell, Id., 1948), 127–29. On contact between Pilipino men and white women from the male perspective, see Carlos Bulosan, *America Is in the Heart: A Personal History* (New York, 1946).

16. Unless otherwise specified, the material for this paper has been derived from a series of thirteen interviews with American wives and Pilipino husbands conducted during 1979 and 1981. Because of the sensitive nature of the material presented, the respondents remain anonymous. The men and women interviewed consider themselves typical of Chicago's "old-timer" Pilipino community. The Filipinos' lives reveal varied marital patterns. Some left wives behind in the islands. Some saw early unions with American women fail. All tried again, and sometimes found greater success—if duration is the measure. Others married once—for life, it seems, since they are now in their late seventies and eighties. So too, while some women married their Pilipino husbands after an earlier divorce, others entered first marriages that endured. The representativeness of these couples lies, therefore, in the diversity of their experiences. Yet it is likely that the West Coast pattern differs sharply. California's legal prohibition against Pilipino-white intermarriage, enacted in 1933, effectively foreclosed the option enjoyed by Chicago couples (see, for example, Iris Brown Buaken, "You Can't Marry a Filipino," and Henry Empeno, et al., "Anti-Miscegenation Laws and the Pilipino," in Quinsaat, ed., *Letters in Exile*, 63–71). The extent, nature, and persistence of interracial unions formed on the West Coast without formal ceremony or legalized in other states have yet to be examined; for a brief memoir of a California interracial marriage, see "Frank Coloma," in Vallangca, *Pinoy: The First Wave*, 86–89.

17. *1940 Census*, 112; ibid., vol. 3, "The Labor Force: Occupation, Industry, Employment, and Income," 874–75.

18. *1940 Census*, 111.

19. Leopoldo T. Ruiz, "Filipino Students in the United States" (M.A. thesis, Columbia University, 1924), 40–47.

20. On the extent and impact of American education in the Philippines, see Encarnacion Alzona, *A History of Education in the Philippines, 1565–1930* (Manila, 1932), and Glenn Anthony May, *Social Engineering in the Philippines: The Aims, Execution, and Impact of American Colonial Policy, 1900–1913* (Westport, Conn., 1980), chs. 5–7.

21. Posadas, "The Hierarchy of Color."

22. Buaken, *I Have Lived with the American People*, 33–38.

23. Ibid., 38; Mariano, *The Filipino Immigrant in the United States*, 10–12.

24. City of Chicago, Department of Development and Planning, *The People of Chicago: Who We Are and Who We Have Been, Census Data on Foreign Born, Foreign Stock and Race, 1837–1970* (Chicago, 1976), 33–39. On ethnic and black settlement, see, for example, Humbert S. Nelli, *Italians in Chicago, 1880–1930* (New York, 1970), and Allan Spear, *Black Chicago: The Making of a Negro Ghetto, 1890–1920* (Chicago, 1967).

25. *1940 Census*, vol. 2, "Characteristics of the Population," 642.

26. David Nasaw, *Schooled to Order: A Social History of Public Schooling in the United States* (New York, 1979), 163.

27. U.S. *1940 Census*, vol. 3, "The Labor Force," 874–75, 898.

28. Posadas, "The Hierarchy of Color."

29. Thomas Lee Philpott, *The Slum and the Ghetto: Neighborhood Deterioration and Middle-Class Reform, Chicago, 1880–1930* (New York, 1978), 189; Spear, *Black Chicago*, 202.

30. Palmer, *Orientals in American Life*, 97; Vallangca, *Pinoy: The First Wave*, 84.

31. Villangca, *Pinoy*, 134.

32. "Minutes of the Board of Directors of Chicago Theological Seminary," September 1926–25 November 1942, Chicago Theological Seminary.

33. Spear, *Black Chicago*.
34. *1940 Census*, 109–10.
35. On the working-class daughters of immigrant families, see Louise Montgomery, *The American Girl in the Stockyards District* (Chicago, 1913), and Leslie Woodcock Tentler, *Wage-Earning Women: Industrial Work and Family Life in the United States, 1900–1930* (New York, 1979), 85–135.
36. *Polk's Chicago (Illinois) City Directory 1928–1929* (Chicago, 1928), 3389. On the "dancing school" milieu in Chicago, see Paul G. Cressey, *The Taxi-Dance Hall: A Sociological Study in Commercialized Recreation and City Life* (Chicago, 1932), especially ch. 7, "The Filipino and the Taxi-Dance Hall," 145–74; and "Anacleto Gorospe," in Vallangca, *Pinoy: The First Wave*, 84–85. Dance halls were also a common form of recreation for the California Pilipinos; see, for example, Benicio Catapusan, "The Filipino Occupational and Recreational Activities in Los Angeles" (M.A. thesis, University of Southern California, 1934), 65–84; Vallangca, *Pinoy: The First Wave*, 50–53; and the fictionalized account set in San Francisco in Precioso M. Nicanor, *Martyrs Never Die* (New York, 1968), 114–23.
37. Palmer, *Orientals in American Life*, 99, 102.
38. The interviewees also recall several marriages between Pilipinos and women of Jewish heritage. In Hawaii, Pilipinos tended to intermarry with Christian women of varied ethnic backgrounds, rather than non-Christian Asian women; see Adams, *Interracial Marriage in Hawaii*, 180.
39. *City of Chicago Directory* I (Chicago, 1950), 206.
40. Similarly, Pilipino members of the predominantly black Brotherhood of Sleeping Car Porters rarely attended union "soirees," in part because their white wives would not have felt comfortable at the black social gatherings. See Posadas, "The Hierarchy of Color."
41: Alfredo N. Munoz, *The Filipinos in America* (Los Angeles, 1971), 118.
42. On the preservation of a hospitality "tradition" by Pilipino men in the United States, see Burt W. Aginsky and Ethel G. Aginsky, "The Process of Change in Family Types: A Case Study," *American Anthropologist* 51 (1949): 611–14; and Ruben R. Alcantara, "The Filipino Wedding in Waialua, Hawaii," *Amerasia* 1 (February 1972): 1–12.
43. This tendency toward the Americanization of "hybridized offspring" was noted as early as 1940 in Catapusan, "The Filipino Social Adjustment in the United States," 86.

24

"We Are that Mythical Thing Called the Public": Militant Housewives during the Great Depression

Annelise Orleck

> "We are that mythical thing called the public and so we shall demand a hearing."
> —Jean Stovel, organizer of a housewives' flour boycott, Seattle, 1936

The last fifteen years have seen a growing literature on women in the 1930s. These new histories have examined organizing among working women of various ethnicities, illuminated women's political networks in the New Deal, and assessed the relationship of women to New Deal social welfare programs. But we still know next to nothing about how poor and working-class housewives fared during the Great Depression. To a large extent our view is shaped by popular imagery of the time, which glorified the self-sacrificing wife and mother. Black-and-white documentary photographs such as Dorothea Lange's portrait of a gaunt migrant woman sheltering her frightened children, novels such as Sholem Asch's *The Mother*, and films such as *The Grapes of Wrath* reinforced the popular view of poor mothers as the last traditionalists, guardians of the beleaguered home. In many ways this idealization of motherhood placed on poor women's shoulders the responsibility for easing the hardships of hunger and joblessness.[1]

In her 1933 book *It's Up to the Women*, Eleanor Roosevelt argued that mothers, through self-sacrifice and creativity, would save their families from the worst ravages of the Depression. There is abundant evidence to show that poor wives and mothers did approach their traditional responsibilities with heightened urgency during the Depression. They did not, however, suffer alone their inability to provide food or shelter for their families; nor did they sacrifice silently for the sake of their husbands and children. Quite the contrary. From the late 1920s through the 1940s, there was a remarkable surge of activism by working-class American housewives.[2]

From New York City to Seattle, from Richmond, Virginia, to Los Angeles, and in hundreds of small towns and farm villages in between, poor wives and mothers staged food boycotts and antieviction demonstrations, created large-scale barter networks, and lobbied for food and rent price controls. Militant and angry, they demanded a better quality of life for themselves and their children. Echoing the language of trade unionism, they asserted that housing and food, like wages and hours, could be regulated by organizing and applying economic pressure.

This was not the first time Americans were treated to the spectacle of housewives demanding food for their families. Since the early nineteenth century, hard times in New York, Philadelphia, and other major cities had moved housewives in immigrant neighborhoods to demonstrate for lower food prices. But never before had Americans seen anything this widespread or persistent. The crisis conditions created by the Depression of the 1930s moved working-class wives and mothers across the United States to organize on a scale unprecedented in U.S. history. By organizing themselves as class-conscious mothers and consumers, they stretched the limits of both working-class and women's organizing in the United States.

Housewives' activism, like that of every other group of Americans during the Depression era, was profoundly influenced by Franklin Roosevelt's New Deal. During the early years of the Depression, prior to the 1932 presidential election, housewives organized to stave off imminent disaster. Their focus was on self-help—setting up barter networks, gardening cooperatives, and neighborhood councils. After 1933 the tactics and arguments used by militant housewives reflected their acceptance of Roosevelt's corporatist vision. By the mid-1930s poor and working-class housewives, like farmers and factory workers, had begun to see themselves as a group that could, by organizing and lobbying, force the New Deal state to respond to their needs.

Press coverage reflected the ambivalence with which many Americans greeted the idea of politically organized housewives. Both mainstream and radical editors took their movement seriously. Housewives' strikes and demonstrations were featured in major newspapers and national magazines. Still, these publications could not resist poking fun at the very idea of a housewives' movement. Writers never tired of suggesting that, by its very existence, the housewives' movement emasculated male adversaries. A typical headline ran in the *New York Times* in the summer of 1935 at the height of housewives' activism nationwide. "Women Picket Butcher Shops in Detroit Suburb," it blared. "Slap. Scratch. Pull Hair. Men Are Chief Victims." A more pointed headline, about Secretary of Agriculture Henry Wallace, ran a few weeks later in the *Chicago Daily Tribune:* "Secretary Wallace Beats Retreat from Five Housewives." Underlying this tone of ridicule was a growing tension over the fact that housewife activists were politicizing the traditional roles of wives and mothers.[3]

In New York City neighborhoods, organized bands of Jewish housewives fiercely resisted eviction, arguing that they were merely doing their jobs by defending their homes and those of their neighbors. Barricading themselves in apartments, they made speeches from tenement windows, wielded kettles of boiling water, and threatened to scald anyone who attempted to move furniture out onto the street. Black mothers in Cleveland, unable to convince a local power company to delay shutting off electricity in the homes of families who had not paid their bills, won restoration of power after they hung wet laundry over every utility line in the neighborhood. They also left crying babies on the desks of caseworkers at the Cleveland Emergency Relief Association, refusing to retrieve them until free milk had been provided for each child. These actions reflected a sense of humor, but sometimes housewife rage exploded. In Chicago, angry Polish housewives doused thousands of pounds of meat with kerosene and set it on fire at the warehouses of the Armour Company to dramatize their belief that high prices were not the result of shortages.[4]

This activity was not simply a reaction to the economic crisis gripping the nation. It was a conscious attempt on the part of many housewives to change the system that they blamed for the Depression. In Seattle in 1931 urban and farm wives orchestrated a massive exchange of timber and fish from western Washington for grain, fruits, and vegetables from eastern Washington. As a result, tens of thousands of families had enough food and fuel to survive the difficult winter of 1931–32. Similar barter networks were established in California, Colorado, Ohio, and Virginia in which housewives gathered and distributed food, clothing, fuel, and building materials.[5]

Understanding their power as a voting bloc, housewives lobbied in state capitals and in Washington, D.C. They also ran for electoral office in numerous locales across the country. In Washington state and in Michigan, housewife activists were elected in 1934 and 1936 on platforms that called for government regulation of food prices, housing, and utility costs. And in Minnesota in 1936, farm wives were key players in the creation of a national Farmer-Labor Party.[6]

These actions were not motivated by desire on the part of poor wives and mothers to be relieved of their responsibilities in the home—although certainly many were attracted by the excitement and camaraderie of activism. These were the actions of women who accepted the traditional sex-based division of labor but who found that the Depression had made it impossible for them to fulfill their responsibilities to the home without leaving it.

Housewife activists argued that the homes in which they worked were intimately linked to the fields and shops where their husbands, sons, and daughters labored; to the national economy; and to the fast-growing state and federal bureaucracies. Mrs. Charles Lundquist, a farmer's wife and president of the Farmer-Labor Women's Federation of Minnesota, summed up this view in a 1936 speech before a gathering of farmers and labor activists.

> Woman's place may be in the home but the home is no longer the isolated, complete unit it was. To serve her home best, the woman of today must understand the political and economic foundation on which that home rests and then do something about it.[7]

The extent and variety of housewives' activism during the Depression suggests that this view of the home was widely accepted by black as well as white women, farm as well as urban women. The housewives' rebellions that swept the country during the 1930s cannot be seen as only spontaneous outcries for a "just price." Like so many others during the Depression, working-class housewives were offering their own solutions to the failure of the U.S. economic system.[8]

Roots of a Housewives' Uprising

This essay focuses primarily on urban housewives' organizing, but it should be noted that farm women played an essential role in Depression-era housewives' activism. Apart from organizing on their own behalf—establishing farmer-labor women's committees and food-goods exchanges with urban women—farm women provided urban women with information about the gap between what farmers were paid and what wholesalers charged. This profit taking formed the basis for activists' critique of what they called "food trusts." Farm wives' activism during the 1920s and 1930s must be studied before a full assessment of this phenomenon is possible. However, because of space limitations, this essay focuses on three of the most active and successful urban housewives' groups: the New York–based United Council of Working-Class Women, the Seattle-based Women's Committee of the Washington Commonwealth Federation, and the Detroit-based Women's Committee against the High Cost of Living.

Greater availability of sources on New York housewives' activism has made possible a deeper analysis of New York than of Detroit or Seattle, both of which merit further study. Still, there is sufficient evidence on the latter two cities to make for a fruitful comparison and to discern some key patterns in working-class housewives' organizing during the Depression.

An examination of these three groups illustrates that although there were some important regional differences in housewives' political style and focus, there were also commonalities. Most significantly, each had a strong labor movement affiliation. Housewives' activism developed in union strongholds, flourishing in the Bronx and Brooklyn among the wives and mothers of unionized garment workers, in Detroit among the wives and mothers of United Auto Workers (UAW) members, and in Seattle among the wives of unionized workers who had begun to argue the importance of consumer organizing during the 1920s.[9]

This union link is important for several reasons. Union husbands' fights for higher wages during the 1910s had resulted in a fairly comfortable standard of living for many families by World War I. But spiraling inflation and the near-destruction of many trade unions during the 1920s eroded the working-class quality of life. By 1929 it had become increasingly difficult, even for families of employed union workers, to make ends meet.[10]

The militance of the Depression-era housewives' movement was an outgrowth of this sudden and rapid decline in working-class families' standard of living. But it was also rooted in women organizers' own experiences in trade unions. There are no statistics detailing exactly how many housewife activists were formerly union members. However, in all the areas where housewives' organizations took hold, it was common for women to work for wages before marriage. And given the age of most leading activists in New York, Seattle, and Detroit, their working years would have coincided with the years of women's labor militance between 1909 and 1920.[11]

Certainly the key organizers of the housewives' movement were all labor leaders before the Depression. In Seattle, Jean Stovel and Mary Farquharson were active in the American Federation of Labor (AFL) before they became leaders of the Women's Committee of the Washington Commonwealth Federation. Detroit's Mary Zuk was the daughter of a United Mine Workers member and was raised on the violent mine strikes of the 1920s. As a young woman, she migrated to Detroit to work on an automobile assembly line and was fired for UAW organizing before founding the Detroit Women's Committee against the High Cost of Living. In New York, Rose Nelson was an organizer for the International Ladies' Garment Workers' Union (ILGWU) before she became codirector of the United Council of Working-Class Women (UCWCW). And the career of the best-known housewife organizer of the 1930s, Clara Lemlich Shavelson, illustrates the importance of both labor movement and Communist Party links. (Only the New York organizers had explicit ties to the Communist Party, although charges of Communist Party involvement were leveled against nearly all the housewife leaders.)[12]

Shavelson's career also roots the housewives' rebellions of the 1930s in a long tradition of Jewish immigrant women's agitation around subsistence issues. Because few immigrant or working-class families in the early twentieth century could afford to live on the salary of a single wage earner, wives, sons, and daughters contributed to the family economy. Clara Lemlich Shavelson's mother ran a small grocery store. Other immigrant women took in boarders, ran restaurants, peddled piece goods, and took in washing or sewing. Their experience with small-scale entrepreneurship gave them a basic understanding of the marketplace that carried over to their management of the home. This economic understanding was deepened by their exposure to unionist principles through their husbands, sons, and daughters and sometimes through their own experience as wage workers.[13]

These experiences nourished a belief among working-class women that the home was inextricably bound in a web of social and economic relationships to labor unions, the marketplace, and government. That view of the home was expressed in a series of food boycotts and rent strikes that erupted in New York; Philadelphia; Paterson, New Jersey; and other East Coast cities between the turn of the century and World War I. Clara Lemlich came of age on Manhattan's Lower East Side, where married women led frequent food boycotts and rent strikes during the first decade of the twentieth century. Long before she made the famous speech that set off the massive 1909 shirtwaist makers' strike—"I am tired of the talking; I move that we go on a general strike!"—Lemlich was aware that the principles of unionism could be applied to community activism.[14]

Blacklisted by garment manufacturers after the 1909 strike, fired from her new career as a paid woman's suffrage advocate after conflicts with upper-class suffragists, Lemlich married printer Arthur Shavelson in 1913 and immediately began looking for ways to channel spontaneous outbursts of housewives' anger into an organizational structure. During World War I the U.S. government made her task easier by mobilizing housewives in many city neighborhoods into Community Councils for National Defense. Now, when housewives decided to protest rapidly increasing food prices, they had an organizational structure to build on and a hall in which to meet. In 1917 and 1919 Shavelson and other community organizers were able to spread meat boycotts and rent strikes throughout New York City by winning support from the community councils as well as synagogue groups and women's trade union auxiliaries.[15]

By 1926, when Shavelson established the United Council of Working-Class Housewives (UCWCH), she was working under the auspices of the Communist Party. However, Shavelson's insistence on organizing women made her a maverick within the party, as she had been in the labor and suffrage movements. The male leadership of the Communist Party expressed little interest in efforts to win working-class wives to the party. And the women who ran the UCWCH put no pressure on women who joined the housewives' councils to also join the party.[16]

Around the same time that the united councils were founded, non-Communist organizers such as Rose Schneiderman of the Women's Trade Union League (WTUL) and Pauline Newman and Fania Cohn of the ILGWU were also trying to bring housewives into the working-class movement. In the twenty years since the 1909 shirtwaist strike—the largest strike by U.S. women workers to that time—these labor organizers had run up against the incontrovertible fact that working-class women lacked the economic power to achieve their social and political aims unless they allied themselves with more powerful groups such as middle-class women or working-class men.[17]

Seeking a way to maximize working-class women's economic power, they decided to organize women both as consumers and as workers. As workers, women were segregated into the lowest-paid, least-skilled sectors of the labor force. Economic deprivation and discrimination in male-dominated labor unions limited their power, even when they organized. But as consumers, U.S. working-class women spent billions of dollars annually. Organized as consumers, even poor women could wield real economic power. By the late 1920s women organizers were ready to try to link the home to labor unions and government in a dynamic partnership—with wage-earning women and housewives as full partners.[18]

That goal brought women organizers into direct conflict with male leaders in the trade union movement and in the Communist Party, who were unwilling to accept the home as a center of production or the housewife as a productive laborer. Nor did they see a relationship between production and consumption. Poor housewives, whatever their political stripe, understood that relationship implicitly. They responded to the neighborhood organizing strategy because they saw in it a chance to improve day-to-day living conditions for themselves and their families.[19] Jean Stovel explained the surge of militance among Seattle housewives this way: "Women," she said, "have sold the idea of organization—their own vast power—to themselves, the result of bitter experience. We are that mythical thing called the public and so we shall demand a hearing."[20]

It is important to distinguish the aims of veteran women's organizers from the aims of the majority of women who participated in housewives' protests. For the most part, these housewives had no intention of challenging the traditional sex-based division of labor. Nor were they interested in alternative political philosophies such as socialism or communism. But, desperate to feed, clothe, and shelter their families, poor women challenged traditional limits on acceptable behavior for mothers and wives. In so doing, they became political actors.[21]

From Self-Help to Lobbying the Government

Between 1926 and 1933 housewives' self-help groups sprang up across the United States. In cities surrounded by accessible growing areas (such as Dayton, Ohio, Richmond, Virginia, and Seattle, Washington), housewives and their husbands created highly developed barter networks. Unemployed workers, mostly male, exchanged skills such as carpentry, plumbing, barbering, and electrical wiring. Women—some workers' wives, others unemployed workers themselves—organized exchanges of clothing and food. These organizations grew out of small-scale gardening collectives created by housewives during the late 1920s to feed their communities.[22]

In Seattle, unemployed families organized quickly in the aftermath of the 1929 stock market crash; but then this was an unusually organized city, described by a local paper in 1937 as "the most unionized city in the country." In 1919 Seattle had been the first city in the United States to hold a general strike. During the 1920s Seattle's labor unions again broke new ground by calling on working-class women and men to organize as consumers. When the Depression hit, Seattle's vast subsistence network was described in the national press as a model of self-sufficiency, "a republic of the penniless," in the words of the *Atlantic*. By 1931–32, forty thousand Seattle women and men had joined an exchange in which the men farmed, fished, and cut leftover timber from cleared land, while the women gathered food, fuel, and clothing. The women also ran commissaries where members could shop with scrip for household essentials. By 1934 an estimated eighty thousand people statewide belonged to exchanges that allowed them to acquire food, clothing, and shelter without any money changing hands.[23]

In larger cities such as New York, Chicago, Philadelphia, and Detroit, self-help groups also sprang up during the early years of the Depression, but housewives there had little chance of making direct contact with farmers. Rather than establishing food exchanges, they created neighborhood councils that used boycotts and demonstrations to combat rising food prices. And, rather than rehabilitating abandoned buildings for occupation by the homeless, as the unemployed did in Seattle, housewives in larger cities battled with police to prevent eviction of families unable to pay their rents.[24]

Tenant and consumer councils in those cities took hold in neighborhoods where housewives had orchestrated rent strikes and meat boycotts in 1902, 1904, 1907, 1908, and 1917.[25] They organized in the same way as earlier housewife activists had done— primarily through door-to-door canvassing. Boycotts were sustained in the latter period, as in the earlier one, with picket lines and street-corner meetings. Even their angry outbursts echoed the earlier housewives' uprisings: Meat was destroyed with kerosene or taken off trucks and thrown to the ground. Flour was spilled in the streets, and milk ran in the gutters.[26]

But although its links to earlier housewives' and labor union struggles are important, the 1930s housewives' revolt was far more widespread and sustained, encompassing a far wider range of ethnic and racial groups than any tenant or consumer uprising before it. The earlier outbursts were limited to East Coast Jewish immigrant communities, but the housewives' uprising of the 1930s was nationwide and involved rural as well as urban women. It drew Polish and native-born housewives in Detroit, Finnish and Scandinavian women in Washington state, and Scandinavian farm wives in Minnesota. Jewish and black housewives were particularly militant in New York, Cleveland, Chicago, Los Angeles, and San Francisco.[27]

The 1930s housewives' movement can also be distinguished from earlier housewives' actions by the sophistication and longevity of the organizations it generated. Depression-era housewives moved quickly from self-help to lobbying in state capitals and Washington, D.C., leaders such as the "diminutive but fiery" Mary Zuk of Detroit displayed considerable skill in their use of radio and print media. Their demands of government—regulation of staple food prices, establishment of publicly owned farmer-consumer cooperatives—reflected a complex understanding of the marketplace and the potential uses of the growing government bureaucracy.

Leaders of these groups also demonstrated considerable sophistication about forming alliances. Shortly after Roosevelt was elected president, hostilities between Communist and non-Communist women in the labor movement were temporarily set aside. AFL-affiliated women's auxiliaries and Communist Party–affiliated women's neighborhood councils worked together to organize consumer protests and lobby for regulation of food and housing costs. This happened in 1933, well before the party initiated its Popular Front policy urging members to join with "progressive" non-Communist groups and well before the Congress of Industrial Organizations extended its hand to Communists to rejoin the labor movement.[28]

This rapprochement highlighted the desperation that gripped so many working-class communities during the Depression. Although charges of being Communists were leveled against housewife organizers throughout the Depression, such accusations did not dampen the enthusiasm of rank-and-file council members. To many non-Communists in the movement, the question of who was Communist and who wasn't did not seem terribly relevant at a time when millions faced hunger and homelessness. Detroit housewife leader Catherine Mudra responded this way to charges of Communist involvement in the Detroit meat strike of 1935: "There may be some Communists among us. There are a lot of Republicans and Democrats too. We do not ask the politics of those who join. . . . All we want is to get prices down to where we can feed our families."[29]

Despite this tolerance of Communist leadership, housewife organizers affiliated with the Communist Party were careful not to push too hard. Party regulars such as Clara Lemlich Shavelson were open about their political beliefs, but they did not push members of the housewives' councils to toe the party line. And they organized as mothers, not as Communists. Shavelson did not use the name Lemlich, which still reverberated among New York City garment workers who remembered her fiery speech in 1909. Instead, she organized under her married name and made sure to point out her children whenever they passed by a street corner where she was speaking.[30]

Seasoned organizers such as Shavelson sought to build bonds between women in the name of motherhood. They understood that when appealed to as mothers, apolitical women lost their fears about being associated with radicalism in general and the Communist Party in particular. Meeting women organizers day after day, in the local parks with their babies, in food markets, and on street corners, shy housewives gained the confidence to express their anger. The deepening Depression hastened such personal transformations. Once all sense of economic security had dissolved, temperamentally conservative women became more open to radical solutions. Sophia Ocher, who was a member of a Mother and Child Unit of Communist organizers in the Bronx, wrote that "work among these women was not difficult for there was the baby, the greatest of all issues, and there were the women, all working-class mothers who would fight for their very lives to obtain a better life for their babies."[31]

In New York, ethnic bonding between women facilitated the growth of housewives' councils. Although many community organizers, including Shavelson, Rose Nelson Raynes, Sonya Sanders, and Sophia Ocher, were Communist Party members, they were also genuine members of the communities they sought to organize, familiar with local customs, needs, and fears. They addressed crowds of housewives in Yiddish as well as English. And, steering clear of Marxist doctrine, they emphasized ethnic and community ties in their speeches, likening housewives' councils to the women's charitable associations traditional in East European Jewish culture.[32]

Conscious of the hardship of poor women's lives, the organizers never hesitated to roll up their sleeves and help out. In one Bronx neighborhood, Sonya Sanders created an entire neighborhood council by winning over one resistant housebound woman. After Sanders came into the woman's house when she was sick, cleaned it, bathed the children, and prepared a kosher dinner for the family, the woman gave up her suspicion of Sanders and became an enthusiastic supporter. She invited all her friends to come to her home and listen to Sanders discuss ways to fight evictions and high prices. Before long a new neighborhood council was born. Of course, successes such as these were predicated on the shared ethnicity of organizer and organized. The ploy would not have worked as well if Sanders had not understood the laws of *kashrut* or known how to cook Jewish-style food.[33]

This strength was also a weakness. As a result of New York's ethnic balkanization, the city's neighborhood councils were not ethnically diverse. Organizers tended to have most success organizing women of their own ethnic group. The UCWCW, founded and run by Jewish immigrant women, was primarily composed of Jewish immigrant housewives; owing to the Communist Party's strength in Harlem, black women were the second largest group; small numbers of Irish and Italian housewives also joined.

"We never intended to be exclusively a Jewish organization," Rose Nelson Raynes recalls.

> But we built in areas where we had strength. Maybe it was because of the background of so many Jewish women in the needle trades, maybe it was because of the concentration of immigrants from the other side, I don't know. But there was a feeling in the Jewish working class that we had to express ourselves in protest of the rising prices.[34]

As in New York, the Detroit and Seattle housewives' actions were initiated by immigrant women of a particular ethnic group—Polish Catholics in Detroit and Scandinavian Protestants in Seattle. Because those cities were less ghettoized than New York, organizers were more successful in creating coalitions that involved black as well as white women, Protestants as well as Jews and Catholics, immigrants and the native-born. However, ethnic differences were not unimportant, even outside New York. For example, American-born Protestants in the Detroit housewives' councils were far less confrontational in their tactics than their Polish, Jewish, or black counterparts. They signed no-meat pledges rather than picketing butcher shops and handed in petitions rather than marching on city hall.[35]

Women had different reasons for joining housewives' councils in the 1930s, but those who stayed did so because they enjoyed the camaraderie, the enhanced self-esteem, and the shared sense of fighting for a larger cause. During an interview in her Brighton Beach apartment, eighty-eight-year-old Rose Nelson Raynes offered this analysis of why the councils inspired such loyalty:

> Women were discriminated against in all organizations in those years and the progressive organizations were no exception. When women joined progressive organizations with men they were relegated to the kitchen. There was a need on the part of the

mother, the woman in the house. She wanted to get out. There were so many things taking place that she wanted to learn more about. So women came to our organization where they got culture, lectures. Some developed to a point where they could really get up and make a speech that would meet any politician's speech today. It came from the need, from the heart. We felt we wanted to express ourselves, to learn to speak and act and the only way was through a women's council.[36]

The Meatless Summer of 1935

Depression-era organizing against high food prices reached its peak during the summer of 1935. Working-class women activists from Communist and non-Communist organizations convened two regional conferences the previous winter, one for the East Coast, another for the Midwest, to coordinate protests against the sales tax and high cost of living. Representatives from AFL women's union auxiliaries, parents' associations, church groups, farm women's groups, and black women's groups attended. By that summer, they had laid plans for the most ambitious women's consumer protest to that time.[37]

It began when the Chicago Committee against the High Cost of Living, headed by Dina Ginsberg, organized massive street meetings near the stockyards to let the meat packers know how unhappy they were with rising meat prices. New York housewives in the UCWCW quickly raised the ante by organizing a citywide strike against butcher shops.[38]

On 22 May women in Jewish and black neighborhoods around New York City formed picket lines. In Harlem, according to historian Mark Naison, the meat strike "produced an unprecedented display of coordinated protest by black working-class women."[39] The strike lasted four weeks. More than forty-five hundred butcher shops were closed down by housewives' picket lines. Scores of women and men around the city were arrested. The New York State Retail Meat Dealers Association threatened to hold Mayor Fiorello LaGuardia responsible for damage to their businesses as a result of the strike. The mayor, in an attempt to resolve the strike, asked federal officials to study the possibilities for reducing retail meat prices.[40]

Raynes, citywide coordinator of the meat strike, describes what happened next.

It was successful to a point where we were warned that the gangsters were going to get us. . . . We decided to call the whole thing off but first we organized a mass picket line in front of the wholesale meat distributors. . . . About three, four hundred women came out on the picket line. It was supposed to be a final action. But . . . instead of being the wind-up it became a beginning.[41]

Housewives across the United States promptly joined in. Ten thousand Los Angeles housewives, members of the Joint Council of Women's Auxiliaries, declared a meat strike on 8 June that so completely shut down retail meat sales in the city that butchers cut prices by the next day. In Philadelphia, Chicago, Boston, Paterson, St. Louis, and Kansas City, newly formed housewives' councils echoed the cry of the New York strike: "Stop Buying Meat until Prices Come Down!"[42]

On 15 June a delegation of housewives from across the country descended on Washington, D.C., demanding that the Department of Agriculture enforce lower meat prices. Clara Lemlich Shavelson described the delegation's meeting with Secretary of Agriculture Henry Wallace: "The meat packers and the Department of Agriculture in Washington tried to make the strikers' delegation . . . believe that the farmer and the drought are to blame for the high price of food. But the delegation would not fall for this. They knew the truth."[43]

The Polish housewives of Hamtramck, Michigan, a suburb of Detroit, did not believe Wallace's explanation, either. A month after the end of the New York strike, thirty-two-year-old Mary Zuk addressed a mass demonstration of housewives gathered on the streets of Hamtramck to demand an immediate reduction in meat prices. When the reduction did not come by that evening, Zuk announced a meat boycott to begin the following day.[44]

On 27 July 1935 Polish and black housewives began to picket Hamtramck butcher shops, carrying signs demanding a 20 percent price cut throughout the city and an end to price gouging in black neighborhoods. When men, taunted by onlookers who accused them of being "scared of a few women," attempted to cross the lines, they were "seized by the pickets . . . their faces slapped, their hair pulled and their packages confiscated. . . . A few were knocked down and trampled." That night Hamtramck butchers reported unhappily that the boycott had been 95 percent effective.[45]

Within a matter of days the meat boycott spread to other parts of Detroit, as housewives in several different ethnic communities hailed the onset of "a general strike against the high cost of living." Jewish women picketed kosher butcher shops in downtown Detroit neighborhoods. Protestant women in outlying regions such as Lincoln Park and River Rouge declined to picket or march but instead set up card tables on streetcorners to solicit no-meat pledges from passing housewives.[46]

Housewives also sought government intervention. Detroit housewives stormed the city council demanding that it set a ceiling on meat prices in the metropolitan area. "What we can afford to buy isn't fit for a human to eat," Joanna Dinkfeld told the council. "And we can't afford very much of that." Warning the council and the state government that they had better act, Myrtle Hoaglund announced that she was forming a statewide housewives' organization. "We feel that we should have united action," she said. "We think the movement of protest against present meat prices can be spread throughout the state and . . . the nation." As evidence, she showed the city council bags of letters she had received from housewives around the country, asking her how to go about organizing consumer boycotts.[47]

Throughout August the meat strikers made front-page news in Detroit and received close attention in major New York and Chicago dailies. The women staged mass marches through the streets of Detroit, stormed meat-packing plants, overturned and emptied meat trucks, and poured kerosene on thousands of pounds of meat stored in warehouses. When these actions resulted in the arrest of several Detroit women, hundreds of boycotters marched on the city jails, demanding the release of their friends. Two hours after her arrest, Hattie Krewik, forty-five years old and a mother of five, emerged from her cell unrepentant. A roar went up from the crowd as she immediately began to tell, in Polish, her tale of mistreatment at the hands of the police. By the end of the first week in August, retail butchers in Detroit were pleading with the governor to send in state troops to protect their meat.[48]

Although without a doubt the butchers suffered as a result of this boycott, the strikers in Detroit, like the strikers in New York, frequently reiterated that the strike was not aimed at retail butchers or at farmers. It was targeted, in Clara Shavelson's words, at the "meat packer millionaires." To prove that, in the second week of August a delegation of Detroit housewives traveled to Chicago, where they hooked up with their Chicago counterparts for a march on the Union stockyards.

Meeting them at the gates, Armour & Company president R. H. Cabell attempted to mollify the women. "Meat packers," he told them, "are not the arbiters of prices, merely the agencies through which economic laws operate." The sudden rise in prices, he explained, was the fault of the Agricultural Adjustment Administration, which had recently imposed a processing tax on pork.[49]

"Fine," Mary Zuk responded. The housewives would return to Washington for another meeting with agriculture secretary Wallace. On 19 August 1935 Zuk and her committee of five housewives marched into Wallace's office and demanded that he end the processing tax, impose a 20 percent cut on meat prices, and order prompt prosecution of profiteering meat packers.[50] Wallace, perhaps sensing how this would be played in the press, tried to evict reporters from the room, warning that he would not speak to the women if they remained. Zuk did not blink. She replied: "Our people want to know what we say and they want to know what *you* say so the press people are going to stay." The reporters stayed and had a grand time the next day reporting on Wallace's unexplained departure from the room in the middle of the meeting.[51] "Secretary Wallace Beats Retreat from Five House-wives," the *Chicago Daily Tribune* blared. *Newsweek* reported it this way:

> The lanky Iowan looked down into Mrs. Zuk's deep-sunken brown eyes and gulped his Adam's apple.
> Mrs. Zuk: Doesn't the government want us to live? Everything in Detroit has gone up except wages.
> Wallace fled.[52]

In the aftermath of Zuk's visit to Washington, *Newsweek* reported housewives' demonstrations against the high price of meat in Indianapolis, Denver, and Miami. The *New York Times* reported violent housewives' attacks on meat warehouses in Chicago and in the Pennsylvania towns of Shenandoah and Frackville. And Mary Zuk, the "strong-jawed 100 lb. mother of the meat strike," became a national figure. The Detroit post office announced that it was receiving letters from all over the country addressed only to "Mrs. Zuk—Detroit."[53]

Although boycotts and strikes continued to be used as a tool in the housewives' struggle for lower prices, the movement became more focused on electoral politics as the decade wore on. Both Shavelson and Zuk used the prominence they'd gained through housewife activism to run for elected office. Shavelson ran for the New York State Assembly in 1933 and 1938 as a "real . . . mother fighting to maintain an American standard of living for her own family as well as for other families." She did not win, but she fared far better than the rest of the Communist Party ticket.[54]

Zuk ran a successful campaign for the Hamtramck city council in April of 1936. Although the local Hearst-owned paper warned that her election would be a victory for those who advocate "the break-up of the family," Zuk was swept into office by her fellow housewives. She won on a platform calling for the city council to reduce rents, food prices, and utility costs in Hamtramck. After her election she told reporters that she was proof that "a mother can organize and still take care of her family."[55]

In some ways what the Hearst papers sensed was really happening. Zuk's campaign represented an express politicization of motherhood and the family. On Mother's Day 1936 seven hundred Zuk supporters rallied outside the city council to demand public funding for a women's health-care clinic, child-care centers, playgrounds, and teen centers in Hamtramck. They also called for an end to evictions and construction of more public housing in their city. The government owed this to mothers, the demonstrators told reporters.[56]

Two years earlier, in Washington state, the Women's Committee of the Washington Commonwealth Federation (WCF) had successfully elected three of its members to the state senate—Mary Farquharson, a professor's wife, and Marie Keene and Katherine Malström, the wives of loggers. Their campaign had been built around a Production-for-Use initiative to prohibit the destruction of food as a way of propping up prices. Such waste, they said, was an outrage to poor mothers in the state, who had been fighting the practice since the beginning of the Depression. The ballot measure also proposed a state distribution system for produce so that farmers could get a fair price and workers' families could buy food directly from farmers. Led by Katherine Smith and Elizabeth Harper, committee members collected seventy thousand signatures to put the measure on the 1936 ballot.[57]

The Production-for-Use initiative failed by a narrow margin, but it made national news as columnists across the country speculated on the impact it might have had on the U.S. economic system. Other WCF campaigns were more successful, however. The most important of these was the campaign to create publicly owned utilities in Washington state. Washington voters were the only ones to approve state ownership of utilities, but voters in localities across the country endorsed the creation of city and county utility companies during the 1930s.[58]

Housewife activists also kept their sights on the federal government during this period. From 1935 to 1941 housewives' delegations from major cities made annual trips to Washington, D.C., to lobby for lower food prices. These trips stopped during World War II but resumed afterward with a concerted campaign to save the Office of Price Administration and to win federal funds for construction of public housing in poor neighborhoods.[59]

The alliance of housewives' councils and women's union auxiliaries continued to grow through the late 1930s, laying the groundwork for two more nationwide meat strikes in 1948 and 1951. These strikes affected even more women than the 1935 action because housewives now had an organizing tool that enabled them to mobilize across thousands of miles: the telephone. "We have assigned fifty-eight women ten pages each of the telephone directory," said one strike leader in Cincinnati. In August 1948 housewives in Texas, Ohio, Colorado, Florida, Michigan, and New York boycotted meat. And during the winter of 1951 a housewives' meat boycott across the country forced wholesalers dealing in the New York, Philadelphia, and Chicago markets to lower their prices. In New York City alone, newspapers estimated, one million pounds of meat a week went begging. Fearing for their own jobs, unionized butchers, then retailers, and finally even local wholesalers called on the federal government to institute price controls on meat.[60]

But even as these actions made front-page news across the country, the housewives' alliance was breaking apart over the issue of Communist involvement. As early as 1933 the Washington state legislature had passed a bill requiring that Seattle take over the commissaries created by the unemployed two years earlier. Conservative politicians claimed that Communists had taken control of the relief machinery in the city and were seeking to indoctrinate the hungry. In 1939 Hearst newspapers charged that the housewives' movement nationwide was little more than a Communist plot to sow seeds of discord in the American home. The Dies Committee of the U.S. Congress took these charges seriously and began an investigation. U.S. entry into World War II temporarily ended the investigation but also quelled consumer protest, because the government instituted rationing and price controls.[61]

Investigations of the consumer movement began again soon after the war ended. During the 1948 boycott housewife leaders were charged by some with being too friendly to Progressive Party presidential candidate Henry Wallace. In 1949 the House Committee on Un-American Activities began investigating the organizers of a 1947 housewives' march on Washington, and in 1950 they were ordered to register with the Justice Department as foreign agents. By the early 1950s national and local Communist-hunting committees had torn apart the movement, creating dissension and mistrust among the activists.[62]

The unique alliance that created a nationwide housewives' uprising during the 1930s and 1940s would not reemerge, but it laid the groundwork for later consumer and tenant organizing. Housewives' militance politicized consumer issues nationwide. "Never has there been such a wave of enthusiasm to do something for the consumer," *The Nation* wrote in 1937. Americans have gained "a consumer consciousness," the magazine concluded, as a direct result of the housewives' strikes in New York, Detroit, and other cities. The uprising of working-class housewives also broadened the terms of the class struggle, forcing male union leaders to admit that "the roles of producer and consumer are intimately related."[63]

Housewives' groups alleviated the worst effects of the Depression in many working-class communities by bringing down food prices, cutting rent and utility costs, preventing evictions, and spurring the construction of more public housing, schools, and parks. By the end of World War II housewives' activism had forced the government to play a regulatory role in food and housing costs. Militant direct action and sustained lobbying put pressure on local and federal politicians to investigate profiteering on staple goods. The meat strikes of 1935 and of 1948 through 1951 resulted in congressional hearings on the structure of the meat industry and in nationwide reductions in prices. The intense antieviction struggles led by urban housewives and their years of lobbying for public housing helped to convince New York City and other localities to pass rent-control laws. They also increased support in Congress for federally funded public housing.[64]

Perhaps an equally important legacy of housewives' activism was its impact on the consciousness of the women who participated. "It was an education for the women," Brooklyn activist Dorothy Moser recalls, "that they could not have gotten any other way." Immigrant women, poor native white women, and black women learned to write and speak effectively, to lobby in state capitals and in Washington, D.C., to challenge men in positions of power, and sometimes to question the power relations in their own homes.[65]

By organizing as consumers, working-class housewives not only demonstrated a keen understanding of their place in local and national economic structures; they also shattered the notion that because homemakers consume rather than produce, they are inherently more passive than their wage-earning husbands. The very act of organizing defied traditional notions of proper behavior for wives and mothers—and organizers were often called upon to explain their actions.

Union husbands supported and sometimes, as Dana Frank argues in her study of Seattle, even instigated their wives' community organizing. However, that organizing created logistical problems, namely, who was going to watch the children and who was going to cook dinner? Some women managed to do it all. Others could not. Complaining of anarchy in the home, some union husbands ordered their wives to stop marching and return to the kitchen. In November 1934 *Working Woman* magazine offered a hamper of canned goods to any woman who could answer the plaint of a housewife whose husband had ordered her to quit her women's council.

First prize went to a Bronx housewife who called on husbands and wives to share child care as "they share their bread. Perhaps two evenings a week father should go, and two evenings, mother." The same woman noted that struggle keeps a woman "young physically and mentally" and that she shouldn't give it up for anything. Second prize went to a Pennsylvania miner's wife who agreed with that sentiment. "There can't be a revolution without women. . . . No one could convince me to drop out. Rather than leave the Party I would leave him." And an honorable mention went to a Texas farm woman who warned, "If we allow men to tell us what we can and cannot do we will never get our freedom."[66] The prize-winning essays suggest that, like many women reformers before them, Depression-era housewife activists became interested in knocking down the walls that defined behavioral norms for women only after they had personally run up against them.[67]

In defending their right to participate in a struggle that did not ideologically challenge the traditional sexual division of labor, many working-class housewives developed a new sense of pride in their abilities and a taste for political involvement. These women never came to think of themselves as feminists. They did, however, begin to see themselves as legitimate political and economic actors. During this period, poor wives and mothers left their homes in order to preserve them. In so doing, whether they intended to or not, they politicized the home, the family, and motherhood in important and unprecedented ways.

Notes

1. For an analysis of the impact of one school of documentary photography on our impressions of poor mothers during the Depression, see Wendy Kozol, "Madonnas of the Field: Photography, Gender, and Thirties' Farm Relief," *Genders* 2 (summer 1988): 1–23.

2. Eleanor Roosevelt, *It's up to the Women* (New York: Frederick A. Stokes, 1933). A less friendly version of this argument can be found in Norman Cousins's 1939 article skewering those who suggested that women who left the home to work were somehow responsible for the ongoing unemployment crisis. See Norman Cousins, "Will Women Lose Their Jobs?" *Current History and Forum*, September 1939, 14–18, 62–63.

3. The *New York Times, Newsweek, The Nation, The New Republic*, the *Saturday Evening Post, Harper's*, the *Christian Century, Business Week*, and *American Mercury* all covered and commented on housewife organizing. The *Chicago Daily Tribune* and the *Detroit Free Press* also provided detailed coverage of housewives' activism in their cities. *Working Woman*, the monthly publication of the Women's Commission of the Communist Party, was invaluable. Although extremely dogmatic in its early years, the magazine is one of the most complete sources available on working-class women during the Depression. The two main archives consulted for this paper were the Tamiment Library in New York City and the Robert Burke Collection in the Manuscripts Division of the University of Washington Library, Seattle. See *New York Times*, "Buyers Trampled by Meat Strikers," 28 July 1935; "Secretary Wallace Beats Retreat from Five Housewives," *Chicago Daily Tribune*, 20 August 1935.

4. See *Working Woman*, April 1931, June 1931, April 1933, June 1935; *New York Times*, 30 January–28 February 1932; *Detroit Free Press*, 6–9 August 1935; *Chicago Daily Tribune*, 18 August 1935.

5. See *The Atlantic*, October 1932; *Collier's*, 31 December 1932; *Literary Digest*, 11 February 1933; *The Nation*, 1 March 1933 and 19 April 1933; *Survey*, 15 December 1932 and July 1933; *Saturday Evening Post*, 25 February 1933; *Commonweal*, 8 March 1933; *Good Housekeeping*, March 1933.

6. *Working Woman*, June 1935; *The Woman Today*, April 1936; *New York Times*, 10 April 1936; *Party Organizer*, September 1935. Meridel Le Sueur describes the radicalization of one of those farm women, Mary Cotter, in her 1940 short story "Salute to Spring," in Meridel Le Sueur, *Salute to Spring* (New York: International Publishers, 1940).

7. *The Woman Today*, April 1936.

8. For selected sources on housewife activism early in the Depression, see *Working Woman*, 1931–35. See also *New York Times*, 23, 30 January; February; 22 March; 22 May; 7 June; 7, 11 July; 13–26 September; 9 October; 7, 21 December 1932; January–February; 23, 30 March; 13, 24 May; 1, 2, 8 June; 2, 31 August; 7, 9, 26 September; 9 December 1933. See also *The Atlantic*, October 1932; *The Nation*, 1 March 1933; 19 April 1933; 14, 18 March 1934; *The New Republic*, 15 November 1933; *Ladies' Home Journal*, October 1934.

9. For information on the links between union activity and community organizing in New York City neighborhoods between 1902 and 1945, see Annelise Orleck, "Common Sense and a Little Fire: Working-Class Women's Activism in the Twentieth-Century United States" (Ph.D. diss., New York University, 1989); on Seattle politics in the post–World War I period, see Albert Acena, "The Washington Commonwealth Federation: Reform Politics and the Popular Front" (Ph.D. diss., University of Washington, 1975); and Dana Frank, "At the Point of Consumption: Seattle Labor and the Politics of Consumption, 1919–1927" (Ph.D. diss., Yale University, 1988).

10. A leaflet distributed by the UCWCW in 1929 noted that "the prices of most essential foodstuffs are still very high, while . . . the wages of those workers still employed, and part time workers, have been cut more and more." See "Working-Class Women, Let Us Organize and Fight" (leaflet, n.d., Tamiment Library).

    A *Working Woman* study in the winter of 1931 reported that even among those workers still employed in the big cities of the United States, income had declined 33 percent, but food prices had decreased only 7 percent. See *Working Woman* 3 (March 1931).

11. Rose Nelson Raynes, one of the chief organizers of the UCWCW, recalls that in 1931, when she first became involved with the organization, most of the women were older than thirty-five. Interview with Rose Nelson Raynes, New York City, 8 October 1987. *New York Times* reports of arrests in antieviction actions and consumer boycotts between 1931 and 1935 show that all the women were married and the vast majority

were between the ages of thirty and forty-two. *Detroit Free Press* accounts of arrests in the 1935 meat strike list the majority as having been between the ages of twenty-eight and forty-eight. In 1932 T. J. Parry (*The Atlantic*, October 1932), writing about members of the food exchanges in Seattle, commented that most of them were "near life's half-way mark or beyond."

12. See *The Woman Today*, July 1936; Mary Farquharson Papers, Burke Collection, boxes 12–14, and folders 30 and 94; and Frank, "At the Point of Consumption."

13. In *The Jewish Woman in America* (New York: New American Library, 1976), 99–114, Charlotte Baum, Paula Hyman, and Sonya Michel review some of the voluminous immigrant literature highlighting the entrepreneurship of Jewish immigrant mothers. See Orleck, "Common Sense and a Little Fire," ch. 1, for a fuller analysis of the literature on working-class women's entrepreneurship, their conception of home, and their involvement in activism around tenant and consumer issues in the first decade of the twentieth century.

14. Paula Hyman makes this point in her essay "Immigrant Women and Consumer Protest: The New York City Kosher Meat Boycott of 1902," *American Jewish History* 70 (September 1980): 91–105. See also *New York Times* for May–June 1902; 13 July–2 September 1904; 30 November–9 December 1906; 26 December 1907–27 Jan. 1908. These sources indicate that many of the women involved were the wives and mothers of garment workers.

15. See *New York Times*, 3, 4, 7–10, 12–15 May; 17 June; 4–6 September 1919. Also see "Women's Councils in the 1930s," a paper presented by Meredith Tax at the June 1984 Berkshire Conference on the History of Women, Smith College, Northampton, Mass. Also see *The Daily Worker*, 23 May 1927.

16. Communist Party women complained consistently in the *Party Organizer* during the 1930s that party men were hindering or ignoring their efforts at organizing women in urban neighborhoods. See particularly the August 1937 issue in which Anna Damon, head of the Communist Party Women's Commission, lashes out at party leaders for undercutting her efforts with black women in St. Louis.

17. See New York Women's Trade Union League, *Annual Reports*, 1922, 1926, 1928; and Summary of Speeches, Women's Auxiliary Conference, Unity House, Forest Park, Penn., 30 June–1 July 1928, New York WTUL Papers, Tamiment Library. See also Mary Van Kleeck Papers, Sophia Smith Collection, Smith College, Northampton, Mass. See also correspondence between Fania M. Cohn and women's auxiliary leaders, Grace Klueg and Mary Peake: Cohn to Klueg, 27 August 1926; 15 January 1927; 3 March 1927; Cohn to Peake, 20 April 1927; Klueg to Cohn, 7 April 1927, in Fania Cohn Papers, New York Public Library.

18. A study by the American Federation of Women's Auxiliaries of Labor estimated in 1937 that U.S. women in union households spent $6 billion annually. See *Working Woman*, March 1937.

19. Robert Shaffer notes that the national Communist Party leadership condemned party feminist theorist Mary Inman particularly for her assertion that the home was a center of production and that housewives did productive labor. See his "Women and the Communist Party, USA, 1930–1940," *Socialist Review* 45 (May–June 1979): 73–118. See also Mary Inman, *Thirteen Years of CPUSA Misleadership on the Women Question* (published by the author, Los Angeles, 1949).

20. *The Woman Today*, July 1936.

21. See Temma Kaplan, "Female Consciousness and Collective Action: The Case of Barcelona, 1910–1918," *Signs* 7 (spring 1982): 545–66.

22. See *The Atlantic*, October 1932; *Collier's*, 31 December 1932; *Literary Digest*, 11 February 1933; *The Nation*, 1 March 1933, 19 April 1933; *Survey*, 15 December 1932, July 1933; *Saturday Evening Post*, 25 February 1933; *Commonweal*, 8 March 1933; *Good Housekeeping*, March 1933.

23. See Parry (note 11); *New York Times*, 7 June, 3 September 1936; *The Woman Today*, July 1936; *Ladies' Home Journal*, October 1934; *Seattle Post-Intelligencer*, 11 January 1937; *American Mercury*, February 1937.

24. *Working Woman*, June–September 1931. For antieviction activity, see *New York Times* almost daily in February, as well as 1, 2, 13 March; 28 May; 7 June; 7 July; 13, 15–18, 20, 26 September; 7, 21 December 1932; 6, 12, 17, 28 January; 1, 22 February; 8, 23, 30 March; 13, 24 May; 1, 2, 8 June; 2, 3 August; 7, 9, 26 September; 9 December 1933.

25. Identifiable links to these earlier events, in addition to Clara Lemlich Shavelson, include Dorothy Moser, another New York activist of the 1930s, who remembers her mother's involvement in the 1917 boycotts. Moser, interview with the author, New York City, 8 October 1987. Judging from the age of the women arrested in New York and Detroit actions (see *New York Times* and *Detroit Free Press*, 1931–35), mostly in their forties, most of the 1930s activists were old enough to remember earlier actions.

26. See Hyman, "Immigrant Women and Consumer Protest," 91–105; and Dana Frank, "Housewives, Socialists, and the Politics of Food: The 1917 New York Cost-of-Living Protests," *Feminist Studies* 11 (summer 1985): 255–85. See also Kaplan, "Female Consciousness and Collective Action."

27. Rose Nelson Raynes, interviews with author, 8 October 1987 and 17 February 1989. *Working Woman*, June, July, and August 1935; *The Woman Today*, July 1936; *New York Times, Chicago Daily Tribune, Detroit Free*

Press, Newsweek, and the *Saturday Evening Post* also provided coverage of housewife actions. See particularly *New York Times,* 28 July; 4, 6, 11, 18, 24, 25 August 1935; *Saturday Evening Post,* 2 November 1935; *Chicago Daily Tribune,* 18, 20, 21 August 1935; *Newsweek,* 17, 31 August 1935.

28. In 1933, pleased with the success of their neighborhood organizing strategy, the UCWCW, the umbrella organization for New York housewives' councils, began working to build a coalition with other New York women's organizations, many of which had previously been quite hostile to anyone with Communist Party affiliations. This was an important turning point in the housewives' movement. (See *Working Woman,* October 1933, December 1933.)

29. *New York Times,* 6 August 1935.

30. "Who Is Clara Shavelson?" (leaflet from her 1933 campaign for New York State Assembly in the 2d Assembly District, courtesy of her daughter, Rita Margulies); interview with daughter Martha Shaffer, 11 March 1989.

31. *Party Organizer* 10 (July 1937): 36.

32. Brighton Beach, Brooklyn, where Clara Shavelson organized, is a perfect example of this strategy. Shavelson built on a highly developed network of Jewish women's religious and cultural associations to create the effective Emma Lazarus Tenants' Council during the 1930s. See Orleck, "Common Sense and a Little Fire," ch. 8.

33. *Party Organizer* 11 (March 1938): 39–40.

34. Raynes interview, 8 October 1987.

35. Information on the New York UCWCW comes from interviews with Raynes, 8 October 1987 and 17 February 1989. Also, both *New York Times* and *Working Woman* coverage of New York City housewives' actions from 1932 to 1937 show that the most consistently militant sections of the city were Jewish immigrant communities. Information on the composition of the Seattle housewives' groups was drawn from membership lists of the Renters' Protection, Cost of Living, and Public Ownership committees of the Women's League of the Washington Commonwealth Federation, Burke Collection, folders 30, 94, 182, 183, 188. Information on the composition of the Detroit housewives' movement comes from the *Detroit Free Press,* 26 July–25 August 1935 when housewife activists made the paper, quite often the front page, almost every day.

36. Raynes interview, 8 October 1987.

37. *Working Woman,* March 1935.

38. *Chicago Daily Tribune,* 18 August 1935; *Working Woman,* August 1935.

39. Mark Naison, *Communists in Harlem during the Depression* (New York: Grove Press, 1983), 149.

40. See *New York Times,* 27–31 May; 1, 2, 6, 10–12, 14–16 June 1935.

41. Raynes interview, 8 October 1987.

42. *Working Woman,* June 1935; *New York Times,* 15, 16 June 1935.

43. *Working Woman,* August 1935.

44. *Detroit Free Press,* 27 July 1935; *New York Times,* 28 July 1935.

45. *Detroit Free Press* and *New York Times,* both for 28 July 1935.

46. *Detroit Free Press,* 29–31 July 1935; *New York Times,* 30 July 1935.

47. *Detroit Free Press,* 1 August 1935; *New York Times,* 4 August 1935.

48. *Detroit Free Press,* 3–5 August 1935.

49. *Chicago Daily Tribune,* 18 August 1935; *Newsweek,* 17 August 1935; *Saturday Evening Post,* 2 November 1935.

50. *New York Times,* 20 August 1935.

51. Ibid.

52. *Newsweek,* 31 August 1935.

53. *Detroit Free Press,* 6–7, 9 August 1935; *Newsweek,* 31 August 1935; *New York Times,* 19 August; 1, 5 September 1935.

54. "Who Is Clara Shavelson?" (see note 30); Martha Shaffer, interview with the author, 11 March 1989; and Sophie Melvin Gerson, interview with the author, 17 February 1989.

55. *Detroit Free Press* and *New York Times,* both for 10 April 1936; *The Woman Today,* July 1936.

56. *The Woman Today,* July 1936.

57. Ibid.; *New York Times,* 7, 13 June; 5, 26 July; 3, 9, 10, 13 September; 1, 9 November 1936; "A Few Honest Questions and Answers about Initiative 119" (handbill, n.d., Burke Collection).

58. "A Few Honest Questions and Answers" (leaflet of the Washington Commonwealth Federation, n.d., Burke Collection). See *The Nation,* 28 November 1934; 19 August 1939.

59. *The Woman Today,* March 1937; *New York Times,* 4 December 1947; 20 May; 20 July; 3–31 August 1948; 24, 26–28 February; 25, 26 May; 14 June; 18 August 1951.

60. Raynes interview, 17 February 1989: *New York Times,* 3, 5, 8–11, 19, 28, 31 August 1948; 24, 26–28 Feb.; 14 June 1951.

61. *New York Times,* 26 February 1933; *The Woman Today,* March 1937; *The Nation,* 5, 12 June 1937; 18 February 1939; *Business Week,* 11 November 1939; *Forum,* October 1939; *The New Republic,* 1 January 1940.

62. *New York Times*, 23 October 1949; 7 January 1950.

63. *The Nation*, 5, 12 June 1937; *The New Republic*, 8 April 1936.

64. *New York Times*, 20, 24, 25 August 1935; 20 May; 20 July; 3–31 August 1948; 24, 26–28 February; 25, 26 May; 14 June; 18 August 1951.

65. Moser interview.

66. *Working Woman*, March 1935.

67. Frank argues that during the 1920s, working-class women in Seattle resisted their husbands' and brothers' calls to consumer action, because they resented their exclusion from meaningful participation in governance and policy making of the labor unions. See Frank, "At the Point of Consumption"; Schaffer interview.

25

Raiz Fuerte: Oral History and Mexicana Farmworkers

Devra Anne Weber

Mexicana field workers, as agricultural laborers, have been remarkable for their absence in written agricultural history. Most studies have focused on the growth of capitalist agriculture and the related decline of the family farm. Concern about the implications of these changes for American culture, political economy, and the agrarian dream has generally shaped the questions asked about capitalist agriculture. If freeholding family farmers were the basis of a democratic society, capitalist and/or slave agriculture was its antitheses. Studies of capitalist agriculture have thus become enclosed within broader questions about American democracy, measuring change against a mythologized past of conflict-free small farming on a classless frontier.

When considered at all, agricultural wage workers have usually been examined in terms of questions framed by these assumptions. Rather than being seen in their own right, they have usually been depicted as the degraded result of the family farm's demise. The most thoughtful studies have been exposés, written to sway public opinion, that revealed the complex arrangement of social, economic, and political power perpetuating the brutal conditions under which farmworkers lived and toiled. As was the case with the history of unskilled workers in industry, the written history of farmworkers became molded by the pressing conditions of their lives. The wretchedness of conditions became confused with the social worlds of the workers. Pictured as victims of a brutal system, they emerged as faceless, powerless, passive, and ultimately outside the flow of history. Lurking racial, cultural, ethnic, and gender stereotypes reinforced this image. This was especially true for Mexican women.[1]

These considerations make oral sources especially crucial for exploring the history of Mexican women.[2] Oral histories enable us to challenge the common confusion between the dismal conditions of the agricultural labor system and the internal life of workers. They enable us to understand the relationship for Mexicanas between the economic system of agriculture and community, politics, and familial and cultural life. Oral histories help answer (and reconceptualize) fundamental questions about class, gender, life and work, cultural change, values, and perceptions neglected in traditional sources. They also provide an insight into consciousness.

In conducting a series of oral histories with men and women involved in a critical farmworker strike in the 1930s, I began to think about the nature of gender consciousness. How does it intersect with a sense of class? How does it intersect with national and ethnic identity? In the oral histories of Mexican women, their sense of themselves as workers and Mexicans frequently coincided with that of the men, and drew upon similar bonds of history, community, and commonality. Yet the women's perceptions of what it meant to be a Mexican or a worker were shaped by gender roles and consciousness that frequently differed from that of the men. This seemed to correspond to what Temma Kaplan has defined as "female consciousness." According to Kaplan,

> Female consciousness, recognition of what a particular class, culture and historical period expect from women, creates a sense of rights and obligations that provides motive force for actions different from those Marxist or feminist theory generally try to explain. Female consciousness centers upon the rights of gender on social concerns, on survival. Those with female consciousness accept the gender system of their society; indeed such consciousness emerges from the division of labor by sex, which assigns women the responsibility of preserving life. But, accepting that task, women with female consciousness demand the rights that their obligations entail. The collective drive to secure those rights that result from the division of labor sometimes has revolutionary consequences insofar as it politicizes the networks of everyday life.[3]

This essay will explore how oral histories can help us understand the consciousness of a group of Mexican women cotton workers (or *companeras* of cotton workers) who participated in the 1933 cotton strike in California's San Joaquin Valley. One was a woman I will call Mrs. Valdez.

Mrs. Valdez and the 1933 Cotton Strike

Mrs. Valdez came from Mexico, where her father had been a *sembrador*, a small farmer or sharecropper, eking out a livable but bleak existence. She had barely reached adolescence when the Mexican Revolution broke out in 1910. With the exception of a sister-in-law, neither she nor her immediate family participated in the revolution.[4] As is the case with many noncombatants, her memories of the revolution were not of the opposing ideologies nor of the issues, but of hunger, fear, and death.[5] Fleeing the revolution, the family crossed the border into the United States. By 1933 she was twenty-four, married with two children, and living in a small San Joaquin Valley town.

The agricultural industry in which she worked was, by 1933, California's major industry. Cotton, the most rapidly expanding crop, depended on Mexican workers who migrated annually to the valley to work.[6] Larger cotton ranches of over three hundred acres dominated the industry. Here workers lived in private labor camps, the largest of which were rural versions of industrial company towns: Workers lived in company housing, bought from (and remained in debt to) company stores, and sent their children to company schools. Work and daily lives were supervised by a racially structured hierarchy dominated by Anglo managers and foremen; below them were Mexican contractors who recruited the workers, supervised work, and acted as intermediaries between workers and their English-speaking employers.

With the Depression, growers slashed wages. In response, farmworkers went on strike in crop after crop in California. The wave of strikes began in southern California and spread north into the San Joaquin Valley. While conducted under the banner of the Cannery and Agricultural Workers Industrial Union (CAWIU), the strikes were sustained largely by Mexican workers and Mexican organizers. The spread and success of the strikes depended on the familial and social networks of Mexican workers as much as, if not more than, the small but effective and ambitious union. The strike wave crested in the cotton fields of the San Joaquin Valley when eighteen thousand strikers brought picking to a standstill. Growers evicted strikers, who established ad hoc camps on empty land. The largest was near the town of Corcoran, where thirty-five hundred workers congregated. The strikers formed mobile picket lines, to which growers retaliated by organizing armed vigilantes. The strikers held out for over a month before a negotiated settlement was reached with the growers and the California, United States, and Mexican governments.

Mexicanas were a vital part of the strike, and about half of the strikers at Corcoran were women. They ran the camp kitchen, cared for children, and marched on picket lines. They distributed food and clothing. Some attended strike meetings, and a few spoke at the meetings. And it was the women who confronted Mexican strikebreakers. In short, women were essential to this strike, though they have been largely obscured in accounts of its history. Mrs. Valdez went on strike and was on the picket lines. She was not a leader, but she was one of the many women who made the strike possible.

Voice and Community

Before examining her testimony, a word is in order about voice and tone as a dimension of oral histories. How information is conveyed is as important as what is said and can emphasize or contradict the verbal message. Conversation and social interaction are a major part of women's lives, and gesture and voice are thus particularly crucial to their communications. The verbal message, the "song" of a story, is especially important for people with a strong oral tradition, which, as Jan Vansina has pointed out, has meaning as art form, drama, and literature. Oral histories or stories are often dramatic, moving with a grace and continuity that embody analytical reflections and communicate an understanding of social relations and the complexities of human existence.

Mrs. Valdez structured the telling of her oral history in stories or vignettes. Most sections of her oral history had distinct beginnings and endings, interrupted only if I interjected a question. She developed characters, villains and heroes, and hardship and tragedy (but little comedy). How this story was constructed and its characters developed embodied her assessment of the conflict.

As she told her story, the characters emerged with voices of their own, each with separate and distinct tones and cadence, perhaps reflecting their personalities to an extent, but more generally expressing Mrs. Valdez's assessment of them and their role in the drama. Strikebreakers, for example, spoke in high-pitched and pleading voices, and the listener understood them immediately as measly cowards. Her rendition of the strikers' voices, offered a clear contrast: Their words were given in sonorous, deep, and steady tones, in a voice of authority that seemed to represent a communal voice verbalizing what Mrs. Valdez considered to be community values.

Mrs. Valdez's sense of collective values, later embodied in collective action either by the strikers as a group or by women, was expressed in what I would call a collective voice. At times individuals spoke in her stories: the grower, Mr. Peterson; her contractor, "Chicho" Viduarri; and the woman leader "la Lourdes," but more often people spoke in one collective voice that transcended individuality. This sense of community as embodied in a collective voice became a central feature of her narrative and permeated everything she said about the strike. This manner of telling underscored the sense of unanimity explicit in her analysis of solidarity and clear-cut divisions.[7] How she told the story underlined, accentuated, and modified the meaning of the story itself.

Beyond her use of different voices, Mrs. Valdez's narrative contains substantial nonverbal analysis of the "facts" as she remembered them. Her voice, gestures, and inflections conveyed both implications and meanings. She gestured with her arms and hands—a flat palm down hard on the table to make a point, both hands held up as she began again. Her stories had clear beginnings and often ended with verbal punctuations such as "and that's the way it was." She switched tenses around as, in the heat of the story, the past became the present and then receded again into the past. Vocal inflections jumped, vibrated, climbed, and then descended, playing a tonal counterpoint to her words.

Mrs. Valdez's memories of the 1933 strike focused on two major concerns: providing and caring for her family, and her role as a striker. How she structured these memories says much about her perceptions and her consciousness as a woman, a Mexican, and a worker. It is striking to what extent her memories of the strike focused on the collectivity of Mexicans and, within this, the collectivity of Mexican women.

Mrs. Valdez's sense of national identity, an important underpinning to her narrative, reflects the importance of national cohesion against a historic background of Anglo-Mexican hostility.[8] Mrs. Valdez vividly recounted the United States' appropriation of Mexican land in 1848 and the Treaty of Guadalupe Hidalgo, which ceded the area to the United States. She drew from stories of Mexican rebellion against U.S. rule in California and the nineteenth-century California guerrillas Tiburcio Vasquez and Joaquin Murieta; the knowledge that Mexicans were working on land that had once belonged to Mexico increased her antagonism toward Anglo bosses. Mrs. Valdez may well have felt the same way as another interviewee, Mrs. Martinez, who, upon arriving at the valley, pointed out to her son and told him, "Mira lo que nos arrebataron los bárbaros ."[9]

Most of these workers had lived through the Mexican Revolution of 1910–20, and they utilized both the experience and legacy within the new context of a strike-torn California. The military experience was crucial in protecting the camp: Often led by former military officers, Mexican veterans at the Corcoran camp constituted a formidable armed security system. Mrs. Valdez remembers that during the strike stories of the revolution were told, retold, and debated. The extent to which Mexicans employed the images and slogans of the revolution helped solidify a sense of community. Workers named the rough roads in the camp after revolutionary heroes and Mexican towns. Even Mrs. Valdez, whose individual memories of the revolution were primarily of the terror it held for her, shared in a collective memory of a national struggle and its symbols: She disdainfully compared strikebreakers with traitors who had "sold the head of Pancho Villa."[10]

Mrs. Valdez expressed a sense of collectivity among Mexicans. There were, in fact, many divisions—between strikers and strikebreakers, contractors and workers, people from different areas of Mexico, and people who had fought with different factions of the revolution or Cristero movement. Yet conflict with Anglo bosses on what had been Mexican land emphasized an identification as Mexicans (as well as workers) that overshadowed other divisions.

The Community of Mexican Women

Mrs. Valdez remembered a collectivity of Mexican women. By 1933 Mexican women were working alongside men in the fields. Like the men, they were paid piece rates and picked an average of two hundred pounds per ten-hour day. Picking required strength, skill, and stamina. As one woman recalled:

> But let me describe to you what we had to go through. I'd have a twelve-foot sack. . . . I'd tie the sack around my waist and the sack would go between my legs and I'd go on the cotton row, picking cotton and just putting it in there. . . . So when we finally got it filled real good then we would pick up the hundred-pound sack, toss it up on our shoulders, and then I would walk, put it up there on the scale and have it weighed, put it back on my shoulder, climb up on a wagon and empty that sack in.[11]

As Mrs. Valdez recounted, women faced hardships in caring for their families: houses without heat (which contributed to disease), preparing food without stoves, and cooking over fires in oil barrels. Food was central to her memory, reflecting a gender-based division of labor. Getting enough food, a problem at any time, was exacerbated by the Depression, which forced some women to forage for berries or feed their families flour and water. Food was an issue of survival. As in almost all societies, women were in charge of preparing the food, and Mrs. Valdez's concern about food was repeated in interviews with other women. Men remembered the strike in terms of wages and conditions; women remembered these events in terms of food. Men were not oblivious or unconcerned, but women's role in preparing food made this a central aspect of their consciousness and shaped the way they perceived, remembered, and articulated the events of the strike.

Mrs. Valdez's memory of leadership reflects this sense of female community. After initially replying that there were no leaders (a significant comment in itself), she named her labor contractor and then focused on a woman named Lourdes Castillo, an interesting choice for several reasons. Lourdes Castillo was an attractive, single woman who lived in Corcoran. She used makeup, bobbed her hair, and wore stylish dresses. Financially independent, she owned and ran the local bar. Lourdes became involved with the strike when union organizers asked her to store food for strikers in her cantina.

In some respects Lourdes represented a transition many Mexican women were undergoing in response to capitalist expansion, revolution, and migration. When the revolution convulsively disrupted Mexican families, women left alone took over the work in rural areas, migrated, and sometimes became involved in the revolution. *Soldaderas*, camp followers in the revolution, cooked, nursed, and provided sexual and emotional comfort. Some fought and were even executed in the course of battle. This image of *la soldadera*, the woman fighting on behalf of the Mexican community, was praised as a national symbol of strength and resistance. Yet it was an ambivalent image: Praised within the context of an often mythified revolution, the *soldaderas* were criticized for their relative sexual freedom and independence. The term *soldadera* became double-edged. When used to describe an individual woman, it could be synonymous with *whore*.

Gender mores in the United States differed from those in rural Mexico. Some changes were cosmetic manifestations of deeper alterations: Women bobbed their hair, adopted new styles of dress, and wore makeup. But these changes reflected shifts in a gender-based division of labor. Women, usually younger and unmarried, began to work for wages in canneries or garment factories, unobserved by watchful male relatives. Some women became financially independent, as Lourdes did, and ran bars and cantinas. Financial independence and a changing gender-based division of labor outside the house altered expectations of women's responsibilities and obligations. Yet these women still risked the approbation of segments of the community, male and female.

According to Mrs. Valdez, during the strike Lourdes was in charge of keeping the log of who entered and left the camp and who spoke at meetings. She was also in charge of distributing food.[12] Lourdes thus reflects women's traditional concern about food, while at the same time she epitomized the cultural transition of Mexican women and the changing gender roles from prerevolutionary Mexico to the more fluid wage society of California. It was precisely her financial independence that enabled her to store and distribute the food. Perhaps Mrs. Valdez's enthusiastic memories of Lourdes suggests Mrs. Valdez's changing values concerning women, even if these were not directly expressed in her own life.

While Mrs. Valdez described the abysmal conditions under which women labored, the women were active, not passive, participants in the strike. Women's networks, which formed the lattice of mutual assistance in the workers' community, were transformed during the strike. The networks helped organize daily picket lines in front of the cotton fields. Older women still sporting the long hair and rebozos of rural Mexico, younger women who had adapted the flapper styles of the United States, and young girls barely into their teens rode together in trucks to the picket lines. They set up makeshift child-care centers and established a camp kitchen.

With the spread of the conflict, these networks expanded and the women's involvement escalated from verbal assaults on the strikebreakers to outright physical conflict. When, after three weeks, growers refused to settle, women organized and led confrontations with Mexican strikebreakers. According to Mrs. Valdez, the women decided that they, not the men, would enter the fields to confront the strikebreakers.[13] They reasoned that strikebreakers would be less likely to physically hurt the women.

In organized groups, the women entered the field, appealing to strikebreakers on class and national grounds—as "poor people" and "Mexicanos"—to join the strike. Those from the same regions or villages in Mexico appealed to compatriots on the basis of local loyalties, denouncing as traitors those who refused.

Exhortations turned to threats and conflict. The women threatened to poison one man who had eaten at the camp kitchen—an indication again of the centrality of (and their power over) food. But women had also come prepared. Those armed with lead pipes and knives went after the strikebreakers. One ripped a cotton sack with a knife. Others hit strikebreakers with pipes, fists, or whatever was handy. Although strikers had felt that the women would not be hurt, the male strikebreakers retaliated, and at least one woman was brutally beaten:

> Las mismas mujeres que iban en los troques . . . que iban en el picoteo. Adentro, les pegaron. Les rompieron su ropa. Les partieron los sombreros y los sacos y se los hicieron asina y todo. Y malos! Ohh! Se mira feo! Feo se miraba. Y nomas miraba y decia "no, no." Yo miraba la sangre que les escurria. [She imitates the strikebreakers in high-pitched, pleading tones:] "No les peguen, déjenlos, no les peguen." [Her voice drops as the voice of the strikers speaks:] "Que se los lleve el esto. . . . Si a nosotros nos esta llevando de frio y de hambre pos que a ellos también. No tienen, vendidos, muertos de hambre!" [Her voice rises as the strikebreakers continue their plea:] "Pos nosotros vivemos muy lejos, venimos de Los Angeles . . . tienes que saber de donde, que tenemos que tener dinero pa' irnos." [Her voice lowers and slows as it again becomes the voice of the strikers:] "Si . . . nosotros también tenemos que comer y también tenemos familia. *Pero no somos vendidos!*"[14]

This passage underlines the importance of the female collectivity. The women went in because it was women's business, and they acted on behalf of the community. Mrs. Valdez implied that the men had little to do with the decision or even opposed it: "Porque las mujeres tenemos más chanza. Siempre los hombres se detenian más porque son hombres y todo. Y las mujeres no. Los hombres no nos pueden hacer nada. No nos podian hacer nada pos ahi vamos en zumba."[15]

The issues of confrontation focused around food. This underlines a harsh reality: Strikebreakers worked to feed their families, and without food strikers would be forced back to work. Her memory reflects the reality of the confrontation but also her understanding of the central issue of the strike. Mrs. Valdez recalls the strikebreakers justifying themselves to the women in terms of the need to feed their families. But the striking women's ultimate rebuke was also expressed in terms of this need: "Si . . . nosotros también tenemos que comer y también tenemos familia. *Pero no somos vendidos!*"[16] Food remained central in her memories. Discussions about the strike and strike negotiations were all couched in relation to food. Her interests as a Mexican worker were considered, weighed, and expressed within the context of her interests as a woman, mother, and wife.

As the strike wore on, conditions grew harsher in the Corcoran camp. Growers lobbed incendiaries over the fence at night. Food became hard to get, and at least one child died of malnutrition.[17] In response to public concern following the murder of two strikers, California's governor overrode federal regulations withholding relief from strikers under arbitration and, over the protestations of local boards of supervisors, sent in truckloads of milk and food to the embattled camp. Mrs. Valdez remembers nothing of federal, state, or local government or agencies, but she remembered the food: "rice, beans, milk, everything they sent in."

At a meeting where Lourdes addressed strikers, food, or lack of food, was juxtaposed against their stance in the strike:

> Pa' [Lourdes] decirles que pasaran hambre.
> "Mira," dice . . . "aunque alcanzemos poquito pero no nos estamos muriendo de hambre," dice. "Pero no salsa. Pero *ninguno* a trabajar . . . aunque venga el ranchero y les diga que, que vamos y que pa'ca. *No* vaya ninguno!" dice.
> "Miren, aunque sea poquito estamos comiendo . . . pero no nos hemos muerto de hambre. Ta viniendo comida . . . nos estan trayendo comida."
> [Mrs. Valdez interjected:] Leche y todo nos daban. . . . Si. Y a todos ahi los que trabajában diciendo que no fueran con ningún ranchero. Que no se creeran de ninqúin ranchero. Que todos se agarraban de un solo modo que nadien, todos parejos tuvieran su voto, parejos.[18]

Mrs. Valdez was clear about the effects of a united front on both sides—that if one grower broke with the others, the rest would follow. [The collective voice speaks:] "No. Y no que no. No. Si nos paga tanto vamos, Y al pagar un ranchero tenían que pagar todos los mismo. Tenían, ves."[19]

Unity and the centrality of women carried over into her recollection of the final negotiations:

> El portuguese [a growers'representative] . . . le dijera que ahí iban los rancheros . . . a tener un mitin en el campo donde estaban todos ahí campados con la Lourdes Castillo y todo.
> "Si," dice. "Ahí vamos a juntarnos todos los rancheros. Y vamos a firmar. Les vamos a pagar tanto. Y vamos a firmar todos para que entonces, sí, ya vayan cada quien a sus campos a trabajar."
> "Si," dice [the strikers' representative], "pero no menos de un centavo. No. No salimos hasta que tengan un . . . sueldo fijo. Todos vamos. Pero de ahí en más ni uno vamos. *Ni uno* salimos del camps." Y todo.[20]

The strike was settled, the ranchers had been beaten, and wages went up.

The Structure of Memory

Mrs. Valdez's account of the strike and women—how she structured her memories—tells us more about why Mexicanas supported the strike than interviews with leaders might have. Without the perceptions of women such as Mrs. Valdez it would be more difficult to understand strike dynamics.

Of particular interest is the fact that she remembers (or recounts) a collectivity among Mexican strikers. In her telling, workers speak in a collective voice and act as a united group. She remembers little or no dissent. In her account, *all* the workers on the Peterson ranch walked out together to join the strike, *all* the women were on the picket lines, and *all* the strikers voted unanimously to stay on strike. Growers, also a united group, spoke with one voice as a collective opposition. The lines between worker and grower were clearly drawn. According to Mrs. Valdez, it was this unity that accounted for the strike's success.

But within this collectivity of Mexicans was the collectivity of women. Mrs. Valdez focused on female themes and concerns about food, caring for their families and, by extension, the greater community. Women were the actors on the picket line, made decisions about the strike, and acted as a unit. It is perhaps this sense of female collectivity and the concern around the issue of food that accounts for why Lourdes was considered a leader, though she is never mentioned by men in their accounts. Men played little part in Mrs. Valdez's narrative; she stated flatly that the women were braver. She remembered female leadership, female participation, female concerns, and a largely female victory. While other interviews and sources may disagree (even among women), it does suggest Mrs. Valdez's reality of the strike of 1933.

What Mrs. Valdez did not say suggests the limitations of oral narratives. She either did not know, could not recall, or chose not to recount several crucial aspects of the story: Like many other strikers, she remembered nothing of the CAWIU, nor of Anglo strike leaders mentioned in other accounts. This was not uncommon, and I discuss elsewhere the implications of this and the nature of Mexican leadership within the strike.[21] The role of the New Deal and the negotiations of the governments—Mexican, United States, and California— play no part in her narrative. The visit by the Mexican consul to the camp, visits by government officials, threats to deport strikers—she recounted nothing about the negotiations that led to the settlement of the strike.

Her memory of the strike thus is limited. But the fact that Mrs. Valdez's memories were so similar to those of other women indicates that hers is not an isolated perception. There are also many points at which the women's memories intersect with the men's. We thus may be dealing with a community memory made up of two intersecting collective memories: the collective memory (history) of the group as a whole, and a collective memory of women as a part of this.

Conclusion

Oral narratives reflect people's memory of the past: they can be inaccurate, contradictory, altered by the passage of time and the effects of alienation. In terms of historical analysis, Mrs. Valdez's oral history, used alone, raises questions. Was there really such unity in the face of such an intense conflict? There were, obviously, strikebreakers. Were there no doubts, arguments? In part she may have been making a point to me. But it may be also indicative of her consciousness, of the things important to her in the event. Mrs. Valdez also remembers a largely female collectivity. Certainly it is clear from other sources that men played a crucial role as well. Yet her focus on women provides information unavailable in other sources, and provides a woman's point of view. It suggests which issues were important to the female collectivity, how and why women rallied to the strike, and how they used their networks within the strike.

So how may an oral history be used? Seen on its own, it remains a fragment of the larger story. Oral narratives must also be read critically as texts in light of the problem of alienation, especially in the United States, where various forms of cultural and historical amnesia seem so advanced. Used uncritically, oral histories are open to misinterpretation and may reinforce rather than reduce the separation from a meaningful past. This is especially true of the narratives of those people usually ignored by written history. Readers may lack a historical framework within which to situate and understand such narratives. The filters of cultural and class differences and chauvinism may also be obstacles. Some may embrace these narratives as colorful and emotional personal statements, while ignoring the subjects as reflective and conscious participants in history.

In the case of the Mexican women farm laborers considered in this essay, oral testimonies are not a complete history, nor can they, by themselves, address the problems of historical amnesia. Used with other material and read carefully and critically, however, such narratives prove crucial to a reanalysis of the strike. They need to be interpreted and placed within a historical framework encompassing institutional and social relations, struggle, and change. But when this is done, testimonies such as that of Mrs. Valdez become a uniquely invaluable source. Used critically, they reveal transformations in consciousness and culture; they suggest the place of self-conscious and reflective Mexican women—and farm-laboring women in general—in the broader history of rural women in the United States.

Notes

1. Portions of this essay appear in Devra A. Weber, "Mexican Women on Strike: Memory, History and Oral Narrative," in Adelida Del Castillo, ed., *Between Borders: Essays on Mexicana/Chicana History* (Encino, Calif.: Floricanto Press, 1990), 161–74.
2. I use the term used by the women themselves. They called themselves Mexicans. Although all had lived in the United States over fifty years, all but one identified themselves as Mexicanas by birth, culture, and ethnicity. The one woman born and raised in the United States, and a generation younger, referred to herself interchangeably as Mexicana and Chicana.
3. Temma Kaplan, "Female Consciousness and Collective Action: The Case of Barcelona, 1910–1918," *Signs* (spring 1982): 545.
4. The sister-in-law is an interesting, if fragmentary, figure in Mrs. Valdez's memory. From Mrs. Valdez's account, the sister-in-law left her husband (Mrs. Valdez's brother) to join a group of revolutionaries, as a *companera* of one of them. When she returned to see her children, she threatened to have the entire family killed by her new lover. It was in the wake of this threat that the family fled to the United States.
5. That these were the main concerns of many Mexicans does not undermine the importance of the revolution in their lives, nor the extent to which the images and symbols of the revolution *later* became symbols of collective resistance, on both class and national scales.
6. By 1933 the overwhelming majority of Mexican workers migrated not from Mexico but from settled communities around Los Angeles or the Imperial Valley, adjacent to the Mexican border. Some came from Texas. The point is that they were not the "homing pigeons" described by growers—people who descended on the fields at harvest and cheerfully departed for Mexico. They were residents, and some of the younger pickers were United States citizens.
7. I want to emphasize that this is *her* analysis. I would disagree with the picture of solidarity; disputes among strikers would, I think, bear this out. Nevertheless, the point is that Mrs. Valdez's historical analysis tells us a great deal about her conception of the strike—and perhaps her conception of what I should be told about it.
8. In Mexico, Mexicans tended to have a greater sense of identity with the town or state they came from than with the country as a whole. These identities were still strong in the 1980s, as were the rivalries that existed between them. It has been argued that the Mexican revolution helped create a sense of national conciousness. One of the primary reasons was its opposition to foreign interests. For those who migrated north, across the Rio Bravo, the sense of opposition to Anglo-Americans was even greater. It was on the border areas, after all, where the corridors of resistance developed, and where many have argued the sense of Mexican nationalism was strongest.
9. "Look at what the barbarians have stolen from us." Interview by author with Guillermo Martinez, Los Angeles, April 1982.
   Note: Having encountered strong objections to using the original Spanish in such a text, a word of explanation is in order. Translating another language—especially if the language is colloquial and therefore less directly translatable—robs the subjects of their voices, diminishing the article as a consequence. This is especially true if, as in this case, the language is colloquial and, to those who know Spanish, manifestly rural and working-class. The original text gives such readers an indication of class and meaning unavailable in a

translation. It also underscores the value of bridging monolingual parochialism in a multilingual and multi-cultural society. In any event, full English translations for all quotations will be provided in the Notes.

10. After his death, Villa's corpse was disinterred and decapitated. His head was stolen in the 1920s, and the incident became a legend.

11. Interview by author with Lydia Ramos. All names used here are pseudonyms.

12. It is unclear whether Lourdes did keep the log. In a brief interview, Lourdes confirmed that she spoke at meetings and distributed food.

13. It is unclear exactly who made this decision. Roberto Castro, a member of the central strike committee, said the strike committee decided that women should enter the fields to confront strikebreakers because the women would be less likely to be hurt. The women remembered no such decision, and said that they made the decision themselves. It is hard to fix definitively the origins of the idea, but this may not matter very much: even if the strike committee made the decision, the action was consistent with spontaneous decisions by women that both antedated and followed this strike. Mexican women in Mexico City and other parts of the republic had taken part in bread riots in the colonial period. They had fought in the revolution. And in California, later strikes, in the 1930s but also as recently as the 1980s, were punctuated by groups of Mexican women invading the fields to confront strikebreakers both verbally and physically. In short, it was a female form of protest women had used both before and after the strike.

14. "The same women who were in the trucks, who were in the . . . picket line . . . these women went in and beat up all those that were inside the fields picking cotton. . . . They tore their clothes. They ripped their hats and the [picking] sacks. . . . And bad. Ohhh! It was ugly! It was an ugly sight. I was just looking and said 'No. No.' I watched the blood flowing from them.

    [She imitates the strikebreakers voice in high-pitched, pleading tones:] 'Don't hit us. Leave them [other strikebreakers] alone. Don't hit them.'

    [Her voice drops as the collective voice of the strikers speaks:] 'Let them be set upon. . . . If we are going cold and hungry then they should too. They're cowards . . . sellouts. Scum.'

    [Her voice rises as the strikebreakers continue their plea:] 'Because we live far away, we come from Los Angeles. . . . We need to have money to leave. . . .'

    'Yes,' she says [her voice lowers and slows as it again becomes the voice of the strikers]. 'We also have to eat and we also have family,' she says. *But we are not sellouts!*'"

15. "Because women take more chances. The men always hold back because they are men and all. But the women, no. The men couldn't make us do anything. They couldn't make us do anything [to prevent us from going] and so we all went off in a flash."

16. "Yes . . . we also have to eat and we also have family. *But we are not sellouts!*"

17. As the local district attorney admitted after the strike, conditions in the strikers' camp were no worse than those of the cotton labor camps. Growers did use the bad conditions, however, to pressure the health department to close the strikers' camp as a menace to public health.

18. "She [Lourdes] was telling them that they might have to go hungry for awhile.

    "'But look,' she said . . . 'they are bringing us food. We'll each get just a little, but we're not going to starve,' she says. 'But don't leave. But don't *anybody* go to work. Even if a rancher comes and tells you "come on, lets go," don't anybody go,' she says.

    "'Look, even if its a little bit, we're eating. But we aren't starving. They're bringing us food.'"

    [Mrs. Valdez interjected:] They brought us milk and everything. Yes, everybody that was working [in the strikers' camp] was told not to go with any rancher. They were told not to believe any rancher. But everyone had to stand together as one. Everyone had an equal vote [in what was decided] . . . equal."

19. "'No. And no [they said]. No. No. If you pay us this much, then we go. And if one [rancher] pays [the demand] then all the ranchers have to pay the same.' They had to, you see."

20. "The Portuguese [a growers' representative] told [the strikers' representative] that the ranchers . . . were going to have a meeting at [the strikers' camp] with 'la Lourdes.'

    "'Yes,' he says. 'We're going to pay you so much. All of us are going to sign so that then all of you can return to your camps to work.'

    "'Yes,' said [the strikers' representative]. 'But not a cent less. No. We won't go until we have a set wage. Then all of us go. But if there is something more [if there is more trouble] *none* of us go. Not even *one* of us leaves the camp.'"

21. Devra Weber, *Dark Sweat, White Gold: California Farm Worker, Cotton, and the New Deal* (Berkeley: University of California Press, 1994).

26

Breaking the Silence: Putting Latina Lesbian History at the Center

Yolanda Chávez Leyva

1994. Marty sits on a mustard-colored flower-patterned recliner in her living room. "What was it like for lesbians when you were young? Did anyone ever talk about it?" I ask her, hoping for a story.

She shakes her head "No," and repeats the phrase that has become so common to me, "Everybody knew, but no one talked about it." She has lived her entire life in a small, now midsized southwestern city where everyone in town knew everyone else. I've seen photographs—young women with short haircuts, jeans rolled up to the ankle, white socks and loafers, all smiles. "Norma García," she begins, "was always in love with Dora. Every time there was a picnic, she'd have me a sing a song for Dora." Then Marty begins singing, "Nunca . . ." "Norma's eyes always teared up when I started singing."

"What happened to the woman she was in love with?" I ask.

"I don't know, she got married. They say she married a gay man. That's what they say." Her voice drifts a bit. "It was harder back then than now."[1]

It is a forty-year-old story told casually one evening in a darkened living room, in part a story of unrequited love, universal in its pathos, yet also much more. It is also a story of silences. Latina lesbians have survived both because of the protection that silence has provided and despite the many limits and compromises it has imposed. Silence has been for us a paradox, both protecting us and harming us. In recent years, Latina lesbians have undertaken to break that silence, their voices singing in intricate harmonies and disharmonies with every word spoken, every poem written, every story told. To remember our history is to draw together the pieces from many continents and from myriad experiences, from those of the fifth-generation Chicana to those of the *recién llegada*, the most recent immigrant. To speak our history is to learn the words that we were called and that we called each other—*marimachas, jotas, tortilleras, manflores, patas, amigas íntimas, cachaperas, primas,* girlfriends, lovers.

It must begin with an understanding that Latina lesbian history—or, more accurately, *histories,* since we are a diverse people—must be looked at on its own terms rather than as simply an extension, or sidebar, to the evolution of white lesbian identity. The trajectory of Latina lesbian histories challenges the models, the chronology, the very language set forth by scholars of white lesbian and gay history. Regional differences, disparate economic opportunities, intersections of racism and sexism, immigrant status, nativity, ethnic affiliation, varying degrees of assimilation, and finally cultural and religious values, often distinct from those of the dominant society, create a unique context for Latina lesbian history. It is within these multiple contexts, then, that we can begin to explore the evolution of Latina lesbian sexuality, community, and political identity.

Despite the emergence over the last two and a half decades of an important body of work documenting the historical evolution of both a modern lesbian identity and the emergence of lesbian communities in the United States, in most histories Latina lesbians remain barely visible, appearing only when we become visible to the white lesbian community. In spite of assurances of cultural sensitivity, scholars present gay and lesbian people of color in marginal roles. We are labeled "subcultures," on the "periphery" of the lesbian community, "constituencies within the gay population."[2] Our history is viewed from afar, through the eyes of others. Latina lesbian history, like the histories of other peoples of color, requires new and creative methodologies—a truer telling of these histories calls for a conscientious effort at what Ann Ducille labels "centering the periphery."[3]

Language becomes an integral tool, and challenge, in any effort to center the periphery. As Ducille points out, there is "a pressing need to revise the language by which people of color are written in our scholarship" (127). The cultural values and assumptions associated with such words as *heterosexual, homosexual, lesbian,* or *gay* make their use problematic. As Madeline Davis and Elizabeth Kennedy disclose in their pathbreaking study of the lesbian community in Buffalo, New York, their narrators "rarely used the word lesbian," preferring to use "butch and femme" or "butch and her girlfriend." With this acknowledgment, Davis and Kennedy go on to define lesbians as "all women in the twentieth century who pursued sexual relationships with other women."[4] The question of who can or should be classified historically as a lesbian and whether sexual contact is a requisite is an ongoing debate within lesbian studies. When applied across cultures, the question becomes even more clouded. Across cultures, even the meaning of words as seemingly obvious as *manhood* or *womanhood* cannot be assumed.

Latinas in the United States, to varying degrees, have been socialized into a system that amalgamates white U.S. values and culture with those of Latin America. This assimilation into white American culture has proceeded at different rates and with different consequences, dependent upon the historical context. How that amalgamation has played out in women's sexual identification is not entirely clear, particularly since the public sexual identities available to women historically have been quite limited. As Donna Guy suggests in her recent article on Latin American gender history, however, women have been able to "maintain various sexual identities disguised within the conformity of roles of daughters, wives, and widows."[5] The task of the historian, then, is to peel back the layers of mystery and mystification that obscure the spectrum of women's true sexual identities.

1972. We're sitting together at the kitchen table. She's sixty years old and she likes to tell stories. "I was just seventeen years old in 1929 and I would go dancing with my husband's sister. She was a wonderful dancer. When we first met I didn't know how to dance at all. She said, 'Don't worry. I'll teach you.' So every Sunday afternoon we'd go to the tardeada and we'd dance. I fell in love with her. I was really in love with her, not my husband. I could hardly wait until Sunday afternoons just to dance with her." She laughs, her eyes twinkle. For a minute she's a seventeen-year-old with beautiful legs and full red lips in the arms of another woman.

Where do we fit into the stories of such women? In another time, would she have spent her life with a woman? What opportunities were available to her to center her life around women? And where does this story fit into lesbian history? It also raises some important questions regarding the acceptability of "being in love" with another woman. The narrator of this story did not consider herself a lesbian, nor did she consider her emotional and erotic feelings toward her sister-in-law as abnormal. Did she consider herself "heterosexual," however? Although scholars often refer to heterosexuality as if its definition were universal, it, like homosexuality, is socially constructed. While we are beginning to understand more clearly the expanded options available to heterosexual men within the Latin American social and cultural system, we know very little about what heterosexuality means to women today, or what it has meant to them historically. If we hear the voices of women at all, often all that we know is what women *said* they felt. It is much more difficult to uncover what the bonds between women truly meant to those women.

What opportunities have been available, historically, for Latina women to develop such bonds? As Oliva Espín points out, Latino culture encourages women to depend heavily on each other rather than on men.[6] In addition, sex-segregated activities, from social activities to church functions, provide opportunities for women to form deep, often intense relationships with each other. In fact, the Catholic Church, so often cited for the ways in which it has limited women's opportunities, may also have created some spaces for women. Without discounting the ways in which religious conventions limited women's ability to be themselves, it is as important to understand the ways in which women maneuvered within such institutions. Since the colonial period, for example, the option to live in all-women religious communities provided an escape from societal restrictions for some women. It is telling that Sor Juana Inés de la Cruz, a Mexican nun who was the most famous writer and thinker of her century, has become an idol for many contemporary Latina lesbians.

1992. At a lesbian house party I meet two women, fairly recent immigrants to the United States. They've migrated here from Mexico because they want to work, and because they want to live more freely as lesbians, although they won't use that word. They are very active in their parish, working in women's groups that organize bazaars and religious processions. "We go to confession every Saturday," María confides. "And every Saturday I tell the priest I love Elisa. The priest says it's good. God wants us to love each other. Then I tell him we have sex. He gets mad and lectures me and tells me to do penance. Then during the week I make love to Elisa. It starts all over again. So the next Saturday, I'm back in the confessional, telling the priest that I love Elisa."

It would be extremely misleading, however, to assume that the Catholic Church was or is the only religious avenue open to women in Latin America. African as well as Native American religions have survived, and even flourished, in Latin America despite ongoing attacks by the Catholic Church. Women have found different options available to them within these systems in which they can express their sexual identities. The work of Cuban writer and folklorist Lydia Cabrera, for example, provides evidence of a strong lesbian presence within Santería from the nineteenth century to the present.[7]

The formation of a sexual identity is a complex, ongoing process that involves both the individual and the community. An individual's sexual identity is but one component that determines a person's place within her community. In turn, sexual identity helps to shape a person's definition of community. A recent survey conducted at a national Lesbiana Latina conference asked women to answer who they thought of when they heard the word *community*: "Latinas, lesbians, homosexuals . . . because they all aptly describe me." "Familia, extended through neighborhoods." "I think of the women that give me support and I think of the Latino community as a whole." "Gays and lesbians." "I see it in layers. Closest to me are other Chicanas with similar experience, then other Chicanos, then other Latinos and lesbians."[8] What these answers reveal are definitions that incorporate very personalized relationships (family, neighborhoods) with sexual identity (gay, lesbian, homosexual), ethnic identity (Chicanas/Chicanos) and as a broader political identity (Latinos).

Remaining within the family and community are vital survival strategies for Latinas struggling to cope with what has often been a hostile, violent, racist outside environment.[9]

In addition, fewer economic opportunities have lessened the avenues available to many Latinas to leave their families. Finally, although the pressure on daughters to remain at home
until marriage has eased in recent years, it continues to be an important consideration when
investigating the ways in which Latinas, particularly lesbians, have negotiated their lives.
When scholars of lesbian history posit that one prerequisite for the formation of a lesbian
identity is the opportunity to leave the family unit, they ignore the possibility that such an
identity can be negotiated with the family unit. Latina lesbian history challenges a number of
other aspects of the Anglo–lesbian paradigm of the emergence of modern lesbian identity:
urbanization, which allows individuals to lead relatively anonymous lives; economic opportunities, which allow women to become self-supporting; a public culture that allows lesbians
to find each other; and finally, the eroticization of individuals by intellectuals who view sexuality as central to a person's identity.[10] These factors take on different meanings and nuances,
not yet fully understood, when we look at Latina lesbian experiences in the United States.

The importance of community, like family, both shapes and is shaped by the interplay
of sexual identity, ethnicity, and gender. Community is yet another paradox that has created spaces for Latina lesbians while at the same time acting as an agent of control. The
desire and need to remain within the community, however individually defined, raises a
number of important issues. What compromises have Latina lesbians made in order to
remain within their communities? In what ways have Latina lesbians created forms of
resistance to that silence? And how has silence allowed lesbians to maintain a place within
their communities? Why was it possible, in the first place, to continue "not talking about
it"? At what moment did lesbianism become such a threat that it was constructed as a
threat to the whole race? Was it when the silence was broken? What happened within families and within communities when that unspoken contract—silence in return for some
type of acceptance—was severed?

One response is that ethnic identity has become a form of sexual control. The construction of lesbianism "as a sickness we get from American women and American culture" works
to control women's sexual behavior by threatening to take away their ethnic identity, by
implicating them as not true Latinas.[11] This construction, a serious threat to many women,
strives to take away lesbianism as an option for women with strong ethnic identities. Well
into contemporary times, women seeking to expand their options continue to face accusations of being too Americanized, *vendidas* (sellouts) or *agabachadas* (a derogatory term for
those who are Anglicized). For example, in the early 1970s women and men engaged in
often heated debates regarding the implications of the nascent Chicana feminist movement,
which called for an analysis of women as an oppressed group and which sought to find solutions to the needs and issues of Chicanas.[12] According to sociologist Alma García, Chicana
feminist lesbians experienced even harsher attacks by cultural nationalists who saw women
solely as wives and mothers.[13] The connections between lesbianism and feminism and the
use of ethnic identity to control women deserve fuller investigation.

*1974. Small, one-story yellow and white houses encircle a bare dirt courtyard. Tiny square cement
porches are surrounded by plants and flowers that, despite the deadening heat, flourish in old coffee
cans painted red and blue and purple. I see four or five children running across the yard, an old
woman sitting on a chair staring at the traffic, and a middle-aged woman hanging laundry on a
sagging clothesline. All around, the desert heat sits heavy. That's where La Sylvia lives—I've heard
about her from the neighborhood kids even before I started seeing her at the gay bar. They hang out
at her house; she listens to them, gives them advice when they ask. She has a steady girlfriend. I see
them most weekends at the bar with Sylvia's best friend, Charlie. La Sylvia and Charlie are always
together. Charlie could almost pass for a man–her lean body in men's clothing, usually jeans, western*

shirts, and boots. Only the hint of breasts reveal her to be a woman. They drink their beers, heads leaning toward each other, telling stories, taking long drags on cigarettes. Sometimes Charlie tells us about all her old girlfriends and La Sylvia just smiles. I'm eighteen years old, dealing with my own emerging identity, and always in awe of these two butch women. Twenty years later I can look back and see how their very look was a form of resistance—without words, they declared their identity in that neighborhood where everyone "just knew" but never really talked about it.

The emergence of a Latina/o lesbian and gay movement in the last twenty-five years has heightened the debate surrounding ethnicity and sexuality. In recent years, for example, the radical right, often with the cooperation of conservative segments of communities of color, has endeavored to place gays and lesbians in opposition to people of color. These efforts have attempted to erase the place of Latina/o lesbians and gay men within our own communities. In response, activists have declared their unwillingness to deny any one part of their ethnic, gender, and sexual identities. This conscious effort to embrace all the separate parts of identity is a hallmark of gay and lesbian political organizing within communities of color.

The history of political organizing incorporating ethnicity and sexuality begins with the inception of the gay rights movement itself. According to John D'Emilio, people of color began organizing separately within a year of the Stonewall riot.[14] In the decade following the 1969 riot Latina lesbians and Latino gay men organized across the United States. El Comité de Orgullo Homosexual Latino-americano (New York City), Comunidad de Orgullo Gay (Puerto Rico), Greater Liberated Chicanos (Los Angeles), and the Gay Latino Alliance (San Francisco) emerged in the early 1970s. By the 1980, Latinas Lesbianas Unidas (Los Angeles), Ellas (Texas), and Las Buenas Amigas (New York City) gave voice to Latina lesbians. In 1987 a group of activists formed LLEGO, the National Latina and Latino Lesbian and Gay Organization.[15]

The genesis of a Latina/o lesbian and gay movement raises important analytical questions. There has been little analysis of the relationship between the civil rights movement within communities of color and organizations of gays and lesbians of color. D'Emilio has suggested that the "rhetoric and politics of such groups as the Black Panthers and the Young Lords" may have inspired, or at least provided a backdrop, for the actions of young gay men of color who participated in the Stonewall riot.[16] Hence, we might question Lillian Faderman's conclusion crediting white "radicals" with "fostering awareness in minority lesbians, who now began to see themselves as a group with lesbian and feminist political interests."[17] This artificial separation of one part of a political identity from another does a disservice to the true history of lesbians and gay men of color. It reflects the distorted vision of Latina lesbians and other lesbians of color that comes across in so many studies of U.S. lesbians. Rather than the true picture, what we see is a mirror image, a reversal of what is really there. Furthermore, if the gay rights movement in this country owes its inspiration to the civil rights movement, how much more can gay people of color themselves claim a connection? How did an understanding of what it meant to be a person of color in the United States influence individuals' understanding of what it meant to be lesbian or gay?

Latina lesbian history puts Latina lesbians at the center. It is a history that challenges scholars to look at the story from a new angle—from the inside looking out rather than from the outside looking in. It calls for new language, new explanations, new ways to understand the evolution of Latina lesbian sexuality, community, and political identity. It is a call "to come to terms with our past in order to develop a better future where we can all grow together."[18]

Notes

1. The names in these stories are pseudonyms.
2. Lillian Faderman, *Odd Girls and Twilight Lovers: A History of Lesbian Life in Twentieth-Century America* (New York: Penguin Books, 1991), 285; John D'Emilio and Estelle Freedman, *Intimate Matters: A History of Sexuality in America* (New York: Harper and Row, 1988), 324.
3. Ann Ducille, "'Othered' Matters: Reconceptualizing Dominance and Difference in the History of Sexuality in America," *Journal of the History of Sexuality* 1, 1 (1990): 107.
4. Madeline Davis and Elizabeth Kennedy, *Boots of Leather, Slippers of Gold: The History of a Lesbian Community* (New York: Routledge, 1993), 6.
5. Donna Guy, "Future Directions in Latin American Gender History," *The Americas* 52, 1 (1994): 9.
6. Oliva Espín, "Cultural and Historical Influences on Sexuality in Hispanic/Latin Women: Implications for Psychotherapy," in Carole S. Vance, ed., *Pleasure and Danger: Exploring Female Sexuality* (Boston: Routledge and Kegan Paul, 1984), 155.
7. Lydia Cabrera, *El Monte; Igbo-Finda; Ewe Orisha. Vititi Nfinda.* (Miami: Ediciones Universal, 1975), 58–59.
8. Lesbiana Latina survey, conducted by Yolanda Leyva at *Adelante con nuestra visó:* First National Latina Lesbian Leadership and Self-Empowerment Conference, Tucson, Arizona, 16–18 September 1994.
9. Ana Castillo, "La Macha: Toward a Beautiful Whole Self," in Carla Trujillo, ed., *Chicana Lesbians* (Berkeley, Calif.: Third Woman Press, 1991), 38.
10. See, for example, Faderman, *Odd Girls and Twilight Lovers*, and Davis and Kennedy, *Boots of Leather, Slippers of Gold*.
11. Oliva Espín, "Issues of Identity in the Psychology of Latina Lesbians," in Boston Lesbian Psychologies Collective, ed., *Lesbian Psychologies: Explorations and Challenges* (Urbana: University of Illinois Press, 1987), 40.
12. See, for example, Sonia A. López, "The Role of the Chicana within the Student Movement," in Rosaura Sánchez, ed., *Essays on La Mujer* (Los Angeles: University of California, Chicano Studies Center Publications, 1977); Alfredo Mirandé and Evangelina Enríquez, *La Chicana: The Mexican American Woman* (Chicago: University of Chicago Press, 1979).
13. Alma M. García, "The Development of Chicana Feminist Discourse, 1970–1980," in Ellen Carol DuBois and Vicki L. Ruiz, eds., in *Unequal Sisters: A Multi-Cultural Reader in U.S. Women's History*, 2d Edition (New York: Routledge, 1990).
14. John D'Emilio, *Making Trouble: Essays on Gay History, Politics, and the University* (New York: Routledge, 1992), 261.
15. Dennis Medina, "Gay and Lesbian Latinos/as: A History of Organizing," in *Nuestra Herencia* (Washington, D.C.: LLEGO, 1994.) See also Gonzalo Aburto, "Abriendo caminos, nuestra contribucion" in the same issue.
16. D'Emilio, *Making Trouble*, 240–41.
17. Lillian Faderman, *Odd Girls and Twilight Lovers: A History of Lesbian Life in Twentieth-Century America* (New York: Columbia University Press, 1991), 285.
18. Liz, "My Name Is Liz (Oral History)," in Juanita Ramos, ed., *Compañeras: Latina Lesbians* (New York: Routledge, 1987), 80.

27

"But We Would Never Talk about It": The Structures of Lesbian Discretion in South Dakota, 1928–1933

Elizabeth Lapovsky Kennedy

"But we would never talk about it" is a refrain in Julia Boyer Reinstein's account of her life that expresses her frustration in trying to explain her life as a lesbian to contemporary lesbians, including her daughter. Boyer Reinstein was born in 1906, on the cusp of the last generation of "new women."[1] She is an "ordinary" bourgeois woman who lived as a lesbian schoolteacher in Deadwood, South Dakota, and Castile, New York, during the 1920s and 1930s; as a married woman in Buffalo, New York, from the 1940s through the 1970s; then again as a lesbian. When I first began recording Boyer Reinstein's life story, I had a simplistic understanding of what "never talking about it" meant. Influenced by gay liberation categories, I stereotyped Boyer Reinstein and her friends as not being "out"—not having the courage to be public. But as her story unfolded, I realized that the phenomenon of being "in the closet" was much more complicated than I had assumed. During the 1920s and 1930s Boyer Reinstein was an active lesbian within a community of lesbian friends. She had few, if any, negative feelings about being a lesbian, and she was "out" to her immediate family, who were supportive of her. Yet she did not publicly disclose being gay. She was always discreet, she never drew public attention to her relationships with women, and, when necessary, she developed convenient covers to use with those outside her immediate family. She never—or at least rarely—talked about being a lesbian, not even to her friends and family. These incongruities challenge the binary opposition of being "in" or "out" and suggest that lesbianism in the early twentieth century took various and complex forms.

This essay explores private lesbianism in Deadwood, South Dakota, during the 1920s and 1930s through the lens of Julia Boyer Reinstein's life story.[2] I am tempted to say this essay documents how Boyer Reinstein constructed her closet, because of the graphic picture such a concept presents and the ease with which it would connect my work with that of some contemporary theorists. However, I am afraid using the term *closet* to refer to the culture of the 1920s and 1930s might be anachronistic.[3] Boyer Reinstein herself uses the concept of the closet today, but she never fails to remind me that neither she nor her friends thought about life in those terms in the past. My goal is to reveal the social formations of the period, to understand in particular how class, Protestantism, and the teaching profession shaped Boyer Reinstein's preference for discretion and secrecy. I hope to reveal how Boyer Reinstein managed discretion in her family and in her profession while still pursuing a rich lesbian social life, and how she and her friends were not interested in bringing lesbianism into the public but in constructing a private world in which lesbianism could flourish.

I am intrigued by these issues because of my recent research on working-class lesbians during the 1930s, 1940s, and 1950s, who had an apparent drive to end the necessity of secrecy, to reveal the closet by breaking out of it.[4] The contrast between Boyer Reinstein and these working-class lesbians highlights that discretion is a distinct social formation and raises provocative questions: Is discretion always oppressive? Is rupturing the closet always liberatory? But before exploring the social construction of discretion in Boyer Reinstein's life, I frame the subject by reviewing scholarship on discreet lesbians in the early twentieth century.

Until now, research on twentieth-century lesbians has focused primarily on the development of a public lesbian identity and has inadequately documented and analyzed the more private forms of woman-to-woman relationships. A variety of factors have conspired to make research on the lives of women such as Boyer Reinstein, who were completely private about their lesbianism, a low priority. First, if lesbian life is not public, it is difficult to identify. Successful discretion leaves few traces for study. The major sources have been autobiographies such as Elsa Gidlow's *Elsa, I Come with My Songs* or personal memoirs such as Boyer Reinstein's where the author/narrator consciously attempts to place the privacy of her past lesbianism in the context of today's public lesbianism.[5] Such sources are extremely rare. Usually personal letters, diaries, and memoirs will continue the pattern of discretion created during a lifetime of "never talking": They express deep love for women, but they leave no traces of how the authors considered themselves in relation to lesbianism. The rarity of the sources tends to present "invisibility" as an individual choice rather than as a social formation.

Second, research on lesbian and gay history was born as part of the gay and lesbian liberation movement and has adopted that movement's emphasis on being out as a path to liberation. This perspective contains an implicitly negative judgment of all those who were not out, no matter the historical period, and in extreme form caricatures those who lived before Stonewall as leading secretive, furtive, and deprived lives.[6] Such an attitude does not encourage probing questions about the social formations that shaped private gay and lesbian living. Queer theory, with its emphasis on deconstruction, has challenged the identity-based politics of gay liberation and its emphasis on being out clearing the way politically for scrutiny of earlier, less public, forms of lesbian identity.[7]

A third reason for the paucity of scholarship on lesbians who led private lives in the early twentieth century is the framework of analysis developed by feminist scholarship on the so-called New Woman. Ironically, the rigorous, detailed research that has done so much to reveal the forces shaping the ferment around women's lives at the turn of the century has developed categories that camouflage some lesbians. The groundbreaking work of Carroll Smith-Rosenberg characterizes the older generation of the New Woman as entering the public sphere while still locating their emotional lives in the female world of love; the younger generation made sexuality an active part of their self-definition and became the heterosexual "sex radical" women of Greenwich Village or "mythic mannish women," the icons of twentieth-century lesbianism.[8] The "mannish" woman was sexually interested in more "feminine" women. By definition, she was not private about her lesbianism; rather, her appearance drew public attention, stigmatizing her in the eyes of the straight world and identifying her to those women who might be interested in connecting with her. In this framework, women who located their lives with other women but who were not mannish or did not associate with mannish women are assumed to be part of the tradition of the first generation of the New Woman: women who did not identify themselves on the basis of their sexuality but who created deeply erotic, though nongenital, ties among women. Such an analysis has the benefit of heightening the importance and power of women's traditions, but at least from the perspective of Boyer Reinstein's life, it underplays the profound effect the sexual revolution had on twentieth-century women. This approach is buttressed by Esther Newton's pioneering study of "mannish women" that explains the appropriation of masculine identity as a way for women to break from the nineteenth-century tradition of women being asexual.[9] Through masculinity, women claimed active sexuality for themselves and expressed interest in other women. This argument suggests there cannot be other forms of lesbianism in the early twentieth century because it would be difficult for women to announce their sexuality.[10]

The existing historical record provides tantalizing glimpses of various ways women were private about their erotic love for women. Some women seem to have eschewed the label of lesbian entirely, and we have no idea how they understood their sexualities. Other women indicated that they considered themselves lesbians but were completely private; for some this was due to the fear of exposure in a hostile environment, while others, including Gidlow and Boyer Reinstein, preferred ambiguity and discretion. Leila Rupp's article "'Imagine My Surprise'" is the classic discussion of the women who gave no recognition to the word *lesbian*.[11] She describes the fragmentary evidence of women who were lifelong couples and who expressed love for each other, women who developed deep crushes on charismatic leaders, and women who had affairs while both or one partner was married, none of whom identified themselves publicly as lesbian. In some cases, anecdotal evidence suggests they were actually offended at being labeled lesbians after the rise of the lesbian feminist movement in the 1970s. Rupp points out that it is wrong to interpret these women as remnants of the nineteenth-century culture. They were, after all, living in a century when women were considered sexual and women identified themselves publicly as lesbians. She explores the irresolvable dilemma of either naming such relationships as "lesbian," despite the subjects' denial of the label, or completely disassociating these relationships from public lesbianism. In the end, Rupp calls for more careful documentation and interpretation.

Boyer Reinstein provides an interesting perspective on these relationships, for which we usually have only fragmentary evidence, and the analytic dilemmas they raise. Her life story raises the possibility that the evidence we have of women who vehemently denied that they were lesbians, even though they formed lifelong couples with other women, should be interpreted as an assertion that their sexuality was not a public matter, rather than as a denial that they had a sexual interest in women. The question is not so much whether they would label themselves as lesbians in public, but whether they privately considered themselves as having sexual/romantic interests in women, and therefore as different from women who were sexually interested in men, and, most important, how they constructed discretion in order to live in a social environment that was hostile to intimate relationships between women.

In her overview of twentieth-century lesbian history, Lillian Faderman provides many examples of women who, like Boyer Reinstein, were conscious of being lesbians but were still extremely circumspect. They also emphasize the custom of never talking about being lesbians. Faderman quotes a woman describing her experience in the late 1930s at the University of Washington:

> Although several of us were in couples, no one ever talked about their love lives. We could unload with problems about families, jobs, money, but not lesbianism. If two women broke up they wouldn't discuss it with the group, though they might have a confidante who was also part of the group. It was our attitude that this sort of relationship was nobody's business. We all really knew about each other of course. But the idea was, "You don't know if someone is a lesbian unless you've slept with her." You didn't belong if you were the blabbermouth type.[12]

Faderman gives another example:

> Sandra, who worked in a Portland department store during the early 1930s, tells us of having been part of a group of eight women—four couples—who went skiing every

winter between 1934 and 1937. "I'm sure we were all gay," she remembers, "but we never said a word about it. Talking about it just wasn't the thing to do. Never once did I hear the L word in that group or a word like it—even though we always rented a cabin together and we all agreed that we only wanted four beds since we slept in pairs."[13]

Faderman, like most scholars up until now, interprets these women's discretion as I originally interpreted Boyer Reinstein's: They were silent because of fear of exposure and consequent oppression. And indeed Faderman might be correct in these cases. She provides evidence that at least some women who were private longed to be more public. However, Boyer Reinstein's life provides yet another possibility.

Julia Boyer Reinstein was born in western New York; six weeks later she and her mother joined her father in Wolesley, Saskatchewan, where he worked as an electrical engineer. When she was one and a half years old, her parents divorced and her mother returned to western New York with Julia, living first in Castile and then in Warsaw. Raised by her schoolteacher mother and by her great-aunt and -uncle, who owned a newspaper in Warsaw, Julia grew up in the bosom of a respected Daughters of the American Revolution family.[14] When Julia was a teenager, her mother married the owner of the general store in Silver Springs; Julia continued to live during the week in Warsaw but on weekends joined her mother and stepfather. Julia remembers her childhood as primarily happy, despite the inevitable discomfort caused by the stigma of her parents' divorce and her unusual height for a girl—Julia claims that by the time she was eleven she had already reached her adult height of six feet. She developed a warm and open relationship with her mother that continued throughout her mother's life.

Part of her parents' divorce agreement was that Julia and her father would have no contact until she was eighteen. He remarried and settled in Deadwood, South Dakota, and became a very successful owner of the Consolidated Power and Light Company, eventually moving in the highest circles of western society.[15] Julia's life was dramatically altered when he contacted her in 1926, when she was twenty. She started spending her summers with him, and after she finished college in 1928 she went to live with him in Deadwood, where she stayed until his premature death on 1 July 1933. (During that period she continued her closeness with her mother through regular visits.)

Julia's father recognized and accepted her lesbianism at their first meeting, when he visited her at Elmira College. Here is how Julia tells the story:

> The second day he saw me, we were both of us in Elmira, and we were talking about me growing up and one of the things he asked me about was about my boyfriends. . . . And I said, "I've had my share of men friends, but they didn't mean anything to me. . . . I don't particularly care for them. If I have to have somebody for a prom or something of that sort I can always get one of the boys from Warsaw, from Cornell or Syracuse or wherever, to come down and be there for the weekend." But I wasn't interested in boys, . . . and I had never met anybody that I cared about enough to even think about getting married, although some of my friends were already getting themselves pinned or engaged or what have you. And my father questioned me a little bit about why I didn't. I said, "They just never interested me, they never interested me." I didn't tell him I was a lesbian. I knew it. Oh, yes, I knew it, I had been playing with it, you see, for two years in Elmira, quite openly at college. . . . But I remember the second afternoon, we were both of us sitting in this hotel room talking, about . . . the girls he had met, and I was telling him about who this one was and who that one was, . . . and he said to me, "They're all alike, aren't they?" And I looked at him and I said, "We're all in college, you know." He said, "You know what I mean." He said, "I've known you were a homosexual . . . practically from the time I met you. You gave yourself away in your letters." See, for about six weeks, from the time my father first called me until I first met him, I wrote him a letter

every day (and of course, I'd love to know what happened to those letters. . . . I imagine he destroyed them, I imagine he did. They certainly weren't in the house when he died). . . . He said, "But it's all right with me."

Julia developed an intense relationship with her father and became the apple of his eye. She believes that in some sense he liked her being a lesbian because she could give him more attention:

Oh yes, in fact, I think he even heaved a sigh of relief, too, in many respects, when he got me out to Deadwood, because he was very adept at turning the fellows that were interested in me away. Well, one thing is he absorbed me so that I was—My life was his life and his was mine there for those years.

She went everywhere with him, to business meetings in big cities and to the wilderness to look for new power plant sites. He was showing off his new daughter. He felt that she had the mind and the reflexes of a man, and appreciated her company. Julia did not consider herself masculine but considered his judgment a compliment.

Julia's lesbian identity continued to blossom beyond the college environment. In Deadwood, South Dakota, she created several different sites of lesbian connections. She had affairs with women when she traveled with her father, she developed flirtations with some of the local girls who were her age, and in 1931 she met another teacher, Dorothy, who became a serious love in her life. Despite these connections her lesbianism remained private, protected by the complex structures of discretion.

Julia remembers her father's business trips as very exciting. She saw new places and met many people, one of whom was Amelia Earhart. Julia's memories of the weekend she met Earhart encapsulate the privilege her father's social position brought her, and also the erotic excitement of meeting other women who might be lesbians.

Well, my father had his own airplane, and of course, when I was out in South Dakota he was . . . acquiring, as president, and managing a string of small electric companies, because in those days the villages would have their own electric plants. And it would serve the area about it, but there was nothing in between . . . . There [were] five in the Black Hills, then there were four in Nebraska, and there was one in Missouri, and there was one in the panhandle and on down. So that he was driving or flying—first driving and then flying—after he got his own plane, a great deal of the time. Of course, that's when I was with him and doing the same thing, being with him at the same time . . . . He conceived the idea that if he had a helicopter he could get to these places without these long drives or having to fly. Because none of these little towns had airports, you see, so he had to land in a field and get off the field. So he announced to me that this one weekend we would be spending the weekend in Rapid City because Amelia Earhart was going to bring a helicopter from Denver up to demonstrate. . . . She represented a helicopter company.
    So she arrived at the hotel, and she and I were assigned to one room and my father had the next room over. Of course, I was terribly excited because [this was] Amelia Earhart, [and] here I was still in college. And she landed at the airport, Rapid City, . . . where my father had his plane. And this very attractive gal got out of this helicopter in a flying suit . . . . Soft-voiced, but it had a timbre to it, and there was a little bit of authority about her. She knew what she was doing, and she spoke with authority. So I was very awed, and I stood in awe all that weekend. I wish now I hadn't . . . . I had thoughts immediately when I saw her, but I put them in the back of my head. . . . Anyway, she arrived up in the afternoon, and we went to the hotel and settled down, and that night we had dinner together. . . . She was talking about her flights, and of course I was listening. . . . And I didn't talk to her about it. She included me in her conversations and asked me about Elmira; [she] knew about Elmira. She was interested in the fact that it was a girls'

school and that it was as old as it was. But the conversation was strictly straight. . . . They talked about motors and all that sort of thing, which I knew nothing about. . . . Well, we sat around in the bar, I remember, that night, but it was very casual. And strangely enough, even though my father introduced her to people there, and they were impressed, it didn't cause any great stir.

We got ready to go to bed, and so I took my shower, got out, she went in, and, of course she came out in pajamas, without a robe. . . . And we chatted. We both had books or things to read and so we went to bed. And she said something about sweet dreams, and I said equally, and she patted me on the shoulder, or on the—not on my head, but on my shoulder, and I lay there half the night wishing to goodness that I had nerve enough to go over and sit on the edge of her bed, but I didn't. . . .

The next morning, . . . I was an early riser so I was out of the bathroom before she got up. When she came out, she was in a bra and shorts, and the shorts were men's shorts . . . yes, they were boxer shorts. And of course, that impressed me immediately, and it gave me a chance to see what her body looked like. And I wanted to be very helpful, I remember I did straighten out her [collar]—She went into slacks and a shirt, and it was a man's shirt. And then we went down to breakfast. And somehow or another we got to talking about the young people, and I don't know, I still don't know, whether—I don't think I mentioned the fact that I was a lesbian, but I think I did probably everything that would let her know that I was. I remember she smoked, and I'd light her cigarettes and things of [that] sort. I was very attentive, but at the same time I was in awe of her, because she was Amelia Earhart.

So we went flying. And of course, it was one of those bubble . . . helicopters. It wasn't very large, and so I was in the back seat. . . . My father and [s]he were flying, and of course then I couldn't say anything, because I just had to listen and be amazed at how she handled it herself. And then [she] showed my father, and, of course, he handled it also. . . . We did the hills all over, and it was the first time I had seen what became Mt. Rushmore from the air. Of course it was just a rock then, but there was talk about doing something to the rock. That was also one of my father's projects. Then . . . we landed and had lunch. And when we went walking . . . where we had lunch at a lodge in the hills, she took hold of my arm—we went arm and arm walking around the woods. . . . I had a feeling of intimacy, but I couldn't, I didn't dare go beyond it. She was still Amelia Earhart. She was personal and yet she was impersonal.

Then we had dinner again, and the three of us sat in our bedroom for the evening, and my father always had a bottle of scotch, and we were drinking some scotch. And when we got ready to go to bed [after my father left] she undressed in front of me and I did likewise, but I didn't dare make a move. I thought, if she's interested and she is a lesbian, and I know she is, she's going to have to make the first move. So I got into bed first, and she came over and sat down on the edge of the bed and talked about the weekend, that she had a pleasant weekend and my father was a great guy. . . . He and she and I had talked about his meeting me, so she knew the story of how we had been separated in my early childhood. And she leaned over and kissed me goodnight. And I wish now, I could have easily put my arms around her, but instead I just put my arm up on her shoulder and she kissed me. And it was, I think back now and I don't know, I don't know, it was more than just a casual kiss, and yet it wasn't an intimate one. But I had the feeling, I went to sleep that night feeling that, well, we knew we were each other is what we were. . . . I felt that that night. But, of course, I couldn't do anything.

So when we got up the next morning, she was getting ready to fly back to Denver. While we were at the airport she always had her arm through mine, or her arm across my shoulder, because she stood fairly tall, but not too tall—she came above my shoulder. And her flesh was just hard, muscular hard. Of course there wasn't any extra on her. When I saw her dressing, I realized she was just a wonderfully organized woman. And she kissed me goodbye when she got into the plane and took off. (My father did not buy [a helicopter] because it flew too slow for him.)

Julia's not exactly sure how, but before that weekend she had heard through her college associates that Earhart was a lesbian. "I knew when my father said we were going to [meet her] I was excited, because I thought, here is a famous lesbian woman that I can meet."

Her memories seventy years later are still vibrant, evoking a concrete sense of Earhart's body and style. They also convey Julia's persistent attempts to establish common ground with Earhart without ever talking about the topic of lesbianism directly, and her strong interest in having an affair with her, despite her shyness in the presence of such an accomplished woman. Julia loved sharing this wonderful meeting with her friends. "I was in seventh heaven. All my friends knew about it, too—that I slept in the same room with her and she kissed me goodnight." Her friends also thought she should have been more forward. A few years later when Julia told her new friend Dorothy about the weekend, Dorothy was disappointed: "Oh dear, you spoiled it. Why didn't you make a move?"

Julia never had any further contact with Amelia Earhart, and her excitement did not lead to impaired judgment about the meaning of the meeting.

> My feeling . . . was . . . that . . . it was primarily a business weekend for her. She had flown up to sell a helicopter, and it was up to her to sell it if she could, and I just happened to be . . . there. [Laughter.] No, I never thought of it [as becoming more serious]. And I don't think my father thought of arranging it as that, he just was taking me to meet Amelia Earhart, he knew I would be interested and he was interested.

For Julia this was just one of many adventures as she came into her womanhood as a lesbian, as a college student, as the daughter of a father who was a prominent citizen and business owner, and as the daughter of a mother who was strongly independent yet part of an established small-town Protestant family. Julia is very clear on how stimulating that period was for her, so that weekend was one among many, rather than one that had a particular lasting effect on her life.[16]

> There were too many other things going on; it was just one of those events. I think back now and realize that I piled and put into those years with my father what lots of people would have put maybe a lifetime into. . . . And it was exciting, and I could talk about it to other people and brag about it. . . . But I didn't think of it as being terribly important. It was just one of those things that was happening to me.

Julia's father never thwarted her lesbian desire; in fact he encouraged it, as long as it remained hidden—like his extramarital affairs. Julia remembers her affairs with other women as an integral part of accompanying her father on his business trips:

> Those years were hectic years, but they were wonderful years. I've often thought about them since then. My father would take me, for instance, to Denver, and he would be with people from the big electric companies, and then we would go out to dinner and go to the nightclub afterwards. And invariably, . . . I knew, one of the women in that ten or fifteen that were at the nightclub with us was the woman he was going to sleep with that night. I would find out which one it was. . . . Invariably, there was a lesbian among them. . . . I would team up with her. . . . I don't know [how he arranged that]. And I never questioned it, I just accepted it. This gal would separate herself from all of the men and women. Some of them were wives and some of them weren't, you know. Some of them were secretaries, some of them were executives from some other place. . . . And then once I met her, of course, why the next time, why you just teamed up again, that's all.

On hearing those stories, at first I assumed that Julia and her friend for the evening would just spend time together without specific sexual intentions. But Julia corrected me and said most often they did have a sexual encounter in the hotel where she and her father were, each in their separate rooms. "See, I was young and it was exciting to me, and they were always older people, older women. They might be in their late twenties or their early thirties or even their forties. Some of them were charming, and some of them became very good friends of mine after my father died and I came back east."[17]

Lillian Faderman documents that in New York City during the 1920s women were beginning to define themselves as sexual beings and were willing to explore sexual relationship with other women.[18] The many rendezvous Julia had during trips indicate this was happening in cosmopolitan centers throughout the United States, including the West. Usually Julia saw the women of these affairs only when she was away from Deadwood with her father, and primarily in the evening. But she did spend full days with some of them. When Julia was in Denver, Bonnie, a married woman who raised terriers, might join her for a day of shopping and for the evening. Julia would even accompany Bonnie to her house to care for the dogs if Bonnie hadn't made any other arrangements, but Julia never met Bonnie's husband.

As Julia matured she became less dependent on her father to arrange her contacts. She could attend a meeting and identify someone she was interested in immediately, as she did with Columbia:

> Oh dear, there was Columbia, who was a secretary to one of the presidents of the electric company for the city of Minneapolis. And she was my age. She was out at a big conference that was held in Rapid City, [a] very big conference, and there were several of the secretaries, because they were supposed to work . . . in the administration part of the conference business area. But I stole Columbia from that area; we barged all over the Black Hills together for five days. Then she came back one summer, she and I took off, went down to one of the local spas in the lower Black Hills and spent a week down there. . . . When I came back East, we carried on a correspondence, and she finally migrated out to the West Coast and I lost track of her. So I never knew what happened to her, but she never married, to my knowledge.

Julia also had continuing contact with a woman who had nursed her back to health when she became sick on one of her father's business trips. "She lived in McCook, Nebraska. And she came up and visited me for about two weeks one summer. She was very much a lady. You would never have known it to look at her that she was a lesbian. Never known it—until she went to bed." Julia also accompanied this nurse on a trip to visit her family in Minnesota. Neither Julia nor any of these partners was ever interested in making their relationships more serious. In fact, she does not call them relationships or affairs, but "escapades," indicating their frivolity. These women had other commitments to family or business. Julia was not in love with them, and to the best of her knowledge none of them wanted something more serious from her. Julia reminisces: "Columbia and I just knew we liked each other, and it was fun being together and that was it." Julia did not consider most of these women lesbians, despite their sexual predilections, nor did they consider themselves as such.

During the period Julia was accompanying her father and meeting women interested in making love with women, she also developed a social life in Deadwood. Julia describes Deadwood as an unusual town. Despite its size and isolation, it was very lively, up-to-date, and open-minded.

> Deadwood was just different. . . . Once a month there was a dinner dance in the hotel— everybody who was anybody went to the dinner dance, and the reservations were limited because the center of the big dining room was cleared so that you could dance in it. . . . The Shriners always had a big ball, and when we had a ball, I want you to know, there was a grand march. You see, it was done properly. The theater was in sections, like the big theaters that were built . . . it would probably hold six hundred to seven hundred people. But it had its grand circles and its boxes, and strangely enough, it had good theater, [which]

would come up from Denver . . . for five nights and then go back down to Denver. There was a lot of social life, and it was cultured, and the library was an excellent library. But our lives were—All I can say is we were just loose-knit . . . , "[doing] pretty much what you wanted to do."

The dress code in Deadwood was quite lax, and allowed space for women who did not want to dress in a typically feminine manner. "See, the thing is, we could dress casually there in slacks, in riding trousers, riding things, so that they didn't think anything about that." But for such public events as dances and theater, women were expected to be fashionably dressed as ladies who could mix in the best society. Julia loved dressing up and was quite good at it. She understands that some of the resentment that her stepmother had toward her was the way she came from nowhere into Deadwood as a very fashionable woman.

> Here I was, coming from the East, with a mother who had dressed me exotically from the time I was a child, and I knew how to dress and be strikingly dressed, differently dressed, and had dressmakers who could . . . make me clothes that fitted me. And my mother, . . . if she saw a pattern she liked and some cloth, she would just like as not turn it over to a dressmaker, who was a wonderful, wonderful dressmaker, who could make me a dress, ship it to me and it would fit me perfectly. Some clothes were always six months to a year ahead of South Dakota, which made me unusual. And I don't blame her [my stepmother] for resenting me. And my father took me, very obviously was showing me off, and I was a brat enough to like it, too.

In this context Julia made friends with several local girls of her age and class. They took advantage of Deadwood's social life, attending the theater and dances. They also went on outings together, sometimes to accompany Julia's father on a short trip, and played bridge with the family. Julia was particularly fond of Dorothea, who was not a lesbian although she had an extended affair with Julia. Julia would have liked to have made it more serious, but Dorothea was not interested. She thought it would be too difficult to lead a life outside of marriage.

Originally, Julia's father wanted her to remain a woman of leisure who accompanied him on his trips, learning about and helping with his business. Once the Depression hit, his perspective was particularly sensible, since there were few jobs available for a young female college graduate. Although Julia was enjoying her life of leisure, she was not completely comfortable in it. When one of her circle of friends who was teaching in a mining camp became sick, Julia applied and was hired to replace her. "I liked it, I liked it. And I thought it was exciting to be living in this little mining camp." Julia was reappointed the second year, after which her father pressured her to leave and return to a life of leisure. She decided to use this time to study in Chicago. Her father, wanting her close by, used his influence to find her a teaching position in Deadwood. She was offered one at the last minute, and she took it.

Julia's mother had insisted that she prepare herself at Elmira College to be a teacher. She remembers her mother saying:

> "I'm going to ask one thing of you—I want you to take enough education courses so that you will qualify for a teacher's license." And evidently, I had looked skeptically at her, because she ended up by saying, "Remember, Julia, that if I hadn't had my teacher's license I never would have been able to have taken care of you and grandma. . . . I had my license and I could teach, and I want you to be able to teach."

In this environment Julia took for granted that she would be competent and independent—and in fact, all the women on her mother's side of the family were. Not only was her mother a teacher, but her great-aunt, who had helped to raise her, had been a teacher in Nebraska before her marriage, and was a suffragist and a member of the Woman's Christian Temperance Union. In time her father, too, came to accept her teaching, and even encouraged her to pursue her master's degree during the summers.

It was while teaching in Deadwood that Julia met Dorothy. This was a turning point in her life, and it was her first serious love. Until this time Julia considered herself isolated from other lesbians. She did not consider her "escapades" as having provided a lesbian friendship or relationship. "And frankly, other than my own personal feeling, and until Dorothy came into my life, I had very little to do with any lesbian people after I left college. See, I was isolated." Thus, in looking back Julia clearly distinguishes between sexual encounters with women and more stable lesbian relationships in a context of continuous contact with lesbians, even if the word was never spoken.

Julia still vividly recalls how she met Dorothy:

> Six or seven [teachers lived in the big hotel in town]. . . . They always went over to the hotel for lunch at noon, and those teachers always came over from the hotel and came in the . . . side door of the school so they had to go past my first grade. I was always assigned to be in the doorway with the first graders as they came in. And there were three or four teachers who came in, and I spotted this one, and I was immediately attracted. She taught Latin and French. It was Dorothy—her blue eyes and her hair. She had dark—her hair was curly, and no matter what she did with it, no matter what she did with it, it curled. No matter how she had it cut or whether it was wet or dry it curled. And she had the most beautiful blue eyes. She was tall, rather slender, and she dressed very nicely—she had wonderful taste. And there was just something about her along with the others, they all came in, in a group, she just was there and that was it. So during that year when I was teaching first grade . . . I got so I didn't go home for lunch, I would go over to the hotel with the girls and the teachers there and have lunch with them, so that I got to know Dorothy. And Dorothy was, she was quiet and she had a wonderful wit, and it was sharp. We liked the same kind of poetry, and the teachers, because there were these seven or eight of them up there, they hung together, they did things together.

Julia and Dorothy began their life together in 1930. Her relationship with Dorothy did not dramatically change Julia's relationship with her father. She continued to travel with him, though to a more limited extent since her teaching job didn't allow her time off during the week. And she no longer had affairs with women on these trips. Now she and her father aided and abetted each other's sexual interests in other ways. She was a cover for her father, just as he was for her. Dorothy's roommate, Helen, became quite smitten with Julia's father, who began an affair with her. Normally he didn't have affairs with women in Deadwood, so he had to be careful.

> What happened was, Helen fell for my father. So for all that winter and spring it was a foursome. Dorothy, Helen, and I would start out in Dorothy's car, my father would start out in his car, we would meet some place or another, and I don't know when my father got home and Dorothy and I didn't care. So it was a nice foursome, it worked out very nicely. And you'll see some pictures of Helen and Dorothy and me and we all were having fun. . . . That's the reason why she's in the pictures, because we were together, the three of us were traveling together a great deal of the time.[19]

Julia was unquestionably protective of her father. She says, "Dorothy and I kind of kept [Helen] under, kept her locked down." Julia's father helped her materially as well. For instance, Dorothy was in a deteriorating relationship with a teacher in Rapid City when she met Julia. A stumbling block to ending the relationship was the fact that the two had bought a car together. Dorothy used the car regularly but did not have the money to buy her partner out. Unknown to Julia and Dorothy, Julia's father went to see Dorothy's partner and paid off the car. He wanted his daughter to be happy.

There were no other lesbians among the teachers in town, but there were three other "odd" couples, which is the term Julia thinks she and her acquaintances would have used back then. She and Dorothy became friends with one such couple who were closest to them in age and class. One of the women was the daughter of a doctor in town. And after college, "she brought [home] this obvious—so obvious that it was too obvious, almost—dyke, and they settled in," Julia recalls. "Then I know there were eyebrows raised." But there were no sanctions. Rather, the doctor bought his daughter a building for a beauty parlor, and in time she and her partner set up a sauna, with a ladies' afternoon once a week. Julia remembers the importance of the sauna to their lives as lesbians:

> Well, they decided that they would start a sauna of their own, so they established a sauna in connection with their hair salon, and it was quite popular with the ladies, because they didn't have to go up to where the big sauna was, which was obviously for men, built for men and masculine. And they [the couple] lived in the apartment, in one of the two apartments upstairs over it, and they rented out the next apartment. Well, when Dorothy, the first year that I went to teach in Deadwood and I met Dorothy, and fell in love with her and she with me, I was having the girls do my hair. And Dorothy said, well she always had somebody in Rapid City do her hair, [but] she would try them, and so we both of us used to go to the sauna together. And of course that led us immediately to the fact that the other two were lesbians, so there were the four of us. We would very often go late in the afternoon for our sauna and then the four of us would have dinner together. Now we talked about everything but being homosexuals. . . . Never talked about it. Maybe occasionally, Heidi [who] was the older of the two of them, Heidi would say, well, I left something good down in Denver . . . something like that, but it was never, we never talked about it. And this is what I keep saying to so many, many people, in that period of time it just wasn't talked about. We knew it existed, we accepted it or didn't accept it, but it was there.

Julia and Dorothy's close group of friends included Helen, and a substitute teacher and her self-employed husband. Julia recalls that this was a forward-looking straight couple who shocked the town of Deadwood when the man had a vasectomy, because he and his wife had two children and didn't want more. Together these friends were adventurous and fun-loving. One of Julia's favorite stories is about the evening they decided to alter a sign by the road leading out of Deadwood. The sign said "Prepare to meet thy God." They climbed the rocks and changed it to "Prepare to make thy goddess." Julia was very happy during this period of her life:

> The second year I taught in Deadwood was kind of a wonderful year, because we [Dorothy and I] were together; my father aided and abetted me. Of course I was aiding and abetting him. And we [Dorothy and I] were both of us talking about . . . starting our master's, and we decided we'd go to Wisconsin instead of Chicago. Helen decided she'd go to Wisconsin and start her master's degree, the three of us would go. That was the year that . . . the couple that had the hair dressing [salon] opened the sauna, and Dorothy and Helen were going to take an apartment, which would have made it much nicer for the three of us. And I knew that it was a bad year for my father, because he began to do some heavy drinking. He was traveling an awful lot, to New York and Chicago and St. Louis, so I knew there was a lot of stress, as far as the Depression, the stock crash happened. But I was in such . . . euphoria is right. Lots of things just went over my head—you know, this was it.

Julia's father died suddenly as the result of an infected tooth, right before she was to leave for Wisconsin for summer school. Two weeks later she left Deadwood permanently.

Julia's life in Deadwood goes against much of the received wisdom about women in this period: her sexual energy; her ability to live an active and full lesbian life while not being public; her Protestant upbringing, which supported as well as repressed her lesbianism; and her positive relationship with her parents. Since this is only one woman's life, we could view it as exceptional and disregard its implications for women's and lesbian and gay history. But her life was not isolated—it involved friendships and relationships with many other lesbians at all stages of her life. Julia has wonderful photographs documenting her friendships, loves, and escapades, and her daughter, Julia Reinstein, has met many of the people in these stories. Julia's life, therefore, can be taken as a starting point for reevaluating or rethinking lesbianism in the 1920s and 1930s

From the perspective of the late twentieth century it is extraordinary that such extensive lesbian activity could remain a private part of an individual's life and not become public. Julia's memories of life in Deadwood suggest that this was possible not only because of her own careful discretion, but also because the complicity of heterosexuals sustained the blurred line between ignorance and knowledge about matters of sexuality. Together these created the interstices where lesbian life could flourish. Julia herself has often wondered how she and her friends managed to live the life they did. Fifteen years ago she and an old friend talked about it:

> The only conclusion we could come to was the families had money. They had social prestige, and we were not too obvious. I think that was it. They may have talked about us behind our backs, and probably did—in fact I know they did, because mother got upset a couple times when somebody made a crack about "Julia not marrying Bob Sterns in Castile," who was five years younger than I and gay. He taught with me in Castile, and I guess we covered for each other. He went around with me and everybody thought we should get married. And a couple people said something to mother about it and made mother angry. But under normal circumstances that was all it was [talk]. We never felt discriminated against.

Julia's discretion, her not being "obvious," was governed by two rules—first, to publicly behave as a respectful heterosexual daughter, to the extent that was possible without marrying, and second, never to talk about lesbianism. While they constructed female-centered lives, Julia and her friends followed most of the social rules of heterosexual society. They socialized with their parents. They played bridge with family members and went to the theater and to the many dances. At these dances she and Dorothy could dance together, because there were usually more women than men and women often danced together. But they also danced with others, including some men. This did not trouble Julia, who loved to dance and loved to dress in the manner of a "proper lady." Good behavior was expected of women of her class, particularly of teachers. She was used to these gender expectations and did not find them terribly confining. For a woman such as Julia, being a lesbian was just one aspect of her life, albeit an important one. Coming out publicly, being more obvious, would have been more of a burden than a freedom. In most ways her discretion did not limit her life or make it unpleasant. By accepting these rules, Julia received all the benefits and privileges of her class. Furthermore, they allowed her to live without stigma.

Proper behavior for a daughter of this class was unquestionably a key ingredient for acceptance. The partner of the doctor's daughter did not follow these rules by the way she looked or behaved, and Julia remembers "there were some eyebrows raised." In time, the town excluded her from its social circles.

> But the one who came up from Denver, she didn't like to play cards and she didn't like social work, she was an outdoors person anyway. . . . She'd just take off and hide. . . .

> And we just accepted it. When there was a party, she just wasn't invited—that was all,
> we knew she wasn't going to come. She wouldn't come, so we never invited her.

Julia is uncertain what happened to this couple, but she knows they did not remain in Deadwood in the bosom of the doctor's family. A few years after Julia left, the couple followed a religious cult to New York City.

What does it mean that Julia and her friends never talked about lesbianism? They felt that the only appropriate setting for the discussion of love between women was in the context of an intimate relationship between lovers. Lesbian couples who were friends rarely talked about lesbianism together. They never talked, for instance, about the four "odd" couples in the town. Julia explains, "Now at that point, even after I got out of college . . . we didn't talk about lesbianism. We just didn't talk about it, and I don't know why. . . . It's very curious." And lesbianism was certainly not talked about with heterosexual people. Although Julia's father and mother knew about her lesbianism and were comfortable with it, giving her freedom and support, they rarely talked about it. Julia thinks that in her entire stay in Deadwood lesbianism was not mentioned in public. She could only recall one vague reference: Once, her group of friends that included the forward-looking straight couple had planned to take some peyote (plans that never came to fruition), and the man wondered about the effect of peyote on "you girls." Nothing more was said, but Julia assumed that he was referring not to their gender but to their lesbian relationships.[20]

Julia and her friends' avoidance of the subject, and even the term *lesbian*, in conversation seems to be a general strategy of all private lesbians. It seems reasonable that lesbians should avoid public discussion of the topic, due to social norms about the privacy of sexuality and the stigma attached to being lesbian. But why would lesbians avoid discussion among friends? Faderman suggests that the prohibition showed whether you could be trusted to keep quiet in the public realm ("You didn't belong if you were the blabbermouth type"). But it seems that the prohibition is even deeper than that. By using the word *lesbian* they would hasten the naming of themselves as a distinct kind of person and the inevitability of emergence in the public world. The consequences of this naming would be dramatic—it would mean losing extensive social privileges, perhaps the most important of which was acceptance by family and society.

Discretion was an organizing principle not simply in Julia's behavior, but also in her family's. Thus, in Deadwood, her father attempted to accept and protect her, and other townspeople willingly ignored or avoided the obvious signs that she was not a typical heterosexual daughter. Her family respected her privacy and supported her pursuit of the life she wanted. This protection is key for keeping lesbianism in the private realm. In effect, it created a buffer zone between Julia and the judgments of the outside world. In addition, the privacy was maintained by other heterosexuals' ignorance or, if they were knowledgeable, their complicity in supporting her parents' position. Julia tries to capture this complicated environment between those who "know" and those who don't.

> Yeah, then there was another couple that I didn't know too well. One of them was obviously
> [lesbian]. She and her father and her uncle worked a very little . . . gold mine. And then they
> had a housekeeper, and I heard some of the women saying disparagingly, "Oh well, she
> probably goes to bed with Andy's father," like that. But the girl and the housekeeper were
> lovers. . . . I knew it, but the rest of the town—see, again, the town was so square that they
> didn't. There was a definite difference between the men who were in the mining game, or
> that kind, and the women who were there because their husbands were there.

Julia assumes that many of the wives in the town were more ignorant than the men. She thinks her stepmother did not suspect her lesbianism, because she was a strict Catholic who had a very limited knowledge about the world or about sexuality or even her own body. At the same time we can assume that there were also people in Deadwood who, like Julia's father and the many women she had slept with in larger cities, were knowledgeable about the existence of lesbianism because the topic was discussed in medical journals, newspapers, theater, and literature of the times. Such people seemed to accept it, as did Julia's father and the father of the woman who owned the beauty parlor, treating it like marital indiscretion. They assumed that sexual life was private and one could do what one wanted as long as one had the power to protect oneself. Those who did not accept sexual relations among women chose to ignore Julia's behavior because they did not intend to challenge the morality and respectability of the daughter of one of the wealthiest men in town. The family's reputation meant that others would not be too critical, and also that the family would stand behind their own, as long as nothing was too obvious. People might have talked or "raised their eyebrows," but nothing much came of it.

Since Deadwood was a relatively new and booming western town, it is possible that it offered more interstices for lesbian life than more traditionally conservative small towns in western New York. But that doesn't seem to be the case. With few additions and variations the same social formations of discretion seem to have been at work for lesbians and heterosexuals when Julia returned to western New York after her father died. Julia was discreet and behaved as a proper lady, she and her friends did not talk about lesbianism, and her mother and stepfather protected her, welcoming her partner, Dorothy, into their house. That system was effective even while Julia was teaching in Castile, New York, a most conservative town (the only town in Wyoming County that forbade the sale of liquor). During this period a new ingredient was added to the construction of discretion: the use of a gay man as a cover. When Julia and Bob, a gay teacher in the same school, became good friends, members of the town assumed they were engaged. Interestingly, this ruse was invented mostly by heterosexuals, either out of their ignorance or their desire to facilitate complicity, rather than by Julia and Dorothy themselves.

Boyer Reinstein's construction of and comfort with discretion was certainly not unique. She had a set of friends who more or less managed their lives in the same way. But there is evidence that similar patterns of discretion existed in the lives of other lesbians in the early twentieth century. Elsa Gidlow, who also recognized her lesbianism at a young age, lived a multifaceted, sexually active life in which her lesbianism was important but quite private. Born in 1899 in England, she forged a lesbian life in Canada as an adolescent and later in the United States (New York and California). Her childhood in a large working-class family was marked by poverty, and as a woman supporting herself in the early twentieth century without an education, she spent many years in poverty. Her goals and accomplishments in the literary world, however, brought her in contact with a middle-class circle of friends with similar interests. Gidlow was always clear about her interests in women but was not public about it. She also had ties with some gay men who fostered her artistic work and offered her support at key times in her life. She never had a community of lesbian friends; she avoided the bars and did not cultivate a "masculine" identity. It was not that she ever denied who she was; she simply did not announce it or discuss it. Her friends respected each other's privacy. In contrasting her early life with the culture of gay liberation, she writes:

> I am not saying it was better then, although in some ways it was more comfortable. Perhaps it was the San Francisco circles we moved in, but it did seem that in those days civilized persons respected one another's privacies. Some may call this elitist. I can only say if live-and-let-live good manners are elitist, let's learn from elitism.
>
> I think it was more comfortable then because we did not have to be ever-conscious of being in somebody's sexual spotlight. However, speaking for myself and other women I

knew intimately, we were *not* repressed and we were not ashamed of our erotic needs. There are too many erroneous assumptions today concerning women of earlier decades. What was important to me and my intimates then, as it continues to be, was not orgasm, but shared loyalties. I and my lesbian friends took it for granted that our primary loyalty and support was to women.[21]

At the core of her characterization of her life is the idea of respect for privacy that was shared by lesbians and heterosexuals in her circle of friends. They simply did not discuss the details of each other's private lives. In addition, Gidlow is questioning the value of identification by sexuality alone, and the stigma that results from being known only as a sexual being. This explanation of how lesbians and heterosexuals constructed discretion is quite parallel to Boyer Reinstein's. The major difference is that Gidlow did not come from a wealthy family and she never developed a close circle of lesbian friends. It was not her family who protected her, but rather the artistic circles that she moved in, reinforcing the common assumption that artists have been traditionally hospitable to homosexuals.[22] This suggests that the structures of discretion are varied and dependent on specific social contexts.

Boyer Reinstein's memories and reflections indicate that the sites of lesbian desire were multiple in the first half of the twentieth century; that they included the rural areas of New York and South Dakota; that they were intertwined with traditional Presbyterian families, even families who were Daughters of the American Revolution; that they were compatible with the profession of schoolteaching. In most cases private lesbians consciously considered themselves sexual beings and built meaningful relationships that included sexuality, but this was only one aspect of their lives. Their lesbianism was hidden at that time, and therefore to history, by complex structures of discretion that played with the fundamental division between public and private in modern American life and allowed them to escape being characterized primarily on the basis of their sexuality. This evidence suggests that in the 1920s and 1930s the social dichotomies of heterosexuality and homosexuality were not yet hegemonic. Concomitantly, the closet was not fully institutionalized. For many segments of the upper class all sexuality was a personal matter; public hints were gracefully ignored. Lesbian liaisons were not much different from heterosexual infidelities. In some contexts the traditions of discretion were very freeing, allowing lesbians to lead lives fully incorporated into the dominant society while still developing woman-centered spaces. But, unlike the protection offered extramarital affairs, such arrangements were fragile, easily disrupted by forces outside an individual's control. In certain situations discretion can become quite restrictive and limiting.

Julia Boyer Reinstein's life dramatically shows these limits. After almost thirty years as an active lesbian, a confluence of circumstances left her isolated, with the traditions of discretion offering her no way out. She started a new teaching job in Buffalo in the 1940s, away from her friends and family, and her girlfriend left her for someone else. It was not easy for her to find other female companionship unless she was willing to become more public, which she was not. In time the pressure from a widower became overwhelming, and she married. Without the interstices created by the protection of family and the good behavior of friends, the "closet" slammed shut, requiring women to embrace the stigma of lesbianism, to live completely hidden lives governed by fear of exposure, or to leave lesbian life completely. In some respects the increasing public presence of lesbians as the century progressed made it less and less likely for a fluid relationship between public and private, knowledge and ignorance, and in and out of the closet to persist.

This rigidity is a concrete manifestation of what is meant by the dichotomy between heterosexual and homosexual becoming hegemonic. Boyer Reinstein's life in South Dakota (like that of Gidlow) is rich with sexual possibility and connections among women, yet it is suffused with discretion. As such it helps us, the descendants of gay liberation and identity politics, to see beyond a dichotomized sexuality, and it allows us to imagine what it might mean to live without the stigma of sexual difference.

Notes

1. The "New Woman" refers to the two generations of women involved in the transition from the nineteenth to the twentieth century. As a result of the nineteenth-century women's movement, women began to enter the public sphere during this period. The New Woman was part of the social changes that began to give women some autonomy in the public sphere. She was struggling for women's right to earn a living, gain an education, control their reproduction, and finally to vote. See, for instance, Carroll Smith-Rosenberg, "Discourses of Sexuality and Subjectivity: The New Woman, 1870–1936," in Martin Bauml Duberman, Martha Vicinus, and George Chauncey, eds., *Hidden from History: Reclaiming the Gay and Lesbian Past* (New York: New American Library, 1989), 264–81.

2. This article is part of a larger research project in which I aim to write the life story of Julia Boyer Reinstein. It is based on more than forty hours of oral history tapes I collected from 1994 to 1996. Of necessity one article can't capture the full complexity of Julia's life. Many interesting and relevant topics must be set aside to focus on the construction of discretion in a specific period of time and location.

3. Although I avoid the term *closet*, my approach is influenced a great deal by the writing of Eve Kosofsky Sedgwick, who has explicated the centrality of the closet to twentieth-century culture. I particularly appreciate the subtlety with which she deconstructs the simple binarism of "in" and "out," showing the contested nature of permissible speech about gayness in American history and of the relationship between knowledge and ignorance in matters of sexuality (*The Epistemology of the Closet* [Berkeley: University of California Press, 1990]).

4. Elizabeth Lapovsky Kennedy and Madeline Davis, *Boots of Leather, Slippers of Gold: The History of a Lesbian Community* (New York: Routledge, 1993).

5. Elsa Gidlow, *Elsa: I Come with My Songs: The Autobiography of Elsa Gidlow* (San Francisco: Booklegger Press, 1986).

6. The power of the gay liberation framework to erase or to caricature as pathetic other interesting forms of lesbian and gay life is worth noting. Throughout my work in lesbian and gay history, I have encountered interesting incidents suggesting that many people who led private gay lives found them completely satisfying, not oppressive, which I puzzled over briefly, then dismissed as examples of false consciousness or lack of appreciation of the benefits of being out. It was particularly hard on middle-class or bourgeois women who had to remain closeted to keep their jobs. In the late 1970s I remember discussing with members of the San Francisco Gay and Lesbian History Project the strange responses of several older lesbians who were loathe to be interviewed. We couldn't understand their claim that they were reluctant to share memories about their lives as lesbians because the secret was part of the beauty or excitement of being lesbian. Similarly, in the early 1990s when I was part of the planning conference for the Stonewall 25 museum exhibitions, I could not quite digest a conversation I heard between Martin Duberman and a curator for the theater collection at one of the museums. They were about the same age, and they were arguing about whether the thirties, forties, and fifties had been oppressive. The curator took the position that, as part of the theater world, in his experience life for gays had been fun, but Duberman viewed the period as extremely repressive, because people were stigmatized and could not be "out." At the time, I was amazed such a disagreement was possible, and I fliply decided the curator had false consciousness or that he liked his oppression.

7. See, for instance, Judith Butler, "Imitation and Gender Insubordination," in Henry Abelove, Michele Aina Barale, and David M. Halperin, eds., *The Lesbian and Gay Studies Reader*, ed. (New York: Routledge, 1993), 307–20; and Shane Phelan, "Becoming Out: Lesbian Identity and Politics," *Signs* 18, 4 (1993): 765–90.

8. Smith-Rosenberg, "Discourses of Sexuality."

9. Esther Newton, "The Mythic Mannish Woman: Radclyffe Hall and the New Woman," in *Hidden from History*, 281–93.

10. Martha Vicinus also points out the problems in this argument, noting that other forms of lesbianism clearly existed in the early twentieth century ("'They Wonder to Which Sex I Belong': The Historical Roots of the Modern Lesbian Identity," *The Lesbian and Gay Studies Reader*, 432–52).

11. Leila Rupp, "'Imagine My Surprise': Women's Relationships in Mid-twentieth Century America," in *Hidden from History*, 395–410.

12. Lillian Faderman, *Odd Girls and Twilight Lovers: A History of Lesbian Life in Twentieth-Century America* (New York: Columbia University Press, 1991), 109.

13. Faderman, 109.

14. In the introduction and the conclusion of this paper I abbreviate Julia Boyer Reinstein's name as "Boyer Reinstein," but in the body of the paper I use "Julia." I discussed the issue of using first or last names with Boyer Reinstein, who said the decision was up to me. The only thing was that she wanted to be called "Boyer Reinstein," rather than "Reinstein," if I decided to use her last name. She has frequently used the double last name, at her husband's suggestion, ever since she was married. He and his mother were worried the Germans would invade the United States during World War II and that they would be high on the list of those likely to be killed. They wanted Julia to use "Boyer Reinstein" on official documents so that, if necessary, she could take her stepchildren, flee to Canada, and go back to using her maiden name. Boyer Reinstein also said she feels that even though she was "Mrs. Reinstein" for a long time, she never completely denied her lesbian side, so "Boyer Reinstein" is more appropriate.

    I switch to "Julia" in the body of the paper, which relies primarily on oral history to better capture the familiarity of that context, and because she refers to many of her friends by their first names. To use their surnames would distort the quality of her recollections (and in some cases, Julia had forgotten the last names).

15. When the company acquired local plants, the plants kept their local names, becoming subsidiaries of Consolidated Power and Light.

16. Julia also met Willa Cather through her father's acquaintances. Cather had a greater impact on Julia's life, encouraging and inspiring her in her works as a historian.

17. I probed during our interviews to determine if any of these encounters were perhaps coerced, in the sense that the partners felt obligated to be with Julia or she with them, but Julia said she was certain they were not. If there wasn't mutual interest, she slept alone or was free to decline. "If I had somebody that I didn't particularly like, I just spent the evening and came back to the hotel, and maybe I would say goodnight to my father out in the hall and walk in my room, and he and his girlfriend walked in their room." I would imagine that having a room next to her father's made it unlikely that anyone would force himself or herself on her.

18. Faderman, *Odd Girls and Twilight Lovers*, 62–93. For other information on women's willingness to explore relationships with women, see Katharine Bement Davis, *Factors in the Sex Life of Twenty-Two Hundred Women* (New York: Harper and Row, 1929).

19. At another point in the interview, Julia mentioned a variation of this arrangement. Julia and her father would leave the house with the pretext of going to some business-related meeting or weekend. Somewhere out of town, they would hook up with Dorothy and Helen. Julia would join Dorothy and Helen would join Julia's father, and they would agree to meet later to return.

20. Julia couldn't remember the name of the group, but she said she was sure it was one in which whites did support work for African Americans.

21. Gidlow, *Elsa*, 302–3.

22. The lesbians who were part of the founding of Cherry Grove, as documented by Esther Newton in *Cherry Grove, Fire Island*, are another interesting group to compare with Boyer Reinstein and her friends. The Cherry Grove women were all upper class; they emphasized discretion and were not part of the tradition of mannish lesbians (*Cherry Grove, Fire Island: Sixty Years in America's First Gay and Lesbian Town*, [New York: Beacon 1993]). They were careful not to be too obvious. Many were married and insisted on being addressed as "Mrs. So-and-so." In New York City they lived very "respectable" lives, but in Cherry Grove, a resort removed from the strictures of everyday life, they were able to live openly as lesbians. But it is possible that their lives away from the resorts were quite similar to Boyer Reinstein's and her friends', a topic worth further exploration. bell hooks' discussion of the treatment of gays and lesbians in mid-century southern black communities suggests that poverty and the need for community solidarity might create structures of discretion in the rural south that are similar to those of Boyer Reinstein ("Homophobia in Black Communities," *Talking Back: Thinking Feminist, Thinking Black* [Boston: South End Press, 1989] 120–26). This phenomenon also deserves further study.

28

Open Secrets: Memory, Imagination, and the Refashioning of Southern Identity

Jacquelyn Dowd Hall

> Some stories simply come and take you, occupy you, make you work out again and again what it is they mean, and the meaning of your own obsession with them.
>
> —Carolyn Steedman, *Past Tense*

> The purpose of all interpretation is to conquer a remoteness, a distance between the past cultural epoch and the interpreter himself. By overcoming this distance . . . the exegete can appropriate its meaning to himself; foreign, he makes it familiar, that is, he makes it his own. It is thus the growth of his own understanding of himself that he pursues through his understanding of others.
>
> —Paul Ricoeur, *The Conflict of Interpretations*

> Me and you, we got more yesterdays than anybody. We need some kind of tomorrow.
>
> —Toni Morrison, *Beloved*

For most of the twentieth century black Americans abandoned the southern countryside in a steady, ever-widening stream. In the 1970s this exodus suddenly turned back upon itself. By 1990 the South had regained a half million black citizens from the cities of the North and West. Many came home not to the booming cities of the Sunbelt, but to the stripped and devastated counties of the rural South.

In *Call to Home*, an uplifting, heartbreaking book about this startling reversal, the anthropologist Carol Stack offers a meditation on the power of place and the gallantry of people who—under the most crushing circumstances—are struggling to remake the South in their own images. Pushed from the Rust Belt that used to be the Promised Land, pulled by the dread and longing with which the South has always filled its daughters and sons, these women and men find themselves on a "redemptive mission"—a mission that confronts them both with the ghosts of a palpable past and with their own emerging sense of who they are and want to be. Earl Hydrick, one of the storytellers in Stack's book, put it this way: When you go home, "you go back to your proving ground, the place where you had that first cry, gave that first punch you had to throw in order to survive." Eula Grant, a day care crusader in eastern North Carolina, says, "You definitely can go home again. You can go back. But you don't start from where you left. To fit in, you have to create another place in that place you left behind."[1]

Call to Home takes seriously the imaginative, performative, and political aspects of a process that social scientists usually see as a one-dimensional response to economic push and pull. The stories told by these return migrants contribute to a powerful literary tradition, a tradition of writing about the South as a longed-for—yet vexed and dangerous— home. Such stories are actions. They send people moving across the country, confounding

Figure 28.1. Katharine Du Pre Lumpkin. *Courtesy of the Southern Historical Collection, University of North Carolina.*

our expectations about migration and modernity. They influence not just individual lives but the unfolding of entire communities.

This essay is about an earlier turn to home. It is a story within a story: first, the story of Katharine Du Pre Lumpkin (Fig. 28.1), a white southerner who, as a sociologist, historian, and autobiographer, allied herself with the cause of racial justice and spent a lifetime trying to reconfigure the South as a place she could call home; second, the story of my entanglement with Katharine and her sisters. At both levels, what interests me is the power of "open secrets" as strategies of cultural amnesia—but also of reticence and love.

Born in Georgia in 1897, Katharine was the youngest of seven children in a dispossessed planter family, a family haunted by defeat, obsessed with race, and determined to win back the pride and power lost in the Civil War. Her father, William, fought with the Confederacy and then rode with the Ku Klux Klan. Reduced to working for the railroad, he moved his family to South Carolina, where he spent his life romanticizing slavery and promulgating the cult of the Lost Cause.[2]

Katharine's childhood was bathed in her father's memories; bittersweet, self-serving, and beguiling, they surrounded human bondage with a noxious golden glow. But memories are stories of experience, not experience itself, and his were shot through with the disquiet caused by Reconstruction, populism, and turn-of-the-century white supremacy campaigns. It took tremendous effort for men such as William Lumpkin to reconcile an early-twentieth-century present of intense racial and class alienation with a "dream replica" of a paternalistic past.[3] Katharine sensed that effort, those rifts and contradictions—and through them she would eventually slip into critical consciousness. She would have her own stories to tell.

It was, moreover, Katharine's mother and her older sister Elizabeth, a popular speaker on the Lost Cause circuit, who effectively carried forward the battle for public memory. William, in the end, became a pathetic figure, a relic of another age. His sons, embarrassed by their father's failure, chased after money. It fell to elite white women gathered in massive voluntary organizations, the most powerful of which was the United Daughters of the Confederacy, to assert their cultural authority over virtually every public representation of the southern past.[4] In their hands, the performance of southern identity secured the identification of southernness with whiteness. But it also carved out for white women a new public space.

Katharine and her sister Grace jettisoned the ideology of white supremacy and expanded that public space. Graduating from college at the end of World War I, each found her way to New York, where Katharine studied sociology at Columbia University and Grace wrote proletarian novels in which she reworked Lumpkin family history to attack every shibboleth that her parents defended. While Grace stayed on in Greenwich Village, weaving new identities from a swirl of sex, art, and revolution, Katharine returned home to lead the Young Women's Christian Association's (YWCA) unprecedented effort to build an interracial student movement in the South.

Eventually Katharine left the South again, first to complete a doctorate at the University of Wisconsin and then to settle in Northampton, Massachusetts. She entered the job market in the late 1920s, just as professionalization, discrimination, and depression combined to push women to the margins of the academy and stamp sociology as a masculine domain. Unable to secure a teaching position, she helped to found alternative institutions: first a Council of Industrial Studies at Smith College whose focus on women, family, and community foreshadowed the new labor history that would emerge in the 1970s; then an independent Institute of Labor Studies that tracked World War II developments in labor relations. The left-wing ferment of the 1930s inspired her to return to intellectual home ground—to the issues of race and region that had animated her work for the YWCA. Writing from the fringes of a New England college community that, as Katharine put it, still imagined southerners "with horns and forked tails," she "came out" as a southerner, first in a book called *The South in Progress* and then, in 1946, in *The Making of a Southerner*, the autobiography that became her major work.[5]

The South has always elicited from its writers and intellectuals what Fred Hobson aptly terms a "rage to explain."[6] Whether they looked back in pride, anger, or sorrow, most white southerners who committed themselves to print shared a belief in the region's categorical *difference* from the rest of the country. Katharine, by contrast, grew up in a family in which a static, unified, iconic South was an article of faith, and she understood all too well that idea's invidious ideological uses. The burden of her work is the essential Americanness of a large, diverse, and conflicted region, a region enmeshed in modernity and shaped by change.

Katharine's project, her lifelong endeavor, was to convince southerners and northerners alike to tell a new story, a story in which the South ceased to figure either as the not-modern—a landscape of nostalgia, a touchstone of yearning and loss—or as the nation's collective unconscious, the repository of American nightmares that America could not face. Both were dream states, and against them she deployed what she called the "plain . . . truths" of revisionism, a new southern history that turned the old tales upside down.[7] She took her cues from a small group of dissenters—men such as W. E. B. Du Bois and C. Vann Woodward—who were on the cusp of overturning the work of U. B. Phillips and William Dunning, towering figures who had forged a North-South consensus around a story of paternalistic slaveholders and the criminal outrages of Reconstruction. But unlike the revisionists—indeed, unlike most historians of the South to the present day—she placed a woman at the center of southern history. Taking herself as her subject, she sought to problematize "whiteness," to denaturalize racism, and to show how race is grounded in the child. Above all, she sought to trace the messy process by which consciousness changes, with all its backward and forward movements, its ground gained and then lost, its beachheads rarely secured once and for all.

Race, writes Dominick LaCapra, is "a feeble mystification with formidable effects." Those effects arise, Tessie P. Liu argues, in part from the historical association between race and kinship, one of the fundamental organizing principles of human societies. Before contact with non-Western peoples, Europeans arranged themselves hierarchically along kinship lines. Power flowed from lineage. A child was marked indelibly by the privileges, entitlements, and stigmas of birth. As Europeans came to define themselves as "white" in contrast to subjugated others, skin color superseded bloodlines as the marker that drew diverse peoples together in a privileged community. Yet the older formulation lived on; assimilated and transformed, it gave emotional power to the metaphor of race as a substance passed on by fathers in legitimate line.[8] It was this potent association between race, home, family, and kindred, this deep structure of racial reasoning, that Katharine used autobiography both to represent and to undo.

When *The Making of a Southerner* appeared in paperback, Katharine chose for the cover a turn-of-the-century image of herself as a child (Fig. 28.2). The girl in the photograph seems incandescent, from her cloud of blond hair to her long lacy dress. Yet there is no remnant here of a treasured plantation past, not a jasmine or a magnolia in sight. A tree splits the scene; the border is patrolled by a dark spiky fence. Weeds brush the child's feet, her hand rests on the edge of a huge wooden barrel half–filled with dead leaves. Swaddled in whiteness yet confined by fences and dwarfed by obelisks, she is a daughter not of the Old South but of the New, now living in rented houses and playing on sad, sparse lawns. She glances to her right with a doubtful, questioning expression. She is poised to step forward, out of the frame.[9]

Katharine's protagonist is this vulnerable, watchful girl, at the mercy of good people who create monstrous systems, drilled in a racism, as she put it, that "takes hold of us . . . through our loyalties, affections . . . [and] ideals." But she is also the writer who claims the authority to tell this tale. Taught to believe that the plantation South was the real South, haunted by the dogma "that but one way was Southern, and hence there could be but one kind of Southerner," Katharine could not, it seemed to her, turn against her "old heritage of racial beliefs" without turning against her own people. In the end, she writes, it was the discovery of a different heritage—that of the "white millions whose forbears had never owned slaves," and the "Negro millions whose people had been held in slavery"—"that drew me to my refashioning."[10]

As Katharine tells it, there were two moments in particular on which her refashioning turned. The first shocked her into color consciousness; the sec-

Figure 28.2. Katharine Du Pre Lumpkin. *Courtesy of the Southern Historical Collection, University of North Carolina.*

ond confronted her with the injuries of class. Together they helped to create a structure of feeling in which new, emancipatory stories could take root and grow.

The first moment occurred when she was six years old. Playing in the yard one summer morning, she suddenly heard a terrible noise. "Sounds," she remembered, "to make my heart pound and my hair prickle at the roots. Calls and screams were interspersed with blow upon blow. Soon enough I knew someone was getting a fearful beating." Peeking in the kitchen window, Katharine saw the family's black cook

> writhing under the blows of a descending stick wielded by the white master of the house. I could see her face distorted with fear and agony and his with stern rage. I could see her twisting and turning as she tried to free herself from his firm grasp.[11]

That "white master," whom Katharine leaves unnamed in her account of this incident, was, of course, her father. The beating was an open secret, omnipresent but never spoken of in the family. There were no repercussions from the outside world.

Eventually, this scene—a tiny woman, a furious man, the thud of a stick on flesh and bone—would reverberate backward, causing Katharine to revise her inherited views of slavery and of the heroism of the Klan. At the time, however, it had a more convoluted result. It made her anxious to distance herself from people to whom such things could be done. To a girl who was herself subject to the disciplinary power of adults, the spectacle of the whipped black woman was horrifying in part because of the dangerous possibilities it represented. Her father, a man for whom chivalry toward women was an article of faith, could do this: He could beat a woman because she was black.[12] "Thereafter," she recalled, "I began to be self-conscious about the . . . signs and symbols of my race position," signs and symbols that policed the line between black and white.[13]

Longing, as all children do, to feel at one with her surroundings, Katharine tried to forget the dissonant image of violence in the kitchen, at the center of family life. But never again could she enfold herself quite so securely in her family's assumptions about the benevolence of patriarchy and the righteous superiority of their race. Never again could her home of origin be so simply a safe, sheltering place. Her confidence had been fissured as if by an earthquake, leaving on one side innocence and trust and on the other mixed feelings, and, faintly at first, the hairline cracks of doubt.[14]

Those doubts were widened in a most unlikely place—on a farm in the poverty–stricken Sand Hills of South Carolina, to which Katharine's family moved in 1909, when she was eleven years old. This sojourn represented William's last desperate attempt to recapture the glories of the plantation past. But three months later he died of throat cancer, leaving his wife and children to make a living on two hundred acres of God–forsaken land.

In the Sand Hills Katharine found herself, for the first time, in close proximity to the black and white rural poor. Freed of her father's influence just as she reached adolescence, she saw things around her that she might not otherwise have seen. She watched the black washerwomen and field hands come and go as strangers—a far cry from the cheerful, devoted slaves that her father's nostalgic stories had conjured up. To be sure, she was used to black poverty, but in the Sand Hills her white playmates were also hobbled by destitution—a destitution that the logic of racial thinking could not excuse or explain.[15]

Katharine had learned the meaning of whiteness—as a metaphor for family, a mark of privilege, and a boundary between herself and others that must, at all cost, be maintained—when she saw her father beat the cook. Now, to that secret imprint of racial violence, she added a perception of grinding *class* inequity—a perception that would, as it grew, denaturalize black poverty. For if white skin was no defense against immiseration, then the poverty of black people could not be blamed on the *racial* inferiority of the poor.

All of these doubts about the rightness of her world, however, might have come to nothing had Katharine chanced to be a student in less dynamic times. In college in north Georgia during World War I, she found herself swept up in the interracial student movement led by the YWCA. In the 1920s, traveling through the Jim Crow South with her black coworkers, she glimpsed the indignities of segregation from their point of view. She also glimpsed a new kind of solidarity, the solidarity that results from political effort, not from an affinity that is supposed to reside naturally in the members of a privileged group. Guided toward a leftist literature in sociology and economics by the YWCA's industrial secretaries, she learned to think of the South not as an icon but as a social system and to apply to it a critique of racism and capitalism that would grow more radical as time wore on.

I first stumbled upon *The Making of a Southerner* in the early 1970s. I was drawn to its mix of empathy and irony, to its gentle tone and elliptical style. Plainness, I thought, has its advantages, especially in a literature of regional self-discovery so given to mournful apologia and Gothic excess. But I was puzzled by the book's obscurity and its silences. It ended abruptly in the 1920s. Who and where was its author, I wondered, by the mid-1940s, when she turned to autobiography as social critique? And what were the lines of interinfluence among these fascinating sisters, each vying with the other to speak for her family and her region's past?

I met Grace before Katharine. I found her in a ramshackle farmhouse near King and Queen Courthouse, Virginia, a crossroads that could barely be called a town. It was early August, the paint was peeling, and the garden behind the house had gone to seed. A bright-eyed woman with wild yellow hair opened the ragged screen door when I knocked. She led me to what seemed less like a living room than a shrine, dominated by a portrait of Jacob Lumpkin, who had settled on crown lands in Virginia early in the eighteenth century. It was Jacob's grave that had drawn her to this place. I learned later that this was the house-with-a-garden of Grace's dreams, the old-fashioned cottage she had tried to conjure up when she lived with her lover (later her husband), Michael Intrator, in a brick walk-up in New York City on East Eleventh Street near Tompkins Square. But to me the house seemed decrepit and lonely drab browns and faded greens, bric-a-brac everywhere, an atmosphere of mildew and must. On the coffee table lay an inscribed copy of *Witness*, the story of her idol Whittaker Chambers, his sojourn in and out of the Communist Party, and his famous accusations against Alger Hiss. With Chambers as her mentor, Grace had joined in the orgy of confession through which former radicals purged themselves of their Communist pasts.[16]

Our conversation was as disconcerting as it was mesmerizing. Grace described her younger self as an innocent abroad, led astray not so much by the engaging young Communists she met in Greenwich Village as by Katharine—who was, she said, "always the radical one." Over and over, Grace had cut herself off from the past—when she left home in the 1920s, when she left the Party in the 1940s, when she moved to the Virginia countryside in the 1950s. Each move deepened her isolation, each required new layers of secrecy and rationalization. By the time I met her, she was so snarled in a web of deception that she had "forgotten" the barest outline of her life.[17]

I could hear the echo of the left-wing passions of the 1920s and 1930s in the voice of this isolated woman who still took herself seriously as a writer and who was absolutely certain of her ideas, however much those ideas now contradicted, even canceled out, the values that had produced her best work. Yet she struck me as an orphaned spirit, sustained, paradoxically, by the thin gruel of a past she had so willfully discarded.

She had always been a storyteller. Once she began to write, she spun her fiction out of autobiographical elements and patched together a personal history from half-truths and suggestions. The details were malleable; what mattered to Grace was artistic control. When I met her she was eighty-three years old. She could no longer drive, she was virtually penniless, and she was in the throes of a reluctant move to a retirement home in South Carolina, where most of her nieces and nephews still lived. The time was long past when she might have been willing or able to peel away the encrusted layers of memory, fantasy, and reality that had settled over what she had to tell. Looking back, I see the impossibility, even treachery, of basing my vision of Grace Lumpkin's life on this encounter in her later years. Still, I am grateful to have met her, twisted as she was by querulousness and resentment, yet clinging valiantly to the rural idyll she had salvaged from the wreck of her marriage, her politics, and her writing career.

Two hours away in Charlottesville, Katharine lived with her companion, Elizabeth Bennett, in a tiny house that they had furnished meticulously. There were books and magazines and polished antiques—all the trappings of a well-educated retired couple eager to stay current in a stimulating college town. No sign of ancestor worship, no atmosphere of mildew and must.

The years that Grace could—or would—only fleetingly conjure up Katharine willingly and vividly recalled. But when I shifted from the 1920s to questions about her relationship to her family and about her own activities after she left the South, she resisted, politely but firmly, with a fixed and practiced resolve.[18] Her reticence went further: Not only were there large areas about which she would not speak, but before she died she purged those same subjects from her papers, destroying not only much of her private correspondence but Grace's diary as well.

In the process, Katharine erased from the narrative of her life her relationship with Dorothy Douglas, a radical economist with whom she had shared her life in Northampton for almost thirty years. Gone were the years when she was cut off from her family, who felt betrayed by her revelations and refused to acknowledge her book. Gone also was what Lillian Hellman called "Scoundrel Time"—the 1950s, when Grace, called before the House Committee on Un-American Activities, had named names, apparently going so far as to finger Dorothy Douglas, thus colluding in a storm of red-baiting that silenced Katharine and shattered the life that she and Dorothy had so carefully built.[19]

Generation, profession, sexuality, and politics—all contributed to Katharine's reserve. She grew up in an era when telling secrets to strangers was not the pastime it has become today. She was trained in an objectivist sociology that denied emotion a role in the public self.[20] She lived her adult life in committed partnerships with women, over a period in which such relationships were medicalized, morbidized, sexualized, and finally celebrated—none of which was commensurate with how she saw herself. She was, moreover, protective of fragile ties to her family in South Carolina, fetters and lifelines that, especially in old age, she had labored to mend. No wonder she had been so ambivalent about being "discovered" by me. Word about my project had gone out on the grapevine. She had talked to old friends on the left about my motives: Was I really interested in them as "southern women activists," an identity they were eager to claim, or did I want to dredge up the charges of Communism that had wrecked their later lives? As with Grace, though for different reasons, the anti-Communism and homophobia of the 1950s had dropped a curtain between then and now. I kept up with Katharine in the years that followed, but our relationship never escaped that legacy: a habit of secrecy, a shadow of fear.

I never lost interest in the Lumpkin sisters, especially in Katharine, who had spent her life in a quest to understand, explain, and change a place that she always saw as home. But I found myself caught in the eddies of what seemed to be irreconcilable desires. I wanted to write about her; I also wanted to befriend her. The very reserve that stymied one desire evoked the other. You could say that I loved her for the secrets she did not want to tell. In the end, I was not courageous—or bloody-minded—enough to write about her while she was alive. And even now, as I take up the dropped threads of that project, my memory of our conversations confronts me with what is so tantalizing and poignant about biography: the feelings of loyalty and responsibility it generates, the intimacy it simultaneously frustrates and invites, the tension it produces between respect for privacy and lust for knowledge, the way it can position even the most respectful author as an intruder, a thief in the houses of the living and the dead.[21]

These dilemmas, moreover, are not limited to biography. They lie at the heart of scholarly procedures. We inherit an idea of truth as a buried secret, always out of reach. Scientists, psychoanalysts, historians—all rely on metaphors of interrogation. Truth lies outside of us, in the other—Mother Nature, the unconscious, the relics of another place and time. We wrest it from them violently.[22]

We can, however, draw on more democratic traditions. We can, for instance, conceive of truth not as a secret to be extracted but as understanding forged in dialogue. Such a conception situates our scholarship "in the realm of symbolic exchange"—exchange between the present and the past, between the scholar and the women about whom and to whom she talks and writes.[23]

As Katharine wrote, she could hear the hurt, disapproving voices of people she loved humming in her ears. For her, those voices personified the resistance that keeps a writer from writing: the withering voice that contests one's authority to interpret the past.[24] As for me, I never sit down to work on this project without feeling the power of open secrets as sites of not knowing as well as knowing and trying to situate myself in the productive, imaginative space between the two.

Katharine ended her autobiography in the mid-1920s in part to avoid calling attention to her sexuality and her politics—each of which would have undercut the moral and political authority of the autobiographical persona she sought to create. Lesbianism and Communism were, for Katharine, "open secrets": prevailing, omnipresent, but unspoken dimensions of her life that for me, writing women's history in the 1990s, it is unthinkable to ignore. There is, however, a big difference between reburying family secrets and perpetuating a tabloid culture of exposé that depends on fixed identities, on a series of either/ors. We *know* that the nuances of sexual difference go well beyond the polarities of gay and straight, well beyond the "was she or wasn't she" in which we have learned to think. But that does not make it any easier to honor silence as a speech act as eloquent as any other or to understand sexuality as an axis of difference in which "difference" encompasses the infinite varieties of desire.[25]

In *Epistemology of the Closet*, Eve Kosofsky Sedgwick argues that since the late nineteenth century same-sex desire has been *the* "open secret" of Western culture. The will to classify and regulate along the axes of homosexual/heterosexual has assumed primary importance—not just for a homosexual minority but for everyone—precisely because of the ways in which it has marked the categories of secrecy and disclosure, knowledge and ignorance. In Katharine's case, I cannot know in advance, perhaps can never know, how sexuality figured in her identity; nor can I ever know the full meaning to her of that other, related "open secret"—Dorothy's (and Katharine's, at least by association) involvement with the Communist Party. What I can do, however, is confront both questions directly. I can also admit the sound of doubt, the crack in the author's self-assurance that breaks the spell of biography—the spell that lies in its promise to reveal whole and hidden truths.[26] Finally, I can suggest that whatever we can or cannot know about these particular women, we do know that southern history, like all modern history, has been crosscut by valiant radicalisms and transgressive identities and desires.

Since *The Making of a Southerner* appeared in 1947, the American South has changed dramatically. Yet the *historiography* of the South remains a story of limits—a story of racism, of white male demagoguery, and of ugly electoral politics. This view of the South and of southern history has served a useful, perhaps invaluable purpose. It has allowed us to externalize and thus to expunge conditions that were American in scope without forfeiting our belief in America as a land of equality, innocence, and success.[27] That strategy, however, has grown tattered, irrelevant, and self-defeating. The last thirty years have exposed the national dimensions of racism, the roots of poverty in the nation's political economy, and the pervasiveness of what W. J. Cash termed the South's "savage ideal"—the mix of individualism, machismo, and violence that drew southern white men together, trumping any possibility of class action or cross-race solidarity.[28] We can no longer muster the political will to address our failings by projecting them onto a distinctive and "unAmerican" region. What we need is what Katharine tried, so long ago, to provide: a history of imagination, of possibility, of people—women and men, black and white—who never quit believing they could create a new place in the place they left behind.

The discipline of history is defined by prohibitions—against doubt, against dialogue, against excess, against utopianism, against self-revelation. As we go about the business of rewriting history, I hope that we will find ways to burst those boundaries, to give those disciplines the slip. To do that, as many have argued, we need new categories and more sensitive analytic tools. But we also need new forms of writing. Writing that exceeds the norms of scholarly representations, writing that speaks, writing that stands its ground, writing that throws and keeps on throwing that punch, writing that seeks not only to represent what was but to bring into being "what has never been."[29]

As for me, this project has become a journey back to the site of my first excursions into oral history, southern history, women's history. It has also allowed me to tack back and forth between memory and imagination, the fragile materiality of the past (the present that is always absent, no matter how anxiuosly we seek it out) and the exigencies of political resolve.[30] A bricolage? A proving ground? A redemptive mission? Certainly, a return. Not to a place I left behind but to a female antiracist tradition that is still in the making and to a way of writing that is beginning to feel like home.

Notes

This essay is drawn from a book-in-progress tentatively titled *Writing Memory: Katharine Du Pre Lumpkin and the Refashioning of Southern Identity*. An earlier version was delivered at a plenary session on "Gendering Historiography" at the Berkshire Conference of Women Historians, Chapel Hill, N.C., 7 June 1996. I am deeply indebted to a circle of ideal readers and friends: Glenda Gilmore, Nancy Hewitt, Robert Korstad, and the members of my writing group, Joy Kasson, Carol Mavor, and Della Pollock.

1. Carol Stack, *Call to Home: African Americans Reclaim the Rural South* (New York, 1996), xvi, 199.
2. Charles Reagon Wilson, *Baptized in Blood: The Religion of the Lost Cause, 1865–1920* (Athens, Ga., 1980), and Gaines M. Foster, *Ghosts of the Confederacy: Defeat, The Lost Cause, and the Emergence of the New South, 1865 to 1913* (New York, 1987).
3. Katherine Du Pre Lumpkin, *The Making of a Southerner* (New York, 1946), 130.
4. Fitzhugh Brundage, "White Women and the Creation of Southern Public Memory, 1865–1950" (unpublished paper in Brundage's possession) 7; and Anastatia Sims, *The Power of Femininity in the New South: Women's Organizations and Politics in North Carolina, 1880–1930* (Columbia, S.C.), 128–54. For African American counter-memories and histories, see David W. Blight, "'For Something Beyond the Battlefield': Frederick Douglass and the Memory of the Civil War," *Journal of American History* 75 (March 1989):

1156–78, and Genevieve Fabre and Robert O'Meally, eds., *History and Memory in African-American Culture* (New York, 1994).

5. Katharine Du Pre Lumpkin, Lecture to a General Audience, 1947, p. 1, Katharine Du Pre Lumpkin Papers, Southern Historical Collection, University of North Carolina at Chapel Hill (hereinafter KDL Papers) (quote); Katharine Du Pre Lumpkin, *The South in Progress* (New York, 1940), and *The Making of a Southerner* (New York, 1946); all subsequent page references are to this edition.

6. Fred Hobson, *Tell about the South: The Southern Rage to Explain* (Boston Rouge, La., 1983), 4.

7. Lumpkin, *The Making of a Southerner*, 206.

8. Dominick LaCapra, ed., *The Bounds of Race: Perspectives on Hegemony and Resistance* (Ithaca, N.Y., 1991), 1; Tessie P. Liu, "Race," in Richard Wightman Fox and James T. Kloppenberg, eds., *Companion to American Thought* (Cambridge, 1995), 564–67. See also Barbara Fields, "Ideology and Race in America," in J. Morgan Kousser and James M. McPherson, eds., *Region, Race, and Reconstruction: Essays in Honor of C. Vann Woodward* (New York, 1982), 143–77.

9. Katharine Du Pre Lumpkin, *The Making of a Southerner, with an Afterword by the author* (Athens, Ga., 1981).

10. Katharine Du Pre Lumpkin, Lecture to Prof. Harlow's Class, spring 1947, p. 8. KDL Papers; Lumpkin, *The Making of a Southerner*, 235–36, 239.

11. Lumpkin, *The Making of a Southerner*, 131–32.

12. For the abuse of black women under slavery, and how its crippling effects were carried forward by blacks and whites alike, see Deborah E. McDowell, "In the First Place: Making Frederick Douglass and the Afro-American Narrative Tradition," in William L. Andrews, eds., *Critical Essays on Frederick Douglass* (Boston, 1991), 192–214; Nell Irvin Painter, "Soul Murder and Slavery: Toward a Fully Loaded Cost Accounting," in Linda K. Kerber, Alice Kessler-Harris, and Kathryn Kish Sklar, eds., *U.S. History as Women's History: New Feminist Essays* (Chapel Hill, N.C., 1995), 125–46; and Jennifer Fleischner, *Mastering Slavery: Memory, Family, and Identity in Women's Slave Narratives* (New York, 1996).

13. Lumpkin, *The Making of a Southerner*, 133.

14. This metaphor is drawn from Susan Cheever, *Home before Dark: A Biographical Memoir of John Cheever by His Daughter* (Boston, 1984), 4.

15. Lumpkin, *The Making of a Southerner*, 151–73.

16. Whittaker Chambers, *Witness* (New York, 1952).

17. Grace Lumpkin interview by Jacquelyn Hall, King and Queen Courthouse, Virginia, 6 August 1974, in interviewer's possession.

18. Katharine Du Pre Lumpkin interview by Jacquelyn Hall, Charlottesville, Virginia, 4 August 1974, Southern Oral History Program Collection, Southern Historical Collection, University of North Carolina at Chapel Hill.

19. Lillian Hellman, *Scoundrel Time* (Boston, 1976).

20. Robert C. Bannister, *Sociology and Scientism: The American Quest for Objectivity, 1880–1940* (Chapel Hill, N.C., 1987), 10.

21. The metaphor of the biographer as burglar was suggested to me by Janet Malcolm, "The Silent Woman I," *The New Yorker*, 23–30 August 1993, 86.

22. Page duBois's *Torture and Truth* (New York, 1991) argues that the idea of truth embedded in our philosophical tradition is intimately bound up with the deliberate infliction of human suffering. The ancient Greeks and Romans routinely tortured slaves as a means of forcing them to speak truly, thus reinforcing the nation that truth was a buried secret and that the body of the "other" was the site from which truth could be produced.

23. Tania Modleski, *Feminism without Women: Culture and Criticism in a "Postfeminist" Age* (New York, 1991), 46.

24. Malcolm, "The Silent Woman I," 124.

25. Eve Kosofsky Sedgwick, *Epistemology of the Closet* (Berkeley, Calif., 1990), 22–29 and passim.

26. Malcolm, "The Silent Woman I," 87.

27. Larry J. Griffin, "Why Was the South a Problem to America?" in Larry J. Griffin and Don H. Doyle, eds., *The South as an American Problem* (Athens, Ga., 1995), 10–32.

28. W. J. Cash, *The Mind of the South* (New York, 1941), 137.

29. Della Pollock, "Performing Writing," in Peggy Phelan and Jill Lane, eds., *Ends of Performance* (New York, 1998); Hayden White, "The Politics of Historical Interpretation: Discipline and De-Sublimation," in *The Content of the Form: Narrative Discourse and Historical Representation* (Baltimore, 1987), 58–82; and Modleski, *Feminism without Women*, 46 (quote).

30. Shannon Jackson, "Performances at Hull-House: Museum, Micro-fiche, Historiography," in Della Pollock, ed., *Exceptional Spaces: Essays on Performance and History*, (Chapel Hill, N.C., 1997).

29

From Servitude to Service Work: Historical Continuities in the Racial Division of Paid Reproductive Labor

Evelyn Nakano Glenn

Recent scholarship on African American, Latina, Asian American, and Native American women reveals the complex interaction of race and gender oppression in their lives. These studies expose the inadequacy of additive models that treat gender and race as discrete systems of hierarchy.[1] In an additive model, white women are viewed solely in terms of gender, while women of color are thought to be "doubly" subordinated by the cumulative effects of gender plus race. Yet achieving a more adequate framework, one that captures the interlocking, interactive nature of these systems, as been extraordinarily difficult. Historically, race and gender have developed as separate topics of inquiry, each with its own literature and concepts. Thus features of social life considered central in understanding one system have been overlooked in analyses of the other.

One domain that has been explored extensively in analyses of gender but ignored in studies of race is social reproduction. The term *social reproduction* is used by feminist scholars to refer to the array of activities and relationships involved in maintaining people both on a daily basis and intergenerationally. Reproductive labor includes activities such as purchasing household goods, preparing and serving food, laundering and repairing clothing, maintaining furnishings and appliances, socializing children, providing care and emotional support for adults, and maintaining kin and community ties.

Marxist feminists place the gendered construction of reproductive labor at the center of women's oppression. They point out that this labor is performed disproportionately by women, and is essential to the industrial economy. Yet because it takes place mostly outside the market, it is invisible, not recognized as real work. Men benefit directly and indirectly from this arrangement—directly in that they contribute less labor in the home while enjoying the services women provide as wives and mothers, and indirectly in that, freed of domestic labor, they can concentrate their efforts in paid employment and attain primacy in that area. Thus the sexual division of reproductive labor in the home interacts with and reinforces sexual division in the labor market.[2] These analyses draw attention to the dialectics of production and reproduction, and to male privilege in both realms. When they represent gender as the sole basis for assigning reproductive labor, however, they imply that all women have the same relationship to it, and that it is therefore a universal female experience.[3]

In the meantime, theories of racial hierarchy do not include any analysis of reproductive labor. Perhaps because, consciously or unconsciously, they are male-centered, they focus exclusively on the paid labor market, and especially on male-dominated areas of production. In the 1970s several writers seeking to explain the historical subordination of peoples of color pointed to dualism in the labor market—its division into distinct markets for white workers and for racial-ethnic workers—as a major vehicle for maintaining white domination.[4]

According to these formulations, the labor system has been organized to ensure that racial-ethnic workers are relegated to a lower tier of low-wage, dead-end, marginal jobs; institutional barriers, including restrictions on legal and political rights, prevent their moving out of that tier and competing with European American workers for better jobs. These theories draw attention to the material advantages whites gain from the racial division of labor. However, they either take for granted or ignore women's unpaid household labor and fail to consider whether this work might also be "racially divided."

In short, the racial division of reproductive labor has been a missing piece of the picture in both literatures. This piece, I would contend, is key to the distinct exploitation of women of color, and is a source of both hierarchy and interdependence among white women and women of color. It is thus essential to the development of an integrated model of race and gender, one that treats them as interlocking, rather than additive, systems.

In this article I present a historical analysis of the simultaneous race and gender construction of reproductive labor in the United States, based on comparative study of women's work in the South, the Southwest, and the far West. I argue that reproductive labor has divided along racial as well as gender lines, and that the specific characteristics of the division have varied regionally and changed over time as capitalism has reorganized reproductive labor, shifting parts of it from the household to the market. In the first half of the century, racial-ethnic women were employed as servants to perform reproductive labor in white households, relieving white middle-class women of onerous aspects of that work; in the second half of the century, with the expansion of commodified services (services turned into commercial products or activities), racial-ethnic women are disproportionately employed as service workers in institutional settings to carry out lower-level "public" reproductive labor, while cleaner, white-collar, supervisory and lower professional positions are filled by white women.

I will examine the ways race and gender were constructed around the division of labor by sketching changes in the organization of reproductive labor since the early nineteenth century, presenting a case study of domestic service among African American women in the South, Mexican American women in the Southwest, and Japanese American women in California and Hawaii, and finally examining the shift to institutional service work, focusing on race and gender stratification in health care and the racial division of labor within the nursing labor force. Race and gender emerge as socially constructed, interlocking systems that shape the material conditions, identities, and consciousnesses of all women.

Historical Changes in the Organization of Reproduction

The concept of reproductive labor originated in Karl Marx's remark that every system of production involves both the production of the necessities of life and the reproduction of the tools and labor-power necessary for production.[5] Recent elaborations of the concept grow out of Engels's dictum that the "determining force in history is, in the last resort, the production and reproduction of immediate life." This has, he noted, "a two-fold character, on the one hand the production of subsistence and on the other the production of human beings themselves."[6] Although often equated with domestic labor, or defined narrowly as referring to the renewal of labor power, the term *social reproduction* has come to be more broadly conceived, particularly by social historians, to refer to the creation and re-creation of people as cultural and social, as well as physical, beings.[7] Thus it involves mental, emotional, and manual labor.[8] This labor can be organized in myriad ways—in and out of the household, as paid or unpaid work, creating exchange value or only use value—and these ways are not mutually exclusive. An example is the preparation of food, which can be done by a family member as unwaged work in the household, by a servant as waged work in the household, or by a short-order cook in a fast-food restaurant as waged work that generates profit for the employer. These forms exist contemporaneously.

Prior to industrialization, however, both production and reproduction were organized almost exclusively at the household level. Women were responsible for most of what might be designated as reproduction, but they were simultaneously engaged in the production of foodstuffs, clothing, shoes, candles, soap, and other goods consumed by the household. With industrialization, production of these basic goods was gradually taken over by capitalist industry. Reproduction, however, remained largely the responsibility of individual households. The ideological separation between men's "productive" labor and women's non-market-based activity that had evolved at the end of the eighteenth century was elaborated in the early decades of the nineteenth. An idealized division of labor arose, in which men's work was to follow production outside the home, while women's work was to remain centered in the household.[9] Household work continued to include the production of many goods consumed by members, but as an expanding range of outside-manufactured goods became available, household work became increasingly focused on reproduction.[10] This idealized division of labor was largely illusory for working-class households, including immigrant and racial-ethnic families, in which men seldom earned a family wage; in these households women and children were forced into income-earning activities in and out of the home.[11]

In the second half of the twentieth century, with goods production almost completely incorporated into the market, reproduction has become the next major target for commodification. Aside from the tendency of capital to expand into new areas for profit-making, the very conditions of life brought about by large-scale commodity production have increased the need for commercial services. As household members spend more of their waking hours employed outside the home, they have less time and inclination to provide for one another's social and emotional needs. With the growth of a more geographically mobile and urbanized society, individuals and households have become increasingly cut off from larger kinship circles, neighbors, and traditional communities. Thus, as Harry Braverman notes:

> The population no longer relies upon social organization in the form of family, friends, neighbors, community, elders, children, but with few exceptions must go to the market and only to the market, not only for food, clothing, and shelter, but also for recreation, amusement, security, for the care of the young, the old, the sick, the handicapped. In time not only the material and service needs but even the emotional patterns of life are channeled through the market.[12]

Conditions of capitalist urbanism also have enlarged the population of those requiring daily care and support: elderly and very young people, mentally and physically disabled people, criminals, and other people incapable of fending for themselves. Because the care of such dependents becomes difficult for the "stripped-down" nuclear family or the atomized community to bear, more of it becomes relegated to institutions outside the family.[13]

The final phase in this process is what Braverman calls the "product cycle," which "invents new products and services, some of which become indispensable as the conditions of modern life change and destroy alternatives."[14] In many areas (for example, health care) we no longer have choices outside the market. New services and products also alter the definition of an acceptable standard of living. Dependence on the market is further reinforced by what happened earlier with goods production, namely, an "atrophy of competence," so that individuals no longer know how to do what they formerly did for themselves.

As a result of these tendencies, an increasing range of services has been removed wholly or partially from the household and converted into paid services yielding profits. Today activities such as preparing and serving food (in restaurants and fast-food establishments), caring for handicapped and elderly people (in nursing homes), caring for children (in child-care centers), and providing emotional support, amusement, and companionship (in counseling offices, recreation centers, and health clubs) have become part of the cash nexus. In addition, whether impelled by a need to maintain social control or in response to pressure exerted by worker and community organizations, the state has stepped in to assume minimal responsibility for some reproductive tasks, such as child protection and welfare programs.[15] Whether supplied by corporations or the state, these services are labor-intensive. Thus, a large army of low-wage workers, mostly women and disproportionately women of color, must be recruited to supply the labor.

Still, despite vastly expanded commodification and institutionalization, much reproduction remains organized at the household level. Sometimes an activity is too labor-intensive to be very profitable. Sometimes households or individuals in them have resisted commodification. The limited commodification of child care, for example, involves both elements. The extent of commercialization in different areas of life is uneven, and the variation in its extent is the outcome of political and economic struggles.[16] What is consistent across forms, whether commodified or not, is that reproductive labor is constructed as "female." The gendered organization of reproduction is widely recognized. Less obvious, but equally characteristic, is its racial construction: Historically, racial-ethnic women have been assigned a distinct place in the organization of reproductive labor.

Elsewhere I have talked about the reproductive labor racial-ethnic women have carried out for their own families; this labor was intensified as the women struggled to maintain family life and indigenous cultures in the face of cultural assaults, ghettoization, and a labor system that relegated men and women to low-wage, seasonal, and hazardous employment.[17] Here I want to talk about two forms of waged reproductive work that racial-ethnic women have performed disproportionately: domestic service in private households, and institutional service work.

Domestic Service as the Racial Division of Reproductive Labor

Both the demand for household help and the number of women employed as servants expanded rapidly in the latter half of the nineteenth century.[18] This expansion paralleled the rise of industrial capital and the elaboration of middle-class women's reproductive responsibilities. Rising standards of cleanliness, larger and more ornately furnished homes, the sentimentalization of the home as a "haven in a heartless world," and the new emphasis on childhood and the mother's role in nurturing children all served to enlarge middle-class women's responsibilities for reproduction, at a time when technology had done little to reduce the sheer physical drudgery of housework.[19]

By all accounts, middle-class women did not challenge the gender-based division of labor or the enlargement of their reproductive responsibilities. Indeed, middle-class women—as readers and writers of literature; as members and leaders of clubs, charitable organizations, associations, reform movements, and religious revivals; and as supporters of the cause of abolition—helped to elaborate the domestic code.[20] Feminists seeking an expanded public role for women argued that the same nurturant and moral qualities that made women centers of the home should be brought to bear in public service. In the domestic sphere, instead of questioning the inequitable gender division of labor, they sought to slough off the more burdensome tasks onto more oppressed groups of women.[21]

Phyllis Palmer observes that, at least through the first half of the twentieth century, "most white middle-class women could hire another woman—a recent immigrant, a working class woman, a woman of color, or all three—to perform much of the hard labor of household tasks."[22] Domestics were employed to clean house, launder and iron clothes, scrub floors, and care for infants and children. They relieved their mistresses of the heavier and dirtier domestic chores.[23] White middle-class women were thereby freed for supervisory tasks and for cultural, leisure, and volunteer activity or, more rarely during this period, for a career.[24]

Palmer suggests that the use of domestic servants also helped resolve certain contradictions created by the domestic code. She notes that the early-twentieth-century housewife confronted inconsistent expectations of middle-class womanhood: domesticity and "feminine virtue." Domesticity—defined as creating a warm, clean, and attractive home for husband and children—required hard physical labor and meant contending with dirt. The virtuous woman, however, was defined in terms of spirituality, refinement, and the denial of the physical body. Additionally, in the 1920s and 1930s there emerged a new ideal of the modern wife as an intelligent and attractive companion. If the heavy parts of household work could be transferred to paid help, the middle-class housewife could fulfill her domestic duties, yet distance herself from the physical labor and dirt, and also have time for personal development.[25]

Who was to perform the "dirty work" varied by region. In the Northeast, European immigrant women, particularly those who were Irish and German, constituted the majority of domestic servants from the mid-nineteenth century until World War I.[26] In regions where there was a large concentration of people of color, subordinate-race women formed a more or less permanent servant stratum. Despite differences in the composition of the populations and the mix of industries in the regions, there were important similarities in the situation of Mexicans in the Southwest, African Americans in the South, and Japanese people in northern California and Hawaii. Each of these groups was placed in a separate legal category from whites, excluded from rights and protections accorded full citizens. This severely limited their ability to organize, compete for jobs, and acquire capital.[27] The racial division of private reproductive work mirrored this racial dualism in the legal, political, and economic systems.

In the South, African American women constituted the main and almost exclusive servant caste. Except in times of extreme economic crisis, whites and Blacks did not compete for domestic jobs. Until World War I, 90 percent of all nonagriculturally employed Black women in the South were employed as domestics. Even at the national level, servants and laundresses accounted for close to half (48.4 percent) of nonagriculturally employed Black women in 1930.[28]

In the Southwest, especially in the states with the highest proportions of Mexicans in the population—Texas, Colorado, and New Mexico—Chicanas were disproportionately concentrated in domestic service.[29] In El Paso nearly half of all Chicanas in the labor market were employed as servants or laundresses in the early decades of the century.[30] In Denver, according to Sarah Deutsch, perhaps half of all Chicano/a households had at least one female member employed as a domestic at some time, and if a woman became a widow, she was almost certain to take in laundry.[31] Nationally, 39.1 percent of nonagriculturally employed Chicanas were servants or laundresses in 1930.[32]

In the far West—especially in California and Hawaii, with their large populations of Asian immigrants—an unfavorable sex ratio made female labor scarce in the late nineteenth and early twentieth centuries. In contrast to the rest of the nation, the majority of domestic servants in California and Hawaii were men: in California until 1890 and in Hawaii as late as

1920.[33] The men were Asian—Chinese and later Japanese. Chinese houseboys and cooks were familiar figures in late-nineteenth-century San Francisco; so too were Japanese male retainers in early-twentieth-century Honolulu. After 1907 Japanese women began to immigrate in substantial numbers, and they inherited the mantle of service in both California and Hawaii. In the pre–World War II years, close to half of all immigrant and native-born Japanese American women in the San Francisco Bay area and in Honolulu were employed as servants or laundresses.[34] Nationally, excluding Hawaii, 25.4 percent of nonagricultural Japanese American women workers were listed as servants in 1930.[35]

In areas where racial dualism prevailed, being served by members of the subordinate group was a perquisite of membership in the dominant group. According to Elizabeth Rae Tyson, an Anglo woman who grew up in El Paso in the early years of the century:

> [A]lmost every Anglo–American family had at least one, sometimes two or three servants: a maid and laundress, and perhaps a nursemaid or yardman. The maid came in after breakfast and cleaned up the breakfast dishes, and very likely last night's supper dishes as well; did the routine cleaning, washing and ironing, and after the family dinner in the middle of the day, washed dishes again, and then went home to perform similar services in her own home.[36]

In southwestern cities, Mexican American girls were trained at an early age to do domestic work, and girls as young as nine or ten were hired to clean house.[37]

In Hawaii, where the major social division was between the haole (Caucasian) planter class and the largely Asian plantation-worker class, haole residents were required to employ one or more Chinese or Japanese servants to demonstrate their status and their social distance from those less privileged. Andrew Lind notes that "the literature on Hawaii, especially during the second half of the nineteenth century, is full of references to the open-handed hospitality of Island residents, dispensed by the ever-present maids and houseboys."[38] A public-school teacher who arrived in Honolulu in 1925 was placed in a teacher's cottage with four other mainland teachers. She discovered a maid had already been hired by the principal.

> A maid! None of us had ever had a maid. We were all used to doing our own work. Furthermore, we were all in debt and did not feel that we wanted to spend even four dollars a month on a maid. Our principal was quite insistent. Everyone on the plantation had a maid. It was, therefore, the thing to do.[39]

In the South, virtually every middle-class housewife employed at least one African American woman to do cleaning and child care in her home. Southern household workers told one writer that in the old days, "if you worked for a family, your daughter was expected to, too."[40] Daughters of Black domestics were sometimes inducted as children into service to baby–sit, wash diapers, and help clean.[41] White-skin privilege transcended class lines, and it was not uncommon for working-class whites to hire Black women to do housework.[42] In the 1930s white women tobacco workers in Durham, North Carolina, could mitigate the effects of the "double day"—household labor on top of paid labor—by employing Black women to work in their homes for about one-third of their own wages.[43] Black women tobacco workers were too poorly paid to have this option, and had to rely on the help of overworked husbands, older children, Black women too old to be employed, neighbors, or kin.

Where more than one group was available for service, a differentiated hierarchy of race, color, and culture emerged. White and racial-ethnic domestics were hired for different tasks. In her study of women workers in Atlanta, New Orleans, and San Antonio during the 1920s and 1930s, Julia Kirk Blackwelder reported that "Anglo women in the employ of private households were nearly always reported as housekeepers, while Blacks and Chicanas were reported as laundresses, cooks or servants."[44]

In the Southwest, where Anglos considered Mexican or "Spanish" culture inferior, Anglos displayed considerable ambivalence about employing Mexicans for child care. Although a modern-day example, this statement by an El Paso businessman illustrates the contradictions in Anglo attitudes. The man told an interviewer that he and his wife were putting off parenthood because

> the major dilemma would be what to do with the child. We don't really like the idea of leaving the baby at home with a maid . . . for the simple reason if the maid is Mexican, the child may assume that the other person is its mother. Nothing wrong with Mexicans, they'd just assume that this other person is its mother. There have been all sorts of cases where the infants learned Spanish before they learned English. There've been incidents of the Mexican maid stealing the child and taking it over to Mexico and selling it.[45]

In border towns, the Mexican group was further stratified by English-speaking ability, place of nativity, and immigrant status, with non-English-speaking women residing south of the border occupying the lowest rung. In Laredo and El Paso, Mexican American factory operatives often employed Mexican women who crossed the border daily or weekly to do domestic work for a fraction of a U.S. operative's wages.[46]

The Race and Gender Construction of Domestic Service

Despite their preference for European immigrant domestics, employers could not easily retain their services. Most European immigrant women left service upon marriage, and their daughters moved into the expanding manufacturing, clerical, and sales occupations during the 1910s and 1920s.[47] With the flow of immigration slowing to a trickle during World War I, there were few new recruits from Europe. In the 1920s domestic service became increasingly the specialty of minority-race women.[48] Women of color were advantageous employees in one respect: They could be compelled more easily to remain in service. There is considerable evidence that middle-class whites acted to ensure the domestic labor supply by tracking racial-ethnic women into domestic service and blocking their entry into other fields. Urban school systems in the Southwest tracked Chicana students into homemaking courses designed to prepare them for domestic service. The El Paso school board established a segregated school system in the 1880s that remained in place for the next thirty years; education for Mexican children emphasized manual and domestic skills that would prepare them to work at an early age. In 1909 the Women's Civic Improvement League, an Anglo organization, advocated domestic training for older Mexican girls. Their rationale is explained by Mario Garcia:

> According to the league the housegirls for the entire city came from the Mexican settlement and if they could *be* taught housekeeping, cooking and sewing, every American family would benefit. The Mexican girls would likewise profit since their services would improve and hence be in greater demand.[49]

The education of Chicanas in the Denver school system was similarly directed toward preparing students for domestic service and handicrafts. Sarah Deutsch found that Anglo women there persisted in viewing Chicanas and other "inferior-race" women as dependent, slovenly, and ignorant. Thus, they argued, training Mexican girls for domestic service not only would solve "one phase of women's work we seem to be incapable of handling" but would simultaneously help raise the (Mexican) community by improving women's standard of living, elevating their morals, and facilitating Americanization.[50] One Anglo writer, in an article published in 1917 titled "Problems and Progress among Mexicans in Our Own Southwest," claimed, "When trained there is no better servant than the gentle, quiet Mexicana girl."[51]

In Hawaii, with its plantation economy, Japanese and Chinese women were coerced into service for their husbands' or fathers' employers. Prior to World War II:

> It has been a usual practice for a department head or a member of the managerial staff of the plantation to indicate to members of his work group that his household is in need of domestic help and to expect them to provide a wife or daughter to fill the need. Under the conditions which have prevailed in the past, the worker has felt obligated to make a member of his own family available for such service, if required, since his own position and advancement depend upon keeping the goodwill of his boss. Not infrequently, girls have been prevented from pursuing a high school or college education because someone on the supervisory staff has needed a servant and it has seemed inadvisable for the family in disregard the claim.[52]

Economic coercion also could take bureaucratic forms, especially for women in desperate straits. During the Depression, local officials of the federal Works Project Administration (WPA) and the National Youth Administration (NYA), programs set up by the Roosevelt administration to help the unemployed find work, tried to direct Chicanas and Blacks to domestic service jobs exclusively.[53] In Colorado, local officials of the WPA and NYA advocated household training projects for Chicanas. George Bickel, assistant state director of the WPA for Colorado, wrote: "The average Spanish-American girl on the NYA program looks forward to little save a life devoted to motherhood often under the most miserable circumstances."[54] Given such an outlook, it made sense to provide training in domestic skills.

Young Chicanas disliked domestic service so much that slots in the programs went begging. Older women, especially single mothers struggling to support their families, could not afford to refuse what was offered. The cruel dilemma that such women faced was poignantly expressed in one woman's letter to President Roosevelt:

> My name is Lula Gordon. I am a Negro woman. I am on the relief. I have three children. I have no husband and no job. I have worked hard ever since I was old enough. I am willing to do any kind of work because I have to support myself and my children. I was under the impression that the government or the W.P.A. would give the Physical [sic] fit relief clients work. I have been praying for that time to come. A lady, Elizabeth Ramsie, almost in my condition, told me she was going to try to get some work. I went with her. We went to the Court House here in San Antonio, we talked to a Mrs. Beckmon. Mrs. Beckmon told me to phone a Mrs. Coyle because she wanted some one to clean house and cook for ($5) five dollars a week. Mrs. Beckmon said if I did not take the job in the Private home I would be cut off from everything all together. I told her I was afraid to accept the job in the private home because I have registered for a government job and when it opens up I want to take it. She said that she was taking people off of the relief and I have to take the job in the private home or none. . . . I need work and I will do anything the government gives me to do. . . . Will you please give me some work.[55]

Japanese American women were similarly compelled to accept domestic service jobs when they left the internment camps in which they were imprisoned during World War II.

To leave the camps they had to have a job and a residence, and many women were forced to take positions as live-in servants in various parts of the country. When women from the San Francisco Bay area returned there after the camps were closed, agencies set up to assist the returnees directed them to domestic service jobs. Because they had lost their homes and possessions and had no savings, returnees had to take whatever jobs were offered them. Some became live-in servants to secure housing, which was in short supply after the war. In many cases domestic employment became a lifelong career.[56]

In Hawaii the Japanese were not interned, but there nonetheless developed a "maid short-age" as war-related employment expanded. Accustomed to cheap and abundant household help, haole employers became increasingly agitated about being deprived of the services of their "mamasans." The suspicion that many able-bodied former maids were staying at home idle because their husbands or fathers had lucrative defense jobs was taken seriously enough to prompt an investigation by a university researcher.[57]

Housewives told their nisei maids it was the maids' patriotic duty to remain on the job. A student working as a live-in domestic during the war was dumbfounded by her mistress's response when she notified her she was leaving to take a room in the dormitory at the university. Her cultured and educated mistress, whom the student had heretofore admired, exclaimed with annoyance: " 'I think especially in war time, the University should close down the dormitory.' Although she didn't say it in words, I sensed the implication that she believed all the [Japanese] girls should be placed in different homes, making it easier for the haole woman."[58] The student noted with some bitterness that although her employer told her that working as a maid was the way for her to do "your bit for the war effort," she and other haole women did not, in turn, consider giving up the "conveniences and luxuries of prewar Hawaii" as their bit for the war.[59]

The dominant group ideology in all these cases was that women of color—African American women, Chicanas, and Japanese American women—were particularly suited for service. These racial justifications ranged from the argument that Black and Mexican women were incapable of governing their own lives and thus were dependent on whites—making white employment of them an act of benevolence—to the argument that Asian servants were naturally quiet, subordinate, and accustomed to a lower standard of living. Whatever the specific content of the racial characterizations, it defined the proper place of these groups as in service: They belonged there, just as it was the dominant group's place to be served.

David Katzman notes that "ethnic stereotyping was the stock in trade of all employers of servants, and it is difficult at times to figure out whether blacks and immigrants were held in contempt because they were servants or whether urban servants were denigrated because most of the servants were blacks and immigrants."[60] Even though racial stereo-types undoubtedly preceded their entry into domestic work, it is also the case that domes-tics were forced to enact the role of the inferior. Judith Rollins and Mary Romero describe a variety of rituals that affirmed the subordination and dependence of the domestic; for example, employers addressed household workers by their first names and required them to enter by the back door, eat in the kitchen, and wear uniforms. Domestics understood they were not to initiate conversation but were to remain standing or visibly engaged in work whenever the employer was in the room. They also had to accept with gratitude "gifts" of discarded clothing and leftover food.[61]

For their part, racial-ethnic women were acutely aware that they were trapped in domestic service by racism, and not by lack of skills or intelligence. In their study of Black life in prewar Chicago, St. Clair Drake and Horace Cayton found that education did not provide African Americans with an entree into white-collar work. They noted, "Colored girls are often bitter in their comments about a society which condemns them to the 'white folks' kitchen.'"[62] Thirty-five years later, Anna May Madison minced no words when she declared to anthropologist John Gwaltney:

> Now, I don't do nothing for white women or men that they couldn't do for themselves. They don't do anything I couldn't learn to do every bit as well as they do it. But, you see, that goes right back to the life that you have to live. If that was the life I had been raised up in, I could be President or any other thing I got a chance to be.[63]

Chicana domestics interviewed by Mary Romero in Colorado seemed at one level to accept the dominant culture's evaluation of their capabilities. Several said their options were limited by lack of education and training. However, they also realized they were restricted just because they were Mexican. Sixty-eight-year-old Mrs. Portillo told Romero, "There was a lot of discrimination, and Spanish people got just regular housework or laundry work. There was so much discrimination that Spanish people couldn't get jobs outside of washing dishes—things like that."[64]

Similarly, many Japanese domestics reported that their choices were constrained because of language difficulties and lack of education, but they, too, recognized that color was decisive. Some nisei domestics had taken typing and business courses and some had college degrees, yet they had to settle for "schoolgirl" jobs after completing their schooling. Mrs. Morita, who grew up in San Francisco and graduated from high school in the 1930s, bluntly summarized her options: "In those days there was no two ways about it. If you were Japanese, you either worked in an art store ['oriental curios' shop] where they sell those little junks, or you worked as a domestic. . . . There was no Japanese girl working in an American firm."[65]

Hanna Nelson, another of Gwaltney's informants, took the analysis one step further, recognizing the coercion that kept African American women in domestic service. She saw this arrangement as one that allowed white women to exploit Black women economically and emotionally and exposed Black women to sexual assaults by white men, often with white women's complicity. She says:

> I am a woman sixty-one years old and I was born into this world with some talent. But I have done the work that my grandmother's mother did. It is not through any failing of mine that this is so. The whites took my mother's milk by force, and I have lived to hear a human creature of my sex try to force me by threat of hunger to give my milk to an able man. I have grown to womanhood in a world where the saner you are, the madder you are made to appear.[66]

Race and Gender Consciousness

Hanna Nelson displayed a consciousness of the politics of race and gender not found among white employers. Employers' and employees' fundamentally different positions within the division of reproductive labor gave them different interests and perspectives. Phyllis Palmer describes the problems the YWCA and other reform groups encountered when they attempted to establish voluntary standards and working hours for live-in domestics in the 1930s. White housewives invariably argued against any "rigid" limitation of hours; they insisted on provisions for emergencies that would override any hour limits. Housewives saw their own responsibilities as limitless, and apparently felt there was no justification for boundaries on domestics' responsibilities. They did not acknowledge the fundamental difference in their positions; they themselves gained status and privileges from their relationships with their husbands—relationships that depended on the perfor-mance of wifely duties. They expected domestics to devote long hours and hard work to help them succeed as wives, without, however, commensurate privileges and status. To challenge the inequitable gender division of labor was too difficult and threatening, so white housewives pushed the dilemma onto other women, holding them to the same high standards by which they themselves were imprisoned.[67]

Some domestic workers were highly conscious of their mistresses' subordination to their husbands, and condemned their unwillingness to challenge their husbands' authority. Mabel Johns, a sixty-four-year-old widow, told Gwaltney:

> I work for a woman who has a good husband; the devil is good to her, anyway. Now that woman could be a good person if she didn't think she could just do everything and have everything. In this world whatsoever you get you will pay for. Now she is a grown woman, but she won't know that simple thing. I don't think there's anything wrong with her mind, but she is greedy and she don't believe in admitting that she is greedy. Now you may say what you willormay [sic] about people being good to you, but there just ain' a living soul in this world that thinks more of you than you do of yourself. . . . She's a grown woman, but she have to keep accounts and her husband tells her whether or not he will let her do thus-and-so or buy this or that.[68]

Black domestics are also conscious that a white woman's status comes from her rela-tionship to a white man, that she gains privileges from the relationship that blinds her to her own oppression, and that she therefore willingly participates in and gains advantages from the oppression of racial-ethnic women. Nancy White puts the matter powerfully when she says:

> My mother used to say that the black woman is the white man's mule and the white woman is his dog. Now, she said that to say this: we do the heavy work and get beat whether we do it well or not. But the white woman is closer to the master and he pats them on the head and lets them sleep in the house, but he ain' gon' treat neither one like he was dealing with a person. Now, if I was to tell a white woman that, the first thing she would do is to call you a nigger and then she'd be real nice to her husband so he would come out here and beat you for telling his wife the truth.[69]

Rather than challenge the inequity in the relationship with their husbands, white women pushed the burden onto women with even less power. They could justify this only by denying the domestic worker's womanhood, by ignoring the employee's family ties and responsibilities. Susan Tucker found that southern white women talked about their ser-vants with affection and expressed gratitude that they shared work with the servant that they would otherwise have to do alone. Yet the sense of commonality based on gender that the women expressed turned out to be one-way. Domestic workers knew that employers did not want to know much about their home situations.[70] Mostly the employers did not want domestics' personal needs to interfere with serving them. One domestic wrote that her employer berated her when she asked for a few hours off to pay her bills and take care of pressing business.[71] Of relations between white mistresses and Black domestics in the period from 1870 to 1920, Katzman says that in extreme cases "even the shared roles of motherhood could be denied." A Black child nurse reported in 1912 that she worked four-teen to sixteen hours a day caring for her mistress's four children. Describing her existence as a "treadmill life," she reported that she was allowed to go home "only once in every two weeks, every other Sunday afternoon—even then I'm not permitted to stay all night. I see my own children only when they happen to see me on the streets when I am out with the children [of her mistress], or when my children come to the yard to see me, which isn't often, because my white folks don't like to see their servants' children hanging around their premises."[72]

While this case may be extreme, Tucker reports, on the basis of extensive interviews with southern African American domestics, that even among live-out workers in the 1960s,

> [w]hite women were also not noted for asking about childcare arrangements. All whites, said one Black woman, "assume you have a mother, or an older daughter to keep your child, so it's all right to leave your kids." Stories of white employers not believing the children of domestics were sick, but hearing this as an excuse not to work, were also common. Stories, too, of white women who did not inquire of a domestic's family—even when that domestic went on extended trips with the family—were not uncommon. And work on Christmas morning and other holidays for black mothers was not considered by white employers as unfair. Indeed, work on these days was seen as particularly important to the job.[73]

The irony is, of course, that domestics saw their responsibilities as mothers as the central core of their identity. The Japanese American women I interviewed, the Chicana day workers Romero interviewed, and the African American domestics Bonnie Thornton Dill interviewed all emphasized the primacy of their role as mothers.[74] As a Japanese immigrant single parent expressed it, "My children come first. I'm working to upgrade my children." Another domestic, Mrs. Hiraoka, confided she hated household work but would keep working until her daughter graduated from optometry school.[75] Romero's day workers arranged their work hours to fit around their children's school hours so that they could be there when needed. For domestics, then, working had meaning precisely because it enabled them to provide for their children.

Perhaps the most universal theme in domestic workers' statements is that they are working so their own daughters will not have to go into domestic service and confront the same dilemmas of leaving their babies to work. A Japanese American domestic noted, "I tell my daughters all the time, 'As long as you get a steady job, stay in school. I want you to get a good job, not like me.' That's what I always tell my daughters: Make sure you're not stuck."[76]

In a similar vein, Pearl Runner told Dill, "My main goal was I didn't want them to follow in my footsteps as far as working."[77] Domestic workers wanted to protect their daughters from both the hardships and the dangers that working in white homes posed. A Black domestic told Drake and Cayton of her hopes for her daughters: "I hope they may be able to escape a life as a domestic worker, for I know too well the things that make a girl desperate on these jobs."[78]

When they succeed in helping their children do better than they themselves did, domestics may consider that the hardships were worthwhile. Looking back, Mrs. Runner is able to say,

> I really feel that with all the struggling that I went through, I feel happy and proud that I was able to keep helping my children, that they listened and that they all went to high school. So when I look back, I really feel proud, even though at times the work was very hard and I came home very tired. But now, I feel proud about it. They all got their education.[79]

Domestics thus have to grapple with yet another contradiction. They must confront, acknowledge, and convey the undesirable nature of the work they do to their children, as an object lesson and an admonition, and at the same time maintain their children's respect and their own sense of personal worth and dignity.[80] When they successfully manage that contradiction, they refute their white employers' belief that "you are your work."[81]

The Racial Division of Public Reproductive Labor

As noted earlier, the increasing commodification of social reproduction since World War II has led to a dramatic growth in employment by women in such areas as food preparation and service, health care services, child care, and recreational services. The division of labor in public settings mirrors the division of labor in the household. Racial-ethnic women are employed to do the heavy, dirty, "back-room" chores of cooking and serving food in restaurants and cafeterias, cleaning rooms in hotels and office buildings, and caring for the elderly and ill in hospitals and nursing homes, including cleaning rooms, making beds, changing bedpans, and preparing food. In these same settings white women are disproportionately employed as lower-level professionals (for example, nurses and social workers), technicians, and administrative support workers to carry out the more skilled and supervisory tasks.

The U.S. Census category of "service occupations except private household and protective services" roughly approximates what I mean by "institutional service work." It includes food preparation and service, health care service, cleaning and building services, and personal services.[82] In the United States as a whole, Black and Spanish-origin women are overrepresented in this set of occupations: in 1980 they made up 13.7 percent of all workers in the field, nearly double their proportion (7 percent) in the workforce. White women (some of whom were of Spanish origin) were also overrepresented, but not to the same extent, making up 50.1 percent of all "service" workers, compared with their 36 percent share in the overall workforce. (Black and Spanish-origin men made up 9.6 percent, and white men, who were 50 percent of the workforce, made up the remaining 27.5 percent.)[83]

Because white women constitute the majority, institutional service work may not at first glance appear to be racialized. However, if we look more closely at the composition of specific jobs within the larger category, we find clear patterns of racial specialization. White women are preferred in positions requiring physical and social contact with the public, that is, waiters/waitresses, transportation attendants, hairdressers/cosmetologists, and dental assistants, while racial-ethnic women are preferred in dirty, back-room jobs as maids, janitors/cleaners, kitchen workers, and nurse's aides.[84]

As in the case of domestic service, who does what varies regionally, following racial-ethnic caste lines in local economies. Racialization is clearest in local economies where a subordinate racial-ethnic group is sizable enough to fill a substantial portion of jobs. In southern cities, Black women are twice as likely to be employed in service occupations as white women. For example, in Atlanta in 1980, 20.8 percent of African American women were so employed, compared with 10.4 percent of white women. While they were less than one-quarter (23.9 percent) of all women workers, they were nearly two-fifths (38.3 percent) of women service workers. In Memphis 25.9 percent of African American women, compared with 10.2 percent of white women, were in services; though they made up only a third (34.5 percent) of the female workforce, African American women were nearly three-fifths (57.2 percent) of women employed in this field. In southwestern cities Spanish-origin women specialize in service work. In San Antonio 21.9 percent of Spanish-origin women were so employed, compared with 11.6 percent of non-Spanish-origin white women; in that city half (49.8 percent) of all women service workers were Spanish-origin, while Anglos, who made up two-thirds (64.0 percent) of the female workforce, were a little over a third (36.4 percent) of those in the service category. In El Paso, 16.9 percent of Spanish-origin women were service workers, compared with 10.8 percent of Anglo women, and they made up two-thirds (66.1 percent) of those in service. Finally, in Honolulu, Asian and Pacific Islanders constituted 68.6 percent of the female workforce, but 74.8 percent of those were in service jobs. Overall, these jobs employed 21.6 percent of all Asian and Pacific Islander women, compared with 13.7 percent of white non-Spanish-origin women.[85]

Particularly striking is the case of cleaning and building services. This category—which includes maids, housemen, janitors, and cleaners—is prototypically "dirty work." In Memphis one out of every twelve Black women (8.2 percent) was in cleaning and building services, and Blacks were 88.1 percent of the women in this occupation. In contrast, only one out of every two hundred white women (0.5 percent) was so employed. In Atlanta, 6.6 percent of Black women were in this field—constituting 74.6 percent of the women in these jobs—compared with only 0.7 percent of white women. Similarly, in El Paso, 4.2 percent of Spanish-origin women (versus 0.6 percent of Anglo women) were in cleaning and building services—making up 90 percent of the women in this field. And in San Antonio the Spanish and Anglo percentages were 5.3 percent versus 1.1 percent, respectively, with Spanish-origin women 73.5 percent of women in these occupations. Finally, in Honolulu, 4.7 percent of Asian and Pacific Islander women were in these occupations, making up 86.6 percent of the total. Only 1.3 percent of white women were so employed.[86]

From Personal to Structural Heirarchy

Does a shift from domestic service to low-level service occupations represent progress for racial-ethnic women? At first glance it appears not to bring much improvement. After domestic service, these are the lowest-paid of all occupational groupings. In 1986 service workers were nearly two-thirds (62 percent) of the workers in the United States earning minimum wage or less.[87] As in domestic service, the jobs are often part-time and seasonal, offer few or no medical and other benefits, have low rates of unionization, and subject workers to arbitrary supervision. The service worker also often performs in a public setting the same sorts of tasks that servants did in a private setting. Furthermore, established patterns of race-gender domination-subordination are often incorporated into the authority structure of organizations. Traditional race-gender etiquette shapes face-to-face interaction in the workplace. Duke University Hospital in North Carolina from its founding in 1929 adopted paternalistic policies toward its Black employees. Black workers were highly conscious of this, as evidenced by their references to "the plantation system" at Duke.[88]

Still, service workers, especially those who have worked as domestics, are convinced that "public jobs" are preferable to domestic service. They appreciate not being personally subordinate to an individual employer and not having to do "their" dirty work on "their" property. Relations with supervisors and clients are hierarchical, but they are embedded in an impersonal structure governed by more explicit contractual obligations and limits. Also important is the presence of a work group for sociability and support. Workplace culture offers an alternative system of values to that imposed by managers.[89] Experienced workers socialize newcomers, teaching them how to respond to pressures to speed up work, to negotiate workloads, and to demand respect from superiors. While the isolated domestic finds it difficult to resist demeaning treatment, the peer group in public settings provides backing for individuals to stand up to the boss.

That subordination is usually not as direct and personal in public settings as in the private household does not mean, however, that race and gender hierarchy is diminished in importance. Rather, it changes form, becoming institutionalized within organizational structures. Hierarchy is elaborated through a detailed division of labor that separates conception from execution, and allows those at the top to control the work process. Ranking is based ostensibly on expertise, education, and formal credentials.

The elaboration is especially marked in technologically oriented organizations that employ large numbers of professionals, as is the case with health care institutions. Visual observation of any hospital reveals the hierarchical race and gender division of labor. At the top are the physicians, setting policy and initiating work for others; they are disproportionately white and male. Directly below, performing medical tasks and patient care as delegated by physicians and enforcing hospital rules, are the registered nurses (RNs), who are overwhelmingly female and disproportionately white. Under the registered nurses and often supervised by them are the licensed practical nurses (LPNs), also female but disproportionately women of color. At about the same level are the technologists and technicians who carry out various tests and procedures and the "administrative service" staff in the offices; these categories tend to be female and white. Finally, at the bottom of the pyramid are the nurses's aides, predominantly women of color; housekeepers and kitchen workers, overwhelmingly women of color; and orderlies and cleaners, primarily men of color. They constitute the "hands" that perform routine work directed by others.

The Racial Division of Labor in Nursing

A study of stratification in the nursing labor force illustrates the race and gender construction of public reproductive labor. At the top in terms of status, authority, and pay are the RNs, graduates of two-, three-, or four-year hospital- or college-based programs. Unlike the lower ranks, registered nursing offers a career ladder. Starting as a staff nurse, a hospital RN can rise to head nurse, nursing supervisor, and finally director of nursing. In 1980 whites were 86.7 percent of RNs, even though they were only 76.7 percent of the population. The LPNs, who make up the second grade of nursing, generally have had twelve months' training in a technical institute or community college. The LPNs are supervised by RNs and may oversee the work of aides. Racial-ethnic workers constituted 23.4 percent of LPNs, with Blacks, who were 11.7 percent of the population, making up fully 17.9 percent. Below the LPNs in the hierarchy are the nurse's aides (NAs), who typically have on–the–job training of four to six weeks. Orderlies, attendants, home health aides, and patient care assistants also fall into this category. These workers perform housekeeping and routine caregiving tasks "delegated by an RN and performed under the direction of an RN or LPN." Among nurse's aides, 34.6 percent were minorities, with Blacks making up 27.0 percent of all aides.[90]

Nationally, Latinas were underrepresented in health care services but were found in nurse's aide positions in proportion to their numbers—making up 5.2 percent of the total. The lower two grades of nursing labor thus appear to be Black specialties. However, in some localities other women of color are concentrated in these jobs. In San Antonio 48 percent of aides were Spanish-origin, while only 15.1 percent of the RNs were. Similarly, in El Paso, 61.5 percent of aides were Spanish-origin, compared with 22.8 percent of RNs. In Honolulu, Asian and Pacific Islanders, who were 68.6 percent of the female labor force, made up 72.3 percent of the NAs but only 45.7 percent of the RNs.[91]

Familial Symbolism and the Race and Gender Construction of Nursing   How did the present ranking system and sorting by racial-ethnic category in nursing come about? How did the activities of white nurses contribute to the structuring? And how did racial-ethnic women respond to constraints?

The stratification of nursing labor can be traced to the beginnings of organized nursing in the 1870s. However, until the 1930s grading was loose. A broad distinction was made between so-called trained nurses, who were graduates of hospital schools or collegiate programs, and untrained nurses, referred to—often interchangeably—as "practical nurses," "hospital helpers," "nursing assistants," "nursing aides," or simply as "aides."[92]

During this period health work in hospitals was divided between male physicians (patient diagnosis and curing) and female nursing staff (patient care) in a fashion analogous to the separate spheres prescribed for middle-class households. Nurses and physicians each had primary responsibility for and authority within their own spheres, but nurses were subject to the ultimate authority of physicians. The separation gave women power in a way that did not challenge male domination. Eva Gamarinikow likens the position of the British nursing matron to that of an upper-class woman in a Victorian household who supervised a large household staff but was subordinate to her husband.[93] Taking the analogy a step further, Ann Game and Rosemary Pringle describe the pre–World War II hospital as operating under a system of controls based on familial symbolism. Physicians were the authoritative father figures, while trained nurses were the mothers overseeing the care of patients, who were viewed as dependent children. Student nurses and practical nurses were, in this scheme, in the position of servants, expected to follow orders and subject to strict discipline.[94]

Like the middle-class white housewives who accepted the domestic ideology, white nursing leaders rarely challenged the familial symbolism supporting the gender division of labor in health care. The boldest advocated, at most, a dual-headed family.[95] They acceded to the racial implications of the family metaphor as well. If nurses were mothers in a family headed by white men, they had to be white. And, indeed, trained nursing was an almost exclusively white preserve. As Susan Reverby notes, "In 1910 and 1920, for example, less than 3% of the trained nurses in the United States were black, whereas black women made up 17.6% and 24.0% respectively of the female working population."[96]

The scarcity of Black women is hardly surprising. Nursing schools in the South excluded Blacks altogether, while northern schools maintained strict quotas. Typical was the policy of the New England Hospital for Women and Children, which by charter could only admit "one Negro and one Jewish student" a year.[97] Black women who managed to become trained nurses did so through separate Black training schools, and were usually restricted to serving Black patients, whether in "integrated" hospitals in the North or segregated Black hospitals in the South.[98]

White nursing leaders and administrators justified exclusion by appeals to racist ideology. Anne Bess Feeback, the superintendent of nurses for Henry Grady Hospital in Atlanta, declared that Negro women under her supervision had no morals: "They are such liars. . . . They shift responsibility whenever they can. . . . They quarrel constantly among themselves and will cut up each other's clothes for spite. . . . Unless they are constantly watched, they will steal anything in sight."[99] Perhaps the most consistent refrain was that Black women were deficient in the qualities needed to be good nurses: They lacked executive skills, intelligence, strength of character, and the ability to withstand pressure. Thus Margaret Butler, chief nurse in the Chicago City Health Department, contended that Black nurses' techniques were "inferior to that of the white nurses, they are not punctual, and are incapable of analyzing a social situation." Apparently Black nurses did not accept white notions of racial inferiority, for Butler also complains about their tendency "to organize against authority" and "to engage in political intrigue."[100] Another white nursing educator, Margaret Bruesche, suggested that although Black women lacked the ability to become trained nurses, they "could fill a great need in the South as a trained attendant, who would work for a lower wage than a fully trained woman."[101] Even those white nursing leaders sympathetic to Black aspirations agreed that Black nurses should not be put in supervisory positions, because white nurses would never submit to their authority.

Similar ideas about the proper place of "orientals" in nursing were held by haole nursing leaders in pre–World War II Hawaii. White-run hospitals and clinics recruited haoles from the mainland, especially for senior nurse positions, rather than hiring or promoting locally trained Asian American nurses. This pattern was well known enough for a University of Hawaii researcher to ask a haole health administrator whether it was true that "oriental nurses do not reach the higher positions of the profession." The administrator confirmed this: "Well, there again it is a matter of qualification. There is a limit to the number of nurses we can produce here. For that reason we have to hire from the mainland. Local girls cannot compete with the experience of mainland haole girls. In order to induce haole nurses here we could not possibly put them under an oriental nurse because that would make them race conscious right at the start. And as I said before, Japanese don't make good executives."[102] Because of the racial caste system in Hawaii, Japanese American women who managed to get into nursing were not seen as qualified or competent to do professional work. The chairman of the Territorial Nurses Association noted that

> before the war [started], our local nurses were looked down [upon] because they were mostly Japanese. . . . The Japanese nurses feel they can get along better with Mainland nurses than local haole nurses. That is true even outside of the profession. I remember hearing a Hawaiian-born haole dentist say, "I was never so shocked as when I saw a white man shine shoes when I first went to the Mainland." Haoles here feel only orientals and other non-haoles should do menial work.[103]

The systematic grading of nursing labor into three ranks was accomplished in the 1930s and 1940s, as physician-controlled hospital administrations moved to establish "sound business" practices to contain costs and consolidate physician control of health care.[104] High-tech medical and diagnostic procedures provided an impetus for ever-greater specialization. Hospitals adopted Taylorist principles of "scientific management," separating planning and technical tasks from execution and manual labor. They began to hire thousands of subsidiary workers, and created the licensed practical nurse (LPN), a position for a graduate of a one-year technical program, to perform routine housekeeping and patient care. With fewer discriminatory barriers and shorter training requirements, LPN positions were accessible to women of color who wanted to become nurses.

The lowest level of nursing workers, nurse's aides, was also defined in the 1930s, when the American Red Cross started offering ten-week courses to train aides for hospitals. This category expanded rapidly in the 1940s, doubling from 102,000 workers in 1940 to 212,000 in 1950.[105] This occupation seems to have been designed deliberately to make use of African American labor in the wake of labor shortages during and after World War II. A 1948 report on nursing told the story of how nurse's aides replaced the heretofore volunteer corps of ward attendants: "In response to this request for persons designated as nursing aides, the hospital discovered among the large Negro community a hitherto untapped reservoir of personnel, well above the ward attendant group in intelligence and personality."[106] One reason for their superiority can be deduced: They often were overqualified. Barred from entry into better occupations, capable, well-educated Black women turned to nurse's aide work as an alternative to domestic service.

In the meantime, RNs continued their struggle to achieve professional status by claiming exclusive rights over "skilled" nursing work. Some nurses, especially rank-and-file general duty nurses, called for an outright ban on employing untrained nurses. Many leaders of nursing organizations, however, favored accepting subsidiary workers to perform housekeeping and other routine chores so that graduate nurses would be free for more professional work. Hospital administrators assured RNs that aides would be paid less and assigned nonnursing functions and that only trained nurses would be allowed supervisory roles. One administrator claimed that aide trainees were told repeatedly that "they are not and will not be nurses."[107]

In the end, the leaders of organized nursing accepted the formal stratification of nursing, and turned their attention to circumscribing the education and duties of the lower grades to ensure their differentiation from "professional" nurses. Indeed, an RN arguing for the need to train and license practical nurses, and laying out a model curriculum for LPNs, warned: "Overtraining can be a serious danger. The practical nurse who has a course of over fifteen months (theory and practice) gets a false impression of her abilities and builds up the unwarranted belief that she can practice as a professional nurse."[108] Hospital administrators took advantage of race and class divisions and RNs' anxieties about their status to further their own agenda. Their strategy of co-opting part of the workforce (RNs) and restricting the mobility and wages of another part (LPNs and NAs) undermined solidarity among groups that might otherwise have united around common interests.

Nursing Aides: Consciousness of Race and Gender   The hierarchy in health care has come to be justified less in terms of family symbolism and more in terms of bureaucratic efficiency. Within the new bureaucratic structures, race and gender ordering is inherent in the job definitions. The nurse's aide job is defined as unskilled and menial; hence, the women who do it are too. Nurse's aides frequently confront a discrepancy, however, between how their jobs are defined (as unskilled and subordinate) and what they actually are allowed or expected to do (exercise skill and judgment). Lillian Roberts's experiences illustrate the disjunction. Assigned to the nursery, she was fortunate to work with a white southern RN who was willing to teach her:

> I would ask her about all kinds of deformities that we would see in the nursery, the color of a baby, and why this was happening and why the other was happening. And then I explored with her using my own analysis of things. Sometimes I'd be right just in observing and putting some common sense into it. Before long, when the interns would come in to examine the babies, I could tell them what was wrong with every baby. I'd have them lined up for them.[109]

The expertise Roberts developed through observation, questioning, and deduction was not recognized, however. Thirty years later Roberts still smarts from the injustice of not being allowed to sit in on the shift reports: "They never dignify you with that. Even though it would help you give better care. There were limitations on what I could do."[110]

She had to assume a deferential manner when dealing with white medical students and personnel, even those who had much less experience than she had. Sometimes she would be left in charge of the nursery and "I'd get a whole mess of new students in there who didn't know what to do. I would very diplomatically have to direct them, although they resented to hell that I was both black and a nurse's aide. But I had to do it in such a way that they didn't feel I was claiming to know more than they did."[111] One of her biggest frustrations was not being allowed to get on-the-job training to advance. Roberts describes the "box" she was in:

> I couldn't have afforded to go to nursing school. I needed the income, and you can't just quit a job and go to school. I was caught in a box, and the salary wasn't big enough to save to go to school. And getting into the nursing schools was a real racist problem as well. So there was a combination of many things. And I used to say, "Why does this country have to go elsewhere and get people when people like myself want to do something?"[112]

When she became a union organizer, her proudest accomplishment was to set up a program in New York that allowed aides to be trained on the job to become LPNs.

While Roberts's experience working in a hospital was typical in the 1940s and 1950s, today the typical aide is employed in a nursing home, in a convalescent home, or in home health care. In these settings, aides are the primary caregivers.[113] The demand for their services continues to grow as treatment increasingly shifts out of hospitals and into such settings. Thus, even though aides have lost ground to RNs in hospitals, which have re-organized nursing services to re-create RNs as generalists, aides are expected to remain among the fastest-growing occupations through the end of the century.[114]

Whatever the setting, aide work continues to be a specialty of racial-ethnic women. The work is seen as unskilled and subordinate, and thus appropriate to their qualifications and status. This point was brought home to Timothy Diamond during the training course he attended as the sole white male in a mostly Black female group of trainees: "We learned elementary biology and how we were never to do health care without first consulting someone in authority; and we learned not to ask questions but to do as we were told. As one of the students, a black woman from Jamaica used to joke, 'I can't figure out whether they're trying to teach us to be nurse's aides or black women.'"[115]

What exactly is the nature of the reproductive labor that these largely minority and supposedly unskilled aides and assistants perform? They do most of the day-to-day, face-to-face work of caring for the ill and disabled: helping patients dress or change gowns, taking vital signs (temperature, blood pressure, pulse), assisting patients to shower or giving bed baths, emptying bedpans or assisting patients to the toilet, changing sheets and keeping the area tidy, and feeding patients who cannot feed themselves. There is much "dirty" work, such as cleaning up incontinent patients. Yet there is another, unacknowledged, mental and emotional dimension to the work: listening to the reminiscences of elderly patients to help them hold on to their memory, comforting frightened patients about to undergo surgery, and providing the only human contact some patients get. This caring work is largely invisible, and the skills required to do it are not recognized as real skills.[116]

That these nurse's aides are performing reproductive labor on behalf of other women (and ultimately for the benefit of households, industry, and the state) becomes clear when one considers who would do it if paid workers did not. Indeed, we confront that situation frequently today, as hospitals reduce the length of patient stays to cut costs. Patients are released "quicker and sicker."[117] This policy makes sense only if it is assumed that patients have someone to provide interim care, administer medication, prepare meals, and clean for them until they can care for themselves. If such a person exists, most likely it is a woman— a daughter, wife, mother, or sister. She may have to take time off from her job or quit. Her unpaid labor takes the place of the paid work of a nurse's aide or assistant and saves the hospital labor costs. Her labor is thereby appropriated to ensure profit.[118] Thus, the situation of women as unpaid reproductive workers at home is inextricably bound to that of women as paid reproductive workers.

Conclusions and Implications

This article began with the observation that the racial division of reproductive labor has been overlooked in the separate literatures on race and gender. The distinct exploitation of women of color and an important source of difference among women have thereby been ignored. How, though, does a historical analysis of the racial division of reproductive labor illuminate the lives of women of color and white women? What are its implications for concerted political action? In order to tackle these questions, we need to address a broader question, namely, how does the analysis advance our understanding of race and gender? Does it take us beyond the additive models I have criticized?

The Social Construction of Race and Gender

Tracing how race and gender have been fashioned in one area of women's work helps us understand them as socially constructed systems of relationships—including symbols, normative beliefs, and practices—organized around perceived differences. This under-standing is an important counter to the universalizing tendencies in feminist thought. When feminists perceive reproductive labor only as gendered, they imply that domestic labor is identical for all women and that it therefore can be the basis of a common identity of womanhood. By not recognizing the different relationships women have had to such supposedly universal female experiences as motherhood and domesticity, they risk essen-tializing gender—treating it as static, fixed, eternal, and natural. They fail to take seriously a basic premise of feminist thought, that gender is a social construct.

If race and gender are socially constructed systems, then they must arise at specific moments in particular circumstances and change as these circumstances change. We can study their appearance, variation, and modification over time. I have suggested that one vantage point for looking at their development in the United States is in the changing divi-sion of labor in local economies. A key site for the emergence of concepts of gendered and racialized labor has been in regions characterized by dual labor systems.

As subordinate-race women within dual labor systems, African American, Mexican American, and Japanese American women were drawn into domestic service by a combina-tion of economic need, restricted opportunities, and educational and employment tracking mechanisms. Once they were in service, their association with "degraded" labor affirmed their supposed natural inferiority. Although ideologies of "race" and "racial difference" justifying the dual labor system already were in place, specific ideas about racial-ethnic womanhood were invented and enacted in everyday interactions between mistresses and workers. Thus ideologies of race and gender were created and verified in daily life.[119]

Two fundamental elements in the construction of racial-ethnic womanhood were the notion of inherent traits that suited the women for service and the denial of the women's identities as wives and mothers in their own right. Employers accepted a cult of domesticity that purported to elevate the status of women as mothers and homemakers, yet they made demands on domestics that hampered them from carrying out these responsibilities in their own households. How could employers maintain such seemingly inconsistent orientations? Racial ideology was critical in resolving the contradiction: it explained why women of color were suited for degrading work. Racial characterizations effectively neutralized the racial-ethnic woman's womanhood, allowing the mistress to be "unaware" of the domestic's relationship to her own children and household. The exploitation of racial-ethnic women's physical, emotional, and mental work for the benefit of white households thus could be rendered invisible in consciousness if not in reality.

With the shift of reproductive labor from household to market, face-to-face hierarchy has been replaced by structural hierarchy. In institutional settings, stratification is built into organizational structures, including lines of authority, job descriptions, rules, and spatial and temporal segregation. Distance between higher and lower orders is ensured by structural segregation. Indeed, much routine service work is organized to be out of sight: It takes place behind institutional walls where outsiders rarely penetrate (for example, nursing homes, chronic care facilities), in back rooms (for example, restaurant kitchens), or at night or other times when occupants are gone (for example, in office buildings and hotels). Workers may appreciate this segregation in time and space because it allows them some autonomy and freedom from demeaning interactions. It also makes them and their work invisible, however. In this situation, more-privileged women do not have to acknowledge the workers or to confront the contradiction between shared womanhood and inequality by race and class. Racial ideology is not necessary to explain or justify exploitation, not for lack of racism, but because the justification for inequality does not have to be elaborated in specifically racial terms; instead it can be cast in terms of differences in training, skill, or education.[120]

Because they are socially constructed, race and gender systems are subject to contestation and struggle. Racial-ethnic women continually have challenged the devaluation of their womanhood. Domestics often did so covertly. They learned to dissemble, consciously "putting on an act" while inwardly rejecting their employers' premises and maintaining a separate identity rooted in their families and communities. As noted earlier, institutional service workers can resist demeaning treatment more openly because they have the support of peers. Minority-race women hospital workers have been in the forefront of labor militancy, staging walkouts and strikes and organizing workplaces. In both domestic service and institutional service work, women have transcended the limitations of their work by focusing on longer-term goals, such as their children's future.

Beyond Additive Models: Race and Gender as Interlocking Systems

As the foregoing examples show, race and gender constructs are inextricably intertwined. Each develops in the context of the other; they cannot be separated. This is important because when we see reproductive labor only as gendered, we extract gender from its context, which includes other interacting systems of power. If we begin with gender separated out, then we have to put race and class back in when we consider women of color and working-class women. We thus end up with an additive model in which white women have only gender and women of color have gender plus race.

The interlock is evident in the case studies of domestic workers and nurses's aides. In the traditional middle-class household, the availability of cheap female domestic labor buttressed white male privilege by perpetuating the concept of reproductive labor as women's work, sustaining the illusion of a protected private sphere for women, and displacing conflict away from husband and wife to struggles between housewife and domestic.

The racial division of labor also bolstered the gender division of labor indirectly, by offering white women a slightly more privileged position in exchange for accepting domesticity. Expanding on Judith Rollins's notion that white housewives gained an elevated self-identity by casting Black domestics as inferior contrast figures, Phyllis Palmer suggests the dependent position of the middle-class housewife made a contrasting figure necessary. A dualistic conception of women as "good" and "bad," long a part of Western cultural tradition, provided ready-made categories for casting white and racial-ethnic women as oppositional figures.[121] The racial division of reproductive labor served to channel and recast these dualistic conceptions into racialized gender constructs. By providing them an acceptable self-image, racial constructs gave white housewives a stake in a system that ultimately oppressed them.

The racial division of labor similarly protects white male privilege in institutional settings. White men, after all, still dominate in professional and higher-management positions, where they benefit from the paid and unpaid services of women. And as in domestic service, conflict between men and women is redirected into clashes among women. This displacement is evident in health care organizations. Because physicians and administrators control the work of other health workers, we would expect the main conflict to be between doctors and nurses over workload, allocation of tasks, wages, and working conditions. The racial division of nursing labor allows some of the tension to be redirected so that friction arises between registered nurses and aides over work assignments and supervision.

In both household and institutional settings, white professional and managerial men are the group most insulated from dirty work and contact with those who do it. White women are frequently the mediators who have to negotiate between white male superiors and racial-ethnic subordinates. Thus race and gender dynamics are played out in a three-way relationship involving white men, white women, and women of color.

Beyond Difference: Race and Gender as Relational Constructs

Focusing on the racial division of reproductive labor also uncovers the relational nature of race and gender. By "relational" I mean that each is made up of categories (for example, male/female, Anglo/Latino) that are positioned, and therefore gain meaning, in relation to each other.[122] Power, status, and privilege are axes along which categories are positioned. Thus, to represent race and gender as relationally constructed is to assert that the experiences of white women and women of color are not just different but connected in systematic ways.

The interdependence is easier to see in the domestic work setting, because the two groups of women confront each other face-to-face. That the higher standard of living of one woman is made possible by, and also helps to perpetuate, the other's lower standard of living is clearly evident. In institutional service work the relationship between those who do the dirty work and those who benefit from it is mediated and buffered by institutional structures, so the dependence of one group on the other for its standard of living is not apparent. Nonetheless, interdependence exists, even if white women do not come into actual contact with women of color.[123]

The notion of relationality also recognizes that white and racial-ethnic women have different standpoints by virtue of their divergent positions. This is an important corrective to feminist theories of gendered thought that posit universal female modes of thinking growing out of common experiences such as domesticity and motherhood. When they portray reproductive labor only as gendered, they assume there is only one standpoint—that of white women. Hence, the activities and experiences of middle-class women become generic "female" experiences and activities, and those of other groups become variant, deviant, or specialized.

In line with recent works on African American, Asian American, and Latina feminist thought, we see that taking the standpoint of women of color gives us a different and more critical perspective on race and gender systems.[124] Domestic workers in particular—because they directly confront the contradictions in their lives and those of their mistresses—develop an acute consciousness of the interlocking nature of race and gender oppression.

Perhaps a less obvious point is that understanding race and gender as relational systems also illuminates the lives of white American women. White womanhood has been constructed not in isolation but in relation to that of women of color. Therefore, race is integral to white women's gender identities. In addition, seeing variation in racial division of labor across time in different regions gives us a more variegated picture of white middle-class womanhood. White women's lives have been lived in many circumstances; their "gender" has been constructed in relation to varying others, not just to Black women. Conceptualizing white womanhood as monolithically defined in opposition to men or to Black women ignores complexity and variation in the experiences of white women.

Implications for Feminist Politics

Understanding race and gender as relational, interlocking, socially constructed systems affects how we strategize for change. If race and gender are socially constructed rather than being "real" referents in the material world, then they can be deconstructed and challenged. Feminists have made considerable strides in deconstructing gender; we now need to focus on deconstructing gender and race simultaneously. An initial step in this process is to expose the structures that support the present division of labor and the constructions of race and gender around it.

Seeing race and gender as interlocking systems, however, alerts us to sources of inertia and resistance to change. The discussion of how the racial division of labor reinforced the gender division of labor makes clear that tackling gender hierarchy requires simultaneously addressing race hierarchy. As long as the gender division of labor remains intact, it will be in the short-term interest of white women to support or at least overlook the racial division of labor, because it ensures that the very worst labor is performed by someone else. Yet as long as white women support the racial division of labor, they will have less impetus to struggle to change the gender division of labor. This quandary is apparent in cities such as Los Angeles, which have witnessed a large influx of immigrant women fleeing violence and poverty in Latin America, Southeast Asia, and the Caribbean. These women form a large reserve army of low-wage labor for both domestic service and institutional service work. Anglo women who ordinarily would not be able to afford servants are employing illegal immigrants as maids at below minimum wage.[125] Not only does this practice diffuse pressure for a more equitable sharing of household work, but it also re-creates race and gender ideologies that justify the subordination of women of color. Having a Latino or Black maid picking up after them teaches Anglo children that some people exist primarily to do work that Anglos do not want to do for themselves.

Acknowledging the relational nature of race and gender and therefore the interdependence between groups means that we recognize conflicting interests among women. Two examples illustrate the divergence. With the move into the labor force of all races and classes of women, it is tempting to think that we can find unity around the common problems of "working women." With that in mind, feminist policy makers have called for expanding services to assist employed mothers in such areas as child care and elderly care. We need to ask, Who is going to do the work? Who will benefit from increased services? The historical record suggests that it will be women of color, many of them new immigrants, who will do the work and that it will be middle-class women who will receive the services. Not so coincidentally, public officials seeking to reduce welfare costs are promulgating regulations requiring women on public assistance to work. The needs of employed middle-class women and women on welfare might thus be thought to coincide: The needs of the former for services might be met by employing the latter to provide the services. The divergence in interest becomes apparent, however, when we consider that employment in service jobs at current wage levels guarantees that their occupants will remain poor. However, raising their wages so that they can actually support themselves and their children at a decent level would mean many middle-class women could not afford these services.

A second example of an issue that at first blush appears to bridge race and ethnic lines is the continuing earnings disparity between men and women. Because occupational segregation, the concentration of women in low-paying, female-dominated occupations, stands as the major obstacle to wage equity, some feminist policy makers have embraced the concept of comparable worth.[126] This strategy calls for equalizing pay for "male" and "female" jobs requiring similar levels of skill and responsibility, even if differing in content. Comparable worth accepts the validity of a job hierarchy and differential pay based on "real" differences in skills and responsibility. Thus, for example, it attacks the differential between nurses and pharmacists but leaves intact the differential between nurses and nurses's aides. Yet the division between "skilled" and "unskilled" jobs is exactly where the racial division typically falls. To address the problems of women service workers of color would require a fundamental attack on the concept of a hierarchy of worth; it would call for flattening the wage differentials between the highest- and lowest-paid ranks. A claim would have to be made for the right of all workers to a living wage, regardless of skill or responsibility.

These examples suggest that forging a political agenda that addresses the universal needs of women is highly problematic, not just because women's priorities differ but because gains for some groups may require a corresponding loss of advantage and privilege for others. As the history of the racial division of reproductive labor reveals, conflict and contestation among women over definitions of womanhood, over work, and over the conditions of family life are part of our legacy as well as the current reality. This does not mean we give up the goal of concerted struggle. It means we give up trying falsely to harmonize women's interests. Appreciating the ways race- and gender-based divisions of labor create both hierarchy and interdependence may be a better way to reach an understanding of the interconnectedness of women's lives.

Notes

Work on this project was made possible by a Title F leave from the State University of New York at Binghamton and a visiting scholar appointment at the Murray Research Center at Radcliffe College. Discussions with Elsa Barkley Brown, Gary Glenn, Carole Turbin, and Barrie Thorne contributed immeasurably to the ideas developed here. My thanks to Joyce Chinen for directing me to archival materials in Hawaii. I am also grateful to members of the Women and Work Group and to Norma Alarcón, Gary Dymski, Antonia Glenn, Margaret Guilette, Terence Hopkins, Eileen McDonagh, JoAnne Preston, Mary Ryan, and four anonymous *Signs* reviewers for their suggestions.

1. Patricia Hill Collins, "Learning from the Outsider Within: The Sociological Significance of Black Feminist Thought," *Social Problems* 33, 6 (1986): 14–32; Deborah K. King, "Multiple Jeopardy, Multiple Consciousness: The Context of a Black Feminist Ideology," *Signs: Journal of Women in Culture and Society* 14, 1 (1988): 42–72; Elsa Barkley Brown, "Womanist Consciousness: Maggie Lena Walker and the Independent Order of Saint Luke," *Signs: Journal of Women in Culture and Society* 14, 3 (1989): 610–33.

2. For various formulations, see Margaret Benston, "The Political Economy of Women's Liberation," *Monthly Review* 21 (September 1969): 13–27; Wally Secombe, "The Housewife and Her Labour under Capitalism," *New Left Review* 83 (January–February 1974): 3–24; Michèle Barrett, *Women's Oppression Today: Problems in Marxist Feminist Thought* (London: Verso, 1980); Bonnie Fox, ed., *Hidden in the Household: Women's Domestic Labour under Capitalism* (Toronto: Women's Press, 1980); and Natalie J. Sokoloff, *Between Money and Love: The Dialectics of Women's Home and Market Work* (New York: Praeger, 1980).

3. Recently, white feminists have begun to pay attention to scholarship by and about racial-ethnic women, and to recognize racial stratification in the labor market and other public arenas. My point here is that they still assume that women's relationship to domestic labor is universal; thus they have not been concerned with explicating differences across race, ethnic, and class groups in women's relationship to that labor.

4. Robert Blauner, *Racial Oppression in America* (Berkeley: University of California Press, 1972); Mario Barrera, *Race and Class in the Southwest: A Theory of Racial Inequality* (Notre Dame, Ind.: University of Notre Dame Press, 1979). See also Mark Reisler, *By the Sweat of Their Brow: Mexican Immigrant Labor in the United States, 1900–1940* (Westport, Conn.: Greenwood, 1976), which, despite its title, is exclusively about male Mexican labor. I use the term *racial-ethnic* to refer collectively to groups that have been socially constructed and constituted as racially as well as culturally distinct from European Americans, and placed in separate legal statuses from "free whites" (cf. Michael Omi and Howard Winant, *Racial Formation in the United States* [New York: Routledge, 1986]). Historically, African Americans, Latinos, Asian Americans, and Native Americans were so constructed. Similarly, I have capitalized the word *Black* throughout this article to signify the racial-ethnic construction of that category.

5. Karl Marx and Friedrich Engels, *Selected Works*, vol. 1 (Moscow: Progress, 1969), 31.

6. Friedrich Engels, *The Origins of the Family, Private Property, and the State* (New York: International Publishers, 1972), 71.

7. Mary P. Ryan, *Cradle of the Middle Class: The Family in Oneida County, New York, 1790–1865* (New York: Cambridge University Press, 1981), 15.

8. Johanna Brenner and Barbara Laslett, "Social Reproduction and the Family," in Ulf Himmelstrand, ed., *Sociology, from Crisis to Science?* vol. 2, *The Social Reproduction of Organization and Culture* (London: Sage, 1986), 117.

9. Jeanne Boydston, *Home and Work: Housework, Wages, and the Ideology of Labor in the Early Republic* (New York: Oxford University Press, 1990), esp. 46–48.

10. Robert W. Smuts, *Women and Work in America* (New York: Schocken, 1959), 11–13; Alice Kessler-Harris, *Women Have Always Worked: A Historical Overview* (Old Westbury, N.Y.: Feminist Press, 1981). Capitalism, however, changed the nature of reproductive labor, which became more and more devoted to consumption activities, i.e., using wages to acquire necessities in the market and then processing these commodities to make them usable (see Batya Weinbaum and Amy Bridges, "The Other Side of the Paycheck," *Monthly Review* 28 [1976]: 88–103; and Meg Luxton, *More than a Labour of Love: Three Generations of Women's Work in the Home* [Toronto: Women's Press, 1980]).

11. Alice Kessler-Harris, *Out to Work: A History of Wage-Earning Women in the United States* (New York: Oxford University Press, 1982).

12. Harry Braverman, *Labor and Monopoly Capital: The Degradation of Labor in the Twentieth Century* (New York: Monthly Review Press, 1974), 276.

13. This is not to deny that family members, especially women, still provide the bulk of care of dependents, but to point out that there has been a marked increase in institutionalized care in the second half of the twentieth century.

14. Braverman, *Labor and Monopoly Capital*, 281. For a discussion of varying views on the relative importance of control versus agency in shaping state welfare policy, see Linda Gordon, "The New Feminist Scholarship on the Welfare State," in Linda Gordon, ed., *Women, the State, and Welfare* (Madison: University of Wisconsin Press, 1990). Frances Fox Piven and Richard A. Cloward note that programs have been created only when poor people have mobilized, and are intended to defuse pressure for more radical change (*Regulating the Poor: The Functions of Public Welfare* [New York: Pantheon, 1971], 66). In their *Poor People's Movements: Why They Succeed, How They Fail* (New York: Pantheon, 1979), Piven and Cloward document the role of working-class struggles to win concessions from the state. For a feminist social control perspective, see Mimi Abramovitz, *Regulating the Lives of Women: Social Welfare Policy from Colonial Times to the Present* (Boston: South End Press, 1988).

15. Abramovitz, *Regulating the Lives of Women*.

16. Brenner and Laslett, "Social Reproduction and the Family," 121; Barbara Laslett and Johanna Brenner, "Gender and Social Reproduction: Historical Perspectives," *Annual Review of Sociology* 15 (1989): 384.

17. Evelyn Nakano Glenn, "Racial Ethnic Women's Labor: The Intersection of Race, Gender, and Class Oppression," *Review of Radical Political Economy* 17, 3 (1985): 86–108; Evelyn Nakano Glenn, *Issei, Nisei, Warbride: Three Generations of Japanese American Women in Domestic Service* (Philadelphia: Temple University Press, 1986), 86–108; Bonnie Thornton Dill, "Our Mothers' Grief: Racial Ethnic Women and the Maintenance of Families," *Journal of Family History* 12, 4 (1988): 415–31.

18. David Chaplin, "Domestic Service and Industrialization," *Comparative Studies in Sociology* 1 (1978): 97–127.

19. These developments are discussed in Carl Degler, *At Odds: Women and the Family in America from the Revolution to the Present* (New York: Oxford University Press, 1980); Susan Strasser, *Never Done: A History of American Housework* (New York: Pantheon, 1982); Ruth Schwartz Cowan, *More Work for Mother: The Ironies of Household Technology from the Open Hearth to the Microwave* (New York: Basic Books, 1983); and Faye Dudden, *Serving Women: Household Service in Nineteenth-Century America* (Middletown, Conn.: Wesleyan University Press, 1983), esp. 240–42. Quoted phrase is from Christopher Lasch, *Haven in a Heartless World: The Family Besieged* (New York: Basic Books, 1977).

20. Brenner and Laslett, "Social Reproduction and the Family." See also Karen Blair, *The Clubwoman as Feminist: True Womanhood Redefined, 1868–1914* (New York: Holmes & Meier, 1980); Barbara Epstein, *The Politics of Domesticity: Women, Evangelism, and Temperance in Nineteenth Century America* (Middletown, Conn.: Wesleyan University Press, 1981); Ryan, *Cradle of the Middle Class*; and Dudden, *Serving Women*.

21. See, e.g., Elaine Bell Kaplan, "'I Don't Do No Windows': Competition between the Domestic Worker and the Housewife," in Valerie Miner and Helen E. Longino, eds., *Competition: A Feminist Taboo?* (New York: Feminist Press at the City University of New York, 1987).

22. Phyllis Palmer, "Housewife and Household Worker: Employer–Employee Relations in the Home, 1928–1941," in Carole Groneman and Mary Beth Norton, eds., *"To Toil the Livelong Day": America's Women at Work, 1790–1980* (Ithaca, N.Y.: Cornell University Press, 1987), 182–83.

23. Phyllis Palmer, in *Domesticity and Dirt: Housewives and Domestic Servants in the United States, 1920–1945* (Philadelphia: Temple University Press, 1990), 70, found evidence that mistresses and servants agreed on what were the least desirable tasks—washing clothes, washing dishes, and taking care of children on evenings and weekends—and that domestics were more likely to perform the least desirable tasks.

24. It may be worth mentioning the importance of unpaid cultural and charitable activities in perpetuating middle-class privilege and power. Middle-class reformers often aimed to mold the poor in ways that mirrored middle-class values, but without actually altering their subordinate position. See, e.g., George J. Sanchez, "'Go after the Women': Americanization and the Mexican Immigrant Woman, 1915–1929," in Ellen Carol DuBois and Vicki L. Ruiz, eds., *Unequal Sisters: A Multicultural Reader in Women's History* (New York: Routledge, 2nd ed., 1990), for discussion of efforts of Anglo reformers to train Chicanas in domestic skills.

25. Palmer, *Domesticity and Dirt*, 127–51.

26. David M. Katzman, *Seven Days a Week: Women and Domestic Service in Industrializing America* (New York: Oxford University Press, 1978), 65–70.

27. Glenn, "Racial Ethnic Women's Labor."

28. U.S. Bureau of the Census, *Fifteenth Census of the United States: 1930, Population*, vol. 5, *General Report on Occupations* (Washington, D.C.: Government Printing Office, 1933), ch. 3, "Color and Nativity of Gainful Workers," tables 2, 4, 6. For discussion of the concentration of African American women in domestic service, see Glenn, "Racial Ethnic Women's Labor."

29. I use the terms *Chicano, Chicana*, and *Mexican American* to refer to both native-born and immigrant Mexican people in the United States.

30. Mario T. Garcia, *Desert Immigrants: The Mexicans of El Paso, 1880–1920* (New Haven: Yale University Press, 1981), 76.

31. Sarah Deutsch, *No Separate Refuge: Culture, Class, and Gender on an Anglo–Hispanic Frontier in the American Southwest, 1880–1940* (New York: Oxford University Press, 1987), 147.

32. U.S. Bureau of the Census, *Fifteenth Census of the United States: 1930, Population*, vol. 5, *General Report on Occupations* (Washington, D.C.: Government Printing Office, 1933).

33. Katzman, *Seven Days a Week*, 55; Andrew Lind, "The Changing Position of Domestic Service in Hawaii," *Social Process in Hawaii* 15 (1951), table 1.

34. U.S. Bureau of the Census, *Fifteenth Census of the United States: 1930, Outlying Territories and Possessions* (Washington, D.C.: Government Printing Office, 1932), table 8; Glenn, *Issei, Nisei, Warbride*, 76–79.

35. U.S. Bureau of the Census, *Fifteenth Census of the United States: 1930, Population*, vol. 5, *General Report on Occupations*.

36. Mario T. Garcia, "The Chicana in American History: The Mexican Women of El Paso, 1880–1920: A Case Study," *Pacific Historical Review* 49, 2 (1980): 327.

37. For personal accounts of Chicano children being inducted into domestic service, see Vicki L. Ruiz, "By the Day or the Week: Mexican Domestic Workers in El Paso," in Vicki L. Ruiz and Susan Tiano, eds., *Women on the U.S.–Mexico Border: Responses to Change* (Boston: Allen and Unwin, 1987); and interview of Josephine Turietta in Nan Elsasser, Kyle MacKenzie, and Yvonne Tixier y Vigil, *Las Mujeres: Conversations from a Hispanic Community* (Old Westbury, N.Y.: Feminist Press, 1980), 28–35.

38. Lind, "The Changing Position of Domestic Service in Hawaii," 73.

39. Ibid., 76.

40. Tucker, "The Black Domestic in the South," 98.

41. Elizabeth Clark–Lewis, "This Work Had an End: African American Domestic Workers in Washington, D.C., 1910–1940," in Carole Groneman and Mary Beth Norton, eds., *"To Toil the Livelong Day": America's Women at Work, 1780–1980* (Ithaca, N.Y.: Cornell University Press, 1987), 200–1. See also life–history accounts of Black domestics, such as Dorothy Bolden, "Forty–two Years a Maid: Starting at Nine in Atlanta," in Nancy Seifer, ed., *Nobody Speaks for Me! Self-Portraits of American Working Class Women* (New York: Simon and Schuster, 1976), and that of Anna Mae Dickson in Wendy Watriss, "It's Something Inside You," in Maxine Alexander, ed., *Speaking for Ourselves: Women of the South* (New York: Pantheon, 1984).

42. C. Arnold Anderson and Mary Jean Bowman, "The Vanishing Servant and the Contemporary Status System of the American South," *American Journal of Sociology* 59 (1953): 215–30.

43. Dolores Janiewski, "Flawed Victories: The Experiences of Black and White Women Workers in Durham during the 1930s," in Lois Scharf and Joan M. Jensen, eds., *Decades of Discontent: The Women's Movement, 1920–1940* (Westport, Conn.: Greenwood, 1983), 93.

44. Julia Kirk Blackwelder, "Women in the Work Force: Atlanta, New Orleans, and San Antonio, 1930 to 1940," *Journal of Urban History* 4, 3 (1978): 349. Blackwelder also found that domestics themselves were attuned to the racial-ethnic hierarchy among them. When advertising for jobs, women who did not identify themselves as Black overwhelmingly requested "housekeeping" or "governess" positions, whereas Blacks advertised for "cooking," "laundering," or just plain "domestic work."

45. Vicki L. Ruiz, "Oral History and La Mujer: The Rosa Guerrero Story," in Vicki L. Ruiz and Susan Tiano, *Women on the U.S.–Mexico Border*, 71.

46. Melissa Hield, "Women in the Texas ILGWU, 1933–50," in Alexander, *Speaking for Ourselve*, 64.

47. This is not to say that daughters of European immigrants experienced great social mobility and soon attained affluence. The nondomestic jobs they took were usually low-paying and the conditions of work often deplorable. Nonetheless, white, native-born, and immigrant women clearly preferred the relative freedom of industrial, office, or shop employment to the constraints of domestic service (see Katzman, *Seven Days a Week*, 71–72).

48. Phyllis Palmer, *Domesticity and Dirt*, 12.

49. Garcia, *Desert Immigrants*, 113.

50. Sarah Deutsch, "Women and Intercultural Relations: The Case of Hispanic New Mexico and Colorado," *Signs: Journal of Women in Culture and Society* 12, 4 (1987): 736.

51. Mary Romero, "Day Work in the Suburbs: The Work Experience of Chicana Private Housekeepers," in Anne Statham, Eleanor M. Miller, and Hans O. Mauksch, eds., *The Worth of Women's Work: A Qualitative Synthesis* (Albany: State University of New York Press, 1988), 16.

52. Lind, "The Changing Position of Domestic Service in Hawaii," 77.

53. Julia Kirk Blackwelder, *Women of the Depression: Caste and Culture in San Antonio, 1929–1939* (College Station: Texas A&M University Press, 1984), 120–22; Deutsch, *No Separate Refuge*, 182–83.

54. Deutsch, *No Separate Refuge*, 183.

55. Blackwelder, *Women of the Depression*, 68–69.

56. Glenn, *Issei, Nisei, Warbride*.

57. Document Ma 24, Romanzo Adams Social Research Laboratory papers, University of Hawaii Archives, Manoa. I used these records when they were lodged in the sociology department; they are currently being cataloged by the university archives and a finding aid is in process.

58. Document Ma 15, Romanzo Adams Social Research Laboratory papers, 5.

59. Ibid.

60. Katzman, *Seven Days a Week*, 221.

61. Judith Rollins, *Between Women: Domestics and Their Employers* (Philadelphia: Temple University Press, 1985), ch. 5; Mary Romero, "Chicanas Modernize Domestic Service" (manuscript, 1987).

62. St. Clair Drake and Horace Cayton, *Black Metropolis: A Study of Negro Life in a Northern City*, vol. 1 (New York: Harper Torchbooks, 1962 [1945]), 246.

63. John Gwaltney, ed., *Drylongso: A Self-Portrait of Black America* (New York: Random House, 1980), 173.

64. Mary Romero, "Renegotiating Race, Class, and Gender Hierarchies in the Everyday Interactions between Chicana Private Household Workers and Employers" (paper presented at the 1988 meeting of the Society for the Study of Social Problems, Atlanta), 86.

65. Glenn, *Issei, Nisei, Warbride*, 122.

66. Gwaltney, *Drylongso*, 7.

67. Kaplan, "'I Don't Do No Windows'"; Palmer, *Domesticity and Dirt*.

68. Gwaltney, *Drylongso*, 167.

69. Ibid., 148.

70. Kaplan, "'I Don't Do No Windows,'" 96; Susan Tucker, "The Black Domestic in the South: Her Legacy as Mother and Mother Surrogate," in Carolyn Matheny Dillman, ed., *Southern Women* (New York: Hemisphere, 1988).

71. Palmer, *Domesticity and Dirt*, 74.

72. "More Slavery at the South: A Negro Nurse," from the *Independent* (1912), in David M. Katzman and William M. Tuttle Jr., eds., *Plain Folk: The Life Stories of Undistinguished Americans* (Urbana: University of Illinois Press, 1982), 176–85, 179.

73. Tucker, "The Black Domestic in the South," 99.

74. Dill, "Our Mothers' Grief"; Glenn, *Issei, Nisei, Warbride;* Romero, "Renegotiating Race, Class, and Gender Hierarchies."

75. From an interview conducted by the author in the San Francisco Bay area in 1977.

76. Ibid.

77. Bonnie Thornton Dill, "The Means to Put My Children Through: Childrearing Goals and Strategies among Black Female Domestic Servants," in La Frances Rodgers-Rose, ed., *The Black Woman* (Beverly Hills: Sage, 1980), 109.

78. Drake and Cayton, *Black Metropolis*, 246.

79. Dill, "The Means to Put My Children Through," 113.

80. Ibid., 110.

81. Gwaltney, *Drylongso*, 174.

82. The U.S. Labor Department and the U.S. Bureau of the Census divide service occupations into three major categories: "private household," "protective service," and "service occupations except private household and protective services." In this discussion, "service work" refers only to the latter. I omit private household workers, who have been discussed previously, and protective service workers, who include firefighters and police, as these jobs, in addition to being male-dominated and relatively well-paid, carry some degree of authority, including the right to use force.

83. Computed from U.S. Bureau of the Census, *Census of the Population, 1980*, vol. 1, *Characteristics of the Population* (Washington, D.C.: Government Printing Office, 1984), chap. D, "Detailed Population Characteristics," pt. 1; "United States Summary," table 278: "Detailed Occupation of Employed Persons by Sex, Race and Spanish Origin, 1980."

84. Ibid.

85. Figures computed from table 279 in each of the state chapters of the following: U.S. Bureau of the Census, *Census of the Population, 1980*, vol. 1, *Characteristics of the Population*, chap. D, "Detailed Population Characteristics," pt. 6: "California"; pt. 12: "Georgia"; pt. 13: "Hawaii"; pt. 15: "Illinois"; pt. 44: "Tennessee"; and pt. 45: "Texas." The figures for Anglos in the Southwest are estimates, based on the assumption that most "Spanish-origin" people are Mexican, and that Mexicans, when given a racial designation, are counted as whites. Specifically, the excess left after the "total" is subtracted from the "sum" of white, Black, American Indian/Eskimo/Aleut, Asian and Pacific Islander, and "Spanish-origin" is subtracted from the white figure. The remainder is counted as "Anglo." Because of the way "Spanish-origin" crosscuts race (Spanish-origin individuals can be counted as white, Black, or any other race), I did not attempt to compute figures for Latinos or Anglos in cities where Spanish-origin individuals are likely to be more distributed in some unknown proportion between Black and white. This would be the case, e.g., with the large Puerto Rican population in New York City. Thus I have not attempted to compute Latino versus Anglo data for New York and Chicago. Note also that the meaning of *white* differs by locale, and that the local terms *Anglo* and *haole* are not synonymous with *white*. The "white" category in Hawaii includes Portuguese, who, because of their history as plantation labor, are distinguished from haoles in the local ethnic ranking systems. The U.S. Census category system does not capture the local construction of race and ethnicity.

86. Computed from tables specified in ibid.

87. The federal minimum wage was $3.35 in 1986. Over a quarter (26.0 percent) of all workers in these service occupations worked at or below this wage level. See Earl F. Mellor, "Workers at the Minimum Wage or Less: Who They Are and the Jobs They Hold," *Monthly Labor Review*, July 1987, esp. 37.

88. Karen Brodkin Sacks, *Caring by the Hour: Women, Work, and Organizing at Duke Medical Center* (Urbana: University of Illinois Press, 1988), 46. Paternalism is not limited to southern hospitals; similar policies were in place at Montefiore Hospital in New York City. See Leon Fink and Brian Greenberg, "Organizing Montefiore: Labor Militancy Meets a Progressive Health Care Empire," in Susan Reverby and David Rosner, eds., *Health Care in America: Essays in Social History* (Philadelphia: Temple University Press, 1979).

89. Susan Porter Benson, *Counter Cultures: Saleswomen, Customers, and Managers in American Department Stores, 1890–1940* (Urbana: University of Illinois Press, 1986). See also the many examples of workplace cultures supporting resistance cited in Karen Brodkin Sacks and Dorothy Remy, eds., *My Troubles Are Going to Have Trouble with Me: Everyday Trials and Triumphs of Women Workers* (New Brunswick, N.J.: Rutgers University Press, 1984); and Louise Lamphere, *From Working Daughters to Working Mothers: Immigrant Women in a New England Industrial Community* (Ithaca, N.Y.: Cornell University Press, 1987).

90. American Nurses' Association, *Health Occupations Supportive to Nursing* (New York: American Nurses' Association, 1965), 6. Reflecting differences in status and authority, RNs earn 20–40 percent more than LPNs and 60–150 percent more than NAs (U.S. Department of Labor, *Industry Wage Survey: Hospitals, August 1985*, Bureau of Labor Statistics Bulletin 2273 [Washington, D.C.: Government Printing Office, 1987]; and U.S. Department of Labor, *Industry Wage Survey: Nursing and Personal Care Facilities, September 1985*, Bureau of Labor Statistics Bulletin 2275 [Washington, D.C.: Government Printing Office, 1987]).

91. For the national level, see U.S. Bureau of the Census, *Census of the Population, 1980*, vol. 1, *Characteristics of the Population*, ch. D, "Detailed Population Characteristics," pt. 1: "United States Summary," table 278. For statistics on RNs and aides in San Antonio, El Paso, and Honolulu, see U.S. Bureau of the Census, *Census of the Population, 1980*, vol. 1, *Characteristics of the Population*, ch. D, "Detailed Population Characteristics," pt. 13: "Hawaii"; and pt. 45: "Texas," table 279.

92. Kathleen Cannings and William Lazonik, "The Development of the Nursing Labor Force in the United States: A Basic Analysis," *International Journal of Health Sciences* 5, 2 (1975): 185–216; Susan M. Reverby, *Ordered to Care: The Dilemma of American Nursing, 1850–1945* (New York: Cambridge University Press, 1987).

93. Eva Gamarinikow, "Sexual Division of Labour: The Case of Nursing," in Annette Kuhn and Ann-Marie Wolpe, eds., *Feminism and Materialism: Women and Modes of Production* (London: Routledge and Kegan Paul, 1978).

94. Ann Game and Rosemary Pringle, *Gender at Work* (Sydney: Allen and Unwin, 1983), 99–100.

95. Reverby, *Ordered to Care*, 71–75.

96. Ibid.

97. Darlene Clark Hine, *Black Women in White: Racial Conflict and Cooperation in the Nursing Profession, 1890–1950* (Bloomington: Indiana University Press, 1989), 6.

98. For accounts of Black women in nursing, see Darlene Clark Hine, ed., *Black Women in the Nursing Profession: A Documentary History* (New York: Pathfinder, 1985); and Mary Elizabeth Carnegie, *The Path We Tread: Blacks in Nursing, 1854–1954* (Philadelphia: Lippincott, 1986). Hine (*Black Women in White*, ch. 7) makes it clear that Black nurses served Black patients not just because they were restricted but because they wanted to meet Black health care needs. Blacks were excluded from membership in two of the main national organizations for nurses, the National League of Nursing Education and the American Nurses' Association. And although they formed their own organizations, such as the National Association of Colored Graduate Nurses, and enjoyed the respect of the Black community, Black nurses remained subordinated within the white-dominated nursing profession.

99. Hine, *Black Women in the Nursing Profession*, 101.

100. Hine, *Black Women in White*, 99.

101. Ibid., 101.

102. Document Nu21–I, p. 2, Romanzo Adams Research Laboratory papers A1989–006, box 17, folder 1.

103. Document Nu10–I, p. 3, Romanzo Adams Research Laboratory papers, A1989–006, box 17, folder 4.

104. This was one outcome of the protracted and eventually successful struggle waged by physicians to gain control over all health care. For an account of how physicians established hospitals as the main site for medical treatment, and gained authority over "subsidiary" health occupations, see Paul Starr, *The Social Transformation of American Medicine* (New York: Basic Books, 1982). For accounts of nurses' struggle for autonomy and their incorporations into hospitals, see Reverby, *Ordered to Care*, and also David Wagner, "The Proletarianization of Nursing in the United States, 1932–1945," *International Journal of Health Services* 10, 2 (1980): 271–89.

105. Cannings and Lazonik, "The Development of the Nursing Labor Force in the United States," 201.

106. Ibid.

107. Reverby, *Ordered to Care*, 194.

108. Dorothy Deming, *The Practical Nurse* (New York: Commonwealth Fund, 1947), 26.

109. Susan M. Reverby, "From Aide to Organizer: The Oral History of Lillian Roberts," in Carol Ruth Berkin and Mary Beth Norton, eds., *Women of America: A History* (Boston: Houghton Mifflin, 1979), 297–98.

110. Ibid., 298–99.

111. Ibid., 298.

112. Ibid., 299.

113. For example, it has been estimated that 80 percent of all patient care in nursing homes is provided by nurse's aides (see Barbara Coleman, "States Grapple with New Law," *AARP News Bulletin* 30, 2 [1989]: 5). In 1988, 1,559,000 persons were employed as RNs, 423,000 as LPNs, 1,404,000 as nurses's aides, orderlies, and attendants, and 407,000 as health aides (U.S. Department of Labor, *Employment and Earnings, January 1989* [Washington, D.C.: Government Printing Office, 1989], table 22). Nurses's aides and home health care aides are expected to be the fastest-growing occupations through the 1990s, according to George T. Silvestri and John M. Lukasiewicz, "A Look at Occupational Employment Trends to the Year 2000," *Monthly Labor Review*, September 1987, 59.

114. Edward S. Sekcenski, "The Health Services Industry: A Decade of Expansion," *Monthly Labor Review*, May 1981, 10–16. For a description of trends and projections to the year 2000, see Silvestri and Lukasiewicz, "A Look at Occupational Employment Trends to the Year 2000."

115. Timothy Diamond, "Social Policy and Everyday Life in Nursing Homes: A Critical Ethnography," in Anne Statham, Eleanor M. Miller, and Hans O. Mauksch, eds., *The Worth of Women's Work: A Qualitative Synthesis* (Albany: State University of New York Press, 1988), 40.

116. Feminists have pointed to the undervaluing of female-typed skills, especially those involved in "caring" work (see Hilary Rose, "Women's Work: Women's Knowledge," in Juliet Mitchell and Ann Oakley, eds., *What Is Feminism?* [Oxford: Basil Blackwell, 1986]).

117. Sacks, *Caring by the Hour*, 165.

118. Nona Glazer, "Overlooked, Overworked: Women's Unpaid and Paid Work in the Health Services' 'Cost Crisis.'" *International Journal of Health Services* 18, 2 (1988): 119–37.

119. Barbara Fields, "Ideology and Race in American History," in J. Morgan Kousser and James M. McPherson, eds., *Region, Race, and Reconstruction: Essays in Honor of C. Vann Woodward* (New York: Oxford University Press, 1982).

120. That is, the concentration of minority workers in lower-level jobs can be attributed to their lack of "human capital"—qualifications—needed for certain jobs.

121. Lenore Davidoff, "Class and Gender in Victorian England: The Diaries of Arthur J. Munby and Hannah Cullwick," *Feminist Studies* 5 (spring 1979): 86–114; Palmer, *Domesticity and Dirt*, 11, 137–39.

122. Michèle Barrett, "The Concept of 'Difference,'" *Feminist Review* 26 (July 1987): 29–41.

123. Elsa Barkley Brown pointed this out to me in a personal communication.

124. Alma Garcia, "The Development of Chicana Feminist Discourse, 1970–1980," *Gender and Society* 3, 2 (1989): 217–38; Gloria Anzaldúa *Making Face, Making Soul—Haciendo Caras: Creative Critical Perspectives by Women of Color* (San Francisco: Aunt Lute Foundation, 1990); Patricia Hill Collins, *Black Feminist Thought: Knowledge, Consciousness, and the Politics of Empowerment* (New York: Allen and Unwin, 1990).

125. Mary Jo McConoway, "The Intimate Experiment," *Los Angeles Times Magazine*, 19 February 1987, 18–23, 37–38.

126. Heidi I. Hartmann, ed., *Comparable Worth: New Directions for Research* (Washington, D.C.: National Academy Press, 1985); Joan Acker, *Doing Comparable Worth: Gender, Class, and Pay Equity* (Philadelphia: Temple University Press, 1989).

30

Telling Performances: Jazz History Remembered and Remade by the Women in the Band

Sherrie Tucker

Scholars and writers in the burgeoning field of jazz studies are critically reevaluating some of the timeworn patterns of how mainstream jazz histories have been written. According to writers such as those anthologized in *Jazz among the Discourses*, jazz scholarship is too "devoted to exalting favored artists," too invested in "campaigns for superiority of genres"; jazz history is too neatly constructed into a misleading "coherent whole" of "styles or periods, each with a conveniently distinctive label and time period"; and, finally, the jazz historical record is too reliant on the very small portion of music that gets made into jazz records.[1]

As someone who does research on all-woman bands, I am heartened by these critiques. The conventional standards for what counts as jazz history make it very difficult to construct historical narratives that include all-woman bands. I would also like to suggest that scholars seeking more complex historical frameworks should take a listen to oral histories of women jazz musicians. The kind of listening I am advocating would not be limited to merely skimming jazzwomen's stories for data to add to the existing historical record, nor would it be geared solely toward the creation of separate women-in-jazz histories. Rather, I believe that through serious study of jazzwomen's oral histories, scholars might learn new narrative strategies for imagining and telling jazz histories in which women and men are both present. Because women who played instruments other than piano were seldom the "favored artists" of the "superior genres," and because they were hardly ever recorded, they have had little access to the deceptive "coherence" of mainstream histories. Therefore, they are uniquely positioned to suggest new frameworks for telling and interpreting jazz history.

Listening to narratives of women instrumentalists might also help jazz scholars to engage in more rigorous gender analysis than has been customary. Women musicians do not tend to construct separate "women's jazz" histories when they talk about their careers, nor do they simply "add themselves in" to dominant historical frameworks. Yet historians aiming to include women seem to be stuck at the crossroads of these two narrative options. Instead, women musicians tend to construct narratives in which they dramatize themselves, at various stages of their careers, as negotiating gendered identities (often in creative ways) as jazz musicians. Indeed, these "telling performances"—the narrations themselves—may prove a rich site for learning about the function of oral history-telling in female artists' construction and maintenance of identities as jazz musicians in a discourse that has historically denied them a place.

Engaged listening to oral histories of women jazz musicians might help historians to reframe jazz history so that it is possible to see "gender" not only as a mode of social organization, but, in Joan Scott's terms, as a "field on which power is articulated."[2] This would involve not only looking at what women did and what men did, but looking at what kinds of masculinities and femininities were performed in specific historical contexts and how they were valued—asking, for instance, which masculinities and femininities were deemed marketable on a national scale and which were relegated to local scenes only. Jazz scholars would do well to examine critically the kinds of gender constructions that have dominated jazz journalism, recording, marketing, and historiography and to ask questions such as: Who is served by the popular construction of the modernist jazz hero as personifying a kind of black masculinity defined (usually by white male writers) as isolated, self-destructive, and childlike?[3] Or by the quintessential jazzwoman as a "girl singer," so often constructed as a bubblehead rather than a knowledgeable professional? Or by the figure of the jazz/ blues singer as the embodiment of stereotypes about black femininity, oversexed and underloved, the musician who is assumed to have no musical knowledge, but

Figure 30.1. Saxophone section, International Sweethearts of Rhythm, publicity photo, 1994. Grace Bayron, fourth tenor (lower left); Helen Saine, third alto (upper left); Rosalind "Roz" Cron, lead alto (center); Vi Burnside, second/jazz tenor (upper right); Willie Mae Wong, baritone (lower right). *Photo courtesy of Rosalind Cron.*

is thought to express, naturally, through her pain, an extra-earthy feminine wisdom that may do the singer no good but which nurtures and entertains listeners?

Clearly the persistence of such problematic representations of race and gender in dominant jazz discourse cover up and damage much more than the history of all-woman bands. Rigorous gender analysis is needed, in conjunction with historically specific, critical analyses of race, racialization, and racism. Again, I suggest that the oral histories of black and white women who played in all-woman bands contain narrative strategies useful to jazz studies scholars in general—not only those of us who write about all-woman bands.

Scratching the Historical Record

When women musicians tell their stories, jazz history tends to come out differently from the usual parade of stars and superlative recordings we often get from mainstream jazz historians. Jazzwomen's stories also have a knack for shaking up the assumptions of an idealistic feminist historiographer who comes along expecting to dig up and celebrate a lost or forgotten jazz sisterhood in such a way as to obliterate sexist practices once and for all. As someone who has spent the last seven years interviewing women who played in all-woman jazz and swing bands of the 1940s, I am so overwhelmed with examples of how women's stories have moved me to rethink and complicate my notions of jazz history and women's history, it is hard to figure out where to start. I "drop the needle," so to speak, on a hot day in June 1994. I am in the Burger King at Washington and Grand in Los Angeles, interviewing Vi Wilson about her half-a-century-and-running career as a jazz bassist. I begin here, over fries and coffee, because it is one of the moments in which I have been most struck with the three-way contrast between how jazz history looks in the mainstream books on the subject, how I, as a feminist jazz historian, imagine it will look, and how jazz history looks when women musicians tell about their lives.

Wilson, who played briefly with the International Sweethearts of Rhythm before switching over to the Darlings of Rhythm in the late 1940s, is telling me about the infrequent but exciting occasions when African American all–woman bands, such as these two or Eddie Durham's All-Star Girls Orchestra, bumped into each other on the road.

Figure 30.2. Violet "Vi" Wilson, publicity photo, circa 1950s. *Photo courtesy of Violet Wilson.*

> Fellas in those days, they had a competition between the Sweethearts and the Darlings. But the Darlings could play. Boy, we would get in jam sessions with them like, whatever town we were in. The fellas, it was a novelty to them to come see these girls play. They said, "Those girls play like men." We'd have a big jam session. Boy, Vi Burnside would really play. And Padjo, we called her Padjo [Margaret Backstrom], she would really play. And, see, the best players, tenor players, were Padjo and Vi Burnside. And Vi Burnside would call Padjo "Lester Young"—I think one was "Lester Young" and the other one was called "Ben Webster." And they'd come shake hands and get on the bandstand. "Let's blow these fellas down!" Oh, we had some good times. . . . And we'd all say, "Let's give them something to talk about!" They'd get up there with the fellas.[4]

Even the most casual reader of jazz history knows that in the mainstream versions women do not tote horns and "blow fellas down" in after-hours jam sessions. Nor are jam sessions coed in dominant versions of history. Jazz is more often portrayed as an exclusive world of male musicians roughing it on the road, tearing it up in legendary jam sessions, waxing creative in clubs, sometimes sharing the spotlight with a lone, begowned female vocalist. Wilson's narrative issues a challenge to the familiar old jazz histories in much the same way that her fondly recalled colleagues gave skeptical male musicians "something to talk about."

And this story also gives feminist historiographers "something to talk about." The coed jam sessions were probably at least as unexpected to me as they would have been to someone working on the assumption that men played instruments and women sang. Presuming that women musicians met with nothing but resentment at every turn, I am surprised that Wilson recalls being welcomed at after-hours jam sessions in strange cities. It astonishes me that the burden of proving to men that women musicians can "really play" is presented here as an occasion for fun, rather than as a perpetual nuisance. Wilson's story in which women musicians square off competitively while amazed men look on, where women take nicknames of men musicians before "blowing the fellas away," issues a challenge to my feminist sensibilities, and tells me I have a great deal to learn from jazzwomen's stories.

I drop the needle again. It is another hot day in June, only this time I am partaking of cranberry juice with two trumpet giants, Jane Sager and Clora Bryant, in Sager's Hollywood trumpet studio. I am enjoying their stories immensely, many of which take up the problem of men's expectations that women musicians are "novelties" and end with the women "blowing them away." Suddenly Sager, who played with many of the major white all-woman bands of the 1930s and 1940s, including those led by Rita Rio and Ada Leonard, regales us with a tale about women musicians "blowing away" quite a different set of unbelievers. While working on vaudeville in the early 1930s, a situation arose where the "tall girls" in the chorus line believed themselves superior to the women musicians in the "all-girl" band, a status that entitled them, they felt, to the best seats on the bus.

> So these girls, when we would be packing up our instruments, they'd go out on the Greyhound and get the best seats. And we'd have to sit over the wheel and bounce and, you know. In the band, we were getting crap. So we weren't going to take it. So what we did, Alice [Raleigh, the drummer] says, "Look, I am going to fix things. You do not have to say a word. Wait till the next show and watch your step because I am going to do something crazy." So she comes to their dance and they're going, "dah, ta-dah, ta-dah, ta-dah," and Alice goes, "one-two-three one-two one-two-three one-two. . . ." Five-four time! And those girls fell on each other, they fell on the stage! I am telling you, after that, they'd say, "Where would you like to sit on the bus?"[5]

While dancers in the chorus line were not exactly the Victorian ideal of traditional womanhood, they were in a more traditional occupation than women drummers or trumpet players in "all-girl" bands. The woman drummer (and Sager in telling this story) proves with humor and panache that women musicians in "all-girl" bands were every bit as important to the success of vaudeville as the glamorous long-legged women of the front line. Indeed, women musicians emerge victorious.[6]

Clora Bryant has an entertaining and amazing story equally unsettling to any remaining feminist assumptions of a "sisterhood" of support for women musicians in a sexist world. While "doing one–nighters up and down the coast" in 1944 with the all-female band from historically black Prairie View College, Bryant found herself playing an army base in Alabama where several male jazz musicians were stationed, including trombonist Jimmy Cheatham and drummer Chico Hamilton. But the competition that ensued was not between male and female musicians, but between women in the audience and women on the bandstand.

> Chico Hamilton was a good-looking guy. He was fine! And he's an egotistical little something anyway. He was a big flirt and it was a small town, and these girls were fighting over who was going to go with him. And we were playing this dance and we were on the stage and we'd had intermission and Chico had introduced himself [to the band] and the whole thing. And after intermission, we're up there playing and all of a sudden we heard a loud commotion and then this bottle—this broad threw this Coke bottle, she was throwing it at the girls! Our front line we had saxophone players and most of them were light girls with long, pretty hair. This broad had thrown a Coke bottle at the band! It just so happened it hit the jukebox and made a loud noise. We all hit the floor. It was something else.[7]

Keeping these three stories in the air is no easy matter. Each stands alone as an expertly crafted and delivered anecdote, each tells of experiences jazzwomen had that are unlikely to have been shared by men, and each is completely different. Yet they all took place in a world historicized as a masculine environment. This juggling act of listening to and learning from women musicians also requires a drastic rethinking of jazz history.

Thanks to the meticulous, groundbreaking work of a small number of researchers and writers devoted to uncovering the histories of women in jazz, we now have a number of what feminist historians call "compensatory" histories. I am grateful to authors such as D. Antoinette Handy, Linda Dahl, Sally Placksin, Frank Driggs, and Leslie Gourse; record producer/historian Rosetta Reitz; and filmmakers Greta Schiller and Andrea Weiss for the extant body of histories of women in jazz. Yet the more I interview women jazz musicians, the more I cannot help but feel that the next step is to find ways of imagining jazz history that include both women and men. I say this as someone who is deeply involved with writing a book on all-woman bands of the 1940s—yet another separate history![8] But even my research on all-woman bands tells me that it is high time to crack open the historical narrative of jazz so that it encompasses the profession as experienced by the women who have been there all along. And the best place to go to learn how to imagine a sphere of jazz history that includes women is the stories of women musicians who already imagine themselves, quite correctly, in jazz history.

Jazz as History

When historian Elsa Barkley Brown urged her colleagues to be more like jazz musicians, she was not talking to jazz historians in particular, but she could have been. Basically, she thought this would be a good idea because history, like jazz,

> is everybody talking at once, multiple rhythms being played simultaneously. The events and people we write about did not occur in isolation but dialogue with a myriad of other people and events. In fact, at any given moment, millions of people are talking at once. As historians we try to isolate one conversation and explore it, but the trick is then how to put that conversation in a context which makes evident its dialogue with so many others— how to make this one lyric stand alone and at the same time be in conjunction with all the other lyrics being sung.[9]

One common theme of the three stories I set in motion in the beginning of this paper is that they all present conversations, dialogues, multiple voices. None of them stakes a claim to a single lyric that can be sung alone. Wilson's story animates a conversation between men who think women players are "novelties" and the women who "blow the fellas away." Sager's pits superior attitudes of dancers against the unrecognized powers of the women who play the tunes. Bryant's demonstrates a contest between women in the audience and women on the band stand. All of these stories contain dialogues missing from mainstream accounts of jazz history.

What if jazz historians were more like women jazz musicians? What if jazz history got told in such a way that we could hear dialogues such as "Women musicians are novelties," "Let's blow these fellas down," "Those women play like men," and so forth? What if the tension, omnipresent in these stories, between a public that assumes that women musicians are "novelties" and women musicians who prove they can "really play" was characterized as a conversation within jazz history, rather than as an inconsequential voice from the margins? What if there was room in the mainstream jazz histories for "conversion" stories, such as this one from Vi Wilson?

We made them respect us because we could blow our instruments. And that was a challenge to them at the same time. Now, with a women's band, it is just a matter of you're all the same sex, and, you know, the best person plays. It doesn't matter. But with men, they always, they have that guard up. "Woman musician, she can't play," you know. Then when we play, that knocks them out. That surprises them. That puts them back in history. Lets them know that women could play just as good as they can. Anytime we walked in, even myself, as a bass player, when I walked in on a set, eyes was raised. When I got through playing, I made a believer out of them.[10]

As Wilson tells it, jazz is a place where women instrumentalists take pride in their work, play just as well as men, and win converts. It is also a world where women are well aware of the powerful belief systems that work against them: the widespread skepticism about their abilities, their reputations as "novelties," and the classic paradoxes of what it means to cross the gender division of labor. In Wilson's history, women know that what they do is considered a "man's job," and when they walk in, men (and sometimes women) will say (or think), "Woman musician, she can't play." And they also know that if they do the job well, they will be said to be good "for girls," or that they "play like men." And they know that even if they "make believers out of them" today, the same battles will have to be fought tomorrow. Her narrative is not one of ultimate triumph over struggle, but one in which struggle is a constant and triumph is cyclical. Wilson's telling of her history, like so many oral narratives of jazzwomen I have interviewed, is a performance that not only renders women visible in a history that erased them, but portrays a savvy understanding of the structures of power that made such erasure possible. Her story also makes what I think is a marvelous intervention into the prevalent notion that women can simply be added into extant versions of jazz history, which are thought to be ungendered. According to Wilson, when men realize that women can play, that puts *the men* back in history.

Jane Sager also told me many stories in which skeptics are convinced, only to be replaced by new skeptics. In one interesting twist on the theme, a skeptic becomes a convert in a most dramatic way, only to be revealed as a perpetual skeptic after all. A white male bandleader hires Sager only after auditioning every male trumpet player in the room first, making her wait in a bar until the wee hours before giving her a chance. Just before the club closes for the night, he calls her to the stand. She outplays the others and gets the job. After playing with the band for a while, however, Sager noticed that the bandleader was watching her closely.

He would follow me around, you know. And he kept waiting for me to get tired. He said, "Aren't you tired?" I said, "Am I supposed to be?" I am holding down a musician's job, it is a man's job, too. But I said, "Why should I be tired?" He said, "Well, I understand that girls menstruate and they do not play so good!" I said, "Ahhh." I said, "I play twice as good when that happens. Where did you get that crazy propaganda?" He followed me around waiting for me to menstruate to see if I would fall over![11]

Cause for More than Celebration

It is tempting to celebrate such stories as recovered bits of women's history, as evidence of women's activity in realms where they were thought not to exist, as proof that women could "really play" in the 1940s. But even then, what we would end up "celebrating" is not a historical nugget tossed to us from jazzwomen of the past, but one story that one writer has selected from hours of others from taped interviews with living sources at particular moments. Women musicians' stories are already shaped by how they perceive the interviewer, and how that perception has influenced decisions over what stories to contribute and what versions of those stories to tell. Even the contents of that vast pool of possible stories most certainly owe a great deal to how women of the 1990s have come to make sense of their careers in the 1940s—not just what happened, but what they remember and how they remember it. As trombonist Helen (Jones) Woods replied when I told her I wanted to tape-record our interview so I could quote her accurately: "As accurately as possible! Be sure to say that. Say you quoted me 'as accurately as she thought she was.'"[12]

And then there is the complicating detail of the interviewer's role in shaping the text that appears before you. In recent years, feminist oral historians have begun to realize that even "celebration" is an executive decision, yet another clue that the relationship between narrator and researcher is rarely an equal one. Usually, as in this case, while it is the narrator who tells the tales during the interview, it is the historian who decides which segments will serve as "something to talk about," and how and in what context to talk about them. The realization that we are not merely benevolent megaphones for "letting women speak for themselves" has sent many a feminist researcher into crisis. While I have certainly lost sleep over this myself, I am ultimately happy to be rid of the fantasy that it is possible for a person to be a conduit. The conduit model fails to notice differences between women (not to mention differences between women and conduits). The assumption that I can be a conduit, channeling voices of jazzwomen to written history, depends upon an assumption that jazzwomen are merely conduits to lived history. Neither assumption seems suitable (or feminist) to me.[13]

Also, while it might feel good to celebrate the fact that Burnside and Backstrom were out there proving that women could "really play" fifty years ago, what does that do for the everyday fact that many female jazz musicians continue to experience the burden of "proving that women can play" whenever they take the stand?[14] As recently as April 1996 Fostina Dixon told the *Washington Post*, "People still come up to me and say, 'You're the first female saxophone player I have ever heard.'"[15] What does celebration do to the fact that mainstream historical narratives that ignore jazzwomen's lives continue to get written? I would like to suggest other ways in which stories of jazzwomen might be even more useful.

There are those who would argue that oral histories and interviews are not particularly useful in jazz historiography. The main criticism, according to Burton Peretti, "asks how any testimony presented decades after the fact could possibly 'clear up' the historical record." Peretti then points out that in jazz history, there is often a lack of hard evidence from the past; thus oral histories become the only way for finding out histories of particular periods, people, and relationships.[16] I would add that this is especially so in the case of jazzwomen's history. Peretti also argues that perhaps more value can come from taking the folklorists' approach of studying oral history narratives as performances. Making a similar case for the value of looking at "textual strategies" and "performance dynamics" in jazz autobiographies, Kathy Ogren argues that "historians need to recognize the possibilities—not merely the limitations—of self–fashioned personas."[17] My interests in studying the ways women jazz instrumentalists tell their stories include my conviction that (1) the memories of living jazzwomen hold much history that is not to be found elsewhere, (2) there is great value in learning how they interpret their own lives, and (3) the shapes jazz history takes when women musicians tell their stories may prove instructive to anyone interested in expanding our repertoire of this thing we call jazz history.

More than an artifact of history, Wilson's story of the coed jam session is an interpretation of history, one that she contributes knowing full well how different it is from dominant ideas about masculine jam sessions and feminine "novelty" acts.[18] The female saxophonists in Wilson's story are well aware that the men who come to hear them and play with them consider them "a novelty." But that doesn't mean the women musicians see themselves as a "novelty." It also doesn't mean that they are able to get rid of the stigma of "novelty" once and for all. The women nickname each other after favorite male tenor sax players, "Lester Young" and "Ben Webster," before proving to the skeptics that women can "really play." They are portrayed as confident and skilled, yet Wilson's repeated insistence that "they would really play" also conveys a historical relationship between women musicians and their ubiquitous doubting public: "Can they play?"

When mainstream jazz histories omit women musicians, it is like saying, "Women musicians, they can't play." When women-in-jazz researchers celebrate the accomplishments of women musicians, it is like saying, "Yes, they can!" (which has been an important argument to assert, since the other side has received so much press). But what if the frameworks of jazz history were to incorporate both sides of the tension, as women musicians so often do when they interpret their careers? What if the scope of jazz history was made wide enough to recognize all the voices Wilson hears from that perpetual after-hours club of fifty years ago: the male skeptics who come to hear a "novelty," the female tenor sax stars who "blow these fellas away," the converts, the next set of skeptics?

Another reason to do more than "celebrate" the stories of women jazz musicians is that "celebration" assumes a kind of "sisterhood" among women that does not always appear in the historical narratives. Many women musicians did not like to play with women. There was some crossing of race lines when black bands such as the International Sweethearts of Rhythm and the Darlings of Rhythm occasionally hired white members who passed as black onstage. For the most part, however, all-female bands, like male bands, were segregated along a black-white binary and played for segregated audiences in the 1920s, 1930s, and 1940s. Jim Crow constructions of whiteness as a "pure" category meant that mixed–race women and women of color who were not African American were more likely to be included in bands on the more inclusive, yet decidedly less privileged, "black" side of the race division. Chinese American Willie Mae Wong (Scott) recalls that she was never required to pass as black to play in black bands in the South and was never harassed by the police for traveling with a black band.[19] Latinas were sometimes coded "white." Some women who were legally black under laws that defined anyone with any black ancestry as black passed as "Spanish" to play in white bands, though it must be said that this kind of passing, and indeed black-to-white passing in general, was quite different from the passing of white women who played with black bands. White alto saxophonist Roz Cron speculated that her presence in the International Sweethearts of Rhythm endangered the black women in the band more than it did herself. "They were the ones that would have suffered. I would have gotten slapped on the wrist and sent home or something."[20] White women could regain white privilege at any time. In order for black women to get work in the most famous and lucrative all-woman bands, they would have to pass as white offstage as well as on, in many areas of their lives. I know of only one white all-woman band in the 1940s whose leader knowingly hired a black musician—and this musician was very light-skinned and had blue eyes. These histories are too complex and too unbalanced to warrant uncritical celebration.[21] A "celebration" of women's stories might also miss the fact that some male musicians were supportive and encouraging of some female musicians, and that men weren't the only people in jazz history who have sometimes been skeptical of women instrumentalists.

Figure 30.3. Sax section, International Sweethearts of Rhythm, After Hours club, Seattle, 1994. *Courtesy of Rosalind Cron.*

Utopian Spaces and Jazz Futures

I would like to close with Clora Bryant's story of jamming in the clubs on Central Avenue, Los Angeles, in the 1940s. This reverie, which she has related to me many times, is an excellent example of how history might be opened up to include unrecorded performances, lesser-known jazz practitioners, and local scenes as sites where we might look if we want to account for lives of both male and female musicians. It also brings me to the topic of jazzwomen's nostalgia, which I see as an area that could be productively explored, again not simply for data nor for proof of participation, but for the conceptual and narrative strategies therein.

During the same period in which Bryant was playing trumpet professionally in all-female combos such as the Queens of Swing, touring all-white towns in the western states where they were often thought to be not merely "novelties" but "exotic," Bryant also spent the time she had in her home base of Los Angeles participating in those now-famous jam sessions with artists such as Wardell Gray, Sonny Criss, Teddy Edwards, and Hampton Hawes. While records, radio broadcasts, and "favored artists" all make appearances in her narrative, Bryant's definition of what counts as jazz history is not dependent on industry support. Her vivid telling of her own engagement with bebop is one of participation, not marginalization.

> I would sit and play Dizzy's record. The first thing that I could play by him was a ballad, "I Can't Get Started," because before that, everybody was doing Bunny Berigan's version. Everybody imitated Bunny Berigan playing "I Can't Get Started." Then when I

heard Dizzy play it, I said, "Wait a minute!" I bought the record and learned it note for note. It was fun. Those were some fun times. I mean the guys, there was a camaraderie that we do not have now. You always knew where you could go and see the best musicians and your friends and hear the best music and get up there and try to play with those people. And you knew you were going to be bopped to death. You know, you knew it was going to be so great! There would be no doubt about it. And you would come out of there and "whew!" I would come out of there with my little trumpet and go home and get the records and I would be in that record player, boy. At that time we had wire recording. Tape wasn't in, but it was wire recording. I had a wire recorder and, man, I would get that and I would try to be playing and I would listen and say, "What was that I was playing?" It was a learning time, and it was a happy time, it was a friendly time, it was a musical time, and it was, you know, it was just something that if you haven't been at that place at that time, you can't explain it.[22]

In her nostalgic portrait of Central Avenue in the 1940s, Bryant evokes a scene in which jazz practice was as serious a calling for those who played with the records as for those who played on the records, for both the known and unknown artists who encountered each other at jam sessions and got "bopped to death." While Bryant is not alone in identifying playing along with records as an important historical site for jazz education and practice, her story is unique because it reveals the participation of women in this important training ground.[23] She portrays herself as a wide-eyed seventeen-year-old, immersed in music and in the technologies that help her to discover what Gillespie is doing and to hone her own skills. Other portions of her narrative explore the kinds of skepticisms, sexisms, and racisms she experienced both on and off the road in her fifty-year career as a jazz musician, but the private sessions with records and public musical collaborations in jam sessions in the clubs of Central Avenue are recalled again and again as utopian spaces for thinking about jazz. And, according to Paul Gilroy, utopian spaces are not just sites for nostalgia, they are important keys to imagining egalitarian futures.[24] If Bryant's account of her participation on Central Avenue in its prime was included in mainstream histories, how might it break up assumptions that serious jazz involvement was out of reach for women trumpet players in the 1940s?[25] How might Bryant's vision of jazz history as something that happens at home as well as in clubs, to underrecorded artists as well as to oft-recorded ones, and to women as well as men, prepare musicians, historians, scholars, and fans to believe in and care about the women trumpet players who arrived later—who are arriving now?

Anyone interested in a more complete account of jazz history, as well as in a more egalitarian jazz future, would do well to listen to jazzwomen's "telling performances." Such stories should be studied carefully for women musicians' myriad tactics for asserting and maintaining identities as jazz musicians: in the business, on the bandstand, and in their memories. If histories were remade to encompass the stories women jazz musicians tell when they talk about their lives, we would know more about jazz and we would know more about women.

Notes

1. Krin Gabbard, "The Jazz Canon and Its Consequences," in Krin Gabbard, ed., *Jazz among the Discourses* (Durham: Duke University Press, 1995), 8–9, 16; Scott De Veaux, "Constructing the Jazz Tradition: Jazz Historiography," *Black American Literature Forum* 25, 3 (fall 1991): 525; Jed Rasula, "The Media of Memory: The Seductive Menace of Records in Jazz History," in Gabbard, *Jazz among the Discourses*, 136, 144.

2. Joan Wallach Scott, *Gender and the Politics of History* (New York: Columbia University Press, 1988), 42–43.

3. See Ingrid Monson's discussion of the gendered dimensions and prevalence of "primitivist ideas of the African American artist unspoiled by culture or civilization" in fanatically well-intentioned jazz prose penned

by white men. Ingrid Monson, "The Problem with White Hipness: Race, Gender, and Cultural Conceptions in Jazz Historical Discourse," *Journal of the American Musicological Society* 48, 3 (fall 1995): 396–422.

4. Vi Wilson, interview by author, 12 June 1994.

5. Jane Sager, interview by author, 10 June 1994.

6. Many jazzwomen, both black and white, who played in the 1920s, 1930s, and 1940s have told me stories in which they distanced themselves from dancers in chorus lines. One musician informed me that chorines were notoriously underpaid and often supplemented their incomes by practicing the "world's oldest profession." Whether or not this was always the case, the widespread public perception of chorines as musical prostitutes would seem to explain why women musicians, who were already fighting against stereotypes of women on the stage as sexually excessive, might wish to distance themselves from such stigmas.

7. Clora Bryan, interview by author, 5 August 1993.

8. Sherrie Tucker, *Changing the Players, Playing the Changes: "All-Girl" Bands during World War II* (Durham: Duke University Press, forthcoming).

9. Elsa Barkley Brown, "Polyrhythms and Improvisation: Lessons for Women's History," *History Workshop Journal* (spring 1991), 84.

10. Vi Wilson, interview by author, 9 November 1993.

11. Jane Sager, interview by author, 2 April 1994. For expanded accounts of this story, see Sally Placksin, *Jazz Women: 1900 to the Present* (London: Pluto Press, 1982), 105–6; and Sherrie Tucker, "Interview with Jane Sager," *Newsletter of the International Women's Brass Conference* 2, 1 (February 1995).

12. Helen (Jones) Woods, interview by author, 20 February 1995.

13. See Sherna Berger Gluck and Daphne Patai, eds., *Women's Words: The Feminist Practice of Oral History* (New York: Routledge, 1991). In her essay "Can There Be a Feminist Ethnography," Judith Stacey worried that if the researcher controls the product, alliance is merely a delusion. And "delusions of alliance" inevitably lead to "betrayal" (113). While I take these concerns to heart, and in fact do often feel closely "allied" with my informants (close enough to worry about "betraying" them), I am also persuaded by Kamala Visweswaran's suggestion that yearning for the lost "innocence" of the conduit is less suitable as a feminist principle than the disappointing specter of betrayal. See Visweswaran, "Betrayal: An Analysis in Three Acts," in Inderpal Grewal and Caren Kapian, eds., *Scattered Hegemonies: Postmodernity and Transnational Feminist Practices* (Minneapolis: University of Minnesota Press, 1994).

14. See any number of reviews of the contemporary all-woman band Diva, including Zan Stewart, "All-Female Band Diva Breaking Stereotypes," *Los Angeles Times*, 16 June 1995, F12.

15. Richard Harrington, "The Rhythm Queens at the Kennedy Center, a Celebration of Women in Jazz," *Washington Post*, 28 April 1996, G1.

16. Burton Peretti, "Oral Histories of Jazz Musicians: The NEA Transcripts as Text in Context," in Gabbard, ed., *Jazz among the Discourses*, 122.

17. Kathy Ogren, "'Jazz Isn't Just Me': Jazz Autobiographies as Performances," in Reginald T. Buckner and Steven Weiland, eds., *Jazz in Mind: Essays on the History and Meanings of Jazz* (Detroit: Wayne State University Press, 1991), 112–14.

18. Writes Douglas Henry Daniels, "The musicians' conception of history and desire to make a contribution needs to be rigorously examined." Douglas Henry Daniels, "Oral History, Masks, and Protocol in the Jazz Community," *Oral History Review* 15, 1 (1987): 143–64.

19. Willie Mae Wong (Scott), interview by author, 3 December 1996.

20. Roz Cron, interview by author, 13 August 1990.

21. For more on the "one-drop rule" and the Jim Crow South, see F. James Davis, *Who Is Black? One Nation's Definition* (University Park: Pennsylvania State University Press, 1991), and Michael Omi and Howard Winant, *Racial Formation in the United States: From the 1960s to the 1990s*, 2nd ed. (New York: Routledge, 1994). For more on how the International Sweethearts of Rhythm negotiated these structures with racially diverse personnel, see D. Antoinette Handy, *The International Sweethearts of Rhythm* (Metuchen, N.J.: Scarecrow Press, 1983) and the documentary by Greta Schiller and Andrea Weiss, *International Sweethearts of Rhythm* (Jezebel Productions, 1986).

22. Clora Bryant, interview by author, 7 October 1990.

23. Paul Berliner includes learning from records as part of his study of the "wide compass of practice and thought that improvisers give to music outside formal performance events." Paul Berliner, *Thinking in Jazz: The Infinite Art of Improvisation* (Chicago: University of Chicago Press, 1994), 15. See also Charles Keil and Steven Feld, "Dialogue 1: Getting into the Dialogic Groove," in *Music Grooves* (Chicago: University of Chicago Press, 1994), 1–31.

24. See Paul Gilroy, "Diaspora, Utopia and the Critique of Capitalism," in *There Ain't No Black in the Union Jack: The Cultural Politics of Race and Nation* (Chicago: University of Chicago Press, 1987). In fact, in Bryant's privileging of playing along with records (rather than passively listening to them) and jam sessions over

gigs, the utopian spaces of her narrative are similar to some of Gilroy's examples of cultural practices that he sees as critiques of capitalism.

25. It is important to note that this work is increasingly being done in jazz oral history archives, though less so in books and films about jazz history. The inclusion of female jazz musicians' narratives in major repositories presents opportunities for jazz historians interested in multivocal approaches, in frameworks that account for both men and women, and in exploring how gender operated in particular times and places in jazz history. Bryant's oral history has been collected by the Smithsonian Jazz Oral History Program (along with those of many other women musicians), as well as by the Central Avenue Sounds Oral History Project at the University of California, Los Angeles. Steven Isoardi's interviews with Bryant and trombonist Melba Liston appear alongside those of male musicians in Clora Bryant et al., ed., *Central Avenue Sounds: Jazz in Los Angeles* (Berkeley: University of California Press, 1998).

31

Japanese American Women during World War II

Valerie Matsumoto

The life here cannot be expressed. Sometimes, we are resigned to it, but when we see the barbed wire fences and the sentry tower with floodlights, it gives us a feeling of being prisoners in a "concentration camp." We try to be happy and yet oftentimes a gloominess does creep in. When I see the "I'm an American" editorial and write-ups, the "equality of race etc."—it seems to be mocking us in our faces. I just wonder if all the sacrifices and hard labor on the part of our parents has gone up to leave nothing to show for it?
—Letter from Shizuko Horiuchi, Pomona Assembly Center, 24 May 1942

Thirty years after her relocation camp internment, another nisei woman, the artist Miné Okubo, observed, "The impact of the evacuation is not on the material and the physical. It is something far deeper. It is the effect on the spirit."[1] Describing the lives of Japanese American women during World War II and assessing the effects of the camp experience on the spirit are complex tasks: Factors such as age, generation, personality, and family background interweave and preclude simple generalizations. In these relocation camps Japanese American women faced severe racism and traumatic family strain, but the experience also fostered changes in their lives: more leisure for older women, equal pay with men for working women, disintegration of traditional patterns of arranged marriages, and, ultimately, new opportunities for travel, work, and education for the younger women.

I will examine the lives of Japanese American women during the trying war years, focusing on the second generation—the nisei—whose work and education were most affected. The nisei women entered college and ventured into new areas of work in unfamiliar regions of the country, sustained by fortitude, family ties, discipline, and humor. My understanding of their history derives from several collections of internees' letters, assembly center and relocation camp newspapers, census records, and taped oral history interviews that I conducted with eighty-four nisei and eleven issei (the first generation). Two-thirds of these interviews were with women.

The personal letters, which comprise a major portion of my research, were written in English by nisei women in their late teens and twenties. Their writing reflects the experience and concerns of their age group. It is important, however, to remember that they wrote these letters to Caucasian friends and sponsors during a time of great insecurity and psychological and economic hardship. In their struggle to be accepted as American citizens, the interned Japanese Americans were likely to minimize their suffering in the camps and to try to project a positive image of their adjustment to the traumatic conditions.

Prewar Background

A century ago, male Japanese workers began to arrive on American shores, dreaming of making fortunes that would enable them to return to their homeland in triumph. For many, the fortune did not materialize and the shape of the dream changed: They developed stakes in small farms and businesses and, together with wives brought from Japan, established families and communities.

The majority of Japanese women—over thirty-three thousand immigrants—entered the United States between 1908 and 1924.[2] The "Gentlemen's Agreement" of 1908 restricted the entry of male Japanese laborers into the country but sanctioned the immigration of parents, wives, and children of laborers already residing in the United States. The Immigration Act of 1924 excluded Japanese immigration altogether.

Some Japanese women traveled to reunite with husbands; others journeyed to America as newlyweds with men who had returned to Japan to find wives. Still others came alone as picture brides to join issei men who sought to avoid army conscription or excessive travel expenses; their family-arranged marriages deviated from social convention only by the absence of the groom from the *miai* (preliminary meeting of prospective spouses) and wedding ceremony.[3] Once settled, these women confronted unfamiliar clothing, food, language, and customs as well as life with husbands who were, in many cases, strangers and often ten to fifteen years their seniors.

Most issei women migrated to rural areas of the West. Some lived with their husbands in labor camps, which provided workers for the railroad industry, the lumber mills of the Pacific Northwest, and the Alaskan salmon canneries.[4] They also farmed with their husbands as cash or share tenants, particularly in California, where Japanese immigrant agriculture began to flourish. In urban areas, women worked as domestics or helped their husbands run small businesses such as laundries, bath houses, restaurants, pool halls, boarding houses, grocery stores, curio shops, bakeries, and plant nurseries.[5] Except for the few who married well-to-do professionals or merchants, the majority of issei women unceasingly toiled both inside and outside the home. They were always the first to rise in the morning and the last to go to bed at night.

The majority of the issei's children, the nisei, were born between 1910 and 1940. Both girls and boys were incorporated into the family economy early, especially those living on farms. They took care of their younger siblings, fed the farm animals, heated water for the *furo* (Japanese bath), and worked in the fields before and after school—hoeing weeds, irrigating, and driving tractors. Daughters helped with cooking and cleaning. In addition, all were expected to devote time to their studies: the issei instilled in their children a deep respect for education and authority. They repeatedly admonished the nisei not to bring disgrace upon the family or community and exhorted them to do their best in everything.

The nisei grew up integrating both the Japanese ways of their parents and the mainstream customs of their non-Japanese friends and classmates—not always an easy process given the deeply rooted prejudice and discrimination they faced as a tiny, easily identified minority. Because of the wide age range among them and the diversity of their early experiences in various urban and rural areas, it is difficult to generalize about the nisei. Most grew up speaking Japanese with their parents and English with their siblings, friends, and teachers. Regardless of whether they were Buddhist or Christian, they celebrated the New Year with traditional foods and visiting, as well as Christmas and Thanksgiving. Girls learned to knit, sew, and embroider, and some took lessons in *odori* (folk dancing). The nisei, many of whom were adolescents during the 1940s, also listened to the *Hit Parade*, Jack Benny, and *Gangbusters* on the radio, learned to jitterbug, played kick-the-can and baseball, and read the same popular books and magazines as their non-Japanese peers.

The issei were strict and not inclined to open displays of affection toward their children, but the nisei were conscious of their parents' concern for them and for the family. This sense of family strength and responsibility helped to sustain the issei and nisei through years of economic hardship and discrimination: the West Coast anti-Japanese movement of the early 1920s, the Depression of the 1930s, and the most drastic ordeal—the chaotic uprooting that occurred during the World War II evacuation, internment, and resettlement.

Evacuation and Camp Experience

The bombing of Pearl Harbor on 7 December 1941 unleashed war between the United States and Japan and triggered a wave of hostility against Japanese Americans. On 8 December the financial resources of the issei were frozen, and the Federal Bureau of Investigation began to seize issei community leaders thought to be strongly pro-Japanese. Rumors spread that the Japanese in Hawaii had aided the attack on Pearl Harbor, fueling fears of "fifth-column" activity on the West Coast. Politicians and the press clamored for restrictions against the Japanese Americans, and their economic competitors saw the chance to gain control of Japanese American farms and businesses.

Despite some official doubts and some differences of opinion among military heads regarding the necessity of removing Japanese Americans from the West Coast, in the end the opinions of civilian leaders, Lieutenant General John L. DeWitt—head of the Western Defense Command—Assistant Secretary of War John McCloy, and Secretary of War Henry Stimson prevailed. On 19 February 1942 President Franklin Delano Roosevelt signed Executive Order 9066, arbitrarily suspending the civil rights of American citizens by authorizing the removal of 110,000 Japanese and their American-born children from the western half of the Pacific coastal states and the southern third of Arizona.[6]

During the bewildering months before evacuation, the Japanese Americans were subject to curfews and to unannounced searches at all hours for "contraband" weapons, radios, and cameras; in desperation and fear, many people destroyed their belongings from Japan, including treasured heirlooms, books, and photographs. Some families moved voluntarily from the Western Defense Zone, but many stayed, believing that all areas would eventually be restricted or fearing hostility in neighboring states.

Involuntary evacuation began in the spring of 1942. Families received a scant week's notice in which to "wind up their affairs, store or sell their possessions, close up their businesses and homes, and show up at an assembly point for transportation to an assembly center."[7] Each person was allowed to bring only as many clothes and personal items as he or she could carry to the temporary assembly centers that had been hastily constructed at fairgrounds, race tracks, and Civilian Conservation Corps camps: twelve in California, one in Oregon, and one in Washington.

The rapidity of evacuation left many Japanese Americans numb; one nisei noted that "a queer lump came to my throat. Nothing else came to my mind, it was just blank. Everything happened too soon, I guess."[8] As the realization of leaving home, friends, and neighborhood sank in, the numbness gave way to bewilderment. A teenager at the Santa Anita Assembly Center wrote, "I felt lost after I left Mountain View [California]. I thought that we could go back but instead look where we are."[9] Upon arrival at the assembly centers, even the nisei from large urban communities found themselves surrounded by more Japanese than they had ever before seen. For Mary Okumura, the whole experience seemed overwhelming at first:

> Just about every night, there is something going on but I rather stay home because I am just new here & don't know very much around. As for the people I met so many all ready, I don't remember any. I am not even going to try to remember names because its just impossible here.[10]

A nisei from a community where there were few Japanese felt differently about her arrival at the Merced Assembly Center: "I guess at that age it was sort of fun for me really [rather] than tragic, because for the first time I got to see young [Japanese] people. . . . We signed up to work in the mess hall—we got to meet everybody that way."[11]

Overlying the mixed feelings of anxiety, anger, shame, and confusion was resignation. As a relatively small minority caught in a storm of turbulent events that destroyed their individual and community security, there was little the Japanese Americans could do but shrug and say, *"Shikata ga nai,"* or "It can't be helped," the implication being that the situation must be endured. The phrase lingered on many lips when the issei, nisei, and the young sansei (third-generation) children prepared for the move—which was completed by November 1942—to the ten permanent relocation camps organized by the War Relocation Authority: Topaz, Utah; Poston and Gila River, Arizona; Amache, Colorado; Manzanar and Tule Lake, California; Heart Mountain, Wyoming; Minidoka, Idaho; Denson and Rohwer, Arkansas.[12] Denson and Rohwer were located in the swampy lowlands of Arkansas; the other camps were in desolate desert or semidesert areas subject to dust storms and extreme temperatures, reflected in the nicknames given to the three sections of the Poston Camp: Toaston, Roaston, and Duston.

The conditions of camp life profoundly altered family relations and affected women of all ages and backgrounds. Family unity deteriorated in the crude communal facilities and cramped barracks. The unceasing battle with the elements, the poor food, and the shortages of toilet tissue and milk, coupled with wartime profiteering and mismanagement and the sense of injustice and frustration, took their toll on a people uprooted, far from home.

The standard housing in the camps was a spartan barracks, about twenty feet by one hundred feet, divided into four to six rooms furnished with steel army cots. Initially each single room or "apartment" housed an average of eight persons; individuals without kin nearby were often moved in with smaller families. Because the partitions between apartments did not reach the ceiling, even the smallest noises traveled freely from one end of the building to the other. There were usually fourteen barracks in each block, and each block had its own mess hall, laundry, latrine, shower facilities, and recreation room.

Because of the discomfort, noise, and lack of privacy, which "made a single symphony of yours and your neighbors' loves, hates, and joys," the barracks often became merely a place to "hang your hat" and sleep.[13] As Jeanne Wakatsuki Houston records in her autobiography, *Farewell to Manzanar*, many family members began to spend less time together in the crowded barracks. The even greater lack of privacy in the latrine and shower facilities necessitated adjustments in former notions of modesty. There were no partitions in the shower room, and the latrine consisted of two rows of partitioned toilets "with nothing in front of you, just on the sides. Lots of people were not used to those kind of facilities, so [they'd] either go early in the morning when people were not around, or go real late at night. . . . It was really something until you got used to it."[14]

The large communal mess halls also encouraged family disunity as family members gradually began to eat separately: mothers with small children, fathers with other men, and older children with their peers. "Table manners were forgotten," observed Miné Okubo. "Guzzle, guzzle, guzzle; hurry, hurry, hurry. Family life was lacking. Everyone ate wherever he or she pleased."[15] Some strategies were developed for preserving family unity. The Amache Camp responded in part by assigning each family a particular table in the mess hall. Some families took the food back to their barracks so that they might eat together. But these measures were not always feasible in the face of varying work schedules; the odd hours of those assigned to shifts in the mess halls and infirmaries often made it impossible for the family to sit down together for meals.

Newspaper reports that Japanese Americans were living in luxurious conditions angered evacuees struggling to adjust to cramped quarters and crude communal facilities. A married woman with a family wrote from Heart Mountain:

> Last weekend, we had an awful cold wave and it was about 20° to 30° below zero. In such a weather, it's terrible to try going even to the bath and latrine house. . . . It really aggravates me to hear some politicians say we Japanese are being coddled, for *it isn't so!!* We're on ration as much as outsiders are. I'd say welcome to anyone to try living behind barbed wire and be cooped in a 20 ft. by 20 ft. room. . . . We do our sleeping, dressing, ironing, hanging up our clothes in this one room.[16]

After the first numbness of disorientation, the evacuees set about making their situation bearable, creating as much order in their lives as possible. With blankets they partitioned their apartments into tiny rooms and created benches, tables, and shelves as piles of scrap lumber left over from barracks construction vanished; victory gardens and flower patches appeared. Evacuees also took advantage of the opportunity to taste freedom when they received temporary permits to go shopping in nearby towns. These were memorable occasions. A Heart Mountain nisei described what such a trip meant to her in 1944:

> For the first time since being behind the fences, I managed to go out shopping to Billings, Montana—a trip about 4 hours ride on train and bus. . . . It was quite a mental relief to breathe the air on the outside. . . . And was it an undescribable sensation to be able to be dressed up and walk the pavements with my high heel shoes!! You just can't imagine how full we are of pent-up emotions until we leave the camp behind us and see the highway ahead of us. A trip like that will keep us from becoming mentally narrow. And without much privacy, you can imagine how much people will become dull.[17]

Despite the best efforts of the evacuees to restore order to their disputed world, camp conditions prevented replication of their prewar lives. Women's work experiences, for example, changed in complex ways during the years of internment. Each camp offered a wide range of jobs, resulting from the organization of the camps as model cities administered through a series of departments headed by Caucasian administrators. The departments handled everything from accounting, agriculture, education, and medical care to mess hall service and the weekly newspaper. The scramble for jobs began early in the assembly centers and camps, and all able-bodied persons were expected to work.

Even before the war many family members had worked, but now children and parents, men and women all received the same low wages. In the relocation camps, doctors, teachers, and other professionals were at the top of the pay scale, earning $19 per month. The majority of workers received $16, and apprentices earned $12. The new equity in pay and the variety of available jobs gave many women unprecedented opportunities for experimentation, as illustrated by one woman's account of her family's work in Poston:

> First I wanted to find art work, but I didn't last too long because it wasn't very interesting . . . so I worked in the mess hall, but that wasn't for me, so I went to the accounting department—time-keeping—and I enjoyed that, so I stayed there. . . . My dad . . . went to a shoe shop . . . and then he was block gardener. . . . He got $16. . . . My sister was secretary for the block manager; then she went to the optometry department. She was assistant optometrist; she fixed all the glasses and fitted them. . . . That was $16.[18]

As early as 1942 the War Relocation Authority began to release evacuees temporarily from the centers and camps to do voluntary seasonal farm work in neighboring areas hard hit by the wartime labor shortage. The work was arduous, as one young woman discovered when she left Topaz to take a job plucking turkeys:

> The smell is terrific until you get used to it. . . . We all wore gunny sacks around our waist, had a small knife and plucked off the fine feathers.
> This is about the hardest work that many of us have done—but without a murmur of complaint we worked 8 hours through the first day without a pause.
> We were all so tired that we didn't even feel like eating. . . . Our fingers and wrists were just aching, and I just dreamt of turkeys and more turkeys.[19]

Work conditions varied from situation to situation, and some exploitative farmers refused to pay the Japanese Americans after they had finished topping beets or picking fruit. One worker noted that the degree of friendliness on the employer's part decreased as the harvest neared completion. Nonetheless, many workers, like the turkey plucker, concluded that "even if the work is hard, it is worth the freedom we are allowed."

Camp life increased the leisure of many evacuees. A good number of issei women, accustomed to long days of work inside and outside the home, found that the communally prepared meals and limited living quarters provided them with spare time. Many availed themselves of the opportunity to attend adult classes taught by both evacuees and non-Japanese. Courses involving handcrafts and traditional Japanese arts such as flower arranging, sewing, painting, calligraphy, and wood carving became immensely popular as an overwhelming number of people turned to art for recreation and self-expression. Some of these subjects were viewed as hobbies and leisure activities by those who taught them, but to the issei women they represented access to new skills and a means to contribute to the material comfort of the family.

The evacuees also filled their time with Buddhist and Christian church meetings, theatrical productions, cultural programs, athletic events, and visits with friends. All family members spent more time than ever before in the company of their peers. Nisei from isolated rural areas were exposed to the ideas, styles, and pastimes of the more sophisticated urban youth; in camp they had the time and opportunity to socialize—at work, school, dances, sports events, and parties—in an almost entirely Japanese American environment. Gone were the restrictions of distance, lack of transportation, interracial uneasiness, and dawn-to-dusk field work.

Like their noninterned contemporaries, most young nisei women envisioned a future of marriage and children. They—and their parents—anticipated that they would marry other Japanese Americans, but these young women also expected to choose their own husbands and to marry "for love." This mainstream American ideal of marriage differed greatly from the issei's view of love as a bond that might evolve over the course of an arranged marriage that was firmly rooted in less romantic notions of compatibility and responsibility. The discrepancy between issei and nisei conceptions of love and marriage had sturdy prewar roots; internment fostered further divergence from the old customs of arranged marriage.

In the artificial hothouse of camp, nisei romances often bloomed quickly. As nisei men left to prove their loyalty to the United States in the 442nd Combat Team and the 100th Battalion, young Japanese Americans strove to grasp what happiness and security they could, given the uncertainties of the future. Lily Shoji, in her "Fern-a-lites" newspaper column, commented upon the "changing world" and advised nisei women:

> this is the day of sudden dates, of blind dates on the up-and-up, so let the flash of a uniform be a signal to you to be ready for any emergency. . . . Romance is blossoming with the emotion and urgency of war.[20]

In keeping with this atmosphere, camp newspaper columns such as Shoji's in *The Mercedian*, *The Daily Tulean Dispatch*'s "Strictly Feminine," and the *Poston Chronicle*'s "Fashionotes" gave their nisei readers countless suggestions on how to impress boys, care for their complexions, and choose the latest fashions. These evacuee-authored columns thus mirrored the mainstream girls' periodicals of the time. Such fashion news may seem incongruous in the context of an internment camp whose inmates had little choice in clothing beyond what they could find in the Montgomery Ward or Sears and Roebuck mail-order catalogues. These columns, however, reflect women's efforts to remain in touch with the world outside the barbed wire fence; they reflect as well women's attempt to maintain morale in a drab, depressing environment. "There's something about color in clothes," speculated Tule Lake columnist "Yuri"; "Singing colors have a heart-building effect. . . . Color is a stimulant we need—both for its effect on ourselves and on others."[21]

The evacuees' fashion columns addressed practical as well as aesthetic concerns, reflecting the dusty realities of camp life. In this vein, Mitzi Sugita of the Poston Sewing Department praised the "Latest Fashion for Women Today—Slacks," drawing special attention to overalls; she assured her readers that these "digging duds" were not only winsome and workable but also possessed the virtues of being inexpensive and requiring little ironing.[22]

The columnists' concern with the practical aspects of fashion extended beyond the confines of the camps as women began to leave for life on the outside—an opportunity increasingly available after 1943. Sugita told prospective operatives, "If you are one of the many thousands of women now entering in commercial and industrial work, your required uniform is based on slacks, safe and streamlined. It is very important that they be durable, trim and attractive."[23] Women heading for clerical positions or college were more likely to heed Marii Kyogoku's admonitions to invest in "really nice things," with an eye to "simple lines which are good practically forever."[24]

Resettlement: College and Work

Relocation began slowly in 1942. Among the first to venture out of the camps were college students, assisted by the National Japanese American Student Relocation Council, a nongovernmental agency that provided invaluable placement aid to 4,084 nisei in the years 1942–46.[25] Founded in 1942 by concerned educators, this organization persuaded institutions outside the restricted Western Defense Zone to accept nisei students and facilitated their admissions and leave clearances. A study of the first four hundred students to leave camp showed that a third of them were women.[26] Because of the cumbersome screening process, few other evacuees departed on indefinite leave before 1943. In that year, the War Relocation Authority tried to expedite the clearance procedure by broadening an army registration program aimed at nisei males to include all adults. With this policy change, the migration from the camps steadily increased.[27]

Many nisei, among them a large number of women, were anxious to leave the limbo of camp and return "to normal life again."[28] With all its work, social events, and cultural activities, camp was still an artificial, limited environment. It was stifling "to see nothing but the same barracks, mess halls, and other houses, row after row, day in and day out, it gives us the feeling that we're missing all the freedom and liberty."[29] An aspiring teacher wrote: "Mother and father do not want me to go out. However, I want to go so very much that sometimes I feel that I'd go even if they disowned me. What shall I do? I realize the hard living conditions outside but I think I can take it."[30] Women's developing sense of independence in the camp environment and their growing awareness of their abilities as workers contributed to their self-confidence and hence their desire to leave. Significantly, issei parents, despite initial reluctance, were gradually beginning to sanction their daughters' departures for education and employment in the Midwest and East. One nisei noted:

> [Father] became more broad-minded in the relocation center. He was more mellow in his ways. . . . At first he didn't want me to relocate, but he gave in. . . . I said I wanted to go [to Chicago] with my friend, so he helped me pack. He didn't say I could go . . . but he helped me pack, so I thought, "Well, he didn't say no."[31]

The decision to relocate was a difficult one. It was compounded for some women because they felt obligated to stay and care for elderly or infirm parents, like the Heart Mountain nisei who observed wistfully, "It's getting so more and more of the girls and boys are leaving camp, and I sure wish I could but mother's getting on and I just can't leave her."[32] Many internees worried about their acceptance in the outside world. The nisei considered themselves American citizens, and they had an allegiance to the land of their birth: "The teaching and love of one's own birth place, one's own country was . . . strongly impressed upon my mind as a child. So even though California may deny our rights of birth, I shall ever love her soil."[33] But evacuation had taught the Japanese Americans that in the eyes of many of their fellow Americans, theirs was the face of the enemy. Many nisei were torn by mixed feelings of shame, frustration, and bitterness at the denial of their civil rights. These factors created an atmosphere of anxiety that surrounded those who contemplated resettlement. "A feeling of uncertainty hung over the camp; we were worried about the future. Plans were made and remade, as we tried to decide what to do. Some were ready to risk anything to get away. Others feared to leave the protection of the camp."[34]

Thus, those first college students were the scouts whose letters back to camp marked pathways for others to follow. May Yoshino sent a favorable report to her family in Topaz from the nearby University of Utah, indicating that there were "plenty of schoolgirl jobs for those who want to study at the University."[35] Correspondence from other nisei students shows that although they succeeded at making the dual transition from high school to college and from camp to the outside world, they were not without anxieties as to whether they could handle the study load and the reactions of the Caucasians around them. One student at Drake University in Iowa wrote to her interned sister about a professor's reaction to her autobiographical essay, "Evacuation":

> Today Mr. _____, the English teacher that scares me, told me that the theme that I wrote the other day was very interesting. . . . You could just imagine how wonderful and happy *I* was to know that he liked it a little bit. . . . I've been awfully busy trying to catch up on work and the work is *so* different from high school. I think that little by little I'm beginning to adjust myself to college life.[36]

Several incidents of hostility did occur, but the reception of the nisei students at colleges and universities was generally warm. Topaz readers of *Trek* magazine could draw encouragement from Lillian Ota's "Campus Report." Ota, a Wellesley College student, reassured them: "During the first few days you'll be invited by the college to teas and receptions. Before long you'll lose the awkwardness you might feel at such doings after the months of abnormal life at evacuation centers."[37] Although Ota had not noticed "that my being a 'Jap' has made much difference on the campus itself," she offered cautionary and pragmatic advice to the nisei, suggesting the burden of responsibility these relocated students felt, as well as the problem of communicating their experiences and emotions to Caucasians.

> It is scarcely necessary to point out that those who have probably never seen a nisei before will get their impression of the nisei as a whole from the relocated students. It won't do you or your family and friends much good to dwell on what you consider injustices when you are questioned about evacuation. Rather, stress the contributions of [our] people to the nation's war effort.[38]

Given the tenor of the times and the situation of their families, the pioneers in resettlement had little choice but to repress their anger and minimize the amount of racist hostility they encountered.

In her article "A La Mode," Marii Kyogoku also offered survival tips to the departing nisei, ever conscious that they were on trial not only as individuals but as representatives of their families and their generation. She suggested criteria for choosing clothes and provided hints on adjustment to food rationing. Kyogoku especially urged the evacuees to improve their table manners, which had been adversely affected by the "unnatural food and atmosphere" of mess hall dining:

> You should start rehearsing for the great outside by bringing your own utensils to the dining hall. Its an aid to normality to be able to eat your jello with a spoon and well worth the dishwashing which it involves. All of us eat much too fast. Eat more slowly. All this practicing should be done so that proper manners will seem natural to you. If you do this, you won't get stagefright and spill your water glass, or make bread pills and hardly dare to eat when you have your first meal away from the centers and in the midst of scrutinizing caucasian eyes.[39]

Armed with advice and drawn by encouraging reports, increasing numbers of women students left camp. A postwar study of a group of a thousand relocated students showed that 40 percent were women.[40] The field of nursing was particularly attractive to nisei women; after the first few students disproved the hospital administrations' fears of their patients' hostility, acceptance of nisei into nursing schools grew. By July 1944 there were more than three hundred nisei women in over a hundred nursing programs in twenty-four states.[41] One such student wrote from the Asbury Hospital in Minneapolis: "Work here isn't too hard and I enjoy it very much. The patients are very nice people and I haven't had any trouble as yet. They do give us a funny stare at the beginning but after a day or so we receive the best compliments."[42]

The trickle of migration from the camps grew into a steady stream by 1943, as the War Relocation Authority developed its resettlement program to aid evacuees in finding housing and employment in the East and Midwest. A resettlement bulletin published by the Advisory Committee for Evacuees described "who is relocating":

> Mostly younger men and women, in their 20s or 30s; mostly single persons or couples with one or two children, or men with larger families who come out alone first to scout opportunities and to secure a foothold, planning to call wife and children later. Most relocated evacuees have parents or relatives whom they hope and plan to bring out "when we get re-established."[43]

In early 1945 the War Department ended the exclusion of the Japanese Americans from the West Coast, and the War Relocation Authority announced that the camps would be closed within the year. By this time, 37 percent of the evacuees of sixteen years or older had already relocated, including 63 percent of the nisei women in that age group.[44]

For nisei women, like their non-Japanese sisters, the wartime labor shortage opened the door into industrial, clerical, and managerial occupations. Prior to the war, racism had excluded the Japanese Americans from most white-collar clerical and sales positions, and, according to sociologist Evelyn Nakano Glenn, "the most common form of nonagricultural employment for the immigrant women (issei) and their American-born daughters (nisei) was domestic service."[45] The highest percentage of job offers for both men and women continued to be requests for domestic workers. In July 1943 the Kansas City branch of the War Relocation Authority noted that 45 percent of requests for workers were for domestics, and the Milwaukee office cited 61 percent.[46] However, nisei women also found jobs as secretaries, typists, file clerks, beauticians, and factory workers. By 1950, 47 percent of employed Japanese American women were clerical and sales workers and operatives; only 10 percent were in domestic service.[47] The World War II decade, then, marked a turning point for Japanese American women in the labor force.

Whether they were students or workers, and regardless of where they went or how prepared they were to meet the outside world, nisei women found that leaving camp meant enormous change in their lives. Even someone as confident as Marii Kyogoku, the author of much relocation advice, found that reentry into the Caucasian-dominated world beyond the barbed-wire fence was not a simple matter of stepping back into old shoes. Leaving the camps—like entering them—meant major changes in psychological perspective and self-image.

> I had thought that because before evacuation I had adjusted myself rather well in a Caucasian society, I would go right back into my former frame of mind. I have found, however, that though the center became unreal and was as if it had never existed as soon as I got on the train at Delta, I was never so self-conscious in all my life.

Kyogoku was amazed to see so many men and women in uniform and, despite her "proper" dining preparation, felt strange sitting at a table set with clean linen and a full set of silverware.

> I felt a diffidence at facing all these people and things, which was most unusual. Slowly things have come to seem natural, though I am still excited by the sounds of the busy city and thrilled every time I see a street lined with trees, I no longer feel that I am the cynosure of all eyes.[48]

Like Kyogoku, many nisei women discovered that relocation meant adjustment to "a life different from our former as well as present way of living" and, as such, posed a challenge.[49] Their experiences in meeting this challenge were as diverse as their jobs and living situations.

"I live at the Eleanor Club No. 5 which is located on the west side," wrote Mary Sonoda, working with the American Friends Service Committee in Chicago:

> I pay $1 per day for room and two meals a day. I also have maid service. I do not think that one can manage all this for $1 unless one lives in a place like this which houses thousands of working girls in the city. . . . I am the only Japanese here at present. . . . The residents and the staff are wonderful to me. . . . I am constantly being entertained by one person or another.
>
> The people in Chicago are extremely friendly. Even with the Tribune screaming awful headlines concerning the recent execution of American soldiers in Japan, people kept their heads. On street cars, at stores, everywhere, one finds innumerable evidence of good will.[50]

Chicago, the location of the first War Relocation Authority field office for supervision of resettlement in the Midwest, attracted the largest number of evacuees. Not all found their working environment as congenial as Mary Sonoda did. Smoot Katow, a nisei man in Chicago, painted "another side of the picture":

> I met one of the Edgewater Beach girls. . . . From what she said it was my impression that the girls are not very happy. The hotel work is too hard, according to this girl. In fact, they are losing weight and one girl became sick with overwork. They have to clean about fifteen suites a day, scrubbing the floors on their hands and knees. . . . It seems the management is out to use labor as labor only. . . . The outside world is just as tough as it ever was.[51]

These variations in living and work conditions and wages encouraged—and sometimes necessitated—a certain amount of job experimentation among the nisei.

Many relocating Japanese Americans received moral and material assistance from a number of service organizations and religious groups, particularly the Presbyterians, the Methodists, the Society of Friends, and the Young Women's Christian Association. One such nisei, Dorcas Asano, enthusiastically described to a Quaker sponsor her activities in the big city:

> Since receiving your application for hostel accommodation, I have decided to come to New York and I am really glad for the opportunity to be able to resume the normal civilized life after a year's confinement in camp. New York is really a city of dreams and we are enjoying every minute working in offices, rushing back and forth to work in the ever-speeding sub-way trains, counting our ration points, buying war bonds, going to church, seeing the latest shows, plays, operas, making many new friends and living like our neighbors in the war time. I only wish more of my friends who are behind the fence will take advantage of the many helpful hands offered to them.[52]

The nisei also derived support and strength from networks—formed before and during internment—of friends and relatives. The homes of those who relocated first became way stations for others as they made the transition into new communities and jobs. In 1944, soon after she obtained a place to stay in New York City, Miné Okubo found that "many of the other evacuees relocating in New York came ringing my doorbell. They were sleeping all over the floor!"[53] Single women often accompanied or joined sisters, brothers, and friends as many interconnecting grapevines carried news of likely jobs, housing, and friendly communities. Ayako Kanemura, for instance, found a job painting Hummel figurines in Chicago; a letter of recommendation from a friend enabled her "to get my foot into the door and then all my friends followed and joined me."[54] Although they were farther from their families than ever before, nisei women maintained warm ties of affection and concern, and those who had the means to do so continued to play a role in the family economy, remitting a portion of their earnings to their families in or out of camp, and to siblings in school.

Elizabeth Ogata's family exemplifies several patterns of resettlement and the maintenance of family ties within them. In October 1944 her parents were living with her brother Harry, who had begun to farm in Springville, Utah; another brother and sister were attending Union College in Lincoln, Nebraska. Elizabeth herself had moved to Minneapolis to join a brother in the army, and she was working as an operative making pajamas. "Minn. is a beautiful place," she wrote, "and the people are so nice. . . . I thought I'd never find anywhere I would feel at home as I did in Mt. View [California], but I have changed my mind."[55] Like Elizabeth, a good number of the thirty-five thousand relocated Japanese Americans were favorably impressed by their new homes and decided to stay.

The war years had complex and profound effects upon Japanese Americans, uprooting their communities and causing severe psychological and emotional damage. The vast majority returned to the West Coast at the end of the war in 1945—a move that, like the initial evacuation, was a grueling test of flexibility and fortitude. Even with the assistance of old friends and service organizations, the transition was taxing and painful; the end of the war meant not only long-awaited freedom but more battles to be fought in social, academic, and economic arenas. The Japanese Americans faced hostility, crude living conditions, and a struggle for jobs. Few evacuees received any compensation for their financial losses, estimated conservatively at $400 million, because Congress decided to appropriate only $38 million for the settlement of claims.[56] It is even harder to place a figure on the toll taken in emotional shock, self-blame, broken dreams, and insecurity. One Japanese American woman still sees in her nightmares the watchtower searchlights that troubled her sleep over forty years ago.

The war altered Japanese American women's lives in complicated ways. In general, evacuation and relocation accelerated earlier trends that differentiated the nisei from their parents. Although most young women, like their mothers and non-Japanese peers, anticipated a future centered on a husband and children, they had already felt the influence of mainstream middle-class values of love and marriage, and in the camps they quickly moved away from the pattern of arranged marriage. There, increased peer group activities and the relaxation of parental authority gave them more independence. The nisei women's expectations of marriage became more akin to the companionate ideals of their peers than to those of the issei.

As before the war, in the camps many Nisei women worked, but the new parity in wages they received altered family dynamics. And though they expected to contribute to the family economy, a large number did so in settings far from the family, availing themselves of opportunities provided by the student and worker relocation programs. In meeting the challenges facing them, nisei women drew not only upon the disciplined strength inculcated by their issei parents but also upon firmly rooted support networks and the greater measure of self-reliance and independence that they developed during the crucible of the war years.

Notes

For their invaluable assistance with this paper, I would like to thank Estelle Freedman, Mary Rothschild, and members of the women's history dissertation reading group at Stanford University—Sue Cobble, Gary Sue Goodman, Yukiko Hanawa, Gail Hershatter, Emily Honig, Susan Johnson, Sue Lynn, Joanne Meyerowitz, Peggy Pascoe, Linda Schott, Frances Taylor, and Karen Anderson.

1. Miné Okubo, *Miné Okubo: An American Experience* (exhibition catalogue) (Oakland: Oakland Museum, 1972), 36.

2. The very first Japanese women to arrive in the United States before the turn of the century were the *ameyuki-san*—prostitutes—of whose lives little is known. For information, see Yuji Ichioka, "Ameyuki-san: Japanese Prostitutes in Nineteenth Century America," *Amerasia Journal* 4, 1 (1977). A few references to the *ameyuki-san* appear in Mildred Crowl Martin's biography, *Chinatown's Angry Angel: The Story of Donaldina Cameron* (Palo Alto: Pacific Books, 1977).

3. In Japan, marriage was legally the transfer of a woman's name from her father's registry to that of the groom's family. Even through the Meiji era there was enormous diversity in the time period of this formalization; it might occur as early as several days before the wedding ceremony or as late as seven or more years later, by which time the bride should have produced several sons and proven herself to be a good wife and daughter-in-law. For a detailed cross-cultural history of the issei women, see Yukiko Hanawa, "The Several Worlds of Issei Women" (M.A. thesis, California State University at Long Beach, 1982).

4. Yuji Ichioka. "*Amerika Nadeshiko:* Japanese Immigrant Women in the United States, 1900–1924," *Pacific Historical Review* 69, 2 (May 1980): 343.

5. Evelyn Nakano Glenn has examined the lives of issei and nisei domestic workers in the prewar period in her study "The Dialectics of Wage Work: Japanese American Women and Domestic Servants, 1905–1940," *Feminist Studies* 6, 3 (1980): 432–71.
6. Sources on evacuation: Robert A. Wilson and Bill Hosokawa, *East to America: A History of the Japanese in the United States* (New York: William Morrow, 1980); Audrie Girdner and Anne Loftis, *The Great Betrayal: The Evacuation of the Japanese-Americans during World War II* (Toronto: Macmillan, 1969); Daisuke Kitagawa, *Issei and Nisei: The Internment Years* (New York: Seabury Press, 1967); Roger Daniels, *The Decision to Relocate the Japanese Americans* (Philadelphia: J. B. Lippincott, 1975).
7. Wilson and Hosokawa, *East to America*, 208.
8. Bettie to Mrs. Jack Shoup, 3 June 1942, Mrs. Jack Shoup Collection, Hoover Institution Archives (hereafter referred to as HIA), Stanford, California.
9. May Nakamoto to Mrs. Jack Shoup, 30 November 1942, Mrs. Jack Shoup Collection, HIA.
10. Mary Okumura to Mrs. Jack Shoup, 30 May 1942, Mrs. Jack Shoup Collection, HIA.
11. Miye Baba, personal interview, 10 February 1982, Turlock, California.
12. Many of the Japanese community leaders arrested by the FBI before the evacuation were interned in special all-male camps in North Dakota, Louisiana, and New Mexico. Some Japanese Americans living outside the perimeter of the Western Defense Zone in Arizona, Utah, and other states were not interned.
13. Miné Okubo, *Citizen 13660* (New York: Columbia University Press, 1946), 66.
14. Chieko Kimura, personal interview, 9 April 1978, Glendale, Arizona.
15. Okubo, *Citizen 13660*, 89.
16. Shizuko Horiuchi to Henriette Von Blon, 24 January 1943, Henriette Von Blon Collection, HIA.
17. Shizuko Horiuchi to Henriette Von Blon, 5 January 1944, Henriette Von Blon Collection, HIA.
18. Ayako Kanemura, personal interview, 10 March 1978, Glendale, Arizona.
19. Anonymous, *Topaz Times*, 24 October 1942, 3.
20. Lily Shoji, "Fem-a-lites," *The Mercedian*, 7 August 1942, 4.
21. "Yuri," "Strictly Feminine," *Daily Tulean Dispatch*, 29 September 1942, 2.
22. Mitzi Sugita, "Latest Fashion for Women Today—Slacks," *Poston Chronicle*, 13 June 1943, 1.
23. Sugita, "Latest Fashion."
24. Marii Kyogoku, "A La Mode," *Trek*, February 1943, 38.
25. From 1942 to the end of 1945 the council allocated about $240,000 in scholarships, most of which were provided through the donations of churches and the World Student Service Fund. The average grant per student was $156.73, which in that era was a major contribution toward the cost of higher education. Source: National Japanese American Student Relocation Council, Minutes of the Executive Committee Meeting, Philadelphia, Pennsylvania, 19 December 1945.
26. Robert O'Brien, *The College Nisei* (Palo Alto: Pacific Books, 1949), 73–74.
27. The disastrous consequences of the poorly conceived clearance procedure have been examined by Wilson and Hosokawa, *East to America*, 226–27, and Girdner and Loftis, *The Great Betrayal*, 342–43.
28. May Nakamoto to Mrs. Jack Shoup, 20 November 1943, Mrs. Jack Shoup Collection, HIA.
29. Shizuko Horiuchi to Henriette Von Blon, 27 December 1942, Henriette Von Blon Collection, HIA.
30. Toshiko Imada to Margaret Cosgrave Sowers, 16 January 1943, Margaret Cosgrave Sowers Collection, HIA.
31. Ayako Kanemura, personal interview, 24 March 1978, Glendale, Arizona.
32. Kathy Ishikawa to Mrs. Jack Shoup, 14 June 1942, Mrs. Jack Shoup Collection, HIA.
33. Anonymous nisei nurse in Poston Camp to Margaret Finley, 5 May 1943, Margaret Finley Collection, HIA.
34. Okubo, *Citizen 13660*, 139.
35. *Topaz Times*, 24 October 1942, 3.
36. Masako Ono to Atsuko Ono, 28 September 1942, Margaret Cosgrave Sowers Collection, HIA. Prior to the war, few nisei had college experience; the 1940 census lists 674 second-generation women and 1,507 men who had attended or were attending college.
37. Lillian Ota, "Campus Report," *Trek*, February 1943, 33.
38. Ibid., 33–34.
39. Kyogoku, "A La Mode," 39.
40. O'Brien, *The College Nisei*, 84.
41. Ibid., 85–86.
42. Grace Tanabe to Josephine Duveneck, 16 February 1944, Conard-Duveneck Collection, HIA.
43. Advisory Committee for Evacuees, *Resettlement Bulletin*, April 1943, 2.
44. Leonard Broom and Ruth Riemer, *Removal and Return: The Socio-Economic Effects of the War on Japanese Americans* (Berkeley: University of California Press, 1949), 36.
45. Glenn, "The Dialectics of Wage Work," 412.
46. Advisory Committee for Evacuees, *Resettlement Bulletin*, July 1943, 3.

47. 1950 United States Census, Special Report.
48. Marii Kyogoku, *Resettlement Bulletin*, July 1943, 5.
49. Kyogoku, "A La Mode," 39.
50. *Poston Chronicle*, 23 May 1943, 1.
51. *Poston Chronicle*, 23 May 1943.
52. Dorcas Asano to Josephine Duveneck, 22 January 1944, Conard-Duveneck Collection, HIA.
53. Okubo, *An American Experience*, 41.
54. Ayako Kanemura, personal interview, 24 March 1978, Glendale, Arizona.
55. Elizabeth Ogata to Mrs. Jack Shoup, 1 October 1944, Mrs. Jack Shoup Collection, HIA.
56. Susan M. Hartmann, *The Home Front and Beyond: American Women in the 1940s* (Boston: Twayne Publishers, 1982), 126. There is some debate regarding the origins of the assessment of evacuee losses at $400 million. However, a recent study by the Commission on Wartime Relocation and Internment of Civilians has estimated that the Japanese Americans lost between $149 million and $370 million in 1945 dollars (between $810 million and $2 billion in 1983 dollars). See the *San Francisco Chronicle*, 16 June 1983, 12.

32

Rethinking Betty Friedan and *The Feminine Mystique:* Labor Union Radicalism and Feminism in Cold War America

Daniel Horowitz

> In a certain sense it was almost accidental—coincidental—that I wrote *The Feminine Mystique,* and in another sense my whole life had prepared me to write that book; all the pieces of my own life came together for the first time in the writing of it.
>
> —Betty Friedan, 1976

In 1951 a labor journalist with a decade's experience in protest movements described a trade union meeting where rank-and-file women talked and men listened. Out of these conversations, she reported, emerged the realization that the women were "fighters—that they refuse any longer to be paid or treated as some inferior species by their bosses, or by any male workers who have swallowed the bosses' thinking."[1] The union was the UE, the United Electrical, Radio and Machine Workers of America, the most radical American union in the postwar period and in the 1940s what historian Ronald Schatz, appreciative of the UE's place in history, has called "the largest Communist-led institution of any kind in the United States."[2] In 1952 that same journalist wrote a pamphlet, *UE Fights for Women Workers,* that the historian Lisa Kannenberg, unaware of the identity of its author, has called "a remarkable manual for fighting wage discrimination that is, ironically, as relevant today as it was in 1952." At the time, the pamphlet helped raise the consciousness of Eleanor Flexner, who in 1959 would publish *Century of Struggle,* the first scholarly history of American women. In 1953–54 Flexner relied extensively on the pamphlet when she taught a course at the Jefferson School of Social Science in New York on "The Woman Question." Flexner's participation in courses at the school, she later said, "marked the beginning of my real involvement in the issues of women's rights, my realization that leftist organizations—parties, unions—were also riddled with male supremacist prejudice and discrimination."[3] The labor journalist and pamphlet writer was Betty Friedan.

In 1973 Friedan remarked that until she started writing *The Feminine Mystique* (published in 1963), "I wasn't even conscious of the woman problem." In 1976 she commented that in the early 1950s she was "still in the embrace of the feminine mystique."[4] Although in 1974 she revealed some potentially controversial elements of her past, even then she left the impression that her landmark book emerged only from her own captivity by the very forces she described. Friedan's portrayal of herself as so totally trapped by the feminine mystique was part of a reinvention of herself as she wrote and promoted *The Feminine Mystique.* Her story made it possible for readers to identify with its author and its author to enhance the book's appeal. However, it hid from view the connection between the union activity in which Friedan participated in the 1940s and early 1950s and the feminism she inspired in the 1960s. In the short term, her misery in the suburbs may have prompted her to write *The Feminine Mystique;* a longer-term perspective makes clear that the book's origins lie much earlier—in her college education and in her experiences with labor unions in the 1940s and early 1950s.[5]

The establishment of an accurate narrative of Betty Friedan's life, especially what she wrote in the 1940s and early 1950s, sheds light on the origins of 1960s feminism. Most historians believe that 1960s feminism emerged from events particular to that decade, but some have argued for a connection between the protest movements of the 1940s and the 1960s.[6] Friedan's life provides evidence of such continuity by suggesting a specific and important connection between the struggle for justice for working women in the 1940s and the feminism of the 1960s. This connection gives feminism and Friedan, both long under attack for a lack of interest in working-class and African American women, a past of which they should be proud.

More generally, understanding *The Feminine Mystique* in light of new information illuminates major aspects of American intellectual and political life in the postwar period. Friedan offered a feminist reworking of important themes in a genre of social criticism, including the notion of a faltering masculine identity. The story of Friedan's life provides additional evidence of the artificiality of the separation of a turbulent 1960s from the supposedly complacent preceding years. Recognition of continuity in Friedan's life gives added weight to the picture that is emerging of ways in which World War II, unions, and those influenced by American radicalism of the 1940s provided some of the seeds of protest movements of the 1960s.[7] At the same time, the continuities between Friedan's labor union activity and her feminism underscore the importance of what George Lipsitz has called "collective memory," the way the experiences of the immediate postwar period later reemerged in unexpected places.[8] Moreover, a new reading of *The Feminine Mystique* sheds light on the remaking of progressive forces in America, the process by which a focus on women and the professional middle and uppermiddle classes supplemented, in some ways replaced, a focus on unions. Finally, an examination of *The Feminine Mystique* reminds us of important shifts in the ideology of the left: from an earlier economic analysis based on Marxism to one developed in the 1950s that also rested on humanistic psychology, and from a focus on the impact of conditions of production on the working class to an emphasis on the effect of consumption on the middle class.

Herstory

In print and in interviews, Friedan has offered a narrative of her life that she popularized after she became famous in 1963.[9] A full biography might begin in Peoria, where Bettye Naomi Goldstein was born on 4 February 1921 and grew up with her siblings and their parents: a father who owned a jewelry store and a mother who had given up her position as a society editor of the local paper to raise a family.[10] My analysis of Friedan's political journey starts with her years at Smith College, although it is important to recognize Friedan's earlier sense of herself as someone whose identity as a Jew, a reader, and a brainy girl made her feel freakish and lonely.[11]

As an undergraduate, she has suggested, her lonely life took a turn for the better. "For the first time," she later remarked of her years in college, "I wasn't a freak for having brains." Friedan has acknowledged that she flourished at Smith, with her editorship of the student newspaper, her election to Phi Beta Kappa in her junior year, and her graduation summa cum laude among her most prominent achievements. She has told the story of how Gestalt psychology and Kurt Koffka (one of its three founders) were critical in her intellectual development.[12]

Friedan has described the years between her graduation from Smith in 1942 and the publication of her book twenty-one years later as a time when the feminine mystique increasingly trapped her. In her book and in dozens of speeches, articles, and interviews beginning in 1963, she mentioned a pivotal moment in her life, one that she felt marked the beginning of the process by which she succumbed. She told how, while in graduate school at Berkeley in the year after her graduation from college, the university's offer of a prestigious fellowship forced her to make a painful choice. Her first serious boyfriend, a graduate student who had not earned a similarly generous award, threatened to break off the relationship unless she turned down her fellowship. "I never could explain, hardly knew myself, why" she turned away from a career in psychology, she wrote in 1963. She decided to reject the fellowship because she saw herself ending up as an "old maid college teacher" in part because at Smith, she said, there were so few female professors who had husbands and children.[13] The feminine mystique, she insisted, had claimed one of its first victims.[14]

After leaving Berkeley, the copy on the dust jacket of *The Feminine Mystique* noted, Friedan did some "applied social-science research" and freelance writing for magazines. Friedan's biography in a standard reference book quotes her as saying that in the 1940s, "for conscious or unconscious reasons," she worked at "the usual kinds of boring jobs that lead nowhere."[15] This story continues in 1947 with her marriage to Carl Friedan, a returning vet who would eventually switch careers from theater to advertising and public relations. She has told of how she gave birth to three children between 1948 and 1956 and the family moved to the suburbs, with these experiences making her feel trapped. Friedan's picture of her years in the suburbs is not one of contentment and conformity.[16] Though she acknowledged her role in creating and directing a program that brought together teenagers and adult professionals, Friedan portrayed herself as someone who felt "freakish having a career, worried that she was neglecting her children."[17] In an oft-repeated story whose punch line varied, Friedan recounted her response to the census form. In the space where it asked for her occupation, she put down "housewife" but remained guilty, hesitant, and conflicted about such a designation; sometimes the story has it that she paused and then added "writer."[18]

Friedan laced *The Feminine Mystique* with suggestions of how much she shared with her suburban sisters. In the opening paragraph, she said that she realized something was wrong in women's lives when she "sensed it first as a question mark in my own life, as a wife and mother of three small children, half-guiltily, and therefore half-heartedly, almost in spite of myself, using my abilities and education in work that took me away from home." Toward the end of the paragraph, when she referred to "a strange discrepancy between the reality of our lives as women and the image to which we were trying to conform," she suggested that she experienced the feminine mystique as keenly and in the same way as her readers. Using the first person plural, she wrote that "all of us went back into the warm brightness of home" and "lowered our eyes from the horizon, and steadily contemplated our own navels." Her work on newspapers, she wrote in *The Feminine Mystique*, proceeded "with no particular plan." Indeed, she claimed that she had participated as a writer in the creation of the image of the happy housewife.[19]

Friedan asserted she embarked on a path that would lead to *The Feminine Mystique* only when, as she read over the responses of her college classmates to a questionnaire in anticipation of their fifteenth reunion in 1957, she discovered what she called "the problem that has no name," the dissatisfaction her suburban peers felt but could not fully articulate. When she submitted articles to women's magazines, Friedan said, editors changed the meaning of what she had written or rejected outright her suggestions for pieces on controversial subjects. Then at a meeting of the Society of Magazine Writers, she heard Vance Packard recount how he had written *The Hidden Persuaders* (1957) after *Reader's Digest* turned down an article critical of advertising. Friedan decided to write her book.[20]

In *"It Changed My Life": Writings on the Women's Movement* (1976), a book that included a 1974 autobiographical article, Friedan suggested some of what she had omitted from earlier versions of her life.[21] Perhaps responding to attacks on her for not being sufficiently radical, she acknowledged that before her marriage and for several years after she participated in radical activities and worked for union publications.[22] She and the friends with whom she lived before marrying considered themselves in "the vanguard of the working-class revolution," participating in "Marxist discussion groups," going to political rallies, and having "only contempt for dreary bourgeois capitalists like our fathers." Without getting much more specific, Friedan noted that right after the war she was "very involved, consciously radical. Not about women, for heaven's sake!" but about African Americans, workers, the threat of war, anti-Communism, and "Communist splits and schisms." This was a time, Friedan reported briefly, when, working as a labor journalist, she discovered "the grubby economic underside of American reality."[23]

"I was certainly not a feminist then—none of us," she remarked in the mid-1970s, "were a bit interested in women's rights." She remembered one incident, whose implications she said she only understood much later. Covering a strike, she could not interest anyone in the fact that the company and the union discriminated against women. In 1952, she later claimed, pregnant with her second child, she was fired from her job on a union publication and told that her second pregnancy was her fault. The Newspaper Guild, she asserted, was unwilling to honor its commitment to grant pregnancy leaves. This was, Friedan later remembered as she mentioned her efforts to call a meeting in protest, "the first personal stirring of my own feminism, I guess. But the other women were just embarrassed, and the men uncomprehending. It was my own fault, getting pregnant again, a *personal* matter, not something you should take to the union. There was no word in 1949 for 'sex discrimination.'"[24]

Though in the 1970s Friedan suggested this more interesting version of her life in the 1940s and 1950s, she distracted the reader from what she had said. She began and ended the 1974 piece with images of domestic life. Even as she mentioned participation in Marxist discussion groups, she talked of how she and her friends read fashion magazines and spent much of their earnings on elegant clothes. Describing what she offered as a major turning point in her life, she told of how, after campaigning for Henry Wallace for president in 1948, all of a sudden she lost interest in political activity. The 1940s and 1950s were a period, she later asserted, when she was fully exposed to what she would label the feminine mystique as she learned that motherhood took the place of career and politics. She gave the impression of herself in the late 1940s as a woman who embraced domesticity, mother-hood, and housework, even as she admitted that not everything at the time resulted from the feminine mystique.[25]

In her 1974 article Friedan filled her descriptions of the late 1940s and 1950s with a sense of the conflicts she felt over her new roles, as she surrendered to the feminine mystique with mixed emotions. She reported how wonderful was the time in Parkway Village, Queens, a period when she experienced the pleasure of a spacious apartment, edited the community newspaper, and enjoyed the camaraderie of young marrieds. Yet, having read Benjamin Spock's *Child and Baby Care*, she felt guilty when she returned to work after a maternity leave. With her move to a traditional suburb, she said, the conflicts intensified. She spoke of driving her children to school and lessons, participating in the PTA, and then, when neighbors came by, hiding "like secret drinking in the morning" the book on which she was working.[26]

Accomplishing practical, specific tasks around the house and in local politics was "somehow more real and secure than the schizophrenic and even dangerous politics of the world revolution whose vanguard we used to fancy ourselves." Friedan remarked that by 1949 she realized that the revolution was not going to happen in the United States as she anticipated, in part because workers, like others, wanted kitchen gadgets. She reported that she found herself disillusioned with what was happening in unions, in Czechoslovakia, and in the Soviet Union, despite the fact that cries about the spread of Communism merely provided the pretext for attacks on suspected subversives. In those days, she continued, "McCarthyism, the danger of war against Russia and of fascism in America, and the reality of U.S. imperial, corporate wealth and power" combined to make those who once dreamed of "making the whole world over, uncomfortable with the Old Left rhetoric of revolution." Using the first person plural as she referred to Margaret Mead's picture in *Male and Female* of women fulfilled through motherhood and domesticity, Friedan wrote, "we were suckers for that apple." It hardly occurred to any of those in her circle, who themselves now wanted new gadgets, that large corporations profited from marketing household appliances by "overselling us on the bliss of domesticity."[27]

The new information Friedan offered in 1974 did not dislodge the accepted understanding of how she became a feminist. Historians and journalists have repeated Friedan's narrative of her life, though they have occasionally offered evidence for an alternative script.[28] In 1983 Marilyn French wrote of Friedan's decision not to "spend her life sorrowing over a lost career: She would embrace the man, the home, the children, and live in a bath of felicity." In 1991 the historian of feminism Donald Meyer skipped over her years as a labor journalist and wrote that Friedan herself was "the exemplary victim of the feminine mystique." Similarly, in his 1993 book *The Fifties*, David Halberstam covered nine years of Friedan's career as a labor journalist with the sentence "Betty Goldstein worked as a reporter for a left-wing paper."[29] Yet data that could have provided a different interpretation has been available for a number of years: in what she published as a Smith student, as a labor journalist, and later as a freelance author; in what Friedan herself said in 1974; and in what her personal papers, opened since 1986, contained.

An Alternative Story: Bettye Goldstein, Class of '42

What the written record reveals of Friedan's life from her arrival at Smith in the fall of 1938 until the publication of *The Feminine Mystique* makes possible a story different from the one she has told. To begin with, usually missing from her narrative is full and specific information about how at college she first developed a sense of herself as a radical.[30] Courses she took, friendships she established with peers and professors, events in the United States and abroad, and her campus leadership all turned Friedan from a provincial outsider into a determined advocate of trade unions as the herald of progressive social change, a healthy skeptic about the authority and rhetorical claims of those in power, a staunch opponent of fascism, a defender of free speech, and a fierce questioner of the social privilege expressed by the conspicuous consumption of some of her peers.[31]

What and with whom she studied points well beyond Gestalt psychology and Koffka.[32] Though Friedan acknowledged the importance of James Gibson, she did not mention his activity as an advocate of trade unions.[33] Moreover, her statement that at Smith there were few role models is hard to reconcile with the fact that the college had a number of them; indeed, she took courses from both James Gibson and Eleanor Gibson, husband and wife and parents of two children, the first of them born in 1940.[34] As a women's college, and especially one with an adversarial tradition, Smith may well have fostered in Friedan a feminism that was at least implicit—by enabling her to assume leadership positions and by encouraging her to take herself seriously as a writer and thinker.

In the fall of her junior year, Friedan took an economics course taught by Dorothy W. Douglas, Theories and Movements for Social Reconstruction. Douglas was well known at the time for her radicalism.[35] In what she wrote for Douglas, and with youthful enthusiasm characteristic of many members of her generation, Friedan sympathetically responded to the Marxist critique of capitalism as a cultural, economic, and political force.[36]

Friedan also gained an education as a radical in the summer of 1941 when, following Douglas's suggestion, she participated in a writers' workshop at the Highlander Folk School in Tennessee, an institution active in helping the Congress of Industrial Organizations (CIO) organize in the South. The school offered a series of summer institutes for fledgling journalists which, for 1939 and 1940 (but not 1941), the Communist-led League of American Writers helped sponsor. For three years beginning in the fall of 1939, opponents of Highlander had sustained a vicious red-baiting attack, but an FBI investigator found no evidence of subversive activity.[37] In good Popular Front language, Friedan praised Highlander as a truly American institution that was attempting to help America to fulfill its democratic ideals. She explored the contradictions of her social position as a Jewish girl from a well-to-do family who had grown up in a class-divided Peoria, gave evidence of her hostility to the way her parents fought over issues of debt and extravagance, and described the baneful influence of the mass media on American life. Though she also acknowledged that her Smith education did "not lead to much action," she portrayed herself as someone whose radical consciousness relied on the American labor movement as the bulwark against fascism.[38]

At Smith Friedan linked her journalism to political activism. She served as editor-in-chief of the campus newspaper for a year beginning in the spring of 1941. The campaigns she undertook and the editorials she wrote reveal a good deal of her politics. Under Friedan's leadership, the newspaper's reputation for protest was so strong that in a skit a fellow student portrayed an editor, perhaps Friedan herself, as "a strident voice haranguing from a perpetual soap-box."[39] While at Smith, a Peoria paper reported in 1943, Friedan helped organize college building and grounds workers into a union.[40] Under her leadership, the student paper took on the student government for holding closed meetings, fought successfully to challenge the administration's right to control what the newspaper printed, campaigned for the relaxation of restrictions on student social life, censured social clubs for their secrecy, and published critiques of professors' teaching.[41] In response to an article in a campus humor magazine that belittled female employees who cleaned the students' rooms and served them food, an editorial supported the administration's censorship of the publication on the grounds that such action upheld "the liberal democratic tradition of the college."[42]

The editorials written on her watch reveal a young woman who believed that what was involved with almost every issue—at Smith, in the United States, and abroad—was the struggle for democracy, freedom, and social justice. Under Friedan's leadership the editors supported American workers and their labor unions in their struggles to organize and improve their conditions. With an advertisement for a dress in which students could "TWIRL AWAY AT TEA-TIME!" on the same page, one editorial asserted that life, liberty, and the pursuit of happiness meant very different things to employers and employees. The inequality of power in America, the editorial argued in good social democratic terms, "has to be admitted and dealt with if democracy is to have meaning for 95% of the citizens of this country."[43]

Above all, what haunted the editorials was the spread of fascism and questions about America's involvement in a world war. In April of 1941 the editors made it clear that the defeat of fascism was their primary goal and one that determined their position on questions of war or peace. In the fall of 1941, after the German invasion of the Soviet Union during the preceding summer, the editors increasingly accepted the inevitability of war even as they made it clear that they believed "fighting fascists is only one part of fighting fascism."[44] Some Smith students responded with red-baiting to the newspaper's antifascism and reluctance to support intervention wholeheartedly, accusing the editorial board of being dominated by Communists, at a time when the Communist Party reached its greatest membership in the years after Pearl Harbor while the United States and the Soviet Union were allies. Though one editor denied the charge of Communist influence, on the paper's staff were students attracted to the political analysis offered by radical groups; this was true of many newspapers at American colleges in these years. In the fall of 1940 one columnist argued against lumping Communists and Nazis together, remarking that Communism was not a "dark terror" but "a precarious scheme worked out by millions of civilized men and women."[45]

When America entered the war in December 1941, the editors accepted the nation's new role loyally, albeit soberly. The central issue for them was how American students, especially female ones, could "contribute *actively* to the American cause." Those in charge of the newspaper found academic life "detached and fruitless." Lamenting student reluctance to make serious sacrifices, the editorial writers were mindful of their privileged positions and retained their commitment to the well-being of working-class women, even when it meant they might have to clean their own rooms or work in campus kitchens. They insisted that any new arrangement not force into unemployment the hundreds of women whose jobs student sacrifice might threaten. By her senior year, Friedan and her peers conveyed a sense that they were chafing against the isolation of Smith College from the world of action and were eager to find ways to act upon their commitments.[46] When she left Smith, she dropped the final *e* from her first name, perhaps a symbolic statement that she was no longer a girl from Peoria.

Betty Goldstein: Labor Journalist

Friedan's experiences at Smith cast a different light on her decision to leave Berkeley after a year of graduate school. The editorials she and her peers had written immediately after Pearl Harbor revealed an impatience to be near the action. A 1943 article in the Peoria paper reported that Friedan turned down the fellowship because "she decided she wanted to work in the labor movement—on the labor press."[47] Another issue doubtlessly affected her decision to leave Berkeley. When her father accused her of immorality while she was home at Christmas vacation, she was so upset that she returned to Berkeley without saying goodbye to him. A few days later, on 11 January 1943, he died at age sixty-one.[48]

The period that Friedan has treated most summarily in her narrative covers the years from 1943 to 1952, when she worked as a labor journalist. Off and on from October 1943 until July 1946 she was a staff writer for the Federated Press, a left-wing news service that provided stories for newspapers, especially union ones, across the nation.[49] Here Friedan wrote articles that supported the aspirations of African Americans and union members. She also criticized reactionary forces that, she believed, were working secretly to undermine progressive social advances.[50] As early as 1943 she pictured efforts by businesses, coordinated by the National Association of Manufacturers, to develop plans that would enhance profits, diminish the power of unions, reverse the New Deal, and allow businesses to operate as they pleased.[51]

At the Federated Press, Friedan also paid attention to women's problems. Right after she began to work there, she interviewed UE official Ruth Young, one of the clearest voices in the labor movement articulating women's issues. In the resulting article, Friedan noted that the government could not solve the problem of turnover "merely by pinning up thousands of glamorous posters designed to lure more women into industry." Neither women, unions, nor management, she quoted Young as saying, could solve problems of escalating prices or inadequate child care that were made even more difficult by the fact that "women still have two jobs to do." Action by the federal government, Friedan reported, was needed to solve the problems working women faced.[52] In the immediate postwar period, she pictured the wife in a union family as more savvy than her husband in figuring out how large corporations took advantage of the consumer.[53] She paid special attention to stories about protecting the jobs and improving the situation of working women, including married ones with children.

For about six years beginning in July 1946, precisely at the moment when the wartime Popular Front came under intense attack, Friedan was a reporter for the union's paper, *UE News*.[54] At least as early as 1943, when she quoted Young, Friedan was well aware of the UE's commitments to equity for women.[55] Friedan's years on *UE News*, which made her familiar with radicalism in the 1940s and early 1950s, provided a seedbed for her feminism. Her writings in the 1940s and early 1950s reveal that although she did not focus on the Soviet Union or on American-Soviet relations, Popular Front ideology shaped the way Friedan viewed American society and politics. As Flexner said of her own work for justice for working-class and African American women from the 1930s to the 1950s, left-wing movements welcomed "an enormous latitude of opinions under a very broad umbrella."[56] Specific political affiliation was not important; what was critical was commitment to a broad range of issues within the framework of a fight for social justice. The end of the cold war makes it possible to look at the left in the 1940s without the baggage of red-baiting. Indeed, the world in which Friedan moved in the 1940s and early 1950s was varied, containing as it did Communist Party members, pacificists, socialists, union activists, fighters for justice for African Americans—and at *UE News*, Katherine Beecher, the grandniece of the nineteenth-century feminist Catharine Beecher.[57]

In the immediate postwar period, the UE fought for justice for African Americans and women.[58] In 1949–50, union activists who followed the recommendations of the Communist Party, torn in the postwar years by bitter internal divisions, advocated the automatic granting of several years of seniority to all African Americans as compensation for their years of exclusion from the electrical industry. If the UE pioneered in articulating what we might call affirmative action for African Americans, then before and during World War II it advocated what a later generation would label comparable worth. Against considerable resistance from within its ranks, the UE also worked to improve the conditions of working-class women, in part by countering a seniority system that gave advantage to men.[59] After 1949, with the UE out of the CIO and many of the more conservative union members out of the UE, women's issues and women's leadership resumed the importance they had had in the UE during World War II, when it had developed, Ruth Milkman has written, a "strong ideological commitment to gender equality."[60]

Beginning in 1946, Friedan witnessed the efforts by federal agencies, congressional committees, major corporations, the Roman Catholic Church, and the CIO to break the hold of what they saw as the domination of the UE by Communists. The inclusion of a clause in the Taft-Hartley Act of 1947, requiring union officers to sign an anti-Communist affidavit if they wished to do business with the National Labor Relations Board, helped encourage other unions to challenge the UE, whose leaders refused to sign.[61] Internecine fights took place within the UE, part of a longer-term fight between radicals and anti-Communists in its ranks. One anti-Communist long active in the union spoke of how a Communist minority "seized control of the national office, the executive board, the paid staff, the union newspaper and some district councils and locals." The division in union ranks had reverberations in national politics as well: In 1948 the anti-Communists supported President Harry S. Truman, while their opponents campaigned for Henry Wallace. In the short term the attack on the UE intensified its commitment to equity for working women, something that grew out of both ideological commitments and practical considerations. Before long, however, the UE was greatly weakened: In 1949 its connection with the CIO was severed and the newly formed and CIO-backed IUE recruited many of its members. Membership in UE, numbering more than 600,000 in 1946, fell to 203,000 in 1953 and to 71,000 four years later.[62]

Reading the pages of *UE News* in the late 1940s and early 1950s opens a world unfamiliar to those who think that in this period Americans heard only hosannas to American exceptionalism. The villains of the publication were Truman, Hubert H. Humphrey, Richard M. Nixon, Walter Reuther, the House Un-American Activities Committee (HUAC), and American capitalists. The heroes included Wallace, Franklin D. Roosevelt, and union leaders who fought to protect the rights and lives of working people. Above all, the paper celebrated ordinary workers, including women and African Americans, who found themselves engaged in a class struggle against greedy corporations and opportunistic politicians.

At *UE News*, from her position as a middle-class woman interested in the lives of the working class, Friedan continued to articulate a progressive position on a wide range of issues. She again pointed to concerted efforts, led by big corporations under the leadership of the NAM, to increase profits, exploit labor, and break labor unions.[63] In 1951 she contrasted the extravagant expenditures of the wealthy with the family of a worker who could afford neither fresh vegetables nor new clothes.[64] Friedan also told the story of how valiant union members helped build political coalitions to fight congressional and corporate efforts to roll back gains workers made during the New Deal and World War II.[65] She drew parallels between the United States in the 1940s and Nazi Germany in the 1930s as she exposed the way HUAC and big business were using every tactic they could to destroy the UE. Friedan hailed the launching of the Progressive Party in 1948.[66] She exposed the existence of racism and discrimination, even when they appeared among union officials and especially when directed against Jews and African Americans. Praising heroic workers who struggled against great odds as they fought monopolies, Friedan, probably expressing her hopes for herself, extolled the skills of a writer "who is able to describe with sincerity and passion the hopes, the struggle and the romance of the working people who make up most of America."[67]

Throughout her years at *UE News*, Friedan participated in discussions on women's issues, including the issue of corporations' systematic discrimination against women. Going to factories to interview those whose stories she was covering, she also wrote about working women, including African Americans and Latinas.[68] In the worlds Friedan inhabited in the decade beginning in 1943, as the historian Kathleen Weigand has shown, people often discussed the cultural and economic sources of women's oppression, the nature of discrimination based on sex, the special difficulties African American women faced, and the dynamics of discrimination against women in a variety of institutions, including the family.[69] Moreover, for the people around Friedan and doubtless for Friedan herself, the fight for justice for women was inseparable from the more general struggle to secure rights for African Americans and workers.[70] As she had done at the Federated Press, at *UE News* in the late 1940s and early 1950s she reported on how working women struggled as producers and consumers to make sure their families had enough on which to live.[71]

Friedan's focus on working women's issues resulted in her writing the pamphlet *UE Fights for Women Workers*, published by the UE in June 1952.[72] She began by suggesting the contradiction in industry's treatment of women as consumers and as producers. "In advertisements across the land," Friedan remarked, "industry glorifies the American woman—in her gleaming GE kitchen, at her Westinghouse laundromat, before her Sylvania television set. Nothing," she announced as she insightfully explored a central contradiction women faced in the postwar world, "is too good for her—unless" she worked for corporations, including GE, or Westinghouse, or Sylvania.[73]

The central theme of the piece was how, in an effort to improve the pay and conditions of working women, the UE fought valiantly against greedy corporations that sought to increase their profits by exploiting women. Friedan discussed a landmark 1945 National War Labor Board decision against sex-based wage discrimination in favor of the UE. Remarking that *"fighting the exploitation of women is men's business too,"* she emphasized how the discriminatory practices that corporations used against women hurt men as well by exerting downward pressure on the wages of all workers. To back up the call for equal pay for equal work and to fight against segregation and discrimination of women, she countered stereotypes justifying lower pay for women: They were physically weaker, entered the workforce only temporarily, had no families to support, and worked only for pin money. She highlighted the "even more shocking" situation African American women faced, having to deal as they did with the "double bars" of being female and African American.[74] Friedan set forth a program that was, Lisa Kannenberg has noted, "a prescription for a gender-blind workplace."[75]

Nor did Friedan's interest in working women end with the publication of this pamphlet. For a brief period she worked as a freelance labor journalist. In the winter of 1952–53 she was probably the author of a series of articles for *Jewish Life: A Progressive Monthly*. These pieces were somewhat more radical in tone than those Friedan had written for *UE News*, in part because her foil was the International Ladies' Garment Workers' Union, whose commitment to women workers and progressive politics was no match for the UE's. She explored the contradiction of a situation where wealthy women dressed in clothes working-class women labored to produce. She told a story of rising profits and declining wages in a union that had, she argued, taken a conciliatory position with employers.[76] Then, in May 1953, she carefully tracked and probably participated in what a historian has said "appears to be one of the first national women's conferences in the postwar era."[77] There Friedan followed discussions of the importance of sharing household duties. She also heard of the efforts of profit-hungry corporations to divide the working class by emphasizing divisions between whites and African Americans as well as between men and women. She again learned of the union's advocacy of federal legislation to lower military expenditures and support programs for child care, maternity benefits, and equal pay.[78]

Friedan's association with the labor movement gave her a sustained education in issues of sexual discrimination and shaped her emergence as a feminist. However, the precise impact of the influence is not clear. If, as some historians have suggested, the UE remained committed to gender equality, then Friedan's years as a labor journalist may well have provided a positive inspiration.[79] In contrast, the historian Nancy Palmer has argued that women in the UE persistently faced difficulties when they articulated their grievances but, in the name of solidarity, were told not to rock the boat.[80] Such a situation might mean that her experience with radical organizations that could not live up to their vision of a just and egalitarian society served more as a negative spur than a positive inspiration. At both the Federated Press and *UE News*, she lost her jobs to men who had more seniority, a general policy issue that had concerned the UE at least since the early 1940s.

The conditions under which she left the Federated Press and *UE News* are not entirely clear. In May 1946, during her second stint at the Federated Press, she filed a grievance with the Newspaper Guild, saying she had lost her job in June 1945 to a man she had replaced during the war. Later she claimed she was "bumped" from her position "by a returning veteran." There is evidence, however, that Friedan had to give up her position to a man who returned to the paper after two years in prison because he refused to serve in the military during what he considered a capitalists' war.[81] Friedan later claimed that she lost her job at the UE during her second pregnancy because the labor movement failed to honor its commitment to maternity leaves. Yet a knowledgeable observer has written that when the union had to cut the staff because of the dramatic drop in its membership, something that resulted from McCarthyite attacks, Friedan "offered to quit so another reporter," a man with more seniority, could remain at *UE News*.[82] Although her experience with unions may have provided a negative spur to her feminism, it also served as a positive inspiration. Friedan was indebted to the UE for major elements of her education about gender equity, sex discrimination, and women's issues.

The reason Friedan left out these years in her life story is now clear. Her stint at the *UE News* took place at the height of the anti-Communist crusade, which she experienced at close quarters. When she emerged into the limelight in 1963, the issue of affiliation with Communists was wracking the Committee for a Sane Nuclear Policy (SANE), Students for a Democratic Society (SDS), and the civil rights movement. In the same years, HUAC was still holding hearings, the United States was pursuing an anti-Communist war in Vietnam, and J. Edgar Hoover's FBI was wiretapping Martin Luther King Jr., ostensibly to protect the nation against Communist influence. Had Friedan revealed all in the mid-1960s, she would have undercut her book's impact, subjected herself to palpable dangers, and jeopardized the feminist movement, including the National Organization for Women (NOW), an institution she was instrumental in launching. Perhaps instead of emphasizing continuities in her life, she told the story of her conversion in order to heighten the impact of her book and appeal to white middle-class women. Or maybe, having participated in social movements that did not live up to her dreams, in *The Feminine Mystique*, whether consciously or not, she was trying to mobilize middle-class readers and thus prove something to the men on the left. When constructing a narrative, she may have adopted a convention that made it difficult to discuss anger, ambition, excitement, and power.[83] Why she did not tell her full story between the early 1970s and the present raises other issues. Some of the explanation lies with her ongoing commitment to accomplishing urgent tasks as a writer and political figure. Perhaps she hoped to write a memoir that would have the impact of her 1963 book. The way a participant remembers events is bound to differ from the way a historian recovers them, largely from written records. Friedan may have come to believe a narrative that outlived the needs it originally fulfilled.

Betty Friedan: Freelance Writer and Housewife

Until 1952, almost everything Friedan published as a labor journalist appeared under the name Betty Goldstein, though she had married in 1947. When she emerged as a writer for women's magazines in 1955, it was as Betty Friedan. Aside from indicating her marital status, the change in name was significant. It signaled a shift from an employee for a union paper who wrote highly political articles on the working class to a freelance writer for mass-circulation magazines who concentrated on the suburban middle class in more muted tones.

Around 1950 the Friedans moved from the Upper West Side of Manhattan to Parkway Village in Queens.[84] Developed to house United Nations personnel from around the world and the families of returning veterans, this apartment complex contained a cosmopolitan mix of people, including diplomats, American Jews, and African Americans.[85] For two years beginning in February 1952, Friedan edited *The Parkway Villager*, transforming it from a chatty source of community news into an activist publication.[86] Beginning in the spring of 1952, she led an extended protest and rent strike, actions she couched in terms of protecting an authentic community from greedy bankers. Something else enriched Friedan's perspective in the years after she stopped working for the UE. Shortly after its 1953 publication in English, Friedan appreciatively read Simone de Beauvoir's *The Second Sex*. Yet when she mentioned this later, she did not point to the book's Marxism or to the author's politics. Instead in *The Feminine Mystique* she hailed its "insights into French women," and in 1975 she stated that from it she learned "my own existentialism."[87]

In the 1950s the Friedans spent many weekends trying to find another place to live that had an authentic sense of community. With other families they explored the possibility of creating a communal group of homes north of New York City.[88] After the birth of a third child in May 1956, the Friedans accepted a more individualistic solution, moving later that year to a stone barn in Sneden's Landing, on the west side of the Hudson in Rockland County, New York, just above the New Jersey border. A year later they settled in nearby Grandview, in an eleven-room Victorian house, which they bought with the help of the GI Bill and some money Friedan inherited from her father.[89]

What Friedan wrote for mass-circulation women's magazines belies her claim that she had contributed to what she later attacked in *The Feminine Mystique*. Joanne Meyerowitz, relying on a systematic analysis of articles in widely read periodicals, has called into question Friedan's assertion that articles such as the ones she wrote and then later attacked fostered the worst kind of cold war ideology that focused on domesticity and togetherness.[90] Meyerowitz has demonstrated that pieces such as the ones Friedan authored actually "expressed overt admiration for women whose individual striving moved them beyond the home," in the process supporting women's work outside the home and women's activity in politics. As a result, Meyerowitz has enabled us to see that mass-circulation magazines, even as they advocated domesticity and femininity, portrayed women as independent, creative, and nonconformist. Moreover, she has demonstrated that Friedan's work, "remarkably rooted in postwar culture," had resonance for contemporaries because it both relied on and reformulated what others had stated.[91]

An examination of Friedan's articles adds weight to Meyerowitz's conclusions.[92] By the mid-1950s Friedan was achieving success as a writer. Sylvie Murray has demonstrated that Friedan drafted, but was unable to get into print, articles that fully celebrated women's political activism, expressed skepticism about male expertise, and described blue-collar and lower-middle-class families, not generic middle-class ones. Yet Friedan was able to sell articles that went against the grain of the cold war celebration by criticizing middle-class conformity. The pieces she published between 1955 and the early 1960s reveal a woman who was thinking about how to find authentic community life, satisfactory motherhood, and a productive career. Friedan critiqued suburban life by drawing a dismal picture of those who conformed, by offering alternatives to conventional choices, and by exploring the strength of cooperative communities.[93] She drew portraits of American women that opposed the picture of the happy suburban housewife who turned her back on a career in order to find satisfaction at home.[94] Friedan also portrayed women accomplishing important tasks as they took on traditionally feminine civic roles, thus implicitly undercutting the ideal of the apolitical suburban housewife and mother.[95] The theme of independent women also emerged in an unpublished piece that was an illuminating precursor of *The Feminine Mystique*. "Was Their Education UnAmerican?" relied on a questionnaire Friedan's Smith classmates filled out for their tenth reunion. She repudiated McCarthyism and upheld academic freedom by showing that, despite exposure to radicalism in college, many of her peers were conservatives who took seriously their obligations as citizens.[96]

In one particularly revealing piece, Friedan prefigured some of the issues she later claimed she began to discover only when she started to work on *The Feminine Mystique*. In "I Went Back to Work," published in *Charm* in April 1955, she wrote that initially she did not think highly of housework or of housewives and felt guilty about what she was doing. Eventually she decided that her commitment to being a good mother was not "going to interfere with what I regarded as my 'real' life." Finding it necessary to be away from home for nine hours a day in order to work, she solved the problem of child care by hiring "a really good mother-substitute—a housekeeper-nurse." In the end, Friedan had no regrets about her decision or apparently about her privileged position. She believed her work outside the home improved her family's situation and acknowledged that her "whole life had always been geared around creative, intellectual work" and "a professional career."[97] A revealing bridge between Friedan's community activity in the 1940s and *The Feminine Mystique* was a 1957 article in *Parents' Magazine*. Here Friedan told the story of a group of women who lived in a housing project an hour from Manhattan and organized a day camp for their children. In the process, the mothers demonstrated their ability to work cooperatively without replicating hierarchical organizations and developed a model for a cross-class summer camp for urban children.[98]

In what ways, then, was Friedan a captive of the feminine mystique? There is no question but that she was miserable in the suburbs. Her emphasis on her captivity may have expressed one part of her ambivalence. Yet though she claimed that she shared so much with her suburban white middle-class sisters in the postwar world, during much of the two decades beginning in 1943 Friedan was participating in left-wing union activity, writing articles that went against the grain of cold war ideology, and living in a cosmopolitan, racially integrated community. During most of the time between her marriage in 1947 and the publication of *The Feminine Mystique*, Friedan combined career and family life. As a woman who worked with her at the Federated Press later noted, at the time Friedan and her female colleagues expected to have professional careers.[99] Caution about the predominantly suburban origins of her book is also in order because Friedan's move to suburban Rockland County in 1956 preceded by only a few months her initial work on the survey for her reunion that was so critical to *The Feminine Mystique*.[100]

To be sure, in the postwar world Friedan experienced at first hand the trials of a woman who fought against considerable odds to combine marriage, motherhood, and a career.[101] Yet in critical ways her difficulties did not stem from the dilemmas she described in her book: lack of career and ambition, a securely affluent household, and absence of a political sensibility. Friedan experienced psychological conflicts over issues of creativity in writing and motherhood.[102] Researching and writing her freelance articles was a laborious process.[103] She had three young children, hardly felt comfortable in the suburbs, had no local institutions to provide a supportive environment for an aspiring writer, and continually faced financial difficulties. Her income from writing articles was unpredictable, a situation exacerbated by the pressure she was under to help support the household and justify the expenses for child care. Tension persisted between the Friedans over a wide range of issues, including who was responsible for earning and spending the family's income. Moreover, she was in a marriage apparently marked by violence.[104]

Rereading *The Feminine Mystique*

Friedan was largely right when she said "all the pieces of my own life came together for the first time in the writing" of *The Feminine Mystique*. The skills as a journalist she had developed beginning as a teenager stood her in good stead as she worked to make what she had to say accessible to a wide audience. Her identity as a Jew and an outsider gave her a distinctive perspective on American and suburban life. Her years at Smith boosted her confidence and enhanced her political education. Her life as a wife and mother sensitized her to the conflicts millions of others experienced but could not articulate. Her education as a psychologist led her to understand the gestalt, the wholeness of a situation, and to advocate self-fulfillment based on humanistic psychology. Above all, her work as a labor journalist and activist provided her with the intellectual depth, ideological commitments, and practical experiences crucial to her emergence as a leading feminist in the 1960s.

Why did a woman who had spent so much energy advocating political solutions focus in *The Feminine Mystique* largely on adult education and self-realization and turn social problems into psychological ones? How did a woman who had fought to improve the lives of African Americans, Latinas, and working-class women end up writing a book that saw the problems of America in terms of the lives of affluent, suburban white women?[105]

Even at the time, at least one observer, Gerda Lerner, raised questions about what Friedan emphasized and neglected. Active in the trade union movement in the 1940s, present at the founding meeting of NOW, and after the mid-1960s one of the nation's leading historians of women, Lerner wrote Friedan in February 1963. "I have just finished reading your splendid book and want to tell you how excited and delighted I am with it. . . . You have done for women," she remarked, "what Rachel Carson did for birds and trees," referring to the author who had warned about the destruction of the environment. Yet, Lerner continued,

> I have one reservation about your treatment of your subject: you address yourself solely to the problems of middle class, college-educated women. This approach was one of the shortcomings of the suffrage movement for many years and has, I believe, retarded the general advance of women. Working women, especially Negro women, labor not only under the disadvantages imposed by the feminine mystique, but under the more pressing disadvantages of economic discrimination. To leave them out of consideration of the problem or to ignore the contributions they can make toward its solution, is something we simply cannot afford to do. By their desperate need, by their numbers, by their organizational experience (if trade union members), working women are most important in reaching *institutional* solutions to the problems of women.[106]

The dynamics of Friedan's shifts in attention from working-class to middle-class women are not entirely clear. At some point after May 1953, when she followed the proceedings at the UE conference on the problems of women workers, Friedan turned away from working-class and African American women, something that undercut the power of *The Feminine Mystique*. An important question is whether the shift from her UE radicalism and focus on working-class women was a rhetorical strategy designed for the specific situation of *The Feminine Mystique* or part of a longer-term deradicalization. Until her personal papers are fully open and extensive interviewing is carried out, and perhaps not even then, we may not know the dynamics of this change. Among the things that call for examination is what role her distinctive and in some ways privileged social position—Peoria, merchant's daughter, Smith College—played in the change in her stance.[107]

Given what Friedan wrote and observed for the UE as late as 1953, the obliteration from *The Feminine Mystique* of the experiences of a wider range of women is quite striking.[108]

After the mid-1950s Friedan never returned to working-class women and labor unions as the primary or even major objects of her attention. In the mid-1950s Friedan may have undergone some deradicalization, although her departure from radical commitments, unlike those of many contemporaries, did not result in her becoming a conservative. Possibly, behind what she wrote in *The Feminine Mystique* was a series of events that burned her out politically and made her skeptical about how seriously American labor unions, even radical ones, took their commitment to advance the cause of women.

Whatever may yet be learned of Friedan's personal life and political journey, along with shifts in her politics and the consequences of McCarthyism, issues of genre, audience, and persona go a long way in explaining why *The Feminine Mystique* did not more accurately reflect her experience. During much of her life, but especially for the ten years beginning in 1953, Friedan thought of herself primarily as a writer, a professional journalist looking for the story that would increase her income and make her career. From her teenage years on, she had developed a keen understanding of her readers and of a variety of genres. Three children and an upper-middle-class life to support, as well as conflicts with her husband over issues of breadwinning, make understandable the change in the focus of her writing that resulted from the necessity to use her skills as a writer to generate income. She cast *The Feminine Mystique*, and her situation in the world it described, as part of an effort to enhance the book's popularity and impact.

With *The Feminine Mystique*, she was writing for a middle-class audience that had certain expectations about social criticism. She and her publishers thought her book might have the same kind of reverberations as William W. Whyte Jr.'s *The Organization Man* (1955) and Vance Packard's *The Status Seekers* (1959).[109] To that list, she might have added David Riesman's *The Lonely Crowd* (1950), on which she drew extensively. What Friedan's book shared with these best-sellers accounts to some extent for her shift in focus from her earlier political positions. Friedan adapted what they had written about suburban, middle-class men to their female counterparts. Like them, Friedan held a mirror up to Americans, both frightening and encouraging them with the shock of recognition. With them, she assumed that the problem resulted from the struggle to enhance identity amid widely experienced affluence, not from the prevalence of poverty or discrimination.[110]

Central to *The Feminine Mystique* was a series of issues about which her male counterparts had also written but on which her history could have given her a different perspective. Like her predecessors, she psychologized social problems and considered identity and mythology but not social structure as the principal impediments to a coherent identity. Friedan followed others with a book that was longer on analysis designed to shock readers than on public policies that provided solutions.[111] Consequently, in her last chapter, she offered "A New Life Plan for Women." Having acknowledged the importance of some policy issues, she ended by emphasizing how women should break the mental chains of the feminine mystique in order to achieve fuller self-realization.[112]

Nonetheless, Friedan's book contained themes that drew on what she had learned in the 1930s, 1940s, and 1950s. *The Feminine Mystique* had two autobiographical narratives. One, which provided its spine and strengthened its appeal, suggested that Friedan herself experienced uncertainty, blocked career mobility, and an identity crisis throughout her adult life.[113] The second, for which Friedan provided the evidence though she kept the plot line and its relevance to her life obscure, involved a concerted effort by men and corporations to suppress the aspirations of women. Throughout her book, although she had the evidence to do so, Friedan drew back from declaring that men—as fathers, husbands, editors, psychologists, social scientists, educators, corporate heads, and advertising executives—had coordinated the postwar counterrevolution against women.[114] Friedan could not highlight this second story for several reasons. As a labor journalist (and later as a nationally known feminist), Friedan argued for building coalitions of men and women to fight for social justice. Any process of deradicalization she had undergone may have impelled her to hedge her discussion of a capitalist conspiracy. More immediately, she may have felt that to have developed the idea of a conspiracy more fully would have undermined the book's impact, given what middle-class women supposedly believed about their situations at the time. Friedan had to hide her own radical past and create a believable persona. Perhaps guessing at how far she might push an audience whose consciousness she wished to raise, she decided that she had to temper her position.

Still, not very hidden in her book was a simplified Marxist view of ideological domination. In the pivotal chapter of her second and more radical narrative, titled "The Sexual Sell," the task she set for herself was to explain the "powerful forces" served by the feminine mystique. What, she asked, undermined the force of feminism and fueled the retreat of women into the privatism of the suburban home? In seeking an answer, Friedan articulated arguments congruent with what she learned from Dorothy W. Douglas and as a labor journalist. Friedan thus provided a bridge between the discussions in radical circles of the 1940s about the problems women faced and the feminism that many women would articulate in the late 1960s. Because of the importance of business in America, she said at the beginning of the chapter, making purchases for the home was the housewives' crucial function. Since women were "the chief customers of American business," she argued, "somehow, somewhere, someone must have figured out that" they would purchase more "if they are kept in the underused, nameless-yearning, energy-to-get-rid-of state of being housewives." Having hinted at the possibility of a conspiracy in which the heads of major corporations decided to mount a campaign to keep women home so they would consume household products, Friedan then ducked the logic of her argument and evidence. "Conspiratorial theories of history," she wrote in a way that differed from her 1940s and early 1950s attacks on the postwar plans of the NAM, were not adequate to explain what she had observed.[115]

Having examined a range of strategies adopted by corporations, Friedan concluded her consideration of the sexual sell by using rhetorical strategies that offered vague hints of larger issues. She suggested that America was a "sick society," not willing to confront its problems or see its purposes in terms commensurate with the ambitions of its citizens, including women.[116] Like the young radicals who wrote the Port Huron Statement for SDS in 1962, Friedan seemed unable to utter the word *capitalism*. Though C. Wright Mills in *The Power Elite* (1956) went farther in exploring how elites operated undemocratically, Friedan provided the evidence for such an analysis and then hinted at what it would mean for a male power elite to suppress women systematically.

This second narrative emerged elsewhere. Without mentioning her version of her own experience, Friedan talked of the transformative power of women's experience in World War II. She wrote at one point that "women were often driven embittered" from their jobs by returning veterans. Ever since the end of World War II, she asserted, "a propaganda campaign, as unanimous in this democratic nation as in the most efficient of dictatorships," had exalted the prestige of housework. Although others would date the counterrevolution against women to the 1920s or 1930s, Friedan focused on the late 1940s, a period linked in her own experience with a time when cold warriors undermined the left and, more specifically, the UE's fight for justice for women. She explored the alienating nature of women's work, not in factories but in suburban homes. She talked about the "devastating" effects of discrimination against women. At one moment, also without mentioning herself, she spoke of women of her generation, who, though not focusing on women's rights, were "still concerned with human rights and freedom—for Negroes, for oppressed workers, for victims of Franco's Spain and Hitler's Germany."[117]

There were other suggestions of a radical analysis. Absent from the book was any hint of a critique of the Soviet Union or a celebration of Cold War America. Indeed, Friedan's phrase "comfortable concentration camp" invoked the antifascism that she had articulated at Smith. In addition, perhaps the call for women to express themselves on public issues was a code for the politics she could not openly express. Rejecting a narcissistic version of self-fulfillment, Friedan instead emphasized that people fulfilled themselves by pursuing "a human purpose larger than themselves."She argued that people developed a healthy identity not through routine work, but by purposeful and committed effort outside the confines of the home. She insisted that it was important to recognize that there were still battles to fight in the United States. Institutions of higher education would have to make provision for people, women especially, whose lives did not fit easily into the pattern of college completion by age twenty-two, followed directly by a career. Drawing on her UE experience, Friedan also briefly mentioned the importance of enabling married women with children to have "the right to honorable competition" by providing maternity leaves, "professionally run nurseries, and the other changes in the rules that may be necessary."[118]

Others will assume the task of rethinking Friedan's post-1963 career in light of new evidence, but several comments are in order. In important ways, *The Feminine Mystique* marked a brief interlude in Friedan's longer-term political commitments. In the early 1950s the UE agenda included many of the commitments that Friedan would return to beginning in the mid-1960s: opposition to government infiltration into social movements, the end of racial and gender segregation and discrimination, commitment to comprehensive social welfare legislation, and opposition to unjust wars.[119] The UE and Friedan (post-1963) shared much that *The Feminine Mystique* lacked, including a commitment to a coalition that included unions, men, and African Americans. To be sure, her aims, language, ideology, and the subjects of her agitation shifted between 1953 and the mid-1960s. Yet in important ways she remained on the left. Full equality for women, she wrote in 1973, "will restructure all our institutions. "[120] One further proof of continuity in her ideology came in *The Second Stage* (1981). Though in important ways more conservative than *The Feminine Mystique*, this book nonetheless offered an analysis of the relationship between women and consumer culture that was more radical than her 1963 book and echoed many of the themes in her writings as a labor journalist.[121]

Friedan's experiences in the 1940s and early 1950s help explain but do not excuse her attack in 1973 on "disrupters of the women's movement" who were constantly advocating "lesbianism and hatred of men" and who did so, she claimed, with the encouragement of the FBI and the CIA. Those who were "pushing lesbianism" in NOW, she wrote, "were creating a sexual red herring that would divide the movement and lead ultimately to sexual McCarthyism." At the same time she distanced herself from her past when questioning those who based their feminism "on a false analogy with obsolete or irrelevant ideologies of class warfare or race separatism."[122] Whatever their origins in her personal experiences and in partisan battles, in complicated ways such remarks connect Friedan's later life with her early experiences with red-baiting, government suppression of radicalism, the dangers of factionalism, and class-based coalition politics. To someone rooted in 1940s radicalism, the identity politics of the 1970s were anathema.

Conclusion

A more complete story of Friedan's past illuminates a wide range of issues in recent American history. Moreover, this fuller story reveals information that enhances our sense of the importance of Friedan's contribution to American feminism. Recognizing the origins of

Friedan's 1963 book reminds us of the way that journalists of the 1950s emerged as social critics who helped shape the consciousness of the next decade.[123] The recovery of her past suggests the importance of thinking of her in comparison with New York intellectuals who, although they did much to shape postwar ideology, generally neglected issues of gender. *The Feminine Mystique* sheds light on important dimensions of gender issues. If Riesman, Whyte, and Packard suggested the troublesome nature of male identity in the 1950s, then we can understand how Friedan gave this theme a twist. "Male outrage," she remarked as she pointed to "the homosexuality that is spreading like a murky smog over" America, "is the result, surely, of an implacable hatred for the parasitic women who keep their husbands and sons from growing up."[124] The homophobia of such a comment is standard for the period. What is also of note is Friedan's promise that the liberation of women would strengthen a male identity that she and others found fragile. From writers such as Whyte and Riesman, Friedan took an analysis that blamed life in the suburbs, jobs in large organizations, and consumer culture for their inability to promote healthy masculinity and then turned this analysis into an argument for women's liberation.

The Feminine Mystique played a critical role in reshaping the ideology and social composition of the American left. Along with others, such as Herbert Marcuse, Friedan was exploring how to ground a cultural and social critique by rethinking the contributions of Freud and Marx. What Marcuse did in *Eros and Civilization: A Philosophical Inquiry into Freud* (1955) Friedan did almost a decade later: respond to the cold war by attempting to minimize her debt to Marx even as she relied on him. For her solutions, if not her analysis, she relied on psychology. In the process, she recovered the lessons of the discipline in which she majored at college, joining others such as Paul Goodman, David Riesman, Margaret Mead, Erik Erikson, and Erich Fromm in using humanistic psychology and neo-Freudianism to ground a powerful cultural critique at a time when other formulations were politically discredited. In her 1963 book Friedan was reshaping American social criticism by focusing not on the working class and the processes of production but on the way changes in consumer culture were reshaping the lives of the middle class.

Friedan was not alone in experiencing what it meant to have a radical past and eventually end up living in the suburbs, cut off from the realities of urban industrial life that once gave radicalism its palpability.[125] The trajectory of her career provides another example of the transition in the media from working-class, ethnically charged cultural representations to largely suburban, middle-class, and deracinated ones.[126] Moreover, the widening division between the working class and the urban poor brought issues of race to the surface in ways that made some of Friedan's analysis outdated. At a time when unions (although not the UE) accommodated themselves to the cold war consensus and Mills was noting the key role of university students and intellectuals in progressive politics, Friedan was arguing that middle- and upper-middle-class white women would replace workers in the vanguard of American social protest.[127] Her image of herself as the frustrated housewife came from a number of sources, including her recognition that the rhetoric of the Old Left shed little light on the realities of millions of American women. The persona of the suburban housewife enabled her to talk about alienation and discrimination in a new setting and in less radical terms.

A reconsideration of Friedan's career deepens our understanding of the relationship of the 1930s, 1940s, and 1950s to the social protests of the 1960s.[128] Her life underscores the difficulty of separating history into neatly packaged decades. Friedan's experiences in the 1940s and 1950s show us once again that life in the years before the 1960s was hardly calm.[129] It reminds us of how issues of Communism and anti-Communism shaped a generation. Friedan's life suggests discontinuities as well as continuities between the Old Left and the protests of the 1960s.[130] If McCarthyism prompted her to hide elements of her past from view, it also made it difficult for her to directly confront her debt to the Old Left, perhaps out of a sense that she may have betrayed a problematic or martyred cause.

Yet her life makes clear how important were World War II, unions, issues of the 1940s, and the fights by radicals for justice for women and African Americans in setting the stage for the reemergence of protests in the 1960s. Robert Korstad and Nelson Lichtenstein have demonstrated that in the 1940s union members and radicals created what E. P. Thompson called a "window of opportunity" in the struggle for civil rights for African Americans. We may come to see that the 1940s offered a somewhat parallel situation for millions of women. Among the forces at work, the roughly similar consequences of which Korstad and Lichtenstein have explored for African Americans, were the war-induced economic boom that created new types and levels of economic opportunities, the wartime entry of millions of women into the workforce and a smaller but significant number into CIO unions, the commitment of agencies of the federal government to women's advancement, the organizational and ideological leadership of the Communist Party, the generation of a "rights consciousness," and the broadening of public discourse. Following the war, the returning veterans and, more significantly, an employer-led offensive closed that window by isolating Communist-influenced leaders, curbing union ambitions, and undermining the Popular Front coalition. The result, Korstad and Lichtenstein's model suggests, was that when feminism reemerged in the 1960s, "it would have a different social character and an alternative political agenda," transformed by the consequences of the lost opportunities of the 1940s.[131]

This revision of Friedan's past sheds light on the history of women and second-wave feminism by enriching our sense of the origins of what happened in the 1960s. It offers vivid proof of the intertwined processes of containment and resistance of women in the 1940s and 1950s.[132] Moreover, it suggests that we think of Friedan, at some crucial points in her life, as a "left feminist" and a crucial link between generations of advocates for women's advancement.[133] American feminism, most historians agree, emerged in the 1960s from two sources: white, professional, and well-educated liberals, including Friedan and a few acknowledged union activists, who relied on a Washington-based approach as they called for national legislation; and a diverse group of women, shaped by the civil rights movement, who worked from the grassroots to develop a more adversarial insurgency.[134] However, if Rosa Parks refused to take a seat at the back of a segregated bus not simply because her feet hurt, then Friedan did not write *The Feminine Mystique* simply because she was an unhappy housewife. Nor was Friedan alone. Gerda Lerner, Bella Abzug, Eleanor Flexner, and Milton Meltzer are among those active in the labor movement in the 1940s who would emerge in the 1960s as people who helped shape post-1963 feminism.[135] Once we recover the stories of their counterparts among middle-class activists across the nation (perhaps, like those discussed above, predominantly Jews) and among working-class and African American women, the importance of the 1940s in the history of American feminism will be clearer.[136]

Friedan's experiences happened in specific contexts, especially the cauldron of labor union activism and even more particularly that provided by the UE. Whatever the accompanying frustrations and however much her focus shifted, her work for the UE shaped her engagement with the issues women faced. Friedan's story suggests that, at least as far as she and some others are concerned, what we have seen as liberal feminism had radical origins. Consequently, it underscores the importance of a reconsideration of the nature of the breach between the proponents of women's rights in the early 1960s and the late-1960s advocates of women's liberation, especially socialist feminists. For Friedan, labor union activity in the 1940s and early 1950s provided the bridge over which she moved from the working class to women as the repository of her hopes as well as much of the material from which she would fashion her feminism in *The Feminine Mystique*.

Notes

Many friends and colleagues at Smith College and in Northampton helped me think through the issues discussed in this article, and I am especially indebted to those who made extensive comments on various drafts: Travis Crosby, Alice L. Hearst, Helen L. Horowitz, Thomas F. Jackson, Gina Rourke, Donald Weber, and Robert Weir. I am grateful to others whose responses to earlier versions sharpened what I have to say: Robert H. Abzug, Lynn Dumenil, Ronald Schatz, and Judith Smith. I am grateful to Jane S. De Hart and Linda K. Kerber for helping me think through a series of key issues when, in response to an earlier draft, they agreed with me on some issues and disagreed on others. Casey Blake and Howard Brick, readers for *American Quarterly*, provided exceptionally thoughtful critiques that contributed considerably to how I framed my argument. Jennifer L. Hootman carried out research into Peoria materials. At Smith, Rachel Ledford and Gina Rourke helped track down materials. From his position at the UE Archives at the University of Pittsburgh, David L. Rosenberg provided important leads. The librarians at Smith College responded to my questions with thoroughness and alacrity and the staff of the Schlesinger Library facilitated my use of the Friedan and Flexner collections. Throughout, Lucy Maddox ably served as advisor and editor. I am grateful to the National Endowment for the Humanities, which awarded me a Fellowship for College Teachers, under whose auspices I did the initial research and writing of this article.

1. Betty Goldstein, "UE Drive on Wage, Job Discrimination Wins Cheers from Women Members," *UE News*, 16 April 1951, 6. My interview of Friedan in 1987 first brought to my attention the possibility of this alternative story, as did the research my colleague Helen L. Horowitz carried out in the late 1980s. The appearance of the article by Joanne Meyerowitz in 1993, cited below, added an important piece of evidence. Because Friedan has denied me permission to quote from her unpublished papers and has not responded to my request that she grant me an opportunity to interview her again or to have her provide answers to my questions, I have not been able to present as full and perhaps as accurate a story as I wished to do.

2. Ronald W. Schatz, *The Electrical Workers: A History of Labor at General Electric and Westinghouse, 1923–60* (Urbana, Ill., 1983), xiii.

3. Lisa Kannenberg, "The Impact of the Cold War on Women's Trade Union Activism: The UE Experience," *Labor History* 34 (spring–summer 1993): 318; Jacqueline Van Voris, interview with Eleanor Flexner, Northampton, Mass., 16 October 1982, 70–71, Eleanor Flexner Papers, Schlesinger Library, Radcliffe College, Cambridge, Mass. [hereinafter cited as FP-SLRC]; [Eleanor Flexner], "The Woman Question" (syllabus for course at Jefferson School of Social Science, 1953–54) 1, 2, 5. For information on Flexner, I am relying on Ellen C. DuBois, "Eleanor Flexner and the History of American Feminism," *Gender and History* 3 (spring 1991): 81–90. On the Jefferson School, see Annette T. Rubinstein, "David Goldway," *Science and Society* 54 (winter 1990–91): 386–89; Daniel F. Ring, "Two Cultures: Libraries, the Unions, and the 'Case' of the Jefferson School of Social Science," *Journal of Library History* 20 (1985): 287–88.

4. Betty Friedan, "Up from the Kitchen Floor," *New York Times Magazine*, 4 March 1973, 8; Betty Friedan, *"It Changed My Life": Writings on the Women's Movement* (New York, 1976), 304.

5. For evidence of the continuing importance of Friedan and her book, see, for example, Elaine T. May, *Homeward Bound: American Families in the Cold War Era* (New York, 1988), 209–17, 219; and Joanne Meyerowitz, "Beyond the Feminine Mystique: A Reassessment of Postwar Mass Culture, 1946–1958," *Journal of American History* 79 (March 1993): 1455–82. For textbooks, see John M. Faragher et al., *Out of Many: A History of the American People* (Englewood Cliffs, N.J., 1994), 2:865, 943; James A. Henretta et al., *America's History*, 2nd ed. (New York, 1993), 2:909, 910, 911, 968; William H. Chafe, *The Unfinished Journey: America since World War II*, 3rd ed. (New York, 1995), 124, 330, 433. A widely used reader in American women's history contains a selection from Friedan's book, introducing its author as "a suburban housewife": Linda K. Kerber and Jane S. De Hart, eds., *Women's America: Refocusing the Past*, 4th ed. (New York, 1995), 512.

6. Kathleen A. Weigand, "Vanguards of Women's Liberation: The Old Left and the Continuity of the Women's Movement in the United States, 1945–1970s" (Ph.D. diss., Ohio State University, 1995) contains the fullest treatment of this continuity, as well as the best bibliography on the issue of women and radicalism in the postwar period. Gerda Lerner, "Midwestern Leaders of the Modern Women's Movement: An Oral History Project," *Wisconsin Academy Review*, Winter 1994–95, 11–15 provides an important corrective to the notion that 1960s feminism emerged spontaneously in that decade and that its leadership was mainly white and middle class. Among the other historians who have suggested such a connection, focusing mostly

on women union activists, peace advocates, proponents of civil rights for African Americans, and radicals, are Susan Lynn, *Progressive Women in Conservative Times: Racial Justice, Peace and Feminism, 1945 to the 1960s* (New Brunswick, 1992); Michael E. Brown et al., *New Studies in the Politics and Culture of U.S. Communism* (New York, 1993); Kannenberg, "Impact," 323; Nancy F. Gabin, *Feminism in the Labor Movement: Women and the United Auto Workers, 1935–1975* (Ithaca, 1990); Dorothy Healey and Maurice Isserman, *Dorothy Healey Remembers: A Life in the American Communist Party* (New York, 1990). Many of the contributors to Joanne Meyerowitz, ed., *Not June Cleaver: Women and Gender in Postwar America, 1945–1960* (Philadelphia, 1994) emphasize how the persistence of adversarial traditions in the 1940s and 1950s provided important bridges to social movements in the 1960s. The same is true of several articles in Linda K. Kerber, Alice Kessler-Harris, and Kathryn K. Sklar, eds., *U.S. History as Women's History: New Feminist Essays* (Chapel Hill, N.C., 1995), especially Joyce Antler, "Between Culture and Politics: The Emma Lazarus Federation of Jewish Women's Clubs and the Promulgation of Women's History, 1944–1989," 267–95 (also in this volume), and Amy Swerdlow, "The Congress of American Women: Left Feminist Peace Politics in the Cold War," 296–312. For Flexner's location of the origins of 1960s feminism in 1940s and 1950s radicalism, see Eleanor Flexner to Pat King, 13 May 1983, FP-SLRC.

7.   See, for example, Robert Korstad and Nelson Lichtenstein, "Opportunities Found and Lost: Labor, Radicals, and the Early Civil Rights Movement," *Journal of American History* 75 (December 1988): 786–811; Maurice Isserman, *If I Had a Hammer: The Death of the Old Left and the Birth of the New Left* (New York, 1987).

8.   George Lipsitz, *Time Passages: Collective Memory and American Popular Culture* (Minneapolis, 1990), 42.

9.   For biographical information, in addition to what Friedan has said in print, I am relying on Kathleen Wilson, "Betty (Naomi) Friedan," *Contemporary Authors*, New Revision Series (New York, 1995), 45:133–36; David Halberstam, *The Fifties* (New York, 1993), 592–98; Marilyn French, "The Emancipation of Betty Friedan," *Esquire* 100 (December 1983): 510, 512, 514, 516, 517; Jennifer Moses, "She's Changed Our Lives: A Profile of Betty Friedan," *Present Tense* 15 (May–June 1988): 26–31; Lyn Tornabene, "The Liberation of Betty Friedan," *McCall's*, May 1971, 84, 136–40, 142, 146; Paul Wilkes, "Mother Superior to Women's Lib," *New York Times Magazine*, 29 November 1970, 27–29, 140–43, 149–50, 157; Marcia Cohen, *The Sisterhood: The True Story of the Women Who Changed the World* (New York, 1988), 25, 54–71, 83–84, 89–99; Lisa Hammel, "The 'Grandmother' of Women's Lib," *New York Times*, 19 November 1971, 52; Friedan, *Changed My Life*, 5–16; Jacqueline Van Voris, interview of Betty Friedan, New York, N.Y., 17 April 1973, College Archives, Smith College, Northampton, Mass. [hereinafter cited as CA-SC]; Daniel Horowitz, interview of Betty Friedan, Santa Monica, Calif., 18 March 1987. As late as 6 November 1995, the date she sent me a letter denying me permission to quote from her unpublished papers, Friedan reiterated key elements of her story. I am grateful to Rachel Ledford for reporting to me on Friedan's 6 November 1995 talk at the Smithsonian Institution, Washington, D.C. Ironically, two biographies aimed at children provide fuller stories than do other treatments (for instance, they are the only published sources I have been able to locate that make clear that Friedan worked for the UE): Sondra Henry and Emily Taitz, *Betty Friedan: Fighter for Women's Rights* (Hillside, N.J., 1990) and Milton Meltzer, *Betty Friedan: A Voice for Women's Rights* (New York, 1985).

10. This article is based on considerable but hardly exhaustive examination of the available written record. When other researchers examine the Friedan papers (including those to which access is still restricted) and are able to carry out extensive interviews, they will be able to offer a fuller exploration of several issues, especially the shifts in Friedan's commitments as a radical at a time of great factionalism, when and how the feminine mystique did or did not trap her, how she interpreted the research on which *The Feminine Mystique* relied, and the pressures Friedan faced from her publisher to shape her 1963 book in certain ways.

11. An examination of what Friedan wrote for her high-school paper reveals someone less lonely than she has often portrayed herself; see articles by Friedan in *Peoria Opinion* from the fall of 1936 until the spring of 1938. For one political piece that reveals an early antifascism, see Bettye Goldstein, "Long, Coughlin, Roosevelt in 'It Can't Happen Here,'" *Peoria Opinion*, 18 September 1936, 8.

12. Friedan, quoted in Wilkes, "Mother Superior," 140; Betty Friedan, *The Feminine Mystique* (New York, 1963), 12.

13. Friedan, *Feminine Mystique*, 70; Friedan, quoted in Wilkes, "Mother Superior," 140. On the paucity of role models at Smith, see Van Voris, Friedan interview.

14. Horowitz, interview.

15. Dust jacket of 1963 copy of *The Feminine Mystique*, author's possession. See also "About Betty Friedan . . . ," biographical note accompanying Betty Friedan, "How to Find and Develop Article Ideas," *The Writer* 75 (March 1962), 13.

16. Friedan, quoted in "Betty Friedan," Charles Moritz, ed., *Current Biography Yearbook 1970* (New York, 1971), 146; Betty Friedan, "New York Women: Beyond the Feminine Mystique," *New York Herald Tribune*, 21 February 1965, 7–15; women's liberation, biographies, individuals, box 4, folder 31, clippings on Betty Friedan, Sophia Smith Collection, Smith College [hereinafter referred to as SSC-SC]; Wilkes,

"Mother Superior," 141; Friedan, quoted in Wilkes, "Mother Superior," 141; Tornabene, "Liberation," 138; and Friedan, " Kitchen Floor," 8.

17. Tornabene, "Liberation," 138. See Betty Friedan, "The Intellectual Pied Pipers of Rockland County," (unpublished paper, written in 1960–61, FP-SLRC, carton 9, folder 347, Friedan Collection, Schlesinger Library, Radcliffe College, Cambridge, Mass. [hereinafter cited as BF-SLRC; unless otherwise noted, the references are to collection 71-62 . . . 81-M23]).

18. Rollene W. Saal, "Author of the Month," *Saturday Review*, 21 March 1964; women's liberation, biographies, individuals, box 4, folder 31, SSC-SC; *Hackensack Record*, 2 May 1963; Class of 1942 folders, Betty Goldstein folder, CA-SC; Friedan, "Kitchen Floor," 8.

19. Friedan, *Feminine Mystique*, 9, 20, 66, 70, 186–87.

20. Horowitz, interview; Betty Friedan, "Introduction to the Tenth Anniversary Edition" of *Feminine Mystique* (New York, 1974), 1–5. For early articles with the themes that would emerge in the book, see Betty Friedan, "I Say: Women Are *People* Too!" *Good Housekeeping*, September 1960, 59–61, 161–62; Betty Goldstein Friedan, "If One Generation Can Ever Tell Another," *Smith Alumnae Quarterly*, February 1961, 68–70.

21. The 1974 article, which in the book was called "The Way We Were—1949," was originally published with some relatively unimportant differences, but with a more revealing title, as Betty Friedan, "In France, de Beauvoir Had Just Published 'The Second Sex,'" *New York*, 30 December 1974–6 January 1975, 52–55. In Horowitz, interview, which covered mainly the years up to 1963, Friedan discussed her move to a radical politics even as she emphasized captivity by the feminine mystique beginning in the Berkeley years. Though Friedan has revealed a good deal about her life, to the best of my knowledge she has not acknowledged in print the full range of reasons she left Berkeley, that she worked for the UE, her authorship of the 1952 pamphlet, and her leadership of the rent strike. Moroever, she has insisted that in the late 1940s and early 1950s she had interest neither in a career nor in women's problems.

22. I am grateful to Judith Smith for helping me to think through this and other issues.

23. Friedan, *Changed My Life*, 6, 8–9.

24. Ibid., 6, 9, 16; Halberstam, *Fifties*, 593; French, "Emancipation," 510. Horowitz, interview, dates the firing in 1952. In the immediate postwar years, the term *feminist* often referred to women who were Republicans, independent businesswomen, and professionals.

25. Friedan, *Changed My Life*, 5, 6–7, 8–9, 15, 16. She gave 1949 as the turning point because she had been asked to do a piece in 1974 on what had happened a quarter of a century earlier; Horowitz, interview.

26. Friedan, *Changed My Life*, 14–16.

27. Ibid., 12, 16.

28. An extensive examination of the letters that Friedan received from women may well reveal the success of her strategy of encouraging her readers to identify with her situation: for an astute examination of these letters, carried out in a different context, see May, *Homeward Bound*, 209–17.

29. French, "Emancipation," 510; Donald Meyer, "Betty Friedan," in G. J. Barker-Benield and Catherine Clinton, eds., *Portraits of American Women: From Settlement to the Present* (New York, 1991), 601; Halberstam, *Fifties*, 593–94. For other problematic accounts, see "Friedan," *Current Biography*, 146; Wilson, "Friedan," 134; Donald Meyer, *Sex and Power: The Rise of Women in America, Russia, Sweden, and Italy* (Middletown, Conn., 1987), 389; Rosalind Rosenberg, *Divided Lives: American Women in the Twentieth Century* (New York, 1992), 138–39.

30. Cohen, *Sisterhood*, 63, and Wilkes, "Mother Superior," 140, briefly draw a picture of Friedan as a college rebel, but to the best of my knowledge, the politics of that rebellion have remained largely unknown.

31. This summary relies on unsigned editorials that appeared under Friedan's editorship, which can be found in *SCAN* from 14 March 1941 to 10 March 1942, 2. Although members of the editorial board held a wide range of opinions, I am assuming that as editor-in-chief Friedan had a significant role in shaping editorials. Friedan placed four editorials in her papers: "They Believed in Peace," "Years of Change and Unrest," "Behind Closed Doors," and "Answer No Answer": carton 7, folder 310, BF-SLRC.

32. For the article she published on the basis on her honors thesis, see H. Israel and B. Goldstein, "Operationism in Psychology," *Psychological Review* 51 (May 1944): 177–88.

33. See James J. Gibson, "Why a Union for Teachers?" *Focus* 2 (November 1939): 3–7.

34. I am grateful to Margery Sly, archivist of Smith College, for providing this information. She has also pointed out that teaching at Smith in Friedan's years were several married female faculty members who had children and that Harold Israel and Elsa Siipola, two of Friedan's mentors, were married but without children.

35. In 1955 Douglas took the Fifth Amendment before HUAC as she was red-baited, and accused of having been a member of a Communist teachers union in the late 1930s. I am grateful to Margery Sly and Jacquelyn D. Hall for providing this information on Douglas. See also Betty Friedan, "Was Their Education UnAmerican?" unpublished article, 1953 or 1954, carton 11, folder 415, BF-SLRC, 3. For Friedan's continued use of Marxist analysis, see Friedan, *Changed My Life*, 110.

36. Bettye Goldstein, "Discussion of Reading Period Material," paper for Economics 319, 18 January 1941, carton 1, folder 257, BF-SLRC, 1, 2, 4, 8. See also "Questions on *Communist Manifesto*" and "Questions on Imperialism," papers for Economics 319, carton 1, folder 257, BF-SLRC.

37. John M. Glen, *Highlander: No Ordinary School, 1932–1962* (Lexington, Ky., 1988), 47–69. I am grateful to Professor Glen for a letter in which he clarified the timing of the league's sponsorship. Meltzer, *Friedan*, 20, says that Friedan's economics professor pointed her to Highlander but identifies that professor as a male; since the only economics course Friedan took was from Douglas, I am assuming that it was she who urged her student to attend the workshop. Meltzer thinks that is a reasonable assumption: Milton Meltzer, phone conversation with Daniel Horowitz, 24 September 1995.

38. Bettye Goldstein, "Highlander Folk School—American Future," unpublished paper, 1941, carton 6, folder 274, BF-SLRC; Goldstein, "Learning the Score," 22–24.

39. "Epilogue of Failure," *SCAN*, 10 March 1942, 2.

40. "Betty Goldstein, Local Girl, Makes Good in New York," clipping from Peoria newspaper, probably 10 December 1943 issue of *Labor Temple News*, carton 1, folder 86, BF-SLRC.

41. "Behind a Closed Door," *SCAN*, 3 October 1941, 2; "Declaration of Student Independence," *SCAN*, 5 December 1941, 1–2; "SCAN Protests Against Censorship," *SCAN*, 5 December 1941, 1; "A Few Hours More," *SCAN*, 10 October 1941, 2; "Review of Philosophy Courses," *SCAN*, 10 March 1942, 2.

42. "The Tatler Suspension," *SCAN*, 7 November 1941, 2; for the article in question see "Maids We Have Known and Loved," *Tatler*, October 1941, 9, 21. When the administration moved against *SCAN*, over a different incident, the editors changed their minds about the earlier suspension of the *Tatler*: *SCAN*, 5 December 1941, 1–2.

43. "Education in Emergency," *SCAN*, 15 April 1941, 2; "The Right to Organize," *SCAN*, 21 October 1941, 2; "Comment," *SCAN*, 14 November 1941, 2; Filene's advertisement, *SCAN*, 21 October 1941, 2. Bettye Goldstein, "For Defense of Democracy," *Smith College Monthly* 1 (October 1940): 11, 12, 28, is a passionate defense of democracy and a warning about the possibility of American fascism.

44. "They Choose Peace," *SCAN*, 22 April 1941, 2; for the minority opinion, see "The Case for Intervention," *SCAN*, 2 May 1941, 2; "War Against Fascism," *SCAN*, 24 October 1941, 2. Placing the editorials written on Friedan's watch in the national context of student politics makes clear that after the Nazi-Soviet pact the student movement was more active and radical at Smith than elsewhere. In addition, the commitment of Friedan and her fellow editors to antifascism and their reluctance to embrace interventionism fully after the German invasion of the Soviet Union suggests that they dissented from the Communist Party position. On the national context see Robert Cohen, *When the Old Left Was Young: Student Radicals and America's First Mass Student Movement, 1929–1941* (New York, 1993), especially 315–37.

45. J. N., "The Red Menace," *SCAN*, 14 October 1941, 2; Neal Gilkyson, "The Gallery," *SCAN*, 21 October 1941, 2.

46. "We Cannot Rejoice," *SCAN*, 9 December 1941, 2; "Our Duty Now," *SCAN*, 12 December 1941, 2; "Campus Cooperatives," *SCAN*, 24 February 1942, 2; "No Change in Emphasis," *SCAN*, 26 September 1941, 2.

47. "Betty Goldstein, Local Girl." Meltzer, *Friedan*, 21, provides explanations for Friedan's decision that do not rely on the standard story.

48. Certificate of Death for Harry M. Goldstein, County of Peoria, State of Illinois, copy in author's possession; Henry and Taitz, *Friedan*, 31. Keeping in mind the problematic nature of such documents, see FBI reports on Betty Goldstein, 1944, carton 1, folder 67, BF-SLRC.

49. To date her work for the Federated Press, see Betty Friedan, job application for Time Inc., 1 July 1951, carton 1, folder 61, BF-SLRC. For information on the Federated Press, see Doug Reynolds, "Federated Press," in Mari Jo Buhle, Paul Buhle, and Dan Georgakas, eds., *Encyclopedia of the American Left* (New York, 1990), 225–27.

50. Betty Goldstein, "Negro Pupils Segregated, Parents Strike; Issue Headed for Courts," Federated Press, 15 September 1943, carton 8, folder 328, BF-SLRC; Betty Goldstein, "Peace Now: Treason in Pious Garb," Federated Press, 16 February 1944, carton 8, folder 328, BF-SLRC; Betty Goldstein, "Well-Heeled 'White Collar League' Seen as Disguised Native Fascist Threat," Federated Press, 16 March 1944, carton 8, folder 328, BF-SLRC.

51. Betty Goldstein, "Big Business Getting Desperate, Promising Postwar Jobs," Federated Press, 19 November 1943, carton 8, folder 328, BF-SLRC; Betty Goldstein, "NAM Convention Pro-War—For War on Labor, New Deal, Roosevelt," Federated Press, 14 December 1943, carton 8, folder 328, BF-SLRC; Betty Goldstein, "Details of Big Business Anti-Labor Conspiracy Uncovered," Federated Press, 11 February 1946, carton 8, folder 328, BF-SLRC. For the larger story, see Elizabeth A. Fones-Wolf, *Selling Free Enterprise: The Business Assault on Labor and Liberalism, 1945–60* (Urbana, 1994).

52. Betty Goldstein, "Pretty Posters Won't Stop Turnover of Women in Industry," Federated Press, 26 October 1943, and Ruth Young quoted in same, carton 8, folder 328, BF-SLRC.

53. Betty Goldstein, "Post War Living: 'Are They Putting Something over on Us?' Mrs. Jones Wonders," Federated Press, 23 January 1946, carton 8, folder 329, BF-SLRC.

54. Job application, 1951.

55. For information on women in the UE see Schatz, *Electrical Workers;* Ruth Milkman, *Gender at Work: The Dynamics of Job Segregation by Sex during World War II* (Urbana, 1987); Kannenberg, "Impact"; Lisa A. Kannenberg, "From World War to Cold War: Women Electrical Workers and Their Union, 1940–1955" (M.A. thesis, University of North Carolina, Charlotte, 1990). Robert H. Zieger, *The CIO, 1935–1955* (Chapel Hill, N.C., 1995), 253–93, assesses the role of Communists in the CIO, including the UE, and discusses the vagueness of the line between sympathy and party membership in unions such as the UE; Ronald L. Filippelli and Mark McCulloch, *Cold War in the Working Class: The Rise and Decline of the United Electrical Workers* (Albany, N.Y., 1994) charts the attack on the UE and discusses the issue of Communist presence in the UE.

56. Van Voris, Flexner interview, 8 January 1977, 16 October 1982, and 11 May 1983, 2, 62, 67, 70–71, 81–82. Helen K. Chinoy, who shared a house with Friedan in the summer of 1944 or 1945, confirmed this judgment that in the 1940s Communist Party membership was not the critical issue among those on the left who identified themselves with a wide range of political positions: Daniel Horowitz, interview with Helen K. Chinoy, Northampton, Mass., 7 October 1995.

57. For Beecher's ancestry, I am relying on James Lerner, interview with Daniel Horowitz, Brooklyn, N.Y., 21 August 1995.

58. For the positive responses of this union and other Communist-led ones to problems of minority and female workers, see Zieger, *CIO*, 87, 255–56.

59. Schatz, *Electrical Workers*, 30, 89, 116–27, 129–30.

60. Milkman, *Gender at Work*, 77–78; see also Kannenberg, "Impact," esp. 311, 315. Nancy B. Palmer, "Gender, Sexuality, and Work: Women and Men in the Electrical Industry, 1940–1955" (Ph.D. diss., Boston College, 1995), more skeptical of women's gains in the UE, focuses on how the construction of gender in labor unions, including the UE, limited women's advances: see esp. ch. 4.

61. Zieger, *CIO*, 251.

62. This summary relies on Schatz, *Electrical Workers*, 167–240. The 1946 quote is from Harry Block in Schatz, *Electrical Workers*, 181. For the impact of the attack on UE on women's issues, see Kannenberg, "From World War to Cold War," 95.

63. Betty Goldstein, "NAM Does Gleeful War Dance to Profits, Wage Cuts, Taft Law," *UE News*, 13 December 1947, 4. What follows relies on the more than three dozen articles signed by Betty Goldstein in the *UE News* from the fall of 1946 until early 1952.

64. Betty Goldstein, "A Tale of 'Sacrifice': A Story of Equality in the United States, 1951," *March of Labor*, May 1951, 16–18, carton 8, folder 334, BF-SLRC. This also appeared in *UE News*, 12 March 1951, 6–7.

65. Betty Goldstein, "It'll Take a Strong Union to End Winchester Tyranny," *UE News*, 7 December 1946, 9; Betty Goldstein, "Fighting Together: We Will Win!" *UE News*, 31 May 1947, 5, 8; Betty Goldstein, "Labor Builds New Political Organization to Fight for a People's Congressman," *UE News*, 23 August 1947, 4.

66. Betty Goldstein, "People's Needs Forgotten: Big Business Runs Govt.," *UE News*, 12 May 1947, 5; Betty Goldstein, "In Defense of Freedom! The People vs. the UnAmerican Committee," *UE News*, 8 November 1947, 6–7; Betty Goldstein, "They Can't Shove the IBEW down Our Throats," *UE News*, 4 September 1948, 6–7; Betty Goldstein, "UnAmerican Hearing Exposed as Plot by Outsiders to Keep Grip on UE Local," *UE News*, 22 August 1949, 4; Betty Goldstein, "New NAM Theme Song: Labor-Management Teamwork," *UE News*, 9 January 1950, 5; Betty Goldstein, "Plain People of America Organize New Political Party of Their Own," *UE News*, 31 July 1948, 6–7.

67. B.G., review of Sinclair Lewis, *Kingsblood Royal, UE News*, 6 September 1947, 7; B.G., review of the movie *Gentleman's Agreement, UE News*, 22 November 1947, 11; B.G., review of movie *Crossfire, UE News*, 9 August 1947, 8–9; Betty Goldstein, "CIO Sold Out Fight for FEPC, T-H Repeal, Rep. Powell Reveals," *UE News*, 17 April 1950, 4; B.G., review of Fielding Burke, *Sons of the Stranger, UE News*, 24 January 1948, 7.

68. These two sentences rely on James Lerner, interview. For treatments of the relationship between Communism and women's issues, see Ellen K. Trimberger, "Women in the Old and New Left: The Evolution of a Politics of Personal Life," *Feminist Studies* 5 (fall 1979): 432–61; Van Gosse, "'To Organize in Every Neighborhood, in Every Home': The Gender Politics of American Communists between the Wars," *Radical History Review* 50 (spring 1991): 109–41; Kannenberg, "From World War to Cold War"; and Weigand, "Vanguards." For her coverage of Latinas, see Betty Goldstein, "'It's a Union that Fights for All the Workers,'" *UE News*, 3 September 1951, 6–7.

69. Though she does not discuss Friedan's situation, the best treatment of the prominent role of women's issues in radical circles in the 1940s and 1950s is Weigand, "Vanguards." In working on *The Feminine Mystique*, Friedan may have been influenced by writings she may have encountered in the 1940s, such as Mary Inman,

In Women's Defense (Los Angeles, 1940) and Betty Millard, "Woman Against Myth," *New Masses*, 30 December 1947, 7–10 and 6 January 1948, 7–20. There is evidence that Friedan was well aware of *New Masses*. Under a pseudonym, she published two articles in *New Masses*: Lillian Stone, "Labor and the Community," *New Masses* 57 (23 October 1945): 3–5; Lillian Stone, "New Day in Stamford," *New Masses* 58 (22 January 1946): 3–5. In identifying Friedan as the author, I am relying on a 22 September 1995 conversation with Kathy Kraft, an archivist at the Schlesinger Library and on a letter in carton 49, folder 1783, BF-SLRC.

70. Chinoy, interview.

71. Betty Goldstein, "Price Cuts Promised in Press Invisible to GE Housewives," *UE News*, 1 February 1947, 7; Betty Goldstein, "Union Members Want to Know—WHO Has Too Much Money to Spend," *UE News*, 26 March 1951, 8.

72. [Betty Goldstein], *UE Fights for Women Workers*, UE Publication no. 232, June 1952 (New York, 1952). To authenticate her authorship, I am relying on the following: Horowitz, interview; James Lerner, interview; Betty Friedan, postcard to author, late August 1995; Meltzer, *Friedan*, 25. Meltzer, who knew Friedan in the 1940s, discusses her work on women's issues at the UE. Friedan may also have written *Women Fight for a Better Life!* (New York, 1953): see Friedan, postcard.

73. [Goldstein], *UE Fights*, 5.

74. [Goldstein], *UE Fights*, 9–18, 26–27, 38.

75. Kannenberg, "Impact," 318.

76. See the following articles in *Jewish Life* by Rachel Roth: "'We're Worse off Every Year,'" 7 (April 1953): 11–14; "A 'Sick' Industry—But the Bosses Don't Suffer," 7 (May 1953): 10–13; "The Price of 'Collaboration,'" 7 (June 1953): 21–24. In identifying Friedan as the author, I am relying on the 22 September 1995 conversation with Kathy Kraft.

77. Kannenberg, "Impact," 318; the conference took place in New York in early May 1953.

78. These issues appear in "Resolution on Job Discrimination," "Resolution on Legislative Action," and "National Conference on the Problems of Working Women," mimeographed documents in carton 8, folder 336, BF-SLRC.

79. Generally speaking, Kannenberg and Schatz emphasize the genuineness of the UE's commitments, despite opposition within the union.

80. Palmer, "Gender, Sexuality, and Work."

81. Betty Goldstein to Grievance Committee of Newspaper Guild of New York, 23 May 1946, carton 8, folder 330, BF-SLRC; Friedan, *Changed My Life*, 9; Mim Kelber, phone conversation with Daniel Horowitz, 16 September 1995, identified the man as James Peck; obituary for James Peck, *New York Times*, 13 July 1993, B7.

82. Meltzer, *Friedan*, 29. For additional perspectives on Friedan's departure from the *UE News*, see Kelber, conversation, and James Lerner, interview. Lerner, who had more seniority than Friedan, worked for the UE for more than forty years, eventually becoming managing editor of *UE News*. He shared an office with Friedan during her years at *UE News* and has noted that the union protected Friedan's position during her first pregnancy: James Lerner, interview.

83. Margery Sly pointed me toward discussions of how women write about themselves, especially Carolyn G. Heilbrun, *Writing a Woman's Life* (New York, 1988), 13, 17, 24, 25; Jill K. Conway, "Introduction," in Conway, ed., *Written by Herself: Autobiographies of American Women: An Anthology* (New York, 1992), x–xi.

84. The precise dates of Friedan's residence in Parkway Village are difficult to nail down, and I am relying in part on the existence in her papers of copies of the Parkway Village newspaper from April 1949 to January 1956; Friedan, *Changed My Life*, 13; Betty Friedan, "Accomplishments," unpublished manuscript, c. 1959, 1, carton 1, folder 62, BF-SLRC, 2, which dates the departure to 1955; *Smith College Bulletin: Alumnae Register Issue* (Northampton, Mass., November 1949, November 1952, March 1956, and November 1958). From the written record, it is possible to determine little, if anything, of Carl Friedan's politics and of his role in shaping his wife's ideology.

85. Roy Wilkins lived there: see "Village Profile: Roy Wilkins," *Parkway Villager*, February 1954, 2.

86. See, for example, the headlines from the May 1952 issue: carton 10, folders 381–85, BF-SLRC.

87. Friedan, *Feminine Mystique*, 10; Friedan, *Changed My Life*, 304–16; Sandra Dijkstra, "Simone de Beauvoir and Betty Friedan: The Politics of Liberation," *Feminist Studies* 6 (summer 1980): 290–303.

88. Betty Friedan, conversation with Daniel Horowitz, Washington, D.C., 29 March 1995.

89. To date these moves, I am relying on a number of sources, including Betty Friedan to Mrs. Clifford P. Cowen, 5 August 1957, carton 7, folder, 313, BF-SLRC; Friedan, "New York Women"; "About the Author," in "New York Women"; "Friedan," *Current Biography*, 146; *Smith College Bulletin*.

90. Friedan, *Feminine Mystique*, 33–68.

91. Meyerowitz, "Beyond the Feminine Mystique," 1458, 1481.

92. For her claim, made before 1963, for the seriousness of her journalism in these magazines, see Friedan, "Accomplishments," 2.

93. Betty Friedan, "Two Are an Island," *Mademoiselle*, July 1955, 88–89, 100–101; Betty Friedan, "Teenage Girl in Trouble," *Coronet*, March 1958, 163–68; Betty Friedan, "The Happy Families of Hickory Hill," *Redbook*, February 1956, 39, 87–90; Marian Stone and Harold Stone [fictitious names], as told to Betty Friedan, "With Love We Live . . ." *Coronet*, July 1957, 135–44. For another article on a suburban development that relied on cooperation, see Betty Friedan, "'We Built a Community for Our Children,'" *Redbook*, March 1955, 42–45, 62–63. Friedan's papers contain information on scores of articles that she was working on; this analysis focuses on those actually published. Sylvie Murray's "Suburban Citizens: Domesticity and Community Politics in Queens, New York, 1945–1960" (Ph.D. diss., Yale University, 1994) ably contrasts the adversarial politics of Friedan's unpublished pieces with the milder tone of her published ones; on the difficulty of getting into print articles on women who were not middle-class, I am relying on Sylvie Murray, phone conversation with Daniel Horowitz, 9 October 1995.

94. Betty Friedan, "The Gal Who Defied Dior," *Town Journal*, October 1955, 33, 97–98; Betty Friedan, "Millionaire's Wife," *Cosmopolitan*, September 1956, 78–87; Betty Friedan, "New Hampshire Love Story," *Family Circle*, June 1958, 40–41, 74–76. An influential book on the origins of 1960s feminism begins with a discussion of Friedan's magazine articles without seeing how they might connect parts of her career: Sara Evans, *Personal Politics: The Roots of Women's Liberation in the Civil Rights Movement and the New Left* (New York, 1979), 3.

95. Betty Friedan, "Now They're Proud of Peoria," *Reader's Digest*, August 1955, 93–97.

96. Friedan, "Was Their Education UnAmerican?" 1–3.

97. Betty Friedan, "I Went Back to Work," *Charm*, April 1955, 145, 200.

98. Betty Friedan, "Day Camp in the Driveways," *Parents' Magazine*, May 1957, 36–37, 131–34.

99. Kelber, conversation.

100. Parkway Village had some suburban characteristics and was marketed on the basis of its suburban qualities: Murray, conversation. Yet Friedan has made it clear that she was happy there: Friedan, *Changed My Life*, 14. Moreover, being in Parkway Village did not involve inhabiting a single-family home or living individualistically among conformists.

101. Especially crucial but nonetheless elusive is the period from May 1953, when she appears to have ended her union work, to 1955, when her first article appeared in a women's magazine.

102. Friedan, "How to Find and Develop Article Ideas," 12–15, has some discussion of these conflicts.

103. This becomes clear through an examination of her files on her freelance work, especially when compared with the files of Vance Packard in the same years.

104. Wilkes, "Mother Superior," 141. On violence in the marriage, see also Tornabene, "Liberation," 138; Cohen, *Sisterhood*, 17–18; Meyer, "Friedan," 608; Myra MacPherson, "The Former Mr. Betty Friedan Has Scars to Prove It," probably 1971, newspaper article from unidentified source, women's liberation, biographies, individuals, box 4, folder 31, clippings on Betty Friedan, SSC-SC.

105. On this problem, see Elizabeth V. Spelman, *Inessential Woman: Problems of Exclusion in Feminist Thought* (Boston, 1988).

106. Gerda Lerner to Betty Friedan, 6 February 1963, box 20a, folder 715, BF-SLRC; quoted with permission of Gerda Lerner. For information on Lerner's participation in the labor movement, the Congress of American Women, and at the founding meeting of NOW, I am relying on Daniel Horowitz, phone conversation with Gerda Lerner, 18 October 1995; Swerdlow, "Congress of American Women," 306.

107. Meltzer, *Friedan*, 23, hints at the limitation that stemmed from her social position.

108. For criticism of Friedan for defining women so narrowly in *The Feminine Mystique*, see, for example, bell hooks, *Feminist Theory: From Margin to Center* (Boston, 1984), 1–15; among the many astute analyses of Friedan's 1963 book, none of which has taken into account accurate information about Friedan's early career, see Rachel Bowlby, "'The Problem With No Name': Rereading Friedan's *The Feminine Mystique*," *Feminist Review* 27 (September 1987): 61–75.

109. Betty Friedan to Scott Fletcher, 29 September 1959, carton 20a, folder 707, BF-SLRC.

110. For a reference to racial discrimination, see Friedan, *Feminine Mystique*, 180.

111. Friedan to Fletcher makes it clear that the germ of the idea that continuing education was a solution came from Betty Friedan, "Business Problems? Call in Plato," *Rotarian* 97 (August 1960): 19, 55–58.

112. Friedan, *Feminine Mystique*, 370, 378.

113. Ibid., 69, 70, 75, 76, 186, 187.

114. See, for example, the discussion of male editors in Friedan, *Feminine Mystique*, 51–54, which Friedan did not connect to the action of male social and behavioral scientists, college and university educators, and corporate executives.

115. Friedan, *Feminine Mystique*, 205–7. In Horowitz, interview, Friedan connected what she wrote in this chapter with her work as a labor journalist. Meyer, "Friedan," 206, briefly discussed Friedan's anticipation of socialist feminism.

116. Friedan, *Feminine Mystique*, 232.

117. Ibid., 100, 185–86, 255–57.

118. Ibid., 309, 333–37, 372, 374, 375.

119. Compare "GEB Presents Union Position to Convention," *UE News*, 23 June 1952, 6–7, and many of the documents in Friedan, *Changed My Life*, 87–145; Friedan, "Kitchen Floor," 33–34.

120. Friedan, "Kitchen Floor," 30.

121. Betty Friedan, *The Second Stage* (New York, 1981), 299–307.

122. Friedan, "Kitchen Floor," 33–34.

123. See, for example, Daniel Horowitz, *Vance Packard and American Social Criticism* (Chapel Hill, N.C., 1994).

124. Friedan, *Feminine Mystique*, 274, 276.

125. I am grateful to Robert H. Abzug for helping me to think through this and other issues.

126. Here I am relying on Lipsitz, *Time Passages*, especially 39–75, and on unpublished papers by Donald Weber and Judith Smith.

127. See, for example, C. Wright Mills, "The New Left," in Irving L Horowitz, ed., *Power, Politics and People: The Collected Essays of C. Wright Mills* (New York, 1963), 247–59.

128. See, for example, Todd Gitlin, *The Sixties: Years of Hope, Days of Rage* (New York, 1987), 11–71.

129. For some examples of this reinterpretation of the 1950s, see Wini Breines, *Young, White, and Miserable: Growing up Female in the Fifties* (Boston, 1992); Brett Harvey, *The Fifties: A Women's Oral History* (New York, 1993); Lary May, ed., *Recasting America: Culture and Politics in the Age of Cold War* (Chicago, 1989).

130. Isserman, *If I Had a Hammer*; Susan Lynn, "Gender and Post World War II Progressive Politics: A Bridge to Social Activism in the 1960s U.S.A.," *Gender and History* 4 (summer 1992): 215–39.

131. Korstad and Lichtenstein, "Opportunities," 787, 800, 811; the Thompson quote appears on 811.

132. May, *Homeward Bound*.

133. I am borrowing the term from DuBois, "Flexner," 84.

134. Jane S. De Hart, "The New Feminism and the Dynamics of Social Change," in Linda K. Kerber and Jane S. De Hart, eds., *Women's America: Refocusing the Past*, 4th ed. (New York, 1995), 539–60. De Hart, 547–48, acknowledges the presence of "a few feminist union activists" but did not so characterize Friedan's earlier career. For the scholarship on the ways women in the 1950s struggled to resist the dominant tendencies of American society in that decade, see Eugenia Kaledin, *Mothers and More: American Women in the 1950s* (Boston 1984); George Lipsitz, *A Life in the Struggle: Ivory Perry and the Culture of Opposition* (Philadelphia, 1988); Susan Ware, "American Women in the 1950s: Nonpartisan Politics and Women's Politicization," in Louise A. Tilly and Patricia Gurin, eds., *Women, Politics, and Change* (New York, 1990), 281–99; Kate Weigand, "The Red Menace, the Feminine Mystique, and the Ohio Un-American Activities Commission: Gender and Anti-Communism in Ohio, 1951–1954," *Journal of Women's History* 3 (winter 1992): 70–94; Amy Swerdlow, *Women Strike for Peace: Traditional Motherhood and Radical Politics in the 1960s* (Chicago, 1993). In their study of the persistence of a women's movement into the 1950s, Leila J. Rupp and Verta Taylor, in *Survival in the Doldrums: The American Women's Rights Movement, 1945 to the 1960s* (New York, 1987), state that in 1955 Friedan was "on the verge of discovering women's inequality in American society for herself" (7).

135. Beginning in the 1940s, Bella Abzug provided legal counsel to workers and African Americans. Milton Meltzer, who knew Friedan when they were both labor journalists, emerged in the 1960s as an author of books on women, African Americans, workers, and dissenters that post-1963 feminists read to their children.

136. On Flexner's work in the labor movement, see DuBois, "Flexner," 84.

33

Between Culture and Politics: The Emma Lazarus Federation of Jewish Women's Clubs and the Promulgation of Women's History, 1944–1989

Joyce Antler

On 22 November 1909 more than two thousand New York women's garment workers, many of them already out on strike, crowded into Cooper Union to vote on an industry-wide action. In the ensuing hours of debate, speakers repeatedly urged caution in deciding whether to take the dramatic step of calling a general strike. Although the audience was more than half female, the only woman speaker was Mary Dreier, president of the New York Women's Trade Union League.

Then a worker called from the floor to be heard; despite complaints, she was permitted to speak. The woman was Clara Lemlich, a twenty-three-year-old who looked so slight that she was described in the next day's press as a teenage "girl." Yet Lemlich, a worker from the Leiserson shop, had been arrested seventeen times and was then recovering from a beating she had received two days earlier. In Yiddish, Lemlich proclaimed: "I am a working girl, one of those who are on strike against intolerable conditions. I am tired of listening to speakers who talk in general terms. What we are here for is to decide whether we shall or shall not strike. I offer a resolution that a general strike be declared—now."[1] As the delegates roared their approval, Benjamin Feigenbaum, the chairman of the meeting, sprang to Lemlich's side and thrust her right arm into the air.[2] "Will you take the old Hebrew oath?" he asked. According to a newspaper account of the strike, "Two and a half thousand right arms shot up. Two and a half thousand voices repeated the Yiddish words: 'May my right [hand] wither from [my] arm if I betray the cause I now pledge.'"[3] By the next evening more than twenty thousand workers had walked out; the strike thereafter became known as the Uprising of the Twenty Thousand. When the strike ended fourteen weeks later, 354 shirtwaist shop owners had signed union agreements. Although not all the workers' demands were met, the agreements generally raised wages, limited weekly work hours, and capped the amount of night work employers could demand. The strike also dispelled the myth that women wage earners could not be organized and, by promoting unionization of the garment industry, helped shape the course of labor organizing in the twentieth century.

For her role in these events, Clara Lemlich has been allotted a place in the annals of labor history and in the history of women workers.[4] What has been ignored, however, is the emblematic quality of her actions in the strike as a female *Jewish* activist, an identity that she would claim all her life and that was particularly represented in the organization she helped to found in the 1940s: the Emma Lazarus Federation of Jewish Women's Clubs (ELF). For forty-five years the ELF stood at the forefront of Jewish women's cultural and political activism, staking out progressive stands on a variety of issues, including the fight against anti-Semitism and racial discrimination, and the promotion of women's rights.

In their unflinching efforts to reconcile the female, radical, and Jewish components of their identity, Clara Lemlich Shavelson and the Emma Lazarus Federation illustrate the multiple, layered, and shifting amalgam of gender and ethnicity revealed on that momentous occasion in 1909 when Lemlich rose at Cooper Union. Lemlich had stood as a woman, a "girl" striker, speaking from the experience, and abuse, of women's work; as a radical labor movement activist, eager to create working-class unity and push the movement forward; and as a Jew, addressing in Yiddish an assembly of Jews who took a Jewish oath to affirm commitment to the radical cause of women. The search to join these three elements would occupy her and many colleagues throughout their lives; together they would create a new kind of American cultural Jewishness, embodied in the Emma Lazarus Federation, which fostered Jewish, feminist, and radical causes.

Although historians have recognized the importance of ethnic ties to the formation of Jewish women's working-class consciousness in the years prior to 1920, they have ignored the continuing cultural and political activities of these women, especially the primary importance to these activities of Jewish content.[5] The paradigm of assimilation has reigned supreme, with scholarly attention focused on the colorful immigrant period and the seeming denial of ethnic consciousness as Jews moved into the mainstream.[6] But the meaning of Clara Shavelson's life, and that of many of her allies, is that she managed to create a bridge that enabled her and others both to maintain their Jewish identity and to use it in a way that built (and built upon) their social and political commitments. In a world in which to be both radical and Jewish meant to be attacked in different ways and to be divided by ideological fissures (that between religion and Communism, for example, or between nationalism and working-class unity), this was no small accomplishment. Even more unusual is the fact that it was built upon a foundation of knowledge in women's history during a period when the subject held little interest even for formally trained academicians. Creating new heroines out of women's experience and promulgating these figures to primarily working-class audiences, the ELF developed an agenda for collective action that linked women's rights and human rights to historical models. In this cultural work the "Emmas" fashioned a Jewish womanhood sensitive not only to issues of class but also to anti-Semitism and racism. Their post-Holocaust political identity sprang, then, both from a newly invigorated gender consciousness and an increasingly salient sense of themselves as Jewish Americans who were proud possessors of a unique cultural heritage.

Examining the federation's multiple interests—including women's history, Jewish culture, civil rights, peace, Israel, the women's movement, and working-class, consumer, and immigrant issues—this essay will suggest that the federation illuminates a model of what I call "linked" identity, combining elements of gender, culture, politics, race, and ethnicity in a flexible, yet unusually engaged, fashion. The federation's simultaneous commitment to creating consciousness and to activism—another example of its "betweenness"—will also be explored.

From Trade Unionism to Jewish Culture: Clara Lemlich Shavelson and the Emergence of the Emma Lazarus Federation of Jewish Women's Clubs

Clara Lemlich Shavelson was born in 1886 in the town of Gorodok in the Ukraine, the daughter of an Orthodox Jewish scholar and grocery-store keeper. The Lemlichs left their home in 1903, fleeing the Kishinev pogrom. After a few months in England, the family arrived in the United States; two weeks later Clara found a job in the garment shops. In 1906 she became one of the founding members of Waistmakers Local 25, affiliated with the fledgling International Ladies' Garment Workers' Union (ILGWU), then largely an organization of male cloak makers. Clara took part in a succession of bitter strikes: in 1907 at Welsen and Goldstein, in 1908 at the Gotham plant, and in 1909 at the Leiserson shop, where she was beaten up while walking the picket line. She was a seasoned strike veteran when the waistmakers gathered at Cooper Union in November 1909.

After the waistmakers' strike, Clara served as a delegate to union conventions, a member of the executive boards of Local 25 and of the Women's Trade Union League, an outspoken socialist, and a tireless organizer of women workers. As a working-class proponent of woman suffrage, she spoke frequently on the importance of the vote and its relationship to the labor movement.

In 1913 Lemlich married Joseph Shavelson, a printer and union activist. The couple had three children, a son and two daughters. Struggling to make ends meet on Joseph's $17-a-week salary, they shared a home with his sister and her family on DeKalb Avenue in Brownsville, Brooklyn, then a Jewish immigrant community with an activist tradition; Clara Shavelson returned to work in a tie shop on the ground floor of her own sister's building when her oldest child was two. She also resumed her organizing activities, becoming a familiar figure on neighborhood street corners. Shavelson's goal was to mobilize housewives around consumer and housing issues that affected the quality of working-class life. In 1917 she participated in a series of citywide riots and a boycott against the high price of kosher meat. In 1919 she helped organize tenants in a rent strike against high housing costs; that same year she became a charter member of the U.S. Communist Party. In 1926 she helped found the United Council of Working-Class Women, a consumer-based group organized to supplement the party's industrial organizing.

In the early 1930s the Shavelsons moved to the working-class community of Brighton Beach, where Clara established the area's first Unemployment Council and organized hunger marches, rent and food strikes, and kitchens for the jobless. She also participated in a neighborhood tenant council named after the Jewish essayist and poet Emma Lazarus. In 1935 the United Council of Working-Class Women became the Progressive Women's Council. Though the council never intended to become exclusively Jewish, most members were Jewish immigrants; like Shavelson, many had been involved in the garment union before marriage. During the Great Depression, the council organized housewives to bring down food and housing costs; a 1935 meat boycott organized by Shavelson and Rose Nelson (Raynes) brought Shavelson to Washington to confront Secretary of Agriculture Henry Wallace and spread to dozens of cities.[7]

In the early 1930s Shavelson ran unsuccessfully for the State Assembly as a member of the Communist Party; she was the only female candidate. It was one of the rare times, her daughter recalled, that her mother purchased a new dress.[8] In 1944, with her husband's health in decline, Shavelson returned to the garment industry as a hand finisher in a cloak shop on Thirty-Eighth Street in New York, joining Local 9. She remained there for almost a decade.

Shavelson was an activist in the fight against fascism as well. In 1934 she attended the first International Women's Congress against War and Fascism in Paris, traveling afterward to the Soviet Union. After her return, she lectured on the Soviet Union to the Progressive Women's Council, which she served as educational director, giving courses on fascism, war, and peace. She became a familiar figure on Brighton Beach street corners, rallying workers against Hitlerism.

At the time of World War II, the Progressive Women's Council, of which Shavelson was then president, merged with the women's clubs of the Jewish People's Fraternal Order (JPFO) of the International Workers Order (IWO), a fraternal benefit insurance company formed after a split in the Workmen's Circle (the Arbeiter Ring) between the "centrist" *Forward* socialists and the left-wing, "progressive" radicals friendly to the Soviet Union; nearly eight thousand of the latter left the Workmen's Circle in 1930 to form the IWO as a "proletarian" fraternal organization.[9] After 1936, aided by the encouragement of the Communist Party, now in its Popular Front phase, the IWO launched a massive recruitment effort among immigrant workers. The party's support of ethnic awareness and pride, coupled with its active campaign against domestic anti-Semitism, made it attractive to Jews; by 1939 they constituted between 40 percent and 50 percent of party membership.[10]

Although not a political or labor organization, the IWO assisted the Congress of Industrial Organization's (CIO) organizing drives and campaigned for unemployment insurance and for aid to Spain. With its health and insurance benefits and its sponsorship of ethnic language schools, summer camps, theater, dance, and other cultural programs, it became the fastest-growing fraternal order in the country. By the end of World War II the IWO counted almost two hundred thousand members in thirteen nationality societies, white and black; the JPFO, with fifty thousand members, was the largest. In addition to its wide variety of benefit programs, many members were attracted by the IWO's multinational, multiracial character and its cutting-edge positions on racial relations and antidiscrimination matters. Even though the majority of rank-and-file members did not belong to the Communist Party (in contrast to major IWO leaders, who did), IWO politics generally mirrored those of the Communist Party.[11]

Clara Shavelson became New York City secretary of the IWO's Women's Division; during the war she organized its knitting circles, first-aid clubs, aluminum-collecting campaigns, and bond rallies. In March 1944 the IWO-JPFO gave birth to an Emma Lazarus Division; that year the IWO published *Emma Lazarus: Selections from Her Poetry and Prose*, edited by Morris U. Schappes, the first collection of Lazarus's work in fifty years.[12] Schappes highlighted Lazarus's dual consciousness as a Jew and an American, a focus that the division adopted. Although earlier women's organizations, including the Brooklyn tenants' group established by Clara Shavelson, had been named after Lazarus, they did not focus on Lazarus's intellectual contributions as an American Jew, as the new division set out to do. Advertising itself as the "home of progressive Jewish women," the division attracted a membership of left-wing, largely Yiddish-speaking women, many of the immigrant generation.[13] Over the next five decades, though she was also an antiwar activist campaigning against the proliferation of nuclear weapons and for improved international relations, Clara Lemlich Shavelson devoted much of her energy to the "Emmas."

In its broad strokes, Shavelson's biography does not differ greatly from those of other women who were instrumental in organizing and leading the Emma Lazarus Division and the ELF. June Croll Gordon, a founder and longtime executive director of the group, was born in Odessa in 1901; she immigrated to the United States at the age of three, and later began working in New York City's needle trades. Gordon became a prominent trade unionist, leading strikes in the textile and millinery unions. By 1935 she was secretary of the Anti-Nazi Federation, helping to arouse public opinion against the Nazis' territorial ambitions. Rose Raynes, who became the ELF's executive director after Gordon's death, came to the United States from Russia when she was ten. Soon employed in garment and millinery shops, Raynes became active in the textile and millinery unions. Like Shavelson, Raynes and Gordon were Communist Party members and officers of the United Council of Working-Class Women and the Progressive Women's Council. All three became targets of McCarthyism. An unsuccessful attempt was made to deport Gordon; Shavelson had her passport revoked. All were called before the House Un-American Activities Committee and harassed by the Federal Bureau of Investigation (FBI).[14]

The Emma Lazarus Division of the JPFO was established by these three women and others with similar backgrounds to combat anti-Semitism and racism, provide relief to wartime victims, and nurture positive Jewish identification through a broad program of Jewish education and women's rights. Founders believed that because of the Holocaust, thousands of women had become "newly aware of themselves as Jewish women," but they urgently needed "history, self-knowledge as Jews, and cultural products" that could sustain the fight against fascism. "Since the attack by Hitler against the Jewish people," Rose Raynes recalled, "we felt that [anti-Semitism] was not only an issue for Europe but for the U.S. as well. We felt that a progressive Jewish woman's organization was the order of the day."[15] Beginning in 1945, the division offered fellowships for works of fiction and history on Jewish themes; it was the first of its many efforts to heighten Jewish identity as a weapon against bigotry. It also supported a home for French war orphans and a day nursery in Israel and championed a broad range of women's issues: full employment for men and women; equal pay for equal work; maternity, unemployment, old age, health, and housing benefits; day nurseries and after-school care; and the inclusion of greater numbers of women in government.

From Division to Federation: Promoting Jewish Women's History

In 1951 the division became the Emma Lazarus Federation of Jewish Women's Clubs, an independent organization. Although links to the progressive left remained, the shift from division to federation marked an important transformation in the group's focus. The change in status was influenced by attacks against the Communist Party and the IWO. In 1951 the New York State attorney general initiated proceedings against the IWO as a subversive institution formed and directed under Communist Party auspices. Although the IWO denied that it used members' funds to support the Communist Party, New York State, aided by J. Edgar Hoover and the FBI, successfully prosecuted the order and forced it to liquidate in 1954. A much-reduced JPFO, without the financial advantages of a fraternal benefit society, reorganized as the Jewish Cultural Clubs and Societies, retaining several thousand members interested in cultural programs in Yiddish and English.[16] While Communist Party leaders played a part in reorganizing IWO constituencies, the Emma Lazarus Division had been moving toward a more independent, woman–centered stance in the 1940s in any case; cold war necessities further advanced its autonomy.

During the politically charged fifties, the ELF did not relinquish its radical commitments, although some leaders broke with the Communist Party. As an organization, the ELF vigorously protested against McCarthyism. The trial of Julius and Ethel Rosenberg, which frequently focused on their left-wing Jewish associations, especially alarmed federation leaders, who believed in the Rosenbergs' innocence.[17] Although she never met Ethel Rosenberg, Clara Lemlich Shavelson spent two years working on her defense committee, recognizing in the accused woman's labor activism and ethnic associations a replica of her own background. As individuals and in some cases, as chapters, many ELF members rallied to the Rosenbergs' (especially Ethel's) support. After their deaths, the Rosenbergs' sons were adopted by Ann Meeropol, who was herself a member of the ELF, and her husband.[18]

Throughout the 1950s the federation emphasized the progressive voice of labor as the hallmark of democracy and called for coexistence with the Soviet Union. While Nikita Khrushchev's startling 1956 revelations about Stalinist terrors and later information about the country's virulent anti-Semitism left ELF members "shocked" and "grieved," publicly its leaders continued to hope that the USSR would return to its earlier encouragement of ethnic minorities. On at least one occasion, a branch delegate protested that the executive board did not condemn anti-Semitism within the Soviet Union as vigorously as it opposed domestic bigotry; the group remained split for many years between those who wanted to break all ties with the USSR and those who continued to support Communism.[19]

Yet the division's unity around cultural work outweighed political differences. By the time the group called its first constitutional convention in 1951 to inaugurate the federation, the Emmas had decided that in the wake of Nazism's terrors, nothing was more important than integrating Jewish heritage into contemporary life. The terrors of McCarthyism, which stigmatized many Jewish radicals as "un-American" Communists, also contributed to the Emmas' desire to claim their own Jewish identity by promoting a progressive, secular Jewish heritage. "Our purpose was to add to the fabric of American culture and democracy by advancing all that is most humane and forward looking in Jewish culture," remarked ELF president Leah Nelson at its third convention in 1959.[20] If Jews were to survive as a people and contribute to the solution of world problems in morally responsible ways, they could not be isolated from the social mainstream.

The federation's emphasis on creating a "culturally enlightened American Jewry" co-incided with the increasing acceptance of cultural pluralism in postwar life. Even as Jews moved ever more forcefully into the American mainstream, many seemed eager not to obliterate their heritage but to identify with it. A so-called Jewish revival, indicated by the construction of synagogues and Jewish social centers, the enrollment of a new generation of youth in Jewish educational programs, and the proclamations of Jewish book, music, and history months revealed the desire of many Jews to connect to Jewish roots as well as the increasing acceptability of such expressions of "Americanized" ethnicity.[21]

Yet the ELF believed that this Jewish revival lacked depth and vision. Arguing that knowledge of Jewish tradition should extend beyond holidays and artifacts to an under-standing of vital Jewish contributions to American history and democracy, the federation sought to promulgate the neglected history of American Jewish women—their contribu-tions to American arts and letters, to abolition and the trade union movements, and to immigration policy—in order to create a framework for positive identification with Jewish culture and for understanding and acting on present problems. This did not mean assimi-lation, the Emmas believed, but its opposite: a reaffirmation of the long history of Jewish participation in American democracy *as Jews* and a recommitment to Jews' moral values and humanistic culture. Both the focus on women and the linkage of women's history to activism distinguished this goal from that of the Jewish Cultural Clubs and Societies, the reorganized JPFO group, whose emphasis lay in encouraging Yiddish culture (*yiddishkeit*) while also supporting progressive Jewish culture in English (for example, by aid to *Jewish Currents* magazine).[22]

In promulgating a secular progressive Judaism without relying on the special qualities of *yiddishkeit*, the Emmas resolved a paradox that had long troubled the immigrant Jewish left. Jewish fraternal organizations had offered cultural programs, sports leagues, and medi-cal services to members in an attempt to serve the interests of an increasingly assimilated Jewish immigrant population and their descendants; Yiddish newspapers began inserting English pages for similar reasons. But the Emmas were unusual in emphasizing a Jewish intellectual tradition that was both militantly secular and progressively American as the best appeal to the post-Yiddish-speaking generation.

In the early 1950s the ELF commissioned biographies of two Jewish women whose achievements they believed symbolized different, though compatible, directions in pro-gressive American Jewish history. The first subject, writer Emma Lazarus (1849–1887), the group's major inspiration, had concentrated on Jewish themes within a broad universalistic setting. The other, Ernestine Rose (1810–1892), social reformer, abolitionist, and suffragist, had focused her energies on many important problems of the day, not especially Jewish ones. Although they had been radicals in their own time, both women's protests were clearly within the American democratic tradition; thus the Emmas selected models who helped ensure their own legitimacy as political and cultural dissenters.

Lazarus was, of course, the writer whose poem "The New Colossus," engraved on a plaque on the Statue of Liberty in May 1903, has helped welcome generations of immigrants to the United States. In the 1950s, however (and, it can be argued, even today), neither Lazarus's Jewish or woman's consciousness had been widely recognized. The standard belief was that Lazarus had become concerned with her Jewishness belatedly, only after the Russian pogroms of the 1880s; her contributions to the cause of women were even less commonly understood.

ELF members believed that Lazarus was an inspiration for both Jewish culture and women's rights. Though not associated with the women's rights movement, Lazarus had helped remove the "veils and screens" of women's lives, with which the "woman-souled poet," as she called herself, had to grope. In the biography of Lazarus that the federation commissioned Eve Merriam to write (to celebrate the anniversary of the Jews' tercentennial in America in 1954), the author comments that "the figure representing work is a woman to Emma Lazarus, not the conventional symbol of a man."[23]

The federation also portrayed Lazarus as a woman who had spoken out forcefully and consistently against anti-Semitism and assimilation, and as a Jew who was concerned not only with what she called a narrow, "tribal" Judaism but also with oppressed peoples the world over. "Until we are all free, we are none of us free" was the Lazarus line most often quoted by the ELF to demonstrate the poet's concern for all humanity.[24]

Lazarus had originally used the line to refer to solidarity with the Jewish people. "When the life and property of a Jew in the uttermost provinces of the Caucasus are attacked," she wrote, "the dignity of a Jew in free America is humiliated. . . . Until we are all free, we are none of us free." Her universalism appeared in a line that stated that Jews should not "become too 'tribal' and narrow and Judaic rather than humane and cosmopolitan." Instead they must concern themselves with the misfortunes of "our unhappy brethren."[25] To the ELF, this "universal scope" coupled with Lazarus's support for Jewish culture and women's freedom made her an admirable symbol of secular, humanistic values.

Ironically, the federation ignored one element in Lazarus's background that, as a left–wing organization, it might have been expected to highlight: her Jewish-based socialism. Lazarus argued, for example, that the root of the "modern theory of socialism" lay in the "Mosaic Code," which established the "principle of the rights of labor" and denied the "right of private property in land. . . . [W]e find the fathers of modern socialism to be three Jews—Ferdinand Lassalle, Karl Marx, and Johann Jacoby."[26] The federation also ignored another major Lazarus theme—her support for a Jewish homeland in Palestine. While the ELF endorsed both formulations, it found Lazarus's leadership in the campaign to promote Jewish culture, aid new immigrants, and fight anti-Semitism both more compelling and more characteristic.

For almost fifty years federation members never tired of presenting Lazarus's ideas to any group that would listen. Every year the Emmas celebrated her birthday with a trip to Liberty Island; they succeeded in having the mayors of New York and Miami declare an Emma Lazarus Day, and later they arranged a commemorative stamp. The true meaning of Lazarus for the federation, however, lay less in these occasions than in the model of action, authority, and leadership that she claimed as a woman, a Jew, and an American. Basing their program on her work, the Emmas hoped to give "leadership to women in Jewish communities in our own time in the same spirit as Emma Lazarus did in hers."[27]

In 1954 the ELF published a biography of Ernestine Rose that it had commissioned Yuri Suhl to write. To the Emmas, Rose represented a model of activism even more than Lazarus, who spoke with her pen. They cited the fact that Susan B. Anthony had named Rose, along with Mary Wollstonecraft and Frances Wright, as the most important early leader of the women's movement, praising her activism on behalf of women's property rights and suffrage.

Unlike Lazarus's, Rose's work did not have a Jewish orientation, yet the federation claimed her as the first Jewish woman reformer in the United States. Born in the ghetto of Piotrkow, in Russian Poland, Rose, the daughter of a rabbi, refused to accept the traditional destiny of young Jewish women. While still a teenager, she took her father to court, protesting his determination to marry her against her will and suing to obtain possession of the dowry her mother had left her. Rose won the lawsuit but returned most of the property to her father. Then, at age seventeen, she left the country, eventually settling in the United States.

Although Rose abandoned the formal practice of religion, she took a "fighting stand" against anti-Semitism, publicly disavowing its presence in her own circle of freethinkers. According to the Emmas, her work on behalf of abolition and women's rights and against anti-Semitism demonstrated the "interrelationships between Jew and non-Jew, Negro and white, men and women." Like Lazarus, she was seen to combine Jewish patriotism with a broader humanism. "Emancipation from every kind of bondage is my principle," they recalled her words. "I go for the recognition of human rights, without distinction of sect, party, sex or color." As she wrote to President Abraham Lincoln during the Civil War, "So long as one slave breathes in this Republic, we drag the chain with him."[28]

The Emmas considered Rose a model for her work in the peace movement; an activist for the Universal Peace Society, founded in Rhode Island, she was a delegate to several international peace congresses. To Rose, women had a special stake in peace crusades: "War is a terrible enemy of man," she observed, "a terrible school. . . . I trust that if every woman touched the sword it would be to sheath it in its scabbard forever."[29] The ELF often quoted these words to legitimate its own work for peace.

Though none received the attention given to Lazarus and Rose, the federation remembered other American Jewish women in its cultural work, spreading biographical reminiscences of Rebecca Gratz, Lillian Wald, Sophie Loeb, Penina Moise, and others. In the early 1950s it commissioned a history of Jewish women in the United States to be published in Yiddish and English but canceled the volume when the draft failed to meet its standards. The ELF debated publishing such a work into the late 1970s.

The federation documented the experience of Jewish women outside the United States as well. In commemorating the tenth anniversary of the uprising of the Warsaw ghetto, it paid tribute to those who had taken part in the antifascist resistance and who had fought for freedom in partisan groups, women such as Niuta Teitelboim, Dora Goldkorn, Zofia Yamalka, Rosa Robota, Mala Zimmetbaum, Regina Fuden, Zivia Lubetkin, Hana Senish, Vitka Kempner, and Frumke and Hentche Platnitksy. To federation members, the courageous stand of the "mothers" of the Warsaw ghetto merged with the traditions of women trailblazers in the United States—"Ernestine Rose, Sojourner Truth, Susan B. Anthony, Emma Lazarus, and the women from the shops and mills like Esther Greenleaf, a shoe worker, and the later immigrants like those of the Triangle Shirt and Waist shop who fought against sweatshop conditions."[30] Moreover, the ELF cited women's heroism in the fight for Israeli independence.

The federation also issued study outlines on themes in general Jewish and Yiddish history and culture, writing on such subjects as bigotry in school textbooks, the Jewish contribution to American law and letters, and Yiddish prose and poetry. In praising the work of Sholom Aleichem and I. L. Peretz, the Emmas singled out these writers' forward-looking, empathic treatment of women in the shtetls of Eastern Europe.

Toward an Inclusive Women's History: Dissidents, Working Women, White Women Reformers, and Black Women

Interested in the broader history of American women, the federation developed curricula on such subjects as the contributions of dissident women from Anne Hutchinson to Ethel Rosenberg and the role of America's working women in the Lowell mills and garment sweatshops. In 1954 it commissioned artist Philip Reisman to do a mural of the 1909 mass meeting at Cooper Union, depicting Clara Lemlich at the center; the five-foot-by-seven-foot painting was donated to the International Ladies' Garment Workers' Union in 1982.

The link between the women's rights and abolitionist movements was of vital interest. In the 1950s and 1960s the ELF prepared study guides on Sojourner Truth, Ida B. Wells, and Harriet Tubman and paid tribute to the leadership of Sarah Douglass, Mary Bibb, Grace Mapps, and France Ellen Harper. The federation also called attention to the contemporary achievements of Rosa Parks, Autherine Lucy, and other black women involved in the civil rights struggle.

Its most important contribution in this area was the pamphlet "Women in the Life and Time of Abraham Lincoln," a reprint of the proceedings of a conference held by the National Women's Loyal League. Formed at a mass rally called on 14 May 1863 by women's rights leaders (including Ernestine Rose) at Cooper Union in New York City, the league assembled over a thousand northern white women abolitionists who pledged to rally women in their states to obtain a million signatures on a petition to endorse the proposed Thirteenth Amendment. Though the league disbanded after the enabling legislation passed, the Emmas believed that it had activated white women and advanced the women's rights movement. They hoped that its work for abolition would challenge contemporary white women (particularly Jewish women) to work for civil rights.

The ELF pamphlet about the Loyal League contained an introduction by Daisy Bates, leader of the desegregation struggle at Little Rock High School. Bates was also the principal speaker at a celebration held at Cooper Union by the federation's New York club in December 1963 to commemorate the hundredth anniversary of the league's founding. Thirteen hundred people joined the Emmas on that occasion to celebrate the unity of white and black women in the common struggle for civil rights.

"Thinking . . . Expressed in Action": The Federation's Campaigns for Human Rights

For federation members, there was nothing pedantic or merely academic in its cultural work. The ELF believed that women's and Jewish history could inspire contemporary thought and policy by providing models of commitment and activism. "Thinking is expressed in action; culture is . . . promoted by projects," remarked Leah Nelson at the ELF's 1959 convention. Executive Director June Gordon used to say that the federation served the Jewish community as a true "university for women"; later she preferred to point to the ELF as a *"Veker"* and a *"Wegweiser"*—a pathfinder and awakener—involving members of other Jewish women's groups, as well as the community at large, in vital actions.[31]

The federation's practical work covered a wide spectrum. Its five-point program, adopted in 1951, established lasting goals. In addition to the promotion of Jewish culture (the "number one project"), these included the elimination of anti-Semitism and racism, the campaign for women's rights, support for the state of Israel, and world peace and consumers' issues.[32]

With the legacy of Emma Lazarus, Ernestine Rose, and the National Woman's Loyal League pointing the way, the federation dedicated much of its efforts over four decades to work on behalf of civil rights. The "Negro question is ours," as one club member put it in 1955.[33] The Emmas acknowledged that while anti-Semitism and racism sprang from common roots and that American Jews and minorities shared the same dangerous enemy—the ultra-Right—oppression in the black community was not only significantly greater than that of American Jews but also could be fueled by Jews' own racism. Consciousness of the impact of racial difference on women's roles and opportunities led the federation to focus on the needs of black women and racial minorities long before the white women's movement turned to these issues in the 1970s.

Its most important leaders, including Clara Shavelson, June Gordon, and Rose Raynes, had been members of the Communist Party at a time when interest in black culture and the promotion of civil rights was actively encouraged; June Gordon herself had married an African American artist, Eugene Gordon. For these reasons, and because of their guiding belief that discrimination in the form of anti-Semitism and that based on racism were deeply linked, the Emmas took on the challenge of promoting racial justice by engaging Jewish women in a joint campaign with blacks. "America's white women have been in semi-hibernation ever since the abolitionist movement," an Emma wrote in the first edition of the group's bulletin, *The Lamp*, in 1952.[34] Through concrete actions, it was time to wake them.

Shortly after its founding, the federation joined in a common statement of principle with the Sojourners for Truth and Justice, a black women's civil rights group. The Emmas made a regular financial contribution to the Sojourners, and the groups met at an annual luncheon.[35] The Los Angeles Emma Lazarus club established a similar relationship with the Southern Region of the California State Association of Colored Women's Clubs, jointly sponsoring an interracial Mother's Day event and other programs; in Miami, Emmas joined with black women in an interracial Mother's Association that worked on civil rights projects. In 1953 several Emmas traveled to Georgia as part of a delegation of black and white women to plead with the governor against the imprisonment of a black woman for the murder of a white man who had attacked her. (Two decades later they would defend black professor Angela Davis against what they considered unjust imprisonment.) By 1956 the Emmas were sending truckloads of food and clothing to Mississippi and joining boycotts and sit-ins. By the 1960s they were working with civil rights groups throughout the country, supporting the Freedom Rides and Freedom Summer, participating in civil rights marches in Washington, D.C., and organizing local demonstrations, rallies, and picket lines.

The Emmas fought segregation in housing and schools in their own communities, lobbying legislators, presenting petitions, and holding forums. They observed Negro History Week with readings, lectures, and joint programs with black organizations, often highlighting the contributions of black and Jewish women to the building of the country.[36] At annual Mother's Day celebrations, they typically honored a black woman active in civil rights. Black women's associations in some regions honored the Emma Lazarus clubs at their own meetings and made contributions to the Emma Lazarus nursery in Israel.

The Emmas believed, however, that more was needed than occasional meetings with African American groups and ceremonial events; they called for "constant contact" and intensive, rather than token, support of black rights. To this end they established ongoing affiliations not only with the Sojourners but also with the National Association for the Advancement of Colored People (NAACP), the National Association of Colored Women, and other groups, and they urged immediate and varied measures to end discrimination and increase opportunities in all arenas. But they warned against a "humanitarian" approach—whites "helping" blacks—rather than a "joint struggle." Jewish women's special task, modeled by the National Woman's Loyal League, was to engage white women and Jews in the civil rights movement.[37]

The federation urged its own members to support equality for blacks by eliminating white supremacist attitudes they might unwittingly hold. In a 1951 position paper on "Racism, Enemy of the Jewish People," the ELF established two principles: first, that blacks suffered greater oppression in the United States than any other people, including Jews, whatever their experience with anti-Semitism; and second, that the main fight against discrimination was the responsibility of whites. While Jews were especially affected by discrimination, since anti-Semitism and racism derived from common white-supremacist roots, the ELF argued that "every Jewish worker who wants to fight for peace and against fascism is hurting that struggle when he doesn't root out . . . every bit of racism in himself."[38]

The Emmas gave examples of how "Jewish nationalism and chauvinism" could feed the idea that Jews were superior to non-Jews—for example, the use of the terms *goyim* and *shikseh*. Such superior attitudes applied with double intensity to blacks: Jews who knew the derogatory meaning of anti-Semitic terms were cautioned against the use of *schvartse* and other stereotypical expressions about blacks. The Emmas voiced special concern for Negro women, who suffered "triple oppression, as women, as women workers, and as Negroes"—discriminated against in industry, they were forced to take menial jobs as houseworkers only to suffer from exploitation by white housewives.

The Emmas considered the campaign to secure passage of the United Nations (UN) Genocide Convention their most important political crusade. In 1963 the ELF initiated a petition campaign for the United States to ratify the Genocide Convention, which had been adopted by the UN General Assembly in 1948 and subsequently signed by seventy-five nations. ELF presented the first four thousand signatures on the petitions to UN Ambassador Adlai Stevenson in December 1963. Two years later, when the twentieth session of the General Assembly signed a new treaty to eliminate all forms of racism, the ELF issued a new petition calling upon the United States to ratify both treaties. In 1966 the federation delivered seven thousand signatures to Ambassador Arthur Goldberg; in 1969 it sent a delegation (including three black women) to present sixty thousand signatures to Senator William Fulbright of the Senate Foreign Relations Committee. The Senate finally ratified the Genocide Convention on 19 February 1986.[39]

The Emmas never abandoned their faith in the potential of culture, and especially history itself, as an agent of change in the battle for human rights. In 1964 a member of the Emma Lazarus Boston club told the ELF national convention of an incident that confirmed this belief:

> At a panel discussion on the relationship of the Jew to the Negro in Roxbury, where there is considerable racial strife, the Jew did not fare so well. One Negro speaker bluntly said that he considered the Jews and the landlord and storekeeper as one who exploits him. The Jew on the panel, a representative of one of our big organizations, didn't elevate the level of the discussion. He started out, "No matter what," facing the Negro, "you still should be grateful that you live in America. You are still better off than if you lived in Russia."
>
> In the general discussion that followed Elizabeth Stern [president of the Boston Emma Lazarus club] took the floor and directed the attention of the audience to our Panel on the wall of that room and said in effect: "Let me show you a different relationship between

Negro and Jew during our Civil War period," and she pointed to Ernestine Rose, Sojourner Truth and all the other characters depicted on the panel. One by one the audience came up to look at the Panel. It was closely scrutinized, discussed, admired by all. Our organization was commended for bringing to light this historical data and for the fashion in which it was presented, and the whole tone of the meeting was changed.[40]

Nor did the federation abandon its conviction that by working for social equality for blacks, its members were expressing their identity as good Jews and good Americans, as Emma Lazarus herself had proclaimed when she highlighted the harmony between America's multiple nationalities and its civic culture. For the Emmas, the civil rights crusade in which they played an early, vigorous, and continuous role was a perfect example of democratic pluralism at its best. Here, for example, is June Gordon's account of the Emmas demonstrating with thousands of black and white women during the historic March on Washington on 22 August 1963:

> At one point in the line of March, as we approached a spot where Lincoln Rockwell's brown-shirted bullies were on the lookout for an opportunity to jeer and make trouble, two young Episcopalian Ministers sprinted up in front of us and declared: "Ladies, pictures are being taken. We want our Bishop to see us leading the Emma Lazarus Contingent." At the same time a fellow Negro marcher chose to walk with us. He moved up front and said to one of our banner bearers: "You must be tired, let me carry it for a while." And so our contingent was headed by Episcopalians; one end of the banner—*on the side where the Nazi hoodlums were lined up*—was carried by a Negro marcher. Looking for Leah Nelson [the ELF president] to call her attention to the gloriously symbolic sight of unity we represented, we spotted her marching behind a banner of a *Catholic* organization. This truly was America.[41]

Because the Emmas believed that anti-Semitism and racism were inherently linked, they recognized that in working for civil rights, they were "not doing something for the black people, but . . . doing something for ourselves."[42] When in the late 1960s relations between blacks and Jews grew strained, the ELF affirmed the historic relationship between the two groups and insisted that differences on specific issues, which they felt had been inflamed by extremists on both sides, not be allowed to tamper with the groups' common interests. In contrast to many Jewish organizations, the Emmas supported affirmative action, community control of schools, and decentralization. Yet occasionally, when they found evidences of black anti-Semitism, they spoke out in protest: In 1967, for example, they called upon the Student Nonviolent Coordinating Committee (SNCC) to revise its "shocking and disturbing" position on Jewish organizations.[43]

From its inception, the federation was vigilant about anti-Semitism. It tracked, and opposed, the resurgence of Nazism through letters, telegrams, resolutions, pickets, and mass meetings; targets for its attacks included neo-Nazi movements in Germany, England, France, Italy, Argentina, and dozens of cities in the United States. The federation also protested the ominous spread of anti-Semitism among the general population; too often, it noted, Jews were discriminated against at public resorts, at schools and colleges, and in the workplace. Quoting Emma Lazarus's protest against anti-Semitism that the word *Jew* was used constantly "even among so-called refined Christians" as a term of opprobrium and was increasingly employed as a verb "to denote the meanest tricks," the Emmas called for actions to protest pernicious stereotyping as well as discriminatory quota systems.[44] But they persistently argued that groups most guilty of anti-Semitic bigotry—at various times, the Ku Klux Klan, the American Nazi Party, the Liberty Lobby, or the Moral Majority—also posed the greatest danger to the rights of racial minorities.[45]

The blind spot in the federation's campaign against anti-Semitism remained the Soviet Union. The absence of a committed campaign against Soviet anti-Semitism was a consequence of the continuing political attachment of a significant number of federation members to the Communist Party; others within the leadership had broken with the party, or had become critical of its actions, because of revelations about Stalinist terror and Soviet anti-Semitism. The last president of the ELF, Rose Raynes, for example, was anti-Stalinist, whereas her second in command, Gertrude Decker, remained loyal to the USSR. This split prevented the executive board from taking a vigorous stand against Soviet brutality and harassment of Jews.[46]

The federation was involved in other issues outlined in its five-point program. From its inception, the ELF supported the cause of peace. At the Emmas' first annual Mother's Day luncheon in 1951, members read poems of peace, commemorating the struggles of women, written by Gerda Lerner. ELF leaders made clear to members that the role of the federation, as a cultural group, was to support existing peace organizations rather than create its own initiatives. ELF clubs cooperated with the Committee for a Sane Nuclear Policy (SANE), the Women's International League for Peace and Freedom (WILPF), and the Committee for World Development and World Disarmament. Within these groups the Emmas endeavored to help make policy as well as support petition drives and fund collections. As in the civil rights arena, they sought to become liaisons to Jewish women's organizations so as to bring these groups into the peace movement.[47]

While ELF shared a common agenda with SANE and other peace organizations, it criticized the minimal involvement of workers and their families in these groups. Here, too, the Emmas claimed a special role: "With our participating in the communities, we reach women from wage-earning families. Through work in the shops and raising this greatly important question in the union, where many of our sisters and their husbands belong, we can help strengthen and expand the peace organizations."[48] From their early interest in the elimination of nuclear weapons to their activities to end the Vietnam War, the Emmas remained involved in questions of war and peace, militarism, and foreign policy.[49]

As a Jewish women's organization, the federation was greatly concerned with the fate of Israel. The ELF was the first Jewish group to establish a day-care center in the new state (for the Jewish and Arab children of working mothers). The Emma Lazarus Nursery in Jaffa, later moved to Tel Aviv, was administered by the women's division of the Agudath Tarbuth L'Am (the Association for People's Culture), which worked mainly with families of immigrants and workers. The federation was the sole support of the nursery, which it considered its "pet project," until 1988, when the facility was forced to close because of the lack of funds. Many members journeyed to Israel specifically to visit the nursery; others knit sweaters for its children. The ELF also raised considerable sums of money for Israel at the time of the 1967 and Yom Kippur wars, and it regularly supported the Red Mogon Dovid.

In addition to holding forums and publishing study guides on Israel, the ELF attempted to focus the attention of peace groups on the need for a constructive stand on U.S. foreign policy in regard to Israel and peace in the Middle East. The federation distinguished its identification with Israel, however, from that of many other Jewish organizations. Its own positions were based on "kinship with the Israeli people and not on Israel as the core of Jewish life," as it understood was the case with other groups; the most vital service the ELF thought it could render to Israel was to heighten cultural identification among American Jews.

Concern for Israel, in any event, reflected the Emmas' class analysis of the Middle Eastern politics of oil, which it believed threatened the security of Israel and its Arab neighbors.

The Emmas questioned whether the success of Arab national liberation movements might not benefit Israel in the long run and worried about the second-class treatment of Arabs within Israel. After the Six-Day War, the federation questioned whether Israel needed all the territory it had won, but demanded that Arab neighbors accept Israel's right to exist without qualification.[50]

In November 1975 the federation adopted a resolution condemning the UN resolution equating "Zionism with racism" as "vicious anti-Semitism . . . directed against all Jews." But controversy erupted when ELF vice president Gertrude Decker declared in a public speech that she was "for the existence of Israel as a progressive State, not a Zionist state in the service of imperialism," and could not support the Israeli government's "discriminatory and *racist* policies." Board members condemned her remarks, and members of one local chapter circulated a petition opposing them.[51]

Promoting the rights and culture of immigrants and supporting consumer interests were also of deep concern. In the 1950s the federation engaged in a vigorous campaign for a statute of limitation against the deportation of foreign-born Americans; it was the only Jewish group to become a founder of the Museum of Immigration on Liberty Island. The ELF spoke out consistently against the high cost of living and for senior citizens' rights and entitlements; many local groups gave substantial support to the farm workers' union.

Women's issues, finally, were always central to federation interests. The ELF worked continuously to bring women's history to a wide public so that the lessons of the past might help shape the present. In the mid-1950s it inaugurated a celebration for the thirty-fifth anniversary of woman suffrage, focusing on women's history. (Twenty years later Congresswoman Bella Abzug addressed another large ELF-sponsored meeting honoring the achievement of suffrage.) After the advent of the new feminist movement in the 1960s, ELF members worked with women's rights organizations on myriad issues (including the Equal Rights Amendment); its International Women's Day celebration was an annual highlight.

The federation identified a host of economic and social problems that affected the lives of women, particularly working women. Far in advance of the times, its 1955 discussion guide, for example, focused on the lack of equal pay for equal work, "double" wage discrimination faced by black women, occupational segregation, unequal job security and promotional opportunities, lack of representation in trade unions and management, and problems of working mothers (day nurseries and after-school care). Issues of educational access and the representation of women in politics, government, and the professions were also highlighted. Here, too, the ELF believed that it could play an important role by representing the needs of working women and implementing programs developed by union members. In addition, the federation hoped to bring a greater consciousness of black women's work, educational, and political situations to women's groups and other organizations to which it was affiliated. It supported these varied goals not only by raising its own members' consciousness through the production of study guides, dramatic presentatations, lectures, exhibits, and other cultural programs but also through a continuing series of demonstrations, marches, picket lines, petition campaigns, celebrations and convocations, and other actions.

"Jewish Culture Does not Limit One": The Elf and Problems of Outreach

Spanning the country, with chapters in New York (Brooklyn, the Bronx, Rochester), New Jersey (Newark, Jersey City, Lakewood, Toms River), California (Los Angeles, San Francisco), and Boston, Chicago, Philadelphia, Detroit, and Miami, the Emma Lazarus

Federation maintained its educational and political activities for close to forty years. Yet almost from the outset, questions of expanding its outreach had been raised. At their peak, some of the largest chapters in New York, Chicago, and Los Angeles had more than a dozen branches, with several hundred members each; other groups were much smaller. Though the organization kept no membership records, the best estimate is that the federation attracted approximately four to five thousand members in one hundred clubs during the 1950s; membership remained fairly stable in the 1960s but fell in later years.

Though no match for Hadassah, with its hundreds of thousands of middle-class members, the ELF boasted an unusually active, committed membership. Like Clara Lemlich Shavelson, June Croll Gordon, and Rose Raynes, most of the original federation members were working-class women who had been associated with the IWO or other progressive, labor-oriented groups. Many had worked in industry and had participated in the trade-union movement; others had been radicalized as housewives and consumers. Most long-time members were Yiddish-speaking. Even when the balance began to shift, with increasing numbers of members speaking only English, leaders advocated the bilingual approach: "The sisters [should] use the language which lends itself with greater ease to [their] verbal or written expression. Never, under any circumstances, should one be preferred over the other."[52] *The Lamp*, the monthly newsletter of the federation, appeared in both languages; meetings were usually conducted in English.

Leaders wondered, however, whether the ELF's relatively narrow membership base was sufficient to support the broad scope of its five-point program. Over the years they urged chapters to reach out to a wider circle of Jewish women. "We must be among women and unite on issues of concern to all women," the Newark club president declared.[53] From the beginning, the federation program appealed to a broader constituency than was reflected in its membership: Regular presentations to Hadassah, B'nai B'rith, synagogue sisterhoods, and similar groups enlarged the ELF's audiences by many thousands. The Brooklyn and Los Angeles chapters were proud of their relationships with Jewish women's assemblies; several clubs enrolled non-Jewish, nonwhite members as well.

Although some ELF members did not want to lose their identity by doing "leg work for other organizations" or adjust their message to suit organizational partners, they realized that because new members were needed to keep the federation growing, so were new methods. "Know parliamentary procedures," advised the Philadelphia delegate to the 1955 ELF convention: "Learn to compromise our old methods without compromising our principles. Find new language—i.e., 'forward-looking people' instead of the word 'progressive.' Use language that is acceptable to others . . . so they will come to listen to us. . . . Emphasize the issues that unite and bring with warmth and friendship our message to others."[54]

While some in the Jewish community dismissed the Emmas as "embittered women" with "heavy Yiddish accents," a number of prominent leaders were pleased to be associated publicly with them.[55] In 1947, when the Emma Lazarus Division was an IWO affiliate, Louise Waterman Wise, president of the Women's Division of the American Jewish Congress and wife of eminent Reform rabbi Stephen S. Wise, took the podium to introduce a public session ("An Evening of Jewish Culture") at the division's First Constitutional Convention, held at Hunter College.[56] Illinois state legislator Esther Saperstein, impressed with the ELF-sponsored biography of Ernestine Rose by Yuri Suhl, joined the Chicago chapter in the 1950s and memorialized Rose's name in the legislature. New York congresswomen Bella Abzug and Elizabeth Holtzman also honored Rose and Lazarus and participated in federation events.[57]

The question of whether the ideas of the federation were too progressive to attract the support of more mainstream Jewish women—or whether subtle changes in language and procedure might win new members—frequently surfaced. At the 1964 ELF convention June Gordon denied that the Emmas could not comfortably speak to a broad audience. "Many, all too many members think we are so far in advance of all other Jewish women in our progressive outlook that it is useless to approach them as prospective members and cultivate their interest in joining the club. This attitude is a disservice."[58] Though some members felt that other women's groups were too "reactionary," Gordon insisted that the federation offered a place for women of varied opinions.

Although new members joined Emma Lazarus clubs primarily for their educational programs, opportunities for sociability and friendship were important. "Even more precious than learning," recalled one Chicago member, was "a warm sisterly relation in the club, sisters we can share our joys and sorrows with—in short you feel a part of a great big noisy family." But most important was the connection to Jewish heritage this member (and many others) made as an Emma. She recalled her initiation to the Emmas at her first club meeting, where she had listened to a program about Chanukah and Emma Lazarus:

> I suddenly became aware that I was part of the struggles and triumphs of the Jewish people. How was it that I could not see it before? Perhaps because I wanted to forget I was a Jew, and thereby avoid facing the grim facts of my people not being accepted as equals even in our country. . . . I have always been interested in culture generally, and I thought at the time that pursuing Jewish culture only is too narrow and limited. . . . My interest was aroused, and I joined the club at the following meeting. Since then, having participated in cultural as well as other projects, it became clear to me that Jewish culture does not limit one, but on the contrary, broadens one's horizon. I became conscious of a feeling of pride in my origin, particularly after reading the works of Emma Lazarus.[59]

Attracting young women who had been uprooted from their Jewish heritage was a continuing source of pride for the ELF.

While certain sections were able to attract new members, including young mothers, the graying of the membership became a major problem. Even though attendance at meetings was high, the ability of aging members to take on demanding campaigns diminished. Still, many ELF women remained vigorous well into their seventies and eighties. Here, too, Clara Shavelson led the way: As she aged along with the federation, Shavelson regularly attended its meetings and participated in its activities. In her seventies, she collected fifteen hundred signatures for the federation's Genocide Convention campaign; the ELF gratefully acknowledged her contributions. Shavelson admitted that although she had been proud of the youthful Clara Lemlich, she thought that Clara Shavelson, a lifetime activist, had accomplished much more. When asked by a student interviewer to talk about the famous 1909 strike, she responded, at age eighty, that "I[n] so far as I am concerned, I am still at it."[60]

After 1968 Shavelson resided at the Hebrew Home for the Aged in Los Angeles, where she participated in political discussions and forums. She died in 1982 at the age of ninety-six. Like Shavelson, many federation members moved to suburban neighborhoods or retirement communities, at a distance from former comrades and Emma clubs. The federation tried to meet the problem by encouraging the formation of chapters in new communities; although Los Angeles was successful in starting suburban clubs, other regions could not adapt as readily to changing residence patterns.

The transformation of women's work, and the women's movement itself, also affected the federation's longevity. By mid-century most Jewish working women did not share a trade union background with the original Emmas, though they might encounter gender discrimination at work and home. While many Jewish women were drawn to the women's movement, it was not as Jewish-identified women that they joined new feminist ranks. Sexism, although a major ELF concern, was not an exclusive one; women's liberationists no doubt found it difficult to identify with the pantheon of federation causes. And while there was an incipient Jewish women's movement in the 1970s, it did not share the Emmas' secularism but rather focused on issues of religious patriarchy.

Despite their lack of political progeny, federation members were not discouraged. Indeed, they were delighted that ideas they had promoted for a quarter of a century were attracting the attention of young feminists. "We did our small part," Rose Raynes commented; now it was time for others to take the lead.[61]

By the end of the 1980s ELF leaders such as Clara Shavelson and June Gordon had passed on, and elderly members could not be replaced. Though some individual clubs in Chicago, Los Angeles, and the Bronx remained, the Emma Lazarus Federation of Jewish Women's Clubs disbanded in 1989.

The Federation and "Betweenness": "A Part of the Whole Multinational Culture of American Life"

For nearly four decades, the federation played a distinct role in Jewish women's organizational life. It was, according to its leaders, the "only Jewish women's organization that encourages mass action, the movement of people," a "progressive organization . . . which meets the needs of those women who are on the move."[62] It had also, over this period, taken its message regarding the significance of Jewish women's history, culture, and ideals to a broad audience of women in more traditional Jewish organizations. At the same time, the Emmas joined successfully with black women and other minorities to work for an end to racism. Though not a peace group, the federation dedicated its energies to programs and education for peace.

All of its varied projects sprang, the Emmas believed, from a dedicated core of Jewish identity. As distinct from Hadassah or synagogue sisterhoods, whose identity focused on Israel or the religious aspects of Judaism, the ELF proudly asserted itself as a secular Jewish group centered in the culture of America and its Jewish population. Much as their ancestors turned to Judaic religious emblems, the Emmas selected a heroine compatible with their own multifaceted identities as secular Jews, women, and Americans. Their primary identification with Emma Lazarus arose from her secularism, which the Emmas associated with a universalist humanism that they argued reflected the essence of Jewish values.

While the Emmas were a Jewish organization, their proud ethnicity did not hamper, but in fact promoted, their identification as women, as workers, and as Americans. As proclaimed in the ELF's first constitution in January 1951, the enhancement of Jewish culture was proposed "as a part of the whole multinational culture of American life." To be Jewish and American was not a contradiction but an interrelationship; as Lazarus's life had implied, "to be a good Jew was to be a better American."[63] Furthermore, gender was as fundamental to the group's identity as were ethnicity and nationality; as we have seen, women's issues and history were woven into all activities of the federation over the course of nearly forty years. Class consciousness was also deeply ingrained within the federation: Like Shavelson, Gordon, and Raynes, most leaders and members came from trade-union backgrounds or had married men who were active in workers' movements. Working-class consciousness distinguished the federation from middle-class Jewish women's organizations and helped shape its theory and practice.

The history of the Emma Lazarus Federation also raises provocative questions about racial identity and sensitivities. From the creation of the Emma Lazarus Division in 1944 to the demise of the federation forty-five years later, members consistently spoke to the necessity of eliminating white racism as well as anti-Semitism. In a series of continuing projects, they directed their efforts practically as well as rhetorically to the support of civil rights, particularly to the task of awakening white women (especially Jewish women) to the cause and allying themselves with black women to improve their situation.

In view of the ways in which the Emma Lazarus Federation amalgamated rather than separated the traditional markers of group identity—class, gender, nationality, ethnicity, and race—the experience of this group sheds light not only on Jewish women's activism in the twentieth century, but also on broader theoretical questions of feminism.[64] As feminists examine the various ways in which race, class, gender, and ethnicity interact and compete for the allegiance of individuals, organizations, and communities, the history of the Emma Lazarus Federation cautions us about the pitfalls of naming "discrete, coherent and absolutely separate" measures of identity.[65] For the Emmas, there was no dichotomy between class and gender, race and ethnicity. In one respect, the group itself represented a "racialized ethnicity," a people with a common ethnic past who came to regard itself as a "race" because of the traumatic experience of the Holocaust, recognizing connections with other victims of genocide and racism.[66]

Like Clara Shavelson, most members of the ELF had begun their organizational lives as trade-union members. Yet while Shavelson in 1909 had spoken her famous words as a worker, the delegates to the Cooper Union meeting offered a Jewish prayer before voting on her strike resolution. Jewish solidarity supported workers' consciousness on that occasion, as it did for all the years in which Shavelson, Gordon, Raynes, and their friends took part in the Jewish People's Fraternal Order of the IWO. These women's participation in the United Council of Working-Class Women, the Progressive Women's Council, and the Women's Division of the IWO illustrates their early recognition of the importance of gender as well as class and ethnic consciousness.

Not, however, until the Holocaust had accomplished its unspeakable horrors did the Jewish component of their identity become most salient. Remembering the women victims who "sang lullabies to console their children while facing the open graves before them," Clara Shavelson and her progressive friends made themselves over into "Emmas," dedicating themselves to promote Jewish culture—albeit a woman-centered "people's" culture—as a "shield" against fascism and genocide. "We dare not forget or forgive . . . the crimes of Nazism," they repeatedly exclaimed.

The coming to consciousness of the Emmas as "racialized" Jews in a way that fully incorporated their identities as women, trade unionists, and Americans illuminates the importance of the Holocaust in shaping Jewish women's experience. Yet it was the microcosmic context of these women's lives over a long period of time—their roles and relationships as comrades in the sweatshops and unions, as housewives in their neighborhoods, on bread and meat picket lines, and as associates in the JPFO and Progressive Women's Council—that provided the fulcrum for their gender-specific response to the Holocaust.

At its twentieth-anniversary convention in 1971, the Emma Lazarus Federation reconsidered its organizational roots. "Why are we calling ourselves a Jewish women's organization?" one delegate asked. "Since we are progressive with our ideology and program to benefit all people, why the separation? Why emphasize our Jewishness?" "Why a woman's organization?" Rose Raynes repeated. "Why the Hadassah, the Pioneer Women, the Council of Jewish Women, the Women's Division of the American Jewish Congress, the Women Strike for Peace, the National Council of Negro Women, the Emma Lazarus Federation?"

In response, the ELF president reaffirmed the importance both of "unity as Jews, unity in variety" and the "special approach" needed to solve women's problems because of pervasive attitudes of "male superiority": "We are a part of American life generally, and of the Jewish community in particular," she reaffirmed, as well as a member of the "family" of women's organizations.[67] In pursuing this aim, the ELF created linkages with groups that complemented its purposes, yet it did not hesitate to criticize allies when they fell short of the mark: peace and women's groups for failure to represent working-class interests; minority organizations for anti-Semitism; "progressive" male Jewish clubs for ignoring the contributions of Jewish women.

Another "unity" in the federation's approach was its elimination of standard dualities between thought and action, history and policy. A cultural organization, the federation was deeply involved in politics: Knowledge isolated from activity had little meaning. The Emmas repeatedly pointed out that culture was a "weapon" in the hard battle against bigotry and complacency. History, put forward on the first line of advance, would shape the present and the future.

Ironically, these dualities were bridged almost effortlessly not by feminist theorists but by the working-class women of the federation—both housewives and paid laborers—women who through their self-styled cultural work made themselves into intellectual activists. Here, too, Clara Shavelson had been a prototype. Growing up in the Ukraine, Clara read late at night after her housework and sewing were done, hiding her books to prevent her father's wrath. In New York, following a full day's work in the garment factory, she studied at the free night school, dreaming of becoming a doctor; when she had time, the public library was a favorite haunt. After Clara married and was busy with children, job, and community organizing, she still made time for several newspapers a day and a book "for dessert."[68]

Such hunger for learning was common to the Emmas, even though they belittled their skills and acknowledged the difficulty of being truly informed on the many issues that concerned them. "Sisters, believe me, it is not an easy task to do research, sit up nights and write outlines," confessed Miriam Silver, of the Bronx Co-ops, ELF's last cultural director. "I am not a professional writer, but I am willing and happy to do my job as long as I know that the material is being utilized."[69]

As demonstrated by these bridgings between theory and practice, Jewishness and universalism, and class, gender, ethnicity, race, and nationality more broadly, the women of the Emma Lazarus Federation cannot easily be ascribed with a fixed identity that framed them as a group apart—coherent, unitary, singular, and unchanging. Identity for the Emmas was neither linear nor static, but rather multiple, loose, fluid, and "linked." As anthropologist James Clifford suggests, when identity is conceived "not as a boundary to be maintained but as a nexus of relations and transactions actively engaging a subject," ethnicity becomes "more complex, less . . . teleological."[70]

Although the group consciousness of the Emmas grew and changed in interaction with historical events, the ability to unite conflicting values, bringing together disparate axes of experience in a new synthesis, remained constant. In many ways, the Emmas resembled the *mestiza* conciousness described by Gloria Anzaldúa as a "consciousness of the borderland" that arises from constantly "crossing over" and thereby "uniting all that is separate . . . breaking down the unitary aspect of each new paradigm." Like the mestiza, the Emmas' struggle to live "between ways," between different cultures, developed into a "tolerance for contradictions [and] ambiguity" and the ability to transcend painfully limiting dualities.[71]

The quality of "betweenness" has long been ascribed to Jewish identity as well. Georg Simmel described the Jew as the perpetual "stranger" who combines "nearness and distance"

in "reciprocal tension"; more recently, Daniel and Jonathan Boyarin have spoken of Jewishness as a "diasporic" identity, a living apart from and among others, "disrupt[ing] the very
categories of identity because it is not national, not genealogical, not religious, but all of these
in dialectical tension with one another."[72] The same kind of "disaggregated" identity—one
that is partial and fluid rather than whole and linear—may apply to gender; the writers suggest the parallel notion of a "diasporized gender identity" that combines difference and
sameness, specialness and universalism, in contradictory, yet positive and empowering, ways.

The Emma Lazarus Federation of Jewish Women's Clubs demonstrates the simultaneity—
rather than the dispersion—of the components of American Jewish female identity in ways
that exemplify these creative tensions. As women, as Jews, as proud members of the working class, as radical activists, and as Americans sensitive to the horrors of race prejudice,
they fought anti-Semitism and pursued their mission of social justice in ways that drew
on the many strengths, as well as the weaknesses, of their shared background and experiences. Their lack of sustained attention to Soviet anti-Semitism was unfortunate—and
ironic, given how often they quoted Lazarus's line "Until we are all free, none of us is free,"
a reference to the plight of Russian Jews.

The Emmas' response to domestic anti-Semitism after the Holocaust and their commitment to antiracist work was, however, continuing and vigorous; both efforts underscore the varied ways in which they joined cultural and political means to reaffirm Jewish
identity even as the pull of assimilation grew ever more powerful. During a period when
few others evidenced interest in women's historical consciousness, moreover, the Emmas
supported innovative research in many areas of women's history, focusing on subjects that
were Jewish and black, working-class and intellectual, American and international; they
linked the production of this knowledge to active involvement in a variety of human rights
campaigns. The contributions of the federation in these arenas helped transform our
knowledge of Jewish culture and politics, and of women's lives, in postwar America.

Rather than accepting the generational trope that posits the denial of ethnic conciousness after the first generation as normative, women's historians would do well to probe the
various patterns, exemplified by the Emma Lazarus Federation, by which ethnic, gender,
class, racial, and national identities were linked in innovative and flexible ways across the
generations. Crossing unsettled boundaries between these markers, the Emma Lazarus
Federation struck out for new frontiers that we, their feminist heirs, are still traversing.

Notes

I would like to thank the editors of *U.S. History of Women's History* for their insightful comments. Special
thanks are also due Kathy Spray, archivist at the American Jewish Archives in Cincinnati, and members of the
Brandeis University Faculty Seminar and Graduate Seminar in Jewish women's history and theory. Paul
Buhle, Morris U. Schappes, and Rose Raynes provided a helpful context about the organization and the Jewish
immigrant left.

1. Louis Levine, *The Women's Garment Workers* (New York: B. W. Huebsch, 1923), 154.
2. According to Morris U. Schappes, Feigenbaum used his knowledge of the Bible and Jewish tradition to
   promote socialist ideas. Among other works, he translated August Bebel's *Women and Socialism* and *Yiddishkeit and Sozialismus* (Jewishness and Socialism) into Yiddish. See Schappes, "Clara Lemlich Shavelson,"
   Jewish Currents 36 (November 1982): 11.
3. Clara Lemlich Shavelson, "Remembering the Waistmakers General Strike, 1909," *Jewish Currents* 36
   (November 1982): 11; also recounted in Paula Scheier, "Clara Lemlich Shavelson: Heroine of the Garment
   Strike of 1909," *Morgen Freiheit*, September 17, 1982. See also Scheier, "Clara Lemlich Shavelson: Fifty
   Years in Labor's Front Line," *Jewish Life* (November 1954): 7–11; Arthur Zipser, "A Labor Heroine," *Daily
   Worker*, 13 August 1982; Miriam Silver, "Clara Shavelson—Heroine of Labor," and tape of Memorial Meet-
   ing for Shavelson, 24 October 1982, both in the Papers of the Emma Lazarus Federation of Jewish Women's

Clubs, American Jewish Archives, Cincinnati (hereafter cited as ELF Papers). Shavelson's biography is drawn from these sources and from one of the few scholarly histories to treat Shavelson's mature activities, Annalise Orleck, "Common Sense and a Little Fire: Working-Class Women's Activism in the Twentieth-Century United States" (Ph.D. diss., New York University, 1990).

4. On the strike, see Meredith Tax, *The Rising of the Women: Feminist Solidarity and Class Conflict, 1880–1917* (New York: Monthly Review Press, 1980), 205–40, and Ann Schofield, "The Uprising of the 20,000: The Making of a Labor Legend," in *A Needle, a Bobbin, a Strike: Women Needleworkers in America*, Joan M. Jensen and Sue Davidson, eds. (Philadelphia: Temple University Press, 1984), 167–82. On Jewish women radicals, see Alice Kessler-Harris, "Organizing the Unorganizable: Three Jewish Women and Their Union," *Labor History* 17 (winter 1976): 5–23. Also of interest are Ruth A. Frager, *Sweatshop Strife: Class, Ethnicity, and Gender in the Jewish Labour Movement of Toronto, 1900–1939* (Toronto: University of Toronto Press, 1992), and Naomi Shepherd, *A Price below Rubies: Jewish Women as Rebels and Radicals* (Cambridge: Harvard University Press, 1993), which, with a few exceptions, concentrates on European women. On radical women generally, see Mari Jo Buhle, *Women and American Socialism, 1870–1920* (Urbana: University of Illinois Press, 1981), and Robert Schaffer, "Women and the Communist Party, USA, 1930–1940," *Socialist Review* 9 (May–June 1979): 73–118.

5. Among major studies in American Jewish women's history, see the pioneering volume by Charlotte Baum, Paula Hyman, and Sonya Michel, *The Jewish Women in America* (New York: New American Library, 1975); Jacob Rader Marcus, *The American Jewish Woman, 1654–1980* (New York: KTAV Publishing House, 1981); June Sochen, *Consecrate Every Day: The Public Lives of Jewish American Women, 1880–1980* (Albany: State University of New York Press, 1981); Sydney Stahl Weinberg, *The World of Our Mothers: The Lives of Jewish Immigrant Women* (Chapel Hill: University of North Carolina Press, 1988); Susan A. Glenn, *Daughters of the Shtetl: Life and Labor in the Immigrant Generation* (Ithaca, N.Y.: Cornell University Press, 1990); Linda Kuzmack, *Woman's Cause: The Jewish Woman's Movement in England and the United States, 1881–1933* (Columbus: Ohio State University Press, 1990); and Faith Rogow, *Gone to Another Meeting: The National Council of Jewish Women* (Tuscaloosa: University of Alabama Press, 1993).

6. See Arthur Hertzberg, *The Jews in America: Four Centuries of an Uneasy Encounter: A History* (New York: Simon and Schuster, 1989), and Edward S. Shapiro, *A Time for Healing: American Jewry since World War II* (Baltimore: Johns Hopkins University Press, 1992). Deborah Dash Moore's study of the children of immigrants, *At Home in America: Second-Generation New York Jews* (New York: Columbia University Press, 1981), offers a different argument. On the question of immigrant generations, see Peter Kivisto and Dag Blanck, eds., *American Immigrants and Their Generations: Studies and Commentaries on the Hansen Thesis after Fifty Years* (Urbana: University of Illinois Press, 1990).

7. On an earlier protest by Jewish housewives, see Paula Hyman, "Immigrant Women and Consumer Protest: The New York Kosher Meat Boycott of 1902," *American Jewish History* 70 (September 1980): 91–105. For an account of the housewives' movement in the Great Depression, see Annalise Orleck, " 'We Are That Mythical Thing Called the Public': Militant Housewives during the Great Depression," *Feminist Studies* 19 (spring 1993): 147–72. See also Mark Naison, *Communists in Harlem during the Great Depression* (New York: Grove Press, 1983), 149–50, for an account of the 1935 meat boycott led by Shavelson and Rose Nelson [Raynes].

8. Tape of Memorial Meeting for Clara Lemlich Shavelson, October 1982, ELF Papers.

9. See, e.g., "Class Struggle in Fraternal Organization," *Daily Worker*, 18 July 1930, IWO Papers, Tamiment Library, New York University (hereafter cited as IWO Papers).

10. Mark Naison, "Remaking America: Communists and Liberals in the Popular Front," in Michael E. Brown, Randy Martin, Frank Rosengarten, and George Snedeker, eds., *New Studies in the Politics and Culture of U.S. Communism*, (New York: Monthly Review Press, 1993), 58–59; Arthur Leibman, *Jews and the Left* (New York: John Wiley and Sons, 1978), 59, 350–51.

11. "Straight from the Shoulder Fraternalism," JPFO Bulletin, IWO Papers. On the IWO, see Arthur J. Sabin, *Red Scare in Court: New York versus the International Workers Order* (Philadelphia: University of Pennsylvania Press, 1993), 10–23; Rose Raynes, Gertrude Decker, Morris U. Schappes, and Annette Rosenthal, interviews by author, February–March 1993. On Jews and American Communism, see Paul Buhle, "Jews and American Communism: The Cultural Question," *Radical History Review* 23 (spring 1980): 9–33; Leibman, *Jews and the Left*; and David Leviatin, *Followers of the Trail: Jewish Working-Class Radicals in America* (New Haven: Yale University Press, 1969).

12. Morris U. Schappes, ed., *Emma Lazarus: Selections from Her Poetry and Prose* (New York: Cooperative Book League, Jewish-American Section, IWO, 1944); the ELF sponsored new editions of the volume in 1978 and 1982. Schappes also wrote an introduction and notes to *An Epistle to the Hebrews by Emma Lazarus*, centennial ed. (New York: Jewish Historical Society of New York, 1987), and he edited, with an introduction, *The Letters of Emma Lazarus, 1868–1885* (New York: New York Public Library, 1949).

13. Founding documents, ELF Papers.

14. Ibid.; Rose Raynes, interview by author, February 1993.

15. Rose Raynes, interview by Paul Buhle, 21 March 1979, Oral History Interviews of the Left, Tamiment Library, New York University.

16. In his book about the case, law professor Arthur J. Sabin describes the prosecution as without parallel in American law and concludes that the IWO had been destroyed for political reasons. See Sabin, *Red Scare in Court*. For further information, see IWO Papers, including "Report of the Officers," IWO, 3–4 February 1951.

17. See, e.g., Leah Nelson, "They Shall Not Die," *The Lamp* 1, 3 (November–December 1952): 4–5.

18. Robert Meeropol, interview by author, May 1993.

19. "Resume of a Discussion by the Executive Committee of the Emma Lazarus Federation on the Destruction of Jewish Culture and Unjust Execution of Jewish Cultural and Civic Leadership," 10 July 1956, ELF Papers; Rose Raynes and Gertrude Decker, interviews by author. See also the discussion of the ELF and the Soviet Jewish question in *Israel Horizons and Labour Israel* 21 (January–February 1974): 2, 28–30.

20. *Proceedings of the Third Convention*, 6–8 February 1959, ELF Papers.

21. On postwar Jewry, see Moore, *At Home in America;* Shapiro, *A Time for Healing;* and Marshall Sklare and J. Greenblum, *Jewish Identity on the Suburban Frontier* (New York: Basic Books, 1967).

22. The Jewish Cultural Clubs and Societies, like the Yiddisher Kultur Farband, supported such institutions as the *Morgen Freibeit* newspaper, *Yiddishe Kultur* magazine, and Camp Kinderland and worked to publish Yiddish books.

23. Cited in ELF Papers; see Eve Merriam, *Woman with a Torch* (New York: Citadel Press, 1957).

24. Study outline on Emma Lazarus, ELF Papers.

25. Schappes, *Epistle to the Hebrews*, 30.

26. Lazarus, "The Jewish Problem," reprinted in Schappes, *Emma Lazarus: Selections from Her Poetry and Prose*, 78.

27. ELF constitution and by-laws, 20–21 January 1951, ELF Papers.

28. Cited in Ernestine Rose study guide, ELF Papers, from Yuri Suhl, *Ernestine L. Rose and the Battle for Human Rights* (New York: Reynal, 1959).

29. Study guide on Ernestine Rose, ELF Papers.

30. Discussion outline, "Women, Heroines of the Warsaw Ghetto," 1951, ELF Papers.

31. Report of June Gordon, Executive Director of the Third National Convention, *Proceedings of the Third Convention*.

32. See, e.g., Miriam Silver, Cultural Report, 4 December 1976, ELF Papers.

33. Report of Ida Sper to the Second National Convention, 23 October 1955, ELF Papers.

34. *The Lamp* 1, 1 (May 1952): 6.

35. Ibid., 6–7.

36. In 1959, for example, under the auspices of the Brooklyn Emma Lazarus clubs, hundreds of blacks and Jews attended a brotherhood meeting at the Eastern Parkway Jewish Center cosponsored by local affiliates of the American Jewish Congress, the NAACP, and the Brownsville Neighborhood Health Council. A new Brooklyn Emma Lazarus club, made up of young mothers, rejected the lecture/meeting format and organized a brotherhood puppet show about changing neighborhoods attended by 1,400 black and white children.

37. See, e.g., address of Leah Nudell, Vice President of the ELF and President of the Los Angeles club, to the Seventh National Convention, 14–16 November 1975, ELF Papers.

38. Speakers Guide, "Racism, Enemy of the Jewish People," ELF Papers.

39. To the Emmas, genocide not only was "actually killing" but also was caused by poverty, starvation, malnutrition, and the social ills that "killed people's spirit." See Miriam Silver, "Helping to Shape a Brighter Future for Our New Generation," 1969, and remarks of Rose Raynes, 9 April 1989, ELF Papers.

40. Report of Eva Mamber, Boston ELF, to the Fifth National Convention, 1964, ELF Papers.

41. Report of the Fifth National Convention, ibid.

42. Rose Raynes, keynote address, Seventh National Convention, 14–16 November 1975, ELF Papers.

43. Press release, 18 August 1967, ELF Papers.

44. *The Lamp* 1, 6 (May–June 1960): 6.

45. In 1959, for example, the ELF sponsored a mass meeting in Union Square that attracted 8,000 Americans who protested a swastika outbreak in West Germany and the United States. At the same time the Brooklyn chapter called a mass meeting with twelve other organizations at which Jackie Robinson spoke. Thus was the fight against anti-Semitism joined, they said, "with the Negro people's struggle for equality." Mollie Ilson, "As I See It," *The Lamp* 6, 12, ELF Papers.

46. Rose Raynes, Gertrude Decker, and Morris U. Schappers, interviews by author.

47. At the urging of the Emma Lazarus Committee in Los Angeles (which included fifteen member clubs), WILPF called a conference of Jewish women's organizations. ELF Papers.

48. Quotation from the Third National Convention, *Proceedings of the Third Convention*.

49. Local branches also supported regional issues: the Los Angeles group, for example, started a cooperative nursery school for Mexican American, Filipino, and Jewish children.

50. When some members of the Jewish community criticized the ELF for a member's anti-Israel statement, leadership disassociated the federation from the member, noting that its firm support for Israel had long been a matter of public record. See letters from Rose Raynes and Morris U. Schappes discussing the incident in *Israel Horizons and Labour Israel* 21 (January–February 1974): 2, 28–30.

51. Undated typescript, ELF Papers.

52. Leah Nelson, President's Report, *Proceedings of the Third Convention*.

53. Shirley Bolton, Newark, N.J., Second National Convention, October 1955, ELF Papers.

54. Helen Lewis, Second National Convention, ibid.

55. See letter of Rose Raynes in *Israel Horizons and Labour Israel* 21 (January–February 1974): 30.

56. IWO press release, 13 November 1947, IWO Papers. See also photos of Louise W. Wise and June Croll Gordon embracing on the stage of Assembly Hall, Hunter College, ELF Papers.

57. Abzug spoke on 25 October 1970, at the ELF's fiftieth anniversary celebration of woman suffrage; on 14 December 1974, she spoke at its celebration of Emma Lazarus's 125th birthday. Holtzman, described as a "twentieth century disciple of Ernestine Rose," was the guest of honor at a 25 March 1974, celebration of Rose.

58. June Gordon, Fifth National Convention, 1964, ELF Papers.

59. Ida Good, "Why I Joined the E.L. Club," *The Lamp* 4, 8 (October 1958): 4.

60. Scheier, "Clara Lemlich Shavelson: Fifty Years in Labor's Front Line," 11; Schappes, "Clara Lemlich Shavelson," 11.

61. Rose Raynes, interview by Buhle.

62. Leah Nelson, address at the Fourth National Convention, 3–5 November 1961, ELF Papers.

63. ELF constitution and by-laws, 20–21 January 1951, ELF Papers.

64. For example, on the problem of class/gender paradigms in women's history, see Nancy A. Hewitt, "Beyond the Search for Sisterhood: American Women's History in the 1980s," reprinted in Ellen Carol DuBois and Vicki L. Ruiz, eds., *Unequal Sisters: A Multicultural Reader in U.S. Women's History* , 2d ed. (New York: Routledge, 1990), 1–14.

65. Biddy Martin and Chandra Talpade Mahanty, "Feminist Politics: What's Home Got to Do with It?" in Teresa de Lauretis, ed., *Feminist Studies: Critical Studies*, (Bloomington: Indiana University Press, 1986), 192.

66. The term is used by Nancy Fraser in "Rethinking the Public Sphere: A Contribution to the Critique of Actually Existing Democracy," in Craig Calhoun, ed., *Habermas and the Public Sphere*, (Cambridge: MIT Press, 1992), 118.

67. Address (unsigned) of Leah Nelson to the Sixth National Convention, 1971, ELF Papers.

68. Scheier, "Clara Lemlich Shavelson: Fifty Years in Labor's Front Line," 8.

69. Miriam Silver, "Report on Culture: Anti-Semitism and Resurgence of Nazism," ca. 1978, ELF Papers.

70. James Clifford, *The Predicament of Culture: Twentieth-Century Ethnography* (Cambridge: Harvard University Press, 1988), 341–42, 344.

71. Gloria Anzdaldúa, "La conciencia de la mestiza: Towards a New Consciousness," in *Borderlands/La Frontera: The New Mestiza* (San Francisco: Sprinter/Aunt Lute Books, 1987), 79. On feminist consciousness and "otherness," see esp. Martin and Mahanty, "Feminist Politics"; Teresa de Lauretis, "Eccentric Subjects: Feminist Theory and Historical Consciousness," *Feminist Studies* 16 (spring 1990): 115–50; Trinh T. Minh-Ha, *Woman Native Other: Writing Postcoloniality and Feminism* (Bloomington: Indiana University Press, 1989); and Shane Phelan, "(Be)Coming Out: Lesbian Identity and Politics," *Signs* 18 (1993): 765–90. Also useful are Barbara Smith, ed., *Home Girls: A Black Feminist Anthology* (New York: Kitchen Table/Women of Color Press, 1983), and Elly Bulkin, Minnie Bruce Pratt, and Barbara Smith, eds., *Yours in Struggle: Three Feminist Perspectives on Anti-Semitism and Racism* (Brooklyn, N.Y.: Long Haul Press, 1984).

72. Kurt H. Wolff, ed., *The Sociology of Georg Simmel* (New York: Free Press, 1950), 408; Daniel Boyarin and Jonathan Boyarin, "Diaspora: Generation and the Ground of Jewish Identity," *Critical Inquiry* 19 (summer 1993): 721.

34

"More than a Lady": Ruby Doris Smith Robinson and Black Women's Leadership in the Student Nonviolent Coordinating Committee

Cynthia Griggs Fleming

Throughout the history of this country, countless African American activists have resisted racism and oppression in a wide variety of ways. A number of these activists were women, and a few of them became famous. Most Americans have at least heard of legendary black women such as Harriet Tubman and Sojourner Truth, who were passionately committed to black freedom. There are many, however, who were never recognized for their achievements and their importance. One such woman was Ruby Doris Smith Robinson, who worked with the Student Nonviolent Coordinating Committee from its earliest days in 1960 until her death at age twenty-five in October 1967.

Robinson was born in Atlanta, Georgia, on 25 April 1942 to Alice and J. T. Smith. She was the second of seven children; the oldest was a girl named Mary Ann, and then came Ruby, Catherine, Bobby, John, Willie, and Gregory.[1] The Smith family owned their own home in Summerhill, the oldest black neighborhood in Atlanta. While Summerhill had its share of crime, it also provided positive experiences for its residents. Mary Ann Smith Wilson, Robinson's older sister, described Summerhill as a "mosaic" that included all kinds of people. Middle-class families lived alongside those who were mired in abject poverty. Wilson also remembered that the community provided a network of support for its youngsters. Schools, churches, and other institutions such as the YMCA sponsored activities and provided encouragement to neighborhood youth while they also protected community youngsters from the worst part of segregation.[2]

In such a warm and supportive atmosphere Ruby Doris Smith Robinson developed a keen sense of social and racial justice. She watched the events of the 1950s—the integration of Little Rock's Central High School, the Montgomery bus boycott—with a growing sense of concern. When she entered Spelman College as a freshman in the fall of 1958, Robinson was excited about the prospect of change in the South's system of segregation. But, Robinson remembered, "I wasn't ready to act on my own." By the next academic year other idealistic black college students in the Atlanta University Center, which served Atlanta University, Gammon Theological Seminary, and Spelman, Morehouse, Morris Brown, and Clark colleges, created the Atlanta Committee on Appeal for Human Rights. The group sponsored its first demonstration on 15 March 1960 at the state capital building—a short distance from their campuses. This was just what Robinson had been waiting for. She enthusiastically joined the Atlanta committee and participated in that first demonstration.[3]

At the same time that Ruby Doris Smith Robinson and her colleagues were protesting segregation in Atlanta, black college students all across the South were engaged in similar activities. It soon became obvious to some that all these student movements could benefit by establishing an organization to coordinate their activities. Accordingly, in April 1960 black student leaders from all over the South met and established the Student Nonviolent Coordinating Committee (SNCC). By early 1961, even as Robinson continued her work with the Atlanta committee, she began to work with this new group, serving SNCC as an activist in the field as well as an administrator in the Atlanta central office.

In May 1966 she succeeded Jim Forman as SNCC's executive secretary. She was the only woman ever to serve in this capacity.[4] Robinson was elected during a particularly emotional and difficult staff meeting in Kingston Springs, Tennessee. The heated debates about strategies and goals that occupied the staff at that meeting were complicated by the serious splits that had developed within the ranks of the staff by this time. Divisions based on gender, race, and status in the organization produced a great deal of suspicion and mistrust. Despite these problems, however, Robinson commanded the respect of the majority of her SNCC colleagues. They admired her unshakeable commitment to the cause of civil rights in general and the Student Nonviolent Coordinating Committee in particular.

While Robinson had the practical experience and the firm commitment necessary to administer SNCC, she faced some unique problems and challenges because of her gender. Like some other female leaders in the organization, she found that her femininity was questioned because she exercised power over men. Furthermore, in the midst of her SNCC work Robinson married (1964) and had a child (1965). This added dimension provoked a great deal of tension in her life as she sought to fulfill the traditional roles of wife and mother as well as the unusual role of female civil rights leader.

SNCC colleagues recognized Robinson's importance. One recalled, "You could feel her power in SNCC on a daily basis." Another insisted, "As a female, she was a pretty powerful person."[5] As SNCC's membership enlarged and its character changed over time, it became increasingly difficult to administer. But Robinson tried. SNCC had always had a flexible view of leadership. Most in the group believed that everyone could be a leader. Whereas this belief served to inspire broad participation by the membership, it also caused serious discipline problems. There were times when some members simply refused to follow orders. Regardless of the existence of such attitudes, Robinson demanded hard work and dedication from all those around her. Jack Minnis, a member of SNCC's research staff, insisted that it was almost impossible to fool Robinson; he had no doubt that she had "a 100 percent effective shit detector." Above all, she made sure that nobody abused the organization's limited financial resources. Stanley Wise, who would later succeed Robinson as executive secretary when she became ill, clearly recalled a particularly illustrative incident. It occurred when a group of field workers came to Atlanta for a meeting.

> She absolutely did not tolerate any nonsense. I remember some people came in there [the Atlanta central office] once from Mississippi. They had driven their car over there and they said they needed new tires. And she pulled out [a card] from her little file. She said, "Listen, I've given you sixteen tires in the last four months. . . . I've sent you four batteries, you had two motors in the car. You're not getting another thing. Now take that car out of here and go on back to Mississippi."[6]

Coworker Reginald Robinson remembered that Robinson could be uncompromising about procedure. "When she became in charge of the payroll and you had reports to do—you had expense accounts to turn [in]. Well, if you didn't do what you were supposed to do, Big Mama [Robinson] would cut your money." Movement colleague Charles Jones succinctly summed up her no-nonsense approach. "You didn't run any games on her." As coworker Worth Long declared, "The office would not have run except for her; and then the field would not have survived." Long recalled her as "a cantankerous person. . . . She's set in her ways, and she's mostly right. . . . She would take a principle[d] stand. . . . She'd argue, and she'd huff and puff too." In the freewheeling discussions that SNCC staff members had about organizational policy, Long remembered Robinson as "a formidable opponent. I wouldn't want to play poker with her."[7] There were indeed many sides to Ruby Doris Smith Robinson. Regardless of what colleagues thought of her administrative techniques and her office demeanor, all agreed that Robinson's actions were always guided by her sincere commitment to SNCC.

Despite her importance to SNCC, however, Robinson has received little attention from scholars and others who are now writing the civil rights movement's story. Has her gender consigned her to obscurity? That is part of the answer. Still another part of the answer, however, is rooted in Robinson's personality and her vision of her role in the movement. Even in childhood, Robinson had been an intensely private and independent person. Her older sister remembered that their parents understood this and accepted it. They knew that "whatever she's going to do, she's going to do."[8] They never expected their daughter to consult them or even inform them of her activities, and she never did.

Robinson so guarded her privacy that she actively discouraged those who wanted to extend special recognition to her for her protest activities. While she understood that such activities themselves attracted a good deal of attention, she absolutely did not want any personal notoriety. Her attitude toward personal publicity became quite obvious in early 1961 when she became part of a SNCC delegation that was jailed in Rock Hill, South Carolina. The SNCC action in Rock Hill grew out of a decision that the group made at its February 1961 meeting. During that meeting, staff members expressed concern about the jail-versus-bail question. All over the South, thousands of black college students involved in protest activities were being arrested. In the majority of cases students posted bail and were released. Increasingly, however, some argued that there were compelling reasons why protestors should start refusing to post bail and should serve out their jail sentences instead.

Tactically, some insisted, those who protested segregation could do the movement a great service by remaining in jail. Clogging the jails with increasing numbers of protesters would put additional pressure on segregation by straining local resources. At the same time, others insisted that attempts to bail black students out of jail were placing a terrible financial burden on local black communities—a burden that could eventually interfere with their will and their ability to continue the fight against segregation. Finally, others argued that the protestors' presence in jail would provide powerful moral reinforcement for their position. The SNCC members attending that February meeting were aware that a group of South Carolina students had already taken a public stand on this issue. On 1 February, just prior to the beginning of the meeting, students from Friendship College in Rock Hill, South Carolina, were convicted of trespassing after they had demonstrated in downtown variety stores and drugstores. The students refused to post bail, and they expressed a determination to serve out their full sentences. Participants in that February SNCC meeting unequivocally expressed their view of the stand taken by the Rock Hill students:

> Their sitting-in shows their belief in the immorality of racial segregation and their choice to serve the sentence shows their unwillingness to participate in any part of a system that perpetuates injustice. Since we too share their beliefs and since many times during the past year we too have sat-in at lunch counters, we feel that in good conscience we have no alternative other than to join them.[9]

Robinson and the others who attended SNCC's February meeting were invigorated by their new stand. They excitedly debated the question of which SNCC members should go to Rock Hill to inaugurate this new policy. Finally the decision was made: Charles Jones,

Charles Sherrod, Diane Nash, and Mary Ann Smith, Robinson's older sister, were selected. But Smith remembered that after she left the meeting she began to have some serious second thoughts about going to jail in Rock Hill. "I started thinking about all the little things I had in the making for next year, you know. Academically—fellowships and what have you." While Smith became increasingly uncertain, Robinson became increasingly excited. "So what happened eventually is Ruby Doris talked it up, and I just bowed out and let her go."[10]

After they protested segregation at Good's Drug Store in downtown Rock Hill, Robinson and the others were arrested. They served thirty-day sentences in the York County jail. As the end of her jail sentence approached, Robinson began to worry that she would be the target of special recognition. She told her sister: "I think the Rock Hillians are planning something for us when we get out. . . . I don't care for the publicity that they'll probably give us when we come out." Robinson clearly did not want any special recognition from anyone. She did not even want family members and friends to celebrate her achievements. "Please don't plan anything for me," she insisted. "I'm no celebrity and you know it."[11]

Despite Robinson's wishes, the *Atlanta Inquirer* had photographers on hand at the airport when she returned from serving her jail time in South Carolina.[12] After her Rock Hill experience, Robinson participated in a number of protest activities over the next few months in Atlanta and other Georgia cities and other states. Regardless of the media coverage that these protests attracted, Robinson continued to shun personal publicity.

Movement colleagues all agreed that Robinson was a team player. She did not want the movement to be affected by individual attitudes and aspirations. This conviction sometimes prompted Robinson to make pointed comments about civil rights veterans who seemed to enjoy the inevitable publicity and notoriety that accompanied their protest activities. She was particularly concerned that the media attention lavished on some could lead to serious distortions and dangerous misrepresentations. Her views of Stokely Carmichael's relationship to the press clearly indicate the depth of her concern. She charged that because of the media attention Carmichael attracted, he had become "the only consistent spokesman for the organization, and he has had the press not only available but seeking him out for whatever ammunition could be found—FOR OUR DESTRUCTION." Because of Carmichael's penchant for attracting press coverage, Robinson half-jokingly and half-seriously christened him "Stokely Starmichael."[13]

Robinson's attempts to stay in the background even in the face of her growing influence in SNCC clearly illustrate one of the conflicts that complicated her life as an activist. Indeed, her gender, race, personal convictions, personality, and position all meant that she would inevitably face conflicts in the environment of the civil rights movement of the sixties. Among the most painful of those conflicts was the issue of her own femininity—a problem that many of her African American female friends shared. Against the backdrop of the peculiar status of black women in American society, black female activists' efforts have routinely been tied to a deemphasis of black femininity. Such a linkage is entirely consistent with negative notions of black femininity that are firmly anchored in the nineteenth century and slavery. One scholar has identified the roots of this negative nineteenth-century notion:

> The slave system defined Black people as chattel. Since women, no less than men, were viewed as profitable labor-units, they might as well have been genderless as far as the slaveholders were concerned. . . . Judged by the evolving nineteenth century ideology of femininity, which emphasized women's roles as nurturing mothers and gentle companions and housekeepers for their husbands, Black women were practically anomalies.[14]

In the popular consciousness, notions of accepted female behavior are inconsistent with popularized views of the black female activist persona. Consequently, one does not think of the fierce "General" Tubman primping in front of a mirror, or the legendary Sojourner Truth worrying about which hat to wear. Of course, women in leadership roles, regardless of race, have often been vulnerable to attacks on their femininity. Yet the experience of black women activists is unique, since it is firmly based in the broader context of negative notions of black femininity in general.

Predictably, as Robinson gained power and influence in SNCC, increasing numbers of her movement colleagues came to identify her by her role in the organization, not her gender. Some insist that part of the perception they have of her is rooted in their view of Robinson's physical appearance. Many remember her as a rather plain woman. She was five feet two inches tall with a stocky build. She had large hips, a small waist, and bowed legs. Because of her build she had a very distinctive walk. Her older sister, Mary Ann, remembered that this earned her the nickname "Duck." Robinson's skin color was medium, and she had a broad nose, relatively large lips, and kinky hair. Because she possessed these characteristics, Charles Jones described her as "practical and black" in terms of attitude and appearance. Coworker Courtland Cox insisted that people in SNCC "didn't view her as a man or woman, they viewed her as a strength." Her friend and coworker Joanne Grant remembered, "I think that everybody accepted her as one of the boys."[15]

A number of Robinson's colleagues were particularly impressed by her commanding voice. Constancia Romilly vividly recalled the impression Ruby's voice made on her. "Ruby . . . was as tough as the men, and as courageous, and her voice was as strong as any man's voice. . . . Yes, she had a—she had a carrying voice, and a very well defined [voice]. When she spoke, you could definitely hear what she had to say." Curtis Muhammad was also deeply impressed by Robinson's voice. He described it as authoritative, masculine, but not too heavy. In his words, "She didn't have a whiny female thing . . . none of that."[16]

Earlier acquaintances who observed Robinson before she began her movement work recalled a demeanor and behavior that were remarkably similar to those she would display as a mature activist. Fellow Spelman College student Norma June Davis remarked that "she [Robinson] seemed so atypical of Spelman, I mean at that point in time. It was amazing that she was even there. She didn't look like a Spelmanite, she didn't dress like a Spelmanite, she didn't act like one." Another early acquaintance, the Reverend Albert Brinson, explained that students at Spelman "were always taught to be a lady. A lady stood back and waited to be waited upon by a man." Brinson thought that Ruby did not fit too well in this atmosphere, since "she was not the ladylike kind. . . . She was rather aggressive."[17]

Robinson was indeed aggressive whenever issues of racial justice were at stake. It seemed to her that there was always so much to be done. When idealistic and enthusiastic students first organized the Student Nonviolent Coordinating Committee in April 1960, they expected that their new committee would function as a coordinating body linking student protest movements in various communities. They soon recognized, though, that this was only the beginning. By February 1961 the group became involved in plotting movement strategy when they made the decision to send the delegation to Rock Hill, South Carolina.

In May 1961, shortly after Robinson and her colleagues finished serving their sentences in the York County jail, SNCC became involved in the Freedom Rides. Although the Congress of Racial Equality organized the rides, SNCC stepped in and provided the volunteers to continue when white resistance threatened to disrupt them. Robinson was one of those volunteers. She was later arrested and jailed for sixty days along with the other Freedom Riders. The riders served the first part of their sentence in the Hinds County jail in Jackson, Mississippi. They were later transferred to Parchman Penitentiary, a large state facility. Robinson's release came on 11 August 1961. By that time SNCC had decided to organize a voter registration campaign in McComb, Mississippi. Once again Robinson was right there. She went door to door urging people in McComb to register.

It seemed that Robinson was always willing to volunteer for the most hazardous movement duty. Furthermore, in such circumstances colleagues could depend on her to be bold, daring, and frequently outrageous. Because of her attitude and her actions, Ruby Doris Smith Robinson soon became a legend—even among the bold and brave young people of the Student Nonviolent Coordinating Committee. Most people who were with SNCC in the early years could recount at least one Robinson story. For example, Julian Bond remembered that when a delegation of SNCC staff members was preparing to board a plane for Africa in September 1964, an airline representative told them that the plane was full, even though they had tickets for that flight. He wanted to know if they would wait and take a later flight. This angered Robinson so much that, without consulting the rest of the group, she went and sat down in the jetway, preventing passengers from boarding the plane, and refused to move. The group was given seats on that flight.[18]

Coworker Michael Sayer particularly remembered Robinson's actions during an important SNCC staff meeting at Waveland, Mississippi, in November 1964. The group confronted some very difficult and emotional issues at that meeting, but the conferees still managed to find time for recreation. After one especially intense and emotional day, "someone suggested we have a football game. And . . . we played tackle football with no equipment. . . . Ruby was quarterback. We played eleven on a side . . . and I was playing the line and she ran over me." Robinson's intensity generally affected everything she did. James Bond, who worked in the SNCC print shop, witnessed still another Robinson incident, which occurred when a group of SNCC staff members went to the airport to meet some of the organization's celebrity supporters in 1963.

> So we went out there and met the first plane which was coming from California, which had Marlon Brando and Tony Franciosa on it. And then we had to go meet a second plane, which had Paul Newman on it. So we took them down to the other gate. . . . Ruby Doris was with us. And as we stood out at the gate waiting . . . the first person to come off the plane was Governor George Wallace. And Ruby Doris went up to him and said, "How are you, Governor?" and introduced herself and said, "I've spent time in your jails." And he said, "Well, I hope they treated you well, and if you're ever back, look me up."[19]

She never did.

Robinson's assertiveness, brashness, and courage were important, but they were not unique. Rather, her actions and her attitude mirror the boldness displayed by many African American women in the movement, and by many others over time. Consider the example of Annelle Ponder. Ponder, a Southern Christian Leadership Conference voter education teacher, was arrested in Winona, Mississippi, in 1963. Fannie Lou Hamer, who was arrested with her, remembered hearing an exchange between Ponder and her white prison guard. He demanded that she use a title of respect when addressing him: "Cain't you say yessir, bitch?" Ponder answered, "Yes, I can say yessir." The guard then demanded that she say it. Ponder's reply: "I don't know you well enough." The guard was so incensed that he beat her. Hamer remembered, "She kept screamin' and they kept beatin' her . . . and finally she started prayin' for 'em, and she asked God to have mercy on 'em because they didn't know what they was doin'."[20]

Then there was the case of Annie Pearl Avery. During the course of a demonstration in Montgomery, Alabama, in 1965, Avery came face-to-face with a white policeman who had a billy club aimed straight at her head. He had already beaten several others. Avery "reached up, grabbed the club and said, 'Now what you going to do, motherfucker?'" Then she slipped back into the crowd of demonstrators. Another activist, Judy Richardson, had more than a verbal confrontation with a policeman. During the course of a demonstration, she kicked an Atlanta policeman in the groin. Richardson explained what prompted her to take such drastic action. "He was mistreating a Black demonstrator, and it forced me to do something."[21]

In an era when American women were regularly told that a woman's place was in the home, women such as Ruby Doris Smith Robinson, Annie Pearl Avery, Judy Richardson, and Annelle Ponder definitely did not conform to contemporary notions of ladylike behavior. The advice offered by diplomat Adlai Stevenson in his commencement address to the class of 1955 at Smith College clearly illustrates contemporary expectations: "The assignment to you, as wives and mothers, you can do in the living room with a baby in your lap or in the kitchen with a can opener in your hand. If you are clever, maybe you can even practice your saving arts on that unsuspecting man while he's watching television. I think there is much you can do . . . in the humble role of housewife."[22]

Even though the behavior of black women activists did not always fit contemporary notions of proper female behavior, it did fit comfortably into an established tradition of black female assertiveness. Yet because of the predominance of broader notions of a woman's place, the actions of Robinson and some of her African American movement sisters brought them into conflict with many who questioned or ignored their femininity. Many, including Robinson, were troubled by this. Her colleague Cynthia Washington explained the frustration that many felt.

> I remember discussions with various women about our treatment as one of the boys and its impact on us as women. We did the same work as men—organizing around voter registration and community issues in rural areas—usually with men. But when we finally got back to some town where we could relax and go out, the men went out with other women. Our skills and abilities were recognized and respected, but that seemed to place us in some category other than female.[23]

The feminine side of their natures was a vital part of all of these women, including Robinson. Indeed, the feminine side of Robinson's nature dictated many of the choices she had made earlier in her life while she was growing up. A number of her SNCC colleagues who knew her only as a legendary freedom fighter and hard-nosed administrator would have been surprised to know that she was a debutante in 1958. She was also one of the head majorettes with the Price High School marching band. Years later, her younger sister Catherine recalled how much Robinson cared about her appearance when she was in high school. She was very concerned about fashion and she had a keen sense of style. She liked wide skirts, wide belts, and sweaters. "She had very expensive tastes. *Very.* She wore nothing cheap. She couldn't stand cheap clothes, and cheap shoes she would not put on her feet." She was concerned that her clothes should flatter her figure.[24]

Her concern about her appearance did not end once Robinson entered the movement. Although she became less inclined to indulge her expensive tastes, she still took a great deal of care with her appearance, sometimes under very difficult circumstances. Movement colleague Connie Curry remembered one particularly illustrative incident that occurred when the SNCC delegation went to Rock Hill, South Carolina, in 1961.

> They all knew that they were going to be arrested and go to jail. And Rock Hill was a very scary place. We got up real, real early that morning. Everybody was ready to go. And Ruby Doris said, "Well, everybody can just sort of sit down and do whatever because my hair is not right, and I'm rolling it, and I'm not leaving until it's curled."

I thought, my God, this woman—she's going to be in jail within two hours. And she had these great big rollers . . . and everybody there just said, "Oh, okay."[25]

Robinson was not really "one of the boys" after all. What is clear is that Ruby Doris Smith Robinson was a woman whose existence called into question a whole range of stereotypes. Because she was an activist, she was not supposed to be "ladylike." Because she was an African American woman, she was not supposed to be feminine.

As she wrestled with the issue of femininity, Robinson was faced with a related problem: relationships between black and white women in SNCC. These relationships were the source of a great deal of tension within the organization at certain times. Part of this tension was rooted in the opposing perspectives of black and white women on some very fundamental issues. Cynthia Washington discussed some of those differences.

During the fall of 1964, I had a conversation with Casey Hayden about the role of women in SNCC. She complained that all the women got to do was type, that their role was limited to office work no matter where they were. What she said didn't make any particular sense to me because, at the time, I had my own project in Bolivar County, Mississippi. A number of other black women also directed their own projects. What Casey and other white women seemed to want was an opportunity to prove they could do something other than office work. I assumed that if they could do something else, they'd probably be doing that.

Washington recognized how hard the work of a project director was, and besides that, "it wasn't much fun." Because of her insider's view, she was at a loss to understand why white women were complaining about their assignments. Their discontent over such issues only convinced Washington "how crazy they [white women] were."[26]

Even as they were conscious of the opposing perspectives of many of their white female colleagues, African American women in the movement were also painfully aware of the differences in the way society viewed them. One black female civil rights worker frankly discussed the resentment. "We've been getting beaten up for years trying to integrate lunch counters, movies, and so on, and nobody has ever paid us no attention or wrote about us. But these white girls come down here for a few months and get all the publicity. Everybody talks about how brave and courageous *they* are. What about us?" Another black female civil rights worker was both angered and amazed. When she was with a group demonstrating at a bus station, "a cop grabbed me by the arm and slapped my face. I don't know why I was surprised, but I really was." She decided to remind him of a basic tenet of southern etiquette. "I looked at him and I say, 'Listen Man, take another look at me. I'm a woman! You don't hit a woman! Didn't they teach you that?' He look kinda sorry, but he say, 'You're a niggah and that's all you are!'" Such a pervasive and negative view was bound to wound black women's sense of themselves. One black female civil rights worker clearly explained how deep those wounds were. White women, she said, did the less glamorous and domestic jobs "in a feminine kind of way, while [black women] . . . were out in the streets battling the cops. So it did something to what [our] femininity was about. We became amazons, less than and more than women at the same time."[27]

African American women's resentment about society's differential treatment of them was further complicated by the issue of physical appearance. Robinson and her African American colleagues came of age in a society that, from its earliest days, had judged African women by a European standard of beauty. Many women of African descent, including Robinson, had only to look in the mirror to see that they could never measure up physically. But many tried, and it was often quite painful.

Zohara Simmons, one of Robinson's SNCC colleagues and a fellow Spelman student, was keenly aware of the European standard of beauty that was idealized by so many. That awareness was born of Simmons's experience on the Spelman campus, a place famous for the "beauty" of its student body. Translation: A fairly high proportion of the students had light skin, keen features, and straight or nearly straight hair. Simmons explained the prevailing view at Spelman in the early sixties.

> First of all, the best of all possible worlds is that you are light as you can be, you have green eyes, or light brown, and you have long straight hair. They [Morehouse students] would be lined up outside your door, trying to get a date. Then you could be paper bag brown or above and have long hair that you have to straighten, you know, that's still real cool, right? 'Cause we were all straightening—tough—in those days. Then, of course, you could be darker and have straight hair, long straight hair. . . . Then the last, of the last category was that you were dark-skinned and you had short hair or medium-length hair, you know?[28]

Having physical features that did not measure up to the white standard of beauty could be painful for black women sometimes. Because she was dark-skinned, Simmons learned that the pain was caused less by white reaction than by black rejection. She insisted, "Some of the Morehouse guys were so nasty to a person who looked like myself. *Overt.* I mean, straight up."[29] Appearance was important, but black women were powerless to change their appearance, at least permanently. Feelings of insecurity about their looks were a terrible burden that African American women were forced to bear. Ruby Doris Smith Robinson had to carry her share of this black women's burden because she was not particularly light-skinned, she had broad features, and her hair was not naturally straight. Like so many African American women of her generation, she wrestled with negative views of who and what she was—views that were popularized by white society and then embraced, at least in part, by black society.

Thus the relationship between black female SNCC staffers and their white female activist colleagues was influenced by black female resentment about American society's history of negative perceptions and treatment of them. At the same time, however, the attitudes of white females also contributed to tension between black females and themselves. American white people, even sympathetic female activists, had all been touched to a greater or lesser extent by the negative black stereotypes so popular in their society. Psychiatrist Alvin Poussaint, in his evaluation of the adjustment of white women volunteers to the rigors of Freedom Summer, found that a number of these women were indeed struggling with racist stereotypes. In Poussaint's estimation, some of them lost that struggle. He identified a syndrome he labeled the White African Queen Complex.

> At the center of this "complex" is probably a tabooed and repressed fantasy of the intelligent, brave, and beautiful white woman leading the poor, downtrodden, and oppressed black man to freedom and salvation. One white female worker told me she sometimes felt like "the master's child come to free the slaves." Another confided, "What an electrifying feeling it is to be worshipped by the Negroes."[30]

Black women bitterly resented this attitude and the condescending behavior that accompanied it.

A further complicating factor in this white female–black female conflict was the issue of class. Many of the white women who worked in the civil rights movement were middle-class or even upper-middle-class. On the other hand, many of the African American activists, including Robinson, were from families with middle-class aspirations but only working-class incomes. Some of these black women had faced very difficult economic circumstances during their lives. Consequently, when middle-class white women doing office work began to complain about being oppressed, Robinson and other black women like her simply lost their patience. Joyce Ladner recalled tense times in the office.

> The impression Ruby conveyed was that . . . white women were always at kind of uneasy peace around her. She didn't mistreat them, but they sure didn't pull that . . . on her. She was the last person they would run to with some complaint about, "Oh, we're poor oppressed, we're poor oppressed white women here. . . ." She'd been in jail and was from a poor background herself. So it was hard for her to have sympathy for a girl from Sarah Lawrence who felt put upon.[31]

Some in the movement charged that even though a preponderance of the white women on the permanent staff were limited to office work, they tried to exert too much influence. Regardless of its accuracy, this perception helped to intensify the conflict. Joyce Ladner clearly recalled this notion. "See, a lot of white women who came into SNCC even though they felt they were discriminated against, in quotes, . . . they still tried to dominate the office. I mean it was a matter of [not] being content anywhere—[even] if you put them in the field. They were white women; that's all that was necessary to know about them."[32] Because Robinson was such a critical part of the central office staff, she found herself in the middle of this complex of feelings and resentments plaguing both black and white women. In retrospect, at least one white female staff member in SNCC understood why Robinson and the other black women were so suspicious. "If I were to put myself in Ruby Doris's head, what I would say is, you know, 'Here comes Dinky Romilly, here comes Mary King. Why are they here? They don't have any intrinsic interest in promoting the rights of black people. They're middle-class white women. . . .' And I can understand that . . . she would be very suspect of that."[33]

In such an atmosphere Robinson exerted her increasing authority. She had to cope with a variety of attitudes, resentments, and behaviors exhibited by white women staff members. At the same time, she had to balance these against the resentments and perceptions of the black women on the staff. In the midst of this she was still dragging around her share of the black woman's burden as she sought to cope with the historical and recent negative assessments of black female morality, femininity, physical appearance, and capabilities.

As Robinson wrestled with questions of femininity and black female–white female tensions, her life was complicated by still another factor. In addition to being a full-time freedom fighter, Ruby Doris Smith Robinson was also a wife and a mother. She married Clifford Robinson in 1964 and gave birth to a son, Kenneth Toure, in 1965. Even though she was totally committed to the movement, her family obligations were also important to her. One of her close movement friends, Mildred Forman, remembered that Robinson was "ecstatic over the baby and the husband." Even though Robinson was already extraordinarily busy with her work in SNCC, Forman felt that motherhood further enriched her life: "I think that was the best thing that could have happened to her, because she just . . . beamed and glowed with the baby." Although motherhood added a unique richness, it also added tasks to Robinson's already overburdened schedule. As she juggled motherhood and movement work, at times the frantic pace of her life caught up with her. Movement colleague and friend Freddie Greene Biddle clearly recalled an incident that graphically illustrated how overwhelming things sometimes became.

> I remember once Ruby came out [of her house] with all these bags and her pocketbook and all this stuff, and we're going to the office, and she's going to drop, uh, Toure . . .

off. . . . Well she's backing out of the . . . driveway and I'm in the car. . . . She had all these bags and stuff and so then all of a sudden she said, "Oh shit!" [I] said "What's wrong?" She's forgotten the baby![34]

As Robinson settled into motherhood, she was still struggling to find a balance between her marital and movement duties. Her husband, Clifford, was also a SNCC staff member. Despite his membership in the organization, however, Clifford's commitment paled in comparison to Ruby's. He freely admitted that he joined the movement only because of his wife's involvement. This disparity in commitment was sometimes the source of a certain amount of tension. Zohara Simmons recalled:

> I can just remember, you know, you run in the office and he's [Clifford] standing there waiting on her to go. And, you know, everybody's saying, "Ruby Doris, so and so and so." And he's saying, "Look, we got to go." And she's saying, "Cliff, wait a minute . . . I got to take care of this." And him stalking off mad. And her saying, "Oh, God . . . later for him, then." I imagine she caught hell when she got home.

But Clifford insisted that the volume of work Ruby did in SNCC did not cause a strain on their relationship, even though "it was going on all the time around the house." Clifford went on to explain, though, that when *he* thought Ruby was doing too much movement work after office hours, "I was there to stop it."[35]

Robinson tried very hard to balance her family relationships and her movement obligations. At the same time, she was confronted by enormous pressures and tensions in SNCC. Her determination and commitment had always given her the strength to cope with all these concerns. As a Freedom Rider, Robinson faced down hostile white mobs. She confronted brutal southern sheriffs and assorted Klan representatives when she canvassed for voter registration. As a powerful leader, Robinson had confronted numerous and strident conflicts in SNCC. But when she was diagnosed with terminal cancer in April 1967, even her strength and determination were not enough. She wanted to continue with the important things in her life: raising her son, caring for her husband, and guiding her beloved Student Nonviolent Coordinating Committee. But the cancer would not let her. Ruby Doris Smith Robinson died on 9 October 1967, at the age of twenty-five.

Many of her SNCC colleagues are convinced that it was not cancer but the frantic pace of her life that killed her. They all remember how Robinson always tried to do everything; her commitment to the civil rights movement did not stop her from trying to be a full-time wife and mother. Furthermore, according to some, the SNCC conflicts were exacerbated because of her gender. It was simply too much for one woman. Despite the conflicts and difficulties that faced her, however, Robinson would not have lived her life any other way. She was a woman who believed that she could and should do it all.

Notes

1. Mary Ann Smith Wilson, interview by author, Atlanta, Ga., 19 November 1989.
2. Ibid.
3. Howard Zinn, *SNCC: The New Abolitionists* (Boston: Beacon Press, 1964), 17.
4. Clayborne Carson, *In Struggle: SNCC and the Black Awakening of the 1960s* (Cambridge: Harvard University Press, 1981), 203.
5. Matthew Jones, interview by author, Knoxville, Tenn., 24 April 1989; Mildred Forman, interview by author, Chicago, Ill., 6 November 1989.
6. Jack Minnis, interview by author, New Orleans, La., 4 November 1990; Stanley Wise, interview by author, Atlanta, Ga., 11 November 1990.

7. Reginald Robinson and Charles Jones, interview by author, McComb, Miss., 28 June 1991; Worth Long, interview by author, Atlanta, Ga., 8 February 1991.

8. Wilson, interview.

9. *Student Voice* 2, February 1961.

10. Wilson, interview.

11. Ruby Doris Smith to Mary Ann Smith, 25 February 1961, in Mary Ann Smith Wilson's private papers, Atlanta, Ga.

12. *Atlanta Inquirer*, 18 March 1961.

13. Carson, *In Struggle*, 230; Mucasa (Willie Ricks), interview by author, Atlanta, Ga., 8 April 1990.

14. Angela Davis, *Women, Race, and Class* (New York: Random House, 1983), 5.

15. Wilson, interview; Robinson and Jones, interview; Courtland Cox, interview by author, Washington, D.C., 16 December 1988; Joanne Grant, interview by author, New Orleans, La., 4 November 1990.

16. Constancia Romilly, interview by author, Atlanta, Ga., 14 June 1991; Curtis Muhammad (Curtis Hayes), interview by author, McComb, Miss., 29 June 1991.

17. Norma June Davis and Lana Taylor Sims, interview by author, Atlanta, Ga., 11 November 1990; Albert Brinson, interview by author, Atlanta, Ga., 10 November 1990.

18. Julian Bond, interview by author, Washington, D.C., 16 December 1988.

19. Michael Sayer, interview by author, New Market, Tenn., 5 May 1990; James Bond, interview by author, Atlanta, Ga., 8 February 1991.

20. Paula Giddings, *When and Where I Enter: The Impact of Black Women on Race and Sex in America* (New York: Morrow, 1984), 290.

21. Ibid., 292.

22. Ibid., 243.

23. Cynthia Washington, "We Started from Different Ends of the Spectrum," *Southern Exposure* 5 (winter 1977): 14.

24. Catherine Smith Robinson and Ruby O'Neal, interview by author, Atlanta, Ga., 3 March 1990.

25. Connie Curry, interview by author, Atlanta, Ga., 10 November 1990.

26. Washington, "We Started from Different Ends," 14.

27. Alvin Poussaint, "The Stresses of the White Female Worker in the Civil Rights Movement in the South," *Journal of American Psychiatry* 123 (October 1966): 403; Josephine Carson, *Silent Voices* (New York: McGraw Hill, 1969), 60; Sara Evans, *Personal Politics: The Roots of Women's Liberation in the Civil Rights Movement and the New Left* (New York: Random House, 1979), 81.

28. Zohara Simmons, interview by author, Philadelphia, Pa., 17 December 1988.

29. Ibid.

30. Poussaint, "The Stresses of the White Female Worker," 404.

31. Joyce Ladner, interview by the author, Washington, D.C., 18 December 1988.

32. Ibid.

33. Romilly, interview.

34. Forman, interview; Freddie Greene Biddle, interview by author, McComb, Miss., 29 June 1991.

35. Simmons, interview; Clifford Robinson, interview by author, Atlanta, Ga., 17 March 1989.

35

To Become an American Woman: Education and Sex Role Socialization of the Vietnamese Immigrant Woman

Gail Paradise Kelly

In late April 1975, 129,000 Vietnamese immigrated to the United States. Before being allowed to settle in this country, they were held in four camps in the United States: Camp Pendleton in California, Fort Chaffee in Arkansas, Eglin Air Force Base in Florida, and Fort Indian Town Gap in Pennsylvania. At the camps, the immigrants received medical examinations and applied for and awaited entry visas. American authorities, aware that many of the refugees had little exposure to American life, took this waiting time, which for many was about six months, to "introduce" the Vietnamese to the country, and teach them behavior deemed minimally necessary for living in an American social setting. Within each refugee camp were scores of programs to do precisely this. They consisted of formal and informal programs, some designed to teach the English language, others offering advice on child rearing and medical care, and still others counseling Vietnamese on how to keep houses clean, buy clothes, and so on. These programs are the focus of this paper. I shall analyze how the camps' formal and informal education programs attempted to mold Vietnamese women into roles thought consonant with American culture, but at variance with ones these women had assumed within the Vietnamese family and society.

Women's Roles in Vietnam

Most Vietnamese women, immigrant and nonimmigrant alike, worked for a living. (Only 14 percent of women refugees reported their occupations as "housewife.")[1] This was just as true of urban, middle-class women as of peasant women or the urban poor. Peasant women worked the land with their families for survival; they also brought in cash income from petty trading. During the 1920s and 1930s rural markets were filled with women selling prepared food, dogs, handicrafts, and the like—usually to other Vietnamese.[2] In villages depending on fishing, women earned a living either in fishing, marketing fish, producing other foodstuffs on household plots, or handicrafts. Poverty obliterated sex role divisions that occurred in richer Vietnamese families. Within upper-class families, however, except among urbanized, Westernized groups, women tended not to be part of economic life. They were sheltered within the household, and their sole function was to produce male heirs for the continuity of the corporate family.

The distinction between women's roles among classes changed drastically as a result of twenty years of warfare and inflation in Vietnam.[3] Peasant women continued, as before, to work as farmers, traders, or craftspeople to sustain the family. Petty trade items changed, as many began to sell Coca-Colas and other Western manufactured items siphoned from American stores. The war, especially after 1964, forced urbanization. Strategic hamlets, the establishment of free-fire zones, defoliation programs, search-and-destroy missions, and programs such as Phoenix, which assassinated countless villagers thought to be Vietcong, made the countryside uninhabitable. Cities such as Saigon, Hue, and Da Nang swelled; Saigon alone tripled its population between 1962 and 1975. Changes in locale brought changes in peasant women's occupations and intensified the pressures of subsistence. Peasant women became bar girls, prostitutes, laundresses, and maids and continued as petty traders in Coca-Cola, cigarettes, liquor and beer, and drugs to urban Vietnamese and the military, both American and Vietnamese. Further, as the toll in death and mutilation among men, mostly of the lower classes who could not afford to buy their way out of military service, increased, women frequently became the sole support of their families, either as heads of households or as the only persons capable of earning a living.[4]

The war appreciably altered the role of middle-class women by bringing incredible inflation to urban areas, which obliterated the buying power of men supporting their families. The American press wrote much about how this inflation led to widespread corruption, including bribery and theft from American military warehouses. Corruption was one outgrowth of the inflation; another result was extensive moonlighting. Men such as Mr. D., whom I interviewed at length, a professor of English at Saigon University, worked three other jobs trying to live in the style to which he and his family were accustomed. Additionally, in his family—and, he claimed, in others of his class in Saigon—not even five male family members working full time at several jobs could produce adequate income. Thus his mother, who, he said, had before 1964 tended solely to the household, began working. She opened a "knitting factory" in the house during the days, employing his sisters, sisters-in-law, and aunts. She had to do this despite the fact that her husband was a highly placed government official, one of her sons was a colonel in the Vietnamese army, another was a businessman, and yet another was a customs official. Other urban families underwent similar experiences, which undermined traditional sex roles within the family and the economy. The war, in short, changed women's roles in all classes. Women became an integral part of the Vietnamese economy, often working as the sole support of the family.

While women's roles within the family changed dramatically as a result of the war, families, themselves survived. The vast majority of Vietnamese who immigrated to the United States came as families. Few refugees, male or female, came alone. Of the 5,849 women who were processed at Fort Indian Town Gap, only 53 immigrated without relations.[5] Further, those families that came usually spanned three generations, and included brothers and sisters and their children, as well as grandparents. Several of these families had over a hundred members. Motivations for leaving Vietnam also reflected the persistence of the family as the basic unit in Vietnamese life. Many refugees whom I interviewed said they immigrated because they feared the new Vietnamese government would harm them because a relative had worked for the Americans.[6]

Vietnamese refugee women, then, were connected to families. Their roles, in reality and by self-definition, were not that of housewife, nor did those roles arise from Confucian notions of womanhood, as camp officials and many Americans working with refugees believed. Occupationally, the majority did not fit into American job categories. For the most part, as I will show in this article, it was assumed that in America they would take on the role of housewife and mother, consistent with American conceptions of sex-role behavior. This was not only assumed but enforced; educational efforts in the camps, including English-language classes, vocational courses, cultural orientation meetings, and printed materials circulated in the camps, were almost without exception directed at resocializing these women into American stereotypic roles.[7]

Adult Education: New Language, New Roles

Within the refugee camps there were two types of organized classroom instruction for adults: English classes and vocational training, both run by professional educators under contract from the U.S. Department of Health, Education, and Welfare (HEW). The "school" had but one purpose—to make Vietnamese more "sponsorable." Under the Indochina Refugee Act, Vietnamese could officially enter the United States only if they had a cash reserve of four thousand dollars per person or if an American family, group, or organization was willing to assume moral and financial responsibility for the immigrant, either as an individual or as a family, for three years. The responsibilities were such that most Americans were reluctant to assume them unless it was clear that those they sponsored would be self-supporting in a relatively short time. The key to being self-supporting was not only that refugees have skills marketable in the United States, but that the refugees be able to speak English, to enable them to get jobs working with and for Americans. About 50 percent of the refugees could speak some English; of these, only about half could carry on a conversation in English.[8]

Camp authorities therefore placed great emphasis, when the refugee camps opened, on language classes for the refugees. Using HEW funds, they contracted with local agencies (in the case of Fort Indian Town Gap, the Pennsylvania State Department of Education; at Fort Chaffee, Fort Smith Community College; at Camp Pendleton, the San Diego County school system) to set up formal instruction, using volunteers wherever possible rather than paid professionals as teachers. Instruction was centered on "survival" English, that is, on teaching only those English skills considered minimally necessary for functioning in the United States. It was directed only to *heads* of households. The decision to teach only heads of households meant that women and children were excluded from class. Camp authorities, school administrators, and teachers believed that men would support their families and women would care for the family at home. The classes, twenty-six in all, were initially flooded with Vietnamese of both sexes and all ages—and were too large to allow adequate individual work on English pronunciation. Thus women and children were told to leave.

This led to a large controversy at Indian Town Gap between the Pennsylvania Commission for Women, which assumed the role of advocate for immigrant women, and school and camp personnel. The latter justified their policies on several grounds: first, they argued that men, not women, would be breadwinners and therefore should have priority; second, that permitting women in class would disrupt the Vietnamese family. Women, they said, might learn the language faster than men, the men would "lose face" because of this, and this in turn, would lead to marital conflicts and divorce. Further, they argued that there were other types of classes for women that would suitably adjust them to American life: classes in birth control, child care, sewing, and cooking, as well as, after September, the Pennsylvania Commission for Women sessions called "Women in America."[9] In short, American sex-role stereotypes were imposed by determining who could go to English class. This broke down several months later as more refugees left the camps and space became available to women.

English classes taught more than language. They were designed to teach immigrants how to live in America, and this involved teaching sex-role behavior. This was clear in the curricular materials used in class, the conduct of class, and teacher attitudes. It was explicit in interviews I had with school personnel.

Two types of curricular materials were used in teaching English at Fort Indian Town Gap: The HEW-developed "Survival" English course, and, as a supplement, the Macmillan 900 English-language texts. The Survival English course, taught at three levels, had sixteen lessons that covered topics such as meeting strangers, finding a place to live, occupations, renting apartments, shopping, "John's interest," and applying for jobs.[10] The first lesson began with greetings and sex identifications. Students were drilled on phrases such as "Hello," "Good afternoon," "My name is . . . " "I'm a man," "I'm a woman," "I'm a boy," "I'm a girl, " "Do you speak English?" Subsequent vocabulary included locations of lavatories, days of the week, numbers, food, time, and job titles. Once vocabulary was introduced as words, lessons centered on the pattern of sentences and conversations. In all but two of the sixteen lessons, the conversations took place between "Mr. Brown" and "Mr. Jones," with Mr. Brown responding to Mr. Jones's questions. For example, Mr. Jones (no doubt the refugee) inquired, in the lesson on numbers, how he might go about buying a house. In the lesson on occupations, Mr. Jones asked what kind of job he might get to support his wife and two children. Mr. Jones said he could work as a room clerk, salesman, cashier, laborer, plumber, bricklayer, cook, cleaning person, secretary, typist, seamstress, or nurse's aide. Women appeared in the dialogues in only two instances: in a lesson on budgeting and shopping, and in a lesson called "Conversation." Both are explicit in delineating male/female roles. In the conversation Miss Jones becomes part of the drill in two places—with the pattern sentence "Miss Jones missed the bus to the Miss Universe competition" and "She is an attractive girl."[11] In the shopping sequences, all levels of English classes made it clear that women could shop only for small items. In the basic classes, teaching persons who knew no English, Mrs. Brown shopped for dresses, shoes, food, aspirin, baby needs, and cosmetics; Mr. Brown, on the other hand, shopped for shirts, houses, cars, and furniture.[12] In the advanced classes this division of labor between the sexes was expanded. "Marie" (no doubt the advanced classes' equivalent of Mrs. Brown) compared prices on food and other commodities, thereby saving her husband *his* hard-earned money. She was wise and would buy nothing but food without consulting her husband, Tim. In the lesson she found out where the cheapest sofa and sewing machine in town could be bought, but took her husband to the stores to decide for them where they should make their purchases.[13]

The Macmillan English Language 900 series, used as a supplement to the Survival English course, was not written specifically for Vietnamese refugees. It is a series of texts designed for non-English-speakers, be they Italian, Arab, Chinese, German, or French. These texts, interestingly enough, are quite different from the materials devised specifically for Vietnamese. Women are not absent in the text, nor so inactive. They travel, they work, go to the doctor, shop, ask questions. Despite this, the roles portrayed for women are quite limited. In unit 1, book 3 (for intermediate students), for example, Judy talks with John about buying a new sofa, not because it is needed, but because it's pretty and a bargain.[14] In unit 2 Barbara and Ella talk about baking a cake for Harry, while Frank and Tom discuss hammers and nails; in unit 4 marriage is discussed, as are bridal dresses; in unit 5 Mr. James buys a house, and Mabel has coffee klatches with her new neighbors; in unit 8, on health and sickness, Dr. Smith and his female nurse give Mrs. Adams advice on her children's health and Mr. Lewis advice on his own health; in unit 9, mother puts the kids to bed and wakes them up while father goes off to work.[15] Designed primarily to teach English, the readers tended to focus less on sex-role depictions than on teaching first- and second-person patterns of speech. "I-you" is more apparent in the text than "he-she."

English-language classes, in short, transmitted, as do many American texts used in schools, stereotypical roles. Women were noticeably absent in class materials. When they appeared, their qualities were reduced to beauty and interest in it, and their roles were that of wife and mother, particularly shopper. It is interesting to note that in the Survival English course, designed specifically for Vietnamese refugees, occupations reserved for American women (typist, seamstress, nurse's aide) were presented as jobs for Vietnamese men. Not only were the programs allocating Vietnamese men into lower-class women's occupations, but they also presented immigrant men with nonoccupational roles traditionally reserved for U.S. women—it is Mr. Jones, in the Survival English course, who finds out where stores are, gets a doctor, selects a church, locates the children's school, and so on. In the Survival English materials, women ventured out of the house only to shop.

While the sex bias evident in the Macmillan 900 series may be unconscious—publishers of children's books and school texts in the United States have explained their past practices in this way—this was not the case in camp-prepared materials. Many camp officials and school personnel were gravely concerned about the stability of the immigrant family and the consequences for individuals and the social order should the Vietnamese family disintegrate. (Some veterans of the Agency for International Development working in the camps believed this had already happened under the stress of the war and was the reason the South Vietnamese government fell. They were determined to reconstruct what they thought was the traditional Vietnamese family among the immigrants, believing this to be the only way for them to survive in America.) Schoolteachers, curriculum coordinators, and administrative and resettlement personnel emphasized time after time the role of education in reinforcing the Vietnamese family and the supremacy of the father, which they assumed was characteristic of both Vietnamese and American families. It was thought that only through the reinforcement and/or reestablishment of patriarchal relations could immigrants "adjust" well to America. And, as the curriculum coordinator of the adult school pointed out to me in one of our lengthy interviews, the school's role was not just to teach English; its mission was to help its students "adjust" to America and live happily there.[16]

The teaching materials were not the only elements in formal English instruction that attempted to rob Vietnamese women of their social and economic roles and put Vietnamese men into lower-class and "female" jobs. In-class instruction also worked in such a manner. An incident in an English class designed for illiterates illustrates this best. This class had more women in it than any other class I observed at Fort Indian Town Gap. (The other classes appeared to be predominantly male; advanced English classes had almost no women in them.) Because the students were illiterate, written materials could not be used. The six-week course had only three units: parts of the body and their names, foods, and jobs. All this was constructed by the teachers with the assistance of the curriculum coordinator. Vocabulary was introduced by pointing to an object or a picture of it and learning the English name for it. When pictures or objects were not available, charade was used. In one class the teacher clucked and flapped his arms like a chicken to introduce the term *chicken*. He then drilled the class on the phrase, "I want some chicken to eat."[17]

The major emphasis in the classroom was on occupations—teaching Vietnamese refugees how to describe their work skills to prospective employers. In class the teacher began with the phrase, "What kind of work do you do?" He then drew stick figures showing different kinds of work—ditch-digging, selling, and so on, naming them all. After introducing phrases like "I am a ditch digger; I am a mechanic," he asked each of his thirty or more students, "What kind of work do you do?" The first student to respond was a young man, obviously a former soldier. He responded by imitating a gun with his fingers and replied, "I rat-a-tat-tat." The teacher corrected him with, "I work with my hands." Next to recite was a middle-aged woman who had lacquered teeth (indicating she came from a rural, lower-class family). She made a motion that looked like casting nets (I found out later she came from coastal Vung-Tau and fished for a living). The teacher responded with, "I am a housewife." The woman looked puzzled. The teacher then drew a stick figure on the blackboard representing a woman with a broom in her hand, inside a house. He repeated "I am a housewife," pointing to the woman. She and the women sitting with her began a lively discussion in Vietnamese and started laughing. The teacher then drilled all the women as a group repeatedly with the phrase "I am a housewife."[18]

English classes were the major formal education provided within the refugee camps. The adult school, however, did offer vocational courses in electricity, plumbing, carpentry, and home economics. All except the home economics class were simultaneously classes in English terminology appropriate to the skills immigrants already possessed. Perhaps this explains the poor attendance at the classes; only five or ten students came regularly. The home economics class, conducted in English without a translator, was the only vocational class that taught skills rather than terminology. It was designed primarily for women, to teach them how to use and maintain appliances found in American homes (electric stoves, refrigerators, mixers, and blenders); how to shop in supermarkets; how to tell the difference between nonprepackaged and prepackaged foods and their nutritional values; and how to cook American-style (to make chili, pickled beets, gingerbread, Jell-o molds, and so on). Attendance at class averaged seven persons, none of whom spoke English.

Formal education in schools was but one means by which immigrants were prepared for living in America. Within the refugee camps, outside the school, similar efforts occurred. The Pennsylvania Commission for Women, believing that the school and camp authorities were inadequately preparing women for life in America, set up a series of programs called "Women in America" to rectify these deficiencies—much to the chagrin, I might add, of camp authorities and school personnel.

"Women in America": A Counter to English Classes?

"Women in America" represented to some extent an alternative to the kind of sex-role socialization evident in the English-language classes. Those who designed it firmly believed in women's rights and fluidity of sex roles, and that Vietnamese women were in a stage of bondage similar to that in nineteenth-century China.[19] The program coordinator, an American woman in her late twenties, had lived for several years in Taiwan, Hong Kong, and Japan and saw the Vietnamese family and women's roles within it in light of her limited observations abroad. To her, it was only recently that these women had stopped having their feet bound. According to her, their role was only to produce male heirs for the family and to accede to their mother-in-law's and husband's wishes within the household where they were confined. She told me that camp authorities, through their educational programs and their practices (specifically the practice of not intervening in known cases of wife beating at Indian Town Gap), reinforced Vietnamese women's traditional roles, which, she believed, were both oppressive and impractical in America.[20] The "Women in America" programs, thus, were set up to explain to immigrant women their roles and rights in the United States.

"Women in America" was initially designed as a series of meetings dealing topically with life in the American family, women's rights (the right to hold property, abortion, birth control, and so on), women at work, and organizations that assist women in whatever they choose to do. What was planned as a series of meetings became six single-evening presentations covering basically the same ground each time. This occurred because few of the same people came to more than one session, either because they had found sponsors and left the camps, or because of lack of interest or difficulty in finding someone to care for their children.

The content of the classes varied in minor ways at each meeting, depending on responses to them. At several meetings discussion centered on snow or shopping, as women, excluded from English-language classes, sought out information about America in general and took the opportunity to meet Americans and ask questions that intrigued them most. Generally, the class organizers tried to cover four topics—family life, women's rights, jobs for women, and women's organizations—each night before allowing refugees to change the subject. The four main topics were presented by four women from the Pennsylvania Commission for Women, who spoke in English with simultaneous translation into Vietnamese. The first speaker covered the family. Her presentation stressed men's participation in housework and child care and was accompanied by pictures of men bathing children, doing dishes, shopping, and so on. There were almost no pictures of women engaged in these tasks. The second presentation told women they had a right to abortion on demand and could divorce their husbands, vote, own property, and work if they chose to. It stressed women's right to plan family size, and said that two children was the desirable number for happy families. The third presentation was on jobs. It told Vietnamese women that while some American women worked, some chose not to work. With the aid of photographs, the speaker surveyed the world of work for women, showing photos of women as bulldozer operators, nurses, teachers, librarians, salesclerks, karate teachers, engineers, corporate presidents, and so on. The person giving the presentation paused when she showed the picture of a nurse at work, and told the class that it was an excellent occupation for women. At this point, a middle-aged immigrant asked if women could be butchers. The response given was that the presenter knew of no woman butchers in America. The final talk was on women's organizations. This was primarily a detailed enumeration of groups such as the YWCA, Planned Parenthood, the National Welfare Rights Organization, and the League of Women Voters.[21]

These classes did indeed present women's roles and work in quite a different light than did other formal education within the camps. Unlike the English-language classes, women were depicted outside the home, with the possibility of financial independence. The series, however, did not have as much an impact as the English-language classes, for no more than thirty-persons attended the meetings each night. Several of those who attended were men who, in the discussions following the presentations, made speeches claiming that men in America had no rights at all. The impact of the programs was all the more limited because there was no real incentive for refugees to attend them or take them seriously. Camp authorities and teachers openly disapproved of the meetings, and ran movies and English classes during the times they were scheduled. Further, camp authorities made it clear to refugees that only by learning English would they adjust well to America. By September, when the "Women in America" series began, area commanders, who were responsible for barrack sections of the camps, pressured adults into going to English-language classes; they did not exert any such pressure for persons to attend the other series. Apparently they resented the classes because they believed "Women in America" would disrupt the Vietnamese family, make Vietnamese men anxious about resettling in America and having to cope with aggressive women, and in the long run would make camp authorities' task more difficult.[22]

The Written Word

A discussion of sex-role socialization for Vietnamese refugees in the camps would be incomplete without considering other parts of camp life. Refugees learned about American life every day by shopping at the camp (usually done by men); going to the various recreation centers in the camp; watching nightly movies; hanging around resettlement agency offices, chatting with American soldiers and refugee workers about snow, Montana, dating, and hot dogs; and reading Vietnamese-language materials circulated within the camp. The most widely circulated and read material at Fort Indian Town Gap was *Dat Lanh* (Good Land), the daily bilingual camp newspaper published by the U.S. Army Psychological Operations Unit. *Dat Lanh* was not merely a news sheet summarizing national, international, and camp events; it was also a journal intended to supplement the work of schools in preparing Vietnamese to live in America. It was the only bilingual reading material at Indian Town Gap, other than camp notices and government documentary information.

Dat Lanh, which began publication on 28 May 1975, carried three types of articles: camp announcements (meeting and meal times, lists of incoming refugees, notices of sponsorships available to refugees, barrack rules, immigration laws), how-to articles (work a telephone, register for a sponsor, buy a car), and informational articles about the United States and its culture. The informational pieces about the United States will be the focus of this section, for in them the newspaper spelled out social behavior expected of persons living in the United States. The informational articles were of two broad types: American history and geography, designed to teach the basics of patriotic identification; and information on social behavior. The history and geography articles appeared almost daily. They consisted of atlas-type descriptions of each of the fifty states and the lives of American presidents. On holidays *Dat Lanh* ran two- or three-page stories explaining the significance of the day, particularly Memorial Day, Flag Day, the Fourth of July, Labor Day, Armed Forces Day, Halloween, and Thanksgiving.

The articles on social behavior were in keeping with the sex–role molding of the English-language classes. Most of these articles, all called "The American Way of Life," were addressed to heads of households, presumably male, and explained tipping in restaurants (when the man takes his family out), getting insurance for *his* car and family, buying *his* family clothes, cars, and houses, and so on. Following these articles were short tips on pregnancy, child care, child health, toys, and so on, addressed to mothers. A front-page article on 31 July for example, was entitled "Attention Mothers," and described mothers' duties in getting health care for their children. Articles of this nature assumed sex-role divisions for the Vietnamese family along stereotypical lines. Other articles openly promoted such sex roles as crucial for Vietnamese to follow if they wished to get along in this country. For example, a *Dat Lanh* front-page article on 7 September 1975 entitled "Men and Women" advised men to take their wives on trips, rise when a woman enters the room, open doors for women, help them push revolving doors since they are not strong enough to push them themselves, pay bills at restaurants, buy tickets, and so on. Further, it told them not to be "frightened" by American women who seem "noisy, aggressive, dominating," and reassured them that most women in America are "quiet, content and gentle" and enjoy being taken care of. The following two issues carried articles on single women's behavior. One of them counseled women on how to find single men. It advised them to join sports clubs, or photography or ballroom dancing classes. Girls should not ask men out, it continued. "In this country the man . . . does the inviting and the planning." The article then pointed out that girls could ask men to their homes for dinner if they really wanted to impress them.

Education, Role Imposition, and Role Reality

This article has described educational efforts directed at Vietnamese immigrants to the United States in one resettlement camp, Fort Indian Town Gap, Pennsylvania, particularly the sex-role behavior taught through both formal and informal education designed for adults. The roles suggested for women had little correspondence with roles Vietnamese had historically assumed in their own country. Through circumstances of social class, war, and inflation, almost all Vietnamese women had worked to support their families, and through their economic contribution they had gained a degree of power within the family, often serving as heads of families. They were not confined to cooking, cleaning, shopping, and child rearing. The education in the camps proposed to take these women out of the workplace and put them back in the home. Access to English classes, initially restricted to adult males, meant that the women were deprived of an opportunity to enter the American workplace. It was men, not women, who were to be taught the language and how to fill out job applications. Women's education was initially confined to birth control, child care, and maternity classes, conducted in Vietnamese, and home economics classes, none of which involved preparation for life outside the house and the family.

When women entered English-language classes that were key to entering the American economy, they found class materials that relegated them to roles in their homes—for women could only shop and budget and marry. They were not expected to work for a living, even though most Vietnamese women had; nor to make decisions. "I am a housewife" was the only role model offered, and that role model was presented in such a manner as to imply that assuming such a role was required for living in America. This role socialization was deliberate. Americans, teachers and camp officials alike, believed in the primacy of the family and women's place as housekeeper. Despite their insistence on teaching these roles, they claimed that such relationships were intrinsically Vietnamese, and that retaining such "Vietnameseness" would facilitate immigrants' adjustment to the country.

Even the camps' definition of "the family" was somewhat of an anomaly, given the way Vietnamese families were broken up through resettlement. Americans defined the family as nuclear rather than extended, and resettled only nuclear families as units. Thus nuclear families within Vietnamese extended families could be settled at different ends of the continent. The solidarity of the Vietnamese family, which depended far more on the trigenerational extended unit than it did upon male supremacy, was therefore not especially preserved.

The Pennsylvania Commission for Women and its representatives, while scarcely able to speak for refugees as a whole or for Vietnamese women in particular, tried to offer a different view of American life for Vietnamese women and their possible role within it. To some extent, their view was more realistic about changes necessary to survive. Vietnamese were being resettled in an American society in an economic recession, during which there were few jobs available to Americans, let alone to immigrants who barely spoke English and possessed few skills. Jobs for which most refugees were qualified were among the lowest-paying in the society. Under American definitions of the nuclear family, the Vietnamese family averaged seven persons. Men working as day laborers and nurse's aides were not likely to earn enough to sustain an entire family, so that women would be forced to work, either to supplement family income or as the sole source of family income. A year after the camps closed, 73 percent of the immigrants who had once been professionals, technicians, managers, and businessmen found themselves blue-collar workers; another 17 percent became clerical and sales personnel. Only 10 percent went into jobs equivalent to those they had held in Vietnam. Most worked in jobs paying minimum wages; many of these jobs were temporary. Yearly incomes were so low that close to 50 percent of all Vietnamese families in the United States received some form of welfare.

While the camp educational programs were a point of entry for Vietnamese into the society and culture of Americans, they did not serve this purpose equally for men and women. Rather, they prepared only Vietnamese men for integration into the U.S. workforce and society. Vietnamese women were not the focus of integrational efforts. "Women in America" alone tried to prepare the women for entry into the U.S. workforce. However, like the other educational efforts, this program impinged upon Vietnamese culture and set U.S. terms for Vietnamese adjustment to the society. The educational programs also fostered the lowering of Vietnamese expectations by preparing men for occupations usually reserved for women in U.S. society. While preparing men for women's roles, they also positioned Vietnamese men to usurp women's roles within the family. The schools taught Vietnamese men to take care of schooling, medical care, shopping, and the like.

English-language programs, *Dat Lanh*, and even the "Women in America" programs, regardless of their points of disagreement, were all directed toward getting Vietnamese to enter the society and culture of Americans regardless of their desires. Most Vietnamese were ambivalent about becoming integrated into American society; they opposed the U.S. resettlement policy, openly expressing their desire to remain Vietnamese within the United States. Of this, Americans were well aware. Article after article in *Dat Lanh* derided Vietnamese unwillingness to leave the "Little Vietnams" of the camps and become Americans. After the camps closed, Vietnamese opposition to U.S. resocialization policies became overt, as they abandoned their original places of resettlement and left the diaspora designed for them, to form their own Vietnamese communities.[23]

Notes

Research for this paper was made possible by grants from the University of Buffalo Foundation; State University of New York at Buffalo Institutional Funds; the SUNY Foundation; and the New York State Council for the Humanities.

1. These statistics are taken from "Refugee Demographic Characteristics," Camp Pendleton, 16 September 1975 (mimeo); "Refugee Statistical Data," Fort Indian Town Gap, Pennsylvania, November 1975 (mimeo).
2. My discussion of women's roles is based on Ngo Vinh Long, ed., *Vietnamese Women in Society and Revolution*, vol. 1, *The French Colonial Period* (Cambridge: Vietnam Resource Center, 1974), and to a lesser extent on Arlene Eisen Bergman, *Women of Vietnam* (San Francisco: People's Press, 1974), and Ngo Tat To, *When the Light Is Out* (Manor: Foreign Languages Publishing House, 1960).
3. Changes in women's roles are discussed in Bergman, *Women of Vietnam*; Tiziano Terzani, *Giai Phong: The Fall and Liberation of Saigon* (New York: St. Martin's Press, 1976). Several interviews I conducted at Fort Indian Town Gap also detailed these changes, particularly: interview with Melvin R. Chapman, area coordinator, Area 5B, Fort Indian Town Gap, Pennsylvania, November 1975 (Mr. Chapman had served with USAID in Vietnam from 1967 to 1975); interview with Duc-Ting-Nguyen, teacher's aide and former university teacher, Fort Indian Town Gap, Pennsylvania, 30 October 1975; interview with Dr. Dao, Chief, Family Planning Clinic, Fort Indian Town Gap, Pennsylvania, October 1975.
4. Interview with Duc-Ting-Nguyen.
5. "Refugee Statistical Data," Fort Indian Town Gap.
6. Interview with Dr. Dao; interview with X (a Vietnamese woman of thirty-five), 26 September 1975, Fort Indian Town Gap; interview with Nguyen-Ngoc-Bich, 15 October 1975; interview with Nguyen Thank Viet, 15 October 1975.
7. My analysis is based on four sources, all obtained in extensive fieldwork at the refugee camps at Fort Indian Town Gap, Pennsylvania, from September to December 1975. These are: (1) curriculum guides, books, and instructional materials used in adult education classes; (2) observations of adult education classes and orientation meetings; (3) interviews with refugee workers, teachers, curriculum specialists, and refugees

who participated in these programs; and (4) an analysis of the contents of *Dat Lanh*, the bilingual daily newspaper of the camp. I believe that the resocialization efforts I observed at Fort Indian Town Gap were quite similar to those at the other refugee centers, since personnel at the camps were remarkably similar and education programs were set up under the supervision of the Department of Health, Education and Welfare and the Indochina Refugee Taskforce in Washington.

8. "Refugee Statistical Data."
9. The school's policy of excluding women from English-language classes initially was discussed in the following interviews: interview with Phyllis Hesser, curriculum coordinator, Adult Education School, Day Program, Fort Indian Town Gap, Pennsylvania, 29 October 1975 and 21 November 1975; interview with Kenneth Adams, superintendent of Schools, Fort Indian Town Gap, Pennsylvania, 25 September 1975; interview with Judy Hansen, Director of Information, Pennsylvania Commission for Women, 29 October 1975.
10. This discussion of English-language curriculum is based on an analysis of survival English materials collected at Fort Indian Town Gap, Pennsylvania (mimeo).
11. Survival English, unit 1, lesson 1, Basic Course (mimeo).
12. Ibid., level II, intermediate, lesson 4, 4.
13. Ibid., advanced English, unit 5, "How to Stretch Your Dollar."
14. English Languages Services, Inc., *English 900, Books 1–3*, 16th ed. (New York: Collier Macmillan, Inc., 1975); book 3, 8.
15. Ibid., book 3, unit 2, 19; unit 4, 38–42; unit 5, 49; unit 8, 77–86; unit 9, 93.
16. This was explicit in interviews with the following people at Fort Indian Town Gap, Pennsylvania: Melvin Chapman; Phyllis Hesser; Jerry Chemiolek, case worker, USCC, 17 October 1975; Peggy Dillon, case worker, USCC, and teacher, Adult Education School, Night Program, 20 November 1975 (she did not agree with this perspective but discussed it at length); Pvt. Richard Lee Blumski, information specialist, U.S. Army, and teacher, Adult Education School, Night Program, 20 November 1975.
17. Classroom observation (taped), Adult Education School, Day Program, Fort Indian Town Gap, Pennsylvania, 30 October 1975.
18. Ibid.
19. Interview with Judy Hansen.
20. Ms. Hansen is not the only person who spoke about camp authorities ignoring wife beating. Melvin Chapman told me in a taped interview that it was camp policy (November 1975).
21. "Women in America," third session, 29 October 1975, Fort Indian Town Gap, Pennsylvania (taped).
22. This attitude was most clearly expressed by Jerry Chemiolek. It was echoed by Phyllis Hessler.
23. Gail P. Kelly, *From Vietnam to America: A Chronicle of the Vietnamese Immigration to the United States* (Boulder: Westview Press, 1978), ch. 7.

36

Changing Women: The Crosscurrents of American Indian Feminine Identity

Rebecca Tsosie

The Blanket Around Her

Maybe it is her birth
which she holds close to herself
or her death
which is just as inseparable
and the white wind
that encircles her is a part
just as
      the blue sky
hanging in turquoise from her neck
oh woman
remember who you are
woman
it is the whole earth

                  —*Joy Harjo*

Laguna novelist Leslie Silko begins *Ceremony* with one word—"Sunrise." The word is simple, yet it encompasses an entire body of culture and thought that revolves around the concepts of birth regeneration, cyclicity, and the union of masculine and feminine elements. Many American Indian worldviews speak of balanced "opposite" forces that combine as a dynamic whole to form the universe. One may extend the metaphor of "sunrise" further in reference to the contemporary "rebirth" of American Indian cultures, perhaps best illustrated in the growing body of literature by American Indian writers. Kenneth Lincoln makes such an analogy in his comprehensive analysis of American Indian literature, *Native American Renaissance*. Interestingly, Lincoln correlates the dynamics of this movement to gender when he writes, "Native Americans are writing prolifically, particularly the women, who correlate feminist, nativist, and artistic commitments in a compelling rebirth."[1]

The "rebirth" is indeed compelling, though perhaps not unexpected. For too long, Indian women have suffered the burden of Euro-American stereotypes. Following the traditional European perceptions of Indian people as "noble savages" or, worse, as "bloodthirsty savages," Indian women have been cast into a similarly bifurcated role: the "noble princess" (Pocahontas) or the more "savage squaw," a loathsome, unintelligent drone. Countless Hollywood epics and dime novels have ingrained these stereotypes in American minds, and even today Indian women are frequently approached in terms of these stereotypes.

Importantly, then, contemporary Indian women writers are speaking out against these stereotypes and affirming their own concepts of femininity and "Indianness." Their artistic expressions frequently lean toward traditional beliefs, deeply rooted in the spiritual essence of tribal worldviews; at other times the same writers speak with an essential understanding of contemporary reality—"Indian" bars, urban ghettos, Ph.D. programs, and Oklahoma powwows. In this seemingly contradictory mixture lies the essence of contemporary Indian literature: the active, forceful unity of the dual worlds in which Indian people *must* survive. Paula Allen comments accurately: "From the meeting of the archaic and the contemporary the facts of her life become articulate, and the fact that modern American Indians are both Indian and American becomes very clear."[2]

Perhaps one could say that "American Indian feminine identity" is itself a myth, for the diversity of tribal systems and worldviews is immense, and the thoughts and feelings of Indian women are equally diffuse. However, contemporary Indian women writers have chosen to express both the diversity of Indian people and the centrality of an Indian ethos that emphasizes life, motion, and balance against the polarized madness of Western technology. They have chosen to stress the critical female principle of the universal cycles, and use this natural power to refute the victimization and oppression that characterizes Western patriarchal power structures. By making these choices, these women writers have established a voice and an identity for the Indian woman that are grounded in the realities of the present rather than the stereotypes of the past.

By objectively considering the social history of American Indian people and the autobiographical experiences of Indian women in conjunction with the current literature, a dynamic portrait of social change, cultural resilence, and lasting power emerges for the American Indian woman. This portrait counters the American myth of the Princess and the Squaw with clarity and dignity, and, one can only hope, with finality.

As Patricia Albers notes in the opening chapter of *The Hidden Half*, the male image of the American Indian has always been dominant in the minds of white observers. The "chief" in feathered regalia, the lithe bison hunter poised above the prey—both images recur in American art and film. The Indian woman, eclipsed by such masculine glory, is either omitted entirely or considered in terms of dichotomous stereotypes—the noble princess or the savage squaw. These images of the Indian woman originated with the bifurcated, ethnocentric observations of early European explorers and traders. Their observations stemmed from the European ideology that Alice Kehoe terms "oppositional dualism," or the stratified, hierarchical Western worldview that perceived the universe as polarized and alienated in a set of opposing categories: "civilized" versus "primitive," "male" versus "female," "Christian" versus "pagan."[3] This worldview was manifested in European society through social castes, gender inequality, and the rigid dichotomy between the public or market sphere, and the private or domestic sphere. Predictably, the entire system was transposed onto Indian societies by the early European observers, creating gender splits and inequalities which were previously unknown, and tainting Indian women with a version of the "pure" versus "fallen" woman categorization that had already been applied to European women.

When applied to women of a more "savage" race, as Indian people were considered to be, this moral categorization assumed significantly more harmful proportions. Rayna Green comments on the long-lasting effects of the princess/squaw stereotype in her article "The Pocahontas Perplex: The Image of Indian Women in American Culture." Green traces the "princess" phenomenon back to traditional European ballads about handsome male adventurers and the beautiful "pagan" (Arabian, Far Eastern) princesses who saved them from the wrath of the "savages" (often at their own personal expense). Green believes that this folktale tradition was transferred to America with the Pocahontas tale and subsequent variations of the story, which eventually came to comprise almost a specific genre of American fiction. The princess was defined by her noble, selfless love for a brave white man. But following the European tradition of oppositional dualism, the princess received a negative counterpart, the squaw, who was sullied by actual reference to sexual liaisons with white men.

Naturally, any vestiges of reality inherent in the social history of white-Indian contact became meaningless for the vast majority of Americans, for whom the stereotypes became "truth." The princess/squaw dichotomy does not even approach the historical realities of Indian women, and may be more closely paralleled with what Rayna Green terms the "virgin/whore paradox" in regard to European women. The primary factor in perceptions of both European women and Indian women became their definition in terms of their relationship with *males*. The Puritan ethic accorded the European woman some status for being a dutiful wife and mother: faithful, submissive, pious, and hardworking. "Bad" women blatantly displayed the opposite traits: promiscuity, assertiveness, disregard for Christian precepts, laziness. It is notable that, whether "good" or "bad," European women were expected to remain confined to the private sphere of love, sex, marriage, and childbirth. Only men could become involved in the public sphere of politics, warfare, and Church authority.[4]

Although the same social dichotomy has been applied to Native American groups from first contact to twentieth-century anthropological studies, the distinction between public and private spheres, not to mention gender role differentiation, often becomes meaningless when applied to traditional Indian systems. As the studies of *The Hidden Half* emphasize, and Paula Allen affirms in *The Sacred Hoop*, gender roles were often flexible and adaptive in traditional Indian cultural systems. Perhaps the most dangerous characteristic of European gender categorizations is the tendency to *rank* duties into hierarchical layers of status, thereby ascribing notions of inferiority to women's domestic duties and superiority to men's roles in politics and warfare. Such value judgments invariably stem from assumptions of the universal attributes of the male-female relationship.[5] Although clearly many Indian societies did subscribe to a degree of task differentiation according to gender, the degree of "importance" attached to these tasks may be a purely European invention. Janet Spector's research on Hidatsa task differentiation reveals the vital role that women played in all phases of the agricultural process.[6] Since the success of the crops often meant the difference between survival and starvation, one might perceive that real status would accrue to competent agriculturalists. In this case, the work of the women complemented the hunting efforts of the men and had equal importance.

Patricia Albers also discusses the native integration of public and domestic spheres in her article on the changing status of Devil's Lake Sioux women.[7] Albers outlines the traditional Sioux ethic, which promoted the ideal relationship between male and female as complementary and based on principles of individual autonomy and voluntary sharing. Because of this ethic, Albers claims that the concept of male dominance was meaningless for the traditional Sioux. However, Albers agrees with many other authors that U.S. government policies that, according to patriarchal Euro-American traditions, recognized only male political leaders and only male adults as head of household eventually altered the traditional system to a certain extent. Paula Allen supports Albers's view with her discussion of the effects of European colonization on the "gynocratic" social and political systems of the Iroquois tribes and the Cherokee.[8] In such groups, the political and social structures were formerly guided by tribal women; however, with the advent of the federal "trust" relationship, Indian groups were forced to follow the Anglo model of government, which specified male leadership. However, Albers disputes the final effects of Anglo patriarchy. For most Indian groups, the spheres remain integrated even today. As Albers comments, despite the preponderance of males on the Devil's Lake Sioux Tribal Council, "to a large extent, tribal politics and domestic politics are the same. . . . The issues that tribal leaders have been faced with in recent years are dominated by domestic concerns that have been critical to both men and women."[9] For many Indian groups, the traditional worldviews, which emphasize a holistic, balanced universe, continue to counter the Euro-American emphasis on hierarchy and dominant/subordinate social roles.

A primary distinction between the definition of women by Europeans and that by Indians was the Indian emphasis on individuality. While Europeans defined women in relation to male figures, American Indians generally perceived women and men as individuals with specific talents, abilities, and clan-sanctioned roles. Because Europeans failed to realize this Native emphasis on individuality, they largely ignored the fact that Indian women often played key roles in all of the major political, religious, and economic institutions of the tribe. In Robert Grumet's article on seventeenth- and eighteenth-century coastal Algonkin women, "Sunksquaws, Shamans and Tradeswomen," he maintains that all major tasks were cooperatively performed by men and women on the basis of ability, and that a "corresponding egalitarian sociopolitical organization" characterized most of the mid-Atlantic Algonkin groups during the colonial period.[10] Likewise, in "Farmers, Warriors, Traders: A Fresh Look at Ojibway Women," Priscilla Buffalohead contrasts the popular notion of Ojibway women as "drudges and slaves to men" with the reality of their dynamic roles in the "political, economic and social life of their communities." In addition to the more expected roles of food gathering, preparation, and child care, Buffalohead finds evidence of Ojibway women as recognized band leaders, medicine women, and warriors. She comments that Anglo officials often chose to ignore these women and deal with male members of the tribe instead. However, in the tribal view, these women were recognized and respected as leaders. Buffalohead concludes that Ojibway society placed a premium value not on gender but on individuality: "Women as well as men could step outside the boundaries of traditional sex role assignments and, as individuals, make group-respected choices."[11]

The social and political power of Indian women was sanctioned by tribal religious traditions that often emphasized the vital role of female deities. Unlike the European Christian religion, guided by an omnipotent male god, most Indian religions revolved around coequal deities who protected their "creations"—earth, sky, animals, crops, and human beings. Because the earth's natural system depends on cyclical regeneration, the "female" aspects of creation were particularly important. Hence, many of the primary deities were perceived as female. For example, Changing Woman in Navajo belief is a powerful creator-figure who is responsible for the growth of the crops and the birth of all new life. Changing Woman is also perceived as a powerful protectress of what she has created. To this day, the ideal of Navajo womanhood is modeled on the characteristics of Changing Woman. Jennie Joe comments on the strong, protective feelings Navajo women have for their land (which is passed down matrilineally through clan ties). Joe associates these strong traditional ties with the present resistance to federal relocation policies, largely organized by Navajo women: "The defensive actions that these women . . . continue to take fit . . . their perceptions of [the] appropriate role for themselves. This concept includes the role of a warrior. For example, most traditional Navajo women have names that contain the word 'baa,' which signifies 'female warrior.' As a female warrior she is expected to fight off . . . whatever poses a threat to the well being of her family and home."[12]

Similarly, the Sioux believe that their Sacred Pipe Religion was given to them by White Buffalo Woman, a female deity who presides over the Four Winds, the primary natural powers of the Great Plains area.[13] To this day, Sioux women are perceived as sacred and powerful. Grace Black Elk, an Oglala Lakota elder and spiritual leader, scoffs at the white feminists who see Indian woman as "slaves to their men." Ward Churchill records her opinions:

The Lakota have no word for "sexist."
  The White man does.
The Lakota does not put his name to his child.
  White men do.
For the Lakota, property is the possession of
  the woman. The generations are the responsibility
  of the woman. Power is thus in the hands of
  women. . . .
Lakota women are the strength of the people.[14]

Most tribes saw the strongest, most active and articulate tribal women as closely paralleling the traditional female deities. Indian women were accorded great status for their achievements in agriculture, hunting, and hide and meat preparation. Indian people felt that such abilities were divinely sanctioned, hence deserving of the utmost respect; Europeans, on the other hand, perceived Indian women as exploited "work drones."[15] Priscilla Buffalohead offers an interesting appraisal of the European attitude toward Indian women: "American Indian women appeared exploited to many nineteenth-century writers if only because their idea of woman, fostered by the privileged classes of Europe and America, was a frail, dependent person in need of protection."[16] And indeed, the nineteenth-century Euro-American ideal of the passive, self-effacing, delicate, useless woman (personified by Lily Bart in Edith Wharton's novel *The House of Mirth*) was *never* observed by American Indians.

The disparity between European and Native American gender perceptions resulted in a continued Euro-American bias that clouded the realities of American Indian women as dynamic, interactive individuals, in favor of the polarized princess/squaw stereotype. These stereotypes prevented any conception of the Indian woman as real, powerful, or even, at times, human. Rayna Green notes, "As some abstract, noble Princess tied to 'America,' and to sacrificial zeal, she [had] power as a symbol. . . . As the Squaw, a depersonalized object of scornful convenience, she [was] powerless. Like her male relatives she [could be] easily destroyed without reference to her humanity."[17] Green associates these dehumanizing stereotypes with the tragic massacre at Sand Creek, and unfortunately history supports her conclusion, with the Baker Massacre of 1870, in which approximately three hundred unarmed Blackfeet women, children, and old people were slain by the U.S. Cavalry, and with the 1890 massacre at Wounded Knee.[18]

The ethnocentric stereotypes of Euro-American explorers and traders were eventually employed by U.S. policy makers and military men to sanction policies of removal and genocide. And the stereotypes, which have persisted to the present day, reached mass acceptance among American people as they were popularized and promoted by nineteenth-century writers.

Perhaps nineteenth-century fiction concerned with Indian women explains more about nineteenth-century Euro-American women than about Indian women; nonetheless, the stereotypes promoted in these early novels became the basis for many popular twentieth-century western stories and movies, and therefore continue to dominate American perceptions of Indian women.

Karen Elliott discusses the role of Indian women in nineteenth-century popular fiction in her doctoral thesis, "The Portrayal of the American Indian Woman in a Select Group of American Novels."[19] Two of the novels she considers were written in the nineteenth-century Romantic tradition, and these further reinforced the noble princess stereotype. Ann Stephen's *Malaeska: The Indian Wife of the White Hunter* and Helen Hunt Jackson's

Ramona were hailed by nineteenth-century do–gooders as charitable contributions to understanding the "Indian plight." In fact, they probably served more to assuage white guilt for the all-too-recent atrocities committed by the U.S. Cavalry on Indian people.

Initially, *Malaeska* provides no departure from the Pocahontas model. Her father is a chief (hence she is a princess); she marries a brave white man against the wishes of her family, and she has a child. Then—unexpectedly—the white hunter dies, after giving instructions to his wife to take the child to his family in Manhattan. After a successful trip (by canoe, of course), she arrives in the city and the white family "allows" her to remain as a nursemaid to her son. Her true identity as his mother is carefully concealed for the shame it would cause—interesting proof of the nineteenth-century taboos against miscegenation. The end of the story is rather predictable: Malaeska dies of a broken heart after her son commits suicide upon learning of his shameful, mixed-breed ancestry. Throughout the novel, several nineteenth-century stereotypes are reinforced. First, Malaeska is noble only by virtue of her marriage to the brave white man; second, Malaeska has no basis in the reality of an American Indian identity—she behaves in the passive, self-effacing, dependent manner of the nineteenth-century Euro-American woman; and finally, the nineteenth-century view of the Indian as the "vanishing American" becomes reinforced, as Malaeska perishes while attempting to become "civilized" and is abandoned by her more "savage" relatives.

The Indian woman receives slightly different treatment in Jackson's *Ramona*, although it is not much better. Ramona is a half-breed, raised by a Spanish woman who keeps Ramona's heritage a secret from her until she falls in love with Alessandro, a young Indian ranch hand. Ramona elopes with Alessandro, and to his "delight, she began to evidence real signs of her Indianness." In other words, she becomes "attuned to nature," and hears "the trees speak . . . the rocks . . . and the flowers," as all "noble savages" do.[20] Ramona and Alessandro live dangerously, preyed upon by evil white men, until Alessandro is murdered. Ramona falls into a deep depression, and, in the tradition of nineteenth-century Romanticism, we await her death from a broken heart. But Ramona is rescued by her handsome Spanish stepbrother, with whom she falls in love and to whom she is duly married. The "Pocahontas perplex" is once again resurrected, along with all the other stereotypes: the helpless woman dependent on males for protection (and even for an existence); the pitiful inability of Indians to make it in the white world; and the ultimate, inevitable demise of savagery (however noble) in the face of civilization. Interestingly, the *Ramona* story is still enacted yearly at a California pageant, and variations of her story and of poor Malaeska's story are still found in contemporary pulp novels and Hollywood productions.

However unfortunate, Ramona and Malaeska remain relatively "good" Indian women. They are not promiscuous, they are not alcoholic, and they both care for white men. Slim Girl, in Oliver La Farge's *Laughing Boy*, presents an alternative image.[21] La Farge's novel was written somewhat later than the previous selections, but the evolution of the Indian woman has been anything but positive. Slim Girl is a product of the boarding school: She has lost her clan and family ties, she has learned to sell her body to white men for money and trinkets, and she manipulates people for her own gain. Aware of her cultural loss, she attempts to reintegrate herself with the Navajo way of life by marrying Laughing Boy—a handsome, naive, and "noble" Indian. Slim Girl finagles a marriage over the protests of Laughing Boy's family, and manages to keep a firm hold on him at her small-town home with the help of small doses of "medicine" (whisky doctored with oranges and sugar). However, Slim Girl continues to prostitute herself to a white man in town—a man who "would have liked to raise her to a position in which he could respect himself if he married her"—because she has learned to depend on the cash income.[22] Although La Farge interjects

Slim Girl's attempts to participate as a Navajo woman through the rituals and art of weaving, Slim Girl never truly succeeds, and just as they are moving back to the reservation for good, she is fatally wounded by a misfired bullet meant for Laughing Boy.

However well-intentioned, *Laughing Boy* perpetuates many of the most deleterious stereotypes of Indians, and particularly of Indian women. La Farge appears to support the notion that an Indian cannot successfully bridge two worlds, that the gentle, beautiful Indian woman who nurtures sheep, corn, and babies will be corrupted by a white world she cannot fit into, and will become the antithesis of a "good Indian"—a promiscuous, manipulative, materialistic creature with no salvation in either the Indian world or the white world. Hence, *Laughing Boy* both romanticizes the noble "blanket Indian" and denigrates the reality of cultural transition for Indian women. At any rate, the racism and sexism inherent in the princess/squaw stereotype lives on in *Laughing Boy*, and Slim Girl ends up the way a lot of good Indians did in the Anglo mind—dead.

Interestingly, *Malaeska*, *Ramona*, and *Laughing Boy* have all been hailed as works that are "sympathetic" to Indians, and therefore of some benefit to their "plight." In reality, however, they all acted to misinform the American public about the true problems and possibilities that faced American Indian people. For example, white education was widely perceived by nineteenth-century Indian leaders as necessary, and although the boarding schools were far from ideal, at one time they were the only option for Indian people who sought to learn how to manage in the white American world. As many tribes learned, complete ignorance of white ways often had profoundly negative effects, since the "Great White Father" frequently had only his own best interests at heart. Unfortunately, white boarding-school teachers often reacted to Indian students in terms of the very stereotypes perpetuated in these novels. This early conditioning often influenced the Indian student's self-perception for the rest of his or her life, a fact that must be considered as we examine the changing self-identity of the American Indian woman. Other issues of importance at this time involved the ongoing dilemmas faced by tribes as they experienced increasing miscegenation, disputes over land rights, and controversies over their own right to practice traditions prohibited by federal assimilation policies.

The scanty, romanticized plots of these early novels seem laughable when compared to the realities of the day. However, it is important to consider that policy makers, influenced by the stereotypical biases of the novels, often applied the same ethnocentric, androcentric attitudes as they formulated Indian policy. The changing realities faced by Indian women become apparent through analysis of autobiographical and biographical works. The real-life experiences of Indian women mediate between the European American stereotypes and the profusion of issues currently addressed in the contemporary literature of American Indian women.

As Gretchen Bataille and Kathleen Sands comment in *American Indian Women, Telling Their Lives*, Indian women's autobiographies are quite different from the male-oriented European autobiographical model, with its emphasis on flamboyant heroism and the dramatic recitation of historical events. The autobiographies of Indian women more closely correlate to the emerging American feminine autobiography, with the same tendency to "sift through their lives for explanation and understanding" in order to "clarify, to affirm and to authenticate" their own roles, as Estelle Jelinek has written.[23] However, the specific tribal orientations of American Indian women clearly receive the primary focus in their autobiographies. Bataille and Sands follow the interpretations of Vine Deloria, Sr. to suggest that "Indian women have been repositories of tradition and concern for spiritual ideals, upholding the stability of the tribe through both spiritual and generative power."[24]

A comparison of autographical experiences from the traditional past with the rapidly modernizing present reveals several important qualities of Indian women's identity that persist into contemporary literature. Among the most important of these themes are the Indian woman's unique relationship to the land, her place within the changing social relationships of her tribe, her perceptions of herself as a traditional Indian woman or as one influenced by nontraditional concepts and values, and finally her honest appraisal of her hopes, dreams, and ever-changing, often painful reality.

The following discussion will include excerpts from Nancy Lurie's *Mountain Wolf Woman* (a study of a Winnebago woman born in 1884), the autobiographies of Anna Shaw (Pima, born in 1898) and Helen Sekaquaptewa (Hopi, born in 1898), and the biography of Acoma potter Lucy Lewis (born in 1890), as examples from a primary period of conflict between traditional tribal values and those of white government authorities. Their experiences will be contrasted with those of a more recent generation of Indian women, including Maria Campbell (Metis), the late Micmac activist Anna Mae Aquash, Jeela Alilkatuktuk (Inuit), and Pawnee-Oto writer Anna Lee Walters.

Mountain Wolf Woman's story tells of the tremendous changes and conflicts that faced the traditional Winnebago culture in the early 1900s, when the Anglo culture was imposed upon them. Mountain Wolf Woman's experience reflects the impermanence of Winnebago life during the years following their successive relocations by the federal government. As Bataille and Sands note, "She was not tied down to a specific geographical location . . . but moved . . . from one location to another" throughout her life.[25] Mountain Wolf Woman exemplifies the transitional phase between traditionalism and adaptive change for Indian people.

The mediating role that Mountain Wolf Woman assumes between old and new is perhaps best illustrated by her conscious involvement with three religions: the traditional Winnebago religion, Christianity, and the Native American Church. As a child, Mountain Wolf Woman was advised by her father to "go cry to the thunders." She relates, "We used to sing and scatter tobacco, standing there and watching the stars and the moon. We used to cry because, after all, we were hungry. We used to think we were pitied."[26] Mountain Wolf Woman observed many of the traditional customs, such as the menstrual taboos, and later participated in the traditional Winnebago ceremonies such as the Scalp Dance and the Medicine Dance. However, her early education at Christian schools had a lasting influence, and when she finally attended the Native American Church, Mountain Wolf Woman found that the synthesis of Indian and Christian ritual beliefs held the greatest meaning for her.

Mountain Wolf Woman's story compares to the experiences of many Indian women who lived during her generation. The pressures to acculturate were tremendous, and many Indians responded as Mountain Wolf Woman did: They utilized parts of the white world in conjunction with their own traditional beliefs and value systems. Nancy Lurie comments that Mountain Wolf Woman saw herself in positive terms, as a link between "the historical life of her people and the future generations."[27] Lurie sees this perception as one generated by her traditional responsibilities as wife, mother, and a woman of her lineage. In contrast, Lurie notes, the men of her same generation were affected negatively as their traditional roles in economic provisioning and political decision making were assumed by paternalistic government agents.

The story of Helen Sekaquaptewa, a Hopi woman born in 1898, illustrates a successful adaptation to two worlds that parallels that of Mountain Wolf Woman. Sekaquaptewa was born in the ultratraditional village of Oraibi, and her family was one of those expelled from the original village by the more "progressive" Hopi for their rigid resistance to white schooling, and Americanization in general. Sekaquaptewa remembers this violent expulsion and her subsequent (forcible) removal to the Bureau of Indian Affairs (BIA) boarding school. Her childhood was plagued by the factional disputes of her people, which carried over even to the boarding school. Sekaquaptewa remembers that the daughters of the "progressives" teased and tormented the "exiles" mercilessly.[28] And to complicate her adjustment to white education, her own relatives began to criticize Sekaquaptewa for becoming too progressive.

The genuine pain of these conflicting worlds and their attendant value systems permeates the entire autobiography. As a small child, Sekaquaptewa was separated from her family for months at a time in an environment of loneliness, dietary change, and exposure to disease that resulted in the deaths of many Hopi children. Sekaquaptewa learned to speak and read English, and developed the "leadership skills" that the Anglo teachers stressed, but when she was sent back to her family, she faced "a household that looked to the elders, not children, for guidance . . . [and] to tradition, not change, for stability."[29] The two environments seemed mutually exclusive, and so, when offered the opportunity to go on to Phoenix Indian School, Sekaquaptewa accepted. She later married a Hopi man from a similar boarding-school background, and details their experiences in the village, where, despite their full-blood Hopi ancestry, they were considered "marginal" Hopi. Eventually, Sekaquaptewa emphasizes, she and her husband were accepted into the Hopi village and into the accompanying round of clan duties. However, the effects of their earlier experiences remained pronounced: Sekaquaptewa and some members of her immediate family converted to Mormonism, though it was practiced in conjunction with Hopi ways, and the family established an alternative residence at a cattle ranch below the mesas, a marked departure from Hopi tradition. Sekaquaptewa sums up the family's attitude: "We chose the good from both ways of living."[30]

Naturally, the reader wonders just how much of Sekaquaptewa's life has been true choice and how much a destiny shaped by the conflicting attitudes and policies of Hopi society and U.S. government officials. However, it is important to remember that throughout this critical period characterized by turbulent, accelerated change, Sekaquaptewa retains a sincere appreciation of her Hopi heritage and invariably practices the older system of ethics and values, even as she pioneers different experiences. In this respect she assumes a role similar to that of Mountain Wolf Woman: as a strong mediating force between generations and conflicting value systems. Importantly, Sekaquaptewa retains her love for the Hopi land and her sense of connection to the matrilineal village of her birth; in that sense, she remains completely "Hopi."

Like Helen Sekaquaptewa, Anna Shaw was born in 1898. However Shaw came from a Christianized Pima family that had, in many respects, already adapted to white ways. Bataille and Sands comment that, in contrast to the forcible removal of Hopi children to the BIA boarding school, "for Pimas, school was an extension of the household—close, filled with friends and kin, approved of by tribal members."[31] Anna Shaw's family supported her progress at school and applauded her graduation from high school (she was the first Indian woman in Arizona to do so). She became the author of two books, *Pima Legends* and her autobiography, *A Pima Past.*

Although Shaw has been criticized for being the "ideal product of the acculturation process advocated in the Indian school system," she stands apart from many other Indians of the same generation by her apparent success in *both* worlds.[32] She and her husband emphasized their Pima identity with pride and did not attempt to conceal it, as other Indians of the time often did for fear of prejudice. Anna Shaw's autobiography seems to prove what popular opinion seeks always to *disprove*—that an Indian can make it in the white world, yet still remain an Indian. That Shaw achieves this goal seems apparent. After her husband's retirement they moved back to the reservation, where she became involved in reviving traditional Pima arts, edited the tribal newspaper, and helped create a museum of Pima culture. Shaw seems to retain a strong appreciation of the value of the traditional ways and the need to pass them on, thereby refuting accusations of "assimilation" while still exercising her right to join the modern world on an equal footing.

It is important to consider Shaw's experiences in a regional and chronological context. The Pima, unlike some other tribes, were located in close proximity to the large urban centers of Phoenix and Tucson. Therefore, they possessed the ability to engage in commerce with the "white world" without necessarily forfeiting their traditional roles. In addition, Shaw completed her education at a time when total assimilation was actively encouraged by BIA teachers. Native ways were often denigrated and suppressed. That Shaw continued to nurture tribal traditions and in fact sought to explain their importance to the American people at large testifies to her confidence in her Pima identity, rather than her compromise to white values.

The story of Acoma potter Lucy Lewis contrasts with the experiences of Mountain Wolf Woman, Anna Shaw, and Helen Sekaquaptewa. Unlike the other three women, Lewis did not attend white schools, nor did she ever learn English or live in an urban setting. In this sense, Lewis illustrates a far older tradition and lifestyle. Lest one equate tradition with a static refusal to permit change, however, Lucy Lewis's story details both her traditional role as a Pueblo woman—the matriarchal head of her family and guarantor of spiritual and traditional continuity—and her radical departure from that role as a widely recognized practitioner of pottery as a fine-art form. Lucy Lewis was the first Acoma woman to experiment with different techniques and more detailed designs, and later, the first to sign her pottery (against the wishes of tribal leaders) and display it at competitive shows such as the Gallup Ceremonials.[33]

Because of her determination to revive an ancient art in a creative, fulfilling way, Lucy Lewis has inspired many other Pueblo women to learn the art of pottery, develop it through individual styles, and receive acclaim and profit for their artistic achievements. At the same time, Lewis has served her children as a source of spiritual and cultural continuity with Acoma tradition. Many of her children have lived away from the Pueblo, and all have been educated in white schools; yet they do not feel threatened by their exposure to the white world because of their strong ties to their Acoma heritage.

It is essential to realize that maintaining one's ties to the traditional past, to the ritual and symbolic structures of one's culture, imparts a significant sense of power. That power includes a sense of identity, connection, and self-confidence. The power may vary according to tribe, gender, or age, but always it is there. In the Acoma tribe, Lewis's daughters explain, the women are inextricably tied to the past through their ritual duties and participation in the ceremonial cycle.

Clearly, each of the women from this generation—Mountain Wolf Woman, Helen Sekaquaptewa, Anna Shaw, and Lucy Lewis—has had a strong and vital connection to the traditional past. Though in some cases they were educated in white schools, converted to Christianity, or pioneered a nontraditional role or art form, all of these women have maintained their tribal identities, clan obligations, and traditional value systems. But what about the following generation? What happens when the "power" becomes transmuted through mixed-blood ancestry, an urban environment, and displacement from tradition? What happens when the "new ways" seem hopelessly and finally irreconcilable with an Indian identity?

Maria Campbell's story centers around conflicts of identity and place that are far more severe than those experienced by the women of previous generations. Campbell, a Metis, or mixed-blood Cree, was born in Canada in the 1940s, arguably even more racist than American society at this time. As a Metis woman, Campbell suffered from both racial and gender oppression. The Metis were victims of discrimination from Canadian whites, as well as from their full-blood Treaty Indian kin, who referred to their mixed-blood relatives as the "Awp-pee-tow-kooson," the "half-people."[34] The Metis held no treaty rights under Canadian law and were forced to eke out a marginal existence poaching wildlife from government parks and squatting on strips of rocky, muskeg-covered land.

As a child, Maria Campbell was teased by white classmates for eating roasted gopher at lunch and for dressing in old, mended clothes. For respite, Campbell dreamed of living in a big city such as Vancouver, a place of "toothbrushes and pretty dresses, oranges and apples."[35] And eventually she did go to Vancouver, as the wife of a young white man who left her there, battered and penniless and with a baby daughter to support. Too proud to return home to her great-grandmother, Cheechum, and her widowed father, Campbell plunged ahead into her dream of wealth and success; she became a high-priced call girl in a house of prostitution. She had money, satin dresses, and jewels, and rich white men paid to "keep" her, but Campbell admits, "Something inside of me died. . . . I had married to escape from what I'd thought was an ugly world, only to find a worse one."[36] Failing to gain an identity that would answer her need for recognition and self-respect, Campbell turned to alcohol and heroin.

Campbell finally realized that by running away from what she was—a half-breed—she was helping to destroy herself. She turned her anger away from herself and toward the society that had labeled Native people into opposing categories, Metis vs. Treaty Indian, to further divide and weaken them. Canadian society has done its best to reduce the number of Native "wards" under its care. And too often the Indian woman has borne the major burden in this process. For example, under the Indian Act of Canada, a Treaty Indian woman loses her status if she marries a white, while a white woman gains Indian status and land if she marries an Indian.[37] The patriarchal biases of white bureaucrats together with the androcentric Christianity of the missionaries have dramatically altered traditional Indian perceptions of women. Campbell summarizes, "The missionaries had impressed upon us the feeling that women were a source of evil. This belief, combined with the ancient Indian recognition of the power of women, is still holding back the progress of our people today."[38]

Although in a sense Maria Campbell returns home to her ancestral past, embarking on a critical reunion trip to see her Cree great-grandmother, she realizes that for the Metis there *is* no "traditional past" with one set of values, rituals, and attitudes. Years of colonial oppression and miscegenation have fragmented the Metis, and the only unity that remains, aside from certain shared cultural attitudes, is a modern, politically centered manifestation of Native solidarity. In the larger sense, then, Maria Campbell's Indian identity is created largely from the shared bitterness, frustration, and poverty of Canada's diverse Native population. This sense of Indianness parallels the pan-Indianism that is apparent in large urban centers such as Los Angeles today, characterized by the unified social consciousness of Indian people who come from various tribes and regions and have varying degrees of Indian blood. But on a more personal level, Campbell seems to merge her identity with that of her Cree great-grandmother, assuming Cheechum's dreams for the rebirth of the Cree people in her own efforts as a political activist. Although the two women are separated by many years and several worlds of experience, they unite in a single spiritual current more ancient than tribal memory or degree of blood. This spiritual current becomes apparent in the modern literature of authors such as Leslie Silko, Joy Harjo, and Louise Erdrich, who are all of mixed Indian and white blood yet demonstrate a tenacious attachment to their tribal heritage and a lyrical appreciation of the deepest qualities of that heritage.

Like their ancestors, contemporary Indian women display strong ties to the spiritual currents of the past and also to the political realities of the present. The contemporary Indian woman faces a bewildering array of misconceptions, prejudices, and problems. Many Indian women in the last few years have refused to accept the status quo of society and have actively resisted through direct political involvement, as Maria Campbell did, and/or through written works that illuminate their concerns.

In the political arena, Indian women who have been through the white educational system can often appreciate the sophistication of the problems that face their people. The real frustration comes from white bureaucracies and Native political organizations built on the white model, which fail to recognize either the traditional power of Indian women or their modern skills as political facilitators. Jeela Alilkatuktuk, an Inuit woman raised in a traditional family but sent to boarding school as a teenager, explains: "I became involved in community affairs and was elected to the Frobisher Bay Hamlet Council at the age of 19. [While] the Council is supposed . . . to run the community for the people . . . in reality the territorial government controls all the money and all the personnel . . . the councils are [largely] powerless."[39] Alikatuktuk relates this powerlessness to the breakdown of traditional political structures, significantly to the loss of position by women. She claims that in traditional times, the most respected persons were the old women, and many women exerted great influence over camp decisions. Now, Alikatuktuk says, white men have transposed an alien political system onto the Inuit people, along with their own negative attitudes about women. She concludes: "One of our greatest losses is that our young Inuit men are copying the white people in their attitude. Where a white woman can walk without fear an Inuit woman is harassed and propositioned."[40] Alilkatuktuk's statement is corroborated by Indian Health Service worker Phyllis Old Dog Cross for the Navajo. Old Dog Cross documents the dramatic increase of rape on the Navajo reservation; formerly almost unheard of among Navajos, who held women in high esteem, rape is now the number-one crime on the reservation. She explains: "For the Indian male, the only route to be successful, to be good, to be right, and to have an identity was to be as much like the white man as he could."[41] The modern conflict between genders, for many Indian groups, has largely resulted from patterns learned from white colonial authorities whose policies destroyed traditional egalitarian systems among Indian people.

Because the various government-controlled agencies have failed to provide Indian people with a structure compatible with traditional beliefs, many young Indians have taken a more militant stance in all-Indian organizations such as the American Indian Movement (AIM). Unfortunately, the effects of patriarchal gender oppression often extend equally to these groups.

In *The Life and Death of Anna Mae Aquash,* Johanna Brand tells the story of a young Micmac woman from Nova Scotia who became involved with AIM during the late 1960s and early 1970s, and was murdered under suspicious circumstances.[42] Anna Mae's story substantiates many of the comments Jeela Alilkatuktuk and Maria Campbell make about the racism and sexism of Canadian officials toward their Indian "wards." Eventually Anna Mae left her poverty-blighted reserve to go to Boston, where she became involved in various Indian-rights organizations, including AIM. Because of her outspoken endorsement of AIM's most militant activities, many Indian people allege, Anna Mae became a prime target in the FBI campaign against "anti-American agitators." When she was murdered, the subsequent investigation was hurried and incomplete, and many Indians became suspicious that there were political motivations for her death. After Anna Mae's death, many Indian women eulogized her as the "Brave-Hearted Woman," a female warrior in an ongoing war of violence, genocide, and oppression. But Brand's biography reveals a far more complex portrait of Anna Mae's struggle.

Brand indicates that Anna Mae was very idealistic about her identity as an Indian woman and could not reconcile her deeply felt spiritual commitments with the realities of alcoholism, fast-moving city life, and mounting political tensions within and around AIM. In part the tensions were gender-based, because although AIM members claimed to have built their organization on traditional Indian precepts and values, it was apparent that some of the male leaders adopted a macho posturing that more clearly reflected the patriarchal Western mind-set than the traditional egalitarianism practiced by most tribes. One reviewer of Beatrice Medicine's *The Native American Woman: A Perspective* quoted a young AIM woman, Kathleen Smith, on her experience at Wounded Knee:

> The AIM leaders are particularly sexist, never having learned our true Indian history where women voted and participated equally in all matters of tribal life. They have learned the white man's way of talking down to women and regarding their position as inferior. Some ... actually don't believe women can fight or think, and gave us the impression that we were there for their use and that we should be flattered to have their children. One man said he was helping Indian unity by having a girlfriend from every tribe. They want to keep women divided and fighting for men's friendship and attention.[43]

Aside from gender differences, however, the goals of Indian activism clearly reflected the unified concerns of all Indian people. Shirley Witt, an Akwesasne Mohawk, wrote of Anna Mae's struggle as representative of many Indians who were tired of seeing their people incarcerated, unemployed, alcoholic, and suicidal in racist border towns, of seeing their children removed to far-off boarding schools and "brainwashed white," and of having brothers and sons recruited for a white man's army that didn't care if they came back alive or not.[44] In the struggle, both genders participated equally. In fact, Witt claims, after many of the male leaders had been jailed or were trying to escape incarceration in the mid-seventies, it was the women "warriors" who formed the stable core of the Indian movement and kept the concerns alive. And their concerns were substantial. Witt offers the statistics of Dr. Connie Uri, Cherokee, who claims that at the Claremore Indian Hospital in July 1974, sterilization surgery was performed on forty-eight Indian women, most in their twenties. The Indian women activists were the first to bring attention to this forcible sterilization of Indian women in government hospitals. Another area of concern at this time involved adoption of Indian children, who were generally placed with higher-income white families rather than families of their own tribal background. The Indian Child Welfare Act has since been passed, modifying such policies to reflect greater tribal control over the placement of Indian children.[45]

Women of All Red Nations (WARN), an all-women Native activist group, was formed as a female counterpart to the American Indian Movement. Currently WARN investigates and calls attention to the various concerns of Indian women. In recent years these have centered around the massive contamination of Indian water by radioactive waste from uranium mines located on Indian land. Winona La Duke, an Anishinabe and founder of WARN, has assembled statistical evidence of the high rate of birth defects on Indian reservations, apparently closely linked to the radioactive contamination of the land and water.[46]

Contemporary Indian women are reasserting the traditional power of their female ancestors in many ways. Many have become strong political leaders for their tribes, such as Ada Deer, Menominee, who was largely responsible for the reinstatement of her tribe to federal status after its disastrous "termination" by the government in 1961.[47] Other women choose to outline their concerns through written works that illuminate the struggles, failures, and triumphs of their people. Interestingly, many of the fictional works written by Indian women are constructed on an autobiographical mode of presentation. Often a central character in the poetry or prose of the Indian woman author will be modeled on the author herself; her experiences become those of the protagonist. Paula Allen describes her novel *The Woman Who Owned the Shadows* in this way. Allen's novel centers around the quest of Ephanie, a half-breed Laguna woman, as Allen is, for an identity that answers modern realities and traditional needs. Allen observes that the novel "leans on the tradition of autobiography," and that Ephanie was constructed from "qualities and, characteristics drawn from her grandmother, mother and herself, as well as fictional elements."[48]

Two concepts are essential in understanding the work of contemporary Indian women writers. The first is to understand the sense of place that permeates their work, as it always has the lives of Indian people. Even among Indian women writers who were born or raised largely in urban environments, there is a strong sense of origin from a specific geographic region, and a concomitant identity which centers around this land. Tribal stories, American Indian autobiographies, and contemporary literature by Indian writers all share this emphasis on "place." However, the Indian women writers perhaps exhibit the most central connections to the land, since, traditionally, the cyclical and regenerative characteristics of the earth were strongly linked to tribal women. To illustrate, Paula Allen refers to the "feminine landscape" of Leslie Silko's novel *Ceremony* with this inclusive remark: "We are the land, and the land is mother to us all."[49] Gretchen Bataille and Kathleen Sands comment similarly on the autobiography of Maria Chona, a Papago woman: "Like all works of American Indian literature [her] autobiography is permeated with a sense of place, the inextricable interweaving of language and landscape, the concept that the land is not merely setting for the story, but that the story is formed and shaped by the land, and the land is given significance and vitality in the language."[50] This summary could be applied equally to the work of Leslie Silko, Joy Harjo, Paula Allen, Luci Tapahonso, and countless other Indian women writers. The land unifies tradition and modern experience to reflect the wholeness of Indian cultures and nations.

However, along with this sense of wholeness and place, there is a troubling sense of loss, of deprivation and sadness. The idealism that many people ascribe to Indian people via traditionalism is countered by the often ugly realities of Indian life on the reservation and in urban areas. Problems such as assault, family violence, alcoholism, incarceration, and murder continually reassert themselves in Indian communities, largely due to widespread socioeconomic deprivation and the significant degree of culture loss (reflected in the loss of tribal languages, rituals, and clan relationships) that now threaten tribal groups. Indian women write consciously of both sides of life—positive and negative—to evoke the power of change and growth for Indian people. The language in the works may be lyrical and delicate, or it may be harsh and tense, as in this paragraph from a forthcoming autobiography by Anna Lee Walters, Pawnee-Oto:

> I have seen handsome people become ugly and disfigured. I have been close when people have been murdered and women raped and given birth. . . . I am familiar with people who have given their children away for a price, cash or a drink. I grew up with children whose parents fought and maimed each other by plan, no accident. I know of men who have given away their daughters.[51]

Walters's work will be an autobiography, but the realism compares to Erdrich's *Love Medicine* and Harjo's poem "The Black Room."

The idealism of tradition and place and the realism of squalid alleys and border-town bars may seem paradoxical and incompatible; but then, oftentimes so is the story of Indian survival and the tremendous adaptability of ancient cultures. Students of contemporary Indian literature might take this cue from Joy Harjo in reference to a modern trickster story told by a prison inmate:

Everyone laughed at the impossibility of it,
but also the truth. Because who would believe
the fantastic and terrible story of all of our survival
those who were never meant
     to survive?[52]

In a metaphorical sense, the diverse works of contemporary Indian women writers combine as a collective whole to generate the rebirth of Native tribal energy and female power. Leslie Silko, Joy Harjo, Paula Allen, and Luci Tapahonso are representative of the many contemporary women writers who have begun to assert this traditional power in written form. Joy Harjo writes that "we exist / not in words, but in the motion / set off by them," summarizing the power inherent in contemporary literary expression.[53]

These women combine modern experience with an ancient past in a unified continuum, rather than a fragmented assembly of parts. This mode of expression mirrors what Paula Allen calls "the traditional tribal concept of time . . . timelessness," and the complementary understanding of "space " as "multidimensionality."[54] This complex understanding of time and space underlies the ritual construction of many Indian worldviews, as Dr. Alfonso Ortiz affirms in *The Tewa World*.[55]

In conjunction with these concepts, many Indian groups perceive the individual as moving within the constant, natural motion of the universe in "dynamic equilibrium."[56] The relationship of an individual to the universe exists as an ancient, vital bond, as Joy Harjo explains:

I am memory alive
not just a name
but an intricate part
of this web of motion,
meaning: earth, sky, stars circling
my heart
    centrifugal.[57]

Similarly, the relationship of the individual to her ancestors is also continuous and alive; Luci Tapahonso writes of a woman who looks into her young daughter's face, "knowing they breathe the same memories, the same blood / dark and wet circulating / forever into time and others."[58]

This sense of connection to the ancient past transcends the modern realities of mixed bloodlines, gender splits, and urban settings, and often appears in modern literature as a surrealist blend of myth and reality. Possibly the best example of this appears in Leslie Silko's novel *Ceremony*. Significantly, in *Ceremony* a great emphasis rests on the female principle of this universal motion, in accordance with the worldview of the matriarchal Laguna people. On a more intricate level, as Paula Allen notes, while *Ceremony* is "ostensibly a tale about a man, Tayo, it is as much and more a tale of two forces: the feminine life force of the universe and the mechanistic death force of the witchery."[59] Allen's comment indicates a major philosophical thread that runs through Pueblo worldviews—the belief that each individual consists of both male and female elements, a balanced unity of "life forces" roughly equivalent to the Asian concept of yin and yang.

Interestingly, Silko chooses to use a male character to illustrate the competing values of the matriarchal Pueblo culture and the patriarchal Euro-American culture. Louise Erdrich uses a similar approach in *Love Medicine*, with Henry Lamartine Jr., a Chippewa newly arrived from the horrors of the Vietnam War. Tayo and Henry Jr. are both Indian men who have been mentally "raped" by a Euro-American culture promotes death and violence and is in direct conflict with the traditional Indian life force. Silko and Erdrich frame the dilemma from a male perspective to reinforce the contemporary realization that the victimization of an individual parallels the victimization of a culture and ethos, and therefore respects no gender boundaries.

Because of this understanding of victimization, which has been an intimate part of American Indian experience (both male and female), contemporary Indian women writers often do not observe the same dichotomy between male dominance and female victimization that white feminist authors do. Even in Joy Harjo's prose poem "The Black Room," which concerns the literal rape of a woman, the rape is much more complex than a physical act, and can be correlated to victimization on a much larger scale:

> Joey had her cornered. Leaned her up against the wall of her room, in black willow shadows his breath was shallow and muscled and she couldn't move and she had no voice no name and she could only wait until it was over—like violent summer storms that she had been terrified of.[60]

When Harjo says "she had no voice no name," she refers to what has been called the "mute zone," the chronically passive victim mentality of those who have had identity (a name) and power (a voice) ripped away from them. Tayo and Henry Jr., though male, have succumbed to this victimization through army indoctrination, much as female rape victims often do through societal judgments ("she asked for it"). For Tayo, the ceremony finally allows him to have a voice. Previously, he has been nearly mute, numbly wading through an existential fog of pain and denial. At the height of his sickness, he perceives the world around him as vague and shadowy; he even sees his own mouth as "an outline . . . like all the other outlines he saw."[61] For Tayo, at this point, the world has no substance, no vitality without the body of tradition and understanding which gives meaning to life.

Tayo learns to transcend the death force of the white witchery by relearning the spiritual power of his Laguna traditions, but Henry Jr. faces a different outcome. Henry Jr. is plagued by memories of the violence and inhumanity of the war he has just experienced. He remembers witnessing the rape of a Vietnamese woman by American soldiers:

> She looked at him. They had used a bayonet. She was out of her mind. You, me, same. Same. She pointed to her eyes and his eyes. The Asian folded eyes of some Chippewas. She was hemorrhaging.[62]

Henry Jr. has witnessed the violent rape of a woman, but he has been similarly victimized by his fellow soldiers, who destroy his own values and perceptions, and leave him "ghost-like," an empty shell of his former self. As his mother realizes: "All his life he did things right, and then the war showed him right was wrong."[63] The European American world that allows the exploitation of women and Third World peoples in its quest for power and gain, and then discards the victims without reference to their humanity, conflicts severely with the traditional Indian ethic of balance and mutual respect. Henry Jr., unlike Tayo, has no traditional healer to turn to, and he takes his own life by drowning himself in the river.

Throughout the works of Indian women writers there is powerful emphasis on transcending victimization to find one's own identity and voice. The initial step in this direction is to define oneself in one's own terms, rather than those of the outer society. For Indian women, this means discarding the Anglo feminine ideal in favor of what Paula Allen in *The Sacred Hoop* appropriately calls "recovering the feminine in American Indian traditions."

Many American women have struggled to counter the nineteenth-century feminine ideal—the beautiful, passive, subordinate woman who received her identity in terms of her affiliation to males. However, even today a feminine ideal persists in ad campaigns and beauty contests. Modern women are encouraged to adopt the makeup, hairstyle, and clothing that society determines to be "feminine." The Virginia Slims woman must always be perfect, always elusive and mysterious. She cannot be real (with a voice, a name, or an occupation) or she would destroy her allure and her commercial worth.

For the American Indian woman, the conflict between a traditional identity and the feminine ideal promoted by Euro-American society has assumed complex dimensions in relation to the contemporary search for identity. Maria Campbell discusses her aspirations to be a beautiful, revered "lady," which ultimately led her into prostitution and drug addiction, and admits: "Dreams are so important in one's life, yet when followed blindly, they can lead to the disintegration of one's soul."[64] Louise Erdrich illustrates the same conflict through June in *Love Medicine*. June searches for an identity that will make her feel good about herself, and, as society has conditioned women to do, she looks to men for this identity. She maintains a thin veneer of physical attractiveness to cover her inner disintegration but realizes sadly that she is "truly empty," and eventually walks to her death in a storm.

In *Ceremony*, Tayo's mother shares a fate similar to June's. Like June, Tayo's mother seeks to establish her identity and importance through men, but eventually she faces reality when, "after she had been with them, she could feel the truth in their fists and in their greedy feeble love-making."[65] She grows to feel marginal and inadequate both with the Indian people, who feels shame for her promiscuity and alcoholism, and with the white men who feel contempt for her, and finally dies a lonely, alcoholic death. Both June and Tayo's mother illustrate the consequences of cultural loss and denial. Erdrich and Silko have countered these tragic images with strong Indian women such as Lulu, Marie, and Albertine in *Love Medicine*, and Ts'eh in *Ceremony*, who embody the strength and resilence of their ancestral cultures, even as they adapt and persist in the face of severe opposition.

Defining a contemporary identity becomes critical in achieving such cultural resilience. As Indian women begin to counter the negative effects of the societally imposed feminine ideal, they start to assert the older values and perceptions that have always allowed Indian women to maintain a sense of autonomy and self-worth. The process of gaining such an identity entails, first, a realization of one's own oppression; second, the release of one's pain and often self-directed anger; and third, the realization of one's individual self-worth through connections to tradition and kin. This process of "going back home" permeates *Love Medicine* through Lipsha's search for his identity and kin, *Ceremony* through Tayo's ritual connection to his traditional past, and Harjo's collection *She Had Some Horses* through Noni Daylight's search for a "voice" and a "self" that can transcend her pain and nihilistic self-denial.

As Noni Daylight realizes, at the root of all pain is fear. For Indian women this may include fear of the cold, anonymous city, fear of going back to the poverty of the reservation, fear of racists and rapists, fear of what the schools will teach the children, fear of what vision the next drink will bring, and fear of what will happen if there *is* no next drink. Noni Daylight lives with that fear. It grips her heart and dries her mouth and leaves her "a dishrag wrung out over bones":

> Noni Daylight is afraid.
> She waits through traffic lights at intersections
> that at four a.m. are desolate oceans of concrete.
> She toys with the trigger; the heartbeat
> is a constant noise. She talks softly
> softly
> to the voice on the radio. All night she drives.[66]

Noni Daylight is striving for *connection*, as are Maria Campbell, June, Tayo, and Lipsha. Noni Daylight seeks a voice, and needs to hear the heartbeat that tells her she is alive. But she cannot truly find her identity until she realizes, "It is not the moon, or the pistol in her lap / but a fierce anger / that will free her."[67] In these final three lines of "Heartbeat," Harjo discovers an important lesson that might be appropriately used by any person seeking to overcome victimization and assert an individual identity: Anger must be used as energy, directed away from the self and worked through, if one is ever to achieve control over one's life. This realization has also received attention in the works of many white feminist writers. It is significant that Paula Allen and Joy Harjo have spoken of the bond that unites all women, regardless of race, in the struggle to overcome the patriarchal oppression and victimization of European American society. Although both have recognized the significant departures between white feminism and traditional Indian beliefs, they choose to focus on the mutualities of women's experience.

A main tenet of modern feminist thought involves discarding the traditional passive role of the female in favor of a more autonomous, active role. This breaks the victim mentality and allows the woman to feel confident about making her own choices and decisions. Adrienne Rich, a white feminist poet, outlines this concept in her acclaimed collection *Diving Into the Wreck*. As critic Helen Vendler writes, "The forcefulness of *Diving Into the Wreck* comes from the wish not to huddle wounded, but to explore the caverns, scars and depths of the wreckage."[68] By taking this active step, one may discard the internalized anger, which, as Rich notes, is often "converted into self-hate and despondency . . . the cause of paralysis."[69] By "paralysis," Rich means the same numb denial that destroys June and Henry Jr. and threatens to destroy both Tayo and Paula Allen's Ephanie in *The Woman Who Owned the Shadows*.[70]

Joy Harjo correlates this "paralysis" with suicides, which often occur through a passive method (drowning, overdose, exposure) because the individual is incapable of making an active decision. In "The Woman Hanging from the Thirteenth Floor Window," Harjo describes a woman who

> . . . knows she is hanging by her own fingers, her
> own skin, her own thread of indecision. . . .
> She thinks she remembers listening to her own life
> break loose, as she falls from the 13th floor
> window on the east side of Chicago, or as she
> climbs back up to claim herself again.[71]

Harjo intentionally leaves the poem's ending ambiguous to indicate that it is the element of choice, the active power in taking the initiative to save oneself, that is the key to survival. That choice is the fundamental theme of the pivotal poem in Harjo's collection, "She Remembers the Future." In this poem, Noni Daylight finally confronts her "other self," the self she has long denied for fear of facing the intense pain and anger that, in fact, *empower* this self. Noni asks the complacent, passive self, which contemplates suicide, "Should I dream you afraid / so that you are forced to save / yourself? / Or should you ride colored horses / into the cutting edge of the sky / to know / that we're alive / we are alive."[72]

For Noni Daylight, the act of unifying the two disparate selves, involves the resolution of her seemingly polarized existence into one entity—her "self." Joy Harjo uses Noni Daylight to illustrate her own belief that the contradictions and polarities that often fragment Indian people must be reconciled into "an order that is harmonious, balanced and whole."[73] This passage from "She Had Some Horses" illustrates the vital resolution of polarity:

> She had some horses.
> She had horses who got down on their knees for any savior.
> She had horses who thought their high price had saved them.
> She had horses who tried to save her, who climbed in her
> bed at night and prayed as they raped her.
> She had some horses.
> She had some horses she loved.
> She had some horses she hated.
> These were the same horses.[74]

Harjo has realized that it is this sense of polarity, as she says, of "good/evil, sun/moon, light/dark," that fragments the modern consciousness into near-insanity.[75] The Western worldview revolves around polarity—Christian/pagan, sacred/secular, male/female, technology/nature—with an attendant imbalance in the judgment that one is superior to its opposite. In the traditional Indian view, as Paula Allen notes, the image of unified balance predominates in the form of the "Sacred Hoop." This view refutes the Western polarity that often seems paradoxical, even to Westerners. For example, a white man once asked an old Tuscarora why the polarities of "good and evil," like those of "genius and insanity," often seemed to be "just a hair's breadth apart." The Tuscarora man answered: "There is no such thing as polarity, except in the frail choice of man. If you take the line between your polarities and curve it into a circle, you would have your own answer."[76] It is this understanding of polarity which forms the core of American Indian worldviews. Today, the resolution of an artificially imposed polarity restores one to the "primordial center," as Betonie explains to Tayo. For Tayo, this means finding the balance between modern life and the older traditions, between the mechanistic forces of technology and the life forces of Laguna tradition.

Contemporary Indian women restore themselves to this balance as they find an identity more appropriate to their unique tribal traditions, one that emphasizes their own special bond to the female life forces of the universe. Because Indian women have always perceived their regenerative qualities in close concert with the earth's cycles, many contemporary Indian women writers use this theme in their work. Chickasaw poet Linda Hogan writes: "I teach my daughters, / that we are women, / a hundred miles of green / wills itself out of our skin. / The red sky ends at our feet / and the earth begins at our heads."[77] Hogan's image might well coincide with a Navajo sand painting that depicts the circular universe, the unbroken continuum of earth and sky, the female deities arched over the land like rainbows, promising rebirth for a new generation.

In Indian tradition, the births of a woman parallel the other births that belong to the land. Luci Tapahonso explores this connection in relation to sunrise, the ultimate rebirth of the natural world. "The first born of dawn woman / slid out amid crimson fluid streaked with stratus clouds / her body glistening August sunset pink / light steam rising from her like rain on warm rocks."[78] And Joy Harjo relates a human birth to the cycles of the land in much the same way:

> . . . the ground spoke when she was born.
> Her mother heard it. In Navajo she answered
> as she squatted down against the earth
> to give birth. It was now when it happened,
> now giving birth to itself again and again
> between the legs of women.[79]

When Harjo writes, "It was now . . . giving birth to itself again and again," she summarizes the temporal continuity of the Indian universe. This ability to include the traditional past with the changing present characterizes the works of American Indian writers. Linda Hogan offers a concise appraisal of this quality:

> No one is much without the earth
> in their hands
> and I pick up the earth,
> touch the people
> the country
> and the things we try to forget.[80]

Indian women writers, in particular, are all too aware of the modern tendency to forget what should not be forgotten: the older traditions, the recent (painful) history, the harsh realism of the modern world. The older Indian people recognized the need to keep memory alive and perfected the art of oral history. Today, the modern written works of many Indian women fulfill a similar function. Joy Harjo emphasizes the value of memory:

> Remember that you are this universe and that this
> universe is you.
> Remember that all is in motion, is growing, is you.
> Remember that language comes from this.
> Remember the dance that language is, that life is.
> Remember.[81]

Harjo correlates language and memory with the motion of life. She emphasizes that the past is the current to the future, but only if we allow it to be. In their respective novels, Silko and Erdrich describe what can happen when memory is allowed to die, when the natural cycles are broken in the modern death of warfare and atomic technology. Just as Lipsha needs to establish his kinship to Gerry Nanapush, June, and Lulu in *Love Medicine*, and Tayo must establish his kinship to his Laguna ancestors and traditions in *Ceremony*, so must we all establish our mutual kinship to the land—to the rocks the Lakota call "Tunkashila" or "grandfather," to the rain-filled clouds which the Hopi call "Kachinas," their spirit ancestors—and to all the living beings that have been born to this land.

This sense of motion, regeneration, and life permeates the work of contemporary Indian women writers. The written expressions of these authors might well be considered a powerful legacy of survival for the next generation. In the combined works of women rests a strong vision for a better future.

In traditional Navajo mythology, a male deity associated with "thought" unites with a female deity associated with "speech" to create the preeminent deity of the Navajo people—Changing Woman.[82] Changing Woman personifies the female life force of the universe, and through her the ritual structure of the Navajo people was born. Similarly, thought and speech combine for a dynamic rebirth of the traditional American Indian cultures and belief systems in the contemporary writings of Native American authors. And American Indian women writers have a vital role in this regenerative process. At the conclusion of *Seasonal Woman*, Luci Tapahonso places herself in this continuum of life, art, and beauty with a final, gentle prayer:

> bless me hills
> this clear golden morning
> for I am passing through again.
> I can easily sing
> for . . . time is mine
> and these ragged red cliffs
> flowing hills and wind echoes
> are only extensions
> of a never-ending prayer.[83]

As Tapahonso realizes, the prayers of generations of people rest in those "ragged red cliffs" and "flowing hills." Their handprints and drawings often remain, etched ghostlike on rock slabs, though their words have long since faded into wind echoes. However, the essence of their prayers remains, giving strength and continuity to a new generation, a generation passing through the dawn—once again.

Notes

1. Kenneth Lincoln, *Native American Renaissance* (Berkeley: University of California Press, 1983), preface.
2. Paula Allen, *The Sacred Hoop* (Boston: Beacon Press, 1986), 160.
3. Alice Kehoe, "The Shackles of Tradition," in Pat Albers and Beatrice Medicine, eds., *The Hidden Half* (Lanham, Md.: University Press of America, 1983), 61.
4. Wendy Martin, *An American Triptych* (Chapel Hill: University of North Carolina Press, 1984), 29–30.
5. Albers and Medicine, eds., *The Hidden Half*, 13.
6. Janet Spector, "Male Female Task Differentiation among the Hidatsa," in Albers and Medicine, eds., *The Hidden Half*, 95.
7. Patricia Albers, "Sioux Women in Transition," in Albers and Medicine, eds., *The Hidden Half*, 175–223.
8. Allen, *The Sacred Hoop*, 41.
9. Albers, "Sioux Women in Transition," 216–17.
10. Robert Grumet, "Sunksquaws, Shamans and Tradeswomen," in Mona Etienne and Eleanor Leacock: eds., *Women and Colonization Antropological Perspectives* (New York: Praeger, 1980), 56.
11. Priscilla Buffalohead, "Farmers, Warriors, Traders: A Fresh Look at Ojibway Women," *Minnesota History* 48 (1983): 242.
12. Jennie Joe, "Keepers of the Earth Bundle: Navajo Women and Forced Relocation" (manuscript, 1986).
13. Allen, *The Sacred Hoop*, 16.
14. Ward Churchill, "Generations of Resistance: American Indian Poetry and the Ghost Dance Spirit," in Bo Scholer, ed., *Coyote Was Here: Essays on Contemporary Native American Literary and Political Mobilization* (Aarhus: SEKLOS, 1984), 168.
15. Albers and Medicine, eds., *The Hidden Half*, 31.
16. Buffalohead, "Farmers, Warriors, Traders," 238.
17. Rayna Green, "The Pocahontas Perplex," *Massachusetts Review* 16 (1975): 713.
18. Vine Deloria Jr., *Of Utmost Good Faith* (San Francisco: Straight Arrow Books, 1971), 156.
19. Karen Sue Elliott, "The Portrayal of the American Indian Woman in a Select Group of American Novels" (Ph.D. diss., University of Minnesota, 1979).
20. Ibid., 136.
21. Oliver La Farge, *Laughing Boy* (Boston: Houghton Mifflin 1929).
22. Ibid., 135.
23. Gretchen Bataille and Kathleen Sands, *American Indian Women, Telling Their Lives* (Lincoln: University of Nebraska Press, 1984), 8.
24. Ibid., 18.
25. Ibid., 76.
26. Jane Katz, *I Am the Fire of Time* (New York: E. P. Dutton, 1977), 28.
27. Bataille and Sands, *American Indian Women, Telling Their Lives*, 74.
28. Ibid., 103.
29. Ibid., 104.
30. Ibid., 109.
31. Ibid., 87.
32. Ibid., 95.
33. Susan Peterson, *Lucy Lewis: American Indian Potter* (Tokyo: Kodansha International, 1984), 40.
34. Maria Campbell, *Halfbreed* (Toronto: McClellan and Stewart, Ltd., 1973), 26.
35. Ibid., 114.
36. Ibid., 116.
37. John Price, *Native Studies: American and Canadian Indians* (New York: McGraw-Hill Ryerson, 1978), 83.
38. Campbell, *Halfbreed*, 144.
39. Jeela Alilkatuktuk, "Canada: Stranger in My Own Land," *Ms.*, February 1974, 8–10.
40. Ibid.

41. Allen, *The Sacred Hoop*, 192.
42. Johanna Brand, *The Life and Death of Anna Mae Aquash* (Toronto: James Lorimer, 1978).
43. Editorial, *Off Our Backs* 11, 2 (1981).
44. Shirley Hill Witt, "The Brave-Hearted Woman," *Akwesasne Notes* 8 (early summer 1976): 16–17.
45. Monroe Price and Robert Clinton, *Law and the American Indian* (Charlottesville: Michie, 1983), 89.
46. Winona LaDuke, "They Always Come Back," in Beth Brant, ed., *A Gathering of Spirits: Writings and Art by North American Indian Woman* (Rockland, Me.: Sinister Wisdom Books, 1984), 62–67.
47. Katz, *I Am the Fire of Time*, 149.
48. Bataille and Sands, *American Indian Women, Telling Their Lives*, 140.
49. Allen, *The Sacred Hoop*, 119.
50. Bataille and Sands, *American Indian Women, Telling Their Lives*, 49.
51. Ibid., 138.
52. Joy Harjo, "Anchorage," in *She Had Some Horses* (New York: Thunder's Mouth Press, 1983), 15.
53. Harjo, "Motion," in *She Had Some Horses*, 54.
54. Allen, *The Sacred Hoop*, 147.
55. Alfonso Ortiz, *The Tewa World* (Chicago: University of Chicago Press, 1969).
56. Allen, *The Sacred Hoop*, 147.
57. Harjo, "Skeleton of Winter," in *She Had Some Horses*, 31.
58. Luci Tapahonso, "Her Daughter's Eyes," in *Seasonal Woman* (Santa Fe, N.M.: Tooth of Time Books, 1982), 13.
59. Allen, *The Sacred Hoop*, 118–19.
60. Harjo, "The Black Room," in *She Had Some Horses*, 25.
61. Leslie Marmon Silko, *Ceremony* (New York: Viking, 1977), 14.
62. Louise Erdrich, *Love Medicine* (New York: Holt, Rinehart and Winston, 1984), 138.
63. Ibid., 227.
64. Campbell, *Halfbreed*, 116.
65. Silko, *Ceremony*, 71.
66. Harjo, "Heartbeat," in *She Had Some Horses*, 37.
67. Ibid.
68. Martin, *An American Triptych*, 191.
69. Ibid., 177–78.
70. Paula Allen, *The Woman Who Owned the Shadows* (San Francisco: Spinster's Ink Press, 1983).
71. Harjo, "The Woman Hanging from the Thirteenth Floor Window," in *She Had Some Horses*, 23.
72. Harjo, "She Remembers the Future," in *She Had Some Horses*, 46.
73. Allen, *The Sacred Hoop*, 167.
74. Harjo, "She Had Some Horses," in *She Had Some Horses*, 64.
75. Allen, *The Sacred Hoop*, 166.
76. Ted Williams, *The Reservation* (Syracuse: Syracuse University Press, 1976), 254.
77. Linda Hogan, *Seeing through the Sun* (Amherst: University of Massachusetts Press, 1985), 44.
78. Luci Tapahonso, "A Breeze Swept Through," in Brant, ed., *A Gathering of Spirit*, 217.
79. Harjo, "For Alva Benson. And for Those Who I Have Learned to Speak," in *She Had Some Horses*, 18.
80. Linda Hogan, *Eclipse* (Los Angeles: UCLA American Indian Studies Center, 1983), 36.
81. Harjo, "Remember," in *She Had Some Horses*, 40.
82. Gary Witherspoon, *Language and Art in the Navajo Universe* (Ann Arbor: University of Michigan Press, 1977), 16.
83. Tapahonso, "A Prayer," in *Seasonal Woman*, 51.

37

Community, Patriarchy, and Individualism: The Politics of Chicano History and the Dream of Equality

Ramón A. Gutiérrez

This essay is an attempt to map in broad, general terms the origins and development of the Chicano movement in the United States from approximately 1965 to the present. As a prolegomenon to a larger research project on this topic, what is sketched below is but a thematic blueprint, devoid of all the baroque embellishments that greater space and time would permit. As a person who was weaned politically on the rhetorical claims of the movement, and as a university professor who has taught courses on Chicano history for well over ten years, the account presented here mixes insider and outsider knowledge drawn primarily from the fields of anthropology, history, literature, and sociology.

Mexican Americans fought in World War II to make the world safe for democracy. Fighting beside other assimilated immigrants, they believed the national promise that when they returned home, the American dream of social mobility and middle-class status would be theirs. The troops returned to what became a period of unprecedented economic growth in the United States. It was in this period, between 1945 and 1960, that America's global economic hegemony was truly consolidated. For white American men the dream was indeed realized. The GI Bill of Rights helped educate many of them. The consumer goods, cars, stocked refrigerators, money to spare, and government loans to educate their children soon followed. But the benefits, the dreams, and the cash were not equitably distributed. Blacks, Mexicans, and persons of Asian ancestry, all legitimately Americans, had been left out. The 1960 census of the United States graphically showed how far the minority populations lagged behind white America.

These realizations were made potent by the peaceful activism of Cesar Chavez, who was trying to win better wages and work conditions for farmworkers; by Reies López Tijerina's attempts to regain lands fraudulently stolen from New Mexico's *Hispanos;* and by the worldwide crumbling of imperialism and the rise of new nationalisms. This complex conjuncture of structural forces was what sparked the Chicano movement. What differentiated the Chicano movement from the civil rights activities of such groups as the League of United Latin American Citizens (LULAC), the American G.I. Forum, or the numerous mutual aid societies that Mexicanos had created to better their socioeconomic situation, was the Movimiento's radical political stance. The civil rights movement of the 1940s and 1950s had sought slow, peaceful change through assimilation, petitions for governmental beneficence, and appeals to white liberal guilt. The Chicanos, largely a contingent of educated students, in a revolution sparked by rising expectations, demanded equality

with white America, called for an end to racism, and asserted their right to cultural autonomy and national self-determination.

Since so much of the ethnic militancy that Chicanos articulated was profoundly influenced by black nationalism, it is important to recall one of the truly poignant insights in
The Autobiography of Malcolm X. Reciting the psychic violence that racism and discrimination had wreaked on African Americans, Malcolm X noted that the most profound had
been the emasculation of black men. In the eyes of white America, blacks were not deemed
men. Thus whatever else the Black Power movement was, it was also about the cultural
assertion of masculinity by young radical men.

Chicanos faced what was undoubtedly a rather similar experience—social emasculation
and cultural negation—by seeking strength and inspiration in a heroic Aztec past. The
Aztec past they chose emphasized the virility of warriors and the exercise of brute force.
Young Chicano men, a largely powerless group, invested themselves with images of
power—a symbolic inversion commonly found in the fantasies of powerless men worldwide, a gendered vision that rarely extends to women.

Equally important to the young Chicano radicals was the construction of a moral
community that was largely imagined as spatial and territorial. Aztlán the legendary
homeland of the Aztecs, was advanced as the territory Chicanos hoped to repossess
someday. Despite the fuzziness of the concept, its imprecise geographic limits, and the
previous claims to the territory that American Indians could justly claim, the dream of
Aztlán sank deep roots.

The idea and theory of internal colonialism flowed quite logically from this spatial
concept of community. Chicanos were an internally colonized population within the
United States. They were socially, culturally, and economically subordinated and territo-
rially segregated by white Anglo-Saxon America. These concepts receive definition in
the works of Rudy Acuña and myself in history, Tomás Almaguer in sociology, Mario
Barrera and Carlos Muñoz in political science, and in numerous cultural productions and
artistic works.[1]

When this analysis was taken from the global to the local, the barrio became its focus.
We see this very clearly in the scholarly works that provide the foundation for Chicano
history: Albert Camarillo's *Chicanos in a Changing Society: From Mexican Pueblos to American Barrios in Santa Barbara and Southern California, 1848–1930*, Richard Griswold del
Castillo's *The Los Angeles Barrio, 1850–1890*, and Ricardo Romo's *East Los Angeles: A History of a Barrio*.[2]

If anything defined the ethics of this moral community, it was the belief in collectivism
and an explicit rejection of individualism.[3] *Chicanismo* meant identifying with *la raza* (the
race or people), and collectively promoting the interests of *carnales* (or brothers) with
whom they shared a common language, culture, religion, and Aztec heritage.

Examining any of the Chicano scholarly or artistic productions between 1965 and 1975
clearly indicates one point. The history of Chicanos was thought to have begun in 1848, at
the end of the U.S.-Mexican War. This date heightened the legacy of Anglo racism toward
Chicanos, for as Armando Navarro would write, "Chicano politics [and history have]
always been imbued with a spirit of resistance toward Anglo-American oppression and
domination." The relationship between Anglos and Chicanos

> was conceived out of a master-servant relationship between the Anglo conqueror and the
> Chicano conquered. The Chicano reacted politically in two ways to the master-servant
> relationship. Some Chicanos collaborated and accommodated the Anglo invader and
> engaged in "ballot box politics." Other Chicanos, however, rejected the conquest and
> resorted to violence, guerrilla warfare and banditry.[4]

The years 1965 to 1969 were the heyday of Chicano activism, largely, though not exclusively, on college and university campuses. Coming from working-class backgrounds and feeling privileged by their college draft exemptions, Chicanos identified with workers and peasants, and indeed, wrote a heroic past of worker struggles and strikes, resistance to Anglo oppression, and indigenous cultural pride.

But all was not well in Eden. By 1969, at the very moment Corky Gonzales was trying to weld a fractured Chicano student movement into a national force, the more radical Chicanas were beginning to see themselves as triply oppressed—by their race, their gender, and their class. "Women students were expected by their male peers to involve themselves actively but in subordination," recalled Adelaida del Castillo. It was not uncommon in those days for the movement's men "to request sexual cooperation as proof of commitment to the struggle, by gratifying the men who fought it."[5] Although the movement persistently had advocated the self-actualization of all Chicanos, the term *Chicanos* still actually meant only males.

Within the Chicano student movement, women were denied leadership roles and were asked to perform only the most traditional stereotypic roles—cleaning up, making coffee, executing the orders men gave, and servicing their needs. Women who did manage to assume leadership positions were ridiculed as unfeminine, sexually perverse, and promiscuous, and all too often were taunted as lesbians. "When a woman leader had a compañero, he was frequently taunted or chided by the other men for failure to keep her under his control," recalled one woman.[6]

A 1970 incident at San Diego State University was particularly telling of the tenor of those days. There women had managed to assume leadership over the campus Chicano student group. When it was announced that Corky Gonzalez was going to visit the campus, an intense debate ensued. "It was considered improper and embarrassing for a national leader to come on campus and see that the organization's leadership was female," recalled one of the campus leaders. "Consequently, the organization decided that only males would be the visible representatives for the occasion. The female chairperson willingly conceded."[7]

The sexism rampant in the Chicano movement was increasingly critiqued in various forms. Marcela Christine Lucero-Trujillo made the point powerfully in her poem "Machismo Is Part of Our Culture."

> Hey Chicano bossman
> don't tell me that machismo is part of our culture
> if you sleep
> and marry W.A.S.P.
>   You constantly remind me,
>   me, your Chicana employee
> that machi-machi-machismo
> is part of our culture.
>   I'm conditioned, you say,
> to bearing machismo
> which you only learned
> day before yesterday.
>   At home you're no patrón
>   your liberated gabacha
>   has gotcha where
>   she wants ya,
>   y a mi me ves cara
>   de steppin' stone.
> Your culture emanates
>   from Raza posters on your walls

> from bulletin boards in the halls
> and from the batos who hang out at the barrio bar.
> Chicanismo through osmosis
> acquired in good doses
> remind you
> to remind me
> that machi-machi-machismo
> is part of our culture.[8]

In the poem "You Cramp My Style, Baby," Lorna Dee Cervantes took the rhetorical language of the Chicano movement, mixed it with elements from Mexican culture, and drew the appropriate sexual lesson:

> You cramp my style, baby
> when you roll on top of me
> shouting, "Viva La Raza"
> at the top of your prick.
> You want me como un taco
> dripping grease,
> or squeezing masa through my legs,
> making tamales for you out of my daughters.[9]

Articles were also beginning to appear in the movement press highlighting the contradiction between racial and sexual oppression in the Chicano movement. Irene Rodarte posed the question "*Machismo* or revolution?"[10] and Guadalupe Valdes Fallis reformulated the question as tradition or liberation.[11] Others such as Anna Nieto–Gómez, Velia García [then Hancock], and Mirta Vidal spoke out about the sexism in the Movimiento and militated for the liberation of women.[12]

Chicano men initially regarded the feminist critique as an assault on their Mexican cultural past, on their power, and by implication on their virility. If Chicanos were going to triumph in their anticapitalist, anticolonial revolt, divisiveness could not be tolerated. Bernice Zamora, in "Notes from a Chicana COED," captured the tug of war that would characterize this period.

> To cry that the *gabacho*
> is our oppressor is to shout
> in abstraction, *carnal.*
> He no more oppresses us
> than you do now as you tell me
> "It's the gringo who oppresses you, Babe."
> You cry "The gringo is our oppressor!"
> to the tune of $20,000 to $30,000
> a year, brother, and I wake up
> alone each morning and ask,
> "Can I feed my children today?" . . .
>
> And when I mention
> your G.I. Bill, your
> Ford Fellowship, your
> working wife, your
> three *gabacha guisas*
> then you ask me to

write your thesis
you're quick to shout,
"Don't give that
Women's Lib trip, mujer
that only divides us, and we have to work
together for the *movimiento*
the *gabacho* is oppressing us!"
Oye carnal, you may as well
tell me that moon water
cures constipation, that
penguin soup prevents *crudas*,
or that the Arctic Ocean is *menudo* . . .[13]

Men responded to the assault on their privileges by resorting to crass name calling, labeling Chicana feminists as *malinchistas*, traitors who were influenced by ideas foreign to their community—namely, bourgeois feminist ideology. One Chicana complained in 1971 that Chicanos viewed the Chicana feminist as "a white, thick calved, lesbian-oriented, eye-glassed gal."[14] Be "Chicana Primero," the men exhorted, asking the women to take pride in their cultural heritage and to reject women's liberation.[15] Adelaida del Castillo, among others, retorted that women were not seeking to dominate the movement. They only sought full equality:

> [T]rue freedom for our people can come about only if prefaced by the equality of individuals within La Raza. Chicanos must be convinced that Chicanas do not wish to dominate, which would be a negation of equality. Their concern is with the liberation of La Raza; the Chicano movement would be enhanced (and perhaps rejuvenated) if men and women were free to be mutually supportive.[16]

Theresa Aragón was but one of the many women who would clearly and unequivocally state that Chicanas, by incorporating feminist demands in their anticolonial revolution, were not dupes of white bourgeois feminists. "The white women's movement at present is not generally aware of or sensitive to the needs of the Chicana," Aragón wrote, and as such, "Chicanas would have to define their own goals and objectives in relationship to their culture, and their own feminist ideology in relation to those goals."[17] Consuelo Nieto argued that while Anglo feminists operated as individuals with individual goals, Chicanas belonged to a community of interest with whom they intended to cast their lot.[18] Class and racial oppression could not be overlooked only to privilege caste oppression. While in some circles "sisterhood was powerful," for the Chicana, perhaps, it was not.

Just as Chicano scholars who were interested in interpreting the history of the Southwest as a history of racial conflict between Anglos and Mexicans explicitly chose 1848 as the beginning of Chicano history, Chicana feminists began reenvisioning a history ordered by a different sense of time. For women it was not the U.S.-Mexican War that was most important. Instead, it was the first major act of conquest in the Americas, Spain's defeat of the Aztec empire.

As far as I can ascertain, Judith Sweeney, in her 1977 historiographic review of literature on Chicanas, was the first person to propose a new chronology for Chicano history. That history, she stated, began in 1519 and could "be divided into three major periods: the colonial period (1519–1821); the nineteenth century (1821–1910); and the contemporary period (1910–1976)."[19] Others writing on Chicanas quickly took up Sweeney's lead. Alfredo Mirandé and Evangelina Enríquez wrote in their 1979 book *La Chicana: The Mexican-American Woman* that the "roots of the Chicana . . . in the United States, date back to the conquest of Mexico in 1519."[20]

A chronology for Chicana history that began in 1519—not 1848—was not an arbitrary act. Rather, it placed the issues of gender and power at the very center of the political debate about the future and the past. By choosing 1519, women focused attention on one of Mexico's most famous women, Doña Marina. Doña Marina was a Maya woman of noble ancestry who befriended Hernán Cortés in 1517. Cortés availed himself of Doña Marina's considerable knowledge of the local political geography and of her knowledge of various indigenous languages. Acting as his mistress, translator, and confidante, Marina helped Cortés to forge local antipathies toward the Aztecs into a fighting force that Cortés successfully unleashed on Tenochtitlán.

In Mexican history Doña Marina, or la Malinche, had always been seen as a villain, as the supreme betrayer of her race.[21] Luis Valdez in his 1971 play *The Conquest of Mexico* depicted Malinche as a traitor because "not only did she turn her back on her own people, she joined the white men and became assimilated."[22] In expressing this sentiment, Valdez, the playwright who generated so much of the popular culture that became identified as Chicano in the 1970s, was simply reiterating what was well-established dogma among Mexican intellectuals. Octavio Paz in his book *The Labyrinth of Solitude* referred to Mexicans as the "sons of Malinche," *hijos de la chingada*.[23] In a long disquisition on the word *chingar*, Paz argued that it meant

> to do violence to another. The verb is masculine, active, cruel: it stings, wounds, gashes, stains. And it provokes a bitter, resentful satisfaction. The person who suffers this action is passive, inert and open, in contrast to the active, aggressive and closed person who inflicts it. The *chingón* is the *macho*, the male; he rips open the *chingada*, the female, who is pure passivity, defenseless against the exterior world. The relationship between them is violent and it is determined by the cynical power of the first and the impotence of the second. The idea of violence rules darkly over all the meanings of the word.[24]

Paz asserted that just as the power and violence of the *macho* or the *gran chingón* was similar to that of the Spanish conquistador, so too the passivity of the violated mother, or *la chingada*, found an analogue in Malinche. "It is true," Paz writes,

> that she gave herself voluntarily to the conquistador, but he forgot her as soon as her usefulness was over. Doña Marina becomes a figure representing the Indian women who were fascinated, violated or seduced by the Spaniards. And as a small boy will not forgive his mother if she abandons him to search for his father, the Mexican people have not forgiven La Malinche for her betrayal.[25]

For activist Chicanas, the historical representations of Malinche as a treacherous whore who betrayed her own people were but profound reflections of the deep-seated misogynist beliefs in Mexican and Mexican American culture. The only public models open to Mexican women were those of the virgin and the whore.[26] If women were going to go beyond them, then they had to begin by rehabilitating Malinche.

The literary vindication of Malinche began with Sylvia Gonzales's poem "I Am Chicana":

> I am Chicana
> Waiting for the return
> of la Malinche,

to negate her guilt,
and cleanse her flesh
of a confused Mexican wrath
which seeks reason
to the displaced power of Indian deities.
I am Chicana
Waiting for the coming of a Malinche
to sacrifice herself
on an Aztec altar
and Catholic cross
in redemption of all her forsaken daughters.[27]

Adelaida R. del Castillo took up the crusade in historical writing, stating in 1977 that "Doña Marina should not be portrayed as negative, insignificant or foolish, but instead be perceived as a woman who was able to act beyond her prescribed societal function, namely, that of being a mere concubine and servant, and perform as one who was willing to make great sacrifices for what she believed to be a philanthropic conviction."[28] Never mind the fine details; what was important to Chicanas was that Malinche was the primordial source of the two concepts that were at the core of the Chicana movement—*mexicanidad* and *mestizaje*. Malinche, noted del Castillo,

is the beginning of the mestizo nation, she is the mother of its birth, she initiates it with the birth of her mestizo children. Even her baptism is significant. She is, in fact, the first Indian to be christianized (catechized and baptized to Catholicism) in her native land, that land which metamorphizes into our mundo mestizo—again she is the starting point! Thus any denigration made against her indirectly defames the character of the . . . chicana female. If there is shame for her, there is shame for us; we suffer the effects of those implications.[29]

Following del Castillo's lead, other women joined the fray. Cordelia Candelaria in 1980 saw in Malinche "the prototypical Chicana feminist." Malinche, claimed Candelaria, embodied "those personal characteristics—such as intelligence, initiative, adaptability, and leadership—which are most often associated with Mexican American women unfettered by traditional restraints against activist public achievement. By adapting to the historical circumstances thrust upon her, she defied traditional social expectations of a woman's role."[30]

Whatever the facts—in the case of Malinche there are dreadfully few—the crafting of a her-story and feminist chronology had shifted the debate away from racism to sexism, away from the male ethos of *carnalismo*, or brotherhood, and *chicanismo*, toward *mexicanidad y mestizaje*. Equally important, by examining the life of Malinche, the "first" Mexican convert to Christianity, attention was given to the role of religion in maintaining female subordination, with its patriarchal God and its phallocentric clergy.[31]

If the aim of the Chicano movement had been to decolonize the mind, as the novelist Tomás Rivera proposed, the Chicana movement decolonized the body. Male concerns over job discrimination, access to political power, entry into educational institutions, and community autonomy and self-determination gave way to female demands for birth control[32] and against forced sterilizations,[33] for welfare rights,[34] for prison rights for *pintas*,[35] for protection against male violence, and, most important, for sexual pleasure both in marriage and outside of it. "La Nueva Chicana," the new woman, shattered the cultural stereotypes and defined herself.[36]

594 Ramón A. Gutiérrez

Of course, this is not to imply that what had traditionally been the "meat and potatoes" of the Chicano movement, that is, an interest in working-class struggles, ceased with the rise of Chicana feminist writing. It did not. The literature on the condition of Mexican American working women remained prolific, dating all the way back to the 1930s.[37] What did change in feminist-inspired Chicana cultural production, even when it examined traditional topics, was the centrality that the intersection of race, gender, and class assumed. The example of the case of Mexican immigration to the United States illustrates the point well. A whole generation of Chicano scholars earned tenure at universities by describing the nature and dimensions of the immigration process. More than half of all of the Mexican immigrants entering the United States since 1945 have been women, but this fact eluded most earlier authors—Mario García being the exception. The works of Vicki L. Ruiz and Susan Tiano, Margarita B. Melville, Rosalinda Gonzalez, Gilbert Cardenas and Estevan Flores, and Rita Simon and Caroline Brettell were important correctives to this oversight.[38]

But even more exciting were the works by women that linked race, class, and gender domination at the workplace with gender domination within the home. Patricia Zavella's splendid work *Women's Work and Chicano Families* studied women cannery workers in the Santa Clara Valley of northern California and showed how mechanization had contributed to female labor segregation and how the labor market reinforced traditional family roles within the household. Vicki L. Ruiz covered very similar terrain in her masterful *Cannery Women, Cannery Lives*, a study of Mexican women's unionization attempts in the California food processing industry.[39]

In addition to these very traditional topics, what was perhaps most revolutionary was that Chicanas began to write and to express a complex inner emotional life. Reflecting in 1970 on the participation of Chicanas in the liberation movement, Enriqueta Longauex y Vasquez stated that while the role of the Chicana previously "has been a very strong one— [it has been] . . . a silent one."[40] But that silence was soon shattered.

> I am here. (do
> you hear me?) hear
> me. hear me
> I am here. birthing
> (yourself) is
> no easy task.
> I am here. (pleading)
> I am here. (teasing)
> I am here. (taunting)
> I am here. (simply)
> I am here.[41]

So wrote Alma Villanueva in her poem "Inside," crafting a female literary voice and birthing a Chicana poetic consciousness.

Unlike Chicanos, who took their sex/gender privileges for granted, Chicanas, as victims of those privileges, realized that an essential part of their literary birthing had to include an exploration of their sexuality. "Our sexuality has been hidden, subverted, distorted within the 'sacred' walls of the 'familia'—be it myth or reality—and within the even more privatized walls of the bedrooms. . . . In the journey to the love of female self and each other we are ultimately forced to confront father, brother, and god (and mother as his agent)," wrote Norma Alarcón, Ana Castillo, and Cherríe Moraga.[42]

Things that formerly were taboo now appeared in print. Arcelia Ponce, in her short story "La Preferida," described how a young girl named Julia had been sexually abused by her father from the age of six to fourteen. Victoria Alegría Rosales vividly recounted the brutal beatings she had received in marriage. Lesbianism, the love that dare not speak its name, was brought out of the closet by Veronica Cunningham in the poem "When All the Yous":

> when all the yous
> of my poetry
> were really
> she or her
> and i could never
> no
> i would never write them
> because
> of some fears
> i never even wanted
> to see.
> how could i have been frightened
> of sharing
> the being
> and me.

In "The Love Making," Cenen writes:

When the swell of your clitoris came bulging into the roll of my sucking tongue, I knew tonight's sweetness would be long. My excited body moved closer into the swelling folds of your labia, rubbing my teeth, my lips, my whole face into your wetness. Your body jumped and turned spasmodically pressing my head between your legs. As I tried to release my head from your grip, my mouth lost your swollen clitoris.

Ana Castillo shattered all Catholic conventions by describing her sexual desire and fulfillment. Here is her poem "Coffee Break":

> 15 minutes
>   They take
>   their morning papers
>   monogrammed mugs
>   to the lounge
>   moaning and groaning
>   of monday monotony
>   & self boredom—
> she
>   does a 2 step down
>   the narrow hall
>   to the small room
>   where toilet paper
>   plugs the keyhole
>   whitewashed windows
>   graffiti wallpaper
>   designed by unknown
>   heroes and scholars—
> A tiny streak
>   of sun leaks
>   through a space
>   of unpainted glass

makes as a spotlight
for 2 talented fingers
creating fast—

ART IN MOTION!
A STAR IS BORN!
SUCH STYLE!
WHAT GRACE![43]

Given the importance that sexuality had in the Chicana feminist movement, it is not coincidental that so much of the writing would dwell on the mother-daughter relationship. The confrontation between two cultures and between two ways of life was often played out as a generational struggle between mothers and daughters. Alma Villanueva expresses this sentiment well in her poem "Blood Root":

I vowed
   to never
      grow up
to be a woman
and helpless
like my mother.[44]

In "Aztec Princess," Pat Mora casts mothers as the persons who were holding back the liberation of women.

Her mother would say, "Look in
the home for happiness. Why do you stare out
often with such longing?" One day,
almost in desperation, her mother said,
"Here. See here. We buried your umbilical
cord here, in the house. A sign that you,
our girl-child, would nest inside."

That night the young woman quietly dug
for some trace of the shriveled woman-to-woman
skin, but all she found was earth, rich earth,
which she carefully scooped into an earthen jar
whispering, "Breathe."[45]

For Tina Benítez, the love/hate relationship that existed between Chicanas and their mothers was the result of the mother's desire to reproduce in her daughter the values of a patriarchal culture. "The mother blocks her desires by telling her what 'good girls' should and should not do," asserted Benítez, "thereby, condemning her to emulate a role of powerlessness."[46] Rina Rocha captured the essence of this sentiment in her poem "Baby Doll":

Mothers can be
jealous gods
Just like
husbands
Unforgiving and demanding.

Saying
naughty girl,

naught ought
to have done that.
Naught, ought
to have said that . . .

And I . . .
am amazed still—
at me!
That I should wait for these
candied coated loving
words of approval
from
jealous gods.[47]

Mothers came to be despised by their Chicana daughters in large part because of their subordination/accommodation to patriarchal power. As mothers who often favored assimilation, they urged their daughters to learn English, to get educated, to marry well (if to wealthy Anglo men, all the better), and, if necessary, to abandon their cultural past.

The generational conflict took its most confrontational and accusatory tones when daughters, be they lesbian or heterosexual, started to assert their sexuality. To an older generation, sex was not a topic for public discussion, and even in private it was not a topic broached comfortably. To daughters, many as participants in the sexual revolution of the 1960s, female sexuality was something to celebrate openly, to talk about, to write about, and to represent in a myriad of open ways. For mothers such behavior was tantamount to the abandonment of Mexicano cultural values and the acceptance of the Anglo ways.[48] Mothers thus accused their daughters of assimilationism; daughters accused their mothers of accommodationism—and here was the problem.

Perhaps the most intense discussion of the mother/daughter relationship yet written was Cherríe Moraga's *Loving in the War Years: Lo que Nunca Pasó por Sus Labios*—the subtitle translates as "what never crossed her lips."[49] Here Moraga returns to a reevaluation of Malinche as the traitor and *chingada*, seeing in her historical dilemmas a way to confront Moraga's own dilemmas in life. Moraga felt betrayed by her mother, because she loved her sons much more devotedly than her daughters. This was complicated further by two additional levels of betrayal. As a lesbian, Moraga felt accused of betraying her race by choosing the sex of her mother as the object of sexual desire. As a *coyota*, the half-breed daughter of an Anglo father and Chicana mother, Moraga saw herself as the daughter of Malinche, suffering her mother's betrayal of her people.

Moraga is wrenched by the multiple levels of contradiction these betrayals create. On one hand, she loves her mother deeply, treasures the closeness family provides, and realizes that the mother-daughter relationship is "paramount and essential in our lives [in which the daughter always] . . . remains faithful a la madre."[50] And on the other hand, she realizes that while the daughter is taught to be faithful to her mother, mothers do not always reciprocate.

Most Chicanas who explored issues of gender and sexuality through reflections on Malinche often cast themselves as the victimized daughters of Malinche. Moraga is unique in that she focuses not on Malinche but on Malinche's mother, comparing her to her own mother. Thus, in the expository parallels, Moraga and Malinche are identical.

Moraga clearly believes that her mother betrayed her by loving her sons much more than her daughters. We see this resentment when Moraga writes:

> If somebody would have asked me when I was a teenager what it means to be Chicana, I would probably have listed the grievances done me. When my sister and I were fifteen and fourteen, respectively, and my brother a few years older, we were all still waiting on him. I write "were" as if now, nearly two decades later, it were over. But that would be a lie. To this day in my mother's home, my brother and father are waited on, including by me. I do this now out of respect for my mother and her wishes. In those early days, however, it was mainly in relation to my brother that I resented providing such service. For unlike my father, who sometimes worked as much as seventy hours a week to feed my face every day, the only thing that earned my brother my servitude was his maleness.[51]

Moraga continues to describe how her mother treated her own father, conforming to Mexican cultural norms that expected feminine subservience to men. When her mother became a wife, the act of treachery was again repeated; favoring her sons, revering her husband, and taking her daughters for granted. "Traitor begets traitor," Moraga writes; like mother, like daughter. Malinche's mother was the first traitor (mother) who begot the second one (daughter).[52]

To assert her Chicana identity and to reclaim "the race of my mother," Moraga breaks free from Malinche and Malinche's mother by choosing to "embrace no white man."[53] She is finally united with the race of her mother through Chicana lesbianism, by loving other women. By refusing to give her sexual loyalty to Chicano men, by refusing to live as a heterosexual, Moraga realizes that, in the eyes of the Movimiento men, she has become a *malinchista*, a traitor. This she proudly accepts, stating at the end of her book that she comes from a long line of *vendidas* (traitors).

If the generational tension in Chicana expression is between mothers and daughters, the generational refuge is between grandmothers and granddaughters. In various essays Tina Benítez, Norma Alarcón, and Diana Fey Rebollero have explored the ways in which "the grandmother/granddaughter relationship gives the Chicana an escape from her gender role expectations enforced by the mother."[54]

To achieve what Tina Benítez believed was a necessary reconciliation with the mother, she proposed that the mother-daughter relationship had to be conceived as evolutionary.

> As a young girl the mother is portrayed as nurturing and loving. However, as the Chicana matures she becomes more critical of her mother and the role she succumbs to. When the mother tries to impose this self-sacrificing role upon her daughter, what emerges from the literature is the daughter/writer's repulsion and rejection of the mother and veneration of the grandmother. As the Chicana strives for a new vision of transformation she turns to the mother for reconciliation and thereby draws strength for the rebirth and empowerment of herself and all Chicana women.[55]

Early explorations of the relationships between mothers and daughters were hostile, but gradually some women came to realize that they could not blame their mothers for what their mothers themselves had not been able to control. Guadalupe Valdes-Fallis reconciled herself with her mother when she acknowledged that her mother had not had any other options open to her. In an autobiographical essay titled "Recuerdo," Valdes stated:

> My story . . . might well be entitled "Mother's Advice." It is a bitter story, written at a time in which I was angry about my own life and about having followed my own mother's counsel. I was trying to make sense of the world, trying to understand why one could follow all of the (cultural) rules and yet end up unhappy. I felt betrayed, trapped and all alone. Until recently, it had not occurred to me that my mother has also been betrayed and trapped. . . . [L]ike so many women, she had also tried to follow rules; to make sense of so

many things that seemed unfair; and to hope that somehow, for her daughters, things would be different. Clearly, my anger was misdirected. My mother gave me what she could. She said, "Marry a man who doesn't drink." Amazingly that, like the mother in "Recuerdo," her formula for happiness was so simple. She focused on the one thing that had made her life unhappy, and she wanted more for me. It seems sad now, that I blamed her for so many years, blamed her because I believed her, blamed her because the formula was not complete and did not bring happiness.[56]

The ultimate solution to this relationship was, according to one Chicana feminist, for mothers to give their love and approval to their daughters freely, and for daughters to relieve their mothers of all the psychic burdens they too had endured. "The choice is to either passively sit and watch our sisters and mother be beaten into the ground, or to help them rise above by giving them the love and support they so often seek from men."[57]

The theme of the individual in our capitalist, postmodern society forms the last section of this historiographic survey. Postmodernism is one of those much-bantered-about but elusive terms. It usually refers "to a certain constellation of styles and tones in cultural works: pastiche; blankness; a sense of exhaustion; a mixture of levels, forms, styles; a relish for copies and repetition; a knowingness that dissolves commitment into irony; acute self-consciousness about the formal, constructed nature of work; pleasure in the place of surfaces; a rejection of history." A postmodern culture is one in which a formerly unified subject is split into his or her constituent parts; in which a single homogeneous style is superseded by a number of heterogeneous fashions. We see this tendency toward frag-mentation, eclecticism, and reflexivity in television advertising and on MTV. But in addi-tion to being a general cultural style, postmodernism is, says Raymond Williams, a general orientation. It is a "structure of feeling" for apprehending and experiencing the world and our place, or placelessness, in it.[58]

In the past five years some Mexican American intellectuals have embraced the subver-sive experimentation of postmodernism to describe the fragmentation of Chicano culture, showing how there never was, nor currently is, one "Chicano movement," with a capital C. Instead, they view the Chicano movement as an eclectic composition of peoples and tradi-tions. In recent years the names of those whose works could be considered postmodern include Gloria Anzaldúa, Guillermo Gómez-Peña, Richard Rodriguez, Renato Rosaldo, and Tomás Almaguer. I will return to them shortly, but before I do, I want to focus first on John Rechy. In 1963, when the thought of a Chicano movement hardly existed, John Rechy exploded onto the American scene with the publication of *City of Night*, an auto-biographical novel that described vividly, through the eyes of a male prostitute, the sexual underworld that pulsated in the very heart of Los Angeles, New York City, Chicago, El Paso, and San Francisco. In *The Sexual Outlaw* and *Rushes*, Rechy further elaborated on "the narcissistic pattern of my life," a life that was governed by the narcotic of "sexmoney." From room to room, from bed to bed, from face to face, at a dizzying pace, Rechy showed us his tricks. In barrooms and back rooms, in rest rooms and parks, and behind bushes that barely concealed, men of every sort played out their own fantasies with him. Men fellated him, they furtively groped and caressed his body, they licked his legs and boots and drank his urine—a scenario that always ended with him mounting his partners and "play[ing] the male role with [these] men."[59]

At the 1989 meeting of the National Association for Chicano Studies, Rechy was finally honored with a panel on his work. But in the 1960s Chicanos refused to acknowledge Rechy as a Chicano or even to accept his novels as Chicano literature. Though his mother was a Mexicana and had raised him the barrios of El Paso, it was his Scottish father who had given him a name and abandoned him and his mother. It was his name, his homosexuality, and the themes he explored in print that excluded him from the community young men defined as Chicano. Ironically, at the very time that he was being rejected by Chicanos, the Texas Hall of Fame inducted him into its ranks as a Chicano author, an identity Rechy has always proudly claimed.

Rechy's novels were intellectual forerunners to postmodernism among Mexican Americans. The themes of marginality, of fractured identities, of suspension betwixt and between worlds were themes he first articulated, but which would not emerge again until 1987. In that year Gloria Anzaldúa's book *Borderlands/La Frontera: The New Mestiza* appeared. The book defies easy classification. It is a combination of history (much of it wrong), poetry, essays, and philosophical gems, in which Anzaldúa describes her fractured identity—an identity fractured by not only the reality of the border between the United States and Mexico, but also by the numerous borders in personal life. Anzaldúa claims to be a *mestiza*, or mixed-blood, lesbian, and we can see the meaning of that in her poem "Del Otro Lado":

> She looks at the Border Park fence
> posts are stuck into her throat, her navel,
> barbwire is shoved up her cunt.
> Her body torn in two, half a woman on the other side
> half a woman on this side, the right side
> And she went to the North American university,
> excelled in the Gringo's tongue
> learned to file in folders.
> But she remembered the other half
> strangled in Aztec villages, in Mayan villages, in Incan villages . . .
>
> She remembers
> The horror in her sister's voice,
> "Eres una de las otras,"
> The look in her mother's face as she says,
> "I am so ashamed, I will never
> be able to raise my head in this pueblo."
> The mother's words are barbs digging into her flesh.
> *De las otras.* Cast out. Untouchable.
> "But I'm me," she cries, "I've always been me."
> "Don't bring your queer friends into my house,
> my land, the planet. Get away.
> Don't contaminate us, get away."
>
> Away, she went away.
> But every place she went
> the pushed her to the other side
> and that other side pushed her to the other side
> of the other side of the other side
> Kept in the shadows of other.
> No right to sing, to rage, to explode . . .
> Always pushed toward the other side.
> In all lands alien, nowhere citizen.
> Away, she went away
> but each place she went
> pushed her to the other side, al otro lado.[60]

In "To live in the Borderlands," she writes,

> means you are neither *hispana india negra española*
> *ni gabacha, eres mestiza, mulata*, half-breed
> caught in the crossfire between camps
> while carrying all five races on your back
> now knowing which side to turn to, to run from; . . .
>
> *Cuando vives en la frontera*
> people walk through you, the wind steals your voice,
> you're a *burra, buey*, scapegoat,
> forerunner of a new race,
> half and half—both woman and man, neither—
> a new gender;
>
> To live on the Borderlands means to
> put *chile* in the borscht
> eat whole wheat *tortillas*,
> speak Tex-Mex with a Brooklyn accent;
> be stopped by *la migra* at the border checkpoints; . . .
>
> To survive the Borderlands
> you must live *sin fronteras*
> be a crossroads.[61]

In her essay "How to Tame a Wild Tongue," Anzaldúa vividly shows, through the example of language, the complexity of Mexican Amercian cultures. She begins by identifying eight forms of Spanish:

> My "home" tongues are the languages I speak with my sister and brothers, with my friends. They are [Pachuco (called *caló*), Tex-Mex, Chicano Spanish, North Mexican Spanish dialect, and Standard Mexican Spanish, with Chicano Spanish] being the closest to my heart. From school, the media and job situations, I've picked up standard and working class English. From Mamagrande Locha and from reading Spanish and Mexican literature, I've picked up Standard Spanish and Standard Mexican Spanish. From *los recién legados*, Mexican immigrants and *braceros*, I learned Northern Mexican dialect. . . .[62]

She then goes on to describe how and when she uses each type, proving the point that the relationship between language and identity is not a neat and easy one, and that Mexican Americans are a complexly stratified group.

Another person who had been extremely influential in the Chicano postmodernist movement is Guillermo Gómez-Peña, a performance artist in San Diego. He identifies himself as "a child of crisis and cultural syncretism, half hippie and half punk. . . . In my fractured reality, but a reality nonetheless, there cohabit two histories, two languages, cosmologies, artistic traditions, and political systems which are drastically counterposed."[63] His ecleticism poignantly emerges in a poem "Good Morning, This Is Radio Latino Spoiling Your Breakfast as Always":

> Alien-ation
> alien action
> alien-ated
> alguién ate it

alien hatred
aliens out there
hay alguién out there
"aliens" the album
"aliens" the movie
cowboys vs. aliens
bikers vs. aliens
the wet-back from Mars
the Mexican transformer & his radioactive torta
the conquest of Tenochtitlán by Spielberg
the reconquest of Aztlán by Monty Python
the brown wave vs. the microwave
invaders from the South
vs. the San Diego Police reinforced by
the Border Crime Prevention Unit reinforced by
your ignorance, dear San Diego . . .[64]

The Pompidou Center in Paris is often given as a splendid example of postmodern architecture, because instead of concealing its wiring, its vents, its plumbing, and its foundations, everything is exposed. In social science writings on Chicanos, Tomás Almaguer's essay "Ideological Distortions in Recent Chicano Historiography" lays open the historiography on Chicanos, exposing the false epistemological closures and the simplistic ideas that he, as well as other Chicano radicals and intellectuals, claimed as their credo in the 1960s. Almaguer argues that, motivated primarily by the desire to challenge the dominant assimilationist model of the 1950s, Chicano radicals embraced a colonial analysis that depicted the history of Chicanos as that of a colonized minority. In this internal colony, racism and economic exploitation were the dominant themes—themes that had been born as a result of the U.S.-Mexican War. Almaguer shows how in the scholarly works of political scientists Mario Barrera and Carlos Muñoz; historians Ricardo Griswold del Castillo, Albert Camarillo, Ricardo Romo, Juan Gómez-Quiñones, Guillermo Flores, and Rudy Acuña; and sociologists such as Joan Moore, Charles Orneales, and Almaguer, colonialism and racism became the dominant themes of their analytic frameworks. These themes cast the present and the past as a conflict between Anglos and Chicanos that politically called for a cultural nationalist movement to crush imperialism.[65]

However strongly these sentiments were felt in the 1960s, Almaguer argues that the analysis was wrong. A cursory examination showed that Native Americans had been ignored. Mexican Americans historically straddled several classes, and in the racial hierarchy Mexicans occupied an intermediate position between Anglos and Indian. In short, much of what had been written was an ideological distortion of the past, fashioned to fit the political tenor of the day.

Alex Saragoza made a similar point.[66] The Chicano radicals of the 1960s chose 1848 as the beginning of Chicano history because that date more conveniently highlighted Anglo-Mexican conflicts "Why did Chicano history not begin in 1836?" Saragoza asks. The answer is simple. During the Texas War for Independence, *Tejanos* and Anglos fought alongside each other as allies. This date complicated the dichotomous them/us racial vision too much and just did not meet their political needs.

Let me conclude by bringing together the various strands that I have tried to weave together here. I began by outlining the shape and dimensions of that political community Chicano radicals forged in the 1960s, turning next to the feminist assault on that vision and the construction of her-story, a story that was rooted in the politicization of the body. Postmodernism fractured all of this into bits, exploded the categories, and left a disordered and disordering vision of the past and the future. Chicano cultural nationalism had a clear vision. However misdirected and obtuse, by defining Anglos and colonialism as the enemies, a plausible strategy for revolutionary change was close at hand. With Chicana feminism, too, the political vision and strategy were clear: Women, unite against your fathers, brothers, and sons to overthrow patriarchy. But what is the political vision of postmodernism, with its emphasis on alienation, despair, confusion, and the layer upon layer of splinterings and fractures?

Twenty years ago Enriqueta Longauex y Vasquez, an early Chicana feminist, uttered the following words:

> The Raza movement is based on brother- and sisterhood. We must look at each other as one large family. We must look at all of the children as belonging to all of us. We must strive for the fulfillment of all as equals, with the full capability and right to develop as humans.[67]

The majority of the persons living in poverty in this country are Chicana single mothers and their children. Chicanas over the age of twenty-five, on the average, complete only 8.4 years of schooling, in comparison to the 13.5 years of their white counterparts. And when the average income of a Chicana-headed household is still only $4,930, the burning issues that sparked the Chicano movement have only intensified and taken a clearer class form.[68] Indeed, if one takes a long view when analyzing what the ultimate impact of the Chicano movement was on the daily lives of ethnic Mexicans in the United States, it was to obscure the class character of the racial order. No matter whether one subscribed to the masculine Chicano vision of the nation with its emphasis on *la raza* (the race) and *carnalismo* (brotherhood) or the Chicana nationalism of feminists who turned to *mestizaje* (race mixture) and *mexicanidad* for inspiration, the imagined community was stratified by region, by class, by generation, by color, and by political persuasions. The various strands of Mexican American activism that did manage to extract social and political concessions from the state and regional capitalists were those segments of the movement that never lost sight of their class character and class aims. Cesar Chavez organized agricultural workers throughout the Southwest through his United Farmworkers of America, militating for better wages and work conditions—concessions his union was able to extract, if only for a short period of time. Reies López Tijerina created the Alianza Federal de Mercedes in northern New Mexico and southern Colorado, and through this organization was able to get Hispano land claims favorably settled. The impact of the struggles that both of these men led are still felt in labor relations and land rights litigation. As for the student component of the movement, perhaps the most significant and enduring legacy were the curricular changes and the creation of Chicano studies programs and departments.

Notes

1. Rodolfo Acuña, *Occupied America: The Chicano's Struggle toward Liberation* (San Francisco, 1972); Ramón A. Gutiérrez, "Mexican Migration to the United States, 1880–1930: The Chicano and Internal Colonialism" (M.A. thesis, University of Wisconsin, 1976); Tomás Almaguer, "Toward the Study of Chicano Colonialism," *Aztlán* 2 (spring 1971): 7–21, and "Historical Notes on Chicano Oppression: The Dialectics of Racial and Class Domination in North America," *Aztlán* 5 (spring–fall 1974): 27–56; Mario Barrera, "Colonial Labor and Theories of Inequality: The Case of International Harvester," *Review of Radical Political Economics*

8 (summer 1967): 7–27, and *Race and Class in the Southwest: A Theory of Racial Inequality* (Notre Dame, Ind., 1979); Mario Barrera, Carlos Muñoz, and Charles Ornelas, "The Barrio as Internal Colony," *Urban Affairs Annual Reviews* 6 (1972): 465–98.

2. Albert Camarillo, *Chicanos in a Changing Society: From Mexican Pueblos to American Barrios in Santa Barbara and Southern California, 1848–1930* (Cambridge, Mass., 1979); Richard Griswold del Castillo, *The Los Angeles Barrio, 1850–1890* (Berkeley, Calif., 1979); Ricardo Romo, *East Los Angeles: A History of a Barrio* (Austin, Tex., 1983).

3. Acuña, *Occupied America*, 230.

4. Armando Navarro, "The Evolution of Chicano Politics," *Aztlán* 5 (spring–fall 1974): 57–84, quotation from 57–58.

5. Adelaida R. del Castillo, "Mexican Women in Organization," in Magdalena Mora and Adelaida R. del Castillo, eds., *Mexican Women in the United States* (Los Angeles, 1980), 7–16, quotation from 10.

6. Ibid., 7–16, quotation from 9.

7. Ibid., 7–16, quotation from 8.

8. Marcela Christine Lucero-Trujillo, "Machismo Is Part of Our Culture," in Norma Alarcón, Ana Castillo, and Cherríe Moraga, eds., *Third Woman: The Sexuality of Latinas*, (Berkeley, Calif.: 1989), 401–2.

9. Lorna Dee Cervantes, "You Cramp My Style, Baby," quoted in Yvonne Yarbro-Berjarano, "The Female Subject in Chicano Theatre: Sexuality, 'Race,' and Class," *Theatre Journal* 38 (December 1986): 402.

10. Irene Rodarte, "Machismo vs. Revolution," in Dorinda Moreno, ed., *La mujer en Pie de Lucha* (Mexico City, 1973).

11. Guadalupe Valdes Fallis, "The Liberated Chicana: A Struggle against Tradition," *Women: A Journal of Liberation* 3 (1974): 20–21.

12. Anna Nieto-Gómez, "Sexism in the Movimiento," *La Gente* 6 (March 1976): 10; Velia Hancock, "La Chicana: Chicana Movement and Women's Lib," *Chicano Studies Newsletter*, Feb.–Mar. 1971, 1; Mirta Vidal, *Chicanas Speak Out* (New York, 1971).

13. Bernice Zamora, "Notes from a Chicana COED," *Caracol* 3 (1977): 19, as quoted in M. Sanchez, *Contemporary Chicana Poetry* (Berkeley, Calif., 1985), 231–32.

14. Una Chicana, "Abajo con los Machos," *La Raza* 1 (1971): 3–4.

15. Enriqueta Longauex y Vásquez, "Soy Chicano Primero," *El Cuaderno* 1 (1972): 17–22, and "The Mexican-American Woman," in Robin Morgan, ed., *Sisterhood Is Powerful* (New York, 1970), 379–84.

16. Theresa Aragón de Valdez, "Organizing as a Political Tool for the Chicana," *Frontiers: A Journal of Women's Studies* 5 (1980): 11.

17. Ibid., 10.

18. Consuelo Nieto, "Interaction of Culture and Sex Roles in the Schools: Chicana Identity and Its Educational Implications" (unpublished paper), quoted in Aragón, "Organizing as a Political Tool for the Chicana," 10.

19. Judith Sweeney, "Chicana History: A Review of the Literature," in Rosaura Sánchez, ed., *Essays on la Mujer* (Los Angeles, 1977), 99–123, quotation from 100.

20. Alfredo Mirandé and Evangelina Enríquez, *La Chicana: The Mexican-American Woman* (Chicago, 1979), 2.

21. T. R. Fehrenhach, *Fire and Blood: A History of Mexico* (New York, 1973), 131.

22. Luis Valdez, "La Conquista de Méjico," *Actos y el Teatro Campesino* (Fresno, Calif., 1971), 131.

23. Octavio Paz, *The Labyrinth of Solitude: Life and Thought in Mexico* (New York, 1961).

24. Ibid., 77.

25. Ibid., 86.

26. Sylvia A. Gonzales, "La Chicana: Guadalupe or Malinche," in Beverly Lindsay, ed., *Comparative Perspectives of Third World Women: The Impact of Race, Sex, and Class* (New York, 1980), 229–50. For a more succinct theoretical statement of the problem, see Evelyn P. Stevens, "Marianismo: The Other Face of Machismo in Latin America," in Ann Pescatello, ed., *Female and Male in Latin America* (Pittsburgh, 1973), 89–102.

27. Sylvia Gonzales, "I Am Chicana," in *Third Woman*, 442.

28. Adelaida R. del Castillo, "Malintzin Tenépal: A Preliminary Look into a New Perspective," in Rosaura Sánchez, ed., *Essays on la Mujer* (Los Angeles, 1977), 124–49, quotation from 126.

29. Ibid., 141. Adelaida del Castillo's essay was also a profound critique of Octavio Paz, *The Labyrinth of Solitude*. See, for example, 413–32.

30. Cordelia Candelaria, "La Malinche, Feminist Prototype," *Frontiers: A Journal of Women's Studies* 5 (1980): 1–6, quotation from 6.

31. Norma Alarcón "Chicana's Feminist Literature: A Re-Vision through Malintzín or Malinche: Putting Flesh Back on the Object," in Cherríe Moraga and Gloria Anzaldúa, eds., *This Bridge Called My Back: Writings by Radical Women of Color* (New York, 1983), 182–90; Rachel Phillips, "Marina/Malinche: Masks and Shadows," in Beth Miller, ed., *Women in Hispanic Literature: Icons and Fallen Idols* (Berkeley, Calif.,

1983), 97–114; Shirlene Soto, "Tres modelos culturales: La Virgen Guadalupe, La Malinche y la Llorona," *fem* 10 (October–November 1986): 13–16.

32. Sylvia Delgado, "Young Chicana Speaks up on Problems Faced by Young Girls," *Regeneración* 1 (1978): 5–7; Kathy Flores, "Chicano Attitudes toward Birth Control," *Imagenes de la Chicana*, first issue, 19–21; Melanie Orendian, "Sexual Taboo y la Cultura?" *Imagenes de la Chicana* 1, 30 (1974). Theresa Aragón de Valdez chronicles a 1971 San Antonio case in which Mexican American women were used as guinea pigs for a birth control experiment without being informed; see "Organizing as a Political Tool for the Chicana," 9.

33. Carlos G. Velez-I, "Se me Acabó la Canción: An Ethnography of Non-Consenting Sterilizations among Mexican Women in Los Angeles," in Magdalena Mora and Adelaida del Castillo, eds., *Mexican Women in the United States* (Los Angeles, 1980), 71–94.

34. Clemencia Martinez, "Welfare Families Face Forced Labor," *La Raza* 1 (January 1972): 41; Mary Tullos and Dolores Hernandez, "Talmadge Amendment: Welfare Continues to Exploit the Poor," *La Raza* 1 (January 1972): 10–11; Anna Nieto-Gómez, "Madres por la justicia," *Encuentro Femenil* 1 (spring 1973): 12–19; Alicia Escalante, "A Letter from the Chicana Welfare Rights Organization," *Encuentro Femenil* 1 (1974): 15–19.

35. Renne Mares, "La Pinta: The Myth of Rehabilitation," *Encuentro Femenil* 1 (1974): 27–29; Josie Madrid, Chata Mercado, Priscilla Pardo, and Anita Ramirez, "Chicanas in Prison," *Regeneración* 2 (1973): 53–54.

36. Viola Correa, "La Nueva Chicana," in Dorinda Moreno ed., *La Mujer en Pie de Lucha* (Mexico City, 1973); Maxine Baca Zinn, "Gender and Ethnic Identity among Chicanos," *Frontiers: A Journal of Women's Studies* 5 (1980): 18–24.

37. Ruth Allen, *The Labor of Women in the Production of Cotton* (New York, 1975 [1933]) and "Mexican Peon Women in Texas," *Sociology and Social Research* 16 (November–December 1931): 131–42. See also Mary Loretta Sullivan and Bertha Blair, "Women in Texas Industries, Hours, Working Conditions, and Home Work," *Bulletin of the Women's Bureau* 126 (1936); Selden C. Menefee and Orin C. Cassmore, *The Pecan Shellers of San Antonio: The Problem of Underpaid and Unemployed Mexican Labor* (Washington, D.C., 1940); Melissa Hield, "Union-Minded: Women in the Texas ILGWU, 1933–1950," *Frontiers* 4 (summer 1979): 59–70. See also George N. Green, "ILGWU in Texas, 1930–1970," *Journal of Mexican-American History* 1 (1971): 144–69; Mario F. Vásquez, "The Election Day Immigration Raid at Lillie Diamond Originals and the Response of the ILGWU," in Mora and Adelaida del Castillo, eds., *Mexican Women in the United States* (Los Angeles, 1980), 145–48; Douglas Monroy, "La Costura en Los Angeles, 1933–1939: The ILGWU and the Politics of Domination," in Magdalena Mora and Adelaida del Castillo, eds., *Mexican Women in the United States* (Los Angeles, 1980), 171–78; Jane Dysart, "Mexican Women in San Antonio, 1830–60: The Assimilation Process," *Western Historical Quarterly* 7 (October 1976): 365–75; Ester Gallegos y Chavez, "The Northern New Mexican Woman: A Changing Silhouette," in Arnulfo D. Trejo, ed., *The Chicanos: As We See Ourselves* (Tucson, 1979): 67–80; Mario García *Desert Immigrants: The Mexicans of El Paso, 1880–1920* (New Haven, Conn., 1981).

38. Vicki L. Ruiz and Susan Tiano, eds., *Women on the U.S.-Mexico Border: Responses to Change* (Boston, 1987); Margarita B. Melville, "Mexican Women Adapt to Migration," in Antonio Rios-Bustamante, ed., *Mexican Immigrant Workers in the United States* (Los Angeles, 1981), 119–26; Gilbert Cardenas and Estevan T. Flores, *The Migration and Settlement of Undocumented Women* (Austin, Tex., 1986); Rita J. Simon and Caroline B. Brettell, eds., *International Migration: The Female Experience* (Totowa, N.J., 1987).

39. Patricia Zavella, *Women's Work and Chicano Families: Cannery Workers of the Santa Clara Valley* (Ithaca, N.Y., 1987); Vicki L. Ruiz, *Cannery Women, Cannery Lives: Mexican Women, Unionization, and the California Food Processing Industry, 1930–1950* (Albuquerque, N.M., 1987).

40. Longauex y Vasquez, "The Mexican-American Woman," 380.

41. Alma Villanueva, "Inside," in *Mother May I?* (San Francisco, 1972), 54.

42. Norma Alarcón, Ana Castillo, and Cherríe Moraga, eds., *Third Woman: The Sexuality of Latinas* (Berkeley, Calif., 1989), 9.

43. Arcelia Ponce, "La Preferida," and Victoria Alegría Rosales, "To All Women Who Have Followed the Same Road as I," in Norma Alarcón, Ana Castillo, and Cherríe Moraga, eds., *Third Woman: The Sexuality of Latinas*, (Berkeley, Calif., 1989), 85–89, 99–100; Veronica Cunningham, "When All the Yous," quoted in Yvonne Yarbro-Berjarano, "The Female Subject in Chicano Theatre: Sexuality, 'Race,' and Class," *Theatre Journal* 38 (December 1986): 402; Cenen, " The Love Making," in Juanita Ramos, ed., *Compañeras Latina Lesbians (An Anthology)* (New York, 1987), 141–43; Ana Castillo, "Coffee Break," in *The Invitation* (Berkeley, Calif., 1979), 19.

44. Alma Villanueva, quoted in Tina Benítez, "The Mother Daughter Relationship," in Lisa Hernández and Tina Benítez, eds., *Palabras Chicanas* (Berkeley, Calif., 1988), 28.

45. Pat Mora, "Aztec Princess," in *Chants* (Houston, Tex., 1984), 28.

46. Benítez, "The Mother Daughter Relationship," 24.

47. Rina Rocha, "Baby Doll," in *Eluder* (Chicago, 1980).

48. Eliana Ortega and Nancy Saporta Sternbach, "At the Threshold of the Unnamed: Latina Literary Discourse in the Eighties," in Asunción Horno-Delgado et al., eds., *Breaking Boundaries: Latina Writings and Critical Readings* (Amherst, Mass., 1989), 2–26.

49. Cherríe Moraga, *Loving in the War Years: Lo que Nunca Pasó por Sus Labios* (Boston, 1983).

50. Ibid., 139.

51. Ibid., 90.

52. Ibid., 103.

53. Ibid., 94.

54. Benítez, "The Mother Daughter Relationship," 25. On the mother/daughter relationship, see also Lucy Guerrero, "Tu Eres Mujer: The Chicana Mother-Daughter Relationship," in Lisa Hernández and Tina Benítez, eds., *Palabras Chicanas* (Berkeley, Calif., 1988), 37–46. On the grandmother/granddaughter relationship, see Barbara Brinson–Pineda, "'Donde Estas Grandma': Chicana Writers and the Rejection of Silence," *Intercambios Femeniles: The National Network of Hispanic Women* 2 (1984); Diana Rebolledo, "Abuelitas: Mythology and Integration in Chicana Literature," *Revista Chicano-Riqueña* 11 (1983): 149–60; Nan Elsasser, Kyle MacKenzie, and Yvonne Tixier y Vigil, eds., *La Mujeres: Conversations from a Hispanic Community* (Old Westbury, N.Y., 1980), esp. 8–42; Adeny Schmidt and Amado N. Padilla, "Grandparent-Grandchild Interaction in a Mexican-American Group," *Hispanic Journal of Behavioral Sciences* 5 (1983): 195; Lisa Hernández, "Canas," in Lisa Hernández and tina Benítez eds., *Palabras Chicanas* (Berkeley, Calif., 1988), 47–50; Norma Alarcón, "What Kind of Lover Have You Made Me Mother?: Theory of Chicanas' Feminism and Cultural Identity through Poetry," in *Women of Color: Perspectives on Feminism and Identity* (Bloomington, Ind., 1985), 75.

55. Benítez, "The Mother Daughter Relationship," 29.

56. Guadalupe Valdes-Fallis, "Recuerdo," *De Colores* (1975): 60–65. For a very similar statement, see Claudia Colindres, "A Letter to My Mother," in Norma Alarcón, Ana Castillo, and Cherríe Moraga, eds., *Third Woman: The Sexuality of Latinas* (Berkeley, Calif., 1989), 73–79.

57. Francesca S. Burroughs, "Joining the Future and the Past," in Lisa Hernández and Tina Benítez, eds., *Palabras Chicanas* (Berkeley, Calif., 1988), 55–57.

58. Todd Gitlin, "Postmodernism: Roots and Politics," in Ian Angus, ed., *Cultural Politics in Contemporary America* (New York, 1988), 347–85, quotation from 347.

59. John Rechy, *City of Night* (New York, 1984), 18, 23, 40.

60. Gloria E. Anzaldú, "Del otro lado," in Juanita Ramos, ed., *Compañeras: Latina Lesbians (An Anthology)* (New York, 1987), 3–4.

61. Gloria Anzaldúa, *Borderlands/La Frontera: The New Mestiza* (San Francisco, 1987), 194.

62. Ibid., 55–56.

63. Guillermo Gómez-Peña, "Documented/Undocumented," *The Graywolf Annual Five: Multi-cultural Literacy* (St. Paul, Minn., 1989), 127–29.

64. Guillermo Gómez-Peña, "Good Morning, This Is Radio Latino Spoiling Your Breakfast as Always," in *La Linea Quebrada/The Broken Line* (San Diego, 1989), 12.

65. Tomas Almaguer, "Ideological Distortions in Recent Chicano Historiography," *Aztlán* 18 (1989): 7–27.

66. Alex M. Saragoza, "The Significance of Recent Chicano-Related Historical Writings: An Appraisal," *Ethnic Affairs* 1 (fall 1987): 24–62.

67. Longauex y Vasquez, "The Mexican-American Woman," 384.

68. See for instance Elizabeth Waldman, "Profile of the Chicana: A Statistical Fact Sheet," in Magdalena Mora and Adelaida R. del Castillo, eds., *Mexican Women in the United States* (Los Angeles, 1980), 195–204.

38

Dependency and Choice: The Two Faces of Eve

Rickie Solinger

Beggars can't be choosers.
—Old saw

For forty years or more the working mother has walked in our world like a lady in a fun house of mirrors, watching one or another of her features now exaggerated, now diminished, nearly always distorted.

—Elizabeth Douvan, 1963

Dependency—as in "the deep, dark pit of welfare dependency"—is the dirtiest word in the United States today.[1] *Choice*—as in the choice to get an abortion—is not so generally reviled as *dependency*, though it does spark more violent controversy. These two words—these groaningly laden concepts—may be the two most powerful abstractions governing women's lives in the United States. As a matter of course, we use these words separately, to refer to apparently discrete arenas, welfare and abortion. But it seems to me that these terms (both their official policy definitions and typical public usage) are actually coupled. Together they binds the lives of women in concrete ways and keep women vulnerable to censure and control.

Dependency and choice refer to each other, directly: they are antitheses that depend on each other for meaning and for the shifting meanings that society has attached to these terms over time. One reason why it seems useful to clarify the relationship between dependency and choice now is that welfare reformers have very successfully named dependency as the disease of poor women. As a result, poor women are more than ever isolated in this country from others, most consequentially from other women. In the interest of reconciling the history, and the concerns of middle-class women and poor women, I want to consider the relationship between these two key concepts and how they have been applied to the lives of women, especially mothers, in two different eras of the twentieth century.

Overview: Dependency and Choice in the 1950s and 1980s

It is a well-known fact that in our recent past, dependency was considered a normative and positive attribute of some white American women. In the 1950s cultural authorities, including psychiatrists, professors, and judges, insisted in every way they could that dependency was a gender–appropriate status for white middle-class wives, mothers, and daughters. These authorities urged other authorities—teachers, parents, employers—to enforce female dependency within the school, the family, the workplace. Along with psychologists and sexologists, parenting experts of that era described such women as dependent on men and the family for self-definition and self-preservation. One popular guide for parents, referring to the family responsibilities of white middle-class women, explained:

"A married woman only has two jobs, one to care for her children, the other to keep a man happy."[2] Femininity indexes in the 1950s invited these women to determine whether they were *dependent enough* to claim status as a "real woman."

Today, of course, the personal trait of dependency is roundly condemned in any adult, especially in poor women tagged as welfare dependents. But whether dependency is generally considered a good thing for white women, as it was in the 1950s, or a bad thing for poor women and many women of color, as it is today, *the core, essential attribute of a person in the state of dependency is the absence of the capacity to make sensible choices.*

Over time, social commentators have been consistent; dependent women can't make good choices. When female dependency was desirable, in the early postwar decades, Midge Decter wrote that young women were "plagued with choices." That was bad because "choice breeds restlessness." Choice also, she wrote, could create "a disruption of the natural order" of the lives of young women, and cause "grave concern" and "domestic crises."[3] In the 1980s, when female dependency on welfare became the target of public vitriol, Gary Bauer described the source of the problem as women's "reckless choices." If women continued irresponsibly to choose divorce and illegitimacy, he observed, "there will either be no next generation, or [there will be] a next generation that is worse than none at all."[4]

Attaching the epithet *dependent* to womanhood, or to groups of women, or to an individual woman has never been enough, of course, to stop women from trying in various ways to control their own lives by making choices. Yet women tagged as dependent, whether in the 1950s or the 1980s, and who exhibited choicelike behavior were accused of dangerous, pathological behavior. They were routinely described as mentally sick or scammers or both.

Perhaps the most frequently quoted book from the earlier period, *Modern Woman: The Lost Sex*, defined the "independent woman," that is, again, a white middle-class woman who made choices for herself against the grain of culturally prescribed femininity, as "a contradiction in terms." Such a woman debased her essential nature by attempting to rival men. Predictably, instead of improving women's lot, this "masculinization" led women into discontent, frustration, hostility, destructiveness, frigidity, and child rejection. The authors of *Modern Woman* argued that when women attempted to exercise independent judgment and choice, they became neurotic feminists. In this era of glorified and mandated dependence, the desire to exercise choice was said to reflect and intensify women's mental illness. The authors suggested mass psychotherapy for women in the United States. Only professional treatment, they argued, could revitalize the natural dependency of American women, and their femininity.[5]

Many nominally dependent girls and women in the 1950s made decisions for themselves, of course. For example, many made choices when they found themselves pregnant in difficult circumstances.[6] Millions throughout the decade sought and got illegal abortions or "therapeutic" hospital abortions.[7] Mary Romm, a psychoanalyst, sounding quite a bit like the authors of *Modern Woman: The Lost Sex*, claimed in a 1954 book on therapeutic abortion that

> the very fact that a pregnant woman cannot tolerate a pregnancy is an indication that the pre-pregnant personality of this woman was immature and in that sense can be labeled as psychopathological. The problem centers on unresolved oedipal situations. Exaggerated narcissism is present in all cases.[8]

In short, any woman who chose to have an abortion demonstrated by that choice that she was sick.

Smaller numbers of white, mostly middle-class, unmarried girls and women found ways to have and keep their children, resisting the intense pressure in those days for this group to relinquish their babies for adoption.[9] Such a person was sure to be condemned for that choice and, because of it, found to be mentally unstable.[10] Many experts on unwed pregnancy in the 1950s believed that all white unmarried women who got pregnant suffered from neurosis. But they held apart a special classification for the ones who chose to keep their babies: psychosis. Again, a dependent female who exercised what looked like reproductive choice revealed the mark of bad sense, bad choice, and pathology. None of these females escaped the censure of experts—physicians, psychologists, and social workers, often lawyers and judges, frequently journalists, who expressed their discomfort with the specter of dependent women making choices.

In the 1950s, work was another arena in which white women charged with making choices were marked as ill or abnormal. In fact, in the 1950s women defined specifically as working "by choice," instead of out of necessity, were "empirically associated" with causing numerous social problems, such as juvenile delinquency and divorce. One of many studies that aimed to measure the (bad) effects of mothers working in the postwar era was called "Employment Status of Mothers and Some Aspects of Mental Illness." The author's findings were complicated, but in the end, he concluded that "if women become employed [that is, choose to work] in order to express neurotic pressures from within their own personalities, then employment of the mother may lead to a breakdown in the quality of family interaction."[11]

Today the choice to get an abortion, become a single mother, or take a job has become so normal for so many women in the United States that these associations of choice and mental illness in our recent past may seem outlandish, or simply quaint. But many women who confronted difficult reproductive or employment issues personally in the 1950s remember how inconsistent and even dangerous it was to mix "choice" with "dependency" in those days.

By the 1980s the capacity of many women to make sensible reproductive and employment choices was recognized, as dependency ceased to modify the life status of every female. Yet women who were poor in the Reagan era were not generally considered able to make sensible choices or to choose without opprobrium, particularly if they were welfare recipients and therefore *dependent*. When such women exhibited choicelike behavior (for example, getting pregnant, staying pregnant, or staying home to take care of their children), they were accused of irresponsible behavior or worse.[12]

Stereotypes associated with the behavior of "welfare mothers" are based on a belief in the incompatibility of dependency and sensible or good choices. More pointedly, the stereotypes explicitly connect dependency and bad choices or scamming. For example, women who receive welfare benefits have been accused of having babies for the sole purpose of making themselves eligible for benefits or for additional benefits. This charge clearly reflects a judgment that such women don't—and can't—make good choices. The same is true for the claims that welfare dependents spend their checks on luxuries while letting their children go hungry, or that they typically stay on welfare for generations, or that they prefer to laze about rather than get a job. By the middle 1970s many middle-class women may have achieved the status of choice makers, but poor women generally remained trapped by a label of dependency that, by definition, excluded them from that status.

Ironically, as many middle-class women sloughed off a number of the trappings of "dependency," most of them did not look back to consider the situation of other women still so entrapped. But whether a woman was "privately" dependent on her husband in the 1950s or "publicly" dependent on welfare in the 1980s, and exercised what looked like choice, her behavior stimulated cultural judgments and public policies designed to stamp out choice, and encouraged legislation that enabled the state to punish women for making choices. In the earlier period, when the behavior of white middle-class women was at issue, sanctions took forms such as antiabortion statutes and prosecutions, the adoption mandate, and misogynistic psychiatric diagnoses and treatment. Later, as poor women of color were targeted, "family caps," welfare time limits, and public denunciations were sanctions of choice.

Many women who attained the status of choice makers in the 1970s and 1980s experienced this achievement as an individual accomplishment. They ignored or slighted the impact of mass movements and economic shifts that relieved them of full dependency status. Women who felt they chose, or personally earned, this new status had some reasonable grounds for defining themselves as independent actors. If a person recognized as having the capacity to make sensible choices cannot be classified as a dependent, then many women who began to make important choices for themselves in the 1970s and 1980s could justifiably claim independence. After all, the experience of making choices in the life-defining realms of sex and employment supported many women's belief that they were operating in the world on a basis more like men. In addition, the consumerist notion of "choice"—that which individuals may exercise freely and independently in the marketplace when they have the resources to do so—supported many women's belief that being able to make choices about their own lives was a hallmark and proof of independence.[13] This last rang especially true as larger numbers of women, both married and single, took on paying jobs and began to earn the money that made their choices possible.[14]

Many men and women in the United States today are so focused on the association of dependency and welfare—and on the assumptions about the bad choices made by dependent women that characterize welfare reform rhetoric and law—that it is difficult to remember how radically definitions and valuations of female dependency have changed since the early postwar decades. So it must be stressed that between 1950 and 1980 Americans did dramatically alter their attitudes regarding the nature of dependency, who we define as dependent, whose dependency we find acceptable, and who in our society has the capacity to make sensible choices on their own behalf.

In this chapter, I will consider the case of shifting attitudes toward working mothers to demonstrate the nature of these changes and to raise questions about the consequences. This case shows clearly that in our recent past, female dependency was widely considered normative and healthy, and female choice was pathologized. By the 1980s dependency was associated with pathology, while choice was considerably normalized, though restricted to women defined by some measure as independent. It is important to note that whichever model of dependency and choice was ascendant, dependency and choice were in a fixed, antithetical relation to each other. Moreover, this relationship between dependency and choice created fertile grounds for justifying the regulation of women's behavior, including the punishment of women who resisted regulation or could not meet its conditions.

Dependency and Choice in the 1950s: Pathology at Work

Defining women's roles in the 1950s has been a particular challenge for writers of women's history in the United States, partly because so many people—including many historians themselves—"remember" the decade through the great, iconic women of that time: TV matrons. The television moms, such as June Cleaver and Harriet Nelson, were always the same, always at home, always lovingly available to their children and husbands. Recently, historians have gone some distance toward showing that for real women, the 1950s was a much more complicated era.[15] They have asked questions about which women actually were housewives and only housewives after World War II. They have considered the ways that real women experienced their domestic roles and meshed them with roles outside their homes. Historians have questioned why cultural authorities at the time exhorted women so often and so threateningly to be first and foremost "good mothers" and "good wives." They have documented the lives of women whose experiences in the 1950s were "nonconforming," for example, the women who streamed into the paid workforce, joined unions, organized and marched for civil rights and against the bomb, and got illegal abortions. They have uncovered aspects of American culture in the 1950s that encouraged women to resist culturally mandated feminine roles and supported the idea that women could and ought to make significant contributions to society as mothers and as workers at the same time.

Two very striking features of the 1950s especially stand out. First, the number of married women with children living at home who took paying jobs escalated rapidly in the 1950s. By the end of the decade, 39 percent of all women with school-age children were in the labor force. Second, the responses to this phenomenon—of white mothers at work—were deeply ambivalent and often hostile.[16] Americans had just recently experienced crisis-driven, "artificially high" levels of female workforce participation during World War II. The number of working mothers with children under the age of eighteen doubled between 1941 and 1945. After it became evident that substantial numbers of white mothers were in the workforce to stay, however, Americans did not simply embrace wage earning for this group. Early in the postwar era, the results of one large poll measuring attitudes toward women working revealed the public's resistance: Three-quarters of the sample believed that "an employer should fire a competent woman whose husband could support her, in preference to an inefficient man who had a family to maintain."[7]

Social commentators and ordinary people talked endlessly about the meaning and the impact of white mothers working. Most were especially worried about the dangers that might befall children, husbands, whole families, and communities if these mothers continued to slight or abandon their domestic stations for paying work. In 1955, for example, *The Ladies Home Journal* warned "the American woman" that "her children will hate her if she works."[18]

Articles in the popular press, academic studies, cocktail conversation, cartoons, and books devoted to the subject of white mothers working often had at their heart a concern about preserving the traditional and antithetical relationship between female dependency and choice. Typically and meaningfully, these various discussions distinguished mothers who *chose* to work from women who had *no choice* but to work. The first group got almost all the attention. Commentators usually ignored the lives of poor and/or minority mothers, who were much more likely to be employed than the white middle-class mothers whose jobs caused so much concern.

Discussion about white mothers working took place, of course, in an era when numerous psychiatrists, psychologists, child-rearing experts, and others were intent on educating the public about the pathologies associated with womanhood and motherhood generally. White middle-class mothers who seemed to have pushed aside their dependent role came in for harsh evaluations. The influential family therapist Nathan Ackerman described the modern family as under the sway of the "dramatized" mother, a woman whose aggressiveness masked the sadness and fear she felt now that it seemed she could no longer "depend safely on the man" of the family.[19] Other therapists observed "hostile onslaughts of these aggressive women" in their offices, often dragging along their "confused, tense," and disturbed children for treatment.[20] Such bad mothers were "ambitious and controlling"[21] and "dominated by a vengeful competitive attitude toward males and by a strong wish to be a man."[22]

Employed white mothers were widely considered a subgroup of this reviled category of aggressive women. This was so despite—and because of—the fact that during the 1950s so many mothers with children between six and seventeen years old were working outside their houses. As *The Saturday Evening Post* editorialized, "With one woman of three in the United States working full or part time outside the home, you'd think the public would accept this as a necessary part of our modern, superproductive life." Yet, the editorial went on, "a lot of people don't accept" working mothers.[23] "The Tangled Case of the Working Mother," a 1961 essay in the *New York Times Magazine*, classified this type as "so suspect in our culture that any new study appearing to link her working with delinquency, school failure, or emotional disturbance in her young, is almost certain . . . to make headlines."[24] Studies also regularly associated these employed mothers with fathers dethroned and pushed, as Ackerman put it, into the shadows—and with feminine dependency denied.

Given this climate, white mothers—especially those associated with the engrossing category of "middle class" in the postwar years—who were deciding whether to take jobs were counseled to make that choice very carefully. They were urged to plumb their motivations with virtually impossible thoroughness. A *New York Times* feature called "Mother's Dilemma: To Work or Not?" listed the questions such a mother should ask herself before seeking employment:

> Do I need the money and for what? Do I make my decisions as a team member of the family? Do I consider husband and children too? Have I balanced the possible cost of financing, training, the physical exertion, and the time factor against the end result of a work experience that may or may not be satisfying and stimulating?[25]

The implication here and elsewhere was that most of these mothers jumped into jobs willy-nilly, and many ended up making poor, selfish, and damaging choices.

In the late 1940s and into the 1950s, academic researchers took up the task of proving that too many women were, indeed, making bad choices when they went out to work. The dozens of studies designed to measure the impact of mothers' employment were constructed on a racially specific base of doubt. Over and over, researchers reflected public skepticism and fielded studies aiming to uncover the contradictions that resulted when natural dependents (that is, white mothers) chose to work. Studies tested whether these mothers who worked and their daughters ended up with diminished femininity, whether working weakened the woman's mothering skills, and whether children whose mothers worked were more likely to get in trouble or do poorly in school.

These postwar studies, based on the responses of white middle-class samples, with all other demographic groups carefully screened out, often yielded uncertain results. No matter what the data appeared to show, however, the researchers underscored continuing worries about the relationship between white maternal employment, juvenile delinquency, and other forms of personal and family "functional disorganization." Many of the studies did pinpoint trouble spots. A sympathetic researcher who believed that daughters of white working mothers could be inspired by their mothers' efforts admitted that all the girls in her study with working mothers scored below normal on the Index of Traditional Femininity.[26] Another study examined the "adjustment" to family life of 302 Missouri girls between the ages of thirteen and eighteen. It found that

> girls whose mothers are employed are, on the average, more poorly adjusted to family life than are those whose mothers do not work and . . . there is greater feeling of lack of love, understanding, and interest between many parents and their daughters if the mother works . . . [and] also . . . greater lack of cooperation and appreciation on the part of the girls in the homes of employed mothers.[27]

In the late 1950s, the Harvard-based researchers Eleanor and Sheldon Glueck provided a summary in "Working Mothers and Delinquency" of one influential profession's assessment of the family problems caused by working mothers:

Psychiatrists . . . view with alarm the growing excursions of young [white] mothers into factory and shop. They are convinced that the economic gain to the family is far too high a price to pay for the loss of emotional stability of the children. They point to the child's repeated traumatic experiences when again and again his mother, the major source and symbol of his security and love, goes off and leaves him yearningly unsatisfied. . . . They speculate that beneath the ostensible economic reason for the mother's leaving the family roof there may be in many cases the deeper motivation of a wish to escape maternal responsibility or a pathologic drive to compete with men.[28]

Like others, psychiatrists linked the harm that befell children of white working mothers to the sick or bad wishes/drives/*choices* of these women. The implication of this and many of the postwar studies was that white mothers, children, and whole families would be healthier, albeit a bit less economically flush, if the mother accepted dependency and eschewed choice.

To be sure, other prominent experts in the postwar era spoke up in defense of white working mothers and tried valiantly to uncouple the subjects of maternal employment and women's pathological choices. But even these defenses of women's choice to work often ended up cautioning women about the dangers or disappointments of choice. A prominent guidebook for modern middle-class women explained,

We are concerned mainly with the woman who has been brought up to feel that she is free, that she has a choice, yet who becomes discouraged and baffled by her actual life . . . because it often seems as though she had no real choice, as though in the end it always boiled down to the one bitter choice: do you want to be an aggressive careerist or a dull housewife.[29]

Psychologist Stella Chess was one of the few mental health experts of the era who attempted to rehabilitate all mothers, in part by downplaying the problematic of choice and by suggesting that families exist in complex contexts. Mothers, Chess argued, are only one element of this context. They can't be saddled with the responsibility for everything that goes wrong in the family, whether they are employed or not. "In analyzing child behavior problems," Chess wrote in a 1964 response to the hundreds of mother-blaming books and articles published in the postwar period "diagnosticians must refrain from automatically assuming that the child's problems stem from the mother's attitude and behavior toward him, and explore other possible influences such as developmental history, socioeconomic circumstances, family and health and educational background."[30]

Between 1945 and 1965, though, the highest-profile pronouncements about the wages of previously fully dependent white mothers going to work were censorious. In this vein, psychiatrist Leo Bartemeier announced in a 1955 *McCall's* article entitled "Is a Working Mother a Threat to the Home?" that

until children are at least six, motherhood is a 24-hour job and one that no one can do for you. A mother who runs out on her children to work—except in cases of absolute necessity—betrays a deep dissatisfaction with motherhood or with her marriage. Chances are, she is driven by sick, competitive feelings toward men, or some other personality problem. She does a grave disservice to her children, although the harm may not show up for years.[31]

Other experts, however, were most concerned about the harm that showed up immediately in the form of juvenile delinquency. Harvard's Eleanor Maccoby referred to "the positive correlation assumed [to exist] between mothers' employment and juvenile delinquency," and remarked that "it is not uncommon to find a judge in a juvenile court delivering a strong reprimand to a working mother and urging her to stay at home."[32] James H. B. Brossard, the author of one of the most influential child development texts of the era, told this vivid story in his widely used and cited volume:

> Ernestine had a part in her school play. Her working mother rushed there in time to see her daughter appear on the stage displaying an atrocious color combination and stockings with two holes showing. Shortly afterwards, the mother withdrew from employment. In her letter to her employer, she wrote that "every growing child needs a mother in the home."[33]

The author of the 1955 *McCall's* article, Elizabeth Pope, began her consideration of the threat posed by white working mothers by naming the force that led many mothers into the workforce: "the seduction of a weekly pay check."[34] The Gluecks used related language in 1957, similarly associating the "choice" to work with illicit temptation and will-less women lacking the capacity to exercise good judgment. "Basically," they wrote,

> the time is ripe for a reassessment of the entire situation. As more and more *enticements* in the way of financial gain, *excitement*, and independence from the husband are offered married women to *lure* them from their domestic duties, the problem is becoming more widespread and acute.[35]

Susan Hartmann is undoubtedly correct in labeling the postwar decades a period of transition regarding women's employment.[36] Periods of transition are often marked by a resurgence of conservatism, that is, aggressive resistance to change. Between 1945 and 1965, although millions of mothers of school-age children in the United States were accepting paid employment, many Americans did not adjust gracefully to this change. During these postwar decades, hefty cultural resources were devoted to disseminating and enforcing messages about the natural dependency of mothers and the pathological essence of their efforts to undermine or slough off that status.

Considerable cultural resources were also—wittingly or unwittingly—devoted to foregrounding the mostly white, mostly middle-income women who went to work "by choice" against other women, often poor and African American, who were defined, when they were noticed at all, as having *no choice* but to work. The work lives of these two groups were often dependent on each other, of course. As Mirra Komarovsky put it, "back of a career mother, there often stands another woman," one she described as "a person of inferior skills."[37]

Dependency, No Choice, and Bad Choice: Shifting the Foreground

The almost exclusive focus in the mass media and academic studies on the white mother's work dilemma came close to eclipsing the situation of "the mother [who] is compelled to work."[38] This was the mother "forced by grim economic necessity to go to the factory or to clean offices while leaving young children in the care of an adolescent daughter." This was the mother "whose every earned penny must be spent in the corner grocery and who returns from her job to do the washing and the cooking and the cleaning for the family."[39] As one researcher put it in 1955, "[T]he overwhelming majority of [such mothers] can't afford to choose."[40] For these women, work was a given. So was their dependency, defined by their race, gender, and class "inferiority" and by their typical status as low-paid domestic service workers. These women were defined as dependents even though they worked day in and day out to support their families.[41] While the bad choices of economically better-off white mothers justified public excoriation, the choiceless status of poor mothers of color justified exploitation in the workplace and elsewhere. White women were perceived as thrusting themselves into the workforce because they were psychologically disturbed, while African American and other women of color were described as fully alienated from the civilized complexities of psychology. For a poor woman, survival issues, some claimed, "superseded attention to her own psychological dilemmas," if, indeed, she had such dilemmas at all.[42]

This perspective was, of course, congruent with prevailing racial distinctions in the realm of sexual misbehavior. Sexually misbehaving white females in the postwar era were diagnosed as psychologically disturbed (because they made the bad choice to engage in nonmarital sexual relations), while African American females were described as sexually impelled by earthy, biologically determined forces that overtook them in the absence of psyche.[43]

Until the Moynihan Report was published in 1965, the employment behavior of African American women was not widely associated with pathology. Social commentators did not believe that poor minority women were capable of making the bad choices that were the hallmark of pathology in that era.[44] (It is possible that not until after 1960—when the rates of domestic service jobs held by African American women began to decline dramatically as other employment opportunities opened up, and white employers had less absolute control over these women—did mainstream commentators began to associate African American women's work lives with bad choices and pathology.)[45] Yet even before the Moynihan Report, experts *were* worried about the social consequences, if not the psychological causes, of maternal employment for minorities. Experts' concerns about what would happen to small African American children whose mothers worked rarely included references to toddlers developing unhealthy anxiety levels and separation traumas.[46] Concerns were more likely to center on the fact that the substitute care that relatives could give to these youngsters with working mothers was "not likely to be adequate."[47]

After approximately 1965, the choicelessness associated with the work and other life experiences of women of color began a process of mutation. Academics and social commentators in the popular media referred less often to these women as having no choice. Now African American women—poor women of color, in general—were accused, as white women had been, of making bad choices. This shift from "no choice" to "bad choices" in the case of women of color was occurring, in zero-sum fashion, as middle–class white women were beginning to win rights to make sensible and depathologized choices for themselves about work, contraception, and abortion. Now poor women of color replaced middle-class working mothers in the foreground of public discussion and concern.

When policy makers and commentators accused poor women of color of making bad choices, the charge was complex. Often it referred to the fact that these women were unemployed. Just as often it referred to the fact that they had jobs while men of color did not. Once women of color were associated with making bad choices, though, the charges spread to cover all the important areas of their lives: work, sex, marriage, family, and motherhood. In 1965 the Moynihan Report enumerated the consequences of these bad choices: African American women were making a mistake by taking jobs and status from black men; they were making a consequential mistake by presiding over families constructed, nonnormatively, as matriarchies. They were making bad choices when they didn't marry and had babies anyway. All these mistakes and bad choices inexorably led African American women (and other poor women of color) deep into welfare dependency.

Culture-of-poverty theory, introduced most prominently by anthropologist Oscar Lewis in *La Vida: A Puerto Rican Family in the Culture of Poverty, San Juan and New York*, a book published one year after Moynihan's report on the black family, provided a richly narrative and decidedly unpsychological explanation for the charge that poor women made bad choices.[48] In the somewhat liberalized political climate of the 1960s, Lewis intended to render "the poor" as legitimate, interesting subjects whose lives were battered by poverty, and to reveal that poverty itself generated a way of life that constituted a unique "culture of poverty." This was a liberal, innovative perspective since "the poor" had previously been constructed as lacking culture.

Despite this intention, however, policy analysts and others read accounts of the culture of poverty as evidence that the folkways of the poor were crude and irresponsibly self-indulgent. The inescapable moral of culture-of-poverty analysis was that the poor became economically disadvantaged because they misbehaved perpetually. Their disorganized hedonism—constructed of bad choices—was both a mark of poverty and that which chained the poor to poverty, generation after generation. Analysts denied or diminished the roles of racism, colonialism, substandard housing, education, medical care, and job opportunities in creating and sustaining poverty. Poverty and the culture it allegedly spawned—the culture of dependency—were seen as the offspring of individual and group irresponsibility or poor choices.

This interpretation of culture-of-poverty theory was successfully popularized at the height of the civil rights movement. For some, culture-of-poverty theory functioned as a justification for resisting institutionalized racial equality. Many politicians, policy makers, academics, and others adapted Lewis's work to justify the position that it was deeply problematic to mount public policy initiatives to ameliorate the lives of the poor. After all, the culturally determined bad choices of poor people themselves caused their lives of endemic, enduring poverty and dependency. This adaptation and application of culture-of-poverty theory was particularly unfair in the case of African American women, who by the mid-1960s were, in very large numbers, making significant and sensible choices in their own interests, even within the context of a violently racist society. These choices included a mass exodus from domestic service jobs once they had other opportunities (in 1960, 39.3 percent of African American women workers were domestics; in 1990, 2.2 percent) and mass participation in the civil rights movement.[49] Nevertheless, that so many African American mothers remained poor in the United States sustained the popularity of culture-of-poverty theory, locking it into the heart of conservative politics for the rest of the twentieth century. It helped consign poor women of color to a status defined by the combination of "bad choices" and "dependency."

In the first two postwar decades, the lives of most mothers were constrained by the culturally mandated association of mothers and dependency and by the related alienation of women from sensible decision making. Yet the different experiences of middle-class white women and poor women of color within these constraints demonstrate a key aspect of the relationship between sexism, racism, and class oppression. When cultural, political, and legal authorities have taken the right to deny all women independence and thus access to self-determining decision making, these authorities have also been able to treat different groups of women differently, depending on the variables of race and class.

In the earlier period, white middle-class women were excoriated for violating the conditions of dependency when they "chose" to work for wages. Those with jobs were more likely to achieve diagnoses of "deviance" for their bad choices than they were to achieve "independence" in the 1950s. On the other hand, social commentators rendered the work lives of mothers of color invisible. Though these mothers were much more likely to work for wages than were white mothers, they did not achieve the status of "independence" either. Social commentators claimed that these mothers worked because their poverty gave them "no choice." This claim obscured the racist and sexist standpoint of the commentators. It also justified the proposition that mothers of color were essentially dependent, no matter whether or how much they worked outside the home. This was so because in the United States the woman constrained from making choices is the same woman who cannot make a good choice. In either case, forced alienation from choice is the fundamental condition of adult "dependency."

The Death of Republican Motherhood: Disconnecting Dependency and Choice

Between the late 1960s and 1980, American culture experienced a phenomenon that can be called "the death of Republican motherhood."[50] During this period, the United States witnessed and participated in a traumatic and very public shattering of what had been widely considered a relatively stable, if racialized, set of concepts defining "mother." Over the course of this scant decade and a half, the landscape became littered with new kinds of mothers. Many mothers in new roles made strong claims that they defined their mother-hood status for themselves by virtue of newly normalized choice, but many others were defined by cultural commentators as occupying a status shaped by the older category, bad choice. All of these mothers' statuses, however, were associated with mothers making choices, often about the relationship between motherhood and work. The American pub-lic struggled in this period to reconcile or reject the validity of this association.

During the 1970s formerly disgraced unwed mothers became simply "single mothers." Legions aimed to become supermoms with high-powered careers and a passel of kids. Moth-ers became murderers of unborn babies, welfare dependents with too many kids, welfare queens, and heads of households in unprecedented numbers. They became mommy-track mothers, American mothers of Third World babies, earthmothers, militant stay-at-home moms, technologically assisted mothers, feminist mothers, lesbian mothers. They became mothers who should put their children in day care because, experts warned, they were unequipped to be good mothers. Alternatively, they became tagged as mothers who selfishly and neglectfully stuck their children in day care.

Not too far into this period, motherhood had become "a very uncertain assignment" in the United States, with no single language or set of criteria to describe the status or to eval-uate women who held it.[51] In 1977 one young woman attending a meeting on the family at Tulane University was reported in the *New York Times* as plaintively asking the panel of experts before her, "I just want to get married and have a child. Is that still okay?" At the same time, other women were deeply engaged in "the fight . . . to win agreement that working women can also be mothers."[52] Still others, of course, were becoming poor, single mothers and facing the charge that nonworking poor women could not afford to be moth-ers and should refrain from having children. Most important, all of these mothers were associated with making choices often called *lifestyle choices*—whether they were rich or poor, white or not. Now choice seemed normalized for mothers; indeed, it was an integral part of becoming a mother in the first place. This was an early and powerful impression created by *Roe v. Wade* and by the liberatory promises of the civil rights and women's movements.[53]

By the early 1970s many women appeared to be choosing their motherhood circum-stances from a menu of options. Contraception and abortion were available to millions of women. Single mothers became heads of households in explosive numbers.[54] Welfare eli-gibility and benefits expanded, stimulating the claim that, in response, poor mothers were illegitimately "choosing" motherhood.[55] Meanwhile, mothers entered the labor force in unprecedented numbers. During the 1970s three out of five people entering the workforce were women. Just as dramatic, between 1950 and 1980 the labor force participation of women went from 35 percent to 52 percent.[56] Many Americans watched the behavior of mothers with alarm. While most would not have put it this way at the time, in retrospect it seems as if some of that alarm had to do with the ways that women were constructing lives for themselves that ignored or denied the 1950s relationship between dependency and choice. Gary Bauer described the great problem these women represented for policy makers as a matter of figuring out "how to get the genie of personal indulgence back into the bottle of legal restraints."[57]

Many Americans in the late 1970s and 1980s expressed their disapproval of women submitting to personal indulgence by supporting "dependency advocates"—spokespersons who repudiated the "rights" and "choice" gains of the 1960s and early 1970s and advocated overturning them. Others remained silent as these advocates attacked women for behaving as if they were no longer dependents. Dependency advocates focused efforts in many policy arenas that affected the lives of girls and women. Some focused on recriminalizing and repathologizing abortion. Others were interested in constraining and punishing teenagers who got pregnant. Still others stressed the importance of defeating the Equal Rights Amendment. Perhaps the most extensive and ultimately most successful effort of dependency advocates was in the area of women and work.

In 1978 Sheila Kammerman of the Columbia University School of Social Work remarked that "underlying all United States policy today affecting families . . . is a pervasive ambivalence about women working."[58] Politicians, policy makers, and conservative commentators in the Reagan era drew on that ambivalence to blunt the impact of feminist- and civil-rights-driven guarantees for women workers. They also focused on reforging the link between dependency and pathologized choices that many women had recently broken. This part was a cynical effort. Many who worked hardest to resuscitate the definition of unemployed poor mothers as dependents making bad choices had generally been hostile to the needs of employed mothers and had participated in efforts to limit their achievements. During Reagan's presidency, these efforts included failing to insist that employers comply with Title VII of the Civil Rights Act of 1964 and providing only weak enforcement of the affirmative action order that prohibited federal contract funds from going to employers who discriminated in employment policies and practices. Despite this lack of support for women workers generally in the 1980s, conservatives used the burgeoning rates of employment among mothers with young children to make the case that the poverty and unemployment of mothers on welfare were their own fault.

Revitalizing Dependency, Repathologizing Choice

Politicians and policy makers used two key strategies in the 1980s to revitalize dependency, this time as a degraded, not normative, condition of (some) women. First, policy makers set about repathologizing "choicelike behavior" for poor, unemployed, single mothers. Second, policy makers constructed an effective policy apparatus to punish poor, unemployed mothers whose receipt of welfare proved that they had made bad choices.

Efforts to repathologize choice were central to redefining dependency as a degraded status. Yet the argument was different now than it had been thirty years before. In the 1950s (white) women were supposed to be dependent. Their independent choices were inconsistent with dependency and therefore were very likely to reflect poor decision making and to carry bad consequences. In the 1980s politicians and others claimed that dependent women (of color) got that way not because of their gender, but because of their bad choices in the face of "opportunity" and "guaranteed equal rights." Those engaged in revitalizing dependency insisted that the choices a woman made while she was dependent were likely to be bad as well because dependency was still inconsistent with sensible choices.

By 1980 poor, unemployed, single mothers of young children were extremely vulnerable to the charge that they were welfare dependents because they had made bad choices. Few Americans who were not on welfare calculated the impact of factors beyond the control of these women that pushed them to accept public assistance. These factors included the lack of appropriate jobs that paid a living wage for women in their situation and the lack of affordable day care, coupled with the fact that in the early 1970s welfare benefits grew faster than wages.[59]

Nevertheless, in the 1980s, after the real value of the welfare check began to plummet, conservative politicians and public policy experts attacked poor mothers with vigor, claiming that their receipt of welfare benefits—their welfare dependency—was built on choices that reflected irresponsibility, even depravity. Lawrence Mead, a politics professor at New York University and a major spokesman for this position, drew a thick bottom line in defining "welfare mothers" during a congressional hearing in the mid-1980s. "I wanted to comment," he said, "on the presumption that the poor are like the rest of us." This, Mead argued, was a misconception. Unlike "us," the poor are "remarkably unresponsive to . . . economic incentives." He found their behavior "a mystery," but suggested an interpretive key: Welfare recipients were "semi-socialized." Unable to make sensible choices, they became wholly dependent on welfare.[60]

The purpose of policy, Mead argued, is "not to expand the freedom of . . . recipients. It is, in fact, to constrict their freedom in necessary ways."[61] In other words, poor women could not and should not exercise choice. Mead and others in the policy arena were emphatic: When poor, unemployed women made unconstrained choices for themselves, the consequences were awful. Gary Bauer admitted in a 1986 report to President Reagan that he could cite no statistical evidence to prove that these unemployed women decided to have babies in order to collect welfare. "[A]nd yet," he claimed, even the "most casual observer of public assistance programs" could perceive this motivation.[62] Revitalizing this thirty-year-old charge—that dependent women were schemers who debased their bodies and degraded motherhood for public money—depended on convincing the citizenry that dependent women were deliberate malfeasants or compulsive miscreants. Either way, their choice to have babies and to stay home with them was constructed as pathological. Many argued that compounding this bad choice was another, though lesser bad choice: the unnatural decision to give birth to babies who would not have proper fathers.[63]

Basically, these charges against poor, unemployed mothers made sense to many Americans because of the fact that these women did not have paying jobs.[64] After all, following the legalization of abortion, the single motherhood of women with decent jobs was far less problematic, morally or otherwise, for most Americans.[65] Economic dependency, caused by bad choices and leading to more of the same, was now seen as *the* core problem of poor unemployed mothers, not racism or sexism or the effects of deindustrialization, or even the absence of a husband, all of which exercised powerful constraints on the opportunities of poor women.[66] Lawrence Mead, Gary Bauer, and Charles Murray met a warm reception in Washington after 1980, when they claimed that eradicating dependency involved aborting the bad choices of poor women, including their choices to have too many children.

While increasing the military budget, granting corporate tax relief, and investing in the private sector, the Reagan administration aimed to "break the cycle of dependency" by reducing the number of choices a poor, unemployed mother could make. For example, the administration eliminated the Comprehensive Employment and Training Act (CETA) and diminished appropriations for the Vocational Education Act that had provided jobs and training options for poor mothers. The U.S. Civil Rights Commission noted early in the Reagan era that

> Federal support for employment and training programs has decreased dramatically, and therefore, special efforts will be needed to provide alternate sources of skills training for poor women unable to gain access to currently available resources. If not, they may find themselves trapped in poverty in spite of their best efforts to avoid or overcome their dependency.[67]

The administration also crafted policies that eliminated a significant amount of public housing stock, raised rents, and reduced federal subsidies for new construction and reha-bilitation of dilapidated housing stock. It slashed fuel assistance programs for low-income households and made it much more difficult for poor women to obtain free legal represen-tation. Very significantly, the administration cut allocations for day care programs at the same time that 36 percent of low-income women and 45 percent of single mothers said they would work if child care was available. For example, Title XX of the Social Services block grant, a major source of day care funding, was cut 21 percent in 1981.[68] Finally, Rea-gan's policies continued the process of reducing the real value of the average Aid For Dependent Children (AFDC) check—between 1970 and 1985, the real value of these ben-efits declined 33 percent—and began aggressively pushing mothers with young or younger children into the workforce.[69]

As housing, employment and training options, and day care programs were liquidated or hobbled in the 1980s, the administration also focused on policy initiatives that would directly punish unemployed poor mothers for the double-barreled bad choice they were accused of making: having a baby and not having a job. (In this climate, Lawrence Mead suggested that "Congress might wish to consider differentiating between married and unmarried mothers, the latter to face more immediate work obligations.")[70] Typically, pun-ishments targeted the reproductive capacity of these mothers and aimed to make any addi-tional bad choices (babies) impossible, at least until the woman got a job, maybe forever.

Hilmar G. Moore, the chairman of the Texas Human Resources Board and the mayor of Richmond, pushed in 1980 for a mandatory policy in Texas requiring sterilization of mothers on welfare.[71] Policy makers in other states designed programs to pay indigent women to put their babies up for adoption, to establish "family caps," and then to pay recipients to use Norplant, a long-acting contraceptive.[72] All of these proposals were pred-icated on the belief that the dependency of an unemployed poor woman canceled out her right to have a baby. Since so many women made the "bad choice" to have a baby despite these strictures (Mead and others were calling this phenomenon "the plague of illegiti-macy"), public policies were needed to constrain their fertility effectively. The point was not only to reduce the number of welfare dependents, but also to punish the women who persisted in behaving as if pregnancy was a legitimate choice for poor women without jobs.

The results of Reagan era policies were very quickly grim. Between 1980 and 1984 the incomes of the bottom one-fifth of American families, a quintile that included 43 percent of African American families, dropped by 9 percent. At the same time, income rose 9 per-cent for the top quintile, a segment that took in only 7 percent of African American fami-lies.[73] The Congressional Research Service reported that 557,000 people became poor because of cutbacks in social programs that Congress approved at the request of President Reagan during the first years of his administration. This was on top of the 1.6 million peo-ple who became poor in 1982 due to the economic recession.[74] In these same years, the percentage of children who were living in poverty rose from 16 percent to 20 percent, a development that brought the number of children in the United States living in households subsisting at or near poverty levels to one in four.[75]

Representative Patricia Schroeder of Colorado reflected on the Reagan administration's cruel treatment of the mothers of these poor children. "I think," she said, "one of the toughest things that's gone on [recently] . . . was the cutting off of the life raft we had thrown to those kind [sic] of women." Poor mothers had been "so excited," according to Schroeder, to have educational and occupational training options available to them. Now those were gone.

> And I don't think there's anything crueler or more dangerous in a society than to say, "Here is the life raft," they climb up and, just as they're ready to enjoy it, you push them back off and say, "Whoops, not yet. We decided we don't have room for you this time."[76]

This politics of reviling and punishing poor mothers for being unemployed while at the same time making it more difficult for them to receive the education and training necessary to secure family-sustaining jobs was a hallmark of the Reagan years. President Reagan himself complained that people unhappy with this policy paradox were simply "sob sisters" unwilling to face reality.[77]

President Reagan's epithet—"sob sisters"—perfectly captured the conservatives' firm determination in the 1980s to clarify welfare as an issue associated with weak women. Opponents of tough (masculine) Reagan policy were cast as emotional, irrational partisans, wallowing in expensive and destructive sentimentality. Also, Reagan administration attacks on "sob sisters" (welfare mothers and others who spoke out in support of these women's needs) were calculated to salvage traditional gender and race ideologies that had been battered by a generation of liberatory legislative, judicial, and policy innovations, and mass movements.[78]

Having lost significant battles in the effort to maintain male supremacy and white supremacy in the generations between 1954 and 1980, Reagan-aligned politicians and policy makers were waging one of their fiercest battles over considerably diminished terrain: the definition of poor women. Many entered this battle as if the fight to constrain the misbehavior of unemployed, poor mothers was the last great legitimate effort of government, and as if winning this battle was crucial to restoring the health of American society.

The conservatives' struggle to define and constrain poor, unemployed mothers was characterized throughout the 1980s by desperate determination and distortion, not unlike that which characterized the reactionary struggles in the United States against school integration and legal abortion. Their determination stemmed in part from the fact that so many traditional features of women's roles had already been effaced.[79] Between 1960 and 1970, for example, the number of female-headed families increased ten times more rapidly than did the number of two-parent families. In 1971, 2.1 million single mothers were employed outside the home; twenty years later, 5.8 million were. By 1980 mothers going out to work, full or part time, had become so normative for women of every class, married and single, that President Carter designated the day before Labor Day as Working Mother's Day.[80] Still, conservatives such as Gary Bauer held out hope that the phenomenon of white mothers working for pay was a temporary aberration caused by "bad economic policy in Washington." He imagined that "with the breaking of inflation, a gradual decline of interest rates, and the return of stability and predictability to the economy," many of these mothers might go back home.

Reagan-era policies defining and constraining poor, unemployed mothers effectively masked the role of large economic forces in creating and sustaining the poverty of these women. Spokespersons ignored causes such as the lack of adequate education and training programs, the fact that a service job paying minimum wage and with no benefits could not support a mother and child above the poverty level, and that real wages had been declining for American workers since 1973. They did not link the decline in high-paying manufacturing jobs and the increase in low-paying service jobs, or poverty policies that forbid poor people to accumulate savings, or the sharp increase in uneven income distribution to the hard time that many mothers had escaping poverty. The only significant cause of women's poverty, now called with a nasty edge *dependency*, was the bad choices of women whose choice making needed to be proscribed.

Dependency and Choice: Underwriting Paradoxes We Can Live With

The extraordinary success of welfare "reformers" in the 1980s and 1990s—culminating with President Clinton and congressional Democrats and Republicans all joining to enact the Personal Responsibility Act in August 1996—reflects the completion of the process of reinstitutionalizing "female dependency" and reaffirming the relationship between dependency and women making bad choices. In addition to welfare "reform," another measure of the long-term success of policy makers in this domain is how effective the dependency/choice antithesis has been in resolving potentially very troubling policy paradoxes regarding the lives of resourceless women.

For the past two decades, many congressional and state politicians have worked hard to ensure that few poor women would have abortions paid for with public funds. At the same time, many of the same politicians have overseen cuts in welfare benefits, including day care subsidies, and have worked to impose family caps and stimulate public censure against "excessively fertile" women. Many Americans have had a hard time understanding how these apparently contradictory policy initiatives can simultaneously serve our national interests. Some feminists and others have adopted the slogan "Life begins at conception and ends at birth" to express their frustration with the impact of these contradictory policies. Yet for an *explanation* of how politicians—and a large segment of the American public—resolve the apparent contradiction or live comfortably with the paradox, one may look at the revitalized relationship between dependency and choice. Today many Americans are convinced that poor women as dependents do not and cannot make good choices. This conviction tends to apply categorically, whether a poor woman chooses to get an abortion that she does not have the money to pay for herself, or if she chooses to have a baby while she is poor. Adapting the perspective of Mary Romm, the 1950s psychoanalyst, policy makers insist that these pregnancy and motherhood choices of poor, dependent women, *whatever the choices are*, "are immature and in that sense can be labeled as pathological." In short, when poor women appear to exercise choice regarding pregnancy and motherhood, they are blamed and blocked, and finally excoriated as bad mothers.

Pregnant teenagers, of course, face similar policy paradoxes. Many of the same politicians and policy makers determined to block this group's access to sex education and safe, effective contraception also champion parental consent laws to constrain the abortion choices of teenagers. These are often the same folks who lament teenage pregnancy and lambaste poor teenage mothers. Again, many Americans live comfortably with apparently contradictory policies that are resolved not by a real belief that dependent girls will stop having sex, but by the conviction that they can be stopped from making choices.

The role that the dependency/choice antithesis plays in making sense of these paradoxical policies illustrates the powerful relationship between welfare politics and reproductive politics today. Far from simply referring to the separate arenas of welfare and abortion, dependency and choice vibrantly interact with each other, depend on each other for meaning, and together shape and justify punitive and constraining public policies, including eugenically based definitions of motherhood.

Dependency and its association with bad choices shape dangerous terrain for women today, just as these concepts did in the past. Today the foregrounded target is the poor unemployed mother, rather than the white middle-class mother of the postwar years. Yet both groups of mothers have suffered substantially because of the kinds of policies these terms have always mandated. We must remember that the protracted struggle for women's rights in this country had at its heart women's determination to disassociate themselves from "dependency" and establish their right to make motherhood and employment decisions on their own behalf. Women struggled for these goals because of the ways they had been constrained and tainted by dependency and bad choice. Remembering women's efforts to change these conditions of their lives may stimulate contemporary female choice makers to feel less comfortable with the slurs regarding dependency and bad choices that are attached to vulnerable women today.

However, if women, particularly poor women at the end of the century, are finally to be disassociated from "dependency" and "bad choices," the task will require more than sharpening the memories of female choice makers. The task will require, at least, the emergence of a vibrant justice movement that unrelentingly demands the conditions of human dignity and independence for all women, including all mothers, in this country. These claims might be made using the same language, and with the same intentions, that the "founding fathers" used in behalf of "free white men" in 1776.

Notes

1. Senator Orrin Hatch, in *Women in Transition, Hearing Before the Committee on Labor and Human Resources, U.S. Senate, 98th Congress, First Session, An Examination of Problems Faced by Women in Transition from Work without Pay to Economic Self-Sufficiency, November 8, 1983* (Washington, D.C.: U.S. Government Printing Office, 1984), 2.
2. David Goodman, *A Parent's Guide to the Emotional Needs of Children* (New York: Hawthorne, 1959), 36.
3. Midge Decter, "Women at Work," *Commentary*, March 1961, 243–50.
4. Gary L. Bauer, *The Family: Preserving America's Future* (Washington, D.C.: U.S. Department of Education, 12 December 1986), 1.
5. Ferdinand Lundberg and Marynia Farnham, *Modern Woman: The Lost Sex* (New York: Grosset and Dunlap, 1947).
6. In this era, unwanted pregnancy itself was often considered a sick choice. See, for example, Stephen Fleck, "Pregnancy as a Symptom of Adolescent Maladjustment," *International Journal of Social Psychiatry* 2 (autumn 1956): 118–31.
7. Rickie Solinger, "A Complete Disaster: Abortion and the Politics of Hospital Abortion Committees, 1950–1970," *Feminist Studies* 19 (summer 1993): 241–68.
8. Mary Romm in Harold Rosen, ed., *Therapeutic Abortion* (New York: Julian Press, 1954).
9. Rickie Solinger, *Wake Up Little Susie: Single Pregnancy and Race before* Roe v. Wade (New York: Routledge, 1993), ch. 5.
10. See, for example, Henry Meyer, Wyatt Jones, and Edgar F. Borgatta, "The Decision by Unmarried Mothers to Keep or Surrender Their Babies," *Marriage and Family Living* 18 (April 1956): 5–6.
11. Lawrence J. Sharp, "Employment Statuses of Mothers and Some Aspects of Mental Illness," *American Sociological Review* 25(October 1960): 714–17.
12. Rickie Solinger, "Poisonous Choice," in Molly Ladd Taylor and Lauri Umansky, eds., *Bad Mothers* (New York: New York University Press, 1997).
13. Ibid.
14. By 1972, among white married women who lived with their husbands, 40.5 percent were employed; among black women in the same situation, 51.9 percent worked. Just a generation earlier, in 1941, only about one

out of ten married women were in the workforce (U.S. Congress, Joint Economic Committee, *Economic Problems of Women, Part 3: Hearings before the Ninety-third Congress, First Session* [Washington, D.C.: U.S. Government Printing Office, 1973], 548).

15. Most important, see Joanne Meyerowitz, ed., *Not June Cleaver: Women and Gender in Postwar America, 1945–1960* (Philadelphia: Temple University Press, 1994).

16. Joanne Meyerowitz, "Beyond the Feminine Mystique: A Reassessment of Postwar Mass Culture, 1946–1958," in Meyerowitz, ed., *Not June Cleaver,* and Susan M. Hartmann, "Women's Employment and the Domestic Idea in the Early Cold War Years," in the same volume, demonstrate that hostility toward working mothers was not ubiquitous. Nevertheless, responses to the swell of mothers in the workforce *were* often hostile.

17. *Womanpower: A Statement by the National Manpower Council with Chapters by the Council Staff* (New York: Columbia University Press, 1957).

18. Agnes Meyer, "Children in Trouble," *Ladies Home Journal,* March 1955, 205.

19. Nathan W. Ackerman, *The Psychodynamics of Family Life: Diagnosis and Treatment of Family Relationships* (New York: Basic Books, 1958), 178–79.

20. Dorothy McGriff, "Working with a Group of Authoritative Mothers," *Social Work* 5 (January 1960): 63–68.

21. Charles Wener, Marion W. Handlon, and Ann M. Garner, "Patterns of Mothering in Psychosomatic Disorders," *Merrill Palmer Quarterly* 6 (April 1960): 165–70.

22. Herbert S. Strean, "Treatment of Mothers and Sons in the Absence of the Father," *Social Work* 6 (July 1961): 29–35.

23. "Is it Too Late to Send Wondering Mothers Back to the Kitchen?" editorial in the *Saturday Evening Post,* 24 January 1959, 10.

24. Dorothy Barclay, "The Tangled Case of the Working Mother," *New York Times Magazine,* 14 May 1961, 75. Also see, for example, *Womanpower,* 54: "The impact of married women's working on the welfare of their children has probably received more widespread attention than any other issue growing out of the increasing employment of women. Many observers have been quick to attribute the reported rise in juvenile delinquency to the absence of working mothers from the home."

25. Helen F. Southard, "Mother's Dilemma: To Work or Not?" *New York Times Magazine,* 17 July 1960, 39.

26. Elizabeth Douvan, "Employment and the Adolescent," in F. Ivan Nye and Lois Wladis Hoffman, eds., *The Employed Mother in America* (Chicago: Rand McNally, 1963), 142–64.

27. Mary Essig and D. H. Morgan, "Adjustment of Adolescent Daughters of Employed Mothers to Family Life," *Journal of Educational Psychology* 37 (1945): 228.

28. Sheldon Glueck and Eleanor Glueck, "Working Mothers and Delinquency," *Mental Hygiene* 41 (1957): 327–52.

29. Sidonie M. Gruenberg and Hilda Sidney Krech, *The Many Lives of Modern Woman: A Guide to Happiness in Her Complex Roles* (Garden City, N.Y.: Doubleday, 1952).

30. Stella Chess, "Mal de Mere," *American Journal of Orthopsychiatry* 34 (July 1964): 613–14.

31. Elizabeth Pope, "Is a Working Mother a Threat to the Home?" *McCall's,* July 1955, 29.

32. Eleanor E. Maccoby, "Children and Working Mothers," *Children* 5 (1958): 83–89.

33. James H. B. Brossard, *The Sociology of Child Development* (New York: Harper and Brothers, 1948), 383.

34. Pope, "Is a Working Mother a Threat?" 29.

35. Glueck and Glueck, "Working Mothers and Dependency," 350, emphasis added.

36. Hartmann, "Women's Employment and the Domestic Ideal in the Early Cold War Years," 84.

37. Mirra Komarovsky, *Women in the Modern World: Their Education and Their Dilemmas* (Boston: Little, Brown, 1953), 191.

38. *Womanpower,* 340.

39. Komarovsky, *Women in the Modern World,* 189.

40. Pope, "Is a Working Mother a Threat to the Home?" 73, quoted Marie Jahoda, Associate Director of the New York University Research Center for Human Relations.

41. In 1960, 39.3 percent of African American women workers were employed in domestic service jobs; 23 percent worked in service jobs outside of private households (Teresa Amott and Julie Matthaei, *Race, Gender, and Work: A Multi-Cultural Economic History of Women in the United States* [Boston: South End Press, 1996], Table 6-1, 158).

42. Alva Myrdal and Viola Klein, *Women's Two Roles: Home and Work* (London: Routledge and Paul, 1956), 151.

43. See Solinger, *Wake Up Little Susie.*

44. Daniel Patrick Moynihan, *The Negro Family: The Case for National Action* (Washington, D.C.: Government Printing Office, 1965). See E. Franklin Frazier, *The Negro Family in the United States* (Chicago: University of Chicago Press, 1939), for an earlier and equally influential treatment of black family dilemmas and "pathologies." This study, in fact, provided the basis of Moynihan's later work.

45. Amott and Matthaei, *Race, Gender, and Work*, 173, show that "between 1930 and 1960 the share of Black women employed in manufacturing jobs almost doubled, while the share in clerical and sales jobs grew eight-fold. These changes finally allowed Black women to move out of private household service, which employed 42 percent of Black women workers in 1950, 39 percent in 1960, and 18 percent in 1970."

46. See, for example, Lois Meek Stolz, "Effects of Maternal Employment: Evidence from Research," *Child Development* 31 (December 1960): 749–82.

47. "Conference Discussion: Working Mothers and the Development of Children," in *Work in the Lives of Married Women* (New York: Columbia University Press, 1958), 186.

48. Oscar Lewis, *La Vida: A Puerto Rican Family in the Culture of Poverty, San Juan and New York* (New York: Random House, 1966).

49. See note 43. See also Paula Giddings, *When and Where I Enter: The Impact of Black Women on Race and Sex in America* (New York: William Morrow, 1984), part 3.

50. I deal with this subject in depth in the final chapter of a manuscript in progress, "The Cost of Choice: How Choice Trumped Women's Rights after Roe v. Wade."

51. C. Christian Beels, "The Case of the Vanishing Mommy," *New York Times*, 4 July 1976, VI, 28.

52. Jon Nordheimer, "The Family in Transition: A Challenge from Within," *New York Times*, 27 November 1977, 1.

53. See Solinger, "Poisonous Choice."

54. Between 1960 and 1977, the number of one-parent families grew two times as fast as the number of two-parent families (Jean Y. Jones, *The American Family: Problems and Federal Policies* [Washington, D.C.: Congressional Research Service, Library of Congress, 1977], 6).

55. Between 1960 and 1970, the value of welfare benefits increased 75 percent (Harriet Ross and Isabel Sawhill, *Time of Transition: The Growth of Families Headed by Women* [Washington, D.C.: Urban Institute, 1975], 98).

56. *Economic Problems of Women*, 4.

57. Bauer, *The Family*, 4.

58. "White House Conference on the Family," Joint Hearings before the Subcommittee on Child and Human Development of the Committee on Human Resources, U.S. Senate, and the Subcommittee on Select Education, Committee on Education and Labor, House of Representatives, 95th Congress, 2d Sess., on Review of Plans for the Proposed White House Conference on Families and Findings of the Carnegie Council on Children's Report Entitled "All Our Children: The American Family Under Pressure," 2 February –3 March 1978, 182.

59. In 1975 the prospects looked good for poor women. According to two policy analysts, "Overall, the picture is one of more favorable income and benefit status for female-headed families in many jurisdictions, and of increasing favor for those families as (1) welfare benefits grow faster than earnings, and (2) female-headed families continue to experience broader categorical eligibility for cash and in-kind programs, and lower tax rates in those programs than husband-wife families" (Ross and Sawhill, *Time of Transition*, 101). Mimi Abramovitz, in *Under Attack, Fighting Back: Women and Welfare in the United States* (Monthly Review Press, 1996), 76, notes that "between 1960 and 1970, the average earnings of workers rose by 48%, while the average AFDC benefits jumped 78%. In the early 1970s, the AFDC grant exceeded the minimum wage in many high-benefit states."

60. *Workfare versus Welfare: Hearing before the Subcommittee on Trade, Productivity, and Economic Growth of the Joint Economic Committee, Congress of the United States, Ninety-ninth Congress, Second Session, April 23, 1986* (Washington, D.C.: U.S. Government Printing Office, 1986), 98.

61. Ibid., 39.

62. Bauer, *The Family*, 24.

63. See, for example, Anthony Brandt, "The Right to Be a Mother," *McCall's*, March 1984, 146.

64. In "The Patriarchal Welfare State," Carol Pateman argues that paid employment has replaced military service as "the key to [male] citizenship." In the 1980s, employment—or economic solvency—was becoming key to female citizenship as well. In Amy Gutman, ed., *Democracy and the Welfare State* (Princeton: Princeton University Press, 1988), 237.

65. See Solinger, "Poisonous Choice."

66. The U.S. Civil Rights Commission asserted in 1983 that "poor women do participate in the labor force. The problem is they are often unable to find work, must work part-time, or the jobs do not pay a wage adequate to support a family" (U.S. Civil Rights Commission, *A Growing Crisis: Disadvantaged Women and Their Children* [Washington, D.C.: U.S. Civil Rights Commission, 1983]).

67. Ibid., 35.

68. *Problems of Working Women: Hearing before the Joint Economic Committee, Congress of the United States, Ninety-eighth Congress, Second Session, April 3, 1984* (Washington, D.C.: U.S. Government Printing Office, 1984),

97; *Barriers to Self-Sufficiency for Single Female Heads of Families: Hearings before a Subcommittee of the Committee on Government Operations, House of Representatives, Ninety-ninth Congress, First Session, July 9 and 10, 1985* (Washington, D.C.: U.S. Government Printing Office, 1985), 179.

69. *Poverty and Hunger in the Black Family: Hearing before the Select Committee on Hunger, House of Representatives, Ninety-ninth Congress, First Session, September 26, 1985* (Washington, D.C.: U.S. Government Printing Office, 1985), 6.

70. See *Barriers to Self-Sufficiency for Single Female Heads of Families*, 509.

71. *New York Times*, 28 February 1980, 16.

72. See, for example, Isabel Wilkerson, "Wisconsin Welfare Plan: To Reward the Married," *New York Times*, 12 February 1991, 16; and Carol Sanger, "M Is for the Many Things," *Southern California Review of Law and Women's Studies* 1 (1992): 15–67.

73. *Poverty and Hunger in the Black Family*, 15.

74. *New York Times*, 26 July 1984, 19.

75. *New York Times*, 29 April 1983, 12.

76. *Economic Status of Women*, 33.

77. *New York Times*, 3 March 1982, 26.

78. See Gwendolyn Mink, "Welfare Reform in Historical Perspective," *Connecticut Law Review* (spring 1994): 882.

79. See Ross and Sawhill, *Time of Transition*, 5.

80. "Single Mothers Struggle with Tiny Paychecks and Little Help," *New York Times*, 31 March 1992, 1; *New York Times*, 30 August 1980, 44; *Economic Status of Women*, 4.

39

Teaching the Differences among Women from a Historical Perspective: Rethinking Race and Gender as Social Categories

Tessie Liu

During the week-long Southwestern Institute on Research on Women seminar in 1989 on teaching women's studies from an international perspective, I experienced several epiphanic moments when a number of my research and teaching preoccupations melded and came into sharper focus. What follows is a progress report on my ruminations on this subject in the years since the seminar. In particular, I would like to share the conceptual inversions and reexamination of received categories through which this problem has led me.

What has emerged from this journey is a clearer vision that feminist scholars not only must talk about diversity, but also must better understand how the differences among women are constituted historically in identifiable social processes. In this paper, I explore the importance of race as an analytical tool for investigating and understanding the differences among women. To do so, we must recognize that race is a *gendered* social category. By exploring the connections between race oppression and sex oppression, specifically how the former is predicated on the latter, we will also gain new insights into the relationship between gender and class.

Epiphanal moments, in many ways, occur only when one is primed for them. The lectures and workshops in the seminar addressed questions with which I had been grappling throughout the academic year. My first set of concerns came out of a graduate course in comparative women's history that I taught at the University of Arizona with a colleague who specializes in Latin American history and women's history. Through the semester, students and instructors asked one another what we were trying to achieve by looking at women's experiences comparatively. Beyond our confidence that appreciating diversity would enrich us personally, as well as stimulate in us new questions to pose to our own areas of specialization, we raised many more questions than those for which we found definitive answers. One set of questions, in particular, troubled me. Throughout the semester, I wondered about the relationship between the kinds of comparisons in which we were engaged and feminist theory more generally. Were we looking for some kind of underlying sameness behind all the variations in women's experiences? Was our ultimate goal to build a unified theory of gender that would explain all the differences among women? Much later, I realized that my questions centered on the status of diversity in feminist theory and politics. Especially troubling to me was the lack of discussion on such questions as these: How do feminists explain the differences among women? Are there contradictions between the focus on differences and the claim to a universal sisterhood among women? How can these tensions be resolved?

The second set of concerns that I brought to this week-long workshop came out of ongoing discussions with my colleagues in the History Department over how to restructure and teach Western civilization if we were to live up to our mandate to incorporate race, class, and gender.[1] Both sets of concerns address the problems of teaching cultural diversity. In this paper, I point out that the intellectual issues raised by adopting a more cross-cultural or international perspective in women's studies parallel the emotional and conceptual hurdles that my colleagues and I encountered in our attempts to integrate race, class, and gender into courses in Western civilization. Further, I suggest that the rethinking required to restructure such courses can be instructive to feminist scholars in offering an opportunity to reassess our own understanding of the relationships among race, class, and gender in feminist analysis.

The mandate to incorporate race, gender, and class into the western civilization curriculum originated as a political move. But even those of us who pushed for this integration did not have a clear idea of the fundamental intellectual changes entailed. We were initially motivated by the wish to establish diversity. This task is most easily accomplished thematically: that is, every so often we add a lecture on women, on African Americans, on Native Americans, and so on, aiming for a multicultural representation. Although it marked a good-faith beginning, this approach is particularly problematic in the context of courses such as those on Western civilization. This attempt to introduce diversity merely sprinkles color on a white background, as Abena Busia commented in her lecture to the summer institute. One unintended but very serious effect of merely adding women, other cultures, or even discussions of class conflict and colonialism without challenging the basic structure of the idea of Western civilization is that non-Europeans, all women, the poor, and all intersecting subsets of these identities appear in the story only as victims and losers.

One problem I had not anticipated was the capacity of my students, who are primarily white and middle-class, for sympathy and yet distance. To put this more starkly: To many students, they themselves embody the universal norm. In their heart of hearts, they believe that *white* establishes not merely skin color but the norm from which blacks, browns, yellows, and reds deviate. They condemn racism, which they believe is a problem out there between racists and the people they attack. Analogously, many male students accept the reality of sexism, feel bad about it for women, but think that they are not touched by it. Even though they sympathize, for these students poverty, racism, and even sexism are still other people's problems. Teaching them, I learned an important lesson about the politics of inclusion: For those who have been left out of the story of Western civilization, it is perfectly possible to be integrated and still remain marginal.

Teaching students to appreciate cultural differences with the aim of promoting tolerance may not be a bad goal in itself, but the mode of discourse surrounding tolerance does not challenge the basically Eurocentric worldview enshrined in Western-civilization courses. At best, tolerance teaches us to accept differences; at worst, it teaches the necessity of accepting what we fear or dislike. In fact, it often encourages an ethnocentric understanding of differences because this form of comparison does not break down the divisions between "us" and "them," between "self/subject" and "other." Most of all, it encourages us to realize that we are implicated in these differences—that our own identities are constituted relationally within them.

Maintaining the divide between "us" and "them," I suspect, is one way of distancing the uncomfortable reality of unequal power relations, which come to the fore once we include those previously excluded. Classically, Western-civilization courses eschew such discussions of power. The purpose of such courses, structured by very Hegelian notions of the march of progress, is to present world history as the inevitable ascent of Europeans. The noted Islamicist Marshall Hodgson aptly described this as the "torch theory of civilization": The torch was first lit in Mesopotamia, passed on to Greece and then to Rome, and carried to northern Europe; ultimately, it came to rest on the North American continent during and after World War II.[2] In this story, Europeans and their descendants bear the torch. The privileged subject is white and male, usually a member of the ruling elite, and the multiple social relationships that sustain his privilege are rarely, if ever, examined.

In light of these complexities, the basic problem in reforming Western-civilization courses changed. Our new problem was how to decenter the privileged white male (and sometimes female) subject—the "I"—in the story of Western civilization, which, not coincidentally, corresponds closely to the subjectivity students have been socialized to develop in relation to the world. We could not possibly modify or reform this strong underlying message with a sprinkle of diversity. The Euro- (andro-)centric viewpoint is embedded in categories of analysis, in notions of historical significance, in beliefs about who the important actors are, and in the causal logic of the story. We cannot integrate race, class, and gender without completely restructuring a course: critiquing foundations, developing new categories, telling a new story. The critical part of the decentering, however, is the painful process of self-examination. Needless to say, the intellectual and emotional hurdles of such a project must not be underestimated. We are teaching against the grain.

African American feminists in the United States have long argued that the historically privileged white male is paralleled in American feminist discourse by the white female subject. The problem is perhaps most explicitly and succinctly articulated in the title *All the Women Are White, All the Blacks Are Men, but Some of Us Are Brave: Black Women's Studies.*[3] Introducing and more fully representing women in all their diversity, although a good-faith beginning, is not sufficient in itself to correct the problems. The problem for Black women, as just one example, lies not just in their initial invisibility, but also in the manner in which they enter the mainstream. The real possibility of black (and other nonwhite) women being brought in as second-class citizens forces us to consider how we as feminists account for and explain the differences among women. What is the status of these differences in feminist theory and politics, especially with respect to the claims of universal sisterhood?

To illustrate the depth of these unresolved problems, let me refer to our discussions on sameness and difference throughout the week-long institute. My personal history is relevant in explaining my reactions. I am an immigrant born in Taiwan to parents who were political refugees from China; my education, however, is completely Western. My feminist consciousness was formed in the context of elite educational institutions, and my specialization is European history. Not surprisingly, I have lived with the contradictions of being simultaneously an insider and an outsider all of my life. The task of explaining why I do not fit anyone's categories is a burden I long ago accepted. All the same, the week's discussions on sameness and difference stirred within me the undercurrents of unresolved issues and brought into clearer focus how much this problem pervades feminist politics.

The first note of disquiet came on the first day when someone in my discussion group used the term "women of color." A Palestinian woman, two Chicanas, and I looked at each other and winked knowingly. All of a sudden we were others, strangers to each other but placed in the same group. We were all at this conference as feminist scholars, as insiders to the movement, yet suddenly we became outsiders because we had this special affiliation. This concept of diversity (however well meant) begs the question: Where is the feminist standpoint in theorizing about the differences among women? Who is the feminist self and, to borrow from Aihwa Ong, "who is the feminist other?"[4] In the previous paragraph, I deliberately used *difference* in the singular rather than *differences* in the plural because I believe that there is an important distinction. *Difference* has become a crucial concept in feminist theory, yet in this context we are tempted to ask, "Different from what or whom?" As "women of color," we were classed together, in spite of our obvious diversity, simply because we are not white. However well-intentioned such acts of inclusion are, they raise the question: Who is doing the comparing? Unless there is an Archimedean point outside social ties from which one could neutrally compare, as feminist scholars we must recognize that all discussions of differences and sameness are themselves inseparable from the power relations in which we live.[5] In this sense, I maintain, there is no true international or cross-cultural perspective. We can view the world only from where we stand.

Failure to recognize this fundamental limitation leads to the kind of ethnocentrism hidden in works such as Robin Morgan's 1984 anthology *Sisterhood Is Global*. Without doubt, Morgan's anthology is an impressive achievement. Covering seventy countries, it provides a wealth of information on women's lives and their legal, economic, and political status. As reviewers Hackstaff and Pierce (1985) point out, however, the implicit argument that women everywhere are fundamentally and similarly oppressed is extremely problematic. In *Sisterhood Is Global*, differences are treated as local variations on a universal theme. As a result, *why* women's experiences differ so radically is never seriously examined. Moreover, the reviewers point out a Western bias implicit in the uncritical and unself-conscious use of crucial terms such as *feminism, individual rights*, and *choice*, which retain definitions developed by Western feminists from industrialized countries, however inappropriate such working definitions may be in other cultural and social contexts. The problem is not only that women in other cultures define *feminism* or *self* in distinct ways that Morgan should have acknowledged. More fundamentally, an unproblematic assumption of common sisterhood overlooks the social reality within which texts such as *Sisterhood Is Global* are created. Morgan's vision of global feminism does not question the relative power and advantages from which feminists in North America and Western Europe claim the authority to speak in the name of others on the oppression of all women.[6]

This curious result—a catalogue of difference in which the relations among those who are different play no role—is symptomatic of a more general problem with what might be called a cross-cultural perspective. The classic anthropological use of *culture* understands the values, beliefs, and politics of various groups and societies as concrete realizations within the compass of human possibility. In an intellectual move with obvious benefits for liberal politics, difference is made a raw fact, irreducible to any hierarchical orderings of evolution or mental progress. A cross-cultural perspective rests on the notion of a transcendental or universal humanness, an essential similarity that makes it possible to understand the beliefs and behavior of others, however strange.[7]

This is a political vision with clear and obvious benefits. In the hands of members of a society that enjoys advantages of wealth and power over those with different cultures, however, it conceals more than it reveals. By not focusing on the unequal distribution of power permeates relations between groups, the liberal humanist discourse elides the necessary discussion of power. To assert that the differences among women conceal an essential sisterhood is not enough; this quick achievement of solidarity comes at the expense of a real examination of the nature of the connections that actually do exist, by virtue of the fact that we occupy different positions in a world inadequately described as a congeries of reified, discrete cultures.[8] Instead, we must understand difference in social structural terms, in terms of interests, privileges, and deprivation. Only then can we see the work required to make sisterhood more than a rhetorical assertion of common substance. The crucial alternative analytical framework, I argue, entails exploring how diverse women's experiences are constituted reciprocally within relations of power.

On these highly charged issues within feminist politics, Charlotte Bunch, our first speaker at the seminar, brought an important perspective on thinking about the differences among women, arguing that we must take differences as the starting point, as the feminist standpoint. In the process of exploring diversity, Bunch assured the audience, the similarities in women's experiences will emerge. For Bunch, however, difference is not opposed to sameness. Rather, recognizing the differences among women should lead us to ask how our different lives and experiences are connected. In contrast to Morgan, Bunch argues that sisterhood is not a natural category, stemming from an organic community. Rather, an international (or cross-cultural or cross-class) sisterhood is constructed out of common political strategies. In this sense, the possibility of sisterhood begins with the recognition that, despite the vast differences that could divide us, our fates are linked and that very connectedness necessitates common action and common solutions. The fact of difference, however, means that a common cause needs to be constructed; it cannot simply be asserted.[9]

Bunch's perspective is wholly consistent with the general goal of understanding differences across cultures. Yet I think that she asks us to investigate and appreciate diversity not just for its own sake, but also for its strategic importance to feminist politics. The goal of studying women's conditions across regions and cultures is not to demonstrate the sameness of women's oppression, but to understand the connections among the different ways in which women are oppressed (and, perhaps, to understand the connection between some women's privileges and others' deprivations). Because the connectedness of experience allows us to formulate strategies for common action, our study of differences must focus on how differences are constituted relationally. As a historian, I interpret these remarks through the possible contributions of my discipline. Methodologically, social history has much to add to the goal of understanding differences relationally. By situating experience as part of specific social processes, social history understands experience as the result of particular actions and actors, actions that establish connections among people and among groups.

In terms of understanding connections, the lessons I have drawn from revising the curriculum for courses on Western civilization are particularly instructive. Moreover, once we change the content of the course from the story of European ascendency to a critical history of European dominance, the global scale and time frame of the modern half of the course (post-1500) offer a framework for thinking through and empirically studying how the differences among women were relationally constituted.[10] This framework is important, I believe, because differences in the world that we have inherited are not neutral facts. The diversity of lived experiences that we encounter today within a single society and among societies around the globe cannot be abstracted from the legacy of colonization, forced contact, expropriation, and continuing inequalities. Of course, the cultures of subjugated peoples cannot be reduced to the fact of their domination alone, any more than the culture of colonizers can be reduced to conquest. Yet no analysis of cultural diversity can be complete without study of the forces that have so fundamentally shaped experience.

In the remainder of this paper, I offer the broad outlines of a conceptual inversion entailed in remaking courses in Western civilization to serve our goal of understanding the differences among women. At present, although within women's studies we speak often of race, class, and gender as aspects of experience, we continue to organize our courses around gender as the important analytical category. This focus is both understandable and logical because, after all, our subject is women. Yet I would like to suggest the usefulness of organizing courses around the concept of race. By understanding how race is a *gendered* social category, we can more systematically address the structural underpinnings of why women's experiences differ so radically and how these differences are relationally constituted.

In order to place race at the center of feminist inquiry, we need first to rethink how we conceptualize race as an analytical category. We tend to think that race is a relevant social category only when we encounter racism as a social phenomenon, in the form of bigotry, for example. Scholars have tried to understand racial hatred by analyzing characteristics such as skin color, skull size, and intelligence, which racist ideology deems important, and much of this scholarship has consisted of testing and refuting racial categories. As a result, scholars have let the ideologues of racism set the agenda for discussions of racism within the academy. Although this work is important, I think the scope is too narrow. I would like to suggest that it is fruitful to inquire into the social metaphors that allow racial thinking, that is, the kind of logic or type of reasoning about human relationships that allows racists to believe in the reality of their categories. In other words, we need to move beyond the belief that racial thinking is purely an outgrowth of (irrational) prejudices, because such a belief in fact exoticizes racism, in the sense that it makes racism incomprehensible to those who do not share the hatred. Rather, as I will specify below, the more radical position holds that race is a widespread principle of social organization.

Once we ask what kind of reasoning about the nature of human relationships allows racists to believe in the reality of their categories, we find racial metaphors in benign situations as well as under conditions of discrimination, overt hatred, and genocide. In other words, even those of us who do not hate on the basis of skin color must realize that racial thinking is disturbingly close to many of the acceptable ways that we conceptualize social relationships. In this sense, placing race at the intellectual center of courses such as those in Western civilization is decentering, for it attempts to break established habits of categorizing in terms of "self" and "other." My ideas on this subject, I should add, are still in the formative stages. I have sketched with broad strokes very complex and nuanced social situations in the hope of capturing simple patterns that have been overlooked. In making bold and overly schematic generalizations, I also hope to provoke opposition and controversy as one way to assess the usefulness of these ideas for further inquiry.

Let me begin with several dictionary definitions of race that I found quite surprising and illuminating. Under the first definition in the *Oxford English Dictionary*, we find *race* as "a group of persons, animals, or plants connected by common descent or origin." As illustrations, the dictionary lists "the offspring or posterity of a person; a set of children or descendants; breeding, the production of offspring; (rarely): a generation." In a second set of usages, it defines *race* as "a limited group descended from a common ancestor, a house, family, kindred." We find as examples "a tribe, nation, or people, regarded as common stock; a group of several tribes or peoples regarded as forming a distinct ethnic stock; one of the great divisions of mankind, having certain peculiarities in common." The last is qualified by this comment: "This term is often used imprecisely; even among anthropologists there is no generally accepted classification or terminology." These definitions are then followed by explanations of the meaning of *race* when applied to animals, plants, and so forth.

It is clear from the first two sets of usages that ideas about descent, blood ties, or common substance are basic to the notion of race. What struck me, in particular, was the second set of synonyms for *race: house, family, kindred*. Louis Flandrin made the reverse discovery when he looked up *famille* in a French dictionary, *Petit Robert*. *Famille* refers to "the entirety of persons mutually connected by marriage or filiation" or "the succession of individuals who descend from one another," that is to say, "a line," "a race," "a dynasty." Only secondarily does *Petit Robert* define family in the way we usually mean, as "related persons living under one roof," "more specifically, the father, the mother, the children." These dictionary definitions, taken all together, suggest that race as a social category is intimately linked to one of the basic ways in which human beings have organized society, that is, by kinship. As Flandrin points out, etymologically, at least in England and France, *race* as a kinship term, usually to denote the patronymic or family name—called literally "the name of the race," *le nom de race*—predated our current usage of the term, which denotes distinct large populations.[11]

Although the specific referent in notions of race is kinship, in order to understand the significance of racial thinking, we need to move beyond these neutral dictionary distinctions. When kinship becomes the key element in a stratified social order, as in dynastic politics or caste systems, the concept of race becomes important. Thus, European society, before actual contact with peoples of different skin tones and different cultures and customs, was organized by racial principles. The operating definition of race was based not on external physical characteristics but on blood ties—or, more precisely, some common substance passed on by fathers. In early modern Europe, when patriarchal rule and patrilineal descent predominated, political power, social station, and economic entitlements were closely bound to blood ties and lineage. Thus race also encapsulated the notion of class. But class in this society was an accident of birth: either according to birth order (determining which rights and privileges the child inherited) or, more generally, according to the family into which one was born (noble or common, propertied or not). The privileges or stigmas of birth, in this system, were as indelible and as discriminatory as any racial system based on skin color or some other trait. The notion of legitimate and illegitimate birth indicates that blood ties did not extend to all who shared genetic material, but only those with a culturally defined "common substance" passed on by fathers.

Understanding race as an element of social organization directs our attention to forms of stratification. The centrality of reproduction, especially in the transmission of common substance through heterosexual relations and ultimately through birth as the differentiating mark of social entitlements, for example, allows us to see the gendered dimensions of the concept of race. For societies organized by racial principles, reproductive politics are closely linked to establishing the boundaries of lineages. In a male-dominated system, regulating social relationships through racial metaphors necessitates control over women. The reproduction of the system entails not only regulating the sexuality of women in one's own group, but also differentiating between women according to legitimate access and prohibition. Considered in these terms, race as a social category functions through controlling sexuality and sexual behavior.

To borrow from Benedict Anderson's insights about the nature of nationalism, racial thinking, as a principle of social organization, is a way to imagine communities.[12] Basic to the notion of race is that an indelible common substance unites the people who possess it in a special community. It is significant that the community described with racial metaphors is always limited; the intent is to exclude in the process of including. Metaphors of common substance simultaneously articulate the quality of relationship among the members of a group and specify who belongs and who does not, asserting a natural, organic solidarity among people whose relations are described as indelible and nonvoluntary. Thus it is not accidental that racial thinking borrows its language from biology, particularly from a systemic vision of the natural world wherein hierarchies, differences, and even struggles are described as functional to the survival and health of the whole.

These core concepts in racial thinking are powerful and flexible. Racial metaphors are rife in other forms of community building. By analogy, kinship terms—*family, brotherhood, sisterhood*, each with its own specific meanings—are often invoked to create a sense of group affiliation; they can be applied to small communities mobilized for political action or to an entire society, in the sense of the body politic. Most notably, such metaphors are central to nationalist movements and nation building, wherein common language and culture are often linked to blood and soil. The invocation of common substance and frequent use of kinship terms to describe the relationships among members of the political community emphasize the indelible and nonvoluntary quality of the ties and deemphasize conflict and opposing interests. The familiarity of racial metaphors, however, should not lead us to overgeneralize the phenomenon. Racial metaphors are used to build particular kinds of communities, with a special brand of internal politics on which I will later elaborate, but we must remember that forms of community building exist that do not draw on racial metaphors. For example, there are communities, even families, conceived as voluntary associations built on common values and commitment to common goals, not on indelible ties.

The power and flexibility of racial metaphors lie, I think, in the malleability of notions of common substance. In the colonial societies that Europeans and their descendants created around the world, the older notion of race articulating a lineage-based system of entitlements and privileges was expanded and became the organizing concept through which Europeans attempted to rule subjugated populations. Only in this context of colonization did skin color become the mark of common substance and the differentiating feature between colonizers and the colonized, and, in many cases, between freedom and enslavement. Of course, the qualities designated as superior had power only because of the military force and other forms of coercion that reinforced the political and social privileges accompanying them.

Although colonial societies in the Americas, Africa, and Asia differed greatly in the taxonomy of racial categories and in the degree to which they tolerated sexual unions between colonizers and colonized, and thus had different miscegenation laws and roles for *mestizos*, the underlying problem of creating a hierarchal system of differentiation was similar. As Ann Stoler notes,

> Colonial authority was constructed on two powerful, but false premises. The first was the notion that Europeans in the colonies made up an easily identifiable and discrete biological and social entity; a "natural" community of class interests, racial attributes, political and social affinities and superior culture. The second was the related notion that the boundaries separating colonizer from colonized were thus self-evident and easily drawn.[13]

As scholars of colonial societies are quick to point out, neither premise reflected colonial realities. The rulers, divided by conflicting economic and political goals, differed even on which methods would best safeguard European (or white) rule. Yet colonial rule itself was contingent on the colonists' ability to construct and enforce legal and social classifications for who was white and who was native, who counted as European and by what degree, which progeny were legitimate and which were not.

Because racial distinctions claim that common substance is biologically transmitted, race as a social reality focuses particular attention on all women as reproducers of human life (as well as the social life of the group) and at the same time necessarily separates them into distinct groups with special but different burdens. To the degree that colonial authority was based on racial distinctions, then, one could argue that colonial authority itself was fundamentally structured in gendered terms. Although in reality there may have been many types of prohibited unions and contested relationships, "ultimately," as Stoler points out, "inclusion or exclusion required regulating the sexual, conjugal and domestic life of both Europeans in the colonies and their colonized subjects," especially in a racially based slaveholding society such as the American South, where the children of a slave woman were slaves and the children of a free woman were free. Under this juridical system, regulating who had sexual access to which group of women involved economic decisions as well.[14]

In colonial societies as different as Dutch Indonesia, British Nigeria, and the American plantation South, we find bifurcated visions of womanhood.[15] Women of European descent became the guardians of civilization. Thus, the Victorian cult of domesticity in the colonial world must be seen in the context of demarcations between groups. Because the structure of colonial race privileges focused particularly on limiting access to European status, the elevation of white women as civilization's guardians also confined them within narrow spheres. As the reproducers of the ruling elite, they established through their daily actions the boundaries of their group identity; hence their behavior came under group scrutiny.

By contrast, the images and treatment of colonized women resulted from more complex projections. On one hand, colonized women were not viewed as women at all in the European sense; they were spared neither harsh labor nor harsh punishment. On the other hand, as the reproducers of the labor force, colonized women were valued as one might value a prize broodmare. Equally, men of European descent eroticized colonized women as exotic, socially prohibited, but available and subjugated sexual objects. In this case, prohibition and availability are intimately connected to desire. Because such unions were socially invisible, the progeny from the union could be denied. Sex, under these conditions, became a personal rather than community or racial matter. In other words, in sexual unions with women from a socially prohibited category, men could step outside the normal restrictions and obligations imposed on sexual activity by shirking responsibility for their progeny.[16]

The same bifurcated images of women appear in European societies as the result of similar processes of creating hierarchy and class distinctions. Students of European history are not used to thinking about race as a relevant category for societies on European soil; these historians, including historians of women, much more readily accept class as the fundamental divide. Yet despite the presence of more democratically oriented notions of meritocracy in industrial society and the dissemination of Enlightenment notions of contractual policy, we should not underestimate the degree to which older (lineage-based) racial thinking rooted in kinship and family alliances remained basic to the accumulation and concentration of capital in propertied families. Racial metaphors (concerns over purity of stock and preservation of social boundaries) pervaded the rationale behind marriage alliances and inheritance. The European upper classes literally thought of themselves as a race apart from the common rabble. Belief in the reality of these social distinctions constructed around biological metaphors pervaded bourgeois imagination and social fears. Respectability centered on domestic virtues defended by the upper-class woman, the angel of the hearth. Just as the bourgeoisie championed its own vision of domestic order as a model for civic order, they feared the disorder and contagion of the working class.

This fear is evident in perceptions of nineteenth-century elite social reformers, particularly on such seemingly neutral subjects as social hygiene. In their studies of English and French attempts to control venereal diseases, historians Judith Walkowitz and Jill Harsin have shown that regulation focused particularly on policing female prostitutes and not their male clients. As Walkowitz has demonstrated for the port cities of England, forcing working-class women who occasionally stepped out with sailors to register on police blotters as prostitutes created a distinct outcast group, in a sense professionalizing these women while at the same time isolating them from their working-class neighbors. The ideological assumptions behind such police actions were more explicitly articulated in the French case. As Harsin shows, police regulations explicitly considered street prostitutes, called *les filles publiques* or public women, the source of contagion. Although ostensibly the problem concerned public health and the spread of venereal disease, the solutions reveal that elite social reformers such as Parent du Chatalet saw poor working-class women not only as the source of disease, but as infectants of civic order, as sources of social disorder.[17]

The improbability that impoverished street prostitutes could threaten civic order demonstrates the power of the biological metaphors that linked questions of physical health metaphorically to the health of the society (of the body politic). The perception of danger bespeaks how the French upper-class imagination represented working-class women. As the dialectical opposite of the pure and chaste bourgeois angel of the hearth, poor women of the streets symbolized dirt and sexual animality. Whether these perceptions accurately reflected real circumstances is immaterial. It is more important for us to see that elite reformers and the police acted as if their perceptions were true, putting into practice elaborate controls that had material effects on the lives of working-class women and, indirectly, on those of upper-class women as well. The perception of danger and disorder rests on the prior social reasoning that I have identified as racial metaphors.

The previous analysis of the relationship between prostitution and public health demonstrates both the malleability and the power of racial thinking to structure the terms of political debates and actions. In recent European history we can find many other examples where racial metaphors provide the basic vocabulary for political discourse. In the latter half of the nineteenth century the imperatives of competition for empire in a world already carved up by Europeans filtered back into European domestic politics in the form of anxiety over population decline and public health. In the eyes of the state, responsibility for the fitness of the nation rested on women's reproductive capacity, their place in the economy, and their role as mothers in protecting the welfare of children (the future soldiers for the empire).[18] Debates over the "woman question," in the form of feminist demands for greater equality within marriage and for political, economic, and reproductive rights, were debated in the context of colonial politics and concerns over the vitality of the master European races. Competition among European nations for colonial empire and their anxieties about themselves as colonizers set the terms for curtailing women's demands for greater freedom of action and autonomy. Antifeminist projects such as economically restrictive protective legislation, bans on birth control, and pronatalist policies went hand in hand with the campaign against women's suffrage.

In the twentieth century, within the European heartland, German National Socialists took these shared assumptions about the relation between national fitness and women's activities to their terrifying extreme. As Gisela Bock's study of women's reproductive rights in Nazi Germany indicates, obsession with race purity and population strength led to a policy of compulsory motherhood with the criminalization of abortion for Aryan women of the superior race and forced sterilization for the inferior races as part of their ultimate extermination.[19] This study of the differential effects of racial policy on women's reproductive rights shocks us into recognizing that the division of women into breeders and nonbreeders is wholly consistent with the logic of racial thinking, whether we encounter such divisions in European dynastic politics or as part of the effort to establish boundaries between the colonizers and the colonized. The most disturbing aspect of racial thinking is that it is *not* limited to the terrifying circumstances of genocide for some and compulsory motherhood for others. It is, in many respects, its very banality that should trouble us.

This brief survey of the common use and implications of what I have called racial metaphors in colonial contexts as well as in the home countries of colonizers, while hardly satisfactory in terms of detail, has at minimum, I hope, suggested an interesting point of departure for rethinking the connections among gender, race, and class. As Bock's study shows us, racism and sexism are not just analogous forms of oppression; institutionalized racism is a form of sexism. One form of oppression is predicated on the other. Racism is a kind of sexism that does not treat all women as the same, but drives wedges between us on the basis of our daily experiences, our assigned functions within the social order, and our perceived interests and mobilization. Although women everywhere have struggled against prescriptive images and have fought for greater autonomy and control, it should not be surprising that, given their different positions within the system and the vastly different material conditions of their lives, women have fashioned different notions of self, have had different grievances against their circumstances, and have often developed different strategies.

Thinking about differences in the ways that I have suggested in this paper requires overcoming very strong emotional and intellectual barriers. We are all products of societies that have taught us to hate others or, worse, to be indifferent to their suffering and blind to our own privileges and to those who labor to provide them. The historical legacy of these differences makes common bonds difficult to conceive. That which divides us may also connect us, but will not easily unite us. Still, if sisterhood beyond the boundaries of class, race, ethnicity, and nation is a meaningful goal, we must try to develop common strategies for change. As a first step, we can become aware that some of the most fundamental differences arise from our distinct locations within a social system that underprivileges all women, but in different ways. To bridge these differences, we must, as Peggy Pascoe has urged, take a candid took at the shameful side, recognizing that we cannot bury the past or wipe the slate completely clean.[20] We can only strive for empathy and mutual understanding. Some of us face the painful process of reexamining our definitions of "self" and "other," and of challenging the categories of analysis and conceptions of historical development that support our intimate vision of ourselves in the world. Others face the equally painful task of letting go of anger, not enough to forget it entirely, but enough to admit the possibility of common futures and joint strategies for transformation.

We cannot fully capture and understand the kinds of differences between women based on race and class by such phrases as "diversity of experiences." By focusing on race as an analytical category in accounting for the differences among women, we are in fact studying race as a principle of social organization and racial metaphors as part of the process of defining hierarchies and constituting boundaries of privilege. The core notion of common substance transmitted through heterosexual intercourse and birth underscores the gendered nature of the concept of race. In a male-dominated society, this concept focuses particular attention on women's activities, on reproductive politics, and, more generally, on control over sexuality and sexual behavior. Understanding this process allows us to see how much the identities of different groups of women in the same society are implicated in one another. Although their experiences of oppression differ dramatically, these differences are nonetheless relationally constituted in identifiable social processes.

Notes

This paper has benefited enormously from Ken Dauber's intellectual support and careful readings. I would also like to thank Karen Anderson, Jan Monk, Amy Newhall, and Pat Seavey for their insights and editorial suggestions.

1. Since 1987 all students earning the Bachelor of Arts and Sciences degree at the University of Arizona have been required to take one course, selected from a designated list, that focuses on gender, class, race, or ethnicity.

2. Marshall Hodgson, "The Interrelations of Societies in History," *Comparative Studies in Society and History* 5 (1963): 227–50.

3. Gloria T. Hull, Patricia Bell Scott, and Barbara Smith, *All the Women Are White, All the Blacks Are Men, but Some of Us Are Brave: Black Women's Studies* (Old Westbury, N.Y.: Feminist Press, 1982).

4. Aihwa Ong, "Colonialism and Modernity: Feminist Representations of Women in Non-Western Societies," *Inscriptions (Journal of the Group for the Study of Discourse in Colonialism)* 3–4 (1988): 79–93.

5. Myra Jehlen, "Archimedes and the Paradox of Feminist Criticism," in Nannerl Keohane, Michelle Rosaldo, and Barbara Gelpi, eds., *Feminist Theory: A Critique of Ideology* (Chicago: University of Chicago Press, 1982);

Chandra Talpade Mohanty, "Under Western Eyes: Feminist Scholarship and Colonial Discourses," *Boundaries* 2, 12–13 (1984): 333–58.

6. Karla Hackstaff and Jennifer Pierce, "Is Sisterhood Global?" *Berkeley Journal of Sociology* 30 (1985): 189–204, reviewing Robin Morgan, *Sisterhood Is Global* (New York: Anchor Press/Doubleday, 1984). See also Ong, "Colonialism and Modernity," and Mohanty, "Under Western Eyes."

7. James Clifford, "On Ethnographic Allegory," in James Clifford and George Marcus, eds., *Writing Culture: The Poetics and Politics of Ethnography* (Berkeley: University of California Press, 1986).

8. For a critique of this view of culture, see Peter Worsley, "Marxism and Culture: The Missing Concept," *Dialectical Anthropology* 6 (1981): 103–23; James Clifford, *The Predicament of Culture: Twentieth Century Ethnography, Literature, and Art* (Cambridge, Mass.: Harvard University Press, 1988).

9. Charlotte Bunch, "Bringing the Global Home," in Charlotte Bunch, ed., *Passionate Politics* (New York: St. Martin's, 1987).

10. Although I am vulnerable, in this move, to the charge that even in the posture of critique, I still privilege a Western perspective, I do so as a politically conscious first step. With regard to my earlier concerns with some of the problems of cross-cultural comparison, a focus on colonialism forces us to keep in the center of our vision the relationship between differences and power.

11. Jean-Louis Flandrin, *Families in Former Times: Kinship, Household, and Sexuality in Early Modern France*, trans. Richard Southern (Cambridge: Cambridge University Press, 1979).

12. Benedict Anderson, *Imagined Communities: Reflections on the Origin and Spread of Nationalism* (London: Verso, 1983).

13. Ann L. Stoler, "Making Empire Respectable: The Politics of Race and Sexual Morality in Twentieth Century Colonial Cultures," *American Ethnologist* 16 (1989): 635.

14. Ibid.

15. For Indonesia, see Jean Taylor, *The World of Batavia* (Madison: University of Wisconsin Press, 1983); for Nigeria, see Helen Callaway, *Gender, Culture, and Empire: European Women in Colonial Nigeria* (London: Macmillan, 1987); for the American South, see Elizabeth Fox-Genovese, *Within the Plantation Household: The Black and White Women of the Old South* (Chapel Hill: University of North Carolina Press, 1988).

16. I am indebted to Ken Dauber for this insight. For European parallels in relationships between upper-class men and working-class women, see Lenore Davidoff, "Class and Gender in Victorian England," in Judith L. Newton, Mary P. Ryan, and Judith R. Walkowitz, eds., *Sex and Class in Women's History* (London: Routledge and Kegan Paul, 1983).

17. Judith Walkowitz, *Prostitution and Victorian Society: Women, Class, and the State* (Cambridge: Cambridge University Press, 1980); Jill Harsin, *Policing Prostitution in Nineteenth Century Paris* (Princeton: Princeton University Press, 1985). For interesting parallels, see Luise White, "Prostitution, Identity, and Class Consciousness in Nairobi during World War II," *Signs* 11 (1986):255–73, and "A Colonial State and an African Petty Bourgeoisie: Prostitution, Property and Class Struggle in Nairobi, 1930–1940," in Frederick Cooper, ed., *Struggle for the City: Migrant Labor, Capital, and the State in Urban Africa* (Beverly Hills, Calif.: Sage, 1983); see also Donna J. Guy, "White Slavery, Public Health, and the Socialist Position on Legalized Prostitution in Argentina, 1913–1936," *Latin American Research Review* 23, 3 (1988): 60–80.

18. Anna Davin, "Imperialism and Motherhood," *History Workshop* 5 (1978): 9–56.

19. Gisela Bock, "Racism and Sexism in Nazi Germany: Motherhood, Compulsory Sterilization, and the State," in Renate Bridenthal, Atina Grossman, and Marion Kaplan, eds., *When Biology Became Destiny: Women in Weimar and Nazi Germany* (New York: Monthly Review Press, 1984).

20. I refer to Pascoe's talk at the Western History Conference in Santa Fe, New Mexico, 1989. See also Pascoe, "At the Crossroads of Culture," *Women's Review of Books* 7, 5 (1990): 22–23.

Selected Bibliographies
African American Women
Compiled by Daina L. Ramey

Anthologies

Abel, Elizabeth, Barbara Christian, and Helene Moglen, eds. *Women Subjects in Black and White: Race, Psychoanalysis, Feminism.* Berkeley: University of California Press, 1997.

Bell-Scott, Patricia, ed. *Flat-footed Truths: Telling Black Women's Lives.* New York: Henry Holt, 1998.

Bobo, Jacqueline. *Black Women as Cultural Readers.* New York: Columbia University Press, 1995.

Crawford, Vicki L., Jacqueline Anne Rouse, and Barbara Woods, eds. *Women in the Civil Rights Movement: Trailblazers and Torchbearers, 1941–1965.* Bloomington: Indiana University Press, 1993.

Giddings, Paula. *"When and Where I Enter": The Impact of Black Women on Race and Sex in America.* New York: William Morrow, 1984.

Gordon, Ann D. et. al. *African American Women and the Vote 1837–1965.* Amherst: University of Massachusetts Press, 1997.

Harley, Sharon. *The Timetables of African-American History; A Chronology of the Most Important People and Events in African-American History.* New York: Simon and Schuster, 1995.

Hine, Darlene Clark, ed. *Black Women in United States Historys:* vols. 1–4, *From the Colonial Times through the Nineteenth Century;* vols. 5–8, *The Twentieth Century;* vols. 9–10, *Theory and Practice.* Brooklyn: Carlson Publishing, 1990.

Hine, Darlene Clark, Elsa Barkley Brown, and Roslyn Terborg-Penn, eds. *Black Women in America: An Historical Encyclopedia.* Bloomington: Indiana University Press, 1993.

Hine, Darlene Clark, Wilma King, and Linda Reed, eds. *"We Specialize in the Wholly Impossible": A Reader in Black Women's History.* New York: Carlson Publishing, 1995.

James, Joy, ed. *The Angela Davis Reader.* Malden, Mass.: Blackwell, 1998.

James, Joy, and Ruth Farmer, eds. *Spirit, Space, and Survival: African American Women in (White) Academe.* New York: Routledge, 1993.

Lerner, Gerda, ed. *Black Women in White America.* 1972. Reprint, New York: Vintage Books, 1992.

Morrison, Toni, ed. *Race-ing Justice, En-Gendering Power: Essays on Anita Hill, Clarence Thomas and the Construction of Social Reality.* New York: Pantheon Books, 1992.

Smitherman, Geneva, ed. *African American Women Speak out on Anita Hill–Clarence Thomas.* Detroit: Wayne State University Press, 1995.

Steady, Filomina, ed. *The Black Woman Cross-Culturally.* Cambridge, Mass.: Schenkman Publishing Company, 1981.

Sterling, Dorothy, ed. *We Are Your Sisters: Black Women in the Nineteenth Century.* New York: W. W. Norton and Company, 1984.

Vaz, Kim Marie, ed. *Black Women in America.* New York: Sage Publications, 1995.

Books

Alexander, Adele Logan. *Ambiguous Lives: Free Women of Color in Rural Georgia, 1798–1879.* Fayetteville: University of Arkansas Press, 1991.

Anderson, Karen. *Changing Woman: A History of Racial Ethnic Women in Modern America.* New York: Oxford University Press, 1996.

Breslaw, Elaine G. *Tituba, Reluctant Witch of Salem: Devilish Indians and Puritan Fantasies.* New York: New York University Press, 1996.

Carby, Hazel. *Reconstructing Womanhood: The Emergence of the Afro-American Woman Novelist.* New York: Oxford University Press, 1987.

Collins, Patricia Hill. *Fighting Words: Black Women and the Search for Justice.* Minneapolis: University of Minnesota Press, 1998.

———. *Black Feminist Thought: Knowledge, Consciousness, and the Politics of Empowerment.* New York: Routledge, 1990.

Davis, Angela Y. *Blues Legacies and Black Feminism.* New York: Vintage Books, 1998.

———. *Women, Race, and Class.* New York: Vintage Books, 1981.

Fox-Genovese, Elizabeth. *Within the Plantation Household: Black and White Women of the Old South.* Chapel Hill: University of North Carolina Press, 1988.

Gaspar, David Barry, and Darlene Clark Hine, eds. *More than Chattel: Black Women and Slavery in the Americas.* Bloomington: Indiana University Press, 1996.

Gordon, Linda. *Pitied but Not Entitled: Single Mothers and the History of Welfare, 1890–1935.* New York: Free Press, 1994.

Hendricks, Wanda. *Gender, Race, and Politics in the Midwest: Black Club Women in Illinois.* Bloomington: Indiana University Press, 1998.

Higginbotham, Evelyn Brooks. *Righteous Discontent: The Women's Movement in the Black Baptist Church, 1880–1920.* Cambridge, Mass.: Harvard University Press, 1993.

Hill, Anita. *Speaking Truth to Power.* New York: Anchor Books, 1998.

Hine, Darlene Clark. *Hine Sight: Black Women and the Re-construction of American History.* Bloomington: Indiana University Press, 1997.

Hine, Darlene Clark, and Kathleen Thompson. *A Shining Thread of Hope: The History of Black Women in America.* New York: Broadway Books, 1998.

Hunter, Tera W. *To 'joy My Freedom: Southern Black Women's Lives and Labors after the Civil War.* Cambridge: Harvard University Press, 1997.

Jones, Jacqueline. *American Work: Black and White Labor since 1600.* New York: W. W. Norton and Company, 1998.

———. *Labor of Love, Labor of Sorrow: Black Women, Work, and the Family, from Slavery to the Present.* New York: Vintage Books, 1985.

King, Wilma. *Stolen Childhood: Slave Youth in Nineteenth-Century America.* Bloomington: Indiana University Press, 1995.

Lee, Chana Kai. *For Freedom's Sake: The Life of Fannie Lou Hamer.* Urbana: University of Illinois Press, 1999.

Lemke-Santangelo, Gretchen. *Abiding Courage: African American Migrant Women and the East Bay Community.* Chapel Hill: University of North Carolina Press, 1996.

Leslie, Kent Anderson. *Woman of Color, Daughter of Privilege: Amanda America Dickson, 1849–1893.* Athens: University of Georgia Press, 1995.

McLaurin, Melton A. *Celia, a Slave.* New York: Avon Books, 1993.

Mink, Gwendolyn. *The Wages of Motherhood: Inequality in the Welfare State, 1917–1942.* Ithaca: Cornell University Press, 1995.

Morton, Patricia, ed. *Discovering the Women in Slavery: Emancipating Perspectives on the American Past.* Athens: University of Georgia Press, 1996.

Neverdon-Morton, Cynthia. *Afro–American Women of the South and the Advancement of the Race, 1895–1925.* Knoxville: University of Tennessee Press, 1989.

Painter, Nell Irvin. *Sojourner Truth: A Life, a Symbol.* New York: W. W. Norton and Company, 1996.

Robinson, Jo Anne. *The Montgomery Bus Boycott and the Women Who Started It: The Memoir of Jo Anne Gibson Robinson,* ed. David Garrow. Knoxville: University of Tennessee Press, 1987.

Robnett, Belinda. *How Long? How Long?: African American Women in the Struggle for Civil Rights.* New York: Oxford University Press, 1997.

Schwalm, Leslie A. *A Hard Fight for We: Women's Transition from Slavery to Freedom in South Carolina.* Urbana: University of Illinois Press, 1997.

Shaw, Stephanie. *What a Woman Ought to Be and to Do: Black Professional Women During the Jim Crow Era.* Chicago: University of Chicago Press, 1996.

Smith, Susan L. *Sick and Tired of Being Sick and Tired: Black Women's Health Activism in America, 1890–1950.* Philadelphia: University of Pennsylvania Press, 1995.

Smith, Valerie. *Not Just Race, Not Just Gender: Black Feminist Readings.* New York: Routledge, 1998.

Stevenson, Brenda. *Life in Black and White: Family and Community in the Slave South.* New York: Oxford University Press, 1996.

Terborg-Penn, Rosalyn. *African American Women in the Struggle for the Vote, 1850–1920.* Bloomington: Indiana University Press, 1998.

Weiner, Marli F. *Mistresses and Slaves: Plantation Women in South Carolina, 1830–80.* Urbana: University of Illinois Press, 1998.

White, Deborah Gray. *Too Heavy a Load: Black Women in Defense of Themselves, 1894–1994.* New York: W. W. Norton and Company, 1999.

———. *Ar'n't I a Woman?: Female Slaves in the Plantation South.* New York: W. W. Norton and Company, 1985.

Williams, Patricia. *The Alchemy of Race and Rights: Diary of a Law Professor.* Cambridge: Harvard University Press, 1991.

Wood, Betty. *Women's Work, Men's Work: The Informal Slave Economies of Lowcountry Georgia.* Athens: University of Georgia Press, 1995.

Wyatt, Gail Elizabeth. *Stolen Women: Reclaiming Our Sexuality, Taking Back Our Lives.* New York: John Wiley and Sons, 1997.

Journal/Anthology Articles

Amott, Teresa. "Black Women and AFDC: Making Entitlement out of Necessity." In Linda Gordon, ed., *Women, the State, and Welfare.* Madison: University of Wisconsin Press, 1990.

Boris, Eileen. "The Racialized Gendered State: Constructions of Citizenship in the United States." *Social Politics* 2, 2 (summer 1995): 160–80.

Farnham, Christie. "Sapphire? The Issue of Dominance in the Slave Family, 1830–1865." In Carol Groneman and Mary Beth Norton, eds., *"To Toil the Livelong Day": America's Women at Work, 1780–1980.* Ithaca: Cornell University Press, 1987).

Fehn, Bruce. "African-American Women and the Struggle for Equality in the Meatpacking Industry, 1940–1960." *Journal of Women's History* 10 (spring 1998): 45–69.

Fulton, DoVeanna S. "Speak Sister, Speak: Oral Empowerment in *Louisa Picquet: The Octoroon.*" *Legacy* 15, 1 (1998): 98–103.

Hammonds, Evelyn. "Missing Persons: African American Women, AIDS, and the History of Disease." *Radical America* 24, 2 (1990): 7–23.

Hanger, Kimberly S. "'Desiring Total Tranquility' and Not Getting It: Conflict Involving Free Black Women in Spanish New Orleans." *Americas* 54 (April 1998): 541–56.

Higginbotham, Evelyn Brooks. "African-American Women's History and the Metalanguage of Race." *Signs* 17 (winter 1992): 251–74.

Johnson, Wittington B. "Free African-American Women in Savannah, 1800–1860: Affluence and Autonomy amid Adversity." *Georgia Historical Quarterly* 76, 2 (summer 1992): 260–83.

Jones, Maxine D. "The Rosewood Massacre and the Women Who Survived It." *Florida Historical Quarterly* 76 (fall 1997): 193–208.

Knapper, Karl. "Women and the Black Panther Party: An Interview with Angela Brown." *Socialist Review* 26, 1–2 (1996): 25–67.

Marks, Carole C. "The Bone and Sinew of the Race: Black Women, Domestic Service and Labor Migration." *Marriage and Family Review* 19, 2 (fall 1995):149–73.

McKnight, Andrew N. "Lydia Broadnax, Slave and Free Woman of Color." *Southern Studies* 5 (spring–summer 1994): 17–30.

Morgan, Jennifer L. "'Some Could Suckle over Their Shoulder': Male Travelers, Female Bodies, and the Gendering of Racial Ideology, 1500–1700." *William and Mary Quarterly* 54 (January 1997): 167–92.

Phillips, Stephanie L. "Claiming Our Foremothers: The Legend of Sally Hemings and the Tasks of Black Feminist Theory." *Hastings Women's Law Journal* 8 (Fall 1997): 401–65.

Ramey, Daina L. "'She Do a Heap of Work': Female Slavery on Glynn County Rice and Cotton Plantations." *Georgia Historical Quarterly* 82, 4 (winter 1998): 707–34.

Ramey, Felicenne H. "Obstacles Faced by African American Women Administrators in Higher Education: How They Cope." *Western Journal of Black Studies* 19, 2 (summer 1995): 113–19.

Scott, Anne Firor. "Most Invisible of All: Black Women's Voluntary Associations." *Journal of Southern History* 56 (February 1990): 3–22.

Shaw, Stephanie J. "Black Club Women and the Creation of the National Association of Colored Women." *Journal of Women's History* 3 (fall 1991): 10–25.

Tate, Gayle T. "Free Black Resistance in the Antebellum Era, 1830 to 1860." *Journal of Black Studies* 28 (July 1998): 764–82.

Venkatesh, Sudhir Alladi. "Gender and Outlaw Capitalism: A Historical Account of the Black Sisters United 'Girl Gang.'" *Signs* 23 (spring 1998): 683–709.

Asian American Women
Compiled by Alice Y. Hom

Anthologies

Aguilar-San Juan, Karin, ed. *The State of Asian America: Activism and Resistance in the 1990s.* Boston: South End Press, 1993.

Chinen, Joyce N., Kathleen O. Kane, and Ida M. Yoshinaga, eds. *Women in Hawaii: Sites, Identities, and Voices.* Honolulu: Department of Sociology, University of Hawaii at Manoa, distributed by University of Hawaii Press, 1997.

Dasgupta, Shamita Das, ed. *A Patchwork Shawl: Chronicles of South Asian Women in America.* New Brunswick, N.J.: Rutgers University Press, 1998.

Eng, David L., and Alice Y. Hom, eds. *Q & A: Queer in Asian America.* Philadelphia: Temple University Press, 1998.

Hongo, Garrett, ed. *Under Western Eyes: Personal Essays from Asian America.* New York: Doubleday, 1995.

Kim, Elaine H., and Eui Young Yu, eds. *East to America: Korean American Life Stories.* New York: New Press, 1995.

Leong, Russell, ed. *Asian American Sexualities: Dimensions of the Gay and Lesbian Experience.* New York: Routledge, 1996.

Lim-Hing, Sharon, ed. *The Very Inside: Writings by Asian and Pacific Islander Lesbians and Bisexual Women.* Toronto: Sister Vision Press, 1994.

Ng, Franklin, ed. *Asian American Women and Gender.* New York: Garland, 1998.

Shah, Sonia, ed. *Dragon Ladies: Asian American Feminists Breathe Fire.* Boston: South End Press, 1997.

Shankar, Lavina Dhingra, and Rajini Srikanth, eds. *A Part, Yet Apart: South Asians in Asian America.* Philadelphia: Temple University Press, 1998.

Tsuchida, John Nobuya, ed. *Reflections: Memoirs of Japanese American Women in Minnesota.* Taipei, Taiwan: Pacific Asia Press, 1994.

Wong, K. Scott, and Sucheng Chan, eds. *Claiming America: Constructing Chinese American Identities during the Exclusion Era.* Philadelphia: Temple University Press, 1998.

Books

Bhopal, Kalwant. *Gender, "Race" and Patriarchy: A Study of South Asian Women.* Aldershot, England: Ashgate, 1997.

Chan, Sucheng. *Hmong Means Free: Life in Laos and America.* Philadelphia, Temple University Press, 1994.

Chow, Claire S. *Leaving Deep Water: The Lives of Asian American Women at the Crossroads of Two Cultures.* New York: Dutton, 1998.

Diggs, Nancy Brown. *Steel Butterflies: Japanese Women and the American Experience.* Albany: State University of New York Press, 1998.

Donnelly, Nancy D. *Changing Lives of Refugee Hmong Women.* Seattle: University of Washington Press, 1994.

Espiritu, Yen Le. *Asian American Women and Men: Labor, Laws and Love.* Thousand Oaks, Calif.: Sage Publications, 1997.

Hayashi, Ann Koto. *Faces of the Enemy, Heart of a Patriot: Japanese American Internment Narratives.* New York: Garland, 1995.

Kessler, Lauren. *Stubborn Twig: Three Generations in the Life of a Japanese American Family*. New York: Random House, 1993.

Kikumura, Akemi. *Issei Pioneers: Hawaii and the Mainland, 1885 to 1924*. Honolulu: University of Hawaii Press, 1993.

Kim, Ai Ra. *Women Struggling for a New Life*. Albany: State University of New York Press, 1995.

Lee, Jid. *From the Promised Land to Home: Trajectories of Selfhood in Asian-American Women's Auto-biography*. Las Colinas, Tex.: Ide House, 1998.

Lee, Joann Faung Jean. *Asian American Experiences in the United States: Oral Histories of First to Fourth Generation Americans from China, the Philippines, Japan, India, the Pacific Islands, Vietnam, and Cambodia*. Jefferson, N.C.: McFarland, 1991.

Lee, Josephine Ding. *Performing Asian America: Race and Ethnicity on the Contemporary Stage*. Philadelphia: Temple University Press, 1997.

Ling, Huping. *Surviving on the Gold Mountain: A History of Chinese American Women and Their Lives*. Albany: State University of New York Press, 1998.

Lowe, Lisa. *Immigrant Acts: On Asian American Cultural Politics*. Durham: Duke University Press, 1996.

Matsumoto, Valerie. *Farming the Home Place: A Japanese American Community in California, 1919–1982*. Ithaca, New York: Cornell University Press, 1993.

Peffer, George Anthony. *If They Don't Bring Women Here: Chinese Female Immigration before Exclusion*. Urbana: University of Illinois Press, 1999.

Sarasohn, Eileen Sunada. *Issei Women: Echoes from Another Frontier*. Palo Alto, Calif.: Pacific Books, 1997.

Tong, Benson. *Unsubmissive Women: Chinese Prostitutes in Nineteenth Century San Francisco*. Norman: University of Oklahoma Press, 1994.

Trask, Haunani-Kay. *From a Native Daughter: Colonialism and Sovereignty in Hawai'i*. Monroe, Me.: Common Courage Press, 1993.

Yu, Diana. *Winds of Change: Korean Women in America*. Silver Springs, Md.: Women's Institute Press, 1991.

Yung, Judy. *Unbound Feet: A Social History of Chinese Women in San Francisco*. Berkeley: University of California Press, 1995.

Journal/Anthology Articles

Abraham, Margaret. "Ethnicity, Gender and Marital Violence: South Asian Women's Organizations in the United States." *Gender & Society* 9, 4 (1995): 450–68.

Agbayani-Siewert, Pauline, and Loring Jones. "Filipino American Women, Work and Family: An Examination of Factors Affecting High Labor Force Participation." *International Social Work* 40, 4 (1997): 407–33.

Alquizola, Marilyn. "The Incorporation of Gender in Minority Discourses: Does the Body Play a Part?" In Gary Okihiro et al., eds., *Privileging Positions: The Sites of Asian American Studies*. Pullman: Washington State University Press, 1995.

Bhattacharjee, Anannya. "The Habit of Ex-Nomination: Nation, Woman, and the Indian Immigrant Bourgeoisie." *Public Culture* 5, 1 (1992): 19–44.

Bhopal, K. "South Asian Women within Households: Dowries, Degradation and Despair." *Women's Studies International Forum* 20, 4 (July 1997): 483–92.

Brock, R. N. "Private, Public and Somewhere In-Between—Lessons from the History of Asian-Pacific-American Women." *Journal of Feminist Studies in Religion* 12, 1 (1996): 127–32.

Chan, Connie S. "Don't Ask, Don't Tell, Don't Know: Sexual Identity and Expression among East Asian-American Lesbians." In Bonnie Zimmerman and Toni A. H. McNaron, eds., *The New Lesbian Studies: Into the Twenty-first Century*. New York: Feminist Press at the City University of New York, 1996.

Chan, Sucheng. "The Exclusion of Chinese Women, 1870–1943." *Chinese America, History and Perspectives*, 1994, 75–125.

Chin-Brandt, Dorothy. "Neither Madame Butterfly nor the Dragon Lady, Rather, Ms. Justice." *Harvard Women's Law Journal* 20 (March 1997): 27–33.

Chow, Esther Ngan-Ling. "Asian American Women at Work." In Maxine Baca Zinn et al., eds., *Through the Prism of Difference: Readings on Sex and Gender.* Boston: Allyn and Bacon, 1997.

Delgado, Gary. "How the Empress Gets Her Clothes: Asian Immigrant Women Fight Fashion Designer Jessica McClintock." In John Anner, ed., *Beyond Identity Politics: Emerging Social Justice Movements in Communities of Color.* Boston: South End Press, 1996.

Dong, Lorraine. "The Forbidden City Legacy and Its Chinese American Women." *Chinese America, History and Perspectives*, 1992, 125–48.

Duleep, Harriet Orcutt, and Seth Sanders. "The Decision to Work by Married Immigrant Women." *Industrial Labor Relations Review* 46, 4 (1993): 677–90.

Espiritu, Yen Le. "The Intersection of Race, Ethnicity, and Class: The Multiple Identities of Second–Generation Filipinos." *Identities: Global Studies in Culture and Power* 1, 2–3 (1994): 249–73.

Geschwender, James A., and Rita Argiros. "On the Proletarianization of Asian-American Women in Hawaii." *Research in Social Movements, Conflicts and Change* 15 (1993): 29–53.

Hanawa, Yukiko. "The 'World of Suzy Wong' and 'M Butterfly': Race and Gender in Asian-America." *Radical History Review* 64 (December 1996): 12–18.

Hassell, M. "Issei Women: Silences and Fields of Power." *Feminist Studies* 19, 3 (fall 1993): 549–69.

Hom, Alice Y. "Addressing Differences: A Look at the 1989 Asian Pacific Lesbian Network Retreat, Santa Cruz." In Gary Okihiro et al., eds., *Privileging Positions: The Sites of Asian American Studies.* Pullman: Washington State University Press, 1995.

Hune, Shirley. "Higher Education as Gendered Space, Asian American Women and Everyday Inequalities." In Carol Rambo Ronai, Barbara A. Zsembik, and Joe Feagin, eds., *Everyday Sexism in the Third Millennium.* New York: Routledge, 1997.

Ikemoto, Lisa C. "The Fuzzy Logic of Race and Gender in the Mismeasure of Asian American Women's Health Needs." *University of Cincinnati Law Review* 65, 3 (1997): 799–824.

Kibria, Nazli. "Migration and Vietnamese American Women: Remaking Ethnicity." In Maxine Baca Zinn and Bonnie Thornton Dill, eds., *Women of Color in U.S. Society.* Philadelphia: Temple University Press, 1994.

Kondo, Doreen. "Women of Color and the Cultural Politics of Identity." *California Sociologist* 14, 1–2 (1991).

Kono, Juliet. "A Sojourner: My Grandmother Sige Oshita." *Hawaiian Journal of History* 26 (1992): 185–206.

Kwong, Peter. "American Sweatshops 1980s Style: Chinese Women Garment Workers." In Cathy J. Cohen, Kathleen B. Jones, and Joan C. Tronto, eds., *Women Transforming Politics.* New York: New York University Press, 1997.

Jensen, Joan M. "Women on the Pacific Rim: Some Thoughts on Border Crossings." *Pacific Historical Review* 67, 1 (1998): 3–39.

Jun, Helen Heran. "Contingent Nationalisms: Renegotiating Borders in Korean and Korean American Women's Oppositional Struggles." *Positions: East Asia Cultures Critique* 5, 2 (1997): 325–55.

Lam, Maivan Clech. "Feeling Foreign in Feminism." *Signs* 19, 4 (1994): 865–93.

Lawsin, Emily Pocincula. "Beyond 'Hanggang Pier Onlu': Filipino American War Brides of Seattle, 1945–1965." *Filipino American National Historical Society Journal* 4 (1996): 50–50G.

Lee, Jee Yeun. "Why Suzie Wong Is Not a Lesbian: Asian and Asian American Lesbian and Bisexual Women and Femme/Butch/Gender Identities." In Brett Beemyn and Mickey Eliason, eds., *Queer Studies: A Lesbian, Gay, Bisexual, and Transgender Anthology.* New York: New York University Press, 1996.

Liang, H. "Fighting for a New Life: Social and Patriotic Activism of Chinese American Women In New York City, 1900 to 1945." *Journal of American Ethnic History* 17, 2 (1998): 22–38.

Ling, Huping. "A History of Chinese Female Students in the United States, 1880s–1990s." *Journal of American Ethnic History* 16, 3 (1997): 81–109.

———. "Surviving on Gold Mountain: A Review of the Success about Chinese American Women." *History Teacher* 26, 4 (1993): 459–70.

Lipat, Christine T., Trinity A. Ordona, Cianna Pamintuan Stewart, and Mary Ann Ubaldo. "Tomboy, Dyke, Lezzie, and Bi: Filipina Lesbian and Bisexual Women Speak Out." In Maria P. Root, ed., *Filipino Americans: Transformation and Identity*. Thousand Oaks, Calif.: Sage Publications, 1997.

Lowe, Lisa. "Work, Immigration, Gender: New Subjects of Cultural Politics." *Social Justice* 25, 3 (1998): 31–41.

Malhotra, Shelly. "Confronting Domestic Violence within Asian Communities." *Sojourner: The Women's Forum*, summer 1993, 13.

Min, Pyong Gap. "Korean Immigrant Wives' Labor Force Participation, Marital Power, And Status." In Elizabeth Higginbotham and Mary Romero, eds., *Women and Work: Exploring Race, Ethnicity, and Class*. Women and Work: A Research and Policy Series, vol. 6. Thousand Oaks, Calif.: Sage Publications, 1997.

Nandi, Proshanta K., and Marilyn Fernandez. "Liberation of Asian American Women: An Uncertain Quest." *International Journal of Sociology of the Family* 24, 1 (spring 1994): 1–22.

Nomura, Gail M. "Significant Lives: Asian and Asian Americans in the History of the U.S. West." *Western Historical Quarterly* 25, 1 (1994): 69–88.

Park, Anna Y. "The Marriage Fraud Act Revisited: The Continuing Subordination of Asian and Pacific Islander Women." *Asian American Pacific Islands Law Review Journal*, February 1993, 29–48.

Shukla, Sandyha. "Feminisms of the Diaspora Both Local and Global: The Politics of South Asian Women against Domestic Violence." In Cathy J. Cohen, Kathleen B. Jones, and Joan C. Tronto, eds., *Women Transforming Politics*. New York: University of New York Press, 1997.

Ting, Jennifer P. "The Power of Sexuality." *Journal of Asian American Studies* 1, 1 (1998): 65–82.

Uchida, Aki. "The Orientalization of Asian Women in America." *Women's Studies International Forum* 21, 2 (1998): 161–75.

Wong, Victoria. "Square and Circle Club: Women in the Public Sphere." *Chinese America, History and Perspectives*, 1994, 127–53.

Wu, Judy Tzu-chun. "'Loveliest Daughter of Our Ancient Cathay!': Representations of Ethnic and Gender Identity in the Miss Chinatown U.S.A. Beauty Pageant." *Journal of Social History* 31, 1 (1997): 5–31.

Yamamoto, Eriko. "Miya Sannomiya Kikuchi: A Pioneer Nisei Woman's Life and Identity." *Amerasia Journal* 23, 3 (1997): 72–101.

Yamane, Nobuyo. "A Nisei Woman in Rural Japan." *Amerasia Journal* 23, 3 (1997): 182–96.

Yung, Judy. "It Is Hard to Be Born a Woman but Hopeless to Be Born a Chinese: The Life and Times of Flora Belle Jan." *Frontiers* 18, 3 (1997): 66–91.

Latinas

Compiled by Mary Ann Villarreal

Anthologies

Acosta-Belen, Edna, ed. *The Puerto Rican Woman*. 2nd ed. New York: Praeger, 1986.

Alarcón, Norma, ed. *Chicana Critical Issues*. Berkeley: Third Woman Press, 1993.

Alarcón, Norma, Ana Castillo, and Cherríe Moraga, eds. "The Sexuality of Latinas" (special issue). *Third Woman* 4 (1989).

Armitage, Susan, and Elizabeth Jameson, eds. *Writing the Range: Race, Class, and Culture in the Women's West*. Norman: University of Oklahoma Press, 1997.

Browne, Irene, ed. *Latinas and African American Women at Work: Race, Gender, and Economic Inequality*. New York: Russell Sage Foundation, 1999.

De la Torre, Adela, and Beatríz Pesquera, eds. *Building with Our Hands: New Directions in Chicana Studies*. Berkeley: University of California Press, 1993.

Del Castillo, Adelaida, ed. *Between Borders: Essays on Mexicana/Chicana History*. Los Angeles: Floricanto Press, 1989.

Del Castillo, Adelaida, and Magadelena Mora, eds. *Mexican Women in the U.S.: Struggles Past and Present*. Los Angeles: UCLA Chicano Studies Research Center Publications, 1980.

Flores, William V., and Rina Benmayor, eds. *Latino Cultural Citizenship: Claiming Identity, Space, and Rights*. Boston: Beacon Press, 1997.

Galindo, D. Leticia, and Marla D. Gonzales, eds. *Speaking Chicana: Voice, Power, and Identity*. Tucson: University of Arizona Press, 1999.

García, Alma, ed. *Chicana Feminist Thought*. New York: Routledge, 1997.

Lopez, Tiffany A., ed. *Growing Up Chicana/o*. New York: William Morrow, 1993.

Martínez, Elizabeth Sutherland. *De Colores Means All of Us: Latina Views for a Multi-colored Century*. Cambridge, Mass.: South End Press, 1998.

Matos Rodríguez, Félix V., and Linda C. Delgado, eds. *Puerto Rican Women's History: New Perspectives*. Armonk, N.Y.: M. E. Sharpe, 1998.

Melville, Margarita B., ed. *Twice a Minority: Mexican-American Women*. St. Louis: C. V. Mosby, 1980.

"Oral History and Puerto Rican Women" (special issue). *Oral History Review* 16, 2 (1988).

Ortiz, Altagracia, ed. *Puerto Rican Women and Work: Bridges in Transnational Labor*. Philadelphia: Temple University Press, 1996.

Rodríguez, Clara. *Latin Looks: Images of Latinas and Latinos in the U.S. Media*. Boulder, Col.: Westview Press, 1997.

Romero, Mary, Pierrette Hondagneu-Sotelo, and Vilma Ortiz, eds. *Challenging Fronteras: Structuring Latina and Latino Lives in the U.S.: An Anthology of Readings*. New York: Routledge, 1997.

Ruiz, Vicki L., ed. *Las Obreras: The Politics of Work and Family*. Los Angeles: UCLA Chicano Studies Research Center Publications, 1999.

Ruiz, Vicki L., and Susan Tiano, eds. *Women on the U.S.-Mexico Border: Responses to Change*. Boston: Allen and Unwin, 1987.

Schlissel, Lillian, Vicki L. Ruiz, and Janice Monk, eds. *Western Women: Their Land, Their Lives*. Albuquerque: University of New Mexico Press, 1988.

Trujillo, Carla. *Living Chicana Theory*. Berkeley: Third Woman Press, 1998.

Books

Amott, Teresa, and Julie Matthaei. *Race, Gender, and Work*. Boston: South End Press, 1996.

Aparicio, Frances R. *Listening to Salsa: Gender, Latin Popular Music, and Puerto Rican Cultures*. Hanover, N.H.: University Press of New England, 1998.

Arrizón, Alicia. *Latina Performance Traversing the Stage*. Bloomington: Indiana University Press, 1999.

Blackwelder, Julia. *Women of the Depression: Caste and Culture in San Antonio, 1929–1936*. College Station: Texas A&M University Press, 1984.

Blea, Irene I. *U.S. Chicanas and Latinas within a Global Context*. Westport, Conn.: Praeger, 1997.

Cabeza de Baca, Fabiola. *We Fed Them Cactus*. Albuquerque: University of New Mexico Press, 1954.

Cantú, Norma. *Canícula*. Albuquerque: University of New Mexico Press, 1995.

Cotera, Marta. *The Chicana Feminist*. Austin: Information Systems Development, 1977.

———. *Diosa y Hembra: The History and Heritage of Chicanas in the U.S.* Austin: Information Systems Development, 1976.

Deutsch, Sarah. *"No Separate Refuge": Culture, Class and Gender on an Anglo-Hispanic Frontier in the American Southwest, 1880–1940*. New York: Oxford University Press, 1987.

Doran, Terry, Janet Satterfield, and Chris State. *A Road Well-Traveled: Three Generations of Cuban American Women*. Fort Wayne, Ind.: Latin American Educational Center, 1988.

Facio, Elisa. *Understanding Older Chicanas*. Thousand Oaks, Calif.: Sage Publications, 1995.

Foley, Neil. *The White Scourge: Mexicans, Blacks, and Poor Whites in Texas Cotton Culture*. Berkeley: University of California Press, 1997.

García, María Cristina. *Havana, USA: Cuban Exiles and Cuban Americans in South Florida, 1959–1994*. Berkeley: University of California Press, 1996.

Gaspar de Alba, Alicia. *Chicano Art Inside/Outside the Master's House: Cultural Politics and the CARA Exhibition*. Austin: University of Texas Press, 1998.

González, Deena J. *Refusing the Favor: Spanish-Mexican Women of Santa Fe, 1820–1880*. New York: Oxford University Press, 1999.

Guerin-González, Camille. *Mexican Workers and American Dreams: Immigration, Repatriation, and California Farm Labor, 1900–1939*. New Brunswick, N.J.: Rutgers University Press, 1994.

Gutiérrez, Ramón. *When Jesus Came, The Corn Mothers Went Away: Power and Sexuality in New Mexico, 1500–1846*. Stanford: Stanford University Press, 1990.

Haas, Lisbeth. *Conquests and Historical Identities in California, 1769–1936*. Berkeley: University of California Press, 1995.

Hardy-Fanta, Carol. *Latina Politics, Latino Politics*. Philadelphia: Temple University Press, 1993.

Henkes, Robert. *Latin American Women Artists of the United States: The Works of 33 Twentieth-Century Women*. Jefferson, N.C.: McFarland, 1999.

Hondagneu-Sotelo, Pierrette. *Gendered Transitions: Mexican Experience of Immigration*. Berkeley: University of California Press, 1994.

Korrol, Virginia Sánchez. *From Colonia to Community: The History of Puerto Ricans in New York City*. Westport, Conn.: Greenwood Press, 1983.

Lucas, María Elena. *Forged under the Sun/Forjada Bajo el Sol: The Life of María Elena Lucas*. Ed. Fran Leeper Buss. Ann Arbor: University of Michigan Press, 1993.

Martin, Patricia Preciado. *Songs My Mother Sang to Me: An Oral History of Mexican American Women*. Tucson: University of Arizona Press, 1992.

Muñiz, Vicky. *Resisting Gentrification and Displacement: Voices of Puerto Rican Women of the Barrio*. New York: Garland, 1998.

Pardo, Mary S. *Mexican American Women Activists: Identity and Resistance in Two Los Angeles Communities*. Philadelphia: Temple University Press, 1998.

Pedraza-Bailey, Sylvia. *Political and Economic Migrants in America: Cubans and Mexicans*. Austin: University of Texas Press, 1985.

Pérez, Emma. *The Decolonial Imaginary: Writing Chicanas into History (Theories of Representation and Difference)*. Bloomington: Indiana University Press, 1999.

Ponce, Mary Helen. *Hoyt Street: An Autobiography*. Albuquerque: University of New Mexico Press, 1993.

Rodríguez, Clara. *Puerto Ricans: Born in the U.S.A*. Westminister, Mass.: Unwin and Heyman, 1989.

Ruiz, Vicki. *From out of the Shadows*. New York: Oxford University Press, 1998.

———. *Cannery Women, Cannery Lives: Mexican Women, Unionization, and the California Food Processing Industry, 1939–1950*. Albuquerque: University of New Mexico Press, 1987.

Sánchez, George. *Becoming Mexican American: Ethnicity, Culture, and Identity in Chicano Los Angeles, 1900–1965*. New York: Oxford University Press, 1993.

Strachwitz, Chris, and James Nicolopulos, eds. *Lydia Mendoza: A Family Autobiography*. Houston: Arte Público Press, 1993.

Weber, Devra. *Dark Sweat, White Gold: California Farm Workers, Cotton and the New Deal*. Berkeley: University of California Press, 1994.

Williams, Norma. *The Mexican-American Family Tradition and Change*. Boston: G. K. Hall, 1990.

Yohn, Susan. *A Contest of Faiths: Missionary Women and Pluralism in the American Southwest*. Ithaca: Cornell University Press, 1995.

Zavella, Patricia. *Women's Work and Chicano Families: Cannery Workers of the Santa Clara Valley*. Ithaca: Cornell University Press, 1987.

Journal/Anthology Articles

Arrizón, Alicia. "Monica Palacios: 'Latin Lezbo Comic.'" *Crossroads* 31 (May 1993): 25.

Benmayor, Rina. "Testimony, Action Research and Empowerment: Puerto Rican Women and Popular Education." In Sherna Berger Gluck and Daphne Patai, ed., *Women's Words: The Feminist Practice of Oral History*. New York: Routledge, 1991.

Boone, Margaret S. "The Use of Traditional Concepts in the Development of New Urban Roles: Cuban Women in the United States." In Erika Bourguignon, ed., *A World of Women*. New York: Praeger, 1980.

Castañeda, Antonia I. "The Political Economy of Nineteenth Century Stereotypes of Californianas." In Michael R. Orñelas, ed., *Between the Conquests*. Dubuque, Iowa: Kendall Hunt Publishing, 1991.

Córdova, Teresa. "Roots and Resistance: The Emergent Writings of Twenty Years of Chicana Feminist Struggle." In Félix Padilla, ed., *Handbook of Hispanic Cultures in the United States: Sociology*. Houston: Arte Público Press, 1994.

Ellis, M., D. Conway, and A. J. Bailey. "The Circular Migration of Puerto Rican Women: Towards a Gendered Explanation." *International Migration* 34, 1 (1996): 31–64.

García, Mario T. "The Chicana in American History: The Mexican Women of El Paso, 1880–1920," *Pacific Historical Review* 49, 2 (1980): 315–37.

Géliga Vargas, Jocelyn A. "Expanding the Popular Culture Debates: Puertorriqueñas, Hollywood, and Cultural Identity." *Studies in Latin American Popular Culture* 15 (1996): 155–73.

González, María C. "Cultural Conflict: Introducing the Queer in Mexican–American Literature Classes." In Linda Garber, ed., *Tilting the Tower: Lesbians, Teaching Queer Subjects*. New York: Routledge, 1994.

González, Yolanda Broyles. "Toward a Re–Vision of Chicano Theatre History: The Women of El Teatro Campesino." In Lynda Hart, ed., *Making a Spectacle: Feminist Essays on Contemporary Women's Theatre*. Ann Arbor: University of Michigan Press, 1989.

Grijalva, Cindy A., and Robert Holman Coombs. "Latinas in Medicine: Stressors, Survival Skills, and Strengths." *Aztlán* 22, 2 (Fall 1997): 67–88.

Harris, Richard J., and Juanita M. Firestone. "Ethnicity, Family Change, and Labor Force Patterns in Texas, 1980–1990." *Hispanic Journal of Behavioral Sciences* 19, 3 (1997): 268–80.

Hernández, Inés. "Sara Estela Ramírez: Sembradora." *Legacies*, 1989, 13–26.

Jones, Correa M. "Different Paths: Gender, Immigration and Political Participation." *International Migration Review* 32, 2 (summer 1998): 326–49.

Korrol, Virginia Sánchez. "On the Other Side of the Ocean: The Work Experiences of Early Puerto Rican Migrant Women." *Carribean Review* 8, 1 (1979): 22–28.

Ledesma, Irene. "Texas Newspapers and Chicana Workers' Activism, 1919–1974." *Western Historical Quarterly* 26, 3 (autumn 1995): 309–31.

Menjívar, Cecilia. "Immigrant Kinship Networks and the Impact of the Receiving Context: Salvadorans in San Francisco in the Early 1990s." *Social Problems* 44 (1997): 104–23.

Oboler, Susanna. "Narratives of National (Be)longing: Citizenship, Race, and the Creation of Latinas' Ethnicities in Exile in the United States." *Social Politics* 3, 2–3 (summer–fall, 1996): 291–315.

Olmedo, I. M. "Voices of Our Past: Using Oral History to Explore Funds of Knowledge within a Puerto Rican Family." *Anthropology and Education Quarterly* 28, 4 (December 1997): 550–73.

Peña, M. Frehill. "Latina Religious Practice: Analyzing Cultural Dimensions in Measures of Religiosity." *Journal for the Scientific Study of Religion* 37, 4 (December 1998): 620–35.

Pessar, P. "Sweatshop Workers and Domestic Ideologies: Dominican Women in the New York Apparel Industry." *International Journal of Urban and Regional Research* 18, 1 (March 1994): 127–42.

Prieto, Yolanda. "Cuban Women in New Jersey: Gender Relations and Change." In Donna Gabaccia, ed., *Seeking Common Ground: Multidisciplinary Studies of Immigrant Women in the United Sates.* Westport, Conn.: Greenwood Press, 1992.

Rich, B. Ruby, and Lourdes Arguelles. "Homosexuality, Homophobia, and Revolution: Notes Toward and Understanding of the Cuban Lesbian and Gay Male Experience." *Signs* 9, 4 (summer 1984), 11, 1 (autumn 1985), 683–99, 120–36.

Rose, Margaret. "The Community Service Organization, 1947–1962." In Joanne Meyerowitz, ed., *Not June Cleaver: Women and Gender in Postwar America, 1945–1960.* Philadelphia: Temple University Press, 1994.

Salas, Elizabeth. "Ethnicity, Gender and Divorce: Issues in the 1922 Campaign by Adelina Otero–Warren for the U.S. House of Representatives." *New Mexico Historical Review* 70, 4 (1995): 367–82.

Segura, Denise. "Chicana and Mexican Immigrant Women at Work." *Gender and Society*, 3, 1 (March 1989): 37–52.

Sosa Riddell, Adaljiza. "Chicanas and El Movimiento." *Aztlán* 5, 2 (1974): 155–65.

Zavella, Patricia. "Reflections on Diversity among Chicanas." *Frontiers* 12, 2 (1991): 763–85.

Native American Women
Compiled by Annette L. Reed

Anthologies

Albers, Patricia, and Beatrice Medicine, eds. *The Hidden Half: Studies of Plains Indian Women.* Washington, D.C.: University Press of America, 1983.

Bataille, Gretchen M., and Kathleen Mullen Sands, eds. *American Indian Women, Telling Their Lives.* Lincoln: University of Nebraska Press, 1984.

Hogan, Linda, ed. *Frontiers: Special Issue on Native American Women* 6, 3 (1981).

Katz, Jane B., ed., *I Am the Fire of Time: The Voices of Native American Women.* New York: E. P. Dutton, 1977.

———, ed. *Messengers of the Wind: Native American Women Tell Their Life Stories.* New York: Ballantine Books, 1995.

Roscoe, Will, ed. *Living the Spirit: A Gay American Indian Anthology.* New York: St. Martin's Press, 1988.

Shoemaker, Nancy, ed. *Negoiators of Change: Historical Perspectives on Native American Women.* New York: Routledge, 1995.

Spittal, W. G., ed. *Iroquois Women: An Anthology.* Ohsweken, Ont.: Iroqrafts, 1990.

Books

Allen, Paula Gunn. *The Sacred Hoop: Recovering the Feminine in American Indian Traditions.* Boston: Beacon Press, 1986.

Bahr, Diana Meyers. *From Mission to Metropolis: Cupeno Indian Women in Los Angeles.* Norman: University of Oklahoma Press, 1993.

Bataille, Gretchen M. *Native American Women: A Biographical Dictionary.* New York: Garland Publishing, 1991.

———. *American Indian Women: A Guide to Research.* New York: Garland Publishing, 1991.

Benedek, Emily. *Beyond the Four Corners of the World: A Navajo Woman's Journey.* New York: Alfred A. Knopf, 1995.

Boyer, Ruth McDonald, and Narcissus Duffy Gayton. *Apache Mothers and Daughters.* Norman: University of Oklahoma Press, 1992.

Buchanan, Kimberly Moore. *Apache Women Warriors.* El Paso: Texas Western Press, 1986.

Canfield, Gae Whitney. *Sarah Winnemucca of the Northern Paiutes.* Norman: University of Oklahoma Press, 1983.

Child, Brenda J. *Boarding School Seasons: American Indian Families, 1900–1940.* Lincoln: University of Nebraska Press, 1998.

Clark, Ella Elizabeth, and Margot Edmonds. *Sacajawea of the Lewis and Clark Expedition.* Berkeley: University of California Press, 1979.

Colson, Elizabeth, ed. *Autobiographies of Three Pomo Women.* Berkeley: Archeological Research Facility, Department of Archeology, University of California, 1974.

Crary, Margaret. *Susette La Flesche: Voice of the Omaha Indians.* New York: Hawthorne Press, 1973.

Crow Dog, Mary, with Richard Erdoes. *Lakota Woman.* New York: Harper Perennial, 1990.

Cruickshank, Julie. *Life Lived like a Story: Life Stories of Three Yukon Native Elders.* Lincoln: University of Nebraska Press, 1990.

Cuera, Delphina. *The Autobiography of Delphina Cuero*. Ed. Florence Shipek. 1970. Reprint, Menlo Park, Calif.: Ballena Press, 1991.

Deer, Ada, and R. E. Simon Jr. *Speaking Out*. Chicago: Children's Press, 1970.

Devens, Carol. *Countering Colonization: Native American Women and Great Lakes Missions, 1630–1900*. Berkeley: University of California Press, 1992.

Farley, Ronnie, ed. *Women of the Native Struggle: Portraits and Testimony of Native American Women*. New York: Orion Books, 1993.

Flood, Renee Sansom. *Lost Bird of Wounded Knee: Spirit of the Lakota*. New York: Scribner Press, 1995.

Foreman, Carolyn Thomas. *Indian Women Chiefs*. Washington, D.C.: Zenger Publishing, 1954.

Green, Rayna. *Native American Women: A Contextual Bibliography*. Bloomington: Indiana University Press, 1983.

———. *Women in American Indian Society*. Indians of North America. Gen. ed. Frank W. Porter III. New York: Chelsea House Publishers, 1992.

Harlan, Theresa. *Watchful Eyes: Native American Women Artists*. Phoenix: Heard Museum, 1994.

Hopkins, Sarah Winnemucca. *Life among the Piutes: Their Wrongs and Claims*. Ed. Mrs. Horace Mann. 1883. Reprint, Bishop, Calif.: Sierra Media Inc., 1969.

Horne, Esther Burnett, and Sally McBeth. *Essie's Story: The Life and Legacy of a Shoshone Teacher*. Lincoln: University of Nebraska Press, 1998.

Hungry Wolf, Beverly. *The Ways of My Grandmothers*. New York: Morrow, 1980.

Jacobs, Margaret D. *Engendered Encounters: Feminism and Pueblo Cultures, 1879–1934*. Lincoln: University of Nebraska Press, 1999.

Jones, David. *Sanapia: Commanche Medicine Woman*. New York: Holt, Rinehart and Winston, 1972.

Klein, Laura F., and Lillian A. Ackerman, eds. *Women and Power in Native North America*. Norman: University of Oklahoma Press, 1995.

Linderman, Frank B. *Pretty-Shield: Medicine Woman of the Crows*. 1932. Reprint, New York: John Day Co., 1972.

Lurie, Nancy. *Mountain Wolf Woman, Sister of Crashing Thunder*. Ann Arbor: University of Michigan Press, 1961.

Mankiller, Wilma, and Michael Mankiller. *Mankiller: A Chief and Her People*. New York: St. Martin's Press, 1993.

Mihesuah, Devon A. *Cultivating the Rosebuds: The Education of Women at the Cherokee Female Seminary, 1851–1909*. Urbana: University of Illinois Press, 1993.

Modesto, Ruby, and Guy Mount. *Not for Innocent Ears: Spiritual Traditions of a Desert Cahuilla Medicine Woman*. Arcata, Calif.: Sweetlight Books, 1980.

Niethammer, Carolyn. *Daughters of the Earth: The Lives and Legends of American Indian Women*. New York: Collier Books, 1977.

Perdue, Theda. *Cherokee Women: Gender and Culture, 1700–1835*. Lincoln: University of Nebraska Press, 1998.

Peterson, Susan. *The Living Tradition of Maria Martinez*. Tokyo: Kodanska International, 1977.

Pitseolak, P. *Pictures out of My Life*. New York: Oxford University Press, 1971.

Potts, Marie. *The Northern Maidu*. Happy Camp, Calif.: Naturegraph, 1977.

Powers, Marla N. Oglala. *Women, Myth, Ritual, and Reality*. Chicago: University of Chicago Press, 1986.

Qoyawayma, Polingaysi Elizabeth White. *No Turning Back: A Hopi Indian Woman's Struggle to Live in Two Worlds*. Ed. Vada F. Carlson. Albuquerque: University of New Mexico Press, 1964.

Reyer, Carolyn. *Cante Ohitika Win (Brave-hearted Women): Images of Lakota Women from the Pine Ridge Reservation, South Dakota*. Vermillion: University of South Dakota Press, 1991.

Ross, Luana. *Inventing the Savage: The Social Construction of Native American Criminality*. Austin: University of Texas Press, 1998.

Sarris, Greg. *Mabel McKay: Weaving the Dream*. Berkeley: University of California Press, 1994.

Schroeder, Susan, Stephanie Wood, and Robert Haskett. *Indian Women of Early Mexico*. Norman: University of Oklahoma Press, 1997.

Shepherd, Alice. *In My Own Words: Stories, Songs, and Memories of Grace McKibbin, Wintu.* Berkeley: Heyday Press, 1997.

St. Pierre, Mark. *Madonna Swan: A Lakota Woman's Story.* Norman: University of Oklahoma Press, 1991.

St. Pierre, Mark, and Tilda Long Soldier. *Walking in the Sacred Manner: Healers, Dreamers, and Pipe Carriers—Medicine Women of the Plains Indians.* New York: Simon and Schuster, 1995.

Stewart, Irene. *A Voice in Her Tribe: A Navajo Woman's Own Story.* Socorro, N.M.: Ballena Press, 1980.

Stockel, H. Henrietta. *Women of the Apache Nation.* Reno: University of Nevada Press, 1991.

Thompson, Lucy [Che-na wah Weitch-ah-wah]. *To The American Indian: Reminiscences of a Yurok Woman.* 1916. Reprint, Berkeley: Heyday Books, 1991.

Tilton, Robert S. *Pocahontas: The Evolution of An American Narrative.* Cambridge: Cambridge University Press, 1994.

Tong, Benson. *Susan La Flesche Picotte, M.D.: Omaha Indian Leader and Reformer.* Norman: University of Oklahoma Press, 1999.

Udell, Louise, ed. *Me and Mine: The Life Story of Helen Sekaquaptewa.* Tucson: University of Arizona Press, 1969.

Van Kirk, Sylvia. *Many Tender Ties: Women in Fur-Trade Society, 1670–1870.* Norman: University of Oklahoma Press, 1980.

Voget, Fred W., assisted by Mary K. Mee. *They Call Me Agnes: A Crow Narrative Based on the Life of Agnes Yellowtail Deernose.* Norman: University of Oklahoma Press, 1995.

Youst, Lionel. *She's Tricky like Coyote: Annie Miner Peterson, an Oregon Coast Indian Woman.* Norman: University of Oklahoma Press, 1997

Journal/Anthology Articles

Albers, Patricia, and William James. "Illusion and Illumination: Visual Images of American Indian Women in the West." In Sue Armitage and Elizabeth Jameson, eds., *The Women's West.* Norman: University of Oklahoma Press, 1987.

Almeida, Deirdre A. "The Hidden Half: A History of Native American Women's Education." *Harvard Educational Review* 67, 4 (1997): 757–71.

Anderson, Karen. "Commodity Exchange and Subordination: Montagnais–Naskapi and Huron Women, 1600–1650." *Signs: Journal of Women in Culture and Society* 11, 1 (1985): 48–62.

Blackwood, Evelyn. "Sexuality and Gender in Certain Native American Tribes: The Case of Cross–Gender Females." *Signs: Journal of Women in Culture and Society* 10 (1984): 27–42.

Blaeser, Kimberly M. "Like Reeds through the Ribs of a Basket: Native American Women Weaving Stories." *American Indian Quarterly* 21, 4 (1997): 555–65.

Brady, Victoria, Sarah Crome, and Lyn Reese. "Resist! Survival Tactics of Indian Women." *California History* 63 (1984): 140–51.

Braund, Kathryn E. Holland. "Guardians of Tradition and Handmaidens to Change: Women's Role in Creek Economic and Social Life during the Eighteenth Century." *American Indian Quarterly* 14 (1990): 239–58.

Brown, Judith K. "Iroquois Women: An Ethnohistorical Note." In Rayna R. Reiter, ed., *Toward an Anthropology of Women.* New York: Monthly Review Press, 1975.

Buffalohead, Priscilla A. "Farmers, Warriors, Traders: A Fresh Look at Ojibway Women." *Minnesota History* 48, 6 (1983): 236–44.

Chato, Genevieve, and Christine Conte. "The Legal Rights of American Indian Women." In Lillian Schlissel, Vicki L. Ruiz, and Janice Monk, eds., *Western Women: Their Land, Their Lives.* Albuquerque: University of New Mexico Press, 1988.

Clark, Jerry E., and Martha Ellen Webb. "Susette and Susan LaFlesch: Reformer and Missionary." In James A. Clifton, ed., *Being and Becoming Indian: Biographical Studies of North American Frontiers.* Chicago: Dorsey Press, 1989.

Dillingham, Brint. "Indian Women and IHS Sterilization Practices." *American Indian Journal* 3, 1 (1977): 27–28.

Dunaway, Wilma A. "Rethinking Cherokee Acculturation: Women's Resistance to Agrarian Capitalism and Cultural Change, 1800–1838." *American Indian Culture and Research Journal* 21, 1 (1997): 155–92.

Fleming, E. McClung. "The American Image as Indian Princess." *Winterthur Portfolio II*, 1965, 65–81.

Frederickson, Vera Mae, ed. "School Days in Northern California: The Accounts of Six Pomo Women." *News from Native California* 4, 1 (fall 1989): 40–45.

Frisbie, Charlotte J. "Traditional Navajo Women: Ethnographic and Life History Portrayals." *American Indian Quarterly* 6 (1982): 11–33.

Green, Rayna. "The Pocahontas Perplex: The Image of Indian Women In Popular Culture." *Massachusetts Review* 16 (autumn 1975): 678–714.

Hauptman, Laurence M. "Alice Jemison: Seneca Political Activist." *Indian Historian* 12, 2 (1974): 15–40.

Holland-Braund, Kathryn E. "Guardians of Tradition and Handmaidens to Change: Women's Roles in Creek Economic and Social Life during the Eighteenth Cenury." *American Indian Quarterly* 14, 3 (1990): 239–58.

Jamieson, Kathleen. "Sex Discrimination and the Indian Act." In J. Rick Ponting, ed., *Arduous Journey: Canadian Indians and Decolonization*. Toronto: McClelland and Stewart, 1986.

———. "Multiple Jeopardy: The Evolution of a Native Women's Movement." *Canadian Ethnic Studies* 13, 1 (1981): 130–43.

Jensen, Joan. "Native American Women and Agriculture: A Seneca Case Study." *Sex Roles: A Journal of Research* 5, 3 (1977): 423–41.

Johnson, David L., and Raymond Wilson. "Gertrude Simmons Bonnin, 1876–1938: 'Americanize the First Americans.'" *American Indian Quarterly* 12, 1 (winter 1988): 27–40.

Kidwell, Clara Sue. "Indian Women as Cultural Mediators." *Ethnohistory* 39, 2 (1992): 97–107.

Klein, Alan M. "The Plains Truth: The Impact of Colonialism on Indian Women." *Dialectical Anthropology* 7, 4 (1983): 299–313.

Klein, Laura F. "Contending with Colonization: Tlingit Men and Women in Change." In Mona Etienne and Eleanor Leacock, eds., *Women and Colonization: Anthropological Perspectives*. New York: Praeger Publishers, 1980.

Knack, Martha E. "Contemporary Southern Paiute Women and the Measurement of Women's Economic and Political Status." *Ethnology* 28 (1989): 233–48.

LaFromboise, Teresa D., Anneliese M. Heyle, and Emily J. Ozer. "Changing and Diverse Roles of Women in American Indian Cultures." *Sex Roles* 22 (1990): 455–76.

Lynch, Robert N. "Women in Northern Paiute Politics." *Signs: Journal of Women in Culture and Society* 11, 2 (1986): 352–66.

Mann, Barbara A. "The Lynx in Time: Haudenosaunee Women's Traditions and History." *American Indian Quarterly* 21, 3 (1997): 423–49.

Mathes, Valerie Sherer. "Native American Women in Medicine and the Military." *Journal of the West* 21, 2 (April 1982): 41–48.

———. "American Indian Women and the Catholic Church." *North Dakota History* 47 (fall 1980): 20–25.

Medicine, Beatrice. "Native American (Indian) Women: A Call for Research." *Anthropology and Education Quarterly* 19, 2 (1988): 86–92.

———. "Indian Women Tribal Identity as Status Quo." In Marion Lowe and Ruth Hubbard, eds., *Woman's Nature: Rationalizations of Inequality*. New York: Pergamon, 1983.

Metcalf, Ann. "Navajo Women in the City: Lessons from a Quarter Century of Relocation." *American Indian Quarterly* 6, 1–2 (1982): 71–89.

———. "From Schoolgirl to Mother: The Effects of Education on Navajo Women." *Social Problems* 23, 4 (1976): 535–44.

Oshana, Maryann. "Native American Women in Westerns: Reality and Myth." *Frontiers* 6 (November 1981): 46–50.

Patterson, Victoria D. "Indian Life in the City: A Glimpse of the Urban Experience of Pomo Women in 1930s." *California History* 71 (fall 1992): 402–31.

Rothenberg, Diane. "The Mothers of the Nation: Seneca Resistance to Quaker Intervention." In Mona Etienne and Eleanor Leacock, eds., *Women and Colonization: Anthropological Perspectives.* New York: Praeger Publishers, 1980.

Round, Phillip H. "There Was More to It, but that Is All I Can Remember: The Persistence of History and the Autobiography of Delfina Cuero." *American Indian Quarterly* 21, 2 (1997): 171–93.

Roundtree, Helen C. "Powhatan Indian Women: The People Captain John Smith Barely Saw." *Ethnohistory* 45, 1 (1998): 1–29.

Shoemaker, Nancy. "From Longhouse to Log House: Household Structure among the Senecas in 1900." *American Indian Quarterly* 15, 3 (1991): 29–38.

———. "The Rise and Fall of Iroquois Women." *Journal of Women's History* 2 (1991): 39–54.

Smith, Sherry L. "Beyond Princess and Squaw: Army Officers' Perceptions of Indian Women." In Sue Armitage and Elizabeth Jameson, eds., *The Women's West.* Norman: University of Oklahoma Press, 1987.

Szasz, Margaret Connell. "'Poor Richard' Meets the Native American: Schooling for Young Indian Women in Eighteenth Century Connecticut." *Pacific Historical Review* 49 (May 1980): 215–35.

Trennert, Robert A. "Educating Indian Girls at Nonreservation Boarding Schools, 1878–1920." *Western Historical Quarterly* 13, 3 (1982): 271–90.

Welch, Deborah. "American Indian Women: Reaching Beyond the Myth." In Colin G. Calloway, eds., *New Directions in American Indian History.* Norman: University of Oklahoma Press, 1988.

Zastro, Leona M. "American Indian Women as Art Educators." *Journal of American Indian Education* 18 (October 1978): 6–10.

Permissions Acknowledgments

Joyce Antler, "Between Culture and Politics: The Emma Lazarus Federation of Jewish Women's Clubs and the Promulgation of Women's History, 1944–1989," from Linda K. Kerber, Alice Kessler-Harris, and Katherine Kish Sklar, eds., *U.S. History as Women's History: New Feminist Essays.* Copyright © 1995 by the University of North Carolina Press. Used by permission of the publisher.

Yamila Azize-Vargas, "The Emergence of Feminism in Puerto Rico, 1870–1930," reprinted with permission of the author and *Radical America*, vol. 23, no. 1, 1989.

Mary H. Blewett, "Deference and Defiance: Labor Politics and the Meanings of Masculinity in the Mid-Nineteenth-Century New England Textile Industry," *Gender and History* 5:3 (1993): 398–415. Reprinted by permission of the publisher.

Jeanne Boydston, "To Earn Her Daily Bread: Housework and Antebellum Working-Class Subsistence," *Radical History Review*, vol. 35 (April 1986): 7–25. Reprinted by permission of Cambridge University Press.

James F. Brooks, "'This Evil Extends Especially to the Feminine Sex': Captivity and Identity in New Mexico, 1700–1846," in Jameson and Armitage, eds., *Writing the Range: Race, Class, and Culture in the Women's West,* University of Oklahoma Press, 1997, 97–121. © 1997 by the University of Oklahoma Press. Reprinted with permission.

Elsa Barkley Brown, "To Catch the Vision of Freedom: Reconstructing Southern Black Women's Political History, 1865–1880," in Ann D. Gordon et al, eds., *African American Women and the Vote, 1837-1965,* University of Massachusetts Press, 1997. Reprinted by permission of the author.

Antonia I. Castañeda, "Gender, Race, and Culture: Spanish Mexican Women in the Historiography of Frontier California," *Frontiers* 11:1 (1990): 8–20. Reprinted by permission of the author.

Ellen Carol DuBois, "Woman Suffrage around the World: Three Phases of Suffragist Internationalism," in Daley and Norton, eds., *Suffrage and Beyond: International Feminist Perspectives,* New York University Press, 1990. Reprinted with permission of the publisher.

Cynthia Griggs Fleming, "'More than a Lady': Ruby Doris Smith Robinson and Black Woman's Leadership in the Student Nonviolent Coordinating Committee," *Journal of Women's History* 4:3, 204–23. Reprinted by permission of Indiana University Press.

Evelyn Nakano Glenn, "From Servitude to Service Work: Historical Continuities in the Racial Division of Paid Reproductive Labor," reprinted by permission of the University of Chicago Press. Originally published in *Signs,* vol. 18, no. 1, 1992.

Linda Gordon, "Black and White Visions of Welfare: Women's Welfare Activism, 1890–1945," reprinted with permission of the *Journal of American History* 78, 1991.

Melanie Gustafson, "Partisan Women in the Progressive Era: The Struggle for Inclusion in American Political Parties," *Journal of Women's History* 9: 2, 1997, 8–30. Reprinted by permission of Indiana University Press.

Ramón A. Gutiérrez, "Community, Patriarchy, and Individualism: The Politics of Chicano History," *American Quarterly* 45 (1993): 44–72. © 1993, the American Studies Association. Reprinted by permission of the Johns Hopkins University Press.

Jaquelyn Dowd Hall, "Open Secrets: Memory, Imagination, and the Refashioning of Southern Identity," *American Quarterly* 50:1 (1998): 109–24. © 1998, the American Studies Association. Reprinted by permission of the Johns Hopkins University Press.

Nancy A. Hewitt, "Beyond the Search for Sisterhood: American Women's History in the 1990s," *Social History*, vol.10 (1985). Reprinted by permission of Taylor & Francis, Ltd.

Evelyn Brooks Higginbotham, "In Politics to Stay: Women Leaders and Party Politics in the 1920s," in Tilly and Gurin, eds., *Women, Politics and Change*, Russell Sage Foundation, 1990. © Russell Sage Foundation. Used with permission of the publisher.

Daniel Horowitz, "Rethinking Betty Friedan and *The Feminine Mystique:* Labor Union Radicalism and Feminism in Cold War America," *American Quarterly* 48 (1996): 1–38. © 1996, the American Studies Association. Reprinted by permission of the Johns Hopkins University Press.

Kumari Jayawardena, "Going for the Jugular of Hindu Patriarchy: American Women Fund-Raisers for Ramabai," in *The White Woman's Other Burden: Western Women and South Asia during British Rule*, Routledge, 1995: 53–62. Reprinted with permission of the publisher.

Susan Lee Johnson, "'Domestic' Life in the Diggings: The Southern Mines in the California Gold Rush," in Matsumoto and Allmendinger, eds., *Over the Edge: Remapping the American West*, University of California Press, 1998. Reprinted by permission of the publisher.

Gail Paradise Kelly, "To Become An American: Education and Sex Role Socialization of the Vietnamese Immigrant Woman," Reprinted by permission of David Kelly.

Elizabeth Lapovsky Kennedy. "'But We Would Never Talk about It': The Structures of Lesbian Discretion in South Dakota, 1928–1933," in Ellen Lewin, ed., *Inventing Lesbian Culture in America*, Beacon, 1996. Copyright © by Ellen Lewin. Reprinted by permission of Beacon Press.

Yolanda Chávez-Leyva, "Breaking the Silence: Putting Latina Lesbian History at the Center," in Zimmerman and McNaron, eds., *New Lesbian Studies*, The Feminist Press, 1996: 145–52. Reprinted with permission of the publisher.

Tessie Liu, "Teaching the Differences among Women from a Historical Perspective: Rethinking Race and Gender as Social Categories," reprinted from *Women's Studies International Forum*, 14:4, 265–76 (1991). Reprinted with permission of the publisher.

Valerie Matsumoto, "Japanese American Women During World War II," *Frontiers* 8:1 (1984): 6–14. Reprinted by permision of the publisher.

Joanne Meyerowitz, "Sexual Geography and Gender Economy: The Furnished-Room Districts of Chicago, 1890–1930," *Gender and History* 2 (1990): 274–96. Reprinted by permission of the publisher.

Devon A. Mihesuah, "'Too Dark to be Angels': The Class System Among the Cherokees at the Female Seminary," *American Indian Culture and Research Journal*, v. 15, no.1 (1991), 29–52. Reprinted by permission of the author.

Alice Yang Murray, "Ilse Women and the Early Korean American Community: Redefining the Origins of Feminist Empowerment," in Song and Moon, eds., *Korean American Women Living in Two Cultures*, Academia Koreana Press. Reprinted by permission of the publisher.

Annelise Orleck, "'We Are that Mythical Thing Called the Public': Militant Housewives during the Great Depression." This article is a revised version of an article originally published in *Feminist Studies*, 19:1 (spring 1993): 147–72, reprinted by permission of the publisher, *Feminist Studies*, Inc.

Peggy Pascoe, "Miscegenation Law, Court Cases, and Ideologies of 'Race' in Twentieth-Century America," reprinted by permission of the *Journal of American History* 83:1 (1996).

Kathy Peiss, "Making Faces: The Cosmetics Industry and the Cultural Construction of Gender, 1890–1930," *Genders* 7, 143–69. Reprinted by permission of the author.

Theda Perdue, "Cherokee Women and the Trail of Tears," *Journal of Women's History* 1:1 (1989): 14–30. Reprinted from *Journal of Women's History* by permission of Indiana University Press.

Barbara M. Posados, "Crossed Boundaries in Interracial Chicago," *Amerasia* 8:2 (1981): 31–52. Reprinted with permission of the publisher.

Vicki L. Ruiz, "'Star Struck': Acculturation, Adolescence, and Mexican American Women, 1920–1950," in West and Petrick, eds., *Small Worlds: Children and Adolescents in America*, University of Kansas Press, 1992. Reprinted with permission of the publisher.

Rickie Solinger, "Dependency and Choice: The Two Faces of Eve," *Social Justice* 25:1 (1998). Reprinted with permission of the publisher.

Contributors

Joyce Antler is Samuel Lane Professor of American Jewish History and Culture at Brandeis University, where she chairs the American Studies Department. Her most recent books include *The Journey Home: How Jewish Women Shaped Modern America* (Schocken, 1998), and the edited volume *Talking Back: Images of Jewish Women in American Popular Culture* (University of New England Press, 1998). She is currently working on a cultural history of Jewish mothers.

Yamila Azize-Vargas earned a Ph.D. from the University of Pennsylvania and is Senior Researcher at the Women's Studies Program at the Cayey Campus of the University of Puerto Rico. Her research has focused on the sociopolitical history of women in Puerto Rico, including issues such as political participation, work, health, abortion, science, education, and sports. She is the author of *La mujer en la lucha* (1979, 1985), one of the first books to chronicle the emergence of the feminist movement in Puerto Rico. She has done extensive work in curricular transformation projects on liberal arts, science, and health. Her current research focuses on women's international migration and work.

Mary H. Blewett, Professor of History at the University of Massachusetts, Lowell, authored *Men, Women, and Work: Class, Gender and Protest in the Nineteenth-Century New England Shoe Industry* (1988), *The Last Generation* (1990), and *We Will Rise in Our Might: Working Women's Voices from Nineteenth-Century New England* (1991). She is completing *Constant Turmoil* for the University of Massachusetts Press, a study of nineteenth-century gender and ethnic relations and labor politics in the southeastern New England textile industry.

Jeanne Boydston is Professor of History and Co-Director of the Graduate Program in United States Women's History at the University of Wisconsin, Madison. She is the author of *Home and Work: Housework, Wages, and the Ideology of Labor in the Early Republic* and co-editor (with Mary Kelley and Anne Margolis) of *The Limits of Sisterhood: The Beecher Sisters on Women's Rights and Woman's Sphere* and (with Nancy F. Cott, Ann Braude, Lori Ginzberg, and Molly Ladd-Taylor) of the second edition of *Root of Bitterness: Documents of the Social History of American Women.*

James F. Brooks is Assistant Professor of History at the University of Maryland, College Park. His monograph, *Captives and Cousins: Slavery, Kinship, and Community in the Southwest Borderlands,* is forthcoming from the Omohundro Institute of Early American History and Culture from the University of North Carolina Press.

Elsa Barkley Brown teaches history at the University of Maryland and is a coeditor of *Black Women in America: An Historical Encyclopedia* (Indiana, 1994). Her articles have appeared in *Signs, Sage, History Workshop Journal,* and *Feminist Studies.*

Antonia I. Castañeda teaches in the Department of History at St. Mary's University. Her current projects include a cultural history of Mestizas in colonial Alta California, a bilingual critical edition of nineteenth-century Californiana narratives, and a cultural history of Tejana farm workers. She is an Associate Editor of the journal *Latina Voces* and is coeditor, with Deena J. González, of *Chicana Matters*.

Ellen Carol DuBois is Professor of History at UCLA. She is the author of *Feminism and Suffrage: The Emergence of an Independent Women's Movement in America, 1848–1969*; *Harriet Stanton Blanch and the Winning of Women's Suffrage* (winner of the 1998 Joan Kelly Price Award from the AHA); and *Woman Suffrage and Women's Rights*.

Cynthia Griggs Fleming was born and raised in Detroit, Michigan. She received her B.A. in history from Knoxville College and her M.A. and Ph.D. in American history from Duke University. A former member of the Peace Corps in Liberia, West Africa, she has published articles in *Journal of Negro History, Phylon, Journal of Women's History, Irish Journal of American Studies* and the *Tennessee Historical Quarterly*. Her biography of Ruby Doris Smith Robinson, *Soon We Will Not Cry*, was published by Rowman and Littlefield. She is currently Associate Professor of Cultural Studies at the University of Tennessee in Knoxville.

Evelyn Nakano Glenn is Professor of Women's Studies and Ethnic Studies at the University of California, Berkeley. Her writings include empirical and theoretical works on race, gender, and class. She is the author of *Issei, Nisei, Warbride: Three Generations of Japanese American Women in Domestic Service* and is the senior editor of *Mothering: Ideology, Experience, and Agency*. Her current project is a comparative study of the race and gender construction of labor and citizenship in three regions, 1870–1930.

Linda Gordon is the Florence Kelley Professor of History and Vilas Distinguished Research Professor at the University of Wisconsin, Madison. She has specialized in examining the historical roots of contemporary social policy debates, particularly as they concern gender and family issues. Her books include *America's Working Women* (1976, revised 1995); *Woman's Body, Woman's Right: The History of Birth Control in America* (runner-up for the National Book Award, 1976, revised 1990); *Heroes of Their Own Lives: The Politics and History of Family Violence* (1988); and *Pitied but not Entitled: Single Mothers and the History of Welfare* (1994). Her latest book, *The Great Arizona Orphan Abduction* (Harvard University Press, 1999), tells the story of how a group of white women organized a 1904 vigilante action against Mexican Americans.

Melanie Gustafson is Assistant Professor of History at the University of Vermont, where she teaches nineteenth- and twentieth-century U.S. history. She is also coeditor of *We Have Come to Stay: American Women and Political Parties, 1880–1960* (University of New Mexico Press, 1999).

Ramón A. Gutiérrez is Professor of Ethnic Studies and History at the University of California, San Diego, where he founded the Ethnic Studies Department, as well as the Center for the Study of Race and Ethnicity. He has written extensively on race and ethnic issues in the Americas, on Indian-white relations in the conquest of America, and on kinship, gender, and sexuality in the Christian West. His contribution in this volume is part of a larger study on the history of the Chicano Movement.

Jacquelyn Dowd Hall is Julia Cherry Spruill Professor of History and director of the Southern Oral History Program at the University of North Carolina, Chapel Hill, for which she received a National Humanities Medal. She is the coauthor of *Like a Family: The Making of a Southern Cotton Mill World* (1987). In 1993 Columbia University Press issued a new edition of her first book, *Revolt Against Chivalry: Jessie Daniel Ames and the Women's Campaign Against Lynching*, with a new introductory chapter and an epilogue. Her articles have appeared in *American Historical Review, Journal of American History, Feminist Studies, Signs, Women's Review of Books, Radical History Review*, and *Southern Exposure*.

Nancy A. Hewitt is Professor of History at Rutgers University. She is the author of *Women's Activism and Social Change: Rochester, New York*, and coeditor, with Suzanne Lebsock, of *Visible Women: New Essays on American Activism*. Her latest book, *Forging Activist Identities: Latin, African American, and Anglo Women in Tampa, Florida*, is forthcoming from University of Illinois Press. A founding editor of *Gender and History*, she currently serves on the editorial board of *Feminist Studies*.

Evelyn Brooks Higginbotham is Professor of African-American Studies at Harvard University. She is the author of *Righteous Discontent: The Women's Movement in the Black Baptist Church, 1880–1920* (Harvard University Press, 1993), which has won book prizes from the American Historical Association, the American Academy of Religion, the Association of Black Women Historians, and the Association for Research on Non-Profit and Voluntary Organizations. Her articles on African American women's history cover such diverse themes as constructions of racial and gender identity, electoral politics, religion, and the intersection of theory and history. Her article "African American Women's History and the Metalanguage of Race," *Signs* (winter 1992) won the Best Article prize of the Berkshire Conference of Women Historians in 1993. She is currently completing a book on African American women and citizenship.

Alice Y. Hom is a Ph.D. candidate in History at the Claremont Graduate University. A recipient of the National Women's Studies Association Lesbian Dissertation Fellowship, Ms. Hom's research focuses on cultural and coalitional politics among lesbians of color. She is the coeditor, with David Eng, of *Q & A: Queer in Asian American* (Temple University Press, 1999).

Daniel Horowitz teaches at Smith College, where he directs the American Studies Program. In *Betty Friedan and the Making of the Feminine Mystique: The American Left, the Cold War, and Modern Feminism* (University of Massachusetts Press, 1998), he has developed more broadly and deeply the full implications of the arguments he first presented in "Rethinking Betty Friedan and *The Feminine Mystique*." Among his other publications are *The Morality of Spending: Attitudes Toward the Consumer Society in America, 1875–1940* (1985) and *Vance Packard and American Social Criticism* (1994).

Kumari Jayawardena was formerly Associate Professor of Political Science at the University of Colombo, Sri Lanka. She is presently a researcher at the Social Scientists' Association, Colombo, where she coordinates a gender history project. She teaches in the Colombo University Women's Studies Program and is the author of *Feminism and Nationalism in the Third World* and *The White Women's Other Burden* (also available from Routledge), and books on several subjects including the ethnic issue in Sri Lanka, the rise of capitalism and the history of the labor movement in Sri Lanka.

Susan Lee Johnson teaches U.S. western history, women's and gender history, and the history of sexuality at the University of Colorado at Boulder. She is the author of *Roaring Camp: The Social World of the California Gold Rush* (W. W. Norton, 2000), and also has published in *Western Historical Quarterly*, *Radical History Review*, and *California History*. Her current work studies Kit Carson's intimate relationships with Arapaho, Cheyenne, and New Mexican women as windows on questions of space, race, gender, nation, and desire.

Gail Paradise Kelly was Professor of Education and Chairperson of the Department of Educational Organization, Administrative of Policy at SUNY, Buffalo. She wrote *From Vietnam to America*, coauthored *Feminism in the Disciplines*, and most recently was a coeditor and contributor *to Emergent Issues in Education: Comparative Perspectives*. She also served a term as president of the Comparative Education Society.

Elizabeth Lapovsky Kennedy was a founding member of Women's Studies at the State University of New York, Buffalo, and is currently professor and head of Women's Studies,

University of Arizona, Tucson. She was trained as a social anthropologist at the University of Cambridge in England and did two years of field work with the Waunan in Colombia, South America. Over the past thirty years Professor Kennedy has worked to build the field of women's studies, pioneered studies of lesbian history, and explored the uses of oral history. She coauthored, with Ellen Carol DuBois, Gail Paradise Kelly, Carolyn W. Korsmeyer, and Lillian S. Robinson, *Feminist Scholarship: Kindling in the Groves of Academe* (University of Illinois Press, 1985), and with Madeline Davis, *Boots of Leather, Slippers of Gold: The History of a Lesbian Community* (Routledge, 1993), as well as numerous articles.

Yolanda Chávez-Leyva is an assistant professor at the University of Texas, San Antonio, where she teaches history. She was born and raised on the Chihuahua-Texas border where she learned the power of memory and keeping stories alive. She has published articles on Latina identity and sexuality, colonial New Mexican widows, and Mexican American women during the Great Depression. She received her Ph.D. from the University of Arizona.

Tessie Liu teaches comparative European history at Northwestern University. In 1994 she published *The Weaver's Knot: The Contradictions of Class Struggle and Family Solidarity in Western France, 1750 to 1914*. Her current research focuses on the role of gender in the historical construction of the concept of race during the French Revolution. She has published articles on race and multiculturalism in women's history.

Valerie Matsumoto teaches history and Asian American studies at the University of California, Los Angeles. She is the author of *Farming the Home Place: A Japanese American Community in California, 1919–1982*, and the coauthor of *Over the Edge: Remapping the American West*.

Joanne Meyerowitz is a professor of history at Indiana University and editor of the *Journal of American History*. She is the author of *Women Adrift: Independent Wage Earners in Chicago, 1880–1930* (1988) and the editor of *Not June Cleaver: Women and Gender in Postwar America, 1945–1960* (1994). She is currently writing a history of transsexuality in the United States.

Devon A. Mihesuah (Oklahoma Choctaw) is professor of history at Northern Arizona University, Flagstaff. She serves as editor of the *American Indian Quarterly* and her publications include *Cultivating the Rosebuds: The Education of Women at the Cherokee Female Seminary, 1851–1909, American Indians: Stereotypes and Realities, Researching and Writing About American Indians*, and the forthcoming *The Roads of My Relations and Other Stories*.

Alice Yang Murray is Assistant Professor of History at the University of California, Santa Cruz, and teaches courses in Asian American history, women's history, and twentieth-century U.S. history. She has edited *What Are the Causes and Consequences of Internment?* (forthcoming from St. Martin's Press) and is currently completing a manuscript on representations of Japanese internment, redress, and historical memory.

Annelise Orleck is the author of *Common Sense and a Little Fire: Women and Working Class Politics in the U.S. and Soviet-Jewish Americans*, and coeditor of *The Politics of Motherhood: Activist Voices from Left to Right*. She is Associate Professor of History and Women's Studies at Dartmouth College. She is now at work on a collective biography of the leaders of the Las Vegas welfare rights movement.

Peggy Pascoe is Associate Professor and Beekman Chair of Northwest and Pacific History at the University of Oregon, where she teaches classes on the history of gender, race, and sexuality, and is currently at work on a book about the history of American laws against interracial marriage.

Kathy Peiss teaches American women's history and cultural history at the University of Massachusetts, Amherst. She is the author of *Cheap Amusements: Working Women and*

Leisure in Turn-of-the-Century New York (Temple University Press, 1986) and *Hope in a Jar: The Making of America's Beauty Culture* (Metropolitan, 1998).

Theda Perdue is Professor of History at the University of North Carolina. Her publications include *Slavery and the Evolution of Cherokee Society, 1540–1865* (1979), *Nations Remembered: An Oral History of the Five Civilized Tribes* (1980), *Cherokee Editor* (1983), *Native Carolinians* (1985), *The Cherokee* (1988), *Southern Women: Histories and Identities* (1992), *Hidden Histories of Women in the New South* (1994), *The Cherokee Removal* (1995) and, most recently, *Cherokee Women: Gender and Culture Change, 1700–1835* (1998).

Barbara M. Posadas is Professor of History at Northern Illinois University. Born in Chicago, the daughter of a Filipino father and a Polish-American mother, she earned her doctorate at Northwestern University. She is the author of *The Filipino Americans* (1999) and the coeditor or *Refracting America: Gender, Race, Ethnicity, and Environment in American History to 1877* (1993). Her articles have appeared in *Chicago History, Labor History, Amerasia*, the *Journal of American Ethnic History*, the *Journal of the Illinois State Historical Society*, and several edited collections. She serves as a member of the editorial boards of *Amerasia*, the *Journal of Women's History*, and the *Journal of the Illinois State Historical Society*, has chaired the Organization of American Historians' Committee on the Status of Minority Historians and Minority History, and is the president of the Illinois State Historical Society (1999–2001).

Daina L. Ramey is Assistant Professor of History and African American Studies at Arizona State University. She received her Ph.D. from the University of California, Los Angeles, in 1998. Her dissertation is entitled, "A Place of Our Own: Labor, Family, and Community Among Female Slaves in Piedmont and Tidewater, Georgia, 1820–1860."

Annette L. Reed (Tolowa) is Assistant Professor of Ethnic Studies at California State University, Sacramento. She received her Ph.D in Ethnic Studies at the University of California, Berkeley, in 1999, and her dissertation provides a tribal history of the Tolowa of northwestern California.

Vicki L. Ruiz is Professor of History and Chair of Chicana and Chicano Studies at Arizona State University. She is the author of *From Out of the Shadows: Mexican Women in Twentieth Century America* and *Cannery Women and Cannery Lives: Mexican Women, Unionization, and the California Food Processing Industry 1930–1950*, and the editor of the journal *Las Obreras: Chicana Politics of Work and Family*.

Rickie Solinger is the author of *Wake Up, Little Susie: Single Pregnancy and Race Before Roe V. Wade* (Routledge, 1992), *The Abortionist: A Woman Against the Law* (Free Press, 1994), and essays about reproductive politics in the United States. She is the editor of *Abortion Wars: A Half Century of Struggle, 1950–2000* (1998). Solinger, who lives in Boulder, Colorado, is completing a book about the consequences of adopting the word "choice" as the signifier of women's autonomy.

Brenda Stevenson is a professor of history and department chair at the University of California, Los Angeles. She is the author of *Life in Black and White: Family and Community in the Slave South* (Oxford University Press, 1996).

Rebecca Tsosie received her J.D. from the University of California, Los Angeles in 1990. After clerking for Vice Chief Justice Stanley G. Feldman, Arizona Supreme Court, she worked as a litigation associate with Brown & Bain in Phoenix. Professor Tsosie spent a year as a Visiting Professor of Law at ASU College of Law before joining the ASU faculty in 1994. She is now actively engaged in writing and speaking on topics which include tribal environmental policy and cultural resources management. She teaches Federal Indian Law, Property, Indian Cultural Property, and Indian Environmental Policy.

Sherrie Tucker received her Ph.D. from the History of Consciousness Program at University of California, Santa Cruz. She is currently Assistant Professor of Women's Studies at Hobart and William Smith Colleges in Geneva, New York. She has spent ten years interviewing women musicians who played in all-woman jazz and swing bands during World War II for her dissertation and book (forthcoming, Duke University Press, 2000). Her recent and forthcoming publications on women and jazz include articles in the *New Grove Dictionary of Jazz* (forthcoming, MacMillan, 2001), *American Music, Black Music Research Journal, Frontiers: A Journal of Women's Studies, Hot Wire: A Journal of Women's Music and Culture, Jazz Now Magazine, Labor's Heritage, Oral History Review, Pacific Review of Ethnomusicology*, and *Women and Music: A Journal of Gender and Culture*. She has conducted interviewers for the Smithsonian Jazz Oral History Program, and is a former jazz radio programmer on KJAZ-FM in the San Francisco Bay Area.

Mary Ann Villareal is a Ph.D. candidate in history at Arizona State University. A recipient of an American Association of University Women's Dissertation Fellowship, Ms. Villareal is completing a study entitled "Cantoras y Cantineras: Tejana Musicians and the Making of Public Space."

Devra Anne Weber is the author *of Dark Sweat, White Gold: California Farm Workers, Cotton, and the New Deal* (California, 1994) and articles on Mexican labor in the United States. She is Associate Professor of History at the University of California, Riverside.

Judy Yung is Associate Professor of American Studies at the University of California, Santa Cruz. She is the author of *Unbound Voices: A Documentary History of Chinese Women in San Francisco* (1999), *Unbound Feet: A Social History of Chinese Women in San Francisco* (1995), and *Chinese Women in America: A Pictorial History* (1986), and coauthor of *Island: Poetry and History of Chinese Immigrants on Angel Island* (1980).

Index